JIM MURRAY'S
WHISKY
BIBLE
2011

**This 2011 edition is dedicated with love and pride to
Finlay James Underwood**

This edition first published 2010 by Dram Good Books Ltd

10 9 8 7 6 5 4 3 2 1

The "Jim Murray's" logo and the "Whisky Bible" logo are trade marks of Jim Murray.

Text, tasting notes & rankings, artwork, Jim Murray's logo and the Whisky Bible logo copyright
© Jim Murray 2010

Design copyright © Dram Good Books Limited 2010

For information regarding using tasting notes from Jim Murray's Whisky Bible contact:
Dram Good Books Ltd, 38 Park Road, Wellingborough, Northamptonshire, UK NN8 4PW
Tel: 44 (0)1933 279709. Or contact us via www.whiskybible.com

A CIP catalogue record for this book is available from the British Library

ISBN: 978-0-9554729-5-4

Printed in England by Stanley L Hunt (Printers) Ltd. Rushden, Northamptonshire
www.stanleylhunt.co.uk

Written by: Jim Murray
Edited by: David Rankin
Design: James Murray, Jim Murray
Maps and Cover Design: James Murray
Production: James Murray, Billy Jeffrey, Dani Dal Molin
Sample Research: Dani Dal Molin, Billy Jeffrey, Julia Nourney
Publicity and Marketing: Mark Hunt

Author's Note
I have used the spelling "whiskey" or "whisky" depending on how the individual distillers
prefer. All Scotch is "whisky". So is Canadian. All Irish, these days, is "whiskey", though
that was not always the case. In Kentucky, bourbon and rye are spelt "whiskey", with the
exception of the produce of the early Times/Old Forester Distillery and Maker's Mark which
they bottle as "whisky". In Tennessee, it is a 50-50 split: Dickel is "whisky", while Daniel's is
"whiskey".

JIM MURRAY'S
WHISKY
BIBLE
2011

DRAM GOOD BOOKS

Contents

Introduction

1066 and all that....! No, it's not one in the eye for Harold. It's once again over a thousand new whiskies in the nose and mouth for Jim.

And in order to ensure that those fit beside the 946 from last year and 1,227 from the edition before (making a staggering total of 3,239 new whiskies I have tasted in the last two years) we have expanded Jim Murray's Whisky Bible by a further 24 pages. That, plus a piece of cunning editing, means that you now get 4,500 tasting notes to carry around and refer to at any given moment.

In the last year or so we have made a point of listening closely to what our loyal readers want. It is pretty divided. Some desire us to carry more whiskies; others want a few less but a bigger font. Some demanded that we change the cover design every year as they were thinking they had already bought it, while others wanted it to stay exactly the same. It was obvious that whatever we did, or didn't do, some would be happy, others not. But now that sales of the 2010 edition brought the overall total of Whisky Bibles sold to over a quarter of a million copies, we thought this was as good as time as any to freshen the image up a bit.

Also this year we have been forced to raise the cover price in Britain and Europe. We had no option: the price of the Bible has gone up by only a pound since the very first edition was launched in 2003 when it was a mere 254 pages covering a piffling 2,000 whiskies. This 2011 edition is now 384 pages, referring to more than twice as many brands. With the extra expenditure of producing a larger book plus the normal but significant rises in printing and paper costs we simply could not subsidise the publication any longer. But we certainly hope you still feel you are getting pretty exceptional value for money: by 2003 standards it should cost £15.10 in terms of number of pages or £21.41 for the whiskies...!!!

And for the traditionalists amongst you wanting to keep your collection of Whisky Bibles uniform (and we know there are many of you!), don't despair. We are printing a special old style cover which can be ordered from our website at a price more or less at cost plus postage and packing. Please see whiskybible.com for details.

So much for the style of the Bible: what of the whiskies this year in it? To be honest, this has been one of the strangest tasting experiences I have had since the Bible was launched. Actually, the strangest... The number of whiskies affected by sulphur is up significantly. So much so, I am over two weeks beyond my deadline, simply because I had to stop so many times for my palate to recover. Not good news. Nor for my waistline. One of the better aids to seeing off sulphur on the palate, I have discovered over the years, is a Red Leicester cheese and tomato sandwich or two. During the course of writing this edition of the Bible I have put on 15 pounds...

But still the number of whiskies scoring 94 and upwards, thus qualifying for the Whisky Bible Liquid Gold Award, runs at almost exactly an identical percentage to that already found in the previous editions. So there is no shortage of fabulous whiskies out there. What I have noticed, however, is that they have tended to be older this year, with the great grand-daddy of them all being the phenomenal 70-year-old Mortlach launched by Gordon and MacPhail. This has run against all I have been saying for the last decade as regards to finding younger whiskies. Maybe it is just a blip. I hope so. Either way, it means bottlers of Scotch as well as buyers of it need to be just a little more circumspect for the time being.

But there is no shortage of good news: as Whisky Bible 2011 shows, there are still plenty of outstanding whiskies to be found. And in Britain, a first: the supermarket giant Sainsbury have picked up the Jim Murray Irish Whiskey of the Year award with their 8-year-old own label from the Cooley Distillery. But World Whisky of the Year went, after years of knocking on the door, to that extraordinary blended Scotch Ballantines 17-years-old, which just seems to have taken the diaphanous and ultra-refined school of scotch to a new level.

Finally, if anyone has that Sheffield United v Millwall programme mentioned in the Review pages and is willing to sell, I shall cross your palm with gold. However, it won't be in liquid form and dating from October 15th 1938...

Jim Murray
The Tasting Room
Wellingborough August 2010

How to Read
The Bible

The whole point of this book is for the whisky lover – be he or she an experienced connoisseur or, better fun still, simply starting out on the long and joyous path of discovery – to have ready access to easy-to-understand information about as many whiskies as possible. And I mean a lot. Thousands.

This book does not quite include every whisky on the market ... just by far and away the vast majority. And those that have been missed this time round – either through accident, logistics or design – will appear in later editions once we can source a sample.

Whisky Scoring

The marking for this book is tailored to the consumer and scores run out just a little higher than I use for my own personal references. But such is the way it has been devised that it has not affected my order of preference.

Each whisky is given a rating out of 100. Twenty-five marks are given to each of four factors: nose (n), taste (t), finish (f), balance and overall complexity (b). That means that 50% of the marks are given for flavour alone and 25% for the nose, often an overlooked part of the whisky equation. The area of balance and complexity covers all three previous factors and a usually hidden one besides:

Nose: this is simply the aroma. Often requires more than one inspection as hidden aromas can sometimes reveal themselves after time in the glass, increased contact with air and changes in temperature. The nose very often tells much about a whisky, but – as we shall see – equally can be quite misleading.

Taste: this is the immediate arrival on the palate and involves the flavour profile up to, and including, the time it reaches maximum intensity and complexity.

Finish: often the least understood part of a tasting. This is the tail and flourish of the whisky's signature, often revealing the effects of ageing. The better whiskies tend to finish well and longer without too much oak excess. It is on the finish, also, that certain notes which are detrimental to the whisky may be observed. For instance, a sulphur-tarnished cask may be fully revealed for what it is by a dry, bitter residue on the palate which is hard to shake off. It is often worth waiting a few minutes to get the full picture of the finish before having a second taste of a whisky.

Balance: This is the part it takes a little experience to appreciate but it can be mastered by anyone. For a whisky to work well on the nose and palate, it should not be too one-sided in its character. If you are looking for an older whisky, it should have evidence of oak, but not so much that all other flavours and aromas are drowned out. Likewise, a whisky matured or finished in a sherry butt must offer a lot more than just wine alone and the greatest Islay malts, for instance, revel in depth and complexity beyond the smoky effects of peat.

Each whisky has been analysed by me without adding water or ice. I have taken each whisky as it was poured from the bottle and used no more than warming in an identical glass to extract and discover the character of the whisky. To have added water would have been pointless: it would have been an inconsistent factor as people, when pouring water, add different amounts at varying temperatures. The only constant with the whisky you and I taste will be when it has been poured directly from the bottle.

Even if you and I taste the same whiskies at the same temperature and from identical glasses – and even share the same values in whisky – our scores may still be different. Because a factor that is built into my evaluation is drawn from expectation and experience. When I sample a whisky from a certain distillery at such-and-such an age or from this type of barrel or that, I would expect it to offer me certain qualities. It has taken me 30 years to acquire this knowledge (which I try to add to day by day!) and an enthusiast cannot be expected to learn it overnight. But, hopefully, Jim Murray's Whisky Bible will help...!

Score chart
Within the parentheses () is the overall score out of 100.
0–50.5 Nothing short of absolutely diabolical.
51–64.5 Nasty and well worth avoiding.
65–69.5 Very unimpressive indeed.
70–74.5 Usually drinkable but don't expect the earth to move.
75–79.5 Average and usually pleasant though sometimes flawed.
80–84.5 Good whisky worth trying.
85–89.5 Very good to excellent whiskies definitely worth buying.
90–93.5 Brilliant.
94–97.5 Superstar whiskies that give us all a reason to live.
98–100 Better than anything I've ever tasted!

Key to Abbreviations & Symbols
% Percentage strength of whisky measured as alcohol by volume. **b** Overall balance and complexity. **bott** Date of bottling. **db** Distillery bottling. In other words, an expression brought out by the owners of the distillery. **dist** Date of distillation or spirit first put into cask. **f** Finish. **n** Nose. **nc** Non-coloured. **ncf** Non-chill-filtered. **sc** Single cask. **t** Taste. ❁ New entry for 2011.
⊙ Retasted – no change. ⊙⊙ Retasted and re-evaluated. **v** Variant

Finding Your Whisky

Worldwide Malts: Whiskies are listed alphabetically throughout the book. In the case of single malts, the distilleries run A–Z style with distillery bottlings appearing at the top of the list in order of age, starting with youngest first. After age comes vintage. After all the "official" distillery bottlings are listed, next come other bottlings, again in alphabetical order. Single malts without a distillery named (or perhaps named after a dead one) are given their own section, as are vatted malts.

Worldwide Blends: These are simply listed alphabetically, irrespective of which company produce them. So "Black Bottle" appears ahead of "White Horse" and Japanese blends begin with "Ajiwai Kakubin" and end with "Za". In the case of brands being named after companies or individuals the first letter of the brand will dictate where it is listed. So William Grant, for instance, will be found under "W" for William rather "G" for Grant.

Bourbon/Rye: One of the most confusing types of whiskey to list because often the name of the brand bears no relation to the name of the distillery that made it. Also, brands may be sold from one company to another, or shortfalls in stock may see companies buying bourbons from another. For that reason all the brands have been listed alphabetically with the name of the bottling distiller being added at the end.

Irish Whiskey: There are four types of Irish whiskey: (i) pure pot still; (ii) single malt, (iii) single grain and (iv) blended. Some whiskies may have "pure pot still" on the label, but are actually single malts. So check both sections.

Bottle Information

As no labels are included in this book I have tried to include all the relevant information you will find on the label to make identification of the brand straightforward. Where known I have included date of distillation and bottling. Also the cask number for further recognition. At the end of the tasting notes I have included the strength and, if known, number of bottles (sometimes abbreviated to btls) released and in which markets.

Price of Whisky

You will notice that Jim Murray's Whisky Bible very rarely refers to the cost of a whisky. This is because the book is a guide to quality and character rather than the price tag attached. Also, the same whiskies are sold in different countries at varying prices due to market forces and variations of tax, so there is a relevance factor to be considered. Equally, much depends on the size of an individual's pocket. What may appear a cheap whisky to one could be an expensive outlay to another. With this in mind prices are rarely given in the Whisky Bible.

Bible Thumping
Gone! Threescore Years & Ten

Was it really 35 years ago that a kindly driver picked up a young hitch-hiker and took him to the very first whisky distillery he had ever seen?

The journey there, on a warm June afternoon and along lonely single-tracked roads offering the most dramatic of Scottish coastal views, was, by very strange coincidence, brought back to me in the most vivid way possible as I typed the introduction a moment ago. Because, by what must be a million to one chance, a Spitfire just flew over my home, its throaty Merlin engine making its guttural mark of respect to the 70th anniversary of the Battle of Britain. Bizarrely, the car in which I arrived at the Talisker distillery in that sun-soaked summer of 1975 also, when cruising in a certain gear, from the front passenger seat appeared to hum that very same unmistakably rich burr. I remember joking about it to the driver: was his a Mark III or Mark IV? And that he listened carefully, eyebrows furrowed, and then burst out laughing when the similarity of the two engines' signature tunes dawned on him. Funny isn't it, when we are able to remember almost every aspect of a life-changing moment, as that trip unquestionably was for me, as if it was yesterday? I have never seen that thoughtful and cheery gentleman again since he dropped me off somewhere or other on the Isle of Skye after we finished the tour: if he is still with us he'll be comfortably in his 70s by now, I guess. I wonder if I shall ever hear from him: it is frustrating when one has been unable to repay a lifetime's gratitude...

So perhaps there is no little irony that should I be somehow transported to that same still house this second to stand at the very spot where I had first witnessed whisky being made, the sounds greeting me would be less evocative of that distant moment than the lone Spitfire which just flew overhead.

Because 35 years ago distilleries were wonderfully noisy, smelly places teaming with blue-smocked life. Talisker, in particular, had a sweet, smoky aura stemming from the peat evident in the steam from the mash and the thick atmosphere which permeated the still house itself. When I was last there the whisky was made in almost reverential silence, just the hiss of the stills adding to the soporific experience. No hob-nailed boots clanging urgently on metal stairs, no voices raised above the daily din of distilling. Extractors meant the air was virtually free of the aroma of lightly smoked spirit, and the Health and Safety people were happy.

It was fitting that the Spitfire should pass overhead as I write this. Because it also reminds me that 35 years ago was the exact halfway point between the Battle of Britain and now. In 1940 it was announced that the following year's distilling season would last just three months. Hogmaney brought a "stampede" to find stocks according to one witness in Glasgow; the price of whisky stocks of all ages rose dramatically and by April 1941 you were unable to buy even a half bottle over the counter. I remember the warehouseman telling me that one or two of the workers had been at the distillery since just after being demobbed as the industry tried to fight its way back to normality. I can't quite recall if he was one of them, but though small in stature and wiry he had that hardness about him and enough life etched into his face to suggest he might.

And that is what fascinates me: then and then and then and now. In other words, just how far have we come in the making of whisky in those 35 years; and just how far had they travelled in the 35 years before? In Kentucky, perhaps not that far. Bourbon making legend Elmer T Lee arrived at what is now Buffalo Trace not long after hostilities ended and the vast majority of distilling and blending practises then are more or less the same as now. A Kentucky distiller from the 1930s and 1940s would not take very long to get used to making whiskey there now and have no problem recognising the whitedog offered him.

The same might be correctly said about his Scottish malt distillery counterpart on the production side. Except the spirit going into the barrel and the whisky coming out of it might have him scratching his head a little. From that perspective things have changed. A lot.

The year 2010 may have been my 35th anniversary of going to my first distillery. But it also marked the 30th anniversary of the beginning my sojourn to all Scotland's distilleries. In 1975 I was a teenage cub reporter on a News Agency earning £15 a week: to tour Scotland I had no option other than to hitch-hike; five years later and I was a young journalist on a British national newspaper seconded to the Glasgow office for the first time, and with a car at my command. It was then I had the opportunity to let my whisky education really begin. And what I found in 1980 – and more or less through to the 1990s – was exactly what I found at Talisker. Distilleries which were sometimes lonely communities operating with large, aging and experienced workforces but with fear. Because the early 80s saw a dramatic cull in Scottish distilleries: a lot of whisky had been made through the 1970s for the blends market but projected sales failed to materialise and the resulting Single Malt Revolution was yet to happen. So a Whisky Loch had formed and inefficient and low grade distilleries were the first to go. If a distillery operated with two stills, there had to be a good argument to keep it operating – even if it produced high class malt. There were mergers, takeovers, job duplication. Since my first visit to Talisker in 1975 the number of people working at the sharp end of whisky making and blending has reduced considerably. And not just in Scotland, but in Kentucky and Canada as well. The whisky world I entered is a vastly different one to that which I inhabit today.

In those passing 35 years the new make produced at many distilleries has changed also. And it would be an act of romanticism over fact to say that it has been entirely for the worse. That's as regard to the spirit. Sadly, the same cannot always be said for the finished article. But without doubt the quirks and foibles at some distilleries, especially those owned by the bigger guys, have been ironed out. There has been a far greater standardisation in style, sometimes brought about because of changes to distilling practices at various distilleries. Now there are gangs of distillery operatives sent to work at different distilleries in the area with slight operational adjustments having been made from distillery to distillery to reduce the risk of mistakes through unfamiliarity. This once could not have happened even in my time because I well remember when a number of the workforce lived in cottages tied to their distilleries, did not own cars and either walked or cycled in to work; indeed some were in such remote areas it was not unusual for them to be unable to receive even a clear television signal and there were not enough lines to have a phone. But then their demands and expectations were less than is the case today, something that was common of that generation be they working in the whisky industry or not. However, this homogenisation within distilleries has not been entirely welcomed with open arms by all blenders I know, but from a practical and cost-saving point of view you cannot fault the logic. And as for the workers: well, there may be fewer of them today but their wages have risen considerably.

But let us return to 1975. And then travel a further 35 years back in time from there: actually, let's make it 36 to a point before World War Two had started. Would the whisky world of 1939 have been closer to that of 1975 than '75 is to today? Most probably. But don't make the mistake in thinking that it would have been the same. The old time workers I met at Talisker would have seen changes to their industry that would have had them muttering darkly about the loss of the good old days in exactly the same way some of the older stagers in Speyside still do today.

For a start, those who worked at a Scottish malt distillery in the 1930s would have seen the vast majority of the new barrels arriving there made from European oak. That changed dramatically as the political maps were redrawn in 1945 and this oak became much harder to source. So Scotland and Ireland turned to Kentucky, who had no shortage of barrels due to their laws preventing the second use of their casks. This meant that aspects of the nose, taste and colour of Scotch whisky changed within a decade. It also meant the extra use of caramel, as less sherry butts were being used, again affecting the flavour and texture of scotch whisky.

Throughout the 1950s distillery workers in Speyside would also have noticed that the whisky they were making was becoming lighter in style. Further archaeological evidence of this was unearthed when Gordon and MacPhail launched their 1938 Mortlach this year, the peat clearly apparent and matching in its smoky weight some 1940s early post war malt from nearby Macallan released a few years back. During the 1950s blenders instructed distillers to more or less ditch peat from the Highland malts so their blends could catch the mood of lighter spirits. As a result, the aroma inside distilleries would have changed perceptibly: you have only to visit Ardmore today to be reminded what it once would have been like.

This lighter malt was increasingly achieved by distilleries closing their own maltings and having malt supplied to them. By doing this distilleries could more likely guarantee the phenol (smoke) level to the spirit. When distillery workers were left to their own devices in operating the kilns, the degrees of smokiness could differ dramatically from one day to the next, depending on who was operating the kiln and how much attention was being paid on the amount of peat added and smoke produced. Inconsistency of spirit from the same distillery was now becoming anathema to blenders. Ordering malt with a pre-set phenol level, achieved by blending peated malt with non-peated malt, was the answer. Blenders I met who had worked in the 1950s told me how the style of certain distillery's malt could change so dramatically that they were uneasy about using it as a set percentage. With the closure of the on-site malting and standardisation of phenol levels life became very much easier for them. But it meant a shrinking workforce: less personnel were required to turn the malt and they joined the coopers as once being mainstays of the distillery but now surplus to requirements. When I listen to brand ambassadors around the world telling enthralled enthusiasts that the whisky they are selling is made exactly the same now as it always was, I cannot help a shake of the head and stifle a wry smile. Scotch whisky is not made the exactly same way now as even when I got my first foot-hold in the industry, let alone generations ago

So here's the rub. If we were able to shoot forward another 35 years into the future, to the year 2045, what will we find? In the highly unlikely event of me still being around, at 87 I'd be older than probably anything even Gordon and MacPhail can come up with. But I should survey many outlines of the whisky world of 2010, though not so much of 1975.

On the production side I don't see a huge amount of changes. Staffing levels have been stripped pretty clean and it's hard to imagine they can get much lower. Technology can only go so far and what automation that is achievable is already largely in place: indeed, some smaller distillers when buying a discarded distillery from a bigger producer are not beyond removing some of it.

It is unlikely that there will be a succession of Superdistilleries built to phase out the small, less commercially viable ones. Well, not if the lesson is learned from Canada where Seagram built the Gimli distillery so it's many smaller ones could be closed to save costs. The idea was that it would produce a number of different styles for the blenders to work from. It simply hasn't happened. Even if smaller distilleries were closed, the huge advent of the whisky tourism industry means that rather than being knocked down or left to rot, they would be bought by companies looking to produce limited amounts for the single malt market and try to make ends meet from visitors.

Because the biggest change, outside maturation, affecting the industry is tourism sparked by the success of Single Malt whisky and the arrival of the internet. When I began trudging around Scotland's distilleries 35 years ago the only way I could get information was by asking those who worked there. Most companies did not have well oiled press and PR machines then; there was no internet to find out this and that at the click of a button. There were no Whisky Festivals in which the company line could be dangled at enthusiasts thirsty for information, understandably intoxicated by the romance of it all. There were not even many visitor centres: Talisker's, for instance, opened in 1988; Ardbeg over a decade later.. The tiny two hovel hamlet that was the scene surrounding the industry when I arrived has now become an ever-sprawling city.

But with the control of information sometimes comes disinformation. And it is that of which I am most wary. There is little more depressing than learning, as I did in Taiwan this year, that a brand ambassador was spouting that sulphur found in sherry butts is an old Scottish tradition. It is not: it was a mistake by the industry, just as was attempts at some distilleries in the 1970s to use stainless steel rather than copper at weak points in the stills to save money. Mistakes recognised and now learned from.

By 2045 the Scotch industry certainly will be flying, unlike that Spitfire. For a start, the irritation of those sulphured sherry and wine butts will have come to an end. Just because we are already seeing that the tarnished casks already emptied are still inflicting sulphur taint as second fills and unless they are removed from the system altogether – an unlikely scenario – they will continue to alter the flavour of whisky they are used for until they have come to the end of their natural lives, which might be another 25 years. But by then there may possibly be a longer-term problem with the casks from Kentucky. The expensive natural seasoning required for a longer life for the barrel has already been reduced: what use is it to a Kentucky distiller using it only once? And what if, during the next 35 years, there is a change of US law which means that virgin oak will no longer be required in order to protect the environment? So will the way whisky is matured in 35 years time have changed radically? Most likely. And because of that, styles and flavours are likely to alter once again.

For while Scotch whisky is based on tradition, it is a tradition that goes through its own evolutionary processes, as does anything needing to survive and thrive. Surely, though, it will be in the industry's best interests to celebrate how whisky got to where it is by telling the story as it really is, warts and all. There is no place for inventing history: for, as I have learned since arriving at Talisker in that vanishing whisky world, the truth is dramatic and fascinating enough.

Review of the Whisky Year

On Saturday October 15th 1938 newly promoted **Millwall Football Club** travelled to the world-famous sporting venue of **Bramall Lane, Sheffield**, to take part in a crucial, top-of-the-table Second Division encounter.

Millwall, the reigning Champions of Division 3 South, had taken the second division by storm having in previous weeks humiliated Manchester City, Football League Champions just two seasons earlier, in front of City's stunned supporters with a sensational 6-1 away victory; then followed this by battering promotion favourites Blackburn Rovers 4-1 in front of nearly 40,000 Millwall faithful (including my own father) at The Den in London. Next, on October 8th, they helped create a record gate which stands to this day at Fulham's Craven Cottage of over 49,000 as the Lions of Millwall, now up to third, travelled to the divisional leaders. Some observers hailed the Fulham-Millwall encounter one of the best second tier games they had ever witnessed and although the Lions led 1-0 at half-time, Fulham fought back to win 2-1 in thrilling fashion. So it was imperative they at least picked up a point the following Saturday on the wide open spaces of Bramall Lane, home of Sheffield United. The Lions, dominating play at will, should have taken a first half lead but Syd Rawlings squandered a penalty. When Walsh finally scored for Millwall with just six minutes remaining it looked as though their constant superiority had been rewarded and a top two position ensured. But with three minutes to go their England international goalkeeper Harold Pearson somehow allowed Hampson's tame shot to squirm under his body for a shock United equaliser entirely against the run of play. And then, with the Lions desperately pressing for a last minute winner, Sheffield broke away and scored through Pickering to make it 2-1. There was not time even for the re-start. Such had been the quality of Millwall's performance in defeat, their manager Charles Hewitt gushed: "Their play had been such a revelation to me....I could not restrain my enthusiasm and admiration, so told the lads that their play had made me proud to be their manager." Had Millwall secured the victory they would have moved into second place and with a game in hand. Instead, United leapfrogged above them and gained promotion at the end of the season. Millwall, crushed by two consecutive cruel defeats, fell back behind the leaders. It was a watershed day for the club, for it took exactly 50 more years before they finally gained promotion to the top flight.

Meanwhile, on that very same autumnal Saturday in October 1938, some 400 miles north of where this high sporting drama was about to unfold, and more or less at the time the Millwall players, still brimming with confidence and intent, pulled into my home railway station of Wellingborough as their steam train rattled them up to Sheffield, a distillery worker went about his morning duties filling casks. He was just one of many employed by the giant Scottish Malt Distillers, the forerunners of Diageo, at the renowned Mortlach distillery, a quite large concern for its day that had been the first to be built in Dufftown and make full use of the new rail link into Speyside. The hefty sherry hogshead, fresh from the Royal Sherry Co in Jerez and marked by the Cardinal de Salis bodega, was already being prepared for its new life and now sported the distillery name roughly stencilled in white as was the allotted new cask number of 2656. On removing the bung, the familiar rich aroma of the fresh sherry would have momentarily greeted him as he inserted the nozzle into the barrel and began pumping the very lightly peated new make into it. Job soon done, he hammered the bung back in, helped weigh the filled butt and finally handed over responsibility for it to his colleagues, who would have soon rolled it with very little ceremony and in the shortest possible time into a nearby warehouse. He then set to work on cask 2657... It is unlikely the distillery manager at the time would have congratulated the filling store man or his colleagues for their efficient and dedicated work, or told them how proud they made him. It was just another whisky production half-day in the remote Scottish highlands. At lunchtime the worker would have gone home thinking little of the casks he had just handled; rather what he intended to do with his precious day and half off, including hopefully seeing Will Hay in his latest film, "Convict 99". On entering his kitchen he hung up his cap and overcoat and tucked into the cooked meal waiting for him. And later, with a soothing pipe on the go, he tended the evening fire as his wife prepared the family dinner, all the while listening to the football results on the radio, noting with satisfaction that local side Aberdeen were continuing their earnest pursuit of the Scottish League title with a 5-2 victory over Ayr. History also does not record what, if anything, he made of the Sheffield United v Millwall result...

Now, as it happens, 40 years of collecting means I have match programmes for 11 of the 12 games Millwall played between September 5th and November 12th 1938. The only one missing is (yep, you guessed it) at Sheffield United.

But what I do now have to mark the day, and against just about all conceivable odds, is some of that Mortlach whisky which was filled into cask 2656. How ironic that an event watched by 27,000 bellowing steelworkers and fully reported in the country's press is today entirely forgotten. Yet an unremarkable, everyday task carried out in the presence of a handful of workmen and a distillery cat at most should lead to one of the biggest whisky events of all time. Because make no mistake: Gordon and MacPhail's launching of their Generations Mortlach 70-year-old on March 11th 2010 cannot even begin to be overestimated in its importance. For a start, it has entirely re-written the textbooks as to regards maturation. This wouldn't be the case if after so long in the barrel it had come out in an undrinkable state with the nose and taste buds registering nothing but oak, which, as the oldest whisky ever bottled, it had every right to do. But it hadn't. It even had the conceit to stand at a near perfect 46.1% abv, when it should have been somewhere, fittingly, in the 30s. So astonishingly good was it, it has even picked up a gong or two in this year's Whisky Bible, including Single Malt of the Year. Of the 1,066 new whiskies tasted for this Bible, it was easily one of the top five. When you consider how many malts fall by the wayside and begin to show signs of decline not long after their 18th summer, some even much earlier, you get to fully appreciate what an extraordinary moment tasting this was. A 20cl sample will put you back £2,500 and a full bottle £10,000, roughly about the same amount paid for all the Millwall players on show on that day. But while all those Millwall legends from yesteryear are sadly no longer with us, the whisky from this freakish Mortlach 1938 cask 2656, this deliciously tangible link to a simpler world, is undoubtedly alive. And very well, indeed. Scotch Single Malt of Year? It is Scotch Single Malt of the last 70 years....

It seems that nearly all the major whisky events in the last year were linked with the past. Or the future. In Kentucky there were separate, lavish celebrations to mark Elmer T Lee's 90th birthday and Parker Beam's 50 year association with Heaven Hill.

And as part of their impressive 10th anniversary celebrations The Whisky Exchange in London unleashed upon us a 42-year-old Japanese single malt from the Karuizawa distillery. I will spare you the painful detail of what Millwall were doing in 1967 when this was distilled (though, as a nine-year-old, I did see them three times that year). But a whisky reaching that kind of age in the broiling heat of Japan is pretty close an achievement as the Mortlach making it to 70 years unscathed; though, indeed, there is more oak evident in the Karuizawa. Not to be outdone, the emerging single malt superpower from India, Amrut, came up with the oldest whisky to make it out of the subcontinent. Seven years may not sound like much, but try visiting Bangalore for a week or two in high summer – which is most of the year – and you might think again.

So the last twelve months will go down in whisky history as the Year of the Oldie. When many of us who have spent a long time in the industry, myself included, have had to reshape our thoughts on ancient whiskies.

But it has been a year of re-birth, too. For there is whisky once more in England after the St. George Distillery in Norfolk launched their first single malt on it reaching three years. However, it hard to imagine the first 70-year-old English malt being unveiled in 2076. Not because it isn't good enough, but it is unlikely they will have any stocks left to keep that long: demand for the whisky is already outstripping supply. But an incident meant those few bottles already released could have gone through the roof in value in a matter of months. Just as I was finishing the tasting of the whiskies for the Bible a fire broke out at the distillery in a small building attached to the warehouse. Smoke was spotted by an alert member of staff just moments before he was going home. Within minutes fire crews were there in force and the warehouse and all its precious contents were saved. On hearing the news I rang the distillery owners to check if they were OK. "Yeah, we're fine. We are just driving back to Norfolk now."

"Oh? Where are you then?"

"Scotland. We have just been visiting Gordon and MacPhail. We've been in Speyside for a couple of days on a fact-finding mission looking into fire security....."

Jim Murray's Whisky Bible Award Winners 2011

Yet again after another thousand whiskies and, seemingly, a hundred thousand sensations; after countless sighs of delight and no shortage of groans of despair; after months of searching the shelves and then my palate I was down to the top three whiskies. They had climbed over remains of 1,063 other assorted drams of all hues and personalities to reach the final base. But now only one could carry on to the very summit and become World Whisky of the Year in the 2011 Whisky Bible.

Some astonishing whiskies had already fallen by the wayside, slain by the singular brutality of genius. How can a 70-year-old single malt with barely a blemish have been cast so deeply into the shadows? Which whiskies can possibly overcome the bipolar beast which is the Octomore Orpheus. How had truly great Ardbegs, Highland Parks and Amruts been left so ruthlessly behind....?

Of course, as is always the case when measuring up the winners, some stood out head and shoulders from the very first moment while others snuck up shyly before slowly confirming their indisputable class. So, as always, the award winners here have been tasted, re-tasted and tasted again by me. First over a number of months, and then over a given couple of days when the palate is entirely clear of any off notes from the lesser whiskies which may in any way dull the shine of the whisky being questioned.

Curiously, two of the three had first come to my attention while the 2010 Bible was being printed. I was at the Buffalo Trace distillery to celebrate Elmer T Lee's 90th birthday and a small group of us were given a preview of the distillery's next batch of special bottlings. Two stood out then. And several months later, when I got to taste them analytically for the Bible, away from the romance of the distillery, that very same pair stood out again. They were the William Larue Weller. And the Thomas Handy rye. For the 2010 Bible, its sister brand Sazerac 18 Rye, had triumphed with the World Whisky Award. The latest version was not quite so bright. Well, if you listen to some who claim to be in the know, they reckon that because a whiskey has been put into a stainless steel container to stop the maturing process every bottling thereafter is exactly the same. Of course that is complete nonsense. They are always very slightly different: it happens with rum; it happens with rye. A number of factors, including the degree of oxidisation and the amount of churning the spirit undergoes before bottling, will have small, but significant, effects on the amount of vital oils included in each bottling. So the degree of sweetness, sharpness and so on may alter almost imperceptibly, but add them all together and you get a slightly different story each time. So the Autumn 2009 bottling of the Sazerac 18 just wasn't quite that of the previous year's. But the Handy...that was another, quite sublime, matter.

And for once the Weller out-rucked the Stag, probably the biggest surprise of them all. It was one hefty bourbon. But the mark of its greatness was that its enormity did not for one moment diminish its complexity or balance. At the distillery I was convinced I was in the presence of greatness. Back in my tasting room, alone, the hairs stood out on the back of my neck as my instincts were confirmed...and then got to know its extraordinary power.

So which of these two monumental whiskeys was it to be? The Weller? Or the Handy? As it turned out, it was neither. As these two slugged it out between them another whisky, delicate and fragile - about as far removed from them in character as you might possibly find - began to make a claim which, in the end, proved irresistible. It was Ballantines 17. A blended scotch which has been sniffing around the top Bible award for a few years now. Recent bottlings had taken it that extra required step. Refined elegance had triumphed over naked beauty...

The Whisky Bible Award Winners 2011

2011 World Whisky of the Year
Ballantine's 17 Years Old

Second Finest Whisky in the World 2011
Thomas H Handy Sazerac Rye (129 proof)
Third Finest Whisky in the World 2011
William Larue Weller (134.8 proof)

SCOTCH

Scotch Whisky of the Year
Ballantine's 17 Years Old
Single Malt of the Year (Multiple Casks)
Octomore Orpheus Aged 5 Years
Single Malt of the Year (Single Cask)
Gordon & MacPhail Mortlach 70
Best Scotch New Brand
Compass Box The Spice Tree
Scotch Blend of the Year
Ballantine's 17 Years Old
Scotch Grain of the Year
Clan Denny Garnheath Aged 40 Years
Scotch Vatted Malt of the Year
Big Peat

Single Malt Scotch

No Age Statement (Multiple Casks)
Ardbeg Corryvreckan
No Age Statement (Runner Up)
The Macallan Oscuro
10 Years & Under (Multiple Casks)
Octomore Orpheus Aged 5 Years
10 Years & Under (Single Cask)
Ardbeg 2000 Lord Robertson of Port Ellen KT
11-15 Years (Multiple Casks)
The Arran Malt 1996 'The Peacock'
11-15 Years (Single Cask)
SMWS 33.77 Aged 11 Years (Ardbeg)
16-21 Years (Multiple Casks)
Highland Park Aged 18 Years
16-21 Years (Single Cask)
Old Malt Cask Lochside Aged 18 Years
22-27 Years (Multiple Casks)
Brora 25 Year Old 7th Release
22-27 Years (Single Cask)
Duncan Taylor Highland Park 1986
28-34 Years (Multiple Casks)
Auchentoshan 1978 Bourbon Cask Ltd Edition
28-34 Years (Single Cask)
Old Malt Cask Auchroisk Aged 34 Years
35-40 Years (Multiple Casks)
Highland Park 1973 Orcadian Vintage
35-40 Years (Single Cask)
G&M Rare Old Convalmore 1975
41 Years & Over (Multiple Casks)
Dalmore Candela Aged 50 Years
41 Years & Over (Single Cask)
Gordon & MacPhail Mortlach 70

Blended Scotch

No Age Statement (Standard)
Ballantine's Finest

No Age Statement (Premium)
The Last Drop
5-12 Years
Johnnie Walker Black Label
13-18 Years
Ballantine's 17 Years Old
19 Years & Over
William Grant's 25 Years Old

IRISH WHISKEY

Irish Whiskey of the Year
Sainsbury's Dún Léire Aged 8 Years

AMERICAN WHISKEY

Bourbon of the Year
William Larue Weller (134.8 proof)
Rye of the Year
Thomas H Handy Sazerac Rye (129 proof)

Bourbon

No Age Statement (Multiple Barrels)
William Larue Weller (134.8 proof)
9 Years & Under
Knob Creek
10-17 Years (Multiple Barrels)
Parker's Heritage Collection Fourth Edition
10-17 Years (Single Barrel)
Willett Aged 17 Years Barrel Proof
18 Years & Over
Evan Williams 23 Year Old

Rye

No Age Statement
Thomas H Handy Sazerac Rye (129 proof)
11 Years & Over
Rittenhouse Rye Aged 25 Years Barrel 19

CANADIAN WHISKY

Canadian Whisky of the Year
Crown Royal Special Reserve

JAPANESE WHISKY

Japanese Whisky of the Year
Karuizawa 1967 Vintage

EUROPEAN WHISKY

European Whisky of the Year
Mackmyra Brukswhisky
European Single Cask Whisky of the Year
The Belgian Owl Aged 44 Months

WORLD WHISKIES

Indian Whisky of the Year
Amrut Intermediate Sherry Matured

*Overall age category winners are presented in **bold**.*

The Whisky Bible Liquid Gold Awards (97.5-94)

Jim Murray's Whisky Bible is delighted to again make a point of celebrating the very finest whiskies you can find in the world. So we salute the distillers who have maintained or even furthered the finest traditions of whisky making and taken their craft to the very highest levels. And the bottlers who have brought some of them to us.

After all, there are over 4,500 different brands and expressions listed in this guide and from every corner of the planet. Those which score 94 and upwards represents only a very small fraction of them. These whiskies are, in my view, the elite: the finest you can currently find on the whisky shelves of the world. Rare and precious, they are Liquid Gold.
So it is our pleasure to announce that all those scoring 94 and upwards automatically qualify for the Jim Murray's Whisky Bible Liquid Gold Award. Congratulations!

97.5

Scottish Single Malt
Ardbeg Uigeadail
Scottish Blends
Ballantine's 17 Years Old
American Straight Rye
Sazerac Rye 18 Years Old

97

Scottish Single Malt
Ardbeg 10 Years Old
Ardbeg Supernova
Brora 30 Years Old
Glenfiddich 50 Years Old
Scottish Blends
Old Parr Superior 18 Years Old
Bourbon
William Larue Weller
American Straight Rye
Thomas H. Handy Sazerac Straight Rye
Japanese Single Malt
The Cask of Yamazaki 1990 Sherry Butt
Nikka Whisky Single Coffey Malt 12 Years
Indian Single Malt
Amrut Fusion

96.5

Scottish Single Malt
Ardbeg 2000 Single Cask Lord Robertson of Port Ellen KT
Ardbeg Corryvreckan
Octomore Orpheus Aged 5 Years Edition 02.2 PPM 140
Port Charlotte PC6
Old & Rare Glencadam Aged 32 Years
Glenfarclas 1962 Family Casks (3rd Release)
Glenfarclas 1979 Family Casks (3rd Release)
Gordon & MacPhail Glen Grant 1958
Private Collection Glenlivet 1959
Glenmorangie Sonnalta PX
Gordon & MacPhail Mortlach 70
Cadenhead's Royal Brackla Aged 16 Years
Old Malt Cask Speyside's Finest Agd 43 Yrs
Scottish Blends
The Last Drop
Bourbon
Blanton's Single Barrel Silver No. 316

Blanton's Uncut/Unfiltered
George T. Stagg
Parker's Heritage Collection Third Edition 2009 "Golden Anniversary"
Japanese Single Malt
Scotch Malt Whisky Society Cask 116.14 Aged 25 Years (Yoichi)
Swiss Single Malt
Säntis Swiss Highlander Dreifaltigkeit
Welsh Single Malt
Penderyn Cask Strength Rich Madeira
Penderyn Port Wood Edition
Indian Single Malt
Amrut Intermediate

96

Scottish Single Malt
Aberlour a'bunadh Batch No. 23
Ardbeg 1974 Single Cask No. 3151
Ardbeg 1977
Ardbeg Kildalton 1980
Ardbeg Provenance 1974
Auchentoshan 1978 Bourbon Cask Matured Limited Edition
Old Malt Cask Auchroisk Aged 34 Years
Brora 25 Year Old 7th Release
Duncan Taylor Collection Brora 1981
Octomore 5 Years Old
The Whisky Agency Bunnahabhain 34 YO
Rare Old Convalmore 1975
The Dalmore Candela Aged 50 Years
Glendronach Single Cask 1992
Glenfarclas Family Casks 1967 Release V
Glenfarclas 105 40th Anniversary Limited Edition 40 Years Old
The Whisky Fair Glenfarclas 40 Years Old
Hart Brothers Glenfiddich Aged 45 Years
Duncan Taylor Collection Glen Garioch 1988 Aged 19 Years
Glenglassaugh 40 Year Old
Old & Rare Glen Grant Aged 31 Years
The Whisky Fair Glen Grant 36 Year Old
Rarest of the Rare Glenlochy 1980
Glenmorangie Truffle Oak
Glen Moray 1986 Commemorative Bottling
Cadenhead's Glenrothes Aged 16 Years

Scotch Malt Whisky Society Cask 93.30 Aged 16 Years (Glen Scotia)
Old Malt Cask Glenury Aged 32 Years
Highland Park 1973 Orcadian Vintage
Duncan Taylor Highland Park 1986
Rarest of the Rare Inverleven 1979
The Arran Malt 1996 'The Peacock'
Lagavulin 21 Years Old
Old Malt Cask Lochside Aged 18 Years
Parkers Whisky Port Ellen 1982 "Pert mELLon" Bottling
A.D. Rattray Pulteney 1982
Rosebank 25 Years Old
Cadenhead's Rosebank Aged 20 Years
The Whisky Fair Springbank Aged 35 Years
Old Malt Cask Tactical Aged 18 Years
Master of Malt Tomatin 19 YO Cask Strength
The Whisky Fair Tullibardine 1976
The Whisky Agency Speyside 39 Year Old

Scottish Vatted Malt
Big Peat

Scottish Grain
Duncan Taylor Collection Port Dundas 1973

Scottish Blends
Ballantine's Finest
Johnnie Walker Gold Label The Centenary Blend 18 Years Old

Irish Pure Pot Still
Redbreast 12 Years Old

Irish Blends
Jameson Rarest 2007 Vintage Reserve

American Single Malt
Stranahan's Colorado Whiskey Batch 11

Bourbon
Buffalo Trace Experimental Collection Course Grain Oak
George T. Stagg (141.4 proof)
Wild Turkey Rare Breed

American Single Malt Rye
Old Potrero Single Malt Hotaling's Whiskey Aged 11 Years Essay MCMVI-MMVI
Old Potrero Single Malt Hotaling's Whiskey Aged 12 Years Essay MCMVI-MMVII
American Straight Rye
Rittenhouse Very Rare 21 YO Barrel 28
Rittenhouse Rye Single Barrel 23 Year Old
Rittenhouse Rye Aged 25 Years Barrel 19

Canadian Blended
Crown Royal Special Reserve

Japanese Single Malt
The Cask of Hakushu 1993 Heavily Peated
Karuizawa 1967 Vintage

Finnish Single Malt
Old Buck Second Release

Swedish Single Malt
Mackmyra Privus 03 Rökning Tillåten

Welsh Single Malt
Penderyn Rich Madeira Limited Edition

Indian Single Malt
Amrut Double Cask

95.5

Scottish Single Malt
The BenRiach 1976
Cadenhead's Benriach Aged 23 Years
Bruichladdich Redder Still 1984
Caol Ila 'Distillery Only'
Adelphi Glenallachie 1973 Aged 36 Years
Norse Cask Glen Grant 1993 Aged 16 Years
Glenmorangie 25 Years Old
Glen Moray 1995 Port Wood Finish
Scotch Malt Whisky Society Cask 77.17 Aged 9 Years (Glen Ord)
Gordon & MacPhail Glenury Royal 1984
Highland Park Aged 18 Years
Highland Park Aged 30 Years
Scotch Malt Whisky Society Cask 4.126 Aged 9 Years (Highland Park)
Scotch Malt Whisky Society Cask 122.16 Aged 15 Years (Croftengea)
Scotch Malt Whisky Society Cask 7.51 Aged 24 Years (Longmorn)
The Macallan Oscuro
Duncan Taylor Collection Macallan 1988
Berrys' Own Selection Port Ellen 1982
Dewar Rattray Port Ellen Aged 24 Years
Old Malt Cask Port Ellen Aged 27 Years
Provenance Port Ellen Over 26 Years
Berry's Own Selection St. Magdalene 1982 Longrow C.V
A.D. Rattray Tamdhu 1967
Old Malt Cask Tamnavulin Aged 20 Years
Tomintoul Agd 12 Yrs Oloroso Sherry Finish Elements of Islay Pe1

Scottish Vatted Malt
Compass Box Flaming Hart
Compass Box The Spice Tree

Scottish Blends
Johnnie Walker Black Label 12 Years Old
William Grant's 25 Years Old

Irish Single Malt
Sainsbury's Dún Léire Aged 8 Years
The Tyrconnell Single Cask

American Single Malt
The Notch Aged 8 Years
Stranahan's Colorado Whiskey Batch 3
Stranahan's Colorado Whisky Batch 17

Bourbon
Blanton's Single Barrel No. 349
Evan Williams 23 Years Old
Parker's Heritage Collection Fourth Edition Aged 10 Years

American Straight Rye
Sazerac Rye 18 Years Old Fall 2007
Sazerac Straight Rye Fall 2009

Canadian Blended
Alberta Premium
Gibson's Finest Rare Aged 18 Years

Japanese Single Malt
Ichiro's Card "King of Hearts"

Belgium Single Malt
The Belgian Owl Single Malt Spirit Aged 44 Months

German Single Malt
Blaue Maus Single Malt 25 Jahre

Swedish Single Malt
Mackmyra Brukswhisky

95

Scottish Single Malt
Aberlour a'bunadh Batch No. 19
Aberlour a'bunadh Batch No. 26
Ardbeg Mor
Cadenhead's Ardbeg Aged 14 Years
Cadenhead's Ardbeg Aged 15 Years
Scotch Malt Whisky Society Cask 33.68 Aged 9 Years (Ardbeg)
Scotch Malt Whisky Society Cask 33.77 Aged 11 Years (Ardbeg)
Scotch Malt Whisky Society Cask 3.148 Aged 9 Years (Bowmore)
Connoisseurs Choice Braes of Glenlivet 1975
Old & Rare Brora Aged 30 Years
Bruichladdich 16 Years Old
Bruichaladdich 1970 Anniversary 125th
Port Charlotte Evolution PC5 Cask Strength
Chieftain's Bruichladdich 19 Years Old
Old Masters Bruichladdich Aged 20 Years
Scotch Malt Whisky Society Cask 53.139 Aged 27 Years (Caol Ila)
Matisse Carpedonich 1972 Highland Malt
Cadenhead's Convalmore 30 Years Old
Duncan Taylor Collection Dallas Dhu 1981
The Dalmore 62 Years Old
Adelphi Dalmore 1990 Aged 17 Years
Dalwhinnie 15 Years Old
Glencadam Aged 10 Years
Glencadam Agd 14 Yrs Oloroso Sherry Finish
Montgomerie's Glencadam 1975
Old Malt Cask Glencadam Aged 21 Years
Glendronach Aged 33 Years
Duthies Glen Elgin 18 Years Old
Glenfarclas 15 Years Old
Glenfarclas 1966 The Family Casks
Glenfiddich 18 Years Old
Glenglassaugh 1973 Family Silver
Glengoyne 1997 Aged 11 Years Single Cask
Old Malt Cask Glen Grant Aged 30 Years
Old Malt Cask Glen Mhor Aged 27 Years
Rarest of the Rare Glen Mhor 1975
Scotch Malt Whisky Society Cask 125.1 Aged 13 Years (Glenmorangie)
Glen Ord 25 Years Old
Berry's Own Selection Glen Scotia 1992
Cadenhead's Glenturret Aged 20 Years
Murray McDavid Highland Park 1989

Scotch Malt Whisky Society Cask 4.143 Aged 20 Years (Highland Park)
The Whisky Agency Highland Park 25 YO
The Arran Malt 1997 Single Cask
Duncan Taylor Collection Knockando 1980
Lagavulin Aged 16 Years
Laphroaig 1/4 Cask
Malts of Scotland Laphroaig 1996
Cadenhead's Longmorn Aged 18 Years
The Macallan 1949 (53 Years Old)
The Macallan 1970 (32 Years Old)
Gordon & MacPhail Macallan 1971
Rarest of the Rare North Port 1981
Scott's Selection North Port 1980
Old & Rare Port Ellen Aged 25 Years
Old & Rare Port Ellen Aged 25 Years
Old Pulteney Aged 17 Years
Rosebank Aged 12 Years
Scott's Selection The Speyside 1991
Da Mhile Organic "New Born" Springbank
Premium Scotch Importers Springbank 1998
Talisker Aged 20 Years
Talisker 57 Degrees North
Old Malt Cask Tamdhu Aged 18 Years
Tomintoul Aged 14 Years
Tullibardine 1986 John Black Selection
Secret Stills Highland 6.1 1988
Wemyss 1990 Highland "Tropical Spice"
Auld Reekie Islay Malt
Master of Malt Islay 12 Years Old
Celtique Connexion Sauternes Agd 13 Yrs
Master of Malt Speyside 50 Years Old Special Reserve

Scottish Vatted Malt
Douglas Laing's Double Barrel Highland Park & Bowmore
Johnnie Walker Green Label 15 Years Old
Norse Cask Selection Vatted Islay 1992 Aged 16 Years
Vintner's Choice Island 10 Years Old
Wild Scotsman Aged 15 Years Vatted Malt

Scottish Grain
The Clan Denny Dumbarton Aged 43 Years
The Clan Denny Garnheath Vintage 1969 Aged 40 Years
Duncan Taylor North British 1978

Scottish Blends
The Bailie Nicol Jarvie (B.N.J)
Chivas Regal 25 Years Old
The Famous Grouse Scottish Oak Finish

Irish Pure Pot Still
Midleton 1973 Pure Pot Still

Irish Single Malt
The Tyrconnell Agd 10 Yrs Madeira Finish
Bushmills Select Casks Aged 12 Years
Bushmills Rare Aged 21 Years

Irish Blends
Jameson

American Single Malt
McCarthy's Oregon Single Malt Agd 3 Yrs
Stranahan's Colorado Whiskey No. 1
Stranahan's Colorado Whiskey No. 23
Bourbon
Ancient Ancient Age 10 Years Old
Cougar Bourbon Aged 5 Years
Willett Aged 17 Years Barrel Proof
Woodford Reserve Master's Collection Four Grain
American Straight Rye
Cougar Rye
Rathskeller Rye
Rittenhouse Very Rare 21 YO Barrel 8
Canadian Blended
Alberta Premium 25 Years Old
Danfield's Limited Edition Aged 21 Years
Wiser's Legacy
Wiser's Red Letter
Japanese Single Malt
The Hakushu Aged 15 Years Cask Strength
Hakushu 1984
Ichiro's Card "Four of Spades"
The Cask of Yamazaki 1993 Heavily Peated
Yoichi Key Malt Agd 12 Yrs "Peaty & Salty"
Yoichi 20 Years Old
Pure Malt Black
Japanese Single Grain
Nikka Single Cask Coffey Grain 1992
Japanese Blended
Royal Aged 15 Years
Finnish Single Malt
Old Buck
Swedish Single Malt
Mackmyra Privus 04 Ratta Virket
Welsh Single Malt
Penderyn
Penderyn Welsh Rugby Union 125th Anniversary Edition
Australian Single Malt
Sullivans Cove 6 Years Old
Indian Single Malt
Amrut Two Continents Limited Edition
Taiwanese Single Malt
Kavalan Solist Fino Sherry Cask

94.5
Scottish Single Malt
Aberlour a'bunadh Batch No. 20
Aberlour a'bunadh Batch No. 29
Cadenhead's Ardbeg 1994
Balblair 1975
The BenRiach Aged 15 Years Pedro Ximinez Sherry Wood Finish
The BenRiach 30 Years Old
Bruichladdich Infinity Third Edition
Single & Single Bunnahabhain 1976 Aged 31 Years Special Edition
Matisse Carpedonich 1972 Highland Malt
The GlenDronach Grandeur Aged 31 Years

The Whisky Agency Glendullan 1981
Glenfarclas Family Casks 1990 Release V
Glenfarclas 1995 45° Heritage Malt Collection
Whisky Doris Ballindalloch
Glenfiddich 15 Years Old
Glen Grant Cellar Reserve 1992
Duncan Taylor Collection Glen Grant 1972
Gordon & MacPhail Glen Grant 1962
The Glenlivet 1973 Cellar Collection
Kingsbury's Finest & Rarest Glenlivet 1978
Murray McDavid Glenlivet 1977 Agd 30 Yrs
Highland Park 1970 Orcadian Vintage
Mackillop's Choice Highland Park 1973
The Arran Malt Sherry Single Cask 1996
The Arran Malt Bourbon Single Cask 1998
The Arran Malt Single Sherry Cask 1998
Lagavulin 12 Year Old
Laphroaig 27 Years Old
Gordon & MacPhail Longmorn 1969
The Whisky Fair Lochnagar 1972
Cadenhead's Strathisla Aged 21 Years
Duncan Taylor Collection Tomatin 1976
Mackillop's Choice Tominoul 1989
Scottish Vatted Malt
John McDougall's Selection Islay Malt 1993
Scottish Blends
Highland Dream 12 Years Old
Irish Single Malt
Green Spot
American Single Malt
McCarthy's
Stranahan's Colorado Whiskey Batch 22
Stranahan's Colorado Whiskey Batch 27
Stranahan's Colorado Whiskey Batch 49
Bourbon
Parker's Heritage Collection
American Straight Rye
Rittenhouse Aged 25 Years Barrel 30
Thomas H Handy Sazerac
Canadian Blended
Royal Reserve Gold
Japanese Single Malt
Ichiro's "Ace of Diamonds" Hanyu 1986
French Single Malt
Kornog Taouarc'h Kentan
Welsh Single Malt
Penderyn bott code Jul 08
Penderyn Madeira
Penderyn Sherrywood Edition
Australian Single Malt
Sullivans Cove Cask Strength
Indian Single Malt
The Ultimate Amrut 2005 Cask Strength

94
Scottish Single Malt
Aberlour 10 Years Old
Scott's Selection Ardbeg 1992
Ardmore 100th Anniversary 12 Years Old
Old Malt Cask Auchentoshan Agd 17 Yrs

Old Malt Cask Auchroisk Aged 33 Years
Balblair 1978
Bladnoch Aged 10 Years
Bowmore 30 Years Old
Exclusive Casks Bowmore 1998 Agd 10 Yrs
Scotch Malt Whisky Society Cask 3.135
Aged 7 Years (Bowmore)
Bruichladdich 1991 Aged 16 Years
Bruichladdich 1993
Bruichladdich Special Edition International
Malt Whisky Festival, Gent 2008
Bruichladdich Infinity Second Edition
Bruichladdich Sherry Edition 1992 "Fino"
Octomore 2_140 Aged 5 Years Edition 02.1
Port Charlotte First Cut 27/05/07
Berry's' Own Selection Bruichladdich 1991
Aged 15 Years
Cadenhead's Bruichladdich Aged 15 Years
Bunnahabhain Aged 18 Years
The Whisky Agency Bunnahabhain 1967
Berrys' Own Selection Caol Ila 2000
Old Malt Cask Caol Ila Aged 26 Years
Old Masters Caol Ila Aged 25 Years
Scotch Malt Whisky Society Cask 53.141
Aged 20 Years (Caol Ila)
The Scotch Single Malt Circle Caol Ila 1982
Duncan Taylor Caperdonich 1972 cask 3246
Duncan Taylor Caperdonich 1972 cask 7422
James MacArthur's Clynelish Agd 12 Yrs
Scotch Malt Whisky Society Cask 26.55
Aged 8 Years (Clynelish)
Chieftain's Dalmore 13 YO Pinot Noir Finish
Old Malt Cask Dalmore Aged 32 Years
Scotch Malt Whisky Society Cask 104.10
Aged 33 Years
The GlenDronach Single Cask 1993
Glenfarclas 1954 The Family Casks
Glenfarclas 1970 The Family Casks
Glenfarclas 1987 Ltd Rare Bottling - No. 13
Glenfarclas 1989 The Family Casks
Glenfiddich 1973 Vintage
Duncan Taylor Glen Garioch 1988
Mackillop's Choice Glen Garioch 1990
Glenglassaugh 21 Year Old
Glengoyne 13 Years Old Single Cask 1995
Glen Grant Cask Strength Aged 17 Years
Old Malt Cask Glen Grant Aged 32 Years
Glenkinchie Agd 15 Yrs The Distillers Edition
The Glenlivet Nadurra Aged 16 Years
Berrys' Own Selection Glenlivet 1982
Old Malt Cask Glenlivet Aged 30 Years
Berrys' Own Selection Glenlossie 1975
Berry's Own Selection Glen Mhor 1982
Glenmorangie 10 Years Old
Glenmorangie Nectar D'or Sauternes Finish
Glen Moray 1962 Rare Vintage Agd 42 Yrs
Glen Moray 1991 Mountain Oak Malt The
Final Release
Cadenhead's Glenrothes-Glenlivet 1994

Scotch Malt Whisky Society Cask 63.22
Aged 18 Years (Glentauchers)
Duncan Taylor Collection Glenugie 1981
Kingsbury Handwriting Highland Park 15 YO
Oklahoma Single Malt Lovers Highland
Park Single Cask Aged 27 Years
Scotch Malt Whisky Society Cask 4.133
Aged 13 Years (Highland Park)
The Arran Malt Pineau des Charentes Finish
Cadenhead's Arran Aged 11 Years
Victoria Single Malt Club Arran 10 Years Old
The Manager's Choice Knockando
Knockdhu 23 Years Old
Laphroaig 18 Years Old
Laphroaig Aged 25 Years
Laphroaig Aged 30 Years
Laphroaig Aged 40 Years
Old & Rare Laphroaig Aged 20 Years
Croftengea Heavily Peated Cask No.1
Distillery Select
Old Malt Cask Lochside Aged 14 Years
Montgomeries Longmorn 1975
Scotch Malt Whisky Society Cask 7.55 Aged
40 Years (Longmorn)
The Macallan 1989
Macallan Cask Strength
The Macallan Easter Elchies Seasonal Cask
Selection Winter Choice 14 Years Old
The Macallan Fine Oak 15 Years Old
Gordon & MacPhail Macallan 1938
Heiko Thieme's 1974 Macallan 65th
Birthday Bottling
The Whisky Agency Miltonduff 1980
Rarest of the Rare Mosstowie 1975
Old Malt Cask Port Ellen Aged 24 Years
The Whisky Fair Port Ellen Aged 25 Years
Longrow Aged 18 Years
The Secret Treasures Springbank 1970
Strathisla Distillery Edition 15 Years Old
Old & Rare Tamdhu Aged 19 Years
Master of Malt Tomatin 19 Years Old
Old Malt Cask Tomatin Aged 31 Years
Tomintoul With A Peaty Tang
Tullibardine 1966
The Whisky Fair Tullibardine 1976
Adelphi's Liddesdale Agd 18 Yrs Batch 1
Smokehead Extra Black Aged 18 Years
Old Malt Cask Speyside's Finest Agd 41 Yrs

Scottish Vatted Malt
Clan Denny
The Famous Grouse 30 Years Old Malt
Sheep Dip 'Old Hebridean' 1990

Scottish Grain
Clan Denny Caledonian Aged 44 Years
Kingsbury Carsebridge 41 Years Old 1964
Duncan Taylor Invergordon 1965 cask 15517
Duncan Taylor Invergordon 1965 cask 15519
Duncan Taylor Invergordon 1965 cask 15528
Loch Lomond 2000 Cask No. 37700

Scottish Blends
  Ballantine's Aged 30 Years
  Black Grouse
  Duncan Taylor Collection Rarest of the Rare
Deluxe Blend 33 Years Old
  Isle of Skye 8 Years Old
  William Grant's Family Reserve
Irish Pure Pot Still
  Redbreast 15 Years Old
Irish Single Malt
  Connemara Cask Strength
  Connemara Turf Mór Small Batch Collection
  Cadenhead's Cooley Aged 15 Years
  Knappogue Castle 1992
  The Whisky Fair Connemara Aged 15 Years
Irish Blends
  Bushmills 1608
American Single Malt
  Edgefield Hogshead
  Stranahan's Colorado Whiskey Batch 8
  Stranahan's Colorado Whiskey Batch 41
  Triple 8 Notch
Bourbon
  Blanton's Single Barrel No. 53
  Blanton's Single Barrel No. 477
  Jim Beam Black Aged 8 Years
  Knob Creek Aged 9 Years
  Old Forester Birthday Bourbon
  Old Taylor Aged 6 Years (Old Bottling)
  Wild Turkey Russell's Reserve 10
American Single Malt Rye
  Old Potrero Essay 10-SRW-ARM-E
American Straight Rye
  Pappy Van Winkle's Family Reserve 13 YO
  Rittenhouse 100 Proof Bottled in Bond
  Rittenhouse Very Rare 21 YO Barrel 14
  Rittenhouse Very Rare 21 YO Barrel 21

  Rittenhouse Very Rare 21 YO Barrel 23
  Rittenhouse Very Rare 21 YO Barrel 27
  Rittenhouse Aged 25 Years Barrel 23
  Rittenhouse Aged 25 Years Barrel 29
Japanese Single Malt
  Scotch Malt Whisky Society Cask 120.05
Aged 17 Years (Hakushu)
  Suntory Pure Malt Hakushu Aged 20 Years
  Karuizawa 1971
  Karuizawa 1979 Aged 24 Years
  Karuizawa 1986 Aged 17 Years
  Shirakawa 32 Years Old Single Malt
  Yamazaki 1984
  The Yamazaki Aged 15 Years Cask Strength
  Nikka Whisky Yoichi 1986 20 Years Old
Japanese Blended
  Nikka Master Blend 12 YO 70th Anniversary
  Nikka Whisky Tsuru Aged 17 Years
  Special Reserve 10 Years Old
German Single Malt
  Sloupisti 4 Years (Cask Strength)
Liechtenstein Single Malt
  Telsington
Swedish Single Malt
  Mackmyra Privus 02 Näsa För Sprit
Swiss Single Malt
  Swissky Exklusiv Abfüllung
  Edition Käser Castle One Single Malt
Welsh Single Malt
  Penderyn bott code Jan 08
  Penderyn bott code Jul 09
Australian Single Malt
  Bakery Hill Classic Malt Cask Strength
Indian Single Malt
  Amrut Peated
  Amrut Peated Cask Strength Ltd Edition
  Stillman's Dram Limited Edition

Scottish Malts

For those of you deciding to take the plunge and head off into the labyrinthine world of Scotch malt whisky, a piece of advice. And that is, be careful who you take your advice from. Because, too often, I hear that you should leave the Islays until you have tackled the featherlight Speysiders and the bolder, weightier Highlanders. This is just complete, patronising nonsense. The only time that rings true is if you are tasting a number of whiskies in one day. Then leave the smoky ones last, so the lighter chaps get a fair hearing.

I know many people who didn't like whisky until they got a Talisker from Skye inside them, or a Lagavulin to swamp their tastebuds with oily iodine. The fact is, you can take your map of malt whisky, start at any point and head in whichever direction you feel. There are no hard and fast rules. Certainly with nearly 3,000 tasting notes for Scottish malts here you should have some help in picking where this journey of a lifetime begins.

It is also worth remembering not to be seduced by age. It is true that some of the highest scores are given to big-aged whiskies. But they are the exception rather than the rule: the truth is that the majority of malts, once they have lived beyond 20 years or so, suffer from oak influence rather than benefit. Part of the fun of discovering whiskies is to see how malts from different distilleries perform to age and type of cask.

Happy discovering.

ORKNEY
ISLANDS
Highland Park
Scapa

Pultney

Clynelish
Brora

Balblair
Glenmorangie
Dalmore
Invergordon
Teaninich
Glenglassaugh
Banff†
Macduff
Glen Ord
Speyside see page 24
Royal Brackla
Knockdhu
Inverness
Tomatin
Glendronach
Glenugie
Glen Albyn
Glen Mhor
Ardmore
Millburn
Glen
Garioch
Speyside Distillery
Royal Lochnagar
Aberdeen
Dalwhinnie
Glenury Royal
Fettercairn
Ben Nevis
Blair Athol
Glencadam
Glenesk†
Fort William
Edradour
North Port
Glenlochy
Lochside
Aberfeldy
Dundee
Glenturret
Perth
Daftmill
Tullibardine
Deanston
Cameronbridge
ch Lomond
Glengoyne
Dumbarton
Rosebank†
Interleven
St. Magdelene
Glenkinchie
†Littlemill
Edinburgh
hentoshan
Glasgow
North British
Strathclyde
Port Dundas

Girvan
Ailsa Bay
Ladyburn

Bladnoch

Key

● **Major Town or City**

▲ Single Malt Distillery

▲ (*Italics*) Grain Distillery

† Dead Distillery

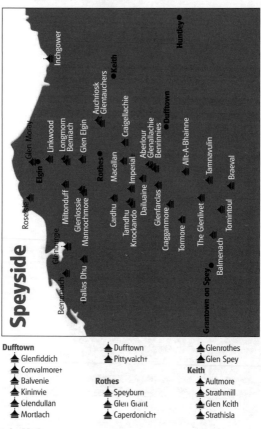

Speyside

Dufftown
🔺 Glenfiddich
🔺 Convalmore†
🔺 Balvenie
🔺 Kininvie
🔺 Glendullan
🔺 Mortlach

🔺 Dufftown
🔺 Pittyvaich†

Rothes
🔺 Speyburn
🔺 Glen Grant
🔺 Caperdonich†

🔺 Glenrothes
🔺 Glen Spey

Keith
🔺 Aultmore
🔺 Strathmill
🔺 Glen Keith
🔺 Strathisla

Single Malts
ABERFELDY

Highlands (Perthshire), 1898. John Dewar & Sons. Working.

Aberfeldy Aged 12 Years bott no. A44103 db **(88.5) n22.5** the signature honey aroma is still there and intact but a subtle smokiness appears to have developed adding extra depth; **t23** busy delivery with the mildly waxy barley having much to say: spice prickle early on followed by some early chocolate toffee; **f21** luxuriant mouthfeel, the honey now tends towards the honeycomb variety and then Canadian, but still plenty of toffee which hushes proceedings; **b22** a lovely whisky which could be improved overnight to true brilliance by simply increasing the strength to the 46% that malt lovers these days expect and a reduction in the colour. A non-chill filtered, non-coloured policy would see this become a Premiership dram in the time it takes to brew the coffee for the marketing meeting which decides it... 40%

⋰ **Aberfeldy Aged 18 Years "Chris Anderson's Cask"** db **(90) n24** brimming with enormous energy and freshness: plays the range from bourbon-rich red liquorice right down to diced kumquat; sharp, angular, bold, salty and very enticing; not a single blemish in distillate or wood...fabulous; **t23.5** sharp delivery with a mouth watering malty juiciness, but also weighty, too, with heavy oaks immediately apparent. Any threatening bitterness is seen off by a light dusting of muscovado and dried dates; **f21.5** bites deep and caramels out; **b22** had the natural caramels just not ticked over a little too exuberantly, this would have headed for a very high score. Aberfeldy in a very unusual light...54.9% 248 bottles.

Aberfeldy Aged 21 Years db **(91) n22** exotic fruit, under-ripe crushed ground cherry and some honey – what else..? **t23.5** sensual delivery that would be recognized and wholly appreciated by fans of Highland Park thanks to the busy honey and semi-hidden waves of smoke; a few oaky touches appear early but enhance in a toasty rather than life-threatening way; the spices rave early on then settle; **f22.5** a gentlemanly exit with its honeyed head held high to the last; no oaky screaming and shouting, just a few bitter-sweet farewells; **b23** a much improved dram which is truer to the Aberfeldy style than earlier bottlings. Very high class malt which confidently underlines this distillery's excellence. 40%

Aberfeldy Aged 25 Years db (85) **n24 t21 f19 b21.** Just doesn't live up to the nose. When Tommy Dewar wrote, "We have a great regard for old age when it is bottled," as quoted on the label, I'm not sure he had as many as 25 years in mind. 40%. 150 bottles to mark opening of Dewar's World of Whisky.

⦂ **A.D. Rattray Aberfeldy 1994** cask no. 4007, dist Jun 94, bott Dec 09 (82) **n20 t23 f19 b20.** All about the big upfront maltiness on delivery which is simply superb. Don't expect the same excellence from the nose and finish, though. 57.3% A.D. Rattray Ltd

Connoisseurs Choice Aberfeldy 1989 Aged 18 Years refill sherry hogshead, dist Sep 1989, bott Oct 2007 (89) **n22 t22.5 f22 b22.5.** A very good distillery in excellent voice. 43%

⦂ **Connoisseurs Choice Aberfeldy 1990** (85.5) **n21.5 t22 f21 b21.** Silky malt but perhaps a bit too much sheen on the vanilla-led finish. 43% Gordon & MacPhail

⦂ **Duthies Aberfeldy 14 Years Old** (86) **n21 t21.5 f22 b21.5.** Clean, almost crunchy barley. A very attractive degree of juiciness, too. 46% Wm. Cadenhead Ltd

Old Malt Cask Aberfeldy Aged 14 Years refill hogshead, dist Jun 94, bott Mar 09 (86) **n21 t21.5 f22 b21.5.** Unusual to see 'Feldy in such an aggressive mood. And, as it happens, this is pretty enjoyable fare if occasionally on the thin side. The semi-thick malt really zaps into the tastebuds but the harsh vanilla has the most profound words. 50%. Douglas Laing. 338 bottles.

⦂ **Old Malt Cask Aberfeldy Aged 26 Years** refill hogshead no. DL 6214, dist Nov 83, bott May 10 (88) **n23** A lovely salty tang to this one, ensuring the barley comes through loud and clear. The good age means the oak has been to work, too, offering a pleasant degree of apricot and under-ripe raspberry, as well as a hint of something slightly more south sea island-ish, as well as something a little less exotic in the form of creamy butterscotch candy; **t23** immediate lift off with that barley rocketing into taste buds; a pleasant marriage of varying sugar tones; **f20** disappointing bitterness from the exhausted oak; **b22** goes swimmingly well until the finale. But loads of quality en route. 50% Douglas Laing. 270 bottles.

ABERLOUR
Speyside, 1826. Chivas Bros. Working.

Aberlour 10 Years Old bott 07 db (94) **n24** the grape is fresh, succulent and sultana-studded; the bourbon element is, well....bourbony, with some lovely liquorice and honey phrases somehow finding a perfect balance with the sherry; **t24** the body is shapely and dying to be caressed with a silky, skimpy grapiness barely covering the naked liquorice-honey beneath; the spiced oak slaloms around the palate without coming to grief showing a balance and poise that astounds; **f22.5** some toffee notes creep in from somewhere and reduce the shine but the vanilla-barley fade is still rather charming; **b23.5** this has been a malt changing slightly in style each time I come to taste a dram of it – which is quite often, as it happens. However, this bottling is about as good as it gets, with the marriage between bourbon and sherry cask as harmonious and angst-free as you are likely to find. The best rendition of this original old distillery bottling I have tasted, without any doubt. Forget all the PR, hype and egos: bottlings like this confirm that this distillery now stands above all others as Chivas' finest. 43%

Aberlour 10 Years Old Sherry Cask Finish db (85) **n21 t21 f21 b22.** Bipolar and bitter-sweet with the firmness of the grain in vivid contrast to the gentle grape. 43%

Aberlour 12 Years Old Double Cask Matured db (88.5) **n22** pretty unsubtle grape but sweet and attractive; **t22.5** serious juice at first drowns the barley but the oaky-spice heralds its return; **f22** delicate barley remnants; **b22** voluptuous and mouth-watering in some areas, firmer and less expansive in others. Pretty tasty in all of them. 43%

Aberlour 12 Years Old Sherry Cask Matured db (88) **n23** dry sherry and make no mistake; **t22** silky, juicy delivery; cramped slightly by a background bitterness; spices take their time but arrive eventually; **f21** double dry finale thanks to both big oak and the sherry influence; **b22** could do with some very delicate extra balancing sweetness to take it to the next level. Sophisticated nonetheless. 40%

Aberlour 13 Years Old sherry cask, hand fill db (84) **n21 t22 f20 b21.** Skimps on the complexity. 58.8%

Aberlour 15 Year Old Double Cask Matured db (84) **n23 t22 f19 b20.** Brilliant nose full of vibrant apples and spiced sultana, but then, after a complex, chewy, malt-enriched kick-off, falls surprisingly flat on its face. 40%

Aberlour 15 Years Cuvee Marie d'Ecosse db (**91**) n22 fresh sherry trace with kumquats and lime for extra zest; t24 beautifully ethereal with the malt drifting in all directions while the fruit offers no weight at all; f22 light vanilla apologetically drifts into the picture. The smoke of old has gone; b23 this always was a deceptive lightweight, and it's got lighter still. It is sold primarily in France, and one can assume only that this is God's way of making amends for that pretentious, over-rated, caramel-ridden rubbish called Cognac they've had to endure. *43%*

Aberlour 15 Year Old Sherry Finish db (**91**) n24 exceptionally clever use of oak to add a drier element to the sharper boiled cooking apple. And a whiff of the fermenting vessel, too. Love it! t22 the sharp fruit of the nose is magnified here ten times for one of the strangest mouth arrivals I've ever come across: the roof of the mouth won't know what's hit it; f23 wave upon wave of malt concentrate; b22 quite unique: freaky, even. Really a whisky to be discovered and ridden. Once you acclimatize, you'll adore it. *43%*

Aberlour 16 Years Old Double Cask Matured bott 2008/01/14 db (**93.5**) n23.5 from the Aberlour 10 school of brilliant noses: the quality of the sherry butts used is as good as you'll find today with their clean, inspirational gently spiced clarity offering sufficient permeability to allow both barley and oak to breath and prosper; t23.5 mouth-cleansing delivery with the clean Sauternes-esque grape polishing every tastebud; the decent weight is just about perfect for its style; again the spices are no more than a distant rumble and the barley breaks out for the relaxed stroll; f23 remains delicate for all the weight; the mild treacle and waxed honey finale satisfies; b23.5 another expression which has been greatly enhanced of late and this one to the . The most improved distillery in terms of house bottlings across the board in recent years? There is a very good case for it. *43%*

Aberlour 18 Years Old db (**91**) n22 thick milkshake with various fruits and vanilla; t22 immediate fresh juice which curdles beautifully as the vanilla is added; f24 wonderful fruit-chocolate fudge development: long, and guided by a gentle oiliness; b23 another high performance distillery age-stated bottling. *43%*

Aberlour 100 Proof db (**91**) n23 beneath this sherried, volcanic start there is something rather sweet and honied. One of the most two-toned noses you'll find in a long while; t23 sweet to begin and honied, too. The maltiness keeps its shape for some time. Between the middle and end an ebulliient spiciness takes hold f22 massively long and fruity; b23 stunning, sensational whisky, the most extraordinary Speysider of them all ...which it was when I wrote those official notes for the bottling back in '97, I think. Other malts have superseded it now, but on re-tasting I stand by those original notes, though I disassociate myself entirely with the rubbish: "In order to savour Aberlour 100 at its best add 1/3 to 1/2 pure water. *57.1%*

Aberlour a'bunadh Batch No. 15 db (**84**) n20 t20 f23 b21. A rogue lightly sulphured cask has taken the edge of this one. A shame. No: bloody annoying!! *59.6%. ncf.*

Aberlour a'bunadh Batch No. 16 db (**87**) n71 t23 f22 b21. For this to happen once is bad for a world-great dram. Twice in a row is close to being the stuff of nightmares. The real shame is that this could so easily have been 2007 Whisky Bible Whisky of the Year, because some of the other casks still bear the hallmark of greatness...I could weep. *59.6%. ncf.*

Aberlour a'bunadh Batch No. 17 db (**88**) n22 t23 f21 b22. If you don't like sherried whiskies, give this one a miss. *60.2%*

Aberlour a'bunadh Batch No. 19 db (**95**) n24 t24 f23 b24. It is a sherried malt such as this that makes my daily encounter with sulphur-ruined dross entirely worthwhile. *59.9%*

Aberlour a'bunadh Batch No. 20 db (**94.5**) n23 quite magnificent sherry: sweet, clean, viscous even on the nose, ebullient, proud and teasingly spiced; t24.5 a perfect translation onto the palate, except for the added bonus of the spices being even more forthcoming and the grapiness having something of the noble rot: outstanding... f23.5 chocolate raisin; b23.5 absolutely all that can be asked of a sherry-matured single malt. *60.5%*

Aberlour a'bunadh Batch No. 22 db (**83.5**) n20 t21 f21.5 b21. Thick grape but a docile mustiness acts as a straightjacket; overall, plenty to get on with, but never sparkles. And such is the high stall Aberlour has set itself in recent years, nothing but the best will do.... *59.3%. ncf. Chivas Bros, Italian market.*

Aberlour a'bunadh Batch No. 23 db (**96**) n24.5 honeycomb, molasses – almost demerera rum style - and that even before we start getting to the myriad layers of sherry. This, in your mind's eye, is how you dream a sherry cask whisky to be: clean, vaguely spiced grape, offering a delicate texture, lightness of touch and yet unfathomable depth...and not a sulphur molecule in sight: well not many, anyway...; t24.5 fabulous double whammy of intense, well-aged bourbon and chunky fruit, both shrill and demanding, colliding head on like two express trains on the same track; the resulting explosion is both enormous and yet seemingly soft, as if in slow motion; burnt raisins abound - the usual fruitcake stuff - and yet the saliva glands are stirred into overdrive by the most gorgeous clean fruit crescendo; f23 long, a slow dissipation of spices, loads of chewy fudge and a very slight sulphur pick up which knocks a mark off.... b24 my word: just so close to being the perfect whisky. There are one or two sherry butts used in this bottling which, individually, must be verging on perfect. Even taking into account my total inability to accept anything sulphurous, I have to say this is a masterpiece of a malt and possibly one less than perfect cask away from being among the top three bottles of Speyside whisky I've ever come across. There is no doubting in my mind that this brand has now become the most eagerly anticipated of not just all Speyside's regular bottlings but the world's. Perhaps part of the fun is that there is a degree of uncertainty to just how good it will be. But when on song this is a whisky searching every liquor store you can to find. This one was just so close to being a world champion... 60.2%

Aberlour a'bunadh Batch No. 25 db (82.5) n21.5 t20.5 f20 b20.5 Oh dear. One or two less than brilliant casks have sneaked in and spoiled the usual party. 60.4%

Aberlour a'bunadh Batch No. 26 db (95) n24.5 bizarre and stunning: picking this up and sniffing absent-mindedly, I genuinely thought it was pot still demerara rum....!!! Absolutely caked in molassed and fruity esters. Sniff deeper and there is a montage of juicy dates and plums ripe enough to explode; on another level we have the ultra rich marriage of Dundee cake and Bakewell Tart. Non-peated malt whisky noses don't get much thicker than this...; t23 oddly, nothing like as towering as the nose: the easily identifiable juicy barley actually does a good job of thinning out the bigger fruit though for a while there is a slight off-key squabble; only towards the middle is balance re-established as milk chocolate notes begin to have a calming effect; f24 brilliant....ffom the most huge nose to something of a civil war on delivery the story ends with a charmingly elegant chocolate mousse and plum pudding mix...; b23.5 another fabulous and enthralling adventure from now one of the truly great brands that is always one of the highlights of the whisky-tasting year to discover. 60.6%

⌐⌐ **Aberlour a'bunadh Batch No. 27** db (82) n21 t21.5 f18.5 b21. More than the odd dud sherry butt. Shame, because some of the intensity of the ginger and Demerara could have made for something ultra special. 60%

⌐⌐ **Aberlour a'bunadh Batch No. 28** db (93.5) n22.5 firm but fruity. A dusty dryness; t24 thrilling delivery: puckering oak and fruit, then a slowly unravelling of liquorice, hickory and mocha; some cherry cake offers the sweeter moments; f23.5 long, remaining massive and intact with jaffa and ginger cakes vying with the chocolate cup cake for supremacy. An iritiatingly dry fade but spices and a late dememara rum surge compensate; b23.5 those of you who like your malts to be quiet in the glass and offer little more than a barley whine, don't even bother. Though there is evidence of a mildly off key sherry butt, such is the uncompromising enormity of all else you cannot be other than blown away. X-rated malt for grownups, with the odd tart amongst class acts. 59.8%

⌐⌐ **Aberlour a'bunadh Batch No. 29** db (94.5) n23.5 rich coffee: very similar to pre-coloured Demerara pot still at seven or eight years; toffee apple and a touch of burnt toast; t24 a degree of puckering dryness suggests good age, then layers of honey of varying thickness and intensity; hickory and crème brulee in the middle ground with a wonderfully moist Lubec marzipan offering the flourish; f23.5 back to the caramel but spices arrive so late they are almost an afterthought. But they work well; b23.5 and indulgent malt lashing on the toffee creams. Assured, with not a single false step from beginning to end. World class. 59.9%

⌐⌐ **Aberlour a'bunadh Batch No. 30** bott Mar 10 db (87.5) n23 a big, fruity signature with succulent dates and dried blackberries; a nipping dryness points towards a particular type of cask; t23.5 now in its element as a huge wave of fruit and honey cascade down upon the taste buds; wonderful weight and structure and a light coppery sheen; f19 a bitter note slowly creeps in, b22 though a renegade cask has slipped through the net, some moments are breathtaking. Oh, what might have been...! 59.8%

Berry's Own Selection Aberlour 1995 bott 09 (85) n21 t22 f21 b21. Plenty of fresh barley and the odd wave of tannin. 46%. Berry Bros & Rudd.

Cadenhead's Authentic Collection Aberlour Aged 12 Years port hogshead, dist 95, bott Sep 07 (92.5) n23 t23 f23.5 b23. A real treat of a Speysider making full use of its bruising, big fruity strength. Everything you could ask of such a cask. 58.2%. 252 bottles.

Cadenhead's Authentic Collection Aberlour Aged 18 Years sherry hogshead, matured in oak cask, dist 89, bott Jun 08 (91) n22 a curiously salty nip to the barley and jackfruit; t23.5 salivating, intense almost petulant barley refuses to play second fiddle to the fruit, which is on a slow burn; shards of honey pepper the proceedings f22.5 back to some salty notes with fabulous vanilla-fruit layering: the elegance is enough to make one swoon; b23 quite simply: wonderful! And for Aberlour fans, a bottling which shows the distillery in a subtly different light. 58%.

⠿ **The Coopers Choice Aberlour 1992 Aged 17 Years** (84) n21.5 t21.5 f21 b20. Clean, grassy, as simplistic as they come. And nothing like its 17 years. *46%*

Duncan Taylor The NC2 Range Aberlour Aged 11 Years dist 95, bott 07 (84.5) n21 t22.5 f21 b20. A brief flowering of charming, sweet, gristy malt gives a fascinating insight into Aberlour thanks to an older cask. *46%. nc ncf.*

⠿ **Milroy's of Soho Aberlour 1991** hogshead, cask no. 101278, dist Sep 91, bott Feb 10 (85) n20.5 t23 f20.5 b21. Just one quick sniff is enough to tell you the cask isn't going to be of much use. So all the workload is borne by the quality of the malt. Thankfully, that is extremely high, so you are treated to a fabulous exhibition of mouth watering barley at its most impressively weighted. A lesser distillery than Aberlour would have buckled. *46% Milroy's of Soho. 314 bottles.*

Old Malt Cask Aberlour Aged 17 Years refill hogshead, cask no. 4275, dist Nov 90, bott May 08 (85.5) n21 t21.5 f22 b21. Even the odd shard of rich barley cannot entirely overcome the tiredness on this. Still mouth-watering and attractive, though, and for those who prefer their martinis dry. *50%. Douglas Laing. 335 bottles.*

Old Malt Cask Aberlour Aged 21 Years refill hogshead, cask no. 3933, dist Oct 86, bott Oct 07 (90) n22 t23 f22.5 b22.5. An ultra-friendly well-mannered malt with not a single degree of aggression. *50%. nc ncf. Douglas Laing. 277 bottles.*

Old Malt Cask Aberlour Aged 22 Years refill hogshead, dist Oct 86, bott Dec 08 (87) n21 docile and shows little of its age. A sprig of ginger and mint offsets the otherwise conservative nose; t22.5 mouth-watering and barley laden; f22 long-ash with a touch of burnt toast bittering up the sugars; a spicy buzz completes the score; b21.5 tasted blind, I'd never have recognised this as Aberlour, except for the sprig o' mint on the nose, perhaps. Composed and steady stuff. *50%. Douglas Laing. 295 bottles.*

Provenance Aberlour Aged 12 Years refill hogshead, cask no. 4254, dist Spring 96, bott Spring 08 (83) n22 t21 f20 b20. Malty, firm blending fodder. *46%. nc ncf. Douglas Laing.*

Scott's Selection Aberlour 1990 bott 07 (86) n21.5 t22 f21 b21.5. A sprig o' mint on the nose sets off a familiar Aberlour, crisp malty, bitter-sweet style. *51.1%*

ABHAINN DEARG
Isle of Lewis, 2008. Working.

⠿ **Abhainn Dearg New Make** db (88) n21.5 t23 f21.5 b22. OK. I admit that the 1,001st new whisky for the 2011 Bible isn't whisky at all, but new make. But, as the Isle of Lewis has made it impossible for me not to visit there by now being an official whisky-making island, I thought it was worth celebrating. The new make in this form is rich, clean and malty but with a much heightened metallic feel to it, both on nose and taste, by comparison to other recently-opened distilleries. This is likely to change markedly over time as the stills settle in. So I had better start looking at the Cal-Mac Ferry timetables to go and find out for myself if it does... *Sample from cask at Whiskyfair Limburg 2010*

ALLT-A-BHAINNE
Speyside, 1975. Chivas Bros. Working.

Chester Whisky & Liquer Co. Allt-A-Bhainne Aged 12 Years dist 96 (78.5) n19 t21 f19 b19.5. One of the weirder whiskies tasted for the 2010 Bible, almost worth collecting in its own right for its oddity alone. Nosed and tasted blind I would have sworn this was from a Holstein still in Germany. Even so, sweet and drinkable but nothing like I would have expected from this distillery. *54.3%*

⠿ **Connoisseurs Choice Allt-A-Bhainne 1995** dist 1995 (88) n21.5 Lincoln biscuit: light, a hint of oil and a sugary coating; t22 fresh barley, lightly salivating as sugar leads the way; f22.5 longer and more complex thanks to the ever-increasing oak participation; b22 almost beautiful in its stark simplicity. *43% Gordon & MacPhail*

Deerstalker Allt-A-Bhainne Aged 12 Years (88) n22 soft barley and toffee fudge; a pleasant ice-cream vanilla touch; t22.5 juicy, lively delivery with a pleasant sugar coating; thickens towards the middle as the oils, vanilla and caramel congregate; f21.5 dogged caramel stalks the tastebuds and hunts down the barley; b22 even though uncoloured, caramel, one presumes naturally extracted from the wood, plays a large part here, especially at the fade. *46%. nc ncf.*

Forbes Ross Allt-A-Bhainne 1992 Aged 15 Years dist 92, bott 07 (84) n22 t22 f20 b20. The fun is all up-front on the charming nose and sweet barley delivery. *43%. Forbes Ross & Co.*

Old Malt Cask Allt-A-Bhainne Aged 17 Years (79) n21 t22 f18 b18. Something distinctly virginal about this 17 year old: it's certainly never seen any wood worth mentioning.... *50%*

Old Malt Cask Allt-A-Bhaine Aged 17 Years refill hogshead, dist Jun 91, bott Dec 08 (84.5) n19.5 t23 f21 b21. For all the evidence of fading glory and slightly over enthusiastic oak, there is much on the punchy, spicy, bourbon-sweetened delivery to celebrate. Almost diametrically opposed to the last Original Malt Cask 17 I tasted from this distillery!! 50%.

Old Masters Allt-A-Bhainne Aged 11 Years cask no. 107158, dist 96, bott 08 **(60.5)** n17.5 t18 f17 b18. Not even the mega barley and spice can save it from the sulphur. 56.9%. James MacArthur & Co. Ltd.

Provenance Allt-A-Bhainne Aged 11 Years refill hogshead no. 4186, dist Autumn 96, bott Spring 08 **(79.5)** n19 t20 f21 b20. Incredible barley, but starkly immature for its age with almost zero oak input. 46%. Douglas Laing.

∵ **Provenance Allt-A-Bhainnne Over 11 Years** sherry cask no. 5439, dist Winter 1997, bott Summer 2009 **(87)** n22 older than its given years with a massive oak-barley head-on smash; t22 pretty chunky for an Allt-a. A deep glossiness to the oak cannot out-perform the barley; f21.5 good, oils keep the toasty barley lingering; b21.5 presumably from a first-fill ex-bourbon cask. 46% nc ncf Douglas Laing & Co Ltd

∵ **Provenance Allt-A-Bhainne Over 12 Years** dist Winter 1997, bott Spring 2010 **(82)** n19 t20.5 f21.5 b20. Curious. The grape appears to neuter any complexity to the big barley, giving the effect of a malt all dressed up but going nowhere. 46% Douglas Laing

∵ **Robert Graham's Allt a Bhainne 15 Years Old** cask no. 13, dist May 92, bott Nov 07 **(92.5)** n22.5 t24 f23 b23. Apparently this little gem has been sitting around Robert Graham's shop in Edinburgh since Christmas 2007. What a crime. With its fresh gooseberries and greengages dipping in and out of the most palate-cleansing barley imaginable it is a must for those looking for an unusual but ultra high quality Speyside. My guess is that when word gets out there'll be none left by the end of Christmas 2010....!! 43% Robert Graham Ltd. 338 bottles.

ARDBEG

Islay, 1815. Glenmorangie Plc. Working.

Ardbeg 10 Years Old db **(97)** n24 more complex, citrus-led and sophisticated than recent bottlings, though the peat is no less but now simply displayed in an even greater elegance; a beautiful sea salt strain to this; t24 gentle oils carry on them a lemon-lime edge, sweetened by barley and a weak solution of golden syrup; the peat is omnipotent, turning up in every crevice and wave, yet never one once overstepping its boundary; f24 stunningly clean, the oak offers not a bitter trace but rather a vanilla and butterscotch edge to the barley. Again the smoke wafts around in a manner unique in the world of whisky when it comes to sheer élan and adroitness; b25 like when you usually come across something that goes down so beautifully and with such a nimble touch and disarming allure, just close your eyes and enjoy.... 46%

Ardbeg 17 Years Old earlier bottlings db **(92)** n23 t22 f23 b24. OK, I admit I had a big hand in this, creating it with the help of Glenmorangie Plc's John Smith. It was designed to take the weight off the better vintages of Ardbeg whilst ensuring a constant supply around the world. Certainly one of the more subtle expressions you are likely to find, though criticised by some for not being peaty enough. As the whisky's creator, all I can say is they are missing the point. 40%

Ardbeg 17 Years Old later bottlings db **(90)** n22 t24 f22 b23. The peat has all but vanished and cannot really be compared to the original 17-year-old: it's a bit like tasting a Macallan without the sherry: fascinating to see the naked body underneath, and certainly more of a turn on. Peat or no peat, great whisky by any standards. 40%

Ardbeg Guaranteed 30 Years Old db **(91)** n24 t23 f21 b23. An unsual beast, one of the last ever bottled by Allied. The charm and complexity early on is enormous, but the fade rate is surprising. That said, still a dram of considerable magnificence. 40%

Ardbeg 1972 Single Cask No. 2738 db **(92)** n23 t23 f23 b23. Charming. Evocative of a storm-lashed Scottish coastal village with peat reek on the wind and enough lightning and thunder to show this is still alive and kicking. 50%

Ardbeg 1974 Single Cask No. 3151 db **(96)** n24 some concentrated lime has been brought in to lighten the peaty load; the oak is pretty full on, yet plays to the Ardbeg rules of not interrupting the complexity of the smoke; t24 the delivery borders on perfection with the oil being no more than a hint, the smoke offering myriad possibilities and the citrus yo-yoing between sweet and sharp: it is impossible not to close your eyes in pleasure with this one... f23.5 some oil arrives at last to give a gliding effect to the more demonstrative themes; smoky butterscotch is to the fore while a few honey notes begin to gain momentum; b24.5 you cannot find fault with a whisky of this calibre: everything is in order, the intensities are large but never booming or vaguely out of control. There are no off notes, nothing dominates yet every single element found within the malt seems to be effortless: maximum in any other whisky...but not here. It is, quite simply, a dram to die for... 47.7%

Ardbeg 1974 Single Cask No. 3160 db **(92.5)** n23.5 surging oak, but the peat runs at varying bitter-sweet levels to compensate. Plenty of saline, coastal notes to remind you of its provenance; t23.5 delicately sweet with - and this is highly unusual – the barley being clearly detached in its juiciness to the rumbling smoke; f23 dries and does so with aplomb as the oak begin to take hold; vanilla and almost a bready, doughy, yeasty attack. The oaks carry on regardless, but the smoke picks up some of the lighter citrus notes to try and maintain balance; b23 brilliant, but the oaky signature shows that the flag to this great Ardbeg is just beginning to be lowered. *49%*

Ardbeg 1974 Single Cask No. 3524 db **(93)** n24 a malt which appears to lie: this doesn't seem to be anything like in its mid thirties simply because the oak is not just genteel but adds only a further depth to the peat rather than working against it; lots of the house citrus and – and here's a curious trick – breath in deeply through the nose a few moments after you have had your proboscis in the glass for a while and the fabulous sensation of fresh grist greets you; t22.5 almost tame on delivery and the slow build up of the smoke and lemon with barley and vanilla getting in on the act; f23 a short, sharp burst of spice and a dull throb of smoke; the vanillas are quite astounding; b23.5 Ardbeg is, by nature, an understated malt. This almost overstates the understatement... *44.9%*

Ardbeg 1974 Single Cask No. 3528 db **(93.5)** n23.5 now starting to head into bourbon territory despite the smoke: even so, it's citrus that is leading the way with some fragments of mothballs; the smoke drifts around, trying to impose, allowing the toast and honey to develop pleasantly; t23 again, and quite improbably for its age, it's citrus on the delivery with the smoke both making a weighty entrance and then again drifting off into a lighter mode; soft salty, oaky notes underscore the age but amid the many layers are some near weightless marmalade and butterscotch tones; f23 long with pastel shades of all the usual Ardbeg suspects, except late on there's an earthier resonance as the peats congregate; b24 ridiculously delicate for its age. Wonderful. *44.3%*

Ardbeg 1977 db **(96)** n25 t24 f23 b24. When working through the Ardbeg stocks, I earmarked '77 a special vintage, the sweetest of them all. So it has proved. Only the '74 absorbed that extra oak that gave greater all-round complexity. Either way, the quality of the distillate is beyond measure: simply one of the greatest experiences – whisky or otherwise – of your life. *46%*

Ardbeg 1978 db **(91)** n23 t24 f22 b22. An Ardbeg on the edge of losing it because of encroaching oak, hence the decision made by John Smith and I to bottle this vintage early alongside the 17-year-old. Nearly ten years on, still looks a pretty decent bottling, though slightly under strength! *43%*

⸭ **Ardbeg 1992 Single Cask No. 772** 1st fill ex bourbon, dist Apr 92, bott Dec 08 db **(86.5)** n22 t22.5 f21 b21. Curious choice of cask. Rare for a distillery bottling not to take off, but this one comes at you with its hands and legs tied The nose suggests there might be some bitterness further down the line. And there is. The citrus is engaging, though. *55.7% 184 bottles*

⸭ **Ardbeg 1995 Single Cask No. 2761** 2nd fill bourbon, dist Dec 95, bott Mar 10 db **(92.5)** n22.5 light coffee; unusually floral, delicate, salty smoke; t24 mouth watering with an immediate citrus kick. Barely discernable oils, but enough to maximise the lighter than normal phenols. A lovely lemon-orange freshness clings to the palate; f23 sharp marmalade with vanilla delving into the increasingly prickly smoke; b23 textbook Ardbeg from the point of view that its complexity can be gauged only after five or six mouthfuls. A shifting sands of a dram.... *53.3% 228 bottles. For Feis Ile*

Ardbeg 1998 Single Cask No. 1189 db **(87)** n22.5 so dense, hard to make neither head nor tail of it. You can peel away the layers, first with the salty crust, next to something vaguely kumquatish and so on. The trouble is, as lovely as this may be, the smoke is rather clumped together; t22 tangy fruit entangled in salt and mocha; again the peat is kind of lumpy; f21 light oils and a light sprinkling of dark sugars; b21.5 this has been a vintage year for very odd new bottlings of Ardbeg. Yes, I've warmed it and reduced with water (anything!); and yes it is enjoyable. But just not up to snuff on the Ardbeg front for me... *54%*

⸭ **Ardbeg 1998 Single Cask No. 1190** toasted oak hogshead, dist May 98, bott Dec 08 db **(88.5)** n21.5 no surprise about the giant tannin-laced oak input: the smoke is not so much dwarfed as submerged. No shortage of chocolate, though; t23 massive: again the oak dominates beyond belief with a whole bunch of natural caramels and Jaffa cakes hanging onto its tail. The smoke appears lost and bewildered as the oils and spices invade; f22 long, tangy orange; b22 it's the oak behaving like some look-at-me merchant on an annoying reality TV show. Pretty and entertaining, but only to a point. The unique personality of Ardbeg is jettisoned and while this is a lovely if rather OTT dram, not for a second is the distillery recognisable. A fascinating experiment, nonetheless. *54.7% 282 bottles. For Feis Ile*

∵ **Ardbeg 1998 Single Cask No. 1275** 1st fill bourbon barrel, dist May 98, bott Oct 09 db (**87**) **n21** dim; **t22** half-hearted vanilla keeps the smoke under control, with a muscovado edge; **f22** delicate vanilla with a soft smoke fade; **b22** enjoyable but lacking a bit of the usual Ardbeg charisma and vitality. *55.4% 252 bottles*

∵ **Ardbeg 1998 Single Cask No. 2763** refill sherry hogshead, dist Sep 98, bott Nov 09 db (**86.5**) **n22 t22 f21 b21.5**. Ardbeg in a straightjacket. The sherry influence tightens every aspect, restricting the usual effortless grace and complexity. As hard an Ardbeg as you'll ever find. 55.6% 270 bottles

∵ **Ardbeg 2000 Single Cask Lord Robertson of Port Ellen KT** cask no. 1217, dist Apr 00, bott May 10 db (**96.5**) **n24** classic busy but relaxed nose: that delicate squeeze of young lemon dancing with such elegant peat confirms that it can be from no other distillery; **t24.5** and there we are: the delivery is at once soft and full of spices which blast you from your chair; again the lemon is quickly in and the phenols melt into cocoa and Demerara....beyond orgasmic; **f23.5** exceptionally long even by Ardbeg standards with the lightest oils to assist. Spices, mocha, citrus and smoke stretch into infinity...; **b24.5** though fun, a number of the distillery bottling casks had left me a little flat. Here though is a cask not just basking in all the finest Ardbegian traditions but taking those unique characteristics and pushing them beyond the distance you thought they might go. And proof, were it needed, that Ardbeg at10 can, as it did one, two and three decades ago, offer something which is the equivalent of a whisky lover's wet dream. Whatever they ask you for this bottling, pay it. Not only is the money going to a great cause. But your experience in whisky will be equally enriched. *53% For Lord Robertson (proceeds donated to Erskine). 202 bottles.*

Ardbeg Almost There 3rd release dist 98, bott 07 db (**93**) **n23 t24 f23 b23**. Further proof that a whisky doesn't have to reach double figures in age to enter the realms of brilliance... *54.1%*.

Ardbeg Blasda db (**90.5**) **n23.5** distant kumquat and lime intertwine with gentle butterscotch tart; it's all about the multi-layered barley and the most vague smokiness imaginable which adds a kind of almost invisible weight; the overall clarity is like that found swimming off a Pacific atoll; **t22.5** sharp barley hits home to almost mouth-watering effect; again there is the most pathetic hint of something smoky (like the SMWS cask, perhaps from the local water and warehouse air), but it does the trick and adds just the right ballast; **f22** soft spices arrive apologetically, but here it could do with being at 46% just to give it some late lift; **b22.5** a beautiful, if slightly underpowered malt, which shows Ardbeg's naked self to glowing effect. Overshadowed by some degree in its class by the SMWS bottling, but still something to genuinely make the heart flutter. *40%*.

Ardbeg Corryvreckan db (**96.5**) **n23** excellent, thick, not entirely un-penetrable – but close – nascent smoke and a vignette of salty, coastal references save the day; **t24.5** amazing: here we have Ardbeg nutshelled. Just so many layers of almost uncountable personalities with perhaps the citrus leading the way in both tart and sweet form and then meaningful speeches from those saline-based, malty sea-spray refreshed barley notes with the oak, in vanilla form, in close proximity. The peat, almost too dense to be seen on the nose, opens out with a fanfare of phenols. It is slumping-in-the-chair stuff, the enormity of the peat taking on the majesty of Cathedral-esque proportions, the notes reverberating around the hollows and recesses and reaching dizzying heights; such is its confidence, this is a malt which says: "I know where I'm going...!" ; **f24** long, outwardly laconic but on further investigation just brimming with complexity. Some brown sugary notes help the barley come up trumps late on but it's the uniquely salty shield to the mocha which sets this apart. Simply brilliant and unique in its effortless enormity...even by Ardbeg standards; **b25** as famous writers – including the occasional genius film director (stand up wherever you are my heroes Powell and Pressburger) – appear to be attracted to Corryvreckan, the third most violent whirlpool found in the world and just off Islay, to boot, - I selected this as my 1,500th whisky tasted for the historic Jim Murray Whisky Bible 2009. I'm so glad I did because many have told me they thought Blasda ahead of this. To me, it's not even a contest. Currently I have only a sample. Soon I shall have a bottle. I doubt if even the feared whirlpool is this deep and perplexing. *57.1%. 5000 bottles.* ☉

Ardbeg Kildalton 1980 bott 04 db (**96**) **n23 t24 f24 b25**. Many years back, when I helped get Ardbeg back on the road, I selected certain years as vintages and created the 17-year-old by using this unpeated version as the heart, with some overly old but highly peated casks to ensure the Ardbeg style flourished and equilibrium was maintained. The one and only recommendation I made that was not carried out, though, was to launch Kildalton as a malt in its own right, showing – uniquely – the inner working of Ardbeg in much the same way as a bourbon cask version does to Macallan. Now, at very long last, they have got around to it. This is better now than when it was 17 years old, and a degree of unbalanced freshness remained (to confirm my suspicions, I have tasted it against the samples I took then). It has developed extra fruit and complexity, making it a breathtaking treat – a masterpiece map of Ardbeg – that no true whisky connoisseur can afford to miss... and proof positive that Ardbeg doesn't need peat to bring complexity, balance and Scotch whisky to their highest peaks.... **57.6%**

Ardbeg Lord of the Isles bott autumn 06 db **(85) n20 t22 f22 b21.** A version of Ardbeg I have never really come to terms with. This bottling is of very low peating levels and shows a degree of Kildalton-style fruitiness. No probs there. More, it's a fact that some of the casks are leaching a soft soapy character noticeable on the nose. Enjoyable enough, but a bit frustrating. **46%**

Ardbeg Mor db **(95) n24** coastal to the point of sea spray showering you, with the smell of salt all the way home until you reach the peat fire. Evocative, sharp with elements of vinegar to the iodine; **t24** one of the biggest deliveries from Ardbeg for yonks; the peat appears way above the normal 50%, thickset and gloriously bitter-sweet, the steadying vanillas carried on the soft oils; **f23** mocha enters the fray with a raspberry jam fruitiness trying to dampen the continuing smoke onslaught; **b24** quite simply Mor the merrier... **57.5%**

Ardbeg Provenance 1974 bott 99 db **(96) n24 t25 f23 b24.** This is an exercise in subtlety and charisma, the beauty and the beast drawn into one. Until I came across the 25-year-old OMC verson during a thunderstorm in Denmark, this was arguably the finest whisky I had ever tasted: I opened this and drank from it to see in the year 2000. When I went through the Ardbeg warehouse stocks in 1997 I earmarked the '74 and '77 vintages as something special. This bottling has done me proud. **55.6%**

Ardbeg Renaissance db **(92) n22.5** sharp and punchy smoke with more than a hint of coke dust, too; the citrus is there but is partially hiding while the phenol level, usually appearing less than it actually is, makes no great secret of its enormity; **t22.5** a stunning delivery both reflecting the sharpness on the nose yet also couched in a light oiliness which aborts all but the first few shockwaves; **f23.5** long, already the vanilla is beginning to bristle and the smoke is moving towards a praline-brushed finale; the bitter-sweet finish could not be better-balanced and just sighs Ardbeg... **b23.5** how fitting that the 1,200th (and almost last) new-to-market whisky I have tasted for the 2009 Bible should be Renaissance...because that's what I need after tasting that lot....!! This is an Ardbeg that comes on strong, is not afraid to wield a few hefty blows and yet, paradoxically, the heavier it gets the more delicate, sophisticated and better-balanced it becomes. Enigmatically Ardbegian. **55.9%.**

··⊹·· **Ardbeg Rollercoaster (90.5) n23** youthful malts dominate; a patchwork of smoke on many different levels from ashy to ethereal: almost dizzying; **t23** again, it's the young Ardbeg which dominates; the delivery is almost painful as you shake your head at the shock of the spices and unfettered peat. A genuine greenness to the malts though some natural caramels do make a smoky surge; **f23** long, buttery in part, limited sweetness; almost a touch of smoked bacon about it; **b21.5** to be honest, it was the end of another long day – and book – when I tasted this and I momentarily forgot the story behind the malt. My reaction to one of my researchers who happened to be in the tasting room was: "Bloody hell! They are sending me kids. If this was any younger I'd just be getting a bag of grist!" This malt may be a fabulous concept. And Rollercoaster is a pretty apt description, as this a dram which appears to have the whisky equivalent of Asperger's. So don't expect the kind of balance that sweeps you into a world that only Ardbeg knows. This, frankly, is not for the Ardbeg purist or snob. But for those determined to bisect the malt in all its forms and guises, it is the stuff of the most rampant hard-ons. **57.3%**

Ardbeg Still Young dist 98, 2nd release bott 06 db **(93) n24 t24 f22 b23.** A couple of generations back – maybe even less – this would not have been so much "Still Young" as "Getting on a Bit." This is a very good natural age for an Ardbeg as the oak is making a speech, but refuses to let it go on too long. Stylish – as one might expect. And, in my books, should be a regular feature. Go on. Be bold. Be proud say it: Ardbeg Aged 8 Years. Get away from the marketing straightjacket of old age... **56.2%.** ncf.

Ardbeg Supernova db **(97) n24.5** moody, atmospheric; hints and threats; Lynchian in its stark black and white forms, its meandering plot, its dark and at times indecipherable message and meaning...; **t24** at first a wall of friendly phenols but only when you stand back and see the overall picture you can get an idea just how mammoth that wall is; there are intense sugary gristy notes, then this cuts away slightly towards something more mouth-fillingly smoky but now with a hickory sweetness; a light oil captures the long, rhythmic waves, a pulse almost; **f24** gentle, sweetening cocoa notes evolve while the peat pulses... again...and again... **b24.5** apparently this was called "Supernova" in tribute of how I once described a very highly peated Ardbeg. This major beast, carrying a phenol level in excess of 100ppm, isn't quite a Supernova...much more of a Black Hole. Because once you get dragged into this one, there really is no escaping... **58.9%**

✥ **Ardbeg Supernova SN2010** bott 2010 **(93.5) n24** youthful, punchy and spicy; vanillas and bananas add a sweetness to the molten peat; **t23.5** an explosion of sharp citrus and grassy malt. Not quite what was expected but the smoke and spices cause mayhem as they crash around the palate: eye-watering, safety harness-wearing stuff; **f23** the oak has a bitter-ish surprise but soft sugars compensate. Elsewhere the smoke and spice continues its rampage; **b23** there are Supernovas and there are Supernovas. Some have been going on a bit and have formed a shape and indescribable beauty with the aid of time; others are just starting off and though full of unquantifiable energy and wonder have a distance to travel. By comparison to last year's blockbusting Whisky Bible award winner, this is very much in the latter category. *60.1%*

Ardbeg Uigeadail db **(97.5) n25** quite simple: perfect. The smoke is dry, something akin to the ash from a cold peat fire; there are hints, though no more, of fruit, possibly sherry. There are hints, though no more, of slightly overdone roasted potato. There are hints, though no more, of coffee-stained old Demerara rum. There are hints, though no more, of sweet grist falling from the mill. There are no hints of perfection: that is stated loud and clear.... **t24.5** from the utter silky brilliance of the delivery to the multi-layered middle this simply oozes complexity, and on a level only a handful of distilleries in the world can even dream of reaching; a molecule or two of over enthusiastic oak takes this away from a full mark, but I am being harsh; the fruit and barley are in an embrace that only the purest of lovers would know... **f23.5** some serious caramel from the cask, and a fruity follow through, perhaps robs the whisky of some of its more intricate notes, but again I am being ultra picky. An unusual oiliness for Ardbeg, though only slight, helps further the finale and encourages some mocha to develop; **b24.5** massive yet tiny. Loud yet whispering. Seemingly ordinary from the bottle, yet unforgettable. It is snowing outside my hotel room in Calgary, yet the sun, in my soul at least, is shining. I came across this bottling while lecturing the Liquor Board of British Columbia in Vancouver on May 6th 2008, so one assumes it is a Canadian market bottling. It was one of those great moments in my whisky life on a par with tasting for the first time the Old Malt Cask 1975 at a tasting in Denmark. There is no masking genius.The only Scotch to come close to this one is another from Ardbeg, Corryvreckan. That has more oomph and lays the beauty and complexity on thick....it could easily have been top dog. But this particular Uigeadail (for I have tasted another bottling this year, without pen or computer to hand and therefore unofficially, which was a couple of points down) offers something far more restrained and cerebral. Believe me: this bottling will be going for thousands at auction in the very near future, I wager. *54.2%*

Ardbeg Uigeadail db **(89) n25** awesome package of intense peat reek amid complex fruitcake and leather notes. Everything about this nose is broadside-big yet the massive oak never once oversteps its mark. A whiff of engine oil compliments the kippers. Perfection; **t22** begins with a mind-blowing array of bitter-sweet oaky notes and then a strangely fruity peat entry; real scattergun whisky; **f20** very odd finish with an off-key fruit element that flattens the usual Ardbeg grand finale; **b22** a curious Ardbeg with a nose to die for. Some tinkering - please guys, as the re-taste is not better - regarding the finish may lift this to being a true classic *54.1%*

Cadenhead's Ardbeg Aged 14 Years dist 93, bott Feb 08 **(95) n22 t24 f24.5 b24.5.** The type of cask which silently sets out why Ardbeg is different to any other whisky in the world. *57.2%*

Cadenhead's Ardbeg Aged 14 Years dist 93, bott Feb 08 **(91.5) n22 t23 f23.5 b23.** Just as one would expect from an Ardbeg. *57.5%. 288 bottles.*

Cadenhead's Ardbeg Aged 15 Years cask no. 1056, dist 94, bott 09 **(92.5) n23** quiet, warm, seaweedy rock pools; orange blossom on the wind... **t23.5** melt-in-the-mouth barley, sweet, juicy and then legions of delicate peat notes marching through...; **f23** silky with a little touch of raspberry preserve to the smoke and vanilla; **b23** typically understated Ardbeg, where everything first appears big, but when analysed is just so delicate and almost coy. Wonderful. *58.1%*

Cadenhead's Ardbeg Aged 15 Years cask no. 1057, dist 94, bott 09 **(95) n23** quiet, warm, seaweedy rock pools which have dried up a bit; spilt pepper on the wind; **t24** melt-in-the mouth barley, sweet, juicy, then legions of spiced up peat notes march through; **f23.5** silky with a few liberal shakes of the pepper pot on a vague fruity note plus smoke and vanilla; **b24.5** virtually peas in a pod, are casks 1056/7. Except this is a spicier cove. And doesn't suffer for it, for those tiny differences add up to a lot. *57.3%*

✥ **Cadenhead's Authentic Collection Ardbeg 1994** bott Feb 10 **(94.5) n23.5** super spiced: a zillion mini explosions on the nose, each of them hitting a nerve. The smoke is dense; **t24** sweetness is at a premium at any point here and after the expected eruption on delivery and scattering of spice, the odd grain of muscovado can be picked up here and there; **f23.5** long, with hickory firming up the peat to a daft degree. And those peppery spices just refuse to fade. Wonderful...; **b23.5** a classy, growling Ardbeg. Just a little attitude here and there, like a superstar having a grouse. *56% Wm. Cadenhead Ltd. 268 bottles.*

Connoisseurs Choice Ardbeg 1991 (93.5) n24.5 unmistakably Ardbeg: a unique combination of salt and smoke, this time in a fruity shell, which boasts a weight and balance that nature has a hard job to explain, but is way beyond the ability of man; **t23.5** light, intrinsically malty and gristy sweet, and then a slow build up of smoke; **f22.5** remains on the sweet side and has to be to see off some rather burnt toasty oakiness; **b23** a superb *whisky unable to live up to the supernatural nose by being merely excellent on the palate. 43%.*

⠴⠂ **Duncan Taylor Collection Ardbeg 1993** cask no. 1724 **(92) n23** classic buzzing peat, nipping and radiating lavender and smoke; **t23.5** bristling delivery: eyes on stalks stuff! The explosive spices clear a path for the smoke and liquorice as its takes a peculiarly bourbon turn for the sweeter; **f23** long, with those white peppers red hot; **b22.5** a tin hat malt; like an abridged version of this year's Cadenhead '94 bottling. *58.9% Duncan Taylor & Co Ltd*

The Exclusive Malts Ardbeg Aged 7 Years cask no. 107, dist Apr 00 **(78.5) n18.5 t21.5 f19 b19.5.** This is Ardbeg? How disappointing. *55.7%. The Creative Whisky Co. 380 bottles.*

Hart Brothers Ardbeg Aged 17 Years dist Feb 91, bott Mar 08 **(92) n23.5 t23 f22.5 b23.** A busy and engaging Ardbeg. *46%. Hart Brothers Limited.*

Old & Rare Ardbeg Aged 36 Years dist Mar 73, bott Apr 09 **(76) n19 t20 f18 b19.** Some serious cowshed moments on the nose: fruity, too. But, frankly, to nose and taste as uniquely weird as any Ardbeg I've come across in over 25 years of worshipping the stuff. Can't help thinking that this might become the stuff of legend in some parts of northern Germany... *44.7%. Douglas Laing. 78 bottles.*

Old Malt Cask Ardbeg Aged 16 Years rum cask no. 3719, dist 91, bott Jun 07 **(88.5) n21.5 t22 f23 b22.** Pretty bitty by Ardbeg standards, with the rum still causing all kinds of unusual dead ends to the norm. Here we have Ardbeg in recognisable, if unique, form. *50%. 346 bottles.*

Old Malt Cask Ardbeg Aged 16 Years rum cask no. 3883, dist Mar 91, bott Sep 07 **(87) n22 t22 f21 b22.** On the sample bottle there was no mention of it, but I have just noticed it was from a rum cask: hand on heart, I didn't know when tasting (in fact, I see there are three of these). But I could think of no other explanation as to why you'd want to finish Ardbeg in rum, well.... *50%. nc ncf. Douglas Laing. 334 bottles.*

Old Malt Cask Ardbeg Aged 16 Years rum cask no. 3893, dist Mar 91, bott Sep 07 **(81.5) n20 t22 f20 b19.5.** Ardbeg in a straightjacket: somehow all the peat and complexity has been locked away inside a flinty wall and simply can't escape. The bitterness on the finish doesn't help either. Drinkable, decent malt....but knowing it's Ardbeg...!! Memo to self (cc Glenmorangie Ltd): never mature Ardbeg in rum casks... *50%. Douglas Laing. 335 bottles.*

Old Malt Cask Ardbeg Aged 17 Years refill hogshead, finished in rum cask, dist Mar 91, bott Oct 08 **(86.5) n21.5 t?? f22 b21.** Enjoyable, juicy, candy-crisp sweet and spicy but relatively flat for an Ardbeg with the higher notes cropped by the rum. *50%. 316 bottles.*

Old Malt Cask Ardbeg Aged 17 Years refill hogshead, dist Mar 91, bott Aug 08 **(90.5) n23.5** brilliant bitter-sweetness on the smoke; a touch of the dryish side about this, too; **t22.5** despite some very early dissolving sugars, remains on the dryish side with a slow-motion development of smoke; the vanilla arrives early and quite sternly; **f22** the oak and smoke continue to trade positions of supremacy; **b22.5** a whispering Ardbeg... *50%. 226 bottles.*

Old Malt Cask Ardbeg Aged 18 Years refill hogshead, dist Mar 91, bott Apr 09 **(86.5) n21.5 t23 f21 b21.** A very different kind of Ardbeg with the oils really showing to maximum effect. Helps the intensity of the delivery, but perhaps not the unveiling of the more complex notes further down the line. Very pleasant, but ordinary by Ardbegian standards. 50%. *357 bottles.*

⠴⠂ **Old Malt Cask Ardbeg Aged 18 Years** refill hogshead no. DL 5440, dist Mar 91, bott Aug 09 **(89) n21** salty and sharp; **t23** juicy: tidal waves of smoky barley with a rich mocha and spice background; **f22** spiced smoky chocolate; **b23** a gentle version which takes time to crank itself up. But worth the wait. *50% Douglas Laing. 208 bottles.*

The Queen of the Moorlands Edition XXII Ourbeg Aged 6 Years cask no. 29, dist 01, bott 07 **(84) n22 t21 f22 b19.** A charming toddler of a malt still trying to find its feet. The sweet peats and oak are delicately displayed but the balance just aint there. Enjoyable and entertaining, as toddlers tend to be, this one was plucked slightly at the wrong time. *58.7%. nc ncf. Wine Shop The Leek and Congleton. 196 bottles.*

Scotch Malt Whisky Society Cask 33.68 Aged 9 Years 1st fill barrel, dist May 98 **(95) n23.5 t23.5 f24 b24.** In bottled form this is perhaps the best example I have seen yet of why Ardbeg makes the greatest whisky in the world. Here there's no peat to talk of, so you get a clear view of the mechanics of the malt. It is like looking at the inner workings of a Rolex, only here time stands still... *57.4%*

Scotch Malt Whisky Society Cask 33.74 Aged 10 Years sherry gorda, dist May 98 **(73.5)** n18 t20 f17.5 b18. Great whisky filled into an absolute rubbish barrel. More like, Good Gorda, What The Hell Was That....??? Or more to the point: Why? *56.6%*

Scotch Malt Whisky Society Cask 33.75 Aged 7 Years 1st fill barrel, dist Sep 01 **(90.5)** n23.5 the background is lightly sugared custard; the foreground is peat – not always the way Ardbeg comes across, preferring, usually, to let those phenols gang up on you. But here the peat is, quite literally, thrust in your face. Still magic, though...; **t23.5** multi-layers of citrus offer the juiciest of starts; the peat begins as a murmur, forms into a rumble and finally crashes upon the tastebuds like a line delivered by James Robertson-Justice; **f21.5** bits and bobs of weak tannin and smoke and natural caramels...in a bit of a maturation no-man's land; **b22** this is a fascinating whisky. It shows, as vividly as can be imagined, the effects of the last two useless, rainy, freezing British summers on maturing whisky stocks: they have taken their toll, for this should be much further advanced after seven years in first fill bourbon. But, that said, not a bad way to bring up my 900th new whisky tasted for Jim Murray's Whisky Bible 2010. *61.5%*

⁙ **Scotch Malt Whisky Society Cask 33.77 Aged 11 Years** 1st fill barrel, dist May 98 **(95)** n23.5 intriguing dusty cocoa on the briny smoke; **t24** jam tart and cream: a lightly oily, fruity edge to this one. Gentle for all the peat and cask strength zap; the middle ground luxuriates in an orangey glow to the smoke; **f23.5** long, more hints and whispers of fruit and bourbon tones while the peat continues its gentle cascade onto the palate; **b24** it's as though this distillery does genius without even trying... *57.3%. 239 bottles*

⁙ **Scotch Malt Whisky Society Cask 33.80 Aged 11 Years** 1st fill barrel, dist May 98 **(86)** n21.5 t22 f22 b20.5. For many distilleries, this wouldn't be a bad dram; it is perfectly flavoursome, enjoyable and chewy. For an Ardbeg, though, this is rather clumsy and ill-defined. *56.5% Scotch Malt Whisky Society. 242 bottles.*

⁙ **Scotch Malt Whisky Society Cask 33.84 Aged 10 Years** 1st fill barrel, dist Sep 99 **(92)** n23 an unusual Ardbeg nose with the peat almost ash dry: spices – all of them smoky – nip at the nose; **t24** powering peat in both ash and oil form. The sugars have that slightly burned feel to them. There is a sublime rhythm and pulse to this one while the bittering oak and confident, gristy sugars offer a superb balance; **f22** remains on the toasty, smoky side; **b23** you get the feeling this is some way above the usual 50ppm phenols! A must have for Smokeheads. *57% Scotch Malt Whisky Society. 243 bottles.*

⁙ **Scotch Malt Whisky Society Cask 33.85 Aged 7 Years** 2nd fill barrel, dist Nov 02 **(84)** n22 t21 f20 b21. I raised an eyebrow on nosing this – until I checked the age. Even so, the bitter notes suggest this may not have been filled into quite the best barrel at the distillery. *60.5% Scotch Malt Whisky Society. 215 bottles.*

⁙ **Scotch Malt Whisky Society Cask 33.86 Aged 10 Years** 1st fill barrel, dist Sep 99 **(89.5)** n23 a beguiling coastal peatiness which, like an Islay storm, builds quickly in intensity; **t23** big sugary drive on delivery followed by some major smoke; plenty of fruits, not least pears – with a damn good dollop of smoky custard; the peats fizz from the first moment; **f21.5** heads into a bitter-sweet siding; **b22** excellent stuff. But runs off the tracks slightly towards the finish. *56.4% Scotch Malt Whisky Society. 243 bottles.*

⁙ **Scotch Malt Whisky Society Cask 33.87 Aged 10 Years** 1st fill barrel, dist Feb 00 **(86.5)** n21.5 t22 f21.5 b21.5. Surprising degree of vanilla. Deliciously smoky and sweet, but fails to engage the usual degree of subtle fruit and complexity. *57.6%. 255 bottles.*

Scott's Selection Ardbeg 1992 bott 07 **(94)** n24 t23 f23.5 b23.5. An exceptionally fine cask, dryer than usual, showing the distillery carried on making a uniquely complex spirit even at a time when massive doubts hang over its future. *51.6%*

ARDMORE
Speyside, 1899. Fortune Brands. Working.

⁙ **Ardmore 25 Years Old** db **(89.5)** n21 decidedly caramel oriented with the smoke thin and crisp; **t23.5** quite brilliant delivery: not only powering, but with an unwavering Demerara and chocolate voice; lightly roasted Blue Mountain benefits from the playful spices; the smoke is little more than a background hum; **f22.5** long with a milky, orangey texture steeling in; **b22.5** a 25-y-o box of chocolates: coffee creams, fudge, orange cream....they are all in there. The nose maybe ordinary: what follows is anything but. *51.4% ncf Beam Global*

Ardmore 100th Anniversary 12 Years Old dist 86, bott 99 db **(94)** n24 t23.5 f22.5 b24. I cannot believe there are still bottles of this still around. It was going to be removed from my guide for having been included for too long, until I was informed that it was still to be had. So I re-tasted it using my new scoring system....and still came to an identical result...!!! Even if by a slightly different route. OK: let's summarise this one more time. Brilliant. Absolutely stunning, with the peat almost playing games on the palate. Had they not put caramel in this bottling, it most likely would have been an award winner. So, by this time next year, I fully expect to see every last bottle accounted for... 40%

Ardmore Fully Peated Quarter Casks db (89) n21 t23 f23 b22. This is an astonishingly brave attempt by the new owners of Ardmore who, joy of all joys, are committed to putting this distillery in the public domain. Anyone with a 2004 copy of the Whisky Bible will see that my prayers have at last been answered. However, this bottling is for Duty Free and, due to the enormous learning curve associated with this technique, a work in progress. They have used the Quarter Cask process which has been such a spectacular success at its sister distillery Laphroaig. Here I think they have had the odd slight teething problem. Firstly, Ardmore has rarely been filled in ex-bourbon and that oak type is having an effect on the balance and smoke weight; also they have unwisely added caramel, which has flattened things further. I don't expect the caramel to be in later bottlings and, likewise, I think the bourbon edge might be purposely blunted a little. But for a first attempt this is seriously big whisky that shows enormous promise. When they get this right, it could – and should – be a superstar. Now I await the more traditional vintage bottlings... 46%. ncf.

Ardmore Traditional Cask db (88.5) n21.5 t22 f23 b22. (For general tasting notes, see above) Not quite what I expected. "Jim. Any ideas on improving the flavour profile?" asked the nice man from Ardmore distillery when they were originally launching the thing. "Yes. Cut out the caramel." "Ah, right...." So what do I find when the next bottling comes along? More caramel. It's good to have influence... Actually, I can't quite tell if this is a result of natural caramelization from the quarter casking or just an extra dollop of the stuff in the bottling hall. The result is pretty similar: some of the finer complexity is lost. My guess, due to an extra fraction of sweetness and spice, is that it is the former. All that said, the overall experience remains quite beautiful. And this remains one of my top ten distilleries in the world. 46%. ncf.

⁘ **Chieftain's Ardmore Aged 17 Years** dist Jun 92, bott 2010 (88.5) n22 deceptively rich smoke; t22 beautiful honey strands to the intense barley, the smoke adds gravitas; f22 long, light oils; buttery barley and a constant smoky, gristy, sugariness ; b22.5 a wonderfully nimble and understated dram. 46% nc ncf Ian Macleod

The Exclusive Malts Ardmore Aged 13 Years cask no. 335, dist Sep 94 (89.5) n21.5 t23 f22.5 b22.5. This is the most enormously peated Ardmore I've ever come across: the phenols plus the tired cask and unusual saltiness makes this pretend to be an 8-year-old Islay. You don't think that once upon a time there was a leaking Laphroaig cask and they emptied it into an old Ardmore cask and forgot to re-mark it Laphroaig and....no, such things don't happen...do they....? 52.5%. The Creative Whisky Company. 324 bottles.

Gordon & MacPhail Ardmore Aged 16 Years dist 91, bott 07 (87) n22 t21.5 f22 b21.5. Hardmore – with a silent "H". Lovely stuff – but every bit lacking in smoke as the previous vintage was groaning with it. 43%

Old Malt Cask Ardmore Aged 12 Years refill hogshead, dist Mar 96, bott Sep 08 (85.5) n22.5 t20.5 f21.5 b21. Billowing smoke, with an earthy, bonfire quality; chewy, malty, pleasantly sweet in part; peppery and gristy. 50%. Douglas Laing. 348 bottles.

Provenance Ardmore Aged 11 Years refill hogshead, dist autumn 96, bott summer 08 (80) n21 t20 f20 b19. I'd like to say this is a third-fill cask. Except it appears to have done the rounds at least once more than that. Pleasant smoke, though. 46%. Douglas Laing.

⁘ **Provenance Ardmore Over 12 Years** refill hogshead no. DMG 5743, dist Autumn 1997, bott Winter 2010 (84.5) n21 t21 f21.5 b21. Light, sweet, playfully smoked; minimum oak interference. 46% Douglas Laing

AUCHENTOSHAN

Lowlands, 1800. Morrison Bowmore. Working.

Auchentoshan 10 Years Old db (81) n22 t21 f19 b19. Much better, maltier, cleaner nose than before. But after the initial barley surge on the palate it shows a much thinner character. 40%

Auchentoshan 12 Years Old db (85) n20 t23 f21 b21. Thicker and more chewy malt than is the norm for a 'Toshan. But don't get this one confused with the astonishing peaty number that was 43%!! The finish is OK, but the delivery is superb. 40%

Auchentoshan 18 Years Old bourbon cask, batch no. L092458 db (87) n21.5 retains its light frame, but bolstered by a new-found bourbon-honey sweetness; t22.5 the oak shows up early, as you might expect from a 'Toshan of this age. But a thick strata of barley and vanilla sponge in syrup sweetness give it an enjoyable polish; f21.5 dries with a wobble, but the late spices come up trumps; plenty of chewy toffee to finish with; b21.5 a much happier soul than previous years, celebrating with an extra dollop of honey. The citrus and almonds promised on the label never quite materialise. 43% ⊙⊙

Auchentoshan 21 Years Old db (93) n23.5 the most unblemished, desirable and surprising of all the distillery-bottled 'Toshan noses: a sprig of mint buried in barely warmed peat, all with an undercoat of the most delicate honeys; t23 velvety and waif-like, the barley-honey theme is played out in hushed tones and unspoiled elegance; f23 the smoke deftly returns as the vanillas and citrus slowly rise but the gentle honey-barley plays to the end, despite the shy introduction of cocoa; b23.5 one of the finest Lowland distillery bottlings of our time. A near faultless masterpiece of astonishing complexity to be cherished and discussed with deserved reverence. So delicate, you fear that sniffing too hard will break the poor thing...! 43%

Auchentoshan 1976 Aged 28 Years cask no. 1115 db (91) n23.5 quite beautiful in its lofty elegance: there are certain toasty ginger cake aromas vying to be top dog amid the citrus and sultana. It succeeds. Softly spiced and vibrant, it grows markedly in stature as it warms in the glass; t22.5 sweet, brown sugar attack recedes as the tannins kick in; the middle offers a metallic coppery sheen which appears to weld the two styles together; f22 simple and gentle with natural toffee and butterscotch; some late jammy fruitiness bids adieu; b23 great to see Auchentoshan hit this kind of heights: it is not the most common of phenomena. Works well in nearly every respect and few Lowlanders reach this degree of excellence when so grey bearded. 47.5%. 156 bottles exclusively for CSN, Calgary.

⁙ **Auchentoshan 1978 Bourbon Cask Matured Limited Edition** db (96) n24.5 a nose which stops you in your tracks: Taiwanese green tea sweetened with a brave and enthralling mix of muscovado sugar and manuka honey. There is essence of Kentucky, too, with a bourbony-liquorice trait while the vanillas head at you with two or three different degrees of intensity. How subtle. How complex. So beguiling, you almost forget to drink the stuff... t24 who could ask for more from a 30-y-o malt? Certainly not I. Because I didn't expect this engrossing seduction of my palate before opening the bottle. Wonderful strands of sweetness of varying types and levels, from the lighter, fragile citrus notes to something sturdier and more honeyed; the middle ground has a few oily moments which allow all the elements to mix without bias or domination: a near perfectly balanced harmony; f23.5 long, lush with the barley now having the confidence to reveal itself while the toasted fudge ensures an attractive and fitting bitter-sweet finale; b24 if there was a Lowlander of the Year, this'd probably wipe the floor with the rest. It's as though someone was in a warehouse, stumbled across this gem and protected it with his life to ensure it was not lost in some blend or other. Whoever is responsible should be given a gold medal, or a Dumbarton season ticket. A tip, by the way. If you ignore on all other requests to do this, please ensure you taste this one at body and not room temperature for full blow-away results. 53.4% 480 bottles

Auchentoshan Classic db (80) n19 t20 f21 b20. Classic what exactly...? Some really decent barley, but goes little further. 40%

Auchentoshan Select db (85) n20 t21.5 f22 b21.5. Has changed shape of late, if not quality. Much more emphasis on the enjoyable juicy barley sharpness these days. 40%

Auchentoshan Three Wood db (76) n20 t18 f20 b18. Takes you directly into the rough. Refuses to harmonise, except maybe for some late molassed sugar. 43%

A.D. Rattray Auchentoshan 1990 cask no. 17285 (86.5) n21 t23 f21 b21.5. A messy nose and confused, vanilla-clad finish is rescued in magnificent fashion by a startlingly bright delivery full of lilting, juicy barley notes.

Cadenhead's Authentic Collection Auchentoshan Aged 17 Years bourbon, dist 90, bott Sep 07 (80.5) n21 t19 f20.5 b20. Soars above the distillery bottling 18-y-o on nose, but at times viciously hot. 59.2%. 252 bottles.

⁙ **The Coopers Choice Auchentoshan 1991 Aged 18 Years** (75.5) n10 t20 f10.5 b19. Virtually nil colour thanks to a third-fill cask and enjoys the corresponding degree of oak complexity. It's pure grist after all these years and a tad feinty, too. Don't come across many of these in the course of a year. 46% The Vintage Malt Whisky Co. Ltd

Duncan Taylor Collection Auchentoshan 1999 cask no. 800003, dist Mar 99, bott Mar 06 (73) n21 t21 f15 b16. After textbook nose and delivery, falls apart alarmingly and bitterly as the balance with oak is lost. 43%. 430 bottles.

⁙ **Duthies Auchentoshan 16 Years Old** (78.5) n19 t21 f19.5 b19. Tangy and somewhat hot. 46% Wm. Cadenhead Ltd

Duthies Auchentoshan 19 Years Old (86) n21.5 t22 f21 b21.5. Mouth-watering, juicy and boasting a lot of natural toffee. 46%. Cadenhead's for Germany.

Kingsbury Celtic Series Auchentoshan 11 Years Old 1984 (86.5) n21 t21 f22.5 b22. Robust, crisp and mega-malt intense. A bit hot, as 'Toshan can oft be, but generates enough crystalline barley towards the end to win the heart over twice-fold. Overall, much younger than its years with the oak barely making a noise. 55.4%. nc ncf. Japan Import System Co. Ltd.

Milroy's of Soho Selection Number One 1991 Auchentoshan Aged 16 Years refill butt, cask no. 485, dist Feb 91, bott Nov 07 **(86) n21 t22 f22 b21.** Competent, attractive and on it's best ultra malty behaviour. With nearly 3,000 bottles from this cask, designated exclusively for miniatures, one assumes, but nothing petit about this bottling. *40%. 2880 bottles.*

Murray McDavid Auchentoshan 1992 (77) n19 t20 f19 b19. Creamy, fruity...but somehow not on the ball. *46%.*

Old Malt Cask Auchentoshan Aged 13 years refill hogshead, dis Dec 95, bott Feb 09 **(86.5) n21 t22 f21.5 b22.** Genuinely enjoyable and showing a deft touch to the barley component. The spices are located where you want them to help counter the juicy onslaught, but also not to an extent that would shut out that source of entertainment. The degree of sweetness if also spot on. Always good to come across a 'Toshan of this calibre. *50%. Douglas Laing. 365 bottles.*

Old Malt Cask Auchentoshan Aged 17 Years refill hogshead no. 4217, dist Aug 90, bott Mar 08 **(94) n23.5 t23.5 f23 b24.** If casks of such brilliance can be located in the 'Toshan warehouses – and they must be in there somewhere – the distillery can do worse than to find them and follow Douglas Laing's lead to up the distillery's profile. A legendary bottling. *50%. Douglas Laing. 295 bottles.*

∴ **Provenance Auchentoshan Over 11 Years** refill hogshead 5586, dist Autumn 1998, bott Autumn 2009 **(86) n22 t22 f21 b21.** Fresh, clean and bursting with triple-distilled lightness. A decent early day dram. *46% nc ncf Douglas Laing & Co Ltd*

Provenance Auchentoshan Aged 12 Years refill hogshead, dist winter 96, bott spring 09 **(73) n18 t20 f17 b18.** Thin, mildly off key. *46%. Douglas Laing.*

Scotch Malt Whisky Society Cask 5.22 Aged 9 Years 1st fill barrel, dist Mar 99 **(92) n22 t23.5 f23 b23.5.** 'Toshan at arguably its best age from this kind of cask. Droolingly brilliant. *60%*

Scotch Malt Whisky Society Cask 5.25 Aged 9 Years refill barrel, dist Jun 99 **(88.5) n22.5** barley bounces around the glass; clean, a tad gristy and very green; **t22.5** every bit as juicy as the nose heralds; a delicate nuttiness combines well with the malt concentrate and soft oil; spicy; **f21.5** remains sweet and delicate, still with a nutty outline to the dominant barley; dries and bitters very slightly as the (improbable) oak intrudes; **b22** a fine, hugely enjoyable example of a (probably) 2nd fill cask allowing a relatively young malt to do its own thing. *57.8%*

Old Malt Cask Auchentoshan Aged 18 Years refill hogshead, dist Aug 90, bott Nov 08 **(83.5) n22 t22 f19.5 b20.** At times unashamedly throat-ripping but plenty of ginger-led fun for those who want to go for the white knuckle ride. *50%. Douglas Laing. 335 bottles.*

Whisky Galore Auchentoshan 1999 (78.5) n19 t21 f19.5 b19. Raw, unrefined and eye-watering. But what fun!! *46%. Duncan Taylor.*

AUCHROISK

Speyside, 1974. Diageo. Working.

Auchroisk Aged 10 Years db **(84)** n20 t22 f21 b21. Tangy orange on the nose, the malt amplified by a curious saltiness on the palate. *43%. Flora and Fauna.*

∴ **Auchroisk The Manager's Choice** bodega sherry European oak, cask no. 11323, dist 1999, bott 2009 db **(84.5) n19 t21.5 f22.5 b21.5.** The astringent nose offers little hope but an entirely different story on delivery. Even though there is the odd spirity weakness on arrival, the thumping barley back-up chased by a light mocha follow through ensures a pleasant few minutes with the glass. *60.6%. 622 bottles.*

Chieftain's Auchroisk Aged 11 Years Medoc Finish (79) n20 t22 f18 b19. Salivating but thin. *43%. Ian Macleod.*

Chieftain's Auchroisk 13 Years Old American/Spanish oak, dist Feb 94 **(84.5) n21 t21 f21.5 b21.** An honest Speysider teaming with lively barley. *43%. nc ncf. Ian Macleod.*

Connoisseurs Choice Auchroisk 1993 (78) n19 t21 f19 b19. Simplistic malt essay of few words. *43%. Gordon & MacPhail.*

Dun Bheagan Auchroisk 17 Year Old port finish, dist Sep 90 **(69)** n18 t17 f17 b17. If ever there was a case to colour and chill-filter, this might be it... *43%. nc ncf. Ian Macleod.*

∴ **Duthies Auchroisk 20 Years Old (63.5)** n16 t16 f16.5 b15. Oops! Should sell well in Germany. *46% Wm. Cadenhead Ltd*

Kingsbury Celtic Series Auchroisk 15 Years Old 1990 (83.5) n21 t20 f21.5 b21. Even at this massive strength, pretty threadbare in terms of complexity and impact although the clarity of the barley late on impresses. *62.8%. nc ncf. Japan Import System Co. Ltd.*

∴ **Kingsbury's "The Selection" Auchroisk 7 Years Old 2002 (81)** n20 t21.5 f19 b20.5. Clean and refreshingly malty. *43% Japan Import System*

Mackillop's Choice Auchroisk cask no. 15576, dist Oct 92, bott May 07 **(87)** n22 t22 f21.5 b21.5 Pavlovian responses usually mean I shudder at the prospect of a single cask Auckroisk of this kind of age. This is above the norm in every respect. *46%. ncf. Iain Mackillop*

Old Malt Cask Auchroisk Aged 16 Years (81) n21 t20 f20 b20. Pear drops and barley. *50%.*

Old Malt Cask Auchroisk Aged 33 Years (94) n22.5 somehow the malt clings on to be the main shareholder with some waves of oak-based fruitiness starting to stir; a few bourbony strands begin to become entangled; **t24** a real surprise mouthful because the body of this is far fuller, richer and oilier than it was when distilled all those years ago. Fabulous, light coating of golden syrup which comfortably sees off the background oak; **f23.5** long, beautifully textured with oaky sinews amid the rich barley; chalky towards the finish but keeps on track; **b24** just a few weeks back I attended the memorial dinner for former J&B Blender Jim Milne, who was in charge when Auchroisk first came on stream. He was always a little disappointed with the frailty and lightness of this malt and had to work punishingly hard to get it up to scratch for when he first unveiled it as a single malt. This stunning OMC is the oldest bottling of this malt I have ever seen, and I am so sorry I did not have a bottle to hand to celebrate his life with his fellow friends. Because had it shown all those qualities and depth 22 years ago, a lot of his problems would have been solved. *47.2%. Douglas Laing*

⁙ **Old Malt Cask Auchroisk Aged 34 Years** refill hogshead 5522, dist Apr 75, bott Sep 09 **(96)** n24 quite superb: a wonderful tangle of delicate floral notes, the faintest dab of citrus and a medley of vanilla-based, weightier oaky tones. All bound together by a nimble barley hand. Not even remotely what I expected...; **t24.5** sensual...there is no other word. The barley is on maximum sweet-sharp mode and brings to the table other delicious issues amid the juiciness, like an over-toasted butterscotch tart and caramelised coffee biscuits...dangerously delicious; **f23.5** long with countless strands of vanilla, each of varying degrees of dryness; **b24** this may not be Whisky of the Year, but it could qualify as "Shock Whisky of the Year"...on two counts. Firstly, is this really 34-years-old...? Hell, I am getting old!!! I remember like yesterday waiting for my local merchant to ring to tell me the first-ever bottling arrived...as a 12 year-old...(the whisky, not me)!!! And secondly, the quality. The blender in charge of Auchroisk during its infant years, Jim Milne, would have given this malt about as much chance of reaching this degree of quality after 34 years as Aberdeenshire winning the County Cricket Championship: none. How one of Speyside's most light and brittle whiskies has not only survived this amount of time in the barrel but actually thrived, showing not a single trace of defamatory over-aging, has to be one of the great malt whisky mysteries of recent years. Astonishing. *50%. 228 bottles.*

Scotch Malt Whisky Society Cask 95.9 Aged 18 Years refill barrel, dist Sep 90 (79) n18 t19 f22 b20. An emaciated malt with some oaky ribs showing. Juicy in part, though. *59.4%*

⁙ **Scotch Malt Whisky Society Cask 95.11 Aged 19 Years** refill barrel, dist Jun 90 (86) n22 t22 f21 b21. Creamy, fruity and, despite the balmy finale, occasionally sharp and lively. *58.2% Scotch Malt Whisky Society. 192 bottles.*

⁙ **Scotch Malt Whisky Society Cask 95.13 Aged 19 Years** refill barrel, dist Jun 90 (87) n20 malty but rather drab; **t22.5** didn't expect that...!! Superb versatility on the delivery with the malt jumping through hoops as it moves rapidly between crunchy and sharp and lightly sugar-coated; **f22** long with an unusual light oiliness for this distillery; **b22.5** puckeringly intense and full of mischief. *60.2% Scotch Malt Whisky Society. 192 bottles.*

Scott's Selection Auchroisk 1989 bott 07 **(83)** n20.5 t21.5 f23 b19. If this were art, which I suppose it is, then as a painting it is the equivalent of hurling paint at a fresh canvas. Neither rhyme nor reason to this, but the honey edge to the barley, especially late on, does impress when given a chance. The finish, seemingly against the odds, does have a certain resonance and spontaneity. *54.7%*

AULTMORE

Speyside, 1896. John Dewar & Son. Working.

Aultmore 12 Years Old db **(86)** n22 t22 f20 b22. Do any of you remember the old DCL distillery bottling of this from, what, 25 years ago? Well, this is nothing like it. *40%*

Connoisseurs Choice Aultmore 1995 (92.5) n24 I know there is no such thing as an exact definition of a Speyside aroma: historically it was lightly smoked and today more are going back to that style. However, if you ask a blender how he would think in terms of a "Speysider", this would just about be it: not just clean and malty, but with a distinctive lemon jam sponge sweetness and freshness. And, for its age, laced with just the correct amount of vanilla. Oh, and for no extra cost, some over-ripe greengages, too... **t23.5** all that barley juice promised on the nose just drips from every tastebud; next come those fruitier notes — pretty hard to make out what exactly — just fruity... but it's all so clean and damned yummy... **f22.5** dries with a dusting of cocoa; **b22.5** Aultmore up to its usual brilliant but simple tricks. *43%. Gordon & MacPhail.*

⋅⋅⋅ Dun Bheagan Aultmore 12 Years Old Sherry Butt Finish dist May 97 **(84)** n22 t22 f19.5 b20.5. Fruity and mildly feisty, the most compelling fun is condensed into the generously rich delivery. A tad thin and a little warming elsewhere. *43%. Ian Macleod*

Dun Bheagan Aultmore Aged 15 Years (76) n19 t19 f19 b19. A bit dense, monosyllabic and bitter. *43%. Ian Macleod.*

Norse Cask Selection Aultmore 1992 Aged 16 Years barrel no. 3839, dist 92, bott 08 **(91)** n23 toffee apples...and those apples are pretty damned green..! t24 tastebuds...we have lift-off...!!!! What a delivery! Spices abound, but while they explode there is no collateral damage, with the barley free to roam unmolested and a natural toffee molasses ensuring a delicate sweetness keeps things in order; f21.5 perhaps over enthusiastic caramels now as complexity levels minimalise; b22.5 what a treat to find Aultmore in this kind of mood. Great fun! *56.8%.*

Old Malt Cask Aultmore Aged 12 Years sherry butt, dist Jan 96, bott Sep 08 **(79)** n20 t21 f18.5 b19.5. Ferociously hot on delivery, you will hunt the grape in vain. Plenty of malt, though. *50%. Douglas Laing. 687 bottles.*

Old Malt Cask Aultmore Aged 18 Years dist Sep 90, bott Jul 09 **(89)** n21 threatening oak... could go either way... t23 selects the spicy, juicy route...and what spices...what juice!! Salivating barley with a touch of bourbony sweet liquorice f22 settles towards a tongue-tickling spice exit, but with plenty of butterscotch to enjoy en-route; b23 a fizzing beaut! *50%.*

⋅⋅⋅ Provenance Aultmore Aged 9 Years sherry butt no. DMG 6211, dist Autumn 2000, bott Spring 2010 **(88)** n22 new mown grass drying in the sun; t22 fantastically juicy with a slow build up of heavier fruit; the middle ground is lush but maltily flighty, too; f22 light vanillas enter but don't break the spell; b22 from a sherry butt it may be, but rarely (thankfully!) does the grape interfere with the bracing malty freshness. *46% Douglas Laing*

Provenance Aultmore Aged 11 Years sherry butt, dist autumn 96, bott summer 08 **(86)** n22.5 t21.5 f21 b21. Perplexing in style, with loads of crystalised brown sugar ensuring a solidity you would hardly expect. The malt is deliciously flinty; crunchy almost. *46%.*

Provenance Aultmore Aged 13 Years sherry butt, dist winter 96, bott winter 09 **(77.5)** n19 t21 f19 b18.5. Tangy with the odd distinctive unhappy note. The colour is excellent but the oak somehow doesn't quite gel. *46%. Douglas Laing.*

Scotch Malt Whisky Society Cask 73.30 Aged 15 Years refill barrel, dist May 92 **(86.5)** n22 t21 f22 b21.5. For a malt with a viperous 60% alcohol after 15 years, this is an incredibly well-mannered dram and not without some bourbony pretensions. Lots of lip-smacking qualities. *60.1%*

Scotch Malt Whisky Society Cask 73.31 Aged 16 Years refill barrel, dist Mar 92 **(91.5)** n22.5 t23.5 f22 b23.5. In shape and style, a twin brother of 70.30, only in execution this is just so much further ahead. A better cask and extra time has moved it on a bit further allowing the oak to have a slightly louder say. Often the time factor can go either way but, in this case, it is a development very much for the better. Make no mistake: this guy is huge and Aultmore at its finest. *9.2%*

Scotch Malt Whisky Society Cask 73.34 Aged 16 Years refill barrel, dist Mar 92 **(81)** n19 t20 f22 b20. Ye Gods! This is hot stuff. Gluey, slightly bourbony nose is followed by a searing delivery. Only when the intense malt and natural caramels settle on the finish does it begin to relax. *58.9%*

Scott's Selection Aultmore 1987 bott 07 **(88)** n22.5 t22 f21.5 b22. It's been some time since I've seen Aultmore bottled at this age. The above average oiliness helps with the length and mouthfeel for this very decent dram. *55.8%*

The Single Malts of Scotland Aultmore 1992 Aged 15 Years small batch, bott Sep 07 **(90.5)** n23 t22 f23 b22.5. A sublime, outwardly simplistic, cleverly understated dram. *46%.*

⋅⋅⋅ The Whisky Agency Aultmore 1990 (82) n21 t21 f20 b20. Once a relatively common malt now in rare supply these days. So a shame that the cask has done little to help this one hit the heights. *56.3%*

BALBLAIR

Highlands (Northern), 1872. Inver House. Working.

Balblair 10 Years Old db **(86)** n21 t22 f22 b21. Such an improved dram away from the clutches of caramel. *40%*

Balblair Aged 16 Years db **(84)** n22 t22 f20 b20. Definitely gone up a notch in the last year. The lime on the nose has been replaced by dim Seville oranges; the once boring finish reveals elements of fruit and spice. It's the barley- rich middle that shines, though, and some more work will belt this up into the high 90s where this great distillery belongs. *40%*

Balblair 1975 db **(94.5)** n24.5 one of the most complex noses in the Highlands with just about everything you can think of making a starring, or at least guest, appearance at some time. That's not a taster's get-out. Nose it and then defy me...For starters, watch the clever bourbon edge alongside the crème brulee and ground cherry topping...hunt the smoke down, also... **t23.5** silk. No, wait....it could be velvet. No, definitely silk. The barley descends in the most gentle manner possible but this does not detract from the intensity: wave upon wave of barley melts upon the tastebuds, varying only in their degree of sweetness; **f23** a few more bitter oak noises, but it remains barley all the way, even at this age. Amazing....; **b23.5** essential Balblair. *46%*

⁘ **Balblair 1978** db **(94) n24** evidence of great antiquity hangs all over this nose, not least in the exotic fruit so typical of such vast aging; there is smoke, too: a delicate peat more common at the distillery in those days is evident and most welcome; **t24** the lush delivery offers up an improbably malty juiciness. But this is almost immediately countered by a spicy oakiness which offsets with great charm the salivating barley chorus and layers of delicate fruit and almost nutty vanilla: not for a second is elegance compromised; **f23** those of you with a passion for older Ballantine's will not be much surprised that this was, in its Allied days, once a vital ingredient: such is the clarity of the vanilla-led silkiness. Again, great age is never in doubt. Towards the very death the wisps of smoke found on the nose make a lingering reappearance; **b23** just one of those drams that exudes greatness and charm in equal measures. Some malts fall apart when hitting thirty: this one is totally intact and in command. A glorious malt underlining the greatness of this mostly under-appreciated distillery. *46%*

Balblair Vintage 1979 dist 79, bott 07 db **(84) n21 t22 f20 b21.** A pretty whisky, but one which refuses to open out entirely despite the barley rich prompting. *46%. nc.*

Balblair 1989 db **(91) n23** a sprinkle of salt has maximised the bourbon intensity; the soft oak benefits, too. But it is the clarity of the barley that makes the hairs stand on end; **t23** superb delivery, with the ultra rich barley showing superb intent; the body is firm and the weight is perfect while the vanilla enters bang on cue; **f22.5** above medium length but hangs on the sweeter elements of the barley longer than anticipated; the soft buttery oak is a wonderful foil; **b22.5** don't expect gymnastics on the palate or the pyrotechnics of the Cadenhead 18: in many ways a simple malt, but one beautifully told. Almost Cardhu-esque in the barley department. *43%*

Balblair Vintage 1989 dist 89, bott 07 db **(89) n22 t23 f22 b22.** The key to this malt is its refreshing qualitiy: the way the oak come on board but the barley wins the day. An excellent journey. *43%. nc.*

⁘ **Balblair 1990** db **(92.5) n24** big, mildly syrupy with figs and pears of exploding ripeness, and a thick layering of barley-oak mix; that there is good age to this is indisputable by the evidence of the nose, as is its extraordinary dexterity and finesse: a nose to spend a good 20 minutes alone with...; **t23.5** fabulous spice explosion on arrival and then a ridiculously soothing massage of lightly sugared oak and gentle fruits; amid all this, the barley is juicy, fresh and almost like a three-year-old in its clarity; **f22** long, lightly waxed and luxuriant; **b23** tangy in the great Balblair tradition. Except here this is warts and all with the complexity and true greatness of the distillery left in no doubt. *46%*

Balblair Vintage 1997 dist 97, bott 07 db **(88) n23 t22 f21 b22.** This is the way I've been wanting to see Balblair at this age for a long, long time. Easily the most true to character distillery bottling for the last 20 years. *43%. nc.*

⁘ **Balblair 2000** db **(87.5) n21.5** gristy and grassy; **t22.5** the freshness on the nose is fully accentuated by a juicy, clean barley delivery; **f21.5** dries markedly towards powdery cocoa; **b22** Balblair without toffee yet still a clever degree of chewy weight for all the apparent lightness. *43%*

⁘ **A.D. Rattray Balblair 1991** cask no. U9/U3U/U **(88) n24** superbly salty and bracing: it is as though the Balblair warehouses have been moved ashore where the stormy seas never cease. One of the most delightful Highland noses of the year; **t21.5** tangy with the malt and lazy fruit really trying to fend off some bitter oak incursions; **f21.5** a touch oily with an injection of late sugars; **b21** the nose perhaps demands too much for the flavours to live up to. By no means your common or garden single malt: a wonderful experience all the same. *46%*

Cadenhead's Authentic Collection Balblair Aged 17 Years bourbon, dist 90, bott Sep 07 **(87.5) n22 t22.5 f21 b22.** One assumes a first full cask at work here with all those neo-bourbon notes around. *56.6%. 192 bottles.*

Cadenhead's Balblair Aged 18 Years bourbon wood, matured in oak cask, dist 90, bott Jun 08 **(92.5) n22 t25 f22.5 b23.** A sublime cask which shows just what this outstanding distillery is capable of. *55.9%. 252 bottles.*

The Creative Whisky Company Balblair 1975 Aged 29 Years (93 .5) n24 t22.5 f24 b23. Almost an off-cut of the original distillery bottling. Very similar, except this is a tad lighter in colour and nature and with a fraction more apparent oak and age. Glorious. *46.2%*

Old Distillery Label Balblair Aged 10 Years (92) n22 oozes class from every pore...and pour: lots of bourbon-cask and barley and a breezy citrus, too; **t23.5** juicy and beautifully busy. Almost impossible to spit, so faultlessly distinctive is the rich barley-bourbon tapestry; **f23** loads of chocolate on the finale with plenty of zingy zestiness and spice to keep the juices flowing despite the move towards a digestive biscuity dryness; some lovely soft oils at the death ensures good length; **b23.5** I'm a sucker for these juicy, big-malted flawless numbers. And this one certainly leaves you sucking hard as you pucker up. A top-notch thirst-quencher. *43%. Gordon & MacPhail.*

Old Malt Cask Balblair Aged 17 Years refill butt 3930, dist Apr 90, bott Oct 07 **(77.5)** n19 t19 f20 b19.5. Not quite the finest oak ever selected for maturation. *50%. nc ncf Douglas Laing. 743 bottles.*

BALMENACH
Speyside, 1824. Inver House. Working.
Balmenach Aged 25 Years Golden Jubilee db **(89)** n21 t23 f22 b23. What a glorious old charmer this is! An essay in balance despite the bludgeoning nature of the beast early on. Takes a little time to get to know and appreciate: persevere with this belter because it is classic stuff for its age. *58%. Around 800 decanters.*

⁙ **Berry's Own Selection Balmenach 1979 (87.5)** n22 polite, almost subdued. Barley for sure, but bread and butter pudding, too...; **t22** intense oak to begin, but always enough sugars to handle the age; **f21.5** the malt fights back amid the half cooked toast; **b22** Auld Balmenach pretty much nutshelled: light and attempting to be barley dominant....but not always achieving. *56.3% Berry Bros & Rudd*

The Càrn Mòr Vintage Collection Braes of Balmenach 2001 barrel, cask no. 800412, dist 01, bott 09 **(85.5)** n20.5 t22 f21.5 b21.5. Light, crisp, sweetly malted and a pleasing spiciness. *46%. The Scottish Liqueur Centre.*

Chieftain's Balmenach 15 Years Old Hogshead **(77)** n19 t21 f18 b19. Fruity and pleasant, but a fraction too over-oaked. *43%. Ian MacLeod.*

Connoisseurs Choice Balmenach Aged 18 Years first fill sherry butt, dist 90, bott 08 **(76)** n19 t20.5 f18 b18.5. Sufficient sulphur to take the shine from the experience. *43%.*

Connoisseurs Choice Balmenach 1991 (88) n22 sweetened oakiness and the vaguest hint of smoke; **t22** chewy, big, busty and lusty with a big oak tang; **f22** various sorts of chocolate confirms the maturity; **b22** firm, steady-as-she-goes malt which would not have improved with further aging. A musty-have though for those who prefer their dram spiced up and chunky. *43%. Gordon & MacPhail.*

⁙ **Connoisseurs Choice Balmenach 1993 (85)** n22 t21.5 f20.5 b21. My glass runneth over with docile vanilla and even more sleepy barley. A few spices and a tang indicate the cask has been taken to its limit. *43% Gordon & MacPhail*

Deerstalker Balmenach Aged 10 Years (90) n22.5 green, young, a fraction gristy, a fraction spent wash: it smells like a distillery... **t22.5** fresh, gently oiled and then a charming build up of barley; **f22** soft vanillas mingle with the malt; **b23** you've nosed the dull Deerstalker 12; you've tasted the mildly dented Deerstalker 18: now get your laughing gear around the best of the lot, the brand-spanking new 10-year-old. Really does show the distillery in a straw-coloured and quite wonderful light...and would do it better still at 46%. *40%. Aberko Ltd*

⁙ **Deerstalker Balmenach Aged 12 Years** bott Apr 10 **(77)** n19 t20 f19 b19. Even more gooseberry-ish than the super-plump gooseberries in my old mum's garden. However, each time I come to this one, I put it back in the pool as something troubled me. Now I finally analyse this, there is, indeed, a detectable odd note: sweetened butyric...? Deerstalker is usually a whisky you can put your hat on for quality. Perhaps not this bottling, alas. *46% Aberko Ltd*

Deerstalker Balmenach Aged 18 Years (86) n22.5 t22 f21 b21. Not quite in the same sparkling mode as many previous Deerstalkers, though the fruitiness does have a spicy tang. *46%. Aberko Ltd*

Old Malt Cask Balmenach Aged 18 Years dist Oct 90, bott Jul 09 **(87.5)** n21 an interesting array of mildly tired oak notes and grassy barley; **t24** a bucking bronco of a kick as far as the barley is concerned: enormous. Takes you through all layers from style and intensity, though the starring roles go to those malt notes tinged with golden syrup: quite wonderful; **f21** altogether more moribund and plain once the oak gains control; **b21.5** excellently weighted and shows some fine touches. *50%. Douglas Laing.*

Provenance Balmenach Aged 8 Years refill hogshead, dist winter 99, bott autumn 08 **(86)** n21 t22 f21.5 b21.5. Clean, simplistic but delightfully malty. *46%. Douglas Laing.*

⁙ **Provenance Balmenach Over 11 Years** refill hogshead 5734, dist Spring 1998, bott Winter 2010 **(78)** n20.5 t20 f18.5 b19. Distilled from helium. Sweet grist. *46% nc ncf*

Scotch Malt Whisky Society Cask 48.12 Aged 8 Years 1st fill barrel, dist Sep 99 **(86.5)** **n21 t22 f21.5 b22.** Warming, spiced, tangy with clipped, firm barley. Quite flawless in its own precise way. *60.6%*

Scotch Malt Whisky Society Cask 48.15 Aged 9 Years 1st fill barrel, dist Sep 99 **(84)** **n20 t21 f22 b21.** A big, rousing dram where the barley dominates despite the caramelised biscuit sheen. Perhaps short on complexity, but doesn't stint a jot on effect. When the alcohol burn subsides, and the vanillas shine rather than glow, the quality of the cask is fully evident. *61.3%*

Scotch Malt Whisky Society Cask 48.16 Aged 8 Years 1st fill barrel, dist Oct 00 **(90)** **n21** slightly ungainly with the oak not quite in alignment with the barley and under-ripe pear; **t23.5** classy, if mildly abrasive, pear drop delivery. Soon gets into a divine malty-mocha stride and the dark sugars build in intensity and suavity; **f22.5** beautifully long and sculpted with the barley re-emerging unscathed while a touch of manuka honey enriches the vanilla; **b23** a beautiful multi-textured dram which at times threatens towards a bitter course but stays on track with a refined, juicy intensity. *58.5%*

THE BALVENIE
Speyside, 1892. William Grant & Sons. Working.

The Balvenie 10 Years Founders Reserve db **(90)** **n23** astonishing complexity: the fruit is relaxed, crushed sultanas and malty suet. A sliver of smoke and no more: everything is hinted and nudged at rather than stated. Superb; **t24** here we go again: threads of malt binding together barely detectable nuances. Thin liquorice here, grape there, smoke and vanilla somewhere else; **f20** Light muscovado-toffee flattens out the earlier complexity. The bitter-sweet balance remains brilliant to the end; **b23** just one of those all-time-great standard 10-year-olds from a great distillery – pity they've decided to kill it off. *40%*

The Balvenie Double Wood Aged 12 Years db **(80.5)** **n22 t20.5 f19 b19.** OK. So here's the score: Balvenie is one of my favourite distilleries in the world, I confess. I admit it. The original Balvenie 10 is a whisky I would go to war for. It is what Scotch malt whisky is all about. It invented complexity; or at least properly introduced me to it. But I knew that it was going to die, sacrificed on the altar of ageism. So I have tried to get to love Double Wood. And I have tasted and/or drunk it every month for the last couple of years to get to know it and, hopefully fall in love. But still I find it rather boring company. We may have kissed and canoodled. But still there is no spark. No romance whatsoever. *40%*

The Balvenie Signature Aged 12 Years batch no. 001 db **(93)** **n25** dried dates and walnuts with a touch of truffle oil. The Melton Mowbray Hunt fruit cake is massaged by demerara while shy strands of liquorice, ginger and chocolate malt add to the brilliance. If anyone wants to know just what a true master blender can do when allowed to get on with it, stick your snout in this and learn.... **t23** watery and delicate, there is a diffused, almost drowned, noble rot feel to this; bolstered by the most delicate spices – again of the fruitcake variety – the malt makes a pretty speech before the custard tart takes over; **f21** disappointing, as it appears to fade just too quickly leaving some vanilla tidemarks; **b24** this whisky was created by Grant's blender David Stewart and bottled to mark his 45 years in the industry. For my money, he's now the best in the business and has been for a little while. But it is a great shame that the marketing guys didn't insist on this being an apposite 45% because, for all the subtle wizardry going on here and the fact that the nose should immediately become the stuff of whisky legend, this is dreadfully underpowered. *40%*

❖ **Balvenie Signature Aged 12 Years** batch no. 003 db **(89)** **n24** nothing like as rich as the first Batch: this aroma is about innuendo and strands. Where once there was powering, fresh-out-of-the-oven fruitcake, now there is more of the mixing bowl with the emphasis on the flour rather than the dried fruit. Even so, there is sufficient orange peel to freshen things up; **t23.5** against the odds the barley shows first, only briefly, mind, before a dizzying welter of fruity blows knocks it from the scene. The mouthfeel is silky but roughens up towards the middle ground; **f19** a hint of discord and fluffy dryness; **b22.5** if you don't taste this at body temperature you are doing both yourself and this whisky a huge disservice. One of the great benefits of Balvenie is that it can shine at virtually any age: at 10 it is truly magnificent – though sadly you'll rarely get the chance to discover this these days – and when a couple of years old still the barley has enough charisma to talk a beautiful game. The fruits have a bitter-sweet effect – literally – by helping to map out a wonderful nose but lessening the value of the finish. Enjoyable whisky all the same and what a pity it isn't at 47%.... *40%*

Balvenie Rum Wood Aged 14 Years db **(88)** **n22** excitable malt; lively almost piercing sugars; **t23** incredible spice delivery, seriously warming and increasingly sensual as the malt fights back; **f21** lots of toffee-barley; **b22** tasted blind I would never have recognized the distillery: I'm not sure if that's a good thing. *47.1%*

The Balvenie Roasted Malt Aged 14 Years (90) n21 a European style of aroma often found in the smaller distilleries being in some ways closed, offering a hard edge and, on another level, showing attractive bitter-sweet conflict; t23 it's the sweet element that shows the more powerful hand, especially with a delicious barley rush, though rabid peppers soon gather all the attention f22 dry at first, a little sinewy but the gradual build up of mocha is sublime b24 Balvenie very much as you've never seen it before: it takes time to settle, but when it does it becomes an absolute, mouth-filling cracker! 47.1%

Balvenie 14 Years Old Cuban Selection db (86) n20 t22 f22.5 b21.5. Unusual malt and tasted blind you wouldn't recognise the distillery in a million years. No great fan of the nose but the roughness of the delivery grows on you; there is a jarring, tongue-drying quality which actually works quite well and the development of the inherent sweetness is almost in slow motion. Some sophistication here, but also the odd note which, on the nose especially, is a little out of tune. 43%

Balvenie 14 Years Old Golden Cask db (91) n23.5 mildly tart: rhubarb and custard, with a vague sprinkling of brown sugar; bourbon notes, too; t23 mouth-watering and zingy spice offer up a big delivery, but settles towards the middle towards a more metallic barley-rich sharpness; f22 soft spices peddle towards the finish and a wave or three of gathering oak links well with the sweetened barley strands; b22.5 a confident, elegant malt which doesn't stint one iota on complexity. Worth raiding the Duty Free shops for this little gem alone. 47.5%

Balvenie 17 Years Old Rum Cask db (88.5) n22 green bananas and oak: curious... t22.5 initially dry with the oak elbowing in first; several levels of barley battle back while some fudge enters the middle ground; f22 remains fudgy, with a touch of oily butterscotch tart, but the emphasis is on the dryer, flaky tart; b22 for all the best attentions of the rum cask at times this feels all its 17 years, and perhaps a few summers more. Impossible not to love, however. 43%

The Balvenie Aged 15 Years Single Barrel db (90.5) n22 candy fruit and barley sugar; t23.5 juicy delivery where the barley leads the way and is soon backed up by sweet enforcements; a powder-dry oakiness ghosts around and a soft fruitiness can likewise be detected; f22.5 long with a clever and astonishingly slow spice development. When it finally arrives, it really lets you know....! b23 sadly, unable to discover which cask this was from or for which market. So one takes this as a generic Balvenie at its new strength. 47.8%

Balvenie New Wood Aged 17 Years db (85) n23 t22 f19 b21. A naturally good age for Balvenie; the nose is lucid and exciting, the early delivery is thick with rich malt. This, though, has sucked out lots of caramel from the wood to leave an annoyingly flat finish. 40%

⁙ **The Balvenie Aged 17 Years Old Madeira Cask** Madeira finish, bott 2009 db (93.5) n24 classically two-toned, with a pair of contrasting tales being told simultaneously yet in complete harmony. One is fruity (especially apple) and ripe and blended with the weighty oak; the other is barley-sweet and refreshing. What a treat...; t23.5 the juicy grape takes the higher ground, joining forces with the juicier barley; some distance below the oak throbs contentedly...; f23 a little oak prickle and a hint of sweet mocha on the vanilla; b23 an essay in deportment. Every aspect appears to have been measured and weighed. Hurry this imperious whisky at your peril. 43%

The Balvenie 17 Year Old Sherry Oak db (88) n23 glorious grape with no off notes: just sherry trifle sweetness with the odd spice kick; t22.5 superbly clean grape even offers an early noble rot flourish; the oaks ensure ballast; f21 long, dry and a touch bitter; b21.5 clean as a nut. High-class sherry it may be but the price to pay is a flattening out of the astonishing complexity one normally finds from this distillery. Bitter-sweet in every respect. 43%

The Balvenie Aged 21 Years Port Wood db (88.5) n22 unusual aroma for a wine-finished whisky: here we are getting distinct ye olde oake signs that are leaning towards the exotic fruitiness of old bourbon casks; t22 salivating and on the money malt-wise with the juicy chewiness appearing a lot fresher than the nose would have you believe; f22.5 busy, multi-layered with some lovely praline amid the soft grape; b22 beautiful, subtle malt. But the fruit element has been reduced considerably, as if the original Port pipes are being used a second or third time round. 40%

The Balvenie Thirty Aged 30 Years db (92) n24 has kept its character wonderfully, with a real mixture of varied fruits. Again the smoke is apparent, as is the panting oak. Astonishing thet the style should have been kept so similar to previous bottlings; t23 big, full delivery first of enigmatic, thick barley, then a gentle eruption of controlled, warming spices; f22 much more oaky involvement but such is the steadiness of the barley, its extraordinary confidence, no damage is done and the harmony remains; b23 rarely have I come across a bottling of a whisky of these advanced years which is so true to previous ones. Amazing. 47.3%

⁙ **The Balvenie Aged 40 Years Batch 1** bott 2010 db (79) n22 t20 f18 b19. The makings of a great nose: a real nutty Dundee cake special. But a bitter let down on the palate. 48.5%

Balvenie 1972 Vintage cask no. 14811 db (82) n20 t22 f20 b20. A tiring, exotic fruited effort which glows rather than shines. 47.3%

The Balvenie 1993 Port Wood db (89) n21 well-weighted but a trifle stifled; t23 much busier arrival, with a lovely roastiness playing off the wine; the spices buzz gorgeously; f22 finds a light-roast Java element; b23 oozes class without getting too flash about it: the secret is in the balance. 40%

BANFF
Speyside, 1863–1983. Demolished.

Cadenhead's Banff 29 Years Old (73) n19 t19 f18 b17. Too heavily oaked: should have been bottled at 25. 52%

Cadenhead's Banff Aged 32 Years dist 76, bott 09 (85) n22.5 t21 f20.5 b21. Valiantly offers all the barley it can muster, and even a touch of defiant sweet grassiness, but the passing years and accumulated oak have the biggest say. 47.1%

Celtic Heartlands Banff 1975 bott 08 (93) n23 sturdy, solid barley fortified with vanilla-oak (and a bit of sap) and citrus; the most delicate drift of smoke; t23.5 big mouth-feel thanks to the suave oils; strawberry jam and cream-Victoria sponge feel; f23 a move towards muscovado-sweetened mocha but elegant with those soft oils ensuring a lengthy tail off; b23.5 pure, unambiguous quality. 48.1%. Bruichladdich Ltd. 449 bottles.

Old & Rare Banff Aged 37 Years dist Mar 71, bott Mar 08 (74) n19 t18 f19 b18. A strange malt: like finding an old piece of music written by Delius, or someone, and finding the whole thing out of key. 53%. ncf. Douglas Laing. 271 bottles.

⁘ **Old & Rare Banff Aged 38 Years** dist Mar 71, bott Aug 09 (86) n22 t21.5 f21 b21.5. Now here's something that might take 38 years to fathom. An old peculiar Banff carrying a tired, bitter oak note which runs directly under the strata of smoke. The result is a very unusual personality which some might find hard to understand. Elsewhere the barley shimmers and there is just enough muscovado sugar to raise a light fruit profile. But it is that almost unique peat-oak combination which will dominate the experience – and entirely baffle - most who encounter this. 53.4% Douglas Laing & Co Ltd. 324 bottles.

Old Malt Cask Banff Aged 32 Years refill hogshead, dist Nov 75, bott Aug 08 (89) n22 oak shavings stirred into custard powder and a tablespoon full of acacia honey for good measure; t23 wonderful layers of sugar-tipped barley head towards an oaky core; f21.5 dries but the threatened oaks don't really overpower and unbalance the malty theme; b22.5 funny how age works on some distilleries and not others. Technically, this probably has too much oak. Yet such is the overall richness and class of this enchanting dram, you can easily forgive its weaknesses. 48.7%. Douglas Laing. 164 bottles.

Old Malt Cask Banff Aged 36 Years refill butt no. 3188, dist Mar 71, bott Sep 07 (88) n22.5 t21 f22.5 b22. Has as many grey hairs as me. But just as sexy. A hint of something smoky on the nose; citrus seeing off the intruding oak on the palate. 50%. Douglas Laing. 451 bottles.

⁘ **The Whisky Agency Banff 1975** (89.5) n23 can't remember the last time I got this amount of honey from a 35-y-o malt which wasn't HP..; an almost pathetic puff of smoke; t23 here we go again...!! Honey in a multitude of guises, though the oak bites hard; vanillas fill the middle ground as does a little pine and eucalyptus; f21.5 oily, with a little liquorice attached to the honey and vanilla; b22 distilled by bees. Matured by squirrels. 44.9%

BEN NEVIS
Highland (Western), 1825. Nikka. Working.

Ben Nevis 10 Years Old db (88) n21 enormously chunky and weighty: for a 10-y-o the oak is thick, but sweetened medley of ripe fruits; t22 an almost syrupy mouth feel: a tad cloying but the malt is something you can so get your teeth into; f23 long with traces of liquorice and hickory; b22 a massive malt that has steadied itself in recent bottlings, but keep those knives and forks to hand! 46%

Ben Nevis 14 Years Old Single Sherry Cask dist Sep 92, bott Jan 07 db (88.5) n21 t22.5 f22 b22.5. Talk about brinkmanship! This sherry butt has been introduced to sulphur. Luckily, its acquaintance was a passing one only, otherwise the marks would have tumbled frighteningly; but they shook hands sufficiently for five or six points to be lost here. That said, the integrity of the actual distillate is so high it comes through as a serious dram to savour. Mind you, I know a few Germans who would do anything for this kind of malt...well almost... 46%. 815 bottles.

⁘ **Ben Nevis 1984 Single Cask** double wood matured cask no. 98/35/1, dist Dec 84, bott Jan 10 db (73.5) n18.5 t19 f17 b19. Formidable sherry and some early grape. But once the sulphur gets hold, it refuses to let go. 56% ncf

⤛ **Ben Nevis 1996 Single Cask** bourbon cask, dist May 96, bott Jan 09 db **(90) n22** malt concentrate man marked by clean, proud oak; **t23** not often you get a delivery this barley entangled. Rich malt head in every direction, enriched by Demerara sugars and a light liquorice: a quasi-bourbony feel to this; **f23** a long, impressive trail of intense malt and lighter vanillas; **b22** a thick-set little gem of a whisky. *56.8% for Swedish Whisky Society TKS*

Ben Nevis 1997 Single Cask double wood matured, dist Feb 97, bott Jul 07 db **(91) n20 t23.5 f24 b23.5.** From the colour, it appears to have been matured with cherries: I have never seen any whisky this ruddy colour in my life. But it tastes a whole lot better than it looks and even appears to see off a sulphurous threat that appears on the nose. Very different and, if in Sweden, worth hunting down. Borders on the mad genius. *46%. ncf. 697 bottles. For Sweden.*

⤛ **Ben Nevis 1997 Single Cask Port Finish for TKS** port bodega butt, double wood matured, dist Feb 97, bott Jul 07 db **(79) n18.5 t22 f18.5 b20.** The quite magnificent rose colouring is not quite matched by the thick, almost impenetrable nose. But things take a turn for the better as the enormity of the fruit makes its mark on delivery. The finish, though, still leaves a little to be desired. *46% ncf For Swedish whisky Society TKS*

⤛ **Ben Nevis 1998 Single Cask** sherry butt no. 358, dist Jun 05, bott Oct 09 db **(67) n16 t17 f17 b17.** Uncompromising sulphur. *46% ncf for Swedish Whisky Society TKS*

⤛ **A.D. Rattray Ben Nevis 1996** cask no. 2214, dist Dec 96, bott Mar 10 **(72.5) n17 t19 f18.5 b18.** Looks like the stillman's watch had stopped when he was working out the cut times. Still, can't say it's not interesting... *58.2% A.D. Rattray Ltd*

Battlehill Ben Nevis Aged 8 Years (80.5) n20.5 t22 f19 b19. A butch, nutty delivery. The malt and oak are barely on speaking terms. *43%. Duncan Taylor.*

Berry's Own Selection Ben Nevis 1996 bott 09 **(86.5) n21.5 t21 f22.5 b21.5.** One of those almost impenetrably dense malty affairs this distillery conjours up from time to time, this one showing some fabulous sweet touches to the barley late on. Serve with a spoon. *56.9%. Berry Bros & Rudd.*

⤛ **The Càrn Mòr Vintage Collection Ben Nevis 1997** hogshead no. 252, dist 1997, bott 2009 **(83.5) n19.5 t22 f21 b21.** Big, busty, at times bruising, but always malty and sweet. *46% nc ncf 1275 bottles.*

⤛ **Dancing Stag Ben Nevis 1996 (89.5) n23.5** so complex and delicate! The odd hint of smoke here and there counters the light, fruity sparkle of the barley; just the mocha note hanging around, too; **t22.5** silky with a puff of smoke arriving early, followed swiftly by busy barley; **f21.5** quietens as the toffee arrives; **b22** a beautifully made and matured whisky. *46% Robert Graham Ltd*

⤛ **Duncan Taylor Collection Ben Nevis 1995** rum cask **(86) n21 t23 f21.5 b21.5.** Almost eye-wateringly juicy. The crisp barley is helped out by a sugary firmness, presumably offered by the rum. Narrow but a joy. *46% Duncan Taylor & Co Ltd*

Duncan Taylor The NC2 Range Ben Nevis 1990 Aged 16 Years (75) n18.5 t20 f18 b18.5. A bitter-sweet affair with the emphasis on the bitter. *46%*

⤛ **The Golden Cask Ben Nevis 1997** cask no. CM141, dist 1997, bott 2009 **(88) n21.5** salt sprinkled on custard; **t22** malty, wonderfully busy with the barley breaking down into an almost bourbon small grain buzz; **f22.5** a mix of malt and chocolate milkshake; **b22** oily textured and tests the palate. *56% The House of MacDuff. 310 bottles.*

⤛ **Malts of Scotland Ben Nevis 1996** sherry hogshead no. 1466, dist Oct 96, bott Jan 10 **(89.5) n22.5** curious: big bodied, but the malt and grape elements, though clear and precise, are pretty lightweight; **t23** the fruity exoskeleton ensures a slow barley build up; **f22** medium length, clean and every bit as dapper as the nose and delivery; **b22** a delicious, quite flawless, experience. *57.1% Malts of Scotland. 192 bottles.*

Milroy's of Soho Ben Nevis 1996 refill sherry butt, cask no. 1670, dist Oct 96, bott Jul 08 **(90.5) n21.5** toasty, for all the hints of fruit; **t22** better delivery than the nose heralds with a confident malt thrust into the building grape; **f24** plateaus superbly with that preserve and toast on the nose now coming through as juicy fig jam with a prickly sweetness reflecting off the stunning oak-fruit sheen: just wonderful... **b23** hard not to be seduced by the rich and silkily-textured finish. A malt of great character. *46%. 198 bottles.*

⤛ **Old & Rare Ben Nevis 1966 Aged 43 Years** dist 1966, bott Nov 09 **(91.5) n23** almost a bourbon feel to this with a roastiness to the sugars of the oak; some fruit around still, as is a dying smokiness; **t22.5** silky: the oak offers a degree of mocha and toasty vanilla; a tad off key, but no damage done; **f24** light spices and soft vanilla; that hint of smoke returns with a light, milk chocolate fade and some lovely late kumquat; **b22** one of those drams which looks as though it just ain't gonna cut it...and then does with a sly flourish. *43.8%*

⤛ **Old Malt Cask Ben Nevis 13 Years Old** refill hogshead no. 5599, dist Nov 96, bott Nov 09 **(91) n22.5** you wouldn't find this nose out of place in Kentucky... **t23.5** chewy, beautifully full bodied and forever building up the Demerara sugar and burnt honeycomb theme; **f22.5** long and vanilla saturated. That sugary sweetness persists to the end; **b22.5** a fabulous cask absolutely bulging with high grade personality. *50% Douglas Laing & Co Ltd. 334 bottles.*

Old Masters Ben Nevis Aged 10 Years cask no. 172, dist 98, bott 08 **(86) n22 t22.5 f20.5 b21.** Typical Nevis thick barley soupiness with the sharpness of the malt and bourbony nose. A real early delight. *579%. James MacArthur & Co. Ltd.*

Provenance Ben Nevis Aged 10 Years Gabriel Meffre wine cask no. 3686 **(84.5) n21 t21 f21.5 b21.** A thin vin fin. *46%. Douglas Laing.*

Provenance Ben Nevis Aged 10 Years refill butt no. 3941, dist winter 97, bott autumn 07 **(81) n18.5 t22 f20.5 b20.** The big, juicy malt sweetness on arrival does its best to overcome some sub-standard oak. *46%. Douglas Laing.*

Provenance Ben Nevis Aged 11 Years sherry finish butt no. 4236, dist winter 96, bott spring 08 **(86.5) n21.5 t22 f22 b21.** Much more like the full-bodied Ben Nevis we know and love. The grape has done a good job adding extra weight. Sweet if borderline cloying. *46%. nc ncf. Douglas Laing.*

⋰⋰ **Provenance Ben Nevis Over 12 Years** refill hogshead no. DMG 6190, dist Autumn 1997, bott Spring 2010 **(80.5) n18.5 t21.5 f19.5 b21.** If you know a whisky bottled this year more uncompromisingly malty, then show me it. *46% nc ncf Douglas Laing*

BENRIACH

Speyside, 1898. The BenRiach Distillery Co. Working.

The BenRiach db **(86) n21 t22 f21.5 b21.5.** The kind of soft malt you could wean nippers on, as opposed to Curiositas, which would be kippers. Unusually for a BenRiach there is a distinct toffee-fudge air to this one late on, but not enough to spoil that butterscotch-malt charm. No colouring added, so a case of the oak being a bit naughty. *40%*

⋰⋰ **The BenRiach Curiositas Aged 10 Years Single Peated Malt** db **(90.5) n23** the thin smoke is losing out to the honey-fudge; **t23** the peat takes a little time to gather its speech, but when it comes it is fine and softly delivered. In the meantime soft barley and that delicious but curiously dampening sweet fudge struts its stuff; **f22** chalky vanillas and a squirt of chocolate like that found on ice cream cones; **b22.5** "Hmmmm. Why have my research team marked this down as a 'new' whisky" I wondered to myself. Then immediately on nosing and tasting I discovered the reason without having to ask: the pulse was weaker, the smoke more apologetic...it had been watered down from the original 46% to 40%. This is excellent malt. But can we have our truly great whisky back, please? As lovely as it is, this is a bit of an imposter. As Emperor Hadrian might once have said: "ifus itus aintus brokus...." *40%*

⋰⋰ **The BenRiach Aged 12 Years** db **(82.5) n21 t20 f21 b20.5.** More enjoyable than the 43% I last tasted. But still a very safe, entirely inoffensive malt determined to offer minimal complexity. *40%*

The BenRiach Aged 12 Years db **(78.5) n21.5 t20 f18 b19.** White peppers on the nose, then goes uncharacteristically quiet and shapeless. *43%*

⋰⋰ **The BenRiach Aged 12 Years Dark Rum Wood Finish** db **(85.5) n21 t22 f21 b21.5.** Does exactly what it says on the tin. More than a decade ago, long before it ever became fashionable, I carried out an extensive programme of whisky maturation in old dark rum casks. So, if someone asked me now what would happen if you rounded off a decently peated whisky in a rum cask, I'd say – depending on time given for the finish and type of rum – the smoke would be contained and there would be a ramrod straight, steel-hard sweetness ensuring the most clipped whisky you can possibly imagine. And this here is exactly what we have... *46%*

The BenRiach Aged 12 Years Matured in Sherry Wood db **(90.5) n22.5** bitter-sweet grape with a chalky, sober dryness; **t23.5** a celebration of velvety fruit offers succulence and unusual clarity; there is enough room for the barley and a delightful latte development; **f22** medium length, continuing on the coffeed theme; even the late custard powder-vanilla oaky influx charms; **b22.5** a treat of a sherried malt: no off notes and a real depth to the grape. *46%*

The BenRiach Aged Over 12 Years "Arumaticus Fumosus" richly peated style, ex-dark rum barrels db **(91) n23** crackingly-hard peat; embers of a crofter's fire; **t23** big entry yet always controlled; the peat is shackled by something non-gristy yet sweet but comes and comes again in waves; the tingling spices are well harnessed; **f22** a Java/Indian medium roast coffee mix with a touch of demerara to lighten it...and the smoke, of course; **b23** very often finishing in rum can sharpen the mouthfeel yet at the same time add a sugary sheen. This little gem is no exception. *46%*

The BenRiach Aged Over 12 Years "Heredotus Fumosus" richly peated style, ex-pedro ximenez sherry butt db **(84) n20 t22 f21 b21.** Perfectly respectable, perfectly drinkable, highly enjoyable and pretty more-ish. But if any whisky was to convince me that latter-day sherry butts and peat make entirely happy bedfellows...this wouldn't be it. *46%*

The BenRiach Aged Over 12 Years "Importanticus Fumosus" richly peated style, ex-port hogshead db **(87) n22** the phenols are hard enough to still be embedded in a New Pitsligo peat stack; **t22** some grudging fruitiness attempts to make inroads into the solid peat base; **f21** some spices chisel their way into the malt; **b22** spill some of this on your foot and you'll break a toe. *Hardicus asius Nailsus. 46%*

⠶ **The BenRiach Aged 12 Years "Importanticus Fumosus"** tawny port wood finish db **(91.5) n23** no matter here had it been finished in Short-eared, Long-eared, Little, Barn or Tawny Port, the peat would have come out tops. The smoke is enormous: owl do they do it....? **t22.5** a peaty custard pie in the mush: enormous impact with more early vanilla than fruit; **f23.5** now the grape begins to get its head above the smoky parapet; a beautiful balance with the smoke, vanilla and minor spices; **b22.5** you'd be a twit not to buy two of 'em. *46%*

The BenRiach Aged 13 Years Maderensis Fumosus Heavily Peated finished in Madeira barrels db **(87.5) n23** dry peat laid on with a trowel but particularly attractive due to the unusual layering of intensity; found hiding amongst these strata is a faint grapiness; **t21.5** no hiding the fruit now as it takes on the smoke for supremacy: a bit of an untidy battle; **f22** settles, possible due to exhaustion. Excellent vanilla calms the squabbling elements and even a touch of liquorice and molasses dives in at the death; **b21** a sharp and wild experience. *46%. nc ncf.*

The BenRiach Aged 15 Years Dark Rum Wood Finish db **(86) n21 t22 f22 b21.** Some malts, when put into a dark rum cask, have a propensity to become enjoyable but pretty sweet. This is one such example. *46%. nc ncf.*

⠶ **The BenRiach Aged 15 Years Madeira Wood Finish** db **(89.5) n22.5** fascinating dry farmhouse cider gives a deliciously unusual edge; **t21.5** as sharp and tangy as they come: the first three or four waves are all about the grape finish, then the barley has a clear run; **f23** settles rather beautifully with the barley and cocoa-dusted oak offering an excellent exit; **b22.5** very much drier than most Madeira finishes you will find around. Once the scramble on delivery is over, this bottling simply exudes excellence. A collector's must have. *46%*

⠶ **The BenRiach Aged 15 Years Pedro Ximinez Sherry Wood Finish** db **(94.5) n25** a delicate PX influence? This is magnificent...can't be... I'll stop and start again...(15 mins later....) Nope, I was right first time: a PX which is subtlety whiskified. Astonishing layering, each one delicate and fragile: vanilla and lime; gooseberry; barley; grape...a buzz of spice. All clean: not a single bitter or off note....wow! This is one of the world whisky noses of the year: absolute perfection; **t23.5** mouth-filling barley then a spreading of a sugary but fruity theme, especially to the roof of the mouth where it sticks on a light oil; in the meantime there is a slow burn of increasing spice; **f22.5** long, absolutely thick with butterscotch barley, framed by a constant drone of spicy, sugared grape; **b23.5** some of the strangest Scotch malts I have tasted in the last decade have been fashioned in PX casks. And few have been particularly enjoyable creations. This one, though, bucks the trend thanks principally to the most subtle of spice imprints. All the hallmarks of some kind of award-winner. *46%*

⠶ **The BenRiach Aged 15 Years Tawny Port Wood Finish** db **(89.5) n21.5** confused and heavy. The fruit has little give; **t23** comes together on the palate with a rare degree of grace. The kicking expected from the fruit never materialises and instead there is a soft malt and firm fruit double whammy; the fruit and nut chocolate arrives earlier than expected; **f22.5** long, with a sustained gracefulness as the malt continues to have an impressive say; a soupcon of furry bitterness at the death; **b22.5** now that really is the perfect late night dram after a bastard of a day. *46%*

⠶ **The BenRiach Aged 16 Years** db **(83.5) n21.5 t21 f20 b21.** How extraordinary: just checked the scoring for its old 43% incarnation...and it's identical right along the line. Which is a shame. Because although maltily enjoyable, if over dependent on caramel flavours, you get the feeling that a full works 46% version would offer something more gripping and true to this great distillery. *40%*

The BenRiach Aged 16 Years db **(83.5) n21.5 t21 f20 b21.** Pleasant malt but now without the dab of peat which gave it weight; also a marked reduction of the complexity that once gave this such a commanding presence. Doubtless next time I come across this it'll be back to its brilliant old self. *43%*

⠶ **The BenRiach Aged 16 Years Sauternes Wood Finish** db **(85) n19.5 t23 f21.5 b21.** One of the problems with cask finishing, is that there is nothing like an exact science of knowing when the matured whisky and introduced wood gel to their fullest potential. BenRiach enjoy a reputation of getting it right more often than most other distillers and bottlers. But here it hasn't come off to quite the same effect as previous, quite sensational, versions I have tasted of the

16-y-o Sauternes finish. No denying the sheer joy of the carpet bombing of the taste buds on delivery, though, so rich is the combination of fresh grape and delicate smoke. 46%

⋙ **The BenRiach Aged 18 Years Gaja Barolo Wood Finish** db (89) n22 clean: bag of semi-sweet wine gums and gristy barley sub-plot; t23 brilliant delivery where the taste buds are washed in something approaching grape juice and barley water; f21.5 bitters and spices out as the oak gets a foothold; b22.5 the delivery gives one of the most salivating experiences of the year. Love it. 46%

⋙ **The BenRiach Aged 18 Years Moscatel Wood Finish** db (92.5) n23.5 one of those sublime noses where everything is understated: the fresh apples and grape, the most delicate of smoke, the jam on toast, the vanilla...; t23.5 textbook delivery: every note clean and clear, especially the juicy fruits melting into the lush barley. A buzz of distant background smoke all helped along by the most subtle of oils; f22 leans towards the vanilla; b23.5 one of those rare whiskies which renews and upholds any belief I have for cask finishing. Superb. 46%

The BenRiach Aged 20 Years db (78) n19 t20 f19 b20. This is big, but not necessarily for the right reasons or in the right places. A big cut of oiliness combines with some surging sugars for a most un-BenRiachy ride. 46% ⊙ ⊙

⋙ **The BenRiach Aged 21 Years "Authenticus" Peated Malt** (85.5) n22 t21.5 f21 b21. A heavy malt, though the smoke only adds a small degree to its weight. The barley is thick and chewy but the oak has a very big say. 46%

⋙ **The BenRiach 25 Years Old** db (87.5) n21.5 sharp and intense: a fruitcake with extra sultanas but the oak bites...; t23 not the most subtle of deliveries: the oak rushes in for an eye wateringly tart and juicy start, but simmers down with hazelnuts and walnut cream cake; on a higher level there is a far more relaxed fruitcake theme pepped up by subtle spice; f21 the spice continues but there is a furry, chalky dryness; b22 the tranquillity and excellent balance of the middle is the highlight by far. 50%

⋙ **The BenRiach 30 Years Old** db (94.5) n24 the fruit, though very ripe and rich, remains uncluttered and clean and is helped along the way by a superb injection of sweetened cloves and Parma Violets; the oak is present and very correct offering an egg custard sub-plot; t24 how ridiculously deft is that? There is total equilibrium in the barley and fruit as it massages the palate in one of the softest deliveries of a 30-y-o around; the middle ground is creamy and leans towards the vanilla; even so, there are some amazingly juicy moments to savour; f23 long, very lightly oiled and mixing light grist and rich vanilla; b23.5 it's spent 30 years in the cask: give one glass of this at least half an hour of your time: seal the room, no sounds, no distractions. It's worth it....for as hard as I try, I can barely find a single fault with this. 50%

⋙ **The BenRiach Single Cask 1970** Pedro Ximinez sherry finish, cask no. 1035 (93.5) n23 the odd soapy tired note is soon swamped by a lightly spiced, massively graped tsunami. Talk about old and new... t24 a quite sublime delivery: buttery barley stands shoulder to shoulder with a feisty, lightly spiced grape. The result is a pulsating encounter which stimulates every working taste bud... f23 long, creamy...a bit like a spiced, fruity iced cream; b23.5 admission time: I was wholly sceptical that a malt like Benriach at this age would have what was needed to carry the load of something so hefty and uncompromising as a PX cask. I suspect the blender probably thought the same thing. But, against the odds I would say, this has worked....and with aplomb. 49.1%. 250 bottles.

⋙ **The BenRiach Single Cask 1975** Tawny port finish, cask no. 4450 db (83) n20.5 t22.5 f19 b21. A massive malt which perhaps I should enjoy more than I do. When the grape is clean it is a sweet thing of wonder. But there is a dull note in there which lets the side down 52.2%. 648 bottles.

The BenRiach 1975 Vintage Single Cask Campaign No. 4 ex port pipe, cask no. 4451, bott Jun 07 db (91) n23 t23 f22 b23. The Port has certainly breathed life into this old 'un. The complexity and enormity of the experience means it takes about 20 minutes to even begin to fathom this one out. 53.9%. 650 bottles.

The BenRiach 1976 hogshead, cask no. 2014, dist 19 Mar 76, bott Jul 08 db (95.5) n24 no doubting its great age for supposedly one of the lighter Speysiders, but the way the butterscotch, rice pudding with a dollop of honey and physalis congregate, oh, and some very light smoke, too, you cannot be other than transfixed; t24 sharp, juicy barley; some oaky extremes are brought under control by varying levels of non-specific juicy, vaguely exotic, fruit and the lightest layer of smoke; f23.5 long, soft custard notes which sit well with the fruit; some late spices confirm the oak and smoke involvement; b24 a classic with memorable barley at its very richest. 50.3%. 200 bottles.

The BenRiach 1976 Vintage Single Cask Campaign No. 4 ex port pipe, cask no. 4469, bott Jun 07 db (90) n22 t22 f23 b23. Good grief! Another BenRiach that is almost redefining cask finishes. This one works a treat, though! 55.5%. 750 bottles.

⁙ **The BenRiach Single Cask 1977** virgin American oak, cask no. 3798 db **(76.5) n21 t19 f18 b18.5.** Proof, were it needed, that there is only so much fun you can have with an old virgin... 43.2%. 292 bottles.

The BenRiach 1977 Muscatel wine barrel, cask no. 1029, dist 15 Apr 77, bott Jul 08 db **(80) n22.5 t20 f19 b18.5.** Superb nose, but on delivery I find this type of malt simply too overpowered by wine with the balance compromised. Doubtless, though, there will wine finish fundamentalists who will drool over it. Good luck to them. 54.9%. 313 bottles.

The BenRiach 1977 hogshead, cask no. 7186, dist 30 Jun 77, bott Jul 08 db **(88) n21.5** mixed messages here: not overly impressive oak but the varying citrus notes delight; **t23.5** fabulously sharp and alive; the barley fans out in all directions, taking a rich malty theme on one hand and also a massively active citric shape on another: breathtakingly beautiful...! **f21** bitter orange and...bitter; **b22** some signs of a cask that was unloved before being filled. Nothing wrong with the spirit which entered into it, though. 51.3%. 237 bottles.

⁙ **The BenRiach Single Cask 1978** Gaja Barolo finish, cask no. 4414 db **(88) n22** huge battle between thumping grape and significant oak; **t22.5** eye-watering in the usual Gaja Barolo style, but here tempered by a very confident butterscotch tart and smoked cheese duet; **f22** dry with pithy grape and quietly unfolding vanillas; **b21.5** a bit leaden footed at times, but where it works it does so splendidly. 51.2% 245 bottles.

The BenRiach 1978 Muscatel wine barrel, cask no. 4412, dist 20 Feb 78, bott Jul 08 db **(77) n21 t20 f17.5 b18.5.** One massive grape impact: for those who like some whisky notes in their wine. 50%. 274 bottles.

The BenRiach 1978 Vintage Single Cask Campaign No. 4 ex moscatel, cask no. 4413, bott Jun 07 db **(81) n22 t21 f20 b18.** My lack of fondness for certain finishes is well documented. Where does this sit in the pantheon of finishes? Very hard to say. Certainly it aint a rip-roaring success. But on the other hand the odd succulence drifts over the palate...but not enough to make it entirely work, sadly. 52.5%. 198 bottles.

The BenRiach 1978 Vintage Single Cask Campaign No. 4 ex tokaji, cask no. 4416, bott Jun 07 db **(88) n23 t21 f22 b22.** Exceptionally rare for this wine style to work with whisky. But here it pulls it off. 52.7%. 246 bottles.

The BenRiach 1979 bourbon barrel, cask no. 10771, dist 5 Dec 79, bott Jul 08 db **(92.5) n23.5** pear drops, sherbet lemons, wooden floors, freshly waxed leather; more pear drops; **t24** stunningly fresh: the barley leaps out at you almost three dimensionally alerting every tastebud alive; more pear drop and shapes itself towards a vague honeycomb note near the middle; **f22** vanilla, butterscotch and custard ensure a degree of conventionality; **b23** I just adore slightly older bourbon casks which give the malt the freedom to express itself. 51.2%.

⁙ **The BenRiach Single Cask 1984** Pedro Ximenez sherry finish, cask no. 1048 db **(90.5) n23.5** peatius fruitus magnificus; **t22.5** chewus significus; grapum sucrus smokum; juicius maximus amazingus; **f22** dullus rubberius primarius; extendos grappa and Cadburyus fruitus and nutus chocolateus; **b22.5** at first just reminded me too much of the Lagavulin PX finish. Enjoyable, but feeling that the peat and sweet grape refuse to be on quite the same wavelength. Massive and enjoyable whisky without a doubt, but a bit like watching your football team winning a game by a decent score without really ever getting into their normal rhythm. In many ways, the 15-y-o version worked far better, I thought. Then remembered that this kind of malt was a mood thing. So held back for another time. Only on a second tasting when in a little darker frame of mind did it all come together... (score on first mood: n22 t21.5 f21.5 b21) 49.2% 279 bottles.

The BenRiach 1984 Tawny port hogshead, cask no. 4046, dist 10 Oct 84, bott Jul 08 db **(91) n23** the peat and grape crash into each other with gay abandon; **t23** good grief.... the tastebuds don't stand much of a chance as thick wine notes and muscular peat slam relentlessly into them; **f22** tries to calm down a bit, showing at first a sharp, angular grapiness then kinder smoke; from start to finish there is a sharpness which is semi-eye-watering; **b23** being slugged around the kisser with a giant kipper and a bottle of port wouldn't have much more effect than a mouthful or two of this. Seriously, head-shaking stuff... 52.4%. 306 bottles.

⁙ **The BenRiach Single Cask 1988** Gaja Barolo finish, cask no. 4424 db **(93.5) n23.5** a rich, weighty bag of tricks with the grape mingling attractively with delicate smoke; **t24** the sharp, intense fruitiness of a mildly unripened grape results in the same salivating tendencies as the 18-y-o version; the most delicate soft smoke imaginable acts as the perfect foil and leads to a fabulous mocha middle; **f22.5** again bitters out but still plenty of life and depth to keep the party going; **b23** superficially, a very similar re-run of the 18-y-o Gaja Barolo. But in reality, much more complex and complete, with the finish intact and the smoke more telling. Another all-round stunner from the wonderful distillery. 54.3%. 322 bottles.

The BenRiach 1988 new wood oak barrel, cask no. 4020, dist 12 Oct 88, bott Jul 08 db **(87)** n20 big oak and vague sugars but not exactly great... t23 huge delivery which arrives in a bit of a tangle but unfolds to reveal the most complex array of sugars I have tasted in a long time; for all that a bitter-sweet affair; f22 various tannins and spices pitch into the muddle b22 what can you quite make of this? If whisky is a work of art, this is pure abstract. 53.6%. 314 bottles.

⋯ **The BenRiach Single Cask 1990** cask no. 970 db **(89.5)** n21.5 clean, heavy vanilla presence; t23 it's salivating, lip-smacking barley all the way with an improbably gristy sweetness retained throughout; f22 the malt continues to an astonishing degree; b22.5 another mind-blowing ultra clean maltfest from this distillery. With Cardhu, Glen Moray and Tomatin, no-one can do malt quite like this. 57.1% 195 bottles.

The BenRiach 1991 claret wine barrel, cask no. 6903, dist 19 Aug 91, bott Jul 08 db **(87)** n22 spiced, pungent and sharp; t20.5 thumping wine hits home: the malt takes a while to find its bearings; f23 settles, relaxes and balances at last; b21.5 blimey! A French wine barrel and not an atom of sulphur to be had anywhere: I must be dreaming. The wine still perhaps over-dominates in places. 52.8%. 311 bottles.

The BenRiach 1994 new wood oak barrel, cask no. 4022, dist 2 Mar 94, bott Jul 08 db **(92.5)** n23.5 vanilla pods and tannin fuse attractively with the maple syrup and natural caramel; some blood orange gets to work in there, too, as it stretches out to embrace a bourbony style; t23.5 superb interplay between firm malt and softened, enveloping, honeyed oak; no shortage of brown sugars at work; f22.5 the barley holds out against the oaky surge – just..!! b23 at this age this has to be the way to go if you want to give your malt a big rich kick and stay away from the shark-infested waters that is today's sherry butt. Major stuff. 54%. 317 bottles.

⋯ **The BenRiach 1994 Limited Release Madeira Finish Aged 15 Years** cask no. 4810, bott Sep 09 db **(87)** n23 richly layered and textured fruit on a bedrock of cement-like barley; t22 good grief! Mouth-watering but the barley is hard enough to crack your teeth f20.5 disappointing compared to the bare-knuckle entertainment of before: a distinctive bitter note; b21.5 gives the impression of having been distilled from granite... 57.1% Exclusive to Kensington Wine Market

The BenRiach 1994 Vintage Single Cask Campaign No. 4 ex port hogshead, cask no. 26, bott Jun 07 db **(89.5)** n21 t24 f24 b21. Good grief....!!! Those of a nervous disposition had better give this one a miss. It's like tasty TNT.... 55.7%. 300 bottles.

⋯ **The BenRiach "Heart of Speyside"** db **(85.5)** n21.5 t22 f21 b21. A decent, non-fussy malt where the emphasis is on biscuity barley. At times juicy and sharp. Just a tease of very distant smoke here and there adds weight. 40%

Birnie Moss Heavily Peated db **(93)** n23.5 peat (dry and sweet); t24 peat (mainly sweet); f23 peat (oily, sweet, but some dryness, too) b22.5 no chance of them being done under the Trade Descriptions Act.... 48%

Cadenhead's Benriach Aged 23 Years dist 86, bott 09 **(95.5)** n24 extravagantly salty barley and oak with a wonderful mulchy, floral sub-strata: a complex aroma to keep your nose occupied for a good half hour; t24 mouth-watering and fresh, honey-crusted barley making a mockery of the passing years. The salt remains visible and works wonders with the slow butterscotch development; f23.5 long with lingering vanilla and absolutely no oak burnt out; b24 how blenders for so long considered this very much a second rate distillery is entirely beyond me. 53.3%

⋯ **The Càrn Mòr Vintage Collection Benriach 1985** barrel no. 5494, dist 2009 **(89.5)** n22.5 a squeeze of lemon on the clean barley; t23 clean, salivating and intensifying in barley input through to the fudgy middle; the citrus plays peek-a-boo throughout and some nut oil adds needed weight; f22 long barley-rich fade with an increasing amount of natural caramels; b22 very attractive in its light citrusy mode. Just don't expect a brooding malt of some 25 years, complete with thick eyebrows and a stoop...this is a dandy, but one which will charm the life out of you. 46% 819 bottles.

Chieftain's Benriach 14 Years Old Medoc finish, dist Sep 93 **(89)** n22 t22.5 f22 b22.5. A gifted wine finish which works well in every respect. 43%. nc ncf. Ian Macleod.

Connoisseurs Choice Benriach 1987 **(82.5)** n20 t22 f20 b20.5. Pretty oak-laden, even for its age. Attractive barley sugar attack, though. 43%. Gordon & MacPhail.

Dewar Rattray Benriach 1990 cask no. 1779, dist Feb 90, bott Nov 07 **(83.5)** n22 t20.5 f21 b20. Delightful, mountainous malt, but complexity at a minimum. 61.5%

Dun Bheagan BenRiach Aged 10 Years **(86)** n21 t22 f21 b22. A delicate, delicious and youthful Benriach in full blending colours. 43%. Ian Macleod.

Duncan Taylor The NC2 Range Benriach Aged 12 Years dist 96, bott 08 **(85.5)** n22 t21 f21.5 b21. Has soaked up no shortage of oak in its dozen years, but the barley and spice fizz, topped with plain chocolate, evens things out. 46%

The Exclusive Malts Benriach Aged 11 Years cask no. 30608, dist Mar 96 (**90.5**) n22 t22.5 f23.5 b22.5. An exceptionally lively and clean version with the barley in highly concentrated form: stunning and one for the purists. *55.9%. The Creative Whisky Company. 317 bottles.*

Old Malt Cask Benriach Aged 18 Years refill hogshead cask no. 4278, dist Feb 90, bott May 08 (**84.5**) n20.5 t22 f21 b21. Elegant, malty and some fine mocha but certainly showing some grey hairs. *50%. Douglas Laing. 204 bottles.*

Old Malt Cask Benriach Aged 19 Years refill hogshead, dist Feb 90, bott Apr 09 (**83.5**) n20 t22 f20 b21.5. It's all about the malty delivery: exceptional balance to the sweetness. Light latte, too. *50%. Douglas Laing. 235 bottles.*

Provenance Benriach Aged 11 Years refill hogshead no. 4074, dist 96, bott 07 (**90**) n22.5 t23 f22 b22.5. For as much as I love their peated style, this is a way in which I adore to see Benriach. When I say this is sublime blending malt, I don't mean that as a put down – quite the opposite. The clarity of barley, the subtlety of the sweetness and extra, manageable, complexity offered by the spice are the kind of things blenders quietly purr about. Also, most likely, from a high quality second fill bourbon cask – which helps. *46%. nc ncf. Douglas Laing.*

⋙ **Provenance Benriach Aged 11 Years** refill hogshead DMG 5740, dist spring 1998, bott winter 2010 (**89**) n23 rarely comes more cleanly malty than this; t23 spot on! The degree of gristy sugars mixing with the blooming oaky vanillas just can't be faulted; weight and mouth-feel tick all the right boxes; f21 heads back towards the vanilla. A degree of toasty bitterness, but the barley is never far away; low level spices kick in at the very death and extend the finale considerably; b22 top rate Benriach, not only at its very maltiest but in an uncommonly excellent cask. For nose and delivery alone, a minor gem of its type showing why some blenders prize this distillery so highly. *46% Douglas Laing & Co Ltd*

Whisky Doris Benriach 12 Year Old cask no. 45757, dist Mar 96, bott Oct 08 (**88**) n22 t22 f23 b21.5. See 52.1% below. Works very fractionally better at this strength as the honey just gets a slightly higher profile and there is less jarring. On the minus side, there is much less character and is a little too suave. *46%*

Whisky Doris Benriach 12 Year Old cask no. 45757, dist Mar 96, bott Oct 08 (**87.5**) n22 a surprising hint of pine and spearmint amid the citrus; a touch of honey lightens it; t21 useful honeyed barley-rich delivery cracks quickly under the oak and then re-asserts itself briefly; f23 really does gather in momentum and intensity to with a rich, oily barley theme. Softens noticeably; b21.5 bit of a stop-start merchant, never quite finding a rhythm. That said, the goods parts really are excellent...! *52.1%*

The Whisky Fair Benriach 33 Year Old dist 76, bott 09 (**84.5**) n21.5 t21.5 f21 b21. Has all the exotic fruit flourishes to mark the years - and a touch of coppery sheen on the palate, but perhaps a fair few splinters, too. *46.2%. The Whisky Fair, Germany.*

The Whisky Fair Benriach 33 Year Old dist 76, bott 09 (**84.5**) n21.5 t21.5 f21 b21. The absolute twin of the 46.2% version, other than a quick, briefly passing explosion of juicy barley. *47.4%. The Whisky Fair, Germany.*

BENRINNES
Speyside, 1826. Diageo. Working.

Benrinnes Aged 15 Years db (**70**) n16 t19 f17 b18. What a shame that in the year the independent bottlers at last get it right for Benrinnes, the actual owners of the distillery make such a pig's ear of it. Sulphured and sicklysweet, this bottling has little to do with the very good whisky made there day in day out by its talented team. Depressing. *43%. Flora and Fauna.*

⋙ **Benrinnes The Manager's Choice** refill American oak, cask no. 8994, dist 1996, bott 2009 db (**89.5**) n21.5 thick, pulpy gooseberry; a bit of a thin, biting note, too, but vanilla-barley layering also attractive; t23.5 excellently active barley really hitting some glorious clean and eye-wateringly sharp notes; for a triple distilled malt, the light, malty oils are a bit of a surprise....and a treat; f22 simplistic like the delivery and thins again. But some attractive powdery oak suggests good cask selection and age...and enough controlled dryness to balance the continuing fresh barley; b22.5 great to see the distillery in this kind of outstanding form. *59.7% 328 bottles.*

⋙ **A.D. Rattray Benrinnes 1996** cask no. 6461, dist Jun 96, bott Sep 09 (**89**) n20 somewhere, amid this soupy fruit, there has to be some whisky...hasn't there...? t22 thundering delivery of the most intense grape and barley imaginable. I say barley...something which offers a juicy element is in there somewhere; quite metallic and spicy, too; f23 settles down from the pell-mell of the nose and delivery and heads in a much more refined cocoa and custard direction. But the lingering burned raisin drifts on forever... b22 the nose has more rum about it than Scotch whisky in many respects. But such is the lack of discipline and shape here, it's bloody impossible to tell what is going on. Just put on a tin hat and go for the bumpy – and undeniably fun – ride. *57% A.D. Rattray Ltd*

The Càrn Mòr Vintage Collection Braes of Benrinnes 2002 hogshead, cask no. 5, dist 02, bott 09 **(80) n19 t21 f20 b20.** An entirely competent example of sweet, malty blending fodder untroubled by oak. 46%. *The Scottish Liqueur Centre.*

⋯ **Connoisseurs Choice Benrinnes 1975 (85.5) n22 t21.5 f20.5 b21.5.** I remember as a nipper going annually to Epsom Downs, close to my Surrey home, on Derby Day in the very early '60s. The two most important things to get my parents to buy me were a) a blue and white quartered riding cap and b) a toffee apple from the fair they used hold there in those days. This reminds me very much of those old-fashioned toffee apples. The stick was made of wood, like that used in lollies. And after chomping through the toffee and apple, I would then give the wood a good gnaw to extract every last piece of flavour. Who would have thought that over 45 years ago this would have been made from Benrinnes casks....? 43% *Gordon & MacPhail*

Old Malt Cask Benrinnes Aged 14 Years sherry cask no. 4428, dist 94, bott Jun 08 **(81) n16 t21 f22.5 b21.5.** Some whiskies just leave you speechless: after the disaster of a nose I feared the worst. Yet the delivery on the palate and follow through is relative bliss. Get past the nose and be charmed! 50%. *Douglas Laing. 661 bottles.*

Old Malt Cask Benrinnes Aged 21 Years refill hogshead, dist Mar 88, bott May 09 **(91.5) n23** a light coating of fried banana and almonds really does lift the barley; **t23** beautiful texture on delivery with the oak offering perfect vanilla on the barley sugar; the malt simply melts on the tongue and a vague saltiness intensifies the sharpness of the grain... **f22.5** long, subtly oiled with almonds and remains remarkably intact and sweet to the end; **b23** heart-warming to see Benrinnes in this outstanding nick and so clean on nose and delivery. A distillery classic. 50%. *Douglas Laing. 276 bottles.*

Provenance Benrinnes Aged 10 Years bourbon finished barrel no. 3940 **(84) n22 t20 f21 b21.** Exceptionally light, thought the squeeze of lemon really lifts it. 46%. *Douglas Laing.*

⋯ **Provenance Benrinnes Over 11 Years** bourbon cask no. 5238, dist Spring 1998, bott Summer 2009 **(84.5) n21 t21 f21.5 b21.** Eye-watering barley in sharp, concentrated form... and with raspberry jam for good measure. Great fun. 46% *nc ncf Douglas Laing & Co Ltd*

Scotch Malt Whisky Society Cask 36.39 Aged 11 Years refill hogshead, dist Apr 96 **(68) n15 t16 f19 b18.** I'd put my house on this being a dud barrel even before spirit was put into it. Rarely do such poor casks slip through the SMWS net. Some decent cocoa on the finish tries to salvage a little pride. 60.8%

Scotch Malt Whisky Society Cask 36.42 Aged 15 Years sherry butt, dist Feb 93 **(83.5) n20 t22.5 f20 b21.** For the all less than subtle fruit involvement – classic early '90s United Distillers style – and stomping spices really it is the big natural caramels which steal the show. 57%

Scotch Malt Whisky Society Cask 36.43 Aged 9 Years 1st fill barrel, dist Sep 99 **(86) n20.5 t23 f21 b21.5.** One for those with a penchant for sweet, eye-wateringly sharp barley. Excellent oak for age, too, though the massive natural caramels flatten the nose somewhat. 59.9%

Scotch Malt Whisky Society Cask 36.44 Aged 20 Years refill butt, dist May 88 **(74.5) n18.5 t19 f18 b19.** Lively, tangy, some interesting cocoa but with its many flaws really would have been better suited to a blend. 60.5%

⋯ **Stronachie Benrinnes Aged 12 Years** 2009 batch **(75.5) n18.5 t20 f19 b19.** Big malt but, technically, not quite at the races. 43% *A.D. Rattray Ltd*

BENROMACH
Speyside, 1898. Gordon & MacPhail. Working.

⋯ **Benromach 10 Years Old** matured in hand selected oak casks db **(87.5) n22** how you might expect a chocolate peat bar to be when grated. The odd blood orange note, too; **t22** a gristy sweetness imparts a delicate smoke which mingles with the vanilla; **f21.5** surprising degrees of sugars see off the worst of a bitter oakiness; **b22** for a relatively small still using peat, the experience is an unexpected and delicately light one. 43%

Benromach 21 Years Old db **(91.5) n22** some exotic fruit and green banana is topped off with a splodge of maple syrup; **t23.5** excellent interplay between the sweeter, barley-rich components and the elegant, spiced oaky backbone; virtually no bite and softened further by an unfurling of vanilla on the middle; **f23** long, oak-edged with a slow, tapering dryness which does nothing to confront the sugared backnotes or even the suggesting of the most delicate smoke; **b23** an entirely different, indeed lost, style of malt from the old, now gone, big stills. The result is an airier whisky which has embraced such good age with a touch of panache and grace. The sweetness has been underlined in the last few seconds by attracting a tiny fruit fly which, whilst writing these notes, has chosen this to dive into and drown in. What a way to go: you could hardly wish for a classier end... 43%

Benromach 22 Years Old Finished in Port Pipes db **(86) n22 t23 f20 b21.** Slightly Jekyll and Hyde. 45%. *3500 bottles.*

Benromach 25 Years Old db **(92) n24** seriously sexy with spices interplaying with tactile malt: the bitter-sweet balance is just so. There is even the faintest flicker of peat-smoke to underscore the pedigree; **t22** an early, surprising, delivery of caramel amongst the juicy barley; **f23** lots of gentle spices warm the enriched barley and ice-creamy vanilla; **b23** a classic old-age Speysider, showing all the quality you'd hope for. *43%*

Benromach Classic 55 Years Old dist 49, bott 04 db **(93) n24 t23 f22 b24.** Only distillery owners G&M could come up with something like this. Scotland had a King in those far off days. In fact, so did the British Empire – and there was still an Empire (just) in 1949. And this has to be a king of aged whiskies because it bears virtually no scars of time. Charlie Hewitt was back as manager of recently relegated Millwall; my parents were in their first year of marriage; Surrey were on the cusp of forming a cricket team to dominate the English game for the next decade and some guy in Scotland, possibly long dead and his name lost to history, laid down one cask that a generation and a half on would delight and astound a lucky few. That's whisky for you. *42.4%. 83 bottles.*

Benromach Cask Strength 1981 db **(91) n21.5** a day out at Margate, only crushed grapes for fish 'n' chips...; **t23** the sherry dives in head first, leaving little doubt about its fruity intent; although less coastal on the palate, there is still a touch of brine to the grape; **f23.5** long, with a soft barley tune being heard just above the grapey symphony; **b23** really unusual with that seaweedy aroma awash with salt: stunningly delicious stuff. *54.2%*

⠿ **Benromach 2002 Sassicaia Wood Finish** db **(86) n21 t22 f21 b22.** Again this entirely idiosyncratic wood-type comes crashing head to head with the smoke to form a whisky style like nothing else. Dense, breathless and crushed, there is little room for much else to get a word in, other than some oak-extracted sugars. A must experience dram. *45%*

Benromach Latitude 57° cask no. 580 db **(73.5) n18.5 t19 f18 b18.** I'm afraid with that sulphur evident it shows the wrong kind of latitude altogether... *57%. 330 bottles.*

Benromach Madeira Wood db **(92) n22** some rolling smoke and chunky dried fruits almost cancel each other out...almost...; **t24** voluptuous body displaying soft oils which coat the mouth with a spot on peat which is at once full and chewy yet light enough to allow the layered fruits full reign; the bitter-sweet balance just couldn't be better; **f23** long with some touches of almost Jack Daniel hickory amid the circling smoke and juiced up fruit; mind-boggling complexity to this for so long... **b23** good grief! If you want a boring, safe, timid malt, stay well away from this one. Fabulous: you are getting the feeling that the real Benromach is now beginning to stand up. *45%*

Benromach Marsala Wood db **(86.5) n21.5 t22 f22 b21.** Solid, well made, enjoyable malt, which in some ways is too solid: the imperviousness of both the peat and grape appears not to allow much else get through. Not a dram to say no to, however, and the spices in particular are a delight. *45%*

Benromach Organic db **(91) n23** massive oak input and the freshest oak imaginable. But sits comfortably with the young pulsing malts. Wow!!; **t23** oak arrives first again, but has enough deftness of touch to allow the rich, mouthwatering malts to prosper; **f22** plenty of vanillins and natural, sweet toffee; **b23** young and matured in possibly first fill bourbon or, more likely, European (even Scottish) oak; you cannot do other than sit up and take notice of this guns-blazing big 'un. An absolute treat! *43%. nc ncf.*

Benromach Origins db **(84.5) n20 t22 f21 b21.5.** You'd think after tasting over 1,250 whiskies in the space of a few months you'd have nosed and tasted it all. But no: here is something very different. Discordant noises from nose to finish, it is saved by the extraordinary richness of the coppery input and a vague smoky richness finishing with cold latte. Very different, indeed. *50%*

Benromach Peat Smoke Aged 6 Years 2nd edition 1st fill bourbon barrel, dist 02, bott 08 db **(92) n22.5** beautiful, sweet, flakey smoke with hickory amid the phenols; **t23.5** intense, soft, complex delivery but the accent very much of a sweet, controlled evolution of refined barley; **f23** medium length and smoky; the oak kicks in with aplomb and sympathy with just the right degree of weight and dryness; **b23** this is Benromach getting it right at every turn, including bottling at such tender years. Proof that excellence can be achieved with first class wood selection and fine work in the still house, rather than simply summers spent in the warehouse. *46%*

Benromach Sassicaia Wood Finish bott 07 db **(86) n23 t20 f22 b21.** Benromach in very different clothing here – in fact, there is no other malt with the elements so portrayed. Particularly pleasing is the beauty of the balance between the soft smoke and the varied oaky tones – very European. The arrival is a little confused (a touch of the Italian tantrums at one point) but it eventually pans out into an attractively sweet, and again softly peated, little charmer. Unique. *45%*

Benromach Traditional db **(89) n24** hard not to adore: young, vibrant, elegantly smoky; gooseberry jam and Arbroath Smokies on an Aberdeenshire breakfast table. Stunning for all its youth; **t22** clean, relentlessly youth barley with no shortage of peat: chewy yet fresh; **f21** thins out not least because of lack of oak but enough around to ensure a chalky vanilla death; **b22** some will regard this way too young. It is just that reason, though, that this malt is such a treat, soaring on the nose and delivery with abandon. Just lovely. And very well made, too. 40%

Bevmo Benromach Single Cask No 704 dist 4/Oct/99 bott Jul 07 db **(74) n17 t20 f19 b18.** Young - very young! Some feints on the nose and a touch of smoke, too. Some grappling caramel also on the finish. Plenty to chew over, but minimal harmony. 43%

BLADNOCH
Lowland, 1817. Working.

Bladnoch Aged 6 Years Bourbon Matured db **(91) n21.5** young, yes. But the soft feints have nothing to do with that; **t22.5** a youthful, oily delivery, not exactly a picture of harmony, gives way to a brutal coup d'etat of ultra intense prisoner-slaughtering barley; **f24** I'm in barley heaven: intense barley-concentrate oils offer a perplexing array of sweet, grassy tones; you simply chew and chew until the jaw aches. Cocoa at last arrives, all with a spiced buzz and a smearing of vanillas. Meanwhile your tongue explores the mouth, wondering what the hell is going on... **b23** ignore the mildly feinty nose and delivery. The fun starts with the late middle, where those extra oils congregate and the taste buds are sent rocking. Great to see a Lowlander bottled at an age nearer its natural best and even the smaller cut, in a roundabout way, ensures a mind-blowing dram. 573%

Bladnoch Aged 6 Years Lightly Peated db **(93) n23** a peat fire just bursting into life; **t23** firm, bitter-sweet; the layering of the peat is awesome, with the youth of the malt adding an extra dimension; some citrus notes help lighten the load; **f23.5** smoky hickory; the vanillas make a feeble entry, a gentle oiliness persists; **b23.5** the peat has nothing to do with the overall score here: this is a much better-made whisky with not a single off-note and the cut is spot on. And although it claims to be lightly peated, that is not exactly true: such is the gentle nature of the distillate, the smoke comes through imperiously and on several levels. "Spirit of the Lowlands" drones the label. Since when has outstanding peated malt been associated with that part of the whisky world...?? 58.5%

Bladnoch Aged 6 Years Sherry Matured db **(73.5) n18 t19 f18.5 b18.** A sticky, lop-sided malt where something, or a group of somethings, conjures up a very unattractive overture. Feints on the palate but no excellent bourbon cask to the rescue here. 56.9%

Bladnoch Aged 10 Years db **(94) n23** lemon and lime, marmalade on fresh-sliced flour-topped crusty bread; **t24** immensely fruity and chewy, lush and mouthwatering and then the most beguiling build-up of spices: the mouthfeel is full and faultless; **f23** long, remains mildly peppery and then a dryer advance of oak. The line between bitter and sweet is not once crossed; **b24** this is probably the ultimate Bladnoch, certainly the best I have tasted in over 25 years. This Flora and Fauna bottling by then owners United Distillers should be regarded as the must-get-at-all-costs Bladnoch. If the new owner can create something even to hang on to this one's coat-tails then he has excelled himself. For those few of us lucky enough to experience this, this dram is nothing short of a piece of Lowland legend and folklore. 43%. *For those of you with a nervous disposition, the author would like to point out that not a single drop of this whisky was spat out during the creation of these tasting notes.*

Bladnoch Aged 15 Years db **(91) n22.5** remnants of zest and barley sit comfortably with the gentle oaks; **t22.5** excellent delivery and soon gets into classic Bladnoch citric stride; **f23** wonderfully clean barley belies the age and lowers the curtain so delicately you hardly notice; **b23** quite outstanding Lowland whisky which, I must admit, is far better than I would have thought possible at this age. 55%.

Bladnoch Aged 15 Years sherry cask no. 1056 db **(81) n17 t22 f21 b21.** Perhaps not the best sherry influence of all time here but the juicy malt experience on the palate compensates for the nose. 46%. ncf.

Bladnoch Aged 15 Years sherry butt no. 2615, dist Jul 92, bott Feb 08 db **(86.5) n19 t23 f22.5 b22.** Maybe not the greatest-ever butt to be filled with Scotch, but there is no denying that the challenge of the enormous delivery and finish makes for some serious and hugely enjoyable dramming. There is something of the thick chocolate mousse late on, and then only after a sherry trifle opening. Have a fork and dessertspoon beside your glass when you pour this monster! And forget the nose – just add this to your collection: it's a rather delicious education... 55%. 550 bottles.

Bladnoch Aged 16 Years "Spirit of the Lowlands" db **(88) n22** vaguely salty, digestive biscuit; very firm and attractive with pleasing barley edge; **t22** salivating and entire: the age doesn't detract from the richness of the barley one iota; **f22** continues in the same vein though the oak does dry things out; **b22** really lovely whisky and unusual to see a Lowlander quite this comfortable at such advanced age. 46%. ncf.

Bladnoch 18 Years Old db **(88.5) n21** dulled with oak; **t23.5** fabulous balance between juicy fruit and juicy barley. The gooseberries are green, fat and splitting at the sides...; **f22** vanilla and a trail of light oil allows the barley an extended stay **b22** the juiciness and clarity to the barley, and especially the big gooseberry kick, early on makes this a dram well worth finding. 55%

⋰ **Berrys' Own Selection Bladnoch 1990 (86) n21.5 t22 f21 b21.5.** Not your typical Bladnoch, with the usual ultra malty personality being moved by a sharper, apple-accented nose and delivery. Angular and entertaining with a touch of severity. 50.4%

Berry's Own Selection Bladnoch 1990 bott 09 **(89) n23** the house style of boiling gooseberries at their piepiest; **t22** light, ultra-clean grassy barley with no more than a hint of vanilla; **f22** one of cleanest finishes you'll find with the barley still dominating, leading with that green fruity, grassy edge; the excellent barley-sugar sees off any threat of bitterness from the oak; **b22** some people will be disappointed with this as an 18-year-old, as it doesn't actually do much. And they might have a point. But on the other hand, how can you not be charmed by something so crystalline. 43%. Berry Bros & Rudd.

Cadenhead's Bladnoch Aged 15 Years dist 92, bott Feb 08 **(87.5) n22 t21.5 f22 b22.** A charming dram that gets better the longer it stays in the palate. 53.5%. 320 bottles.

Cadenhead's Bladnoch Aged 17 Years dist 92, bott 09 **(92.5) n23.5** doesn't come much cleaner with the accent on barley and a sherbet citrus buzz; **t23.5** eye-wateringly salivating: this is 3-D barley; **f22.5** a touch of vanilla and mocha rounds off the fun; **b23** an exceptional cask full of charisma and quality. 55.1%

⋰ **Chieftain's Bladnoch 16 Years Old** hogshead, dist Nov 92, bott 2009 **(84.5) n21 t21.5 f21 b21.** Distilled during its lighter body phase, this still juicy offering holds up well, though the slightly sawdust-like oakiness does play the most prominent role. 48% nc ncf Ian Macleod

⋰ **Connoisseurs Choice Bladnoch 1993 (88.5) n22.5** big oak, but buttery and floral enough to command a balance; **t21.5** quietly spoken barley offers a decisive intensity to counter the drier oak; **f22.5** surprisingly long, revealing the soft oiliness hinted at elsewhere is very real. A late chewiness offers excellent sweet-dry interplay; **b22** one of those drams which on the oaky face of it shouldn't work..but deliciously does. 43% Gordon & MacPhail

John McDougall's Selection Bladnoch 1990 cask no. CM101, dist 90 **(83.5) n22 t21 f20 b20.5.** Clean and crammed with big malt. But on the hot and thin side. 54.2%. House of Macduff. 260 bottles.

John McDougall's Selection Bladnoch 1990 cask no. CM124, dist 90 **(92) n23.5 t23 f22.5 b23.** Just wonderful malt, showing Bladnoch in a clear and excellent light. The structure and layering is sublime. 53.3%. House of Macduff. 240 bottles.

Old Malt Cask Bladnoch Aged 15 Years refill hogshead no. 4241, dist Apr 08 **(86) n21.5 t22.5 f21 b21.** Even and refreshing with some chewy natural caramel at the death. 50%. nc ncf. Douglas Laing. 364 bottles.

Old Malt Cask Bladnoch Aged 16 Years refill hogshead, cask no. 4446, dist Mar 92, bott Jun 08 **(86.5) n21.5 t22 f21.5 b21.5.** Lovely malt in so many ways. Yet you do get the feeling that it is reaching the limit of its range at this kind of age. 50%. Douglas Laing. 295 bottles.

Private Cellar's Selection Bladnoch 1993 bott 07 **(86.5) n22 t23 f20 b21.5.** Soft, sensual, a little syrupy, perhaps, but seriously sexy. 43%

Scotch Malt Whisky Society Cask 50.33 Aged 17 Years refill barrel, dist Jul 90 **(83.5) n20 t21 f21.5 b21.** Malt and citrus aplenty. A bit hot. 55.9%

Scotch Malt Whisky Society Cask 50.38 Aged 16 Years refill hogshead, dist Oct 92 **(78.5) n20 t20 f18.5 b19.** Technically decent, refreshing distillate, but the evidence points towards a cask left out in the rain too long between fillings. 54.4%

Scotch Malt Whisky Society Cask 50.39 Aged 16 Years refill hogshead, dist Oct 92 **(89) n22** crisp barley with a mildly starchy, cassava undertone; **t23** gorgeous, salivating malt is stretched even further by a vague saltiness and that wonderfully distinctive cassava; the lightest oil carries with it a gentle throb of spice; **f22** dries, but not with a hint of over-oakiness. Chalky but dusted with sweetened vanilla; **b22** fascinating: same distillate as 50.38, but not denigrated by a sub-standard cask. Here the malt is given perfect support and the difference is spell-binding. By comparing the two, what a great way for whisky students to discover the negative impact of dodgy cask on very good malt. 56.1%

Wilson & Morgan Barrel Selection Bladnoch Aged 18 Years rum finish, dist 90, bott 08 **(93) n22.5** dense, barely penetrable with the sugar and barley combining to offer toffee apple and jelly babies; **t24** whoosh...!!! The barley is so concentrated and firm, the sugars so crisp and brittle, you feel your teeth are in danger of being chipped; thick, almost gloopy but the barley is sharp and juicy enough to offer a salivating arm which nigh makes the eyes water... f23 long, very long and wonderfully sweet. The barley really does appear polished and crisp to the very last; b23.5 a glittering malt whose delivery is nothing short of sublime. *51%*

BLAIR ATHOL
Highlands (Perthshire), 1798. Diageo. Working.

Blair Athol Aged 12 Years db **(77) n18 t19 f21 b19**. Thick, fruity, syrupy and a little sulphury and heavy. The finish has some attractive complexity among the chunkyness. *43%. Flora and Fauna range.*

⠿ **Connoisseurs Choice Blair Athol 1995 (76) 20 t20 f18 b18**. Clean and malty. But straight as a dye. Zero complexity. *43% Gordon & MacPhail*

Old & Rare Blair Athol Aged 32 Years dist Jun 76, bott Aug 08 **(86.5) n22 t22.5 f21 b21**. Belies its years in any number of ways, not least in how the oak is so easily accommodated. Hugely enjoyable, especially on the lightly smoked, gingerbread nose and early Parkin Cake delivery, and even though not one to exactly raise the pulse there is a very agreeable degree of complexity. *55.4%. Douglas Laing. 119 bottles*

Old Malt Cask Blair Athol Aged 9 Years sherry butt, dist Sep 99, bott Mar 09 **(81) n19 t20 f21 b21** Sweet, warming and clean. *46%. Douglas Laing.*

Old Malt Cask Blair Athol Aged 10 Years sherry butt, dist Dec 98, bott Jul 09 **(73) n18 t20 f17 b18** More Blair Witch. *50%. Douglas Laing.*

Old Malt Cask Blair Athol Aged 18 Years (89.5) n21.5 tinned tangerines and salmon sandwiches...it must be a Sunday afternoon in the 60s... t22 huge malt sweetens by the second with only a trace of the salty edge to the nose; f23.5 unravels with some barley sugar but it's the perfect texture to the oils which wins the day... b22.5 borders on cloying and over-indulgent – gets away with it. As sweet and malty as this distillery gets. And, to be honest, seriously enjoyable. *50%. Douglas Laing.*

⠿ **Old Malt Cask Blair Athol Aged 35 Years** refill hogshead no. 5572, dist Oct 74, bott Oct 09 **(86) n21 t22 f22 b21**. from the days when Bells ruled the distillery...what the bloody hell was going on here? Was this some attempt to create an Islay-style malt? If so, they failed..... spectacularly. No: I think just mucky, overworked stills at play here. Enormous and bordering on the manic. Thick, incomprehensible...but magnificent fun! *50% Douglas Laing. 217 bottles.*

Premier Barrel Blair Athol Aged 9 Years sherry cask **(77) n19 t20 f19 b19**. Curious whisky: it is rare to find one that does so little. An old cask means the oak aint around while the abundance of light malt yields minimal complexity. *46%. Douglas Laing. 776 bottles.*

Premier Barrel Blair Athol Aged 10 Years sherry cask **(78) n18 t20 f20 b20**. A very sweet and simple barley-fest. The oak is mainly conspicuous by its absence. *46%. 651 bottles.*

Provenance Blair Athol Aged 10 Years sherry butt, dist autumn 99, bott autumn 08 **(85) n20 t22 f21.5 b21.5**. Beautifully spiced, chewy and juicy for all its weight. *46%. Douglas Laing.*

Provenance Blair Athol Aged 11 Years sherry Butt 3937, dist 95, bott 07 **(74.5) n19.5 t19 f18 b18**. Not great. *46%. nc ncf. Douglas Laing.*

Provenance Blair Athol Aged 12 Years sherry butt, dist Jul 95, bott 08 **(86.5) n22 t21.5 f21.5 b22**. Lots of biscuity moments on nose and palate with fruit shortcake taking the leading role. *46%. nc ncf. Douglas Laing.*

BOWMORE
Islay, 1779. Suntory. Working.

Bowmore 12 Years Old db **(91) n22.5** light peats, the air of a room with a man sucking cough sweets; sweet pipe smoke; t23.5 soft, beautiful delivery of multi-layered peats; lots of effervescent spices and molassed sugars; spices abound; f22.5 much drier with sharper berries and barley; the peat still rumbles onwards, but has no problems with the light, sawdusty oaks; b23.5 this new bottling still proudly carries the Fisherman's Friend cough sweet character, but the coastal, saline properties here are a notch or three up: far more representative of Islay and the old distillery style. Easily by far the truest Bowmore I have tasted in a long while with myriad complexity. Even going back more than a quarter of a century, the malt at this age rarely showed such relaxed elegance. Most enjoyable. *40%*

Bowmore 12 Years Old Enigma db **(82) n19 t22 f20 b21**. Sweet, molassed and with that tell-tale Fisherman's Friend tang representing the light smoke. This Enigma hasn't quite cracked it, though. *40%. Duty Free.*

Bowmore 15 Years Old Darkest db **(74) n18 t18 f19 b19**. An improvement on the dreadful original. Just. *43%.*

Bowmore 15 Years Old Mariner db **(79) n19 t21 f19 b20**. There are two ways of looking at this. As a Bowmore. Which is how I have marked it. Or a something to throw down your neck for pure fun. Which is probably worth another seven or eight points. Either way, there is something not entirely right here. *43%. Duty Free.*

⁘ **Bowmore Aged 17 Years** db **(77) n18 t22 f18 b19.** For all the attractiveness of the sweet fruit on delivery, the combination of butt and cough sweet makes for pretty hard going. *43%*

Bowmore 18 Years Old db **(79) n20 t21 f19 b19.** Pleasant, drinkable Fisherman's Friend style – like every Bowmore it appears around this age. But why so toffee-dull? *43%.*

Bowmore 25 Years Old db **(86) n21 t22 f21 b22.** Not the big, chunky guy of yore: the age would surprise you if tasted blind. *43%*

Bowmore 30 Years Old db **(94) n23** intense burnt raisin amid the intense burnt peat; a deft rummy sweetness strikes an improbable chord with the sweetened lime; the oak is backward coming forward but binds beautifully with both peat and fruit; **t24** near flawless delivery showing a glimpse of Bowmore in a form similar to how I remember it some 25 years ago. The peat, though intense - much bigger than you will find today - does have a hint of the Fisherman's Friend about it, but not so upfront as today. For all the peat this is clean whisky, moulded by a craftsman into how a truly great Islay should be; **f23** dries sublimely as the oak contains the peat and adds a touch of coffee to it in unsugared form. Gentle oils cling tightly to the roof of the mouth but it is at once gentle yet enormous; **b24** frankly, a Bowmore that no Islay scholar should be without. Shows the distillery at its most intense yet delicate; an essay in balance and how great oak, peat and fruit can combine for those special moments in life. Unquestionably one of the best Bowmores bottled this century. *43%*

Bowmore 1971 Vintage 34 Years Old sherry cask db **(86) n23 t22 f20 b21.** Loses it on the finish. But one for those who like their whisky big and with splinters aplenty. *51%. 960 bottles.*

Bowmore Legend db **(88) n22** big peat fire; dry, but really attractively so; **t22.5** Ok, Fisherman's Friend cough sweet maybe, but the countering barley and brown sugar sweetness appears to dissipate the worst of the effect: the result is big peat, very evenly spread; **f22** gentle finale with a vanilla flourish; **b22.5** not sure what has happened here, but it has gone through the gears dramatically to offer a substantial dram with both big peat and excellent balancing molasses. Major stuff. *40%*

⁘ **Bowmore Tempest Aged 10 Years Small Batch Release No.1** db first fill bourbon, bott 2009 **(87) n22.5** attractive salty kick to the gentle smoke: about as coastal as it comes. Welcome traces of citrus and lavender, too; **t22** tangy, with a pretty full-bodied layering of thick, stubby vanillas: dates and Demerara almost outweigh the shy smoke; a few saintly spices bubble away in a most contented and friendly manner; **f21** pretty full on caramel fudge with just a touch of creamy mocha to soften things slightly; just enough smoke to get through to the final moments; **b21.5** a very different Bowmore which is perhaps too dependent on the fudgy character. When given a chance, its coastal attributes are set off to excellent effect. *55.3%*

⁘ **Adelphi Bowmore 2001 Aged 8 Years** sherry butt, cask no. 1126, bott 2010 **(89.5) n23.5** fantastically crisp and roasty aspect to the barley: almost like chocolate malt but made all the better thanks to a beautiful smoky crust. Impressive... **t22.5** like the nose, firm and malt-studded. And again the smoke drifts on a slightly different plane, bringing with it some pretty significant sweetness; the middle ground lightens towards that chocolate again, only this time spiced; **f21** a touch of forgivable oak bitterness, but gristy sugars do their best to compensate; **b22.5** now why can't more bottlings of Bowmore be this wonderful? *59.9% Adelphi Distillery Ltd. 583 bottles.*

A.D. Rattray Bowmore 1991 sherry butt, cask no. 2060, bott Nov 08 **(85.5) n21 t22.5 f20.5 b21.5** Dry, ashy, sooty, with an excellent thick, fruity swirl and flourish; but ultimately over bitters out. *56.2%*

⁘ **A.D. Rattray Bowmore 1996** cask no. 960028, dist Mar 96, bott Mar 10 **(90) n23** custard and smoke: a clean and attractive combination; **t23** sweet delivery but the bite and spice are a treat; **f22** soft oils and a touch of smoky chocolate mousse; **b22** now that's much more like it!! Memories of Bowmore from 30 years ago: assertive but with a touch of poise. Exemplary. *46% A.D. Rattray Ltd*

Alchemist Bowmore Aged 9 Years dist Apr 98, bott Aug 07 **(75.5) n18.5 t19 f19 b19.** Sweet and slightly off centre. *46%. nc, ncf.*

Berry's Own Selection Bowmore 1989 bott 08 **(89) n22** very light peat plays hide-and-seek amid the honey and butterscotch; **t23** superbly weighted: golden syrup with a few pinches of peat stirred into it. Add some salt and zingy vanilla and your tastebuds are really worked over; **f22** bittering vanilla but the peat now enters a spicy mode; **b22** technically, Berry's 1994 bottling is a superior whisky. But here you just have to admire the structure and complexity. *53.5%. Berry Bros & Rudd.*

Berry's Own Selection Bowmore 1994 bott 08 (86.5) n21 t22.5 f21.5 b21.5. A must for those looking for something very sweet and moderately smoky yet exceptionally clean. *53.5%. Berry Bros & Rudd.*

Berry's Own Selection Bowmore Aged 11 Years (84) n20 t23 f21 b20. To see Bowmore like this from a second- (or even third) - filled bourbon cask makes for interesting tasting: such is the mouthwatering malt intensity, and so retiring is the peat, this could almost pass for lightly smoked Speyside. *56.2%. Berry Bros & Rudd..*

Cadenhead's Authentic Collection Bowmore Aged 14 Years bourbon, dist 93, bott Sep 07 (87.5) n22 t21.5 f21.5 b21.5. Entertaining and energetic, the peat is out of the traps in double quick time, followed by liquorice. Do look out for the chocolate on the nose. Delicious, even if the oak isn't entirely at home. *63.9%. 162 bottles*

Cadenhead's Bowmore Aged 15 Years dist 92, bott Feb 08 (87) n22.5 t21 f22 b21.5. Slightly aggressive at times but a real treat. *54.4%. 333 bottles.*

Cadenhead's Bowmore Aged 15 Years dist 92, bott Feb 08 (84.5) n21 t21 f21.5 b21. Bit of a hothead for all its charming and beguiling ways. *55%. 343 bottles.*

⋯ **The Coopers Choice Bowmore 1998 Aged 10 Years** (85) n20 t21 f22.5 b21.5. After an inconsequential nose and delivery the smoked chocolate of the middle ground is an absolute treat! *46% The Vintage Malt Whisky Co. Ltd*

The Creative Whisky Company Exclusive Malts Bowmore Aged 10 Years cask no. 60105, dist Apr 97 (89.5) n21 t23 f22.5 b23. Hugely enjoyable, teeth-baring, malt that has been very well made. *56.9%.*

Dewar Rattray Bowmore Aged 17 Years cask no. 2058, dist Jul 91, bott Sep 08 (89) n22 t23 f21.5 b22.5. Not the kind of whisky you want to land on your desk when you are desperately trying to finish a book: this isn't a tale that can be unravelled in a few minutes. There isn't a single element of this malt which is straightforward. From nose to finish something is not right about this. Yet, so much of it works so well that you can forgive it its trespasses. It's as if cognac, rum and sherry cask have all been at work on this one, each leaving unfinished business. If I had £100 for every Bowmore I'd tasted over the years I'd be a pretty wealthy guy. But I have never come across anything with a signature like this. *55.9%.*

Dewar Rattray Bowmore 1990 cask no. 261, bott Jun 07 (86.5) n20 t22 f22.5 b22. For those who prefer their peat sweet and a bit nippy. Excellent cocoa on the finale. *54.1%*

⋯ **Douglas of Drumlanrig Bowmore Aged 11 Years** refill hogshead no. LD 5593, dist Sep 98, bott Oct 09 (88) n22.5 clean grist with light, sweet smoke untroubled by oak; t22 think of new make with just enough clear vanilla to soak up the more youthful edges; f22 medium length with the barley and smoke having all the final words; b21.5 beautifully made, minimum fuss and spic and span. *46% Douglas Laing. 210 bottles.*

Duncan Taylor Collection Bowmore 1982 cask no. 85030 (82) n20.5 t20 f21 b20.5. Had to laugh when I lined up this latest bunch of DT Bowmores. Talk about déjà vous...!! It was like opening up a packet of Fisherman's Friends, that cough sweet style unique for a while at this distillery. And I thought: didn't DT do something like this last year? Well, on consulting my notes, yes they did. And here are half a dozen more or so from the same batch – peas from the same pod. The thing is, you can't not like them. Nor do they blow you away: they simply offer a quite different whisky style, one that no other distillery has done before or since. *50.1%*

Duncan Taylor Collection Bowmore 1982 cask no. 85031 (86.5) n21.5 t23 f21 b21. By far and away one of the best casks in the set: everything is a tad sharper and more intense. The barley is truly salivating and there is even a thread of honey woven through the smoke and liquorice. Lovely. *52.1%*

Duncan Taylor Collection Bowmore 1982 cask no. 85032 (83) n20 t21 f21 b21. A bit of a hot-head, this. The nose is a dullard, but a bit of zip on the palate compensates and really cranks out the cough sweet side of things. *53.7%*

Duncan Taylor Collection Bowmore 1982 cask no. 85057 (86) n23 t22 f20 b21. We have moved on a few casks and the whisky has moved on in style, slightly, too. To nose, some real butterscotch on the cereals and smoke ensure a touch of class and there is shades of demerara and liquorice on delivery before the finish bitters and flattens. *53.5%*

Duncan Taylor Collection Bowmore 1982 cask no. 85060 (83.5) n21 t21 f20.5 b21. Pure, unadulterated Fisherman's Friend cough sweet. *55.4%*

Duncan Taylor Collection Bowmore 1982 cask no. 85062 (85.5) n20.5 t22 f21.5 b21.5. Some bourbony liquorice and redcurrant. Oh, and Fisherman's Friend. *57.1%*

Duncan Taylor Collection Bowmore 1982 cask no. 85063 (77.5) n19.5 t22 f17.5 b18.5. Cough sweet. But the oak really does it some damage. *55.8%*

Duncan Taylor Collection Bowmore 1982 cask no. 85064 (84) n21 t22.5 f20 b20,5. Slightly in the style of 85032 but with a touch of extra citrus and finesse. *54.9%*

Duncan Taylor Collection Bowmore 1982 cask no. 85068 **(84)** n21 t21 f21 b21. A fleet of Fishermen's Friends: sweet, but absolutely uncompromising in the cough sweet department. 53.8%

Duncan Taylor Collection Bowmore 1982 cask no. 85072 **(83.5)** n20 t21.5 f21 b21. A bit of a softie, but sticks to the cough sweet script for all the best vanilla-led intentions. 50.4%

⋯ **Duncan Taylor Collection Bowmore 1982** cask no. 85162 **(78)** n19.5 t20 f19 b19.5. Date drawn: 9.9.9. But no need to call the Fire Brigade as the smoke is easily doused. 50.5%

⋯ **Duncan Taylor Collection Bowmore 1982** cask no. 378770 **(80.5)** n19 t21 f20 b20.5. A rough hewn blighter and one of the Fishermen's Friend variety. 50.6%

Duncan Taylor Collection Bowmore 1987 cask no. 18053 **(83)** n20.5 t21.5 f20 b21. Pretty limited beyond the bizarre cough sweet characteristic of that period. 52.4%

⋯ **Duthies Bowmore 17 Years Old (86.5)** n20 t22.5 f22 b22. Unusually crisp for a Bowmore with the smoke little more than an afterthought. Adore the clarity of the barley and the almost husky crunchiness. Worth seeking. 46% Wm. Cadenhead Ltd

Exclusive Casks Bowmore 1998 Aged 10 Years American oak **(94)** n24 now this is a charmer: amid the heather there is that familiar hint of Fishermen's Friend cough sweet, but it appears to have been calmed by honey: noses don't come any healthier than this...and certainly one not to be sneezed at; **t23.5** mouth-watering and stunningly fresh: the vanilla from the cask melts into the phenols while the barley sugar offers perfect weight and balance; **f23** hickory and unbelievably mellow smoke drift off towards a chocolaty finale; **b23.5** a gold nugget of a cask that is worth a trip to the walled city for alone... 52.7%

Hart Brothers Bowmore Aged 10 Years dist Apr 98, bott Jun 08 **(85)** n21.5 t21 f21.5 b21. Sweet, simplistic but with a pleasing degree of peat ash. 46%. Hart Brothers Limited.

Hart Brothers Bowmore Aged 11 Years dist Apr 97, bott Oct 08 **(77)** n20 t20 f18 b19. Interesting farm yard nose. But, overall, a bitter experience. 46%. Hart Brothers Limited.

Hart Brothers Bowmore Aged 18 Years dist May 90, bott Jun 08 **(86.5)** n22 t22 f21 b21.5. Very pleasing malt with a distinctively fresh, fruity edge to the smoke. 46%.

⋯ **James MacArthur's Old Masters Bowmore 1996 Aged 13 Years** cask no. 960003, bott Nov 09 **(87.5)** n22 decent mixture of thick and lighter, punchy phenols; **t22** a hint of chocolate marzipan at the well smoked heart of this; **f21.5** a touch of bitterness to the oak; **b22** attractively sweet and viscous. 58.8% James MacArthur & Co Ltd

⋯ **The John Milroy Selection Bowmore 21 Years Old** dist 1987, bott 2009 **(84)** n21 t21.5 f20.5 b21. Heads down for the absolutely unique "Hughsey" style of Victory V and Parma Violet smokiness. 45% Berry Bros & Rudd

⋯ **The John Milroy Selection Bowmore 22 Years Old (85.4)** n21 t22 f21 b21.5. Very lightly smoked and with myriad forms of sugared toast. 48.4% Berry Bros & Rudd

⋯ **Kingsbury's Bowmore 1997 (87)** n21.5 more Bow-less than Bow-more...the peat is little more than a whisper, very much outshouted by the barley; **t22** excellent mouthfeel with the juicy barley brushing aside the lightest of smoky strokes; **f21.5** a soft smoky burr to the developing cocoa; **b22** those looking for a smoky experience will feel a little short-changed. But a well made and attractive malt nonetheless. 57.4% Japan Import System

Kingsbury's 'The Selection' Bowmore 7 Years Old dist 01, bott 07 **(82)** n20.5 t21 f20 b20.5. Docile, sweet and very clean. Could have done with being at cask strength. 43%.

Kingsbury's Single Cask Bowmore Aged 19 Years dist Dec 87, bott Aug 07 **(85.5)** n21 t21.5 f22 b21. Right out of the Fisherman's Friend school of Bowmore, but in crisp, attractive form. 46%. Japan Import System.

⋯ **Mackillop's Choice Bowmore 1989 Sherrywood** dist Apr 89, bott May 07 **(86)** n21 t22.5 f21 b21.5. So outrageously cough-sweetish, it appears to be a quite brilliant -and at times, delicious - parody of its own unique Fisherman's Friend style...!! 57.4% Iain Mackillop & Co. Ltd

⋯ **Malts of Scotland Bowmore 1995 Clubs** sherry butt no. 113, dist May 95, bott Nov 09 **(81.5)** n20.5 t20 f21 b20. Peat and anthracite nose but with an attractively sweet and mildly sticky pay off. 56.7% Malts of Scotland. 192 bottles.

Master of Malt Bowmore 26 Years Old bott 09 **(88)** n21.5 uniquely Bowmore: a hickory-sweetened mixture of Fisherman's Friends and kippers; **t21** weird: there is no other word for it. The cough sweet peat appears to be drowned in a tidal wave of sweet, nondescript fruit. For a moment there is silence on the palate...then spices break out... **f23.5**...and at last we have serious whisky. Beautiful texture to the oaky vanilla and phenols materialise in various degrees of intensity and sweetness and dryness: a fabulous fade.... **b22** now that's something completely different: the nose and early delivery has you checking the paper for the date: nope, it really isn't April 1st. Where the hell is all that sweetness coming from...? Then it starts to settle towards something recognisable as very good whisky and from then onwards you are served up a minor treat. 53.4%. Master of Malt.

Old Malt Cask Bowmore Aged 15 Years refill hogshead no. 3972, dist Mar 92, bott Nov 07 (88) n21.5 t22.5 f22 b22. Plenty of cough sweet. But here there's so much more.... *50%. Douglas Laing. 357 bottles.*

Old Malt Cask Bowmore Aged 18 Years refill hogshead no. 4237, dist Oct 89, bott Apr 08 (90) n23 t22 f22 b23. Truly glorious Bowmore with any number of twists and turns. Not exactly textbook, but there are so many brilliant asides... *50%. nc ncf. Douglas Laing. 318 bottles.*

Old Malt Cask Bowmore Aged 21 Years refill hogshead, dist Jun 87, bott Sep 08 (88) n21.5 some surprising gristiness for one so old; gentle smoke and mildly floral; t23 delicate in the extreme though the peat does get chunkier as the oak gathers weight; f21.5 bitter marmalade and a light, silky smoke; b22 a cask taken as far as it dare go but the light radiation of peat is lovely. *50%. Douglas Laing. 229 bottles.*

Old Malt Cask Bowmore Aged 25 Years refill hogshead, dist Mar 83, bott Mar 08 (75) n18.5 t18 f19.5 b19. Twentyfive years????? All that cough sweet and bugger all else...???.... nooooooooooo!!!! *50%. nc ncf. Douglas Laing. 259 bottles.*

Old Malt Cask A Fine Cigar's Pleasure Bowmore Aged 9 Years refill hogshead (84) n21 t21 f22 b21. Lots of natural caramel wrapped in chocolate. *50%. Douglas Laing. 354 bottles.*

⁙ **Old & Rare Bowmore Aged 22 Years** sherry finished hogshead, dist Nov 87, bott Apr 10 (80) n19 t20 f21 b20. Fisherman's Friend concentrate. *56.1% nc ncf. 244 bottles.*

⁙ **Premier Barrel Bowmore Aged 9 Years** (80) n19 t20 f21 b20. When I tell people that I remember the days, 20 years ago, when Bowmore was sold by Oddbins as a five-year-old, I tend not to be believed. Especially when I explained it was a more than enjoyable dram. Here is something which reminds me a little of those days, though, for all its simplistic charm, this doesn't have quite the same cut and dash. *46% nc ncf Douglas Laing & Co Ltd. 362 bottles.*

Premier Barrel Bowmore Aged 9 Years (83.5) n21.5 t22 f20 b20. Pleasantly sweet before running out of legs. *46%. Douglas Laing. 302 bottles.*

Premier Barrel Bowmore Aged 9 Years (89) n22.5 soft evening garden perfumes amid the delicate smoke; t23 sweet malt and smoke delivery which soon conjours up something fuller yet teasing and controlled; the molassed sweetness really does strike a cord with the peat; f21.5 some oils enter the fray; b22 a beautiful, creaseless malt. *46%. 383 bottles.*

Premier Barrel Bowmore Aged 10 Years (78.5) n19 t20.5 f19 b19. If it's a Premier barrel then it must be non-league spirit...*46%. nc ncf. Douglas Laing. 382 bottles.*

Provenance Bowmore Aged 8 Years hogshead no. 3866-3887, dist winter 98, bott autumn 07 (89) n23 t22.5 f21.5 b22. Sn untaxing but complex malt. Lovely stuff. *46%. Douglas Laing.*

Provenance Bowmore Aged 8 Years Gabriel Meffre wine cask no. 3895, dist winter 98, bott autumn 07 (82) n21 t21 f20 b20. What an interesting one-off (one-hopes) experiment! *46%.*

Provenance Bowmore Aged 9 Years hogshead cask nos. 4109, 4110 dist winter 98, bott winter 08 (88.5) n22 t23 f22 b21.5. Minimal input from the cask maximizes the malt. And this is pretty good stuff, even if much younger than the age suggests. Refreshing. Sweet. Fun. Absolutely love it!! *46%. nc ncf. Douglas Laing.*

⁙ **Secret Stills 4.9 Islay 1991** bott 2008 (89.5) n23 no secret about this being a top-notch nose: the peat is controlled and quite refined, the citrus is little more than an echo, the sugars in total harmony with the vanillas and a speck or two of salt just to up the tang a little; t22.5 a distant murmur of cough sweet gives the game away regarding identity, but to the foreground there is a relaxed gristy sweetness with the smoke melting on the tongue; f22 weightier as the oaks and spices roll in; b22 the perfect malt for those who like smoky but not heavily peated whisky. The style tells me this is likely to be from one distillery only. And though it is a secret, and I thought I just heard a door creak behind me, I am certain this has all the hallmark of a B... aarrrhhhh......!! *45% Gordon & MacPhail.*

Scotch Malt Whisky Society Cask 3.135 Aged 7 Years 1st fill barrel, dist Oct 00 (94) n24 t23.5 f23 b23.5 As some of us in the game have long suspected: if it can be this good at 7 years – the kind of age preferred by our forefathers – why let it get into a greybeard stage? Keep these kinds of bottlings coming, guys!!! *58%*

Scotch Malt Whisky Society Cask 3.138 Aged 10 Years refill butt, dist Feb 98 (89) n23 t23 f21 b22 Oh, what might have been had this been filled into a top quality cask? *57.2%*

Scotch Malt Whisky Society Cask 3.139 Aged 10 Years refill butt, dist Feb 98 (83) n22 t21.5 f19 b20.5. Sharp and awkward, what would have been a very good dram – the spirit is excellent – has been limited by a so-so cask. *56.5%*

Scotch Malt Whisky Society Cask 3.140 Aged 10 Years refill butt, dist Feb 98 (85.5) n22.5 t22 f20 b21. Some wonderful peaty touches. But again the cask has spoken. And not wisely. *56.4%*

Scotch Malt Whisky Society Cask 3.146 Aged 9 Years refill hogshead, dist Feb 99 (78) n19 t21 f19 b19. Prepare to be underwhelmed. *60.1%*

Scotch Malt Whisky Society Cask 3.147 Aged 10 Years refill hogshead, dist Feb 98 **(85)** n20 t21.5 f21.5 b22. A spiced up bottling which really gets the tastebuds tingling. The peat conjures up some hickory and cocoa amid the sweeter demerara. *57.3%*

Scotch Malt Whisky Society Cask 3.148 Aged 9 Years refill hogshead, dist Feb 99 **(95)** n23.5 now this is a classy nose: some lavender amid the soft peat and a touch of bourbon for good measure; t24 thick and chewy, the smoke arrives as the very best peaty malts tend to: slowly and with a build up that allows the other sides of its personality to shine. Bourbony liquorice and cocoa haunt the middle ground; f23.5 long, with that smoky cocoa hanging onto an oily slick; some velvety muscovado balances out the drier vanillas b24 the kind of excellent and intrinsically structured malt which will re-assert where this distillery was 30 years ago...this is actually a twin sister cask to 3.146, being one cask number along. It is worth getting both to see how the line between success and failure can be so fine... *59.8%*

Scotch Malt Whisky Society Cask 3.149 Aged 10 Years dist Feb 98 **(86.5)** n22 t23 f20.5 b21. An up and down, no frills bottling. The oak has intervened enough only to as act as a gentle foil to the clean, softly honeyed peat which though bigger than many Bowmores is entirely non aggressive. *56.4%*

Scotch Malt Whisky Society Cask 3.150 Aged 18 Years refill hogshead, dist Aug 90 **(91.5)** n22 some knotty oak is unpicked by lemon-zesty smoke; t23.5 light and juicy. The mouth-watering freshness embraces the hickory-tipped smoked with ease; f23 long, much drier with vanilla replacing the citrus within the delicate smoke; b23 charming and delicate with just the right dose of sweetness where needed. *54.5%*

Scotch Malt Whisky Society Cask 3.151 Aged 18 Years refill hogshead, dist Aug 90 **(84)** n20 t20.5 f22.5 b21. Sharp, malty, zesty, sometimes bracing. *56.2%*

⋯⋯ **Scotch Malt Whisky Society Cask 3.155 Aged 21 Years** refill hogshead, dist Dec 87 **(88.5)** n22 passion fruit and peat...an unlikely, but lovely combination...; t22.5 the nature of the exotic fruit is a bit of a giveaway regarding the age while the strained cough mixture note equally spills the beans on the distillery; f22 some vanilla is added to the unusual mix; b22 for those who like their peat – or cough sweets - a little exotic... *49.1% 214 bottles.*

⋯⋯ **Scotch Malt Whisky Society Cask 3.160 Aged 10 Years** 1st fill barrel, dist May 99 **(86)** n21 t22 f21.5 b21.5. Malty with a surprising hint of mango. The smoke is lethargic, distant and little more than an echo. *60.1% Scotch Malt Whisky Society*

⋯⋯ **Scotch Malt Whisky Society Cask 3.161 Aged 11 Years** refill sherry butt, dist Feb 99 **(85)** n21 t22.5 f21 b21. Juicy, fruity, lightly smoked and no shortage of zip and nip. Surprising degree of oak, too. *58.4% Scotch Malt Whisky Society. 204 bottles.*

⋯⋯ **Scotch Malt Whisky Society Cask 3.162 Aged 17 Years** 2nd fill hogshead, dist Sep 92 **(78.5)** n20 t21 f18 b19.5. Get the feeling that this is not firing on all cylinders, in spite of its early decadence. Thin, biting and a little unforgiving. *56% Scotch Malt Whisky Society. 209 bottles.*

Scott's Selection Bowmore 1990 bott 07 **(86.5)** n21.5 t22 f21.5 b21.5. Sweet, at times nutty, with pretty decent peat for a Bowmore. Pussycat malt and what it loses on lack of complexity it makes up for with style, clarity and confidence. Enjoy. *52%*

⋯⋯ **Single & Single Bowmore 2000 Aged 8 Years Limited Release (81.5)** n21.5 t22 f18 b20. Stereotypical, decent quality, young-ish peated Islay early on, but then let down on the finish. Almost Caol Ila-esque in its early, lightly oiled, approach. *46% South Africa*

Whisky-Doris Bowmore 1994 The Dram (86.5) n21.5 t22 f21.5 b21.5. Lots of sweet barley on the gently oiled delivery; a tad bitter from the oak. *46%*

The Whisky Fair Bowmore 10 Year Old dist 98, bott 09 **(93)** n23 beautiful mocha attached to the chunky, salty malt; t24.5 mouth filling: every sinew of the sweet barley can be tasted and chewed. But the malt and cocoa fill the middle ground with unblemished brilliance; f22.5 slows down as the vanilla takes a firmer grip but still that smoky, sugared cocoa has a long way to go; b23 simply and beautifully made whisky matured in a cask which gives full view to the malt. *59.8%. The Whisky Fair, Germany.*

⋯⋯ **Whisky Galore Bowmore 2002** (87.5) n22.5 gristy, guttural smoke. No attempt at refinement or even great complexity: just honest, relatively young Bowmore with a natural barley sweetness; t22 like the nose, there are no pretensions here and all is based on simplicity: the smoke does have a degree of citrus to lighten it, though; f21 the oak eases in to offer a little green tea bitterness; b22 Ah-ha!! I see the Whisky Galore brand is back. There are those who probably still have a touch of the vapours when the name is mentioned, as a decade or so ago it was well, a bottle of caramel with some whisky in it. Well, of course it wasn't, but that's how it sometimes seemed. Not anymore. Lessons have obviously been learned. And for those who produce a natural tick whenever the name is mentioned...it is safe to come out now...!!! If this bottling is anything to go by, then go buy: for you are getting malt very much as nature intended. Except for the impurity of that irritating splash of water, taking it down to 46%, of course. *46%*

Wilson & Morgan Barrel Selection Bowmore 1997 Extra Strength bott 07 **(89) n22 t23 f22 b22.** Peaty, despite the nose. *50%*

BRAEVAL
Speyside, 1974. Chivas. Working.

Connoisseurs Choice Braes of Glenlivet 1975 (95) n23.5 the antiquity of the malt has pointed it in the direction of a mild exotic fruitiness, but never to the extent that the oak even thinks about dominating, so the barley gets a fair hearing. Diluted lemon helps keep the aroma fresh and keen; **t24.5** spit.....???? Not likely: not when a malt of this age absolutely refuses to show wrinkles and sprints around the tastebuds in a lemon-yeasty tracksuit; the barley and vanilla harmonise effortlessly in its wake; **f23.5** how can a malt so light carry on for so long? Obviously the chocolaty oak has something to do with it, as well as the growing spice. But delicate oils appear to also keep the show going, with not an off or bitter note to be had. What a charmer..... **b23.5** an astonishing time capsule of a dram. We are tasting a malt made within months of the distillery being opened, nearly 35 years on. The result is one of the malts of the year: how it has survived so flawlessly should keep connoisseurs in heated debate for a very long time. Spectacularly elegant and beautiful. And an all time Braes classic, never to be forgotten. *43% Gordon & MacPhail*

The Cärn Mör Vintage Collection Braes of Glenlivet 1989 hogshead, cask no. 997, dist 89, bott 09 **(88) n22.5** beautiful clean barley with the lightest speck of smoke; **t22** juicy, crisp barley and light spices; **f21.5** oily, slightly sweet vanilla; **b22** charming, simplistic but beautifully made malt. *46%. The Scottish Liqueur Centre.*

Deerstalker Braeval Aged 10 Years bott Sep 07 **(92) n23 t23.5 f22.5 b23.** For Speyside lovers, this bottling (see details above) is an absolute must. A hard distillery to find, Deerstalker has the habit of bottling it at this age in near perfect fettle. A backwater blinder. *40%. Aberko.*

Deerstalker Braeval Aged 15 Years (83) n20.5 t22 f20 b20.5. By contrast to the 10-y-0, this is flat and uninspiring. It could be the extra oak, there might be a touch of toffee. Dazzles briefly on delivery. *46%. ncf. Aberko.*

Dun Bheagan Braeval Aged 13 Years Manzanilla sherry butt, dist Jun 95 **(83) n20 t23 f20 b20.** One of those curious malts which needs some serious adjustments of the tastebuds to help come to terms with the uncompromising character. The dishevelled nose puts you on guard and it possibly four of five mouthfuls to really get into this one. At first the character again appears all over the shop, and of no particular style, but the richer fruits to guarantee a sumptuous and divinely bitter-sweet backbone. The fade is just too bitter, though. *46%. Ian Macleod Distillers Ltd.*

Duncan Taylor Collection Braes of Glenlivet 1989 cask no. 1070 **(91) n22.5** has shrugged off the years with a mighty malty cloak; no shortage of butterscotch, either; **t23** brilliantly crisp and erudite in its malty qualities; salivating and lively before the drier middle approaches; **f22.5** shows a more austere timbre, but the finesse remains beyond doubt; **b23** quietly complex and classy. *50.3%*

Old Malt Cask Braeval Aged 12 Years sherry butt, dist Jul 96, bott Sep 08 **(88) n20** a tad thin and uncertain; **t23** made its mind up now...going for it big time with a huge battering ram of juicy, crusty barley and crisped sugars **f22.5** outstanding follow-through of gentle spices and ever sweetening barley; light fruity edges support the late oak; **b22.5** makes the nose something of a liar. An ultimately fine dram with a tale to tell. *50%. 665 bottles.*

⬩ **Old Malt Cask Braes of Glenlivet Aged 20 Years** refill hogshead no. DL 5717, dist May 89, bott Dec 09 **(84.5) n22 t20 f21.5 b21.** The oak has much to say, some of it a little bitterly. But the oratory of the malt is much more uplifting. *50% Douglas Laing*

⬩ **Premier Barrel Braeval Aged 10 Years** sherry cask, dist Sep 99 **(77) n18.5 t21 f18.5 b19.** Grapey and....I bet this'll be as popular in Germany as Joachim Loew... *46% 582 bottles*

⬩ **Premier Barrel Braeval Aged 11 Years** (79.5) **n20 t20.5 f19 b20.** Everything about this screams that it is a competent dram made to bulk up the malt content – and maltiness – in a blend. *46% nc ncf 180 bottles*

Provenance Braeval Aged 10 Years sherry butt, dist summer 98, bott autumn 08 **(73) n18 t19 f18 b18.** Some grand barley does its best to negate the lightly sulphured flaws. *46%.*

BRORA
Highland (northern), 1819–1983. Diageo. Closed.

Brora 25 Year Old 7th Release bott 08 db **(96) n24** even with the lowest peating levels you ever have nosed from this distillery, the aura of beauty is unmistakable: the soft phenol molecules appears to be perfectly matched with the oak ones. Meanwhile fragile citrus ensures a youthful charm; somewhere there is a hint of bourbon; **t24.5** superb barley kick off, absolute waves of juices running about the palate, and still the smoke holds back, no more than a background murmur; as the middle fills, that bourbon on the nose become more pronounced with shades of honeyed liquorice; **f23.5** long, with the sugars hanging in there allowing the vanillas to form very slowly; **b24** as the distillery closed in March 1983, if memory serves me correctly, this must be coming to the end of the road for the true 25-year-old. Those looking for the usual big peat show might be disappointed. Others, in search of majesty, sophistication and timeless grace, will be blown away. *56.3%*

Brora 30 Years Old Special Releases 2006 db **(92) n23 t24 f22 b23.** Showing a degree of age decay but even so the sheer beauty of this malt leaves you gasping. *55.7%*

Brora 30 Years Old Special Releases 2007 db **(88.5) n21.5** smoke, hickory and some tired oak notes; **t23.5** excellent arrival of sweet peat and almost sweeter oak; lush, not overly complex but does what it can with minimum fuss and maximum effect; **f21.5** the soft oils and smoke can't entirely blot out the unwelcome off-oak notes; **b22** not in the highest echelons of old Broras with a degree of lactic being milked from the oak. But close your eyes, concentrate on the more delicate smoke tones – especially on arrival – and still be amazed. *55.7%. 2,958 bottles.*

Brora 30 Years Old db **(97) n24** that stunning Brora farmyard again, perhaps with a touch of extra fruit this time round. Beautiful structure, layering and harmony; **t25** Gosh! Perfect or what? How can something be this old yet offer such a gristy sweetness? Chewy, smoky, barely oaky but 100 okay-dokey; **f24** some late peat spice buzz adds a bit of bite to the smoke-fuelled serenity of this dram. A touch of something citrus helps thin out the layers; **b24** here we go again! Just like last year's bottling, we have something of near unbelievable beauty with the weight perfectly pitched and the barley-oak interaction the stuff of dreams. And as for the peat: an entirely unique species, a giant that is so gentle. Last year's bottling was one of the whiskies of the year. This even better version is the perfect follow-up. *56.4%*

Chieftain's Brora 26 Years Old oloroso sherry butt, dist Dec 81 **(92.5) n24 t22 f23.5 b23.** On delivery there is a fear that the great nose of the work will be undone. But hang on in there: the ending is a happy one. *48%. Ian Macleod Distillers Ltd.*

⋯ **Duncan Taylor Collection Brora 1981** cask no. 291 **(96) n23.5** playful and succulent, the smoke enjoys equal billing to the citrus and cherry cake; **t24.5** we are talking near perfect weight, sweetness, injection of oil, control of smoke, slow infusion of cocoa, almonds and other delicate flavours and involvement of spice....; **f23.5** hard to know where the middle ends and the finish begin...like some kind of lightly peated orgasm; a very light degree of oaky bitterness, but it is a trifle; **b24.5** you won't ever want to wash your glass again after tasting this one. *51.3%*

Duncan Taylor Collection Brora 1981 cask no. 1424 **(92) n22.5** one of the most peat-less Brora noses of all time; makes up for it with a lovely mixture of foresty, floral tones, honey and maple syrup, **t23** as soft and delicate as this can ever get· the barley flows around the palate on a wave of nectar; **f22.5** ridiculous clarity for a malt so old: barley and soft sugars link convivially with the vanilla; **b23** graceful, charming, entirely unexpected. That's why I love this job so much... *54.5%*

⋯ **Old & Rare Brora Aged 28 Years** sherry cask, dist Jun 81, bott Nov 09 **(91) n23** buzzing, nipping peat with a real farmyard feel; **t22.5** at first a wave or two of crusty molasse sugar, giving way to an earthy peatiness; **f23** the vanillas arrive in force, but the smoke drifts around on an oily carpet; **b22.5** a beautifully dirty tasting whisky: you will have to taste it to see exactly what I mean...! *57.4% Douglas Laing. 93 bottles.*

Old & Rare Brora Aged 30 Years dist Oct 76, bott Sep 07 **(87) n22 t22 f21.5 b21.5.** For all the strength, it refuses to be anything other than a lullaby dram. *55.1%. ncf. 104 bottles.*

Old & Rare Brora Aged 30 Years dist Oct 76, bott Apr 07 **(95) n23 t24 f24 b24.** Once more a dram from a distillery that leaves you spellbound. No descriptors entirely do justice. And as I am just completing this edition and space is at a premium, I'll not even try. *57.5%. 109 bottles.*

BRUICHLADDICH
Islay, 1881. Bruichladdich Ltd, Working.

Bruichladdich 10 Years Old db **(90) n22** beautifully clean and zesty, the malt is almost juvenile; **t23** sweet, fruity then malty charge along the tastebuds that geets the mouth salivating; **f23** the usual soft vanilla and custard but a bigger barley kick in the latter stages; **b22** more oomph than previous bottlings, yet still retaining its fragile personality. Truly great stuff for a standard bottling. *46%*

Bruichladdich 12 Years Old 2nd Edition db **(88) n23** big barrage of fruit; crisp barley beautifully integrates with oak; **t22** an uneven, mildly uncertain, delivery due to the grape being out of sync with the big barley; give it about eight-ten seconds and they have found a delicious degree of harmony; **f22** long with the intense, chiselled flavours still slightly at odds, but calming down with some oils; **b21** a similar type of wine involvement to "Waves", but this is oilier in the old-fashioned 'Laddie style and lacks a little of the sparkle. The fruit on the finish is outstanding, though, and I don't think you or I would turn down a third glass... 46%

Bruichladdich 15 Years Old 2nd Edition db (86) **n22 t23 f20 b21.** Delicious, as usual, but something, possibly fruity, appears to be holding back the show. 46%

Bruichladdich 16 Years Old bourbon cask db (89) **n22.5** sweet barley hangs from sturdy oak beams; **t22.5** remains firm yet sweet with a charming honeyed streak; again the oak plays a major role but its obvious dry input remains contained; **f22** dries further, with vanilla replacing the honey; some superb spices; **b22** plucked from the cask in the nick of time. In this state rather charming, but another summer or two might have seen the oak take a more sinister turn. 46%

Bruichladdich 16 Years Old bourbon/Chateau d'Yquem cask db (95) **n24** if you've got a good half an hour to spend, try using it intelligently by sticking your nose in this for a while: the grape is sweet and sultana juicy; the understated spices somehow hit just the right point to satisfy grape, oak and barley in one hit: some achievement... **t23.5** sweet, as the nose suggests, but the arrival is not all about grape. That sweetness also contains pristine barley.... **f23.5** just so soft and subtle with the vanillas offering a discreet escort to the barley-grape marriage; **b24** possibly the most delicate and understated of all the truly great whiskies of the year. Not one for the ice and water brigade. 46%

Bruichladdich 18 Years Old bourbon/cognac cask db (84.5) **n23.5 t21 f20 b20.** Big oak-spice buzz but thin. Sublime grapey nose, for sure, but pays a certain price, ultimately, for associating with such an inferior spirit... 46%

Bruichladdich 18 Years Old bourbon/opitz cask db (80.5) **n19 t22 f19.5 b20.** Dry, complex; at times oak-stretched. 46%

Bruichladdich 18 Years Old 2nd Edition bourbon/jurancon db (86) **n22 t21.5 f21 b21.5.** Plenty of fruit, including medium ripe greengages and slightly under-ripe grape. Juicy and sweet in the right places. 46%

Bruichladdich Flirtation Aged 20 Years 2nd Edition db (86) **n21 t22 f22 b21.** Hi sugar! A Laddie for those with a sweet tooth. 46%

Bruichaladdich 1970 Anniversary Bottling 125th bourbon cask, mature enhanced in zind humbrecht selection de grains noble pinot gris alsace white wine casks db (95) **n24 t24 f23 b24.** An unbelievably complex malt that defies time. A must- experience malt. 40.1%

Bruichladdich "Golder Still" 1984 bourbon cask, db (88.5) **n22 t23 f22 b21.5.** A huge amount of natural caramels leached from the oak does the joint job of ensuring extraordinary softness and eroding the higher notes. Still, there is enough eye-rolling honey and spice to keep anyone happy and the rich bourbony character on delivery really is dreamy stuff. 51%

Bruichladdich Blacker Still 1986 sherry cask db (87) **n21 t22 f22 b22.** Mildly flawed but you can forgive it its trespasses on account of its utterly juicy deliciousness. 50.7%

⸬ **Bruichladdich Black Art 19 Aged Years 1989** bourbon/wine casks db (78.5) **n20 t21.5 f19 b18.** Good grief...!! What was all that about? About as much balance as England and West Ham goalkeeper Robert Green trying to catch a tame shot. You have to admire the ruthless grape delivery, but the remainder is pretty shapeless and without a coherent plan...a bit like Mr Green's team mates... 51.1% nc ncf 6,000 bottles

Bruichladdich "DNA" 37 Years Old 80% bourbon/20% sherry cask, aged in Le Pin wine casks db (87) **n23.5** a beautiful, if potentially dodgy, counter between some gray-haired oak and pre-pubescent grape; **t22** nothing is settled with this one: the oak charges about in one direction, grapey waves soothes in another. A real flavour factory, especially with some light mocha in the middle ground, but don't look for a story here; **f20.5** a bit bitter, furry and nibbling; **b21** balance..? What balance...? Actually, somehow, this crazy thing does find some kind of equilibrium... 41%

Bruichladdich 1989 db (75.5) **n20 t19 f17.5 b19.** Ouch! 52.9%. Special bottling for Alberta.

Bruichladdich 1990 Aged 18 Years db (85.5) **n22.5 t21 f21 b21.** Enlivened by citrus and emboldened by soft salt. 46%

Bruichladdich 1990 Aged 18 Years cognac cask db (81.5) **n20.5 t21 f20 b20.** Wouldn't be a far greater benefit to the spirit world if Cognac was matured in a Bruichladdich cask...? 46%

Bruichladdich 1991 Aged 16 Years Chat Margaux finish db (94) **n23** fingers of grape essence tease and play with the crisp malt; there is almost a frailty to the spices; **t22** quite simply one of the finest deliveries of any non-peated Islay I have ever encountered; or any other whisky, come to that. The perfection of the juicy grape, the élan, as it glides over the barley is something you are likely never to forget; words, I'm afraid, could simply never do it justice; **f22.5** dries and reverts to a spiced attack as the vanilla gets little more than a foothold; **b23.5** a true Premier Cru malt...I have been almost certainly the most outspoken critic of whisky finishes: trust me, if they were all like this, you would never hear the merest clack of a dissenting typing key from me again... 46%

Bruichladdich 1993 db **(94) n23.5 t24 f23 b23.5.** As far as I can remember, or am aware, I had never tasted a Sassicaia-finished whisky before. And, as luck would have it, I have now tasted two in one day. On this evidence it would be entirely fair to argue that these tastebud-exploding finishes are Italy's greatest contribution to the whisky world....!! 50.2%. Special bottling for Alberta.

Bruichladdich 1994 db **(87) n22 t22 f21.5 b21.5.** Bravo to Bruichladdich for demonstrating to the Taiwanese that you don't have to have your whisky coloured to death to experience a very substantial dram. 54.9%. Taiwan.

Bruichladdich 1994 Full Strength db **(90) n21.5 t23 f22 b23.5.** Not dissimilar to the stunning Sassicaia, except a tad fatter. Just brilliant! 56.5%

Bruichladdich Valinch Blandola 1994 bourbon/Chateau d'Yquem casks, dist Sep 94 db **(87) n21.5** musty, dusty grape; **t22.5** a confused early delivery but pans out with a really complex fruit-toffee delivery with a touch of coffee and, finally, juicy barley; **f21** vanilla and a dry, furry grapiness; **b22** a bit muddled here and there but, like the distillery and staff, no shortage of personality. 55.3%. Available only from Bruichladdich's distillery shop.

Bruichladdich "Kosher" 1994 Aged 12 Years db **(85.5) n22 t21 f21 b21.5.** Clean. What else, my dear? 46%

Bruichladdich 1998 db **(89) n22 t22.5 f22.5 b22.** A truly unique signature to this but absolute class in a glass. 46%

Bruichladdich 1998 bourbon/oloroso cask, dist 98 db **(87.5) n22.5** splatted grape shows a fresh, juicy character; **t22.5** two or three waves of tart grape crash against the tastebuds before a more delicate spicy shadow forms, followed by richer barley; **f21** a lazy, custard cream biscuit sweetness dwindles towards a remarkably dry finale; **b21.5** surprisingly conservative. But, joy of joys, not an atom of sulphur to be found...!! 46%

Bruichladdich 1998 bourbon/Manzanilla cask, dist 98 db **(82.5) n21 t21 f20 b20.5.** Fruity. But bitter where it should be sweet. 46%

⚬ **Bruichladdich 2001 The Resurrection Dram 23.10.01** bourbon cask, dist 2001, bott 2009 db **(90.5) n23** so subtle! Spiced sultana on malt, laced with golden syrup; **t23** grist dissolves in the mouth: molten (fruitless) barley again with a sugary sheen. Simplistic, but beautifully effective; **f21.5** long, vanilla-led, spiced and a little bitter; **b23** now, be honest. How can you not have a first class Resurrection in the Bible....? 46% 24,000 bottles

Bruichladdich Full Strength Special Edition - The International Malt Whisky Festival, Gent 2008 db **(94) n23 t23.5 f23 b24.5.** The only thing more beautiful than this I came across for the first time at Gent was the girl selling my books. Both are enough to dive you inSanne with desire. 56.5%. nc, ncf.

⚬ **Bruichladdich Islay Barley 2004 Valinch** fresh sherry butt db **(89.5) n22.5** positively porridgey, complete with brown molten sugar; someone's tipped a sherry trifle into this one, too...; **t24** waaaowww...!! That is some delivery: the thickest, most uncompromising Laddie of the year. Forget about sticking a spoon in it: this could easily accommodate a pitch fork. The fruit plays along with the porridge character and there is fudge, sundry spices, and tannin-shaded barley; **f21** quite bitter, but the mocha effect works well; **b22** yet another quite fabulous bottling form Bruichladdich, this one really cranking up the flavours to maximum effect. Having said all that, call me mad if you will...but seeing as this is Islay barley, would it not have been a good idea to shove it into a bourbon barrel, so we could see exactly what it tastes like? Hopefully that is on its way... 57.5%

Bruichladdich Infinity Second Edition bourbon/rioja db **(94) n24 t24 f23 b23.** Wasn't it Daffy Duck who used to put on his cape and shout: "Infinity and Beyond" ? Oh, no... it was Buzz Lightyear. Anyways, he must have been thinking of this. And there's certainly nothing dethspicable about this one... 52.5%

⚬ **Bruichladdich Infinity Third Edition** refill sherry tempranillo db **(94.5) n24** the smokiness appears to have a life of its own: still cured bacon, as in previous Infinities (actually can there be such a thing....?) but perhaps a touch of Bavarian smoked cheese, perhaps, as a side dish, next to a freshly diced apple? I adore the lack of oils on the nose; the teasing dryness compensated by a distant fruit freshness; **t24** and its more of the same: just so dry, the palate is parched in seconds. The smoke is ashy, the vanilla is powdery, the malt gristy.... just flakes of flavour wafting into every crevice like snow falling on a silent day; **f23** long, with the inevitable build up of dry, powdery spices which match the vanilla for weight and impact; **b23.5** I dare anybody who says they don't like smoky whisky not to be blown away by this. Go on...I dare you... 50%

∵∵ **Bruichladdich Laddie Classic Edition 01** db **(86)** n22 t21 f21.5 b21.5. Easy going with intense malt and natural caramels in pretty equal shares. 46% *Multi Vintage*

Bruichladdich Legacy Series 3 Aged 35 Years db **(91)** n22 t22.5 f23.5 b23. So they managed to find a whisky exactly the same age as Ladie distiller Jim. 40.7%

Bruichladdich Links "Carnoustie" 14 Years Old db **(78)** n19 t20 f19 b20. Hits some unexpected rough. 46%

Bruichladdich Links K Club Ireland "16th Hole" 14 Years Old bourbon/syrah, dist 92, bott 07 db **(93)** n23 t23 f23 b24. I quite like this, though as hard as I try I can't quite love it. The spices offer great entertainment value and the juiciness on delivery is astonishing, but..... My tongue is investigating every crevice in my mouth with some urgency, so I know it's complex – and very unusual, but..... It's gossamer light. It kind of teases you. It's playful. But it's not beautiful. Is it...? Third mouthful in and I'm getting hooked. Oh, sod it! I've just upped it from a 86 to 93. What can I do? I'm in love... 46%. *nc ncf. 12,000 bottles.*

Bruichladdich Links "Torrey Pines" 15 Years Old db **(89.5)** n23 t22.5 f22 b22. As clean as the perfect tee shot from the 15th... 46%

∵∵ **Bruichladdich Organic 2003 Anns An T-Seann Doigh** bourbon db **(84.5)** n22 t22 f20 b20.5. Thick barley carrying soft smoke. A slight bitterness threads in and out of the proceedings. 46% *nc ncf 100% Scottish barley*

Bruichladdich Redder Still 1984 db **(95.5)** n23.5 t24 f23.5 b24.5. Now it's finding whiskies like this that I became the world's first-full time whisky for. I dreamed of discovering drams which stretched my tastebuds and spoke to me with eloquence, charisma and unmistakable class. This is one such whisky: the style is highly unusual; the cleverness of the layering almost unique. This is the kind of near flawless whisky for which we were given tastebuds. Oh, and a nose... 50.4%

Bruichladdich "The Resurrection" bourbon cask, dist 01 db **(90)** n23 sharp, striking, salty oak and a light yet firm smokiness: beautifully coastal; t22.5 sweet, soft and the peat simply glides over the buds; f22 some chocolate mint to keep the smoke company; b22.5 from the distillery that brings orgasms (see PC6), no doubt about the surrection here... 46%

Bruichladdich Rocks db **(82)** n19 t22 f20 b21. Perhaps softer than you'd imagine something called "rocks"! Beautiful little malty charge on entry. 46%

∵∵ **Bruichladdich Sherry Classic Fusion: Fernando de Castilla** bourbon/Jerez de la Frontera db **(91)** n23 a warm oaky spiciness adds attitude to the otherwise clean grape barley mix; a real dank warehouse backdrop to this one; t23 a barley-grape see-saw which moves effortlessly into a dry winey middle; the malt when apparent appears youthful and lithe; f22 some late prickly spice helps to really emphasise the subtlety of the oak; b23 what a fantastically stylish piece of work! I had an overwhelming urge to sing Noel Coward songs while tasting this: for the Dry Martini drinkers out there who have never thought of moving on to Scotch... 46%

∵∵ **Bruichladdich Sherry Edition 1992 Aged 17 Years "Fino"** bourbon/fino sherry db **(94)** n23.5 dry, suety, spotted dick; in the background, dried dates lurk deliciously; wonderful balance; t24 fabulously subtle malt-generated sweetness sits comfortably with a much drier, juicier sub-plot; the mouthfeel hovers around perfection with just enough light oil to grease the roof of the mouth and keep the barley in the ascendancy; f23 lots to chew here as the vanillas offer a custardy edge, though sugars – whilst present - are at a premium. Again we are back to the dregs of dried dates; b23.5 exceptionally good: a rare showing of Fino at its most sophisticated and unblemished. 46% *nc ncf*

∵∵ **Bruichladdich Sherry Edition 1992 Aged 17 Years "Pedro Ximinez"** bourbon/PX db **(83)** n22 t22 f18.5 b20.5. Semi-puckering delivery: my word, that grape really does fly relentlessly at the taste buds. Probably the hardest sherry type to get right and here it works pretty well for the most part. 46% *nc ncf*

Bruichladdich 16 Years Old bourbon/Chateau Haut Brion cask db **(81.5)** n21 t21.5 f19 b20. fruity and busy for sure. But just not the kind of wine barrel effect that does much for me, I'm afraid, not least because of the background buzz on the palate. 46%

Bruichladdich 16 Years Old bourbon/Chateau Lafite cask db **(89)** n24 yet another nose where the grape appears almost three dimensional in its ability to offer the cleanest of fruits...and somehow sharpen the barley element for all those years in cask; t22.5 absolutely melt-in-the-mouth: deliveries rarely come softer or so dripping in grape. The spices which form belatedly towards the middle are of a servile nature; f21.5 perhaps too soft here, as the grape, though delicate, somehow appears to dominate and desired late complexity doesn't materialise; b21.5 ridiculously soft. Could just do with an injection of something to propel it into greatness. 46%

Bruichladdich 16 Years Old bourbon/Chateau Lafleur cask db **(92.5)** n23 a real floral dustiness to the grape; delicate spice prickle; t23.5 barley tries to make a brief statement before the microphone is snatched away by bristling fruit; the mouthfeel is a bit like a dissolving sugar candy; **f23** some oak gets a word in, but can barely make itself heard against the barley; **b23** so luminous on the palate, it's positively Lafleurescent... *46%*

Bruichladdich 16 Years Old bourbon/Chateau Latour cask db **(84.5) n21 t21.5 f21 b21.** Enjoyable. But there is a strange aggression to the spice which doesn't altogether sit as comfortably as it might. The fruit heads off into not just grapey but citrus territory, but there is a always a but about the direction it takes... *46%*

Bruichladdich 16 Years Old bourbon/Chateau Margaux cask db **(78.5) n20.5 t20 f19 b19.** Not 1st Cru Bruichladdich, I'm afraid. *46%*

Bruichladdich 21 Years Old oloroso sherry cask db **(76.5) n18.5 t21 f18 b19.** Oops! *46%*

Bruichladdich WMD II - The Yellow Submarine 1991 db **(75) n20 t19 f18 b18.** This one just doesn't have the balance and sinks. *46%*

Bruichladdich X4 db **(82) n18 t22 f21 b21.** Frankly, like no new make I have ever come across in Scotland before. Thankfully, the taste is sweet, malty and compact: far, far better than the grim, cabbage water nose. Doesn't really have the X-Factor yet, though. *50%*

⋰ **Bruichladdich X4 +3 Quadruple Distilled 3 Aged Years** bourbon db **(86) n21.5 t22 f21 b21.5.** It is as if the sugars in the barley have been reduced to their most intense form: this is all about huge barley of eye-watering intensity. A novel and not unattractive experience. *63.5% nc ncf 15,000 bottles*

Bruichladdich X4 2007 db **(86.5) n18 t23 f23.5 b22.** Taste slowly with the eyes closed and just let that silky-soft oil coat the palate/palette until you find yourself giving an involuntary whimper. That's what happens when your tastebuds are being seduced and screwed by something of naked, bold beauty. And at 65.4% even the outwardly ugly can be beautiful... *65.4%. 2008 festival bottling.*

⋰ **Bruichladdich XVII Aged Years "The Seventeen" Rum Cask** bourbon/renegade rum db **(92) n23** typical rum "clipped" nose; this one with just a shade of soft, dry rubber typical of certain Guyana (especially Enmore) or Barbados marks; a rather lovely lemon tint to the vanilla works a treat; **t23.5** super dry delivery, too, with the sugars taking time to arrive. When they do, they weld with the barley attractively; formidable balance between the barley and spices while a light sprinkling of salt seems to up the spicy oak input to counter the sugars; **f22** mainly dry and attractively layered with short, sweet bands; **b23.4** no shortage of sophistication here. Always good to see the casks of drier, more complexly structured rums being put to such intelligent use. My sample doesn't tell me which rums casks were used, but I was getting vivid flashbacks here of Ruby-Topaz Hummingbirds flitting from flower to flower in the gardens of the now closed Eigflucht distillery in Guyana in the long gone days when I used to scramble around the warehouses there. That distinctive dryness though is pure Enmore, though some Barbadian rum can offer a similar effect. Something very different and a top quality experience for late at night or to get the taste buds aroused as dinner is prepared. *46% nc ncf*

Octomore 5 Years Old db **(96) n23.5** seeing how Octomore is actually a farm on Islay, it is rather fitting that the massive peat here yields a distinctly farm-yardy aroma. Yet this is curiously low on peat reek for a dram boasting phenomenal phenols at 131 parts per million – Ardbeg is about 50; the much smokier PC7 is just 40. That said, obviously peaty, yet an age-related lemon lightness, too...and a herd of cattle...; **t24.5** the oils are absolutely perfect, as is the slow unfurling of the myriad strata of peat; those youthful, zesty, citrus notes have been enriched with a perfect degree of golden syrup; a near-perfect sprinkling of spice enriches further...; **f24** a wonderful array of vanillas lighten not just the peat but the sweetened mocha which is now making its mark. Long, relaxed and very assured for a malt so young... **b24** forget about the age. Don't be frightened by the phenol levels. Great whisky is not about numbers. It is about excellent distillation and careful maturation. And here you have a memorable combination of both... *63.5%*

⋰ **Octomore 2_140 Aged 5 Years Edition 02.1** bourbon cask, bott Jun 09 db **(94) n23** a snug nose of tight, thick peat: needs a chainsaw to cut through it; **t24** surprisingly sweet delivery with more than a hint of citrus: a massive gristy surge which is about as mouth-watering as heavily peated malt ever gets; **f23** long with some vanilla at last getting into the act; some excellent late mocha and marzipan thins the smoke; **b23** talk about a gentle giant: as though your taste buds are being clubbed to death by a ton of smoky feathers. *62.5% nc ncf 15,000 bottles*

⋰ **Octomore Orpheus Aged 5 Years Edition 02.2 PPM 140** bourbon/chateau Petrus, bott 2009 db **(96.5) n24** when you clean out the ashes of fire that had been fed 100% by peat, that morning after the night before task, this is what you get. Well, partially. You will have to have one hand in the grate, the other around a glass of Petrus....; **t24.5** let's get this right:

140ppm phenols? Check. 61%abv? Check. How then, can the landing on the palate be like jumping onto a bed of feathers? The Demerara-gristy sweetness helps. So does the smoke, which envelopes the mouth. But the peat is also dry and that means a magnificent balance with those gristy sugars, so all seems to be in harmony. Brilliant! **f23.5** long, and just a gentle wind down of all before. Maybe a bit of extra fruit visible later on, as well as some Liquorice Allsorts; **b24.5** a standing ovation for this massive performance....the quite perfect way to bring up my 900th new whisky for the 2011 Bible. Everything works; the age and freshness of the barley, the controlled enormity of the smoke...even the entirely sulphur-free wine barrel. For those with a lot of hair on their chest...and want even more. *61% 15,000 bottles.*

Port Charlotte Evolution PC5 Cask Strength db **(95) n24 t23 f24 b24.** A bit like a David Lynch movie: you are caught in the dazzling genius of it all, not exactly knowing what is going on, yet never doubting that you are experiencing something very special; and only at the very end does the plot make any sense at all. One thing is for certain: even the most experienced peat whisky lovers are unlikely to have encountered anything quite like this....simply because Port Charlotte offers a style of peating different from any other not only on Islay but in the world. *63.5%. 6,000 bottles.*

Port Charlotte First Cut 27/05/07 bourbon cask no. 007, dist 28 May 01, bott May 07 db **(94) n23 t24 f24 b23.** Great whisky, even if it does, through youth, struggle slightly to get its legs and balance. For best results, leave in the glass to settle and oxidise for a while before tasting. A malt for extremists. *61.5%*

Port Charlotte PC6 db **(96.5) n24.5** ohhhhhh... arrrrrrrrhh..... mmmmmmmmmmm..... oh, the peat, the peat..... yessssss...., oh my god......mmmmmmmm..... ohhhhhhh.... **t24** first you get the smoky... ooooohhhhhhh... arrrrrrrrr..... then the sweeter... mmmmmmmmm..... arrrrooooohhhh.... **f24** it finishes with a more gentle arghoooo...... mmmmmmmm..... oooophhhhhh..... arrrrrrrrr.... **b24** not many whiskies have a truly unmistakable nose.... and....., but this is, this........ is....... this..... mmmmmmm..., arrrrrhh. Ohhhhhhhh........ *61.6%*

Port Charlotte PC7 dist 01 db **(93.5) n24** dry. The most profound peat fire ashes: not for peaty amateurs... **t24** a few drops of sweetness added; a liquorice/molassed melt to the massive smoke: the phenols seems a lot higher than the 40ppm they talk about; **f22** drops down a gear or two as some bitterness creeps in, as does a secondary fizz to the spice; **b22.5** not quite as orgasmic as last year, sadly. But should still be pretty stimulating... *60.5%*

·⁖· **Port Charlotte PC8** bourbon, dist 2001, bott 2009 **(88) n22** the bourbon and smoke appear to be rather too in cahoots; **t23** beautifully rounded with the smoke taking off. But the oak is very caramel-centric and lacks complexity; **f21** cartloads of natural caramel; some injury time spice; **b22** enjoyable, but muted by PC standards. *60.5% 30,000 bottles.*

Berrys' Own Selection Bruichladdich 1988 cask no. 1879, bott 07 **(84.5) n21 t22 f20.5 b21.** The kind of neat and tidy cask which blenders used to enjoy for its powers of simply malty persuasion. *56.4%. Berry Bros & Rudd.*

Berry's Own Selection Bruichladdich 1991 Aged 15 Years (94) n24 greengages, honey, salt and a vague smokiness combine for something rather wonderful; **t24** a stunning honey thread weaves through the crystal-clear barley; threatens to be mouthwatering, but prevented at the last minute by drier vanilla. The weight and delicacy of the sweetness defy the odds. 'Laddie, you feel, unplugged...; **f23** raspberry jam raps itself around that renegade peat; **b23** unexpected little gems like this make you feel so lucky to do this job... *46%.*

Cadenhead's Authentic Collection Bruichladdich Aged 15 Years bourbon hogshead, dist 92, bott Sep 07 **(94) n23 t23.5 f23.5 b24.** Exemplary 'Laddie with such clever sweetness that for not a single moment is the balance lost on either nose or palate. *55.5%. .26% whisky*

Chieftain's Bruichladdich 19 Years Old hogshead, dist Apr 89 **(95) n23.5 t24 f23.5 b24.** Weirdly enough, although this doesn't come from the distillery, I'd choose this cask as being perhaps the closest thing I could find to the absolute textbook 'Laddie. A must-have Islay. *50%.*

Eidora 9 Port Charlotte 6 Years Old bourbon cask, dist 01, bott 07 **(86.5) n21 t23.5 f21.5 b20.5.** Certainly enjoyable and worth the ride for the ultra intense peat and shock factor alone. However, here is a malt bottled at the wrong time, when the oaks and the malt were not quite in sync and, therefore, the vital balance had been compromised. The same can't be said for the PC6, which has been masterfully engineered. All that said, still well worth the experience: nose, taste a decent mouthful and hold on tight... *66.5%. Slowdrink, Germany.*

The Golden Cask Bruichladdich 1992 cask no. CM114 **(93) n23.5** barley dipped in runny honey; **t24** more honey on delivery, this time engulfing strands of coconut; the spices arrive early and are consistent; the cocoa arrives later and is beautifully controlled and met in the middle with a hint of molasses; **f22.5** much drier finish with the odd sign of a tiring cask. But that is mere detail: the vanillas, remaining strands of honey and lightly pulsing spice are good enough; **b23** a quite truly golden cask... *54.2%. 223 bottles.*

•⇒• **Hart Brothers Bruichladdich Aged 15 Years** dist Dec 94, bott Apr 10 **(89)** n22 firm, lightly salted barley but with just a hint of smoke on the breeze; t23 intense but always clean and fresh malt, again with that lightly salted, marginally smoked feel, but now with cream and jam sponge in the middle ground; gristy barley sugar throughout; f22 spices up very late on; b22 a delight of a near flawless bottling. *46% Hart Brothers, for the Whiskyfair Limburg 2010*

Japan Import System Bruichladdich Classic (83.5) n22 t20.5 f21 b20. Thick, oily almost Caol Ila in style; sweet, delicate but niggardly in complexity. *46%*

•⇒• **Malts of Scotland Port Charlotte 2001** sherry hogshead, cask no. 829, dist Dec 01, bott Mar 09 **(93.5)** n23 when worlds collide: dense grape....impenetrable peat....not for the faint hearted...; t23.5 my taste buds have just been lost under a deluge of....errr...something. Seeing that the book has to be finished this year, I'll try and take a stab at what: errr... sherry... errr... peat....errrr.... f23 no, not technically the soundest finish, but then this is all about the experience...and does it ever end...? b23 if this was any more weighty and solid it'd probably have its own gravity... *66.2% Malts of Scotland. 96 bottles.*

•⇒• **Malts of Scotland Port Charlotte 2001** bourbon barrel, cask no. 967, dist Dec 01, bott Feb 10 **(91)** n23.5 bonfires and smoked Hungarian sausage; t22.5 sweet, fabulously grist-malty delivery with excellent early buttery-vanilla layering; f22 back to the bonfires as the ash comes through; the degree of smoke drifts and wafts around the palate while the degree of sweetness likewise pulses: how very clever....; b22 impossible not to enjoy. Unless you don't like peat.... *60.2% Malts of Scotland. 192 bottles.*

•⇒• **Malts of Scotland Port Charlotte 2001** sherry hogshead, cask no. 833, dist Dec01, bott Feb 10 **(73.5)** n18.5 t20 f17 b18. Strange, isn't it. Cask 829 works a treat. This one... well, doesn't. That's present day sherry butts for you. Like playing Russian roulette. Only with significantly more than one bullet in the chamber... *61.6% Malts of Scotland. 192 bottles.*

Old Malt Cask Bruichladdich Aged 13 Years refill hogshead, cask no. 3700, dist Nov 93, bott Jun 07 **(89)** n22 t22 f22.5 b22.5. The kind of whisky you could drink all day every day: dangerous stuff! *50%. nc ncf. Douglas Laing. 345 bottles.*

Old Malt Cask Bruichladdich Aged 14 Years refill hogshead no. 3826, dist Nov 93, bott Dec 07 **(89)** n22 t22.5 f22.5 b22. There isn't a blender in Scotland who wouldn't give his left nostril for a malt of this unerring intensity. Not exactly shabby as a single malt, either. Finishes? Who needs 'em...? *50%. nc ncf. Douglas Laing. 352 bottles.*

Old Malt Cask Bruichladdich Aged 15 Years refill hogshead, dist Nov 93, bott Nov 08 **(91)** n22.5 huge citrus lead: the barley is clean and delicate; t23 lively lemon energises the barley and salty oaks; f22.5 delicate barley, more citrus and some wonderful chocolate mint on the fade; b23 very similar to the old Invergordon bottlings at this age. *50%. Douglas Laing. 353 bottles.*

Old Malt Cask Bruichladdich Aged 18 Years refill hogshead, dist Nov 89, bott Aug 08 **(76)** n20 t21 f17 b18. Sweet, fat and juicy early on. But never gets into a stride and the finish is rather inevitable. *50%. Douglas Laing. 350 bottles.*

Old Malt Cask Bruichladdich Aged 19 Years refill hogshead, cask no. 3839, dist Feb 88, bott Aug 07 **(84)** n21 t21.5 f21.5 b20. Clean, juicy malt: that's the start and end of it. *50%. nc ncf. Douglas Laing. 328 bottles.*

Old Malt Cask Bruichladdich Aged 20 Years refill hogshead 4065, dist Feb 88, bott Feb 08 **(86)** n21 t22.5 f21 b21.5. Charming whisky which ramps up the barley big time. Perhaps a shade oversweet in part but the tongue is puckered to the utmost. *50%. nc ncf. Douglas Laing. 341 bottles.*

Old Masters Bruichladdich Aged 19 Years cask no. 1882 dist 88, bott 08 **(86.5)** n21 t22.5 f21 b22. Softly oiled in the classic 'Laddie style and a natural step on from the original old 10-year-old which graced the distillery and island for so many years. *54%. James MacArthur & Co. Ltd.*

Old Masters Bruichladdich Aged 20 Years cask no. 1883, dist 88, bott 08 **(95)** n24 classic 'Laddie of the old school: big, salty malt style; t23.5 unusually viscous but the malts carry on pressing home that salty, malty theme and not without an attractive early sweetness. Chewy and just lightest hint of burnt fudge; f23.5 long, still persistently oily and the fudge just keeps on amassing a bigger molassed style; b24 a beautiful version of the old-fashioned peatless Bruichladdich 10, which was once the most popular malt on the island. Twice as old and twice as intense. An indisputable must-have malt for the Islayphile, whether you are peathead or not, for this is one of the true classic Islays of the year. *52.6%. James MacArthur & Co. Ltd.*

•⇒• **Port Sgioba Private Cask Port Charlotte Aged 8 Years** refill sherry hogshead no. 826/2001, dist Dec 01, bott Mar 10 **(93.5)** n24 how can some be at the same time enormous, and yet on another level feather-light in its touch? Sherry and peat have a history of occasionally becoming unhappy barrel fellows. But not here. Both the grape and smoke are pristine and confident. They are both full bodied, but not for a second shout the other aspect down. Frankly, brilliant... **t24** it's not just the unlikely marriage of juicy grape and intense peat that works here, but the weight also. All three combine memorably – and to jaw-aching, lip-smacking effect. Black cherry tops off the thickest of the smoke; hickory softens the middle ground; **f22.5** although only eight, tires a bit at the death with a shadow of oaky bitterness visible, but the peaty smog fills in the cracks while the lingering sugars ensure fair play; **b23** this is a cask from the whisky syndicate, FOAH...Friends Over A Hogshead. This is not to be confused the blackmailing syndicate, FOAB...Friends Over A Barrel. However, kidnap a few cases of this and you'll be able to hold these guys to ransom: this is priceless whisky, believe me.... *66% Bruichladdich for Friends Over A Hogshead (FOAH) Syndicate*

Provenance Bruichladdich Aged 11 Years refill hogshead no. 3870, dist Autumn 1995, bott Autumn 2007 **(92.5) n23 t23 f23.5 b23**. Such an unusual malt: rarely does anything come on the market so clean and refreshing. It is as though the mash has been injected with alcohol without any of that yeasty stuff reducing its fresh sweetness. A brilliant one off! *46%*.

Scotch Malt Whisky Society Cask 23.59 Aged 14 Years refill hogshead, dist Apr 93 **(83) n20 t21 f21 b21**. The tobacco smoke nose warns of an unusual 'Laddie, and so it proves with a real sharpness to the barley that is mildly out of character. *52.1%*

Scotch Malt Whisky Society Cask 23.61 Aged 7 Years refill butt, dist Nov 01 **(77) n18 t20.5 f18.5 b20**. A very odd cask of whisky. The strength is pretty weird, for a start. But there is something, some kind of off note, on the nose I don't exactly recognise (pretty unusual), but every sinew of my instinct tells me it's not quite right. There is also a suspicion that the powering spirit perhaps helps mask other off notes. The phenols are attractive to taste in a plain, girl-next-door way while ugly to sniff; but the warning lights come on again for the finish. *68.2%*

The Whisky Fair Bruichladdich Aged 17 Years bourbon hogshead, dist 90, bott 07 **(92) n23 t23.5 f22.5 b23**. Now this is exactly how a bourbon cask Bruichladdich should be. Not at this age, perhaps, but who gives a toss? *57.9%. The Whisky Fair.*

BUNNAHABHAIN
Islay, 1881. Burn Stewart. Working.

⋰ **Bunnahabhain 12 Years Old** db **(80) n19 t21 f20 b20**. Pleasant in its own clumsily sweet, smoky way. But unrecognisable to the masterful, salty Bunna 12 of old. *43.3% nc ncf*

Bunnahabhain Aged 16 Years Manzanilla Sherry Wood Finish db **(87) n20.5** big, fruity and ungainly; **t23** eye-watering stuff: a wave of salty grape-juice comes hurtling at you and right behind comes a second wave of sweeter barley which thumps you with equal force; **f21.5** definitely an off-key note, but there is so much happening with the grape, ultra dry vanilla and soft cocoa tones...oh, and salt...you hardly get a chance to notice; **b22** the kind of undisciplined but fun malt which just makes it up as it goes along... *53.2%*

⋰ **Bunnahabhain Aged 18 Years** db **(94) n24.5** chestnut colour and, fittingly, roast chestnut on the fruitcake nose: the health-conscious might say there is too much salt in the mix, but it works perfectly here...; **t24** outstanding oloroso with the clean, faultless grape dripping of the salty barley; the oak again offers a nutty background, while Demerara sugars form a crisp counter to the invading salt; burnt raisin underscores the fruitcake character; **f22.5** light mocha, as a very slight bitterness steels its way in; **b23** a triumph for the sherry cask and a reminder of just how good this distillery can be. It's been a long time since I've enjoyed a distillery bottling to this extent. *46.3%*

Bunnahabhain Aged 18 Years (Older Bottling) db **(85.5) n22.5 t22 f20 b21**. Much better nose than of old, but still the malt dies an unnatural death at an earlier stage of its life than it should. Again caramel appears to be a suspect as the early, juicy delivery, after a few citrus circuits, vanishes with nothing to take its place. *43%*

⋰ **Bunnahabhain XXV Aged 25 Years** db **(91.5) n23** hard to imagine a more coastal aroma than this: the grape tries to get a word in edgeways but the salt has formed a crusty doorway; what fruit does get through is top quality; **t23** excellent arrival, the grape forcing the pace but with a tell-tale tang of saltiness; busy with a sneaky arrival of malt through the middle; **f22.5** chocolate fruit and nut....and salt; **b23** an intense and fun-packed malt for those who like a fine sherry and a sea breeze. *46.3%*

Bunnahabhain XXV Aged 25 Years db **(93) n22** some serious coastal saltiness here...and grape; **t24** big saline kick as the oak offers some early latte; mouthwatering barley also impresses, topped off with brown sugar and damson tart; **f23** more milky coffee with an oatcake side dish; **b24** a fruity Bunna, but jam-packed with all the big barley-salt notes which set this distillery apart. One of the few bottlings around at the moment that us Bunna Old Timers can hold up and say: "Yeah, this is the business." Quite superb. *43%*

⋰ **Bunnahabhain Darach Ùr Batch no. 1** db **(87) n21.5** a real fruit and barley soup; **t22.5** a wall of flavours hit the palate on entry, but it is the near impenetrability of the barley mouth feel amid soft fruit which catches the eye; **f21** bitters and fault lines show; **b22** almost milkshake thick. Not exactly a technical triumph but high marks for entertainment value! 46.3%

🔹 **Bunnahabhain Toiteach** db (78) n19 t21 f19 b19. Cloying, sweet, oily, disjointedly smoky. Had you put me in a time capsule at the distillery 30 years ago, whizzed me forward to the present day and given me this, it would have needed some serious convincing for me to believe this to be a Bunna. 46%

🔹 **Adelphi Bunnahabhain 1968 Aged 41 Years** sherry butt, cask no. 12401/3, bott 2010 **(84)** n22 t21 f20 b21. A procession of sticky treacle notes stave off the staves. Every one of those 41 years is on show. 41.2% Adelphi Distillery Ltd. 719 bottles.

🔹 **Adelphi Bunnahabhain 1997 Aged 11 Years** sherry butt, cask no. 5368, bott 2009 **(93.5)** n23.5 they've caught some kippers in the Sound of Islay....; **t23.5** beautiful mouth feel with the peat offering both soft smoke and sharper, more biting earthiness; some lovely muscovado sugars throughout; **f24** the degree of excellent nip and bite one would demand from its age; the smoke continues on its own, literally sweet, way; **b22.5** a beautifully made Bunna where the peat has a life of its own. A gem of a bottling. 58.6%. Adelphi Distillery Ltd. 610 bottles.

🔹 **A.D. Rattray Bunnahabhain 1974** cask no. 7111, dist Jul 74, bott Dec 09 **(81.5)** n21.5 t20 f19 b20. Silky and savoury. But the big oakiness has bitten just a little too deep. That said, there is a sharpness to the barley which bites back rather beautifully. 44.3% A.D. Rattray Ltd

🔹 **A.D. Rattray Bunnahabhain 1974** cask no. 5448 **(85)** n21.5 t22.5 f20 b21. Dense, brooding and a tad cloying. Huge presence in the glass and you can chew this stuff until your jaw aches. But doesn't really open up enough to ever get to know the true personality....a veritable Heathcliffe of a malt. 53.7% A.D. Rattray Ltd

Cadenhead's Chairman's Stock Bunnahabhain Aged 28 Years bourbon hogshead, dist 79, bott Sep 07 **(86)** n22 t22.5 f20 b21.5. Salty and tangy with some startling orangey notes. A tad furry, too. 45.8%. 168 bottles.

Celtic Heartlands Bunnahabhain 1973 bott 08 **(91)** n20 a touch of lactic coming through... **t24** wow..!! didn't expect that...!!! Near perfect delivery with the intense malt funnelled directly into the tastebuds through the sexy oils which accompany this. A gossamer delivery of accompanying sugars is then overtaken by sea salt...; **f23.5** the complexity doesn't even begin to diminish, though now we have a touch of mocha landing and an upping of the molasses to counter the intrusion of the saltier, drier oak...and then, bizarrely, a quick flash of orangey citrus.... **b23.5** the tired, slightly through-the-wood nose warns you of the worst... then the delivery blows you away....!! 46.1%. Bruichladdich Ltd. 669 bottles.

Chieftain's Bunnahabhain 10 Years Old cask no. 3207, dist Sep 97 **(89)** n22.5 t22 f22 **b22.5**. The new look Bunna in its most naked form: and pretty tasty, too! 46%. nc ncf. Ian Macleod Distillers. Danish Market.

Chieftain's Bunnahabhain Peated 10 Years Old hogshead, dist Sep 97 **(92)** n22.5 t23.5 f23 b23. Enough to make Edvard Munch scream in ecstasy....historic, really, because with this bottling Bunna has indubitably arrived as a top-rank Islay peated malt...!! 56.1%. nc ncf. Ian Macleod Distillers. Norwegian market.

🔹 **Douglas of Drumlanrig Bunnahabhain Aged 9 Years** refill hogshead no. LD 3844, dist Dec 99, bott Oct 09 **(88)** n22 malt 'n' salt; **t22.5** lightly oiled sweet malt; **f21.5** strands of vanilla...clinging to malt; **b22** quite possibly the maltiest whisky I have tasted this year. 46% Douglas Laing. 180 bottles.

Dun Bheagan Bunnahabhain Aged 10 Years Manzanilla Finish (86) n22 t22 f20 b22. Distinctive fruity bite to this. 46%. Ian Macleod.

🔹 **Dun Bheagan Bunnahabhain 14 Years Old Medoc Finish** dist Apr 95 **(88)** n22 something of the rose garden about this one; even a little earthy; **t22** chewy and juicy with excellent salt/oak and fruit interplay; **f22** remains intact throughout with a very attractive vanilla and liquorice fade; **b22** A very steady malt. 46% nc ncf Ian Macleod

🔹 **Dun Bheagan Bunnahabhain 24 Years Old** barrel, dist Jun 85 **(92.5)** n23 fruit pastels (especially the green ones) but really it is the barley dominating with citrus, salt and surprising smoke always there or thereabouts; **t23.5** classic Bunna body: thick malt and a hint of a something saline. But gentle waves of chocolaty peat are anything other than the norm for this distillery at the time...; **f23** long with a wonderful, light peppery residue. Mocha appears to hang around forever... **b23** amazingly, I holidayed in the old workman's cottage above the distillery a month or two after this was distilled. And I do remember being told of a peated run as a complete one-off that had been made just prior to my arrival....and tasting some of the still virtually new make in one of the warehouses. Miraculously, one of the casks has, some quarter of a century later, turned up in my tasting lab. It appears to have fared better than I over the years... 48.1% nc ncf Ian Macleod

Duncan Taylor Collection Bunnahabhain 1970 cask no. 4073 **(79) n21 t21 f18 b19.** Hanging on for grim life to any last vestiges of its old self. Curious to think: it was malt from this vintage of Bunna that made up the 12-y-o stuff I used to drink at the distillery when I first stayed there. Let's just say it was then in its prime... *40.3%*

Duncan Taylor Collection Bunnahabhain 1970 cask no. 4075 **(81) n20.5 t20 f20.5 b20.** Clung like a limpet to retain its whisky life. In so doing has taken on nougat and honey clothing with just enough depth and sharpness to the barley to see off the mounting resin. Yet, for all its best effort, unwieldy and inelligent. *40.2%*

⫶ **Kingsbury's Bunnahabhain 11 Years Old 1997 (84.5) n21 t22 f20 b21.5.** For all the charming, ashy smokiness found on this, it is a malt which still lacks conviction. Somehow the salty, rich body, which used to be such a vibrant part of this distillery's DNA, is missing. So, attractive as this may be - and it is well worth a visit - for a Bunna you can't help thinking that there perhaps should be so much more.... *54.5% Japan Import System, Celtic Series.*

⫶ **Malts of Scotland Bunnahabhain 1976** sherry butt no. 6388, dist Nov 76, bott Mar 09 **(93.5) n24** astonishing: the clarity of the grape cocks a snook at appalling butts which ended up in the warehouses a decade later. This is exemplary stuff: cucumber spiciness sits so well with the fragile vanillas and lightly sweetened sherry note. One of the great noses of the year... **t23.5** deft fruit delivery on the palate actually gets the juices up and running; something you'd hardly expect of a 33-y-o Bunna! Everything comes into play early on: the barley, grape and oak but only towards the middle, as the drying begins, does a cedar wood and red liquorice complexity kick in...; **f23** for all the obvious late spiced oak and gathering dryness, a stubborn barley sit in ensures a high quality finale; **b23** ridiculously good for its age. *52% 96 bottles*

Murray McDavid Mission Bunnahabhain 1966 oloroso sherry **(86) n21 t23 f20 b22.** Creaks a fair bit, but never goes snap... *40.3%. 500 bottles.*

Old & Rare Bunnahabhain Aged 34 Years dist May 74, bott Sep 08 **(93.5) n23** the real deal with sherry: a mixture of burst sultana with suet sprinkled with salt and vanilla; **t23** oak takes little time to show, but is roundly seen off by a real old juicy fruitcake, in which liquorice and molasses have been added with abandon; **f24** long and stunningly weighted with this beauty getting sweeter by the moment as the oak, astonishingly, abates, allowing the sultana to return with gristy barley and a wonderful interplay of salt and peppers: one of the finest Bunna finishes for a while; **b23.5** ah, pride of my heart, my own love.... *58.3%. 333 bottles.*

Old Malt Cask Bunnahabhain Aged 11 Years refill hogshead no. 3699, dist Jun 96, bott Jun 07 **(70.5) n17 t19 f17 b17.5.** Matured in a dreadful, stale cask. *50%. nc ncf. 340 bottles.*

Old Malt Cask Bunnahabhain Aged 11 Years refill hogshead no. 3936, dist Sep 96, bott Oct 07 **(81.5) n18 t22.5 f20 b21.** Malty, almost yeasty in places. *50%. 320 bottles.*

Old Malt Cask Bunnahabhain Aged 12 Years (80.5) n20 t21 f19 b20.5. A knackered old cask hasn't done much to add to the attractive early barley kick. *50%*

⫶ **Old Malt Cask Bunnahabhain Aged 13 Years** refill hogshead no. DL 5811, dist Sep 96, bott Feb 10 **(81) n20 t21 f20 b20.** Gristy, malty, a molecule of smoke here and there. Pleasant but never quite reaches second gear. *50% Douglas Laing & Co Ltd. 347 bottles.*

Old Malt Cask Bunnahabhain Aged 19 Years dist Feb 90, bott Jul 09 **(73.5) n18 t19 f18 b18.5.** Typical Bunna sherry cask of the era. Alas. *50%. Douglas Laing.*

Old Malt Cask Bunnahabhain Aged 30 Years refill butt, dist Dec 78, bott Apr 09 **(87) n23.5** if you can imagine an old sherry butt sitting in a Jerez bodega just inches from the sea and drinking in salty air for three decades...well, there you have it... **t20.5** dry and angular with burnt raisin and toast making heavy going of it; **f22** blossoms deliciously as the sweeter barley notes emerge and some sultanas chip in; **b21** ground to a halt on delivery just through old age, but there's still some fabulous life to be found. *50%. Douglas Laing. 566 bottles*

⫶ **Premier Barrel Bunnahabhain Aged 12 Years (80.5) n19.5 t21 f20 b20.** Simplistically malty but with a tang and twang. *46% nc ncf Douglas Laing. 310 bottles.*

Provenance Bunnahabhain Aged 7 Years Gabriel Meffre wine cask no. 3706, dist winter 99, bott summer 07 **(84.5) n21 t21.5 f21 b21.** Rosy, rounded and spiced. *46%. Douglas Laing.*

Provenance Bunnahabhain Aged 8 Years refill hogshead cask no. 4073, dist 99, bott 07 **(89) n22.5 t22.5 f22 b22.** Beautiful, lively, malt. *46%. nc ncf. Douglas Laing.*

Provenance Bunnahabhain Aged 9 Years refill hogshead, dist winter 99, bott winter 08 **(79.5) n18.5 t20 f21 b20.** I have spent many a summer at Bunna. And from the early '80s got to know its whisky uncommonly well, at all ages and in all casks. It was never like this, though; a mixture of sweet, sticky barley and an assortment of vague off notes. *46%. Douglas Laing.*

⫶ **Provenance Bunnahabhain Over 11 Years** refill hogshead no. DMG 5812, dist Autumn 1998, bott Winter 2010 **(77) n18 t20 f19 b19.** Juicy in part. But thinner than you might expect. *46% Douglas Laing & Co Ltd*

Scotch Malt Whisky Society Cask 10.66 Aged 11 Years refill hogshead, dist Aug 97 **(91)** n23.5 a light, bonfire-esque smoky bacon signature leaves little doubt about the use of peat; still delicate enough for the subtly oaky backbone of liquorice and toasted hazelnut; **t23** sweet, malty, mildly oily and youthful delivery with a slow build up of smoky kippers; **f22** half-hearted spices make little impression of the peat and oak-led cocoa; **b22.5** this 10.66 is one in the eye for those who don't like smoky Bunnas: altogether now: "Westering Home with peat in the air...." *57.3%*

Scotch Malt Whisky Society Cask 10.67 Aged 11 Years refill hogshead, dist Aug 97 **(82)** n20.5 t20.5 f21 b20. An example of an indifferent cask doing nothing to help the malt. Thin, with only the peat holding this one together as the oak involvement is woefully sketchy. *59.9%*

⠿ **Scotch Malt Whisky Society Cask 10.69 Aged 11 Years** refill hogshead, dist Dec 97 **(79)** n18.5 t22 f19 b19.5. One of those highly peated Johnnies from Bunna which, for what it badly lacks in technical quality, makes up for with a quite extraordinary smoky grunt. *55.4% Scotch Malt Whisky Society. 276 bottles.*

Signatory Vintage Peated Bunnahabhain 1997 cask no. 5355, dist 04 Dec 97, bott 04 Feb 08 **(69)** n14 t19 f18 b18. An escapee. A reject which got away, surely? The nose is a crash site. But the intensity of the peat makes for something palatable at least and compensates... at times impressively. *46%. 852 bottles.*

⠿ **Single & Single Bunnahabhain 1976 Aged 31 Years Special Edition** sherry cask no. 592 **(94.5)** n23.5 one of those noses where the many varied fruit, spice and malt elements merge into a single, delicious, soup....which has been lightly seasoned...; **t24** the delivery is also a case of dazzling bitter-sweet notes breasting the tape together; no overall victor, though the spices work particularly well, while the malt appears to absorb a pruney fruitiness easily; **f23.5** long, date and walnut cake and a late sprinkle of salt; **b23.5** Bunna has long held a special place in my heart and when you taste this you'll discover why its malt was quite so special during the early and mid 80s. The question is: in 31 years time, is it likely you will find a Bunna of this quality emptied from a sherry butt? *47.9% Single & Single, South Africa.*

⠿ **The Single Malts Of Scotland Bunnahabhain Aged 29 Years** dist 1979, bott Aug 09 **(87)** n23 a beautiful mishmash of vanilla and coriander with some salty orange pith thrown in for good measure; **t22** the mouthfeel is outstanding though some aggressive oak does its best to interfere a little way in. The intense, fruit-edged barley keeps the malt on course but that is one struggle going on; **f20.5** fades as soon as the oak gains the inevitable upper hand and dries intensely; **b21.5** not a malt usually noted for staying the course and this one struggles gamely over the line. Some delightful moments amid the fading light, but it is the nose which really shines. *44% Speciality Drinks Ltd*

The Whisky Agency Bunnahabhain 32 Year Old fino cask, dist 76, bott 08 **(92.5)** n23 dry, nutty: mainly marzipan. Elegant, delicate; **t24** beautiful crystalline and delicate sweetness frames the salty barley, **f22.5** dries as the oak invades and the nuttiness returns, **b23** this is one very sophisticated dram. *53.7%. The Whisky Agency, Germany.*

The Whisky Agency Bunnahabhain 34 Year Old dist 74, bott 08 **(96)** n24 a salty coffee surround, but the core of the aroma is deepest, cleanest, oldest oloroso; **t24.5** the nose in flavour form: absolutely identical...but of glorious intensity; **f23.5** more oak here, as to be expected, and the coffee moves up a gear...as to be expected; pure textbook old oloroso matured; **b24** as magnificent and mighty as The Paps which looked down upon this whisky being made and matured... *59.3%. The Whisky Agency, Germany.*

The Whisky Agency Bunnahabhain 35 Year Old dist 73, bott 08 **(78)** n17 t21 f19 b21. Tastes better than its noses, which is hardly difficult. *50.1%. The Whisky Agency, Germany.*

⠿ **The Whisky Agency Bunnahabhain 1967** sherry cask **(94)** n23.5 moist Jamaican ginger cake dappled with salt and orange peel; **t24** oak all the way, but so invigorating are the sugars and fruits that never for a moment does it pose a threat to the general excellence; **f23** the silky texture continues, even as the drier vanillas arrive. A burned raisin bitterness, too, but the molasses negate the effects; **b23.5** impossible not to be mesmerised by. *40.5%*

The Whisky Fair Bunnahabhain Aged 30 Years Artist Edition Bourbon hogshead, dist 77, bott 07 **(82.5)** n21.5 t22 f19 b20. An exotic fruit merchant. Short changes you on the complexity, though. *43%. Germany.*

CAOL ILA

Islay, 1846. Diageo. Working.

Caol Ila Aged 8 Years Unpeated Style dist 99, bott 07 db **(93.5)** n23 t24 f23 b23.5. Oh well, here goes my reputation...honest opinion: on this evidence (backed by other samples over the years) Caol Ila makes better straight malt than it does the peated stuff. Sorry, peat lovers. This should be a, if not the, mainstay of the official Caol Ila portfolio. *64.9%*

Caol Ila Aged 8 Years Unpeated Style 1st fill bourbon, dist 00, bott 08 db **(91.5) n23** a touch maltier than the previous bottling; salty digestive biscuit; **t23** beautifully refreshing with a real puckering, salty tartness to the barley; I seem to remember citrus here last year. But this time we have butterscotch and toffee; **f22.5** long, very delicately oiled with the vanillas and toffee in decent harmony; **b23** a bit more of a pudding than last year's offering, but delicious dramming all the way. *64.2%*

⁖ **Caol Ila Aged 10 Years "Unpeated Style"** bott Aug 09 db **(93.5) n24** a beautiful medley of pear and lime with a thin spread of peanut butter for good measure...not exactly what one might expect...!!! **t23.5** the barley is just so juicy from the kickoff: the citrus on the nose reappears, though any hopes of pear vanishes; the barley, so rarely heard in a Caol-Ila grows in confidence and intensity as the delivery develops; **f23** not as oily as you might expect, allowing extra oak to emerge; **b23** always fascinating to see a traditional peaty Islay stripped bare and in full naked form. Shapely and very high class indeed. *65.4% Only available at the Distillery.*

Caol Ila Aged 12 Years db **(89) n23** a coastal, salty biting tang (please don't tell me this has been matured on the mainland!) with hints of rockpools and visions of rock pipits and oystercatchers among the seaweed; **t23** enormously oily, coating the palate with a mildly subdued smokiness and then a burst of gristy malt; **f21** caramel and oil; **b22** a telling improvement on the old 12-y-o with greater expression and width. *43%*

Caol Ila Aged 18 Years db **(80) n21 t20 f19 b20.** Another improvement on the last bottling, especially with the comfortable integration of citrus. But still too much oil spoils the dram, particularly at the death *43%*

Caol Ila 1979 db **(74) n20 t19 f17 b18.** So disappointing. I could go on about tropical fruit yada, yada, yada. Truth is, it just conks out under the weight of the oak. Too old. Simple as that. *58.6%*

⁖ **Caol Ila 1997 The Manager's Choice** db **(93.5) n24** dry, ashy peat sweetened less by grist but mango chutney; **t23.5** now the grist does arrive and sharpens up quickly: a barley juiciness sets in as Lincoln biscuit/garibaldi dunked in peat hogs the middle ground; hickory and liquorice begin the form....; **f23** a tad dusty but the liquorice and smoke hold sway; **b23** when this malt is not enveloped in in taste bud-clogging oil, it really can be a little special. Here's further proof. *58%*

Caol Ila Distillery Bottling bott May 07 db **(88) n24 t22 f20 b22.** Like most bottlings from this distillery, it's a dram that refuses to run a natural path. Never lives up to the nose, but still enough to delight Islay lovers. *58.4%*

Caol Ila 'Distillery Only' bott 07 db **(95.5) n24 t24 f23.5 b24.** Caol Ila is the third hardest distillery to get to in Scotland: however should you do so some time soon you can reward yourself by picking up a bottle of this. I can say honestly that the journey will be very much worthwhile... *58.4%. 5,000 bottles. Available only from the Caol Ila Distillery shop.*

A.D. Rattray Caol Ila 1995 cask no. 10035 **(92) n24** breathtakingly attractive and complex: delicate portions of salt, smoke and apple blossom mix charmingly; **t23.5** absolutely brilliant: not a hint of oil on delivery, allowing the gristier barley notes to shine; the smoke is almost a distant rumble of thunder; **f21.5** the oak begins to bitter out; late oils form and the vanilla punctuates the smoke frequently; **b23** the nose and delivery is pure textbook. *60.4%*

Alchemist Caol Ila Aged 10 Years dist Oct 96, bott Sep 07 **(85) n21.5 t21 f21.5 b21.** Silky and lazily smoked, appears even younger than its relatively tender years. *46%. nc, ncf.*

Berry's Own Selection Caol Ila 1991 cask nos. 486/487, bott 07 db **(93) n23 t23 f23 b24.** One of the few Caol Ilas this year to really get my pulse racing. *51.8%.*

Berry's Own Selection Caol Ila 1995 bott 08 **(93) n23** anthracite and peat mix in an ash-dry heavenly manner; **t24** really outstanding weight to the delivery: the smoke has a lot to say, but doesn't shout, the sub barley notes are of the juiciest variety and the oak offers some red liquorice to the table: a real soup of malt with the dryness and sweetness inter-twining to magnificent effect; **f23** gentle, oily smoky butterscotch; dries as the ashes return and the vanillas kick in; **b23** now that's the way a Caol Ila of this age should behave... *58.9%. Berry Bros & Rudd.*

⁖ **Berrys' Own Selection Caol Ila 2000 (94) n23.5** a beautiful mix of banana skins and dry, cindery peat: exceptionally fine in its style; **t23.5** playfully aggressive delivery with the sweetness of the barley interlocking with the much drier smoke; the middle ground is like smoked draff biscuits; **f23.5** medium length but with a citrus swirl lightening the intensity of the smoke....just so delicate and precise; **b23.5** benefits hugely from the limited oils present. This is the way I love to see Caol Ila, rather than in its oily, shapeless form. A classic. *58.9%*

Bladnoch Forum Range Caol Ila Aged 16 Years hogshead, cask no. 3869, dist 11 Mar 91, bott 28 Jun 07 **(86.5) n21.5 t22.5 f21 b21.5.** From the farmyard school of peaty whisky this is big stuff eschewing the normal oily style but boasting an almost rummy- sugary-flintiness at times. *59%. ncf. Bladnoch Forum.*

Cadenhead's Caol Ila Aged 17 Years dist 91, bott Feb 08 **(85.5) n22 t22.5 f19.5 b21.5.** Dry, rasping malt. Excellent complexity but a less than sympathetic cask has curtailed the class. *53.4%. 338 bottles.*

Cadenhead's Caol Ila Aged 17 Years dist 91, bott Feb 08 **(89) n22 t23 f22 b22.** It is amazing what a good quality cask can do to a whisky. Taste this beside Cadenhead's 53.4% and see what I mean... *55.4%. 361 bottles.*

Cadenhead's Authentic Collection Caol Ila Aged 22 Years bourbon hogshead, dist 84, bott Feb 07 **(92) n22 t24 f23 b23.** Ultra complex? Hardly. Something I've never come across before? Most probably not. A genuinely well made whisky that has matured as well as might be expected for its age and makes all the right noises? Most certainly. *55.5%. 246 bottles.*

Cadenhead's Authentic Collection Caol Ila Aged 23 Years bourbon hogshead, dist 84, bott Sep 07 **(89) n22.5 t22.5 f22 b22.** Delicate and boasting some impressive strata, this is the other side of the coin to the Whisky Society's 23-y-o for example. *56.3%. 258 bottles.*

⫶ **Cadenhead's Authentic Collection Caol Ila 1984** bott Feb 10 **(88) n21** smoky, but strangely under-ripe: not the cleanest...; **t23** didn't expect that...!! Wow!! An absolute explosion of sweetly confectioned smoke, with boulders of oak and spice...and all this played out in the most juicy barley imaginable; **f21.5** confirms the nose's message that all is not technically right, but the pulsing spices and smoke is pretty disarming; **b22.5** while the nose may not be particularly alluring, what follows next is sheer joy. *55.5% Wm. Cadenhead Ltd. 250 bottles.*

⫶ **The Càrn Mòr Vintage Collection Caol Ila 1983** hogshead no. 4801, dist 1983, bott 2009 **(87.5) n21.5** a nose which simply can't make up its mind: concentrated vanilla pod against sweetened peat...neither wish to win the battle; **t23** works well enough here as the initial waves ignore the nose and come through as rich barley. The smoke and vanilla play catch up, but with the phenols always ahead; **f21** a bit tired as the oak shows a more bitter side; **b22** an intriguing battle between vanilla and peat... *46% nc ncf 1203 bottles*

⫶ **Cask Strength Caol Ila 1998** **(73) n19 t19 f17 b18.** I tasted this a month or so apart from the CC Caol Ila, as it had been filed in the wrong place. But we can safely assume it is from the same batch of casks. *58.8% Gordon & MacPhail*

Chester Whisky & Liqueur Co. Caol Ila Aged 13 Years dist 95 **(84) n22 t21.5 f20 b20.5.** Excellent ashy dryness to the smoky nose and soft oils on delivery. *50.6%*

Chieftain's Caol Ila Aged 12 Years hogshead **(77) n19 t20 f19 b19.** Pleasant and plodding in its own way, but has little to say. *43%. Ian Macleod.*

Chieftain's Caol Ila 12 Years Old Rum Finish (83) n22 t20 f20 b21. Slightly too oily and thick to fully take advantage of the proffered rum influence. But the peat is more polished than it might be. *46%. Ian Macleod.*

Chieftain's Caol Ila 24 Years Old hogshead, dist Apr 84 **(89.5) n24** brilliant! A wonderful mixture of very deeply cut, high density peat reek offers that farmyard manure edge, sweetened by a light gristiness; **t23** punchy, juicy, spicy and big; the sweetness is of the sugared rather than honeyed variety; **f21** vanilla and fading smoke; **b22.5** the guys at Ian Macleod must have been sitting on this one with a little smile on their faces. Great mischief and fun on nose and delivery. By the way: anyone who has ever made or cleared out a peat fire will be touched by this one. *48%. nc ncf. Ian Macleod Distillers.*

Connoisseurs Choice Caol Ila 1993 (81) n21 t20 f21 b19. The nip and bite to the nose is hardly matched by the supine, oily delivery to the palate. *40%.*

Connoisseurs Choice Caol Ila 1994 (72) n17 t19 f18 b18. Misses the target: just never feels right either on nose or palate. *40%. Gordon & MacPhail.*

Connoisseurs Choice Caol Ila 1995 (91.5) n23.5 gristy, excellent sweet-dry balance to the smoke; **t22** touches of citrus help break up the peaty dominance; **f23** clean, minimal oils and chalky oaks; still the citrus-peat combination works superbly; **b23** I have been drinking Connoisseurs Choice Caol Ila since the days when the stuff in the bottle came from the original distillery which, I'm afraid, rather dates me. But I have to say, that this brand always seems to get the most out of this malt. Another excellent bottling. *40%. Gordon & MacPhail.*

⫶ **Connoisseurs Choice Caol Ila 1998 (74.5) n19 t20 f17.5 b18.** The odd blast of liquorice. But the finish is far from great. *43% Gordon & MacPhail*

⫶ **The Coopers Choice Caol Ila 1981 Aged 28 Years (83.5) n23 t21 f20 b20.5.** Oily and old, the malts work exceptionally hard to keep the whisky's integrity against the marauding oak. Success is only partial. *46% The Vintage Malt Whisky Co. Ltd*

⫶ **The Coopers Choice Caol Ila 1992 Aged 17 Years (90.5) n22.5** oily and monosyllabic for the most part, a little vanilla battles through after 17 years, but enough to generate some serious sophistication; **t23** sweet, but with a half-hearted spice jab to the palate; the oils are well ordered and carry the barley away from the background smoke; the oak in the meantime goes through a number of vaguely fruity lives; **f22.5** some citrus battles through on the coat-tails of the vanillas; **b22.5** the distillery at its most disarmingly erudite. Though it makes little attempt to offer more than its smoke and oil early on, the degrees of sweetness and slow are quite charming. *46% The Vintage Malt Whisky Co. Ltd*

Demijohn Caol Ila 1991 Single Malt (91) n23 t23 f22 b23. Tip top Caol Ila at its gristiest. *46%. Demijohn Ltd, UK.*

Dewar Rattray Caol Ila 1984 cask no. 1358, dist Mar 84, bott Nov 07 **(89.5)** n23 t23.5 f21 **b22.** Oiled up and full of big, chewy, personality. Excellent stuff. *58%*

Dewar Rattray Cask Collection Caol Ila Aged 22 Years cask no. 6264, dist 12 Dec 84, bottled 25 Jun 07 **(89.5)** n24 t21 f22.5 b22. An above average Caol Ila which offers much more complexity than you might expect from this distillery. A true gentle giant which does show a touch of creaking age, but more than compensated for by the brilliance of the nose. *57.7%. 221 bottles for Willow Park, Calgary.*

⠿ **Douglas of Drumlanrig Caol Ila Aged 11 Years** refill hogshead no. LD 5218, dist Sep 97, bott May 09 **(85.5) n21.5 t22 f21 b21.** Just about the perfect whisky for those looking for a peaty – but not too peaty – dram with soft oils to make the friendliest of glides down the gullet. *46% Douglas Laing. 287 bottles.*

Dun Bheagan Caol Ila Aged 15 Years hogshead, dist Jun 93 **(86.5)** n22.5 t22 f21 b21. From the slightly slithery, oily school of Caol Ila. The dry nose and sharp delivery are a treat, though. *50%. Ian Macleod Distillers Ltd.*

Dun Bheagan Caol Ila 16 Years Old Medoc finish, dist March 91 **(82)** n20 t21 f20 b21. Pleasant and easy going, but, if anything, rather too clean and sanitised. What's up, Medoc..? *46%. nc ncf. Ian Macleod.*

Duncan Taylor Collection Caol Ila 1981 cask no. 2932 **(91)** n22.5 t23 f22.5 b23. This year has seen the best releases for a long time of lightly- or un-oiled Caol Ila and this is among the finest. *53.8%*

⠿ **Duncan Taylor Collection Caol Ila 1981** cask no. 3491 **(86.5)** n20.5 t21 f23 b22. Attractively sweet and spicy with the rampaging sugars compensating for the mild excesses of the old oak. Pleasantly complex mocha, too. *55.2%*

Duncan Taylor Collection Caol Ila 1982 cask no. 2736 **(91)** n22 evening primroses amid the peat; **t23** the fabulous sweet and lush phenols counter the drier oaks with aplomb; **f22.5** spicy, soft and with some excellent custard tart to balance the ashier peats; **b23.5** very complex and excellently balanced. *55.4%*

Duncan Taylor Collection Caol Ila 1982 cask no. 2741 **(84)** n20.5 t21 f21.5 b21. Full-flavoured. But never less than sharp and hot. *55.9%*

⠿ **Duncan Taylor Collection Caol Ila 1984** cask no. 6275 **(87.5)** n23 the nose is pure fun: almost a self parody of a big, salty Islay...; **t20.5** begins sweetly and brightly but hits a sharp, almost bitter note in midstream; **f22** sweet, malty, gloriously smoky notes come galloping to the rescue like white blood cells to a wound. The finish is transformed back to something closer to what the nose promised...; **b22** a real character of a dram. *53.8% Duncan Taylor & Co Ltd*

Duthies Caol Ila 13 Years Old (90.5) n23 ridiculously young and gristy: even a touch of the Port Ellens at 10 years old here, but without the body; **t23** sweeter and smokier than a smoked sweet thing; **f22** makes the most of the gentle oils to further the cause of lightly smoked sugar cane; **b22.5** young and green (in every sense) for its age. But a sweet, refreshing delight. *46%. Springbank Distillers for Germany.*

Exclusive Casks Caol Ila 1980 Aged 28 Years American oak **(92)** n23.5 for its age, exceptional: wonderful, earthy, evening hedgerows and garden. There really is cowslip and farmyards at play; pastoral; **t24** excellent sweet and sharp delivery, some really astonishing clarity to the juicy barley for a malt of this age; oils up for the middle, **f22** vanilla and cocoa slip through the oiliness; **b22.5** you never quite know what you are going to get from this distillery. This one's a winner. *50.5%. Chester Whisky & Liqueur Co.*

Hart Brothers Caol Ila Aged 11 Years dist Aug 96, bott Jun 08 **(84.5) n21.5 t21 f21 b21.** A quiet dram, happy to rumble along with gentle peat and dry vanilla. *46%.*

⠿ **James MacArthur's Old Masters Caol Ila 1995 Aged 14 Years** cask no. 10042, bott May 10 **(85.5) n21 t22 f21 b21.5.** Stereotypical Caol Ila unplugged which makes an enjoyably peaty noise without having any meaningful lyrics. *58.4% James MacArthur & Co Ltd*

⠿ **The John Milroy Selection Caol Ila 29 Years Old (84) n21.5 t20.5 f21 b21.** Such is the antiquity here, the peat is breaking down seemingly into constituent parts and heading back towards its floral past. Some exotic fruit tries to get off the ground but is smothered by smoke. Painfully enjoyable and a fine example of a whisky that had once seen better days. *57.2% Berry Bros & Rudd*

Kingsbury's Caol Ila 1984 24 Years Old Cask Strength (92) n23.5 outstandingly clean nose for its age: wonderful coke and peat mix to the smoke but still retaining green shoots of sweet barley; the oak is specific and shows great clarity on the vanilla; **t23.5** beautifully bitter-sweet, showing just the right amount of oaky age-wear. The peat is deft and very lightly oiled; **f23** strains of butterscotch accompany the long delicately smoked finale; **b22.5** classy little cask. 53.2%. Japan Import System.

Kingsbury's Finest & Rarest Caol Ila 1982 (90.5) n23 smoky bacon crisps; a wonderfully nagging nip to the phenols; **t23** assertive and sharp. The barley appears to send short, sweet blasts of grassiness independently of the rampaging smoke: some trick; **f22** salivating to the end, for all the best attention of drying vanillas; **b22.5** another tip-top Caol Ila from Kingbury. 58.9%. Japan Import System.

Kingsbury "The Selection" Caol Ila 6 Years Old 2000 (85) n21 t22 f21.5 b21.5. Not as peaty as you might expect, allowing the grassy citrusy notes full voice. Charming. And perhaps one of the most refreshing drams of the year! 43.0%. nc ncf. Japan Import System Co. Ltd

⮞ **Kingsbury's "The Selection" Caol Ila 8 Years Old 2000 (86.5) n21.5 t22 f21 b22.** Lovely stuff, indeed. Celebrates its youthful simplicity by getting the balance of banana and vanilla amid the peat spot on. 43% Japan Import System

⮞ **Mackillop's Choice Caol Ila 1990 Sherrywood** dist Feb 90, bott May 07 **(91.5) n22.5 t24 f22.5 b22.5.** Curious, though magnificently enjoyable whisky. All Caol Ila at this time was made for blending. So what was the point of putting it into sherry wood unless it was destined for an excessively old blend, like Old Parr? Here you can see that both the natural oil of Caol Ila and the sherry have ganged together to entirely fill in any peaks or troughs so, an early smoky crescendo apart, this is as even as it comes. 56.3% Iain Mackillop & Co. Ltd

⮞ **Malts of Scotland Caol Ila 1998** bourbon hogshead no. 12374, dist Dec 98, bott Mar 09 **(88) n21.5** quite tight and confined with the smoke and oak fighting the same territory; **t21.5** like the nose, the delivery appears restricted with everything working within a crisp, sugary frame; **f23.5** at last throws off the shackles as a light oiliness unfurls, bringing with it a much more relaxed maltiness and a lighter, ashy, peatiness; **b22** takes a little time to find its feet, but leads you on a smoky dance when it finally does. 60.9% Malts of Scotland. 96 bottles.

Murray McDavid Mission Caol Ila 1984 gold series, bourbon/grenache Vincent Le Grand **(91) n24 t22 f23 b22.** The big question is: is it an Islay or a French rock pool? I'm sure this is near the Singing Sands... 54.1%

Norse Cask Selection Caol Ila 1991 Aged 16 Years hogshead cask no. 3871, dist 91, bott Aug 07 **(93) n23 t24 f22.5 b23.5.** One of the best Caol Ilas I have come across for a long time. Devoid of that limiting oiliness which usually does it so much damage on the complexity front, this has enough about it for the real Caol Ila to come through, citrus and all. Wonderful. 59.2%. nc ncf. Qualityworld, Denmark. 288 bottles.

Old & Rare Caol Ila Aged 28 Years dist Feb 79, bott Mar 07 **(93) n24 t23 f22 b24.** Great to see a CA with this kind of attitude. One of the rare un-oily versions and worth investigating for its delicate but unrestricted beauty. A recent Caol Ila classic. 54.6%. 272 bottles.

Old & Rare Caol Ila Aged 28 Years dist Feb 79, bott Sep 07 **(90) n22 t23 f22 b23.** This was my 900th whisky for this edition and it hasn't let me down, finish apart. Loads of character from a relatively lightly peated version. 54.2%. Douglas Laing, exclusively for The Whisky Shop, Edinburgh. 261 bottles.

Old Malt Cask Caol Ila Aged 12 Years dist Sep 96, bott Jul 09 **(88) n22** pepper, smoky style; **t22** soft at first, then ker-pow-fizz...!! Those peppers on the nose bite... **f22** smoky and sweet; **b22** sweet, but with attitude. 50%. Douglas Laing.

Old Malt Cask Caol Ila Aged 12 Years refill butt no. 4104, dist Sep 95, bott Jan 08 **(86) n21.5 t22 f21 b21.5.** Lots of smoke and gristy sweetness but limited oak balance for its age. 50%. Douglas Laing. 743 bottles.

Old Malt Cask Caol Ila Aged 12 Years refill hogshead, cask no. 4445, dist Feb 96, bott Jun 08 **(91) n23 t22.5 f22 b23.5.** Oh, if only all Caol Ilas were like this! 50%.

Old Malt Cask Caol Ila Aged 17 Years rum barrel no. 3807, dist Mar 90, bott Aug 07 **(86) n21 t23 f21 b21.** Very drinkable with the peat clear, crisp and clean. Lovely stuff. 50%. Douglas Laing. 243 bottles.

Old Malt Cask Caol Ila Aged 17 Years rum barrel, cask no. 3898, dist Mar 90, bott Sep 07 **(84.5) n20 t22 f21.5 b21.** Well spiced, clean, standard fare. 50%. Douglas Laing. 182 bottles.

Old Malt Cask Caol Ila Aged 17 Years claret wine barrel, cask no. 4055, dist Mar 90, bott Dec 07 **(73) n18 t20 f17 b18.** It's not that often you get sulphur bringing down massive peat...!! 44.1%. Douglas Laing.

⮞ **Old Malt Cask Caol Ila Aged 18 Years** refill hogshead no. DL 5556, dist Mar 91, bott Oct 09 **(84) n21.5 t21 f20.5 b21.** Feathered peat and enjoyable pit. 50% 327 bottles.

Old Malt Cask Caol Ila Aged 19 Years claret finish, bott 09 **(82) n20 t21 f21.5 b20.5** For a cask finish, especially wine, to work well, the barley, oak and fruit have to somehow integrate to reach a harmony. It is always more much difficult when big peat is thrown in the mix. This one shows you just how difficult it can be. *50%. Douglas Laing.*

Old Malt Cask Caol Ila Aged 25 Years refill hogshead, dist Jan 84, bott Apr 09 **(84) n21.5 t22 f20 b20.5.** Attractively floral in part and well weighted. But showing distinct sign of fatigue. *50%. Douglas Laing. 309 bottles.*

⋄⋄⋄ **Old Malt Cask Caol Ila Aged 26 Years** refill hogshead no. DL 6207, dist Jan 84, bott May 10 **(94) n23** the liquorice and hickory sits well with the smoke; a hint of honeycomb helps disguise the ravages of old age so well that you can't actually see any...; **t24** sublime: the honey sits in immediately and, in its holding role, allows the liquorice and smoke to raid every crevice of the palate; light vanillas help form the middle ground, underlining the high quality of the cask; **f23.5** not a single trace of bitterness marks this out not only as a rare cask, but a truly classic Caol Ila; **b23.5** usually a distillery which ages like a smoker. This, though, is a cracker of a dram: one of the best old 'uns from the Sound of Islay for a very long while. *50% 268 bottles*

Old Malt Cask Caol Ila Aged 27 Years bourbon barrel, cask no. 3896, dist Nov 79, bott Sep 07 **(86) n22 t22.5 f20 b21.5.** Quite lovely malt, not least because it heroically does its best to overcome the creaking of the cask. One of the few Caol Ilas around to show a sea-weedy, coastal quality, but time catches up with it in the end. *50%. nc ncf. Douglas Laing. 240 bottles.*

Old Malt Cask Caol Ila Aged 29 Years refill hogshead, dist Feb 79, bott Aug 08 **(93) n24** a rare case of where delicate smoke and exotic fruit combine; the label offers age and the nose dishes it out but showing style every step of the way; **t23.5** every bit as soft as the nose, possibly more so; those exotic fruits are persistent early on before the ashy phenols make their mark; some elegant liquorice adds weight and age; **f22.5** now really has dried out but remains intact with no negative notes from the assembling oak **b23** melts on the nose and mouth and shows that even big Islays like this can be purring, graceful pussycats even after the best part of three decades. A classic. *50%. Douglas Laing. 238 bottles.*

⋄⋄⋄ **Old Malt Cask Caol Ila Aged 30 Years** refill butt, cask no. 5731, dist Nov 79, bott Jan 10 **(89) n22.5** fresh, perky barley; green banana and sugared smoke; **t23** a softy, with a youthful barley streak; the oak arrives with a forceful jolt midway through but is nudged out again once the sugars reform; **f21.5** chewy, well smoked vanilla; **b22** refuses to grow up and show its age. So bravo for that!! *50% Douglas Laing & Co Ltd. 266 bottles.*

Old Masters Caol Ila Aged 12 Years dist 95, bott Jul 08 **(87.5) n22.5 t22 f21.5 b21.5.** About as subtle as a punch in the chops. If you are looking for structure and delicate tendencies, forget it. If it's peat you want... *59.8%. James MacArthur & Co. Ltd.*

Old Masters Caol Ila Aged 13 Years cask no. 10046, dist 95, bott 08 **(92) n23.5** wonderful sweet/dry sibling battle on the peaty side; **t22.5** the sugars arrive first making a friendly landing site for the weighty ashy smoke which follows; **f23** long, peat-laden vanilla and still those playful sweet-drier notes interplay; **b23** a quite beautifully constructed malt. *59.8%.*

Old Masters Caol Ila Aged 25 Years cask no. 731, dist 82, bott 07 **(94) n23 t23 f24 b24.** This is Caol Ila at its very best. *55.5%.*

Old Masters Caol Ila Aged 26 Years cask no. 733, dist 82, bott 08 **(86) n22.5 t21.5 f21 b21.** Some lovely lavender mingles charmingly with the smoke on the nose, but a big thrust of natural caramel limits the complexity of the salty but gentle palate. *55.2%. James MacArthur*

Provenance Caol Ila Aged 8 Years dist winter 98, bott winter 07 **(88) n20 t23 f23 b22.** Another warts-and-all bottling from a well used cask (to put it mildly) – and you can only applaud its naked beauty. *46%. Douglas Laing.*

Premier Barrel Caol Ila Aged 9 Years (84.5) n21.5 t22 f21 b20. Enjoyable, ultra simplistic malt from a well used cask. Might have profited from being cask strength in order to really pump up and exploit those juicier notes. *46%. Douglas Laing.*

Provenance Caol Ila Aged 10 Years refill barrel no. 4297, dist spring 98, bott spring 08 **(86.5) n20 t22.5 f22 b22.** Plenty of chocolate to keep the smoke company. A bit flat in part, nose especially, but a chewy cove that'll entertain the tastebuds more than enough. Decent sweetness throughout. *46%. nc ncf. Douglas Laing.*

Provenance Caol Ila Aged 11 Years dist Sep 97, bott Jul 09 **(89.5) n23** clean and in perfectly smoky order; **t22** simplistic maybe, but the sweetness to smoke ratio is superb; **f22.5** the lack of usual oils from this distillery allow the vanilla, citrus and smoke each to have separate personalities; **b22** a spot on cask. *46%. Douglas Laing.*

Provenance Caol Ila Aged 11 Years refill hogshead, dist summer 97, bott winter 09 **(88) n23** wonderful complexity to the smoke alone: works on both sweet and dry levels; **t22** a touch of oil, but enough to ensure the barley has a say in proceedings and the slightly sugary word is spread; **f21** bitters out slightly; **b22** sweet and delicious. *46%. Douglas Laing.*

⋄⋄⋄ **Provenance Caol Ila Over 12 Years** refill hogshead no. 5720/5721, dist Autumn 1997, bott Winter 2009 **(80.5) n21 t20.5 f19 b20.** Regulation Caol Ila from a blending cask. *46%*

Scotch Malt Whisky Society Cask 53.128 Aged 19 Years refill hogshead, dist Dec 89 **(91)** n22.5 attractive, but some oak nip unsettles the otherwise embedded peat; **t23** big custard tart and the inevitable silky smoke and gentle bite: a very handsome combination; **f22.5** the sweetness continues with some intriguing marzipan getting in amid the chocolate-smoke; **b23** a high quality malt that is confident and comfortable with itself. 56.1%

Scotch Malt Whisky Society Cask 53.129 Aged 19 Years refill hogshead, dist Dec 89 **(88.5) n23.5** fabulous quasi-bourbony depth to the smoke; the profound saltiness also lifts this above the norm; **t22** again the oaks punch hard, but the silky oils act as a buffer; delicate sweet, grassy barley thread to the smoke; some cocoa in towards the late middle; **f21** bitters out a little too enthusiastically; **b22** doesn't quite end with the same panache as it starts, but still a good 'un. 55.2%

Scotch Malt Whisky Society Cask 53.130 Aged 9 Years refill hogshead, dist Nov 99 **(90)** n23.5 much more flaky smoke: drier, less oily, more ashy than the old Caol Ila style; **t21.5** nips and bites, not least because of the extraordinary alcoholic strength; but the peat is always to the fore (not always the case with this distillery) and accentuated; **f22.5** one of the driest Caol Ila finishes I have encountered in bottled form. Invariably there is a cocoa powder dusting to this; **b22.5** Caol Ila. But few of you would recognise it if tasted blind. The peated George T Stagg of the whisky world.... 68.2%

Scotch Malt Whisky Society Cask 53.131 Aged 9 Years refill hogshead, dist Nov 99 **(83)** n21 t20 f21 b21. Take away the big alcohol kick and it's just a little too plain and ordinary: not a patch on it's twin cask 53.130. 67.9%

⁙ **Scotch Malt Whisky Society Cask 53.134 Aged 9 Years** refill hogshead, dist Nov 99 **(91)** n23 a delight for its sheer simplicity: a real smoke thump, but never all consuming, allowing the barley-side of the malt to be heard; **t23** crisp barley offers smoke of varying levels of sweetness and youthful intensity. Just so clean and almost sparkles on the palate; **f22.5** excellent burst of mocha attaches itself to the well-behaved smoke; **b22.5** when a whisky is this well made and matured in such an exemplary cask, you cannot ask for too much more. 67.3% Scotch Malt Whisky Society

⁙ **Scotch Malt Whisky Society Cask 53.136 Aged 17 Years** refill hogshead, dist Jan 92 **(92.5) n23** freshly squeezed lemon on peated grist; **t23.5** breathtakingly refreshing, clean and vibrant with alternating smoke and juicy barley waves; **f23** long, a slow building of oils and a little bourbony liquorice adding lustre; **b23** don't you just love it when whisky is this damned simple... 55% Scotch Malt Whisky Society. 256 bottles.

⁙ **Scotch Malt Whisky Society Cask 53.137 Aged 17 Years** refill hogshead, dist Jan 92 **(79)** n20 t22 f18.5 b19.5. Pleasantish - soft. But, frankly, a little dull... 56.2% Scotch Malt Whisky Society. 284 bottles.

⁙ **Scotch Malt Whisky Society Cask 53.139 Aged 27 Years** refill hogshead, dist Feb 82 **(95) n24** the smoke appears to have given up any attempt at the macho stuff and acceded to the graceful and dulcet tones of lightly honeyed vanilla and toffee apple; on a deeper level you can find some earthier notes with a tantalising hint of cucumber; **t24** a beautiful natural fudge delves into the smoke at regular intervals ensuring a delicate layering of sugared barley amid the peat; every facet to this is rounded and elegant and even the spices - which descend about a third of the way in - are on tip-top behaviour; **f23.5** every bit as graceful as all that has gone before with a gentle, artful mocha attaching to the dying rays of the peat; **b23.5** the stuff of whisky genius... 55.2% Scotch Malt Whisky Society. 256 bottles.

⁙ **Scotch Malt Whisky Society Cask 53.141 Aged 20 Years** refill hogshead, dist Dec 89 **(94) n24** fabulous multi-dimensional nose: ultra-ripe greengages meet bananas head on; elsewhere, several layers of barley offer gristy sugars and the most delicate smoke notes: sublime... **t23.5** every bit as fresh and invigorating as the nose promises with an initial soft barley introduction, then wave upon wave of Demerara, followed by hickory-tipped phenols; **f23.5** so long, yet proudly continues along the same complexly smoked lines, always with a hint of something citrusy up its sleeve...; **b23** a spot on barrel: the type you dream of from this distillery...but so rarely find. 52% Scotch Malt Whisky Society. 259 bottles

The Scotch Single Malt Circle Caol Ila 1982 cask no. 2724, dist Apr 82, bott Oct 08 **(94)** n23.5 two pronged: from one side comes a distinctly, grey, ashy, dead peat fire; from the other a fizzing barley, sweet, salivating monster...; **t24** eye-watering delivery, and it's not about the strength: the barley is sharp and piercing: first blood to the monster. The waves are sweet and relentless until the middle is reached. Milky Way candy bar meets that ashy element and all is sweetness and dust; **f23** elegant, peaceful and refined it may be, but by comparison with what's gone before this, relatively drab as the peated vanillas fade; **b23.5** hardly one for those with a heart condition. Big, rousing. Beautifully made and matured.And bloody delicious. 62.7%. German market.

Scott's Selection Caol Ila 1982 bott 08 **(86)** n23 t21.5 f21 b21. The nose gets top billing where the smoke churns out with a sweet, Madeira cake twist. The remainder, though, is reduced by tired, burnt, toasty oak. 60.6%. Speyside Distillers.

Scott's Selection Caol Ila 1982 bott 08 **(76.5)** n20 t19.5 f18 b19. Oily and austere, despite the smoke and strength. 61.2%. Speyside Distillers.

Scott's Selection Caol Ila 1984 bott 07 **(78)** n18 t22 f17 b19. The nose baffled me for a bit: it was something I had come across before. Then it clicked – rainy or wet patches in a leaking Islay warehouse. Not exactly how things should be and the finish confirms that not all is tickety-boo. 54.1%

⠿ **The Secret Treasures Caol Ila 1990** oak cask no. 4721, bott no. 165, dist Apr 90, bott Sep 07 **(86)** n21.5 t22.5 f21 b21. Adore the intriguing lack of smoke on this guy. The peat is little more than a shadow of its normal self, and that works brilliantly, while the citrus is intriguing. But the lack of smoke means there is less to disguise the warts on the oak itself. 43% Haromex Development GmbH, Germany. 443 bottles.

The Single Malts of Scotland Caol Ila 1991 Aged 16 Years bott Sep 07 **(90)** n23 t23 f22.5 b22.5. Complex, genuinely well balanced and enticing. 57.5%. Speciality Drinks.

The Single Malts of Scotland Caol Ila 1982 Aged 25 Years bott Sep 07 **(91.5)** n20.5 t23.5 f23 b25. Astounding: rarely do you get a nose which sends out such clear signals, then an experience on the palate which contradicts almost completely. This is great Caol Ila. But for the nose, a possible award-winner. 54.7%. Speciality Drinks.

The Whisky Agency Caol Ila 26 Year Old dist 82, bott 09 **(85.5)** n21 t22 f21 b21.5. Softly oiled, lightly smoked and very pleasant without ever bothering about complexity. 63%.

The Whisky Agency Caol Ila 27 Year Old dist 82, bott 09 **(87)** n21 sooty: as much coal dust as there is peat reek; t23 sharp, eye-watering, juicy barley pierces the softer, sleepier smoke; f21 a slight off note towards the finish, as though the oak isn't too happy; b22 this one was probably on the way down and was plucked from the cask in the nick of time. Some great moments, but a few dodgy ones too. 62.4%. The Whisky Agency, Germany.

The Whisky Agency Caol Ila 27 Year Old Rum Finish dist 82, bott 09 **(80.5)** n20 t21 f19.5 b20. A disappointingly tart, closed and very average bottling from this normally first-class bottler. 50%. The Whisky Agency, Germany.

Whisky Doris Caol Ila 1992 dist 92, bott 09 **(85.5)** n22 t21 f21.5 b21. A very pleasant, medium- sweet and safe Caol Ila which doesn't overly depend on its natural oils and accentuates some gristy qualities. 46%

The Whisky Fair Caol Ila Aged 23 Years bourbon, dist 84, bott 07 **(92)** n23 t23 f22 b24. An excellent bottling devoid of the usual spoiling oiliness. Not overly complex in variety of flavours, but certainly in the way they are delivered. 55.9%. Germany.

The Whisky Society Caol Ila 1984 Aged 23 Years bott Sep 07 **(84.5)** n21.5 t22 f20 b21. Enjoyable dramming, but really doesn't show or even begin to hint at the great age it has achieved. 57%. Speciality Drinks.

Wilson & Morgan Barrel Selection Caol Ila 18 Years Old Cask Strength dist 89, bott 07 **(85)** n21 t22 f21 b21. A pleasant if perfunctory Islay showing the occasional neat touch. 53.2%

Wilson & Morgan Barrel Selection Caol Ila Aged 20 Years dist 88, bott 08 **(76)** n19 t20 f18 b19. You know that grating sound when the bagpipes first start up? Yep, as off key as that... 46%

⠿ **Wilson & Morgan Barrel Selection Caol Ila 20 Years Old** cask no. 4224/4225, dist 1988, bott 2008 **(90.5)** n23 how soft can a full-bodied peatiness be? The sub plot of lilacs helps....; t22.5 elegant and delicate, the soft coating of Demerara blends superbly with the billowing smoke; f22.5 light spices and a touch of cocoa trumpets the playfully oaky finale; b22.5 absolutely charming. 46% Wilson & Morgan

Wilson & Morgan Barrel Selection Caol Ila 23 Years Old dist 84, bott 07 **(82)** n21 t21.5 f19 b20.5. Hard not to believe that this isn't related in some way to the Whisky Society bottling of the same age. Not quite so sweet. 46%

⠿ **Wilson & Morgan Barrel Selection Caol Ila 25 Years Old** cask no. 3133, dist 1984, bott 2009 **(89)** n23 some really sexy milk chocolate mixes in with a cut-grass freshness which is unusual for a Caol Ila. Actually, rather than newly cut grass, think the stuff that dried out in the sun for a few days to make hay... t22.5 sweet, surprisingly juicy, barley barely troubled by smoke; f21.5 the oak makes a drying entry; b22 a dram that's making hay in many ways... 46% Wilson & Morgan

Wilson & Morgan barrel Selection Caol Ila 1995 refill butt, bott 08 **(87)** n22 floral with trace smoke at the most delicate, almost puniest level; t22.5 the phenols, bizarrely, are the first to show, offering a hint of camp coffee; salty; f21 rather typically fades and bitters as the oak takes command; b21.5 for those who like their peat to tease them.. 46%

Wilson & Morgan Barrel Selection Caol Ila 1996 bott 08 **(79.5)** n20.5 t21 f19 b19. A old cask filled for blending has somehow turned up as a single malt. 48%

⫶⫶ **Wilson & Morgan Barrel Selection Caol Ila 2000** cask no. 310262/310269, dist 2000, bott 2010 **(87.7)** n22 peat and mocha in dapper doses; t22 juicy, young with a developing sweet lemon character; f21.5 oaks out quietly; the smoke remains shy; b22 steady, clean and delicate. 48% Wilson & Morgan, Limited Edition

CAPERDONICH
Speyside, 1898. Chivas. Mothballed.

Cadenhead's Chairman's Stock Caperdonich Aged 27 Years bourbon hogshead, dist 80, bott Jun 08 **(76.5)** n20 t20 f18.5 b18. Something of the wallpaper glue about this one. 56.8%.

⫶⫶ **Connoisseurs Choice Caperdonich 1972 (83)** n20.5 t18 f22.5 b20. A very strange creature, this: a kind of topsy-turvy dram which actually repairs itself after apparently being inflicted by fatal oaky damage. The initial intensity of the oak is such that you actually close your eyes and shudder. But so good is the sherry that the grape softens the blow to the extent that a beautiful mocha finish makes you just about purr. A real oddity...and not without moments of magic. 46% Gordon & MacPhail

⫶⫶ **Connoisseurs Choice Caperdonich 1994 (88)** n22 pretty clean barley with a blancmange and floral subplot; t22.5 perfectly attractive, juicy malt with myriad levels of sugar and light oak f21.5 light and sawdust-like but still enough lingering barley to make a impact; b22 an unusual Caper, as this one appears to have the guts to go the distance. Quality. 46% Gordon & MacPhail

Duncan Taylor Collection Caperdonich 1968 cask no. 2608 **(86.5)** n22 t22 f21 b21.5. I don't believe it! 56% at 40-years-old! Well, yes it's true. And this Victor Meldrew of a malt, curmudgeonly, cantankerous and fiery despite having one foot in the grave, still has some style, albeit bourbony, despite the flat cap-ing finale. 56%

Duncan Taylor Collection Caperdonich 1970 cask no. 4376 **(84.5)** n22 t21.5 f21 b20. A drowsy ride along barley sewn on oaky ground. 42.3%

Duncan Taylor Collection Caperdonich 1970 cask no. 4377 **(86.5)** n21.5 t22.5 f21.5 b21. Punchier, weightier, tellingly more intense than 4376 and for a while a real malty treat. But still the complexity is at a premium and we are finding Caper at its most simplistic and undemanding, taking into account the whisky's great age. Some flakes of chocolate do help at the end. 45.9%

Duncan Taylor Collection Caperdonich 1970 cask no. 4381 **(82.5)** n20 t21 f21.5 b20. Some sharp barley and waxy vanilla, but you get the feeling this was once a hot whisky, which may explain the limited development on its sister casks. 46.8%

Duncan Taylor Collection Caperdonich 1972 cask no. 3246 **(94)** n24 t23 f24 b23. Any number of distilleries reach the "exotic fruit" stage of old age, but none seem to master the genre with such panache as Caper. What a treat! 46.5%

Duncan Taylor Collection Caperdonich 1972 cask no. 6712 **(85)** n20 t22.5 f21.5 b21.5. Some quite lovely movements to this old classic, especially in the exotic fruit department, but ultimately closer in style to 7435 than 3246, alas. 51.3%

Duncan Taylor Collection Caperdonich 1972 cask no. 7421 **(87)** n22.5 rhubarb and custard with an extra big dollop of vanilla; t22.5 massive delivery. The sweet malt and silky fruits are backed to the hilt by aggressive, OTT, spiced-out oaks. You know that its too old and too much – but the effect is so, well, kapowering!!, you are happy to let it go; f21 dries to a toasty desert; b21 Oooh, so borderline!! I have given this one the benefit of the doubt. The march of the oak towards the late middle and finish is relentless. 55.6%

Duncan Taylor Collection Caperdonich 1972 cask no. 7422 **(94)** n23.5 has moved from rhubarb to a much more exotic style befitting its age; leathery and bourbony, too: a much more intense and classy nose than its sister cask; t24 held on the palate, you are immediately aware of the depth of flavours here: again there is a spicy, bourbony thrust, fattened out by molasses and a hint of liquorice then as the middle approaches the barley saunters through; f23 so very long: chewy and muttering dark sugars and burned honeycomb. The vanillas are no more than decoration; b23.5 tasted against its sister cask, 7421, here is a display of how one barrel can absorb the years and come out positively gleaming, while the other is tarnished and hanging on to its fading beauty grimly. This is truly stunning malt. 54.8%

⫶⫶ **Duncan Taylor Collection Caperdonich 1972** cask no. 7449 **(81)** n21 t22 f18.5 b19.5. Old Capers – especially from this bottler - have in recent years shown an astonishing beauty once the tell-tale exotic fruit kicks in. This one bears all the hallmarks of a whisky which has gone through the back of greatness, with those fruits now faded and much drier, more substantial – and unforgiving – oak taking its place. The first few bars of the delivery, though, remains a definite treat. 47.8% Duncan Taylor & Co Ltd

Lonach Caperdonich 1969 (83.5) n22 t21 f20 b20.5. Curious. Nothing like the famed ancient Caper fruitfest I imagined I'd get. Instead, we have a malt which has been submerged in oak, but has retained enough oxygen in the form of barley to keep alive. Just. *42.4%*.

Lonach Caperdonich 1969 (89.5) n22 barley aplenty and even outweighs the south Pacific fruit...which is a good sign thing... **t23** plenty of integrity on the malt which makes a cushioned impact: superb... **f22.5** melted vanilla ice cream over pears and butterscotch tart; **b22** a beautiful Speysider which has withstood the ravages of time: wonderful. *40.6%*.

Lonach Caperdonich 1969 bott 08 **(80) n20.5 t20.5 f19 b20.** Malty but fading fast. *44.7%*.

Lonach Caperdonich 1970 (78.5) n21 t20 f18.5 b19. You can almost hear the fingernails screeching as this malt tries to grip frantically on to the right side of the aging process. God, it has my sympathy... *43.3%. Duncan Taylor.*

⋰⋰ **Matisse Carpedonich 1972 Highland Single Malt** bott Jul 09 **(94.5) n23.5** soft exotic fruit, but over ripened gooseberries enjoy equal star billing; **t24** the whisky spiders have been busy producing the finest silk from sugar almond barley touched by acacia honey; **f23.5** an almost inevitable mocha to this with golden syrup and malt shake add the lingering sweetnes; **b23.5** sometimes these exotic fruit types are a bit of a let down; others are the very reason why whisky was invented. This, comfortably, falls into the latter. *47.5% Matisse Spirits Co Ltd*

⋰⋰ **Matisse Carpedonich 1972 Highland Single Malt** cask no. 7447, bott Jul 09 **(92.5) n24** battling sharpness: almost kiwi fruity, but sweetened by lime and liquorice; **t23.5** again, an immediate impact which brings a tear to the eye: barley in concentrate form; the oak is sugared vanilla pods; citrus abounds; **f22.5** after all that work, no wonder it begins to feel tired; **b22.5** a more aggressive version of the 47.5% cask. In your face, but pays the price in sophistication. Fabulous, though! *50.5% Matisse Spirits Co Ltd*

⋰⋰ **Matisse Carpedonich 1972 Highland Single Malt** cask no. 7448, bott Jul 09 **(95) n24** inevitable exotic fruit, rather simplistic other than the extra spices; a surprising puff of something peaty; **t24** good grief! I wasn't joking about the spices on the nose as they seer into the palate without asking for an invite; the barley is clean, rich and salivating with sugared almonds and vanilla filling the middle ground; **f23.5** elegant with a slow denouement of light smoke and golden syrup; **b23.5** I've said it before and I'll say it again: had Caper been half this quality a malt when in its vital three to five years, it wouldn't now be part of a copper works. The most sophisticated of Matisse's three exceptional casks. *49.7% Matisse Spirits Co Ltd*

Old Malt Cask Caperdonich Aged 34 Years refill hogshead, cask no. 4296, dist Dec 73, bott May 08 **(77.5) n21 t19.5 f18 b19.** Does its best to start brightly but soon becomes evident this is pretty shagged out (very lightly smoked) whisky. *41.5%. Douglas Laing. 267 bottles.*

Old Malt Cask Caperdonich Aged 40 Years refill hogshead, cask no. 3920, dist Feb 67, bott Oct 07 **(74.5) n18.5 t18 f19 b19.** It's strange how 40-year-old sounds older than 1968 vintage: a message for us all there, I think. However, this one simply does feel older... *42.9%. 133 bottles.*

Provenance Caperdonich Aged 11 Years hogshead, cask no. 4200, dist summer 96, spring 08 **(73.5) n18.5 t18 f19 b18.** Excessively thin, malty. Yep, Caperdonich all right... *46%.*

Provenance Caperdonich Aged 12 Years refill hogshead, dist spring 96, bott winter 08 **(81.5) n22 t20.5 f20 b19.** An uncommon Caper at this age, but a good example of a malt which flatters to deceive – and why the owners despaired so. The under-ripe greengage nose is attractive but the thinness of the body underwhelms. *46%. Douglas Laing.*

⋰⋰ **Provenance Caperdonich Over 12 Years** refill hogshead no. DMG 5569, dist Spring 1997, bott Autumn 2009 **(85) n22.5 t21.5 f20 b21.** While it might be fair to say that this, as Caper has a tendency to do, lacks substance; what it does do, it does very well. The barley is light and precise, the malt dissolving before being able to take the complexity much further. But, for all that, a refreshing dram for an early part of the day and better for its age than much of the stuff that came from this distillery over the previous three decades. By coincidence, the day before I tasted this I happened to see part of the distillery dismantled. Sad. *46% Douglas Laing*

Whisky Doris Caperdonich 36 Year Old cask no. 7425, dist Nov 72, bott Feb 09 **(89.5) n22** no shortage of oak, but the honey is big enough to see it off; **t22.5** beautiful mouthfeel and weight. Again the oak really does try to shout as loudly as possible, but those acacia honey notes succeed in intervening; **f23** at its best now with the drier oak involvement settling for a subtler, more chocolaty approach which works well with that persistent honey; **b22** a must for lovers of Crunchie bars or just those with a sweet tooth who like to chew the toothpicks. *54.4%*

The Whisky Fair Caperdonich 1972 refill sherry hogshead, dist Nov 72, bott Aug 08 **(93.5) n22.5** the usual exotic fruit, except now with a faint ginger incursion; **t24** there we go: a mixture of youthful Caperdonich's fire and brimstones alongside the mature whisky-of-the-world Caperdonich's ability to strike a suave, intelligent lushness embracing those juicy fruits, titillating spices and, again, a hint of something gingery; **f23** back to the vanilla, but the light trickle of barley oils ensures a balanced finale; **b24** just fantastic... *48.3%.*

CARDHU

Speyside, 1824. Diageo. Working.

Cardhu 12 Years Old db **(90) n23** just about the cleanest, most uncluttered, pure, sweet malt you will ever find, a touch of apple, perhaps, giving an extra dimension; **t24** again the malt is pure and rich, just a thread of oak adding some dryness and depth; **f21** vanilla and malt; **b22** a classic: welcome back! *40% (see also Cardhu Pure Malt)*

CLYNELISH

Highlands (Northern), 1968. Diageo. Working.

Clynelish Aged 15 Years "The Distillers Edition" double matured in oloroso-seco casks Cl-Br: 169-1f, bott code L6264CM000 03847665, dist 91, bott 06 db **(79) n20 t20 f19 b20**. Big in places, distinctly oily in others but the overall feel is of a potentially brilliant whisky matured in unsympathetic barrels. *46%*

�„⋅ **Clynelish The Manager's Choice** first fill bourbon American oak, cask no. 4341, dist 1997, bott 2009 db **(90.5) n22.5** friendly barley which is both intense and relaxed but the oak is a little uptight by sending out some major natural caramels; **t23** puckeringly sharp barley helped by breathtakingly clean oak. A little spice nip, but simply underlines the barley's credentials; **f22.5** custardy vanilla but still it is the barley which dominates with a profound clarity; **b22.5** excellent cask selection. Everything is geared towards accentuation the untarnished richness of the malt. *58.5% 232 bottles.*

⋙⋅ **A.D. Rattray Clynelish 1997** cask no. 4664, dist Apr 97, bott Dec 09 **(87) n22** dry custard tart....with the emphasis on the tart; **t22** a light honey topping to the delicate barley-vanilla; **f21.5** mildly bitters; **b21.5** a very pleasant sheen throughout. *59.4% A.D. Rattray Ltd*

Cadenhead's Authentic Collection Clynelish Aged 17 Years bourbon, dist 90, bott Sep 07 **(86.5) n22 t21 f22 b21.5**. Hugely intense malt which is blemish-free and improves wave upon wave. *51.2%. 204 bottles.*

⋙⋅ **Cadenhead's Authentic Collection Clynelish 1993** bott Feb 10 **(86) n21 t22 f21.5 b21.5**. Very enjoyable malt, though sharp and citrusy by Clynelish standards. Just a bit of attitude from the cask, I feel... *56.8% Wm. Cadenhead Ltd. 315 bottles.*

The Cárn Mór Vintage Collection Clynelish 2003 hogshead, cask no. 2223, dist 03, bott 09 **(78.5) n22 t20 f18 b18.5**. Lovely nose but all the signs of a cask that would add little in 60 years, let alone six... *46%. The Scottish Liqueur Centre.*

Chieftain's Clynelish 14 Years Old hogshead, cask no. 15103, dist Nov 92 **(85.5) n22 t21.5 f21 b21**. Big malt though playing down the normal sweetness. *46%. nc ncf. Danish Market.*

⋙⋅ **Connoisseurs Choice Clynelish 1994** **(85.5) n21.5 t22 f21 b21**. Pleasingly dry with the odd honeyed note quickly counter-balanced. *43% Gordon & MacPhail*

The Creative Whisky Company Clynelish 1994 Aged 11 Years ex-sherry **(64) n16 t17 f15 b16**. Entirely jiggered by sulphur. *53.3%*

Dun Bheagan Clynelish 13 Years Old hogshead **(79) n20 t21 f19 b19**. Some pleasant shards of honey and butterscotch cannot disguise the relatively hot nature of this one. *46%*

Dun Bheagan Clynelish Aged 17 Years butt, dist Dec 90 **(89) n23.5 t23 f21 b22.5**. There is no silencing a fine distillery and here it crows effortlessly. Beautiful. *46%.*

Duncan Taylor The NC2 Range Clynelish 1993 (88.5) n21.5 like sticking your head in a florist's; **t23** wonderful build up of ultra clean barley sugar and muscovado; **f22** barley remains crisp and neat; **b22** simple yet high quality malt. *46%*

Duncan Taylor The NC2 Range Clynelish 1994 (87.5) n22.5 mown grass and haylofts; **t22** firm, juicy barley; **f21.5** you know that toffee you get in the middle of Everton mints... **b21.5** a strange one this: has all the scaffolding for a exceptional malt, but not quite enough Brix. *46%*

⋙⋅ **Duthies Clynelish 14 Years Old (74) n17 t19 f18 b18**. The nose is a good indicator of what is to follow. *46% Wm. Cadenhead Ltd*

⋙⋅ **Finest Whisky Clynelish 37 Years Old 80 Proof (89.5) n22.5** stewed rhubarb in thick custard; **t23.5** early wave of fresh barley followed by a thick, but short-lived puff of peat; the middle ground is coffee-cream biscuit with a firm sugary lip; **f22** an aged sheen to this with the barley remaining crunchy and firm; **b21.5** no doubting its antiquity. Hangs on stoically against the gathering oaks and has plenty in reserve. *46% Speciality Drinks Ltd. Bottled for TWE's 10th Anniversary.*

⋙⋅ **The Golden Cask Clynelish 1997** cask no. CM146, bott 2009 **(91) n22** dry oak amid the honey; **t23** superb delivery: some waspish oak-spice livens up the butterscotch and vanilla middle; **f22.5** mocha and plenty more oak; **b22.5** has aged ahead of its time. But the result is a lively treat. *58.2% The House of MacDuff. 255 bottles.*

Gordon & MacPhail Cask Strength Clynelish 1997 (91.5) n23 the barley is stark but the fruity punchiness is something to get your nose round. The coal dust adds just-so weight;

t22.5 crisp and juicy on one level, abounding with spice and oak on another; f23 dipped in cocoa powder for a drying finish to the long barley-rich theme; b23 plenty of class and more age than you would expect. 59.7%

⋙ **James MacArthur's Fine Malt Selection Clynelish Aged 12 Years** cask no. 11828, bott May 10 (94) n24 spot-on nose: a light citrus note melts into the summer garden lavender ...one of the most exquisite perfumes for any malt aroma this year. Delicate butterscotch represents the understated oak; t23 very clever: all kinds of fresh fruit and barley notes, but none of them sweet. The oak forms a drier boundary inside which there are numerous juicy elements, but none really pushing it with the sugars: a rare case of being malty, but without the usual barley water effect; f23 elongated by a soft oil, a return of the pastry-dominant butterscotch but an intense and tapering barley; b24 an excellent cask from a fabulous and still under-rated distillery: not a single hint of bitterness, yet no OTT sweetness, either. Of a style once common, now a bit of a rarity these days. 45% MacArthur & Co Ltd for the USA market

⋙ **Kingsbury's "The Selection" Clynelish 7 Years Old 1999** (81.5) n20 t21 f20 b20.5. Fresh, malty, uncomplex. 43% Japan Import System

Lombard's Jewels of Scotland Clynelish 1982 Aged 21 Years (88) n21 t23 f22 b22. A busy and quite joyous bottling. 50%. Lombard Brands.

⋙ **Malts of Scotland Clynelish 1982** bourbon hogshead no. 5895, dist Dec 82, bott Jan 10 (91) n22.5 hardly surprising this is from a bourbon barrel: bourbon is perhaps the main theme. Toasty and full of Demerara rum and hickory notes; t23.5 those sugary notes really pound through, meeting the unforgiving barley with a whack. Salivating early on then a subtle wave of spice as the oak thuds home; f22.5 back to the hickory and a touch of liquorice, too. How wonderfully bourbony...in a malty kind of way...; b22.5 uncompromisingly delicious. 51.5% Malts of Scotland. 192 bottles.

⋙ **Malts of Scotland Clynelish 1996** sherry butt no. 8245, dist Oct 96, bott Mar 09 (69) n17.5 t17.5 f17 b17. I remember the day this was distilled very well: it was my son James' 10th birthday. Sadly, the spirit was filled into a less than memorable cask. 58.1% 96 bottles.

Norse Cask Selection Clynelish 1995 Aged 12 Years sherry butt no. 12773, dist Dec 95, bott Nov 08 (69) n17.5 t18.5 f16 b17. Sulphured. 57.3%. Qualityworld for WhiskyOwner.com

⋙ **Old Malt Cask Clynelish Aged 14 Years** refill hogshead no. DL 5724, dist Jun 95, bott Jan 10 (81) n21 t22 f18 b20. Malts as underdeveloped for its age as this tend to be all upfront on delivery and struggle on the finish. This one is true to type. 50% Douglas Laing & Co Ltd.

Old Malt Cask Clynelish Aged 20 Years bott 09 (92.5) n22 typically honeyed and lightly fruited; t23 fine delivery with a real richness to the radiating malt; f24 continues on this theme for ever and a day, perhaps with some natural caramels turning up, too. Juicy with the final fade is just so beautifully estery; b23.5 an excellent must-have example of typically classy from this great distillery. 50%. Douglas Laing.

Old Malt Cask Clynelish Aged 24 Years dist Apr 83, bott May 07 (88) n22 t23 f21 b22. Elegant and clean. 50%. Douglas Laing. 305 bottles.

Old Malt Cask Clynelish Aged 36 Years refill hogshead, cask no. 3913, dist Mar 71, bott Sep 07 (83) n22 t20.5 f20 b20.5. Bruised and battered by some severe oaky beatings, there is just enough pep in the barley for a final sweet, malty hurrah. 44.6%. nc ncf. 191 bottles.

Old Malt Cask Clynelish Aged 38 Years refill hogshead, dist Mar 71, bott Mar 09 (91) n23 stylish to the point of being quietly majestic: the anthracite smoke really does offer a beautiful backdrop to the surprisingly clear barley and murkier citrus; the complexity, though, and in particular the weight is fabulous.. t23.5 brilliant delivery which falls somewhere between silk on one hand and intensely lively barley on the other. There is the odd oaky phrase which announces an unmistakable tiredness from age (the odd bit of exotic fruit here and there), but countering it is that juicy barley thrust and, just like the nose, the most subtle of not necessarily peaty smoke; f22 plenty of vanilla custard as a sweetness begins to outweigh those signs of age; finally dries to a chalky dustiness; b22.5 an absolute class act which grows on you with every single, ultra-complex mouthful. Unusually, the obvious age wrinkles somehow add to the charm. 47.9%. Douglas Laing. 145 bottles.

Old Masters Clynelish Aged 10 Years dist 97, bott May 08 (86.5) n21.5 t22 f22 b21. Not the usual honeyed style, but every bit as mouth-watering as it should be with an attractive soft cocoa finale. 57.8%. James MacArthur & Co. Ltd.

Provenance Clynelish Aged 10 Years dist 96, bott 07 (86) n22 t21.5 f21.5 b21. A dram closer to 10 months than 10-years in style: a cask that's seen much of life has contributed minimally, except for the filtering out of some of the more volatile qualities. That said, they certainly don't come much more mouth-watering or barley-laden than this. 46%. Douglas Laing, exclusively for Edinburgh University Water of Life Society. 240 bottles.

Provenance Clynelish Over 10 Years refill hogshead no. DMG 5236, dist Autumn 1998, bott Summer 2009 **(92.5) n23** porridge topped with melting brown sugar; some coal dust hangs around; **t23.5** always fresh and energetic on the palate without ever going on the attack: the barley is duo-toned with a wonderful interplay between crisp barley and an altogether more yielding maltiness; **f23** dries as the oak makes its polite and elegant entry; something lightly smoked simmers in the background; **b23** shows what an excellent malt can do in a less than excellent cask. *46% Douglas Laing & Co Ltd*

Provenance Clynelish Aged 11 Years hogshead, cask no. 4187 & 4188, dist autumn 96, bott spring 08 **(88) n22** grassy with coal gas and lime; **t22.5** every bit as juicy as the nose suggests: malt at its cleanest; **f22** straight-laced barley with a smidgeon of vanilla and butterscotch; **b21.5** Clynelish at its most simple, clean, elegant and malty. *46%. Douglas Laing.*

Provenance Clynelish Over 12 Years refill hogshead no. DMG 5609, dist Autumn 1997, bott Autumn 2009 **(84.5) n22 t21 f20.5 b21.** Unusual degree of citrus for the distillery. *46%*

Provenance Clynelish Over 12 Years refill hogshead, cask no. 6057, dist spring 1998, bott spring 2010 **(92.5) n23** lemon squeezed on honey-sweetened pancakes; **t23.5** clean barley, light and sensuously juicy; **f23** more citrus as the vanilla adds weight. Clean and very classy; **b23** a dream of a bottling revealing unambiguously through the medium of a well used but intact cask the distillery's brilliance. The citrus here combines with the honey quite charmingly but there is always that richer, bigger, more complex picture. *46% Douglas Laing & Co Ltd*

Scotch Malt Whisky Society Cask 26.55 Aged 8 Years 1st fill barrel, dist Nov 99 **(94) n24 t24 f23 b23.** Almost an exact imprint of how you imagine the finest Clynelish to be. Both spooky and spanking and the blueprint by which all other such bottlings should be measured. A serious contender for young whisky of the year. *62.4%*

Scotch Malt Whisky Society Cask 26.56 Aged 8 Years refill barrel, dist Nov 99 **(90.5) n22.5 t23 f22.5 b22.5.** A wonderful dram, if lacking the sparkle, devilment and indisputable élan of the 26.55. Amazing the difference a cask can make. *61.8%*

Scotch Malt Whisky Society Cask 26.63 Aged 12 Years refill butt, dist Oct 96 **(85.5) n22.5 t22.5 f19.5 b21.** Fabulous nose: not entirely unlike the inside of a fruit-scented wooden trinket box. The delivery briefly sparkles but the finish is sub-prime. *54.9% 580 bottles.*

Scotch Malt Whisky Society Cask 26.61 Aged 25 Years refill hogshead, dist May 83 **(92) n23.5** exquisite soft smoke and honey makes for what, nosed blind, appears a low voltage Highland Park; **t24** even better delivery with a spicy fizz helping to seriously ramp up the soft acacia honey notes and playful phenols. Fabulous mouthfeel with the oak steady and sturdy, but on very best behaviour; **f22** cocoa dependent; **b22.5** at times simply irresistible and with a sprig of heather this could be top-notch HP. *55%*

Scotch Malt Whisky Society Cask 26.62 Aged 26 Years refill hogshead, dist May 83 **(92) n23** an attractive combination of over-ripe tangerine and delicate smoke; **t23** a chunky, big-bodied delivery with shards of Demerara sugar ducking and weaving with the thin smoke cloud; **f23.5** the smoke lingers as late spice and latte arrives; **b22.5** sounds odd, I know, but there is a touch of blue fruit mould, especially to nose and delivery, to this...but it's actually attractive and sits with the gentle smoke very comfortably. *55% 155 bottles.*

Scotch Malt Whisky Society Cask 26.67 Aged 25 Years refill sherry butt, dist Dec 84 **(86.5) n21.5 t22 f21 b22.** The oak makes some heavy demands which the barley just about resists. But at times it's touch-and-go. *48.9% Scotch Malt Whisky Society. 60 bottles.*

The Scotch Single Malt Circle Clynelish 1995 cask no. 12780, dist Sep 95, bott Aug 08 **(88) n21** barley concentrate and vanilla; **t23** big early barley and honey mix, then a slow, irreversable penetration of bourbony-sweet, spiced oak; **f22** much drier as the oaky element takes control; **b22** impressive, well-made malt with a particularly well-balanced entry. *60.6%. German market.*

The Single Malts of Scotland Clynelish 1992 Aged 15 Years bott Sep 07 **(84) n21.5 t21.5 f20 b21.** Just so much natural caramel! *46%. Speciality Drinks.*

The Whisky Agency Clynelish 14 Years Old dist 1995, bott 2010 **(88) n21.5** fruity, a light dab of coal smoke and oak; **t22.5** salivating marmalade and manuka honey; **f22** more fruity sugars with a surprising lack of age; **b22** great fun: get the feeling this one is still warming up. *48%*

The Whisky Agency Clynelish 27 Year Old dist 82, bott 09 **(90) n22** serious heather honey; **t22.5** firm barley-oak delivery, with pulsing, spiced honey arriving in nearby waves; **f22** long with vanilla and salt; **b22.5** holds its age stupendously: like a Highland Park without the peat. *53.9%. The Whisky Agency, Germany.*

Whisky-Doris Clynelish 1997 dist 97, bott 07 **(86.5) n21.5 t22 f21.5 b21.5.** Thickset and malty, the usual freshness is missing. That said, this is wonderful stuff, especially if you like an American malt shake-style whisky. *59%*

The Whisky Society Clynelish 1992 Aged 15 Years bott Sep 07 **(89)** n23 t23 f21 b22. A kind of sophisticated, handsome brother to the Single Malts bottling. *58.5%. Speciality Drinks.*

Wilson & Morgan Barrel Selection Clynelish Aged 12 Years marsala finish, dist 96, bott 08 **(84.5)** n23 t21.5 f19 b21. Wow...!! Well, that's different. This is quite massive with about as much prickle as you might find at a porcupine convention. There has been a touch of sulphur involved somewhere, but the sulphur stick must have passed through like and an express as the damage is manageable. The nose is just one salivating chorus of sultana fruitcake and the intensity on the palate is something else besides. The marauding chocolate later on is pretty telling, too. For those who never detect sulphur, or perhaps even like it, you might mark this one well in the 90s... *58.6%*

Wilson & Morgan Barrel Selection Clynelish 1996 bott 08 **(79.5)** n20.5 t20 f19 b20. Dry, occasionally to the point of austerity, and locates far too many cul-de-sacs. *46%*

COLEBURN
Speyside, 1897–1985. Diageo. Closed.

Connoisseurs Choice Coleburn 1981 (81) n21 t21 f19 b20. Usual thin, hot stuff from Coleburn but benefits from a big malt kick. Way above the norm. *43%*

The Whisky Agency Coleburn 26 Year Old dist 83, bott 09 **(88.5)** n22 light, clean, citrusy malt: the epitome of Speyside style; **t23** juicy, clean, salivating barley sees off the growing oaky attention with a sugar candy barley-sugar, chocolate lime infusion; **f21.5** cocoa and vanilla...the oaky bitterness is expected, threatens and then is headed off... **b22** Coleburn is a rare whisky. A thoroughly enjoyable Coleburn is rarer still. So here's one you've just got to go and track down... *49.5%. The Whisky Agency, Germany.*

CONVALMORE
Speyside, 1894–1985. Closed.

Convalmore 1977 bott 05 db **(91)** n23 t23 f22 b23. Must be blended with Botox, as there is no detrimental ageing to either nose or delivery. A quite lovely and charming whisky to remember this lost – and extremely rare - distillery by. *57.9%. 3900 bottles.*

Cadenhead's Convalmore 30 Years Old dist 77, bott Sep 07 **(95)** n23.5 t24 f23.5 b24. The strength for the age is unbelievable: this appears a throwback, to a time 25 years ago when I was tasting this at full strength and full of vitality. It's been a ling time since I was hit by Convalmore like this; thinking about it, I really cannot remember this distillery showing to such near perfection in the past at all. Just amazing. *61.6%. 240 bottles.*

Connoisseurs Choice Convalmore 1984 (88.5) n23 the house style, curiously plasticy and fruity, still intact: delicate and unusual hint of fried yam and softened passion fruit all slightly confused by coke smoke; **t22** juicy, outwardly thin and missing meat in the middle but compensated by beautiful, bitter-sweet layering of clean malt; **f21** cocoa powder and peppers compensate for the vanishing sweetness and body; **b22.5** one of the younger Convanmores to have found its way on the market of late, having been distilled shortly before its fatal closure. This is crisper than older expressions, yet celebrates the finesse so often found from the older versions. An historic treat. *43%. Gordon & MacPhail.*

Old Malt Cask Convalmore Aged 30 Years dist Oct 76, bott Apr 07 **(88)** n23 t22 f21 b22. A charming and unusual expression of this rare malt. *44.1%. Douglas Laing. 192 bottles.*

Old Malt Cask Convalmore Aged 32 Years refill hogshead, cask no. 4246, dist Oct 75, bott Apr 08 **(89.5)** n23 tangerines and barley for a simple but wonderfully effective duo; **t22.5** silky, malty, more citrus to ensure a fresh, lively element seeing off the vanilla; **f22** runs out of gas slightly and retires meekly but with no little elegance; **b22** almost too charming to be true. *50%. nc ncf. Douglas Laing. 202 bottles.*

⌐∞⌐ **Rare Old Convalmore 1975 (96)** n24.5 that coal dust character which pops up in this distillery from time to time is more evident than usual here and works pretty well with the watery kiwi fruit and greengage tart; a sprig of lavender pays homage to the oak; one of the great noses of the year....; **t24** wow!! A real sprinkling of light peat, clearer than usual, adds a lovely weight to the surprisingly agile barley which sets the ball rolling; there is also the most delicate of spicy threads imaginable, too; **f23** the light peaty dusting continues and dovetails well with the drier vanillas and spices; husky barley ensures an improbable freshness; **b24.5** a caressing, ambient dram: certainly shows great age but does it in a style and manner which demands total respect. A true classic and yet another example of a distillery lost to us hitting heights of which other can only dream. *43% Gordon & MacPhail*

Scott's Selection Convalmore 1975 bott 07 **(91)** n22 t23 f23 b23. A malt determined to keep its head below the parapet. But once you make the effort to notice it, its quiet but unmistakable quality is there to admire. *46%*

CRAGGANMORE

Speyside, 1870. Diageo. Working.

Cragganmore Aged 12 Years db **(81.5) n**20 **t**21 **f**20 **b**20.5. I have a dozen bottles of Cragganmore in my personal cellar dating from the early 90s when the distillery was first bottled as a Classic Malt. Their astonishing dexterity and charm, their naked celebration of all things Speyside, casts a sad shadow over this drinkable but drab and instantly forgettable expression. 40%.

Cragganmore Aged 14 Years The Distillers Edition finished in port casks, dist 93, bott 07 db **(85) n**22 **t**21 **f**21 **b**21. The tightly closed fruit on the palate doesn't quite match the more expansive and complex nose. 40%.

⁘ **A.D. Rattray Cragganmore 1997** cask no. 1491, dist Mar 97, bott Mar 10 **(88) n**22.5 cut grass, clean barley and celery; **t**22 juicy, spicy and brimming with barley; **f**21.5 light oils circle and lengthen the vanilla **b**22 an excellent Speysider showing why blenders love this stuff. 46% A.D. Rattray Ltd

⁘ **Berry's Own Selection Cragganmore 1997 (93.5) n**24 ultra complex with a beguiling collection of barley and oak notes interlinking to outstanding sweet-dry effect; no shortage of floral notes, too, but it's that delicate, lemon-tinged manuka honey which really wins it; **t**24.5 a beautiful, textbook, delivery with not a single note out of sync; the barley is delightfully salivating and clean and the sugars simply melt-in-the-mouth; just the lightest of spice buzzes ensures the oak offers more than just butterscotch; **f**22 perhaps a little on the dry side; **b**23 to be honest, I have just tasted a whole raft of pretty substandard malts. To come across something as technically excellent as this is as much a relief as it a joy...a go get bottling. 58.6% Berry Bros & Rudd

Cadenhead's Authentic Collection Cragganmore Aged 18 Years sherry butt, dist 89, bott Sep 07 **(88) n**21.5 **t**22.5 **f**22 **b**22. Battling with old age very effectively. 58.5%. 594 bottles.

Duthies Cragganmore 15 Years Old (84) n20.5 **t**22 **f**20.5 **b**21. Does its best in a tight cask. 46%. Cadenhead's for Germany.

Kingsbury's Cragganmore 1989 18 Years Old Cask Strength **(84.5) n**21.5 **t**23 **f**20 **b**20. Big, intense barley with massive early maple syrup kick. Fades as the bitter-ish oak takes charge. 54.8% Japan Import System.

Kingsbury's Single Cask Cragganmore Aged 17 Years dist Sep 89, bott Aug 07 **(75.5) n**19 **t**20 **f**17.5 **b**19. Lots of "Nourishment" chocolate energy drink. But a few flaws along the way, especially at the brutal death. 46%. Japan Import System.

Kingsbury Celtic Series Cragganmore 14 Years Old 1989 (84.5) n21 **t**21.5 **f**21 **b**21. Puffing a bit and creaking with oak. The barley though ensures a soft centre. 58.9%. nc ncf.

Murray McDavid Mission Cragganmore 1985 Aged 21 Years bourboun/syrah enhanced in Guigal Côte Rôtie **(82) n**23 **t**21 **f**19 **b**19. When they say bourbon, they aren't kidding: parts of this is pure Kentucky, especially on the glorious nose. But the truth is that it's gone through the wood and after the brain-blowing entry, things slip downhill. 56.5%. nc ncf. 665 bottles.

Norse Cask Selection Cragganmore 1993 Aged 14 Years hogshead, cask no. 001979, dist 93, bott Dec 07 **(89) n**22 **t**23 **f**21.5 **b**22.5. Wonderful to see this distillery on such great form. 60.5%. nc ncf. Qualityworld, Denmark. 276 bottles.

⁘ **Old Malt Cask Cragganmore Aged 20 Years** refill hogshead no. DL 5577, dist Oct 89, bott Oct 09 **(87) n**22.5 delicate and complex with a light dusting of cocoa on the cucumber and vanilla; **t**22 juicy malt delivery; leaking some oak, but the barley is easily big enough to cope; **f**21 the barley gives way to the drying vanillas; **b**21.5 another first-class malt from this outstanding distillery. Here the oak is taken as far as is comfortable. 50% 317 bottles.

Scotch Malt Whisky Society Cask 37.43 Aged 15 Years sherry butt, dist Mar 93 **(83.5) n**20 **t**20.5 **f**22 **b**21. A big, ungamely clodhopping brute of a malt. Even so, the marriage between bourbon and grape makes for some (mildly sulphured) nose. Once past the at times entertaining mess of a delivery excellent blood orange notes emerge. 60.4%

Scotch Malt Whisky Society Cask 37.38 Aged 16 Years refill barrel, dist Apr 92 **(85.5) n**21.5 **t**21 **f**21.5 **b**21.5. At times delicate and complex...but tired, also. Would love to have tasted this six years ago... 55.7%

⁘ **Scotch Malt Whisky Society Cask 37.44 Aged 16 Years** 1st fill sherry butt, dist Mar 93 **(79) n**22 **t**20 **f**18 **b**19. A real pea-souper of a dram which for all the rich, fruity promise on the nose, doesn't begin to live up to on the palate. 56% Scotch Malt Whisky Society

CRAIGELLACHIE

Speyside, 1891. Dewar's. Working.

Berrys' Own Selection Craigellachie 1994 cask no. 1057, bott 07 **(84) n**20 **t**21 **f**22 **b**21. Distinct similarities between this and SMWS bottling 44.36. There is a sulphury element to the nose and early delivery which has nothing to do with casks - and then, after a confused start, a much more harmonious, slightly cocoa-infused finale. However, here the cask is a little more worn and allows the barley a clearer say. 56.4%. Berry Bros & Rudd.

Cadenhead's Craigellachie Aged 14 Years dist 94, bott 09 **(91)** n23 always love it when I see that old Craigellachie peat smoke molecule signature – and there it is...accompanied by kumquats and crème brule; **t24** absolutely brilliant arrival: as top notch as I've ever experienced from this distillery at this age even in blending samples, **f21.5** a catch: bitters out late on with a shade too much enthusiasm; **b22.5** can't have it all: the indifferent, though not unpleasant, finish is the devil's trade off for some earlier heaven. 56.5%

⌁ **The Càrn Mòr Vintage Collection Craigellachie 1999** barrel no. 137, bott 2009 **(74.5)** n19 t20 f17.5 b18. Another half-cocked Craigellachie. Just no oak inspiration at all. 46% nc ncf. 1041 bottles.

Dewar Rattray Craigellachie 1991 cask no. 6924, dist Aug 91, bott Sep 07 **(91)** n24 t23 f22.5 b22.5. Helps confirm my suspicions that the spirit made here in the early 90s tailed off slightly in quality as the decade progressed. This is just brimming with the character that made me fall slightly in love with this distillery back in the early 80s. A treasure. 60.7%

⌁ **Hart Brothers Craigellachie Aged 11 Years** dist Dec 97, bott Nov 09 **(74)** n18 t19 f19 b18. An inert cask means the malt is acting half its age. Juicy, though. 46% Hart Brothers.

⌁ **Premier Barrel Craigellachie Aged 10 Years** sherry cask **(86)** n21 t22 f21.5 b21.5. An understated little charmer, this. The delicate, salivating barley and playful spice appear to wander around the palate hand-in-hand. Even a hint of smoke here and there. 46%

⌁ **Provenance Craigellachie Over 10 Years** sherry finished butt no. DMG 5813, dist Summer 1999, bott Winter 2010 **(76.5)** n19 t20 f18 b18.5. Sharp, a little abrasive and never quite finds its rhythm. 46% Douglas Laing.

Provenance Craigellachie Aged 11 Years refill hogshead, cask no. 4256, dist Autumn 96, bott Spring 08 **(85)** n21 t22 f21 b21. Sharp, clean malt softly oil-coated and spiced. 46%. nc ncf. Douglas Laing.

Scotch Malt Whisky Society Cask 44.36 Aged 14 Years refill hogshead, dist Feb 94 **(85)** n21 t19 f23.5 b21.5. One of those malts you'll either love or hate. Though most probably both during the space of about three minutes. Fractious and ill-disciplined for the most part, there are still some wonderfully garbled cocoa notes at the finish which are quite superb. 46%

Scotch Malt Whisky Society Cask 44.39 Aged 15 Years refill barrel, dist Aug 93 **(91)** n22.5 Finest Kentucky....like a young bourbon achieving sweet-vanilla maturity; **t23** a beautiful balance on delivery between juicy barley and intense vanilla; a dollop of molasses ensures a fine sweetness; a charming soft lemon freshness also hits the right note; **f22.5** long, oaky butterscotch and red liquorice flourish combine effortlessly with the fudgy sugars; **b23** some serious bourbon notes to this, from first nosing right through to the dying embers of oak on the finish. 58.1%

Scotch Malt Whisky Society Cask 44.40 Aged 9 Years refill butt, dist Aug 99 **(89.5)** n22 circles planet bourbon in a grapey capsule; **t23.5** almost oafishly intense, duffing up the tastebuds with a blistering bourbony-oak attack; some juicy barley-sultana enters as a sub plot; **f22** a major cocoa incident; **b22** as mouth-watering as you might expect from a malt of this age, and the odd zingy injection. But grapey remnants and a big vanilla surge minimally limit the range of the higher notes and complexity. 58.5%

DAILUAINE
Speyside, 1854. Diageo. Working.

⌁ **Dailuaine 1997 The Manager's Choice** db **(87.5)** n21.5 intriguing... t23 wow!!! Well, what do you know: a Dailuaine going on a charm offensive. On one hand the big malty body thumps into the taste buds, then several layers of honey wash over the wounds. Superb...; **f21** tails off rather too quickly towards the bittering oak; **b22** one of the most enjoyable (unpeated!!) Dailuaines I've come across in an age. There is the usual distillery biff to this, but not without a honeyed safety net. Great fun. 58.6%

Dailuaine Aged 16 Years bott lot no. L4334 db **(79)** n19 t21 f20 b19. Syrupy, almost grotesquely heavy at times; the lighter, more considered notes of previous bottlings have been lost under an avalanche of sugary, over-ripe tomatoes. Definitely one for those who want a massive dram. 43%

⌁ **Cadenhead's Authentic Collection Dailuaine-Glenlivet 1989** bott Feb 10 **(85.5)** n21 t21.5 f22 b21. Dense, malty and hot it may be; showing all the elegance of a one-legged giraffe, certainly; as technically brilliant as a Sunday League pub player on the Inter Milan training ground, for sure. But just one of those fabulously eccentric drams you cannot help but love. 56.5% Wm. Cadenhead Ltd. 256 bottles.

⌐ **Harris Whisky Co. Dailuaine Aged 10 Years "Bright Young Things"** cask no. cask 000090, dist May 00, bott Jul 10 (86) n21.5 t22 f21 b21.5. The barley shines and the sugar sparkles. So, yes, it is certainly bright. *46% Harris Whisky Co. 304 bottles.*

Hart Brothers Dailuaine Aged 11 Years dist Mar 97, bott Jun 08 (74) n16 t20 f19 b19. Typically feinty, though some of the oils do have a scarred attractiveness. *46%*

⌐ **Old Malt Cask Dailuaine Aged 27 Years Old** refill hogshead no. DL 5809, dist Feb 83, bott Feb 10 (93.5) n23 bloody hell...smoke!!! And we're not talking a couple of ppms, either. Sweet, almost a touch of cloves, to dance with the phenols; t24 probably the best delivery from this distillery I've come across in 20 years. Not only is the peat chewy, but there are sumptuous waves of Demerara blending in perfectly; the middle is entirely consumed with vanilla and barley, with the smoke drifting around the back of the palate: what a treat... f23 the usual distillery leaden-footed lushness works to good effect here as the smoked honey goes the full length... b23.5 don't get me wrong. I am not just marking this up because it is a peaty malt. There are any number in this book which have underwhelmed me, as you can see. No, this is all about the sublime marriage between the smoke and varying sugary notes. A real journey of a dram...what a discovery!! *50% nc ncf Douglas Laing & Co Ltd*

Old Malt Cask Dailuaine Aged 34 Years refill hogshead, cask no. 3976, dist Nov 73, bott Dec 07 (89.5) n23.5 t22 f22 b22. Some malts just don't work at this age...this one very clearly does. Lovely! *50%. Douglas Laing. 238 bottles.*

Provenance Dailuaine Aged 9 Years sherry butt, dist autumn 99, bott autumn 08 (67) n15 t19 f16 b17. Badly made and matured. *46%. Douglas Laing.*

⌐ **Provenance Dailuaine Over 9 Years** refill hogshead no. DMG 6213, dist Summer 2000, bott Spring 2010 (87.5) n22.5 the usual ballsy, thick malt with a light citrus edge to the vanilla; t22 coats the mouth with a mildly thuggish maltiness, seemingly all knuckles against the floor and little finesse. But the odd sharp note offers something that resembles layering; f21.5 slapped on barley vies with the simple vanilla; b21.5 I know one or two blenders who are not great fans of this stuff. And I remember one distillery manager at Dailuaine telling me many years back that he'd made "better spirit elsewhere." But this isn't half bad, and appears to enjoy its mildly quirky maltiness. *46% nc ncf Douglas Laing*

⌐ **Provenance Dailuaine Over 10 Years** sherry butt no. DMG 5747, dist Autumn 1999, bott Winter 2010 (84.5) n20.5 t22 f21 b21. Pleasant and at its best when the honeyed barley is showing, as opposed to the grape. *46% Douglas Laing*

⌐ **Scotch Malt Whisky Society Cask 41.42 Aged 23 Years** refill hogshead, dist May 86 (85) n22 t22 f20 b21. Big, uncomplicated, thumping malt. Perfect for bulking up in blends, and not bad here as a tart, malty mouthful. *57.2% Scotch Malt Whisky Society. 220 bottles.*

DALLAS DHU
Speyside, 1899–1983. Closed. Now a museum.

Dun Bheagan Dallas Dhu 26 Years Old sherry butt, dist April 81 (92) n24 t23.5 f22 b22.5. Delightful stuff. Not exactly textbook as it lurches about the palate, but the messages sent are lovely ones. *50%. nc ncf. Ian Macleod.*

Duncan Taylor Collection Dallas Dhu 1981 cask no. 389 (90) n21.5 a curious mixture of acacia honey and dry, mildly soaped pummace stone; t21.5 honeyed silk - and then a screeching delivery of nippy spices; settles in the middle to something more comfortably vanilla and cocoa; f24 now really comes into its own as the barley finds a foothold to ensure a charming complexity to the vanilla and mocha. Sheer class; b23 until the finale, it's difficult to know where this one is going. Or even that it is Dallas Dhu, as this is a much wilder, kick ass version than most... *55.1%*

Duncan Taylor Collection Dallas Dhu 1981 cask no. 419 (95) n24 t24 f23 b24. It's almost as if this old distillery is sending a message: forget about me being a bloody museum...just fire up my stills again!!! Just marvellous...indescribable...a thing of total beauty! *57.9%*

Duncan Taylor Collection Dallas Dhu 1981 cask no. 421 (91) n22 barley leads the vanilla; t23.5 beautiful, sharp barley retains some unblemished youth; f22.5 remains mouth-watering but the vanilla slowly invades; b23 another outstanding malt from this lost distillery. *55.8%*

Duncan Taylor Collection Dallas Dhu 1981 cask no. 422, dist Apr 81 (85.5) n20.5 t22 f21.5 b21.5. Clean and delightful, but an extra dose of natural caramel reduces the brightness. *53.3%*

Duncan Taylor Collection Dallas Dhu 1981 cask no. 432 (90) n22 t23 f22 b23. The notes for cask 421 will just about do for this. Rare as hen's teeth do two barrels play so similar a tune after all these years, even when sitting side by side. This is a tad duller thanks to the fractionally stronger vanillins and caramel. But still you wouldn't say no to a fourth glass... *55.7%*

Cadenhead's Chairman's Stock Dallas Dhu Aged 27 Years bourbon hogshead, dist 79, bott May 07 (89) n23 t22 f22 b22. This distillery never fails to amaze me. Yes, the oak is a little too emboldened but such is the chemistry of the barley and butterscotch foreground, you have to be impressed. *59.2%. 198 bottles.*

Old Malt Cask Dallas Dhu Aged 36 Years refill hogshead, cask no. 4106, dist Apr 71, bott Jan 08 **(89.5) n23 t22.5 f21.5 b22.5.** Few Speysiders appear to embrace old age with such open arms as DD. *46.2%. Douglas Laing. 151 bottles.*

Old Malt Cask Dallas Dhu Aged 36 Years refill hogshead, cask no. 3802, dist Mar 71, bott Aug 07 **(82) n21 t20.5 f20 b20.5.** Heads in the direction of exotic fruit, but doesn't quite have the legs to get there. *42.3%. nc ncf. Douglas Laing. 181 bottles.*

Old Malt Cask Dallas Dhu Aged 37 Years refill hogshead, cask no. 3927, dist Apr 70, bott Nov 07 **(93) n24 t23.5 f22.5 b23.** A malt which simply defies its enormous age. Just how much longer we'll be able to find gems like this from the distillery is anyone's guess. *50%. nc ncf.*

DALMORE
Highand (northern), 1839. Whyte and Mackay. Working.

The Dalmore 12 Years Old db **(90) n22** mixed dates: both dry and juicy; **t23** fat, rich delivery with a wonderful dovetailing of juicy barley and thick, rumbling fruit; **f22.5** lots of toffee on the finish, but gets away with it thanks to the sheer depth to the barley and the busy sherry sub-plot; **b22.5** has changed character of late yet remains underpowered and with a shade too much toffee. But such is the quality of the malt in its own right it can overcome any hurdles placed before it to ensure a real mouth-filling, rumbustious dram. *40%*

⋅⋰⋅ **The Dalmore Dee Dram 12 Years Old** db **(63.5) n15.5 t17 f14 b16.** Words fail me...*40%*

The Dalmore 15 Years Old db **(83.5) n21 t21 f20.5 b21.** Another pleasant Dalmore that coasts along the runway but simply fails to get off the ground. The odd off note here and there, but it's the blood orange which shines brightest. *40%*

⋅⋰⋅ **The Dalmore 18 Years Old** db **(76.5) n19 t21 f18 b18.5.** Heaps of caramel and the cask choice might have been better. *43%*

The Dalmore 21 Years Old db **(87) n22** just how many citrus notes can we find here? Answers on a postcard … on second thoughts, don't. Just beautifully light and effervescent for its age: a genuine delight; **t23** again, wonderfully fruity though this time the malt pushes through confidently to create its own chewy island: fabulous texture; **f20** simplifies towards toffee slightly too much in the interests of great balance. A lovely coffee flourish late on; **b22** bottled elegance. *43%*

The Dalmore Forty Years Old db **(82) n23 t20 f19 b20.** Doubtless my dear friend Richard Paterson will question whether I have the ability to spot a good whisky if it ran me over in a ten ton truck. But I have to say here that we have a disappointing malt: I had left this too late on in writing this year's (2008) Bible as a treat. But it wasn't to be. A soft delivery: but of what? Hard to exactly pin down what's going on here as there is so much toffee and fruit that the oak and barley have been overwhelmed. Pleasant, perhaps, but it's all rather dull and passionless. Like going through the motions with an old lover. Adore the sherry-trifle/toffee mousse nose, though... *40%*

The Dalmore 50 Years Old db **(88) n21** buxom and bourbony, the oak makes no secret of the antiquity; **t19** oak again arrives first and without apology, some salty malt creaking in later. Ripe cherries offer a mouthwatering backdrop; **f25** comes into its own as harmony is achieved as the oak quietens to allow a beautiful malt-cherry interplay. Spices arrive for good measure in an absolutely has-it-all, faultless finish: really as much a privilege to taste as a delight; **b23** takes a while to warm up, but when it does becomes a genuinely classy and memorable dram befitting one of the world's great and undervalued distilleries. *52%*

⋅⋰⋅ **The Dalmore Candela Aged 50 Years** db **(96) n25** there you go: that's the next half hour to 45 minutes taken up...trying to unravel this one. Fresh fruity frame, but the picture in the middle is far more difficult to understand. Dates – both dried and juicy – mingle with finest quality Lubec marzipan paste (sans chocolate) while a few spices nip in to say 'hullo'; clean, relaxed...and very sprightly for its age; **t24** immediate onrush of oaks, offset by a cherry sauce and later plain chocolate fondant to ensure any bitterness is kept in check; elsewhere an improbable layering of barley juice and fruit again makes a mockery of the age; **f23.5** for a whisky reaching half a century, curiously reserved with the oaks now really starting to get a degree of bitterness generated; a thin line of chocolate and raisin helps keep that bitterness at acceptable levels; **b23.5** just one of those whiskies which you come across only a handful of times in your life. All because a malt makes it to 50 does not mean it will automatically be great. This, however, is a masterpiece, the end of which seemingly has never been written... *50% (bottled at 45%) Whyte & Mackay. 77 bottles.*

⋅⋰⋅ **The Dalmore Selene 58 Years Old** cask no. 1781/1782 dist Jun 51 db **(87.5) n23** the oak let's you know it has been around a while; eggnog and spiced spotted dick make an unlikely backdrop combination; **t22** the oak bites with a viciousness that is enough to cause the eyes to close; the middle ground fills with chocolate caramel and spices begin to really kick in; **f21** tired and monumentally oaky but enough natural caramels to ensure a light finish; the spices keeps the whisky ticking pleasantly **b21.5** a fascinating experience, but in terms of quality, though very good indeed for its range alone, not in the same league as the Dalmore 50 or 60-y-o. A great present for anyone born in 1951, or supporters of Queen of the South marking the 60th anniversary of their winning the Scottish Div 2 title. But as a whisky spectacle: great nose, decent delivery and then after that...you are on your own. *44% Whyte & Mackay. 30 bottles.*

The Dalmore 62 Years Old db **(95) n23** PM or REV marked demerara potstill rum, surely? Massive coffee presence, clean and enormous, stunning, topdrawer peat just to round things off; **t25** this is brilliant: pure silk wrapping fabulous moist fruitcake soaked in finest oloroso sherry then weighed with peat which somehow has defied nature and survived in cask all these years. I really cannot fault this: I sit here stunned and in awe; **f24** perfect spices with flecks of ginger and lemon rind; **b24** if I am just half as beautiful, elegant and fascinating as this by the time I reach 62, I'll be a happy man. Somehow I doubt it. A once-in-a-lifetime whisky – something that comes around every 62 years, in fact. Forget Dalmore Cigar Malt – even I might be tempted to start smoking just to get a full bottle of this. *40.5%*

The Dalmore 1263 King Alexander III db **(86) n22 t22.5 f20 b21.5.** Starts brightly with all kinds of barley sugar, fruit and decent age and oak combinations, plus some excellent spice prickle. So far, so good...and obviously thoughtfully and complexly structured. But then vanishes without trace on finish. *40%*

The Dalmore 1974 db **(83.5) n23) n22 t21 f20 b20.5.** Extremely odd whisky: on one hand there is a big fruity thrust, presumably from sherry, on the other is over-tired oak. It's a bit of a mess as balance is never quite attained. There are enough highlights in this muddle to make for an interesting experience. Definitely different. *42%*

The Dalmore 1980 db **(81.5) n19 t21 f20.5 b21.** Wonderful barley intensity on delivery does its best to overcome the so-so nose and finale. *40%*

⋰∴ **The Dalmore 1981 Amoroso Sherry Finesse** amoroso sherry wood cask db **(85.5) n21 t22 f21.5 b21.** A very tight, fruity, dram which gives away its secrets with all the enthusiasm of an agent under torture. Enjoyable to a degree...but bloody hard work. *42%*

⋰∴ **The Dalmore Mackenzie 1992** American oak/port pipes, bott 2009 db **(88.5) n23** a dripping nose: dripping of fresh grape juice, that is. Mostly clean, with a slow unveiling of delicate spices and further fruit notes, especially a well disguised kiwi; really very seductive, indeed... **t22** on one level a sharp, almost metallic delivery, crushed fruit stone, at first finding it hard to hit a rhythm; on the other, immediately soft, creamy and luxuriant. Finally some vanillas get a grip and the fruit now has somewhere to go; **f21** after a short bitter burst, settles towards a gentle sherry trifle finale; a late furry bitterness develops.... **b22.5** I suppose you could say that such is the influence of the grape that this is a tad one dimensional. But such is the grim state of wine casks in the industry today, one is forgiven for falling on bended knee and kissing the bottle. Though even this isn't without its sulphury failings... *46%*

The Dalmore Cabernet Sauvignon db **(79) n22 t19 f19 b19**. Too intense and soupy for its own good. *45%*

Dalmore The Gran Reserva db **(78.5) n22 t19.5 f18 b19**. Pleasantish, but after tasting this against the Adelphi bottling...well, it's a bit of a miss-match to put it politely. Writing this on the men's Final's Day at Wimbledon, it is like pitting Roger Federer against Baldrick. As for the finish...well, is there one...? *40%*

Adelphi Dalmore 1990 Aged 17 Years sherry butt, cask no. 7327, dist 90, bott 07 **(95) n24 t24 f23 b24.** Truly magnificent, un-sulphur-blemished sherried whiskies are now so rare, that when one like this turns up it automatically hits classic status. One of the finest sherry bottlings I have come across in a very long time. I feel the hand of Gonzalez Byass at work here, and somehow one of their very finest got away... *59.7%. 590 bottles.*

⋰∴ **A.D. Rattray Dalmore 1999** cask no. 3080 **(86.5) n21.5 t23 f20.5 b21.5**. With all that intense malt and gooseberry running about, there will be a few blenders wanting to get their hands on this stuff. *59.1 A.D. Rattray Ltd*

Berrys' Own Selection Dalmore 1997 cask nos. 16634/16635, bott 07 **(88.5) n22 t22.5 f22 b22.** About as sweet as you can take - a very good whisky. *46%. Berry Bros & Rudd.*

Chester Whisky & Liquer Co. Dalmore Aged 10 Years dist 99 **(84) n21.5 t21.5 f21 b20.** Evidence of feints backed up by the oiliness and near black hole-like mass of this blighter. Prisoners barely taken as the molten Rollo toffee/chocolate sticks to all corners of the palate. Enjoyable and fun, but not without its flaws and hardly one for the purest. *54.8%*

Chieftain's Dalmore Aged 10 Years hogshead **(78) n19 t21 f19 b19**. A bit of a sweaty armpit nose and the malt meanders aimlessly, if sweetly and fruitily, around the palate. *58%.*

⦂⦂ **Chieftain's Dalmore 13 Years Old Pinot Noir Finish** dist Jun 96, bott 2010 **(94)** n23 a curious phenol note to this is neither peaty nor coal-dusty. But it appears to give the grape an extra degree of weight and thrust. Some lovely bourbony sweetness to this, too; **t24** a deliciously schizophrenic and stunning delivery: on one hand it appears light and incapable of complexity, yet elsewhere moody barley grows in intensity and the fruits begin to thicken wonderfully; **f23.5** long and lingers with a tingling but profound spiciness that tags on to the ever intensifying barley; there is an unusual coffee and cola union towards the finish. But this is ground-breaking stuff all the way... **b23.5** bravo!! A wine finish which appears be in total sympathy with the malt. Not sure whether to drink it or mount it on the wall.... Definitely worth hunting down as this is a minor classic in its own right. *56.7% nc ncf Ian Macleod*

⦂⦂ **Chieftain's Dalmore Aged 14 Years Rum Finish** dist Dec 95, bott 2010 **(85.5)** n22 t21 **f21.5 b21.** A very tight example of rum at work. Usually you get a clipped sugary style. Here a dry Demerara-style cask appears to have been used which happily squeezes every spare bit of sweetness out of it, even though there a few oils to spare. Conservative, enjoyable and just a little bit different. *46% Ian Macleod*

Connoisseurs Choice Dalmore 1992 (81) n20 t21 f20 b20. Sweet, sticky and spiced, without offering much in the way of form or format. Not the distillery at its finest. *40%.*

Duncan Taylor Collection Dalmore 1990 Aged 17 Years cask no. 7325 **(93)** n22.5 t24 f23 **b23.5.** Enough to make you swoon. Genuinely underlines the greatness of the Dalmore in a way the distillery bottlings sadly, these days, very rarely do. *55.5%*

Duncan Taylor Collection Dalmore 1990 Aged 17 Years cask no. 7328 **(89)** n23 t22 f22 **b22.** Slightly tight but that can mean some serious pleasure along the way.... *56.9%*

Duncan Taylor Collection Dalmore 1990 cask no. 7329 **(87)** n22 gosh! Now there's a nose: a fleck of lavender further invigorates the weighty oiled and sugared vanilla; **t23** sweetly spiced; again the oils from a generous, shall we say daring, cut give this malt a real wide body, allowing the malt to stick to the palate for a real chew; **f20.5** the downside to the slight feints kick in with the odd, flawed wobble on the barley; **b21.5** brimming with esters and quite a few acceptable feints and spice this is absolutely enormous whisky which might equally appeal to rum freaks. *56.7%*

Old Malt Cask Dalmore Aged 19 Years dist Apr 90, bott Jul 09 **(83)** n20 t22 f21 b20. Pleasant but perhaps over sweet. *50%. Douglas Laing.*

Old Malt Cask Dalmore Aged 32 Years refill hogshead dist Dec 76, Apr 09 **(94)** n23 nutty, green fig and fresh boxwood: soft, sublime and even boasting a whiff of smoke; **t24** brilliant delivery of the highest standard: the malt is thick but delicate enough to show its fresh, juicy colours; soft spices intermingle with the muscovado sugars; mildly overcooked butterscotch tart; **f23** natural caramels abound, but in no way interfere with the further development of that now very crisp barley; **b24** quite a triumph of age over probability. Oh, if only the distillery bottlings were regularly this fresh and breathtaking. *50%. Douglas Laing. 306 bottles.*

Old Masters Dalmore Aged 12 Years cask no. 5603, dist 97, bott 09 **(90)** n22 minty with huge clean, intense barley and leather back up; **t23** salivating and deliciously sharp on delivery it then heads off on many quieter paths including liquorice-honey, muscovado sugar and something involving mocha with a sprig of mint; **f22.5** chocolate mint chip; **b22.5** if they were to make a Scottish Mint Julip... *59.8%. James MacArthur & Co. Ltd.*

Scotch Malt Whisky Society Cask 13.41 Aged 11 Years refill butt, dist Dec 96 **(62)** n16 **t16.5 f14 b15.5.** I absolutely dread to think how bad the sulphur must have been first time round...one can assume only that the chairman of the panel was getting "citrus"... *62.4%*

DALWHINNIE
Highlands (central), 1898. Diageo. Working.

Dalwhinnie 15 Years Old db **(95)** n24 sublime stuff: a curious mixture of coke smoke and peat-reek wafts teasingly over the gently honied malt. A hint of melon offers some fruit but the caressing malt stars; **t24** that rarest of combinations: at once silky and malt intense, yet at the same time peppery and tin-hat time for the tastebuds, but the silk wins out and a sheen of barley sugar coats everything, soft peat included; **f23** some cocoa and coffee notes, yet the pervading slightly honied sweetness means that there is no bitterness that cannot be controlled; **b24** a malt it is hard to decide whether to drink or bath in: I suggest you do both. One of the most complete mainland malts of them all. Know anyone who reckons they don't like whisky? Give them a glass of this – that's them cured. Oh, if only the average masterpiece could be this good. *43%*

Dalwhinnie Aged 17 Years Distiller's Edition finished in oloroso casks, dist 90, bott 07 db **(83.5)** n23 t21 f19.5 b20. Yes, very pleasant and all that. And the nose really does radiate some finer, deftly smoked, honey tones. But the oloroso does a pretty thorough job of flattening out the development on the palate. Enjoyable, certainly. But I'd just love to know what this was like had the grape not become involved. *43%*

DEANSTON
Highland (Perthshire), 1966. Burn Stewart. Working.

Deanston 6 Years Old db (83) n20 t21 f22 b20. Great news for those who remember how good Deanston was a decade or two ago: it's on its way back. A delightfully clean dram with its trademark honey character restored. A little beauty slightly undermined by caramel. *40%*

Deanston 12 Years Old db (74) n18 t19 f18.5 b18.5. It is quite bizarre how you can interchange this with Tobermory in style; or, rather, at least the faults are the same. *46%. ncf.*

⋰⋱ **Deanston Aged 12 Years Un-Chill Filtered** db (71) n18 t18 f17 b18. Someone told me I would enjoy this new version of Deanston 12 far more than the old un-chill filtered one, which I didn't care for at all. They were wrong. *46.3%*

Deanston Aged 12 Years Un-Chill Filtered db (84.5) n21 t21.5 f21 b21 A decent, attractive Deanston which is a definite step in the right direction. Nutty for sure, but some attractive barley sweetness flits about the palate. A wide cut at work here, one feels, but plenty to chew on. *46.3%*

Deanston 1967 casks 1051-2, filled Friday 31st Mar 67 db (90) n23 the very faintest hint of peat rubs shoulders with high fluting honey and polished pine floors; t23 the loud oak influence is perfectly tempered by rich barley concentrate. Sweet towards the middle with hints of honey and peat; f21 spiced and softening towards vanilla; b23 the oak is full on but there is so much class around that cannot gain control. A Perthshire beauty. *50.7%*

⋰⋱ **Deanston Virgin Oak** db (90) n22.5 does exactly what it says on the tin: absolutely brimming with virgin oak. To the cost of all other characteristics. And don't expect a bourbon style for a second: this is sharp-end tannins where the sugars have their own syrupy point of entry; t23 now those sugars dissolve with some major oak attached: many years back, I tasted a paste made from roasted acorns and brown sugar....not entirely dissimilar; f22.5 continues to rumble contentedly in the oakiest possible manner....but now with some fizzy spice; b22 quirky. Don't expect this to taste anything like Scotch... *46.3%*

Old Malt Cask Deanston Aged 12 Years refill hogshead, cask no. 4422, dist Mar 86, bott Jun 08 (75.5) n18.5 t20 f18.5 b18.5. A rare chance at commercial level to analyse a single cask of a malt not remotely happy with itself. The delightful, sweet malt fanfare on delivery apart, it groans its off-key discontent at every chance. *50%. Douglas Laing.*

⋰⋱ **Old Malt Cask Deanston Aged 15 Years** refill butt DL 6043, dist Jun 94, bott Apr 10 (76) n18 t21 f18 b19. Huge, almost immeasurable, barley. But found technically wanting. *50% nc ncf Douglas Laing & Co Ltd. 391 bottles.*

Old Malt Cask Deanston Aged 16 Years refill hogshead, dist Dec 92, bott Mar 09 (90) n21.5 honey scraped onto pencil shavings; t23.5 hick honey mingles superbly with spices and marmalade; juicy and pulsing with sweet barley; f22.5 good length, the oils calming and soft butterscotch drifts off with the vanillas; b23 distinctly a cut above for this distillery of late: indeed, much more what this place was about 20-odd years ago. *50%. 330 bottles.*

DUFFTOWN
Speyside, 1898. Diageo. Working.

Singleton of Dufftown 12 Years Old db (71) n18 t18 f17 b18. A roughhouse malt that's finesse-free. For those who like their tastebuds Dufft up a bit... *40%*

Cadenhead's Dufftown Aged 19 Years sherry butt, dist 88, bott Feb 08 (86) n21.5 t22 f21 b21.5. Dufftown at its friendliest. Enough sugar to give a an area the size of Wales diabetes, perhaps. But by this distillery's usually duff standards, there is something enjoyable here, especially on the bourbony nose, an impressive theme it keeps going to the very last. A must-get bottling. *53.5%. 243 bottles.*

Cadenhead's Dufftown Aged 31 Years dist 78, bott 09 (84) n21.5 t21.5 f21 b20. No surprise about the syrupy fruit. Behaves itself to offer a pleasant chewy dram. *48.6%*

⋰⋱ **Connoisseurs Choice Dufftown 1997** (81) n20 t22 f21 b21. Sticky, syrupy and one-dimensional for sure. But the malt is rich and intact. Not at all bad. Indeed, honestly enjoyable. *43% Gordon & MacPhail*

⋰⋱ **The Golden Cask Dufftown 1979** cask no. CM144, bott 2009 (77) n19 t22 f17 b19. No matter how golden the cask is, if it's from Dufftown chances are it's going to be a little tarnished. *54.8% The House of MacDuff. 282 bottles.*

⋰⋱ **Kingsbury's "The Selection" Dufftown 7 Years Old 1999** (81) n19 t21 f20 b21. Big oils, intense malt, hints of Demerara and, in this form, quite decent fun. *43% Japan Import System*

Old Malt Cask Collection Dufftown Aged 14 Years refill butt, dist Aug 94, bott Oct 08 **(84.5) n19 t22 f21.5 b21.** Syrupy and spicy. Faintly trashy and certainly not one to take home to your parents, but some nice curves in some of the right places and a sweet heart. *50%.*

Old Malt Cask Collection Dufftown Aged 28 Years sherry cask, dist May 80, bott Oct 08 **(80) n18 t22 f21 b19.** An outrageous dram. Rumbustious, rollicking, uncouth, more oak than a Henry VIII battleship and a few more explosions, too. And dirtier than the filthiest Jolly Jack Tar. But for its myriad faults, it's fun, by gum! 50%. Douglas Laing. *302 bottles.*

Old Malt Cask Dufftown Aged 30 Years refill hogshead, dist Mar 77, bott Apr 07 **(82) n22 t21 f20 b20.** A bit on the hot side it may be, but one can only admire how it's kept its truculent attitude after all these years. *50%. Douglas Laing. 303 bottles.*

Private Cellar Dufftown 1985 bott 07 **(88.5) n23 t23 f20.5 b22.** OK, it's happened: a Dufftown I like. I'll turn a blind eye to the rough landing; but eually I can't praise the nose and delivery highly enough. Good stuff!! *43%. Speyside Distillers.*

⠿ **Provenance Dufftown Over 11 Years** rum finished cask no. DMG 5169, dist Autumn 1997, bott Spring 2009 **(74) n18 t19 f18 b19.** Malty, a tad spicy but always muddled. A little too nutty for its own good. *46% nc ncf Douglas Laing & Co Ltd*

Provenance Dufftown Aged 12 Years Sherry Finish dist winter 95, bott winter 07 **(86) n21 t22 f21 b22.** From a distillery that is so often a dud, this has more than its fair share of charming, even delicate, moments in a very attractive clean barley theme – despite the sherry intervention. And it's not often you can say that – with or without the sherry! *46%*

EDRADOUR
Highland (Perthshire), 1837. Signatory. Working.
Edradour Aged 10 Years db **(79) n18 t20 f22 b19.** A dense, fat malt that tries offer something along the sherry front but succeeds mainly in producing a whisky cloyingly sweet and unfathomable. Some complexity to the finish compensates. *43%*

Edradour Ballachin #1 The Burgundy Casks db **(63) n17 t16 f15 b15.** A bitter disappointment in every sense. Were the Burgundy casks sulphur treated? I'd say so. Something completely off-key here. A shocker. *46%*

Edradour Ballachin #2 Madeira Matured db **(89) n22** stonking peat which takes absolutely no prisoners; **t22** if there was any fruit there it is soon crushed by the intense smoke; **f23** a fleeting degree of something fruity; **b22** on the nose and entry I didn't quite get the point here: putting a massively peated malt like this in a Madeira cask is a bit like putting Stan Laural into bed with Marylyn Munro. Thankfully doesn't come out a fine mess and the Madeira certainly has a vital say towards the beautifully structured finale. It works! I feel the hand of a former Laphroaig man at work here. *46%*

FETTERCAIRN
Highland (Eastern), 1824. Whyte and Mackay. Working.
Fettercairn 12 Year Old db **(66) n14 t19 f16 b17.** If the nose doesn't get you, what follows probably will...Grim doesn't quite cover it. *40%*

Fettercairn 1824 db **(69) n17 t19 f16 b17.** By Fettercairn standards, not a bad offering. Relatively free from its inherent sulphury and rubbery qualities, this displays a sweet nutty character not altogther unattractive – though caramel plays a calming role here. Need my arm twisting for a second glass, though. *40%*

Old Malt Cask Fettercairn Aged 33 Years (85.5) n19 t23 f22 b21.5. Funny how some malts get better as they reach their Darby and Joan years. Some 23 years ago, I probably would not have much enjoyed the experience, sampling this as a 10-year-old. And whilst this has some distinctly weird and rough edges, it also now possesses serious character, too. Certainly, there is a charming fruitiness and silky delivery which is worth the entrance fee alone. As are the spices and balancing sweetness. *50%*

The Whisky Agency Fettercairn 34 Year Old dist 75, bott 09 **(75.5) n18 t17.5 f21 b19.** A sweet, nutty finish compensates for some of the earlier crimes against the tastebuds. *57%.*

GLEN ALBYN
Highland (Northern) 1846–1983. Demolished.
Old Malt Cask Glen Albyn 35 Years Old dist 26 Sep 69, bott Jul 05 **(90) n24** a star-studded aroma for something this ancient: the oak weaves delicate vanilla patterns around the apple-honey-barley lead. As aromas go, a veritable gold nugget for its age; **t23** early barley absolutely rips through the tastebuds helped along the way by a glossy sweetness and a puff of smoke and cocoa; **f21** the drying oak lays claim with tolerable force; **b22** understandable signs of longevity, but overall this is simply wonderful. *50%. Douglas Laing. 229 bottles.*

Rarest of the Rare Glen Albyn 1979 cask no. 3960, dist Dec 79, bott Mar 06 **(91) n23** melon and barley play host to a clever, nose-nipping spiciness. So relaxed: supreme confidence here; **t23** the incredibly fresh, salivating barley intertwines with glorious vanilla to give a drier tier to the delicately sweet malt; **f22** some chalky vanilla and mocha but the barley holds true; **b23** of Scotland's disappearing malts, this is going with flourish. *57.3%. Duncan Taylor. 244 bottles.*

GLENALLACHIE
Speyside, 1968. Chivas. Working.

Glenallachie 15 Years Old Distillery Edition db **(81) n20 t21 f19 b19**. Real battle between nature and nurture: an exceptional sherry butt has silk gloves and honied marzipan, while a hot-tempered bruiser lurks beneath. *58%*

⋅∺⋅ **Adelphi Glenallachie 1973 Aged 36 Years** bourbon hogshead, cask no. 1873, bott 2010 **(95.5) n24** wears exotic fruit of antiquity like a Lord wears his robes. An injection of green apple takes it away from the norm for these kind of old whiskies, suggesting a devilment and youth which, frankly, it never sported in the years it originally had the chance; here's a surprise though; a playful few molecules of peat...; **t23.5** silky and soft, as opposed to steely and hard when a quarter of a century younger. There is a buzz nipping at the back of the throat suggesting great composure and spice; in fact it is the distillery bite which no number of years can even out. But in these lush surroundings it now works rather well; **f24** graceful and long, retaining that rock-hard exoskeleton, but inside it softens as that light peat returns with charming degrees of cocoa, vanilla and barley. Not a bitter note; not a single hint of disharmony....astonishing.... **b24** a whisky which really makes you laugh inwardly and outwardly. Like nearby Caperdonich, this malt was way too harsh and thin for enjoyment in its prime years. Now in great age, it takes on the Elder Statesman mantle like to the warehouse born. Some whiskies are born great. Some achieve greatness. Others have greatness thrust upon them (usually by marketing departments). Trust me when I tell you that this one fluked it. But hats off to a 24 carat stunner all the same...and what a way to bring up my 500th new whisky of the 2011 Bible...!!! *48.1% 201 bottles.*

Cadenhead's Authentic Collection Glenallachie Aged 17 Years dist 89, bott Feb 07 **(88) n22 t23 f21 b22**. The best Glenallachie bottled? Certainly I have never tasted a superior expression and for once I have to say this is a malt that unquestionably delights. *58.5%.*

The Cärn Mör Vintage Collection Braes of Glenallachie 1992 barrel, cask no. 587, dist 92, bott 09 **(82) n20 t21 f21 b20**. Thin and malty in the typical house style. No off notes, but no real development, either. *46%. The Scottish Liqueur Centre.*

Dewar Rattray Glenallachie 1995 cask no. 1258, dist Mar 95, bott Nov 07 **(85.5) n21 t22 f21.5 b21.** I'm as shocked as I am impressed. A few years back the distillery manager of Glenallachie told me that he thought it was capable of producing pretty decent whisky. The look I gave him was the kind of double take Laurel and Hardy stooge James Finlayson would have been proud of. Well, just as Stan Laurel once famously did, perhaps its time for me to eat my hat. 'Cos this aint half bad. Not great, just not bad. I thought tasting this at 60% abv would see me rushed to hospital with my throat ripped out. Not a bit of it: the malt is intense and clean and although asking for complexity on top might be taking the piss, you just can't deny that this is one enjoyable, ultra malty dram. Half eaten hats off to Glenallachie. *60.7%*

Duncan Taylor The NC2 Range Glenallachie 1995 **(82.5) n21 t20 f21.5 b20**. Fortune favours the brave, obviously!! I had thought about the prospects of suing DT for the likely disintegration of my teeth on tasting this bottling. But instead I found a genuinely friendly malt, not the usual jet fuel one associates with this distillery, which clearly basks in its simplistic role as a pure maltfest. *46%*

⋅∺⋅ **The John Milroy Selection Glenallachie 11 Years Old** hogshead, dist 1999, bott 2010 **(84.5) n20.5 t22 f21 b21**. Clean, malty blending fodder this may be but you cannot but marvel at the degree of vanilla. *56.4% Berry Bros & Rudd*

Old Malt Cask Glenallachie Aged 38 Years dist Feb 71, bott May 09 **(72) n20 t17 f17.5 b17.5**. I don't think they had quite got to grips with the stills 38 years ago, or the casks: typical of the period in being spectacularly off key almost to the point of vulgarity. *50%.*

Provenance Glenallachie Aged 9 Years refill hogshead, dist spring 99, bott autumn 08 **(79) n20.5 t20.5 f19 b19.** Clean, malty, gristy, slightly yeasty, well made, under-matured (from the point of view of being in an over-aged cask) blending fodder. *46%. Douglas Laing.*

GLENBURGIE
Speyside, 1810. Chivas. Working.

Glenburgie Aged 15 Years bott code L00/129 db **(84) n22 t23 f19 b20**. Doing so well until the spectacularly flat, bitter finish. Orangey citrus and liquorice had abounded. *46%*

Duncan Taylor The NC2 Range Glenburgie 1996 Aged 11 Years (86.5) n22 t22 f21.5 b21. Youthful, slightly raw, ultra-clean...the barley appears to be gleaming on both nose and palate. Superficial development, perhaps, but as a good old fashioned slap around the tastebuds...well, it doesn't come much better! 46%

⇜ **The Golden Cask Glenburgie 1983** cask no. CM145 (92.5) n23 burned honeycomb infused with crushed leaves; earthy and floral; t23.5 punchy delivery, again with a touch of honey but also red liquorice and muscovado sugar; teasing Danish marzipan plays with the spices; f23 fruitier finale, sharp and full of vigour to the very chocolatey end; b23 I have been well known over the years for telling people at tastings that Burgie is a malt which Allied should have done much more with when they owned it. And I hoped Chivas would now open doors for it. Grab a bottle of this, and you'll see why.... 57.7% The House of MacDuff. 224 bottles.

Gordon & MacPhail Distillery Label Glenburgie 10 Years Old (77) n20 t20 f18 b19. Sweet, toffeed and dull. 40%

Gordon & MacPhail Rare Vintage Glenburgie 1963 (86) n20.5 t22 f22.5 b21.5. For all its chewiness and enormity, as lovely as the spiced fruit and liquorice is: you can't get over the fact that just a too much oak has entered the system. Still, those lingering coffee and walnut cake notes are a delight. 43%

⇜ **Kingsbury's Hand Writing Label Glenburgie 23 Years Old** dist 1980 (89) n23 earthy, even with a touch of grated carrot. But all aroma roads lead to something a touch bourbony; t23 profoundly juicy despite the big bourbony oak statement with honey-softened hickory filling the middle ground; f21 dries in the manner expected; b22 I can see this doing some great work in an older blend as this is multi-faceted. Even as a singleton, and despite the age impact, it is a busy little gem. 54.4% Japan Import System

⇜ **Old Malt Cask Glenburgie Aged 20 Years** dist Sep 89 (90) n22 mid range barley with excellent oak-sugar balance; t23 just stunning delivery with the most mouth-watering of Speyside deliveries; the fifth and sixth flavour waves are uncluttered citrus; f22.5 custardy vanillas and powdery oak; b22.5 one of the great Speyside distilleries deserving a much wider field of appreciation. Well done, Laing brothers, for giving people a chance to discover this little gem. 50% Douglas Laing

Old Malt Cask Glenburgie Aged 20 Years dist May 89, bott Jul 09 (91) n22 butterscotch, but with a touch of the antique about it.. t23 supremely juicy with a huge charge of barley rolling back the years; a grassy, sugary sweetness compliments perfectly; f22.5 drier, spicier, subtler; b22.5 hardly a gray hair...! 50% Douglas Laing

⇜ **Provenance Glenburgie Over 11 Years** refill hogshead no. DMG 6001, dist Autumn 1998, bott Spring 2010 (86) n21.5 t22 f212 b21.5. Coats the taste buds in barley with a trowel. Juicy and lively all the way. 46% nc ncf Douglas Laing & Co Ltd

Provenance Glenburgie Aged 12 Years refill hogshead, dist spring 96, bott autumn 08 (81) n20.5 t21.5 f19 b19. Pear-drops, anyone? 46%. Douglas Laing.

GLENCADAM

Highland (Eastern), 1825. Angus Dundee. Working.

Glencadam Aged 10 Years db (95) n24 crystal clarity to the sharp, ultra fresh barley. Clean, uncluttered by excessive oak, the apparent lightness is deceptive; the intensity of the malt carries its own impressive weight and the citrus note compliments rather than thins. Enticing; t24 immediately zingy and eye-wateringly salivating with a fabulous layering of sweet barley. Equally delicate oak chimes in to ensure a lightly spiced balance and a degree of attitude; f23 longer than the early barley freshness would have you expecting, with soft oils ensuring an extended, tapering malty edge to the gentle, clean oak; b24 sophisticated, sensual, salivating and seemingly serene, this malt is all about juicy barley and balance. Just bristles with character and about as puckeringly elegant as single malt gets....and even thirst-quenching. My God: the guy who put this one together must be a genius, or something... 46%

⇜ **Glencadam Aged 12 Years Portwood Finish** db (89.5) n22.5 oaky vanillas manage to shape this attractively while delicate, clean grape bends this towards a subtle fruit and custard effect: soft, playful and teasing; t22.5 attractive marriage of those drier vanillas promised on the nose with that fragile fruit; for all the softness there is a playful nip to be had, too; a youngish barley flashes keenly about the taste buds; f22 a rumble of prickly spice and cocoa but that clean fruit, as light as it is, lasts the distance; b22.5 after coming across a few disappointing Port finishes in recent weeks, just wonderful to experience one as you would hope and expect it to be. 46%

⇜ **Glencadam Aged 14 Years Oloroso Sherry Cask Finish** bott May 10 db (95) n24 pinch me: I'm dreaming. Oloroso exactly how it should be: classically clean with a dovetailing of dry and sweeter grape notes which are weighty, but not heavy enough to crush the lighter barley and vanillas from adding to the sumptuous and elegant mix; **t23.5** mouth-filling with firstly fat grape then a second flavour round of spices and custardy vanillas; **f24** much drier now with the accent on the barley but still that light spice persists, actually increasing in weight and effect as it goes along; **b23.5** what a total treat. Restores one's faith in Oloroso whilst offering more than a glimpse of the most charming infusion of fruit imaginable. *46%*

Glencadam Aged 15 Years db **(90.5) n22.5** soft kumquats mingle with the even softer barley. A trace of drier mint and chalk dust points towards the shy oak. Harmonious and dovetails beautifully; **t23** sharp, juicy barley - almost fruity - fuses with sharper oak. The mouth-watering house style appears to fatten out as gentle oils emerge and then give way for a spicy middle; **f22** long, with those teasing, playful spices pepping up the continued barley theme. Dries as a 15 year old ought but the usual bitterness is kept in check by the prevailing malt; **b23** the spices keep the taste buds on full alert but the richness and depth of the barley defies the years. Another exhibition of Glencadam's understated elegance. Some more genius malt creation.... *46%*

Glencadam Aged 15 Years db **(84) n19 t22 f22 b21.** The first distillery-bottled Glencadam I can remember thanks to new owners and the brakes are never taken off. The middle and early finale are really quite sublime with that glorious malt-intense signature that offers the kind of irresistible drive and style to the tastebuds that Frank Lampard gives to Chelsea...and it's worth getting just for that. But something, a roasty caramel maybe, is holding back on the start and finish: oh, what might have been! Delicious all the same! *40%*

⬩⬥ **Glencadam Aged 21 Years "The Exceptional"** bott May 10 db **(81) n21.5 t22 f17.5 b20.** For a little distillery with a reputation for producing a more delicate malt this is one big whisky. Sadly, the finish is out of kilter, for the delivery is a knife and fork job, offering some extraordinary variations on a fudgy-maple syrup theme which promises much. *46%*

Glencadam 25 Years Old Single Cask cask no. 1002, dist Apr 83, bott Dec 08 db **(76.5) n20.5 t21 f16 b19.** One of those "oh what might have been" casks. Or, if you are German or Swiss, one of the best experiences you will have for a very long time. Those who can't pick up sulphur will have a new love in their lives. The rest of us will continue to sob quietly.... *46%*

Cadenhead's Authentic Collection Glencadam Aged 25 Years bourbon hogshead, dist 82, bott Sep 07 **(87.5) n22 t21 f21 b21.5.** Starts beautifully but naturally tails off. A lovely experience, though. *51.2%. 150 bottles.*

⬩⬥ **Glencadam Single Cask 1978** cask no. 2335, bott no. 554, dist Apr 78, bott Mar 09 db **(93.5) n24** this is very much how a sherry cask should be. Regard: intense nutty fruitcake. You will observe the dappling effect of the spices. Note how this gives great vitality to the whisky after 30 years and the manner in which none of the constituent parts dominate. For those who have joined the whisky industry in the last 15 years, please also take note that contrary to what you may think is the norm and perfectly acceptable, sulphur is playing no part in the proceedings; **t24** melt-in-the mouth grape. The controlled muscovado and juicy date sweetness fuse and allow a build up of playful spice and vanillas; natural caramels seep into the mix, as does a biscuity malt character; **f22.5** despite the grape's enormity, there is still room for the oak to flourish and, mingling with the grape, creating a blood orange bitterness to balance with the continuing sugars; **b23.5** a fabulous distillery which is coming out of the shadows since its confidence-sapping Allied days and is now putting Brechin on the map. Its secret is that the malt is of a consistently high standard; one willing and able to get the best out of any cask type used. Some malts can't handle sherry, failing to get their personality across. This one appears able to do just that without batting an eyelid. *46% nc ncf 615 bottles*

Connoisseurs Choice Glencadam 1987 (87.5) n23 fulsome and fruity with a distinctive blood orange and grape theme; **t22** silky delivery with malt and fruit dished out in equal measures; the house spice kicks in playfully and enlivens the chalky middle; **f21** lots of spice still, but lightly duller at the death as the cocoa bites; **b21.5** charming and fruity. *43%.*

Dewar Rattray Glencadam 1990 cask no. 5981, dist Oct 90, bott Nov 07 **(86.5) n21.5 t22 f21.5 b21.5.** Hot whisky from some charmless oak. But, oddly enough, the fire and brimstone personality works amazingly well with the barley. *59.6%*

Dun Bheagan Glencadam 20 Years Old Hogshead (80) n20 t19 f21 b20. For all its age it remains hot stuff. The honey influence will win friends, though. *48%*

Montgomerie's Glencadam 1975 (95) n23.5 t23.5 f24 b24. A gem of a malt: compact and defies the years like a film star. Possesses the clarity of a 10-year-old choirboy and the body of 32-year-old nymph. *46%. Montgomery & Co. Ltd.*

Montgomerie's Glencadam 1990 cask no. 5990, dist Aug 89, bott Mar 08 **(87) n24.5 t21.5 f20 b21.** Taste-wise, the oak has gone through the barley. But the nose is simply exceptional, one of the best malts of the year, and the delivery is no mug, either. *43%.*

⋄ **Old & Rare Glencadam Aged 32 Years** sherry cask, dist Apr 77, bott Oct 09 **(80) n19 t22 f19 b20.** Thick grape. A bit on the minty side here and there. But a furry dryness, too. *54.9% Douglas Laing & Co Ltd. 296 bottles.*

Old & Rare Glencadam Aged 32 Years dist Apr 77, bott Jul 09 **(96.5) n25** bulging with yielding bourbon: all those gorgeous brown sugar, liquorice and antique furniture notes are just soft watercolours, but together form something tangible and magnificent; so delicate it is nigh-on perfect...actually, with that crushed Malteser chocolate candy to boot, it is perfect...25 points it is; **t24** again the delivery is at once soft yet profound: a nanosecond of barley and then we are engulfed by a gently rolling river of light...well...everything....!! Honeycomb dipped in milk chocolate, barley which is almost three dimensional in its delicate sharpness; molten demerara; molten praline....; **f23.5** not so much short as just fades away. Where does the middle end and the start begin...? A bit like a massive orgasm, you are not sure where the beginning, middle and end exactly is...you know it's just something special you immerse into and you don't want it to go away...it's a thing that 32-year-olds have a tendency to do to you.. **b25** from Brechin to Bardstown in 32 years: brilliant! Worth getting just to nose alone... *58.6%. Douglas Laing.*

Old Malt Cask Glencadam Aged 21 Years dist Jun 85, bott Apr 07 **(95) n24 t24 f23 b24.** A true gem of a cask with a nose that, alone, could seduce a eunuch. *50%.*

Provenance Glencadam Aged 11 Years hogshead, cask no. 3938, dist Winter 1995, bott Autumn 2007 **(76.5) n18 t19.5 f20 b19.** You know when you find an interesting whisky....well, you won't here... *46%. Douglas Laing.*

⋄ **Single & Single Glencadam 1991 Aged 16 Years (81.5) n21 t21.5 f19 b20.** Decent barley sharpness but elsewhere there is a constant drone of caramel like bagpipes at a haggis convention. *46% Single & Single. South Africa.*

The Whisky Fair Glencadam Aged 32 Years sherry wood, dist 74, bott 07 **(83) n22 t22 f19 b20.** Some lovely red berry fruits are crushed latterly under oak. *57.3%.*

GLENCRAIG
Speyside, 1958. Allied. Silent.

⋄ **Rare Old Glencraig 1975 (87.5) n22.5** a soothing mixture of exotic fruit and more prosaic rhubarb tart; **t22** what was once background caramel leaking from the oak has now become the main theme; soft spices offer a puckering depth; **f21.5** just enough barley to manage the major oak on show; **b21.5** signs are showing that the Glencraigs are reaching the end of their natural range. *43% Gordon & MacPhail*

Rarest of the Rare Glencraig 1974 cask no. 2923 **(89) n22.5** the fruitiness suggests very good age; but also clean and delicate with the barley offering little more than sweetness: a curious old and new feel to this; **t22** immediate firm barley followed by clean vanilla: for its age simple and elegant, with just enough citrus to ensure freshness; **f22.5** quite estery with a metallic, coppery edge to the barley; plenty of natural caramels represent the oak; **b22** such an elegant dram which feels very at home with its age. After all these years, a bottling worth waiting for. *40.9%. Duncan Taylor.*

Rarest of the Rare Glencraig 1974 cask no. 2929 **(89.5) n22.5** very similar to its sister cask bottled by DT with a fruitiness suggesting that we are entering the autumn of the cask. But attractive every step of the way; **t23** fabulous arrival with the barley and natural caramels herding together. The lightest hint of liquorice and hickory ensures a deft sweetness; **f22** long, still intact with absolutely no negative oak and even a few spasms of spice for good measure; **b22** Rarest of the Rare, alright; the smallest sample I have ever been sent for the Whisky Bible. Must have gone out on April 1". Come on guys. give me — and the whisky — a chance!! *40.8%. Duncan Taylor.*

Scotch Malt Whisky Society Cask 104.10 Aged 33 Years refill barrel, dist Jun 74 **(94) n24 t23 f23.5 b23.5** I chose this to be the 1,000th whisky tasted for the 2009 edition simply because this really is one of the rarest whiskies in the world. Indeed, the first new commercial bottling I have tasted for five years. So you hope against hope that it will be a classic. And it most certainly is. For God's sake, re-install them stills...!!!! *45%*

Scotch Malt Whisky Society Cask 104.12 Aged 34 Years refill barrel, dist Jun 74 **(91) n22.5** school custard with a high sugar content; the surprisingly pleasant aroma of distant slightly rotting tangerines; **t23.5** wow!! The barley is still making a stand after all these years, with a brittle barley-sugar theme successfully preventing the oak from getting too aggressive; natural caramels and a small cocktail of exotic fruit; the dissolving mouth-feel also makes for a spot-on malt; **f22** finally the oak has its say, but a lingering muscovado sweetness sees off any bitter excesses; **b23** not quite in the same league as 104.10, but confirms what a fabulous make this was. *48.4%*

GLENDRONACH
Highlands, 1826. BenRiach Distillers. Working.

Glendronach 12 Years Old db **(92) n22** some pretty juicy grape in there; **t24** silky delivery with the grape teaming with the barley to produce the sharpest delivery and follow through you can imagine: exceptionally good weight with just enough oils to make full use of the delicate sweetness and the build towards spices and cocoa in the middle ground is a wonderful tease; **f22.5** dries and heads into bitter marmalade country; **b23.5** an astonishingly beautiful malt despite the fact that a rogue sherry butt has come in under the radar. But for that, this would have been a mega scorer: potentially an award-winner. Fault or no fault, seriously worth discovering this bottling of this too long undiscovered great distillery 43%

☆ **The GlenDronach Aged 12 Years "Original"** db **(86.5) n21 t22 f22 b21.5.** One of the more bizarre moments of the year: thought I'd got this one mixed up with a German malt whisky I had tasted earlier in the day. There is a light drying tobacco feel to this and the exact same corresponding delivery on the palate. That German version is distilled in a different type of still; this is made in probably the most classic stillhouse on mainland Scotland. Good, enjoyable whisky. But I see a long debate with distillery owner Billy Walker on the near horizon, though it was in Allied's hands when this was produced. 43%

Glendronach Original Aged 12 Years Double Matured db **(88) n23** dense, ripe plummy fruit: serious touches of fruitcake, complete with brown sugars. Oak does give a vanilla topping but barley also punches through. Some coal smoke buzzes around, too. Needs some time to get the full story; **t21** some serious infighting here, some of it off-key, between grape and grain. The grape wins but is not entirely unbloodied as the mouthwatering barley has some juicy moments; **f22** the lull after the storm; much more measured doses of bitter marmalade and vanilla, softening towards a gentle spice within the cocoa. Very different; **b22** vastly improved from the sulphur-tainted bottling of last year. In fact, their most enjoyable standard distillery bottling I've had for many years. But forget about the whisky: the blurb on the back is among the most interesting you likely to find anywhere. And I quote: "Founder James Allardice called the original Glendronach, 'The Guid Glendronach'. But there's no need to imitate his marketing methods. The first converts to his malt were the 'ladies of the night' in Edinburgh's Canongate!" Fascinating. And as a professional whisky taster I am left wondering: did they swallow or spit... 40%

Glendronach 15 Years Old db **(77.5) n19 t18.5 f20 b20.** The really frustrating thing is, you can hear those amazingly brilliant sherry butts screaming to be heard in their purest voice. Those alone, and you could, like the 12-y-o, have a score cruising over 95 mark. I can't wait for the next bottling. 46%

Glendronach 15 Years Old db **(83) n20 t22 f20 b21.** Chocolate fudge and grape juice to start then tails off towards a slightly bitter, dry finish. 40%

☆ **The GlenDronach Aged 15 Years "Revival"** db **(88.5) n22** almost impenetrably thick malt, further strengthened by an oak-muscovado exoskeleton; **t23** again the malt takes on massive form; the fruit marches along as a sub-plot; **f21.5** vanilla and malt, a slightly bitter finale; **b22** unambiguously Scottish.... A fantastically malty dram. 46%

Glendronach 18 Years Old db **(87) n22** rhubarb and custard – both the sweet and the candy; this is underpinned by a real resonance to the oak, and undermined by a subtle evidence of a less than helpful sherry butt; **t21.5** a dry delivery with the sweet grape taking its time to get a grip; **f22** lightly overdone toast and fruit preserve...smoothed over with a knife that had previously dipped into the pot of chocolate spread; **b21.5** apart from those dead few seconds on delivery and the obvious mild flaw, this is really lovely stuff – just so good to see this distillery back in harness. But you know that even better is to come... 46%

☆ **The GlenDronach Aged 18 Years "Allardice"** db **(83.5) n19 t22 f21 b21.5.** Huge fruit. But a long-running bitter edge to the toffee and raisin sits awkwardly on the palate. 46%

☆ **The GlenDronach Grandeur Aged 31 Years** db **(94.5) n23.5** dry, mildly peppery vanilla; crushed golden raisin counter-plot; **t24** spice-dusted grapes explode on the palate on entry; the mouth-feel plays a key role as the early lushness carries the fruit only so far before it begins to break up, allowing a fabulous spicy complexity to develop; **f23.5** beautiful intertwining between those golden raisins and coffee. The spices are never far away....; **b23.5** just one hell of an alpha sherry butt. 45.8%

Glendronach Aged 33 Years oloroso sherry db **(95) n24 t24 f23 b24.** Want to know what sherry should really nose like: invest in a bottle of this. This is a vivid malt boasting spellbinding clarity and charm. A golden nugget of a dram, which would have been better still at 46%. 40%

☆ **The GlenDronach Single Cask 1971** oloroso cask no. 483 **(80) n20 t22 f19 b19.** Plenty of marmalade to be getting on with here. But the finish is tight and bitter. 494% 544 bottles.

Glendronach Single Cask 1992 cask no. 401 db **(96) n24** more than a hint of Demerara rum to the rich, sherried nose. Molasses sweeten the high roast Java while the barley screams to make itself heard; the oak has a slightly unusual, mossy earthiness adding to the overall enormity; **t23.5** the palate is swamped in luxuriant, lush sugar-coated burnt raisins; wave upon wave of spice explode on the back of the tongue and roof of the mouth. A big, sugary coating gives a distinct crispness to the rigid malt; **f24.5** the coffee, so well defined on the nose, returns here with even more molasses to sweeten it up. Excellent soft oils coat the roof of the mouth, ensuring a long fade as busy spices continue their lively assault. The juicy barley finale offers a welcome lightness and balance; **b24** ultra distinctive with that firm sheen offering a very unusual dimension. However, the unmistakeable rum character on a sherry theme really makes for a memorable and massive malt which never quite tastes the same twice and alters in weight and complexity considerably depending on heat and time applied. Outrageously excellent. The distillery at its most complex. *60.2%. BenRiach Distillers exclusively for Parkers Whisky.*

∷ **The GlenDronach Single Cask 1992** oloroso butt no. 1140 db **(93.5) n23.5** sharp, incisive grape with tannins running amok. Under all this, some barley stirs... **t24.5** quite beautiful grape, almost three dimensional in its shape, form and structure. Clean, intact, marginally juicy but relaxed enough to allow both the barley and vanilla a free run; **f22.5** plenty of coffee notes to give that usual rummy character which so often attaches itself to Glendronach. Some very late fuzzy bitterness...; **b23** yes, it is feeling a little tired. Yes, it occasionally lurches about the palate as if under the influence of its own fumes. But we are talking a sherry butt under 20 years old with only the odd sulphur molecule in sight, before the Bodegas went insane with the stuff. Or so it appears to my poor, jaded taste buds as I near the end of this Bible. A relative wonder to behold.... *57.2% 598 bottles*

∷ **The GlenDronach Single Cask 1993** oloroso butt no. 523 db **(94) n23.5** salted sherry; malted Mysore; **t24.5** succulent sugars; spine-tingling spices; gregarious grape, magnificent mocha; **f22.5** more Mysore; savoury staves; vanishing vanilla; **b23.5** sulphurless. Sophisticated. Sensational. *60.4% 634 bottles*

Glendronach Single Cask 1994 cask no. 2311 db **(91.5) n21.5** almost playfully light; fragile barley embraces the oak and the two fuse so that after a while it is difficult to distinguish where one note starts and the other ends. A lazy nuttiness perfectly compliments the bittersweet tone; **t23** mouthwatering barley pounds the tastebuds relentlessly from the start, bringing with it delicate oaky shades for extra weight and depth. A lively character with a fiery temperament when cool but at body temperature relaxes allowing the barley to reach searing levels of intensity. The biting, salivating sharpness of the malt nigh brings tears to the eyes; **f23.5** there is a minty chocolate edge to this, as well as hazelnuts and vanilla. For all the obvious lightness there is considerable length with the barley dovetailing comfortably with the oak, as ever, for the final say; **b23.5** about the closest I have ever tasted to the long defunct 12-year-old bourbon cask Glendronach, a legendary single malt in the old Allied armoury. A malt which really needs to be warmed to body temperature to see it in its full glory and form, one quite unique to this little-known distillery. Fascinating and fabulous. *59.4%. BenRiach Distillers exclusively for Parkers Whisky.*

∷ **Glendronach Single Cask 1996** oloroso butt, cask no. 193 db **(88.5) n22** you'd be hard pressed to find an old Demerara rum with this degree of salty, fruity intensity; **t23.5** taste buds coated with several layers of sherry tar, each about three inches thick: eye-watering in intensity, a middle ground of coffee and chocolate crèmes lightening the load; **f21** more coffee, but a little on the burnt side; **b22** an almost frightening whisky. The ferocity of the sherry might have some hiding behind their sofas. *59.4% 399 bottles*

∷ **Dun Bheagan Glendronach Aged 34 Years** hogshead, dist Jun 75 **(88.5) n22** you'd be hard pressed to find an old Demerara rum with this degree of salty, fruity intensity; **t23.5** taste buds coated with several layers of sherry tar, each about three inches thick: eye-watering in intensity, a middle ground of coffee and chocolate crèmes lightening the load; **f21** more coffee, but a little on the burnt side; **b22** an almost frightening whisky. The ferocity of the sherry might have some hiding behind their sofas. *47.8% Ian Macleod*

Duncan Taylor Collection Glendronach 1975 cask no. 706 **(87.5) n22.5** brittle barley on the nose, encased by sugar, sprinkled Bakewell tart crust; **t22** almost crystalline in its delivery: the barley is rock hard while the myriad sugar notes seep out offering varying intensity; **f22** vanilla and caramelised ice cream cones; **b21.5** maybe at 25 years you might be looking for a touch more variance. But on the other hand, what it does it does very well... *51.4%*

∷ **Old Malt Cask Glendronach Aged 14 Years Old** refill butt, cask no. DL 5671, dist May 95, bott Jan 10 **(85) n21.5 t21.5 f21 b21.** Salty, tangy, lively, oddly coastal-style. Barley dominates but sugars not far behind. *50% Douglas Laing & Co Ltd. 240 bottles.*

GLENDULLAN (see also below)

Speyside, 1972. Diageo. Working.

Glendullan Aged 8 Years db **(89) n20** fresh, gingery, zesty; **t22** distinctly mealy and malty. **f24** brilliant – really stunning grassy malt powers through. Speyside in a glass – and a nutshell; **b23** this is just how I like my Speysiders: young fresh and uplifting. A charming malt.

⌐ **Glendullan The Manager's Choice** European oak, cask no. 12718, dist 1995, bott 2009 db **(93.5) n24.5** just a near flawless nose: an absolute perfection of balance between purring barley and fresh fruit, especially apples. Just love the new-mown hay... in fact, everything about this, especially that mix of old and new characteristics ...; **t23.5** intriguing combination of ripening fruit and young-ish make: has a suet pudding feel but with the extra addition of thick sultana and reduced plum sauce; **f23** a long, leviathan of rich fruit, dappled with barley and vanilla; **b22.5** a bit like finding a perfectly preserved old Merc with low mileage: performs as beautifully as it does effortlessly and offers a priceless symmetry between simplicity and style. Whoever chose these casks deserves a medal struck. And take this one at body temp only. *58.7% 635 bottles.*

Singleton of Glendullan 12 Years Old db **(87) n22** significant oak hides some of the Jamaican ginger; **t22** a gutsier barley character with stifled honey and the oak dives in again; **f21** dry with a slight return of ginger; **b22** much more age than is comfortable for a 12-y-o. *40%*

Connoisseurs Choice Glendullan 1993 (88) n22 t22 f22 b22. Usually, because of the wood policy, you never quite know what you are going to get from this distillery. Pretty decent cask yet you have very pleasant, untaxing up and downer simply because of the extra oil on the body. *43%. Gordon & MacPhail.*

⌐ **Hart Brothers Glendullan Aged 11 Years** dist Jun 98, bott Sep 09 **(61) n17 t18 f12 b15.** A very poor cask. Simple as... *46% Hart Brothers*

Old Masters Glendullan Aged 12 Years cask no. 5059, dist 97, bott 09 **(85) n21.5 t22 f20.5 b21.** Decent, thoroughly enjoyable, simplistic malt with a good, refreshing zing to the barley delivery. *56.1%. James MacArthur & Co. Ltd.*

Provenance Glendullan Aged 12 Years refill hogshead, dist summer 96, bott autumn 08 **(80.5) n21.5 t20 f19 b20.** Very happy to steer a malty course, causing minimum wake. *46%.*

Scotch Malt Whisky Society Cask 84.11 Aged 11 Years refill hogshead, dist Sep 97 **(89) n21** dry, oak dominated; **t22** excellent, juicy delivery which makes a lie of the nose: resounding barley notes are thick and subtly sweetened; the middle has an oaky threat but soft mocha's to the rescue; **f23.5** beautiful chocolate mint, soft spice, and a reprise of the juicy barley...fabulous; **b22.5** after such an ordinary nose the complex beast which follows simply stuns. *58.6%*

⌐ **Scotch Malt Whisky Society Cask 84.12 Aged 12 Years** refill hogshead, dist Sep 97 **(92.5) n23** the gentle feed of delicate watermelon and under-ripe papaya suggests a malt older than its years; **t22.5** amazingly light delivery, almost apologetic and takes a while for oils to build and the malts to begin to offer a distinct weight and chewiness; **f24** now goes in to overdrive as those fledgling fruity notes return, but with enough substance to take on the gathering vanilla and spice; **b23** a rare malt where the finish trumps all else. *59.1% 296 bottles.*

⌐ **The Whisky Agency Glendullan 1981 (94.5) n23.5** freshly diced celery complete with peppery kick; green under-ripe gooseberry; a hint of smoke; **t24** so salivating! Spices tumble around the palate as the barley goes into overdrive; still the fresh fruit and veg echo, though now some pink raspberry joins in, too; rarely to whiskies produce so much juice and spice for quite so long: exceptional; **f23.5** long, sharp and barley at its most jagged and angular; **b23.5** it is nigh impossible to find a cask of such age that could be any fresher and revitalising. Track down a bottle of this at all costs. Fabulous!! *49.6%*

GLENDULLAN (see also above)

Speyside, 1898–1985. Closed.

Glendullan 1978 Rare Malt db **(88) n23** exceptional piquancy to this with the quietness of the oak shattered by a lemon-citrus shrill. Genuinely wonderful; **t22** a lovely, tart start with that citrus making a crashing entry but the oak barges in soon after and coffee is soon on the menu; **f21** more coffee and lemon cake, though it by now a very small slice; **b22** Sherlock Holmes would have loved this one: he would have found it lemon-entry. *56.8%*

GLEN ELGIN

Speyside, 1900. Diageo. Working.

Glen Elgin Aged 12 Years db **(89) n23** blistering, mouthwatering fruit of unspecified origin. The intensity of the malt is breathtaking; **t24** stunning fresh malt arrival, salivating barley that is both crisp and lush: then a big round of spice amid some squashed, over-ripe plums. Faultless mouthfeel; **f20** the spice continues as does the intense malt but is devalued dramatically by a bitter-toffee effect; **b22** absolutely murders Cragganmore as Diageo's top dog bottled Speysider. The marks would be several points further north if one – rightly or wrongly – didn't get the feeling that some caramel was weaving a derogatory spell. Brilliant stuff nonetheless. States Pot Still on label – not to be confused with Irish Pot Still. This is 100% malt... and it shows! 43%

Cadenhead's Glen Elgin Aged 30 Years dist 78, bott 09 **(92) n23** no doubting the age. Suet pudding and curiously salted bread pudding provide the curious complexity; **t24** ginger and honey really beef up the cut glass barley. Layer upon layer of delicious stuff with always a thread of sweetness to be found in every one; **f22** bitters slightly as the oak interjects but still retains a juicy freshness to the last; **b23** worthy of this excellent distillery. 49.1%

Connoisseurs Choice Glen Elgin 1995 (91) n22.5 t23 f22.5 b23. An essential Glen Elgin: textbook excellence. If only this malt could be more easilly found. 46%. Gordon & MacPhail.

Duncan Taylor The NC2 Range Glen Elgin 1991 (72) n17 t18 f17 b17. A United Distillers' sherry "butt", one assumes. Say no more... 46%

⁙ **Duthies Glen Elgin 18 Years Old (95) n24.5** oh my word...this promises to be a little special....; one of the most delicate noses I have come across this year landing with all the impact of a budgie's down feather during a good moult. With a wonderfully floral edge, the sweeter elements are provided by a freshly opened biscuit tin. Truly fabulous...; **t24** melts in the mouth, in much the same manner that the aroma lands on the nose; just layer upon layer of grist and lightly toffeed honey...and then a light coat of liquorice; **f23** even though the oak pokes through to bitter out, the burnt Demerara maintains the balance sublimely; **b23.5** spellbindingly beautiful... 46% Wm. Cadenhead Ltd

Old Malt Cask Glen Elgin Aged 16 Years refill hogshead no. 3927, dist Jun 91, bott Oct 07 **(88) n22 t22 f22 b22.** Fair degree of complexity. 50%. Douglas Laing. 287 bottles.

Old Malt Cask Glen Elgin Aged 24 Years bott Jul 09 **(83) n21.5 t21 f20 b20.5.** One of my favourite Speyside distilleries here feels the oaky pace. Pleasant natural caramels. 44.9%.

Old Masters Glen Elgin Aged 17 Years cask no. 2598 dist 91, bott 08 **(91.5) n23.5** ultra-clean sherry coats every aspect of this lightly spiced nose; **t23.5** lush, freshly-crushed grape moving on to lightly spiced sultana. There is a barley sub-plot here; **f22** slightly bitter burnt toast; **b22.5** benefits from an unusually beautiful sherry influence. How rare is that these days...? 54.6%. James MacArthur & Co. Ltd.

GLENESK
Highland (Eastern), 1897–1985. Closed.

Duncan Taylor Collection Glenesk 1981 cask no. 932 **(57) n14 t15 f14 b14.** I say! Sulphur, anyone? 54.3%

Duncan Taylor Collection Glenesk 1981 cask no. 933 **(84) n22 t20 f21 b21.** I say! Sherry anyone? 56.9%

Duncan Taylor Collection Glenesk 1983 cask no. 4930 **(89.5) n22** chugging, thick, two-tone fruit –one mildly nondescript, the other offering physalis while the barley is fit and healthy; **t23** now that is rather lovely. Hot, perhaps, but in its way it helps accentuate the depth to the barley while allowing the more juicy, tangy notes free reign; **f22** some lovely latte towards the finish, a touch creamy; **b22.5** by far the best Glen Esk I've tasted in years. Perhaps not the most complex, but the liveliness and clarity are a treat. 52.1%

Duncan Taylor Rare Auld Glenesk 26 Years Old sherry cask, dist Feb 81, bott Dec 07 **(82.5) n20.5 t21 f20.5 b20.5.** I say! Sherry and sulphur, anyone..? 56.9%. Whisky-Doris.

GLENFARCLAS
Speyside, 1836. J&G Grant. Working.

Glenfarclas 8 Years Old db **(86) n21 t22 f22 b21.** Less intense sherry allows the youth of this malt to stand out. Mildly quirky as a Glenfarclas and enormous entertainment. 40%

Glenfarclas 10 Years Old db **(80) n19 t20 f22 b19.** Always an enjoyable malt, but for some reason this version never seems to fire on all cylinders. There is a vague honey sheen which works well with the barley, but struggles for balance and the nose is a bit sweaty. Still has distinctly impressive elements but an odd fish. 40%

Glenfarclas 105 Cask Strength 10 Years Old db **(91) n22** perfect fresh sherry influence; clean, intense, charismatic, fruity and precise; **t23** rather confusing as the might of the malt and sherry battle for supremacy: takes time to settle and the drier oak helps enormously to accentuate the honied qualities of the malt; **f23** a fine, layered oak seeing off the sweeter honeycomb theme for a distinguished finale; **b23** this, for various reasons, has been a regular dram of mine for over 20 years. It has been at its very best in recent bottlings, though the nose here doesn't quite hit the heights. 60%

Glenfarclas 12 Years Old db **(89) n22** oops! Nothing like its usual near brilliant self early on, but some golden strands of honey compensate handsomely; **t23** recovers superbly to offer lashings of the trademark honeycomb amid a riot of gentle oaky spice; the light sprinkling of muscovado sugar is sublime, as is the crushed raisins; **f22** more burned honeycomb and some subtle extra oak offers dry vanilla; **b23** from this sample just the odd cask has tarnished the usual brilliance, but it's still good enough to offer moments of Speyside most glorious. *43%*

Glenfarclas 15 Years Old db **(95) n23** such is the intensity of the fruit and sugar-rich barley, there is an element of medium ester Jamaican pot still rum to this, a feeling intensified by an orangey-oak influence that seems greater than 15 years. The top-shelf sherry, though, is of a classical type rarely found these days, though common 30 years ago; **t24** succulent and stupendous. Barley sugar shows first then a sherry input that borders on intense but dissipates as the spicy oak digs in; **f24** long, chewy, a tad oily and fades with a wonderful coffee-vanilla combination and a late surge of something bourbony; **b24** Eureka!!! The 15-y-o back to how I can remember it in the past. Some of you may have been scared away by some less than impressive recent bottlings. It's safe to come back because now it has been returned to its position as one of Scotland's most sublime malts. The quality of the sherry is astonishing; its interaction with the barley is a wondrous joy. Go find and get... *46%*

Glenfarclas 17 Years Old db **(93) n23** just so light and playful: custard powder lightens and sweetens, sultana softens, barley moistens, spice threatens...; **t23** the relaxed sherry influence really lets the honey deliver; delightfully roasty and well spiced towards the middle; **f23** when I was a kid there was a candy – pretend tobacco, no less! – made from strands of coconut and sweetened with a Demerara syrup. My, this takes me back...; **b24** an excellent age for this distillery, allowing just enough oak in to stir up the complexity. A stupendous addition to the range. *40%*

Glenfarclas 21 Years Old db **(83) n20 t23 f19 b21.** A chorus of sweet, honied malt and mildly spiced, teasing fruit on the fabulous mouth arrival and middle compensates for the blips. *43%.*

Glenfarclas 25 Years Old db **(88) n22** a heavy, impervious nose with the sherry and oak providing a cleanly-built wall; **t23** much softer with an immediate mouthwatering delivery full of prime, sweet barley and then toasted raisins; **f21** soft vanilla; fruitcake and cream; **b22** an distinct improvement on previous bottlings with the finish here having much more to say. *43%*

Glenfarclas 30 Years Old db **(85) n20 t22 f21 b22.** Flawed yet juicy. *43%*

᷾ **Glenfarclas Aged 40 Years** db **(76.5) n18.5 t21 f18 b19.** Recently, on radio somewhere, I was asked what some of the great Scottish whisky moments can be. My reply included sitting at the Glenfarclas distillery with a freshly opened bottle of 40-year-old. The one I had in mind wasn't at all like this, which for all its magnificence in the earliest moments of delivery is, with its furry dry-bitterness on finish, far from representative. I will need to re-taste for next year, as this, hopefully, is a freak. *46%*

Glenfarclas 40 Years Old Millennium Edition db **(92) n23 t23 f23 b23.** An almost immaculate portrayal of an old-fashioned, high-quality malt with unblemished sherry freshness and depth. The hallmark of quality is the sherry's refusal to dominate the spicy, softly peated malt. The oak offers a bourbony sweetness but ensures a rich depth throughout. Quite outstanding for its age. *nc ncf.*

Glenfarclas 50 Years Old db **(92) n24** Unique. Almost a marriage between 20-y-o bourbon and intense, old-fashioned sherry. Earthy, weighty stuff that repays time in the glass and oxidization because only then does the subtley become apparent and a soft peat-reek reveal itself; **t23** an unexpected sweet – even mouthwatering - arrival, again with a touch of peat to add counter ballast to the intense richness of the sherry. The oak is intense from the middle onwards, but of such high quality that it merely accompanies rather then dominates; **f22** warming black peppers ping around the palate; some lovely cocoa oils coat the mouth for a bitter-sweet, warming and very long finish; **b23** Most whiskies cannot survive such great age. This one really does bloom in the glass and the earthy, peaty aspect makes it all the more memorable. It has taken 50 years to reach this state. Give a glass of this at least an hour's inquisition, as I have. Your patience will be rewarded many times over. *44.4%*

Glenfarclas 1952 The Family Casks (3rd Release) plain hogshead, cask no. 1713 db **(81) n20.5 t20 f20.5 b20.** For a curious moment there is an almost hoppy bitterness to this one: a dram for the Campaign For Real Whisky. Just too much oak for greatness, I'm afraid. *47.3%*

Glenfarclas 1953 The Family Casks cask no. 1678, sherry butt db **(87) n23** fruit spirit: cherry and raspberry brandy softened by burnt honeycomb; **t21** excellent malt delivery then a sinus-attacking wave of oak; **f22** recovers superbly for a tangy grapey finale; **b21** myriad battles are fought to keep the oak in check. Most are won. *53.7%. 480 bottles.*

Glenfarclas 1954 The Family Casks cask no. 444, sherry butt db (**94**) **n22** more oak than an Elizabethan man-of-war. Except this is far from sunk... **t24** oak scorches into the back and roof of the mouth; countering muscovado tries to douse the flames. The ensuing battle is fabulous.. **f24** long, ultimately on the dry and mildly bitter side, but not before some mocha and Melton cake have made their fabulous marks, as well as marmalade and cherry preserve; **b24** simply defies time and belief. Carries the scars of 52 summers, for sure. But with the same pride a legionnaire would wear his trophies of combat. *52.6%. 406 bottles.*

Glenfarclas 1955 The Family Casks cask no. 2211, sherry butt db (**88**) **n23** medium roast Brazilian and crushed hazelnuts adds complexity to dried dates; **t21** big oak start, off balance slightly but stabilised by a pinch of Demerara; **f22** recovers for an impressive finale with outstanding vanilla camp coffee; **b22** a proud dram gallantly hanging on to its last sweet traces. *46.1%. 545 bottles.*

Glenfarclas 1956 The Family Casks cask no. 1758, sherry butt db (**83**) **n24** amazingly similar to the '58 but with a shot of extra oak; **t21** short oloroso blast, soft oils and spice; dries quickly; **f19** pretty well oaked and bitters up; **b19** great nose but relentless oak. *47.3%. 435 bottles.*

Glenfarclas 1957 The Family Casks (3rd Release) sherry hogshead, cask no. 2 db (**91.5**) **n25** the perfect oldie nose: medium roast, un-ground Blue Mountain coffee beans merging blissfully with a super-rich Dundee cake magnificently beyond its sell by date and all topped with what first appears to be sherry trifle, but on further inspection is old, nutty oloroso of the highest order; **t22.5** improbable, sweet, mouth-watering delivery for a second or two but then the oak rushes in....and some. There is a spicy counter, but the middle ground dries and thinks about offering a eucalyptus layer or three; **f22** some molasses help dispel the more fundamental oaky themes and we are left with a kind of slightly burned honeycomb and spice; **b22** to mark my 50th birthday in 2007, I had planned on buying a cask of Glenfarclas 1957 and bottling it. Sadly, I was simply too busy to make it happen; had I done so this might possibly have been the cask I chose. It is a couple of summers past its best – well, probably more. But back in '07, I might just have been able to prevent some of the oaky excess. Then again, maybe not. What cannot be denied is that the nose would probably be Nose of the Year for this Bible, were there such an award. And that even though, like the rest of us from that vintage, it has seen better days, there is no denying that this is less a whisky but more of a life experience. And it is certainly as good and privileged a way I can think of wrapping up all my new whiskies for 2010, this being something like number 920 (actually I have lost count – we'll have to do a final tally by computer), because astonishing whiskies like this don't grow on trees: they simply mature in bits of them....if they are very, very lucky... *46.2%*

Glenfarclas 1958 The Family Casks cask no. 2245, sherry butt db (**88**) **n24** outrageous aroma for its age: walnut oil coated on ripe greengage and mildly burnt Dundee cake and sprinkled with demerara...swoon!..; **t22** lush, juicy delivery then, after about ten seconds, in comes the oak. With a vengeance... **f20** brown sugars try to head off the oak's excesses; **b22** keeps its head above the oaky water - just. *51.6%. 455 bottles.*

Glenfarclas 1959 The Family Casks (3rd Release) sherry hogshead, cask no. 3227 db (**79.5**) **n23 t20 f17.5 b19**. Huge gooseberry and grape. But appears to have suffered from a little renovation work. *50.9%*

Glenfarclas 1960 The Family Casks (3rd Release) sherry hogshead, cask no. 1768 db (**91**) **n24** attractively stewed oak with the sherry offering both lighter juice and depth; the odd big, ripe cherry moment, too; **t23** puckering sharpness to the fruitcake; somewhere in the recipe are a few spoonfuls of molasses and again those cherries; **f21.5** predictably tires at the end, though the odd milk-coffee note sympathises; **b22.5** retains a fabulous degree of life for its age. *44.6%*

Glenfarclas 1961 The Family Cask (3rd Release) sherry hogshead, cask no. 1322 db (**79**) **n20 t23 f17.5 b19**. Fat and full with the grape leading from the front though the bitterness does seem rather over rampant and not entirely oak related: a touch of déjà vous... *52.2%*

Glenfarclas 1962 The Family Casks (3rd Release) sherry hogshead, cask no. 2647 db (**96.5**) **n25** good grief...!!! Had this been marked a 25-year-old Demerara Pot Still rum, I would have believed them. The fruit and oak have fused together to form one rich, semi-sweet, breathtakingly spiced, coffee-enriched, marmalade-lightened thing of brain-exploding beauty. Nose-wise: perfection... **t24** the oaks make all the running, being of the big toasty nature you would expect. But those rich and still juicy fruits also play a magnificent part in forming the early balance and high-class flourish; **f23.5** when those sweeter notes dissolve you are left with a big burnt toast and torched raisin wedge of oak; **b24** the age takes its toll late on, which is to be expected. But up until the finish you nose this one until your nostrils bleed and close your eyes and swallow something a little special. Do I normally advocate spitting...? Not this time.... *52%*

Glenfarclas 1963 The Family Casks cask no. 4098, sherry butt db **(87)** n24 stunningly floral with crushed, dank petals, marzipan and hickory...phew!! t22 dry and spiced for all the grape; f19 a tad too oaked; bitter; b22 borderline. The oak really is big, but the grape holds out – just. The nose is a different matter. *56.7%. 420 bottles.*

Glenfarclas 1964 The Family Casks cask no. 4717, sherry butt db **(92)** n23 signs of creaking oak but clean, sweetish oloroso stands firm; t24 juicy, tangy marmalade and spice; f22 gentle, refined finale with grape in ascendant; b23 a gentleman dram which speaks quietly despite the obvious power at hand. *53.1%. 415 bottles.*

⊰⊱ **Glenfarclas The Family Casks 1965 Release V** cask no. 4362, bott May 10 db **(91.5)** n24 classic fruitcake nose...this one with high percentage of overcooked cherry. There is a toasty, spicy oak imprint, but such is the clarity and intensity of fruit that this is one for those who dream of sherried Speysiders of the old school; t23.5 after the brief silky grape opening score, all kinds of spices ping around the palate as the grape goes to work injecting a muscovado sugar balance; the oak drills deeply into the palate and nearly goes OTT. But those big fruits and sugars keep the delivery and middle ground intact; f21.5 finally dries and bitters out with a stain of coffee; b22.5 as silky a whisky as you might ever find. Needs a minimum half hour in the glass to open properly. *51.9%*

Glenfarclas 1966 The Family Casks cask no. 4177, sherry butt db **(95)** n25 faultless. Exactly how you dream a 40 year old sherry butt should be. Curves everywhere, not a jagged edge, just caresses, hints, whispers and innuendoes. A king – or perhaps queen - among casks; t23 surprising lightness with some raspberry amid the juicy grape; f23 soft honey and spice. Absolutely no evidence of oaky deterioration; b24 how fitting this whisky is the same colour as Alan Ball's hair. Because there is no greater way of toasting the memory of the man who was 1966. *51.5%. 514 bottles.*

⊰⊱ **Glenfarclas The Family Casks 1967 Release V** cask no. 5110, bott May 10 db **(96)** n24 cuts a nutty dash to seriously underscore the big fruitcake quality here; no shortage of bourbon, orange peel and liquorice characteristics, either; t24.5 like sneezing, tasting this is something it's impossible to do with your eyes open....helped by an extraordinary alcohol kick of its age, the soupy intense kumquat, over-ripened banana and sherry (as it is sherry you get here, not grape...!!) form an indestructible alliance, refusing to allow even 43 years of oak to make any kind of telling impact, other than to offer a tame and friendly vanilla frame in which the fruit can take centre stage; elsewhere brown sugars and spices adorn the picture and the odd little liquorice bourbon feature makes a cameo appearance; f23.5 the milky cocoa makes a much later start than you'd expect, thanks to the bullying fruit; tangy orange peel and banana milkshake sticks to the very end; b24 one of those whiskies once tasted, never forgotten. A malt which hasn't grown old gracefully: it has simply become a fruity Lothario, seducing every taste bud in sight. And taking it by force if it has to.... *60.8%*

Glenfarclas 1968 The Family Casks cask no. 1316, sherry butt db **(84)** n21 t20 f22 b21. Despite the massive strength for its age, has a slightly metallic resonance. *65.1%. 483 bottles.*

Glenfarclas 1969 The Family Casks (3ʳᵈ Release) sherry hogshead, cask no. 3188 db **(92.5)** n22.5 such intensity, this really needs a few minutes in the glass to breath and unravel. Eventually a mega thick, nutty, almost primeaval oloroso emerges: the barley has vanished but some toasty, flakey oak guarantees some serious dryness; for a moment there even appears to be a kind of mild sulphur whiff – it's a 1969, so surely can't be...can it...? t24 a sherry/oak duo is dolloped on delivery, but the salivating grapey raisiny notes begin to spread and thin and eventually an initial bitter-dryness is evened out; wonderful demarara, mocha and hickory fill the middle ground as a quasi-bourbony character momentarily takes hold; f22.5 a gentle dark sugared sweetness pervades while burnt raisin offer a fruity edge to the vanilla; bitters out...strange.... b23.5 even taking into account what appears a minor fault, this is not a dram you can knock back in a couple of minutes. Treat this malt as you would a first growth Bordeaux and you will be amply rewarded. *55.6%*

Glenfarclas 1970 The Family Casks cask no. 566, sherry butt db **(94)** n24 Jamaica Ginger Cake doused in beautifully clean oloroso; t23 massively mouth-filling with heavyweight fruit punctuated by lazy spice; f23 back to the moist ginger again with black peppers and molassed sugar in equal measures; b24 seriously elegant and complex malt that shows not a single blemish despite the extraordinary great age. A Glenfarclas Great. *53.6%. 497 bottles.*

Glenfarclas 1971 The Family Casks cask no. 140, sherry butt db **(93)** n24 Demerara rummy with enormous depth: bitter-sweet heaven with slow build up of big fruit; t24 sandalwood, toffee and berry fruit; f22 thins quite fast, allowing in the vanilla; b23 a noble dram. *57.1%. 459 bottles.*

Glenfarclas 1972 The Family Casks cask no. 3546, sherry butt db **(83)** n21 t21 f21 b20. Dry, a tad dull and much more natural toffee here. *51.1%. 645 bottles.*

Glenfarclas 1973 The Family Casks cask no. 2578, sherry butt db **(92) n24** ginger and honeycomb; **t22** soft, yielding grape; usual spices abound; **f23** vanilla stirs up the complexity; **b23** a more gentle expression than most from the mid 70s: one for the faint hearted. 58.8%. 457 bottles.

Glenfarclas 1974 The Family Casks cask no. 5786, sherry butt db **(93) n23** salty and seasoned; **t23** wonderful orangey-grapey-spicy infusion; Warming spices become positively vicious; **f23** some old citrus sinks deeply into the vanilla; the pugilistic spices are positively puckering; **b24** what a real brawling dram! A kind of Oliver Reed of malts; shows that touch of class despite those rough diamond edges. 60.8%. 555 bottles.

Glenfarclas 1975 The Family Casks cask no. 5038, refill hogshead db **(92) n23** chunky marmalade with the oak at full throttle; **t22** dry yet salivating. Only a wonderful stratum of juicy grape absorbs the blows; **f24** so long, so spicy: so get stuck in...!! **b23** dry yet balances wonderfully. Another spicy number. 51.4%. 187 bottles.

Glenfarclas 1976 The Family Casks cask no. 3111, refill butt db **(92) n23** wallows in a Dundee cake fruit richness, complete with nuts and perhaps with a curl of butter; **t23** melts on impact to leave a grapey residue. Burnt raisin and plump sultana dominate; **f23** dries with a suety dryness but barley water and a sprinkle of silver sugar maintains the balance; **b23** no whisky that's 30 years old has any right to be this juicy and fresh. A malt to take your time over. 49.4%.

Glenfarclas 1977 The Family Casks cask no. 61, refill butt db **(90) n22** slight, crushed sultana; **t23** wonderful amalgam of barley sugar and grape juice: light, but on a waxy body; **f22** delicate banana custard; **b23** a class, understated act from nose to finale. 59%. 582 bottles.

Glenfarclas 1978 The Family Casks (3rd Release) plain hogshead, cask no. 626 db **(88) n22** attractive rhubarb and custard topped with barley sugar; **t21.5** fizzing barley and fizzier oak; **f23.5** settles down majestically for a really classy display of boiled sweets and low sugared chocolate with the malt really gathering a head of steam; **b22** the oak grabs hard early on but lets go gently to allow the barley to escape unscathed. 57.6%

Glenfarclas 1979 The Family Casks (3rd Release) plain hogshead, cask no. 2216 db **(96.5) n24.5** the oak makes all kind of fruity noises not unlike a Grenadian breakfast table and is bolstered further by honey roast nut and trifle sans sherry; of it's style, not far off perfect... **t24** dissolves on impact: soft but not to the point of subjugation as there are firmer, ultra-clean, juicy barley notes springing forward to develop a malty theme, but one which is caked in delicate honey; the oak is always showing but refuses steadfastly to cross the line of good taste and manners; **f24** an unbelievably civilised winding down. Full of gentle, sweet, cocoa notes, the oak certainly has a bigger role, but one it carries off with aplomb; **b24** proof, not that it was ever needed, that this quite brilliant distillery does not need sherry to bolster its quality. On this evidence, there could be an argument put forward that sherry actually detracts from the greatness of the distillate. At 30 years there appears to be a marriage forged in heaven between the honey-rich barley and the oak. But to achieve this kind of style and depth, it is the raw spirit which must stand up and be counted. Game set and match against those who reckon Glenfarclas a one trick pony: if this isn't proof that the foundations of complexity aren't laid by the make, then I have no idea what is. 50.6%

Glenfarclas 1980 The Family Casks cask no. 1942, refill sherry butt db **(80) n19 t21 f20 b20.** Soft toffee apple, but not entirely flawless. 50.1%. 681 bottles.

Glenfarclas The Family Casks 1981 Release V cask no. 58, bott May 10 db **(88.5) n22.5** dense. Sherry trifle, with extra custard; **t23** sharp delivery with the barley and fruits crammed into the first few crashing waves; a tad salty and tangy with the middle ground giving way to an orgy of Fruit Pastilles; **f21** flaky vanilla, the most bitter orange...continues on its eclectic way...., **b22** as cluttered and intricate as a Victorian sitting room. And in its own way, just as classically beautiful, too. 50.9%

Glenfarclas The Family Casks 1982 Release V cask no. 633, bott May 10 db **(87) n23** classy, classy, classy....!!! Firm, clipped, sugary: similar to rum cask influence but with an extra semi-ripe greengage fruitiness; **t22.5** more of the same; a re-run of the nose with those vaguely fruited sugars dissolving around the palate; **f20** a tad thin and bitter; **b21.5** a long way from the Glenfarclas norm, but an enjoyable diversion! 54.2% 216 bottles.

Glenfarclas 1983 The Family Casks cask no. 50, refill hogshead db **(88) n20** tight, a tad untidy; **t22** firm barley which slowly blossoms into a wonderful, bitter-sweet spicefest; **f24** better balance as the barley shines and muscovado sugar sorts out the oak; **b22** a sunshine after a rainy afternoon malt 56%. 302 bottles.

Glenfarclas 1984 The Family Casks cask no. 6028, plain hogshead db **(93) n23** citrus!! What's all this about? Nostrils-full of barley....; **t23** more citrus on delivery with soft, mildly chalky oak dovetailing with the grassy, mouth-watering barley; **f23** lemon then a light dusting of cocoa; **b24** at first I thought I had been poured malt from the wrong distillery until I saw the cask type. By no means the first non-sherry Glenfarclas, but perhaps the most lemony-fresh and palate-cleansing at this age. So, so lovely! *51.3%. 267 bottles.*

Glenfarclas 1985 The Family Casks cask no. 2826, refill sherry hogshead db **(91) n23** apple crumble and near cinnamon; **t23** lush, warmed plum pudding on a caramel base; **f22** custard pie and light spice; **b23** what a tart! And a fruity one at that... *46.3%. 329 bottles.*

Glenfarclas 1986 The Family Casks cask no. 3434, refill sherry puncheon db **(87) n22** fruity, but with nip and bite; **t22** the spices initially rise above the laid-back sherry-toffee theme; some honeycomb notes counter the drier oaks; **f21** genuinely lethargic finale with very light oak; **b22** the fight on the nose and delivery isn't matched by the sleepy follow through. *56.5%. 521 bottles.*

Glenfarclas 1987 Limited Rare Bottling - Edition No. 13 cask no. 6806 - 6809, dist Dec 87, bott Sep 08 db **(94) n24** ultra clean grape mixes beautifully with polished wooden floors; there is also a wonderful walk on part of botanicals sans juniper; **t23.5** lush, sharp delivery; a hint of blood orange and some momentarily raging spice; vanilla holds the middle ground; **f23.5** that classy fruit/barley/oak balance continues to the end with a hint of very late hickory; **b23** the grape grazes serenely around the tastebuds without a single note of discord. Simply delicious malt whisky which brings the major elements into play without any major conflict. *46%.*

Glenfarclas 1988 Quarter Casks cask no. 251 - 261, dist Jan 88, bott Feb 08 db **(91) n23 t23.5 f22 b22.5.** Chocolate fruit and nut bar lovers will be happy with this one, as will devotees of unspoiled sherry casks. *46.1%. German market. 1,478 bottles.*

Glenfarclas 1989 The Family Casks cask no. 11721, sherry butt db **(94) n23** almost identical to the 1990 bottling; **t24** see 1990 **f23** slight change here with more of a molassed, old bourbon accent here, otherwise identical; **b24** the 1989 and 1990 could be twins born a year apart – astonishing! *60%. 600 bottles.*

⸭⸭ **Glenfarclas The Family Casks 1990 Release V** cask no. 5095, bott May 10 db **(94.5) n23.5** big clean grape, but the coffee aspect hints of dark rum, too; **t24.5** juicy, beautifully sweetened and structured grape; strata of Lubec marzipan and elsewhere a butterscotch-barley intrigue; **f23** long with the fruit mingling confidently with a busy, peppery spice; always Demerara sugars keep the spices and vanillas in very good shape; **b23.5** you will dream of dusty bodegas if you drink this late at night. Massive sherry, but excellent balance and complexity, too. The delivery and early complexity ranks among the best whisky moments of the year. Strikingly gorgeous. *56.5% 459 bottles.*

Glenfarclas 1991 The Family Casks cask no. 5623, sherry butt db **(92) n24** exemplary display of highly complex fruit and toffee tones; some over-ripe cherry, a touch salty and some crushed pine nut; **t23** mildly aggressive arrival, mainly thanks to early spices; again complexity rules and the brief raspberry stratum is a treat; **f22** simplifies out with the natural toffee; **b23** an entrancing malt which has your tastebuds on full alert. *57.9%. 613 bottles.*

Glenfarclas 1992 The Family Casks cask no. 264, sherry butt db **(89) n23** wonderful marmalade and botanicals; **t22** the fruit is voluptuous, the body curvy and soft; **f22** long, traces of cocoa and massive chewing power; **b22** big, gutsy, oily stuff. *55.5%. 669 bottles.*

⸭⸭ **Glenfarclas The Family Casks 1993 Release V** cask no. 3942, bott Apr 10 db **(72) n17.5 t19.5 f18 b18.** All over the place. The black sheep of the family.... *59.7% 566 bottles.*

Glenfarclas 1993 Premium Edition Limited Rare Bottling oloroso sherry casks, cask no. 29 & 30 distilled Feb 93, bott Dec 08 db **(75.5) n18 t20 f18.5 b19.** Lots of grape and chocolate. But one of these casks just wasn't right to begin with. *46%. German market. 3,600 bottles.*

⸭⸭ **Glenfarclas The Family Casks 1994 Release V** cask no. 3629, bott Apr 10 db **(86) n22 t21 f22 b21.** So dripping in clean, rich sherry that all barley traces have been expunged. Eye-watering, lightly spiced, entirely sulphur-free, and, even if a little heavy -handed here and there, in its more lucid moments of a style now almost unique to this distillery. *59.3% 609 bottles.*

Glenfarclas 1995 45° The Heritage Malt Collection sherry cask, dist Nov 95, bott Sep 06 db **(94.5) n24** blood orange, teasing spice, vanilla pods and even a touch of barley: who could ask for more...? **t23.5** salivating and fresh, the grape pulses with ripeness; **f23.5** long with much more barley apparent, though the grape never loses its sheen; a touch of toffee with a hint of mocha; **b23.5** exceptional. Absolutely everything you could demand from a sherried malt of this age. Not a single off note and the freshness of comparative youth and complexity of years in the cask are in perfect harmony. *45%. Spain.*

Glenfarclas 1996 Premium Edition matured in sherry casks, cask no. 678 & 679 dist Feb 96, bott Sep 08 db **(75) n17.5 t20 f18.5 b19.** Plenty of excellent grape. But spoiled by the obvious fault. I am told that quite a number of Germans actually enjoy sulphured casks. Then this should be right up their strasse. *46%. German market.*

Glenfarclas 1997 Cask Strength Premium Edition matured in sherry casks, cask no. 642 - 648, dist Feb 97, bott Mar 09 db **(77.5) n18.5 t20 f19.5 b19.5.** In their defence, the quality of some of the casks that have gone into this are so good, it may have been possible to have missed the obvious problem. But it is there, and unmistakably so 55.5%. *German market.*

Glenfarclas 105 40th Anniversary Limited Edition 40 Years Old dist 68, bott 08 db **(96)** n24 hickory, basil and any number of thick ye olde bourbony notes collide head on with faultless fruit; t24 this is massive: you have to count to three to get your breath back and only then can you start getting to grips with the complexities that have been delivered on your palate: again lots of bourbony tones and some countering middle-aged and old notes. The sherry is surprising down at heel to the rich molasses and honeycomb....and there's that basil again...; f24 just so long with all that had gone on before winding down like a clock. A memorable experience... b24 I have had quite a few 105s over 33 of those 40 years. And not a single one was quite like this. Quite magnificent! 60%

Cadenhead's Chairman's Stock Glenfarclas Aged 34 Years bourbon hogshead, dist 73, bott Sep 07 **(84)** n21 t22 f20 b21. Big oak character. 43.7%. 198 bottles.

⟫ **Kaleu's Own #2 Private Edition Glenfarclas Aged 20 Years** hogshead, cask no. 2116, dist Feb 89, bott Jul 09 **(77)** n19.5 t22 f17.5 b19. Big, malty, eye-wateringly tart but the suspicion, confirmed on nose and finish, is that the cask itself could be a little more sympathetic. 58.5%

⟫ **Kaleu's Own #3 Private Edition Glenfarclas Aged 12 Years** hogshead, cask no. 1372, dist Mar 97, bott Jul 09 **(85.5)** n21.5 t21.5 f21.5 b21. A rare chance to dissect a Glenfarclas. Matured in what looks like a decent quality third fill bourbon barrel we can see just how excellently constructed this malt is, and even locate the deftest smoke. 54.8%

⟫ **Kingsbury's Finest and Rarest Ballindalloch 34 Years Old 1971** **(84.5)** n22.5 t21.5 f20 b20.5. More oak than a Tudor battleship. But there are some enjoyable marmalade notes to form the ballast. 51.2% Import System.

Old Malt Cask Glenfarclas Aged 42 Years dist Jun 66, bott 08 **(92)** n23 familiar hickory-bourbony flag is waved; t22.5 early oak threatens dominance but the oloroso springs back into play with lusty and wonderfully clean fruitiness; f23 for a while there is a hint of barley, but this is soon lost in a vanilla-led onslaught of fruity-bourbony notes which provide a softness beyond belief for such great age; b23.5 another beautiful Glenfarclas which absolutely defies the years. 48.8%. Douglas Laing.

Scotch Malt Whisky Society Cask 1.137 Aged 14 Years refill hogshead, dist Sep 93 **(85)** n21.5 t21 f21.5 b21. Barley concentrate in concentrated form. Pretty hot stuff. 58%

Scotch Malt Whisky Society Cask 1.144 Aged 15 Years dist Sep 93 **(86.5)** n22 t22.5 f20 b22. Plenty of malty biff about the nose and the sharp delivery warms and entertains. 57.6%

⟫ **Scotch Malt Whisky Society Cask 1.147 Aged 39 Years** refill hogshead, dist Feb 70 **(93)** n23.5 a big oaky signature but the fruit has managed to maintain a degree of freshness; delicate smoke and butterscotch fills in the background; t23.5 quite enormous: the taste buds are placed on full alert as a succession of big, noisy flavours bombard every inch of the palate. The fruits manage to keep the bigger oaks at bay, allowing the middle ground to be occupied by a milkshakey mocha; f23 the odd sharp splinter here and there, but the excellence of the mocha and spice ensures a classic finale; b23 proving that you aren't always going to seed at 39...... 53.5% 124 bottles.

⟫ **Scotch Malt Whisky Society Cask 1.154 Aged 40 Years** refill hogshead, dist Feb 70 **(77)** n21 t18.5 f19 b18.5. A great number of people enjoy this nougat-rich style of over-matured malt, especially when the creosote kicks in. And though it has the odd, fleeting, enjoyable moment, I can't say I'm a great fan. If 1.147 was the SMWS's Brazil of their 1970 bottlings, then this is their Italy... 43.4% 61 bottles.

⟫ **Scotch Malt Whisky Society Cask 1.146 Aged 42 Years** refill hogshead, dist Dec 66 **(70.5)** n23 t20 f17.5 b18. If you invest in this one, do so for the fabulous nose. Elsewhere the oak is shot, a thin sweet fudgy thread keeping this one alive. So just breathe in the glorious gooseberry and butterscotch tart and enjoy. 44.4% 76 bottles.

Whisky Doris Ballindalloch dark sherry cask, dist 66, bott 07 db **(94.5)** n24 t24 f23 b23.5. A sherry butt to make even a perfectionist swoon. 51.3%

The Whisky Fair Glenfarclas 40 Years Old oloroso sherry cask, dist 66, bott 07 **(96)** n23.5 t24.5 f24 b24. A type of cask and style lost to us. Tasted blind you really wouldn't be able to tell between the oloroso or a near faultless 20-year-old bourbon. A magnificent experience. And probably this organisation's greatest ever bottling. 52.4%. The Whisky Fair, 150 bottles.

GLENFIDDICH
Speyside, 1887. William Grant & Sons. Working.

Glenfiddich 12 Years Old db **(79)** n20 t21 f19 b19. Attractively malty in part, but caramel dulls a dram already struggling to come to terms with the oaky imbalance. A real 40 watt bulb. 40%

Glenfiddich 12 Years Old Toasted Oak Reserve (92.5) **n22.5** the oaky building blocks to this are firm and substantial; just enough natural sweet caramel and spice to balance; traces of apple, pear and other soft fruit; **t23.5** much softer delivery than you might imagine from the nose with barley – which was invisible on the nose – making the first impression; again there is a soft fruit moment followed by a wonderful oak development which is at once dry and spicy but by no means out of sync with its surrounds; **f22.5** much drier with rhubarb tart (unsweetened) offering the background notes to that wonderful barley and custard finale; **b24** another bottling to confound the critics of Glenfiddich. This is as fine an essay in balance, charm and sophistication as you are likely to find in the whole of Speyside this year. Crack open a bottle...but only when you have a good hour to spend. 40%

Glenfiddich Aged 12 Years Special Reserve (see Glenfiddich 12 Years Old)

Glenfiddich Caoran Reserve Aged 12 Years db (89) **n22.5** barley breezes in and there is a "did I really see that?" flicker of smoke, too..; **t22** sweet, buzzing malts and some vanilla-lashed oak; **f21.5** traces of muscovado sugar balance the soft spice and custardy finale; **b23** has fizzed up a little in the last year or so with some salivating charm from the barley and a touch of cocoa from the oak. A complex little number. 40%

⋄∷⋄ **Glenfiddich Rich Oak Over 14 Years Old** new American & new Spanish oak finish db (90.5) **n23** fascinating: there is a nod towards Japanese oak in the naked wood profile here. Toned down, though, by a huge pithy kumquat presence. That this is virgin oak there can be no doubt, so don't expect an easy ride; **t22** soft oils help for a quiet landing: like lonely oaks falling in a forest...there is a brief sensation of passing barley. Then it returns again to a number of oak-laden notes, especially the spices which move towards a creamy mocha territory; **f23.5** possibly the best phase of the experience. The vivid, surging oak has cooled and some barley oils mingle in a relaxed fashion with the sweetening, very mildly sugared mocha; **b22** from the moment you nose this, there is absolutely no doubting its virgin oak background. It pulls towards bourbon, but never gets there. Apparently European oak is used, too. The result is something curiously hinting at Japanese, but without the crushing intensity. Delicious, thoughtful whisky and one to tick off on your journey of malt whisky discovery. Though a pity we don't see it at 46% and in full voluptuous nudity: you get the feeling that this would have been something really exceptional to conjure with. 40% William Grant

Glenfiddich 15 Years Old db (94.5) **n23** such a deft intermingling of the softer fruits and bourbon notes...with barley in there to remind you of the distillery; **t23** intense and big yet all the time appearing delicate and light; the most apologetic spices help spotlight the barley sweetness and delicate fruits; **f24.5** just so long and complex; something of the old fashioned fruit salad candy about this but with a small degree of toffee just rounding off the edges; **b24** if an award were to be given for the most consistently beautiful dram in Scotland, this would win more often than not. This under-rated distillery has won more friends with this masterpiece than probably any other brand. 40%

Glenfiddich Aged 15 Years Cask Strength db (85.5) **n20 t23 f21 b21.5.** Improved upon the surprisingly bland bottlings of old, especially on the fabulously juicy delivery. Still off the pace due to an annoying toffee-ness towards the middle and at the death. 51%

⋄∷⋄ **Glenfiddich Distillery Edition 15 Years Old** db (93.5) **n24.5** banana skins, but there is no slip up here as the aroma spectrum moves from ultra fat sultanas on one side to dried coconut on the other. You'll find countless other reference points, including lightly salted celery and even molten candle wax. Quite astonishing and, even with its spice nip, one of the great whisky noses of 2010; **t24** my word!! Just so lively...enormous complexity from the very first mouthful. The mouthfeel is two-toned with heavier fruit not quite outstripping the flightier barley. All kinds of vanilla – both dry and sweet – and a dusty spiciness, too; **f22** tones down rather too dramatically, hedging much more towards the more docile banana-vanilla elements; **b23** had this exceptional whisky been able to maintain the pace through to the finish, this would have been a single malt of the year contender - at least. 51% ncf William Grant

Glenfiddich Aged 15 Years Solera Reserve (see Glenfiddich 15 Years Old)

Glenfiddich 18 Years Old db (95) **n23.5** the smoke, which for long marked this aroma, appears to have vanished. But the usual suspects of blood orange and various other fruit appear to thrive in the lightly salted complexity; **t24.5** how long are you allowed to actually keep the whisky held on the palate before you damage your teeth? One to really close your eyes and study because here we have one of the most complex deliveries Speyside can conjour: the peat may have gone, but there is coal smoke around as the juicy barley embeds with big fat sultanas, plums, dates and grapes. Despite the distinct lack of oil, the mouthfeel is entirely yielding to present one of the softest and most complete essays on the palate you can imagine, especially when you take the bitter-sweet ratio and spice into balance; **f23** long, despite the miserly 40% offered, with plenty of banana-custard and a touch of pear; **b24** at the moment, the ace in the Glenfiddich pack. If this was bottled at 46%, unchilfiltered etc, I dread to think what the score might be... 40%

Glenfiddich 21 Years Old db (86) n21 t23 f21 b21. A much more uninhibited bottling with loads of fun as the mouth-watering barley comes rolling in. But still falls short on taking the hair-raisingly rich delivery forward and simply peters out. 40%

Glenfiddich 30 Years Old db (91.5) n23.5 the usual custard trifle but with a bit of extra bourbon tipped on for good measure; t23.5 again a big early dose of rich honey-hickory bourbon then softer fruits including blackberries; f21.5 a tad tired; chalky and dry; b23 one assumes this is a new vatting because, finale apart, here everything appears to be just that much sharper and cleaner than the last version I officially tasted. 40%

Glenfiddich Rare Collection 40 Years Old db (86.5) n22.5 t23 f20 b21. A quite different version to the last with the smoke having all but vanished, allowing the finish to show the full weight of its considerable age. The nose and delivery are superb, though. The barley sheen on arrival really deserves better support. 43.5%

Glenfiddich 50 Years Old db (97) n25 we are talking 50 years, and yet we are still talking fresh barley, freshly peeled grape and honey. Not ordinary honey. Not the stuff you find in jars. But the pollen that attracts the bees to the petunia; and not any old petunia: not the white or the red or pink or yellow. But the two-toned purple ones. For on the nose at least this is perfection; this is nectar.... t24 a silky delivery: silky barley with silky, watered down maple syrup. The middle ground, in some previous Glenfiddich 50-year-olds a forest of pine and oak, is this time filled with soft, grassy barley and the vaguest hint of a distant smoke spice; f24 long, long, long, with the very faintest snatch of something most delicately smoked: a distant puff of peat reek carried off on the persistent Speyside winds, then a winding-down of vanillas, dropping through the gears of sweetness until the very last traces are chalky dry; b24 for the record, my actual words, after tasting my first significant mouthful, were: "fuck! This is brilliant." It was an ejaculation of genuine surprise, as any fly on the wall of my Tasting Room at 1:17am on Tuesday 4th August would testify. Because I have tasted many 50-year-old whiskies over the years, quite possibly as many as anyone currently drawing breath. For not only have I tasted those which have made it onto the whisky shelves, but, privately, or as a consultant, an untold number which didn't: the heroic but doomed oak-laden failures. This, however, is a quite different animal. We were on the cusp of going to press when this was released, so we hung back. William Grant blender David Stewart, whom I rank above all other blenders on this planet, has known me long and well enough to realise that the surrounding hype, with this being the most expensive whisky ever bottled at £10,000 a go or a sobering £360 a pour, would bounce off me like a pebble from a boulder. "Honestly, David," he told my chief researcher with a timorous insistence, "please tell Jim I really think this isn't too oaky." He offered almost an apology for bringing into the world this 50-year-old babe. Well, as usual David Stewart, doyen of the blending lab and Ayr United season ticket holders, was absolutely spot on. And, as is his want, he was rather understating his case. For the record, David, next time someone asks you how good this whisky is, just for once do away with the Ayeshire niceness installed by generations of very nice members of the Stewart family and tell them: "Actually, it's bloody brilliant if I say so myself! And I don't give a rat's bollocks what Murray thinks." 46.1%

Glenfiddich 1955 Vintage cask no. 4221 db (93) n23 pumped up oak, but deflated somewhat by the subtle nuances of the barley which, somehow, have enough breeziness to breathe a doughy freshness into the proceedings; t23 brilliant, entirely schizophrenic, delivery of honey-oak and big spice, all on a base of a coppery sheen: very much the sma' still character to this one; f23 long, lush with drying, oak-vanilla and still that wonderful barley/coppery gloss. Oh, and a dribble of smoke bleeding into the late honey; b24 a real surprise package, because even without sherry or peat to hide behind there is enough complexity and, at times, utter brilliance to dazzle the most demanding of commentators. And, believe me; this is one sample I didn't spit.... Over 50 years old and quite majestic. Truly classic stuff. 52.6%

Glenfiddich 1958 Vintage cask no. 8642 db (78) n23 t18 f18 b19. Oak can be such an unforgiving master. Fabulous old oloroso nose, though. 46.3%

Glenfiddich 1959 Vintage cask no. 3934 db (89) n23 big age here: this one is creaking with oak and oloroso but the harmony is excellent. Pans out with spiced toffee apple and dates: superb; t22 stunning delivery with big fruit at first then several layers of spice over the burned fudge; the oak is less than discreet but does limited damage; f22 long, toasty and a fade of cremated raisins; some lovely esters last the pace; b22 from the year Jacky Cox led Ayr United to the old Scottish Second Division Championship, something equally as rare! Glenfiddich showing something of a rummy side to its character with lots of copper and ester in the mix. The oak is profound, but sits comfortably in the scheme of things. One for late at night, closed eyes and memories of long-lost days at Somerset Park. 48.1%

Glenfiddich 1964 Vintage cask no. 13430 db **(80)** n22 t22 f17 b19. The nose is pure bourbon – and very old bourbon at that. Wobbles a bit in both aroma and delivery but for all its oaky over- zestfulness – and even a touch of the soaps (especially on the finish) – you still cannot help but enjoy this one. To say it is a character is something of an understatement...!! 45.6%

Glenfiddich 1973 Vintage cask no. 9874 db **(94)** n23 citrus - made from concentrate: hard as nails nose really pumps out the barley-fruit marriage; t23 mouth-filling, luxuriously mouthwatering and barley, fruit and spice all at full throttle; f24 the oak is driven like a stake through the barley, but there is a fabulous molassed edge to it. The late viscosity carries a delightful hint of liquorice. Wow!; b24 I've been tasting these special casks from this distillery since before my hair went grey. I've sampled some good 'uns. This is possibly the best of the lot. 48.1%

Glenfiddich Vintage Reserve 1973 cask no. 9874 **(92)** n23 very few Glenfiddich casks of this age stand quite so tall: wonderful hot-cross bun theme, even with a sliver of salted butter; the fruit-barley element excels; t23 exquisite delivery and mouth-feel: the oak is pounding at the door but that glorious fruit/bourbon/barley core refuses to budge; some wonderful strands of smoke disappear into the middle's demerara depths f22 appears for a while to be sliding under the oak, then bucks up as the honey-barley breathes fresh life back into it; b24 whisky picked at its very ripest! The juices are still flowing despite a massive oak threat. But such is the sheer élan and fruit and sweet edges that an astounding and beautiful experience is assured. 46.5%

Glenfiddich 1976 cask no. 16389 bott 07 db **(87)** n23.5 apricots and pears, all under a dollop of custard, sees off the encroaching oaks; finely tuned and finely balanced, the bitter-sweet ratio is just about spot on and the clarity at body temp is excellent; look close enough and you might even find the most delicate flicker of smoke; t22 a few splinters early on are overcome by intense barley and vanilla; mouth-watering at first, and a tad spicy; the middle sees the oak gaining ground fast; f20 just a shade too oaky for its own good, but some fruit does counter; b21.5 bottled in the nick of time. The vast majority of Glenfiddichs crash and burn by this age: it is not a malt, peaking in age as it does in the 15 to 18 region, that can usually stand up to great years in the cask. Here it manages it, just, and for good measure offers a truly memorable nose. 474%. Exclusively for Willow Park, Calgary

Glenfiddich Vintage Reserve 1976 cask no. 516, bott 07 db **(93.5)** n23 t24 f23 b23.5. I still say that Glenfiddich is not naturally disposed to old age. However, the odd ancient gem crops up...and this is one. 51.9%. 549 bottles.

⸭ **Hart Brothers Glenfiddich Aged 45 Years** 1st sherry hogshead filled, dist Sep 64, bott Oct 09 **(96)** n25 what a wonderful marriage of over-ripe dates, mid roast Mysore coffee, blackened banana and the fruitiest of old Demerara pot still rum-seasoned fruitcake... Perfection, it has to be said... t24 the oak shows up early but immediately states that it shall go so far and not encroach on the overall balance. Just as well because the balance between the sharpness and richness of toasted raisin is spot on; there is burnt toast sweetened with plum jam and Demerara-lightened coffee; f23 an understandable degree of bitterness – a mixture of that toast again and cocoa – but offset by a fabulous burnt fudge sweetness; b24 to think this was distilled in 2 BR: 2 Before Ramsey, that is 1964...two years before England first won the World Cup. Now, having spent the last half hour being blown away by this, I leave my tasting lab to watch England take on the Germans in the hope (never expectation) that we might continue on course to do it again. This time, though, with some of the finest malt Scotland is currently able to offer. How ironic is that....? 55.6% Hart Brothers Ltd

GLEN GARIOCH
Highland (Eastern), 1798. Suntory. Working.

Glen Garioch 8 Years Old db **(85.5)** n21 t22 f21 b21.5. A soft, gummy, malt – not something one would often write about a dram of this or any age from Geary! However, this may have something to do with the copious toffee which swamps the light fruits which try to emerge. 40%

Glen Garioch 10 Years Old db **(80)** n19 t22 f19 b20. Chunky and charming, this is a malt that once would have ripped your tonsils out. Much more sedate and even a touch of honey to the rich body. Toffeed at the finish. 40%

Glen Garioch 12 Years Old db **(88.5)** n22 gooseberries and fudge....and a touch of smoke...!!!!; t23 mouth filling with a delicious degree of sharp maltiness; f21.5 toffees out, though a little smoke drifts back in; b22 a significant improvement on the complexity front. The return of the smoke after a while away was a surprise and treat. 43%

Glen Garioch 15 Years Old db **(86.5)** n20.5 t22 f22 b22. In the a bottling I sampled last year the peat definitely vanished. Now it's back again, though in tiny, if entertaining, amounts. 43%

Glen Garioch 21 Years Old db **(91)** n21 a few wood shavings interrupt the toasty barley; t23 really good bitter-sweet balance with honeycomb and butterscotch leading the line; pretty juicy, busy stuff; f24 dries as it should with some vague spices adding to the vanilla and hickory; b23 an entirely re-worked, now smokeless, malt that has little in common with its predecessors. Quite lovely, though. 43%

Glen Garioch 1797 Founders Reserve db **(87.5)** n21 fruit toffee fudge; t22 some fizz on delivery followed by a rampaging barley juiciness; much lighter and softer than the strength indicates; f22.5 excellent mocha accompanies the fruit with aplomb; b22 impressively fruity and chewy: some serious flavour profiles in there. 48%

Glen Garioch 1958 db **(90)** n24 what a brilliant, heady, almost eccentric mix of once chunky peat, once vivid malt and now beautifully varnished oak; t21 loses its early balance but settles on a waxy honey thread to complement the slowly reasserting peat; f23 elegance in abundance as the oak plays lip-service to the sweet, chewy malt. Just so charming! b22 the distillery in its old clothes: and quite splendid it looks! 43%. 328 bottles.

Duncan Taylor Collection Glen Garioch 1988 Aged 19 Years cask no. 1559 **(96)** n24.5 t24 f23.5 b24. I knew there must have been a reason I got up this morning...it was to discover this irresistible, slightly feisty, sublimely-structured malt!!! Oh, joy! 55.4%

Duncan Taylor Collection Glen Garioch 1988 cask no. 1560 **(86)** n22 t22 f21 b21. Seriously enjoyable, long and some insanely rich barley. But by comparison to its twin – cask 1559 – just rather flat and docile. Such is the difference a cask can make. 55.5%

Duncan Taylor Collection Glen Garioch 1988 cask no. 1988 **(94)** n23 sexy peat is understated yet, despite a fruity presence, offers the lead and background: intriguing... t24 pure old-fashioned Geary in the way the peat pulses through, but the final delivery is near orgasmic as the sultana fruits and smoke combine with an irresistable rough edge and bite: mind-blowing... f23 long, slick, for all the nip and bite and wave upon wave of ever-sweetening smoke; ultimately a slightly over-burned fruit cake; b24 glorious whisky with attitude. A must get malt: simple as that! 54.4%

Lonach Glen Garioch 1989 cask no. 8426 **(89.5)** n22 the vanillas are lost amid delicate gristy-sweet tones; t23.5 near perfect mouthfeel: no oil to speak of, allowing the barley to fizz and zip around, landing soft and/or thumping blows to different taste buds; f22 a gentlemanly fade with the barley and vanilla taking turns to lead the way; b22 another wonderful Geary! 53.3%. Duncan Taylor.

⏤ **Mackillop's Choice Glen Garioch 1990** dist Apr 90, bott Feb 10 **(94)** n23 well, what do you know? A touch of dark, earthy peat.... a throwback to the days when their kiln was still working (and I'd throw on some of the turf) I assume; t24 big, uncompromisingly full bodied with wonderful thick malt; touches of light smoke and cocoa work wonderfully together; best of all, though, is the house style of nip and pinch on the palate...just love it! f23.5 long with a light citrus flourish to the half-hearted spice and smoke; b23.5 almost brings a tear to the eye when I find a ye-olde style Geary with a touch of smoke. A bit rough and ready, but absolutely gorgeous! And a type of Geary I haven't tasted in years. 56.6% Iain Mackillop & Co. Ltd

Mackillop's Choice Glen Garioch 1990 cask no. 10291, dist Dec 90, bott Jan 07 **(84)** n21 t22 f21 b20. Usual 'Geary bite, passion and fun . But the fruity notes and the trace peat don't somehow gel with the oak in a way you hope it might. 57.1%. Iain Mackillop & Co. Ltd

Old Masters Glen Garioch Aged 19 Years cask no. 1536 dist 88, bott 08 **(93)** n23 outstanding toffee apple and burnt raisin aroma; spotted dog pudding and custard; t24 firm barley arrives first with multi-layers of brown molasses and dried dates; never less than huge, yet always controlled; f23 long and refined: it is like picking very old fruitcake from between the teeth; b23 Old Master by name and nature! 53.1%. James MacArthur & Co. Ltd.

Provenance Glen Garioch Aged 12 Years refill hogshead, cask no. 4072, dist 95, bott 07 **(87.5)** n22 t22 f21.5 b22. There is an older generation who will appreciate certain aspects of this one. 46%. nc ncf. Douglas Laing.

⏤ **Scotch Malt Whisky Society Cask 19.44 Aged 20 Years** refill hogshead, dist Oct 88 **(79)** n21 t20 f19 b19. Thin with a touch of the malty paint stripper about it. 53.3% 251 bottles.

GLENGLASSAUGH
Speyside, 1875. Scaent Group. Working.

Glenglassaugh 21 Year Old db **(94)** n23.5 elegant and adroit, the lightness of touch between the citrus and barley is nigh on mesmeric: conflicting messages of age in that it appears younger and yet you feel something has to be this kind of vintage to hit this degree of aloofness. Delicate and charming...; t24.5 again we have all kinds of messages on delivery: the spices fizz around announcing oaky intentions and then the barley sooths and sweetens even with a degree of youthful juiciness. The tastebuds are never more than caressed, the sugar-sweetened citrus ensuring neither the barley or oak form any kind of advantage; impeccably weighted, a near perfect treat for the palate; **f22.5** white chocolate and vanilla lead the way as the oak begins to offer a degree of comparative austerity; **b23.5** a malt which simply sings on the palate and a fabulous benchmark for the new owners to try to achieve in 2030...!! 46%

⋯ **Glenglassaugh 26 Years Old** db **(78.5) n19 t21.5 f18.5 b19.5.** Industrial amounts of cream toffee here. Also some odd and off key fruit notes winging in from somewhere. Not quite the gem I had hoped for. 46%

Glenglassaugh 30 Year Old db **(89) n23** the grape of noble rot stands haughtily beside the oak without blot; **t23** fruity, silky, if in some places a little flat. Lots of dried dates, demerara, chocolate raisins, a little of this, a little of that... **f21** against every wish, drifts away incoherently, mumbling something coffee-ish; **b22** sheer poetry. Or not... 43.1%

Glenglassaugh 40 Year Old db **(96) n24.5** the kind of oak you'd expect at this age – if you are uncommonly lucky or have access to some of the most glorious-nosing ancient casks in all Scotland - but there is so much else on the fruity front besides: grape, over-ripe yam, fat cherries...And then there is a bourbony element with molassed hickory and sweetened vanilla: wake me, I must be dreaming...on second thoughts, don't; **t24.5** pure silk on delivery. All the flavours arrive in one rich wave of consummate sweetness, a tapestry celebrating the enormity of both the fruit and oak, yet condensed into a few inches rather than feet; plenty of soft medium roast Jamaican Blue Mountain and then at times mocha; on the fruity front there is juicy dates mulched with burned raisin; **f23** the relative Achilles heel as the more bitter, nutty parts of the oak gather; **b24** it is as if this malt has gone through a 40-year marrying process: the interlinking of flavours and styles is truly beyond belief. One of the great world whiskies for 2010 44.6%

Glenglassaugh 'The Spirit Drink' db **(85) n20 t22 f21.5 b21.5.** A pretty wide margin taken on the cut here, it seems, so there is plenty to chew over. Richly flavoured and a tad oily, as is to be expected, which helps the barley to assert itself in midstream. The usual new make chocolaty element at work here, too, late on. Just great to see this distillery back in harness after all these years. And a great idea to get the new spirit out to the public, something I have been encouraging distilleries to do since my beard was still blue. Look forward to seeing another version where a narrower cut has been made. 50%. 8,160 bottles.

Glenglassaugh 'The Spirit Drink That Blushes to Speak Its Name' db **(85) n22 t21.5 f21 b21.** Not whisky, of course. New make matured for a few months in wine barrels. The result is a Rose-looking spirit. Actually takes me back to my early childhood – no, not the tasting of new make spirit. But the redcurrant aroma which does its best to calm the new make ruggedness. Tasty and fascinating, though the wine tries to minimalise the usual sweetness you find in malt spirit. 50%

Glenglassaugh 1973 Family Silver db **(95) n23 t24 f24 b24.** From first to last this whisky caresses and teases. It is old but shows no over-ageing. It offers what appears a malt veneer but is complexity itself. Brilliant. And now, sadly, almost impossible to find. Except, possibly, at the Mansefield Hotel, Elgin. 40%

⋯ **Adelphi Glen Garioch 1990 Aged 19 Years** bourbon hogshead, cask no. 2697, bott 2009 **(83) n21.5 t21 f20 b20.5.** Pretty one dimensional malt, but helped along the way with a nod towards a pleasing bourbony sweetness. 53.8% 234 bottles.

Berrys' Own Selection Glenglassaugh 1983 bott 07 **(89.5) n22 t22 f23 b22.5.** Drag off the shelf and buy: it's a diamond. 46%. Berry Bros & Rudd.

Cadenhead's Authentic Collection Glenglassaugh Aged 23 Years sherry butt, dist 84, bott Sep 07 **(79) n19 t21.5 f19 b19.5.** At its better moments much closer to Demerara pot still rum in style than malt. One assumes the sherry butt is authentically from the old distillery owners, taking into account its obvious 's' fault. 52.5%. 612 bottles.

Dewar Rattray Glenglassaugh 1986 cask no. 162, bott Jun 07 **(75.5) n18 t21 f18 b18.5.** Sulphur all over this one like a rash. Massive injection of orangey citrus tries to compensate. Memo to new owners: don't put your spirit into sulphur-screwed sherry butts. 53.4%

⋯ **Highland Malt Glenglassaugh 31 Years Old 1978** bott 2009 **(87) n23** from the polished leather and boiled candy school of aged sweetness: **t22** immediate oaky impact but weathered by the sharpness of barley which rages ages the age; **f20.5** pretty tired and rickety; **b21.5** a cask on the brink. But enough life left in there, just, for some excellent moments. 44.6% Speciality Drinks Ltd, bottled for TWE's 10th Anniversary

⋯ **Old Malt Cask Glenglassaugh Aged 25 Years** sherry butt, cask no. DL 5362,dist Jul 84, bott Jul 09 **(71) n17.5 t20 f16.5 b17.** Bottled in Rotarua, new suspects... 50% 616 bottles.

Wilson & Morgan Barrel Selection Glenglassaugh 23 Years Old dist 84, bott 07 **(91.5) n23 t23 f22.5 b23.** The best 'Glassaugh for a little while and even able to overcome a minor glitch. A real gentle giant, which is more of a giant than it is gentle. 46%

GLENGOYNE

Highlands (Southwest), 1833. Peter Russell. Working.

Glengoyne 10 Years Old db (90) n22 beautifully clean despite coal-gas bite. The barley is almost in concentrate form with a marmalade sweetness adding richness; t23 crisp, firm arrival with massive barley surge, seriously chewy and textbook bitter-sweet balance; but now some oils have tucked in to intensify and lengthen; f22 incredibly long and refined for such a light malt. The oak, which made soft noises in the middle now intensifies, but harmonises with the intense barley; an added touch of coffee signals some extra oak in recent bottlings; b23 proof that to create balance you do not have to have peat at work. The secret is the intensity of barley intermingling with oak. Not a single negative note from first to last and now a touch of oil and coffee has upped the intensity further. 40%

∴ **Glengoyne 12 Years Old** db (91.5) n22.5 salty, sweet, lightly fruity; t23 one of the softest deliveries on the market: the fruit, gristy sugars and malt combine to melt in the mouth: there is not a single hint of firmness; f23 a graduation of spices and vanilla. Delicate and delightful...; b23 the nose has a curiously intimate feel but the tasting experience is a wonderful surprise. 43%

Glengoyne 12 Years Old Cask Strength db (79) n18 t22 f19 b20. Not quite the happiest Glengoyne I've ever come across with the better notes compromised. 57.2%. nc ncf.

∴ **Glengoyne 12 Years Old Scottish Merchant's Choice 1996** sherry hogshead no. 3447 db (88.5) n22 pots of marmalade; t23 lush, quite wonderful dovetailing between juicy barley and no less juicy grape; f21.5 dries and bitters slightly but enough vanilla to cope; b22 high quality sherry influence. 57.8%

∴ **Glengoyne 13 Years Old Single Cask 1995** European oak sherry hogshead no. 2082, dist Oct 95 db (94) n24 just one of those fabulous, weakening of the knees, moments you used to get in the warehouse many years ago: a 12 to 15 whisky maturing in a top form oloroso butt...the bung is pulled out and you stick your nose in the barrel. You used to get...this. But very rarely now, alas. That unique slightly burnt raisin, slightly concentrated orange pith, dank heavy mixture with a custardy oakiness and a sweeter, fresher edge. Priceless.... t24 just awe inspiring. Almost a perfect weight on the palate as those burnt raisins and sultanas battle it out, with that orangey fruitcake background which this kind of malt demands; f23 a touch bitter. Just burnt raisin in excess, or was a sulphur stick waved around here for a second or two thirteen years ago....? I'll go with the raisins...; b23 for those of you wandering what a 1990s non sulphured sherry butt tastes like – and I am sure some of your still don't know for certain – grab some of this. And just jump into that glass: it's safe and wonderful! 56.1% Ian Macleod

∴ **Glengoyne 16 Years Old Single Cask 1993 American** oak sherry hogshead no. 899 db (86) n22 t22 f21 b21. Hold the front page, for here's the amazingly good news: sherry hogshead used...no sulphur. The not quite such good news is that the grape is so dominant, not much else gets a look in. Some lovely coffee notes to cling on to, and all-in-all a dram worthy of a second glass. 53.9% for Dr Jekyll's Pub, Oslo

Glengoyne 17 Years Old db (86) n21 t23 f21 b21. Some of the guys at Glengoyne think I'm nuts. They couldn't get their head around the 79 I gave it last time. And they will be shaking my neck not my hand when they see the score here...Vastly improved but there is an off sherry tang which points to a naughty butt or two somewhere. Elsewhere mouth-watering and at times fabulously intense. 43%

∴ **Glengoyne 18 Years Old Ambassador's Choice 1990** bourbon cask no. 2850, dist Nov 90 db (92) n23 thick natural caramels offer clean barley, oranges and a number of delicate sugars; t23.5 excellent barley layering on delivery: sweet despite some prickle and nip. Mouthwatering yet creamy...this is a complex hombre; f23 remains big and returns to those caramels on the nose; b22.5 I am assuming that the Ambassador who chose this isn't Scotland's Ambassador to England. No, I think they mean the guy who turns up wearing a kilt at some whisky festival or other and tells you Glengoyne/ Talisker/ Glenmorangie, or whoever he (or she) is representing, is the dog's. Well, take a bow Mr Glengoyne Ambassador: you obviously know your casks. This is a charmer with hobnail boots. 59.9%

Glengoyne 21 Years Old db (90) n21 closed and tight for the most part as Glengoyne sometimes has a tendency to be nose-wise, with the emphasis very much on coal gas; t22 slow to start with a few barley heads popping up to be seen; then spices arrive with the oak for a slightly bourbony feel. Gentle butterscotch and honey add a mouth-watering edge to the drier oaks; f24 a stupendous honey thread is cross-stitched through the developing oak to deliver near perfect poise and balance at finish; b23 a vastly improved dram where the caramel has vanished and the tastebuds are constantly assailed and questioned. A malt which builds in pace and passion to delivery a final, wonderful coup-de-grace. Moments of being quite cerebral stuff. 43%

Glengoyne 21 Years Old Sherry Edition db **(93)** n22 heavy, nutty oily, slightly sweaty and not entirely faultless. When warmed the full, brooding oloroso gamut comes into play. Seriously big, if somewhat cumbersome; **t24** much sweeter arrival than you might have thought possible from the nose, and less sticky too. The richness of the oloroso coats every crevice and a playful spice teases while a mollased, toasted oaky/barley sub plot develops delightfully; **f23** not dissimilar to an excellent Demerara rum on the finish with no shortage of coffee-tinted roasty notes on the death. A real chew; **b24** the nose at first is not overly promising, but it settles at it warms and what follows on the palate is at times glorious. Few whiskies will match this for its bitter-sweet depth which is pure textbook. Glengoyne as few will have seen it before. *43%*

⋰⋱ **Glengoyne 23 Years Old Single Cask 1986** European oak sherry butt no. 399 db **(85)** n22 t22 f21 b21. Though from a sherry cask, fascinating just how many bourbon attributes sneak onto the nose. An enjoyable malt, but not without the odd flaw. *53.6%*

⋰⋱ **Glengoyne 40 Years Old** db **(83)** n23 t21 f19 b20. Thick fruit intermittently pads around the nose and palate but the oak is pretty colossal. Apparent attempts to reinvigorate it appear to have backfired. *45.9%*

Glengoyne 1988 Aged 19 Years Single Cask Pedro Ximinex butt, cask no.718 db **(92)** n23 t21.5 f24.5 b23. The delivery is a bit too glutinous, but on the finish the story can be told: and in what detail!! A whisky to smear over your partner's body. Or anyone consenting you fancy, really... *58.3%. German Market.*

Glengoyne 1989 Single Cask Billy's Choice Amontillado hogshead, cask no. 1202 db **(65.5)** n15 t17 f16.5 b17. You genuinely shudder with this one. Seriously, sulphurously grim. *54.1%*

Glengoyne 1989 Single Cask Robbie's Choice ruby port hogshead, cask no. 328 db **(89)** n21.5 sandalwood and crushed petal (yes, really....!!); **t22** proud grape struts its stuff; sweet and spicy; **f23** genuinely sophisticated with bitter cocoa putting the final touches to the oily juices; **b22.5** Robbie 1, Billy 0. *55.1%*

Glengoyne 1990 Aged 17 Years Single Cask Amontillado butt, cask no. 1523 db **(63)** n14 t17.5 f15.5 b16. The grape fights bravely against the sulphur, but it's a bloodbath. *56.3%.*

Glengoyne 1992 Aged 16 Years Single Cask refill hogshead, cask no. 2078, dist Sep 92 db **(87)** n21 a strange one: both generous and niggardly at the same time, the rich barley being kept down by some sharp, unhelpful oak notes; **t22** not quite a faultless delivery but there are all kinds of sugar-spangled barley themes going on. Light shards of almond found amid the growing spice; sharp, at times eye-watering; **f21.5** dries allowing a few cracks to show. But those sweeter elements keep out the worst; **b22.5** have to admit: than the nose suggests: at times a sugar sprinkled (mildly flawed) charmer... *52.3%*

Glengoyne 1993 Aged 14 Years Single Cask American oak, sherry hogshead, cask no. 832 db **(90)** n23 t22 f22.5 b22.5. I suppose a curmudgeon would grumble about there being too much sherry. Perhaps. But then I would counter argue that in this day and age to find a cask so not screwed by sulphur is in itself something to truly celebrate. *59.6%*

Glengoyne 1993 Aged 14 Years Single Cask Pedro Ximinex hogshead, cask no. 876 db **(91.5)** n23.5 t23 f22.5 b22.5. For those of us who are rapidly losing confidence in whisky held in sherry (and from what I understand I am by no means alone), here is something to restore your faith. Well, a little bit, anyway.... *57.9%. German Market.*

Glengoyne 1993 Aged 15 Years Single Cask oloroso sherry hogshead, cask no. 845, dist Apr 93 db **(92.5)** n24 unmistakable oloroso mixed with blood orange; dense with a fudge border; **t22.5** juicy, winey arrival and then a slow leaking of spices; even becomes a bit sharp and semi-aggressive; **f23** some barley actually gets a word in as the camp coffee begins to melt into the burnt raisin; **b23** sherry as it used to be and a strange choice for the Germans, as they appear to be the one nation that can cope with the sulphur with minimum fuss. *55.5%. German market.*

Glengoyne 1996 Aged 11 Years Single Finish Cask La Nerthe cask finish db **(88)** n21.5 t21.5 f22.5 b22.5. Beautifully textured and weighted: a real delight. *52.5%. German Market.*

⋰⋱ **Glengoyne Port Cask Finish 1996** db **(74)** n17 t20 f18.5 b18.5. Decent fruit on delivery, but elsewhere proof that in whisky there is no such thing as any port cask in a storm... *46% Ian Macleod*

Glengoyne 1997 Aged 11 Years Single Cask European oak sherry hogshead, cask no. 2692, dist Jun 97 db **(93)** n24 huge, and I mean gigantic, sherry. Almost something of the old fashioned nut brown ale to this one, except this is also dripping with noble rot grape. Of the barley you cannot hear a squeak; **t23** sherry, anyone? For the first few waves that's all that can be found, as it crashes with a feather-light softness against the tastebuds; the early sweetness is slowly replaced by a much more down to earth spice and a bit of a salty edge, too; **f24** a glorious sherry-led sunset, but now the grape has thinned to allow all manner of spices and demerara-sweetened mocha notes to show; the body changes too, from silk to a pleasant bit of rough; **b23** I bet you 20 years ago I might have given this a 89 or so. However, such has been the damage done by the influx of sulphur-ruined or -damaged sherry butts into the industry, and so wide their rotting net, that you just have to give the rare, wonderful specimens such as this a standing ovation. The first two or three mouthfuls are overwhelming: when your tastebuds adjust you will be in for a rare treat. *56.3%*

Glengoyne 1997 Aged 11 Years Single Cask cask no. 2725, dist Jun 97 db **(95) n24** absolutely cracking first-fill bourbon cask thumping out zesty vanilla, red liquorice and barley as though its life depends on it; **t24.5** you almost swoon, such is the piled high, unrelenting intensity to the barley: this is concentrated barley concentrate. To the power of ten. Wonderful golden syrup-dipped strands of oak tie in beautifully; **f23** long, delicately spiced, with a light oiliness further expounding the virtues of liquorice-led bourbony notes; **b23.5** taking into account that Norway has to be the most expensive place on this planet, this still will have been worth twice whatever price was asked for it. *56.5%. Bottled for the Oslo Whisky Festival*

Glengoyne 1999 Single Cask Deek's Choice refill hogshead, cask no. 16 db **(83.5) n20.5 t21.5 f21 b21.** Crisp, juicy barley and emerging vanilla. Some bitter orange, too. *60.9%*

Glengoyne 'Glen Guin' 16 Year Old Shiraz Finish db **(79) n18.5 t20 f19.5 b20.** Some oily depth here. *48%*

Glengoyne Burnfoot db **(84) n21 t21 f21.5 b21.** A clodhopping bruiser of a malt. Good honey, though. *40%. Duty Free Market.*

❖ **Berrys' Own Selection Glengoyne 1999** cask no. 500781 **(83.5) n21.5 t21.5 f20.5 b20.** A plodding though pleasant malt. *46% Berry Bros & Rudd*

The Càrn Mòr Vintage Collection Glengoyne 2000 hogshead, cask no. 438, dist 00, bott 09 **(76.5) n18.5 t18.5 f19.5 b19.** Even taking into account its age, there should be a lot more offered than this. Settles only when the natural caramels kick in late on. *46%.*

Hart Brothers Glengoyne Aged 12 Years dist Jun 95, bott May 08 **(85.5) n22 t22 f20.5 b21.** Magnificently clean and malty. But too much a straight bat and the finish is smothered by natural caramel. *46%. Hart Brothers Limited.*

❖ **Malts of Scotland Glengoyne 1972** sherry butt no. 3195, dist Sep 72, bott Jun 09 **(85) n22.5 t22 f20 b20.5.** The marmalade is perhaps a tad too bitter. Elsewhere the honey and spice delights. *52.8% Malts of Scotland. 192 bottles.*

❖ **Malts of Scotland Glengoyne 1973** bourbon barrel no. 677, dist Feb 73, bott Jun 09 **(92) n24** magnificent! Has started on the road to old aged exotic fruit, but been diverted somewhere along the line and ended up on a much more floral route. Even some crushed, lightly salted macadamia nut. With a tiny dollop of acacia honey for good measure, it just needs a good half hour even before tasting...; **t23** how can something approaching 40 years of age be this juicy? Well, except probably my neighbour. But that apart, the barley has no problem fending off the close attentions of the oak and makes a complex fist of it; **f22.5** does dry now but still enough soft honey to do the job; **b22.5** Glengoyne + very good bourbon barrel = excellence. Usually. *55.1% Malts of Scotland. 192 bottles.*

❖ **Malts of Scotland Glengoyne 1997** sherry butt no. 582, dist Feb 97, bott Jun 09 **(62) n16 t15.5 f15 b15.5.** Sulphur, anyone? *57.2% Malts of Scotland. 192 bottles.*

❖ **Malts of Scotland Glengoyne 1998** sherry butt, cask no. 1131, dist Apr 98, bott Feb 10 **(77.5) n19 t20.5 f19 b19.** Sumptuous grape. But very tight with a furry buzz. Much better than cask 1132. The thing is: would Brian Eno's Subtlety Spectrograph have spotted the difference? *54.8% Malts of Scotland. 192 bottles.*

❖ **Malts of Scotland Glengoyne 1998** sherry butt, cask no. 1132, dist Apr 98, bott Feb 10 **(70.5) n18 t19 f16.5 b17.** Beautiful colour. *55.2% 192 bottles.*

Old Malt Cask Glengoyne Aged 10 Years Gabriel Meffre wine cask no. 3686, dist Dec 96, bott Jun 07 **(75.5) n18 t20 f19.5 b18.** Sweet in part, but simply doesn't gel. *50%. Douglas Laing. 303 bottles.*

Old Malt Cask Glengoyne Aged 11 Years Bourbon Finish dist Jun 96, **(83) n21 t21 f20 b21.** Intense barley sugar, though a bit of a fuzzy note. Even, so, in a different league to the Wine Finish. *50%. Douglas Laing.*

❖ **Old Malt Cask Glengoyne 13 Years Old** refill hogshead no. DL 5727, dist Dec 96, bott Jan 10 **(89) n22** grassy....drying hay; **t22** flinty barley just hardens further; **f23** unusually long for a Glengoyne with a delicate oiliness helping to maximise the muscovado sugars and tangy spice; **b22** solid as a rock. Not exactly complex, but when you get top quality barley all the way it doesn't need to be. Fabulous spices towards the end, though. *50% 311 bottles.*

❖ **Provenance Glengoyne 10 Years Old** refill hogshead no. DMG 5737, dist Autumn 1999, bott Winter 2010 **(86.5) n20.5 t23 f21.5 b21.5.** Malty – almost with a Horlicks creaminess – but not that many other tricks. Not one to say no to. *46% Douglas Laing & Co Ltd*

Provenance Glengoyne Aged 10 Years refill hogshead, dist autumn 97, bott summer 08 **(82.5) n19 t22.5 f21 b20.** Soaring, intense barley. Given a better cask, and this would have been some dram. *46%. Douglas Laing.*

⋯∷⋯ **The Whisky Agency Glengoyne 1972** sherry cask **(90) n21.5** uncompromising oak. A little Demerara lightens things a little; **t22.5** a bit of a mess as the oak tries to play big shot; some decent oils and sharp fruit: for those who like a bit of the rough stuff; **f24.5** one of the great finishes of any OAP malt this year: the chocolate fruit and nut needs experiencing for believing...; **b22** the oak gets tossed around the palate like logs on a raging river. Amazingly finds something to cling to at the end. An amazing malt you are unlikely to forget in a hurry. *63.5%*

GLEN GRANT
Speyside, 1840. Campari. Working.
Glen Grant db **(87) n21.5** young barley, new-mown grass and a smudge of toffee; **t23** huge flavour explosion led by juicy, young malt. Soft spices reveal an oaky interest, too; **f21** over-laced with caramel; **b21.5** this is a collector's malt for the back label alone: truly one of the most bizarre I have ever seen. "James Grant, 'The Major'" it cheerfully chirrups, "was only 25 when he set about achieving his vision of a single malt with a clear colour. The unique flavour and appearance was due to the purifiers and the tall slender stills he designed and the decision to retain its natural colour...." Then underneath is written: "Farven Justeter Med Karamel/Mit Farbstoff"" Doh! Or, as they say in German: "Doh!" Need any more be said about the nonsense, the pure insanity, of adding colouring to whisky. *40%*

Glen Grant 5 Years Old db **(89) n22.5** dry and herbal with crushed celery, grist, agave, a sprinkle of pepper; **t22** crisp, firm barley with the sweetness handcuffed by a quick spurt of vanilla; semi-serious spice; **f21.5** clean, late oils and warming peppers; **b23** elegant malt which has noticeably grown in stature and complexity of late. *40%*

Glen Grant 10 Years Old db **(88) n22** fine, flinty grain, quite hard and with limited oak interference; **t22** really mouthwatering, clean and fresh: not an offnote in sight; **f22** gentle, almost half sleeping, just malt and a faint buzz of oak; **b22.** a relaxed, confident malt from a distillery that makes great whisky with effortless charm and each mouthful seems to show that it knows it. And on re-taste it appears a honey and spice element has been upped slightly. *40%*

Glen Grant 15 Years Old Cask Strength Limited Edition Cask no.17163 dist Feb 92, bott Sep 07 db **(86) n20 t23.5 f21 b21.5.** Such a frustrating bottling: thumping caramel makes its mark on both the nose and finish. Glen Grant is, for me, unquestionably one of the truly great distilleries of Scotland. And this should have been a cask soaring into the 90s score-wise because elsewhere the stunning oak-spice and layered bourbon-esque honey is truly brilliant. But caramel, either added, or naturally leaking from the cask, has flattened the beginning and end, leaving memories of those fabulous waves of rich, sweet barley to haunt you. *59.9%*

⋯∷⋯ **Glen Grant Aged 16 Years** bott Mar 10 db **(91.5) n23** a lovely under-ripe banana sharpness to this while the malt snuggles up to the crunchy green apple; a playful molecule of smoke wafts around; **t23.5** salivating, fresh, slightly green ...and that's just the first few nano-seconds of the delivery! Next comes a lengthy, relaxed wave of oilier barley, with a coppery, honeyed depth; tangy vanilla fills the middle ground; **f21.5** medium length, more oils and barley but with a degree of bitterness; **b22** again the finish doesn't do justice to the earlier jousting on the nose and palate. The label talks about orchard fruits, and they are absolutely spot on. Apples are order of the day, but not sure about the ripe bit: they appear slightly green to me...and that suits the nature of the crisp malt. A gorgeous whisky I fully expect to see improve over coming batches: it's one that has potential to hit superstar status. *43%*

⋯∷⋯ **Glen Grant Cask Strength Limited Edition Aged 17 Years** cask no. 17152, dist Feb 92, bott May 09 db **(94) n23.5** handsomely elegant and bolstered with an embracing degree of old-fashioned Speyside smoke, this nose demands some study. Curiously salty and studded with dried orange peel, the grain is not exactly its usual crisp self: maybe a degree of toffee has something to do with this; **t24** the initial note on delivery is crisp barley. But this is soon smothered by a sweet, warming, lightly oiled smokiness which brings with it a degree of cocoa. On another level there is toffee fudge and honeycomb: together one is left salivating, with the tongue dementedly pounding the roof of the mouth; **f23.5** continues along the very long road, the sweetness fluctuating with a hint of molasses here and liquorice there; **b23** the nose suggests there maybe some added caramel; the whopping bourbon notes suggests it could be natural. Either way, strip a little toffee away and you might be left with what would have been a contender for Scotch single malt of the year. The balance and artistry beggars belief. Glen Grant distillery really is capable of producing some of the most monumental malt moments you can find on the whisky shelves today. *58.8% 360 bottles.*

Glen Grant Cellar Reserve 1992 bottled 08 db **(94.5)** n23 a beguiling array of crisp barley and crystalised sugary notes; if a nose can be crunchy and brittle, then this really is it; **t24** the tastebuds virtually swoon under this glorious bathing of barley and sugar; unbelievably juicy and mouth-watering for its age, the oak is there to ensure backbone and fair play and does nothing to subtract from the most graceful notes, except perhaps to pep up slightly with a teasing spiciness; **f24** long, with more playful spices and a chocolate fudge lending weight to the glassy barley edge; one to close the eyes to and be consumed by; **b23.5** one of the great world distilleries being revealed to the us in its very finest colours. They tend to be natural, with no colourings added, therefore allowing the extraordinary kaleidoscope of subtle sweetnesses to be deployed and enjoyed to their fullest. I defy you not to be blown away by this one, especially when you realise there is not a single big base note to be heard.... *46% nc, ncf*

⇜ **Glen Grant 170th Anniversary** db **(89)** n23.5 light and spiky for all the obvious fruitiness. Loads of warm sultana underpinning a butterscotch/vanilla spine. A little sharp and prickly in places, like fruit pastille candy, and just a hint of something that might appeal to the Germans...; **t23.5** immediately busy with a dual personality of (house style) juicy, crunchy barley and a spicier, much fruitier alter-ego; **f20** a tell-tale fuzzy bitterness to the finale reveals an Achilles heel; **b22** the odd mildly sulphured cask has slipped through the net here to reduce what was shaping to be something magnificent. Still enjoyable, though. *46%*

⇜ **Glen Grant The Major's Reserve** bott Mar 10 db **(85.5)** n21.5 t23 f20 b21. Forget about the so-so nose and finish. This is one of those drams that demands you melt into your chair on delivery, such is the fresh beauty of the malt and stunning honeycomb threads which tie themselves around every taste bud. Pity about the ultra dry, puffy, caramel-rich finish, but apparently nearly all the sherry butts have now been used up at the distillery. Thank gawd for that. *40%*

Adelphi Glen Grant 1985 Aged 22 Years bourbon hogshead, cask no. 10184, dist 85, bott 08 **(87.5)** n20 just dull, dull, dull... **t23** just exciting, exciting, exciting...the delivery is caked in muscovado sugar and light, fruity barley. But the 62.1 abv ensures that the impact maximises the effect; **f22.5** long, aided by the most gentle of oils and burned fudge; **b22** a classic example of a dull nose leading you up the garden path....which is quite apposite seeing as it's Glen Grant... *62.1%. 167 bottles.*

⇜ **A.D. Rattray Glen Grant 1985** cask no. 12364, dist Sep 85, bott Mar 09 **(90.5)** n22.5 some major toffee apple moments, there... **t23** wow!! What a spicy little animal we have here: some serious viscosity adds to that toffeed effect on the nose and the ability to give those warming spices a damned good chew.. **f22.5** simmers down and thins to reveal a malty tail; **b23** can't help feeling that there is something at play here regarding those old rummagers that used to clatter about the stills. A different kind of Glen Grant, but eternally wonderful. *55.8% A.D. Rattray Ltd*

⇜ **Berrys' Own Selection Glen Grant 1972 (90)** n24 old, for sure. But the barley-honey notes are so faint and beautifully interwoven amid the more vigorous vanillas that it's a hard one to put down...; **t23** relatively full bodied by GG's standards with soft oils helping the toasty-spiced butterscotch barley to have a big say; **f21** some cocoa does its best to cover the thickening oak; **b22** a bit gruff and throaty at the finale, but at this age it has every right to be. A beautiful dram: why can't they all be this charming? *51.8% Berry Bros & Rudd*

Berrys' Own Selection Glen Grant 1973 cask no. 6643, bott 07 **(83.5)** n20.5 t21.5 f21 **b20.5.** No shortage of signs of life as the marmalade-fruit cuts a sharp figure on the palate. Decently honeyed, too, but just a few signs of oaky degradation reveal that the game was up for this cask in terms of possible improvement. *46%. Berry Bros & Rudd.*

Berrys' Own Selection Glen Grant 1993 cask no. 121908, bott 07 **(88.5)** n21 t23 f22.5 b22. Unusually fat and weighty for a GG. But really clean, delicious fun! *53.8%. Berry Bros & Rudd.*

Cadenhead's Authentic Collection Glen Grant-Glenlivet Aged 18 Years bourbon barrel, dist 89, bott May 07 **(90)** n22 t23 f22 b23. Beautiful malt that is much fruitier than it has any right to be. *60.8%. 204 bottles*

Cärn Mör Glen Grant 1993 hogshead, cask no. 121910, dist 93, bott 09 **(87.5)** n22 clean, intense malt; **t23.5** the lightest, cleanest, grassiest, juiciest of barley: **f20.5** the usual old cask bitter-ish pay off... **b21.5** to be honest, I would have been willing, just from the nose alone, to have bet that this would be a tired, bitter finish. From this kind of third-time around cask you are unlikely to get much else. But the virgin freshness to the barley on both nose and delivery is worth the compromise. *46%. The Scottish Liqueur Centre.*

The Coopers Choice Glen Grant 1977 Sherry Wood Aged 30 Years (91) n22 t23 f23 b23. Quite beautiful whisky. *46%. sc ncf. The Vintage Malt Whisky Co.*

Distillery Malt Glen Grant 1990 (88) n22 t23 f21 b22. Only a slight bitterness to the finale detracts from an otherwise excellent malt. *40%. Gordon & MacPhail.*

Duncan Taylor Collection Glen Grant 1970 cask no. 3490 **(89) n20.5 t21.5 f23.5 b23.** The nose and delivery leaves you thinking this is a malt for the scrapyard. But the fabulous recovery leaves you gasping. *49.7%*

⠿ **Duncan Taylor Collection Glen Grant 1970** cask no. 3492 **(85.5) n21 t22.5 f21 b21.** Retains a touch of the debonair despite the obvious oak intrusion. But now the grey temples have been lost in a sea of white... *49.1% Duncan Taylor & Co Ltd*

Duncan Taylor Collection Glen Grant 1970 cask no. 3494 **(88) n21** a real sprig of heather and distant peat among the dominant oaks; **t22.5** a sweeter delivery than the nose heralds, emphasising the intensity and clean-cut nature of the barley. Some butterscotch reinforces the middle segment; **f22** long, spiced, vaguely smoked and dries with a genuine nod towards elegance; **b22.5** only exceptionally well made spirit can absorb oak with such seemingly effortless aplomb. Classy stuff. *49.9%*

Duncan Taylor Collection Glen Grant 1970 cask no. 3496 **(84.5) n20.5 t20 f22.5 b21.5.** Charming old buffer of a dram, showing great age and, from the lack of backbone, infirmity. Knows its way around the palate, though, and enough citrus-lined barley gathers for a delicious middle and finish. *44%*

Duncan Taylor Collection Glen Grant 1972 cask no. 1641 **(85) n21 t22 f21 b21.** A decent, honest malt that has seen the odd summer too many, but the big oaks still – just – play second fiddle to the bustling barley. *53.5%*

Duncan Taylor Collection Glen Grant 1972 cask no. 1643 **(83.5) n19 t21 f22 b21.5.** Improves markedly after an uncomfortable start on the nose and delivery. The middle veritably hums with ultra-intense barley. *53.4%*

Duncan Taylor Collection Glen Grant 1972 cask no. 3890 **(94.5) n23.5 t24 f23.5 b23.5.** I know people who swear blind they loathe bourbon. Hate the stuff with a passion. And then eulogise over top-quality ancient single malts. I'd love to be there when they taste this.... *57.7%*

Duncan Taylor Collection Glen Grant 1972 cask no. 8948 **(85.5) n21.5 t22.5 f20.5 b21.** Barley and gooseberries fight off the spicy oaks. Almost. *46.2%*

Duncan Taylor Collection Glen Grant 1972 cask no. 8950 **(88) n22** gooseberries being boiled; elsewhere a jam tart is being baked; **t23** beautifully soft delivery with the oils really coming to the fore to ensure the softest of landings for the butterscotch malt; salivating and mildly supine; **f21.5** chalky vanilla as the oak takes a gentle hand; **b21.5** the barley and oak have reached a pleasant understanding. *45%.*

Duncan Taylor Collection Glen Grant 1974 cask no. 16574 **(86.5) n21 t22 f22.5 b21.** At times a seeringly hot, though by no means unpleasant. Massively malty, sharp and no shrinking violet. *55.6%.*

⠿ **Duncan Taylor Collection Glen Grant 1974** cask no. 16575 **(92) n23.5** almost a touch of slivovitz to this with plum tart and honeydew melon for good measure; the odd peat molecule drifts about; **t24** melt-in-the-mouth acacia honey followed by a virile volley of barley. Mocha descends into the middle ground; **f22** an oaky burst is quickly spent and the vanilla-barley keeps position..; **b22.5** another Glen Grant which somehow fights off the obvious age to show some serious quality. *51.5% Duncan Taylor & Co Ltd*

Duncan Taylor Collection Glen Grant 1974 cask no. 16576 **(85) n22 t21 f21 b21.** Malty, clean, juicy, vanilla-flecked but ultimately runs out of ideas. *48.4%.*

Duncan Taylor Collection Glen Grant 1974 cask no. 16577 **(81) n21 t19 f21 b20.** Vaguely similar in style to cask 16574, but thinner, hotter and generally lacking its charisma. *54.5%.*

Duncan Taylor Collection Glen Grant 1974 cask no. 16578 **(82.5) n21 t20 f21.5 b20.** A cheery, unsophisticated dram which slaps the barley on as paste might be brushed onto wallpaper. Thin, but some buttery notes help out at the death. *52.2%.*

Duthies Glen Grant 13 Years Old (74.5) n18 t21.5 f17 b18. Sparkles on the palate for a few moments, but the remainder is hard work. A style which might be appreciated by certain sections of the German whisky market. But in pure technical terms, a real disappointment. *46%.* Cadenhead's for Germany.

⠿ **The Golden Cask Glen Grant 1997** cask no. CM142, bott 2009 **(86.5) n22 t22 f21 b21.5.** Beautifully distilled and so juicy. Just lacking some oaky back up. *56.5% The House of MacDuff.* 224 bottles.

Gordon & MacPhail Distillery Label Glen Grant 25 Years Old (93) n24.5 the type of nose it takes hours to fully measure: a soupcon of smoke helps entangle one of the most complex noses of the year even further, making for a dense undergrowth of creamed rice, over-ripened greengages. A pithy orangey note and, above all, a thickness to the barley attained usually only by sticking your head in a mash tun. Beyond glorious... **t23** silky and sweet, the usual brittleness takes a little time to develop, so until then enjoy the porridge and molten brown sugar... **f22.5** long, prickly and spiced with the oaks showing an aging dryness plus a hint of medium roast Mysore coffee; **b23** the type of malt us long-in-the-tooth whisky specialists dream off, but too rarely find. The nose, though, defies belief. *43%*

⋅※⋅ **Gordon & MacPhail Distillery Label Glen Grant 1993** (92.5) **n23** outwardly simple: sniff longer and more delicately and be astonished by its butterfly-like weight of malt; **t23.5** crisp and malty, yet at the same time soft and vanilla-clad; does sweetness ever come so gossamer-like...? **f23** long, with a gathering of light oils to add a malty lustre to the delicate oak; **b23** eye watering: both in its juicy effect and also for its sheer beauty.... *40%*

Gordon & MacPhail Rare Vintage Glen Grant 1958 (96.5) **n24** it's as though a blender – one of those noisy things you find in a kitchen, as opposed to a quiet, saintly soul located in a whisky lab – has been deployed to hurtle together in microscopic form a pot peuri of mashed, sun-kissed fruit and a complex array of vanilla notes. The result is curiously light if intense, if that makes sense: but that is exactly what you will find. The oak is controlled and elegant, the degree of sweetness to dryness absolute textbook stuff; **t24** if you want an essay in finesse, then just take a small mouthful of this: the rich, plummy fruits have been liberally doused in muscovado sugar and the vanillas have a toasty edge. The results is a delivery which frankly defies years as well as description. Astonishing. **f24** you might expect this to be the Achilles heel: sure this dram must have a flaw somewhere, and the build up of oak at the death has to be where you find it. Right? Wrong! Here we have the oaks collecting for sure, but they have been so well impregnated with those stunningly sweet fruity tones, any bitterness is entirely eradicated. Long, lush and lasting... **b24.5** virtually no grey hairs on this 50-year-old which has embraced half a century with an unbelievable degree of finesse and grace. One of the truly great Glen Grants – indeed, Speyside malts – of recent years, this is textbook stuff as to regard how to showcase enormous age with virtually no blemishes to speak of. One of the all time great Old Timers. And if you can't afford Glenfiddich 50-year-old at £10,000 a throw, then settle for this one that is just half a point and £9,850 behind... *40%*

Gordon & MacPhail Rare Vintage Glen Grant 1962 (94.5) **n22.5** overcooked fruitcake with oak where the almonds should be; **t24** oh, my word!! Pure silk and near perfection on delivery as the intense barley gets caught up in some sumptuous treacled spice; the majestic middle makes no secret of the age, but such is lightness of touch and the quiet benevolence of the liquid fruit makes one almost purr out loud...; **f24** long, lingering, deft, raisiny and sugared barley but with vanilla aplenty; **b24** almost faultlessly weighted and a wonderful example of where great oak is used to add nothing but a positive slant. A stunner. And cements my belief, along with the amazing 1958 vintage, that G&M understand this distillery in a way the more recent blender(s) of the previous owners never came close to. *40%*

Harris Whisky Co. Glen Grant Aged 35 Years cask no. 6650, dist Jul 73, bott Sep 08 (87) **n20.5** heavily oaked but some golden syrup tries to rescue the situation; **t22** an incredible transformation from the nose; yes, the oak is there is stave-loads, but the delivery is almost explosive as the spiced sugars erupt immediately on delivery; surprisingly malty and juicy middle, considering; **f22** some better behaved and more sensible mocha calms things down; **b21.5** an injection of sugar concentrate helps negate the overenthusiastic oak. Not one for those looking for a sedate dram... *57.5%. 100 bottles.*

⋅※⋅ **Hart Brothers Glen Grant Aged 11 Years** dist Oct 97, bott Sep 09 (79) **n20 t22 f18 b19**. From the slightly tobacco-flecked nose through the big, pleasant sugars on the palate to the unevenly bitter finish, there is something altogether odd about this one. *46% Hart Brothers Ltd*

Kingsbury's Single Cask Glen Grant Aged 12 Years dist Jul 96, bott Jul 08 (84) **n21.5 t22 f20 b20.5**. Hard nosed and hard arsed. Little give but the crunchy barley offers some juicy sweetness. *46%. Japan Import System.*

Kingsbury "The Selection" Glen Grant 11 Years Old 1996 (87.5) **n22 t22.5 f21 b22**. The delicate sweetness of the intense malt ticks every box. *43.0%. nc ncf. Japan Import System*

Lonach Glen Grant 31 Years Old (84) **n21 t22 f21 b20**. Exceptionally firm barley for its age; enjoys a sugar-coated lustre and good depth. *42.3%.*

Lonach Glen Grant 35 Years Old (83) **n20 t21 f21 b21**. Creaks a bit, but some lovely barley sugar and liquorice. *41.8%. Duncan Taylor.*

Lonach Glen Grant 1969 (83) **n20 t19.5 f23 b20.5**. One small sip for man; one giant leap for oak-kind. *52.3%. Duncan Taylor.*

Lonach Glen Grant 1969 (87) **n21** the exotic fruit shows age, but some niggardly oak refuses to allow it an elegant flourish; **t21** juicy, fruity but with splinters everywhere; **f23** at last evens out with a stunning fanning out of soft Java coffee notes and glorious spices; silky, beautifully textured and rich...and goes on and on...and on... **b22** talk about an over-aged malt. Far too old. Yet such is the enormity of the fruit and barley character, it somehow sees off the excesses of the oak which spoils the start and offers instead a very late alternative. A rare style, indeed. *51.7%. Duncan Taylor.*

Montgomerie's Glen Grant 1990 (84.5) n21.5 t22 f20 b21. Another well used cask allowing the malt a pretty open platform. 46%. Montgomery & Co. Ltd.

Norse Cask Selection Glen Grant 1993 Aged 16 Years hogshead cask no. 121914, dist 93, bott May 09 (95.5) n23.5 beautiful custard poured over barley pie; not a single hint of an off note. Pure gold...literally... t25 just about the perfect – no, sod it!!! - absolutely perfect latter-day non-sherried Speyside delivery: the most intense, complete, perfectly sweetened, juicy and gloriously dense malt massages the tastebuds, adding just a pinch of salt and spice to ensure all is on full alert. It can hardly get better... f23 all that went on before, but now in nostalgic sepia tones with an extra squirt of vanilla from the oak for good measure... b24 a truly great cask from a great distillery: this, surely, is what drinking single malt Scotch should be about... 57.8%. Qualityworld for WhiskyOwner.com, Denmark.

Old Malt Cask Glen Grant Aged 12 Years Gabriel Meffre wine cask no. 3899, dist Jun 95, bott Sep 07 (92) n22 t23 f23.5 b23.5. OK, I admit it: a wine cask which works....and a French one at that!! No sulphur. No grapey flatness. A flimsily clad comtesse of a dram beckoning you towards an evening of elegance and pleasure. 50%. nc ncf. Douglas Laing. 300 bottles.

⋅⋅⋅ **Old Malt Cask Glen Grant Aged 14 Years** refill hogshead no. DL 5980, dist Oct 95, bott Mar 10 (84) n21 t22 f20 b21. Sharp, sough dough and massive malt. 50% 339 bottles.

Old Malt Cask Glen Grant Aged 18 Years sherry butt no. 4280, dist Mar 90, bott May 08 (84.5) n21.5 t22 f219 b21. Juicy for its age with a degree of bite, too. The odd blemish, however. 50%. nc ncf. Douglas Laing. 665 bottles.

⋅⋅⋅ **Old Malt Cask Glen Grant Aged 20 Years** sherry butt no. DL 5971, dist Mar 90, bott Mar 10 (73) n18 t19 f17 b19. Sweet, honeyed. But a sherry butt let down by a dose of you-know-what.... 50% Douglas Laing & Co Ltd. 362 bottles.

Old Malt Cask Glen Grant Aged 22 Years bourbon barrel no. 4242, dist Sep 85, bott Apr 08 (92) n23.5 t22.5 f23 b23. A contented cask which gleefully celebrates its Kentucky origins. Sweet, but the panache of the oaky fight-back leaves you drooling. 50%. nc ncf. 265 bottles.

Old Malt Cask Glen Grant Aged 30 Years sherry hogshead no. 3745, dist Dec 76, bott Jul 07 (90) n22 t23 f22.5 b22.5. What was once a classic butt has been singed by age, but the brilliance still exudes. 50%. Douglas Laing. 228 bottles.

Old Malt Cask Glen Grant Aged 30 Years sherry butt no. 4295, dist May 78, bott May 08 (95) n23.5 ancient oak but with a honeycomb theme; t24 wow!! Was I right about the honeycomb on the nose...!! Pure Crunchie candy bar. Burnt honey, some wonderful cocoa, a touch of spice and then barley in the most concentrated form imaginable. A real bourbony theme now with red liquorice...astonishing... f23.5 a warm finale with a cough sweet edge indicating more ancient oak; a hint of hickory and molasses...genius!! b24 have to admit, on first nose though, this was a gonner. But given the chance to breathe, it comes back to life...and how..!! A blueprint for how great 30-year-old and over whiskies should be. 45.9%

Old Malt Cask Glen Grant Aged 32 Years sherry butt, dist Dec 76, bott Mar 09 (94) n23.5 dismisses its age with contemptuous ease, helped along the way by the slickest, cleanest oloroso imaginable; a background wisp of smoke helps bump up the already considerable complexity; t24 exactly as the nose heralds: clean, thick, grape with some wonderful spicy talons; a touch of bourbony liquorice is also present. It is as if a younger and older top rate cask have been vatted together; f23 the spices gently pulse as the fade is a slow de-intensification of the oloroso; some natural caramel also comes into play; b23.5 an old school sherry butt. And just like old schools, tends to be far more correct and exacting in standards. The flavour of a nearly lost world. 50%. Douglas Laing. 266 bottles.

⋅⋅⋅ **Old Malt Cask Glen Grant Aged 34 Years** refill hogshead no. DL 5597, dist Apr 75, bott Nov 09 (90) n23.5 exotic fruit and ginger is a giveaway regarding age; t23 the barley remains improbably crisp and clean despite some softly fruited oaky attention; f21.5 a tad tangy; b22 at this age almost a relative to neighbouring Caper. But just that little more crunchy. 50% Douglas Laing & Co Ltd. 278 bottles.

Old & Rare Glen Grant Aged 31 Years sherry cask, dist Dec 76, bott Feb 08 (96) n24 t23.5 f24 b24.5. A near impeccable cask, even after all these years. Few distilleries did sherry as well as Glen Grant during this period. A contender for Scotch of the Year without question. 58.6%. nc ncf. Douglas Laing. 196 bottles.

Provenance Glen Grant Aged 11 Years hogshead no. 4133, dist autumn 96, bott winter 08 (84.5) n21 t21 f21.5 b21. Absolutely clean, juicy straight down the line GG with not an oaky deviation. 46%. Douglas Laing.

⋅⋅⋅ **Provenance Glen Grant Over 12 Years** refill hogshead no. DMG 5736, dist Autumn 1997, bott Winter 2010 (83.5) n21 t21.5 f20 b21. Gristy and dry, but a little reined in by the cask. 46% nc ncf Douglas Laing & Co Ltd

Provenance Glen Grant Aged 12 Years refill hogshead, dist autumn 96, bott winter 08 **(86) n20 t22 f22 b22.** Recovers spectacularly from a dodgy nose to a real clean barley salvo. Lots of spice and barley sugar. *46%*

Scotch Malt Whisky Society Cask 9.44 Aged 11 Years refill hogshead, dist Apr 97 **(85.5) n22.5 t21 f21 b21.** Attractively malty but makes a point of not making a point. *59.4%*

The Single Malts of Scotland Glen Grant 1972 Aged 35 Years bott Sep 07 **(86) n22 t21 f22 b21.** Big, sweet, intense whisky staying just on the right side of stodgy. The barley-sugar concentrate on the nose delights. *54.9%. Speciality Drinks.*

The Whisky Fair Glen Grant 36 Year Old sherry hogshead, dist 72, bott 09 **(96) n24** not so much that the oloroso here is huge, but it is the overall shape and impact that really takes the breath away. Faultlessly clean: sherry from the old school which embraces the oak with dignity; **t24** a mirror image of the nose on delivery, except perhaps there is more juicy fruit than you might expect. This moves in the middle ground first towards an eggy fruitcake and then one accompanied by milky coffee; **f24** long, sweetening as the molasses and raisin gets to work; **b24** this, in a bottle, is the very point of sherried malt whisky. *56.3%*

GLENGYLE
Campbeltown, 2004. J&A Mitchell & Co. Working.

Kilkerran Single Malt db **(80) n19** very young, slightly Shredded Wheaty, a touch of tobacco leaf, mint and some heavy oils; **t20** ungainly arrival with big barley, big oils, big natural caramel; **f21** settles towards a light, slightly sweeter and gristier fade; **b20** Glyngyle's first offering doesn't rip up any trees. And maybe the odd flaw to its character that you won't see when the distillery is fine-tuned. But this is the first-ever bottling from this brand new Campbeltown distillery and therefore its chances of being a worldbeater as an untried and untested 3-y-o are pretty slim. I will be watching its development with relish. And with heart pounding... *46%. Available exclusively from distillery direct from cask.*

Kilkerran Single Malt bott 22 May 07 db **(84) n20 t21 f22 b21.** Sadly, I was out of the country and couldn't attend the Coming of Age of Kilkerran, when its first casks turned three and became whisky. Very kindly, they sent me a bottle as if I was there and, therefore, these are the notes of the very first bottling handed out to visitors. Interestingly, there is a marked similarity in distillery style to the 46% bottling in that the malt offers a crescendo of quality. This is only three year old whisky, of course, and its fingerprints will alter as it spends longer in the cask. *62%. nc ncf.*

Kilkerran 'Work in Progress' db**(88) n22.5** youthful, malty and a pinch of salt creeping into this one.. **t22** a simple malty delivery is the prologue to a simple, barley-rich tale. Dries to a surprising degree after the initial quick burst of barley sugar with the vanillas kicking hard, followed even by some spice; **f21.5** lots of natural caramel with the malt; **b22** doing very well. *46%*

GLEN KEITH
Speyside, 1957. Chivas. Mothballed.

Glen Keith 10 Years Old db **(80) n22 t21 f18 b19.** A malty if thin dram that finishes with a whimper after an impressively refreshing, grassy start. *43%*

⊹ **Cadenhead's Authentic Collection Glen Keith-Glenlivet 1996** bott Feb 10 **(85) n21 t22.5 f20.5 b21.** What I suspect is a third fill cask has kept the oak at arm's length, allowing the very lightly peated malt to show its eye-watering sharpness to enjoyable effect. *54.2% Wm. Cadenhead Ltd. 303 bottles.*

⊹ **Connoisseurs Choice Glen Keith 1968 (86) n21 t21 5 f22 b21.5.** Becomes much more relaxed and enjoyable when it throws off any pretence of being a good old-fashioned Speysider and revels in its newly-found bourbony-ness. The spirit from this distillery was much thinner back in the 60s than the malt made in its latter years. So it has embraced the oak with both hands, making this a must find for those who enjoy a good Heaven Hill... *46%*

⊹ **Malts of Scotland Glen Keith 1990** bourbon barrel no. 13678, dist Mar 90, bott Jan 10 **(83.5) n20.5 t22 f21 b20.** Chunky and packed thick with barley. A curious creamless Oreo biscuit finish. *52.1% Malts of Scotland. 192 bottles.*

Old Malt Cask Glen Keith Aged 18 Years refill barrel, dist Mar 90, bott Dec 08 **(93.5) n23** distant peat secures a thicker back note than you might normally expect and a touch of extra marmaladey sweetness, too: quite lovely; **t24** brilliant delivery, with a real mixed bag of sweets for beginners. A wonderful blending of molassed, fudgy sugars is lightened by a thinner, honeyed edge. All this is almost perfectly integrated with the thickest sweet barley imaginable. Fabulous; **f23** long, medium weighted and absorbs the developing oak with open arms; in the background a ghost of a smoky trace ensures a light spice and subtle weight; **b23.5** this has never been one of the sexy Speysiders, but now and again a superb bottling rears its head – and here's the best of the lot. Occasionally a peated version was produced here by Chivas. Though this isn't peaty, as such, there is a subtle, smoky echo to this one which does it no harm whatsoever. A distillery classic and must have. *50%. Douglas Laing. 259 bottles.*

⁘ **Old Malt Cask Glen Keith Aged 20 Years** refill hogshead no. DL 5992, dist Mar 90, bott Mar 10 **(79.5) n19 t21.5 f19 b20.** Stodgy though pleasantly sweet. Don't expect too much complexity, though. *50% Douglas Laing & Co Ltd. 257 bottles.*

GLENKINCHIE
Lowland, 1837. Diageo. Working.

Glenkinchie 12 Years Old (66) n16 t19 f18 b18. The nose is a disaster with more off notes than I can begin to count. Never have I come across a more sorry Classic Malt since the range was launched. Luckily - or unluckily for the market – this is from a bottling for Canada with half the label in French. One for the guillotine. *43%*

Glenkinchie Aged 15 Years The Distillers Edition Amontillado finished, dist 92, bott 07 db **(94) n23.5** clean, creamy, unhindered grape; **t24** soft delivery, but the slow-motion evolvement of spice is almost something to marvel at; **f23** returns to a creamier place, drier, nuttier, chewier... **b23.5** now this is absolutely top class wine cask finishing. One of my last whiskies of the night, and one to take home with me. Sophisticated, intelligent and classy. *46%*

Glenkinchie 20 Years Old db **(85.5) n21 t22 f21.5 b21.** When I sampled this, I thought: "hang on, haven't I tasted this one before?" When I checked with my tasting notes for one or two independents who bottled around this age a year or two ago, I found they were nigh identical to what I was going to say here. Well, you can't say its not a consistent dram. The battle of the citrus-barley against the welling oak is a rich and entertaining one. *58.4%*

⁘ **Glenkinchie 1992 The Manager's Choice** db **(78) n19 t22 f18 b19.** Has a lot going for it on delivery with a barley explosion which rocks you back in your chair and has you salivating like a rabies victim. But the rest of it is just too off key. *58.1% Diageo*

Cadenhead's Glenkinchie Aged 21 Years dist 87, bott 09 **(89) n22** pine fresh; **t23** bristling oak kept in place by muscovado sugar-almonded barley; **f22** long, assisted with a soft oil which keeps the vanilla moving; **b22** has no right to be excellent whisky, yet somehow is... *51.6%*

⁘ **Malts of Scotland Glenkinchie 1975** sherry hogshead no. 2968, dist Aug 75, bott Mar 09 **(91) n23.5** the kind of sherry butt which brings a tear to an aging man's eye. This is the way they were...and always should have been; **t23** the immediate honey/liquorice impact is heart- and palate-warming; layer upon layer of indulgent, lightly spiced bourbon character on a bed of pithy grape; the barley remains alive and salivating, though... **f22.5** drier but with a decent line in chocolate-covered grape; **b22.5** oloroso meets Kentucky to stunning effect... *57.2% Malts of Scotland. 96 bottles.*

Secret Stills Lowland 5.1 1987 (86.5) n22 t22 f21.5 b21. Certainly a secret in seeing the distillery in this light: unquestionably a first. Rich and full nose and delivery balances fruit and floral attractively. Though seeing off the age, the growing fruity, coppery edge, flattens somewhat. *45%. Gordon & MacPhail.*

THE GLENLIVET
Speyside 1824. Chivas. Working.

The Glenlivet Aged 12 Years db **(79.5) n22 t21 f18 b18.5.** Wonderful nose and very early development but then flattens out towards the kind of caramel finish you just wouldn't traditionally associate with this malt, and further weakened by a bitter, furry finale. *40%* ⊙ ⊙

The Glenlivet Aged 12 Years Old First Fill Matured db **(91) n22.5** unmistakable oak influence, edging the light barley towards a soft, red liquorice, Kentuckian feel. Gentle but never docile and the malty freshness exuberates; **t22.5** a real barrel-full of apples early on with a gathering sweet edge. Always the barley is in control, though the oaky influence is never far behind; **f23** long, with an almost apologetic build up of spices again underlying the barrel type. The barley remains true but it is the elegance of the delivery which raises the hairs; **b23** a quite wonderful whisky, far truer to The Glenlivet than the standard 12 and one which really every malt whisky lover should try once in their journey through the amber stuff. Forget the tasting notes on the bottle, which remain unhelpful and bear little relation to what is inside. A gem of a dram. *40%* ⊙ ⊙

The Glenlivet 15 Years of Age db **(80) n19 t21 f20 b20.** There is an undeniable charm to the countless waves of malt and oak. But don't expect much in the way of complexity or charisma. *40%* ⊙

The Glenlivet Nadurra Aged 16 Years American oak bourbon, bott code LR10039 db **(94) n23.5** bristling and busy, a little spicier than I expected but with some freshly ground stem ginger lightened by muscovado sugar and the odd gristy note; **t24** a voluptuous delivery with near perfect mouthfeel. The flavour profile never quite sits still: the spices signalled on the nose arrive very early and are quickly followed by ginger nut biscuit and a red liquorice bourbon sweetness; **f23** long, lightly oiled and a growing malt confidence. A touch of caramel shortens the effect; **b23.5** how curious: when I first nosed this one I thought: "hmmmm, stem ginger". Then looking up my previous entry saw ginger was included there, too. This time, though, the chocolate is conspicuous by its absence and a more bourbon character prevails. Remains the "must have" official Glenlivet for me to pour guests. 48% ☉☉

⁜ **The Glenlivet Nadurra 1991** batch no. 0809A, bott Aug 09 db **(89) n22.5** an oaky buzz and nip; some Fox's chocolate ginger usually seen in younger versions; implausibly fresh for its age yet showing just the right texture for an old un: how paradoxical; **t23** quite exemplary and juicy delivery: light oils fill the palate and allow the slow release of tangy blood orange, softly honeyed malt and some unmistakable Kentucky characteristics though toffee does start thickening things; **f21** long with more barley, toasted mallow and spot of liquorice; not a single sign of bitterness or tiredness from the casks; the caramel builds in intensity; **b22.5** ah, had they only been a little more circumspect with the caramel... 48%

⁜ **The Glenlivet Nadurra 1991** batch no. 0310B, bott Mar 10 db **(78) n19 t22 f18 b19.** A sulphurous sherry butt or two leaves you wondering what might have been. 48% Chivas

The Glenlivet Aged 18 Years bott Feb 10 db **(91) n22** attractive mixture of honeycombed bourbon and fruitcake; **t23.5** oh...just didn't expect that...!! Fabulous, honey-sweet and slightly sharp edge to the barley: excellent weight and mouthfeel with the honeycomb on the nose making slow but decisive incursions; **f23** a very slight technical flaw drops it half a point, but there is no taking away from the improbable length of the dissolving honey and barley...some gentle chewing is required, especially with the late juices and vanilla arriving; **b23** a hugely improved bottling seriously worth discovering in this form. Appears to have thrown off its old shackles and offers up an intensity that leaves you giving a little groan of pleasure. 43% Chivas ☉☉

The Glenlivet Archive 21 Years Old batch no. 0508B bott Nov 08 db **(87.5) n22** weighty and fibrous. Thick layers of honeyed fruit: not what I was expecting or how I remember it. Lumbering but attractive despite the odd flaw; **t23.5** fabulous arrival and mouthfeel: arguably the silkiest on the market. Soupy but you can't not love the interplay between barley and deep honeycomb while the spices set it all off beautifully; some liquorice notes fill the middle; **f20** the degree of flattening caramel – be it added or natural – is quite a shock and the building bitterness doesn't help, either; **b22** forget the nondescript finish: just settle down and be royally entertained by the enormity and panache of the big honey arrival. 43%

⁜ **The Glenlivet Archive 21 Years Old** batch no. 1109D, bott Dec 09 db **(86.5) n22.5 t23 f20 b21.** Against the undisputed glory of a 60-second purple patch on delivery when the thick fruit, honey, spice and weight are in total harmony, the rest is comparatively humdrum with a very slight flaw helping to restrict the development to take this to where it belongs. 43%

The Glenlivet XXV 25 Years Old batch no. 50416, bott Oct 08 db **(91) n23** think about all those clichés of Christmas cake and sherry trifle and fruit and nut cake and Demerara sugar....well you have all that plus possibly a cask that just shouldn't be in there... **t24** is that a perfect delivery? Possibly. The weight and mouthfeel are exceptional, the sugars refined – or unrefined, to be precise – and the kumquat and spice are singing from the same hymn sheet. Then, towards the middle...a dull, bitter furriness... **f21.5** blast! A less than perfect cask is making itself heard late on...better take another mouthful and get back to the delivery... **b22.5** possibly the ultimate non-peated late night dram. One cask away from a massive score and a certain award... 43% ☉☉

⁜ **The Glenlivet 1973 Cellar Collection** bott Oct 09 db **(94.5) n24** luxurious stewed sultanas in a custard tart; yet for a malt heading towards 40, improbable grist, too: clean, complex, thick and simply spellbinding... **t24** just melts into the taste buds with the freshest, cleanest, juiciest charm you could possibly imagine, yet always with a nibbling spice dancing around the side of the tongue; **f23** a touch of oaky bitterness, but a mere detail: the late oils are sympathetic and contain a surprising degree of vanilla; **b23.5** for Glenlivet lovers, I point you towards something a little special... 49% Chivas

Adelphi Glenlivet 1978 Aged 29 Years bourbon hogshead, cask no. 13503 **(89.5) n22 t22.5 f22.5 b22.5.** A real touch of class. 52.1%. 193 bottles.

Berrys' Own Selection Glenlivet 1971 cask no. 6450, bott 07 **(77) n18 t20.5 f19 b19.5.** Some old casks work. Some don't. This one cannot for the life of it make up its mind as to whether it wants to or not. 46%. Berry Bros & Rudd.

Berry's' Own Selection Glenlivet 1972 Aged 32 Years **(86) n19 t23 f22 b22.** A fascinating cask which cherishes its vitality. 46%. Berry Bros & Rudd.

Berry's' Own Selection Glenlivet 1974 Aged 32 Years (84) n19 t22 f21 b22. A well-mannered dram offering barley-sugar in all the right places. But has a few bags under the eyes. 46%.

Berry's Own Selection Glenlivet 1975 bott 08 (87.5) n22 barley juice led; t23 excellent sharpness to the barley, salivating and mildly spiced; a glossy metallic sheen and light demerara sweetness; f21 happy to embrace vanilla when you want it to do a little more; b21.5 typically non-committal, as this distillery has a tendency to be, but has that little touch of class. 46%.

Berry's Own Selection Glenlivet 1977 bott 08 (85) n21 t21 f22 b21. Very even: silky-soft with massive vanilla. 46%. Berry Bros & Rudd.

⁂ **Berrys' Own Selection Glenlivet 1982** (94) n24 leathery, fruitcake and marzipan, and attractively oaked; something of the pre-coloured Demerara rum to this one, too; t23.5 one of those big raisin and fudge numbers which bite deep and smuggle some mocha into the act for extra intensity; still that pot still rum richness; f23 dries as the oak makes a thundering but, thankfully, Christmas cake intense speech; b23.5 for all the flying sawdust, still one hell of a bottling. And if you happen to have a love for high quality old Demerara rum, then this will be a double whammy for you. 52.2% Berry Bros & Rudd

Cadenhead's Glenlivet Aged 19 Years port, dist 88, bott Feb 08 (85) n19 t23.5 f21 b21.5. As Port accented casks goes, this is unique. The nose is all over the place, the finish feels like a dreary caramel convention but the fruity, spicy delivery is eye-closingly superb. Very, very strange. 56.7%. 269 bottles.

Celtic Heartlands Glenlivet 1975 bott 08 (85) n21.5 t21.5 f21 b21. oak in as many guises as you can imagine here. Bit OTT on that front, to be honest, but you cannot be blown away by some aspects of the bourbon intensity. 51.2%. Bruichladdich Ltd. 450 bottles.

⁂ **The Coopers Choice Glenlivet 1997 Aged 12 Years** (82.5) n21.5 t21 f19.5 b20.5. A typically juicy but weightless example of its blending style. 46% The Vintage Malt Whisky Co.

⁂ **The Coopers Choice Glenlivet 1998 Sherry Wood Aged 11 Years** (78.5) n18.5 t21 f19 b20. At times, there are wonderful signs of true grapeness, backed by a spicy chorus. But undone somewhat by you-know-what.. 46% The Vintage Malt Whisky Co.

Duncan Taylor Collection Glenlivet 1968 cask no. 5246, bott 08 (86) n20 t23 f21.5 b21.5. Rolls its sleeves up to reveal oaky muscles from the very first sniff. And splinters and sawdust are flying in the fray that follows. But the enormity of the compensating honey is mind-blowing, as are the spices. If you are going to go down, it might as well be fighting... 53.6%

Duncan Taylor Collection Glenlivet 1968 cask no.7601 (90.5) n23 marzipan and lemon jelly; t22.5 crunching oak soon dissipates as the fabulously sweet barley evolves; so mouth-watering....!!! f22.5 the clean juices, which make a mockery of the 40 passing years cling the cocoa-dusted end; b23 allow to settle in the glass for a good 20 minutes and the rewards are wonderful. 49.9%

⁂ **Duncan Taylor Collection Glenlivet 1970** cask no. 2002 (87) n22.5 you almost need a spoon to get the Intensely thick fruitiness out of the glass; t23 like cask 2017 but probably twice as concentrated with a mercurial maple syrup quality fighting off the oak, f19.5 just too well aged; b21.5 were it not for the resistance of the fruit and syrup, this would be a goner. But the battle to keep a grip on life is fascinating. 54.3% Duncan Taylor & Co Ltd

Duncan Taylor Collection Glenlivet 1970 cask no. 2009 (83.5) n21 t21 f21.5 b20. Eye-watering oak offers ample evidence of a few summers too far. The middle, though, broadens out as some bitter-sweet barley counters beautifully, before crushed without pity by the wooden weight at the death. 52.6%

⁂ **Duncan Taylor Collection Glenlivet 1970** cask no. 2017 (85.5) n22.5 t22 f20 b21. Radiates the classic exotic fruit old age charm on nose and delivery, but the middle and finish creak a bit. 50.9% Duncan Taylor & Co Ltd

Duncan Taylor Collection Glenlivet 1970 cask no. 2020 (88) n22.5 effortlessly complex. And by that I mean it's a bit lazy...; t22 sharp, mouth-watering, punchy barley; f22 soft oils stretch out the toffee- sweetness; b21.5 beautiful whisky, but never appears to break sweat. 53.6%

⁂ **Gordon & MacPhail Distillery Label Glenlivet 15 Years Old** (88) n22.5 weighty, malty with a soft, oily sheen upping the intensity; t22 beautiful poise with just a touch of nuttiness to the barley; f22 coconut strands dipped in golden syrup; b22 sturdy with lots of malty weight and an unusual degree of oil. 43% Gordon & MacPhail

Gordon & MacPhail Distillery Label Glenlivet 21 Years Old (88.5) n22 almost thick with fruit, crushed juicy sultana in particular; t23 spiced sherry trifle-type fruitiness but with some fudgy caramel keeping development relatively muted; silky and revels in its age; f21.5 lots of natural caramel but surprisingly lacking ambition after the outstanding start; b22 always merits a refill. 43%

Gordon & MacPhail Rare Vintage Glenlivet 1965 (87) n22.5 textbook "oldie" nose with spicy splinters but a countering blancmange sweetness; vanilla dominates as the malt oxidizes in the glass; **t21.5** lush delivery with soft barley and hints of blood orange and then a gradual heaping on of the oak, at times a touch bitter; **f22** delicate maple syrup sweetness blends in with the most parched oakiness to charming effect; **b21** takes the oak to the limit but somehow works. *40%*

Gordon & MacPhail Station Series Duirinish Glenlivet 1991 refill sherry hogshead 48288, bott Feb 07 **(86.5) n21 t22 f22 b21.5.** Thick malt backed up by ultra soft fruit. Some oaky indulgence, but all very well mannered. *46.0%. nc ncf. Japan Import System Co. Ltd.*

Kingsbury's Finest & Rarest Glenlivet 1978 (94.5) n23.5 a dusting of molasses on a vague fruitiness which hints at that exotic style old malts crave for...but hasn't quite reached; some definite papaya, though; however it is the improbable gristy, fresh malt which wins hearts and minds; **t24** succulent, soft, silky landing on the palate. The malts are at the vanguard, but in many guises. Again a light molassed sheen appears to be attached but after 29 years still the malts are improbably salivating; a faint milky cocoa notes floats towards the middle as do some simmering oaky spices; **f23** still long, clean and elegant. The vanillas are now out in force, offering a milky-custard fade and light flecks of cassava. Effortlessly graceful to the very end of the tapering finish; **b24** does and says all the right things for its age. Premier class malt. *52.6%. Japan Import System.*

Kingsbury's Single Cask Glenlivet Aged 15 Years dist May 93, bott Jun 08 **(79) n21 t20 f18 b18.** Bitter-sweet. But mainly bitter: certainly not as the distiller intended... *46%.*

Lonach Glenlivet 1968 (83) n21.5 t21 f20 b20.5. A malt on the periphery of exhaustion craves some understanding and indulgence here. It deserves it for its big malt statement alone. *40.1%. Duncan Taylor.*

Lonach Glenlivet 1968 bott 08 **(85.5) n23 t21.5 f20 b21.** Some lovely molassed sugar helps save it from the oaky trap door. It's all about the gorgeous nose, though. *41.4%.*

Lonach Glenlivet 1968 (90.5) n22.5 bourbony; red liquorice; **t23** really nubile delivery: unsugared gooseberry and raspberry, tart up the stroking barley; **f22** custard cream biscuits with some faint, oily citrus; **b23** by far and away the star turn of the three new Lonach Glenlivets. Belies its age impeccably. *44.8%. Duncan Taylor.*

Murray McDavid Mission Glenlivet 1977 Aged 30 Years bott 07 **(94.5) n24.5 t23 f23.5 b23.5.** Now here's a conundrum. The label says "Cask Type: Bourbon". Yet I have tasted enough Glenlivets over the years to put my house on this once being filled into a first fill sherry. My guess is that it was then transferred at some stage into bourbon, possibly because the butt was needed elsewhere, or to stop it from tiring. If this really has matured for 30 years in a bourbon cask and come out like this, then we have a new type of whisky on our hands....I look into my crystal ball and see a long chat with Jim McEwan.... And on the subject of crystal, this is a gem for collectors everywhere. *51.7%. 270 bottles exclusively for Willow Park, Calgary.*

꒰꒰ **Old Malt Cask Glenlivet Aged 13 Years** sherry butt no. DL 5537, dist Apr 96, bott Oct 09 **(68) n16 t18 f16.5 b17.5.** The grape fights valiantly against the sulphur. *50% Douglas Laing & Co Ltd. 432 bottles.*

Old Malt Cask Glenlivet Aged 17 Years bourbon cask, dist Apr 92, bott Jul 09 **(90.5) n23** hints of ginger in plain chocolate; some flatter oaky notes, too, but comfortably controlled; **t23** caramelised ginger again, but superbly supported by lively malt. Excellent spice prickle; **f22** vanillas out, but the barley sweetness lingers; **b22.5** amazing how lovely this distillery can be in the right cask and with no colouring. Grab this dazzler if you see it. *50%. Douglas Laing.*

Old Malt Cask Glenlivet Aged 18 Years rum cask, dist Sep 90, bott Sep 08 **(85) n20 t22 f21.5 b21.5.** Well made and delivers on the maltiness. *50%. Douglas Laing. 272 bottles.*

Old Malt Cask Glenlivet Aged 27 Years refill hogshead 3842, dist Apr 80, bott Aug 07 **(83.5) n21 t21.5 f21 b20.** Oak-tanged but quite gentle for all the obvious wear and tear. *50%. nc ncf. Douglas Laing. 222 bottles.*

Old Malt Cask Glenlivet Aged 30 Years refill hogshead, dist Jun 78, bott Apr 09 **(94) n23** dull yet intriguing pulsing of oak and barley. Clean and sophisticated in its lightness of touch; **t24** the distillery's traditional mixture of vanilla and barley are in force. But here with a degree of oiliness and weight no longer found in Glenlivet, alas. It means that not only does the barley flex its juicy muscles to the max, but the sugary layers never get out of control; **f23** eye-watering elegance as the barley intensity decreases notch by notch, allowing the drier, chalkier vanillas the final word; teasing spices wrap up a job superbly done; **b24** from the days when The Glenlivet had body enough to cope with 30 years with nothing more than a shrug. Glorious. *50%. Douglas Laing. 205 bottles.*

꒰꒰ **Old Malt Cask Glenlivet Aged 30 Years** refill hogshead no. DL 5438, dist Aug 79, bott Aug 09 **(93.5) n24** seemingly strangulated by oak, a more careful look under the natural caramels reveals a few molecules of smoke trying to escape as well as a deliciously elegant lychee/papaya hybrid; **t23.5** some soaring oak but there is always the backdrop of prickly barley...and that wonderful echo of smoke; **f23** holds out without further oak damage with a touch of smoky chocolate mousse – lightened by a sprinkling of muscovado sugar - as a final flourish; **b23** textbook complexity and benefits with being lightly warmed in the glass for a good 15-20 minutes before nosing and tasting. *50% Douglas Laing & Co Ltd. 217 bottles.*

⁙ **Old Malt Cask Glenlivet Aged 32 Years** refill hogshead no. DL 5969, dist Jun 77, bott Mar 10 **(89.5) n21** sherbet lemon; **t23** fizzy barley with charming sweet-sharp interplay; **f22.5** drier vanilla with the odd, leathery strand of hickory and honeycomb; **b22.5** limited complexity for its age but maximum early juiciness. *50% Douglas Laing & Co Ltd. 280 bottles.*

Old Masters Glenlivet Aged 12 Years cask no. 906680, dist 96, bott 08 **(82) n22 t21 f19 b20.** Sharp, tasty barley but the feeling is that not all is well with the cask *57.8%.*

Old Masters Glenlivet Aged 30 Years cask no. 1975, dist 78, bott 08 **(85) n22 t22 f20.5 b20.5**. A malt of two halves: the nose shows signs of enormous age with its hints of exotic fruit, but works pleasantly, as does the juicy malt arrival with its delightful, eye-watering zinginess. After that the splinters are harder to remove though some praline does ensure the overall experience is an enjoyable one. *57.6%. James MacArthur & Co. Ltd.*

⁙ **Private Collection Glenlivet 1959 (96.5) n24.5** sure; there is oak, and plenty of it. But that is not a problem when there is a veritable basket of juice-oozing fruit to soften the blow. The mix between delicate kiwi and greengage is a treat, and this in turn blends in with the ripe dates and figs. Beyond wonderful **t24** fabulous: 50-years-old and still the juice spills all over the taste buds on arrival before a delicately sweetened natural caramel and lazy oak fizz toss some weight in there; **f24** long and now those spices take shape; they thin and fizz while the vanillas carry a light coating of barley; **b24** how reassuring it is to know I can still find a world-class whisky older than any of the women in my life.... lithe, velvety textured, juicy, caresses the tongue...yes, and this 50-year-old whisky does all those things, too.... *47.5% Gordon & MacPhail*

Scotch Malt Whisky Society Cask 2.72 Aged 22 Years refill hogshead, dist Aug 85 **(89) n21 t24 f21.5 b22.5** Showing the first signs of grey hairs: wisely bottled in time. *56.9%*

Scotch Malt Whisky Society Cask 2.74 Aged 15 Years refill hogshead, dist May 93 **(89.5) n22.5** a neo-bourbon displaying forests of sweet oak and thick barley: if it was sitting on a fence, it'd be an oaky one....; **t22.5** fat, tart and juicy with waves of hickory-led oaky influence; **f22** much more subtle: rhubarb and custard with minimum sugar; **b22.5** attractively shaped and curves in all the right places. *57.2%*

Scott's Selection Glenlivet 1971 bott 07 **(85) n19 t23.5 f21 b22**. The serious wrinkles on the nose are flattened out on the palate to a pretty decent degree. For a few glorious moments we are treated to a fanfare of honeycombe concentrate, but it's all pretty knife-edge stuff. *55%*

Scott's Selection Glenlivet 1977 bott 07 **(86.5) n21 t22 f22 b21.5**. Wholly enjoyable with stout barley tendencies; sweet and chewy. *50.8%*

Wilson & Morgan Barrel Selection Glenlivet Aged 30 Years cask no. 13501, dist 78, bott 08 **(84.5) n21 t22 f20.5 b21**. Very much in the Glenlivet mould for older bottlings: starts off at a cracking pace on the barley and soft fruits and then flags as the vanillas drive home. *46%*

GLENLOCHY
Highland (Western), 1898–1983. Closed.
Rarest of the Rare Glenlochy 1980 cask no. 2454 **(96) n24** verging on the perfect nose for a malt of this age: honey on several levels, mainly acacia, but some manuka creeps in; there are friendly polished oak floors, a dab of smoke, toasting mallows and orange peel.... mmmm...!! **t24.5** followed by the near perfect delivery: the sweetness is governed by the sharpness of the barley which still has the most important lines; even the spices are two-toned, one definitely of an oaky hue, the other, one suspects, having some kind of smoky root; **f23.5** a mixture of soft fruit and barley has no problems with the mallow-like vanilla finale; **b24** this does what it says on the tin: this really is the rarest of the rare. I do not often see this stuff either in bottled form or privately through a whisky year. It makes hen's teeth look pretty two-a-penny. But then one must ask the question: why? Any distillery capable of making malt this good should still be working, rather than being turned into a small hotel. (Jim Murray and all at Dram Good Books Ltd would like to assure readers of a nervous disposition that no whisky was spat out during the tasting of this sample.) *54.8%. Duncan Taylor.*

GLENLOSSIE
Speyside, 1876. Diageo. Working.
⁙ **Glenlossie The Manager's Choice** first fill bourbon American oak, cask no. 14098, dist 1999, bott 2009 db **(92.5) n23.5** a delicate trace of lime to the barley: what an understated, fragile, uber sexy nose...; **t23.5** unusual in that the first wave on delivery appears to be a

thin, oily note. This is promptly followed by the young barley water, threatening a sharpness but dampened by the lightest scattering of icing sugar; mouth watering and youthful; **f23** even with the custard powder arrival, never a hint of anything that is remotely non kindergarten; **b22.5** one of the most impressive examples of Speyside malt, apparently not even out of nappies but treating you to a spectacular display of barley in all its beauty. Confirmation, barely needed, that with Clynelish, this has to be Diageo's most under-rated distillery. *59.1% 207 bottles.*

⁘ **Berrys' Own Selection Glenlossie 1975 (94)** n23.5 exquisite Lossieness: soft contours of exotic fruit sharpened by a livelier zestiness but with a brittle maltiness just below the surface. Custard topping completes the experience for those who remember Zoom ice lollies...; **t24** pure Lossie-mouth: as delicate as the nose despite the obvious early oak prickle. This soon loses ground to the stupendous lush barley which evolves on a lightly oiled bed of muscovado sugars; **f23** those oils ensure a real length to this one with the oaks reforming, as they have every right, but never at a cost to the overall elegance; vanilla and barley dominate the fade; **b23.5** a quite magic cask, despite the obvious signs of age. Miss at your peril. *49.8% Berry Bros & Rudd*

Cadenhead's Glenlossie Aged 14 Years port, dist 93, bott Feb 08 **(91.5)** n22.5 t23.5; **f22.5 b23**. Colossal Lossie...!! The 777th whisky specially tasted for the 2009 edition...and my word, did it take off!! *57.6%. 267 bottles.*

⁘ **Cadenhead's Authentic Collection Glenlossie-Glenlivet 1993** bott Feb 10 **(78)** n21 t21 f18 b18. A bit of a head scratcher, this. Where did those lightly smoked cabbage notes come from? When pitched in with a wine cask fruitiness, the result is a real hit and miss affair with more misses than hits. *55.8% Wm. Cadenhead Ltd. 265 bottles.*

The Cärn Mör Vintage Collection Glenlossie 1984 sherry butt, cask no. 2537, dist 84, bott 09 **(73)** n18 t19 f18 b18. Sulphur-affected cask. *46%. The Scottish Liqueur Centre.*

⁘ **Old Malt Cask Glenlossie Aged 16 Years** sherry butt no. DL 5530, dist Sep 93, bott Sep 09 **(77.5)** n20 t20.5 f18 b19. A lightweight gristiness. *50% Douglas Laing & Co Ltd. 541 bottles.*

Scotch Malt Whisky Society Cask 46.17 Aged 15 Years refill barrel, dist Sep 92 **(83.5)** n20 t22 f20.5 b21. A refreshing wallpaper paste / lemon drop combo. *53.5%*

Scotch Malt Whisky Society Cask 46.18 Aged 15 Years refill barrel, dist Sep 92 **(86)** n21 t21 f22.5 b21.5. Outwardly a light, delicate malt but one which eventually glows with intensity. *51.6%*

The Spirit Safe Cask Glenlossie Vintage 1993 Aged 13 Years hogshead no. 1168, bott 07 **(87)** n21.5 t22 f22 b21.5. Really unusual stuff this: a Lossie the like of which you will find rarely. For all its obvious shortcomings, a flip side to a feinty dram is that you can often get some real complexity in there, too. I could either have marked it low as a purist or thought: what the hell...enjoy! Guess which I chose... *46%. nc ncf. Celtic Whisky Compagnie. 383 bottles.*

GLEN MHOR
Highland (Northern), 1892–1983. Demolished.

Glen Mhor 1976 Rare Malt db **(92.5)** n23 pure barley sugar but any excess sweetness is trimmed by a luxuriant oaky-vanilla thread that is dipped in honeydew melon; **t24** the delivery on palate edges close to perfection as the natural barley lushness is pricked by oak-induced spice. Oak is very often a detracting factor in an old malt: here it adds depth to the effortless elegance and adds sophistication to the sweetness; **f22** long, lithe and lengthened by a surprising puff of peat popping up from nowhere; **b23.5** you just dream of truly great whisky sitting in your glass from time to time. But you don't expect it, especially from such an old cask. This was the best example from this distillery I've tasted in 30 years....until the Glenkeir version was unleashed! If you ever want to see a scotch that has stretched the use of oak as far it will go without detriment, here it is. What a pity the distillery has gone because the Mhor the merrier... *52.2%*

⁘ **Berry's Own Selection Glen Mhor 1982 (94)** n24 wow! Now there's a nose for me to start the day with: need all the old nose buds in full working order for this one. It's like being in a honey- and peat-selling florists...who have orange blossom on special offer...; **t23.5** again, it's all about the honey: just one soft layer after another but of ever altering intensity. Luckily weighed down by a hint of smoke, otherwise it would all float off...; **f23** long, touch of lingering smoke to the honey-sweetened mocha; **b23.5** the best start I've had to a Bible tasting day...and it's late August. Although it is obvious that the oaks are just beginning to crack, everything about this malt is right. *46% Berry Bros & Rudd*

⁘ **Cadenhead's Glen Mhor 1982** sherry cask, bott Feb 10 **(88)** n22 the oak is in the process of getting its pension but enough crisp barley for an interesting development; **t22** immediate spice fizz softened by a juicy, vaguely fruity second string; **f22** still the unmistakable sign of OTT oak, but some lovely zest, too; **b22** firm and spicy. Enough oak to fell a charging rhino, yet somehow the fruity richness of the barley lightens and brightens to make for a lovely dram. *56.8% Wm. Cadenhead Ltd. 236 bottles.*

Gordon & MacPhail Distillery Label Glen Mhor 1980 (77) n19 t21 f18 b19. A lesser Mhor. *43%*

⸫ **Old Malt Cask Glen Mhor Aged 27 Years** refill hogshead no. DL 5420, dist Aug 82, bott Aug 09 **(95) n24** peat-smoked oak; vanilla cream Swiss roll...simply gorgeous; **t24** smoked-spiced delivery with several layers of lime and caramelised ginger; juicy and improbably sensuous with the peat returning to fill the middle rather nimbly; **f23.5** tires but there is enough Demerara to see off the worst of the oak; the smoke-laden spice is a constant – rather delicious – noise to the very end and helped by a very light oil; **b23.5** more time on its dial than Big Ben. But plenty of the smoky spice of life... this is astonishingly good. *50% Douglas Laing & Co Ltd*

Old Malt Cask Glen Mhor Aged 32 Years refill hogshead no. 4208, dist Dec 75, bott Mar 08 **(85.5) n22 t21 f21 b21.5.** Lovely whisky for its age with the barley having to be at its sharpest to keep out the oak. None of the peat that helps make the RoR the true classic, it has but sufficient charisma and malty depth to ensure a lush and lovely experience. *44.1%. Douglas Laing. 137 bottles.*

Rarest of the Rare Glen Mhor 1975 cask no. 4034 **(95) n24.5 t24 f22 b23.5.** Mhor or less a miracle it has survived intact after so many years. A great way by which to remember the distillery, as this really is priceless stuff in terms of both scarcity and excellence. I can imagine this changing hands for lots of money in the not too distant... *43.5%. Duncan Taylor.*

Rarest of the Rare Glen Mhor 1975 cask no. 4035 **(85) n21 t22 f21 b21.** Exceptionally gentle to the point of being docile. At one stage, threatens to go down the dramatic olde worlde exotic fruit road, decides against it and, a few spice prickles apart, glides to the finish line. *40.2%*

Rarest of the Rare Glen Mhor 1975 cask no. 4041 **(85.5) n21 t21.5 f22 b21.** Never quite know what you are going to get from this batch of casks. They can be ordinary or stupendous. Here we have something of a halfway house, though tending towards the Mhor ordinaire. Wallpaper pasty in part but the crystal brown sugar edge to the barley is quite a treat. Very drinkable and for its age in pretty good nick. Just don't expect to be blown away by the complexity. *40.6%*

GLENMORANGIE

Highland (Northern), 1843. Glenmorangie plc. Working.

Glenmorangie 10 Years Old db **(94) n24** perhaps the most enigmatic aroma of them all: delicate yet assertive, sweet yet dry, young yet oaky: a malty tone poem; **t22** flaky oakiness throughout but there is an impossibly complex toastiness to the barley which seems to suggest the lightest hint of smoke; **f24** amazingly long for such a light dram, drying from the initial sweetness but with flaked almonds amid the oakier, rich cocoa notes; **b24** you might find the occasional "orange variant", where the extra degree of oak, usually from a few too many first-fill casks, has flattened out the more extreme peaks and toughs of complexity (scores about 89). But these are pretty rare – almost a collector's item – and overall this remains one of the great single malts: a whisky of uncompromising aesthetic beauty from the first enigmatic whiff to the last teasing and tantalising gulp. Complexity at its most complex. *40%*

Glenmorangie 15 Years Old db **(90.5) n23** chunky and fruity: something distinctly sugar candy about this one; the barley's no slouch, either; and, just to raise the eyebrows, just the faintest waft of something smoky...; **t23** silky, a tad sultry, and serious interplay between oak and barley; a real, satisfying juiciness to this one; **f22** dries towards the oaky side of things, but just a faint squeeze of liquorice adds extra weight; **b22.5** exudes quality. *43%*

Glenmorangie 15 Years Old Sauternes Wood Finish db **(68) n16 t18 f17 b17.** I had hoped – and expected – an improvement on the sulphured version I came across last time. Oh, whisky! Why are you such a cruel mistress.....? *46%*

Glenmorangie 18 Years Old db **(87.5) n22** freshly sliced lime, mildly under-ripe gooseberry...and malt; **t22.5** beautiful, almost crisp delivery of barley tinged with sharp fruit; **f21** duller vanillas and a soft latte flourish; **b22** much more like it! The citrus has made a welcome and much needed return. *43%*

Glenmorangie 25 Years Old db **(95.5) n24** it's strap yourself in time: this is a massive nose with more layers, twists and turns than you can shake a thief at. Soft, mildly lush Lubec marzipan is sandwiched between fruit bonbons and myriad barley tones. Worth taking half an hour over this one, and no kidding... **t24** the clarity on the nose is matched here. Every single wave of flavour is there in crystal form, starting, naturally, with the barley but this is soon paired with various unidentified fruits. The result is salivation. Towards the middle the oak shows form and does so in various cocoa-tinged ways; every nuance is delicately carved, almost fragile, but the overall picture is one of strength; **f23.5** medium length with the cocoa heading towards medium roast Java **b24** every bit as statesmanlike and elegant as a whisky of this age from such a blinding distillery should be. Ticks every single box for a 25-year-old and is Morangie's most improved malt by the distance of Tain to Wellingborough. There is a hint of genius with each unfolding wave of flavours with this one: a whisky that will go in 99/100 whisky lover's top 50 malts of all time. And that includes the Peatheads. *43%*

Glenmorangie 30 Years Old db **(72) n17 t18 f19 b18.** From the evidence in the glass the jury is out on whether it has been spruced up a little in a poor sherry cask – and spruce is the operative word: lots of pine on this wrinkly. *44.1%*

Glenmorangie 1977 db **(92) n24 t23 f22 b23.** Excellent, but a trifle underpowered....what would this have been like at 46%...??? Shows little of its great age as the oak is always subservient to the sweet barley and citrus. *43%. Exclusively at Harrods.*

Glenmorangie Artisan Casks db **(93) n23** the evening flowers that marked this brand's nose for so long is out. Earthy, dank and cool bluebell woods are in. You can almost hear the jays cackling. For all the extra weight, strands of citrus provide the light entertainment; **t23.5** quite lovely: the barley almost throbs with intensity backed by teeming, busy oak notes; **f23** more greatly weighted than last year, thanks not least to some late spices and a return to a soft earthy feel; **b23.5** if whisky could be sexed, this would be a woman. Every time I encounter Morangie Artisan, it pops up with a new look, a different perfume. And mood. It appears not to be able to make up its mind. But does it know how to pout, seduce and win your heart...? Oh yes. *46%*

Glenmorangie Astar db **(88) n21** it is as though someone has got hold of the grist, picked out all the sugary bits and added it to an oaky dough; **t23** rarely does spice arrive so early or with such force; doesn't last that long as a massive sugary avalanche hits the palate; **f22.5** bitters out as the oak takes hold; only at the death is barley injected – and then with some concentration – into the proceedings; **b22** decidedly strange malt: for quite a while it is as if someone has extracted the barley and left everything else behind. A star is born? Not yet, perhaps. But perhaps a new breed of single malt. *57.1%*

Glenmorangie Burgundy Wood Finish db **(72) n17.5 t19.5 f18 b18.** Sulphured whisky de table. *43%*

Glenmorangie Burr Oak Reserve db **(92) n24 t24 f22 b22.** Fades on the finish as a slightly spent force, but nose and arrival are simply breathtaking. Wouldn't be out of place in Kentucky. *56.3%*

Glenmorangie Cellar 13 Ten Years Old db **(88.5) n22** the richer bourbon note of old has been replaced by much finer, drier layers of oak thanks mainly to a shyer deployment of barley; **t22.5** no less delicate on delivery: the thing feels as though it is about to crumble and fall at any second; **f22** gosh...it hardly seems possible but it is getting even more delicate still: again it is wafer-thin oak that dictates with an almost apologetic honey-butterscotch sub-plot; **b22** oh, if only I could lose weight as efficiently as this appears to have done... *43%*

Glenmorangie Elegance db **(92) n22** quite herbal and soothing; **t24** the thinnest layer of icing sugar coats the silk-soft malt; every bit as gentle as the nose suggests; **f22** medium to short with some attractive rolling vanilla; **b24** a surprise package that is not entirely dissimilar to the Golden Rum, only a tad sweeter. *43%*

⋯ **Glemorangie Finealta** db **(84.5) n21 t22 f20.5 b21.** Plump and thick, one of the creamiest malts around. For what it lacks in fine detail it makes up for in effect, especially the perky oaky spices. *46%*

Glenmorangie Lasanta Sherry Finish db **(79) n19 t21 f19 b20.** Bugger. Some sulphur has crept in here. Not a lot. Some may even struggle to find it. But there is enough working behind the scenes to completely throw the show and flatten the experience. *46%*

Glenmorangie Madeira Wood Finish db **(78) n19.5 t20.5 f19 b19.** One of the real problems with wine finishes is getting the point of balance right when the fruit, barley and oak are in harmony. Here it is on a par with me singing in the shower, though frankly my aroma would be a notch or two up. *43%*

Glenmorangie Margaux Cask Finish db **(88) n22** dark, a bit moody and the odd vinegar note. But, overall, impressive; **t22** soft with a soupy barley-grape feel; **f22** sweet at first, bitters up; **b22** even taking every whisky with an open mind, I admit this was better than my subconscious might have considered. Certainly better than the near undrinkable Ch. Margaux '57 I used to bring out for my birthday each year some 20-odd years ago... *46%*

Glenmorangie Nectar D'or Sauternes Finish db **(94) n23** delicate cinnamon on toast and a drizzle of greengage and sultana; **t24** equally refreshing and dense on the palate as the bitter-sweet battle goes into overdrive; excellent weight and body; **f23** remains clean and precise, allowing some custard onto the apple strudel finale; **b24** great to see French casks that actually complement a whisky – so rare! This has replaced the Madeira finish. But there are some similar sweet-fruit characteristics. An exercise in outrageously good sweet-dry balancing. *46%*

Glenmorangie Quinta Ruban Port Finish db (92) **n24** typical Morangie complexity, but the grape notes added act almost like a prism to show their varied hues; **t23** fruit and spice about as the oak goes in search of glory: barley stands in its way; **f22** light, deftly sweetened and juicy to the end; **b23** this replacement of the original Port finish shows a genuine understanding of the importance of grape-oak balance. Both are portrayed with clarity and confidence. This is a form of cask finishing that has progressed from experimentation to certainty. *46%*

Glenmorangie Sherry Wood Finish db (84) **n23 t21 f20 b20.** Stupendous clean sherry nose, then disappoints with a somewhat bland display on the palate. *43%*

Glenmorangie Signet db (93) **n23** huge oak, doubtless coming from the virgin casks but it works wonderfully, as, rather than overpower, it appears to fuse with the malt. The result is thick, toasty bitter-sweet, with almost a marmalade hit; **t23.5** oooophh!! One hell of a hit with again the oak storming in as if about to wallop you, then holding back becalmed by a chocolate malt insurgence; unquestionably oilier than usual allowing all the elements a platform to stick around; **f23** lengthy, with chocolate now the main theme, both, it appears, from the oak and barley. Genuinely delicious...a bit like praline spread on toast... **b23.5** as there is a Morangie Traditional, then this has to be Morangie Untraditional. An entirely different direction for this malt with an oiliness for a Glenmorangie the like of which I have never seen before and a thick oak intensity unique not just to the distillery but any other Highland malt I can think of. And a tip: drink at cask strength, a fraction above room and not quite body temp...and after it has breathed in the glass for about 20 minutes. Then, believe me, you are in for one hell of a show!! *46%*

Glenmorangie Sonnalta PX db (96.5) **n24.5** now this works: has that heavy-handed feel of a sweet sherry butt (or five) at work here, usually the kiss of death for so many whiskies. But an adroit praline sub-plot really does the trick. So with the malt evident, too, we have a three-pronged attack which somehow meshes in to one. And not even the merest hint of an off-note...goodness gracious: a new experience...!!! **t23** Neanderthal grape drags its knuckles along the big vanilla floor before a really subtle light Columbian coffee kick puts us back on course; sharper vanillas from some awkward oak threatens to send us off course again but somehow it finds a settled, common ground; **f25** now goes into orgasmic overdrive as Demerara sugar is tipped into some gorgeous, cream-lightened mocha. This is obviously to wash down the Melton Hunt cake which is resplendent in its grape and roast nut finery... phew!!! It is, unquestionably, the perfect whisky finish... **b24** this one passed me by. If they told me anything about this chap, I'd forgotten. It absolutely groans from the lucid sweet grape and I discover it's actually Pedro Ximinez. Brave. Foolhardy, even. Because over the last decade of studying whiskies matured in that sugary beast the experience has usually ended in tears. Not here, though. This is a gamble that has handsomely paid off: Glenmorangie as you've never seen it before. Probably Scotch malt as you've never seen before. But after buying one bottle, you'll be wanting to see it again. A giant among the tall stills. *46%*

Glenmorangie Traditional db (90.5) **n22** orange blossom, barley sugar and chalk dust; **t23** delicate delivery revelling in gentle complexity: really playful young-ish malt makes for a clean start and middle; **f22.5** soft mocha notes play out a quiet finish; **b23** an improved dram with much more to say, but does so quietly. *57.1%*

Glenmorangie Truffle Oak db (96) **n24** a significant aroma: big, powering oak yet controlled with no sign of bitterness or tiredness. Some golden syrup on the barley is toned down by age. If you can find a flaw or off-note, e-mail me; **t24** bloody hell!!! Now the golden syrup comes out to play, but the intensity of that plus the barley fair takes the breath away. Something very breakfast-cerealy about this experience. But for grown ups...; **f25** burning embers of honey-nut cereal last forever. Keeping them company are varying shades of golden to molassed sugar. One of the longest un-peated finishes you'll ever find; **b23** the Glenmorangie of all Glenmorangies. I really have to work hard and deep into the night to find fault with it. If I am going to be hyper-critical, I'll dock it a mark for being so constantly sweet, though in its defence I have to say that the degree of sweetness alters with astonishing dexterity. Go on, it's Truffle oak: make a pig of yourself...!! *60.5%*

Glenmorangie Vintage 1975 db (89) **n23** clementines! It must be Christmas...; **t23** improbably clean malt for something so aged, then a layer or three of fruit and spiced vanilla; **f21** bitters out as an oaky trench is found; **b22** a charming, fruity and beautifully spiced oldie. *43%*

Scotch Malt Whisky Society Cask 125.1 Aged 13 Years dist May 93 (95) **n24 t23 f24 b24.** Just a peach of a cask that re-defines fruitiness as far as whisky is concerned. *51.2%*

Scotch Malt Whisky Society Cask 125.2 Aged 11 Years designer hogshead, dist Jun 95 **(90) n21 t23 f23 b23.** Very sweet but countered by wonderful spice. Another chance to see the distillery in a light it has rarely been seen in before. *53.5%*

Scotch Malt Whisky Society Cask 125.19 Aged 13 Years 1st fill hogshead, dist Jun 95 **(86.5) n21.5 t23.5 f20 b21.5.** What can you say? Glenmorangie owns the SMWS. So therefore one would assume that this, with all the casks available, would be the pinnacle of Glenmorangie's 13-y-o whiskies. Somehow I don't think so. Certainly an attractive dram, well made from a noble family and having enjoyed a privileged upbringing in a top quality cask. There is spice. There is malt – lots of malt, in fact. There is oak. There is a well-balanced sweet-dry interchange...but. And the but is the butt, or the cask to be precise. It is too good. Too much for 13 years because the massive degree of natural caramels have started to wear the edges off the finer notes you would expect to find from this wonderful distillery. So there is a rumbling dullness in the undergrowth where the higher notes should be singing from the top branches. Lovely stuff. But not lovely enough... *56.3%*

Scotch Malt Whisky Society Cask 125.20 Aged 13 Years dist Jun 95 **(91) n22.5** predominantly oaky notes, a variety of them and the majority of them keeping the barley at bay. But the odd few are uplifting and gently sweetened in a custardly manner, too... **t23** another silk-soft delivery from a 'Morangie, but that's due mainly to that custard tendency to dictate things; some fabulously juicier barley notes also up the flavour amps; some spiffing spices really get going; **f22.5** reverts to a more conservative cocoa-rich haven, but still bangs out a decent barley theme; **b23** many of the points made about 125.19 could apply here, except a trilling sweetness takes it up several extra notches and the complexity enters another stratosphere. *56.2%*

Scotch Malt Whisky Society Cask 125.21 Aged 13 Years 1st fill hogshead, dist Jun 95 **(86) n22 t22 f21 b21.** Part of any performer's art is to know when to milk the silence: it can be so much more effective than just saying something because you are there. And so, too, with whisky casks. Here we have a great cask, but too much of it: we need the silence, just as in 125.19, to make the piece work to its fullest potential. Good whisky? Certainly. Enjoyable? undoubtedly. Annoying? Massively. Now here's an idea. Three casks. All from the same distillery. And same age. What if I, and other whisky lovers, had been able to monitor a first fill bourbon against a second fill and then third fill and listen to the effect those silences would have had. Now that would have been fun... *56.4%*

⋯❄ **Scotch Malt Whisky Society Cask 125.26 Aged 16 Years** dist May 93 **(83) n23.5 t21.5 f19 b19.** Fabulous, rich chocolate-caramel bourbon nose....then on the palate a severe case of over-aging. *52.2% 243 bottles.*

⋯❄ **Scotch Malt Whisky Society Cask 125.35 Aged 16 Years** sherry butt, dist Feb 94 **(68) n14 t19 f17 b18.** Very thoughtful of the SMWS to throw in a cask to show its members why sulphur-treated casks are close on undrinkable. Sadly, as my 600th new whisky for the 2011 edition....a serious party pooper. *52.1% 367 bottles.*

⋯❄ **Scotch Malt Whisky Society Cask 125.39 Aged 18 Years** dist Feb 92 **(85) n20 t22.5 f21 b21.5.** A kind of 125.26 in reverse: here the nose is dull and unrewarding but the delivery sparks into life with the most intense orangey-bourbon arrival imaginable. Pretty close to the edge, though, and another summer might have been one too many. *55.7% 234 bottles.*

GLEN MORAY
Speyside, 1897. La Martiniquaise. Working.

Glen Moray Classic 8 Years Old db **(86) n20 t22 f21 b23.** A vast improvement on previous bottlings with the sluggish fatness replaced by a thinner, barley-rich, slightly sweeter and more precise mouthfeel. *40%*

Glen Moray 12 Years Old db **(90) n22.5** gentle malt of varying pitch and intensity; **t22** a duller start than it should be with the vanilla diving in almost before the barley but the juicy, grassy notes arrive in good time; **f23** long, back on track with intense malt and the custardy oak is almost apologetic but enlivened with a dash of lime: mmmmm... pure Glen Moray! **b22.5** I have always regarded this as the measuring stick by which all other malty and clean Speysiders should be tried and tested. It is still a fabulous whisky, full of malty intricacies. Something has fallen off the edge, perhaps, but minutely so. Still think a trick or two is being missed by bottling this at 40%: the natural timbre of this malt demands 46% and no less.... *40%*

Glen Moray 16 Years Old db **(74) n19 t19 f18 b19.** A serious dip in form. Drab. *40%*

Glen Moray 16 Years Old Chenin Blanc Mellowed in Wine Barrels db **(85) n20 t22 f22 b21.** A fruity, oak-shaded dram just brimming with complexity. *40%*

Glen Moray 20 Years Old db **(80) n22 t22 f18 b18.** With so much natural cream toffee, it is hard to believe that this has so many years on it. After a quick, refreshing start it pans out, if anything, a little dull. *40%*

Glen Moray 30 Years Old db (92.5) n23.5 it's probably the deftness of the old-fashioned Speyside smoke in tandem with the structured fruits that makes this so special; t23.5 for a light Speysider, the degree of barley to oak is remarkable: soft, oil-gilde d barley is met by a wonderful, if brief, spice prickle; f22.5 deft layering of vanilla and cocoa; a sprinkle of muscovado sugar repels any darker oak notes; b23 for all its years, this is comfortable malt, untroubled by time. There is no mistaking quality. *43%*

Glen Moray 1959 Rare Vintage db (91) n25 t23 f21 b22. They must have been keeping their eyes on this one for a long time: a stunning malt that just about defies nature. The nose reaches absolute perfection. *50.9%*

Glen Moray 1962 Very Rare Vintage Aged 42 Years db (94) n23 t24 f23 b24. The first temptation is to think that this has succumbed to age, but a second and a third tasting reveal that there is much more complexity, integrity and balance to this than first meets the tastebuds. The last cask chosen by the legendary Ed Dodson before his retirement from the distillery: a pretty perceptive choice. A corker! *50.9%. sc.*

Glen Moray 1984 db (83) n20 t22 f20 b21. Mouthwatering and incredibly refreshing malt for its age. *40%*

Glen Moray 1986 Commemorative Bottling cask 4698 db (96) n25 t24 f23 b24. Ed Dodson hand-picked this cask from the warehouse to mark the opening of the distillery's visitor centre in late 2004. Ed has now retired but – and this bottling proves the point entirely – he should be brought back to the distillery, as Elmer T. Lee has at Buffalo Trace, and be given his own named brand. You simply cannot buy the experience and natural feel Ed has for Glen Moray. This astonishing single cask proves the point with a delicious and unforgettable eloquence. *64.4%. ncf.*

Glen Moray 1989 db (86) n23 t22 f20 b21. Doesn't quite live up to the fruit smoothie nose but I'm being a little picky here. *40%*

Glen Moray 1991 Mountain Oak Malt The Final Release dist 15 Mar 91, bott 5 Feb 07 db (94) n24 t24 f23 b23. Another Scotch malt masquerading as bourbon. Massive and quite beautiful. Until the 1986 edition was released, the previous Mountain Oak was the best Glen Moray I had ever happened upon – and if memory serves me correctly that had a decidly bourbony bent, too. This is up there among the distillery's best ever. *58.6%. 1,158 bottles.*

Glen Moray 1992 Single Cask No 1441 sherry butt db (74) n17 t21 f18 b18. Oops! Didn't anyone spot the sulphur ...? *59.6%*

⋯ **Glen Moray 1995 Port Wood Finish** bott Dec 09 db (95.5) n23 a surprising liquorice base to the healthy spiced fruit; t24 vivid grape: clean, intense and, for a while, dominant. The oak surges back with a few tricks of its own, the most impressive being a liquorice-hickory thrust and a soothing custardy topping. Meanwhile, the grape offers spice and a sheen; f24.5 a wonderful array of spicy chocolate and raisin notes that appear to continue indefinitely. Needs to be tasted to be believed. b24 possibly the most satisfying wine finish of the year. *56.7%*

Glen Moray 1995 Single Sherry Cask sherry butt db (56) n15 t14 f13 b14. So stunned was I about the abject quality of this bottling, I even looked on the Glen Moray website to see if they had said anything about it. Apparently, if you add water you find on the nose "the lingering soft sulphury smoke of a struck match." Well, here's the news: you don't need water. Just open the bottle and there's Rotorua in all it's stink bomb finery. And errr...hullo, guys...some further news: that means it's a bloody faulty, useless cask. And has no right to be put anywhere near a bottling hall let alone set loose in a single bottling. This, quite frankly, is absolutely rank whisky, the type of which makes my blood boil. I mean, is this really the best cask that could be found in the entire and considerable estate of Glen Moray..???? Am I, or is it the whisky world going mad...? *59.6%*

Glen Moray Classic db (86.5) n22 t21.5 f21.5 b21.5. I once rather witheringly described this as being short of ideas if memory serves me correctly... (having just dived in to the 2008 Bible, I see my memory has, indeed, served me correctly). Now the idea appears to be to give it a fruity outer coat and it works well. The nose is the star with a wonderful, clean barley-fruit tandem, but what follows cannot quite match its sure-footed wit. *40%*

Glen Moray Mountain Oak Final Release dist 91 db (82) n23.5 t21 f18.5 b19. A malt which reminds me of the sequel to the film Elizabeth: you look forward to something of distinctly high class for a very long time and then, when it arrives, you can only look on aghast as your dreams are dashed. No, this whisky doesn't have anything quite so ludicrously ridiculous as the dramatically mountainous Scottish backdrop to Fotheringhay castle, Mary's prison for days, not years as the film depicts and which was in reality set on the very flattest Northamptonshire countryside heading towards the Fens; or outlandish age issues such as good Queen Bess discussing having children by which time, historically, she was in her mid 50s. But for those who enjoyed the much tighter, historically true first Elizabeth, you will know what I mean. There was something truer, tighter, less fanciful about the first bottling, with the bourbon edge filtering down in perfect synchronization. Here the bourbony nose is sublime. But once it hits the palate it's all imagery and OTT. This should sell well in Hollywood. 58.6%

⠿ **Glen Moray Wine Cask Edition** bott Sep 09 db **(83.5) n20 t23 f20 b20.5.** When in full flow this is just bursting with some of the juiciest fruit you are likely to encounter. But a familiar bitter buzz – not as bad as some, thankfully, but still enough – brings down the value. How sad. 59.7%

Cadenhead's Glen Moray Aged 15 Years sauternes wood, dist 92, bott Jun 08 **(92.5) n22.5 t24 f23 b23.** I am slowly coming to the conclusion that a non-sulphured sauternes cask, with all spice and oak-defeating sweetness that is so elegantly offered, is about as good as any wine cask you'll find for whisky maturation. This is an object lesson in exactly how it should be done. 46%. 320 bottles.

⠿ **Duncan Taylor Collection Glen Moray 1975** cask no. 64 **(89) n22.5** thinks about the exotic fruit possibility but takes the malty-oaky finesse option....; **t23** silky barley with now a rich, creamy fruitiness followed by a burst of vanilla and thin honey; **f21.5** an elegant succession of bourbon tones; **b22** for a malt not renowned for its backbone, withstood 35 years with remarkable ease. 52.7%

Duncan Taylor The NC2 Range Glen Moray 1991 Aged 16 Years **(86) n22 t22 f21 b21.** Ultra pleasant malt, entirely untaxing and plays upon the most simple of barley themes. 46%

Kingsbury's 'The Selection' Glen Moray 7 Years Old hogshead, cask no. 56 & 57, dist Mar 01, bott Jun 08 **(82) n19 t22 f21 b20.** The third-fill cask allows the malt full, though not entirely unblemished scope. Would have been more effective at full strength, though. 43%. Japan Import System. 870 bottles.

Mackillop's Choice Glen Moray cask no. 4065, dist Sep 92, bott Jul 07 **(78.5) n21 t19.5 f19 b19.** A bitter-sweet experience in every sense. The over-used cask allows the barley some early play, but some of the more bitter components of the oak are heard a touch too loudly. 43%. Iain Mackillop & Co. Ltd.

Murray McDavid Glen Moray 1992 bourbon/madeira **(88) n23 t20 f22 b23.** The rich malt canvas of the Glen Moray gives the Madeira an unrestricted medium to do its stuff. 46%

Old Malt Cask Glen Moray Aged 16 Years **(85.5) n22 t22.5 f20 b21.** Both the nose and delivery are swamped with superb malt, though the finish is on the bitter side. 50%

Old Malt Cask Glen Moray Aged 16 Years refill hogshead 4068, dist Nov 91, bott Dec 07 **(85) n22 t21.5 f20.5 b21.** Huge malt à la Glen Moray house style. 50%. nc ncf. 340 bottles.

⠿ **Scotch Malt Whisky Society Cask 35.30 Aged 9 Years** 1st fill barrel, dist Feb 00 **(87) n23.5** diced apple and rhubarb pie; closer to bourbon than scotch; **t22** powering malt and bourbony Demerara suddenly hit a thick vanilla wall; **f20** a little bitter and bready; **b21.5** strange one: starts off like a train, deliciously confident then gets slightly derailed. 60.4% Scotch Malt Whisky Society. 215 bottles.

⠿ **Scotch Malt Whisky Society Cask 35.38 Aged 9 Years** 2nd fill ex chardonnay, dist May 00 **(68.5) n18 t18 f16 b16.5.** Starts badly...and gets worse. 60% 265 bottles

⠿ **Scotch Malt Whisky Society Cask 35.39 Aged 9 Years** fill chardonnay barrique, dist May 00 **(58.5) n15 t15 f14 b14.5.** Someone's going to have to give the panel a crash course in identifying sulphur. Jesus....what on Earth were you thinking of...??? Actually, why bother? I have recently taken up archery. Please allow those responsible for this debacle of a bastard bottling to be my targets...and I promise to make it a long, slow, painful death... 594% Scotch Malt Whisky Society. 250 bottles.

Scotch Malt Whisky Society Cask 35.23 Aged 10 Years 1st fill barrel, dist Mar 98 **(87) n21.5 t22 f22 b21.5** Good, enjoyable rather simple malt which, knowing the what the Society has to choose from regarding this distillery, must be seen as something of a slight disappointment. 59.8%

Scotch Malt Whisky Society Cask 35.26 Aged 10 Years 1st fill barrel, dist Mar 98 **(90) n22** slightly ungainly, not least because the oak is trying to take a big chunk out of the malt...and fails; distinctive soft cedar wood and vanilla combine attractively; **t23** the malt is layered and offers itself in flimsy gossamer form through to thick concentrate; balances well between sweet and sharp; **f22.5** moves back towards a more bourbony edge with shimmering dark sugared coating and a late touch of leather; **b22.5** where bourbon and malt collide... 58.8%

Scotch Malt Whisky Society Cask 35.27 Aged 10 Years 1st fill hogshead, dist Mar 98 **(81.5) n21 t20 f21.5 b19.** Warming, with the usual big malt theme. But, compared to 35.26, the impact of the oak is far less benign and only a gentle butter-toffee quality helps soften the experience. 58.4%

⠲ **Scotch Malt Whisky Society Cask 35.34 Aged 13 Years** new charred oak, dist Mar 96 **(87) n22** kumquats and figs, but just a little crushed and stifled; **t23** thick and searingly hot barley/red liquorice; chewy in a vaguely but not quite bourbony kind of way; **f20** unravels towards a burnt toast bitterness; **b22.5** almost stunning...but not quite. For that you'll have to mosey on down to bottling 35.35. *57% Scotch Malt Whisky Society. 281 bottles.*

⠲ **Scotch Malt Whisky Society Cask 35.35 Aged 13 Years** new charred oak, dist Mar 96 **(93.5) n24** Buffalo Trace at nine years? A Wild Turkey, maybe? Either way, this is all about the cask...just liquorice and honey engulfed vanillin....and a whole bowl of kumquats. A rye mash bill? Might as well be for the intrinsic fruitiness...; **t23.5** yeee-haaar..y'all find some of that darned barley in that honeyed liquorice ye ken... **f23** well...if this ain't a virgin cask with all that orangey stuff an' all, or as near as damned close to it as possible, then I'll be a five-legged racoon.... **b23** when then distillery manager Ed Dodson took some time out to work in Kentucky, I wonder if he came back determined to create a Glen Moray bourbon... if so, he succeeded. And some...!! *56.6% Scotch Malt Whisky Society. 252 bottles.*

⠲ **Scotch Malt Whisky Society Cask 35.31 Aged 19 Years** 1st fill barrel, dist Jan 90 **(76.5) n20 t18 f19 b19.5.** The odd lemon note here and there. But distinctly hot and rough around the edges. *58.4% Scotch Malt Whisky Society. 231 bottles.*

⠲ **Scotch Malt Whisky Society Cask 35.41 Aged 35 Years** refill hogshead, dist Jan 75 **(84) n22 t21.5 f20 b20.5.** The citrus is out in force, but it's a case of damage limitation against the marauding oak. Some pretty major moments, though. *56.1% 179 bottles*

GLEN ORD
Highland (Northern) 1838. Diageo. Working.

Glen Ord Aged 12 Years db **(81) n20 t23 f18 b20.** Just when you thought it safe to go back....for a while Diageo ditched the sherry-style Ord. It has returned. Better than some years ago, when it was an unhappy shadow of its once-great self, but without the sparkle of the vaguely-smoked bottling of a year or two back. Nothing wrong with the rich arrival, but the finish is a mess. I'll open the next bottling with trepidation... *43%*

Glen Ord 25 Years Old dist 78 db **(95) n24** the most narrow seams of peat offer backbone to deeply impressive arrays of fruits, including kumquats, unripe figs and greengages. The oak is firm, as is the malt; **t24** nectar-plus!! The astonishing mouthfeel is matched only by the perfectly presented fruit, mainly a citrussy affair, that battles for supremacy against grassy malt and spiced oak. Waiting in the wings is wonderfully gentle smoke. A faultlessly choreographed production; **f23** slightly more simplistic here thanks to some caramel being sucked from the oak, but the spices continue as does a fruity tang; **b24** some stupendous vatting here: cask selection at its very highest to display Ord in all its far too rarely seen magnificence. *58.3%*

Glen Ord 28 Years Old db **(90) n22** malt and mint bound together by soft liquorice and dark fudge; **t23** delightful barley-sugar theme that forms a stupendously rigid middle with the most delicate hints of smoke and coffee. The body weight is perfect; **f22** amazingly long finale with lashings of cocoa to go with the mollassed sugar and powering barley; **b23** this is mega whisky showing slight traces of sap, especially on the nose, but otherwise a concentrate of many of the qualities I remember from this distillery before it was bottled in a much ruined form. Blisteringly beautiful. *58.3%.*

Glen Ord 30 Years Old db **(87) n22** shaped by oak, there is a peppery element to the floral thrust; **t21** molten barley spearheads the arrival before a cumbersome oakiness interferes. Plenty of spice and underpinning sweetness; **f23** settles down for a really long and delightful finish with a glorious interaction between delicate, velvety barley and vanilla. Charming; **b21** creaking with oak, but such is the polish to the barley some serious class is on show. *58.8%*

⠲ **Glen Ord 1997 The Manager's Choice** db **(93.5) n24** oh my word....what have we here...? Just the most enticing little fruit pastel number you could ask for, and all played out on the softest malty field imaginable. Genuinely complex and enticing with the nose being teasingly caressed; **t23.5** then, just to shock, a real injection of bite and nip on delivery with a tangy blood orange thread which follows from the nose; **f23** custard powder oakiness with some late hickory and toffee; **b23** when given the chance, Glen Ord offers one of the fruitiest drams on the market. Here it is in its full blood orange element. A beauty! *59.2%*

Singleton of Glen Ord 12 Years Old db **(83) n21 t22 f20 b20.** Pleasant with some attractive blood orange notes. But, overall, it's all rather flat and fails to take off the way it should. *40%*

Cadenhead's Authentic Collection Ord Aged 12 Years bourbon hogshead, matured in oak cask, dist 96, bott Jun 08 **(91.5) n22.5 t24 f22.5 b22.5.** Massive malty: perfect for blending, superb as a singleton. *58.2%. 210 bottles.*

The Cärn Mòr Vintage Collection Glen Ord 2004 hogshead, cask no. 55, bott 09 **(84) n22 t21.5 f20 b20.5.** Beautiful citrus and barley though always new makey. 46%.

Old Malt Cask Glen Ord Aged 18 Years sherry finish dist Jan 89, bott Feb 07 **(90) n24** multiple layers of barley and sultana dovetail with lemon-ginger and oak. Sublime; **t23** more mouth-watering on delivery than any 18-year-old has a right be to; again it's the barley and grape at full play, with the very lightest wisps of smoke. The oak crashes in mid stream; **f21** lots more oak, this time with a natural toffee/dried date edge **b22** just shows how stupendous this distillery can be when left to its own devices. 50%. 808 bottles.

Provenance Glen Ord Aged 11 Years dist mar 98, bott Jul 09 **(83) n21 t21.5 f20.5 b20.** Attractive, simple malty but standard Ordie for an oft recycled cask. 46%. Douglas Laing.

⟨≈⟩ **Provenance Glen Ord Over 11 Years** refill hogshead no. DMG 5570, dist Spring 1998, bott Autumn 2009 **(86) n21 t22 f21.5 b21.5.** A distinct, lightly fruity edge to the delicious gristy barley. The oak plays only a minor role. 46% Douglas Laing & Co Ltd

Provenance Glen Ord Aged 12 Years refill hogshead no. 4243, dist Spring 96, bott Spring 08 **(84.5) n21.5 t22 f20 b21.** Pure grist with a squirt of lemon juice. 46%. nc ncf. Douglas Laing.

Signatory Vintage Glen Ord 1998 8 Years Old (86) n21.5 t22 f21 b21.5. Lots of banana milkshake and barley with this simple but very attractive number. Suffers a little from reduced strength. 43%. USA.

Scotch Malt Whisky Society Cask 77.16 Aged 21 Years refill hogshead, dist Aug 87 **(84) n20.5 t23 f20 b20.5.** Hmmm. Either we have a malt which boasts juniper on the nose. Or this was bottled after some gin was and someone didn't change the filters. Some attractive celery notes, too. Sweet and malty early on; bland at the death. 55.8%

Scotch Malt Whisky Society Cask 77.17 Aged 9 Years refill hogshead, dist Mar 00 **(95.5) n24** beauty without a blemish: diced green pear freshens the oak; the most distant speck of smoke and acacia honey of the thinnest most delicate kind; **t24** didn't expect that: surely the taste can't be as pure as the aroma...it is!! Again, one is soothed with a beautiful acacia honey coating to the gristy barley; again there appears a semi-hidden hint of something vaguely smoked; **f23.5** custard tart with a spot-on degree of white sugar; the oak offers nothing more than weight and a balancing dryness; **b24** just one of those unspoiled drams that offers everything with crystal clarity: not a mark, an off note or blemish. Almost virginal in its delivery. 53.6%

Singleton of Glen Ord 32 Year Old db **(91) n23.5** some dreamy, creamy sherry...and very little evidence of age decline; **t23** sharp and juicy punch with toasty oak making its move soon after; plenty of marmalade going round; **f22** sweetens slightly with a touch of barley entering the fray, then oak and finally a furry, orangey feel; **b22.5** delicious. But if ever a malt has screamed out to be at 46%, this is it. 40%

GLENROTHES
Speyside, 1878. Edrington. Working.

The Glenrothes 1978 dist Nov 78, bott 08 db **(90.5) n23** over-ripe gooseberries mixed with dry tobacco; suet pudding and vanilla pods: attractively intriguing; **t23** relaxed, lush barley coats the mouth with a muscovado sugar edge; **f22** mushy sultana and toasty oak; **b22.5** sheer – and delicious – entertainment. 43%

The Glenrothes 1979 Single Cask No. 13458 db **(68) n18 t19 f15 b16.** Wrecked by sulphur. In whisky terms, tragic. 57%

The Glenrothes 1979 Single Cask No. 13459 db **(75) n20 t20 f17 b18.** This twin cask to 13458 has also seen a sulphur stick at work, but it wasn't kept inside anything to lie so long. Even so, enough damage to the finish undoes the promising big fruit start. 56.6%

⟨≈⟩ **The Glenrothes 1988 Vintage** bott 2010 db **(74) n18.5 t19 f18 b18.5.** For all the obvious high quality sugars present, it still can't overcome the Spanish imposition. 43%

The Glenrothes 1994 dist Oct 94, bott 07 db **(77) n19 t20 f19 b19.** The citrus appears as promised on the label, but sadly a few unadvertised sulphured butt-related gremlins are present also. 43%

⟨≈⟩ **The Glenrothes 1998 Vintage** bott 2010 db **(73.5) n20 t19 f16 b18.5.** Talk about bitter-sweet.....!!! 43%

⟨≈⟩ **The Glenrothes Alba Reserve** db **(87.5) n22** muted honey and spices rising from the flattish nosescape; **t22** silky, malty delivery with some toffee turning up in the middle ground; **f21.5** decent length with more of the same and just a hint of a liquorice flourish; **b22** you know that very smartly groomed, unfailingly polite but rather dull chap you invariable get at dinner parties...? 40%

⟨≈⟩ **The Glenrothes John Ramsay** bott 2009 db **(89.5) n22.5** almost a touch of the Highland Parks about this, only without the smoke. The honey has a pronounced softness, as does the toffee and very mildly floral vanilla notes; **t23.5** spices begin sparring from the first nanosecond: absolutely contrary to everything the nose has been telling you. And these are micro spices: tiny, busy little things like you sometimes get from the small grains kicking off in bourbon; in the middle ground you get your first clear sighting of unruffled barley; **f21.5** back to a lightweight, sweetening toffee; **b22** elegant and charming. What else did you expect....? *46.7% 1400 bottles.*

⸬ **The Glenrothes Robur Reserve** db **(81.5)** n20.5 t22 f19 b20. With the youthful barley prominent early on, one of the sweetest distillery bottling from Glenrothes I've come across. Bitter cask fade, though. *40%*

The Glenrothes Select Reserve db **(80)** n17.5 t22 f20.5 b21. Flawed in the usual Glenrothes sherry places, but the brilliance of the sharp barley wins your heart. *40%*

⸬ **The Glenrothes Three Decades** bott 2009 db **(90.5)** n23.5 to say this is somewhat fruity is like saying that Everest is a pretty large mountain....works rather beautifully because there is a pugnacious element to this and, under the softer grape, a message comes through on the oaky spice suggesting that this might be happy to rip your head off... **t24** fabulous delivery with the double whammy of intense but controlled oak and grape concentrate; **f21.5** a touch of bitter marmalade and something a little salty, too; **b22.5** not without a minor blemish here and there, but the overall magnitude of this allows you to forgive quite easily. The distant sulphur apart, a stunner. *43% Duty Free exclusive*

Adelphi Glenrothes 2000 Aged 8 Years sherry hogshead, cask no. 2414, dist 00, bott 08 **(71)** n16 t19 f18 b18. A crying shame because I suspect this was a decent butt before being fatally treated with the S-word. *58%. 309 bottles.*

⸬ **A.D. Rattray Glenrothes 1990** cask no. 35468, dist Nov 90, bott Mar 09 **(90)** n23.5 a molecule of smoke adds a touch of weight to the gooseberries and custard; **t22.5** maple syrup on yoghurt; **f22** long, delightfully textured with still that light syrup tinge to the custard; **b22** am I alone in preferring ex-bourbon Glenrothes to the sherried variety? This one exudes effortless charm. *49.9% A.D. Rattray Ltd*

Cadenhead's Authentic Collection Glenrothes Aged 16 Years rum butt, dist 90, bott Feb 07 **(96)** n24 t23 f25 b24. You don't many of these to the dozen. A very different shape and delivery from most malts with the balance at times slipping and sliding like a one-legged man on a skate... and then suddenly everything falls wondrously into shape. A malt that shows that the line between madness and genius is so very thin...and genius this genuinely is... *57.3%.*

Cadenhead's Glenrothes Aged 17 Years sherry butt, dist 90, bott Feb 08 **(82.5)** n19.5 t20 f22 b21. The faintest of sulphur traces makes for some moments of awkwardness, but the tightness of the grain and grape are at times truly extraordinary. *57.7%. 395 bottles.*

⸬ **Cadenhead's Authentic Collection Glenrothes-Glenlivet 1994** bott Feb 10 **(94)** n23.5 subtle and delicate; gently spiced bourbon edge; **t24** superb...absolutely perfect mouthfeel and weight with the barley zipping around with purpose and intensity; the development is slow but aided by the most gentle of sugary inputs and embraces the almost inevitable cocoa middle warmly; **f23.5** the spices are a long time coming but fizz and nip playfully when they arrive. The cocoa continues, at times sweetened by late grist; **b23** you really can't ask for much more than that from this distillery. Not a single fault. *53.8% Wm. Cadenhead Ltd. 244 bottles.*

Chieftain's Glenrothes 7 Years Old sherry hogshead **(78)** n19 t20 f21 b18. Mon sherry!! The grape has drowned out any evidence of whisky on the nose and delivery or any semblance of balance. But the complexity of the coffee-led fightback is wonderful. Puckeringly dry, though. *53.1%. nc ncf. Ian Macleod Distillers.*

⸬ **The Coopers Choice Glenrothes 1999 Port Wood Finish Aged 10 Years (76)** n18.5 t21 f18.5 b18. The pinkness of the Port is almost a parody of the type, as there really cannot have been any other colour in the whisky to mingle with it. Though a ten year old, the input of the previous barrel had been next to non-existent in that the barley has all the traits of a three-year-old. You certainly don't find samples like this every day... *46%*

D&M Aficionados' Club Bottling Glenrothes Aged 20 Years cask no. 100107, dist May 87 **(88.5)** n20 t23 f23 b22.5. At first I gave this a so-so score: the traces of lactic on the nose didn't endear me. But it is simply one of those drams that demands further and further research. Until you have to at last admit; damn it, this is superb stuff!! *46%. nc ncf.*

Dun Bheagan Glenrothes 12 Years Old sherry finish **(79)** n20 t21 f19 b19. A cleanish, sound sherry cask but short changes in the complexity department. *43%. Ian Macleod.*

Duncan Taylor Collection Glenrothes 1968 cask no.13498 **(79.5)** n20.5 t22 f18 b19. The creosotey finish confirms perhaps a little too much has been asked of the cask. But its early answer is bright and honeyed. *48.2%*

Duncan Taylor Collection Glenrothes 1969 cask no. 12889 **(88.5)** n22.5 am I in Kentucky, sticking my head into some 12-year-old samples? It kind of appears that way as liquorice and Demerara out-manoeuvre the more problematic piny oak notes; **t21.5** early signs aren't encouraging as some big oak punches come raining in. But the barley has stature enough to recover; **f22.5** remains juicy and now gathers a Fox's party Rings-type biscuity sweetness; some late hickory takes us back to Kentucky; **b22** very similar to 12890, except here, on the nose and sometimes elsewhere, this has managed to find a bourbony edge to the oak encroachment. Because of this the body feels fuller and healthier. *46.5%*

Duncan Taylor Collection Glenrothes 1969 cask no. 12890 **(85.5) n21 t21 f22.5 b21** Fascinating to compare this to the DTC 1970 I have just tasted. So many similarities that they appear closely related. But here the oak has delved deeper and upset the vital balance. Pleasant and thoroughly enjoyable and the muscovado-sweetened mocha finish is quite lovely. But you know this cask has crossed the Rubicon. Just. *45.5%*

Duncan Taylor Collection Glenrothes 1970 cask no. 10557 **(93) n23.5** barley-enriched apricot; **t23** like dipping into a bag of mixed boiled sweets with the odd eye-watering sharp one among them: a vague fruitiness meets the sharp barley head on; **f23.5** more salivating over the barley until late on; the vanilla arrives apologetically; **b23** always endearing to find a malt some 40-year-old with this kind of playful persona and so little bothered about oak. Charismatic and full of mouth-watering fun. A minor classic of its type. *42.3%*

⠿ **Duthies Glenrothes 15 Years Old (85.5) n22** a hint of eggnog to the barley; **t21.5** dry delivery with tight but not OTT oak having an early impact; **f22.5** spreads out and relaxes with sugary malt development; **b22.5** high quality Speysider. *46% Wm. Cadenhead Ltd*

Mackillop's Choice Glenrothes cask no. 100107, dist May 87, bott Jul 07 *For tasting notes see D&M Aficionados Club bottling.* Presumably this has come from a split cask. *46%. ncf. Iain Mackillop & Co. Ltd.*

Old & Rare Glenrothes Aged 22 Years dist Feb 85, bott Aug 07 **(91.5) n24.5 t22.5 f22 b22.5.** As good as it is on the palate, it has a problem living up to the astonishing nose. But, there again, so would about 99% of all known whiskies. *56%. Douglas Laing. 277 bottles.*

Old Malt Cask Glenrothes Aged 10 Years Gabriel Meffre wine cask no. 3705, dist Nov 96, bott Jun 07 **(88) n21 t23 f22 b22.** Not a totally dissimilar animal to the OMC Glen Grant 12. Only less finesse and lot more spice. *50%. Douglas Laing. 348 bottles.*

Old Malt Cask Glenrothes Aged 12 Years refill butt, dist May 96, bott Feb 08 **(77) n19 t20 f19 b19.** Give me a prod when something happens...zzzz. *50%. Douglas Laing. 657 bottles.*

Old Malt Cask Glenrothes Aged 14 Years red wine cask, bott 09 **(88) n21** even before knowing this was from a red wine cask, there was a threatening red wine thinness to the barley; complex, though; **t22.5** and the wine is confirmed on the palate with the thin, shaky start. Then it all takes off: the grape and barley at last fuse and harmony is achieved –and some impressive weight; **f22.5** no problems here with a light, sweet juicy element to the cocoa and swirl of smoke; **b22** begins jerkily a bit like a train in a shunting yard before heading off on a frictionless journey. *50%. Douglas Laing.*

Old Malt Cask Glenrothes Aged 16 Years Rum Finish dist Nov 90, bott Mar 07 **(92) n23** for all the obvious rum involvement it is probably the bourbon oakiness that holds sway; excellent weight and balance – slightly Jamaican in style; **t22** warm, biting and at once bracing delivery with a massive barley surge that battles against the peppers; **f24** settles down for something a little special with a glorious marriage of coffee and spice which only sets the scene for the delicate but distinctive echoes of rum and real – or imaginary Jackfruit. Beautifully oiled and quite superb; **b23** a malt that lives long on the finish and in the memory. Wonderful! *50%. Douglas Laing. 318 bottles.*

Old Malt Cask Glenrothes Aged 18 Years refill hogshead, dist Nov 90, bott Apr 09 **(84) n18 t21.5 f22.5 b22.** The broken nose is compensated by the fino, if slightly fizzy, malty recovery. Delicious Maltesers at the death. *50%. Douglas Laing. 295 bottles.*

Old Malt Cask Glenrothes Aged 28 Years sherry finished butt 3901, dist Apr 79, bott Sep 07 **(92) n23.5 t23 f23 b22.5.** Now that's how a sherried Glenrothes should be...!! *50%. nc ncf. Douglas Laing. 311 bottles.*

Old Malt Cask Glenrothes Aged 32 Years refill hogshead, dist Dec 75, bott Aug 08 **(92) n24** stick your beak in this one for a good fifteen minutes: changes colours so many times but at its best a sublime citrus note dovetails with vanilla which has set up camp in a field of honeyed barley; **t22.5** beautiful weight; seemingly light but the barley begins to gather intensity; a slight salty tinge sharpens things up further; **f22.5** the most pleasant vanilla fade you'll taste for a while; some natural fudgy caramels add a chewy quality; **b23** first class bottling just dripping with quiet dignity. *50%. Douglas Laing. 253 bottles.*

Old Masters Glenrothes Aged 12 Years Old cask no. 826089, dist 94, bott 07 **(91) n23** very clean and rich sherry with a honeyed, plummy aside; **t23** outstanding oloroso effect with an immediate build up of spice; the oak then suggests something a lot older; **f22**

almost a bourbony-style vanilla alongside grape; **b23** bit of an oddity this: begins life as uncompromising and rare unspoiled sherry... and finishes as something from Kentucky! Fabulous. *51.9%. James MacArthur for USA only.*

Private Cellar's Selection Glenrothes 1986 bott 07 **(93) n22 t23.5 f24 b23.5.** A real, honest-to-goodness gem of a dram. And not a sherry butt in sight...!!! *43%*

Provenance Glenrothes Aged 11 Years refill hogshead 4075, dist 96, bott 07 **(85.5) n21.5 t22 f21 b21.** Pleasant, grassy, untaxing Speyside fare. *46.0%. nc ncf. Douglas Laing.*

Provenance Glenrothes Aged 12 Years refill hogshead, dist autumn 96, bott autumn 08 **(85.5) n20 t21 f23 b21.5.** Elegant if simple malt where somehow less is more: the clean barley delivery mutates into a light custard tart and bourbon biscuit as if in slow motion. *46%. Douglas Laing.*

Provenance Glenrothes Aged 12 Years sherry finished butt no. 3808, dist summer 95, bott summer 07 **(89) n22.5 t21.5 f22.5 b22.5.** Smoky Glenrothes! Whatever next! Tasted blind, I would have sworn this to be a Caol Ila. *46%. Douglas Laing.*

Scotch Malt Whisky Society Cask 30.55 Aged 15 Years refill hogshead, dist Jul 92 **(86.7) n21.5 t22 f21.5 b21.5.** An enjoyable workaday malt with a blue collar. Honest Joe feel to it. *57.5%*

Scotch Malt Whisky Society Cask 30.59 Aged 16 Years refill hogshead, dist Jul 92 **(90) n22** simplistic, faultless, clean barley in a healthy oak surround; **t23** more of the same, especially on delivery where soft vanilla notes merge gracefully with the much bigger sweet malts; the middle ground fills with butterscotch and butter shortbread; **f22.5** very long, using the limited soft oils to full capacity. Again it's malt all the way, enlivened with a light spice prickle, and delicate vanillas; **b22.5** now this is how I remember Glenrothes all those years ago before it was launched as a single malt and went all sherryfied (and not always for the better). A high quality, big malty number perfect for blending and when in this form a well made, if untaxing, dram. *55.1%*

Scott's Selection Glenrothes 1986 bott 08 **(84) n21.5 t19.5 f22 b21.** Decidedly on the hot side, but otherwise solid and occasionally sweet with a generous late middle barley development. *52.2%. Speyside Distillers.*

GLEN SCOTIA
Campbeltown, 1832. Loch Lomond Distillers. Working.

Glen Scotia 12 Years Old db **(73.5) n18 t19 f18 b18.5.** Ooops! I once said you could write a book about this called "Murder by Caramel." Now it would be a short story called "Murder by Flavours Unknown." What is happening here? Well, a dozen years ago Glen Scotia was not quite the place to be for consistent whisky, unlike now. Here, the caramel is the only constant as the constituent parts disintegrate. *40%* ⊙⊙

Glen Scotia 1999 heavily peated, cask no. 518, dist 23 Jul 99 db **(92) n22** moist marzipan adds a sweet, nutty element to the pre-pubescent, vaguely Bowmore-style peat. Deliciously young; **t23** fresh, enormously sweet and surprisingly oily for this distillery: but, for all this, it is stunningly balanced and charismatic; **f23** dries very impressively; there is an imperious flourish to the peaty signature; **b24** this is pretty big and quite beautifully made malt. Forget the age. Enjoy a touch of class. *45%*

Glen Scotia 1999 heavily peated, cask no. 525, dist 23 Jul 99 db **(85) n21 t22 f22 b20.** Tasty, but relatively blunt, nothing like so together or complex as cask 518. *45%*

Glen Scotia Cask No. 78 american oak, dist 31 May 99, bott 24 Apr 07 db **(85) n22 t22 f20 b21.** Juicy and chewy; perhaps a slight conflict when the oak gets close and personal. *45%.*

Glen Scotia Cask No. 337 dist 23 Jul 99, bott 25 Apr 07 db **(86.5) n21 t22 f22 b21.5.** The thin smoke has almost a tobacco feel. Decent, but you have the feeling it is underperforming a little. *45%. nc ncf. 325 bottles.*

⋰⋰ **A.D. Rattray Glen Scotia 1977** cask no. 985 **(92) n23.5** no doubting the cask type with the grape in dominant and, essentially, clean form: clean enough for the barley and the vaguest hint of salt and smoke to peep through; **t23** astonishing firepower for an oldie: not all of it is technically brilliant and the spices derive more from distillation than maturation. But such is the huge quality of the sherry butt this malt has been housed in for the last 30-odd years that the rougher edges are softened and the grape pushes the boundaries. Molasses and dates offer up a burned fruitcake feel, but there is also seared ginger and a light hint of smoke in there somewhere, too; **f23** long, almost powder dry vanilla pepped up by the remaining layers of grape; **b22.5** proof that a first class barrel can take a third class distillate and turn it into something top quality... *57% A.D. Rattray Ltd*

⋰⋰ **A.D. Rattray Glen Scotia 1992** cask no. 1, dist Mar 92, bott Dec 09 **(64) n15 t17 f16 b16.** If anyone wants to see why I am so unforgiving of sulphured casks or experience the change in sherry cask quality I have seen in the last 30 years, then I strongly suggest you buy a bottle of this and Rattray's superb '77 bottling and simply compare... 59.4% A.D. Rattray Ltd

Berry's Own Selection Glen Scotia 1992 bott 08 **(95) n24** a heavy, weighty plug of dry peat: almost certainly the moss here was cut from very deep in the trench. An acrid acidic bite to the peat should not be confused with any off notes from the cask – of which there are none. This is a rare, natural state and one once found sometimes with Ardbeg samples from the 1960s in particular; **t24** a to-die-for delivery: the sweetness proffers a wonderful sharpness; natural caramels are light and attracts rich barley...and then, of course, that dull, throbbing smoke; **f23.5** spices which had formed in the middle ground have a louder say and the deftly sweetened vanilla sees us out; **b23.5** from among the earliest days of smoked Scotia (well since World War II, certainly), here's a peaty nugget. I bet Berry's very own Dougie McIvor made a pact with the devil for his beloved Charlton to be relegated to their natural place in the third tier of English football in exchange for getting hold of a cask like this. A good bit of business, Dougie, my son...see you soon at The Valley!! 55.7%. Berry Bros & Rudd.

⋯ **Cadenhead's Authentic Collection Glen Scotia 1992** bott Feb 10 **(78) n18.5 t21 f18.5 b20.** Juicy and sizzling: pretty much on the mark for the distillery at this period of its history. 52.1% Wm. Cadenhead Ltd. 260 bottles.

⋯ **Duncan Taylor Collection Glen Scotia 1991** cask no. 71375 **(73.5) n19 t19 f17.5 b18.** Malty firewater. 57.6% Duncan Taylor & Co Ltd

Duthies Glen Scotia 17 Years Old (80.5) n20 t21 f19 b20.5. Busy, mouth-watering...and yet. Definitely not quite the best wood a spirit has ever been filled into. 46%.

The Exclusive Malts Glen Scotia Aged 15 Years cask no. 424, dist Jan 92 **(90) n22 t23 f22.5 b22.5.** Truly delightful stuff. 53.4%. The Creative Whisky Company. 241 bottles.

Exclusive Malts Glen Scotia 1992 Aged 16 Years dist 92 **(89.5) n20** less than flawless; some rough edges and technically unsound...yet attractive in a gritty kind of way; **t24** hot-ish, hard as granite and yet reaches the middle have exploded all kinds of malt bombs around the palate and winning you over in the process; some flinty fruity notes, too; salivating and intensely satisfying; **f23** more blandly defined fruit and barley sugar, sprinkled with some oaky cocoa; b22.5 an imposing malt impossible not to love: a real rough diamond... 52.1%.

⋯ **Hart Brothers Glen Scotia Aged 16 Years** 1st fill sherry hogshead, dist Dec 92, bott Dec 08 **(68) n17 t18.5 f15.5 b17.** Having run through an entire treasure of whisky lab terms in my head, the word which most succinctly sums this one up is.....''weird''. 46% Hart Brothers Ltd

Kingsbury's Glen Scotia 1992 (86.5) n21 t22.5 f21.5 b21.5. Something of the Sugar Frosties about this: a sweet, malty cereal feel – and a bit crunchy, too. But the most impressive quality is its intense Kentucky kick, perhaps due to the heady mix of muscovado and soft cocoa. 66.2%. Japan Import System

The MacPhail's Collection Glen Scotia 1992 Aged 15 Years dist 92, bott 07 **(75) n18 t20 f18.5 b18.5.** Around this period Scotia were at times having all kinds of problems with their distillate and, to boot, were filling into poor casks. Here's proof. 43%. Gordon & MacPhail.

Old Malt Cask Glen Scotia Aged 15 Years sherry butt 4080, dist Mar 92, bott Dec 07 **(76.5) n19 t19.5 f19 b19.** Pretty flat. 50%. nc ncf. Douglas Laing. 707 bottles.

Old Malt Cask Glen Scotia Aged 16 Years refill hogshead, cask no. 4436, dist Mar 92, bott Jun 08 **(90.5) n23.5** big, bourbony overture: powering burnt honey and leather but the malt's in there, too...; **t22.5** superb intensity: the malt really does come alive; **f22** settles with crème caramel with a barley/muscovado sugar sprinkling; **b22.5** a delight from first to last. 50%. nc ncf. Douglas Laing. 257 bottles.

Old Malt Cask Glen Scotia Aged 17 Years bott 09 **(92.5) n23** gloriously anarchic; **t23.5** typically lively with booming bourbony notes: rips into your throat with glee; **f23** a few spices liven up the vanillas **b23** fabulous fun: if this doesn't shake some life into your tastebuds, nothing will. 50%. Douglas Laing.

Scotch Malt Whisky Society Cask 93.30 Aged 16 Years refill barrel, dist Mar 92 **(96) n23 t24.5 f24 b24.5.** I think if someone had asked me to describe or create in the glass exactly how I would envisage the very best malt from this distillery made during that period of its history and put it into concentrated form, I'd have to say this would just about be it exactly. Rarely does a whisky come up, to the nearest nuance, how it sits in your mind. A strange and wonderful experience. One of the whiskies of the year and from what most would consider an unlikely source. 64.5%

Scotch Malt Whisky Society Cask 93.31 Aged 16 Years refill barrel, dist Mar 92 **(92) n22.5 t23.5 f23 b23.** Superb, seductive whisky in its own right but shows and Lord Mayors come to mind. 65.5%

Scotch Malt Whisky Society Cask 93.34 Aged 16 Years refill butt, dist Mar 92 **(93) n24** oatmeal stout meets nut brown ale....it's like the bottle skip of an old boozer in the '70s with a few emptied cream sherries for good measure; **t23.5** sweet 'n' spicy delivery from the off with more than a hint of those brown Liquorice Allsorts towards the middle; malty despite all the lumpenly sherried razzamatazz; **f22.5** much more sober and sensible – though still pretty extrovert – with a lovely sweet lilt to the malty, stouty burnt fudge fade; **b23** not the kind of dram you happen upon too often in a year. Or career. Technically a mess, as the flavours never conform to either type or a set pattern. But this helter-skelter ride is pure fun. Hold on to your hats...and this gloriously idiosyncratic malt's coat-tails... 55.1%

Scotch Malt Whisky Society Cask 93.35 Aged 17 Years refill hogshead, dist Apr 91 **(81.5)** **n19.5 t21 f21 b20.** Abrasive and never quite happy with the oaky environment in which it has been held for the last 17 years. The malt, once past the hot gluey notes, is huge, though, and the finish displays loads of natural caramels. 58.9%

GLEN SPEY
Speyside, 1885. Diageo. Working.

Glen Spey Aged 12 Years db **(90)** **n23** the kind of firm, busy malt you expect from this distillery plus some lovely spice; **t22** mouthwatering and fresh, a layer of honey makes for an easy three or four minutes; **f22** drier vanilla, but the pulsing oak is controlled and stylish; **b23** very similar to the first Glen Spey I can remember in this range, the one before the over-toffeed effort of two years ago. Great to see it back to its more natural, stunningly beautiful self. 43%. Flora and Fauna range.

Cadenhead's Authentic Collection Glen Spey Aged 13 Years bourbon hogshead, dist 95, bott Jun 08 **(84.5)** **n20 t22 f21.5 b21.** Identical nose to the Dewar Rattray bottling of same year, but this is glossier on the palate and homed in a better cask. 58.8%. 246 bottles.

Connoisseurs Choice Glen Spey 1995 (76) **n19 t19 f19 b19.** Vapid blending fodder. 43%.

Dewar Rattray Glen Spey 1995 cask no. 422, dist Apr 95, bott Mar 07 **(81)** **n20 t21.5 f19.5 b20.** A bantamweight packing a big punch. 59%

Old Malt Cask Glen Spey Aged 17 Years bourbon finished barrel 3900, dist Feb 90, bott Sep 07 **(85)** **n20.5 t21 f22 b21.5.** Juicy malt leads the way. Safe whisky. 50%. nc ncf. Douglas Laing. 293 bottles.

⁖ **Old Malt Cask Glen Spey Aged 32 Years** refill hogshead no. DL 5523, dist Dec 76, bott Sep 09 **(90.5)** **n22.5** here we go: first rate exotic fruit, though given a dab of allspice just to ginger it up; **t23** way beyond being recognisable as a Glen Spey: the light oils proudly carry the liquorice and burnt honey of major age, but all with a light sugary sheen; **f22.5** much drier, but the buttery toast still doesn't show negative traits to the aging; **b22.5** fruity exoticism all the way....wonderful! 50% Douglas Laing & Co Ltd

⁖ **Old Malt Cask Glen Spey Aged 32 Years (87)** **n23** rose petals and vanilla: delicate to the point of disintegration; **t21.5** a brief arrival of light, juicy barley and lime, quickly met by dried banana; **f21** almost a papery vanilla moistened by a spot of oil; **b21.5** for one of the lightest malts on Speyside this has withstood the test of time with apparent ease. This must have been one hell of a good cask for it not to have inflicted any telling damage. Naturally it is the vanillins which have the greatest say, but they dovetail gracefully with the softest of oils offered and half-hearted limey sugars. The rose petal nose is also a surprising bonus. 54.5% Speciality Drinks Ltd. Anniversary Selection.

GLENTAUCHERS
Speyside, 1898. Chivas. Working.

The Cärn Mör Vintage Collection Glentauchers 2006 barrel, cask no. 9, dist 06, bott 09 **(85)** **n22 t21 f21 b21.** A three year-old still in its new make nappies thanks to absolute minimum oak input. Shows the high quality malty distillate at its most naked. And refreshing. 46%. The Scottish Liqueur Centre

⁖ **Chieftain's Glentauchers 17 Years Old Pinot Noir Finish** dist Sep 92, bott 2010 **(82.5)** **n21.5 t21 f19.5 b20.5.** Had to laugh: as I poured this, the label was facing the other way. Saw the colour and thought: "Must be a Chieftain's"...!! Just a little too cramped and frantic for the grape to take full effect while the spicy oak bites deep at the death. 50% nc ncf Ian Macleod

Dun Bheagan Glentauchers Aged 15 Years hogshead, dist Sep 92 **(85)** **n22 t22 f20 b21.** Some really wonderful barley and citrus touches to this but a bitter finish undermines some of the good work. No doubt a better cask would have produced a sparkling gem. 43%.

Duncan Taylor Collection Glentauchers 1990 cask no. 14435 **(91)** **n22.5 t23 f22.5 b23.** Odd: when I first nosed this against the DT 46%, I thought it'd get slaughtered. But slow consideration and a few mouthfuls later, and there really is no contest. And the malt floored by a devastating knockout blow....is the 46%....Taste this and, like me, wonder why the hell this has never been brought out as a regular top-quality single malt. 57.6%

Duncan Taylor The NC2 Range Glentauchers 1990 Aged 16 Years (85.5) n22 t21 f21 b21.5. A soft, malt-dominated bottling with enough soft fruit nuances to keep it alive and ticking. 46%

Gordon & MacPhail Distillery Label Glentauchers 1991 (83) n21 t22.5 f19.5 b20. Hardly does this under-rated distillery justice: the nose is lagged down by a vague lactic note from some exhausted oak while the finish is thin and unhappy. Yet the show is saved by a genuinely vivid barley dash on delivery. 43%

Old Malt Cask Glentauchers Aged 12 Years dist Nov 94, bott Feb 07 (88) n22 t23 f21 b22. Fabulous blending whisky that doubles up as an unerring single malt of crisp substance. 50%. 354 bottles.

Old Malt Cask Glentauchers Aged 13 Years refill hogshead, dist Nov 95, bott Feb 09 (87) n22 gristy malt with a squeeze of lemon; t22 the citrus-barley combo keeps the salivating going; f21.5 a dab of vanilla and scorched toast; b21.5 simple, clean, elegant and very drinkable. 50%. Douglas Laing. 334 bottles.

Provenance Glentauchers Aged 8 Years sherry butt, dist summer 00, dist autumn 08 (85.5) n21.5 t22 f21 b21. Another 'Tauchers bottling struggling against indifferent oak. Thankfully there is enough of the trademark low-key complexity and biscuity barley to ensure a pleasant time. 46%

-:::- **Provenance Glentauchers Over 9 Years** refill cask no. DMG 5706, dist Autumn 2000, bott Winter 2009 (80) n20.5 t20 f19 b19.5. An essay in bantamweight gristiness. 46%

Scotch Malt Whisky Society Cask 63.20 Aged 18 Years refill barrel, dist Dec 89 (88) n21.5 t22.5 f22 b22 From a entirely underrated distillery that usually thanks you for bottling at a younger age, comes a malt of serious distinction...and one that probably thanks you for even bottling in at all. 54.7%

Scotch Malt Whisky Society Cask 63.22 Aged 18 Years refill barrel, dist Dec 89 (94) n22.5 woodworking sheds: a sawdusty quality dries the sharp, scratchy barley; t24 for a malt so brittle, rarely is a delivery quite as soft as this: on one hand the barley is hard enough to chip at your teeth, on another the understated lush sweetness appears to graft itself to the salivating, juices; mild peppers spice matters up further while some custard and sugared rice pudding invade the middle ground; f23.5 medium to long in length but it's barley and chewy hay all the way with a mildly overcooked vanilla still having the sugary wherewithal to see off any oak; b24 a minor gem from Speyside which does much to show the subtle but incisive qualities of this wonderful distillery. The first to third tastings won't do the trick on this one: only after the fourth or fifth mouthful can you really unravel the intricate plot. What a treat!! 53.8%

-:::- **Scotch Malt Whisky Society Cask 63.25 Aged 20 Years** refill barrel, dist Dec 89 (84.5) n22 t22.5 f20 b20. The citrus notes are hugely desirable and ensure a zestiness to the barley. But just a little too over aged. 55% Scotch Malt Whisky Society. 211 bottles.

GLENTURRET

Highlands (Perthshire), 1775. Edrington. Working.

Glenturret Aged 8 Years db (88) n21 some sma' still randomness; t22 silky honey, a few feinty oils perhaps, but attractive; f23 honey overdrive with spice; b22 technically no prizewinner. But the dexterity of the honey is charming, as this distillery has a tendency sometimes to be. 40%

The Glenturret Aged 10 Years db (76) n19 t18 f20 b19. Lots of trademark honey but some less than impressive contributions from both cask and the stillman. 40%

The Glenturret Aged 15 Years db (87) n21 t22 f22 b22 A beautifully clean, small-still style dram that would have benefitted from being bottled at a fuller strength. A discontinued bottling now: if you see it, it is worth the small investment. 40%

Glenturret 1991 Aged 15 Years cask no. 638 db (82) n20 t21 f21 b20. Honeycomb and chocolate: liquid fruit jelly. Heavyweight stuff and at times a little stodgy. 55.3%

Glenturret 1992 Aged 14 Years cask no. 855 db (72) n18 t19 f17 b18. A tad feinty and never quite finds the right key despite the best efforts of the honey and spice. 59.7%

Glenturret 1993 cask no. 840 db (83.5) n21 t20 f21.5 b21. I'm afraid the heat on this one isn't simply down to the giant strength. This is hot whisky but with some attractively sharp notes. 59.5%

Cadenhead's Glenturret Aged 20 Years dist 87, bott Feb 08 (95) n24 t24 f23 b24. Brilliant: absolutely bloody brilliant!! Why can't the distillery bottling be this damn good!!! 51.6%

The MacPhail's Collection Glenturret Aged 10 Years dist 97, bott 07 (83.5) n20 t19 f23 b21.5. After a rocky, off-balanced start settles down to impart that rich, rather attractive copper-honey sharpness which appears unique to this distillery. 40%. Gordon & MacPhail.

Old Malt Cask Glenturret Aged 19 Years refill hogshead, dist Sep 89, bott Mar 09 **(91) n23** slivers of honey attach to nutty, barley notes: coppery, light and delicate; **t23.5** mouthwatering, intense barley again shows that vein of honey; the usual metallic tingle is there, but there is also some unexpected pomegranate juice, too; **f22** long, with the usual small still metallic edge usually found on Glenturret, but also slightly pithy with a lime-vanilla fade; **b22.5** one of the few bottlings of late which shows off the Glenturret character to its fullest degree. And at the higher quality found in the early 1990s. A must get malt. *50%. 298 bottles.*

Old Masters Glenturret Aged 14 Years cask no. 188 dist 93, bott 07 **(90) n22 t23 f22.5 b22.5.** Ah-ha! A Glenturret just like what I remember from the good ol' days! Honey by the hive-load. *56.9%. James MacArthur & Co. Ltd.*

Signatory Vintage Glenturret 1992 13 Years Old sherry butt **(74) n19 t19 f18 b18.** Sulpher. *43%. USA.*

GLENUGIE
Highland (Eastern). 1834–1983. Closed.
Duncan Taylor Collection Glenugie 1981 cask no. 5158 **(94) n23 t23 f24 b24.** Sightings of Glenugie are about as common as instances of Gordon Brown leaving those around him in helpless mirth. But, unlike politicians, this distillery never seems to let you down. The rule of thumb is: find a bottle of Glenugie and you'll find liquid gold. This is no exception. In fact, it's probably the best of the lot! *51.5%*

Old & Rare Glenugie Aged 26 Years dist Mar 82, bott Mar 08 **(87.5) n22 t22 f22 b21.5.** Distilled towards the last days in the life of this distillery. By then it was getting a reputation for making hot whisky, and a mouthful of this is enough to give third degree burns to your oesophagus for a year or two. But if you can ride it, and overcome the OTT sherry, then you can enjoy some history. *58%. Douglas Laing. 117 bottles.*

Old Malt Cask Glenugie Aged 26 Years bourbon cask, dist Mar 82, bott Oct 08 **(92.5) n23.5** that nagging hint of ginger – a kind of unofficial Glenugie Trademark – enlivens the thin citrus. Beautifully understated and absolutely zero over encroachment of the oak; **t23.5** another old Trademark, the oils, arrive in force, allowing the bold barley to stick benignly to the palate; the sweetness is of almost perfect weight; **f22.5** an enchanting ending with light spices making their mark on the vanilla; **b23** it is possible I have tasted more bottled versions of Glenugie over the years as anyone else out there. And although it has made many of its usual statements, the manner in which they have been delivered opens new ground; the softest Glenugie and possibly most elegant of them all. *50%. Douglas Laing. 265 bottles.*

Old Malt Cask Glenugie Aged 27 Years bourbon cask, dist Mar 82, bott Mar 09 **(86) n21.5 t21 f22.5 b21.** Pleasantly and intensely malty. A tad thin for the real Glenugie purists and showing a hot streak, too. But seriously enjoyable from first to last, especially last. *50%*

⠿ **Rare Old Glenugie 1970 (90.5) n24** classic old age exotic fruit but so much more: the barley is intact and whether you describe gooseberries as exotic....certainly one of the most delightful old timer noses of the year **t22.5** what was once a thin delivery has, over the years, turned into a crisp one: the barley is ridiculously juicy for a 40-y-o and the oak continues to chip in with the fruit; **f22** returns to its more metallic roots....; **b22** running across a Rare Old classic like this is certainly a true perk of the job... *43.5% Gordon & MacPhail*

GLENURY ROYAL
Highland (Eastern), 1868–1985. Demolished.
Glenury Royal 36 Years Old db **(89) n22** sawdusty and spiced: a busy nose where the barley offers little more than a shadow; **t23.5** improbably juicy and mouth-watering with barley sugar concentrate; the clarity of the malt appears to bring out the best in the brown sugar accompaniment; the middle gets a bit overly dry, though; **f21.5** the barley lingers sweetly – and has to: the oak is pretty toasty and profound; soft, slightly burnt fudge notes go well with the overcooked butterscotch tart; the final fade is almost that of pot still Demerara rum; **b22** with so much dark, threatening oak around, the delivery defies belief or logic. Cracking stuff!! *57.9%*

Glenury Royal 36 Years Old db **(89) n21** oak interference damages the fruit balance; **t23** starts worryingly dull then takes off to fabulous heights on fresh, beautifully textured barley; **f22** begins to fall out of sync as some heavyweight hickory is driven home, but lightens with a succession of gentle waves of cocoa; **b23** an undulating dram, hitting highs and lows. The finish, in particular, is impressive: just when it looks on its last legs, it revives delightfully. The whole package, though far from perfect, is pretty astounding. *50.2%*

Glenury Royal 50 Years Old dist 53 db **(91) n23** marvellous freshness to the sherry butt; this had obviously been a high quality cask in its day and the intensity of the fruit sweetened slightly by the most delicate marzipan and old leather oozes class; a little mint reveals some worry lines; **t24** the early arrival is sweet and nimble with the barley, against the odds, still having the major say after all these years. The oak is waiting in the wings and with a burst of soft liquorice and velvety, understated spice beginning to make an impression; the sweetness is very similar to a traditional British child's candy of "tobacco" made from strands of coconut and sugar; **f22** masses of oak yet, somehow, refuses to go over the top and that slightly molassed sweetness sits very comfortably with the mildly oily body; **b22** I am always touched when sampling a whisky like this from a now departed distillery. *42.8%*

Gordon & MacPhail Rare Old Glenury Royal 1972 (90) **n22 t23 f22 b23**. A thumping malt showing good age but wears it effortlessly. Just beautiful. *40%*.

Gordon & MacPhail Rare Old Glenury Royal 1984 (95.5) **n25** playful coal and peat smoke drifts around the astonishing fruit soup of greengage, physalis and kiwifruit: mind-blowing in the most subtle and understated way possible...it is hard to imagine it getting much better than this flawless display: **t24** the velvet-clad delivery couches burnished barley, gleaming on the palate with the honey radiating a controlled sweetness and lightly fizzing smoke and oak; **f23** dries with the odd burnt toast twinge; **b23.5** Royal and Ancient...another lost distillery comes back to haunt those with the wrecking ball. *43%*

Old Malt Cask Glenury Aged 32 Years refill hogshead, dist Mar 76, bott Oct 08 (96) **n23.5** tense, marriage between thickset barley and confident oak; a squeeze of lime relieves the pressure; elsewhere there is a sweet, diluted Port Ellen style smokiness which adds to the beauty; **t23.5** melt-in-the-mouth barley leaves in its wake a smouldering chocolatey smokiness; the middle ground is mainly oak, but in such a wonderfully docile form that you feel like applauding; meanwhile the barley spreads, as does that chocolate; **f24.5** long, sweet in just the right muscovado manner and still that chocolate mousse-type cocoa lingers; **b24.5** imagine a night of passion consisting solely of long fingernails running over your body and little else, except maybe your head being massaged at the same time. Teasing, beautiful, delectable; impossible not to release a sigh of pleasure when nosing and tasting - and a serious contender for World Whisky of the Year. *50%. Douglas Laing. 37 bottles.*

Rarest of the Rare Glenury Royal 1984 cask no. 3047 (86.5) **n22 t22 f21 b21.5**. Loads of custardy notes on nose and finish. The body is pretty thin for its age, with the oaks offering a gentlemanly hand and not much more until the dry finale. The sugars are like those which melt on hot porridge. Elegant, delicate and refuses, point blank, to say boo to a goose. *49.3%. Duncan Taylor.*

HAZELBURN (see Springbank)

HIGHLAND PARK
Highland (Island–Orkney), 1795. Edrington. Working.

Highland Park 8 Years Old db (87) **n22** firm young, honied malt with food coke/peat smoke; **t22** silky honey and excellent complexity for a malt so young; **f22** complex layers of vanilla and soft peat at first then caramel grabs hold: shame; **b21** a journey back in time for some of us: this is the orginal distillery bottling of the 70s and 80s, bottles of which are still doing the rounds in obscure Japanese bars and specialist outlets such as the Whisky Exchange. *40%*

Highland Park Aged 12 Years db (91) **n22.5** a lighter version than the last few I've enjoyed this year: less honey with more barley to the fore. Almost younger in style though the soft smoke does add the weight demanded; **t23.5** here it comes into its own with a style unlike any other malt in the world: first you get the silky coating. Just as you purr from that and you settle into the malty attack, from nowhere a subtle honey edge descends. An unusual, brief sharpness retreats, allowing room for the most delicate of smoke; **f22** only half-serious vanilla and lazy citrus continue to give the feel of a younger than normal malt; **b23** no heather. The lightest sprinkling of peat. A youthfulness hangs to it. Disappointing HP? Not a bit of it!! Because the complexity still keeps you mesmerised. *40%*

Highland Park Aged 15 Years db (92) **n23** nosed blind, and at this relatively unusual age, there could be only one distillery: the honey-smoke balance and intensity is unique; **t22.5** soft, dissolving honey finds a mint humbuggy kind of middle to offer toffee and spice; **f23.5** some real length to this finale with the usual myriad honey notes going through their repertoire but a further polishing with Demerara and smoke and then buffed with lime, appears to up the charm; **b23** immeasurably better than the last time I came face to face with this. *40%*

Highland Park 16 Years Old db (88) **n23** softly softly strains of oranges, honey and vanilla; **t23** mouthwatering and delightfully weighted barley with soft nuances of liquorice and smoke; **f20** toffee-vanilla: just a little too quiet; **b22** I tasted this the day it first came out at one of the Heathrow whisky shops. I thought it a bit flat and uninspiring. This sample, maybe from another bottling, is more impressive and showing true Highland Park colours, the finish apart. *40% Exclusively available in Duty Free/Travel Retail.*

Highland Park Aged 18 Years db (95.5) n23.5 a thick dollop of honey spread across a layer of salted butter; in the background the ashes of a peat fire are emptied; t24 eye closing beauty: immediate glossy impact of rich, vaguely metallic honey but upped in the complexity stakes by the subtle intense marbling of peat; the muscular richness, aided by the softness of the oil ensures that maximum intensity is not only reached but maintained; f24 long continuation of those elements found in the delivery but now radiating soft spices and hints of marzipan; b24 if familiarity breeds contempt, then it has yet to happen between myself and HP 18. This is a must-have dram. I show it to ladies the world over to win their hearts, minds and tastebuds when it comes to whisky. And the more time I spend with it, the more I become aware and appreciative of its extraordinary consistency. The very latest bottlings have been astonishing, possibly because colouring has now been dropped, and wisely so. Why in any way reduce what is one of the world's great whisky experiences? Such has been the staggering consistency of this dram I have thought of late of promoting the distillery into the world's top three: only Ardbeg and Buffalo Trace have been bottling whisk(e)y of such quality over a wide range of ages in such metronomic fashion. Anyway, enough: a glass of something honeyed and dazzling calls... *43%* ☉

Highland Park 21 Years Old db (85.5) n22 t21.5 f21 b21 Massively honeyed. But also the feeling that there is a fair bit of stuff way beyond the 21 mark here, such is the magnitude of the oaky impact. Enjoy at this strength for now; in future will be at 40%, their guys tell me. *47.5%*

Highland Park Aged 25 Years db (79) n20 t21 f19 b19. I had to look twice at the sample here. And pour twice. The flattest HP 25 of all time. The sherry is dull and mainly lifeless and if caramel has been kicked out of the brand, some of the charmless variety must have made it from the cask. Also a strange bitterness descends....Pleasant-ish. But easily one of the most disappointing versions of this I have come across anywhere. *48%*

Highland Park Aged 30 Years db (95.5) n23.5 a very different nose to before with now the emphasis on a gamut of pastel shades of citrus, pink grapefruit and lime at the fore. But, of course, there are the soft shades of smoke and honey..; t23 the gentle embers of smoke add further weight to the metallic, coppery sharpness which shows this dram is still alive and kicking; f24.5 busy, ever more intense layering of vanilla and cocoa (indeed, not entirely unlike the milky chocolate you could find on lollies in the 1980s), but the smoke and honey simply cannot be repressed; b24.5 one of the whiskies of the year: embarrasses the 25-year-old with its astonishing balance and near perfect shape in every department. A whisky for the gods...but only if they are worthy... *48%*

Highland Park 40 Years Old db (90.5) n20.5 tired and over-oaked but the usual HP traits are there in just enough force to save it from failing with an extra puff of something smoky diving in to be on the safe side; t22.5 even after 40 years, pure silk. Like a 40-year-old woman who has kept her figure and looks, and now only satin stands in the way between you and so much beauty and experience...and believe me: she's spicy..; f24 amazing layering of peat caresses you at every level; the oak has receded and now barley and traces of golden syrup balance things; b23.5 I have to admit to picking splinters from my nose with this one. Some of the casks used here have obviously choked on oak, and I feared the worst. But such is the brilliance of the resilience by being on the money with the honey, you can say only that it has pulled off an amazing feat with the peat. Sheer poetry... *48%*

❖ **Highland Park 1964 Orcadian Vintage** refill hogshead, bott 2009 db (90.5) n23 a spiced up marriage of light smoke, vanilla and soft fruits. For once the trademark honey is nowhere to be seen...; t22 soft and immediately smoky – almost chunkily so – and though there is a raisin and burnt toast shape to this, the silk is never for a moment compromised; f23 the oak makes for a slightly eye-watering finish but there are residual sugars to not only lighten the burden but make for a refreshing finale which vanishes, fittingly, in a puff of smoke....; b22.5 at times you think the old oak is going to sink without trace, taking the whisky with it. But such is the pedigree of the HP make, that it not only fights back but regains control. An honour to experience. *42.2% 290 bottles.*

❖ **Highland Park 1968 Orcadian Vintage** refill casks, bott 2009 db (88.5) n20 thumping staves of oak; t23.5 tangy with all kinds of curled up orange peel; a huge, unexpected wave of oily, caramelised barley; f23 some fabulous sugar and chocolate toffee moments, b22 the spicy oak has taken too firm a grip for true greatness. But some of the passages offer wonderful moments of contemplation. *45.6% 1550 bottles.*

❖ **Highland Park 1970 Orcadian Vintage** db (94.5) n23.5 much smokier than present day HP...would love to have nosed the new make 40 years ago: it would have been massive; helped along here with a squeeze of blood orange; t24 splinters on delivery – in both senses

- but the silky malt-honey body is able to absorb everything thrown at it; the degrees of sweetness run from honey, through light sugars to subtle Lubec marzipan: sublime; **f23.5** long, again with a distinctive orangey note clinging to the sweet, lightly smoked barley: elegant...; **b23.5** most other malts would have disintegrated under the weight of the oak. This takes it in its stride, and actually uses the extra vanilla to excellent effect. Memorable. *48%*

⬩⬩⬩ **Highland Park 1973 Orcadian Vintage** bott 2010 db **(96) n24** what could be better than a standard HP nose, complete with all that delicate smoke and honey? An HP nose with a decent smidgeon of high quality bourbon! Well that's what those extra years in the cask has gone and given you...; **t25** mouth-watering barley enters the arena hand-in-hand with the most pristine acacia honey. Directly behind is two-tone smoke: one firm, lightly peated and spiced, the other a softer, billowing safety net; the middle ground concerns molten manuka honey and muscovado sugar thickened with vanilla...and then the lightest hint of mocha....frankly, perfect....; **f23** lighter, lengthy with toffee and liquorice; **b24** now that, folks, is Highland Park and make no mistake! *50.6%*

⬩⬩⬩ **Highland Park 1990** bott 2010 db **(90) n23** a sprig of lavender (probably in lieu of standard heather) dovetails jauntily with ubiquitous honey and a puff of smoke; **t23** sublime delivery: an almost perfect degree of oil to help the honey slither into its rightful place at the head of the flavour queue with some toffee vanilla not far behind. Just a hint of soapiness; **f22** long, with a buzzing smokiness...and late toffee pudding; **b22** much more like it....!! *40%*

⬩⬩⬩ **Highland Park 1994** bott 2010 db **(87) n23** ah-ha!! Recognisable light smoke and honey sparked by that uniquely enigmatic sweetness....; **t22** toffee-raisin thread to the honey; **f20.5** inexplicably vanishes off radar; **b21.5** I am not sure what is happening here. HPs of this vintage should be soaring into the comfortable 90s. But again the finish is dull and the usual complexity of the malt is vanishing behind a murky veil. *40%*

⬩⬩⬩ **Highland Park 1998** bott 2010 db **(85) n22 t22 f20 b21.** They must have special Orcadian spiders to spin a silk this fine. But, though pleasant, disappointing by HP standards as it never gets to spread its wings. The whisky, that is: not the spider. *40%*

⬩⬩⬩ **Highland Park Earl Magnus Aged 12 Years** 2nd edition db **(76.5) n18.5 t21 f19 b19.** Tight and bitter 2nd edition. *55%*

⬩⬩⬩ **Highland Park Earl Magnus Aged 15 Years** 1st edition db **(76.5) n20 t21 f17.5 b18.** Tight and bitter. *52.6% 5976 bottles.*

⬩⬩⬩ **Highland Park Hjärta** db **(79.5) n18.5 t22 f19 b20.** In part, really does celebrate the honeycomb character of Highland Park to the full. But obviously a major blemish or two in there as well. *58.1% 3924 bottles.*

⬩⬩⬩ **Highland Park New Make Spirit Drink** dist Feb 10, bott Mar 10 db **(85.5) n21 t22 f21 b21.5.** Really had to smile when I saw this. Some 15 or 16 years I ago, I remember sitting in the distillery manager's office at HP discussing whisky trends with the then incumbent. I told him that I couldn't understand why every distillery did not sell new make. People drank white spirit...in fact, I explained that, annoyingly, vodka and white rums were going up in popularity big time. Why not new make whisky in Scotland...and White Dog in Kentucky...to show white spirit could have a personality, too? His answer, as far as I remember, centred around people expecting a whole lot more if the bottle had the Highland Park, or some other famous distillery, brand visible. My counter argument was that you could find chocolate and sauces with household whisk(e)y brand names: new make would not damage a distillery's reputation. And I particularly argued that HP was a prime example of new make which should do well because of the very soft peat that you pick up on the nose. Well, now it has happened: here is new make HP. Ironically, this sample doesn't have the degree of smoke normally associated with the distillery; and it has been reduced to 50%. Why not just have it at natural strength? This one doesn't boast the usual degree of ultra rich texture of new make HP – even when reduced – and though sweet, malty and enjoyable, with its few extra metallic molecules not exactly how I recently tasted new make HP in a blending lab. A curious choice. *50% Venture Whisky Ltd*

⬩⬩⬩ **A.D. Rattray Highland Park 1995** cask no. 1479, dist Jul 95, bott Sep 09 **(89.5) n23** some perky peat hits some hands on honey...; **t23** again the honey smothers the taste buds but there is a sublime smoked spiced sub plot which really ramps up the complexity; **f21.5** caramel flattens the fade somewhat; **b22** pity about the natural toffees. But don't drink this one where there may be bears about... *57.5% A.D. Rattray Ltd*

⬩⬩⬩ **A.D. Rattray Highland Park 1998** cask no. 5789 **(84.5) n21.5 t22 f19.5 b21.** Something of the lightly smoked sugar almonds about this one. *46% A.D. Rattray Ltd*

Cadenhead's Highland Park Aged 17 Years dist 92, bott 09 **(87) n23** a beautiful salty lilt to the standard honey and vague smoke; **t22.5** controlled honeyed sweetness to delivery; **f20** a touch of cask tang and bitterness; **b21.5** nose and delivery are the essence of HP. *64%*

Cask Strength Highland Park 1995 (89) n22 t22 f22 b23. Not immediately recognisable as from Orkney. What is genuinely amazing is that here we have a not entirely spotless cask, yet despite the odd trace of it, we still have a true corker. *57.2%. Gordon & MacPhail.*

D&M Aficionados' Club Bottling Highland Park Aged 22 Years cask no. 369, dist Feb 85 **(76.5)** n18 t20 f19.5 b19. The stillman must have dozed off when he'd reached the cut off point.... *43%. nc ncf. US by Angus Dundee.*

Duncan Taylor Collection Highland Park 1968 cask no. 3466 **(76)** n19.5 t19 f18 b19.5. The poor old chap just faded away... *40.9%*

Duncan Taylor Collection Highland Park 1986 cask no. 2251 **(82.5)** n19 t22.5 f20 b21. The tiredness on the nose and finish is compensated for by the exemplary HP character on delivery. *53.3%*

Duncan Taylor Collection Highland Park 1986 cask no. 2252 **(86)** n22 t22.5 b20.5 f21. Oh brother!! This sister cask also reveals different degrees of wear and tear but the spicy injection and the thicker layering of honey appears to see off the worst excesses. *55.7%*

Duncan Taylor Collection Highland Park 1986 cask no. 2254 **(89.5)** n21 a touch of pine amid the citrus; t23 early oak makes you fear the worst, but the honey/lemon-barley recovery is outstanding; big delivery and has no hesitation to shout its points when need be; f23 really takes off here as some very belated, and laid back, phenols dovetail with the mocha sweetened by honeycomb; the spice buzz is relentless; b22.5 bit of a Lazarus malt, this... *55.7%*

·:·· **Duncan Taylor Collection Highland Park 1986** cask no. 2318 **(96)** n24 exemplary: intense, cut-it-with-a-knife barley and smoke combination with the usual honeyed sweetness tempered by a warming floral note and bitter marmalade; t24 my word!! What a body....just feel those curves!!! Look at the way the tongue finds all that honey! A touch of salt makes it a little sultry and sweaty, too.... f24 a long, lingering, sweet, pulsing finish. As you might expect... b24 just about all you could ask for from an HP, and even a little more besides. *54.2%*

Duncan Taylor Collection Highland Park 1987 cask no. 1529 **(86.5)** n21.5 t22.5 f21 b21.5. Enjoyable, for sure. But you can't get past the fact the oak has too big a toe hold here. Even so, the shinier edges on the first delivery certainly do reveal some talented honey and there is a good smoke-cocoa element, too. *50.4%*

Duncan Taylor Collection Highland Park 1991 cask no. 8088 **(91)** n21.5 smoke apart, natural caramels even out some of the hoped-for complexity; t23 stunning, lush body with loads of spice prickle and then an ever-waxier feel to the smoked honey malt; f23.5 chewy barley with first class bitter-sweet layering and strands of cocoa to show a touch of age; long and one to slump back in the armchair and relish; b23 a stand up and be counted malt with much to say about itself. *55.2%*

Duncan Taylor Collection Highland Park 1991 cask no. 8089 **(83.5)** n21 t20.5 f21 b21. A hotter, sharper version of cask 8089 where the murderous natural caramels have disposed of the smoky body. *54.6%*

·:·· **Duthies Highland Park 17 Years Old (92.5)** n23 a curious touch of tobacco on the usual smoky-honey aroma: quite light and salty, too, with the heather/bracken in concentrate form; t23.5 something of the honeyed throat pastel as it sits in the mouth and massages all it touches; f23 long, lightly oiled and continues with the acacia honey buzz... b23 if you don't like this, you might as well turn to Cognac. Or meths. This is magnificent. *46%*

·:·· **James MacArthur's Old Masters Highland Park 1998 Aged 12 Years** cask no. 5712, bott May 10 **(86.5)** n22.5 t22 f20.5 b21.5. Marginally less sympathetic cask than its twin, 5712, injecting a fair degree of natural caramel which tones down the smoky complexity. Pleasant, though, and well spiced. *57.3%*

·:·· **James MacArthur's Old Masters Highland Park 1998 Aged 12 Years** cask no. 5713, bott Apr 10 **(87.5)** n23 watch out for the playful smoke; t22.5 a little bit of fizz and crackle can be heard over the usual honeyed melody; f20 a tad bitter; b22 at times, full of typical Highland Park mischief. *57.8%*

Kingsbury Handwriting Highland Park 15 Years Old (94) n23.5 t24.5 f22.5 b23.5. Memorable, magnificent malt for those who prefer theirs distilled by bees. *61.5%. nc ncf.*

Lonach Highland Park 1984 (88) n22 vanilla, honey and smoke; t22 honey, smoke and vanilla; f22 vanilla, smoke and...honey...b22 not the most complex HP, but is, delightfully, exactly what it says on the tin... *50.9%. Duncan Taylor.*

Mackillop's Choice Highland Park 1973 cask no. 8395, dist Jun 73, bott Jun 07 **(94.5)** n24 t22.5 f24 b24. Just so wonderfully HP...!!! *43%. Iain Mackillop & Co. Ltd.*

Montgomerie's Highland Park 1992 (91) n23 t23 f22.5 b22.5 This wonderful distillery nutshelled. *46%*

Murray McDavid Highland Park 1989 sherry/port **(95)** n23 t24 f24 b24. My tastebuds, having recovered from the unpleasant shock of having to analyse not one but two

Dufftowns, have been amply rewarded by this truly magnificent malt. Stunningly haphazard, but everything – through either luck or design – falls into place gloriously. *46%*

Oklahoma Single Malt Lovers Highland Park Single Cask Aged 27 Years cask No 8294 **(94) n23.5 t23.5 f24 b23.** A HP that stuns the senses. A real coup by the Oklahoma club. I suggest you join up today!! *56.1%*

Old & Rare Highland Park Aged 29 Years sherry finish dist 1978, bott 07 **(90) n22 t22 f23 b23.** Creakier than a sinking ship, but somehow rides the tidal waves of time. *56.7%. Douglas Laing. 328 bottles.*

Old & Rare Highland Park Aged 30 Years dist Mar 78, bott Aug 08 **(74.5) n19 t19 f18.5 b18.** A real shame. There appears to be an astonishing degree of honey to this. But something has crept in to spoil the party. Any guesses what....? *55.1%. Douglas Laing. 302 bottles.*

Old Malt Cask Highland Park Aged 11 Years refill hogshead 3975, dist Feb 96, bott Nov 07 **(87) n21.5 t22 f21.5 b22.** Doesn't try to be anything other than soufflé light, despite the peat. *50%. Douglas Laing. 367 bottles.*

Old Malt Cask Highland Park Aged 11 Years (81) n19 t21.5 f20.5 b20. Some great honey-intense moments are undermined by sub standard wood. *50%. Douglas Laing.*

⊹∹ **Old Malt Cask Highland Park Aged 12 Years** refill hogshead no. DL 5611, dist Sep 97, bott Nov 09 **(87.5) n22** unusual mixture of coal dust and crushed green leaves; **t22** the honey missing on the nose romps over the taste buds, but always with that slightly ungainly vegetable note in tow; **f21.5** attractive spices and more smoke; **b22** some trademark HP characteristics, but absolutely refuses to conform to the norm. *50% Douglas Laing. 222 bottles.*

⊹∹ **Old Malt Cask Highland Park Aged 13 Years Old** refill hogshead no. DL 5732, dist Sep 96, bott Jan 10 **(92) n23** a little salt 'n' pepper on the honeydew melon; **t24.5** as near enough perfect for a HP of this age: the honey is layered and blended with roasted sugars and then a fabulous spice development rumbles along like a minor earthquake; **f22** an element of bitterness points to a less than perfect cask. But the spirit put into it must have been close to perfection; **b22.5** oh...yes...!!! *50% Douglas Laing & Co Ltd. 325 bottles.*

Old Malt Cask Highland Park Aged 15 Years dist Feb 94, bott Jul 09 **(88) n21.5** a wisp of smoke rescues some stretched oak; **t22** sharp barley and a big salt kick; some bite and light oils here, too; **f22.5** a few friendly, sweeter notes tie up the moodier, meaner elements: excellent complexity; **b22** lovely stuff with just the right degree of attitude. *50%.*

Old Malt Cask Highland Park Aged 23 Years refill butt no. 3805, dist May 84, bott Aug 07 **(93) n23.5 t23 f23 b23.5.** Solid for all its softness, beautifully crafted and charming. 70cl of pure elegance. *50%. Douglas Laing. 655 bottles.*

⊹∹ **Old Malt Cask Highland Park Aged 26 Years** sherry hogshead no. DL 5596, dist Mar 83, bott Nov 09 **(93) n24** wonderfully clean grape of the old school and still enough space for the obligatory honey and smoke; an unusual sprig of mint adds to the fun; **t23.5** now it enters the realms of fantasy whisky with a thick, viscous delivery. Some chewy cream toffee helps give a fudge and raisin middle; **f22.5** more fudge, more raisin...and a late injection of smoke; **b23** a long way from the normal clichéd HP. Delightfully different. *50% 294 bottles.*

Old Malt Cask Highland Park Aged 30 Years refill butt no. 4190, dist Mar 78, bott Mar 08 **(85.5) n21 t22 f21 b21.5.** No doubting here about the vintage. As ever, honey dives in to the rescue. And the smoke helps with the camouflage. *50%. Douglas Laing. 477 bottles.*

⊹∹ **Premier Barrel Highland Park Aged 11 Years (90.5) n23.5** smoke...tick; honey.... tick....; mosses and bracken....tick....HP on the sample label...tick...; **t23** those stunning strata of honey edge out the smoke for top billing; **f22** bitters slightly but some smoky spice kicks in; **b22** an Orcadian odyssey... *46% nc ncf Douglas Laing & Co Ltd. 180 bottles.*

Private Cellar Highland Park 1988 bott 07 **(86.5) n22 t22 f21.5 b21.** No shortage of honey and slightly more body to this than the common or garden HP. But the smoke fails to really make itself heard to give us the usual, recognisable distillery character. That said, effortlessly drinkable and delicious. *43%. Speyside Distillers.*

Provenance Highland Park Aged 10 Years (91) n22 t24 f22.5 b22.5. A slightly usual view of a great distillery. *46%. Douglas Laing.*

Provenance Highland Park Aged 10 Years refill hogshead, dist autumn 98, bott autumn 08 **(87) n22** the lightness of the oak gives the peat a clear road; **t21.5** lively and bracing with a salty tang; **f22** long, sweetens and really comes into its own as the smoke re-emerges; late vanilla and soft chalk; **b21.5** good, delicate malt, for all the smokiness. *46%. Douglas Laing.*

Provenance Highland Park Aged 10 Years dist Sep 98, bott Jul 09 **(89) n21.5** distant, dank peat reek on a cold, rainy Scottish day; well, any day in Scotland, really... **t23** quintessential HP with the smoke and heather really in just-so proportions. But the delicate honey plays the starring role, as is often the case; **f22** a light spice buzz alongside the salty vanilla; **b22.5** a common and garden HP treat. *46%. Douglas Laing.*

⋯ **Provenance Highland Park Over 11 Years** refill hogshead no. DMG 5744, dist Summer 1998, bott Winter 2010 **(85) n21.5 t22 f20.5 b21.5.** Light, lilting and sweet, even the most delicate smoke has a strangely refreshing quality to it. *46% Douglas Laing & Co Ltd*

⋯ **Rare Old Highland Park 1973** (78.5) **n21.5 t20 f18.5 b19.5.** Loses the battle against the oak. *43% Gordon & MacPhail*

Scotch Malt Whisky Society Cask 4.124 Aged 8 Years 1st fill barrel, dist Apr 99 **(93.5) n23 t23.5 f22.5 b24** It is a sad fact that my grey beard testifies to the fact that I have been around long enough to remember the days when Highland Park came only as an 8 year old. It was pretty spectacular, as 8 year olds went, though some caramel on the finale did it few favours. Never, though, did it present itself in this mind-boggling and truly awesome manner: this is the kind of 8 year old that other distilleries loathe: how can they expect to pack so much depth into so few years? This is a malt to savour from a distillery that has somehow begun to improve on its long established highest standards...and remind you, in the most glorious fashion possible, that a malt doesn't have to be a greybeard to achieve true brilliance. *59.8%*

Scotch Malt Whisky Society Cask 4.126 Aged 9 Years 1st fill barrel, dist Apr 99 **(95.5) n23.5 t24.5 f23.5 b24.** There can't be that many of us grizzled old grey-beard sods left who can remember when the only HP you could find was not a million miles from this timeless bottling. Every bottling and tasting note of HP you find these days bangs on about the heather. Often you feel that the way people see it is 1% reality 99% cliché. How many people have actually nosed and tasted the stuff, I wonder? Well, for a start not that many HP bottlings these days have the heather there to be found, simply because of the enormity of the age and the degree of oak or sherry influence. This one does, just like it once usually did – it is much easier to indentify when younger. And how many people have actually nosed and tasted heather, as I and a (very) few others I know have (or had, for those now departed) done? Again, not that many, I would pretty safely guess. So always take HP tasting notes from people you have barely heard of with a pinch of salt...and heather. You can take it from me, though, that this is a classic of our time....and of times past. *60.7%*

⋯ **Scotch Malt Whisky Society Cask 4.141 Aged 10 Years** 1st fill bourbon barrel, dist Apr 99 **(89.5) n22** whispering haystacks and crumbled German caramelised biscuit; **t23.5** crisp, clean, crunchy barley with more of that beautiful caramelisation...not so much the trademark honey but more brown sugars; **f22** thins and bitters a little; **b22** never tries to oversell itself or shout its worth. This is subtlety and quiet construction on the palate. But don't bother looking for the smoke. *58.9% Scotch Malt Whisky Society. 253 bottles.*

Scotch Malt Whisky Society Cask 4.132 Aged 13 Years refill hogshead, dist Nov 95 (78.5) **n21.5 t20 f18 b19.** Malty, a tad smoky but hot and showing wear and tear from an unsympathetic cask. Pretty niggardly fare. Surprised it was picked. *57.6%*

Scotch Malt Whisky Society Cask 4.133 Aged 13 Years refill hogshead, dist Nov 95 **(94) n23** lime juice sprinkled over grassy barley and the most delicate, semi-erotic peat imaginable....what a tease!.... **t24** a graceful delivery with the malt landing in sweet, mildly juicy waves before there is a warming, biting spice sensation; light peat dots itself around the palate like sentries on duty and light liquorice mingles with watered manuka honey; **f23.5** the elegance continues with a slow fade of smoke and a build up of butterscotch. All is concluded in slow motion and with near perfect sweet-dry ratio between barley and oak with not a single hint of bitterness **b23.5** now that's much more like it!

Scotch Malt Whisky Society Cask 4.127 Aged 19 Years sherry butt, dist Nov 88 (84.5) **n21 t21 f21.5 b21.** HP 9-y-o bourbon cask 1; HP 19-y-o sherry butt 0. Game abandoned due to total mis-match in quality....and this is pretty decent, if overly sweet. *58.1%*

Scotch Malt Whisky Society Cask 4.131 Aged 20 Years sherry butt, dist Nov 88 (93.5) **n23.5** a deeply enjoyable fug of smoke and weighty grape; the oak is a bit more than a bystander; **t24** what a clever boy: a big delivery, but those chunky notes are somehow fed to the tastebuds in bite-size nibbles; the grape is pure sultana and when the barley kicks in becomes just so salivating...; **f23** Cadbury's Fruit and Nut candy bar....but without the nut; **b23** heavy-handed grape gets the better of the gentle smoke throughout. The result is a light fug both on nose and palate. The sharper barley notes, touched by liquorice, do help allow fresher tones to develop. Big and chewy. And fantastic...! *60%*

⋯ **Scotch Malt Whisky Society Cask 4.143 Aged 20 Years** refill hogshead, dist May 89 **(95) n25** if you want to know what HP should nose like, then go no further: grab one of these. The barley is shadowed by the lightest shade of lemon; the smoke is little more than suggestion and elsewhere other charming notes drift in and out, especially the glorious, honeyed, crushed gorse petal; **t24.5** so it naturally follows that what happens on the palate is the nose in liquid form: here the honey really does play a more significant part but the barley simply melts in the mouth while the smoke threatens something spicy, but never quite makes it. Single malt whisky at its most gentle...; **f22.5** perhaps because of the fragility of the body and flavours it is inevitable that a slight bitterness form the cask eventually makes itself heard....though those spices do finally form; **b23** one of those truly great whiskies that makes me want to take it home at the end of the day. HP as it should be... *51.4% 241 bottles.*

⁙ **The Whisky Agency Highland Park 25 Years Old** dist 1985, bott 2010 **(95) n23.5** so honey and heathery is this that it could almost be a send up of itself; **t24** now the honey is in league with maple syrup...sweet or what!!! **f24** settles down with an apologetic degree of peat creeping in through the back door. But the honey buzzes along delightfully; **b23.5** an HP do it yourself kit: honey – check. Heather – check. Soft smoke – almost. Go for it....!! *48%*

The Whisky Fair Highland Park Aged 19 Years bourbon hogshead, dist 88, bott 07 **(89) n22 t23 f22 b22.** If this is from the same cask as the 46% version, here is proof positive how extra strength helps. The oily intensity of the honey is sufficient to see off the budding oak bitterness, And how....!!!! *55.7%. Germany.*

The Whisky Fair Highland Park Aged 19 Years Artist Edition bourbon hogshead, dist 88, bott 07 **(85) n21.5 t22 f20 b21.5.** All the usual honeyed suspects, but a tad oak bitter. *46%. Germany.*

IMPERIAL

Speyside, 1897. Chivas. Silent.

Imperial Aged 15 Years "Special Distillery Bottling" db **(69) n17 t18 f17 b17.** At least one very poor cask, hot spirit and overly sweet. Apart from that it's wonderful. *46%*

Battlehill Imperial 1998 (86.5) n22 t21.5 f21.5 b21.5. Lovely stuff, full of natural caramels – a bit like a Tunnocks with a kick. Perfect blending malt which shows attractively as a single. Impressed. *43%. Duncan Taylor.*

⁙ **Berrys' Own Selection Imperial 1989 (86) n22.5 t21.5 f21 b21.** Textbook blending Speysider: the oak has had limited impact on the barley-rich nose and delivery but makes a bitter contribution at the death. Always juicy and attractive, though. *46% Berry Bros & Rudd*

Cadenhead's Chairman's Stock Imperial-Glenlivet Aged 29 Years bourbon hogshead, dist 1977, bott May 07 **(92) n22 t24 f23 b23.** Imperial by name and nature. *54.7%.*

⁙ **Cask Strength Imperial 1997 (72) n18 t19.5 f17 b17.5.** An empire in revolt... Not a great cask. *61.6% Gordon & MacPhail*

⁙ **Duncan Taylor Collection Imperial 11 Years Old (87.5) n23.5** absolutely pristine barley sets the heart a flutter; **t22** same again on delivery with the malt in almost three dimensional mode: early on it doesn't come cleaner, then the oaky bitterness clogs the middle; **f20.5** light and bitter; **b21.5** worth finding for the nose and delivery alone. *46% Duncan Taylor & Co Ltd*

Duncan Taylor Collection Imperial 1990 cask no. 353 **(75.5) n19 t20 f18 b18.5.** Uninspiring blending fodder. *53.9%*

Duncan Taylor Collection Imperial 1990 cask no. 357 **(88.5) n22 t23 f21.5 b22.** Much more like it! The malt is thick and clean while the cask has contributed positively with soft peppers: this may be related to cask 353, but this is from another planet quality-wise. *53.4%*

Duncan Taylor Collection Imperial 1990 cask no. 358 **(93) n23 t23 f23.5 b23.5.** A bit of an edge to this one: some nip and bite and a wave or three of charming bourbon. My kind of malt. And the best Imperial bottled this year by a significant margin. *52.2%*

Duncan Taylor Collection Imperial 1990 cask no. 359 **(84.5) n20 t22.5 f21 b21.** Complexity? Forget it: just go for the ultra-malty ride. *53.1%*

Duncan Taylor Collection Imperial 1990 cask no. 443 **(92) n22.5** custard powder on butterscotch. All on a bed of rich barley... **t23.5** simply caresses the tastebuds with long fingernails coated in honey-sweetened barley; spices fizz around to ensure a degree of belligerence to what could be simply too relaxing; **f23** long with the barley melting into the vanilla in many improbable shades of sweetness; **b23** a superbly made malt. Imperial often gets a bad press for its quality and occasionally perceived blandness. Nonsense! I have always rated this distillery, and here you can see why. This is simply fabulous. *55%*

Duncan Taylor Collection Imperial 1990 cask no. 445 **(91) n23** eyebrows raise as you immediately spot you are in for a treat: real depth to the clean malt; **t23** a wonderful gooseberry phase to this adds the perfect light fruit edge to the barley; **f22.5** thins as the vanilla arrives, but that lightly sweetened, vaguely fruity malt hangs about to the end with a touch of cocoa and butterscotch at the death; **b22.5** quite adorable. *53.1%. Duncan Taylor.*

Duncan Taylor Collection Imperial 1990 cask no. 446 **(86) n21.5 t22 f21.5 b21.** A sharper, thinner, but no less malty version of cask 443. *53.7%*

Duncan Taylor Collection Imperial 1990 cask no. 448 **(88.5) n22.5** a touch gluey but the barley is crisp with a sugared edge; bourbony; **t23** lilting barley goes through the sweetness gears without so much as a judder; eye-watering sharp, refreshing and salivating; **f21** oak bites quickly as the body quickly thins; **b22** fades too quickly but a malty charmer. *55.7%*

Duncan Taylor Collection Imperial 1990 cask no. 449 **(86.5) n21.5 t22 f21.5 b21.5.** Excellent barley theme and tense, at times, too. Plus a fine bourbony skit at the finish. A tad hot here and there, maybe. *53.4%. Duncan Taylor.*

⠿ **Duncan Taylor Collection Imperial 1990** cask no. 450 **(83.5) n22 t21.5 f19.5 b20.5.** Clearly not a malt designed for a second decade in the cask, this has all the exotic fruit oakiness of a whisky twice its age. Stylish early on, it descends into something pretty sawdusty, though. *53.9% Duncan Taylor & Co Ltd*

⠿ **Duncan Taylor The NC2 Range Imperial Aged 13 Years (86) n22 t22 f21 b21.** Charming, grassy, citrusy, ultra fresh Speysider. *46%*

Duncan Taylor The NC2 Range Imperial 1994 (84.5) n22 t22 f20 b20.5. Starts brightly with all kinds of clean, attractive Speysider phrases, but steadfastly refuses to open up. *46%*

Duncan Taylor The NC2 Range Imperial 1996 dist 96, bott 07 **(85) n21.5 t22 f20.5 b21.** Typical Imperial of its type: loads of wonderful, salivating barley to start and then no further development. Even so, charmingly attractive. *46%. nc ncf.*

⠿ **Gordon & MacPhail Distillery Label Imperial 1991 (83) n22 t21 f20 b20.** Lots of suet pudding with some nagging bitterness at death. Seriously easy going beside. *43%*

Provenance Imperial Aged 12 Years refill hogshead, dist summer 96, bott spring 09 **(84.5) n22 t21.5 f20 b21.** Light, airy, malty. Juicy barley early on delivery. *46%. Douglas Laing.*

Provenance Imperial Aged 12 Years refill barrel, dist spring 96, bott winter 08 **(88) n22** a shapely body with some toasty, soft smoke elements; **t23** some pulsing, salivating malt assisted by a clever sweetness carried on the oils; **f21.5** dryer with vanilla substituting for the barley; a touch bitter late on **b21.5** tasting this and another Prov. Imp. 12 together, the difference a good cask can make is clearly defined. *46%. Douglas Laing.*

Whisky-Doris Imperial 8 Years Old dist 18 Dec 98, bott 19 Oct 07 **(83) n20.5 t22.5 f20 b20.** Pleasantly malted but no special awards to the oak. *55.1%. Whisky-Doris.*

INCHGOWER
Speyside, 1872. Diageo. Working.

⠿ **Inchgower 1993 The Manager's Choice** db **(84.5) n21 t21.5 f21 b21.** Like your malts subtle, delicate, clean and sophisticated? Don't bother with this one if you do. This has all the feel of a malt that's been spray painted onto the taste buds: thick, chewy and resilient. Can't help but like that mix of hazelnut and Demerara, though. You can stand a spoon in it. *61.9%*

Cadenhead's Inchgower Aged 18 Years dist 89, bott Feb 08 **(76) n20 t19 f18 b19.** Evidence of peat on the nose but this mess of a malt never comes close to finding any rhythm or balance. Not an entirely hopeless case as there are some attractive, sharper elements to this but please don't look for anything inspiring; really for those who like a bit of rough. *57.6% 790 bottles.*

Connoisseurs Choice Inchgower 1993 (87.5) n21 a touch dirty, but some non specific phenols and grizzled malt ensures something interesting; **t22** chewy with the malt arriving in varying degrees of sweetness; excellent weight and flavour waves come thick and fast; **f22.5** long with some fudgy, maple syrup sweetness topping the more bitter oak very pleasantly, indeed; **b22** finding decent Inchgowers has been far from an easy task in recent years. Good ol' G&M have come to the rescue here, though, with a bottling bursting with character. *43%. Gordon & MacPhail.*

Duncan Taylor The NC2 Range Inchgower 1992 Aged 15 Years (86.5) n21 t22 f22 b21.5 Inchgower at its most respectable with lashings of clean, often sweet malt. Zero complexity, but you can't have everything: if you see the bottle, just buy the bloody thing because you might not get one in this delightful form again for a while. *46%*

Old Malt Cask Inchgower Aged 21 Years refill hogshead 3434, dist Jun 86, bott Dec 07 **(80.5) n22 t21 f18 b19.5.** The cask isn't the greatest, which is a shame because whilst decent malt from this distillery is getting increasingly more difficult to chance across, there was enough honey on the nose and delivery to hope-against-hope that I might just have found one. *50%. nc ncf. Douglas Laing. 240 bottles.*

Old Malt Cask Inchgower Aged 34 Years dist Sep 74, bott Jul 09 **(91) n23** a balmy evening garden with honeysuckle sweetening the damp earthiness; violets and bluebells, too; **t22** chunky, lightly smoked, sweet and sprightly spiced; some liquorice amid the mushy cashews; **f23** chewy dates; lightly molassed; **b23** dating from the days when the distillery was in its pomp. And it shows. *50%. Douglas Laing.*

Scotch Malt Whisky Society Cask 18.26 Aged 23 Years refill hogshead, dist Feb 85 **(76.5) n18 t19 f20 b19.5.** Some decent malty blows, but just so uninspiring and at times reveals itself as a not particularly well made whisky. *48.3%*

⠿ **The Whisky Agency Inchgower 1974** (87.5) n22 mildly feral but with an elegant oakiness; t22 fiery and full bodied, there is an usual thickness to the body for its age; f21.5 liquorice and drying oak; b22 a teamed beast. 57.3%

INVERLEVEN
Lowland, 1938–1991. Demolished.

Gordon & MacPhail Distillery Label Inverleven 1990 (87) n20 oddball stuff. Butyric, lemon-zesty, a touch of something juniper-ish...and in the background the faintest sound of smoke... t23 the early malty delivery melts away towards the no less juicy citrus. As the middle approaches a phenolic element is introduced, a background weight which appears to see off the worst of any off notes the nose suggests might be on their way and offers an understated spicy buzz; f22 long, vaguely smoked; light yet still plenty to chew over; more, lasting, hints of a jenever; b22 absolutely unique version from this lost distillery: if I was a gambling man I'd say that this was filled into an old Laphroaig or Ardbeg cask, for there is a delicate smoky element that was never intended during mashing. Odd, also because the nose reveals a mild, butyric flaw...as well as unmistakable hints of gin/jenever. But as soon as it hits the tastebuds...my, oh my..!!! 40%.

⠿ **Gordon & MacPhail Distillery Label Inverleven 1991** (93.5) n24 beautifully clean, flawless, barley emboldened by a dash of tangerine; distant lavender quietly underscores the age; t23.5 some really beautiful, understated threads of honey give this star quality; f22.5 no major faults that such an age might threaten; b23.5 handled the aging process with an accomplished performance. Surprisingly suave: one of the surprise packages of the year. 40%

Rarest of the Rare Inverleven 1978 cask no. 1878, bott 08 (90.5) n22.5 crushed grapefruit and orange pith: just so clean; t23 soft barley at first, still showing those fruity elements, then a slow building on firmer, oakier foundations; f22.5 long, sensual, almost perfectly weighted with exquisite bitter-sweet qualities; b22.5 Inverleven never, ever, showed this kind of balls when younger and still alive. If it had, the distillery still might be standing. Hang on a minute... Allied...maybe not. 45.5%. Duncan Taylor.

Rarest of the Rare Inverleven 1979 cask no. 5666 (96) n23.5 more than an element of Kentucky as the sweeter oak notes sing freely. Lightened by clean citrus and mashed barley; t24 spellbinding delivery: clean with a sublime concert of sweet-dry notes as the oak and barley harmonize with astonishing clarity for all the big age; there is even a wonderfully soft oil to help the flavours glide along; f24.5 one of the most elegant finishes of the year: rather than simply fade and die like any good Lowland malt should do, this one actually comes to a crescendo, with all the aspects found on the early delivery now being delivered in heightened, concentrated form. Even when it does decide enough is enough, the final fade is as long as a Scottish midsummer evening... b24 easily one of the best lowlanders I've come across in the last five years oozing nothing but sheer class. Beautifully made, wonderfully casked and no less than stunning in the glass. 56.2%. Duncan Taylor.

Rarest of the Rare Inverleven 1979 cask no. 5667 (88) n21.5 respectable oak involvement: the barley holds together well; t22.5 salivating, prickly barley; clean with slow oaky vanilla leak; f22 long, oils up gently but the barley refuses to cede to the drying, mocha-flaked vanilla; b22 simply splendid stuff. 57%. Duncan Taylor.

ISLE OF ARRAN
Highland (Island–Arran), 1995. Isle of Arran Distillers. Working.

⠿ **The Arran Malt 8 Years Old Pinot Noir Finish** db (79.5) n19 t21 f19.5 b20. Pleasant enough. But just seems to lack the trademark Arran balance and has a few lopsided moments to boot, especially at the death. 50% Isle of Arran Distillers

⠿ **The Arran Malt 8 Years Old Pomerol Wine Finish** db (87) n19 another Arran which strains against a fruity muzzle; t23.5 that's much more like it!! All the harmony missing on the nose arrives in buckets as the trademark thickness of body takes on the spiced grape without missing a beat. Beautiful...; f22 much drier, as it should be, but the chalkiness of the oak hardly makes a dent on the barley-grape surface. Just a slight wobble on the finish; b22.5 Full bodied and lush. 50% Isle of Arran Distillers

The Arran Malt Under 10 Years Old db (89) n22 limp, lush barley of the butterscotch variety; t23 those stunning soft oils are working overtime to spread the sweet barley; f22 long, biscuity and balanced; b22 this one's kicked its shoes and socks off... 43%

The Arran Malt Aged 10 Years L140206 db (93) n23 charming, delicate; varying citrus notes hand-in-hand with rich, butterscotch-barley; the odd youthful note thins things out; t24 the palate coated in caressing oils, to which stick the cleanest and most profound barley. You can chew your jaw off here; f23 developing vanillas dovetail with some of those younger new-makish notes but still cannot escape the clutches of the fat barley. Some fizzing spice decides to make an appearance; **b23** at last! The distillery feels confident enough to put an age statement to their malt, although it's been good enough to do that for the last four or five years. This bottling of some of Arran's first casks entertains and delight. It won't be long before the world's malt connoisseurs add Arran to their list of must haves. Because if it's character and quality you want, it's here by the malt shiel load. *46%. ncf.*

The Arran Malt 12 Years Old db **(85)** n21.5 t22 f20.5 b21 Hmmmm. Surprise one, this. There must be more than one bottling already of this. The first I tasted was perhaps slightly on the oaky side but otherwise intact and salt-honeyed where need be. This one has a bit of a tang: very drinkable, but definitely a less than brilliant cask around. *46%*

⊱ **The Arran Malt 1995 Open Day 2010** db **(86.5)** n23 t21.5 f21 b21. Clean and fruity, but one of the most tightly cramped Arran's I've ever encountered! You get the feeling that the various elements in this malt are just going through a transitional period and that another year before – or after – might have seen a more relaxed and expansive result. *51.4%*

⊱ **The Arran Malt 1996 'The Peacock' Icons of Arran** bott 2009 **(96)** n24.5 oh my word: what a shame I have only three or four months to write this book: the degree of complexity will take that time to unravel. Both floral and fruity in almost perfect doses, the white pepper perfectly balances the light saltiness. The big weight is deceptive as the delicate sultana and perry sub plot appears to give more air and space to the overall picture. Outstanding...; **t24.5** what a delicate creature this is: the juicy grape appears to be apparent on a couple of levels, sandwiching the honey and hickory bourbon notes between them; **f23** long, now with that hint of pear on the nose re-surfacing as the finish nestles somewhere between butterscotch tart and buttered toast; **b24** yet again this outstanding distillery delivers the goods: one of the most outstanding malts of the year and certainly one of the most complex. I would not be surprised if this was overlooked by some of you new to whisky: if you have not already discovered the faultless beauty on offer (not a single off note or hint of discord to be had from first to last!!) go back and try again with your palate as clean and unsullied as this magnificent malt demands and deserves. I've not yet spoken to the Arran guys about this, but would happily bet my house that this is a sublime mix of top bourbon cask and faultless sherry. As fabulous as this distillery unquestionably is, they will be hard pressed to keep this standard going... *46%*

⊱ **The Arran Malt 1996 Single Cask** sherry butt, cask no. 1596, bott 2009 db **(88.5)** n22 a slight bubblegum effect to this, though the fruit appears closely tied up with weightier oak elements; **t23** wow....!!! Now that's some delivery with the grape forming the most delicious degree of juiciness to perfectly match the natural glossy oiliness. The oaks are no pushover, either. The spicy crescendo is expected and doesn't disappoint...; **f21** very dry with distinct signs of assertive over-oakiness; **b22.5** excellent whisky. But no doubt the oak is a tad too domineering and the points here would have been higher if bottled a couple of years earlier. *54.4%*

The Arran Malt Sherry Single Cask 1996 cask no. 1860, dist 27 Nov 96 bott Jan 08 db **(94.5)** n23 t23.5 f24 b24. Blazingly beautiful: outwardly big sherry but in fact just so delicate....one of the great Arrans. *56.2%. 233 bottles. Bottled for The Nectar, Belgium.*

The Arran Malt Single Bourbon Cask 1996 ex-bourbon barrel cask no. 2092 db **(71)** n17 t19 f17 b18. Not the greatest cask ever to grace Arran. *54.4%*

The Arran Malt Single Bourbon Cask 1996 cask no. 2125 dist Dec 96, bott Jun 07 db **(91.5)** n23 t22.5 f23 b23. All you could ask from a bourbon cask – plus a dollop of something extra. *53.8%. 205 bottles.*

The Arran Malt Single Sherry Cask 1996 ex-sherry butt cask no. 1760 db **(85)** n22 t20.5 f21.5 b21. Pretty top heavy with the malt having to battle through the grape. Lots of liquorice, though. *57.3%*

⊱ **The Arran Malt Sherry Single Cask 1997** ex-sherry hogshead no. 410 db **(88.5)** n23 coastally complex: decidedly seaweedy, but not so much that the light layering of fresh grape and barley cannot be clearly detected. High class stuff.... **t22** dry delivery with the barley forcing its way through a surfeit of grape skin and tannin; **f21.5** surprising degree of vanilla; **b22** elegant. *52.2%*

⊱ **The Arran Malt Sherry Single Cask 1997** ex-sherry hogshead no. 435 db **(89)** n22.5 clumsy with the salt and grape tripping over each other; **t23** sharp and massively salty delivery with the fruit being almost three dimensional; moves off into a malty middle ground; **f21.5** lots of natural caramels; **b22** lively and showing a pleasing edginess. *52.5%*

⊱ **The Arran Malt Sherry Single Cask 1997** ex-sherry hogshead no. 517 db **(86.5)** n22 t22 f21 b21.5. The occasional clap of thundering, salty malt, but the fruitiness tones the intensity down towards the middle and finish. *53.5%*

⌁ **The Arran Malt Sherry Single Cask** cask no. 819, dist Jun 98, bott Jun 09 db **(91)** **n23** wild strawberry; crushed, under-ripe green grape and a hint of something vaguely kiwi-fruitish. And, despite all this, the clarity is such that the malt is as plain as day...; **t24** fabulously crisp and assertive: golden sugar sprinkled spiced sultana...with the spices hotting up as the salivating qualities multiply; **f22** dulls down as the natural base caramels dig in; **b22** a thumpingly good sherry cask with not a single off note detectable. *57.7%*

⌁ **The Arran Malt 1997 Single Cask** sherry hogshead no. 965, bott 2010 db **(93.5)** **n24** fat with the oils evident. The grape quickly latches on to them, as do the drier vanillas: beautifully complex; **t24** the type of malt which massages: initially sweet and rotund, but a few sleepy waves give way to something a little more charismatic as salt and spice begin to make some profound speeches; mouth filling and chewy all the way; **f22.5** thins out somewhat abruptly, but perhaps that is inevitable considering the type of body on offer on delivery and through to the middle stages; **b23** for those who like their grape a little seasoned. A celebration of what a good, untarnished sherry butt should be all about. What a star...!! *55% Isle of Arran Distillers. Belgium.*

⌁ **The Arran Malt 1997 Single Cask** sherry hogshead no. 1318, bott 2009 db **(95)** **n24** a clever marriage of salty oak and dryish grape with an almost orange blossom sweetness providing the balance: elegant in the extreme; **t24.5** so delicate that you are frightened to move it around the mouth in fear it might snap! Just a light sprinkling of icing sugar seems to see off any oaky excess; at times angular at others sleek, the complex components are forever moving around, the degree of sweetness fading and brightening like the star it is; **f23** for a malt so dry, the finish is longer than first appears. It is the tight vanilla which hangs on longest, though; **b23.5** the kind of sophisticated malt you could drop an olive into...but don't..!! *52.5% Japan.*

⌁ **The Arran Malt 1997 'The Rown Tree' Icons of Arran** bott 2010 db **(77.5)** **n18.5 t22 f18 b19.** The key here is balance and harmony. And this, unusually for an Arran, possesses little of either. The bitter finish confirms the unhappiness hinted at on the nose. Someone was barking up the wrong tree when putting this one together and the malt, in this form, even for all the sweet, bright moments on delivery, is ready for the chop. *46% Isle of Arran Distillers*

⌁ **The Arran Malt 1998 Single Cask** sherry butt no. 452, bott 2009 db **(93.5)** **n23.5** textbook stuff. Not a sulphur atom in sight as the clean, thick-ish grape mixes delightfully with a prickling spice and barley; **t24** a salty delivery with a fabulous texture to the creamy grape and sweeter barley. Spices throb fore and aft but it's that complex texture which really wins the day: one of the best sherried whisky mouthfuls I have encountered this year; **f23** hollows out as the vanilla gets a grip. Ever tasted spiced chocolate? Here it's in liquid form; **b23** wonderfully assertive yet always pays respect to the salty sub-plot. Complex, elegant and never short of character. A charmer bordering on the old school. *56.3% USA.*

⌁ **The Arran Malt 1998 Single Cask** bourbon cask no. 650, bott 2009 db **(89)** **n21.5** a bit of attitude to this: some vanilla-oak nip and a hint of fast distillation; **t23** zippy and thinner than the norm for this distillery, it papers over the cracks with a beautiful lift off of layered malt and citrus-fused vanilla. The spices, though, have the greatest say; **f22** bitter-sweet with a real cocoa depth to the finish; **b22.5** lacking the usual weight and showing signs of an impatient stillman, still this malt turns cartwheels on the taste buds. An entertainer. *57.6% USA.*

⌁ **The Arran Malt 1998 Single Cask** bourbon cask no. 673, bott 2009 db **(87.5)** **n21** elements of bourbon and blood orange; **t22** the citrus-barley theme helps tame the more energetic vanillas; **f22.2** lots of vanilla and chocolate; **b22** many of the same attributes as cask 650; and my suspicion about some rapid distillation has been confirmed. *55.7% Norway.*

The Arran Malt Bourbon Single Cask 1998 cask no. 671 db **(94.5)** **n24** superb tangerine topping to the oak-thickened malt: sublime... **t24** weight of malt and mouth delivery rarely gets better than this: just a soupcon of oil coats the tastebuds allowing this perfect sharp'n'sweet barley a perfect footing. The oak has arrived in just the right numbers to both add a drier element and a spicy base line; **f23** lightens as the citrus notes reappear and thin the vanilla; **b23.5** my gut instinct is that Arran is just about at its best at 10-11 years in bourbon cask, and here is a bottling which does little to change my mind. Brilliantly made malt in a very fine bourbon cask. What a superstar. *58%*

The Arran Malt Bourbon Single Cask 1998 cask no. 675 db **(85.5)** **n22 t20.5 f22 b21.** Similar, beautifully made malt to 671 (above) but the cask is more fragile and offers flattening caramels where the livelier citrus ought to be... *57.5%*

The Arran Malt Bourbon Single Cask 1998 cask no. 682 db **(88.5)** **n22** soft vanilla, a hint of marmalade and plenty of natural caramel and barley; **t21.5** busy delivery with early spices and some sharp barley; the middle slips into neutral; **f23** readjusts as some drier oak notes arrive, somehow engaging the sharper barley tones in the process. Long and intriguingly complex; **b22** at times conservative, there is enough life in the cask to lift the barley. *46%*

The Arran Single Sherry Cask 1998 cask no. 24 dist Jan 98, bott Feb 07 db **(88) n22 t22 f22 b22.** A wonderful example of how very good whisky is made. *58.7%. 669 bottles.*

The Arran Malt Single Sherry Cask 1998 ex-sherry butt cask no. 89 db **(89) n23** whatever sherry this was from, it was dry... **t23** sexy, super-spiced grape from the off; vanilla soon develops; **f21** fattens; **b22** clean and classy. *56.9%*

The Arran Malt Single Sherry Cask 1998 ex-sherry butt cask no. 84 db **(72) n18.5 t19 f16.5 b18.** Nope...! *56%*

The Arran Malt Single Sherry Cask 1998 cask no. 724 db **(73) n17 t20 f18 b18.** Massive – and what otherwise would certainly have been outstanding - sweet grape juice tries to fight off the worst of the sulphur excesses. But it is asking too much. *57.3%*

The Arran Malt Single Sherry Cask 1998 cask no. 353 db **(94.5) n25** made and matured in Grenada...? Ginger and allspice at the double...; kiwi fruit and papaya add to the tropical theme. But somehow there is room for honey in there, too: light, watered manuka and soft toasted honeycomb...one of the noses of the year, for sure; **t23.5** much more bite and spite on the delivery than the silky nose, but then there had to be. Early delivery really juicy with the barley – which hardly features as an aroma – making an early statement before the countless waves of soft, diced fruit cocktail take hold; an annoying bitterness creeps in slightly upsetting the papaya cart; **f22.5** that bitterness continues but still cannot entirely dampen the lush, fruitier tones which fade gracefully; **b23.5** oh, it is just so rare to come across sherry butts unspoiled by sulphur these days I could weep for joy when I find one like this. I immediately nosed its partner (724) afterwards and could thrash myself with a thorned twig because it is a complete negative of it. *53%*

The Arran Malt Single Sherry Cask 1998 cask no. 450 db **(91.5) n22.5** pretty well oaked for age; the grape is fat and fulsome; **t23** big, thumping fruit; just like cask 89 the spices go into overdrive; slowly citrus follows through; **f23** rhubarb tart and custard; the lightest sprinkling of muscovado sugar; **b23** absolutely top-notch. Just underlines this distillery's class. *53.6%*

∴ **The Arran Malt 1999 Vintage 15th Anniversary Edition** finished in amontillado, bott 2010 db **(92.5) n24** quite outstanding: sherry as you demand it shows on the nose. Clean, confident, a hint of sultana only as this is dry, yet always with enough finesse for the barley to come through loud and clear: an absolute treat..; **t23.5** salivating from the off with a glittering delivery of fresh grape and spice. Waves of vanilla punch through and there is a fabulous malty flourish towards the middle. But those spices continue to pulse...; **f22.5** drier, with vanilla pods and a buttery residue; **b22.5** there is no mistaking excellence. And here it appears to flow freely. *54.6% Isle of Arran Distillers*

∴ **The Arran Malt 2005 Single Cask "The Peated Arran"** bourbon cask no. 116 bott 2009 db **(89) n22.5** some burnt toast on the peat; **t22** sweet, gristy smokiness. Rampaging vanilla kicks in with a twist of bitter lemon; **f21.5** oily, disjointed, dry but naggingly smoky; **b22** for its tender years, it works uncommonly well. *57.7%*

The Arran Malt Ambassador's Choice db **(87.5) n22** attractive, if a touch too dense as there seems little air for the barley fruit and oak to breathe; **t22** the tightness on the aroma is not part of your imagination: delivery is also claustrophobic, thanks mainly to the vastness of the tannins; **f21.5** barley, liquorice and a light hint of apricot; **b22** so heavy with oak I was amazed I could pick the nosing glass up... *46%*

The Arran Malt Bourgogne Finish db **(74) n18 t19 f18 b19**. Arran Malt Vinegar more like...! *56.4%*

The Arran Malt Chianti Classico Riserva Cask Finish db **(85) n19 t23 f21 b22.** Mamma mia: there eeza poco zolfo ina mia malto!! Butta chicco d'uva, ee eez eccellente! *55%*

The Arran Malt Fino Sherry Cask Finish db **(82.5) n21 t20 f21 b20.5.** Pretty tight with the bitterness not being properly compensated for. *50%*

The Arran Malt Fontalloro Wine Cask Finish db **(84.5) n20 t22 f21.5 b21.** For a wine cask, the malt really does sing. *55%*

The Arran Malt Lepanto PX Brandy Finish db **(85) n22 t22 f20 b21.** Tight, unusually thin for an Arran, but some lovely sweet fruit amid the confusion. Pretty oaky, too. *59%*

The Arran Malt Madeira Wine Cask Finish db **(77.5) n19 t21 f18.5 b19**. The odd exultant moment but generally flat, flaky and bitter. *50%*

The Arran Malt Moscatel Cask Finish db **(87) n22 t21.5 f22 b21.5.** Arran is pretty full bodied stuff when just left to its own devices. In this kind of finish it heads towards an almost syrupy texture. Luckily, the grape effect works fine. *55%*

∴ **The Arran Malt 'Original'** db **(80.5) n19 t22 f19.5 b20.** Not the greatest bourbon casks used here. *43%*

The Arran Malt Pineau des Charentes Cask Finish db **(94) n22.5** wispy barley clouds in a bright, sweet-grapey sky; **t24** succulent and spicy. Delivery is first class, allowing full weight to the grassy barley before those fuller, fruitier notes close in. The spices are fabulously subtle and mildly puckering; **f23.5** a real chocolate dessert helped by the slow build up of soft oils; **b24** I may not be the greatest fan of cask finishes, but when one comes along like this, exhibiting such excellence, I'll be the first to doff my hat. 55%

The Arran Malt Pinot Noir Cask Finish db (73.5) **n18 t19 f18 b18.5**. A less than efficient cask from the Germans who produced it. Plenty of off key moments on nose and taste, but it does enjoy a too brief, barely redeeming Bird's Angel Delight chocolaty moment. 50%

The Arran Malt Pomerol Cask Finish Bordeux wine casks db (86.5) **n20 t23 f22 b21.5**. Although the cask is very marginally flawed, the relentlessness of the sweet, juicy grape and barley is a sheer delight. The odd cocoa note does no harm either. 50%

The Arran Malt Premier Cru Bourgogne Cask Finish db (86) **n21 t22 f21 b22**. An entertaining dram which some would do somersaults for, but marks docked because we have lost the unique Arran character. 56.4%

The Arran Malt Robert Burns 250 Years Anniversary Edition db (91.5) **n22.5** mainly floral with just a light touch from the barley; **t23.5** unusually light and flighty in body: most unArran...!! A dusting of castor sugar softens the vanilla even further: juicy, a touch spicy and quite wonderful; **f22.5** a few oils had formed towards the middle and follow through to the end. Again it is barley dominant with a squeeze of something citrussy; **b23** curiously, not that far away from the light Lowland style of malt produced in the 60s and 70s in Burns' native Lowlands. Not the usual Arran, but shows that it can change personality now and again and still be a total charmer. 43%

The Arran Malt St. Emilion Cask Finish Grand Cru Classé wine casks db (89) **n24** huge aroma: thick grape and big fruitcake. The vanillas have a toasted feel to them; crisped hazelnut, too; **t22** almost too big and busy as the intensity of the grape and the roastiness of the oak clash. But a fabulous river of sweet barley flows freely enough once it gets past the early dam; **f21.5** muscovado and grapey sugars see off some threatening bitterness but it is still a bit on the heavy side; **b21.5** not the best balanced whisky you'll ever pour. But such is the sheer force of flavours, you have to doff your beret... 50%

The Arran Malt Sassicaia Wine Cask Finish db (92.5) **n22.5 t23.5 f23 b23.5**. Unquestionably one of Arran's better wine finishes. 55%

The Arran Malt Sauternes Finish db (84) **n21 t22 f20 b21**. Strap yourself in for this one: eye-watering sultana and 240 volts of spice. Choked with oak, though. 56%

The Arran Malt Tokaji Aszu Wine Cask Finish db (83) **n20 t21.5 f21 b20.5**. Pleasant enough, but the wine dulls the more interesting edges. 55%

Isle of Arran 'Jons Utvalgte' Aged 7 Years db (87) **n22** intense malt with trace vanilla; **t21.5** tangy malt thickens; **f22** a touch of spiced butterscotch and vanilla adds relief to the full on barley; **b21.5** The clean intensity of the malt is soup-like. 46%. Norway.

⌐∷⌐ **A. D. Rattray Cask Collection Arran Aged 12 Years** puncheon no. 96.723, dist Jul 96, bott Nov 08 **(64) n15 t17 f16 b16**. Does its best to put a sweet face on things, but fatally held below the alcohol line by sulphur. 46%

A.D. Rattray Arran 1996 cask no. 723 **(71.5) n17.5 t18 f18 b18**. Oops. A dodgy, sulphury, cask has slipped through the very early Arran net. 55.7%

Berrys' Own Selection Arran 1996 cask no. 462, bott 07 **(77) n18 t21 f19 b19**. I'd put any money on this cask having sat empty in the sun and rain for a few months before being filled. A pity as the malt itself is/was complex. 54.6%. Berry Bros & Rudd.

Berrys' Own Selection Arran 1996 cask no. 1507, bott 07 **(85) n21 t22 f21 b21**. Simple. 46%.

Cadenhead's Authentic Collection Arran Aged 11 Years fino sherry hogshead, dist 96, bott May 07 **(94) n23 t24 f23 b24**. Arran can always be relied on for beauty, though not always complexity This has both = and in buckets. 56%. 330 bottles.

Master of Malt Arran 12 Years Old Cask Strength (91.5) **n22 t22 f24 b23.5**. This is towards the finish exactly how I imagine whisky from this distillery should be. Uncanny. 55%.

Norse Cask Selection Arran 1996 cask no. 2108 **(73.5) n17.5 t20 f18 b18**. Hot whisky thanks to a very poor cask. 58.3%. Qualityworld, Denmark.

Norse Cask Selection Arran 1996 Aged 11 Years puncheon cask no. 1637, dist 96, bott Sep 07 **(82.5) n21 t21 f20.5 b20**. Sharp and juicy but not helped by poor oak. 56.5%. nc ncf. 577 bottles. Qualityworld, Denmark

Old Malt Cask Arran Aged 11 Years refill hogshead no. 3931, dist Dec 95, bott Oct 07 **(87.5) n22 t21 f22.5 b22**. Pretty simplistic, but just works wonderfully. 50%. nc ncf. 355 bottles.

Old Malt Cask Arran Aged 12 Years refill puncheon, dist Sep 96, bott Dec 08 **(73) n18 t19 f18 b18**. Furry, flat and out of sorts. 50%. Douglas Laing. 687 bottles.

Premier Barrel Arran Aged 12 Years (81) **n22 t21 f19 b19**. Fine, malty nose and a juicy delivery but the cask cracks rather. 46%. Douglas Laing. 369 bottles.

Provenance Arran Aged 9 Years sherry hogshead no. 4271, dist autumn 98, bott spring 08 **(84.5) n21.5 t21 f21 b21.** Light, malty and clean. *46%. nc ncf. Douglas Laing.*

Provenance Arran Aged 10 Years refill hogshead, dist summer 98, bott autumn 08 **(90) n22** simple yet ultra-attractive sweet malt with just the right amount of custard powdered on; **t23** the barley sugar really is so attractive; intense and not a single note out of place; **f22.5** a touch of oil lengthens matters and helps the malt and vanilla gel; **b22.5** this distillery appears to manage excellence effortlessly. *46%. Douglas Laing.*

Provenance Arran Aged 11 Years refill hogshead, dist spring 97, bott winter 09 **(87) n21** a tad light this by Arran standards, with the oak ensuring a good bite; **t22** fizzy, lively delivery with the oak having a real go at the barley's dominance; **f22.5** for a while that threatened, austere oak wins, but then comes a final and irresistible cavalry charge of rich barley.... **b21.5** not the distillery's finest hour, but enough in there to enjoy and savour. *46%. Douglas Laing.*

⋅⋅⋅ **Provenance Arran Over 12 Years** refill hogshead no. DMG 5998, dist Summer 1997, bott Spring 2010 **(91) n22.5** toasty with attractive bourbon elements, especially the zesty orange bit; **t23** beautifully silky arrival with a big oak agenda but barley oozing every other available pore; **f23** long, full of liquorice and hazelnut oil. Improbably soft for its age with more bourbon notes evident on the attractive sheen; **b22.5** a superb offering which nutshells the distillery at this age pretty well. *46% Douglas Laing & Co*

⋅⋅⋅ **Scotch Malt Whisky Society Cask 121.32 Aged 9 Years** refill hogshead, dist Jan 00 **(88) n22** jagged, ragged and maltily gruff; **t23** how can you not adore this delivery...? There is a massive, salty mouth watering explosion with barley hitting every crevice; there is a salty tang, too **f21** evidence of light oil but also surprisingly bitter; **b22** Malty, salty and tasty. But perhaps a bit too course by Arran's high standards to make this a classic. *56.3% Scotch Malt Whisky Society. 313 bottles.*

Scotch Malt Whisky Society Cask 121.28 Aged 11 Years refill butt, dist Jan 98 **(91.5) n23** sublime light fruitcake; a kind of mix between a cherry Madeira and undercooked Dundee... **t23.5** enormous delivery of malt with a real cocoa and dark cherry back up; there is a superb spice fizz which helps accentuate the lightness of the vanilla against the backdrop of raisins and prunes. This is Arran at its most absorbing and delicious... **f22** the late honeycomb fade is a very unusual aspect of this distillery, and one that sits well with the richness of body; yet more cherry cake...with plenty of cherries and the molassed excellence of a Melton Hunt cake; **b23** were this not for the very slightest of sulphury tangs on both nose and finish in particular this might have been one of the best Arrans yet. Even despite the blemish the delicate sophistication of the sherry is monumentally impressive. *53.3%*

⋅⋅⋅ **Scotch Malt Whisky Society Cask 121.36 Aged 12 Years** refill hogshead, dist Apr 97 **(85) n22 t22 f21 b20.** For those looking for a fruity-coffee combo. *57% Scotch Malt Whisky Society. 224 bottles.*

Victoria Single Malt Club Arran 10 Years Old sherry refill, cask no. 374, dist 98, bott 08 **(94) n23.5** although from refill sherry, there is almost a bourbony character to this, with substantial oaky toffee and spice and a dab of red liquorice; the grape appears in top toffee-apple guise; **t24** the malt cascades in the juiciest form, giving just a cursory nod to some soft fruit; vanilla arrives early for a 10-year-old and that playful bourbony feel starts again... **f23** long, a little sharp and still able to keep the saliva buds on full alert; **b23.5** always one of the better experiences of whisky tasting when you come across an in-form Arran like this. *55.8%. Canada.*

ISLE OF JURA
Highland (Island–Jura), 1810. Whyte and Mackay. Working.

Isle of Jura 5 Years Old 1999 db **(83) n19 t23 f21 b20.** Absolutely enormously peated, but has reached that awkward time in its life when it is massively sweet and as well balanced as a two-hour-old foal. *46% The Whisky Exchange*

Isle of Jura 10 Years Old db **(80.5) n19 t21 f20 b20.5.** For a distillery located pretty close to the startling Paps of Jura, how can anything be this flat....? *40%*

Isle of Jura Mountain of Gold 15 Years Old Pinot Noir cask finish db **(67.5) n15 t18 f17 b17.5.** Not for the first time a Jura seriously hamstrung by sulphur - for all its honeyed sweetness and promise: there are some amazingly brilliant casks in there tragically wasted. And my tastebuds partially crocked because of it. Depressing. *46%. 1366 bottles.*

Isle of Jura Mountain of Sound 15 Years Old Cabernet Sauvignon finish db **(81) n20 t21.5 f19.5 b20.** Pretty quiet. *43%*

Isle of Jura The Sacred Mountain 15 Years Old Barolo finish db **(89.5) n21.5** tight, not exactly on song but enough salty, sultry, sherry-esque notes to keep you amused; **t24** good grief...! Didn't expect to be confronted by this beauty...the entire mouth is engaged from kick off with the fresh grape appearing to really attack the roof. The barley and spice intermingle firstly among themselves and then interweave with the salty wine effect. The result is clean, juicy, a textbook balance of sugars to oak, and, overall, is absolutely first class; **f21.5** dulls down as toffee creeps in but not without a fight from the (very late on furry) grape, spice and deft mocha: after all the excitement it's all over too quickly...I believe some people will recognise that feeling... **b22.5** hoo-bloody-rah! One of the three from this series has actually managed to raise my pulse. Not, it must be said, without the odd fault here and there. But there really is a stunning interaction between the grape and barley that sets the nerves twitching: at its height this is about as entertaining a malt as I've come across for some time and should be on everyone's list for a jolly jaunt for the taste buds. Just when I was beginning to lose faith in this distillery... *43%*

Isle of Jura 16 Years Old db (78.5) **n19 t20.5 f19 b20.** I had hoped that this dram would have moved on from the last few lacklustre glasses I quaffed here and there. Nope. Still flatters to deceive with the odd honeyed turn, but nowhere near enough breeziness to pull itself away from the doldrums. The odd feint doesn't help, either. *40%*

Isle of Jura 21 Years Old Cask Strength db (92) **n22** something hard and grainy against the ultra-clean fruit; **t24** fabulous mouth arrival, just such a brilliant fruit-spice combo held together in a malty soup; **f23** long and intensely malty; **b23** every mouthful exudes class and quality. A must-have for Scottish Island collector ... or those who know how to appreciate a damn fine malt *58.1%*

Isle of Jura 30 Years Old db (89) **n22.5** a touch of orange peel and mildly overcooked yam: soft, intriguing and pepped up further by the beginnings of a few sweet bourbony notes; **t22.5** the delivery flutters onto the palate. It's a pretty delicate encounter, perhaps softened by a touch of cream toffee but there is enough life in the juicy citrus and layered barley to get the tongue exploring; spices soon begin to pop around the palate as some vanilla encroaches; **f22** chewy, toffeed, fat and still a touch of spicy feistiness; **b22** a relaxed dram with the caramel dousing the higher notes just as they started to get very interesting. If there is a way of bringing down these presumably natural caramels – it is a 30 years old, so who in their right mind would add colouring? – this would score very highly, indeed. *40%*

Isle of Jura 40 Years Old finished in Oloroso sherry wood db (90) **n23** a different species of Jura from anything you are likely to have seen before: swamped in sherry, there is a vague, rather odd smokiness to this. Not to mention salty, sea-side rockpools. As a pairing (sherry and smoke), the odd couple... which works and doesn't work at the same time. Strange... **t22** syrupy sweet delivery with thick waves of fruit and then an apologetic 'ahem' from the smoke, which drifts in nervously. Again, everything is awkward... **f22** remains soft and velvety, though now strands of bitter, salty oak and molasses drift in and out; **b23** throw the Jura textbooks away. This is something very different. Completely out of sync in so many ways, but... *40%*

Isle of Jura 1974 db (87.5) **n23 t22.5 f20.5 b21.5.** Stick your nose in this and enjoy those very first outstanding moments on delivery. *42%*

⋰ **Jura Boutique Barrels Vintage 1995** bourbon Jo finish db (89.5) **n24.5** just how beautiful is that orange blossom? Could easily be mistaken for a high class bourbon...; **t23.5** busy and lively enough to delight a million mouth nerve endings: the layering of the bourbon-rich oak is a wonder to behold; some lovely chocolate fudge, honeycomb and praline bond beautifully; **f20** ...but the finish is a disappointment as the heavier distillation oils kick all else out of sync; **b21.5** there are moments when you wonder if you have a possible malt of the year on your hands. Then the slip shows.... Even so, one of the more memorable whiskies of the 2011 Bible. *56.5%*

⋰ **Jura Boutique Barrels Vintage 1999** heavily peated, bourbon Xu finish db (84) **n21.5 t21 f20.5 b21.** Pretty peat. But not in the same league as the Prophecy, simply because the base spirit is nowhere near as good. *55%*

Jura Elements "Air" db (76) **n19.5 t19 f18.5 b19.** Initially, I thought this was earth: there is something strangely dirty and flat about both nose and delivery. Plenty of fruits here and there but just doesn't get the pulse racing at all. *45%*

Jura Elements "Earth" db (89) **n23.5 t22 f21.5 b22.** I haven't spoken to blender Richard Paterson about these whiskies yet. No doubt I'll be greeted with a knee on the nuts for declaring two of these as duds. My guess is that this is the youngest of the quartet by a distance and that is probably why it is the best. The peat profile is very different and challenging. I'd still love to see this in its natural plumage as the caramel really does put the brakes on the complexity and development. Otherwise we could have had an elementary classic. *45%*

Jura Elements "Fire" db (86.5) **n22.5 t21.5 f21 b21.5.** Pleasant fare, the highlight coming with the vaguely Canadian-style nose thanks to a classic toffee-oak mix well known east of the Rockies. Some botanicals also there to be sniffed at while a few busy oaky notes pep up the barley-juiced delivery, too. Sadly, just a shade too toffee dependent. *45%*

Jura Elements "Water" db (**73.5**) n18.5 t19 f18 b18. What a shame. Oranges by the box-full trying to get out but the mouth is sent into puckering spasm by the same sulphur which spoils the nose. *50%*

⋰ **Jura Prophecy** profoundly peated db (**90.5**) n23.5 something almost akin to birchwood in there with the peat and salt; there is a wonderful natural floral note as well as coastal elements to this one; t23 impressively two-toned: on one side is the sharper, active barley and peat offering an almost puckering youthfulness and zest; on the other, a sweeter, lightly oiled buzz...a treat; f22 thins as the vanillas enter; b22 youthful, well made and I prophesize this will be one of Jura's top scorers this year.... *46%*

Jura Superstition db (**86**) n21 t22 f20 b23. A rare case of where the whole is better than the parts. A malt that wins through because of a superb balance between peat and sweeter barley. Distinctive to the point of being almost unique. *45%*

Jura Superstition db (**75**) n18 t21.5 f17.5 b18. The last time I had Superstition it was still at 45% and a pretty enjoyable dram...with a few flaws but a hell of a lot of character. Then this.....THIS...!!! First you have to come to terms with a nose uniquely blended from feints and peat; then for a few glorious moments on delivery it threatens to burst out into a honeyed, vaguely smoky rhapsody in gold. But instead of taking me on a thrilling journey, we are shunted off into a multi-story car park....with the exit barriers stuck. This is a dead end whisky. If it's flavour and excitement you are looking for, forget Superstition and try some Super Stilton (white, of course) with Dickenson and Morris Pork Pie (made at Melton only, naturally) and a pint of Grainstore Cooking or (if you must have your dose of caramel) Phipps IPA. Now that is what your taste buds are really for.... *43%*

Connoisseurs Choice Jura 1992 (**89**) n23 t22.5 f21.5 b22. If only all Jura were this expressive and clean. *43%. Gordon & MacPhail.*

⋰ **Connoisseurs Choice Jura 1995** (**76.5**) n19.5 t19.5 f18.5 b19. Pretty faithful to the default Jura style. *43% Gordon & MacPhail*

⋰ **Dun Bheagan Isle of Jura 12 Years Old Manzanilla Finish** dist Jun 97 (**87.5**) n23 various spices of a different hue spring at you from every direction but all find themselves embedded in fruit wine gums; t22 wonderful clarity to the duel layered barley and fruit juice; f20.5 bitters out; b22 one hell of a box of tricks before the finish. Certainly one of the better examples of spirit from the distillery for the last year or so and a much better cask would have seen this score handsomely in the 90s. *43% Ian Macleod*

⋰ **Duncan Taylor Collection Jura 1990** cask no. 6401 (**81.5**) n20.5 t22.5 f18.5 b20. Adorable malt delivery, if a little short-lived. *52.4% Duncan Taylor & Co Ltd*

Old Malt Cask Jura Aged 15 Years (**89**) n22.5 t23 f21.5 b22. Just shows what Jura sans caramel can do: absolutely brimming with life, vitality and charm. *50%. Douglas Laing.*

Old Malt Cask Jura Aged 16 Years refill hogshead no. 3841, dist Feb 91, bott Aug 07 (**79.5**) n19 t21 f19.5 b20. Plenty of harley and sugars in there do battle with the oak. *50%. nc ncf. Douglas Laing. 332 bottles.*

Old Malt Cask Jura Aged 16 Years refill barrel, dist Oct 92, bott Apr 09 (**91.5**) n24 absolutely beautiful malt: clean, the very lightest trace of sweet peat and seasoned with salt and a dab of allspice; t23.5 salivating and juiced up, the barley reveals a wonderful clarity while the smoke drifts around lightly stroking the tastebuds. The most subtle oils makes a gentle experience softer still... f22 touches of vanilla and still that lazy phenol; a hint of bitterness is the evidence of a cask under any stress; b22 ah...if only more Juras were like this... *50%. Douglas Laing. 323 bottles.*

⋰ **Old Malt Cask Jura Aged 18 Years** refill hogshead, cask no. 5977, dist Mar 92, bott Mar 10 (**73**) n17 t19 f18 b19. This distillery does have the propensity to make one shudder. *48.8% Douglas Laing & Co Ltd. 328 bottles.*

Old Masters Isle of Jura Aged 15 Years cask no. 1934, dist 92, bott 07 (**88.5**) n22 t23 f21 b22.5 Just about an action replay of the OMC 15 above. I can't believe the two aren't closely related and for a while warehouse mates. *53.9%. James MacArthur & Co. Ltd.*

Provenance Jura Aged 11 Years refill hogshead, cask no. 3710, dist Nov 95, bott summer 07 (**80.5**) n19 t21 f20.5 b20. Ultra sweet barley. *46%. nc, ncf. Douglas Laing.*

Scotch Malt Whisky Society Cask 31.18 Aged 20 Years refill hogshead, dist Apr 88 (**89**) n21.5 under-ripe gooseberry crushed in the fingers; t23 some wonderful elements to this, especially the coarseness to the malt and salty oak which battle viciously at times for supremacy; at other times tight and restricted in direction; f22.5 big late, delicious chocolate surge; b22 a Jekyll and Hyde distillery at the best of times and here you get a feel of that in just one bottle. A fine, salty tang, though; like taking a mouthful of the Atlantic. *56.2%*

Scott's Selection Isle of Jura 1989 bott 07 (**90**) n22.5 t23 f22 b22.5. Now that was an enjoyable Jura!! *59.6%*

KILCHOMAN

Islay, 2006. Working.

Kilchoman Autumn 2009 Release db (85) n21 t22.5 f20 b21.5. Still to completely find it's legs: a youthful malt is trying desperately hard to hit the high notes, but falling short. Or perhaps I should say flat as the fruit here is acting like caramel in dumbing down the more complex notes you know are in there somewhere...especially in the final third. Like the Inaugeral Release there is a feinty element to this, not all of it bad, but certainly marks the nose and finish. Also a charming gristiness: you feel as though you are standing there watching the barley being dried. But as yet doesn't quite have the early excellence that Arran, for instance, boasted. But these are early days in the distillery's life. And, for me, anything drinkable at all is a bonus... 46%

Kilchoman Inaugural Release db (87.5) n21 the smoke lurks around like a detective under a streetlamp: trying to look casual but can be easily seen. A distant but distinct feintiness gives a mildly off kilter oiliness, but things are lightened by an effusive citrus note; t23 the coppery evidence of a new still soon makes its mark but the fanning out of the phenols towards a vaguely hickory style, all underscored by sultry fruit notes, makes for a gentler experience than might have been earlier predicted on arrival; f21.5 bitters out slightly as both the effect of the feints and stills combine; some very late spice has the last word; b22 not by any means perfect but what could have been something of a bumpy ride has been helped along by some very good casks: like an excellent football referee, you don't notice it, but not only is it there, it makes the best of what is on offer. Not even remotely a great whisky. But a very promising start. 46% nc ncf

KNOCKANDO

Speyside, 1898. Diageo. Working.

Knockando 1994 Aged 12 Years db (86) n22 t22 f21 b21. An usually light bottling for Diageo. Here you get full exploration of the attractive, malty skeleton. But Knockando has a tendency towards dryness and the casks here oblige rather too well. A delicate dram all the same. 43%

Knockando Aged 12 Years dist 95 db (71.5) n16 t19 f18 b18.5. If there was an award for Worst Nose of the Year, this must be somewhere in the running. 43%

Knockando Aged 18 Years sherry casks, dist 87 db (77) n19 t21 f18 b19. Bland and docile. Someone wake me up. 43%

Knockando 1990 db (83) n21 t22 f20 b20. The most fruity Knockando I've come across with some attractive salty notes. Dry, but a little extra malty sweetness these days. 40%

Knockando The Manager's Choice Spanish sherry European oak, cask no. 800790, dist 1996, bott 2009 db (94) n23.5 I think my staff have poured me the wrong stuff: they've opened up some pot still Demerara, right...? Wrong. No, definitely from the Knockando sample. Well, well, well...let's just say it's a fruity, sugary, rich start on the nose....; t25 actually, I don't care if this is rum or whisky. When you get flavours this beautifully defined, a body this sublimely structured...it really doesn't much matter. Oozes fruity, beautifully natural sweetened quality and complexity; f22 a slight bitterness on the finish where, for the first time, there is a very minor blemish, but the array of sugars still make for something memorable...and absolutely 100% nothing like I have ever tasted from any previous Knockando....; b23 I have been in the Demerara region Guyana, crawled around a rum warehouse at a rum distillery and opened a cask of rum which has less rum characteristics than this rumbustuous chappie. Quite a rum do. 58.6% 599 bottles.

Duncan Taylor Collection Knockando 1980 cask no. 1910 (93) n24 t23.5 f23.5 b24. The one reservation I have always held about this malt is its degree of dryness. Here is a rare example of the barley offering sufficient sweetness to see it into great age. Now this really is sophistication. 49.1%

Duncan Taylor Collection Knockando 1980 cask no. 1911 (84.5) n21.5 t22 f20 b21. Relatively dull except for the odd juicy moment. Not bad but very much the poorer relation. 46.7%

Old Malt Cask Knockando Aged 14 Years bourbon barrel, dist Sep 94, bott Jan 09 (83.5) n19 t22.5 f21 b21. Very sweet for a Knockando with a big barley sugar theme, despite the misfiring nose. 50%. Douglas Laing. 357 bottles.

Provenance Knockando Over 9 Years sherry butt no. DMG 5738, dist Summer 2000, bott Winter 2010 (77) n18 t21 f19 b19. Sweet. But no cigars to the stillman. 46% Douglas Laing & Co Ltd

Provenance Knockando Over 9 Years sherry butt no. DMG 5442, dist Summer 2000, bott Summer 2009 (82) n19 t22 f21 b20. A vuvuzela of a whisky: one long, continuous malty note. 46% Douglas Laing & Co Ltd

KNOCKDHU

Speyside, 1894. Inver House. Working.

AnCnoc 12 Year Old db (90) n22 an aggressive pepperiness bites deep into the usual grassy maltiness and coal smoke. Excellent depth and complexity, though slightly more aggressive, if younger, in style than of old; t23 absolutely fabulous, near-perfect, malt arrival, perhaps the most clean, yet intense of any in Scotland. The complexity is staggering with not only multi-layers of malt but a distant peat and oak infusion; f22 deliciously spicy; b23 if there is a more complete 12-year-old Speyside malt on the market, I have yet to find it. A malt that should adorn a shelf in every whisky-drinking home.

AnCnoc 13 Year Old Highland Selection db (85) n21 t23 f20 b21. A big Knockdhu, but something is dulling the complexity. 46%

AnCnoc 16 Years Old db (90.5) n22 a comfortable marriage of gentle, zesty barley and softer oak-induced liquorice and vanilla; as it warms and oxidizes a move towards bourbon is detected with some toast and honey in evidence; t23 luxurious, deftly oiled delivery with the bourbon effect really taking hold: liquorice and hickory give extra depth to the soft brown sugars; f22.5 decent length with more sugared barley and spice develops before unwelcome toffee takes up valuable space and reduces the complexity; drier vanillas are allowed to take full control; b23 ignore the tasting notes on the label: it is a much better whisky than it suggests... 46%. nc ncf.

AnCnoc 26 Years Old Highland Selection db (89) n23 profound. Everything is big, but perfectly proportioned: massive grapey fruit and malt concentrate; t22 pure Knockdhu: intense malt carrying some beautiful spices and an obscure but refreshing fruit; f23 the lull after a minor storm: rich vanilla and echoes of malt; b21 there is a little flat moment between the middle and finish for which I have chipped off a point or two. That apart, superb. 48.2%

AnCnoc 30 Years Old db (85) n21 pipe smoke, old leather armchairs and a sprig of mint: this seems older than its years; t23 wonderfully thick malt, beefed up in intensity by drawing in as much oak as it comfortably can; the honeycomb and molassed sweetness adds a lovely touch; f19 big natural caramel and some pretty rough-stuff oak; b22 seat-of-the-pants whisky that is just on the turn. Still has a twinkle in the eye, though. 49%

An Cnoc 1993 db (89) n22 butterscotch on shortbread pastry and barley sugar interweaves attractively with the trademark soft honey note and the very lightest whiff of something vaguely smoky; t21 surprising oak charge arrives early, bringing with it spices and soft oils; f24 it's the finish that makes this one with a late – and highly unusual – intervention of citrus to help lighten the oaky load and emphasise the richness of the barley; b22 quite an odd one this. I have tasted it a couple of times with different samples and there is a variance. This one takes an oakier path and then invites the barley to do its stuff. Delicious, but underscores the deft touch of the standard 12-year-old. 46%

AnCnoc 1994 db (88.5) n22.5 yessiree, some real ol' Kentuck' in that thar nose...but the barley is full on, too; t22.5 toffee apple delivery with some juicy barley and lazy spice; f21.5 crème brulee and butterscotch, helped along with vanilla: dessert anyone...? b22 coasts through effortlessly, showing the odd flash of brilliance here and there. Just get the feeling that it never quite gets out of third gear... 46%. ncf.

AnCnoc 1995 db (84.5) n21 t22 f20.5 b21. Very plump for a Knockdhu with caramel notes on a par with the citrus and burgeoning bourbon. Some barley juice escapes on delivery but the finish is peculiarly dry for the distillery. 46%

Knockdhu 23 Years Old db (94) n23 t24 f23 b24. Pass the smelling salts. This is whisky to knock you out. A malt that confirms Knockdhu as not simply one of the great Speysiders, but unquestionably among the world's elite. 57.4%.

Harrods Knockdhu Aged 12 Years (84) n19 t23 f21 b21. One can assume only that caramel (or an exceptional dull sherry cask) has been added here because it is otherwise impossible to find such a flat nose from a Knockdhu. However, the arrival on the palate is bliss, with dates combining with glossy honey and marzipan, but again the finish is only a dull echo of what it should be. Shackled greatness. 40%.

LAGAVULIN

Islay, 1816. Diageo. Working.

Lagavulin 12 Years Old 7th release, bott 07 db (92.5) n23 t23 f23 b23.5. Brooding, enigmatic and just pulsing with quiet sophistication. A dram to drink quietly so all can be heard in the glass... 56.4%

Lagavulin 12 Year Old 8th release, bott 08 db (94.5) n24 heady mixture of coal dust and peat reek, quite dry but not without some fried banana sweetness in the most delicate terms possible; t24.5 a lightly oiled landing allows the peats to glide around the palate with minimal friction; a light dusting of hickory powder works well with the big, but by no means brooding phenols; the sweetness levels are just about perfect; **f22.5** surprisingly short with a dull toffee flourish to the smoke; **b23.5** sensational malt: simply by doing all the simple things rather brilliantly. 56.4%

Lagavulin Aged 16 Years db (95) n24 t24 f23 b24. Much more like the Lagavulin of old with unfettered development and delivery. Befitting the great distillery this unquestionably is. Forget some previous disappointing bottlings: this is the real thing! 43%

Lagavulin Aged 16 Years The Distillers Edition PX cask, dist 91, bott 07 db (83) n22 t21 f20 b20. I have oft stated that peat and sherry are uncomfortable bed-fellows. Here, the two, both obviously from fine stock and not without some individual attraction, manage to successfully cancel each other out. One is hard pressed to imagine any Lagavulin this dull. 43%

Lagavulin 21 Years Old bott 07 db (96) n24.5 t24 f23 b24.5. This is rough and ready malt of extraordinary character. It would be easy to dismiss this as off-key and unbalanced. To be honest, I did on the first to third tastings. But something about it bothered me: I was being too pedantic and failing to see the whisky for what exactly it is. So I tried again, clearing my mind in the process. I was rewarded handsomely. This is not a malt that is for those looking for a handsome time of it: this is Islay malt warts and all and almost brought me back to where I came in over a quarter of a century ago. It somehow encapsulates the stormy disposition of the island and its closeness to nature. For those of you who have struggled with this, let me show you my first notes before I twigged what this was all about and tuned in on the right wavelength. It shows what happens when you are tired and you are hunting on the wrong frequency.... (80) n19 t20 f22 b19 Big peat and grape rarely work comfortably together and here we a have malt which struggles from the nose to finish to make some kind of sense of itself. There will be some Islayphiles who will doubtless drool at this and while certain aspects of the finish are quite excellent the balance never appears to come into focus. 56.5%

◦∵◦ **Lagavulin The Manager's Choice** bodega sherry European oak cask no. 4446, dist 1993, bott 2009 (4th and final release) db (91) n24 not sure I've ever seen the pounding smoke from a Lagavulin quite this soft. Gently peated butterscotch tart with just a light teasing of pine; **t22.5** fingers of smoke caress the palate; light oils and a slow integration of cream toffee notes; **f22.5** the toffee becomes quite chewy while the delicate smoke clings to the roof of the mouth **b22** a lot more toffee and oil than I expected. But the quality is beyond question: tastes like it's from the days when Lagavulin was a 50ppm merchant. 54.7% 597 bottles

LAPHROAIG
Islay, 1815. Fortune Brands. Working.

Laphroaig 10 Years Old db (91) n22 less intense smoke; **t24** much silkier delivery than usual with the sweetness all up front as the peat dovetails in and out of the barley – more complex; **f22** a drier finale with a shade more caramel; **b23** I discovered these 20cl 43% bottlings just after it was announced they were to be phased out. I also noticed that the whisky inside them had a slightly different character from the standard bottlings... 43%

◦∵◦ **Laphroaig 10 Years Old Cask Strength** batch no. 001 bott Feb 09 db (91.5) n22.5 like a throbbing 6 litre engine below a still bonnet, you are aware of the peaty power waiting to be unleashed; **t23.5** a stunningly sublime, slightly watered muscovado sugar coating ensures the dry, phenolic explosion conjures myriad variances on a theme; **f23** a quite beautiful milk chocolate quality dovetails to excellent effect with the smoke; **b22.5** a Groundhog Day of a malt with the waves of smoke starting identically but always panning out a little differently each time. Fascinating and fun. 57.8%

Laphroaig 10 Years Old Original Cask Strength (with UK Government's Sensible Drinking Limits boxed on back label) db (92) n22 a duller nose than usual: caramel reducing the normal iodine kick; **t24** recovers supremely for the early delivery with some stunning black peppers exploding all over the palate leaving behind a trail of peat smoke; the controlled sweetness to the barley is sublime; **f23** again there is a caramel edge to the finish, but this does not entirely prevent a fizzing finale; **b23** caramel apart, this is much truer to form than one or two or more recent bottlings, aided by the fresh, gristy sweetness and explosive spices. Wonderful! 55.7%

Laphroaig Aged 15 Years db (79) n20 t20 f19 b20. A hugely disappointing, lacklustre dram that is oily and woefully short on complexity. Not what one comes to expect either from this distillery or age. 43%

Laphroaig 18 Years Old db (94) n24 multi-layered smokiness: there are soft, flightier, sweeter notes and a duller, earthier peat ingrained with salt and leather; **t23.5** perhaps it's the big leg-up from the rampant hickory, but the peat here offers a vague Fisherman's Friend cough sweet quality far more usually associated with Bowmore, except here it comes in a milder, Demerara-sweetened form with a few strands of liquorice helping that hickory to a gentler level; **f23** soft oils help keep some late, slightly juicy barley notes on track while the peat dances off with some spices to niggle the roof of the mouth and a few odd areas of the tongue; **b23.5** this is Laphroaig's replacement to the woefully inadequate and gutless 15-year-old. And talk about taking a giant step in the right direction. Absolutely brimming with character and panache, from the first molecules escaping the bottle as you pour to the very final ember dying on the middle of your tongue. This is as noisily Islay as a sky-blackening invasion of White-fronted Geese or rain pelting against your cottage windows. Relentlessly first class. 48%

Laphroaig Aged 25 Years db **(94) n23** the clean - almost prim and proper - fruit appears to have somehow given a lift to the iodine character and accentuated it to maximum effect. The result is something much younger than the label demands and not immediately recognisable as Islay, either. But no less dangerously enticing... **t24** the grapes ensure the peat is met by a salivating palate; particularly impressive is the way the sweet peat slowly finds its footing and spreads beautifully; **f23.5** no shortage of cocoa: a kind of peaty fruit and nut chocolate bar... **b23.5** like the 27-y-o, an Islay which doesn't suffer for sherry involvement. Very different from a standard, bourbon barrel-aged Laphroaig with much of the usually complexity reined in, though its development is first class. This one's all about effect - and it works a treat! 40%

Laphroaig 27 Years Old sherry cask, dist 80, bott 07 db **(94.5) n24** the sherry is ridiculously clean considering the vintage yet neither fruit nor smoke cloud the way of the other – a fabulous freak of its type, perhaps, but more likely to be the result of great distilling and cask selection... **t23.5** again, a collector's item to find sherry of this age coming across so fresh and intense, especially with such major peat to deal with; the result is clear bright and rich and just full of that unique Melton Hunt Cake roasty fruitiness; wonderfully spiced throughout; **f23** delicate viscosity clinging to every crevice in your mouth. Dark coffee, though never bitters out and moves into mocha mode: a real chewy dram; **b24** one of the better examples of big sherry and big peat working in close harmony without the usual bristling stand off. A real class act. 57.4%. nc. 972 bottles.

Laphroaig Aged 30 Years db **(94) n24 t23 f23 b24.** The best Laphroaig of all time? Nope, because the 40-y-o is perhaps better still... just. However, Laphroaig of this subtlety and charm gives even the very finest Ardbeg a run for its money. A sheer treat that should be bottled at greater strength. 43%

Laphroaig Aged 40 Years db **(94) n23 t24 f23 b24.** Mind-blowing. A malt that defies all logic and theory to be in this kind of shape at such enormous age. The Jane Fonda of Islay whisky. 43%

Laphroaig 1/4 Cask db **(95) n22** burning embers of peat in a crofter's fireplace; sweet intense malt and lovely, refreshing citrus as well; **t24** mouthwatering, mouth-filling and mouth-astounding: the perfect weight of the smoke has no problems filling every crevice of the palate; builds towards a sensationally sweet maltiness at the middle; **f24** really long, and dries appropriately with smoke and spice. Classic Laphroaig; **b25** a great distillery back to its awesome, if a little sweet, self. Layer upon layer of sexed-up peatiness, this is the closest to how I remember it some 30 years ago! 48%

A.D. Rattray Laphroaig 1996 cask no. 7290 **(81) n19.5 t21 f20.5 b20.** Long finish, but should have quit whilst it was ahead... 60.3%

⋅⋰⋅ **A.D. Rattray Laphroaig 1998** cask no. 80044, dist Mar 98, bott Mar 09 **(88.5) n23** pure peat ash.... **t22.5** I know this is a 60+% abv cask, and that might give the impression of upping the peat levels. But believe me...this is very smoky: I've even had to turn off the alarms in my lab....; no shortage of sugars here, as well; **f21** when the vanillas finally break through, everything appears comparatively tame....; **b22** the usual phenol level for Laphroaig is 35ppm. This appears to be a little higher. Well, actually, a lot higher.... Had the previous UK government known you could have this amount of fun legally, they would have banned it. 61.6%

Berry's Own Selection Laphroaig 1990 bott 08 **(73) n17 t20 f18 b18.** Both nose and finish are disasters. Though there is a brief sweet peated revival on delivery, it is not enough to save this from being a rare Berry's dud. 55.6%. Berry Bros & Rudd.

Berry's Own Selection Laphroaig 1998 bott 09 **(87) n21.5** dry, spluttering peat fires; **t22** finely tuned peat-liquorice combo; **f21.5** reverts to drier self through the late signature of weak golden syrup; **b22** simple but effective. 58.7%. Berry Bros & Rudd.

Chieftain's Laphroaig 1997 chateau la Nethe finish, dist Oct 97 **(77) n19 t20 f19 b19.** Dull and off key. The nose even has a weird stale beer touch to it... I really fail to see how a classic distillery such as this needs the help of an obscure French vineyard..... ! An irritating way to mark the 800th new whisky of the book. 46%. nc ncf. Ian Macleod.

⁖ **The Cooper's Choice Laphroaig 1999 Aged 10 Years** refill butt no. 4211, bott 2009 **(85.5) n22; t22 f20 b21.5.** Playful, gristy smoke, light and shy to the point of being a little timid. Let down a little by the bitter finale. Pleasant enough, but goes through the paces a little. *46% nc ncf The Vintage Malt Whisky Co. Ltd.*

The Creative Whisky Company Exclusive Malts Laphroaig 1998 Aged 8 Years cask no. 103, dist Dec 98 **(90) n22 t23 f22.5 b22.5.** A bruiser for its age. *53.7%.*

⁖ **Duncan Taylor Collection Laphroaig 1997** cask no. 56363 **(88) n22** green tea, grist and peat ash; **t22** nervy start with little rhythm, but fun when the smoke and spices really get a grip; **f22** moves towards a hickory-Demerara-cocoa finale; **b22** a pea from the same pod as cask 56441, but more sweet cocoa and better balance. *54.7%*

⁖ **Duncan Taylor Collection Laphroaig 1997** cask no. 56441 **(86.5) n21.5 t21.5 f22 b21.5.** After the powder-dry nose, seriously sweet. Decent complexity. *54.8%*

⁖ **Duthies Laphroaig 11 Years Old (85) n22 t21 f21 b21.** A smidgen oilier than the norm with some citrus scattered among the peaty ashes. *46% Wm. Cadenhead Ltd.*

Exclusive Casks Laphroaig 1996 Aged 12 Years (79.5) n22 t20 f18.5 b19. The charming nose gives a subtle hint of the impending fire waters to be overcome. This is bloody hot stuff...! *52.4%. Chester Whisky & Liqueur Co.*

⁖ **Hart Brothers Laphroaig Aged 18 Years** dist Apr 90, bott Jun 08 **(90.5) n23.5** salty, cindery peat; a butterscotch flourish; **t23** superb delivery with excellent degree of citrussy sweetness to vanilla and smoke: classy layering; **f22** long, dries, back with a salty tang, a touch of liquorice but the malt remains intact; **b22.5** high quality whisky with effortless complexity. *46%. Hart Brothers Limited.*

⁖ **The John Milroy Selection Laphroaig 10 Years Old** hogshead, dist 1998, bott 2009 **(85.5) n22.5 t21.5 f20.5 b21.** After the dry, demure, if vaguely citrusy, nose, this becomes engulfed in attritional in-fighting between the smoke and vanilla. *60.4% Berry Bros & Rudd.*

⁖ **Kingsbury's Laphroaig 11 Years Old 1998 (93.5) n23** wow! Creamy peat....!!! So clean... **t24** soft, docile delivery followed by a fabulous thickening of treacle-sweetened Laphroaig cream-rice; the middle fills with all kinds of chocolate fudge; **f23.5** the smoke and chocolate continue their uniquely creamy way **b23** a Laphroaig chocolate bar. Beautiful. And very different. *61.8% Japan Import System Celtic Series*

Kingsbury's Laphroaig 1990 18 Years Old Cask Strength (86) n22 t21.5 f21.5 b21. The tight, ashy nose – with circling light citrus - is followed by the most cramped of deliveries where the hot barley grunts firm peat. Only towards the finish, where some natural caramels soften and sweeten, is there any room for complexity; but in finding it, a slight bitter oak note is revealed, too. *53.9%. Japan Import System.*

⁖ **Malts of Scotland Laphroaig 1996** bourbon hogshead, cask no. 5382, dist Jan 96, bott Mar 09 **(95) n23.5** when you aren't expecting a sherry cask – as I wasn't – the fresh and intact grape fair knocks you off your seat; **t24** outstanding mouth-feel, with the grape managing to absorb the wilder punches of the thick smoke; the middle ground is a comfortable but complex mix of juicy date, busy sugars...and peat....; **f23.5** very long with a thunder rumble of smoky spices and building vanillas and butterscotch; **b24** this is a very classy bottling. I can see the Islayphiles fighting to the death over each and every bottle of this classic Laphroaig. *58.5%*

⁖ **Malts of Scotland Laphroaig 1998** sherry butt, cask no. MoS 15, dist Dec 98, bott Jul 09 **(85) n22 t21 f21 b21.** Oily, sulkily peated and more tart than tartan. Sulphur-free, though, and a pat on the back for that alone. *55.5% 192 bottles.*

Montgomerie's Laphroaig 1990 (86.5) n22 t22 f21 b21.5. Laphroaig can from cask to cask be a touch lethargic. Here is one such dram. Loads of citrus and grist, this would have made decent blending fodder. But for those not looking to be shaken to their boots and want to be charmed instead, here you go. *46%. Montgomery & Co. Ltd.*

Montgomerie's Laphroaig 1990 cask no. M586, dist Oct 90, bott Jun 07 **(86) n22 t22 f20.5 b21.5.** Sweet, buxom smoky malt softly oiled and spiced in the right places. *46%.*

⁖ **Old & Rare Laphroaig Aged 20 Years** dist Mar 89, bott Aug 09 **(94) n23.5** both firm and rounded in its starchy vanilla opening; the smoke has faded over time and now appears happily integrated with the friendly oak; **t24** jam tart sweetness followed by a few waves of gristy peat and cocoa; **f23** just a succession of soft smoky vanilla plopping against the taste buds; even the mocha cannot be bothered to be anything other than perfectly sweetened; **b23.5** so comfortable, it's smoking a peaty pipe and wearing slippers. Brilliant. *58.1% Douglas Laing & Co Ltd. 174 bottles.*

Old Malt Cask Laphroaig Aged 12 Years refill hogshead, dist Oct 96, bott Feb 09 **(76.5) n18 t20.5 f19 b19.** What little influence the cask has is not particularly positive. *50%.*

⁖ **Old Malt Cask Laphroaig Aged 13 Years** refill hogshead, cask no. DL 5612, dist Oct 96, bott Nov 09 **(85) n21 t22 f21 b21.** a very competent cask. Laphroaig offers arguably the driest of all Islay's peaty noses. And this one is dry even by this distilleries own standards. Excellent for a cold, rainy night, though....but there is a touch of the Bowmores in style on the finish. *50% Douglas Laing & Co Ltd. 313 bottles.*

Old Malt Cask Laphroaig Aged 13 Years refill hogshead, dist Sep 94, bott Nov 07 **(87) n22 t22 f21 b22.** A dram not in the mood for complexity.... *50%. nc ncf. 370 bottles.*

Old Malt Cask Laphroaig Aged 13 Years refill hogshead, cask no. 4419, dist Sep 94, bott Jun 08 **(88.5) n23** dry, sooty; **t22** reluctantly sweeter at first, then the malty sugars blossom; **f21.5** dries, vanilla; **b22** clean, delicate and undemanding. *50%. nc ncf. 333 bottles.*

Old Malt Cask Laphroaig Aged 13 Years refill butt no. 3701, dist Apr 92, bott Jun 07 **(82) n21 t22 f19 b20.** Big peat but the bitterness reveals the end of a cask. *50%. 688 bottles.*

Old Malt Cask Laphroaig Aged 15 Years refill hogshead, cask no. 4066, dist 92, bott Dec 07 **(84.5) n21.5 t21.5 f20.5 b21.5.** Fragile oak but the complex peats are a treat. *50%. Douglas Laing.*

Old Malt Cask Laphroaig Aged 15 Years refill hogshead no. 3932, dist Apr 92, bott Oct 07 **(85) n20 t21.5 f22 b21.5.** Attractive, softly oiled and negotiates some less than perfect oak with complex aplomb. *50%. nc ncf. Douglas Laing. 343 bottles.*

Old Malt Cask Laphroaig Aged 15 Years refill hogshead, dist Mar 93, bott Aug 08 **(90) n22.5** busy with a decent peat prickle; **t23** beautiful oils link the sweeter gristy notes with the more lavish honeyed oak; beautifully paced and balanced; **f22** liquorice and a touch of hickory dry proceedings and add the required ballast; **b22.5** a malt which benefits from a good quality cask to match the even higher distilling: a delightful and complex experience. What a shame the distillery's own 15-y-o could not match this. *50%. Douglas Laing. 352 bottles.*

Old Malt Cask Laphroaig Aged 16 Years refill butt, dist Apr 92, bott Jan 09 **(75) n17 t19.5 f19.5 b19.** Sweet, fat, rather shapeless and never quite gets its act together. *50%. Douglas Laing. 691 bottles.*

Old Malt Cask Laphroaig Aged 18 Years refill hogshead no. 3974, dist Nov 89, bott Nov 07 **(88.5) n23 t21.5 f22 b22.** A lightweight in some ways but the seduction is wonderful. *50%. nc ncf. Douglas Laing. 288 bottles.*

Old Malt Cask Laphroaig Aged 18 Years (84.5) n21 t22 f20.5 b21. Pleasant, light, gristy malt. Does its best not to be noticed. *50%. Douglas Laing*

Old Malt Cask Laphroaig Aged 18 Years (89) n22.5 dry, ashy, tight: fabulous...! **t22** firm barley is backed by a tat-a-tat strafing of spices on the tastebuds; some citrus lightens things; **f22** the spice grumbles on, as do those sharp, almost fresh-cut grassy, notes; **b22.5** hard to believe the age of this guy. Take the one away and you'd believe it: absolutely no oak spoiling the show. *50%. Douglas Laing.*

Old Malt Cask Laphroaig Aged 18 Years refill hogshead, dist Nov 89, bott Aug 08 **(92.5) n23.5** beautifully interlaced sweetness and dryness to the peat: a sprig of lavender and a small cube of chocolate fudge helps lighten the earthier backbone; **t23.5** quite beautiful delivery with the peat a constant, a regular full but not over demanding presence; again the sweet-dry delicate liquorice delivery pushes all the right buttons; **f22.5** a very even fade, again with the peat taking the lead and pulsing gently to the finish; a few delicate dark sugars balance the vanillas: technically spot on for the age; **b23** classic for age and distillery. *50%. Douglas Laing. 229 bottles.*

Old Malt Cask Laphroaig Aged 19 Years rum barrel no. 3804, dist Mar 88, bott Aug 07 **(90) n23 t22 f22.5 b22.5.** Rum finishes do have curious ability to kick things around and produce attitude. No exception here with this very different slant on sweet peat. A one-off classic. *50%. Douglas Laing. 324 bottles.*

⠿ **Old Malt Cask Laphroaig Aged 20 Years** sherry hogshead, cask no. DL 5699, dist Mar 89, bott Dec 09 **(70) n16 t19 f17 b18.** A dose of the sulphurs, I'm afraid. *50%. Douglas Laing & Co Ltd. 286 bottles.*

Old Malt Cask Laphroaig Aged 20 Years sherry hogshead, dist Mar 89, bott Apr 09 **(91) n23** a liberal dose of cream sherry gives the aroma real weight especially with the oak not willing to be outperformed; **t22** thick grape-smoke delivery, though perhaps missing rhythm early on; **f23.5** re-settles superbly for the best part of the experience with all three major players – grape, smoke and oak – interacting with a degree of suavity; **b22.5** weighty yet works with an improbable degree of harmony given the major players looking for top billing. *50%. Douglas Laing.259 bottles.*

Old Malt Cask Laphroaig Aged 21 Years refill hogshead, dist Nov 87, bott Jan 09 **(77.5) n20.5 t20 f18 b19.** Aggressive in part despite the sugary mask. *50%. 439 bottles.*

Old Malt Cask Laphroaig Aged 21 Years rum barrel, dist Mar 88, bott Apr 09 **(84) n21 t20.5 f21.5 b21.** Very sharp, very sweet and very brittle; the smoke gets lost somewhere along the way, re-emerging late on....very. *50%. Douglas Laing. 311 bottles.*

Premier Barrel Laphroaig Aged 7 Years dist May 01, bott Feb 09 **(83.5) n23.5 t21 f19 b20.** Despite the tired, bitter cask finish, this is one to simply stick your snout in. *46%. Douglas Laing. 366 bottles.*

Premier Barrel Laphroaig Aged 7 Years (85.5) n20.5 t22 f22 b21. From an unprepossessing nose comes a malt with a lot to say for itself. The peat is orderly and the fudge on the finish is a smoky delight. *46%. Douglas Laing. 370 bottles.*

Premier Barrel Laphroaig Aged 8 Years (85.5) n22 t21.5 f21 b21. Decent, gristy fare. *46.0%. nc ncf. Douglas Laing. 374 bottles.*

Premier Barrel Laphroaig Aged 9 Years (89.5) n23 t23 f21.5 b22. Some of the elements which make this up are pure, unadulterated joy....and I think the age is the key. *46%.*

Provenance Laphroaig Aged 8 Years refill hogshead no. 3868-3869, dist autumn 98, bott autumn 07 **(88) n22.5 t23 f21 b21.5.** Bit of a mixed up kid but really lovely. *46%.*

Provenance Laphroaig Aged 8 Years refill hogshead no. 4203, dist summer 99, bott spring 08 **(88) n22 t22.5 f22 b21.5.** Very similar to the previous Prov Laphroaig. Quality identical, characteristics similar but reaches same point from slightly different direction. *46%. nc ncf.*

Provenance Laphroaig Aged 8 Years refill hogshead, dist spring 01, bott spring 09 **(88) n21** non-committal but delicate; **t23** deft integration of muscovado sugars and smoke with a stunning liquorice follow through; **f22** a slow rising of spices adds an edge to the dusty but sweet smoke; **b22** lots of whisky to get your tastebuds round despite the limited oak influence. But clean and compelling throughout with just the right amount of oomph. *46%.*

Provenance Laphroaig Aged 10 Years refill hogshead, dist autumn 98, bott winter 09 **(87.5) n21** is there a cleaner, lighter Laphroaig...? **t22.5** the entire outline of the malt is bounded by sweet, gristy sugars; the inner notes are pillow-soft peat; **f22** stays on its most gentle course despite the vanillas getting a bit frantic; **b22** a real pussycat. *46%. Douglas Laing.*

Robert Burns Laphroaig 9 Years Old (90.5) n24 t22.5 f22 b22 A whisky beyond its years. *53.6%. TasTToe, Belgium. 87 bottles.*

❧ **Scotch Malt Whisky Society Cask 29.82 Aged 10 Years** refill hogshead, dist Jun 99 **(91.5) n23.5** wonderful. No off notes. No threat of bitterness further down the line from a sub standard cask. Just an excellent salty vanilla/sweet smoke interplay, helped along by the softest of oils....; **t23** my prayers were answered: on the nose I suspected and then fervently hoped the delivery would include some peaty spice prick'e to ensure the oils don't dominate. Textbook stuff: everything I had hoped for and just a hint of hickory means more; **f22.5** now the oils get a grip, but the lightly salted coastal theme is played to the very long end; **b22.5** the detailed blueprint for how a 10-year-old Laphroaig might be expected to taste for age and bourbon cask type. *56.4% 297 bottles.*

Scotch Malt Whisky Society Cask 29.67 Aged 16 Years refill butt, dist Oct 91 **(84) n21 t23 f19 b21.** Appears to be some grape flouncing about with the massive peat. Not exactly a marriage in heaven, but the shear enormity of it all makes for a tale to tell over dinner. Oh, some gooseberry pops up from time to time, by the way... off-key off-beat and actually at times unpleasant; this most likely is a faulty cask. "Love it or hate it..." their advertising blurb went (without crediting or paying me, the swine!). In this case, like me, you'll probably do both. Whoever is choosing the Laphroaig casks needs a kick up the arse. *53.5%*

Scotch Malt Whisky Society Cask 29.66 Aged 18 Years refill butt, dist Nov 89 **(83.5) n21.5 t20 f21 b21.** Hmmm! Nothing like the quality I'd expect...Overly aggressive. *53.7%*

Scotch Malt Whisky Society Cask 29.68 Aged 18 Years refill butt, dist Nov 89 **(90.5) n22.5 t23 f22.5 b22.5** The balance between sweet and dry is rarely better. There is no mistaking this distillery's fingerprint of excellence. *54%*

Scotch Malt Whisky Society Cask 29.74 Aged 18 Years refill hogshead, dist Oct 90 **(85) n21 t22 f21 b21.** Pleasant, sweet, lightly peated and a tad monotonous. *51.5%*

Scotch Malt Whisky Society Cask 29.75 Aged 18 Years refill hogshead, dist Oct 90 **(90.5) n21.5** salty, lightly smoked and teasingly unbalanced; **t23.5** absolutely jives on the palate with a lively flurry of nibbling, sharp peaty notes partnered by a sweet muscovado-barley theme. Surprisingly salivating; **f22.5** even the old-grand-dad vanillas have a spring to their step; **b23** top rank entertainment from a cask which is the antithese of its fuddy-duddy stay-at-home sister 29.74. *51.5%*

Scotch Malt Whisky Society Cask 29.76 Aged 18 Years refill hogshead, dist Oct 90 **(84.5) n21.5 t21.5 f21 b20.5.** Rotund, sweet and caramel-clad. *51.3%*

❧ **Scotch Malt Whisky Society Cask 29.83 Aged 20 Years** refill butt, dist Nov 89 **(78.5) n20 t22.5 f17 b19.** OK, I like it....sort of. And for some of you out there, that won't be enough. You'll be demanding to know why I'm not swooning just being in the same company as this stuff. Sure, it's sassy and dazzling and tripping over itself with all kinds of meaningful fruity-peaty stuff on delivery; and the mouth feel, the oils the sweetness ratio are spot on and such like. But there was a warning on the nose about the cask. Not sulphur. Just a poor cask. And the finish confirms it. Sorry: it's a bit of a dud. *52.2% 561 bottles.*

The Whisky Agency Laphroaig 8 Year Old dist 01, bott 09 **(89) n22** a Highland hearth; **t23** crisp barley at first, sweet smoke with a light salty tang; **f22** oils out slightly while the phenols take their time to disperse; **b22** exactly the kind of young, near flawless dram you should have in your hand at a ceilidh...and in the other, a woman of a similar description. *59.1%. The Whisky Agency, Germany.*

⟬ **The Whisky Agency Laphroaig 11 Years Old** dist 1998, bott 2010 **(86.5) n21.5 t22.5 f21.5 b21.** A lovely, if rather half-cocked whisky. All the fruit is there, the oils are in place and the smoke is ashy and delicate. But needs the missing ingredient of oak to bring it all together. *59.6%*

The Whisky Agency Laphroaig 12 Year Old dist 96, bott 09 **(81) n23 t21 f18 b19.** Superb nose with all kinds of complex ashy possibilities. But the cask errs on the unfriendly side with a disappointing degree of bitterness. *56.9%. The Whisky Agency, Germany.*

The Whisky Agency Laphroaig 18 Year Old dist 90, bott 08 **(88) n22** clean barley, clean smoke and good balance between oils and ash; **t22** again, more battles between bitter-sweet and oils and ash...beautifully made malt, that's for sure; **f22** the oils win as the vanillas are absorbed; **b22** not entirely complex of the flavour front, but certainly in composition and structure. *56%. The Whisky Agency, Germany.*

The Whisky Fair Laphroaig Aged 9 Years refill sherry butt, dist 88, bott 07 **(92) n24 t23 f22.5 b22.5.** A kind of bigger more full-on version of Tasttoe. Wonderful. *56.7%.*

The Whisky Fair Laphroaig 1998 bott 09 **(82) n21 t20 f21 b20.** Peaty and pleasant. But far too fat, oily, sweet and graceless for greatness. *57.1%. The Whisky Fair, Germany.*

LINKWOOD
Speyside, 1820. Diageo. Working.

Linkwood 12 Years Old db **(79) n21 t22 f17 b19.** Not a patch on previous bottlings, with the usual clarity lost to a very confused fruit-caramel theme. Especially on the finish. *43%*

Linkwood 26 Year Old Port Finish dist 81, bott 08 db **(85) n20 t24 f20.5 b20.5.** Can't say that either nose or finish do it for me. But the delivery is brilliant: the enormity and luxurious sweetness of the grape leaves you simply purring and rolling your eyes in delight. *56.9%*

Linkwood 26 Year Old Rum Finish dist 81, bott 08 db **(89.5) n23.5** sharp, flinty; enticing nose prickle; **t23.5** lots of juice, then a touch of spruce as the oak kicks in; the sweetness is delicate and softer on development than many rum finishes; **f21** becomes dependent on cream toffee; **b21.5** a real touch of the rum toffee raisin candy to this one. *56.5%*

Linkwood 26 Year Old Sweet red Wine dist 81, bott 08 db **(89) n22.5** punchy, salty and lively; distinct sherry-custard trifle; wine and oak together spin out the spice; **t23** perky delivery, again with spice to the fore; juicy grape and a lively layering of oak; **f21** dulls out slightly as it sweetens, again with a cream toffee softness; **b22** juicy, spicy: doesn't stint on complexity. *56.5%*

Linkwood 1974 Rare Malt db **(79) n20 t21 f19 b19.** Wobbles about the palate in search of a story and balance. Finds neither but some of the early moments, though warming, offer very decent malt. The best bit follows a couple of seconds after – and lasts as long. *55%*

A.D. Rattray Linkwood 1983 cask no. 5711 **(86) n21 t22.5 f21.5 b21.** Very sweet: white sugar cubes dropped into a whisky toddy. Pleasant and well spiced. *53%*

Berry's Own Selection Linkwood 1993 bott 07 **(83) n20.5 t21 f21 b20.5.** Malty, if standard, stuff. *46%. Berry Bros & Rudd.*

⟬ **Cadenhead's Authentic Collection Linkwood-Glenlivet 1989** port wood, bott Feb 10 **(90.5) n22.5** a back-seat fruitiness allows the malt and spice to do the driving. Pretty weighty for a Linkwood; **t23** a fabulous chewathon on delivery with the oak adding extra degrees of weight yet never compromising the understated sweetness; there is a vague pulpy fruitiness, too....more skin than meat; **f22.5** long with a rich and very deep degree of medium roast Java coffee; **b22.5** a genuine degree of complexity to this one. Beautiful. *55.4%. 256 bottles.*

Chieftain's Linkwood Aged 13 Years French oak **(72) n19 t18 f17 b18.** Overly sweet and latterly furry. *43%. Ian Macleod.*

Chieftain's Linkwood 15 Years Old fino sherry finish, dist Oct 92 **(71) n19 t18 f19 b19.** The incongruous strands of peat appear only to make this an even more muddled dram than usual. *46%. nc ncf. Ian Macleod Distillers.*

⟬ **The Coopers Choice Linkwood 1995 Aged 13 Years (89) n22.5** just can't get enough of that grassy barley; **t22.5** mouth-watering, crisp with just enough give for the gristy sugars to meet the light vanilla; **f22** lots of natural but attractive caramel; **b22** delightful and delicate. *46% The Vintage Malt Whisky Co. Ltd*

Dewar Rattray Linkwood 1996 cask no. 3982, dist May 96, bott Mar 07 **(73) n18 t18 f19 b18.** Yet another dud from Linkwood. When are the Independents going to give younger malts from this distillery the widest berth possible? *57.7%*

⋰⋱ **Dun Bheagan Linkwood Aged 12 Years** hogshead, dist Dec 97 **(82) n20.5 t21.5 f19.5 b20.5.** Above average spirit let down by a below average cask. *43% Ian Macleod*

Dun Bheagan Linkwood 1993 14 Years Old bourbon cask no. 4702, dist April 93, bott 07 **(76) n18 t20 f19 b19.** If all the whiskies I tasted were this sweet I wouldn't have any teeth left by the time I'd finished writing the book... *56.1%. Ian Macleod Distillers. 300 bottles.*

Dun Bheagan Linkwood 1993 14 Years Old bourbon cask no. 4704, dist April 93, bott 07 **(84.5) n21 t21 f21 b21.5.** Distinctly more malt punching through the sugars. Attractively spiced, too. *56.6%. Ian Macleod Distillers. 306 bottles.*

⋰⋱ **Fine Old Malt Whisky Linkwood 1973** bourbon cask **(80) n21 t20 f19 b20.** Here and there a graceful cameo is performed, especially by the odd highfaluting, debonair barley note. But this one is simply several summers past its best. *49.7% Speciality Drinks Ltd. Bottled for TWE's 10th Anniversary.*

⋰⋱ **Gordon & MacPhail Distillery Label Linkwood 15 Years Old** (62.5) n16 t16.5 f15 b15. The trouble with bottling a 15-year-old from this distillery is that it falls right into the middle of the timeline when they were having a nightmare with their casks...and my word: doesn't this one just prove it..!! *43% Gordon & MacPhail*

Gordon & MacPhail Linkwood 1972 (87) n22 t22 f21 b22. No yield to this hard-as-nails but fun bottling. *43%. Rare Vintage range.*

Hart Brothers Linkwood Aged 10 Years dist Feb 98, bott Mar 08 **(91.5) n23 t22.5 f23.** Now some serious complexity as the oak wakes up and begins to create butterscotch and salt patterns...so the salivation continues... **b23** I had almost given up hope of seeing a Linkwood as good as this again. A ray of malty sunshine. *46%. Hart Brothers Limited.*

⋰⋱ **James MacArthur's Fine Malt Selection Linkwood Aged 12 Years** bott Apr 10 **(87.5) n23.5** if you are looking to discover what is meant by a "clean, grassy Speysider"...then you can do no better than this...especially if you are looking for a "nibble of citrus", too...; **t22** clean... grassy and very...errr...Speysidey; **f20.5** annoyingly bitter oak, but offset by late spice; **b21.5** a reminder that when Linkwood is good, it can be quite charming... *40% For Harry's Pub Sweden.*

Kingsbury Finest & Rarest Linkwood 32 Years Old 1973 bourbon cask **(92.5) n24 t23 f22.5 b23.** Absolutely charming old malt at the limit of its powers. *49.5%. nc ncf.*

⋰⋱ **Kingsbury's "The Selection" Linkwood 7 Years Old 1999** (84.5) n21.5 t21.5 f20.5 **b21.** Clean, light, refreshing and entirely non-taxing. *43% Japan Import System*

⋰⋱ **Malts of Scotland Linkwood 1989** bourbon hogshead no. 1826, dist Apr 89, bott Jan 10 **(79.5) n20 t21.5 f18.5 b19.5.** Malt, initially sweet, but a tad tangy. *53.5%. 192 bottles.*

Northern Light Linkwood 1995 Cask Strength port finish cask no. Q8311 **(77) n18.5 t19 f20 b19.5.** The nose is straight from the sweaty armpit school; the cloying sweetness takes some time to unravel. *51.2%. Qualityworld. Denmark.*

Old Malt Cask Linkwood Aged 10 Years refill hogshead DL3539, dist Dec 1996, bott Apr 2007 **(75.5) n19 t19 f18.5 b19.** Not a bad dram. No off notes, other than the actual Linkwood persona. Just doesn't really say or do anything. *50%. nc ncf. Douglas Laing.*

⋰⋱ **Old Malt Cask Linkwood Aged 13 Years** bourbon cask no. DL 6309, dist May 97, bott May 10 **(88) n23** excellent and quite elegantly clean malt; crisp and citrusy in the occasional house style; **t22** much more richly textured than many examples from this distillery, with the story being exclusively about the malt; **f21.5** love those late spices; **b21.5** a beautiful, unassuming Speysider. *50% Douglas Laing. 276 bottles.*

Old Masters Linkwood Aged 18 Years cask no. 2011 dist 89, bott 07 **(86) n21 t22 f21.5 b21.5.** If in search of a decent, pretty unspoiled Linkwood, you could do a lot worse than this. Still oversweet and shapeless, but that's Linkwood for you. *50.1%. James MacArthur & Co. Ltd.*

Old Malt Cask Linkwood Aged 25 Years refill hogshead, dist Apr 83, bott Oct 08 **(84.5) n22 t21.5 f21 b20.** Proof that whiskies can be too sweet. This one is like molten sugar bedeviled by spice. Have to say its enjoyable, but you can get too much of a good thing...!! *50%.*

Provenance Linkwood Aged 11 Years bourbon barrel, dist spring 97, bott autumn 08 **(81.5) n20 t21 f20.5 b20.** Sugared almonds. Untaxing. *46%. Douglas Laing.*

⋰⋱ **Private Collection Linkwood 1959 (90)** n23.5 that peculiar hint of tinned tomatoes you sometimes get with pre-historic casks, especially sherry butts, is on full view here; also a hint of advocaat and cream strawberry sponge; **t22** lush, but as it melts in the mouth, a few splinters are left high and dry; some major bourbon-style fingerprints all over this one; **f22.5** bitters, but saved by a very lightly sugared, creamy mocha; **b22** one of those which from the nose you know exactly how it is going to taste. And that means a lot of oak. Even so, a most agreeable very late night dram. *45% Gordon & MacPhail*

Scotch Malt Whisky Society Cask 39.65 Aged 11 Years refill barrel, dist May 96 **(82.5) n20** t22 f20 b20.5. Malty, clean, sweet, citric, simple: the stuff of blends. 54.6%

Scotch Malt Whisky Society Cask 39.69 Aged 26 Years refill hogshead, dist Oct 82 **(87.5)** n21.5 sharp barley; sharper oak; t22 delightfully juicy, salivating and clean; f22 attractive dusting of latte b22 easy going and delicate. 55.8%

Scotch Malt Whisky Society Cask 39.70 Aged 26 Years refill hogshead, dist Oct 82 **(83) n20.5 t21.5 f21 b20.5.** Typical Linkwood maltiness; typical Linkwood unsympathetic cask. 55.9%

⋙ **Scotch Malt Whisky Society Cask 39.72 Aged 26 Years** refill hogshead, dist Oct 82 **(85) n21.5 t23 f20 b20.5.** Perfectly enjoyable sweet malt delivery – even with a degree of early richness and fizz - but dulls out at the end considerably. 54.6% *Scotch Malt Whisky Society. 230 bottles.*

⋙ **The Secret Treasures Linkwood 1996** oak cask no. 8761, bott no. 372, dist Oct 96, bott Sep 07 **(89.5) n22.5 t22.5 f22 b22.5.** An aging second fill or young third fill cask allowing the barley to do its stuff. Charming. 43% *Haromex Development GmbH, Germany. 492 bottles.*

⋙ **The Whisky Agency Linkwood 1973 Aged 36 Years (91.5) n22.5 t24 f22 b22.5.** Droolingly beautiful. 49.9%

LITTLEMILL

Lowland, 1772. Demolished.

Littlemill Aged 8 Years db **(84) n20 t22 f21 b21.** Aged 8 Years, claims the neck of the dumpy bottle, which shows a drawing of a distillery that no longer exists, as it has done for the last quarter of a century. Well, double that and you'll be a lot closer to the real age of this deliciously sweet, chewy and increasingly spicy chap. And it is about as far removed from the original 8-y-o fire-water it once was as is imaginable. 40%.

Littlemill 1964 db **(82) n21 t20 f21 b20.** A soft-natured, bourbony chap that shows little of the manic tendencies that made this one of Scotland's most-feared malts. Talk about mellowing with age... 40%

Berry's' Best Lowland Littlemill 12 Years Old (71) n17 t19 f17 b18. Astonishingly tame by Littlemill standards. But, though bad form to speak ill of the dead, pretty naff. 43%

Connoisseurs Choice Littlemill 1991 (73.5) n19 t18 f18.5 b18. Remind me never to wallpaper a room when I have a bottle of this with me. A momentary lapse of concentration could be disastrous for my insides...and the plaster. Yep: pure Littlemill! 43%. *Gordon & MacPhail.*

Dun Bheagan Littlemill Aged 21 Years Sherry Finish (74) n20 t19 f17 b18. Mutton dressed as lamb. 46%. *Ian Macleod.*

⋙ **Hart Brothers Littlemill Aged 16 Years** dist Feb 92, bott Dec 08 **(77.5) n18 t20.5 f18 b20.** Among some of the last Littlemill ever made, this isn't too bad with lots of light barley notes and not a single tooth in site, though you can see it is intrinsically flawed. Curiously, there is almost a touch of German malt to this, which is hardly surprising when you consider the type of still they were using. 46% *Hart Brothers Ltd*

⋙ **Hart Brothers Littlemill Aged 20 Years** dist Oct 88, bott Dec 08 **(71.5) n18 t19 f16.5 b18.** Sweet. Firm. But...well...weird. Collectably so, I'd say...!! 46% *Hart Brothers Ltd*

⋙ **Malts of Scotland Littlemill 1990** bourbon barrel no. 915, dist Mar 90, bott Jan 10 **(91)** n23 really not what I expected at all: a clean gristiness giving excellent weight to the quasi Canadian corn-oak notes. Adorably curious... t23 now this is too good to be true: the taste buds simply salivate to the reverberating malt; a few dud oak notes but easily overcome by the marzipan; f22.5 more of Lubek's best with a little spice, too...; b22.5 Sukinda Singh has somehow bagged himself an eminently drinkable Littlemill. As if to prove, against the odds, that such a thing exists. He sometimes amazes me, that bloke. How does he do it...? 54.3% *Malts of Scotland. 192 bottles.*

Murray McDavid Littlemill 1991 Aged 16 lot 07-1700 **(76.5) n18 t20 f19 b19.5.** The aroma gleefully strips all living flesh – and hair – from your nostrils. The big barley back up works for a while. 46%. *Norway. 480 bottles.*

Old Malt Cask Littlemill Aged 16 Years refill hogshead no. 4064, dist Oct 91, bott Jan 08 **(80.5) n18 t20.5 f21 b21.** Anorexic, naked barley. Relatively friendly and embracing by Littlemill standards. 50%.

Old Malt Cask Littlemill Aged 16 Years refill hogshead no. 3840, dist Mar 91, bott Aug 07 **(77) n18 t19 f20.5 b19.5.** Douglas Laing must be employing a Littlemill tamer among their staff. Another, clean, malty inoffensive if strictly limited bottling. 50%. *Douglas Laing. 332 bottles.*

Old Malt Cask Littlemill Aged 17 Years refill hogshead, dist Mar 92, bott Mar 09 **(72) n18** t19 f16 b17. Sweet barley but the finish is bitter: the kind of badly produced malt this distillery was once a byword for. 50%. *Douglas Laing. 320 bottles.*

⋄ **Old Malt Cask Littlemill Aged 18 Years** refill hogshead no. DL 6201, dist Nov 91, bott May 10 (**68.5**) n18 t18 f15.5 b17. Can you imagine....? I am tasting this directly after the 18 year old Lochside. Probably what the term "from the sublime to the ridiculous" was invented for..... *50% Douglas Laing. 174 bottles.*

Old & Rare Littlemill Aged 19 Years dist Mar 90, bott Mar 09 (**76**) n19 t20 f18 b19. Some of the old distilled-from-razors faults are there, but the extra zeal on the barley has helped iron out the worst of the kinks over the years. *55.4%. Douglas Laing. 333 bottles.*

Scotch Malt Whisky Society Cask 97.11 Aged 18 Years 1st fill barrel, dist Mar 90 (**76.5**) n18.5 t19 f19 b19. Thin, hot, a little jammy fruitiness at the death. But there goes the last of my enamel: a barium meal of a malt. *56%*

Scotch Malt Whisky Society Cask 97.13 Aged 18 Years 1st fill barrel, dist Mar 90 (**78.5**) n18.5 t19 f20 b20. Morbidly pleasantish concentrated barley sweetness: the perfect malt for fire-eaters fresh out of matches. *55.6%*

Scotch Malt Whisky Society Cask 97.16 Aged 18 Years 1st fill barrel, dist Mar 90 (**83.5**) n19.5 t22 f21 b21. Much better cask than the norm, allowing the barley to churn out some juicy notes and no little natural caramel and vanilla. But still a traditional Littlemill viciousness to the bite. *56.4%*

Scotch Malt Whisky Society Cask 97.17 Aged 19 Years 1st fill barrel, dist Feb 90 (**88.5**) n21 sabre-toothed and fair warning of what is coming; t23.5 barley in its most explosive and concentrated form, even offering a degree of citrus and sweetness; the bite is more entertaining than damaging but hold on to your seats, this is some ride...; f22 some tight and mildly bitter oak but the huge barley hangs on in there; b22 what great fun!! Almost like a long-lost old baddie we have come to love. Massive entertainment for the palate. *58.7%*

⋄ **Scotch Malt Whisky Society Cask 97.19 Aged 19 Years** 1st fill barrel, dist Mar 90 (**84**) n21.5 t21.5 f20 b21. Classic glue and paint stripper combo dissolves your teeth in seconds. For masochistic malt lovers with a sense of danger... *55.6% Scotch Malt Whisky Society. 80 bottles.*

⋄ **Scotch Malt Whisky Society Cask 97.20 Aged 19 Years** 1st fill barrel, dist Mar 90 (**87.5**) n21 a light corn whisky style normally found in Georgia, USA...; t22.5 delicate (now there's a term I never expected to use under this distillery) barley delivery which plays quietly with the gathering sawdusty oak; f22 soft vanillas and natural caramels calm down a threatening spice attack but still enough barley around for a pleasant finish; b22 much better behaved. Even a touch of elegance from this one. Hang on: it's Littlemill...I must have swallowed a few by mistake.... *54.4% Scotch Malt Whisky Society. 48 bottles.*

Scott's Selection Littlemill 1990 bott 07 (**77.5**) n18 t19 f21 b19.5. For those who like chillied barley. How many ways are there of describing paint stripper? *57%*

LOCH LOMOND

Highland (Southwestern), 1966. Loch Lomond Distillers. Working.

Craiglodge sherry wood cask 139, dist 26 Mar 98 db (**72**) n17 t19 f18 b18. Cloying, off-key, rough...and they're the good points. The nose of sherry and smoke don't gel and it never recovers. *45%*

Craiglodge Peated Cask No.137 Distillery Select sherry hogshead, dist 26 Mar 98, bott 9 May 07 db (**85**) n18 t24 f21 b22. Good grief!! Have you even been run over and then re-trampled on by a sherry-peat steam roller? Well, now I know for a fact I have. I've been in this game a long, long time. But I haven't, ever, encountered anything quite like this.... The sherry (oloroso presumably) must still have been slightly sloshing around the bottom of the butt when the big, smoky whisky was filled into it. The result is a nose that defies description but demands witnesses so the tale can be passed on to future generations and an arrival to the palate which at once amazes, charms and, ultimately, mugs. To be honest, the sheer gloss on the arrival is stunning and unquestionably beautiful but there are many issues left unresolved on the madcap (iron in the spirit-style) finish. There are only 150 bottles of this. Get one. Because you will have something to discuss at dinner parties for the rest of your life... *45%. 150 bottles.*

Croftengea cask no. 24, dist 22 Jan 98 db (**87**) n22 pungent young peat, bracing, clean and even mildly salty; t22 refreshing barley with coffee/smoke double act; f21 vanilla and dry toast; b22 what a difference a cask makes: entirely together and charming. *45%*

Croftengea American Oak Cask No. 32 dist Jan 97, bott Jun 07 db (**91**) n21.5 t23.5 f23 b23. A tad off key, but the enormity of the sweet oils and peat just wins your heart. This is big, mildly flawed, but stunningly enjoyable whisky. *45%. 410 bottles.*

Croftengea Heavily Peated Cask No.1 Distillery Select sherry butt, dist 3 Mar 03, bott 10 May 07 db (**94**) n23 t24 f23 b24 Fabulous knife and fork malt that doesn't even try to look pretty on the plate....let alone the palate. *45%. 885 bottles.*

Glen Douglas Cask No. 1 Distillery Select madeira puncheon, dist 23 Sep 02, bott 08 May 07 db **(89) n22 t21 f23 b23.** Not exactly firing on all cylinders, with the odd note way out of tune. But very different... and delicious. *45%. 910 bottles.*

Inchfad 2001 Heavily Peated cask no. 665 dist 14 Feb 01 db **(80) n20 t21 f19 b20.** Pretty atypical of this particular malt. Missing the fruity peat kick that comes with the big peat. In fact, what big peat? An underwhelming example. *45%*

Inchfad 2001 Heavily Peated cask no. 666, dist 14 Feb 01 db **(87) n22 t23 f21 b21.** One cask on and so much more in tune. From the same distillate, but an excellent example of how a better quality cask can allow the malt to thrive. Perhaps the cask numbers are the wrong way round...!! *45%*

Inchfad Cask No. 27 Distillery Select American oak, dist 15 Mar 01, bott 3 May 07 db **(90) n22 t23 f22 b23.** A beautiful malt that shows stunning maturity; very individualistic. *45%. 375 bottles.*

Inchfad Cask No. 4359 Distillery Select freshly charred American oak, dist 18 Dec 02, bott 2 May 07 db **(83) n20 t22 f20 b21.** A tad new- makey though the barley is slapped on thick and to eye watering effect. *45%. 445 bottles.*

Inchmurrin Madeira puncheon cask no. 1, dist May 02, bott Apr 07 db **(78.5) n17.5 t21 f20 b20.** A brave and almost successful attempt to disguise that Inchmurrin is by far the worst of the Loch Lomond styles. *45%. 685 bottles.*

Inchmurrin American oak cask no. 414, dist Jan 03, bott Apr 07 db **(68.5) n16.5 t18 f17 b17.** The last time I saw I saw a nose this badly broken I was covering boxing in Nigeria over 30 years ago. Hardly a knockout. *45%. 450 bottles.*

Inchmurrin 12 Years Old db **(86.5) n21.5 t22 f21.5 b21.5.** A significantly improved dram which is a bit of a malt soup. Love the Demerara injection. *40%* ☉ ☉

Inchmurrin Cask No. 1 Distillery Select Madeira puncheon, dist May 02, bott Apr 07 db **(86) n20 t22 f22 b22.** Some lovely oils paint a chewy, beautifully well-balanced malt. The nose drops it down a few points, but worth a go for the curvy body alone. Look forward to seeing a second cask of this one day. *45%. 685 bottles.*

Inchmurrin Organic Cask No. 3946 Distillery Select organic French oak, dist 28 Jul 00, bott 01 May 07 db **(74) n19 t19 f18 b18.** Another poor French cask accounts for a promising malt. In terms of whisky, they should be outlawed. *45%. 410 bottles.*

⋯ **Inchmurrin Single Cask Distillery Select** Madeira puncheon no. 1, dist May 02, bott Apr 07 db **(74.5) n18 t21 f17.5 b18.** Malty and fulsome. But feinty, too. *45% Loch Lomond Distillers. 685 bottles.*

⋯ **Loch Lomond 18 Years Old** db **(78.5) n19 t21 f19 b19.5.** A demanding, oily malt which is a long way from technical excellence but is no slouch on the chocolate nougat front. *43%*

Loch Lomond 21 Years Old db **(89.5) n22.5** a real chunky fella with all kinds of melted fruit and chocolate bar properties; a few oily nuts, too..., **t23** the usual fruitcake feel to this, plus the Demerara sugar topping; **f22** light oils carry vanilla and cocoa; **b22** a little while since I last tasted this, and pretty close to exactly how I remember it. Seems to revel in its own enormity! *43%* ☉ ☉

⋯ **Loch Lomond Copper Pot Still 1966** db **(92) n23** the naturalness of the interplay between clean, fresh grape and a bournony, kumquat-studded oak is enough to make you purr....; **t23.5** soft and sensual delivery, the grape entwines itself around the palate but without ever offering pressure; light spices and more tannin-enriched vanilla supply the weight; **f23** lightly sweetened barley, but still those spices fizz and the delicate mocha is a further treat...; **b22.5** shows remarkably little wear and tear for its great age. A gentleman of a whisky. *45%*

Loch Lomond Gavin's Single Highland Malt dist 96, bott 07 db **(90.5) n23 t23 f22.5 b22.** Ester-fuelled and fabulous. *45%. nc ncf.*

Loch Lomond No Age Statement db **(74.5) n18 t20 f18 b18.5.** Still feinty and out of sync, though the lively sugars try to compensate. *40%* ☉ ☉

⋯ **Loch Lomond Single Highland Peated Malt** db **(74) n16.5 t20 f19 b18.5.** Feints and peat simultaneously: not something you happen upon very often. Thankfully. *46%*

Duncan Taylor The NC2 Range Rhosdhu 1995 Aged 11 Years (79.5) n18 t21 f20 b20.5 The feinty nose is compensated for somewhat, and logically, by the enormity of the body and corresponding oils. *46%*

Scotch Malt Whisky Society Cask 122.16 Aged 15 Years (Croftengea) refill barrel, dist Sep 92 **(95.5) n24.5 t24 f23 b24.** Now this Croftengea is the kind of stuff I work with in the lab. And it is sublime....the finest I think Loch Lomond produces on the malt front. In fact, in this form forget just the distillery: there aren't many malts on earth which can touch this. *59.4%*

LOCHSIDE

Highland (Eastern), 1957–1992. Demolished.

Connoisseurs Choice Lochside 1991 refill bourbon barrel, dist 91, bott 08 **(68)** n18 t19 f15 b16. Sweet delivery and nutty at first. Then nasty. *43%. Gordon & MacPhail.*

Old Malt Cask Lochside Aged 14 Years dist Oct 90 **(94)** n24 bedazzling with a rare firmness to the barley and lucid grassy presence which suggests a whisky considerably younger; **t23** every bit as mouthwatering and charming as the nose suggests with a delicate digression from the barley towards a neat cocoa influx; **f23** really beautifully balanced with a light infusion of vanilla and toast – and a dash of marmalade? – to make for a serene finale; **b24** when a distillery capable of making whisky this good is lost to us for ever, I could almost weep. *50%.*

⚬⚬ **Old Malt Cask Lochside Aged 18 Years** refill hogshead no. DL 6303, dist Oct 91, bott Jun 10 **(96)** n24 attractively floral with fabulous citrus byways; **t24** the arrival is one of the most delicate caresses: although there is an immediate oily film, it is never thick enough to keep at bay an astonishing mosaic of delicate sugar tones and barley in imperious richness; the middle ground hints at wonderful bourbon-style liquorice and hickory **f24** continues on its journey into the outer suburbs of Kentucky; now a few extra caramel and Demerara notes kick in and a few spices, too...just bloody magnificent; **b24** another reason to weep at the loss of this distillery. Frankly, you will be hard pushed to find a malt and cask so easily in tune at this age... *50% Douglas Laing. 289 bottles.*

⚬⚬ **The Whisky Agency Lochside 1981** sherry **(86)** n21 t22.5 f21 b21.5. Not exactly 100% free from treated cask interference, but at least here the grape adds a richness that its sister cask can only dream of and, despite the eye-watering sharpness, burnt fruitcake acridness has enough in reserve to leave you demanding a refill to your glass. *55.5%*

⚬⚬ **The Whisky Agency Lochside 1981** sherry **(82)** n18 t21 f22 b22. Even though the sulphur does its level worst, such is the enormity of the chocolate, honey and toffee on show here that it is actually (once past the nose and early delivery) a very pleasant experience. *54%*

LONGMORN

Speyside, 1895. Chivas. Working.

Longmorn 15 Years Old db **(93)** n23 curiously salty and coastal for a Speysider, really beautifully structured oak but the malt offers both African violets and barley sugar; **t24** your mouth aches from the enormity of the complexity, while your tongue wipes grooves into the roof of your mouth. Just about flawless bitter-sweet balance, the intensity of the malt is enormous, yet – even after 15 years – it maintains a cut-grass Speyside character; **f22** long, acceptably sappy and salty with chewy malt and oak. Just refuses to end; **b24** these latest bottlings are the best yet: previous ones had shown just a little too much oak but this has hit a perfect compromise. An all-time Speyside great. *45%*

Longmorn 16 Years Old db **(84.5)** n20.5 t22 f21 b21. This was one of the disappointments of the 2008 edition, thanks to the lacklustre nose and finish. This time we see a cautious nudge in the right direction: the colour has been dropped fractionally and the nose celebrates with a sharper barley kick with a peppery accompaniment. The non-existent (caramel apart) finale of yore now offers a distinct wave of butterscotch and thinned honey...and still some spice. Only the delivery has dropped a tad...but a price worth paying for the overall improvement. Still a way to go before the real Longmorn 16 shines in our glasses for all to see and fall deeply in love with. Come on lads in the Chivas lab: we know you can do it.... *48%*

⚬⚬ **Adelphi Longmorn 1992 Aged 17 Years** bourbon hogshead, cask no. 48430, bott 2010 **(86.5)** n22 t22 f21 b21.5. Exceptionally stodgy for a Longmorn and at times seems like a convention for dark sugars. Even so, a little bitter at the death, though some half-hearted mocha tries to make amends. *53.9% 186 bottles.*

Berrys' Own Selection Longmorn 1992 cask no. 62551, bott 07 **(87.5)** n21.5 t22 f22 b22. Caught in the nick of time this malt really has some brinkmanship complexity going on...! *46%. Berry Bros & Rudd.*

Berry's Own Selection Longmorn 1996 bott 08 **(91.5)** n22 the waft of smoke is an eye-opener so far as in bottled form. The barley and oak share equal billing backstage; **t22.5** delicate barley and vanilla with light peat and cocoa gaining ground towards the middle; **f23.5** lightly oiled finale ensures excellent length and that delicate smoke just teases away. The controlled degree of sweetness is spot on.. **b23.5** now that Benriach is no longer a part of Chivas, will we be seeing more delightfully smoked Longmorns like this, only officially? *56.7%. Berry Bros & Rudd.*

Cadenhead's Longmorn Aged 18 Years bourbon wood, matured in oak cask, dist 90, bott Jun 08 **(95)** n24 t24 f23 b24. This has obviously matured in one hell of a cask. A triumph. *58.3%. 186 bottles.*

Càrn Mòr Vintage Collection Longmorn 1996 hogshead, cask no. 156794, bott 09 **(82.5)** n20 t21 f21.5. Malty, gristy almost, and exceptionally young in style for its age. Not entirely representative of this distillery's usually excellent output. **b20** 46%.

Chieftain's Longmorn 13 Years Old white port finish, dist April 94 **(88)** n22 t22.5 f21 **b22.** I hadn't read that this was a Port finish before nosing and nearly fell off my chair when I first stuck my nose in this. There appears to be something very un-Longmornish in its smokiness, too, so this really is a collectors' item. Juicy, clean and a bit off the wall. *43%. nc ncf. Ian Macleod.*

◦❖◦ **The Coopers Choice Longmorn 1997 Aged 12 Years (88)** n23 rotund, with some oils clinging to the barley essential to broadening its scope and bringing on board the meatier elements; **t22** again those oils play a vital role: this time marrying the juicier barley to the maple-esque sugars; **f21.5** clean vanilla; **b21.5** a dram which will never over tax you. But what it does do, it accomplishes with a degree of style. *46% The Vintage Malt Whisky Co. Ltd*

Dun Bheagan Longmorn Aged 11 Years Madeira Finish (82) n21 t22 f19 b20. A pretty whisky but, for all its mildly fruity make-up, lacks personality. *43%.*

Duncan Taylor Collection Longmorn 1973 cask no. 8916 **(82.5)** n21.5 t21 f19.5 b20.5. Some lovely barley-sugar, citrus-minty moments cannot disguise a malt that is getting a stitch. Even so, there is the odd phrase of advanced complexity here, on the nose especially. *46.9%*

◦❖◦ **Duthies Longmorn 19 Years Old (93.5)** n24 one of those glorious noses which appears to have so much intensity, yet always understated and in control. Naturally, the vanillas hold the largest hand but the delicate custardy sweetness balances perfectly with a greengage barley and marshmallows... scrummy; **t23.5** ditto the delivery... hugely intense, just somehow relaxed and refined. Again the vanillas lead the way, helped along by biscoito de polvilho which simply melts in the mouth; **f23** more of the same, now with a little extra dryness **b23** the Longmorn of your dreams. For its age, just about faultless. *46% Wm. Cadenhead Ltd*

◦❖◦ **Gordon & MacPhail Distillery Label Longmorn 30 Years Old (86)** n21 t23.5 f21.5 **b20.** Mind the very serious splinters amid the orange peel. Almost a parody of an over-the-top, over-aged malt. But strangely, and against all odds, it retains fragments of pure, indisputable deliciousness. *43% Gordon & MacPhail*

◦❖◦ **Gordon & MacPhail Longmorn 1969 Cask Strength** refill butt no. 5305, bott 2009 **(94.5)** n24.5 spellbinding infusion of fruit, coffee and some thick bourbony notes. Sheer class; **t23.5** punchy oak delivery, some seriously stavey moments, but burnt raisin and Demerara-sprinkled fruitcake makes for a eye-watering but, frankly, fabulous experience; **f23** long with more mocha and overcooked, raisin-burned fruitcake; **b23.5** every year I pray a malt like this turns up. And because of the quality of recent sherry butts, this kind of experience is not going to just get rarer but within a decade will be only a part of the memory. Enjoy while you still can. *57.7% Gordon & MacPhail for TWE's 10th Anniversary*

◦❖◦ **James MacArthur's Old Masters Longmorn 1997 Aged 13 Years** cask no. 156791, bott Oct 09 **(86.5)** n20.5 t22.5 f21.5 b22. Despite the limitations of the cask, this is sweet and malty and at times the chocolate fudge hits the spots. You fancy a bit of smoke has crept in there, too. *56.9%*

◦❖◦ **Kingsbury's Finest and Rarest Longmorn 26 Years Old 1980 (88)** n22.5 slightly tart but the elderflower and butterscotch is superb; **t23** mouth watering, lightly sugared barley helps keep control of the usual big oak spice kick; **f20.5** dries towards a milky mocha; **b22** never settles for the easy ride at any given time. Busy and beautiful. *52.6% Japan Import System*

Kingsbury's Finest & Rarest Longmorn 1980 (89) n21.5 showing some major woodiness but butterscotch compensates; **t23.5** superb delivery with a spicy edge to the layered honey; **f22** natural caramels and vanillas fill in the oaky cavities; **b22** the big oak is well contained in this chunky, stylish bottling. *52.6%. Japan Import System.*

Montgomeries Longmorn 1975 cask no. 3967, dist Mar 75, bott Jul 08 **(94)** n23 peaches and honeydew melon served with a custard topping; **t23** a few pine nuts tend to point towards good age, as does the fruit element which is a little more exotic than the nose; the spices freshen things up and the silk to the barley is divine; **f24** for all the obvious oak, this holds out with consummate ease: the vanillas are chattering and busy but the barley enriched latte is sweetened with a lump of Demerara; **b24** this is exactly how you want to find your old whisky: showing age but the grey hairs are confined to the temples and the sophistication is effortless. *46%. Montgomerie's & Co. Ltd.*

Old Malt Cask Longmorn Aged 14 Years refill hogshead, dist Oct 94, bott Dec 08 **(83)** n20 t23 f19 b21. The thin, unpromising nose is reflected in the stingy finish. However, it is impossible not to be amazed by the beauty of the rich malt delivery which is far more in keeping with the distillery's hallmark. *50%. Douglas Laing.352 bottles.*

Old Masters Longmorn Aged 12 Years cask no. 156777, dist 96, bott 08 **(85) n22 t21.5 f20.5 b21**. Natural caramels have a big say on this otherwise malty affair. *60.1%. James MacArthur & Co. Ltd.*

Old Malt Cask Longmorn Aged 19 Years refill hogshead, dist Apr 89, bott Sep 08 **(88) n22** butterscotch with a lemon drizzle: beautifully clean; **t23** just as juicy as the nose suggests with multi-layered barley offering a degree of sharpness, too; **f21** lots of vanilla; bitters out; **b22** there is sometimes no keeping an excellent distillery down. *50%. Douglas Laing. 313 bottles.*

Provenance Longmorn Aged 10 Years bott 09 **(79) n20 t20 f19 b20** Pleasant. Sweet but surprisingly dull. *46%. Douglas Laing.*

⁖ **Provenance Longmorn Over 10 Years** refill hogshead no. DMG 5575, dist Summer 1999, bott Autumn 2009 **(86) n21 t22.5 f21 b21.5**. Thank heavens someone was willing to bottle this distillery at something other than a pensionable age. This one enjoys some serious sugary gloss to the intense barley. *46% Douglas Laing & Co Ltd*

Provenance Longmorn Aged 11 Years hogshead DMG ref. 3963, dist 96, bott 07 **(75) n18 t19 f19 b19**. Not sure about some of the cask policy at this time. More dud wood. *46%. nc ncf. Douglas Laing.*

Provenance Longmorn Aged 12 Years hogshead no. 4199, dist autumn 95, bott spring 08 **(88) n22 t22 f22 b22**. A well-made, fresh malt where barley remains king. *46%.*

Scotch Malt Whisky Society Cask 7.52 Aged 18 Years refill hogshead, dist Sep 90 **(75.5) n17.5 t20.5 f18.5 b19**. A gruesome nose. And, considering the distillery and age, pretty sweet and anaemic on the palate, too. *56.4%*

⁖ **Scotch Malt Whisky Society Cask 7.58 Aged 19 Years** refill barrel, dist Feb 90 **(87) n22** vanilla ice cream, complete with caramelised cornet; **t22** bright barley start is tempered with a quick surge of oak and massive spice; **f21.5** an oaky rumble lightened by shards of sweet barley; **b21.5** a recently excellent cask still with plenty to enjoy but on its way down. *51.5% Scotch Malt Whisky Society. 188 bottles.*

⁖ **Scotch Malt Whisky Society Cask 7.59 Aged 20 Years** refill barrel, dist Feb 90 **(79.5) n21 t20 f19 b19.5**. Snatched from oaky jaws just a little too late... *48.7% Scotch Malt Whisky Society. 185 bottles.*

Scotch Malt Whisky Society Cask 7.44 Aged 23 Years refill hogshead, dist Oct 84 **(90) n22 t24 f21.5 b22.5** Now this really is how to grow old gracefully... *57.3%*

Scotch Malt Whisky Society Cask 7.45 Aged 23 Years refill hogshead, dist Oct 84 **(86) n21.5 t22 f21 b21.5**. Hugely enjoyable, exceptionally well spiced to the point of being hit, but lacks the vital spark that took otherwise similar 7.44 to greatness. *57.7%*

Scotch Malt Whisky Society Cask 7.51 Aged 24 Years refill hogshead, dist Oct 84 **(95.5) n24** the oak involvement is considerable though controlled, giving a decidedly bourbon slant to the still firm barley; **t24.5** that same bourbon character announces its arrival early: a leathery-liquorice edge to the muscovado sugars which prime and prep the thick, dogged malt; for all the complexity, remains refreshingly juicy; **f23.5** wonderfully long with many a fudge note and dried date for good measure; **b23.5** brilliant whisky from one of the great distilleries. The malt is entirely intact despite the obvious bourbony intentions of the oak. Very much the best of both worlds. *57.4%*

⁖ **Scotch Malt Whisky Society Cask 7.60 Aged 24 Years** refill hogshead, dist Nov 85 **(89) n22** the vanilla-barley relationship is simply so complex...; **t22** juicy, salivating barley with no shortage of oaky pep and natural caramels; **f22** long with this oak-barley battle going to the end, entirely unresolved; **b23** one of those where a little bit of over-aging is not a bad thing. *52.3% 220 bottles*

⁖ **Scotch Malt Whisky Society Cask 7.56 Aged 25 Years** refill hogshead, dist Oct 04 **(88.5) n22** no shortage of cedar wood; **t23.5** enormous! Fabulous strands of manuka honey seeing off an attempted oaky coup. The spices are pounding and ceaseless; **f21** the fragile malt has difficulty keeping the oak in check, but manages...just; **b22** a big whisky that is taken as far as it can by the oak. Saved, beautifully so, by the honey.... *56.8% Scotch Malt Whisky Society. 193 bottles.*

⁖ **Scotch Malt Whisky Society Cask 7.57 Aged 25 Years** refill hogshead, dist Oct 84 **(86) n21.5 t22 f21.5 b21**. Another strikingly attractive malt and very much along the same lines as 7.56. However, here the oak is just a fraction too striking for greatness, though again the spices, softened by natural caramels, are a treat. *58.7% Scotch Malt Whisky Society. 243 bottles.*

⁖ **Scotch Malt Whisky Society Cask 7.55 Aged 40 Years** 1st fill sherry butt, dist Dec 68 **(94) n24** oaky woodiness – the inside of old mahogany drawers comes to mind – but my goodness: just how clean is that intense grape? One of those great Chivas casks of the 1960s being tested to its utmost; **t24.5** silk. No, silk just isn't this sleek and embracing. The taste buds are sent into mouth watering spasms as the oak and grape fight out the most seemly of battles. Neither wins...neither try as this is as harmonious as you could pray for; some stunning medium roast Mysore coffee threads its way through the ripe plum; **f22.5** as usual the end shows a degree of over oaked bitterness. But still the oloroso sooths and caresses; **b23** even though it is obvious that the oak has a little too much to say, such is the high standing of the sherry butt that not only is it capable of withstanding the onslaught but offers enough to ensure complexity. *54.9% 451 bottles*

The Spirit Safe Cask Longmorn Aged 11 Years dist 95 **(89) n21 t23 f22 b23**. A malt which will thank you enormously for allowing to breathe in the glass for about 20 minutes before nosing and drinking. *46%. Celtic Whisky Compagnie.*

⠶⠶ **The Whisky Society Longmorn 1990** bott Oct 08 **(92) n23.5** big bourbony infusion of decaying kumquat and old leather...wonderful! **t23** hold on to your hats as the first layer of enamel is scorched off by a searing spice attached to the molassed sugars; **f23** quietens and the barley is back on track, against a lightly molassed emulsion and lightly charred vanillas; **b22.5** a dram to bring a tear to the eye...for many reasons! *58% Speciality Drinks Ltd*

THE MACALLAN
Speyside, 1824. Edrington. Working.

The Macallan 7 Years Old db **(89) n23** beautifully clean sherry, lively, salty, gentle peppers; **t23** mouth-filling and slightly oily. Some coffee tones intertwine with deep barley and fruit; **f21** unravels to reveal very soft oak and lingering fruity spice; **b22** an outstanding dram that underlines just how good young malts can be. Fun, fabulous and in recent bottlings has upped the clarity of the sherry intensity to profound new heights. *40%*

The Macallan 10 Years Old db **(91) n23** oloroso appears to be the big noise here, but clever, almost meaty, incursions of spice offer an extra dimension; fruity, yet bitter-sweet: dense yet teasingly light in places; **t23** chewy fruit and the old Macallan silk is back: creamy cherries and mildly under-ripe plum ensures a sweet-sour style; **f21.5** traces of vanilla and barley remind us of the oak and barley, but the fruit reverberates for some while, as does some annoying caramel; **b23.5** for a great many of us, it is with the Mac 10 our great Speyside odyssey began. It has to be said that in recent years it has been something of a shadow of its former great self. However, this is the best version I have come across for a while. Not perhaps in the same league as those bottlings in the 1970s which made us re-evaluate the possibilities of single malt. But fine enough to show just how great this whisky can be when the butts have not been tainted and, towards the end, the balance between barley and grape is a relatively equal one. *40%*

The Macallan 10 Years Old Cask Strength db **(85) n20 t23 f22 b21**. Enjoyable and a would give chewing gum a run for its money. But over-egged the sherry here and not a patch on the previous bottling. *58.8%. Duty Free.*

The Macallan 12 Years Old db **(88) n22.5** classic Macallan nose, taking off on a one way sherried flight; **t22.5** a sweeter, fresher sherry delivery than of recent times with an almost PX kick to this early on; lots of toffee nougat fills towards the middle; **f21** the sherry and caramel become confused; **b22** great to see a Macallan so clean. Really enjoyable, but the development is too stunted to make this a true classic. *40%*

The Macallan 12 Years Old Sherry Oak Elegancia db **(86) n23 t22 f20 b21**. Promises, but delivers only to an extent. *40%*

The Macallan 18 Years Old db **(87) n24** near perfection as to regard the sherry: soft, oloroso led, the most playful spice prickle with the balance of sweet and dry almost faultless: stick your nose in this and abide a while... **t22** soft, silky...but without backbone. Limited development and caramel appears to outwit the malt; **f20** pretty dull and lifeless, caramel apart: I really can't get my head around this... **b21** an entirely underpowered dram. The body doesn't even come close to matching the nose which builds up the expectancy to enormous levels and, by comparison to the Independents, this at 43% appears weak and unrepresentative. Why this isn't at 46% at the very least and unambiguously uncoloured, I have no idea. *43%*

⠶⠶ **The Macallan 18 Years Old** dist 1991 db **(87) n22** some seriously old-fashioned Macallan oloroso in finest, most expansive form...but a nagging light off-note just detectable; **t22.5** the delivery through to the middle is just a succession of juicy, mega rich grape; but in the background... **f21** a touch of Mysore enriches the fruit further...then a slight furry, bitter note...; **b21.5** honestly: I could weep. Some of the sherry notes aren't just textbook...they go back to the Macallan manuals of the early 1970s. But the achievable greatness is thwarted by the odd butt of you know what... *43% Imported by Remy Cointreau, USA*

The Macallan 25 Years Old db **(84.5) n22 t21 f20.5 b21**. Dry with an even drier oloroso residue; blood orange adds to the fruity mix. Something, though, is not entirely right about this and one fears from the bitter tang at the death that a rogue butt has gained entry to what should be the most hallowed of dumping troughs. 43%

The Macallan 30 Years Old db **(93) n22.5** a few notes from the lactic-forming, tired parts of butt but these are comprehensively outweighed by the rich sherry and busy spices; **t23.5** lavish, peppy-spiced oloroso thumps headfirst into every tastebud going; as it settles towards the vanilla-clad middle, the grapes take on a much cleaner, juicier form; **f23** long, honey and liquorice add up towards a rich bourbon-esque finale which gamely counters the thick fruit; the late chocolate topping is almost too good to be true; **b24** a grizzled and weary malt it may outwardly appear... but so much closer and more time-consuming inspection there is no questioning its lineage: Macallan at its most traditional. And brilliant! 43%

The Macallan 40 Years Old dist 10 May 61, bott 9 Sep 05 db **(90) n23** no shortage of oak, as you might expect. But nutty, too (chestnut pure, to be precise). The scope is broadened with a distracted smokiness while oak maximizes the longer it stays in the glass; **t23** soft and yielding, with a lovely dovetailing of vanillins and delicate sherry. The grape appears to gain control with a sweet barley sidekick before the oak recovers; **f22** soft oils formulate with some laite and slightly salted, Digestive-style biscuit. Gentle spices delight; **b22** very well-rounded dram that sees off advancing years with a touch of grace and humour. So often you think the oak will take control, but each time an element intervenes to win back the balance. It is as if the dram is teasing you. Wonderful entertainment. 43%

The Macallan 50 Years Old dist 29 Mar 52, bott 21 Sep 05 db **(90) n25** we all have pictures in our minds of the perfect grandmother: perhaps grey-haired and knitting in her rocking-chair. Or grandfather: kindly, gentle, quietly wise, pottering about in the shed with some gadget he has just made for you. This, then, is the cliched nose of the perfect 50-year-old malt: time-defying intensity and clarity; attractive demerara (rum and sugar!) sweetened coffee, a tantalizing glimpse at something smoky and sensationally rich grape and old fruit cake. So that the sweetness and dryness don't cancel each other out, but complement each other and between them tell a thousand tales. Basically, there's not much missing here... and absolutely all you could wish to find in such an ancient Speysider...; **t23** dry delivery with the oak making the early running. But slowly the grape and grain fights back to gain more than just a foot-hold; again telling wisps of smoke appear to lay down a sound base and some oily barley; **f19** now the oak has taken over. There is a burnt-toast and burnt raisin bitterness, lessened in effect marginally by a sweeter vanilla add-on; **b23** loses it at the end, which is entirely excusable. But until then it has been one fabulous experience full of passion and complexity. I nosed and tasted this for over an hour. It was one very rewarding, almost touching, experience. 46%

The Macallan 55 Years Old Lalique II db **(90.5) n23.5 t21 f23.5 b22.5.** Even after all these years, whisky never loses its ability to amaze me. It is the norm that smoke in a malt tends to bale out regarding its intensity as the years pass. And that as the oak increases during that time it becomes impossible to delineate or recognize the forms and characters that give a particular whisky a style or shape. Here neither has happened to a degree where you cannot recognise this for exactly what it is: a classic post war Macallan, complete with all its peaty zest and articulation. Remember, when this was distilled, Elizabeth II had still to become Queen, Winston Churchill was Prime Minister and the very year this was put into cask director David Lean was making films about breaking the sound barrier, let alone man reaching the moon. This is liquid history: a bygone style of Speyside from a bygone age - a gem of a wrinkly. 40.1%

The Macallan 1824 db **(88) n24** welcome to the true, traditional nose of Macallan. Oloroso, ladies and gentlemen. But not just any old oloroso: this is more or less exactly how I remember it form the mid-70s, radiating the rind of kumquats and blood orange juice in pretty equal measure; and as well as grape we have greengages absolutely bursting from their skins. There is a 'but', a very slight mustiness...but it is so far outweighed by the grapey symphony, it is to be contemptuously ignored... **t23.5** not surprisingly, the delivery and first five or six waves are of grape in varying forms of juiciness, sweetness, weight and brilliance... but there is, eventually, a bitterness, too...; **f19** that background noise on the nose cannot be ignored any longer...it is now biting deep into the finish; **b21.5** absolutely magnificent whisky, in part. But there are times my job is depressing...and this is one of them.. 48%

The Macallan 1851 Inspiration db **(77) n19.5 t19.5 f19 b19.** Flat and uninspirational in 2008. 41%

The Macallan 1937 bott 69 db **(92) n23** an outline of barley can eventually be made in the oaky mist; becomes better defined as a honeyed sweetness cuts in. Fingers of smoke tease. When nosing in the glass hours later the fresh, smoky gristiness is to die for ... and takes you back to the mill room 67 years ago; **t22** pleasantly sweet start as the barley piles in – even a touch of melon in there; this time the oak takes second place and acts as a perfect counter; **f24** excellent weight with soft peat softening the oak; **b23** a subtle if not overly complex whisky where there are few characters but each play its part exceptionally well. One to get out with a DVD of Will Hay's sublime Oh Mr Porter which was being made in Britain at the same time as this whisky and as Laurel and Hardy were singing about a Lonesome Pine on the other side of the pond; or any Pathe film of Millwall's FA Cup semi-final with Sunderland. *43%*

The Macallan 1937 bott 74 db **(83) t19 t24 f20 b20.** It's all about the superb, silky initial mouth impact. *43%.*

The Macallan 1938 bott 73 db **(90) n21** hint of apple blossoms on oak; **t23** stupendous balance and poise as the barley rolls, wave after wave over the palate bringing with it a sweet sugar-almond biscuity quality; **f23** fabulous finish of great length. Spices dovetail with an almost perfect barley-oak charm; **b23** no hint of tiredness here at all: a malt that has all the freshness and charisma yet old-world charm and mystery of Hitchcock's The Lady Vanishes, which was made at the same time as this whisky. *43%*

The Macallan 1938 (31 Years Old) dist 38, first bott 69, re-bottled 02 db **(83) n20 t22 f20 b21.** Some wonderful trills of barley early on but the oak dominates. *43%.*

The Macallan 1939 bott 79 db **(90) n23** pleasing peaty edges to the thick malt; a touch of hickory for extra weight and Highland Park-esque heather-honey; **t22** spot on barley gives an unmolested mouthwatering performance; the oak tags on reluctantly drying towards cocoa at the middle; **f22** the integrity is kept as the oak backs off and little wisps of smoke re-surface; some brown sugar keeps the bitter-sweet pot boiling; **b23** enormous complexity confidence to a whisky distilled at a time of uncertainty; one to accompany the original Goodbye Mr Chips, though the whisky seems nothing like so faded. *43%*

The Macallan 1940 bott 75 db **(83) n20 t22 f21 b20.** Easily the most modern style discernible from this distillery; a Macallan recogisable as an ancestor of today's famous dram, even with one or two warts apparent. *43%*

The Macallan 1940 (37 Years Old) dist 40, first bott 77, re-bottled 02 db **(91) n22** not dissimilar to an old sherried Irish of this era with the barley having a firm, crisp, almost abrasive quality. Rather lovely especially with the most subtle wisps of peat imaginable; **t23** bracing, full-on barley where the flintiness from the nose is transferred perfectly to the palate; a touch of spice and hint of smoke towards the middle; **f23** clean, long finale where the barley pulsates its rock hard message; **b23** blind-tasting I would have declared this Irish, though slightly mystified by the distant hints of peat. Hard to believe that something so sublime could have been made by a nation under siege. Obviously nothing can distract a Scotsman from making great whisky ... *43%*

The Macallan 1945 (56 Years Old) cask 262, bott 02 db **(89) n22** extraordinary to the point of improbability: the sherry is fresh and keeping at bay logjams of chunky oak, though the fruitiness burns off the longer it remains in the glass; the smoke hovers and soars like pin-prick eagles on the wing; **t23** battling oak fizzes against the sweeter, mouthwatering barley; the fruit is subtle though there is a pineapple sharpness amid the still lush grape; **f22** really impressive, slow development of peat that offers no spice but a smoky overlay to the oak; **b22** how can a whisky retain so much freshness and character after so long in the cask? This game never ceases to amaze me. *51.5%*

The Macallan 1946 Select Reserve db **(93) n25** does peat arrive any more delicately than this? The sherry, barley and oak offer perfect harmony: perfect and faultless; **t23** teasingly mouthwatering and fruity. Crushed sultanas cruise with the peat; **f22** the oak makes inroads at the expense of the barley. Remains chewy and tantalisingly smoky, though; **b23** I have never found a finer nose to any whisky. Once-in-a-lifetime whisky. *40%*

The Macallan 1946 (56 Years Old) cask 46/3M, bott 02 db **(84) n21 t21 f20 b22.** The most peat-free '46 I've come across yet *44.3%*

The Macallan 1948 (53 Years Old) cask 609, bott 02 db **(77) n18 t21 f19 b19.** Drinkable, but showing some major oaky cracks. *45.3%*

The Macallan 1948 Select Reserve db **(75) n22 t19 f17 b17.** What a fabulous nose! Sadly the package trails behind the '46. *40%*

The Macallan 1949 (53 Years Old) cask 136, bott 02 db **(95) n23** wonderfully lively fruit interwoven with waxy, polished wooden floors and acacia honey; a touch of salt sharpens it further; **t24** nothing extinct about this old Scottish volcano as oak-led spices assert their grip on the tastebuds while soft, sultry sherry tries to act as placator; **f24** oaky-cocoa/liquorice and intense barley; remains mouthwatering yet spicy for seemingly hours; **b24** hold on to your trilbies: this punchy malt knows exactly where it is going. What a year: Carol Reed made the incomparable The Third Man and Macallan can come up with something like this. Oh, to swap Orson Welles for H. G. Wells and his time machine. Sheer, unrepeatable class. *49.8%*

The Macallan 1949 (52 Years Old) cask 935, bott 02 db **(82)** n23 t21 f19 b19. Faded and slightly tired, it has problems living up to the heaven-made nose. *41.1%*

The Macallan 1950 (52 Years Old) cask 598, bott 02 db **(83)** n22 t22 f18 b21. Charmingly delicate peat but probably about two or three summers past being a truly excellent whisky. *46.7%*

The Macallan 1950 (52 Years Old) cask no. 600, bott 02 db **(91)** n20 the early fruit quickly evaporates to leave a clear path for the oak; **t24** stunning sherry: the grape absolutely sparkles yet is soft enough to allow through a tidal wave of malt, on which peat is sensuously surfing; **f23** spices from the middle carry through as does the chewy peat. Some fabulous undercurrents of burnt raisin and healthy malt continue; **b24** only two casks apart, but this is almost a mirror image of the first, in the sense that everything is the other way round... *51.7%*

The Macallan 1951 (51 Years Old) cask 644, bott 02 db **(93)** n23 a minor fruitfest with withering grapes and raisins the main attraction but over-ripe greengages and raspberries bulk up the sub-plot: needs this to see off the firm oak. A gentle, barely discernible peatiness drifts over it all with absolutely no signs of over-aging; **t24** fascinating detail to the barley: it is fresh and still mildly gristy at first but the sherry builds a dark path towards it. All the time the sherry remains clean and in harmony; some confident peat weaves a delicious path through the complexity; **f23** unrefined brown sugar digs in with the barley to see off the encroaching oak; the most delicate wafts of peat imaginable caress the senses; **b23** a malt instantly recognisable to Macallan lovers of the last two decades. Simply outstanding. *52.3%*

The Macallan 1952 (50 Years Old) cask no. 627, bott 02 db **(80)** n20 t20 f21 b19. Good, clean sherry but it all seems a little detached *50.8%*

The Macallan 1952 (49 Years Old) cask 1250, bott 02 db **(74)** n19 t19 f18 b18. Ye olde weirde Macallane. *48%*

The Macallan 1953 (49 Years Old) cask no. 516, bott 02 db **(92)** n22 a shade meaty with the oak offering a big counter to the thumping sherry and delicate smoke; **t24** full sherry alert as the fruitcake richness goes into overdrive, as do the spices; **f23** some medium roast Santos lightens the oak while enrichening the barley; **b23** deliciously big and unflinching in its Christmas pudding intensity. *51%*

The Macallan 1954 (47 Years Old) cask 1902, bott 02 db **(77)** n19 t18 f21 b19. The line between success and failure is thin: outwardly the '53 and 54 are similar but the 53 controls the oak much tighter. I love the coffee finale on this, though. *50.2%*

The Macallan 1955 (46 Years Old) cask 1851 49, bott 02 db **(88)** n21 more burnt raisins and apples; **t22** the tastebuds get a good spicy peppering as the barley rootles about the palate; the sherry is clear and intact; **f23** amazingly long with the oak falling short of its desired palate domination; **b22** close call: one more Speyside August and this dram would have been matchwood. *45.9%*

The Macallan 1958 (43 Years Old) cask 2682, bott 02 db **(86)** n17 t22 f24 b23. One fears the worst from the sappy nose but the taste is sheer Highland Park in its honey depth. *52.9%*

The Macallan 1959 (43 Years Old) cask 360, bott 02 db **(79)** n19 t21 f19 b20. The oak is giving the malt a good hiding but it just hangs on to a delicious sub-plot. *46.7%*

The Macallan 1964 (37 Years Old) cask 3312, bott 02 db **(86)** n24 t22 f20 b20. butterscotch and honey: a real chewing whisky if ever there was one. *58.2%*

The Macallan 1965 (36 Years Old) cask 4402, bott 02 db **(91)** n22 pretty well oaked but wonderful balance from blood oranges; **t23** again lovely mouthfeel as the fabulously balanced and lush barley hits the palate; fruit and oak are dished out in even measures with the spice: this is top notch whisky; **f22** after the big bust comes the ample arse: heaps of chewy barley fortified by sultanas and raisins; **b24** if this was a woman it would be Marilyn Monroe *56.3%*

The Macallan 1966 (35 Years Old) cask 7878, bott 02 db **(83)** n21 t22 f20 b20. A malt which never quite works out where it is going but gives a comfortable ride all the same. *55.5%*

The Macallan 1967 (35 Years Old) cask 1195, bott 02 db **(93)** n23 top notch uncompromised sherry with some lovely nutty touches; **t24** the sherry deftly flicks each individual tastebud while the burnt fudge offers a bitter-sweet distraction; **f23** coffee ice cream but a whole lot warmer as the spices pop about the mouth. Vanilla and raisins gather around the spicy centrepiece; some lovely salt towards the finale; **b23** this is what happens when you get a great sherry cask free of sulphur and marauding oak: whisky the way God intended. Unquestionably classic Macallan. *55.9%*

The Macallan 1968 (34 Years Old) cask 2875, bott 02 db **(92)** n23 lemon curd tart and barley; **t23** full frontal barley with a grape chaperone; **f22** continues to mouthwater now with late cocoa adding depth and finesse; **b24** possibly the most sophisticated and delicate malt in the pack despite the strength. *51%*

The Macallan 1968 (33 Years Old) cask 5913, bott 02 db **(84) n17 t23 f22 b22.** Flawed genius: how can a whisky with such a poor nose produce the goods like this? 46.6%

The Macallan 1969 cask 9369 db **(75) n19 t18 f20 b18.** One of those ungainly sherry butts that swamps everything in sight. 52.7%

The Macallan 1969 (32 Years Old) cask no. 10412, bott 02 db **(76) n18 t20 f18 b20.** One small sip for man, one ordinary vintage for Macallan. Splinters. anybody? 59%

The Macallan 1970 (32 Years Old) cask no. 241, bott 02 db **(95) n23** another heavyweight but this time with some honey and ripe fig to offer complexity; passable impersonation of ancient bourbon blended with old Demerara rum; **t24** quite massive with strands of brown sugar bringing out the best of the grape; **f23** very long and so subtle: the barley and vanilla stretch a long distance with some natural toffee rounding things off; **b25** Brazil win the World Cup with the finest team and performance of all time, my girlfriend born there soon after and Macallan receive a butt from Heaven via Jerez. 1970 was some year ... 54.9%

The Macallan 1970 (31 Years Old) cask no. 9033, bott 02 db **(81) n20 t20 f22 b19.** A butt bottled on its way down. 52.4%

The Macallan 1971 (30 Years Old) cask no. 4280, bott 02 db **(86) n21 t22 f22 b21.** Imagine the trusty 10 years old from about 1980 with a grey beard ... 56.4%

The Macallan 1971 (30 Years Old) cask 7556, bott 02 db **(91) n22** delicate salt helps develop the barley; **t22** vivid barley with rather soft sherry and then spice; **f24** lengthy, subtle end with waves of rich sherry carrying a Demerara sweetness and coffee; **b23** a complex dram that is comfortable with its age. 55.9%

The Macallan 1972 (29 Years Old) cask no. 4041, bott 02 db **(92) n23** hell's teeth!!! This is probably what an explosion in a bodega would smell like. The most awesomely powerful sherry I can probably ever remember on a whisky, much more one dimensional than cask 4043, though; **t24** that trademark coffee-ness is there (in this case something of a heavy roast Costa Rican) then some tomato and burnt raisin; **f22** bitter and slightly nutty as the oak begins to gain some control; **b23** once, I would have hated this type of malt. But I have come across so many sulphur-tainted casks over recent years that I have learned to have fun with monsters like this. Snatched from an awesome clutch of butts. 49.2%

The Macallan 1972 29 Years Old cask 4043, bott 02 db **(93) n25** well, it has to be said: a quite faultless nose. The spices are entirely in true with the perfect sherry-oak balance. This is big stuff, but perfectly proportioned: seems almost a shame to drink it ...; **t24** stupendous spice-plum-giant-boiled-Italian-tomato: enormous with a waft of smoke through the middle; **f21** slightly bitter as the oak nibbles but still lots of complexity; **b23** the sherry butt used for this was a classic: the intensity of the whisky memorable. If, as Macallan claim, the sherry accounts for only 5% of the flavour, I'd like to know what happened to the other 95.... 58.4%

The Macallan 1973 (30 Years Old) cask 6098, bott 03 db **(93) n23** the grape is brittle and nestles behind barley and honey; some ripe pears add to the freshness; **t24** the honey is at the vanguard of a brilliant display of intense, sugarcoated barley; **f23** the sweetness vanishes to leave the more mouthwatering, grassy malt elements; **b23** a superbly chosen cask for those with a sweet tooth in particular. If you know any women who claim not to like whisky, seduce them with this. 60.9%

The Macallan 1989 cask no 552 db **(94) n23 t23 f24 b24.** There are countless people out there who cut their whisky teeth 20 years ago on Macallan. Battle to get a bottle of this and the grey hairs will return to black, the eyesight will improve and your clothes will fit more easily. This is timewarp Macallan at its most dangerously seductive. 59.2%

Macallan Cask Strength db **(94) n22** cranked up, sweet, clean sherry; **t24** absolutely spot on delivery with grape concentrate, thickened further by intense barley. Wonderful spices arrive on cue; **f24** long, with the tastebuds storm-lashed by juicy sherry for some time. And still those spices rock....; **b24** one of those big sherry babies; it's like surfacing a massive wave of barley-sweetened sherry. Go for the ride. 58.6%. USA.

The Macallan Easter Elchies Seasonal Cask Selection Winter Choice 14 Years Old db **(94) n24** you can almost picture the butt before it was filled: large, dripping with dampness inside and smelling as sweet as a nut. Nothing has changed in 14 years, except some exquisite marmalade and honeycomb has been added; **t24** sizzling spices cut rapier-like through the intense grape; juicy barley seeps through the wounds; **f23** lilting, rich-textured natural caramel and vanilla; **b23** from a faultless cask and one big enough to have its own Postcode... 54%. Exclusive to visitor centre.

The Macallan Estate Reserve db **(84) n22 t22 f20 b20.** Doh! So much juice lurking about, but so much bitterness, too. ....grrrrr!!!! 45.7%

The Macallan Fine Oak 8 Years Old db **(82.5) n20.5 t22 f20 b20.** A slight flaw has entered the mix here. Even so, the barley fights to create a distinctive sharpness.

However, a rogue sherry butt has put paid to any hopes the honey and spice normally found in this brand. 40%

The Macallan Fine Oak 10 Years Old db (90) n23 finely tuned and balanced: everything on a nudge-nudge basis with neither fruit nor barley willing to come out and lead: really take your time over this to maximise the entertainment; t22.5 brimming with tiny, delicate oak notes which just brush gently, almost erotically, against the clean barley; f21.5 drier, chewier and no less laid-back; b22 much more on the ball than the last bottling of this I came across. Malts really come as understated or clever than this. 40%

The Macallan Fine Oak 12 Years Old db (92) n24 moist dates and quartered lime; gristy barley perfectly countered by roasted hazelnut and sweetened cocoa: an aromatic triumph; t23 thin acacia honey brushed over the emboldened malt; lightweight at first and gradually more chewy; still, though, it is a fine gristiness which prevails; f22.5 a touch of bitterness as the oak clears its throat but the dexterity of the vanilla allows the sweet a clear path to the finish; b22.5 a star of a malt, altered in style slightly since its launch, offering such clever nuances as the picture, always on a theme, changes from moment to moment. It's the ultra complex nose, though, which takes star billing. 40%

The Macallan Fine Oak 15 Years Old db (94) n24 vanilla holds the key here, with the oak bridging the gap between the myriad soft fruit notes and the angular barley; surprisingly, a deft trail of something smoky is also evident; the first time I have seen this in the FO15 since the very first bottlings; t24.5 ye Gods! Not quite perfection, but its going for it big time: the molten brown sugars simply melt into the gentle fruit while the deft oils carry the barley; some rising spice may indicate very distant smoke; f22 unquestionably a duller finale than when first launched; there is now a telling degree of treacle caramel seeping in from somewhere which is trampling and flattening all around it; b23.5 the finish may have knocked it down a point. But considering that the last time I came across this, in Canada I think, the bottling had been sulphur ruined, this rates as the best and most exciting comeback since Queen of the South's heroic and unforgettable effort in the Scottish Cup Final against Rangers this year. Remains a quite stunning dram; a Queen of the Speyside. 43%

The Macallan Fine Oak 17 Years Old db (84) n21 t21 f21 b21. A curious, pleasant but not entirely convincing addition to the Fine Oak family, having neither the 15-year-old's outrageous complexity or the deftness of the 18. An expression too far? 43%

The Macallan Fine Oak 18 Years Old db (84) n20 t23 f20 b21. The surprisingly bland nose and finish is partly compensated for by the intensity of the honey barley on delivery. Some non-firing cylinders are evident. 43%

The Macallan Fine Oak 21 Years Old db (82.5) n21 t22 f19.5 b20. How dull! No off notes. No sulphur. Granted. But just no character, either. Get past the lovely, honeyed energetic barley on delivery and then there is a void. Unrecognisable from the excellence of previous bottlings. 43%

The Macallan Fine Oak 25 Years Old db (90) n22 coal dusty: the plate of old steam engines; a speckle of raisin and fruitcake; t23.5 despite the early signs of juicy grape, it takes only a nanosecond or two for a much drier oak-spiced spine to take shape; the weight is never less than ounce perfect, however; f22 puckering, aged oak leaves little doubt that this is a malt of advanced years, but a few liquorice notes ensure a degree of balance; b22.5 the first time I tasted this brand a few years back I was knocked off my perch by the peat reek which wafted about with cheerful abandon. Here the smoke is tighter, more shy and of a distinctly more anthracitic quality. Even so, the sweet juiciness of the grape juxtaposes gamely with the obvious age to create a malt of obvious class. 43%

The Macallan Fine Oak 30 Years Old db (91) n22 oak. And lots of it. Leaves of barley makes the canopy a lot more attractive; t23 big oak delivery, but just like the nose there is a pause before much sweeter elements arrive. Here some honeycomb works wonders; f22.5 a natural fire-break occurs and a Demerara-burnt fudge sweetness sees the malt reach a comfortable conclusion; b23.5 a malt once famed for its refusal to take the oaky path has now led us into a forest. Thankfully, there are enough nuances to the barley to ensure complexity and balance; satisfies pretty high expectation. 43%

The Macallan Fine Oak Master's Edition db (91) n23 one of the most delicate of all Macallan's house noses, depending on a floral scented theme with a sweetish malty tinge to the dank bracken and bluebells; t23 so salivating and sensual! The tastebuds are caressed with sugar-coated oaky notes that have a devilish buzz about them; f22 more malt and now vanilla with a bitter cocoa death... b23 adorable. 42.8%

The Macallan Fine Oak Whisky Maker's Selection db (92) n22 good age with the oak determining a dry course; the barley carries delicate grape; t23 distinctively Speyside-style with an early avalanche of spice; there is a barley-juiced fruitiness and perhaps a fino touch, too; **f23** long, with all the vanilla you'd expect from such a well oaked dram; the clean-ness of the barley and grape is stunning, as is the light oily sheen that carries the dim sweetness; **b24** those who cannot see Macallan in anything other than chestnut oloroso will be having sleepless nights: this is a dram of exquisite sophistication. The ultimate pre-prandial dram with it's coy, mildly cocoaed dryness, set against just enough barley and fruit sweetness here and there to see off any hints of austerity. Some great work has gone on in the lab to make this happen: fabulous stuff, chaps! *42.8%. Duty Free.*

Macallan Gran Reserva Aged 12 Years db **(92) n23** massive cream sherry background with well matured fruit cake to the fore: big, clean, luxurious in a wonderfully old-fashioned way. Oh, and a sprinkling of crushed sultana just in case the grapey message didn't get across... **t24** a startlingly unusual combination on delivery: dry yet juicy! The ultra fruity lushness is dappled with soft spices; oak arriving early-ish does little to alter the path of the sweetening fruit; just a hint of hickory reveals the oak's handiwork towards the middle; **f22** dry, as oloroso does, with a vaguely sweeter edge sparked by notes of dried date; the delicate but busy spices battle through to the toffeed end; **b23** well, you don't get many of these to the pound. A real throwback. The oloroso threatens to overwhelm but there is enough intrigue to make for a quite lovely dram which, as all good whiskies should, never quite tells the story the same way twice. Not entirely without blemish, but I'm being picky. A Macallan soaked in oloroso which traditionalists will swoon over. *45.6%*

The Macallan Gran Reserva 1981 db **(90) n23 t22 f22 b23**. Macallan in a nutshell. Brilliant. But could do with being at 46% for full effect. *40%*

The Macallan Gran Reserva 1982 db **(82) n21 t22 f20 b19**. Big, clean, sweet sherry influence from first to last but doesn't open up and sing like the '81 vintage. *40%*

The Macallan Millennium 50 Years Old (1949) db **(90) n23 t22 f22 b23**. Magnificent finesse and charm despite some big oak makes this another Macallan to die for. *40%*

⁙ **The Macallan Oscuro** db **(95.5) n24.5** the cleanest, most juicy grape dripping into a puddle of molten muscovado sugar: amazed I have not been attacked by wasps while nosing this; it would be too much on its own, but there is a sprinkling of spice to balance things beautifully; **t24** and there you go: golden sultanas, ripe fig, exploding greengages and that muscovado sugar and spice again....unreal...; **f23** just a little bitter, but probably from the oak which until now had hardly got a look in; some toasty vanilla makes a late entry but that juicy, lightly spiced fruit just keeps on going; **b24** oh, if all sherried whiskies could be that mind - and taste bud-blowingly fabulous...! *46.5%*

The Macallan Select Oak db **(83) n23 t21 f19 b20**. Exceptionally dry and tight; and a little furry despite the early fruitiness. *40%*

The Macallan Whisky Makers Edition db **(76) n19 t20 f18 b19**. Distorted and embittered by the horrific "S" element... *42.8%*

The Macallan Woodlands Limited Edition Estate Bottling db **(86) n21 t23 f21 b21**. Toffee towards the finish brings a premature halt to a wonderfully mollased early delivery. *40%*

Alchemist Macallan Aged 10 Years bourbon barrel, dist Oct 97, bott Oct 07 **(83.5) n20 t21.5 f21 b21**. A malty haze. Sweet, grassy but supine. *46%. Alchemist Beverage Co.*

Cadenhead's Authentic Collection Macallan Aged 19 Years sherry butt, dist 87, bott Sep 07 **(78) n18.5 t21 f19 b19.5**. Honey and grape strains against the sulphur input. Pity: it would have been a classic. *52.5%. 672 bottles.*

⁙ **Cadenhead's Macallan-Glenlivet 1989** bott Feb 10 **(87.5) n22.5** sharp. Fruit Pastilles; **t22** massive wave of grist. The softest fruit attachment; **f21** delicate spice and a hint of milk chocolate before drying; **b22** malty and even. *52.1% Wm. Cadenhead Ltd. 168 bottles.*

⁙ **The Càrn Mòr Vintage Collection Macallan 1988** hogshead no. 9171, bott 2009 **(85) n22 t22.5 f20 b20.5**. Crisp, clean citrus on the nose and delivery, backed up by juicy barley. But the oak bitters a little. *46% nc ncf 1048 bottles*

Duncan Taylor Collection Macallan 1969 cask no. 6846 **(88) n21 t22.5 f22 b22.5** Oak bangs on the door like the Grim Reaper. Just creeps over the line in terms of both strength and quality. Balances beautifully considering the big oak threat which never quite goes away. The late syrup and mocha is almost taking the piss. *40.4%*

Duncan Taylor Collection Macallan 1987 cask no. 9796 **(91.5) n23 t23 f22.5 b23**. Wonderful Macallan revealing some pretty deep insights into its rich personality. *57.4%*

Duncan Taylor Collection Macallan 1988 cask no. 8426 **(95.5) n24.5 t24.5 f23 b23.5**. One of the great Macallans of recent times. Grab a bottle and defend to the death... *53.3%*

Duncan Taylor Collection Macallan 1989 cask no. 3025 **(90.5) n24 t23 f21.5 b22**. If a whisky ever says less to say more, this is it. *48.7%*

Duncan Taylor Collection Macallan 1990 cask no. 18222 **(87.5) n22** sweetened ginger nut biscuit with light fruits; **t23** silky, malty start. The oils kick in, as does a more aggressive oakiness; **f21** the sugars are leeched out and soften the leaden, oak-vanilla impact; **b21.5** quite a confused and confusing malt, not quite sure what it wants to be, or where it wants to go. Luckily, it works out attractively. *54.1%*

Duncan Taylor Collection Macallan 1991 cask no. 21437 **(92.5) n23** a real butterscotch-marzipan mix; **t23.5** the barley goes on a sugary spree, helped by the lightest of oils...and more butterscotch; **f23** the wonderful barley clarity on the palate continues even as slightly salty vanilla begins to creep in; **b23** no doubting the quality on offer. *52.8%*

Duncan Taylor Collection Macallan 1991 cask no. 21439 **(86) n22 t21 f22 b21.** Acacia honey escorts the barley and the interaction with the oak on the finish is pleasing, as is the intensity. But at times a little on the hot side. *55.1%*

⭐ **Duncan Taylor Collection Macallan 1991** cask no. 9714 **(89) n22.5** perfectly structured malt. A little citrus adds to the clean, rounded forms; **t22.5** beautiful arrival: fresher than you could think a near 20-y-o whisky could be; the malt layers out and thickens; **f21.5** the oak remains in the background but does add a late bitter marmalade quality; **b22.5** a well used bourbon cask but in excellent form. *55.3% Duncan Taylor & Co Ltd*

Duncan Taylor The NC2 Range Macallan 1990 (82.5) n21 t21.5 f20 b20. No shortage of natural caramels follow the banana-vaguely smoked lead. *46%*

Duncan Taylor The NC2 Range Macallan 1995 (87) n22 freshly printed colour magazine; **t22** freshly crushed barley; **f21** freshly sprinkled vanilla; **b22** fresh. *46%*

Gordon & MacPhail Speymalt Macallan 1938 (94) n25 can this really be over 65-years of age? How, after all these years, does the dynamic of the millroom fit so comfortably with pulped citrus and lavender? And, lurking at the very back, almost wishing not to be noticed, a waft of the softest peat imaginable. I have spent over half an hour nosing this. I cannot fault it. True legend...; **t22** an oaky barrage doesn't auger well, but soon it runs out of ammunition. It doesn't take long for accompanying spices and following barley-sugar and burnt honeycomb to unite and link with the pithy orange which has kept the oak in check from the off; **f23** amazingly, the oak remains on the retreat and now we get to the real serious bit. Soft peats return to offer little more than a smoky echo but the sweetness continues for dozens more waves. There is a lingering dryness, totally in sympathy with the leading malt but, most of all, the tangy orange remains sharp and delicious; **b24** when a malt is bottled at this near unbelievable age you expect the worst. And, even if it doesn't come, you have to be hyper-critical because such whisky doesn't come cheap and tasting notes written in awe of age rather than giving a true, honest assessment of its quality is not worth the ink used to print it. So, I have taken a long time to study this. And to find fault. Naturally, there are faults: every whisky has them, and at this age is expected to have more than most. But was it the quality of the wood they used in those days, or the peat involvement? Somehow, this malt has come through the best part of seven decades without any fatal flaws. The nose, in fact, is perfect. And although it wobbles on the palate on the start of its journey, by the end you cannot but be astounded. This is nature-defying whisky, very much like the 62-year-old Dalmore. Few people will be lucky enough ever to taste this. But those that do will be one of the truly privileged. And that includes me. *41.4%*

Gordon & MacPhail Speymalt Macallan 1950 (91) n24 a swirl of peat beds down into the firm barley; the fruit is masterful with blood orange lightened by plums and juicy sultana. Oak is present but refuses to unbalance the delightful tranquillity and weight; **t22** wonderfully fruity pulse but there is still a gristy youth hanging on in there, allowing a subtle touch of peat to weave into the fabric. Again the oak holds back from doing any damage and the off wave of tangy kumquat is there to be found; **f22** does it's best to take an oaky route, but hasn't the heart to do it. Instead, light barley recovers to mingle playfully with the vanilla. Dry and sawdusty, but always in tune and balanced; **b23** I always taste these ultra-ancient whiskies with trepidation. Nature suggests that they should not be that good as barley – even with the aid of sherry – can see off only so much oak. But fortified with a delightful touch of peat, this holds itself together like an old Shakespeare first in original buckskin. It creaks. It's delicate. But take the time and handled carefully, this will amaze you. *43%*

Gordon & MacPhail Speymalt Macallan 1967 (93) n23 t24 f22 b24. A mighty classy malt which has withstood the years with aplomb. *40%*

⭐ **Gordon & MacPhail Speymalt from Macallan 1971 (95) n23.5** weak honeycomb, weak barley, weak smoke, weak red liquorice, stewed fruit....yet all comes together for a powerful dose of yesteryear; **t24.5** silky, melt-in-the-mouth malt is backed by light sultana juiciness; a few reminders of the timber but so very politely done and has much to do with the spices; **f23.5** there is almost an inevitability to the fruit and nut chocolate finale...and the accentuating of the spice; **b23.5** one of most genteel and elegant whiskies of the year: a true classic. Remember to lift the glass with your little finger sticking out... *43% Gordon & MacPhail*

Gordon & MacPhail Speymalt Macallan 1998 (73.5) n18.5 t19 f18 b18. The off key sulphur notes say rather more than it should about stocks of maturing Speyside malt right now... 43%

Gordon & MacPhail Station Series Kyle of Lochalsh Macallan 1996 refill sherry hogshead no. 11069, bott Feb 07 (92) n22.5 t23.5 f23 b23. Exactly how you dream a Macallan to be when un-molested by a poor sherry butt – or sherry at all, come to that. Should you ever be passing Tokyo... 46%. nc ncf. Japan Import System Co. Ltd. 377 bottles.

The Golden Cask Macallan 1999 cask no. CM120, dist 99, bott 07 (83.5) n21 t23 f19 b20.5. The intensity of the honeycomb on delivery is an absolute treat. 57%. House of Macduff. 283 bottles.

Hart Brothers Macallan Aged 15 Years dist Dec 92, bott Jun 08 (77.5) n18 t22 f19 b19.5. What a shame! Loads of sweet juice and for a moment it really takes off with spices in tow. But dries and tightens. 46%. Hart Brothers Limited.

⋙ **Hart Brothers Macallan Aged 17 Years** 1st fill sherry butt, dist Jun 91, bott Jul 08 (88.5) n22.5 succulent grape; a little clove and spice; t23 sultana and apple juice; malt and vanilla begin to build a more solid foundation; f21 spices; a bitter vanilla and grape note; b22 light bodied for a Macallan but wonderfully juicy! 46% Private bottling for Whisky World.

Heiko Thieme's 1974 Macallan 65th Birthday Bottling cask no. 16807 dist 25 Nov 74 bott Jul 08 (94) n23 the clarity of the sherry takes some believing: this malt has obviously been in a good clean home for the last 34 years: not a single off note and the balance between grape, oak, spice and sweetened tomato puree is exceptional...; t23 the arrival is sharp, both in terms of barley and grape. At first it looks shocked to have escaped the cask, or is hunting around for the alcohol to tie it together. But soon it finds harmony, helped along the way by a stunning chocolate and raisin middle which leads to some sweetening molasses; f24 now enters into a class of its own. We all know about the fruitcake cliché: well here it is in glorious roasted raisin brilliance. Melton Hunt cake and trifle combined; the length makes a mockery of the strength. And it looks as though someone forgot to go easy on the burnt cherry. The vanillas are deft, the coffees are medium roast; b24 this is not whisky because it is 38%abv. It is Scottish spirit. However, this is more of a whisky than a great many samples I have tasted this year. Ageism is outlawed. So is sexism. But alcoholism isn't....!! Try and become a friend of Herr Thieme and grab hold of something a little special. 38% 238 bottles.

Kingsbury "The Selection" Macallan 8 Years Old 1998 (85) n23 t21.5 f22 b22. Simple, delicate and very tasty. 43%. nc ncf. Japan Import System Co. Ltd.

⋙ **Kingsbury's Single Cask Macallan Aged 17 Years 1991** (86) n22 t22 f21 b21. Attractive ginger gives the malt an extra lift. 46% Japan Import System

Murray McDavid Macallan Aged 16 Years bourbon/Madeira, dist 90, bott 07 (84.5) n21.5 t22 f20 b21. A curious malt: it ticks many boxes yet somehow the overall sum is less than its parts. 46%. nc ncf. 1974 bottles.

Norse Cask Selection Macallan 1991 Aged 17 Years hogshead cask no. CM703, dist Jul 91, bott Jul 08 (85) n21.5 t22 f20.5 b21. Dusty in a few places, but the delivery sparkles bright barley. 57%. Qualityworld for WhiskyOwner.com, Denmark.

Northern Light Macallan 1995 Cask Strength bourbon cask no. Q583 (83.5) n21 t21.5 f20 b21. The gristiness on nose and palate leaves little doubt about the age. 57.5%. Qualityworld, Denmark.

Old & Rare Macallan Aged 20 Years sherry cask, dist Sep 87, bott Feb 08 (89) n21 t23 f22.5 b22.5. A really fun, intense whisky absolutely bursting with attitude and intent. 54.4%. nc ncf. Douglas Laing. 187 bottles.

Old & Rare Macallan Aged 28 Years dist Oct 78, bott Sep 07 (84) n19 t22 f21.5 b21.5. The sun may have set on the nose, but streaming rays of honeyed barley are breaking through the oaky clouds. 52%. Douglas Laing. 219 bottles.

Old & Rare Macallan Aged 30 Years sherry finish (86) n21 t22 f21.5 b21.5. Works impressively with some coconut on the nose and buzzing oak-drenched spices on the delivery. The malt remains delightfully intact. 53.2%. Douglas Laing.

Old & Rare Macallan Aged 30 Years bott 09 (88.5) n22 big oak, but a teasing wisp of smoke on the barley; t22 juicy barley and a light coppery sheen; f22.5 the oak bites but there is a lovely spice buzz, too b22 a creaky old 'un, this. More ancient on the palate than its 30 years but a fair degree of juicy charm, too. 45.1%. Douglas Laing.

Old Malt Cask Macallan Aged 15 Years rum cask no. 3874, dist Dec 91, bott Sep 07 (89) n21 t23 f22.5 b22.5. A really classy Macallan showing an usual gait and weight. 50%. nc ncf. Douglas Laing. 346 bottles.

Old Malt Cask Macallan Aged 15 Years dist Jun 93, bott Jul 09 (83) n20.5 t22.5 f19 b21. Far from perfect, but for a while the vivid sweetness of the noble rot grape hinted on the nose shines on the palate, too. 50%. Douglas Laing.

Old Malt Cask Macallan Aged 16 Years bourbon cask no. 3737, dist Mar 91, bott Aug 07 **(81) n21.5 t20 f19.5 b20.** Firm barley and clear enough to show traces of smoke. *50%. Douglas Laing. 336 bottles.*

Old Malt Cask Macallan Aged 18 Years refill hogshead, dist Aug 90, bott Feb 09 **(84) n20.5 t21 f21.5 b21.** Even with the dab of peat this one carries, it is pleasant and enjoyable rather than inspiring as a Macallan of this vintage hopefully should be. *50%. 292 bottles.*

Old Malt Cask Macallan Aged 19 Years (78.5) n19 t19.5 f20 b20. Off key malt, a touch of sweet spice...19-years-old...?!?!?... zzzz...wake me up when something happens... *50%*

Old Malt Cask Macallan Aged 19 Years rum finish refill hogshead, finished in rum cask, dist Nov 89, bott Nov 08 **(89.5) n22.5** clean with barley sugar; **t22.5** sweet delivery; a slow barley encroachment still cannot entirely dislodge the sugary middle, though some building vanilla adds good weight; a fine peppery spice completes the treat; **f22** not a single bitter or off note: just more of the same; **b22.5** classic crisp rum finishing. Excellent. *50%. Douglas Laing. 277 bottles.*

∴ **Old Malt Cask Macallan Aged 19 Years** refill hogshead no. DL 5603, dist Sep 90, bott Nov 09 **(92) n23** a wonderful concoction of grass and grape; **t23** fresh, spiced juiciness but the malt is almost crystal clear; excellent array of light sugars and grist; **f23.5** long, pulsing spices with the grape juicy to the end; **b22.5** a total joy. *50% Douglas Laing. 347 bottles.*

Old Malt Cask Macallan Aged 20 Years rum cask no. 3873, dist Sep 87, bott Sep 07 **(87) n23.5 t21 f21.5 b21.5.** Sweet, if confused, on the palate. But some real moments of joy, though bourbon appears to have more weight than rum. *50%.nc ncf. Douglas Laing. 312 bottles.*

Old Malt Cask Macallan Aged 20 Years Wine Finish refill hogshead, finished in wine barrel, dist Oct 08 **(85) n21 t21 f21.5 b21.5.** Sweet, grapey, enjoyable. But could have been devised and matured in East Anglia of England rather than the Highlands of Scotland. *50%. Douglas Laing. 274 bottles.*

Old Malt Cask Macallan Aged 21 Years refill hogshead no. 3847, dist Apr 86, bott Aug 07 **(85.5) n21.5 t22.5 f20 b21.** Attractive malt full of intense barley riches but which is denied of greatness at the death as natural toffee goes into overdrive. *50%. Douglas Laing. 319 bottles.*

Old Malt Cask Macallan Aged 22 Years claret wine barrel no. 3800, dist Apr 85, bott Aug 07 **(86.5) n22.5 t22 f21 b21.** Takes off elegantly but never quite makes it into the stratosphere. Big grape and spice early on compensates and the depth to the layering ensures a high quality experience. *50%. Douglas Laing. 292 bottles.*

Old Malt Cask Macallan Aged 23 Years Rum Finish refill hogshead, finished in rum cask, dist Apr 85, bott Oct 08 **(86) n22.5 t21.5 f21 b21.5.** Scented but not quite soapy on the nose and a stirring, almost thirst-quenching juiciness on delivery. *50%. Douglas Laing.*

Old Malt Cask Macallan Aged 24 Years refill hogshead, dist Apr 85, bott Apr 09 **(93.5) n23** a beautiful bourbon come Canadian oaky sweetness; **t24** glorious honey and butterscotch with a few slices of lime for extra liveliness; the background is a demure gooseberry and pecan tart, rounded off by maple syrup; **f23** a little drier – well, it had to be, with a pulsing echo of the previous round, but a drier vanilla exit; **b23.5** how can a whisky be this sweet but not for a second either cloying or over the top? I defy anyone to say a bad word against this classic dram. *50%. Douglas Laing. 281 bottles..*

Old Malt Cask Macallan Aged 30 Years sherry cask no. 3885, dist May 77, bott Sep 07 **(67.5) n17.5 t18 f15.5 b16.5.** Oh dear. I would not expect sulphur from a cask of this vintage. But there it is: indisputably so. Has the cask been finished (in every sense, alas) on a new, tainted, butt, I wonder...? *50%. nc ncf. Douglas Laing. 263 bottles.*

Premier Barrel Macallan Aged 10 Years (78.5) n19 t21.5 f19 b19. Just checking in the dictionary the definition of the word "Premier" *46%. Douglas Laing.*

Premier Barrel Macallan Aged 11 Years (86.5) n21.5 t22 f21.5 b21.5. A beautiful example of a well used barrel giving the distillery a chance to show its credentials: the barley is gristy-sweet and carried on a coppery-sharp oiliness. *46%. Douglas Laing. 376 bottles.*

∴ **Premier Barrel Macallan Aged 12 Years (86) n21.5 t22 f21.5 b21.** Pleasant, malty, but not much tread left in the barrel. *46% nc ncf Douglas Laing. 180 bottles.*

Premier Barrel Macallan Aged 16 Years bourbon finish **(80) n21 t20.5 f18.5 b20.** Slightly more Conference North. *46%. Douglas Laing. 335 bottles.*

Private Cellar's Selection Macallan 1987 bott 07 **(84.5) n20.5 t21 f22 b21.** Clean, lush malt. Evidence of small still intensity, sweet, almost sharp barley and serious chewability. *43%*

Provenance Macallan Aged 8 Years hogshead no. 3837-3838, dist Autumn 1998, bott Summer 2007 **(85.5) n21 t22 f21.5 b21.** Makes little attempt to blind you with complexity, but it's a clean, fresh, malty number well performed. *46%. Douglas Laing.*

Provenance Macallan Aged 9 Years refill hogshead nos. 4076 & 4077, dist 98, bott 07 **(88) n23 t22.5 f20.5 b22.** Spot on nose and delivery. *46%. nc ncf. Douglas Laing.*

Provenance Macallan Aged 9 Years refill barrel nos. 4269 and 4270, dist Autumn 98, bott Spring 08 **(87.5) n21.5** clean, steady barley; **t22.5** fine barley-spice interplay; slow dissolving of gooseberry in the gentle oil; **f21.5** some major treacle toffee at the death; **b22** a playful, teasing complexity. 46%. nc ncf. Douglas Laing.

Provenance Macallan Aged 11 Years refill hogshead, dist winter 97, bott autumn 08 **(78.5) n20 t21 f18.5 b19.** Low key with the barley working flat out against the bitter oak. 46%.

⋅⋙⋅ **Provenance Macallan Over 12 Years** refill hogshead no. DMG 6191, dist Autumn 1997, bott Spring 2010 **(89) n23** refreshing, clean, and malty to infinity; **t22** juicy, salivating barley: a mixture of grist sweetness and weak golden syrup; **f22** remains of the simplistic but delightful fresh barley trail; **b22** quite literally a breath of fresh air.... 46% Douglas Laing

Provenance Macallan Aged 16 Years rum finished barrel no. 3903, dist spring 91, bott autumn 07 **(79.5) n20 t20.5 f20 b19.** A rum cove, and make no mistake. There appears to be something smoked on the nose, but fails to find a rhythm or balance as the finish appears incomplete. 46%. Douglas Laing.

Scotch Malt Whisky Society Cask 24.100 Aged 11 Years sherry butt, dist Jun 96 **(73) n18 t19 f18 b18.** A disappointing way to bring up the century. 59.5%

Scotch Malt Whisky Society Cask 24.101 Aged 23 Years refill hogshead, dist Apr 85 **(90) n21.5 t23.5 f22 b23** High quality mix of suet pudding and farmhouse cake. 52.8%

Scotch Malt Whisky Society Cask 24.104 Aged 18 Years sherry butt, dist May 90 **(68.5) n17 t18.5 f16 b17.** Nothing more to say than what has already been said on 24.106... 56.9%

Scotch Malt Whisky Society Cask 24.106 Aged 12 Years sherry butt, dist Jun 96 **(64.5) n17 t17.5 f14 b16.** How the hell did such a grotesquely sulphured monster as this blag its way past the tasting panel? A absolute shocker. 58.9%

Scotch Malt Whisky Society Cask 24.107 Aged 12 Years sherry butt, dist Jun 96 **(77) n20 t19 f19 b19.** Juicy with some green fig sweetness. Remnants of what once must have been a great butt before the sulphur stick got to work. 58.6%

⋅⋙⋅ **Scotch Malt Whisky Society Cask 24.110** 1st fill sherry butt, dist May 90 **(77) n19 t21 f18 b19.** Can the panel try to avoid sulphur tainted casks if you don't mind? I mean: I know this isn't as heavily treated as some but, surely, the trick for the members is to select for them one that's free of sulphur, right? Thank you. 57.1% Scotch Malt Whisky Society

Scott's Selection Macallan 1989 bott 07 **(78.5) n21 t20.5 f19 b18.** Malty, clean but boring. 48.3%

The Single Malts of Scotland Macallan 1990 Aged 17 Years bott Sep 07 **(83.5) n19 t22 f21.5 b21.** The butterscotch and barley on the palate compensates for the tired nose. 46%

Speymalt Macallan 1988 (88) n22 seriously citrussy; **t22.5** as light, juicy, grassy and lemon-sharpened as the nose suggests; **f21.5** dulls down as the vanillas move in; **b22** a real Speyside feel to this one. 43%. Gordon & MacPhail.

Speymalt Macallan 1999 (72.5) n19 t19.5 f16 b18. Juicy early on but dulls as the flaws become apparent. 43%. Gordon & MacPhail.

The Whisky Fair Macallan Aged 14 Years Artist Edition sherry, dist 93, bott 07 **(86.5) n21.5 t22 f21.5 b21.5.** Splendidly gristy, juicy and mouth-watering but seriously underdeveloped for its age. 50%. Germany.

Wilson & Morgan Barrel Selection Macallan 16 Years Old Cask Strength dist 91, bott 07 **(89.5) n21.5 t23.5 f22 b22.5.** At first an easy one to overlook, such is its outwardly cumbersome nature. But slow reflection repays you handsomely. 58.6%

Wilson & Morgan Barrel Selection Macallan Aged 20 Years dist 88, bott 08 **(79) n21 t20 f19 b19.** Very tight. 46%. Wilson & Morgan.

Wilson & Morgan Barrel Selection Macallan 1998 Marsala Finish bott 08 **(82) n20.5 t21 f20.5 b20.** Juicy yet dry and restrained. 46%. Wilson & Morgan.

MACDUFF

Speyside, 1963. Dewar's. Working.

Glen Deveron Aged 10 Years dist 95 db **(86) n19 t23 f23 b21.** The enormity of the third and fourth waves on delivery give some idea of the greatness this distillery could achieve perhaps with a little more care with cask selection, upping the strength to 46% and banning caramel. We'd have a malt scoring in the low to mid 90s every time. At the moment we must remain frustrated. 40%

⋅⋙⋅ **Glen Deveron Aged 15 Years** db **(88.5) n22** the vaguest hint of smoke curls around the foot of the honey; **t22.5** one of the most delightful signatures of a Macduff is the softness of textures and a hint of honey lurking somewhere in close proximity. No disappointments here; **f22** more lush, light sweetness but more than a hint of toffee; **b22** for those who like whisky to caress rather than attack their taste buds. 40%

⁘ **Berry's Own Selection Macduff 1984 (91.5) n22.5** anyone with a passion for Crunchie chocolate bars will appreciate this one...; **t24** ...and on delivery, too, as the honeycomb makes a spectacularly grand entrance, flanked by rich barley and butterscotch; **f22.5** some creaking oak, for sure, but the soft oils and continuing watering golden syrup makes amends.. **b22.5** MacDuff at its very best and the kind of wonderful dram which can compensate for watching your team lose in the Play Off semi-finals. *52.2%*

Berry's Own Selection Macduff 1991 bott 08 **(88) n23** raspberry jam buffeted by an almost pathetic degree of smoke: beautiful... **t22** light textured and major emphasis on juicy barley. Some major oak keeps a distance; again the faintest smoke imaginable; **f21** vanilla led; **b22** quite an unusual type of malt which needs three or four mouthfuls to get the measure of. *46%. Berry Bros & Rudd.*

Càrn Mòr Vintage Collection Macduff 2005 hogshead, cask no. 23, dist 05, bott 09 **(78) n19 t21 f19 b19.** Sweet malt on delivery, otherwise not picked at the best moment of its early life cycle. *46%. The Scottish Liqueur Centre.*

⁘ **Connoisseurs Choice Macduff 1989 (82) n19 t21.5 f20.5 b21.** Not even its best attempts to rack up the honey can entirely overcome the slight technical flaw in the distillate. Plenty to chew over, though...literally! *43% Gordon & MacPhail*

Duncan Taylor Collection Macduff 1968 cask no. 8544 **(85.5) n22 t21 f21.5 b21.** Diluted maple syrup sweetens enormously in a bid to keep the oak honest. Has served its time well, but not as complex as something of this magnificent age might be. *45.2%*

Duncan Taylor Collection Macduff 1968 cask no. 8550 **(89.5) n21.5 t22.5 f22.5 b23.** On the nose, it looks as though 8544 will have what it takes, but in this game you never know for certain. Wonderful grace and imagination even after all these years. *49.1%*

Duncan Taylor Collection Macduff 1969 cask no. 3668 **(86.5) n22.5 t21 f21.5 b21.5.** Lovely malt showing some knots of age but having the grace and wherewithal to allow the more elegant barley notes to take a bow. *40.8%*

⁘ **The Golden Cask Macduff 1984** cask no. CM143, bott 2009 **(86.5) n22 t22 f21 b21.5.** Some glorious strands of golden syrup and coconut with some late mocha, too. *55% The House of MacDuff. 326 bottles.*

Lonach Macduff 1969 (92) n23 t23 f23 b23. Uncompromised star quality throughout. One of those malts that makes writing this book so rewarding...!! *40.6% Duncan Taylor.*

Old Malt Cask Macduff Aged 17 Years rum finished barrel no. 3905, dist Oct 90, bott Oct 07 **(88.5) n22 t23 f22 b21.5.** There are rum finishes and then there are rum finishes. Now let me tell you ladies and gentlemen: that was a rum finish... *50%. nc ncf. 150 bottles.*

Old Malt Cask Macduff Aged 19 Years dist Mar 90, bott Jul 09 **(69) n17 t18 f17 b17.** MacDuff without the Mac. *50%. Douglas Laing.*

Old Malt Cask Macduff Aged 40 Years bourbon finished barrel no. 3904, dist Jun 67, bott Sep 07 **(85.5) n21.5 t19 f23 b22.** Coffee walnut cake with plenty of coffee and walnuts. Essentially a dram that's absorbed too much oak. But somehow that creamy coffee effect saves the day and makes for a lovely long finish. *50%. Douglas Laing. 227 bottles.*

Old Masters Macduff Aged 17 Years cask no. 1418 dist 90, bott 08 **(68.5) n16 t18 f17 b17.5.** Duff by name and nature. Noses do come worse than this...but not that often. *57.8%. James MacArthur & Co. Ltd.*

Scott's Selection Macduff 1978 bott 07 **(84.5) n20 t21 f22.5 b21.** Macduffed up by oak it may be, but enough honeyed barley clings on to give the odd clout of its own. *44.4%*

The Single Malts of Scotland Macduff 1991 Aged 16 Years (88) n23 t22 f21 b22. A malt on the very edge, but the pervading oily sweetness just guarantees excellence. *59.6%. sc. Speciality Drinks, UK.*

MANNOCHMORE

Speyside, 1971. Diageo. Working.

Mannochmore Aged 12 Years db **(84) n22 t21 f20 b21.** As usual the mouth arrival fails to live up to the great nose. Quite a greasy dram with sweet malt and bitter oak. *43%.*

⁘ **Mannochmore 1998 The Manager's Choice** db **(71.5) n18 t18 f17.5 b18.** A very bad cask day... *59.1%*

⁘ **Chairman's Stock Mannochmore 1982** claret wood, bott Feb 10 **(91.5) n22.5** very firm, crisp barley with the most lethargic smokiness; **t23** juicy, firm and, as the sugars build, hardens by the second; **f23** a distinct touch of green tea attaches itself to the vanilla and spice; about as crunchy as malt gets; **b23** quite excellent whisky with a mind of its own. *58.4% Wm. Cadenhead Ltd. 221 bottles.*

Connoisseurs Choice Mannochmore 1990 (85) n20 t22 f21 b22. Perhaps overly sweet and slightly featureless. *46%. Gordon & MacPhail.*

Duncan Taylor The NC2 Range Mannochmore 1996 Aged 10 Years (76.5) n20.5 t19 f18 **b19**. Mannoch-less. Overly sweet. Otherwise has little or nothing to say. *46%*

The Exclusive Malts Mannochmore Aged 16 Years cask no. 6600, dist May 92 **(84.5)** n20.5 t22 f21 b21. Decent barley sugar but one-dimensional. *53.8%. 234 bottles.*

Old Malt Cask Mannochmore Aged 18 Years refill barrel, dist Feb 91, bott Apr 09 **(91)** n22.5 just a touch of resin to the grist; refreshing, though, thanks to a citrus sub plot; **t23** sublime melt-in-the-mouth gristy delivery which makes no apology for its big malty theme; a dab of coconut water lightly sweetens the grassy middle; **f22.5** citrus returns, almost apologetically; vanilla intertwines with the barley; **b23** modest in its intentions and delicate, it is never less than charming. *50%. Douglas Laing. 288 bottles.*

Scotch Malt Whisky Society Cask 64.15 Aged 15 Years refill barrel, dist Jun 92 **(88.5)** n21.5 t23 f22 b22 Excellent in-your-face delivery; neat touches elsewhere. *57.1%*

Scotch Malt Whisky Society Cask 64.18 Aged 24 Years refill butt, dist Dec 84 **(93.5)** n23 subtle floral notes sit wonderfully with the lemon curd tart and butterscotch ...delicate and yummy...; **t24** such a crisp delivery: a surprise, really. The barley is sharp and mouth-watering: simple, but just so right... **f23.5** back to the butterscotch; the barley is right behind. Clear and crystalline to the very end; **b23** rarely are we let down by this distillery. And this is a particular cracker, even if the tale it tells is oft told. *56.3%*

MILLBURN
Highland (Northern), 1807–1985. Demolished.

Millburn 1969 Rare Malt db **(77)** n19 t21 f18 **b19**. Some lovely bourbon-honey touches but sadly over the hill and declining fast. Nothing like as interesting or entertaining as the massage parlour that was firebombed a few yards from my office twenty minutes ago. Or as smoky... *51.3%*

Cadenhead's Millburn 31 Years Old (88) n22 an attractive sprinkling of fresh sawdust over the very softest of peats and custard tart; **t23** lush malt coats the mouth before a bombardment of spicy oak keeps the barley at bay; **f21** an oaky echo; **b22** a rumbustuous, red-hot affair which is ensuring the distillery is not disappearing with a whimper. Now a must have cask: decent bottlings of any of the old Inverness distilleries are few and far between. *52.3%*

MILTONDUFF
Speyside, 1824. Chivas. Working.

Miltonduff Aged 15 Years bott code L00/123 db **(86)** n23 t22 f20 b21. Some casks beyond their years have crept in and unsettled this one. But some real big salty moments to savour, too. *46%*

⸭ **The Càrn Mòr Vintage Collection Miltonduff 1998** hogshead no. 3620, bott 2009 **(87)** n21.5 clean, under-developed gristy malt; **t23** stunningly beautiful malt with sheen due not lesst to the soft oils and delicate citrus sub plot; **f21** long malt before a vague tired oak bitterness creeps in; **b21.5** An outstanding example of just how well Miltonduff is made and how astonishly clean and juicy it's malt can be...and why so highly prized by blenders. Even in that exhausted old cask, the 24-carat quality of this under-rated distillery sparkles. *46% nc ncf 1224 bottles*

Dewar Rattray Miltonduff 1980 cask no. 12499, dist Sep 80, bott Nov 07 **(91)** n23 t23 f22.5 **b22.5**. If there is such a thing as whisky vintages, for the record I always thought that the era around 1982 was about the best MD I ever found. This busy, tight, aggressive little classic helps prove the point. *51.9%*

Duncan Taylor Collection Miltonduff 1999 **(86)** n22 t22.5 f20.5 b21. A delightful, though more vanilla-accented and curiously underpowered version of the WG '99. *40%*

The Exclusive Malts Miltonduff Aged 11 Years finished in Chateauneuf du Pape wine cask no. 5566, dist Mar 96 **(63)** n15 t17 f18 b18. The only thing created here is another French wine casked nightmare. Where the hell did that nose come from...? *54.1%. 327 bottles.*

⸭ **The Golden Cask Miltonduff 1998** cask no. CM140, bott 2009 **(74)** n18 t19 f18 b19. Dry, tight, bitter. *57% The House of MacDuff. 258 bottles.*

James MacArthur's Fine Malt Selection Miltonduff Aged 12 Years bott May 08 **(86)** n21.5 t21.5 f22 b21. Clean with big malt surge. Much younger than a 12 in many ways, but no bad habits either. *43%. James MacArthur & Co. Ltd.*

Lonach Miltonduff 1966 **(79.5)** n22 t19 f19.5 b19. Both the oak and barley are polished: a malt feeling its age. *40%. Duncan Taylor.*

Old Malt Cask Miltonduff Aged 12 Years refill hogshead, dist Mar 96, bott Sep 08 **(79.5)** n19.5 t19 f21 b20. Recovers with a malty-vanilla flourish after an uncertain, off-key start. *50%. Douglas Laing. 357 bottles.*

Old Malt Cask Miltonduff Aged 17 Years refill hogshead no. 3890, dist Sep 90, bott Sep 07 **(84.5) n22 t21 f20.5 b21.** Malty with bitterish tendencies. 50%. Douglas Laing. 216 bottles.

Old Malt Cask Miltonduff Aged 28 Years refill hogshead, dist Sep 80, bott Feb 09 **(92) n24** eye-closing, purr-inducing stuff: a stick of very lightly salted celery beside a glass of sweet orange juice. Cut up on the plate is a beetroot sans vinegar. Somewhere else some honey is spread on toast... Captivating, delicate, multi-complex and never less than sublime... **t23** much more oak involvement on delivery than the nose, but the barley is deftly applied and there is a gracious sweetness underpinning it all; **f22** oatcakes and distant vanilla: the oak plays an important but controlled role. **b23** doesn't quite live up to the nose: it is hard to see how it might. Nosing must constitute at least 60% of the experience with this whisky, though it's no disappointment in the glass, either, showing elegance throughout. 44.5%

Old Masters Miltonduff Aged 13 Years cask no. 5563, dist 96, bott 09 **(81) n19 t21 f20.5 b20.5.** Not all the heat is generated by the alcohol. By no means unpleasant but its scope is limited. 57.2%. James MacArthur & Co. Ltd.

Private Cellar's Selection Miltonduff 1987 bott 07 **(86) n21.5 t22 f21 b21.5.** A sturdy yet rotund old stager which fails to quite develop as it might towards the finale. The early fruit-edged barley does have some distinctively attractive elements. 43%

Provenance Miltonduff Aged 11 Years refill hogshead, dist winter 98, bott spring 09 **(74) n19 t19 f18 b18.** Sweetish, but never begins to gel. 46%. Douglas Laing.

Scotch Malt Whisky Society Cask 72.21 Aged 11 Years refill hogshead, dist Oct 97 **(90) n23** easy integration of light barley, vanilla and spiced yam; something of a light, youngish Guyanese pot still rum, too.; **t22.5** soft and bulging with gristy barley freshness and pounding spice, though tires and dries towards the middle; **f22** regains a second wind as a light oiliness helps stretch the sweeter notes over the exposed oak; **b22.5** refined and delicate but makes a big early statement. 56%

Scott's Selection Miltonduff 1988 bott 08 **(83) n21 t22 f20 b20.** A pleasing malt with its entire emphasis on the early barley kick. 54.3%. Speyside Distillers.

⟶ **The Whisky Agency Miltonduff 1980 (94) n23** chocolate orange and figs; **t23** stunning delivery and mouth feel; spot on oils lift the barley and fruit soup; light salt sharpens and intensifies; **f24** superbly long fade with the oak displaying a sweetened liquorice, fitting charmingly with the barley **b24** a cracking malt comfortable with its age and underscoring this distillery's latent talent. 49%

Whisky-Doris Miltonduff 8 Years Old dist 6 Jun 99, bott 19 Oct 07 **(84.5) n22 t21 f21.5 b21.** Clean, malty, attractive: a mildly fiery up and downer. 55.7%. Whisky-Doris.

Whisky Galore Miltonduff 1999 (87.5) n21.5 t22.5 f21.5 b22. Absolutely top hole MD for this age. Simplistic maybe. But as fresh as a nibble on the ear. 46%. Duncan Taylor.

MORTLACH
Speyside, 1824. Diageo. Working.

Mortlach Aged 16 Years db **(87) n20** big, big sherry, but not exactly without a blemish or two; **t23** sumptuous fruit and then a really outstanding malt and melon mouthwatering rush; **f22** returns to heavier duty with a touch of spice, too; **b22** once it gets past the bold if very mildly sulphured nose, the rest of the journey is superb. Earlier Mortlachs in this range had a slightly unclean feel to them and the nose here doesn't inspire confidence. But from arrival on the palate onwards, it's sure-footed, fruity and even refreshing ... and always delicious. 43%

Mortlach 32 Years Old dist 71 db **(88) n22 t22 f22 b22.** Big and with attitude.... 50.1%

Adelphi Mortlach 1990 Aged 17 Years sherry butt, cask no. 5945, dist 90, bott 08 **(86.5) n21 t21.5 f22.5 b21.5.** Competent and attractive for this distillery during this less than glorious period. A touch of smoke on the nose, lively spice and a lid kept on the sweetness makes for a lovely dram. 57.5%. 516 bottles.

⟶ **A.D. Rattray Mortlach 1990** cask no. 5950 **(79) n20 t20 f19 b20.** Monotoned malt syrup. 58.6% A.D. Rattray Ltd

⟶ **Berrys' Own Selection Mortlach 1989** cask no. 5141, bott 2010 **(89.5) n23** not what I was expecting by a long shot: excellent weight to the malt with the sugars in support rather than swamping; even the vanillas have a smartness about them, especially with the light orange blossom attachment....unusually impressive....; **t22.5** a beautiful turn of malt on the palate with there being a splendid countering between malt and vanilla and malt and light salt; **f22** very equal vanilla again with the barely sweetened barley just hanging in there; **b22** there you go. Proof they exist: you can get seriously decent Mortlach after all. Well done Doug McIvor for unearthing this rarity. I mean, it is Mortlach isn't it Doug...? Or were you so shell-shocked by Charlton's 4-0 mauling at the Lions' Den of Millwall, you went and put the wrong labels on....???? 46% Berry Bros & Rudd

Berrys' Own Selection Mortlach 1991 cask no. 4227, bott 07 **(66) n17 t16 f15 b16.** A classic example of the old United Distillers wine-treated casks. I need say no more. *56.4%. Berry Bros & Rudd.*

Cadenhead's Mortlach Aged 19 Years sherry butt, dist 88, bott Feb 08 **(78.5) n19 t21.5 f19 b19.** Some decent oily grape. *576%. 664 bottles.*

Chieftain's Mortlach Aged 15 Years sherry wood **(69) n17 t18 f17 b17.** This sweet and sulphurous effort is one 69 I don't like... *46%. Ian Macleod.*

⸛ **The Coopers Choice Mortlach 1990 Sherry Wood Aged 18 Years** sherry butt no. 4421, bott 2009 **(57) n14 t15 f14 b14.** Grimly sulphured for all the big grape breast-beating. *46% nc ncf The Vintage Malt Whisky Co. Ltd.*

Dewar Rattray Mortlach 1991 cask no. 4238, dist May 91, bott Nov 07 **(80) n19 t20 f20.5 b20.5.** Clumsy, sweet, chewy and with a certain brown-sugared charm. *55.5%*

Duncan Taylor The NC2 Range Mortlach 1993 (81) n21 t20 f20 b20. A steady, no frills, malty Speysider. *46%*

Duthies Mortlach 16 Years Old (88.5) n22.5 unusually clean aroma for this distillery with a lovely, intense fruity theme; **t22.5** genuinely juicy with barley concentrate on the rampage; **f21.5** drier, vanilla-led; **b22** easily one of the more enjoyable Mortlachs on the market. *46%. Cadenhead's for Germany.*

⸛ **Duthies Mortlach 21 Years Old (74) n19 t19 f18 b18.** Tight, bitter and confined, with little scope for manoeuvre. *46% Wm. Cadenhead Ltd*

The Golden Cask Mortlach 1994 cask no. CM115 **(76) n19 t20 f18 b19.** Syrupy and though sumptuous and hearty, enough of the mud from the cask sticks...especially on the finish. *55.1%. House of Macduff. 305 bottles.*

⸛ **The Golden Cask Mortlach 1994** cask no. CM148, bott 2009 **(86) n21 t22 f21 b22.** Above average for the distillery with a balanced oaky dryness to the usual thick, sweet barley. *57.5% The House of MacDuff. 329 bottles.*

⸛ **Gordon & MacPhail Distillery Label Mortlach 21 Years Old (84) n21 t22 f20 b21.** Attractive, well weighted, malty and competent. *43% Gordon & MacPhail*

⸛ **Gordon & MacPhail Generations Mortlach 70** dist 1938 **(96.5) n24** the oak tried to play hardball but fails: instead a light bourbony touch arrives, which in turn is softened by a surprising turn of frutiness. Mainly figs and gooseberry but with a spoonful of chocolate mousse to keep it company. Meanwhile the most delightful and delicate smoke drifts aimlessly around....; **t24** the palate is treated to something unique and extraordinary: 70-y-o oak. But rather than trying to take over the show it is instead quite content to let the softest possible body allow the sultanas and playful smoke have the lion's share of the limelight; various thin brown sugars ensure the desired sweetness is maintained; **f23.5** long and at last some spices; small, fizzing and pernickety. The smoke continues its perambulations around the palate; the fruits remain subtle with the vaguest hint of something exotic and the vanillas are light and fragile; **b25** this is most probably the least likely whisky you are able to encounter. To stay 70 years in the barrel and remain intact after all that time defies logic. To actually go several stages further and become one of the world's most stupendous whiskies of the year defies belief. It is a freakish situation, where the body of the malt and the state of the cask must have been at a million to one state of readiness to have received and complimented each other over so long a period. Remember, when this was distilled, there had only ever been one world war. The whisky itself confirms how peat was used to a far greater scale in the average Speyside distillery than is the case today. And how the sherry casks, so clean and unspoiled, could add fruitiness and oak in just so amounts. It is impossible to have selected anything more spectacular to mark my 999th "new" whisky for the 2011 Bible: the 2012 edition will be hard pressed to trump this. But for those of you lucky enough ever to try it, once you have emptied the glass, DON'T wash it. Allow the aroma to grow for the next hour or two. If I scored the nose then, it would be a 25. Talk about "Rage,rage against the dying of the light".... *46.1%*

⸛ **Hart Brothers Mortlach Aged 18 Years** 1st fill sherry butt, dist Jun 90, bott Dec 08 **(58) n15 t16 f13 b14.** Uncompromisingly sulphured. *46% Hart Brothers Ltd*

⸛ **Kingsbury's Mortlach 15 Years Old 1989 (61) n15 t16 f15 b15.** Grim, even by Mortlach's undemanding standards. *56.7% Japan Import System Celtic Series*

Northern Light Mortlach 1988 Cask Strength cask no. Q125 **(86.5) n22 t22 f21 b21.5.** Thoroughly pleasant with some delightful orangey notes on the nose and seriously thick spiced malt on the delivery and middle. Well spiced, complex and the kind of dram that demands a refill. *59.2%. Qualityworld, Denmark.*

⸛ **Old & Rare Mortlach Aged 17 Years** dist Sep 92, bott Nov 09 **(87.5) n22** a rare subtlety (by Mortlach standards) to the sugars works a treat here, breaking up the usual porridge rather well; **t23** very decent weight, with a light liquorice, semi-boubony thread to the developing oils; big, thick layering, but well measured and attractive; **f20.5** bitters out as expected, but not with too much pain; **b22** my Pavlovian response to first seeing this was that it should be, preferably, bottled under "Old and Extinct". But, I have to say, I'm delightfully surprised with this one which is helped along the way by taking a buccaneering rummy route on the old flavour portfolio rather than its usual hopeless Speyside malt gubbins. Don't mind a second glass of this at all. *56.1% Douglas Laing & Co Ltd. 28 bottles.*

⁂ **Old Malt Cask Mortlach Aged 12 Years** refill butt no. DL 5559, dist Sep 97, bott Nov 09 **(72.5) n19 t19 f17 b17.5.** A brown sugar fest on delivery. *50%. 365 bottles.*

⁂ **Old Malt Cask Mortlach Aged 12 Years** sherry butt no. DL 6074, dist Sep 97, bott Apr 10 **(71) n18 t18 f17 b18.** Pretty unforgiving. I think I need some SMWS 76.67... *50% Douglas Laing & Co Ltd. 330 bottles.*

Old Malt Cask Mortlach Aged 15 Years sherry butt no. 3934, dist Sep 92, bott Oct 07 **(88) n22.5 t22 f21.5 b22.** A bit of a typically cloying pup for this distillery but, untypically, there are no off notes and balance is pretty satisfying. *50%. Douglas Laing. 671 bottles.*

Old Malt Cask Mortlach Aged 16 Years sherry cask, dist Sep 92, bott Jan 09 **(81.5) n20.5 t22 f19 b20.** The old-fashioned trifle, grapey nose survives a sulphur scare, as does the initial, thick delivery. And even for a while we have a bit of a sultana festival. But that dreaded off note can't escape the finale, as is so often the case... *50%. Douglas Laing.*

Old Malt Cask Mortlach Aged 16 Years sherry butt, dist Sep 92, bott Dec 08 **(73.5) n18.5 t19 f18 b18.** Grapey, sweet, lush...and flawed. *50%. Douglas Laing. 582 bottles.*

Old Malt Cask Mortlach Aged 19 Years Gabriel Meffre red wine cask, dist Mar 89, bott Sep 08 **(85) n22 t21 f21 b21.** Pretty acceptable version of a malt which struggles from bottling to bottling. Here there are an extra few spoonfuls of Demerara on the Dundee cake and the big, fig biscuit chew ends up with a bit of Jammy Dodger. Silky but laid on with a trowel. *50%. Douglas Laing. 359 bottles.*

⁂ **Old Malt Cask Mortlach Aged 21 Years** refill hogshead no. DL 6126 **(73) n17 t19 f19 b18.** Do you know, I wondered if I was being a little harsh on the Mortlachs....was I guilty of a personal dislike affecting my scores? Then I found this one, mis-filed amongst the Longmorns and nosed it thinking it was from that excellent Speyside distillery. I shrank back in horror and surprise until I took a closer look at the bottle, to realise what had happened. And it just underlined, in the most garish neon, what second rate whisky this distillery is continuously guilty of producing. Sorry. But it had to be said. *50% Douglas Laing & Co Ltd*

Old Masters Mortlach 1989 Aged 16 Years cask no. 969 **(77) n19 t20 f19 b19.** Furry, bitter, harsh and hot: one of the better Mortlachs from this period... *56.5%. James MacArthur.*

Provenance Mortlach Aged 12 Years refill hogshead, dist summer 96, bott spring 09 **(81) n18 t20.5 f22 b20.5.** Treacle-sweet; recovers well with a bit of barley bite and spice, even, after the poor nose. *46%. Douglas Laing.*

Sassenach's Dram Whisky Club Mortlach 14 Year Old (83.5) n22 t21 f20 b20.5. Excellent fresh, grassy barley on nose. *46%. Exclusively for Sassenach's Dram Whisky Club Ltd.*

Scotch Malt Whisky Society Cask 76.57 Aged 8 Years 1st fill barrel, dist Jun 99 **(81.5) n20 t21 f20.5 b20.** Clumsy, sweet and cloying: must be Mortlach. *60.2%*

Scotch Malt Whisky Society Cask 76.62 Aged 9 Years refill barrel, dist Jun 99 **(85) n21.5 t22.5 f21 b20.** Last week I was at the dentist. Time to go back: it's like sucking on molten barley-flavoured sugar. Decent juiciness, though. *59.4%*

⁂ **Scotch Malt Whisky Society Cask 76.67 Aged 10 Years** 1st fill barrel, dist Jun 99 **(80) n20 t20.5 f19.5 b20.** Saccharine sweet. Kind of pleasant, in the same way that certain medicines are when you are a kid....even complete with mandatory bitter finish. *58.7% 243 bottles.*

Scotch Malt Whisky Society Cask 76.63 Aged 12 Years refill barrel, dist Sep 96 **(84) n21 t21.5 f20.5 b21.** Sweet and moderately hot. But some excellent oak absorbs the worst excesses and allows an attractively malty dram to flourish. *60.3%*

⁂ **Scotch Malt Whisky Society Cask 76.70 Aged 15 Years** 1st fill sherry butt, dist May 94 **(72) n19 t18 f17 b18.** Thick, glutinous, hot.... One for me to take home....now creosote has been outlawed. *59% 627 bottles.*

⁂ **Scotch Malt Whisky Society Cask 76.71 Aged 20 Years** 1st fill sherry butt, dist Aug 89 **(59) n15 t15 f14 b15.** One assumes this was bottled by the Society only to give its members an idea of what sulphured, truly awful whisky tastes like. *60.1% 606 bottles.*

Scotch Malt Whisky Society Cask 76.58 Aged 23 Years refill hogshead, dist Apr 85 **(83.5) n22 t20 f21.5 b20.** Wonderful nose, full of intensely malty, slightly fruity possibilities. But hopes of greatness are dashed by the cloying, furry delivery. *60%*

Scotch Malt Whisky Society Cask 76.59 Aged 23 Years refill hogshead, dist Apr 85 **(79) n20 t19 f20 b20.** Seriously hot whisky: and I'm not talking about the strength. Some less than delicate sugar-coated barley bails it out. At Whisky Fairs (usually in German-speaking lands) I am amazed by how many tell me they count Mortlach among their favourites. The fact that the SMWS have bottled three casks of the stuff must mean there is a big demand out there. I am at a loss: I really must be missing something. *61.8%*

⟫ **Scotch Malt Whisky Society Cask 76.66 Aged 23 Years** refill hogshead, dist Apr 86 **(74.5)** n19.5 t20 f17 b18. The odd spice mixed in with the sugars. *59.1%*

Scott's Selection Mortlach 1990 bott 07 **(84.5)** n20 t22.5 f21 b21. A collector's item: a lightly peated Mortlach. Some charm on delivery and the smoke helps disguise an unhelpful cask. *56%*

Whisky Tales Mortlach 16 Years Old sherry cask, dist 91, bott 07 **(72)** n20.5 t22 f16 b17.5. It's the finish that tells the most telling tale, and as is often the case with this distillery it's a grizzly one involving sulphur. *56.2%. nc ncf. 349 bottles. Germany.*

Wilson & Morgan Barrel Selection Mortlach Aged 18 Years Old butt no. 4422, dist 90 **(74.5)** n18 t19 f19 b18.5. A typically mucky, lightly sulphured affair from this distillery. Oddly enough there is a strawberry jam attractiveness late on. *56.8%. Wilson & Morgan.*

MOSSTOWIE
Speyside, 1964–1981. Two Lomond stills within Miltonduff Distillery. Now dismantled.

Rarest of the Rare Mosstowie 1975 cask no. 5811 **(94)** n25 egg noggin, several squirts of vanilla essence, crumpled rose petals and a stunning mixture of citrus and berry fruit. Whisky of this age just doesn't get better on the nose... t23.5 soft, almost playful barley thickened slightly by a backbone of diluted maple syrup; very delicate fruit naturally intertwines; f22 a degree of bitterness reminds you of the great age here; b23.5 given that these chaps don't happen along too often, I thought it'd be the perfect way to celebrate 999 whiskies for this edition (an even rarer Glencraig is lined up next). And I have been perfectly rewarded: a much better bottling than the last I tasted, this has remained intact from nose to finish and apparently revels in its rarity. The best I have tasted from these lost stills for over a decade. Actually, thinking about it....ever. *48.5%. Duncan Taylor.*

Rarest of the Rare Mosstowie 1975 cask no. 5816 **(90.5)** n23 peaches and custard; a light flicker of mango t23 soft with the barley dissolving on impact; the vanillas begin with an equally deft touch but show they mean business by the middle; the early soft, peachy fruits dissolve with the barley f22 thins and spices out but the custard remains b22.5 talk about getting old gracefully... *48.4%. Duncan Taylor.*

Rarest of the Rare Mosstowie 1975 cask no. 5817 **(81)** n21.5 t21.5 f19 b19. Pleasant, malty but hot and skeletal. *47.7%. Duncan Taylor.*

⟫ **Rare Old Mosstowie 1979 (84.5)** n21.5 t21 f21 b21. Edging inextricably well beyond its sell by date. But there is a lovely walnut cream cake (topped off with brown sugar and spices) to this which warms the cockles. Bless... *43% Gordon & MacPhail*

NORTH PORT
Highland (Eastern), 1820–1983. Demolished.

Brechin 1977 db **(78)** n19 t21 f18 b20. Fire and brimstone was never an unknown quantity with the whisky from this doomed distillery. Some soothing oils are poured on this troubled – and sometimes attractively honeyed – water of life. *54.2%*

Connoisseurs Choice North Port Brechin 1982 bott 08 **(79.5)** n21 t21 f18.5 b19. Although the oak has left a bitter mark, there is a jaunty fruitiness to this on both nose and delivery which speaks well of the barley. *43%. Gordon & MacPhail.*

Private Cellar North Port 1982 bott 07 **(89.5)** n24 t22 f21.5 b22. An over-aged malt which, having reached greatness against the odds, has begun a descent. Even so, the fabulous nose and big barley oomph makes this dram a very enjoyable place to be. *43%. Speyside Distillers.*

Rarest of the Rare North Port 1981 cask no. 775 **(93.5)** n23 oh, you fruity thing...kumquats and pears with a splash of custard...and even something vaguely smoky; t24 North Port....??? Really....????? The delivery is sublime; just the right degree of oil and then a slow release of delicate sugars and a build up of intense barley. Wonderful...!!! f23 wondrous layering of vanilla, lemon and butterscotch. Long, confident and just so classy; b23.5 Rarest of the Rare all right...!! Easily the finest North Port I have come across in bottled form. This may have been a throat-ripping monster in its youth, but in old age it really has reached a point of true charm and charisma. Stunning – and one hell of a shock! *52.9%. Duncan Taylor.*

Rarest of the Rare North Port 1981 cask no. 779 **(95)** n24.5 candyfloss, old-fashioned sweetshops, old-fashioned leather handbags; syrup-coated coconut, Niederegger marzipan... mmmmm!!! t24.5 no less beautiful on delivery: the weight of the softly sugared coating is sublime, but better still there is spice and warmer vanilla notes for contrast; for all this the barley is never lost, is heard early and gets louder towards the middle; **f22.5** still delightful, but by comparison with the just about perfect delivery, the finale is so much thinner with the malt clinging onto the vanilla the best it can; **b23.5** the old Brechin distillery is in danger of getting a good posthumous name for itself...this is what great whisky is all about. 56.5%.

Scott's Selection North Port 1980 bott 07 **(95) n23.5 t24.5 f23.5 b23.5.** Brechin, the home of North Port, must be where they make London buses: you wait a lifetime for a fantastic bottling...then two come along at once.... The Rarest of the Rare bottling really was the finest I had tasted – until five minutes later when I encountered this. My job never ceases to amaze me. Who knew that east coast malt could be this damned good...???? 48%

OBAN

Highland (Western), 1794. Diageo. Working.

Oban 14 db **(84) n20 t22 f21 b21.** Slick and fruity, you can close your eyes and think of Jerez. Oban seems a long way away. A very decent dram. But I want my old, bracing, mildly smoky, fruitless Oban back!! Those who prefer malts with a sheen, sweet and with enormous fruit depth won't be disappointed. 43%

Oban Aged 15 Years The Distiller's Edition db finished in Montilla Fino casks, dist 92, bott 07 **(90) n22.5 t23 f22.5 b22.** This isn't all about complexity and layering. It's about style and effect. And it pulls it off brilliantly. 43%

Oban Aged 15 Years The Distiller's Edition db finished in Montilla Fino casks, dist 93, bott 08 **(91.5) n22** nutty, tight, a little musty; **t24** much more assured: the dryness of the grape sports beautifully against the obviously more outgoing and sweeter barley: excellent balance between the two; **f22.5** perhaps the Fino wins, as it dries and embraces the oak quite happily; **b23** delicate and sophisticated whisky. 43%

PITTYVAICH

Speyside 1975–1993. Demolished.

Pittyvaich Aged 12 Years db **(64) n16 t18 f15 b15.** It was hard to imagine this whisky getting worse. But somehow it has achieved it. From fire-water to cloying undrinkability. What amazes me is not that this is such bad whisky: we have long known that Pittyvaich can be as grim as it gets. It's the fact they bother bottling it and inflicting it on the public. Vat this with malt from Fettercairn and neighbouring Dufftown and you'll have the perfect dram for masochists. Or those who have entirely lost the will to live. Jesus.... 43%. Flora and Fauna.

Old Malt Cask Pittyvaich Aged 16 Years refill hogshead no. 3886, dist Oct 90, bott Sep 07 **(71) n17.5 t18 f18 b17.5.** Drinkable. But you'll wonder why you bothered: another nothing dram from Speyside's ugly duckling. 50%. Douglas Laing. 345 bottles.

Old Malt Cask Pittyvaich Aged 18 Years sherry butt, dist Jun 90, bott Jan 09 **(76) n18.5 t21 f17.5 b19.** If you find a more uncompromisingly sweet malt this year, let me know. 50%

Provenance Pittyvaich Aged 12 Years refill hogshead no. 4255, dist Autumn 95, bott Spring 08 **(78) n20 t20 f19 b19.** Thin, hot-ish, niggardly barley with minimal development: which means for a Pittyvaich not bad at all... 46%. nc ncf. Douglas Laing.

Rarest of the Rare Pittyvaich 1979 cask no. 5635 **(87) n22.5** a delicate Pittyvaich? The barley appears untroubled by the normal gluepot vapours which have taken a day off; **t23** I'm waiting for my throat to be ripped out and it hasn't happened. A bit like Wylie Cyote jumping up and down on the ACME dynamite to see if it works, I take another mouthful and am very pleasantly surprised – no, make that shocked - that the huge malt actually caresses the tastebuds and brings with it a mild sugary edge to the natural caramels. Ye gods...!! This is Pittyvaich and actually very pleasant stuff... **f20** much more like it at the death with a thin gluey fade; **b21.5** I had to check the bottle for this one. Was this really Pittyvaich? Could it be that this mouth-filling, ultra-delicious beast is the prodigy of one of the world's most hopeless distilleries? It appears it is.....!!!! The finish is up to scratch, though.. 48.3%. Duncan Taylor.

Rarest of the Rare Pittyvaich 1979 cask no. 5636 **(79) n21 t20 f19 b19.** Just when for a fleeting second you think the beast may have been tamed, you suddenly – and painfully – realise it hasn't. In this case with a momentary spasm of agony through a rear tooth. At moments like that, there is almost a begrudging respect. 54%. Duncan Taylor.

Rarest of the Rare Pittyvaich 1979 cask no. 5640 **(81.5) n21 t21 f19 b20.5.** Big, rollocking barley flattened by natural caramels; hot and graceless with a splintering finish. But still much better than the norm. 50.2%. Duncan Taylor.

Scotch Malt Whisky Society Cask 90.11 Aged 19 Years refill barrel, dist Mar 90 **(75.5) n20 t20 f17 b18.5.** Thin and impoverished, though the oak does its level best to beef up the barley: one can only imagine with a horror bordering on morbid fascination what this must have been like 19 years ago.... 54.9%

PORT ELLEN
Islay, 1825–1983. Closed.

Port Ellen 1979 db **(93) n22** mousy and retiring; a degree of oak fade and fruit on the delicate smoke **t23** non-committal delivery but bursts into stride with a series of sublime, peat-liquorice waves and a few rounds of spices; **f24** a surprising gathering of oils rounds up the last traces of sweet barley and ensures an improbably long – and refined – finish; **b24** takes so long to get out of the traps, you wonder if anything is going to happen. But when it does, my word...it's glorious! *57.5%*

Port Ellen 28 Years Old 7th Release bott 2007 db **(92.5) n22.5 t23 f24 b23**. This has now taken about as much oak as it can comfortably absorb. There are splinters in every segment but such is the all round brilliance of this malt, it appears to take it all in its stride, even allowing some citrus strains to be heard. It's the stuff that brings a tear to the eye... *53.8%*

Port Ellen 29 Year Old 8th release, dist 78, bott 08 db **(90.5) n23** plenty of oak ensures the lemon/vanilla aspect outweighs the smoke and barley; **t22.5** barley and butterscotch make a hesitant landing before a huge wave of oak and smoke crashes down upon it; **f22.5** relatively short compared to bygone days. The vanilla remains the main theme, with drying oaky pulses and soft oils developing; a final, defiant trademark gristiness ensures enough sweetness covers the journey...gosh, it's the kind of thing to bring a tear to the eye... **b22.5** all great dynasties come to an end, and Port Ellen, at this kind of vintage, is reaching its. Quite simply, this was a whisky designed for blending but was capable of so much more and in its own distilling lifetime was never recognised as such. Only after its demise was its genius formally acknowledged. Here, in this bottle, we have a whisky crooning to us in much the way that an old great singer might in his or her dotage for one last time to a loving crowd experiencing the full gamut of bitter-sweet emotion. For the glory and charisma is still there to cast you under its spell, but some high notes are missed, the timing not quite what it was; yet still we stand and applaud because we recognise it exactly for what it is: beauty and genius still, but fading beauty; receding genius. Something which only those of us, ourselves now of a certain vintage, can remember as being that unique, almost naked, celebration of Islay malt whisky it once so beautifully and so gloriously was. *55.3%*

Berrys' Own Selection Port Ellen 1982 cask no. 2030/2035, bott 08 **(95.5) n24 t24 f23.5 b24.** If you are to never taste a Port Ellen again and remember it in all its deft glory, then you could do a lot worse than this. *46%. Berry Bros & Rudd.*

⋅⋅⋅ **Chieftain's Port Ellen 27 Years Old** hogshead, dist May 82, bott 2009 **(92) n24** stunning cocoa and spice intro to this. The peat is obviously about but tries not to dominate and even takes a back seat to the lemon curd tart; **t23** busy delivery with spice and smoke on equal terms with the unusually early mocha; **f22.5** lingering smoke and a real cranking up of the drier vanilla; **b22.5** one of the best new Port Ellens I have tasted this year. *56.8% nc ncf*

⋅⋅⋅ **Connoisseurs Choice Port Ellen 1982 (89.5) n23.5** floaty peat with still a hint of grist, lightened further by a twist of lemon; **t23** stays on its ultra-light course. That lemony grist shows first, then a slow after-you, after-me build up of smoke and oak; **f21.5** slightly spicy and bittering oak; **b21.5** every aspect is gentle and understated. Wonderful. *43%*

Dewar Rattray Cask Collection Port Ellen Aged 24 Years cask no. 2488 dist 13 Oct 82 bott 17 Sep 07 **(95.5) n24 t24 f23.5 b24.** Of all the Port Ellen bottlings this year, this has to be about the best. It is a near faultless example of a great distillery held for a very long time in a near perfect cask. *60.6%. 188 bottles.*

The Golden Cask Port Ellen 1982 cask no. CM105, dist Oct 82, bott Oct 07 **(84.5) n21 t22.5 f20 b21.** A most curious Port Ellen which from nose to finish appears to be giving its all while handcuffed. The oak influence is not the best. But there are some lovely moments, especially as it reached a honey-tipped crescendo; and also briefly as the salty-vanilla searches for those sweeter notes. But it all seems somewhat muted with the peating and overall complexity levels down. *51%. House of Macduff. 355 bottles.*

⋅⋅⋅ **The Golden Cask Port Ellen 1983** cask no. CM155 **(74) n17 t20 f18 b19**. Sadly, more the yellow cask.... *51.8% The House of MacDuff*

Norse Cask Selection Port Ellen 1979 Aged 28 Years hogshead ref no. QW1311, dist 79, bott Dec 07 **(93) n23 t24 f22.5 b23.5.** A wonderful bottling which has a dash of something unexpected and previously unspotted each time you taste it. *53.6%. nc ncf. Qualityworld, Denmark. 277 bottles.*

Norse Cask Selection Port Ellen 1983 Aged 24 Years hogshead cask no. CM016, dist 83, bott Jul 08 **(92) n22** pure farmyard – or impure – with the sweetish smoke blanketing some building peppers and hickory; **t23.5** dazzlingly sweet at first, with a sugar candy softening of the tastebuds before the smoke strikes; a burst of peppers is restrained as a light toffee-raisin fills the middle ground; **f23** chewy, a return of spice and a touch of hickory. The smoke is never more than an accompaniment; **b23.5** a very different PE, here in a form I'd say is unique. The story chops and changes from one minute to the next and though perhaps technically challenged from time to time, the result is as intriguingly different as it is enjoyable. *52.5%.*

Old & Rare Port Ellen Aged 25 Years dist Apr 82, bott Sep 07 **(95) n23.5 t24.5 f23 b24.** Simply fabulous. *54.8%. Douglas Laing, exclusively for The Whisky Shop, Edinburgh. 226 bottles.*

Old & Rare Port Ellen Aged 25 Years dist 82, bott Jan 08 **(95) n24 t24 f23 b24.** Were it not for the semi-brittle finale this would have been in the play offs for world whisky of the year. Utter joy. *57.7%. Douglas Laing. 300 bottles.*

Old & Rare Port Ellen Aged 30 Years dist Sept 78, bott Jan 09 **(91.5) n21.5** thickset with peat and dusty burnt toast; **t23** the first half dozen or so waves are gorgeously weighted with smoke and molasses and bolstered by a superb sharpness; **f24** long, satisfying, a touch of salt and mocha while a few lime notes thin out the weighty smoke and vanilla; **b23** has stemmed the march of time impressively. *52.5%. Douglas Laing.*

⁙ **Old & Rare Port Ellen Aged 30 Years** dist May 79, bott Oct 09 **(92.5) n24** creaks and reeks with antiquity: pine, heather and honey have by now replaced the more pungent elements of the peat smoke; **t23** a Demerara-sweetened oak kick then the missing smoke from the nose rushes in like a silver screen hero untying the maiden bound to the tracks as the train thunders towards her. But here the smoke appears to release the cocoa and sugars before the oaky express claims everything before it. Complex, chewy and wonderfully balanced; **f22.5** vaguely smoked vanilla; **b23** seen off the years with rare aplomb. *52.1% ncf Douglas Laing. 190 bottles.*

⁙ **Old Bothwell Single Cask Port Ellen 1979** cask no. 7087, bott Jul 10 **(82) n19 t22.5 f20 20.5.** Plenty of citrus, but a case of too much oak limiting the charm. *54.9% Old Bothwell Wine & Spirits Co. Ltd*

⁙ **Old Bothwell Single Cask Port Ellen 1982** cask no. 2852, bott Aug 10 **(84) n20 t22.5 f20 b21.5.** Silky, buttery and the smoke just a little shy with the peat offering an ashy dryness. Some most un-PE nip and bite here. *63.2% Old Bothwell Wine & Spirits Co. Ltd*

Old Malt Cask Lochnagar Aged 19 Years sherry butt, dist May 90, bott Jul 09 **(85) n22.5 t21 f21 b20.5.** certainly no shortage of honey, or chocolate fudge. But it is all rather swimming in natural caramels. *50%. Douglas Laing.*

Old Malt Cask Port Ellen Aged 24 Years refill butt no. 3915, dist Nov 82, bott Sep 07 **(94) n23.5 t23.5 f23 b24** Enchanting. *50%. Douglas Laing. 476 bottles.*

Old Malt Cask Port Ellen Aged 25 Years refill hogshead no. 3651, dist Apr 82, bott Jul 07 **(81.5) n20 t20 f21 b20.5.** Big spices...in fact this one is pretty hot. *50%.*

Old Malt Cask Port Ellen Aged 25 Years cask no. 4112, dist Nov 82, bott Jan 08 **(83) n20 t20.5 f21.5 b21.** Oily and full of citrus. *50%. nc ncf Douglas Laing. 589 bottles.*

Old Malt Cask Port Ellen Aged 25 Years refill butt no. 4244, dist Nov 82, bott Apr 08 **(77) n19.5 t20 f18.5 b19.** Great whisky in a poor barrel. *50%. nc ncf Douglas Laing. 506 bottles.*

Old Malt Cask Port Ellen Aged 25 Years sherry cask no. 3639, dist Feb 82, bott Aug 07 **(65.5) n16.5 t17 f16 b16.** Very severe sulphur. Bugger. *50%. nc ncf Douglas Laing. 594 bottles.*

Old Malt Cask Port Ellen Aged 26 Years dist May 82, bott Oct 08 **(87) n23** citrus (and creosote!) is woven throughout the sweet, peaty fabric; **t22** big oaky demeanor, but the lightly sweetened phenols still possess charm and depth; **f20.5** the peat fades as dry vanilla takes over; **b21.5** sees off the oaky challenge. *50%. Douglas Laing.*

Old Malt Cask Port Ellen Aged 26 Years refill hogshead, dist May 82, bott Oct 08 **(86) n20 t23 f21 b22.** A bit hot and oily. But this is much better than the slightly murky nose shapes up. The delivery is dense and beautifully peated. *50%. Douglas Laing. 263 bottles.*

Old Malt Cask Port Ellen Aged 26 Years sherry cask no. 4447, dist 82, bott Jun 08 **(80) n18 t21.5 f20.5 b20.** Sulphur stained, perhaps. But the gooseberries amid the peat makes for something unique and just about collectable. *50%. Douglas Laing. 721 bottles.*

⁙ **Old Malt Cask Port Ellen Aged 26 Years** refill butt no. DL 5398, dist Sep 82, bott Jul 09 **(92) n23** lively, tingling peat. An eggy cake batter offers sweetness; **t23** civilised delivery with gently intensifying malt and a few useful spices pinging around; **f22.5** the smoke drifts into the butterscotch finale; those light spices persist; **b23.5** a beautiful buzz to this one. *50% Douglas Laing. 712 bottles.*

Old Malt Cask Port Ellen Aged 27 Years refill butt no. 3887, dist Dec 79, bott Sep 07 **(84.5) n21.5 t22 f20.5 b21.** Lovely, gentle whisky, but there gets a point, even for malts as outstanding and unique as Port Ellen, where they become too old and begin an inexorable path downwards. *50%. Douglas Laing. 589 bottles.*

⁙ **Old Malt Cask Port Ellen Aged 27 Years** refill hogshead, dist Apr 82, bott Nov 09 **(83.5) n21 t21 f20.5 b21.** Not the first, and by no means the last PE to have slipped over the oaky edge. *55.2% Douglas Laing for the Whisky Fair, Germany*

Parkers Whisky Port Ellen 1982 "Pert mELLon" Bottling bott 07 **(96) n24 t25 f23 b24.** Don't know about "Pert Mellons". But this is so arousing in so many other ways. A true classic. *56.8%. Parker's Whisky, UK. 220 bottles.*

Port Ellen Aged 25 Years Single Cask Butt No 2036 (87) n24 t22.5 f20 b20.5. An odd one, this. Starts off like a train, cocking a gristy snook at its age. Then just flattens out under a welter of toffee blows. *58.1% Bottled by Bladnoch Distillery 638 Bottles*

Provenance Port Ellen Aged 23 Years refill butt no. 3402+3403, dist Spring 1983, bott Winter 2007 **(88.5) n23 t21 f22.5 b22.** Weird how a malt, which gets a whopping 88-plus mark is a little disappointing. But that just shows the quality we have come to expect from this tragically lost distillery. *46%. nc, ncf. Douglas Laing.*

Provenance Port Ellen Aged 24 Years dist 83, bott 07 **(86.5) n22 t22 f21 b21.5.** Attractive sweet-dry balance; breathtakingly laid-back for its age. *46%. nc ncf. Douglas Laing.*

Provenance Port Ellen Aged 24 Years refill butt no. 4114, dist spring 83, bott winter 08 **(86) n22 t22 f21 b21.** Attractive citrus, lethargic smoke and signs of a slightly tiring cask. *46%. nc ncf. Douglas Laing.*

Provenance Port Ellen Aged 24 Years refill butt no. 4127, dist spring 83, bott winter 08 **(93) n23.5 t24 f22 b23.5.** Takes a few mouthfuls to genuinely recognise the grace and suavity on display. *46%. Douglas Laing.*

Provenance Port Ellen Aged 25 Years sherry butt, dist winter 83, bott autumn 08 **(90) n23.5** an idyllic rock pool nose: the peat is firm yet restrained in its overall effect; a sprig of mint confirms the antiquity; **t22.5** some intriguing coconut cake amid the medium-layered peat; predominantly sweet, and barley can be found as well as smoke; **f21.5** lightly smoky; just bitters out a little; **b22.5** a lovely cask on the edge of its age range. *46%. Douglas Laing.*

Provenance Port Ellen Aged 25 Years (93.5) n23 t23 f24 b23.5. Now this is closer to what I really expect from a Port Ellen 25, though it does have some unusual attributes. A controlled explosion of masterful beauty and a must for Port Elleners. *46%*

⋯⋮⋯ **Provenance Port Ellen Over 26 Years** sherry butt no. DMG 5746, dist Spring 1983, bott Winter 2010 **(95.5) n24** a wall of aroma: fruit and smoke in just about equal proportions, as is the sweetness against the drier vanillas. An all evening experience; **t23** surprising degree of early oak, but this soon dissipates for the fruit and smoke to resume their dominance; **f24.5** long, silky, burnt raisin and sultanas, Demerara sugars and smoky caresses to the very end; **b24** strikingly beautiful whisky. *46% nc ncf Douglas Laing*

⋯⋮⋯ **Provenance Port Ellen Over 27 Years** refill butt no. DMG 6101, dist Spring 1983, bott Spring 2010 **(89) n22** dry oak tightening around the more delicate peat; a real bonfire feel to this nose; **t22** a very soft oil base helps the barley and smoke merge in intensity and, aided by a blast of full on orange, see off the drier oak; **f22.5** sweeter vanilla and late gristiness; **b22.5** the Port Ellens I have tasted this year look as though age is beginning to tell. This one narrowly maintains its integrity. *46% nc ncf Douglas Laing*

The Queen of the Moorlands Rare Cask Port Ellen 1982 bott 07 **(90) n23 t22 f22 b23.** One of those whiskies you really have to take your time over and concentrate on. Take straight, without thinking; you might not be too excited. Peruse it, and you might just be very pleasantly surprised... *46%. nc ncf. The Wine Shop, Leek & Congleton, and Islay Whisky Shop.*

Signatory Port Ellen Distilled 1982 Aged 25 Years dist Apr 82, bott Sep 07 cask no 1136 **(92.5) n24 t23.5 f22 b23.** After 25 years and sporting such a peaty countenance it is hard to believe a whisky could be quite so elegant and refined. But this is all about charm. And a sense of loss and regret. *46%*

⋯⋮⋯ **Wilson & Morgan Barrel Selection Port Ellen 27 Years Old** cask no. 2347, dist 1982, bott 2010 **(87.5) n23** powdery peat; excellent sweet-dry balance with the vanillas just seeming to convey a little lime; **t22.5** sweet, icing sugar sweetness then an immediate spice impact; oily and vanilla-tame through the middle; **f20** traces of bitter oak; **b22** the odd phrase in this is glorious. But the oak is just negating the more complex moves. *61.3% Wilson & Morgan*

The Whisky Fair Port Ellen Aged 25 Years sherry wood, dist 82, bott 07 **(94) n23 t24 f23 b24.** An enchanting malt which captures many of the delicate – and powerful – facets of this late distillery's personality. *59.6%*

PULTENEY

Highland (Northern), 1826. Inver House. Working.

Old Pulteney Aged 12 Years db **(85) n22 t23 f19 b21.** There are few malts whose finish dies as spectacularly as this. The nose and delivery are spot on with a real buzz and panache. The delivery in particular just bowls you over with its sharp barley integrity: real pulse-racing stuff! Then...toffee...!!! Grrrr!!! If it is caramel causing this, then it can be easily remedied. And in the process we'd have a malt absolutely basking in the low 90s...! *43%*

Old Pulteney Aged 15 Years db **(91)** n21 pretty harsh and thin at first but some defter barley notes can be detected; t24 an attention-grabbing, eye-wateringly sharp delivery with the barley in roasty mood and biting immediately with a salty incision; the barley-sugar effect is mesmerising and the clarity astonishing for its age; f23 long, with those barley sugars working overtime; a slight salty edge there but the oak behaves impeccably; b23 only on about the fourth or fifth mouthful do you start getting the picture here: enormously complex with a genuine coastal edge to this. The complexity is awesome. *54.9%*

Old Pulteney Aged 17 Years db **(95)** n22 some weaker oak notes that shows signs of fatigue. But these are offset by evidence of praline and the most delicate puff of smoke; t24 amazingly sweet, as though the barley has ganged up with the oak and pooled its sugars. To balance, drier vanilla and even the odd bourbony liquorice note can be detected; f25 now this is where this malt comes into its own. In fact, this is one of the finishes of the year thanks to the slow burn with the transition from clear, slightly salted barley with a dollop of maple syrup to something running the gamut of milky chocolate notes. One of the longest finishes to be found with the transformation in flavour taking place in super slow-mo so every single nuance can be captured by the tastebuds. In style, unique. In terms of pleasure, absolutely mind-blowing. This is, quite simply, perfection... b24 an improvement on last year's wheezy bottling that defies belief: indeed, if there was a Jim Murray Award for Most Improved Whisky of the Year, this would walk it. And confession time: like a Victorian murderer visiting the scene of his crime, I returned to this malt having originally given it 86. However, for some reason – and a reason that became so apparent when the magnitude of this whisky's astonishing finale got through my thick skull – something kept nagging at me that I might have been very wrong about this one. Now, at 11.23pm, I have taken time out I should be spending in bed to see if justice is being done. It wasn't. Hopefully it is now. This truly is a world great whisky. *46%*

Old Pulteney Aged 21 Years db **(90.5)** n21.5 salty, chalky and citric; t24 what a lovely delivery: lemon and lime fused with barley sugar and chocolate caramel; has almost the character of a candy with a soft centre as the flavours spread around the palate; a flavour profile far removed from the dowdy nose; f22 back to more toffee caramel with a dusting of mildly salted grist; b23 maybe it's just my imagination, but it appears as though some of these distillery bottlings have been worked on over the last year to 18 months, Here's another example of a so-so bottling not so long ago showing some real zeal and class. Surprisingly light for a malt that can scrap like the best of them, but this really is a lovely surprise dram. *46%*

Old Pulteney Aged 23 Years bourbon db **(84)** n20 t22 f21 b21. For all its great age there is a lethargy to this malt which doesn't quite work on the nose but does on the body. Intense malt, but at this age perhaps the complexity should be higher. *46%*

Old Pulteney Aged 23 Years sherry db **(89)** n22 Party Ring biscuits and the softest of crushed raisin; t22 wonderful bitter-sweet/barley-sherry balance; an unusual style and mouthfeel with spices prominent early on; f22 again, superbly relaxed delivery of fruit before the coffee cream; dries with aplomb; b23 highly stylish. Not a single note out of tune. *46%*

Old Pulteney 30 Years Old db **(92)** n23.5 fabulous mix of Jaffa cake and bourbon, seasoned by a pinch of salt; t23.5 an early, unexpected, wave of light smoke and silkier oak gives immediate depth. But stunning, ultra-juicy citrus and barley ensures this doesn't get all big and brooding; f22 thinner and oakier with a playful oak-spice tingle; plenty of vanilla controls the drier aspects; b23 I had to laugh when I tasted this: indeed, it had me scrambling for a copy of the 2009 Bible to check for sure what I had written. And there it was: after bemoaning the over oaking I conjectured, "As Pulteney has the fascinating tendency to radically shift style over not too long a period, I can't wait for the next instalment." And barely a year on, here it is. Pretty far removed from last year's offering and an absolute peach of a dram that laughs in the face of its 30 years.... *45%*

⇢ **Old Pulteney Isabella Fortuna** cask no. WK499, bott 2010 db **(91.5)** n23 reminiscent of a breakfast I had in Grenada some years back: lots of slightly green banana, the lightly sweetened oiliness of mixed diced nuts and a light coastal saltiness in the air: just so wonderfully fresh...; t23.5 wow! Pulteney rarely comes more unambiguously malty than this. For all the bite of the salt and oak – which is more a little nip and nibble, to be fair – it is the barley which shines proudest of all; both sweet and sharp in equal measures; f22.5 a touch tangy; b22.5 over the 30-odd years I have been tasting whisky from this distillery I have noticed that its quality simply continues rising, unlike a number of other whiskies I could name. Here's further proof. *52% 18,000 bottles.*

A.D. Rattray Old Pulteney 1982 cask no. 502 **(90) n23** any more coastal and you'd expect to see an albatross sitting atop a lighthouse singing sea shanties...salty, with a distant buzz of peat reek being tossed around by the shoreline breeze. Pretty malty, too... **t24** faultless weight to the delivery and the manner in which the barley unfolds in dream-like fashion allows the sweeter notes to flourish, including the most vague smoky, spicy ones; **f21.5** annoyingly bitters out as the timbers begin to shiver. **b22** you really can't keep an excellent distillery down... *47.7%*

·::· **A.D. Rattray Pulteney 1982** cask no. 504, dist Apr 82, bott Mar 10 **(96) n24** good god! An albatross on a light house singing a sea shanty...; **t23.5** more early oak than the last Rattray '82 I sighted, but extra fruitcake, too, and this one has a fair degree of salt and Demerara in the recipe. Gorgeously handsome honeycomb fills the middle ground with the build up of something coffee-related there, too...; but still that coastal feel is never far from the surface; **f24.5** on this evidence I might just try salt in my coffee...not to mention more chocolate honeycomb, burnt raisin... and an albatross...; near perfection!! **b24** magnificent malt from a quite magnificent distillery. Easily one of the highlights of the Scotch whisky year. *53.5%*

·::· **Cask Strength Old Pulteney 1995 (85) n22 t22.5 f19 b21.5.** Big, toe-curling fruit. But not without the odd maturation flaw. And curious lack of the normal coastal breeze. *60.5%*

Duncan Taylor Collection Pulteney 1977 cask no. 3976 **(88) n21 t23 f22 b22.** No doubting the class on show here. *55.9%*

Duncan Taylor Collection Pulteney 1989 cask no. 10260 **(91) n22 t24 f22 b23.** Displays all the lucidity and verve missing from the distillery bottling at this age. *58%*

Duncan Taylor Collection Pulteney 1989 Aged 18 Years cask no. 10259 **(85) n21 t21.5 f21.5 b21.** The oak this excellent spirit was put into was not quite up to the mark. A shame. There is evidence enough that a better cask would have resulted in a belter. As it is, there is enough energy and charisma to make for a genuinely enjoyable dram. *57.1%*

Gordon & MacPhail Old Pulteney Aged 15 Years (87.5) n22 lemon cupcakes; **t22** salivating mix of fresh, clean barley and thickening fruit; **f21.5** drier: the lightness of the spirit allows the oak to gain a bitter hand. But the clarity of the malt acts as a healthy buffer; **b22** juicy and zesty. *40%. Gordon & MacPhail.*

Kingsbury's 'The Selection' Pulteney 7 Years Old cask no. 800120 & 800121, dist Jun 01, bott Jun 08 **(83.5) n21 t21.5 f20 b21.** Gristy, sweet and very light. *43%. Japan Import System. 658 bottles.*

·::· **Rare Vintage Old Pulteney 1974 (83) n21 t20 f21 b21.** Sadly, even the great distilleries can radiate their untarnished brilliance for only a finite time. Some lovely old brown sugars seeing off the oaky excess here, but still a malt that needs a Zimmer to move about the taste buds. *43% Gordon & MacPhail.*

Scotch Malt Whisky Society Cask 52.18 Aged 7 Years refill barrel, dist Jun 01 **(89) n22** rain-dampened woollen sports jacket; salty; **t23.5** a fabulous riot of fresh, juicy flavours: the barley is spruced up with a salty tang and a light spice buzz helps point towards the sweetish oaks; **f21.5** loses its way slightly as the barley and oak fail to agree terms; some surprisingly chalky vanilla for its age; **b22** I have long been a champion of bottling at this age: this is a good example as to why. *66.3%*

ROSEBANK
Lowland 1840–1993. Closed. (But if there is a God will surely one day re-open.)

Rosebank Aged 12 Years db **(95) n24** strands of honey and honeycomb entwine around a softly herbal, but enormously weighted maltiness: the type of nose you can stick your head in and wallow about for a few minutes; **t24** this has to be near perfection in regard to texture and not far off with the way the honeypolished malt trips around the palate with an almost apologetic spiciness for accompaniment. Just so accomplished and breathtaking; **f23** long, more honeycomb, with hints of liquorice and soft herbs; **b24** infinately better than the last F&bottling, this is quite legendary stuff, even better than the old 8-y-o version, though probably a point or two down regarding complexity. The kind of whisky that brings a tear to the eye...for many a reason.... *43%. Flora and Fauna.*

Rosebank 22 Years Old Rare Malts 2004 db **(85) n22 t23 f19 b21.** One or two Rosebank moments of joyous complexity but, hand on heart, this is simply too old. *61.1%*

Rosebank 25 Years Old db **(96) n24.5** smoke? From a Rosebank? Well, it's there. My nostrils don't lie to me that much. Grapey fruit? From a Rosebank? Well something is happening in that direction. Either by smoke or mirrors: and there is no question of the smoke...Complex? Don't even start me on that one. The kind of nose that takes 20 minutes of your time. You'll find rose petal and dried dates and chestnut puree...and still you won't be much more in the know... **t23.5** it doesn't just hit the palate, it caresses it with the nubile fingers of young lady and the talons of an eagle: the malt stands erect and proud, yet with a deft smoke and a slight oily complexion; **f24** this is ridiculous; no whisky has the right to be this good at the death. The smoke is now there in terms that can be recognised and appreciated, the soft oils of the body cloak and caress; the exuberance of the malt/fruit fantasy just continues to evolve and not only that with the company of the odd pinch of something cocoa-rich being added; the shifts between sharp barley and softer, more toasty natural sugars become more dramatic: I am almost exhausted just trying to fathom the unfathomable... **b24** I had to sit back, take a deep breath and get my head around this. It was like Highland Park but with a huge injection of sweetened chocolate on the finale and weight – and even smoke – from a Rosebank I had never quite seen before. And believe me, as this distillery's greatest champion, I've tasted a few hundred, possibly thousands, of casks of this stuff over the last 25 years. Is this the greatest of all time? I am beginning to wonder. Is it the most extraordinary since the single malt revolution took off? Certainly. I have just looked at my watch: these tasting notes have taken one hour and 21 minutes to compile....where has the time flown, where have I been? Do I endorse it? My god, yes! *61.4%*

Cadenhead's Rosebank Aged 16 Years dist 91, bott Feb 08 **(93) n23.5 t24 f22 b23.5.** Class never lies.... *55.7%. 230 bottles.*

Cadenhead's Rosebank Aged 20 Years dist 89, bott 09 **(96) n24.5** pretty close to the perfect nose: not only clean and not an off note from distillate or cask, but the barley shimmers with that vital degree of honey sweetness; salt and lime adds the delicate fizz; **t24** the clarity on the nose is every bit as evident here: the barley appears to be carved from honey and set in golden syrup; **f23.5** sherry trifle...without the sherry... **b24** even at this ridiculous age a distillery which peaked so young, this is legendary whisky for the annals... and to tell your grandchildren you once tasted. *52.1%*

⋄⋄ **Cask Strength Rosebank 1991 (67) n18 t18 f15 b16.** A rare disaster from G&M...and Rosebank: not something you would have seen coming. Has this spent time in a sherry butt? Because some sulphur is seeping in from somewhere. And that on top of a ghastly butyric note. Oh dear....taste buds ruined, that's my tasting over for the day... A shocker. *55.3%*

Chieftain's Rosebank 18 Years Old sherry butt, dist Feb 90 **(91) n22** complex: a steady stream of discreet oaky-vanilla notes offer differing degrees sweetness and saltiness; occasionally a deeper, dryer gust crowds the barley out altogether; **t23.5** superb delivery with vast amounts more juicy barley concentrate and lightly spiced fudge, natural caramels well up towards the middle; **f23** if anyone remembers that old syrup-treated coconut that passed for kiddies tobacco in the early '60s, you'll appreciate this: funny I never went on to smoke, really...especially as there is the very lightest dab of something phenolic here, too; **b23.5** perhaps not quite in the element of when the malt was a decade younger, but this is unquestionably made of the very finest stuff. Wonderful, and once opened the type of bottle that empties quickly.. *46%. Ian Macleod Distillers Ltd.*

Connoisseurs Choice Rosebank 1991 (85.5) n22 t22 f20.5 b21. Disappointing. I visited the distillery in its final days and was aware that something less than the best casks available were being sent there. Here is a typical victim of the United Distillers policy at the time; the malt shows every sign of trying to stretch itself but is thwarted. Promising, but ultimately frustrating malt which still shows enough class on delivery especially to add to any collection. *43%. Gordon & MacPhail.*

Hart Brothers Rosebank Aged 17 Years dist Jun 90, bott Mar 08 **(92) n23.5 t23 f22.5 b23.** Just one of those lovely malts which ticks all the right boxes. And look at the tasting notes for the Montgomerie's 1990 below: tasted a month or two apart and without note comparison...consistent whisky, or what! *46%. Hart Brothers Limited*

⋄⋄ **Hart Brothers Rosebank Aged 18 Years** dist Jun 90, bott May 09 **(91) n23** light honey sweetens the oak and barley theme; **t23.5** a delightful dollop of lemon curd sharpens the lush barley; **f22.5** a plethora of vanilla notes, always with a lightly sugared coating; **b22** about as soft and sweet as a Lowlander gets. Glorious. *46% Hart Brothers Ltd*

Montgomerie's Rosebank 1990 (88.5) n22.5 t22.5 f22 b22. Much fresher than its age might suggest: a gentleman dram. *46%. Montgomery & Co. Ltd.*

Montgomerie's Rosebank 1990 cask no. 1756, dist Jul 90, bott Jun 07 **(92.5) n23.5 t23.5 f22.5 b23.** Busy and beautifully biting. *46%*

Old Malt Cask Rosebank Aged 17 Years refill hogshead no. 3740, dist Jun 90, bott Jul 07 **(85) n20 t22.5 f21 b21.5.** An up and down Rosebank leaning on its malty weight, but still finding some lively fruit from somewhere. You get the feeling of a solidly-made malt. *50%. 283 bottles.*

Old Malt Cask Rosebank Aged 18 Years refill butt, dist Feb 90, bott Sep 08 **(87) n21** gooseberry and marmalade topped with delicate grist; **t22** much younger delivery: not even close to 18 years in stature: but that said, the always mouth-watering, slightly fizzy delivery builds slowly in understated intensity; **f22** longer than expected with the vanilla dissolving into the barley; **b22** outwardly appears a little on the thin and shy side, the victim of a sluggish old cask. Slow investigation reveals something a whole lot more charming, however. *50%.*

Old Malt Cask Rosebank Aged 19 Years refill butt, dist Feb 90, bott Feb 09 **(88) n22** sugar-sprinkled barley-vanilla... enticing; **t22.5** beautifully salivating and lays on the barley sugar thickly, though in a multitude of thin layers; **f21** back to untaxing vanilla; **b22.5** definitely on the simplistic side. But it does clean, sweet maltiness...and does it well!! *50%. 374 bottles.*

Old Malt Cask Rosebank Aged 19 Years refill butt, dist Feb 90, bott Mar 09 **(89) n22** light, honey-drizzled barley; **t23** brilliant arrival with an almost Highland Park-style honey and spice beat to the clean malt **f21.5** dries a little too austere, a point, maybe, but loads of chewing on the way; **b22.5** Rosebank doesn't always convert to old age with grace. Here, though, it has embraced a sweet character with relish. *50%. Douglas Laing. 444 bottles.*

⋯ **Old Malt Cask Rosebank Aged 19 Years** refill butt no. DL 5700, dist Feb 90, bott Dec 09 **(89.5) n22.5** the odd atom of phenol perks up an already lively citrus-engaged barley theme; **t23** salivating and lightly spiced, the roll call of honey is well attended; **f22** custard and rhubarb....while those light spices fizzle... **b22** almost impossible not to be charmed by this one. Playful and expansive. *50% Douglas Laing & Co Ltd. 670 bottles.*

⋯ **Old Malt Cask Rosebank Aged 19 Years** refill hogshead no. DL 5360, dist Jun 90, bott Jul 09 **(79) n20 t21 f19 b19.** Curiously sullen for a Rosebank with huge natural caramels at work. *50% Douglas Laing & Co Ltd. 327 bottles.*

Scotch Malt Whisky Society Cask 25.45 Aged 16 Years refill hogshead, dist Jul 91 **(92) n22.5 t23.5 f23 b23** Heavenly malt which tries to out-honey Highland Park...and just about succeeds. Those busy, lively spices, similar to the small grain in certain bourbons means Kenrtucky meets Falkirk. *53.5%*

Scotch Malt Whisky Society Cask 25.49 Aged 17 Years refill barrel, dist Jul 91 **(88.5) n21.5** heading towards Kentucky... **t22.5** scrummy mouthfeel with some very early cocoa notes laying the foundation for the gathering malts; juicy but something of a chocolate candy to this one; **f22.5** those bourbony notes are underlined with the big roasty fudge kick and a cascade of drier vanilla; the spices gather pace; **b22** having spent probably twice as long in the cask than it's optimum period, it can be forgiven for its limited complexity. But its character is still without a blemish. *56.1%*

Scotch Malt Whisky Society Cask 25.48 Aged 18 Years refill hogshead, dist Nov 90 **(77) n19 t20 f18 b19.** A rare very ordinary cask from this distillery. The nose and underlying dull bitterness suggests this was filled into less than excellent wood. *59.9%*

⋯ **Scotch Malt Whisky Society Cask 25.54 Aged 18 Years** refill barrel, dist Jul 91 **(85.5) n21.5 t22 f21 b21.** Fails to roll out the usual Rosebank honeyed carpet. Chirpy, but a less than sympathetic cask reduces the charm. *54.6% Scotch Malt Whisky Society*

The Single Malts of Scotland Rosebank 1991 Aged 16 Years small batch, bott Sep 07 **(80) n20 t20 f20 b20.** Rosebank in a form I have never seen before: no great notes, no bad ones, little complexity...just thick, enjoyable malt. Weird. *46%. Speciality Drinks.*

The Whisky Society Rosebank 1991 Aged 16 Years bott Sep 07 **(89) n21.5 t23.5 f21.5 b22.5.** I must admit, I didn't see Rosebank hang on to its brilliance for quite so may years. Just so alluring. *56.1%. Speciality Drinks.*

ROYAL BRACKLA
Speyside, 1812. Dewar's. Working.

Royal Brackla Aged 10 Years db **(73) n18 t20 f17 b18.** A distinct lowering of the colours since I last tasted this. What on earth is going on? *40%*

Cadenhead's Royal Brackla Aged 15 Years rum barrel, dist 92, bott Feb 08 **(93) n22 t24 f23 b23.5.** Brimming with personality and tension. Really fun, high quality whisky. *57.3%.*

Cadenhead's Royal Brackla Aged 16 Years rum barrel, dist 92, bott 09 **(96.5) n24** just a puff of smoke adds weight to the coconut concerto; **t24.5** simply breathtaking: while the barley fairy melts in the mouth, friendly spices adds complexity to the growing cocoa and coconut; the middle ground begins to take on a cheerful bourbony disposition; **f24** long, very faintly oiled with a light maple syrup massaging the vanilla and delicate liquorice; **b24** another quite awesome cask from Cadenhead's. After tasting the Rosebank, I cannot remember the last time I ever tasted two successive 96-ers: I have been spoiled... *54.7%*

Premier Barrel Royal Brackla Aged 9 Years (86) n20 t22.5 f22 b21.5. Deliciously one-dimensional. Excellently made, not a single off-note but the oak has barely made a mark. About as easy-drinking a whisky as you'll ever find. *46%. Douglas Laing. 374 bottles.*

Provenance Brackla Aged 9 Years dist winter 99, bott winter 08 **(84.5) n20 t22 f21 b21.5.** Oily, malty, juicy, refreshing, deftly spiced, Reisling-looking.....and amoebically simple. *46%.*

Provenance Royal Brackla Aged 12 Years refill hogshead no. 4267, dist Autumn 95, bott Spring 08 **(86) n21.5 t22 f21 b21.5**. Attractively malty and gentle. *46%. nc ncf. Douglas Laing.*

ROYAL LOCHNAGAR
Highland (Eastern), 1826. Diageo. Working.

Royal Lochnagar Aged 12 Years db **(84) n21 t22 f20 b21**. More care has been taken with this than some other bottlings from this wonderful distillery. But I still can't understand why it never quite manages to get out of third gear...or is the caramel on the finish the giveaway...? *40%*

⚜ **Royal Lochnagar 1994 The Manager's Choice** db **(89.5) n23** a lovely fruit cocktail containing guava and lychee amid the grapey orange; **t23.5** sensual delivery with the barley at first forming an oily base then a subtle layering of oak and light fruits; **f21.5** mallow and mocha...but the toffee drowns out the higher notes; **b21.5** much more intense and heavyweight than the norm. Also a bit of toffee on the finish brings down the marks slightly. Great stuff, even so. *59.3%*

Royal Lochnagar Selected Reserve db **(89) n23** superb oloroso, clean and spicy with apples and pears; **t23** stupendous spice lift-off which really starts showing the malts to great effect; **f21** the malts fade as the toffee progresses; **b22** quite brilliant sherry influence. The spices are a treat. *43%*

The Cärn Mör Vintage Collection Royal Lochnagar 1986 hogshead, cask no. 1109, dist 86, bott 09 **(77) n20.5 t19 f18.5 b19**. Though this appears to be from the same batch as the Duncan Taylor bottlings, this one isn't in the same league. The slightly lactic nose does offer plenty of small still richness. But the delivery, though malty, errs on the bitter side. *46%.*

Duncan Taylor Collection Royal Lochnagar 1986 cask no. 942 **(87.5) n22.5** soft, clean with a small still metallic note. Attractive; **t22** juicy malt has some real body lurking about; **f21.5** thins, custardy and then a late metallic, malty tang; **b21.5** one of the better Lochnagars on the market, showing elegance. *56.4%. Duncan Taylor.*

Duncan Taylor Collection Royal Lochnagar 1986 cask no. 948 **(89) n23** a bourbony edge to this one with a dash of honey and salty butter. Pretty understated and sexy; **t22** immediate sweet-tart start with loads of barley shovelled in. Excellent shape and body; **f22** the metallic edge is there but the vanilla and barley adds stature and length; **b22** a more lush, richer version than cask 942 and almost as good as has been seen from this distillery for a while. For the best try cask 951. *56.9%. Duncan Taylor.*

Duncan Taylor Collection Royal Lochnagar 1986 cask no. 951 **(92) n21.5** light, buttery yet curiously coastal; **t24** much more vim and vigour on delivery with an immediate chalky-barley impact then that small still metallic sharpness you might expect; juicy, with spot-on oils that help spread the just-so sweetness; **f23** fabulous light mocha latches on to the sweet barley and vanilla; **b23.5** the bitter-sweet balance is exemplary. Quite the little star. *53.8%.*

⚜ **Duncan Taylor Collection Royal Lochnagar 1990** cask no. 356 **(75.5) n17.5 t19 f20 b19**. There are constant reminders here that the quality of this malt from this period can be variable. While the nose and delivery are technical train wrecks, just occasionally that small still charm attempts some damage limitation. *54.3%*

⚜ **Duthies Royal Lochnagar 10 Years Old (89.5) n23** gosh!! Does malt get any fresher than this? Amazingly lively and effervescent; **t22.5** a tad on the hot side but the ultra refreshing lemony malt is stunning: not a dull moment...; **f22** perhaps the odd touch of second-rate cask, but still that citrussy malt abounds; **b22** now that was fun... *46%*

Harris Whisky Co. Royal Lochnagar Aged 12 Years cask no. 519, dist Jul 96, bott Sep 08 **(89) n23** gosh! How complex is this...??? Curiously herbal: alongside the more basic citric notes, this is a wonderfully delicate fanfare; **t23** mouth-watering. Although the emphasis is on the fabulous barley and all its varying degrees of sweetness, again there is a herbal infusion which cranks up the complexity meter; **f21** falls flat on its face as the oak bites a little too bitterly after the vanilla takes hold; **b22** big delivery of citrus on the nose and palate paves the way for a really charming malt. A very different Lochnagar. *46%. Harris Whisky Co.*

Norse Cask Selection Royal Lochnagar Aged 12 Years Fino sherry butt no. 520, dist Jul 96, bott Nov 08 **(83.5) n20.5 t22.5 f20 b20.5**. An attractive smudge of malty honey through the middle, but the bitter finish unsettles the balance. *57.6%.*

Norse Cask Selection Royal Lochnagar 1977 Aged 29 Years cask no. DL863 **(75) n20 t19 f18 b18**. A touch of soap on the nose and pencil shavings on the palate. But there is still some glossy barley to be had. *50.4%. WhiskyOwner.com, Denmark.*

Old & Rare Lochnagar Aged 21 Years sherry cask **(91) n24** brilliant! A spoonful or a pinch of everything ranging from grape to bourbon – except smoke. A half hour with your nose poked in this can rarely be better spent...; **t22.5** honey and grape arm-wrestle for supremacy.... **f22** the sherry wins – just – but is immediately thumped by some bitter-ish oak; **b22.5** this little guy has come of age impressively. *53.1%. Douglas Laing.*

⋰ **Old Malt Cask Lochnagar Aged 13 Years** refill butt no. DL 6290, dist Jun 97, bott Jun 10 **(89) n22.5** perky barley of the most mouth-watering grassy variety....; **t23** ...and exactly the same again on delivery: there is even a big spice injection which is hardly the norm for a Lochnagar; **f21.5** the usual sma' still coppery tang; **b22** an excellent malt with which to check that your taste buds are alive and well... *50% Douglas Laing. 380 bottles.*

Old Malt Cask Lochnagar Aged 32 Years refill hogshead, dist Jan 77, bott Jan 09 **(92.5) n23.5** well, well...gentle but unmissable smoke on a Lochnagar...if you know where to look!! Mildly leathery and creaking. But for its age...pretty impressive; **t23.5** excellent sheen to the barley and even a puff of smoke; melting sugars ward off and perfectly even out the oak; works exceptionally well; genuinely mouth-filling; **f22.5** wonderful fade, with lime and figs adding to the vanilla and muscovado; the tell-tale metallic edge is there but blunted by the busy barley; **b23** far, far better than I expected: the malt has stayed the course and, perhaps above all other similar distilleries, really does radiate the fact that the stills are circumferentially challenged...Rounds off an above average year for bottled Lochnagars: Great stuff!! *47.7%. Douglas Laing. 74 bottles.*

⋰ **Premier Barrel Royal Lochnagar Aged 11 Years** dist Jun 98 **(86.5) n21.5 t22 f21.5 b21.5.** Fresher than a new-grown daisy. And sweeter, too. *46% Douglas Laing. 270 bottles.*

Provenance Lochnagar Aged 9 Years sherry butt no. 3804, dist Winter 1998, bott Summer 2007 **(75.5) n18.5 t19 f19 b19.** Guess what's up with the cask... *46%. Douglas Laing.*

⋰ **Provenance Royal Lochnagar 12 Years Old** refill hogshead no. DL 5245, dist Summer 1997, bott Spring 2010 **(89) n23** let me grab that sample bottle again: it is Lochnagar! With smoke...?? Virtually not a jot of oak present, so it's sweet, lightly phenolic barley all the way.... lovely!! **t23** again, just the most mouth watering, oak-free experience you might ever have. The peat simply swirls about the taste buds, adding a bit of spice here and there and even some fizzing kiddies' purple Love Heart candy kicks in; **f21.5** barley and not much else; **b21.5** the serious limitations of the cask means this won't run off with many prizes. But a very unusual touch of smoke on this helps paper over the cracks and contributes to a delightful experience where the malts pull in many delicious directions. If you see it, grab it. A real collector's item. And one to be drunk... *46% Douglas Laing & Co Ltd*

⋰ **The Whisky Fair Lochnagar 1972 (94.5) n23.5** apricots and almonds make for a sexy overture; **t23.5** beautiful oils heighten the bitter-sweet delivery; sharp kumquat and then a grassy bourbon sweet quickly followed by vanilla; **f23.5** a little cocoa on the vanilla an though it dries, does so with panache; **b24** a phenomenal cask which shows both the small still character and a distillery and cask absolutely on top of its game. *50.7%*

Wild Scotsman Royal Lochnagar Aged 12 Years hogshead, cask no. CM118, dist 96, bott 08 **(85) n21 t21 f21.5 b21.5.** An attractively lightweight, refreshing dram with the older cask allowing some of the richer barley notes full scope. *46%. House of Macduff.*

ST MAGDALENE
Lowland, 1798–1983. Closed.

Linlithgow 30 Years Old dist 73 db **(70) n18 t18 f16 b18.** A brave but ultimately futile effort from a malt that is way past its sell-by date. *59.6%*

Berry's Own Selection St. Magdalene 1982 bott 08 **(95.5) n24** not sure honey gets any more subtle than this while the fretwork of the barley against the oaky-vanilla accompaniment is simply astonishing; an insanely teasing smokiness is also just detectable; **t22.5** surprisingly, the oak is first to show and it takes a little while before the barley begins to get the upper hand; it does so as the actual mouthfeel changes shape and moves towards a more silky delivery; also a faint smoky weight begins to form; **f25** now the oak is fully integrated and the finale is breathtaking in its charm and depth. Like a pastel-coloured sunset, one flavour merges into the next. There is a frappe-mocha signature to the final movements, its glory underlined by the sparing use of muscovado sugar and vanilla: spellbinding and in every way perfect; **b24** when you get an old whisky from a dead distillery, you pray for something a little special; those prayers have been answered. Glorious: you have died and St Magdalene is waiting at the gates of heaven... *46%.*

Old Malt Cask Linlithgow Aged 24 Years dist Dec 82, bott May 07 **(90) n22 t23 f22 b23.** This distillery may sound as if it has a lisp, but rarely do you get such malty clarity from the mouth. Best I have tasted from here for a very long time. *50%. Douglas Laing. 303 bottles.*

Old Malt Cask St. Magdalene Aged 25 Years refill butt no. 4282, dist Oct 82, bott May 08 **(83.5) n22 t20 f21 b20.5.** The intriguing aroma has a few scars of battle over the last quarter of a century, and is the highlight of this light and malty dram. *50%. nc ncf. 378 bottles.*

Old Malt Cask St Magdalene Aged 26 Years refill butt, dist Sep 82, bott Oct 08 **(90)** **n23** the oak is deft and lands on the vibrant citrus notes like snowflakes.... **t22.5**...and like snowflakes this simply melts on the tongue, such is the delicateness of the barley and gentle lemon; clean, allowing the barley to be seen with no problem; **f22** a light fluttering of vanilla adds a chalky dimension; **b22.5** simply beautiful. *50%. Douglas Laing. 511 bottles.*

SCAPA

Highland (Island–Orkney), 1885. Chivas. Working.
Scapa 12 Years Old db **(88) n23** honeydew melon, soft salt and myriad styles of barley: really complex with a sprinkling of coal dust on the fruit; **t22** truly brilliant mouth arrival: the most complex display of malt and cocoa, the fruit is ripe figs with a thread of honey; **f21** a slight bitterness with some developing toffee, but the malt stays the distance; **b22** always a joy. *40%*
Scapa 14 Years Old db **(88) n22** toasted oak, butterscotch and lime; **t22.5** fresh barley for its age, a few bands of light oak but some fruity notes towards the drying middle **f21.5** chalky but some toffee interferes with the usual sweeter finale; **b22** enormous variation from bottling to bottling. In Canada I have tasted one that I gave 94 to: but don't have notes or sample here. This one is a bit of dis-service due to the over-the-top caramel added which also appears to douse the usual honeyed balance. Usually, this is one of the truly great malts of the Chivas empire and a classic islander. *40%*
Scapa 16 Years Old db **(81) n21 t20.5 f19.5 b20.** The label fires the first warning: "A smooth and full bodied single malt". Which is why I am so disappointed. I don't want that from this magnificent, truly great distillery: that is not what Scapa is all about. On the nose, on delivery and finish I get caramel. I should be getting salt and honey. I should be getting petulant, chocolaty oak under a bitter-sweet assault of beguiling complexity. I should be getting, even from my tasting table 700 miles away, the sea-spray and winds of Orkney stabbing into my face. For it to be so tamed and toothless is a crime against a truly great whisky which, handled correctly, would be easily among the finest the world has to offer. Why has this apparently been subjected to such large doses of caramel? It is flat, allowing only a teasing shadow of the massive honey lurking beneath. Due to the cruelly unsympathetic management of Scapa in its benighted days of Allied, there are tragically few casks for Chivas to sell. So, please, can we taste the real Scapa...? It is far too rare and precious to dish out in this toned-down, populist fashion: the whisky lover has moved away from what was acceptable in the 1980s. Uncoloured. Un-chillfiltered and at 46%, these days please. A whisky which will live long in the memories of all those who try it. And, fittingly, at last do the distillery the justice it has long since deserved. *40%*
⸰⸬⸰ **Scapa 'the' Orcadian 16 Years Old** db **(87.5) n22** honey offering both density to the body yet a lightness of touch; distant smoke alongside a squeeze of satsuma and shake of salt; **t22** silky and gently spiced on delivery; a citrus and toffee follow through; a hint of honey lurks; **f21.5** the softness of touch persists though one is left waiting for the oak which seems unable to battle through the toffee-honey soup; **b22** a thin wisp of honey is key to the weight and balance of this malt. *40% For the Swiss market*
Gordon & MacPhail Scapa Aged 15 Years dist 93, bott 08 **(88.5) n22** tangy oak and barley mix: cleaner than you might expect; **t22** a tangle of vanillas and golden syrup with the odd sharp barley note; **f22.5** some late-in-the-fray spices is met by butterscotch and crème brûlée; **b22** oh, had this been a bit nearer natural strength... *40%. Gordon & MacPhail.*
Old Malt Cask Scapa Aged 14 Years refill hogshead no. 3888, dist Oct 93, bott Dec 07 **(71.5) n20 t18 f16.5 b17.** Bitter, hot: struggling from a poor cask. *50%. nc ncf. Douglas Laing. 339 bottles.*
Old Malt Cask Scapa Aged 14 Years refill hogshead, cask no. 4440, dist Oct 93, bott Jun 08 **(87) n21** Cox's? **t22.5** Pink lady? **f21.5** definitely Crab; **b22** there is a distinct Calvados fruitiness to this which is both enthralling and quite baffling and out of kilter with the distillery style. Can't say it's not enjoyable, though! *50%. nc ncf. Douglas Laing. 370 bottles.*
Old Malt Cask Scapa Aged 15 Years refill hogshead, dist Sep 93, bott Oct 08 **(87) n22.5** granny's handbags; a pleasant leather-mint mix; **t22** sharp oak delivery; immediate sweet barley counter; juices up well; **f21** back to oaky caramel: burnt fudge and then dries; **b21.5** a curious creature: lighter than its years, yet oaky fingerprints everywhere. *50%.*
⸰⸬⸰ **Old Malt Cask Scapa Aged 15 Years Old** refill hogshead no. DL 5245, dist Oct 93, bott Jun 09 **(85) n22 t22 f20 b21** Though this falls away towards the end, there is a resounding salty edge to the barley to ensure a full-flavoured, slightly piquant experience. *50%*
Old Malt Cask Scapa Aged 16 Years dist Apr 91, bott May 07 **(88) n20 t22 f24 b22.** Busy with major spice. The finish is memorable. *50%. Douglas Laing. 335 bottles.*

⠿ **Old Malt Cask Scapa Aged 16 Years** refill hogshead, cask no. DL 5728, dist Oct 93, bott Jan 10 **(81) n20 t22.5 f18.5 b20.** Exceptionally tart and quite oily. *50%*

Provenance Scapa Aged 11 Years refill hogshead, cask no. 3845, dist winter 95, bott summer 07 **(83.5) n21 t21 f20 b21.5.** Pleasant, malty, suety, but somehow lacking the standard Scapa complexity. *46%. nc ncf. Douglas Laing.*

Provenance Scapa Aged 12 Years refill hogshead DMG no. 4111 dist Oct 95, bott 08 **(86) n21.5 t23 f20 b21.5.** Beautiful malts make for a superbly nubile and juicy display the dull finish. *46%. nc ncf. Douglas Laing.*

Provenance Scapa Aged 12 Years refill hogshead no. 3255, dist 94, bott 07 **(91.5) n23 t23 f22.5 b23.** A genuinely classy malt with compartmentalised characteristics each showing to excellent effect. *46%. nc ncf. Douglas Laing.*

SPEYBURN

Speyside, 1897. Inver House. Working.

Speyburn 10 Year Old db **(82) n20 t21 f20.5 b20.5.** A tight, sharp dram with slightly more emphasis on the citric. A bit of toffee on the finale. *40%*

Speyside 12 Years Old db **(85) n22 t22 f20.5 b21.5** Copious honey and malt on delivery. Simplistic, effective but a tad bitter on finish. *40%*

Speyburn Aged 25 Years db **(92) n22** crisp barley sits well with the chalky oak; **t24** beautiful soft honey helps thicken up the malt; exceptional mouth feel as an extra touch of maple syrup helps keeps the oak in check; a real coppery tanginess to this, too; **f23** a thin spread of marmalade on buttered toast; **b23** either they have re-bottled very quickly or I got the diagnosis dreadfully wrong first time round. Last year I wasn't overly impressed; now I'm taken aback by its beauty. Some change. *46%*

Speyburn Bradan Orach db **(76.5) n19 t20 f19.5 b18.** Fresh, young, but struggles to find a balance. *40%*

Connoisseurs Choice Speyburn 1977 (84) n20 t22 f21 b21. Creaks its way through the oaky gears with enough malty panache to leave you wanting more. *43%.*

⠿ **Old Malt Cask Speyburn Aged 18 Years** refill hogshead, finished in rum cask, dist Jan 90, bott Oct 08 **(84) n22.5 t21 f20.5 b20.** Speyburns at this kind of age are pretty rare in bottled form, so it's always a treat to come across a very different character. The green tea characteristic isn't exactly one I have come across in the lab with this distillery at 15 years and onwards, either. Pleasing, but perhaps too many lumps of sugar in it to lift it to greatness. *50%.*

SPEYSIDE

Speyside, 1990. Speyside Distillers. Working.

Drumguish db **(71) n17 t19 f17 b18.** This whisky could only improve. And, thankfully, it has. Even so, a long, long way to go on this. The nose is still flawed and, despite an injection of barley early on, it flatlines its way from the fourth taste wave to the end. *40%*

Speyside 10 Years Old db **(81) n19 t21 f20 b21.** Plenty of sharp oranges around; the malt is towering and the bite is deep. A weighty Speysider with no shortage of mouth prickle.

Speyside 12 Years Old db **(85) n22 t22 f20.5 b21.5** Copious honey and malt on delivery. Simplistic, effective but a tad bitter on finish. *40%*

Speyside 15 Years Old db **(75.5) n18 t19.5 f19 b19.** So much malt, so little complexity. Lots of caramel on the finish. *40%*

Cadenhead's Speyside Aged 15 Years dist 94, bott 09 **(92.5) n23** almost HP in its lazy-smoked honey; **t24** sweet, mouth-watering barley with a wonderful spice sub plot; **f22.5** the vaguest layer of smoke again before yet more honey and a much drier vanilla sign off; **b23** Speyside as in as fine nick as you've ever seen it. What are Cadenhead's doing...? Tipping honey into the casks...? Seriously, chaps: well done you for finding a classic from this notoriously temperamental distillery. *64.6%*

The Càrn Mòr Vintage Collection Speyside 1995 sherry butt, cask no. 18, dist 95, bott 09 **(85.5) n21.5 t22.5 f20 b21.5.** Some serious biscuity maltiness to this one, even sporting a gentle citrus freshness. Much better than some of what was around at the distillery at the time. *46%. The Scottish Liqueur Centre.*

⠿ **Dancing Stag 17 Years Old Speyside** dist 1992 **(92.5) n23** a beautiful mix of garibaldi biscuit dunked in coffee and dank caramelized biscuit; a miniscule touch of smoke can be found in the background; **t23.5** astonishing texture, helped along the way by liberal doses of golden syrup, molasses and hickory; elsewhere some burnt Dundee cake chips in, complete with nuttiness; **f23** long, robust with the molasses really taking hold, followed by a spiced up vanilla fade; **b23** the oldest and probably finest whisky I have ever encountered from this distillery. *46% Robert Graham Ltd*

Hart Brothers Speyside Aged 13 Years dist Jun 95, bott Oct 08 **(85) n19 t22.5 f22 b21.5.** Very simple malt. Built entirely around its mega-malty theme there is some serious juiciness. The feints on the nose come to help by adding extra oil and depth to the finish. 46%.

⌁ **Malts of Scotland Speyside 1993** sherry butt, cask no. 636, dist Oct 93, bott Jul 09 **(93.5) n23** sharp, unsugared gooseberries and slightly under-ripe redcurrants; the thinnest stratum of smoke weaves through the remaining grapey fruit; **t24.5** eye-watering, and not just because of the strength. The barley comes out and carelessly bounds around like fox cubs with their mum; a thicker fruit fudge offers a more sombre note; **f23** the fudge continues to dominate at the death, though there is a Demerera and cherry jam edge to the late butterscotch; there is a very late dry, furry note but... **b23** I am now looking at this distillery in a whole new light. Well, not quite. But this is a rare specimen, to be sure. *61.7% 192 bottles.*

Scott's Selection The Speyside 1991 bott 07 **(95) n23.5 t24 f23.5 b24.** Taste this and weep. This is what Speyside could have tasted like for all these years if the equipment had been run correctly. In whisky terms, tragic. And, gosh. Was it really 14 years ago I drove through the Scottish snow to be there at the warehouses to see the spirit from these new stills turn to whisky on the day of their 3rd birthday? I predicted great things at the time. On this evidence, I was right. And was equally right to feel the alt's development the greatest disappointment of my whisky career. But when it comes to things mechanical, there is no accounting for human error. And I would be lying if I didn't admit to feeling a pang of vindication. *60.4%*

SPRINGBANK
Campbeltown, 1828. J&A Mitchell & Co. Working.

Hazelburn Aged 8 Years 3rd Edition (triple distilled) bott 07 db **(89) n22 t22.5 f22 b22.5.** Somewhat effete by comparison to last year's big malty number. Here there is a shade more accent on fruit. Very light, indeed. 46%

Longrow Aged 10 Years db **(78) n19 t20 f19 b20.** Seeing as I was one of the first people alive ever to taste Longrow from its very first bottling and used to track down – in my comparative youth – every expression thereafter (and still have some in my personal collection), you could say I am a fan. But this has completely bemused me: bereft not only of the usual to-die-for smoke, its warts are exposed badly, as this is way too young. Sweet and malty, perhaps, and technically better than the marks I'm giving it – but this is Longrow, dammit! I am astonished. 46%

Longrow Aged 10 Years 100 Proof db **(86) n20 t23 f22 b21.** Still bizarrely smokeless – well, maybe a flicker of smoke as you may find the involuntary twitching of a leg of a dying fly – but the mouthfeel is much better here and although a bit too oily and dense for complexity to get going, a genuinely decent ride heading towards Hazelburn-esque barley intensity. Love it, because this oozes class. But where's the ruddy peat...? Oi, mister. I want my peat back...!! 57%

Longrow Aged 14 Years db **(89) n25** a strap-on-to-the-head aroma with so many barley-peat nuances at so many levels it almost defies comprehension; and it wouldn't be a Longrow if there wasn't some salty goings on, too; **t21** mildly tart delivery with the smoke and oak refusing to gel; **f21** where the hell is the peat on the nose? No shortage of natural toffee, though; **b22** hard to get a bearing on this one. The nose, though... *46%. nc ncf.*

Longrow Aged 18 Years db **(94) n23.5** the smoke comes in almost as an afterthought: most un-Longrow like; attractively farmyardy and agricultural; **t23** sharp, raspberry jam mingles with the barley and a puff of something more hickory-like than peat; **f24** long, gentle oils, an indistinct fruit element returns but more barley sugar now and a denouement of vanilla and natural fudgy caramels; **b23.5** determined to hide its light under a bushel...but fails. The most subtle and sophisticated Longrow I've come across in 20 years... 46%

Longrow C.V db **(95.5) n25** a beautifully balanced smoke alternating between light, top-soil peats and coke; some praline ups the ante; sublime: quite faultless; **t24** dissolves on impact with the peats melting first, followed by molassed barley and mocha; **f22.5** low key, it allows the vanillas to begin to dominate as the smoke drifts off; **b23.5** a master-class in the art of subtle peat use. 46%

Longrow Gaja Barola Wood Expression Aged 7 Years db **(91.5) n23.5 t22.5 f23 b22.5.** Taking this one is like running around an asylum claiming you're Napoleon. But I have to admit; it's fun! An accidental classic that is unlikely to be repeated...even if they tried..!! 55.8%

Springbank Society Aged 9 Years Rum Wood bott Mar 07 db **(93.5) n23 t23.5 f23 b24.** A mere pup by Springbank standards. For once its comes through as a real winner in these tender years, doubtless aided by the mercurial charms of the rum and even an unexpected touch of smoke to make for one of the most complex and entertaining drams of the year. Don't expect anything too green, though... 60.2%

Springbank 10 Years Old db **(89)** n22 a real young and old supershow, with soft, adolescent tones from the barley and something much more brooding from the oak. Intriguing...; **t22.5** ditto the delivery: a slight molassed feel to the juicy barley but the oak is dry and firm; outstanding spices, too; **f22** some shards of citrus and lemon drop gives a lovely contrasting sharpness to the sweet barley; **b22.5** now that's much more like it!! The last bottling I had really was all over the show. This is still slightly Bambi-ish. But there is some real meat here, too. On this showing, I am beginning to change my mind about younger Springbanks.... 46%

Springbank Aged 10 Years (100 Proof) db **(86)** n21.5 t22 f21 b21.5. Trying to map a Springbank demands all the skills required of a young 18th century British naval officer attempting to record the exact form and shape of a newly discovered land just after his sextant had fallen into the sea. There is no exact point on which you can fix...and so it is here. A shifting dram that never quite tastes the same twice, but one constant, sadly, is the bitterness towards the finale. Elsewhere, it's one hell of a journey....! 57%

Springbank 11 Years Old Madeira Wood Expression db **(88)** n23 more like a smoked cream sherry: delicious and very different; **t22.5** the lush nose turns into an equally lush delivery with lots of phenols kicking around the medium sweet barley; **f21.5** takes a strange turn, but there again this is strange stuff...struggles to find a relaxed rhythm, though the vanillas do their best; **b21** Madeira perhaps as you've never seen it before: don't go thinking Glenmorangie or Penderyn with this one. As big as the fruit is, the smoke outguns it. 55.8%

Springbank 15 Years Old db **(87.5)** n22 furry grape and Oreo biscuit; **t21.5** the silk texture helps move along the grape; a few dry notes perhaps from a less than top butt but the malt regains the moment; **f22** bitter-sweet with a chalky depth to the oak; **b22** pity again about the light sulphur kick which is louder on the palate than nose. Even so, there are so seriously graceful sherry moments. 46%

Springbank Rum Wood Expression 16 Years Old dist Jun 91, bott Aug 07 db **(93.5)** n23.5 t23.5 f23 b23.5. A wonderful malt brought to you by the people who actually created the category and described to you by the guy who originally discovered and invented it! Work that out...OK, I'll tell you. In 1991 in a warehouse in Springbank a (then) young whisky writer (one of just five in the world at that time) spotted a couple of strange looking casks. On investigating, it was found they were former rum casks which had been completely forgotten about and overlooked. We opened the casks and I spotted the whisky had turned a shade of green. And so the legend was born. So good was the whisky that Springbank repeated the trick...and from the date of distillation I am assuming this is some of the whisky that was filled into rum to try to recreate this astonishing Green Whisky. However, after eight years it appears these were emptied into bourbon casks. So no green. But brilliant malt, nonetheless. And the meeting of an old friend for whom I'm partly responsible... 54.2%. 6,000 bottles.

Springbank 18 Years Old db **(89.5)** n23 another dense offering, but here the fruit is playing a bigger role with blood orange and under-ripe fig adding to the barley Not perfect but there is so much going on... **t22** cautiously salivating. There is a buzz from the cask, but the barley ignores this and sings its own song, alternating between sharp and juicy; **f22.5** that chocolate mousse finale that appears to not be uncommon from this distillery these days; **b22** it's amazing that even at 18 years of age, you get the overwhelming feeling that this malt has barely cleared its throat.... 46%

Springbank Vintage 1997 refill sherry, batch no. 1, bott Jun 07 db **(85)** n21.5 t23 f20.5 b21. I'm not sure if malt of this age comes much thicker or intense. Not exactly a pristine sherry butt, this, but the grape and spice are graceful enough. 55.2%

Springbank 1997 Vintage batch no. 2 db **(87)** n21 so dense it's hard to pick out individual nuances: just one very thick wall of intense malt and oak so heavy it makes a lump of lead look like a helium balloon; **t22.5** taste buds are flattened under the weight of the thick barley; just like on the nose there is a dense oak feel, too but also tons of natural caramels and a shot of cocoa; **f22.5** that cocoa really comes into its own now and sweetens along the way into mousse-like qualities; a little butterscotch is stirred in for extra balance; **b22** less a drink, more of a three course dram. You get the feeling the cut was a little wider here than the norm. Seriously hard work, but ultimately worth it. 54.9%

⁙ **Springbank Vintage 1998** cask no. 08/263, bott Jun 09 db **(92)** n24 strewth! You know how generations of Australian batsmen have chipped away single-mindedly at English bowlers for hours on end over the years....well you need that kind of dedication to get through the seemingly impregnable sherry here. When you do, you'll pick up some pretty amazing notes, perhaps the pick of the bunch being a glorious meeting of dried dates, Mysore coffee and molasses. And then you get to the grape itself, which helps form a Melton Hunt cake structure but with some pretty well cooked raisins....but there's plenty more to discover, so

I don't see you declaring before the end of the second day on this one...; **t23** how roasty is that...? Grape in both fresh juicy form and more bitter, pleasantly burned. More bite than the 46% abv would have you think its capable of and soothing hickory fills the middle ground; **f22.5** long. Some molassed dregs keep the finish away from anything too bitter; **b22.5** when I started trying to unravel this one my beard was still black..... *53.3% 612 bottles*

➳ **Springbank 2000** cask no. 240, dist Oct 00, bott Apr 09 **(90) n23** a beautiful alloy of concentrated barley and thickish, condensed, oak and a much younger personality: barley still wet behind the ears and, though a little fruity, still waiting for its nuttiness to drop...; **t23.5** again we have a concentrated display with the barley topped by all kinds of molten sugars so the pulses are sweet, vibrant and often; yet another strata offers a degree of bourbon honeycomb and hickory and this is interwoven with a thinner, pre-pubescent barley. Elsewhere are chewy, burnt raisin notes...some mixture...; **f21.5** a little salty tang to this and a tad furry, too; **b22** not your average eight- or nine-year-old Springbank and certainly not your average malt. Tuck in: there's a little bit for everyone in this one...except smoke lovers! *48% Specially bottled for Lia and Koos den Boef Vlaardingen. 110 bottles.*

Berry's Own Selection Springbank 1993 bott 09 **(83.5) n22 t21 f20 b20.5.** Doesn't quite live up to the lively, lovely pear drop nose. Emotionless fare. *46%. Berry Bros & Rudd.*

Cadenhead's Authentic Collection Springbank Aged 11 Years cream sherry butt, dist 96, bott Sep 07 **(58) n14 t15 f14 b15.** Put it this way: the sulphur is so aggressive on the nose, I decided to make this my last tasting of the day even before I put it to my lips. *56.3%.*

➳ **Cadenhead's Authentic Collection Springbank 2001** cognac cask, bott Feb 10 **(73.5) n18 t21 f17 b17.5.** Uptight, wet-behind-ears, uncouth, bitter and displaying a marked inferiority complex. Though a tad smoky and offering a superficial charm, sadly a poor representative of Springbank in the way we know and love it. *58.5% Wm. Cadenhead Ltd*

Chieftain's Springbank 37 Years Old cask no. 1343 **(89.5) n21.5 t23.5 f22 b22.5.** Gripping so tight for life there are splinters everywhere. On nose, delivery and finish are clear signs that this has had a few summers too many. But on the other side of the coin comes a beautifully sweet, still ridiculously well defined barley theme *43%. nc ncf. Ian Macleod Distillers.*

Da Mhile Organic "New Born" Springbank dist Jun 92, bott Sep 07 **(95) n24 t23 f24 b24.** A roaring success on account of the gripping complexity despite the full-on sherry: a rare combination. This is the only whisky I know with a photo of a baby on the label: Danny, the first grandchild of organic whisky producer John Savage Onstwedder, There is absolutely nothing childish about this malt, though, and I think Danny will be a happy chap when he cracks open his bottle on his birthday in 2025. I just hope by then this kind of classic sherry cask will not be a bottled memory. *56.4%. nc ncf. 153 bottles.*

➳ **Duthies Hazelburn 9 Years Old (93.5) n23** get some concentrated barley...then concentrate it: you'll probably end up with this....; oak is huge, too. But just get that barley....; **t23.5** firm, mouth-puckering barley radiating a delicately sugared juiciness; **f23.5** the oak, which is always hanging thickly around the nose and delivery but without detracting from the barley's, at last gets its ten minutes of fame, with the toasty sugars a perfect joy; **b23.5** pure star quality. *46% Wm. Cadenhead Ltd*

➳ **Duthies Springbank 12 Years Old (84.5) n21.5 t21 f21 b21.** Malty, sweet and enjoyable but with a limited degree of the usual background saltiness. *46%*

Glenkeir Treasures Springbank Aged 17 Years dist Dec 89, bott Nov 07 **(84.5) n20 t22 f20.5 b22.** Now this is a bit of a strange one. Yes, the butterscotch is lovely while the honey tones are as good as you'll get on any Springbank....but. Some odd notes from what I presume was not quite the finest cask of all time. *50.1%. The Whisky Shop, Edinburgh. 272 bottles.*

Founder's Reserve Springbank Aged 17 Years (86) n22 t22 f21 b21. Another Springbank which sets off at an excellent pace with barley riches galore and then tires towards the end. Delicious in part, but the natural vanillas and caramels are simply too much to take it on to greatness. *46%. Japan Import System.*

Kingsbury's Single Cask Springbank Aged 14 Years dist Jun 93, bott Aug 07 **(87) n22 t22 f21 b22.** Another very even, if undercooked, vanilla-rich offering from this distillery. *46%.*

Old Malt Cask Springbank Aged 11 Years refill hogshead no. 4245, dist Oct 96, bott Apr 08 **(81.5) n21 t21.5 f20 b19.** In many ways nearer 11 months than 11 years....still, the malt is intense and sweet but don't bother going in search of oak. *50%. nc ncf. 358 bottles.*

Old Malt Cask Springbank Aged 15 Years refill hogshead, dist Jun 93, bott Oct 08 **(85.5) n21.5 t21.5 f21 b21.5.** Big, enjoyable malt, sharp and happy to keep sweetness to a minimum. A thorough oaky buzz, too. *50%. Douglas Laing. 365 bottles.*

Old Malt Cask Springbank Aged 18 Years cask no. 3964, dist Dec 07 **(84.5) n21.5 t22 f20 b21.** A pleasant, barley-sweet kind of guy, but missing the unspoken salty tang that is part of the distillery's fabric. *50%. Douglas Laing. 353 bottles.*

Premium Scotch Importers Springbank 1998 small oak cask **(95) n24.5** a sublimely sexy package: concentrated barley with bourbony concentrated oak. The explosive mix takes you into a land of heady fruit: peaches and guava thickened by toasty molasses, even maybe a hint of PVC phenols; **t24** the tongue-curling effect of the delivery confirms the big oak presence. But the malt has it under control and dishes out plenty of piercingly sharp notes to compensate; spices form in the middle ground, first shyly and then have a freer role; **f23** liquorice and chocolate gives way to chocolate lime; **b23.5** the problem with Springbank is that it is such an enormous malt it needs big age or at least a major reaction with oak to bring the best out of it. So many malts up to the age of about 18 struggle to really be heard: the oak and barley cancel each other out. That has long been my theory and this wonderful, full-throttled bottling from Springbank filled into small casks to maximise the oak influence – a form of premature aging – goes a way to prove it. The best independent Springbank I have tasted in yonks. *53.3%. Premium Scotch Importers Pty Ltd, Australia.*

Scotch Malt Whisky Society Cask 27.68 Aged 18 Years refill hogshead, dist Dec 89 **(92.5) n23 t23.5 f23 b23** Just so complex!! *52.7%*

Scotch Malt Whisky Society Cask 27.69 Aged 18 Years refill hogshead, dist Dec 89 **(77) n20.5 t19 f19 b18.5.** Entirely out of key and sorts. *52.8%*

Scotch Malt Whisky Society Cask 27.73 Aged 12 Years refill hogshead, dist May 96 **(87.5) n22** I never thought I'd come across a Springbank, that most complex of malts, this clean and uncluttered on the nose: attractive, though; **t21.5** juicy, sharp-ish, thick barley bolstered by one dimensional oak; **f22** medium length with good oil developing sweetness to the barley; **b21.5** dense, simplistic but effective. *55.5%*

Scotch Malt Whisky Society Cask 27.74 Aged 12 Years refill hogshead, dist May 96 **(82.5) n20 t23 f19.5 b20.** decent distillate, and the wave of sweet barley just after initial delivery is superb. But an indifferent cask. *57%*

⋅⋅⋅ **Scotch Malt Whisky Society Cask 27.75 Aged 12 Years** refill hogshead, dist May 96 **(90.5) n23.5** beyond intriguing: polished floors much older than the given 12 years, citrus ranging from diluted lemon to mildly furry old orange! The sugars seem to appear in caramelised biscuit crumb form and there, mega-intriguingly, is even a light strata of vague smoke; and then on another hand there is something of the under-ripe new make about this...a bit like a lad who still has that bumfluff he is refusing to shave ....astonishing....; **t23** the hint of smoke on the nose is there – to say in force would be overstating it – but wearing less of a malty niqab; most Springbanks under 15 tend to flail around a bit and this one doesn't exactly get into a groove, either, but there is a disarming beauty to the juicy barley and there is even a Bowmore-style Fisherman's Friend cough sweet tang to the late middle ground...; **f22** never had a Springbank finish like this in 30 years...; **b22** strictly for those who have a good hour or so. Springbanks at this age are not meant to be quite so absorbing or smoky....and had I not been told otherwise, I would have had this down as coming from another distillery entirely. *59%*

Scotch Malt Whisky Society Cask 126.1 Aged 11 Years (Hazelburn) sherry butt, dist Jul 97 **(85) n22 t20 f23 b20.** Doubtless some people will be wondering why I haven't given this 96 points and some kind of award. Well, here's the reason: granted, it is wonderful to come across a sherry butt that has not even the slightest trace of sulphur. But when the sherry is this dominant, and from a distillery like Springbank, it needs at least another decade for the oaks to start making a significant contribution and begin to sort out the balance. This is a bit like tasting a 1986 Chateaux Latour just a few years after bottling: it needed time to reach its optimum complexity but wasn't granted it. So we have a grape-soaked malt not without charm and with no little Columbian coffee. And molasses. But no shape or direction. A fantastic cask: but one emptied way, way too soon... *56.7%*

⋅⋅⋅ **The Secret Treasures Springbank 1970** sherry cask no. 1344, dist May 70, bott Sep 07 **(94) n23** exotic fruit is only half the story; soft peat mingles with over-ripe banana; **t24** brilliant delivery: all at once full and yielding yet firm, too. Equally the balance is sublime with the darker, oakier notes which threat over-age immediately met by a lighter, more lively fruitiness again, with smoke just drifting around binding the two; **f23.5** long, decadent, a procession of vanillas of varying sweetness, chocolate mousse and that most delicate of peats bringing with it, inevitably, some spices; **b23.5** should you need further confirmation that Springbank ages with almost uncanny beauty, here it is. *43% Haromex Development GmbH, Germany. 489 bottles.*

The Whisky Fair Springbank Aged 35 Years sherry wood, dist 71, bott 07 **(96) n24 t24 f24 b24.** A true golden oldie. Quite sensational. *59%. Germany.*

The Whisky Society Springbank 1992 Aged 15 Years bott Sep 07 **(87) n21.5 t22 f21.5 b22.** some big malt moments makes for a big dram, but never quite settles. *52.6%. Speciality Drinks.*

STRATHISLA

Speyside, 1786. Chivas. Working.

Strathisla 12 Years Old db (87.5) **n22.5** the smoke evident on the last few tastings of this has been largely usurped by a heavy fat-sultana grapiness. Back to its old heavyweight self of a few years back, except the malt-fruit balance is kinder to the nose and the merest whiff of smoke is still detectable; **t23.5** thick, sweet barley swamps the tastebuds early on but slowly nudged aside by the trademark sweet sultana; engaging chocolate honeycomb towards the middle; **f20** duller than before with some big caramels kicking in and the unmistakable furry signature of the odd dud sherry butt; **b21.5** still a big, chewy dram which is about as heavy in body as you are likely to find anywhere in Speyside. Very enjoyable, though you know deep down that some fine tuning could take this guy easily into the 90s. 43%

Strathisla Distillery Edition 15 Years Old db (94) **n23** flawlessly clean and enriched by that silky intensity of fruity malt unique to this distillery; **t23** the malt is lush, sweet and every bit as intense as the nose; a touch of toffeespice does it no harm; **f24** just so long and lingering, again with the malt being of extraordinary enormity: these is simply wave upon wave of pure delight; **b24** what a belter! The distillery is beautiful enough to visit: to take away a bottle of this as well would just be too good to be true! 53.7%

Cadenhead's Authentic Collection Strathisla Aged 21 Years Port hogshead, matured in oak cask, dist 87, bott Jun 08 (94.5) **n23** a dreamy creaminess: much more Spanish than Portuguese on the grape front. Soft and elegant; **t24** immediate soft spice impact, all couched in juicy grape, a few waves of juicy barley and....there's that creaminess again... **f23.5** medium, but with no oak threat whatsoever; gentle fruit all the way, oh except for the creamy mocha... **b24** quite outstanding. Though, puzzlingly, more Cream Sherry than Port... 57.1%. 216 bottles.

Duncan Taylor Collection Strathisla 1967 cask no. 1886 (93) **n22.5 t23.5 f23 b24**. In some places a twin to the Lonach of the same age and strength. Just less oak and more barley sheen. But the overall difference is amazing. This is one sexy 40-year-old. 46.4%

Duncan Taylor Collection Strathisla 1967 cask no. 2716 bott 08 (86) **n21 t21.5 f22 b21.5**. Quite delicious with its waves of natural caramel and honey-tipped barley. But with oak, there is a fine line between excellence and very, very good, as this is. For those who want their first-class whisky to shows its age. 48.6%

Duncan Taylor Collection Strathisla 1967 cask no. 2721 (88) **n24.5** roasted hazelnuts lightened by kumquats and lime; the merest dab of honey is brilliantly balanced by a fleck or two of salt: stunning... **t22** toasted honeycomb splintered with oak; a distinctive old bourbon charm; **f20** tires as the oak is driven home; **b21.5** doesn't live up to the pin-up nose but the bourbony aspects are attractive. 48.3%. Duncan Taylor.

Gordon & MacPhail Distillery Label Strathisla 25 Years Old (89) **n22.5** a hickory/ Demerara double bill should point towards a bourbony nose, but it doesn't due to the chalkier, drier oak notes; **t22.5** wonderful presentation of varying dark sugars with enough barley to ensure a mouth-watering middle; the antiquity is told through the sheen; **f22** much drier, spicier and though creaking, by no means decrepit.; **b22** beautifully crafted, the aging process, apparently threatening, has ultimately been kind. 40%. Gordon & MacPhail.

Gordon & MacPhail Distillery Label Strathisla 30 Years Old (91) **n23** a forest of oak, but sunlight dapples through thanks to a chocolaty presence; almost old Jamaica rum-like in its estery qualities; **t23.5** too old...too old...? Nope...It survives. The oak does take you to the precipice, but such is the magnificence of the crystaline Demerara you are hauled back just as the footing gives way; some blood orange and spices further the fun; **f22** a wonderful fade of cappuccino tops off a wonderful experience; **b22.5** old age doesn't equal great whisky – fact. But here, when there is a degree of drama involved, my word: it can be so enjoyable...!! 43%.

Gordon & MacPhail Distillery Label Strathisla 40 Years Old (84.5) **n23 t21 f20 b20.5**. Excellent exotic fruit nose, but the oak has taken too firm a grip here. 43%

⋯ **Gordon & MacPhail Distillery Label Strathisla 1997** (85.5) **n21.5 t22 f21 b21.** Strathisla offering all its full blown viscosity. 43%

Lonach Strathisla 1967 (88) **n22 t22.5 f21.5 b22.** One of those guys which stands on the oaky precipice, but doesn't jump. 46.4%. Duncan Taylor.

Lonach Strathisla 1968 (92) **n22.5 t23.5 f23 b23.** Age defying stuff. Wonderful. 43.7%.

Murray McDavid Mission Strathisla 1967 bourbon/grenache banyuls (85) **n22 t21 f21 b21.** From the school of exotic fruit via bourbon college. Has just about controlled on the oak, but needed a few fruit salad/black Jack nails to help keep the lid on. 43.6%. 300 bottles.

Norse Cask Selection Strathisla 1997 Aged 12 Years hogshead cask no. 47819, dist 97, bott May 09 (86) **n22 t22 f21 b21.** Malty, juicy and chocolaty. But a bit on the fizzy side, showing a cask not quite on its full game. 57.7%. Qualityworld for WhiskyOwner.com, Denmark.

Old Malt Cask Strathisla Aged 18 Years refill hogshead, dist Mar 91, bott Mar 09 **(85) n22** t22 f20 b21. Juicy, regulation Strathisla in full blending colours. *50%*.

Provenance Strathisla Aged 11 Years refill hogshead, dist winter 96, bott autumn 08 **(86)** n20.5 t22 f21.5 b22. The nose suggests a flagging cask but the delivery is pure Strathisla with the malt intense and gently sweetened to the point of excellence in part. *46%. Douglas Laing.*

⋰ **Rare Vintage Strathisla 1953 (82.5)** n22 t20 f20.5 b20. Resounding oaks from start to finish but just enough brown sugars to limit the damage. But the hints of pine and creosote tell their own story. *43% Gordon & MacPhail*

⋰ **Rare Vintage Strathisla 1963 (89)** n22 oak tries to take an instant stranglehold, orange blossom lightens the load; t22.5 sharp, over the top oak offers a worrying intro, but the recovery is sublime with a cool minty sweetness ushering in praline and spicy fruitcake; f22.5 the oak has been repelled, leaving behind layers of soft vanillas; b22 a Lazarus of a dram, which on more than one occasion looked dead in the glass. Give it a good fifteen minutes between pouring and tasting....and no bloody water!!!. *43% Gordon & MacPhail*

The Whisky Agency Strathisla 42 Year Old dist 67, bott 09 **(91)** n23 when the citrus gets this intense we are talking very serious age...; t22 the initial oaky wall crashes as the barley piles on the buttery pressure: this is some battle... f23.5 a peace treaty is signed and the vanillas sweeten, the weight of the oak reduces and the barley shines unmolested...and spices come out to play; b22.5 this is great whisky on the very edge. Just as much a battle as a dram but the overall effect is startlingly attractive. *44.5%. The Whisky Agency, Germany.*

⋰ **The Whisky Fair Strathisla 1967 (88.5)** n23 a huge orange affair: marmalade and kumquat on heat; t22 sharp and tangy: the oak is not shy coming forward; some pleasant mocha fills the middle; f21.5 oily and vanilla-rich; b22 a valiant, if somewhat orangey, attempt to stay the course over 40 plus years. Doesn't quite entirely succeed. *43%*

STRATHMILL
Speyside, 1891. Diageo. Working.

Berrys' Own Selection Strathmill 1974 cask no. 1212, bott 07 **(92.5)** n23 t21.5 f24.5 b23.5. Oozes a sensuality that those who are charmed by only the most delicate whiskies will find fatally alluring.... *46%. Berry Bros & Rudd.*

The Càrn Mòr Vintage Collection Strathmill 1990 hogshead, cask no. 2400, dist 90, bott 09 **(86)** n21.5 t22 f21 b21.5. So malty and clean it just screams "Speyside" at you... *46%.*

Old Malt Cask Strathmill Aged 16 Years dist Jan 93, bott Jul 09 **(80)** n19 t20 f21 b20. One of the great undiscovered Speysiders. But here it feels pretty restricted and bound in its own natural caramel. *50%. Douglas Laing.*

Old Malt Cask Strathmill Aged 18 Years cask no. 4071, dist Oct 89, bott Jan 08 **(73)** n18 t18.5 f19.5 b18. A real shame: the whisky has matured from distillate not quite up to scratch for this usually excellent distillery and in a cask which do few favours. *50%.*

Old Malt Cask Strathmill Aged 30 Years refill hogshead no. 4070, dist Apr 77, bott Dec 07 **(88)** n22 t21.5 f22.5 b22. Outstanding old Strathmills appear to be in season. *50%. nc ncf.*

Old Malt Cask Strathmill Aged 35 Years dist May 74, bott Jul 09 **(89)** n23 there we have it: geriatric whisky with the heart of a teenager. Plodding exotic fruit gives the age away, but in the heart of it is some years-defying juicy barley; t21.5 bit of an oaky smack in the kisser. But it doesn't take long for that irrepressible barley to breathe fresh, pulsating life back into the proceedings; f22.5 a minor oil spillage from somewhere, but it helps the barley and developing cocoa gel happily; b22 I am astonished how delicate, lightweight malts like these survive 35 years. Well, usually they don't truth be told. And this one's managed it by the skin of its cask. A real gray-haired charmer, though. *47.4%. Douglas Laing.*

TALISKER
Highland (Island–Skye), 1832. Diageo. Working.

Talisker Aged 10 Years db **(93)** n23 Cumberland sausage and kipper side by side; t23 early wisps of smoke that develop into something a little spicier; lively barley that feels a little oak-dried but sweetens out wonderfully; f24 still not at full throttle with the signature ka-boom spice, but never less than enlivening. Some wonderful chocolate adds to the smoke; b23 it is wonderful to report that the deadening caramel that had crept into recent bottlings of the 10-y-o has retreated, and although that extraordinary, that wholly unique finale has still to be re-found in its unblemished, explosive entirety, this is much, much closer to the mark and a quite stupendous malt to be enjoyed at any time. But at night especially. *45.8%*

Talisker 12 Years Old Friends of the Classic Malts db **(86)** n22 t21.5 f21 b21.5. Decent, sweet, lightly smoked...but the explosion which made this distillery unique - the old kerpow! - appears kaput. *45.8%*

Talisker Aged 14 Years The Distillers Edition Jerez Amoroso cask, dist 93, bott 07 db **(90.5) n23** lively, spiced and warming; zaps a few white hot holes through the fruit; **t23** a salivating mixture of big fruit and intense barley; although the usual explosiveness has been muted the effect is no less delicious; **f22** a few whimpering spices make their way through the thick crusts of grape and barley; **b22.5** certainly on the nose, one of the more old-fashioned peppery Taliskers I've come across for a while. Still I mourn the loss of the nuclear effect it once had, but the sheer quality of this compensates. 45.8%

Talisker Aged 20 Years db **(95) n24 t24 f23 b24.** I have been tasting Talisker for 28 years. This is the best bottling ever. Miss this and your life will be incomplete. 62%

Talisker 25 Years Old db **(92) n23.5** slightly fragmented with the smoke going it alone from the clove-clad oak; a touch of toffee; **t24** hold on tight; it's going in...like a munitions dump going off with spices exploding around every crevice in the palate. Only one distillery in the world is capable of this... **f22.5** strangely lethargic: cream toffee everywhere and dousing the peaty fun; a few strands of honey intertwine with citrus and vanilla, too; **b22.5** fabulous stuff, even though the finish in particular is strangely well behaved. 58.1%

Talisker 25 Year Old bott 08 db **(92) n23** lazy smoke drifts over a scene of light citrus and slowly forming ancient oaks; **t23.5** soft vanillas arrive first, then a wave of muted peppers stinging only playfully as the sweet barley unfolds just so charmingly; **f22.5** the oaks really are revving up, but the sweet barley provides the balance; peat and citrus provide an unlikely fade; **b23** busy and creaking but a glass or two of this offers some classy entertainment for the evening. 54.2%

Talisker 30 Years Old db **(84) n21 t22 f20 b21.** Talisker as perhaps never seen before: virtually no peat to make a significant contribution and caramel aplenty on the finish. Some teasing citrus and almost apologetic spice make a decent double act. The oak creaks a bit, but is kept docile enough. Talisker...but very, very different. 50.7%

Talisker 30 Year Old bott 08 db **(89) n21** very tired oak; **t23.5** who would have believed it....? The delivery shows no woody failings whatsoever, but silky-soft barley, with a touch of toffee, and a slow-motion deployment of half-hearted smoke: just the right degree of sweetness and chewiness; **f22** remains soft with the toffee-vanilla dominant; **b22.5** this malt seriously defies the nose, which gives every indication of a whisky about to peg it. The softness of the experience is memorable; 49%

Talisker 57 Degrees North db **(95) n24** salty, smoky, coastal, breezy. The distillery's location in a nose... **t24.5** peat encased in a muscovado sugar, in the same way a fly might be enveloped in amber, melts to allow the slow blossoming of a quite beautiful and peaty thing...; **f23** some welcome whip and bite; the smoke and vanillas hang in there and even the odd hint of mocha puffs around a bit; **b23.5** a glowing tribute, I hope, for a glowing whisky... 57%

⫶⫶ **Hart Brothers Talisker Aged 15 Years** dist Dec 93, bott Jul 09 **(49) n15 t15 f07 b12.** An elementary mistake: I thought the geology around Talisker was known for its iron, not sulphur. 51.7% Hart Brothers Ltd

⫶⫶ **Old Malt Cask Tactical Aged 10 Years** refill hogshead, cask no. 5704, dist Dec 99, bott Dec 09 **(84.5) n21 t22 f20.5 b21.** Talisker, at its maltiest, sweetest and least fiery. 50%

Old Malt Cask Tactical Aged 18 Years refill hogshead, dist Dec 90, bott Apr 09 **(96) n24.5** classic ground black peppers: really sneezable stuff. Those peppers have been shaken onto an almost floral salad with that typical old Talisker style of being neither sweet nor dry, heavy nor light...yet smoky and spicy; **t23.5** veerrrroooom...!!!! We have lift off as those spices go into orbit, peppering – in both senses – the tastebuds with pin-prick attacks; the sweetness seems like pure barley concentrate; **f24** some serious subtlety here as the countless strata of barley, pepper, thinned maple syrup and vanilla duck and weave: **b74** talk about taking you back in time. A style lost to the present day distillery bottling, though this one is a tad sweeter than normal. No other distillery can offer this particular, spectacular, package on nose and tastebuds. 50%. Douglas Laing. 152 bottles.

⫶⫶ **Scotch Malt Whisky Society Cask 14.17 Aged 20 Years** refill hogshead, dist Mar 89 **(90.5) n23.5** white peppers tickle and bite; the kippery smoke appears to carry sugars into the air; salty and unambiguously coastal; **t23** surprisingly sweet arrival, soft, well groomed and a little oily; some unexpected Lubec marzipan and jaffa cake orange before some light spices arrive; **f22** the usual lift off is missing and instead we have slightly bitter vanillas **b22** beautifully distilled but for all its class the usual explosion is muted. 57.2%

TAMDHU
Speyside, 1897. Edrington. Working.

Tamdhu db **(84.5) n20 t22.5 f21 b21.** So-so nose, but there is no disputing the fabulous, stylistic honey on delivery. The silkiest Speyside delivery of them all. 40%

Tamdhu Aged 18 Years bott code L0602G L12 20/08 db **(74.5) n19 t19 f18 b18.5**. Bitterly disappointing. Literally. 43%.

Tamdhu 25 Years Old db **(88) n22** citrus showing now a more orangey based style to the lemon of its youth; **t22** typically fat and intense; the barley eventually escapes the gravitational pull of the oils to offer a wonderful barley sweetness; **f21** dried dates vanilla; **b23** radiates quality. 43%

❖❖ **A.D. Rattray Tamdhu 1967** cask no. 9, dist Jan 67, bott Sep 09 **(95.5) n23.5** talk about pick 'n' mix...!!! Not so much fruity bonbons. But fruity bourbons... **t24** ye-ha! If I ain't in ol' rib-eye steak sizzling Kentuck....no, hang on a mo: I'm in the heart of Mars Bar-frying Speyside...! What are all these hickory and chocolate honeycomb flavours doing here....? And these strung out juicy, over heated grapes. I'm confused...; **f23** some burnt raisin...but is that from the sherry or just thick barley and sugar on the oak....???? **b24** A.D Rattray have been coming out with some stunners of late. But this one almost takes the corn biscuit...or is it sherry-raisin type Garibaldi ...???? 46.5%

Cadenhead's Tamdhu Aged 18 Years dist 91, bott 09 **(85) n20 t22.5 f21 b21.5**. A bit of attitude on the nose, but mainly dealt with by the tsunami of sweet barley on delivery. 58.3%

❖❖ **The Càrn Mòr Vintage Collection Tamdhu 1991** hogshead, cask no. 35093, bott 2009 **(85) n21 t22 f21.5 b21.5**. Well, if that doesn't clean the palate with an uncomplicated malty blast, nothing will.... 46% 1159 bottles.

Dewar Rattray Tamdhu 1990 cask no. 10139, dist Jun 90, bott Nov 07 **(84.5) n20 t21 f22 b21.5**. Tamdhu at its maltiest: attacks with all teeth gnashing. This is a wild boy from this usually docile distillery. 62.9%

❖❖ **The Golden Cask Tamdhu 1991** cask no. CM123, bott 2008 **(91) n22** banana sandwich; **t24** explosive barley. Within about two seconds you are hit not just by faultlessly clean barley, but also spices which, for a brief moment, take a layer off the skin of your mouth. Sharp, eye-watering fresh grass and green apples. It's beautifully insane; **f22.5** calms for a pleasant and gentle butterscotch and spice warm-down; **b22.5** another golden malt from the Golden Cask. While the nose and finish may be pretty standard, the delivery makes the hairs on the back of your neck stand up. 55% The House of MacDuff. 535 bottles.

Lonach Tamdhu 1968 (91.5) n23 t23.5 f22 b23. It is strange how some malts displaying the "exotic fruit" style of age just don't work, while others, like this one, just make you roll your eyes in delight. The trick, I think, is that the oak doesn't degenerate to bitterness, and there is not a hint of it here. 40%. Duncan Taylor.

❖❖ **Old & Rare Tamdhu Aged 19 Years** dist Dec 89, bott Sep 09 **(92.5) n24** some black pepper gives the nearly faultless grape some hostility; **t24.5** if you could see me...or hear me.... I am actually sighing, such is the absolute beauty of the marriage between the flawless grape and cherry and the dense but well controlled vanillas; **f21.5** a late bitter and furry note; **b22.5** the distillery had some critics in later years. But I well remember when its make really was of a very decent standard...and this confirms it. 57.1% Douglas Laing & Co Ltd. 235 bottles

Old & Rare Tamdhu Aged 19 Years sherry cask, dist Dec 89, bott Mar 09 **(94) n24** like being tipped head first into a sherry butt in the good old days before sulphur: pristine grape of the noble rot variety and somehow, vitally, some barley makes itself heard; **t24** a wondrous concoction on delivery: that flawless grape is there, but fizzed up by spices and muscovado sugars, and a hint of molasses for good measure; the barley reappears towards the middle; **f22.5** relatively sedate with more dependency on vanillas; **b23.5** Douglas Laing appear to have hit a rich seem of massive, memorable Tamdhus. Just one of those must-have drams. 55.8%

❖❖ **Old & Rare Tamdhu Aged 20 Years** dist Dec 89, bott Dec 09 **(81) n21 t21.5 f18.5 b20**. With its initial big grapey blast, does everything in its power to hit the high spots, but the faulty sherry butt won't allow it. 55.6% Douglas Laing & Co Ltd. 232 bottles.

Old Malt Cask Tamdhu Aged 17 Years refill hogshead, dist Dec 91, bott Apr 09 **(84.5) n22 t21.5 f20 b21**. Good, honest, malty, lightly oily Speyside malt, though showing more like a 10-year-old. 50%. Douglas Laing. 320 bottles.

Old Malt Cask Tamdhu Aged 18 Years sherry hogshead, dist Dec 89, bott Sep 08 **(95) n24** syrupy sherry - oloroso at its bichamin thickest – clogs the nose...but it is all rather wonderful. Can't spot much in the way of barley, though. But when the sherry is this clean and fine, and the oak is making all the right noises, who cares....? **t24** huge toasted raisins still dripping with juice make for an initially one-dimensional, though thanks to the seeping sweetness, enjoyable experience; silky, with a wonderful build up of crystalised muscovado sugars and anciently over-ripened greengages; **f23.5** long, remains silky and then a slow burn of spices as the mocha begins to build and take quiet control. Still those fruits linger **b23.5** a steamroller of a dram, the sherry crushing everything in its path. Initially not a purists' dream, as complexity takes a backseat, but there is a slow dawning of myriad bitter-sweet complexities – though mainly sweet. It's like an old, clean, unsulphured Macallan cask of yesteryear has rolled down the hill and landed in the warehouse of Tamdhu. One for sherry lovers of the original Macallan school...*50%. Douglas Laing. 268 bottles.*

Provenance Tamdhu Aged 11 Years refill hogshead no. 4253, dist Spring 97, bott Spring 08 **(87) n22** diced apple and marzipan; **t22** double-toned malt with a firmer edge to the softer, sweeter element; **f21.5** waxy honey and more barley layering; **b21.5** so simplistic, but so charming. *46%. nc ncf. Douglas Laing.*

TAMNAVULIN
Speyside. 1966. Whyte and Mackay. Closed.

Tamnavulin 1966 Aged 35 Years cream sherry butt db **(91) n24** cleanest sherry imaginable: thick, glutinous nose with cream soda and toffee; **t22** enormous delivery of oak and toffee raisin; **f23** thins out to allow complexity to evolve, which it does with a fudgy chewiness; **b22** for those who love great old sherry, this is an absolute. Perhaps too much sherry to ever make it a true great, but there is no denying such quality. *52.6%*

Connoisseurs Choice Tamnavulin 1990 (82.5) n20 t22 f20.5 b20. Chugs along pleasantly and maltily enough, but with an annoying lack of enterprise or complexity for a dram normally so good. *43%. Gordon & MacPhail.*

The Exclusive Malts Tamnavulin Aged 39 Years cask no. 3665, dist Nov 68 **(81) n21 t20.5 f19.5 b20.** Decent, honest old malt which, frankly, is several summers past its prime. *40.4%.*

Master of Malt Tamnavulin 15 Years Old (93) n23.5 t23.5 f23 b23. Shows a little age at the death but that can be forgiven for its overall beauty. *40%. Master of Malt, UK.*

Master of Malt Tamnavulin 16 Years Old Cask Strength (90.5) n22 t23 f23 b22.5. At first, not too sure about this one. Then just wears you down with its non-stop enormity. And bloody niceness! *55.1%. .*

⫶⫶ **Old Malt Cask Tamnavulin Aged 18 Years** refill hogshead no. DL 6044, dist Dec 91, bott Apr 10 **(87) n21.5** despite a distant touch of butyric, there is enough Parma Violet and dank bluebell to keep anyone happy; **t22** a little bitter due to the cask, the intense barley fights back; **f21.5** custard powder sticking to the oils; **b22** you get the feeling that in a top cask, this would have been a stunner. Wish we could see more of this distillery in the market place. *50%*

Old Malt Cask Tamnavulin Aged 20 Years dist May 89, bott Jul 09 **(95.5) n24** just wonderful barley: it comes at you from all directions and in varying degrees and forms of sweetness (and dryness); **t24** oh my gosh...even better on palate where the intensity of that barley defies belief. Arrives in a beautiful mix of lush grassy sharp tones and sweeter, more sugar-tinged higher notes; the tongue simply cannot stop working against the palate, such is the richness and controlled intensity; **f23.5** a few citrus notes creep in before the oak has a chance to establish its vanilla and cocoa-mined territory; **b24** as healthy a specimen of Speyside 20-years-old as you are likely to find. A corker. *50%. Douglas Laing.*

Old Malt Cask Tamnavulin Aged 30 Years bourbon barrel no. 3947, dist Jun 77, bott Oct 07 **(91) n22 t23.5 f22.5 b23.** Forceful but no violence to the tastebuds. *50%. 210 bottles.*

Old Malt Cask Tamnavulin Aged 40 Years refill hogshead, dist Nov 68, bott Mar 09 **(86) n21.5 t21 f22 b21.5.** Not quite in the same league as the formidable OMC 30-y-o of last year. Yet though the oak leaves little doubt about the age there is a melodic sweetness, of the old fashioned boiled sweet school, that ensures the barley gets a good hearing. Pleasantly spiced and in better nick than some 40-year-olds I know....I don't mean whisky. *43.1%. 261 bottles.*

Scott's Selection Tamnavulin 1977 bott 07 **(90) n22.5 t23 f22 b22.5.** Just beautiful. *50.8%*

TEANINICH
Highland (Northern), 1817. Diageo. Working.

⫶⫶ **Berry's Own Selection Teaninich 1973 (83.5) n22 t21 f20 b20.5.** Even accounting for the strength, thinner than you might expect with the timid malt entirely subservient to the oak. Some lovely leathery-honey notes here and there, though. *41.8% Berry Bros & Rudd*

Duncan Taylor The NC2 Range Teaninich 1996 Aged 11 Years (82) n21.5 t21 f20 b20.5. From such an old, well-used cask, this has as much newmake about it as matured whisky. *46%*

Lombard Brands Teaninich 12 Years Old Single Malt (85) n21 t22 f21 b21. An agreeable, chewy malt with some good barley sugar. But it feels as though someone left the hand brake on... *43%. Lombards Brands.*

Old Malt Cask Teaninich Aged 36 Years refill hogshead no. 3914, dist Feb 71, bott Sep 07 **(85.5) n21.5 t22 f21 b21.** Enjoyable, but the oaky wrinkles can't quite be smoothed despite a spirited barley attack. Missing the honey and fruit of the Samorali bottling. *50%.*

Scotch Malt Whisky Society Cask 59.38 Aged 25 Years refill hogshead, dist Nov 83 **(91) n23.5** superb subtle citrus gives the barley and polished wooden floors a lift: a real feel of age and elegance here; **t23** typical Teaninich in all its sugar-barleyed splendour, but somehow keeping the sweetness on acceptable levels; also that strange indefinable, vague oaky hint of something fruity but in underdeveloped form... **f22** putting on its PJs, as this is getting a bit tired. The vanillas are attractive, though, and hang on to enough sweetness to keep the barley active; **b22.5** hard to imagine this one getting through another summer or two without losing some excellence. 54.8%

⁘ **The Secret Treasures Teaninich 1984** sherry cask no. 5950, bott no. 250, dist Nov 84, bott Sep 07 **(88.5) n23** a plate of freshly diced kumquats mingles with a playful spice buzz; **t22.5** mouth-watering, juicy and refreshing. If the barley could show more it would be superstar stuff; **f21** a slight marmalade bitterness; **b22** oh, the irony of finding an untainted sherry butt...and it's in Germany! Actually, not entirely without taint, but it arrives only at the very end. Otherwise a really lovely – and unusual – bottling. 43% Haromex Development GmbH, Germany. 774 bottles.

TOBERMORY
Highland (Island–Mull), 1795. Burn Stewart. Working.

⁘ **Ledaig 10 Years Old** db **(85) n21.5 t22 f20 b21.5.** Some gorgeous and beautifully weighted peat at play here, showcased in full glory on the nose and delivery. Has to paper over some cracks towards the finish, though. 46.3%

Ledaig Aged 10 Years db **(63) n14 t17 f15 b17.** What the hell is going on? Even Gulliver on all his weird and wonderful travels would not have come across such a strange world as the one I am on while trying to come to terms with the whisky of Tobermory. Butyric and peat in a ghoulish harmony on nose and palate that is not for the squeamish. 43%

Ledaig Aged 12 Years db **(90) n23** serious farmyard aromas – and as someone who spent three years living on one, believe me....borderline butyric, but somehow gets away with it, or at least turns it to an advantage; **t23.5** the staggering peat on the nose is no less remarkable here: chunky, clunking, entirely lacking poise and posture. And it obviously doesn't give a damn...; **f21.5** strange gin-type juniper amid the smoke; **b22** it has ever been known that there is the finest of lines between genius and madness. A side-by-side comparison of the Ledaig 10 and 12 will probably be one of whisky's best examples of this of all time... 43%

⁘ **Tobermory 10 Years Old** db **(73.5) n17.5 t19 f18 b19.** The last time I tasted an official Tobermory 10 for the Bible, I was aghast with what I found. And didn't taste again for the remainder of the day, I remember. So I prodded this sample I had before me of the new 46.3% version with all the confidence Wile E Coyote might have with a failed stick of Acme dynamite. No explosions in the glass or on my palate to report. And though this is still a long way short, and I'm talking light years here, of the technical excellence of the old days, the uncomplicated sweet maltiness has a very basic charm. The nose and finish, though, are still very hard going. 46.3%

Tobermory Aged 10 Years db **(67.5) n16 t17 f17.5 b17.** People say to me: "Jim, you must really love your job. It has to be the best in the world." Well, yes I do. And yes it most probably is. But as Newton would have told you: "for every action there is an equal and opposite reaction." Well today I have been a bit lucky, because I have been tasting some nectar, and occasionally where I hadn't expected it. This morning, when planning my day ahead, I had included the tasting of Tobermory as my treat for a tough day. Last time I officially tasted it, it had blown me away with its brilliance. I had tasted the odd so-so bottling in the last six months whilst on my travels, admittedly. But I didn't come prepared for this, a less than brilliantly made malt totally bereft of character or charm. I have no idea what has happened here. I must investigate. Frankly, I'm gutted. 40%

Tobermory Aged 15 Years Limited Edition db **(72.5) n17 t18 f19 b18.5.** Another poorly made whisky: the nose and delivery tells you all you need to know. 46.3%

⁘ **Berrys' Own Selection Ledaig 2005** cask no. 900008 **(86) n21 t22.5 f21.5 b20.5.** A massively fruity/peaty number that, though engrossingly enjoyable and at times stops you in your tracks with the odd big surprise, struggles to find the rhythm and harmony to take it up a notch. 62.7% Berry Bros & Rudd

Cadenhead's Authentic Collection Ledaig Aged 11 Years bourbon hogshead, matured in oak cask, dist 97, bott Jun 08 **(81) n19 t21.5 f19.5 b21.** Lovely peat. But, technically, not quite the greatest malt ever made. 57.7%. 234 bottles.

Cadenhead's Tobermory Aged 13 Years sherry butt, dist 94, bott Feb 08 **(65) n15 t19 f18 b19.** No amount of barley bristle and attitude can save this from the cask....and possibly some strange work on the still. 59.6%. 681 bottles.

⁘ **The Càrn Mòr Vintage Collection Tobermory 1994** sherry butt, cask no. 5125, bott 2009 **(88.5) n21.5** thin sugared barley; **t23** thickens up dramatically, but it's still sugared barley all the way; **f22** some vanillas begrudgingly get to work; **b22** a sweetie. Literally! 46%

Chieftain's Ledaig 10 Years Old cask no. 800004, dist Mar 97 **(69.5) n16 t18 f18.5 b17.** Doubtless there will be those who will dance around claiming this to be the best thing since England won the World Cup (No, honest they did...). Well, sorry. But to me this is badly made whisky where only huge peat does a job of making it potable. You can drink it and enjoy it if you don't care about the niceties. But there is something about this which sets my purest nerves on edge. *61.3%. nc ncf. Ian Macleod.*

⌐ **Chieftain's Ledaig 12 Years Old Acolon Wine Finish** dist Mar 97, bott 2010 **(75) n18 t20 f18 b19.** Mutton dressed as spam. *55% Ian Macleod*

⌐ **Duthies Ledaig 13 Years Old (80) n19 t21 f20 b20.** Ultra sweet and busy with the peat pleasantly reducing the effects of a less than brilliant distillate. *46% Wm. Cadenhead Ltd*

Old Malt Cask Tobermory Aged 13 Years refill hogshead no. 4069, dist Apr 94, bott Dec 07 **(86) n20.5 t22 f22 b21.5.** Clean, well made and overflowing with juicy barley. *50%. nc ncf.*

Old Malt Cask Tobermory Aged 14 Years (86) n20 t23 f21.5 b21. One of the most enjoyable Tobermorys I have come across for a little while: the nose is naff and the complexity is at a premium. Oh, and it's as hard as nails and has absolutely no give and it's pretty hot whisky, too. But you can't help being rocked by the sheer vibrancy and concentrated form of the barley which gives the tastebuds a rare old work over. Nobody's idea of a classic, but absolutely great fun. *50%*

⌐ **Old Malt Cask Tobermory Aged 14 Years** sherry butt, cask no. 5993, dist Feb 96, bott Mar 10 **(81.5) n20 t21 f20 b20.5.** Even with a sherry overcoat, still presents itself in too sugary and ill-disciplined a fashion. *50% Douglas Laing & Co Ltd. 677 bottles.*

Private Cellar Tobermory 1995 bott 08 **(86) n21 t22 f21.5 b21.5.** Enjoyable, essentially honeyed and enjoys a coppery richness. *43%. Scott's Selection.*

Provenance Ledaig Aged 8 Years (86) n21 t23 f21 b21. Thundering peat but new-makey and a tad feinty. An early juice-fest, though. *46%.*

Whisky-Doris Tobermory 35 Years Old dark sherry cask, dist 21 Dec 72, bott 25 Feb 08 **(93) n23.5 t23 f23.5 b23.** This is almost grotesquely over-the-top in terms of its sherry input that it seems almost a parody of the style. But having just tasted a couple of pretty horrendous samples, I am embracing this like a long lost lover and willing, no, demanding, to be seduced. I know this is not the score I'd normally give a whisky like this, but what the hell...I'm only human...! *49.4%.*

⌐ **The Whisky Fair Tobermory 8 Years Old** dist 2001, bott 2010 **(86.5) n22 t21 f21.5 b22.** A model lightly peated island whisky: Twiggy. *60.9%*

Wilson & Morgan Barrel Selection Tobermory 1995 Port Finish bott 08 **(84.5) n21 t21.5 f21 b21.** Eye-wateringly sharp fruit pierces the taste buds. A modicum of smoke confuses the issue further. *46%.*

TOMATIN
Speyside, 1897. Working.

Tomatin 12 Years Old db **(85.5) n21 t21.5 f22 b21.** Reverted back to a delicately sherried style, or at least shows signs of a touch of fruit, as opposed to the single-minded maltfest it had recently been. So, nudge or two closer to the 18-y-o as a style and shows nothing other than good grace and no shortage of barley, either. *40%*

⌐ **Tomatin Aged 15 Years** ex bourbon cask, bott 2010 db **(86) n21 t22 f21.5 b21.5.** One of the most malty drams on the market today. Perhaps suffers a little from the 43% strength as some of the lesser oak notes get a slightly disruptive foothold. But the intense, juicy barley trademark remains clear and delicious. *43% Tomatin Distillery*

Tomatin 18 Years Old db **(88) n22.5** a real clean sherry statement; **t22** a bit of a finuesque kick to this, then the oily malts grab the fruit and slowly assimilate it into a fruity maltshake **f21.5** unbelievably gentle and demure; **b22** what a well-mannered malt. As though it grew up in a loving, caring family and behaves itself impeccably from first nose to last whimpering finale; *43%*

Tomatin Aged 18 Years db **(85) n22 t21 f21 b21.** I have always held a torch for this distillery and it is good to see some of the official older stuff being released. This one has some serious zing to it, leaving your tastebuds to pucker up - especially as the oak hits. *40%*

⌐ **Tomatin Aged 18 Years** sherry finish, bott 2010 db **(92.5) n22.5** busy, thick milkshake maltiness with a touch of fruitcake; **t23.5** cream sherry: creamy + sweet barley + fruity = cream sherry...; **f23** very long with a touch of controlled spicy fizz to the proceedings. But that indomitable barley signature sings to the end; **b23.5** finished in quite superior sherry butts. A malt brimming with character and quality. What a treat! *46% ncf Tomatin Distillery*

⌐ **Tomatin Aged 21 Years** created using 6 refill American oak casks and the 7th an ex sherry butt, bott 2009 db **(81) n22 t22.5 f18.5 b19.** A clattering, chattering, cluttering malt never once getting into rhythm to tell a coherent story. The sherry-pitched nose is jumbled but attractive; the delivery is at first rampant and entertaining but the middle and finale fall away, with the odd negative note at the death. A good one to pour your friends while they are blindfolded: this will confuse them. *52% Tomatin Distillery. 2400 bottles.*

Tomatin 25 Years Old db **(89) n22** the trademark Tomatin 25 citrus nose – plus perhaps a dash of exotic fruit - proudly attacks and teases... **t23** but we have a different lad on the palate: starts gently with the citric, mouth-watering maltiness but where once it famously vanished for a while, now a regiment of spices go on the attack; soft oils ensure a rich presentation; **f21.5** a becalmed finale with the malt having found its voice again; **b22.5** not a nasty bone in its body: understated but significant. *43%*

Tomatin 30 Years Old db **(91) n22** if there was a hint of the exotics in the 25-y-o, it's here, five years on, by the barrel load. Evidence of grape, but the malt won't be outdone, either; **t23** silky and sultry, there is every suggestion that the oak is thinking of going too far. Yet such is the purity and intensity of the malt, damage has been repaired and/or prevented and even at this age one can only salivate as the soft oils kick in; **f23.5** probably my favourite part of the experience because the sheer deliciousness of the chocolaty finale is awesome; **b22.5** malts of this age rarely maintain such a level of viscosity. Soft oils can often be damaging to a whisky, because they often refuse to allow character to flourish. Yet here we have a whisky that has come to terms with its age with great grace. And no little class. *49.3%*

Tomatin 40 Years Old db **(89.5) n21.5** a few oaky yawns because this old guy's feeling a bit tired; **t22** for all the oak intrusion, for all the burntish honeycomb, for all the old aged spices coming through, for all the first-rate impression of a high-class old bourbon, somehow, eventually, it's the malt which really catches the eye; **f23** still oily after all these years and though the oak tries to get a bit tough, it doesn't stand a chance: the sweet malt, and those oils see to that; **b23** not quite sure how it's done it, but somehow it has made it through all those oaky scares to make for one very impressive 40-y-o!! Often it shows the character of a bourbon as a Zimmer. *42.9%*

⭑ **Tomatin 1997** 1st fill bourbon, bott 2009 db **(93.5) n23.5** cranked up orangey notes. Some real bourbon DNA but without the heavier oakiness. Intense barley and oak mix with limited room for further complexity development; **t24** seat gripping time as those citrus notes add a piquancy to the spices which let rip. Not a single dull moment with the sugars radiating the odd concentrated Demerara moment; **f23** even with the arrival of some calming vanilla, this still pulses on the palate; **b23** another outlandishly beautiful malt from this underrated distillery. Had they mixed in a few second fill casks into this, the complexity would have been fearsome and the stuff of legend. *57.1% Tomatin Distillery. 244 bottles.*

⭑ **Tomatin 1999** refill American oak, Tempranillo finish, bott 2009 **(92) n22** nutty, tight. Enclosing oak and fruit stone – something of the slivovitz about this; **t23.5** good morning taste buds...!!!! Wow! Now this one has got their attention. Improbably lively following on from the dullish nose with the fruit notes still ricocheting around the palate. The spices are marked but by no means brutal; **f23** absolutely exemplary cocoa...with a touch of cherry perhaps; **b23.5** looking for something different? Want some fun? Give this a whirl around the palate. Fabulous. *57.1% 302 bottles*

⭑ **The Càrn Mòr Vintage Collection Tomatin 1987** hogshead no. 509, bott 2009 **(87.5) n22.5** beautiful, lightly peated grist; **t22** beautiful, lightly peated grist...that's been distilled...; **f21** soft puffs of smoke help see off the more bitter oak notes **b22** for those of you who don't like their peat to have any intensity. Simple...but had this been in better wood the score would have been a lot higher. *46% nc ncf 1065 bottles*

Celtic Heartlands Tomatin 1967 bott 08 **(78) n19 t21 f18 b20** Decent malt kick but less than kind cask input. *47.7%. Bruichladdich Ltd. 523 bottles.*

Connoisseurs Choice Tomatin 1988 refill American hogshead dist Dec 88, bott Nov 08 **(84.5) n21 t22 f20.5 b21.** Malty and sweetens brightly towards the middle. *43%.*

Duncan Taylor Collection Tomatin 1965 cask no. 20942 **(88) n22.5 t22.5 f21.5 b21.5.** At the very death it is the oily malt which really sings. You feel like applauding... *52.1%*

⭑ **Duncan Taylor Collection Tomatin 1976** cask no. 6818 **(94.5) n23.5** a well weighted honeycomb-nutmeg mix; just the odd molecule of peat evident while the oak gives the first overture to what might have become a bourbon melody; **t24** just eye-closingly beautiful arrival of a honey and spice enriched butterscotch tart; then one wave after another of a delicately oiled bourbon-style sweetness, alternating between Demerara sugars and liquorice; **f23.5** long with the oak upping in vanilla yet still there remains a charming barley fade, untainted by age; **b23.5** flawless. *50.8%*

Hart Brothers Tomatin Aged 15 Years dist Jan 93, bott Jun 08 **(81) n20.5 t21 f19 b20.5.** Malty though it is, every evidence that this one's gone through the top: lactic nose, bitter finish. *46%.*

James MacArthur's Fine Malt Selection Tomatin Aged 12 Years cask no. 12391, dist 95, bott 07 **(85.5) n21 t22 f21 b21.5.** Absolutely down the middle, sweet-ish, non-fussy Tomatin at its malty simplistic. And pretty lovely for it, too. *43%. James MacArthur & Co. Ltd.*

Mackillop's Choice Tomatin 1978 dist Jan 78, bott May 08 **(84.5) n23.5 t20 f20.5 b20.5** To taste, leaks oak badly. But the nose is something else: dried, pithy tangerine; the grassiest of barleys; the oak is equally gentle, radiating soft cassava; any more delicate and it'd crack. *46%.*

Master of Malt Tomatin 19 Years Old (94) n23.5 t23 f24 b23.5. In this form it out-Cardhus Cardhu in the stunningly clean, ultra-rich malty stakes! Almost stereotypical Speyside at its most magnificent. *40%. Master of Malt, UK.*

Master of Malt Tomatin 19 Years Old Cask Strength (96) n24 t24 f24 b24. Quite simply astounding: this is how 19-year-old whisky should be. *57.6%. Master of Malt, UK.*

Norse Cask Selection Tomatin 1989 Aged 15 Years (85) n21 t21 f22 b21. Exceptionally oily and creamy with massive chewiness to both barley and fruit. Big stuff. *57.7%.*

Norse Cask Selection Tomatin 1996 Aged 7 Years (79) n20 t21 f19 b19. I must be one of the biggest advocates for young malt going. But this narrowly misses the mark, perhaps by being, despite the obvious youth on the nose, a tad too advanced for its years. The big malt thrust on arrival is wonderful, but it is far flatter than one might otherwise expect. *50%.*

Northern Light Tomatin 1990 Cask Strength cask no. Q1324 **(86.5) n21.5 t21.5 f22 b21.5.** Barley delicious, but definitely on the bourbony side of malty. *53.2%. Qualityworld, Denmark.*

Old & Rare Tomatin Aged 32 Years dist Dec 75, bott May 08 **(91.5) n24 t23 f22 b22.5.** The nose touches genius while the remainder is simply outstanding. *57.7%.*

Old Malt Cask Tomatin Aged 31 Years refill hogshead no. 3923, dist Dec 75, bott Oct 07 **(94) n23.5 t24 f23.5 b23.** Age just drips off this one. Yet somehow the malty backbone is unbent and the quality undented so there is not a single hint of degeneration. Superb. And about as malty as a malt gets. *50%. Douglas Laing. 296 bottles.*

Private Cellar's Selection Tomatin 1988 bott 07 **(80.5) n20 t20 f20 b20.5.** Creaky and feeling its age but the honeycomb is superb. *43%*

The Scotch Single Malt Circle Tomatin 1976 cask no. 19085, dist Nov 76, bott Jan 08 **(89.5) n23** another quietly extravagant nose with all kinds if bourbony sighs and whimpers blending beautifully with toasted mallows; **t23** gentle, oak-extracted caramels bolt onto the trademark barley and help radiate those docile sugars far and wide; **f21.5** a graceful exit despite the build up of a drier tier; **b22** needs a bit of time in the glass to oxidise and see off some of the worst of the oak. But the low voltage sweetness is simply charming. *49.6%.*

Scott's Selection Tomatin 1976 bott 08 **(87.5) n23** more than a nod in the direction of bourbon with lemon curd tarts in there, too; **t21.5** the reflex action is too much oak. But there is a wonderful compensating sweet lilt which really does give the malt full power; **f22** pretty long with butterscotch blending with the chalky oak; **b21** the malty notes scream Tomatin and handle the oak sometimes more comfortably than others. *50.9%. Speyside Distillers.*

Whisky Doris Tomatin 43 Year Old cask no. 20950, dist Nov 65, bott Mar 09 **(87) n22** carrot cake and marzipan; **t22** a befuddled delivery: the juicy barley tries to take the lead but doesn't quite have the strength or willpower; a few zingy spice and honey notes dive in, then its pretty thick up to and including the middle; **f21.5** lots of oak, but just enough sweetness lends a restraining hand; **b21.5** not a great 43-year-old: far too much oak for that. But the spice and honey intervention makes for a battle royale. *48.2%*

The Whisky Fair Tomatin Aged 22 Years bourbon hogshead, dist 84, bott 07 **(86.5) n22 t21.5 f22 b21.** Custard tart...and a lot of malt on the nose. Then it's malt all the way. Absolutely minimal attempt at complexity, some vague citrus apart, and here the oils gather sufficiently enough to hinder further development. Delicious, though....!! *48.1%. Germany.*

The Whisky Fair Tomatin Aged 22 Years bourbon hogshead, dist 84, bott 07 **(86.5) n22 t21.5 f22 b21.** Mein got!!! A just about identical dram. Perhaps an extra shake of the sugar spoon and a fraction less oil, but it's pretty minimal. Another lovely dram. *48.9%. Germany.*

The Whisky Fair Tomatin 43 Year Old dist 65, bott 09 **(93) n22.5** soft biscuity-shortbread aroma with just a touch of welcome citrus in the background; **t24** some serious Jaffa Cake to this one: the barley speaks first, and makes a surprisingly juicy fist of it, then a slow move towards orange and spice, with a background grated chocolate balance; **f22.5** soft oils have been conjured from somewhere and they help soften the vanilla and barley fade; **b24** slightly overstretched age-wise for certain, but still has enough charm and sophistication, helped along by soft orange and cocoa, to make for an improbably beautiful dram which defies the ages. *48.1%. The Whisky Fair, Germany.*

TOMINTOUL

Speyside, 1965. Angus Dundee. Working.

Tomintoul Aged 10 Years db (78) n20 t19 f20 b19. The true character has been lost under an avalanche of caramel. 40%

Tomintoul Aged 12 Years Oloroso Sherry Finish Limited Edition db (95.5) n24 pronounced Oloroso suggests fresh, untainted butts of outstanding quality; some apple juice dovetails with the grape. About the cleanest sherry nose I have seen in a long time; t24 big malt delivery that perfectly and unexpectedly counters the sherry; at times gloriously bitter-sweet with the accent, rightly, being on the juicy barley; as near as damn-it perfect weight and then a tidal wave of spice; f23.5 that excellent spice delivery rounds off the malty-sherry marriage beautifully. Wonderfully long and seductive with the finish remaining busy and balanced; b24 perhaps it is the voluptuousness of the body which works to best effect here: the mouth is filled with a just-so amount of oil to make the soft sherry, firmer oak and balancing sweet barley notes really harmonise. The label claims the sweetness comes from the sherry. It doesn't: the sherry (nose apart) is dry, the barley sweetens. Even so, a huge leap in quality from the standard 10 and a thrilling reminder of just how good an excellent clean-sherry-influenced whisky can be. 40%.

Tomintoul Aged 14 Years db (95) n24 curiously, there is a sea-weed saltiness attached to this one: not exactly what you expect to find from a malt made and (I think) matured in the centre of the Scottish Highlands. But it adds a compellingly attractive - if eyebrow raising – element to this delicately framed and gently structured, lightly honeyed malt fest. The oak splendidly keeps within the spirit of the style; t24 just how many variations on a honeyed theme can you get? Here I count at least five, each wave coming in after the other with just the odd nip and tuck or expansion of its intensity; the very faintest smoke is detectable and just when the natural caramels appear to be getting too excited, the malt re-establishes itself; f23 medium length, but sheer quality all the way: Bird's custard mixing dreamily with drier, playfully spiced, oaky vanillas. The lightest of oils spreads the grassy, sharper malts to ensure a wonderful lightness of touch; b24 not a single weakness: no bitterness, no off notes, no caramels other than those naturally from the oak, no sulphur. Just magnificent whisky bottled exactly the way it is meant to be. An absolute corker from this little-known but outstanding distillery and one of the most delicately complex distillery bottlings of the year. 46%

Tomintoul Aged 14 Years Limited Edition cask no. 1664, dist 02 May 94, bott Jun 08 db (92.5) n23 sliced cucumber sets the mark for the freshness to this; serious complexity here with a warming spice prickle offset by a light marmalade sweetness; t23 ripping spices ensure the entry is noticed; the tastebuds are then pummelled by a legion of varying barley tones... f23 even a hint a vague fruitiness now as the vanillas, gentle spices and crisp barley all lay claim to the finale; b23.5 "The Gentle Dram" coaxes the label..Yeah, right...!!! 46%. nc ncf. 300 bottles.

Tomintoul Aged 16 Years db (88.5) n22 beautifully weighted and lightened by a citrus and pear mix; t23 outstanding control to the sweetness on delivery with the barley really striking home; f21 chewy and a build up of toffee; b22 once more has changed shape slightly, but the quality never wavers. 40%

Tomintoul Aged 27 Years db (87) n22 pretty thick aroma with a decent spread of marmalade and even a hint of something smoky; t22.5 dullish delivery, perhaps colour-related, but develops slowly, first mouth-wateringly, towards an attractive sweetness that is barley rather than fruit induced; f21.5 cream toffee and vanilla with some playful spices stirring the pot; b21 the last time I saw a colour like this was on antique expert David Dickinson's face. Still, lots of charm and character to go round...and on the whisky, too. 40%

⋅∴⋅ **Tomintoul Aged 33 Years** bott 2009 (90.5) n21 not promising. A little touch of resin, even drying creosote....; some incongruous orange blossom lightens the load; t23.5 improbably juicy delivery. Whisky marmalade and figs melt in with the sweetened vanilla and intense barley; f23 long with barley-thickened molasses. A hint of kumquat at the death; b23 didn't see that coming; thought it was almost dead in the bottle on nosing. A Lazarus of a malt. 43%

Tomintoul 1976 bott 07 db (93.5) n22.5 double-whammy of exotic fruits and honeyed vanilla points to the unmistakable influence of very old bourbon casks. A vague hint of lavender adds to the potpourri. A malt that reeks of great age from every pore, but with the most subtle dusting of peat on the wind; t23.5 an immediate statement of ancient classicism with every nuance of controlled antiquity filling the mouth. Wonderfully juicy, yet a languid smokiness adds both weight and helps keep in line the oaky waves. Fabulous interaction between the oak and barley but the great age is driven home by the spicier, drier riches that cling to the understated oiliness so typical of Tomintoul; f23.5 long and at times improbably lush with the malts having a distinct say before settling below the sea of gentle smoke and oak. Late drying vanilla and cocoa charms and redresses the vaguely fruity sub-plot; b24 it is in the balance that victory is achieved: malts like this so often topple off the cliff into the oaky forest of age, and this one has clung gamely on to safety. Any understandable worries from the nose that this could be too old are dispelled once the subtlety, charm and unexpected liveliness of the whisky becomes apparent on the palate. Truly great whisky which, paradoxically, both celebrates and belies the years and in the most complex manner imaginable. Supreme stuff! 40%

Tomintoul With A Peaty Tang db (94) n23 takes me back to my early teens, spending schooldays working on a farm: pure farmyard with an earthy yet fruity punch. The sort of complex nose that almost makes you forget to drink the stuff...almost...; t24 a gentle coating of vaguely sweet peat that multiplies in intensity; salivating yet chewy. Some liquorice and hickory notes make their drying mark; f23 distinctly gristy and unusually dry for a smoky malt. Long, luscious and not a little oaky late on; b24 a bit more than a tang, believe me! Faultlessly clean distillate that revels in its unaccustomed peaty role. The age is confusing and appears mixed, with both young and older traits being evident. 40%.

⋅⋅⋅ **Mackillop's Choice Tomintoul 1966 Sherrywood** dist Oct 66, bott May 07 (87) n22.5 t21.5 f21.5 b21.5. Filled into an above average sherry butt even for its day, this malt was never going to have a problem in making 40 years. Just. 41.5% Iain Mackillop & Co. Ltd.

Mackillop's Choice Tominoul 1989 cask no. 5990, dist Aug 89, bott Mar 08 (94.5) n23 t24.5 f23 b24. It will take a good five or six mouthfuls to get the measure of this. Once you do, this essay in complexity will be a dangerously hard bottle to put down... 43%.

Norse Cask Selection Tomintoul 1992 Aged 15 Years hogshead cask no. CS059, dist Aug 95, bott Jul 08 (90) n22.5 it's usual rampant self with lots of busy, small, salty – almost curiously coastal – detail, but with oak and citrus leading; t24 a delivery to savour: absolutely hits the palate at full speed with an almost challenging intensity to the barley; f21.5 lightly oiled vanilla and malt, but some bitterness from the cask; b22 though it finishes slightly off course, so much else about this is just so wonderful. 55.5%. Qualityworld for WhiskyOwner.com

Old Malt Cask Tomintoul Aged 33 Years refill hoghead, dist Sep 75, bott Apr 09 (86) n22 t21 f22 b21. The oak is heavy, at times cumbersome, but the greater weight is lifted by a curious molten sugared thread and juniper. The lightest oils all help lessen the burden. Really enjoyable, especially when that late puff of smoke materialises. 43.6%. Douglas Laing. 151 bottles.

⋅⋅⋅ **Old Malt Cask Tomintoul 36 Years Old** refill hogshead no. DL 5733, dist Jun 73, bott Jan 10 (86.5) n24 t20 f21.5 b21. Sadly, the oak has taken hold and has way too big an agenda on the palate despite the malty sweetness. But the nose is an entirely different matter with its lavender and lime freshness and mercurial spices. 45.9% Douglas Laing. 215 bottles.

⋅⋅⋅ **Old Malt Cask Tomintoul Aged 40 Years** refill hogshead no. DL 6215, dist Jan 70, bott May 10 (90.5) n22.5 from the exotic fruit school. But with some spices tacked on; t23 classic oldie refusing to die! Some honeyed coconut has entered the fray to see off the weightier oaks; the oils are wonderful; f22.5 long, with the oak creaking back in, but enough honey and syrup to do the job; b22.5 you just can't keep a great whisky down! 50% 168 bottles

TORMORE
Speyside, 1960. Chivas. Working.
Tormore 12 Years Old db (75) n19 t19 f19 b18. For those who like whisky in their caramel. 40%

Tormore Aged 15 Years "Special Distillery Bottling" db (71) n17 t18 f19 b17. even a supposed pick of choice casks can't save this from its fiery fate. 46%

D&M Connoisseurs' Club Bottling Tormore Aged 15 Years cask no. 2258, dist Feb 92 (75.5) n18 t19 f20.5 b18. Honeyed but also a tad feinty. 43%. nc ncf. US by Angus Dundee.

Mackillop's Choice Tormore cask no. 2258, dist Feb 92, bott Jul 07 (79) n19 t21 f20 b19. No off notes, very good barley, for a Tormore; exceptionally pleasant. But less body than a Burke and Hare dug grave. 43%. Iain Mackillop & Co. Ltd.

Provenance Tormore Aged 12 Years dist winter 96, bott winter 09 (82) n20 t21 f21 b20. Malty, pleasant, clean and entirely untaxing; excellent by Tormore standards. 46%.

⋅⋅⋅ **Scotch Malt Whisky Society Cask 105.12 Aged 25 Years** 1st fill sherry hogshead, dist Sep 83 (93.5) n23 rasping bourbon; t23.5 excellent brown sugars playing around with soft spices; f24 a fabulous coating of mocha still allows the bourbon and barley full depth; superbly weighted and helped by a delicate oil; b23 the best bottled Tormore I have tasted in a very long while....and by a distance. 55.8% Scotch Malt Whisky Society

⋅⋅⋅ **Scotch Malt Whisky Society Cask 105.13 Aged 26 Years** 1st fill sherry hogshead, dist Sep 83 (82) n24 t21 f18 b19. OK, so the taste is on the thin side; and the finish hardly sets the pulse racing, either. But I didn't expect a stupendous nose like this from a Tormore. With those wonderful variants of pear and kumquat, this is one worth nosing...but don't bother with the drinking bit. 56% Scotch Malt Whisky Society

TULLIBARDINE

Highland (Perthshire), 1949. Tullibardine Ltd. Working.

Tullibardine 1966 cask no. 3509, bott 08 **(94) n24** toffee apple concentrate. Pot still Demerara at its most ancient and rich; black treacle and further layering of cooked apple. There are some splinters here, but do little or no damage. Dense, immense and slow navigation required: give this at least ten minutes nosing before finally tasting; **t24** silky, immense oloroso and then a soft display of supine spices; layers of black treacle tart as well as manuka Honey; also a coppery edge to this, as though the still had just had some work done; **f22.5** long and understandably bitter as the 42-y-o oak begins to make some sort of noise; the rich grape and soft honey cushions the worst of this, though; **b23.5** this sister cask of the now legendary '66 World Cup edition has moved on considerably from that '06 bottling. Now we have a malt masquerading as a very old, and it must be said, fine cask of pre-caramelised Demerara rum. Not that there is any caramel, of course: the gushing intensity of the obvious first fill oloroso ensures that such nasty stuff is never needed. No matter how you look at it, this is astonishing whisky, the type of which may be a long time coming round again. Few casks can so majestically endure so many summers, even those as short and minimalist as Scottish ones: this must have been a near perfect sherry butt. For either sherry or Tullibardine lovers, an investigation of the next flight to Calgary will be a must. *49.9%. Exclusively for Willow Park, Calgary.*

⟐ **Tullibardine 1968** hogshead no. 130, bott 2008 db **(85) n23.5 t21.5 f19 b21.** The ravages of time are here for all to see, especially towards the middle and finish. But the nose (like the first few clean waves of the delivery) is a treat. The oak is thick, but there is something of the summer night garden to the sweet floral chorus. *40.3% sc 252 bottles.*

Tullibardine 1975 hogshead cask no. 1009, bott Mar 07 db **(85) n22 t20 f22 b21.** Begins life as a garibaldi biscuit, suddenly overwhelmed by a forest of uncompromising oak and finishes life as a high quality Java/Blue Mountain mix latte. *52.7%*

Tullibardine 1986 John Black Selection ex sherry hogshead cask no. 697 db **(95) n25 t24 f22 b24.** There is good reason why John Black has long been one of the most respected distillers in Scotland. This is liquid, 92 proof why....And though he may not have made it, there's now no doubt he knows what a stunning whisky should nose and taste like. *46%.*

⟐ **Tullibardine 1988 John Black Edition 4** bott 2008 db **(91.5) n23.5** gosh!! How about this for ultra ripe figs and greengages? Wonderfully spiced, honeyed - in an intriguingly understated style - and clean for good measure. One of those you leave the empty glass to give any room's aroma a touch of class to for a few days... **t23** the grape cascades onto the taste buds in a thick, dizzying regiment of fruitiness, by no means all grape, either. The spices hinted at on the nose are here ramrod hard and unyielding; **f22.5** the intensity on delivery fades quite dramatically to leave an almost new-makey cocoa residue. Surprising... and delicious...; **b22.5** An altogether superior and much more complex animal to J B's disappointing No 3 Selection. *46%*

Tullibardine 1988 bott 07 db **(89.5) n23 t23 f21.5 b22.** Just great whisky which has moved up a noticeable notch in age since it was first brought out as a vintage. What fun! *40%*

Tullibardine 1988 cask no. 556, bott 08 db **(79) n20 t20.5 f19 b19.5.** A steady-as-you-go-Joe, a bit strait-laced and tight and even at full strength refusing to come out of its corner to fully entertain. Lots of early juicy barley, though. *55.1%. Exclusively for Willow Park, Calgary.*

Tullibardine 1992 cask no. 239 bott 08 db **(90.5) n22 t23.5 f22 b23.** A masterful bottling which outshines another Tully found in the Canadian market, the cask 737. I don't think it is the later bottling which assists: more, this is from a better bourbon cask and the extra degree of alcohol plays to its strengths in every respect. *53.8%. Exclusively for Willow Park, Calgary.*

Tullibardine 1992 cask no. 737, bott Dec 07 db **(88) n22 t22.5 f21.5 b22.** Sound malt with a touch of attitude. *46%. 269 bottles for Victoria Whisky Festival 2008.*

Tullibardine 1992 cask no. 1871 (1st fill Bourbon barrel) db **(93) n24 t22 f24 b23.** There are first fill bourbons and first fill bourbons...this one probably came from a cask that held a bourbon for a dozen years or more, so measured is the oaky influence. The nose is whisky heaven. *46%. nc ncf sc. 270 bottles.*

⟐ **Tullibardine 1992 Rum Finish** bott 2009 db **(89.5) n22** caramelized...but without the toffee, if you see what I mean...; **t23** crunchy, sugar-coated barley helped along the way with a lovely sheen; **f22.5** a mildly sweetened vanilla flourish; **b22** cracking stuff! *46%*

⟐ **Tullibardine 1993** bott 2009 db **(91.5) n22** a touch of yeast underlines the ultra-light, delicate side of an otherwise weighty nose; **t23.5** a quietly weighty body but, like the nose, it is the lightness of touch with the barley which makes for a juicy and attractive malt; **f23** long with those softly spoken oils coming through with the oaked-up vanilla; **b23** intrinsically sweet barley. But spellbindingly charming all the way. *40%*

Tullibardine 1993 John Black's Selection 3 sherry cask no. 10022, bott Jun 07 db **(82.5)** n21 t21 f20.5 b20. The odd juicy edge but otherwise surprisingly dull. *577%. 259 bottles.*

⊰ **Tullibardine 1993 Moscatel Finish** bott 2007 db **(92.5)** n23.5 has the rare knack of belting out its rich, raunchy Moscatel roots, yet allows both oak and barley a pretty free hand: excellent...; t23.5 wonderful sweet and sharp delivery with some really major grape insurgence. Almost something of the liquid honey-filled cough sweet about the delivery; f23 simmers down for an elegant, oaky, slightly mocha-stained retreat; b22.5 this really is how wine casks should integrate. A minor stunner. *46%*

Tullibardine 1993 Muscatel Wood Finish hogshead cask db **(91)** n23 t22 f23 b23. Seriously classy whisky which really does exploit a wine finish to the nth degree. And very different. *46%. nc ncf.*

⊰ **Tullibardine 1993 Oloroso Sherry Finish** bott 2008 db **(89)** n23 now that is oloroso!! Deep, unblemished grape with just a pinch of ginger spicing up the malt; t23 outstanding mouthfeel with the grape offering both soft juiciness and lively kick; f21 purely an age thing as toasty dryness bites; b22 almost a trip down Memory Lane: once a pretty standard sherry butt, but now a treat. *46%*

⊰ **Tullibardine 1993 Pedro Ximenez Sherry Finish** bott 2009 db **(87)** n21 clean with waxy floorboards; t23 much better with excellent spice offering vibrancy to the thick dollop of grape; f20.5 big, weighty toffee-apple...but without the apple... b22.5 sticky and enjoyable. *46%*

⊰ **Tullibardine 1993 Port Finish** bott 2008 db **(83.5)** n21.5 t21 f20 b21. A bumbling, weighty kind of dram with indistinct shape and purpose, even to the extent of displaying a more bourbony gait than a fruity one. Enjoyable, decently spiced but limited in scope. *46%*

Tullibardine 1993 Rum Finish cask no. 15016, bott Mar 07 db **(81)** n21 t20 f20 b20. Thin and miserly on development. Crisp barley, though. *46%*

⊰ **Tullibardine 1993 Sauternes Finish** bott 2008 db **(84.5)** n22 t22 f20 b20.5. Sleepy and soft with the expected major grape input. Yet rather flattens out too early and to too great a degree. Pleasant, but a little disappointing, too. *46%*

Tullibardine 1994 hogshead cask no. 677 db **(88)** n23 relaxed and floral. Citrus undertones cranks up the complexity; t22 evenly weighted barley with a delicate flourish; f21 thins out slightly complexity-wise, perhaps because of the lethargic sherry; b22 such a fragile thing for something that has spent time in a sherry hogshead. *46%. nc ncf sc. 352 bottles.*

⊰ **Tullibardine Aged Oak** bott 2009 db **(86)** n21.5 t21 f22 b21.5. Aged oak maybe. But early on this is all about the malt which is faultless. Major oaky buzz later, but all about attractive simplicity. *40%*

⊰ **Tullibardine Pure Pot** new make db **(90.5)** n24 t23 f21.5 b22. Pure delight! Not whisky, of course, but a great example of how new make malt should be. *69%*

Tullibardine PX Finish dist 93, bott 08 db **(85)** n23 t22 f20 b20. A big, at times bone-hard, whisky which, like many which have spent time in Pedro Xeminez casks, have found it difficult to acquire the kind of balance hoped. The nose offers great promise with a real old-fashioned fruitcake flourish but after the melt-in-the-mouth delivery gets past the barley lead, the degree of bitterness outweighs the growing soft fig notes. For equilibrium, needed less – or more – time in cask: we'll never know. *46%*

Tullibardine Vintage Edition Aged 20 Years dist 88, bott 08 db **(86)** n22 t22 f21 b21. The malt sparkles on the nose and delivery. Fades as caramels kick in. *46%*

⊰ **A.D. Rattray Tullibardine 1990** cask no. 6105, dist Sep 90, bott Sep 09 **(91.5)** n23 a beautiful gooseberry and soft bourbon buzz: a very recognizable, elegant distillery character; t23 biscuity, complete with soft oils, and a light citrus thread; f23 ridiculously clean with the naked barley sauntering to the finish line; b22.5 you know, for some reason Tullibardine has its fair share of detractors. Or at least I often hear it criticised. I have absolutely no idea why. Here is another malt of exceptionally high quality. *59.1%*

Cadenhead's Tullibardine Aged 18 Years sherry butt, dist 89, bott Feb 08 **(78.5)** n19 t21 f19 b19.5. An impressive barley crescendo in there somewhere. *56.8%. 266 bottles.*

⊰ **Duthies Tullibardine 16 Years Old (87)** n22 light, Canadian-style (but without the colouring!) with a touch of gooseberry; t22 the barley is almost elasticated and stringy, getting everywhere; f21 standard dry vanillas; b22 delicate, malty and beautifully assembled. *46%*

The Golden Cask Tullibardine 1989 cask no. CM127, dist 89 **(86)** n21.5 t22 f21 b21.5. A thick, lolling malt with some outrageously intense barley and shards of honey. The oak does bite now and again but the soft liquorice sub-plot ensures something to chew over. *56.7%.*

The Queen of the Moorlands Rare Cask Tullibardine 1994 Edition XV hogshead no. 676 **(89)** n23 t21 f23 b22. Pretty wild, and it has nothing to do with the strength. The delivery is scrambled but finds a rhythm late on and genuinely impresses. *57.7%.*

Scotch Malt Whisky Society Cask 28.19 Aged 18 Years refill hogshead, dist Jun 90 (**86**) n22 t21 f21.5 b21.5. Serious, malty top dressing for any well-aged blend. Would add decent oak, too. 53.4%

Scotch Malt Whisky Society Cask 28.21 Aged 18 Years refill hogshead, dist Jun 90 (**88.5**) n21.5 green tea and dried marzipan; t23 surge of rich, playfully honeyed, biscuity barley on lush but gentle oils; f22 heaps of toasty vanilla; b22 thick enough to make a malty milkshake from: a honeyed insertion enriches the still mildly juicy but typically intense barley. 54.8%

Scott's Selection Tullibardine 1989 bott 07 (**85**) n20 t22 f21.5 b21.5. Wonderful sharp, eye-watering fruit effect to this deliciously salivating version. 55.4%

The Whisky Fair Tullibardine 1976 dark sherry, dist 76, bott Sep 08 (**96**) n24 noses like an old Bristol dockyard warehouse of the mid 1970s (and that's bloody good, believe me); t24.5 spices, as there should be. Grape in prime fruitcake mode, as it should be. Remnants of barley making a brave, lightly juicy, but ultimately futile fight, as it should be. Middle ground occupied by a light coffeeish oakiness, as it should be. Yep, all the excellent bits present and correct; f23.5 sublimely light, even allowing a delicate Jaffa Cake and fig fade... b24 you see, when you nose and taste this you get some idea of the unutterable paucity of the indefensible, sulphur-screwed bollocks which passes for an embarrassing percentage of sherry cask whisky today.... 54.1%. The Whisky Fair.

The Whisky Fair Tullibardine 1976 light sherry, dist 76, bott Sep 08 (**94**) n24 a lilting golden syrup sweetness is a perfect accompaniment for the grape; t24 stunning delivery: barley and grape are of equal status, and there's that watered-down syrup again; vanillas just find enough room to squeeze into the middle ground; f23 wonderfully robust barley refuses to be brow-beaten by the fruit; b23 absolutely not a single sign of age damage. Superb malt. 54.3%.

UNSPECIFIED SINGLE MALTS (Campbeltown)

Cadenhead's Campbeltown Malt (**92**) n22 a touch of cordite to the barley; t24 as explosive as the nose suggests as the taste bud-ripping barley produces a pyrotechnic display. Gung-ho spices kick in with the advancing oak; f23 long, enormous depth to the spices while eye-watering orange rind completes the complexity; b23 on their home turf you'd expect them to get it right...and, my word, so they do!! 59.5%

Cadenhead's Classic Campbeltown (**92**) n23 balance at a premium but, my word, the salty liveliness of the malt is worth a few extra minutes to enjoy; t24 you can drown in your own saliva, so mouth-watering is the barley; a touch of salt accentuates the enormity; f22 pretty mainstream by comparison, with boring ole salty vanilla tucking in; b23 what a dram! Must be what they gave Lazarus... 50%

Chieftain's The Cigar Malt 11 Years Old Chateau la Nethe finish, cask no. 90951, dist Aug 95, bott Jul 07 (**82**) n20 t21 f20 b21. A few spent matches for the cigar evident. Not being a smoker, I'll take their word for this being a Cigar Malt. Mind you, whatever happened to the old Pipe and Slippers dram...? "Splash of soda, dahling?" "Thank you dear." "Let me just get the paper for you to read with your whisky, I've just ironed it for you. Dinner will be ready in 10 minutes. Steak and kidney pie: your favourite, dahling. Is that all right? If not I have some pork chops in the fridge, they wouldn't take a jiffy." "Yes, thank you dear, the pie will be fine. Oh, and Mildred...." "Yes dear?" "You put in a touch too much soda. Top me up with the whisky, there's a good thing." "Of course, dearest. Sorry." Ah... those were the days... 53.5%. nc, ncf. Ian MacLeod. 293 bottles. South African market.

Wemyss "The Almond Tree" Campbeltown Single Malt Vintage 1970 bott Jan 07 (**88**) n22.5 t22 f21.5 b22. Absolutely no doubting the age of this one. Indeed, this is one almond tree that is creaking with oak. 46%. Wemyss Vintage Malts. 165 bottles.

UNSPECIFIED SINGLE MALTS (Highland)

Adelphi Breath of the Highlands 1972 Aged 35 Years bourbon barrel, cask no. 1753, dist 72, bott 07 (**90.5**) n22 t23 f23 b23. Fcuking hell...!! Where oh where did they dig this one up from? This is 35 going on 53. Totally over the top, seriously a one-off among the 1500 whiskies I have tasted this year: no other has this type of fingerprint. And you know what...I love it!!! From the last days of psychedelia a bit of a psychedelic dram...Give it to me, baby...yeah, nice 'n' rough... 51.7%. 130 bottles.

Asda Extra Special Highland Single Malt 12 Years Old (**79.5**) n21.5 t21 f18 b19. Performs well with a chunky body until it bitters dramatically at the finale. 40%

Cadenhead's Classic Highland (**82**) n19 t22 f21 b20. The trace of fusel oil on the nose guarantees a big delivery. Highly malty! 50%

Cadenhead's Highland Malt (90) n22 malt concentrate; t23 ditto for the delivery; soft oaks and apple develop countering complexity; f22 hard, fresh barley, vanilla and malt milkshake all the way; b23 does barley come any more pure or intense than this...? 60.2%

Celtique Connexion 1990 Armagnac Finish dist 90, bott 08 (86) n21.5 t22 f21 b21.5. Clean, firm, pretty hard-nosed but sweet and never less than enjoyable. 46%

Celtique Connexion 1990 Sauternes Finish dist 90, bott 07 (91.5) n22 t23 f23 b23. Magnifique! 46%. Celtic Whisky Compagnie.

Celtique Connexion 1992 Quart de Chaume Finish dist 92, bott 07 (85.5) n19.5 t23 f21 b22. The nose is less than welcoming and the finish, though offering cocoa aplenty, confirms all is not hunky-dory. However, there is sufficient charm and juiciness on the delivery make for some real fun. 46%. Celtic Whisky Compagnie.

Celtique Connexion 1994 Monbazillac Finish dist 94, bott 07 (90) n22.5 t22 f23 b22.5. Takes a bit of getting used to, as flavours are not exactly subtle. But once your taste-buds acclimatise, its pretty damn decent. Impressed! 46%. Celtic Whisky Compagnie.

Celtique Connexion 1994 Vin de Paille Finish dist 94, bott 07 (71) n17.5 t18 f17.5 b18. Ooh-la-la!! La soufrer!!! 46%. Celtic Whisky Compagnie.

Celtique Connexion Highland Single Malt Aged 14 Years Vin de paille du Jura Finish dist Oct 92, bott Jan 07 (93) n25 t23 f22 b23. Fruity, busy...and very different. 46%. nc ncf.

Co-Operative Group Single Highland Malt Aged 12 Years (86.5) n21.5 t22 f21.5 b21.5. Rich, honeyed and chewy. Overplays the toffee game slightly, but genuinely enjoyable. 40%

Dun Bheagan Highland 8 Years Old (88) n22.5 lively, energetic, weighty oak for age; t22 chewy, a wonderful kaleidoscope of sweetness building on the malt and set off by a sharp bite; f21.5 toffee and honeycomb; b22 just damned decent drinking. 43%. Ian Macleod Distillers.

⋰⋱ **Duncan Taylor Majesty Single Highland Malt 30 Years Old** (93.5) n22.5 some grand old age brings out the exotic fruit and a squirt of liquorice...and a dash of smoky creosote; t24 a real shock as fresh barley goes on a salivating orgy; gristy sugars everywhere plus some watered golden syrup...beautiful...almost youthfully so; f23.5 long, with the syrup holding out until the vanilla takes control; b23.5 the nose suggests a malt past its sell by date. The reality on the palate is anything but. A thrilling way to mark the 800th new whisky for Bible 2011. 40%

Glenandrew Aged 10 Years (83.5) n22 t21 f20 b20.5. Soft chewy toffee. 40%.

Glen Burn Single Highland Malt (81) n20 t20 f21 b20. Pleasant, gentle if simplistic pub fodder. 40%. Glen Burn Distillers

Glenfinnan Highland Scotch Single Malt Over 12 Years Old (84) n22 t23 f19 b20. Starts beautifully with citrus and rose petals among other delights. But then stops dead just as you pass the middle. Damn!! 40%. Celtic Whisky Compagnie, France.

Glen Torran Highland Single Malt 8 Years Old (75) n17 t21 f18 b19. Sparkles briefly on arrival, helped along the way by lovely spice. But the caramel on the nose and finish does it in. 40%. Roderick & Henderson for London & Scottish International.

Glen Turner Single Highland Malt Aged 12 Years L616656B (84) n22 t23 f19 b20. There's a really lovely malt trying to escape there, but its wings are clipped by some over hefty caramel on the finish. But the nose and delivery sing beautifully and are joyously mouthwatering. I feel a Bible-thumping trip to France coming on....they must realize that because Cognac has spent the last few decades using caramel as a crutch for its own lack-lustre spirit, it doesn't mean to say that Scotch needs it. Absolutely the contrary! Right, down from my soapbox. 40%. Glen Turner Distillery for La Martiniquaise, France.

Glen Turner Single Highland Malt Aged 12 Years (85) n21.5 t22.5 f20 b21. Pleasant enough. 40%. Glen Turner Distillery for La Martiniquaise, France.

Glen Turner Single Highland Malt Aged 18 Years L532556A (87) n21 t22 f21 b22. A wonderfully clean and characterful malt that lays it on thick with the barley but, again, could do with keeping the caramel at bay. 40%. Glen Turner Distillery for La Martiniquaise, France.

Glen Turner Single Highland Malt Aged 18 Years (83) n19 t23 f20 b21. Some serious honey doing the rounds here and the fruitiness is at times impressive. But the nose and finish testifies that odd dodgy cask has been tipped into this, too. 40%. Glen Turner Distillery for La Martiniquaise, France.

Matisse Aged 15 Years Highland Single Malt (83.5) n22 t21 f20 b20.5. Lots of toffee with fruit. Has rather upped the toffee delivery of late. 40%. Matisse Spirits Co. Ltd.

⋰⋱ **Matisse 19 Year Old Highland Single Malt** bott Oct 09 (85) n22 t21.5 f21 b21.5. Even flavoured and tempered: a safe, malty, lightly fruity dram. 46% Matisse Spirits Co Ltd

⋰⋱ **Matisse 1996 Single Cask Highland Malt Special Scottish Parliament Edition** bott Apr 10 (90) n23 marzipan with sugared eggs and flour: like an uncooked cake; t23 beautifully clean and refreshing: lemon juice freshens further thick, malty middle; f22 a quite astonishing degree of natural caramel and malt concentrate; b22 the nose wants to make you run your fingers around the inside of the glass and devour whatever you get....a whisky far too good to be wasted on mere politicians. *58.6% Matisse Spirits Co Ltd. 222 bottles.*

McClelland's Highland Single Malt (80) n21 t20 f19 b20. Easy going – until the bitter finish kicks in. *40%*

Sainsbury's Single Highland Malt Aged 12 Years (82.5) n21.5 t21 f20 b20. Enjoyable, but has lost its old complexity and now displays big cream fudge. *40%. Sainsbury's, UK.*

Secret Stills Highland 6.1 1988 (95) n23.5 t23.5 f24 b24. Absolutely beautifully made malt which has spent some 20 years in a perfect cask. Truly adorable. *45%. Gordon & MacPhail.*

Tantallan 10 Years Old Highland Single Malt (86) n21.5 t22.5 f21 b21. Has kept impressively to its massively malted principles with a squirt here and there of fruit, too. But let down slightly by the bitterness of the odd tired bourbon barrel. *40%* ☉ ☉

⊰⊱ **Wemyss 1989 Single Highland "The Fruit Bowl"** refill hogshead, bott Sep 09 **(89.5) n22.5** light, flighty malt; stewed cooking apple; **t23** full mouth feel with chunky malt and many stratum of juicy figs sweetened with molasses; **f22** malty and mildly metallic **b22** mild mannered and meandering. *46% Wemyss Malts Ltd. 331 bottles.*

⊰⊱ **Wemyss 1990 Single Highland "Tropical Spice"** refill butt, bott Sep 09 **(95) n24.5** wow!! Now this makes you sit up and take notice. No sitting on fences here: a full broadside of intense oaky spice softened, yet thickened by an ultra rich fruit-barley combo of white knuckle intensity. The type of nose which takes a good hour to circumnavigate....; **t24** the delivery is no less intimidating with a highly unusual charge of rich, sweet fruit and a much drier, austere almost, oakiness; the treacle candy is a treat; through all this the malt is never less than salivating; **f23** long, playful background spice and sweetened hickory; **b23.5** a peach of a barrel. Highly unusual in character and never seemingly the same any two times you taste it. *594% Wemyss Malts Ltd. 767 bottles.*

Tesco Highland Single Malt 12 Years Old (87) n22 t22 f21 b22. A quite lovely malt displaying no shortage of character and charm. *40%. Tesco, UK.*

Wilson & Morgan House Malt cask no. 4082 – 4090 **(85) n21 t21.5 f21 b21.5.** A big-peated, lusty, big-hearted, highly enjoyable chap who eschews subtlety for effect. *43%*

⊰⊱ **Wilson & Morgan Sherry Cask Malt "Highland Heart"** cask no. 4446/4448/4450, dist 2001, bott 2009 **(75.5) n18 t22 f17 b18.5.** For a while the golden honey flies high and handsomely. Then a familiar sherry off note breaks my lowland heart. *43%*

UNSPECIFIED SINGLE MALTS (Island)

⊰⊱ **Adelphi's Fascadale Aged 10 Years Batch 2** bourbon hogshead, bott 2010 **(86.5) n22.5 t21.5 f21 b21.5.** Punchy, peaty, and attractively aggressive. *46% 3746 bottles.*

Chieftain's The Auld Alliance Flora Macdonald First Edition 15 Year Old Island Malt St. Emilion finish, dist Apr 92 **(83.5) n22 t21 f20 b20.5.** Curious how the fruit barely shows on the smoky nose. Certainly makes up for it once it hits the palate! *50%. Ian Macleod.*

Chieftain's The Auld Alliance Flora Macdonald Second Edition 15 Year Old Island Malt Chateauneuf Du Pape finish, dist Apr 92 **(89) n23 t21 f23 b22.** Normally I find peat and wine a bit like baked beans and eggs or soup and wine: they just weren't meant to be. However, I have to begrudgingly admit that, after a few early pratfalls, it works pretty damn well... *47%.*

Dun Bheagan Island Single Malt Aged 8 Years (93) n23 t24 f23 b23. As beautiful as a Scottish isle. *43%. Ian Macleod Distillers.*

Dun Bheagan Island 8 Years Old (83) n21 t21.5 f19.5 b21. Pleasant and although honeyed, no buzz. *43%. Ian Macleod Distillers.*

⊰⊱ **Macleod's Island (85) n21 t22 f21 b21.** A soft, toffee-fudged affair. Easy drinking. *40%*

Master of Malt Orkney 12 Years Old (91) n23.5 now if you really want to know what heather smells like, invest in a bottle of this: rarely do you come across it in such unabridged form....even if it's Scapa!!; seriously botanical all round; **t23** thick malt, a touch of light honey; **f21.5** long, toffeed; **b23** yet another gem from the Master of Malt (fudgy finish apart). His portfolio is pretty damned impressive, I must say. *40%. Master of Malt, UK.*

UNSPECIFIED SINGLE MALTS (Islay)

⊰⊱ **Adelphi's Liddesdale Aged 18 Years Batch 1** sherry butt, bott 2010 **(94) n23.5** crisp, brittle, crumbly peat partnering a more succulent fig and date fruitiness; **t24** glorious delivery, with the fruit thick and jammy, then wave upon wave of manuca honey. Elsewhere, spices dance and the peat rumbles; **f23** a tad bitter, both in a marmalade and burnt way, but now hickory and vanilla rise above the smoke; **b23.5** an exceptional Islay where complexity and balance are the key. *46% Distillery Ltd. 2962 bottles.*

⊰⊱ **Asda Extra Special Islay Single Malt 12 Years Old (91) n23** classic peat ash and citrus-tinged smoke; **t23** fabulous liquorice and Demerara-sweetened peat; toffee vanilla is in no short supply, either; **f22.5** cough sweet, spices and toffee; **b22.5** a high quality Islay from the old traditional school. *40%*

Auld Reekie Islay Malt (95) n24 t24 f23 b24. My last whisky of the day and a dram I shall be tasting all the way to when I clean my teeth. On second thoughts...I'll do them in the morning. Only kidding. But this is a must have dram for Islayphiles: true genius. *46%*.

⟶ **Berrys' Reserve Islay (86.5) n21.5 t22.5 f21 b21.5.** Fat, sweet, chewy and particularly pleasing on delivery. Decent nip, too. *46% Berry Bros & Rudd*

Blackadder Peat Reek (88) n23 t22 f21 b22. A clean, very gentle giant. *46%. Blackadder International.*

Cadenhead's Classic Islay (91) n23 t23 f22 b23. I admit: totally baffled by this one. Just can't read the distillery at all: a completely different take on any of them: kind of Ardbegian, but a Lahphraogish blast and a hint of Caol Ila's oils. Yet it is all, yet none of them. Oddly enough, it reminds of Port Ellen when about eight years old. But, obviously, can't be. Classic, indeed! *50%*

Cadenhead's Islay Malt (84) n22 t21 f20 b21. Fat, well enough peated but lacks ambition and complexity. *58%.*

Chieftain's The Auld Alliance Prohibition Wine Cask 16 Year Old Islay Malt Chateauneuf Du Pape finish, dist Dec 90 **(84) n22.5 t20.5 f21 b20.** There are certain aspects here that are impressive, the bothie fire ashes on the nose for a start. But I well remember learning over 25 years ago from an Ardbeg old timer (even then) that you used wine casks only to store the whisky when it came to peat, never to give extra flavour. I'm particularly reminded of those wise words right now... *46%. Ian Macleod.*

⟶ **Classic of Islay Single Malt Cask Strength (81) n20 t22 f19 b20.** Fat, smoky, oily, very sweet, tight. Enjoyable, but lacking character development due mainly to the casks. *58%*

Dun Bheagan Islay 8 Years Old (92) n22.5 fresh and clean, the peat taps out a smoky tattoo; **t23.5** again, a certain youthfulness allows the barley to really pulse; some excellent gristy sweetness ensures a wonderful succulence; **f23** drier but layered with the oak offering a butterscotch edge – smoked, of course; **b23** spot on. *43%. Ian Macleod Distillers.*

Dun Bheagan Islay 8 Years Old (Canada Release) (87) n22 t21.5 f22 b21.5. Incredibly soft: at times the constituent parts appear to have blurred. *43%. Ian Macleod Distillers.*

⟶ **Dun Bheagan Islay Vintage 2000 (88) n22** dry, powdery peat ashes; **t22.5** opens up on delivery with a charge of molasses and hickory. The smoke is lazy and drifts without shape; **f21.5** more hickory, vanilla and burnt toast tang; **b22** a plodding malt which reveals its considerable charms in slow motion. *43% Ian Macleod for Canadian Market.*

⟶ **Elements of Islay Ar2 (90.5) n22** dry, dusty smoke, some real singed toast to this one; **t23.5** a peppery explosion on delivery, then a beautiful, molassed sweetness coats the mouth; **f22.5** long, a touch of brine on the hickory and smoke; **b22.5** sunshine one minute, storms the next...yep: this whisky about sums up the elements of Islay quite succinctly. *60.5%*

⟶ **Elements of Islay Cl1 (85.5) n21 t22.5 f21 b21.** Molassed Fisherman's Friend cough sweet. Where have I tasted this style before? Simplistic, but a real meal. *62.9%*

⟶ **Elements of Islay Lp1 (91) n23** the entire shape is hewn from smoked grape; **t23.5** thick, juicy multi-layered with more than a single strata dedicated to mocha; the peat is windblown; **f22** dries with dates and molasses keeping the balance; **b22.5** a big, fruity Islay with few pretensions of subtlety. *58.8% Speciality Drinks Ltd*

⟶ **Elements of Islay Pe1 (95.5) n24** absolutely classic dry, peat ash but enlivened by the most subtle heather and lavender; **t24.5** if you heard a distant sigh on the 29th July 2010, it was me tasting this. Again, most of everything I am looking for: a touch of honey to enrich the peat, barley offering attractive juiciness, a countering dryness from the smoke...; **f23.5** long with the inevitable vanillas entering with an almost perfect degree of weight and sweetness; confirmation that the cask element of Islay is quite perfect; **b23.5** this is a fabulous, nigh faultless, example of the purest element of Islay: its whisky... *58.7% Speciality Drinks Ltd*

Finlaggan Islay Single Malt 10 Years Old (82) n21 t21 f20 b20. Beautiful citrus notes mildly tempered with smoke: an enormous improvement from the caramel-ruined previous "Lightly Peated" bottlings. *40%. The Vintage Malt Whisky Co.*

Finlaggan "Old Reserve" Islay Single Malt (79.5) n19 t21 f19 b20.5. A smoky shadow of its once great self. *40% The Vintage Malt Whisky Co. Ltd.* ⊙ ⊙

The Ileach Islay Single Malt (85) n20.5 t22 f21 b21.5. Not the dram it was. Once near faultless, now a highly smoked hotchpotch. Not without its lovely moments, but pray the next bottling is nearer its magnificent old self. *40%* ⊙ ⊙

Islay Storm (76) n19 t20 f19 b18. More of a drizzle. *40%. C.S. James & Sons.*

Islay Storm 12 Years Old (81) n20 t21 f20 b20. Some lovely spice emphasis the seaweed kick. Decent oak weight, too. *40%. C.S. James & Sons.*

McClelland's Islay Single Malt (88) n22 delicate yet confident smoke; t22 light at first then livens as the smoke kicks in; f22 beautifully long and clean with tapering Fisherman's Friend; b22 no mistaking which distillery this little beaut is from: Bowmore anyone? 40%.

Macleod's Islay (84.5) n21 t22 f20.5 b21. Considering the raging bull of a malt this used to be, this appears to have been snipped in its prime. Toffee and coffee have as much impact as the peat, which offers more smoke than depth. 40% Ian Macleod ⊙ ⊙

Master of Malt Islay 12 Years Old (95) n23.5 t23.5 f24 b24. Actually, I lie. There is barely any peat at all, save for a gust of peat reek which hovers unspectacular above the stunning honey notes and then muscles in hardly noticed when no-one's looking. Those on the prowl for a massively peated dram will be disappointed. Those hunting a very gently, almost covertly, smoked malt which appears completely relaxed with its honeycomb and barley constitution and its dependency on complexity will be delighted. A treasure of a find. 40%.

Milroy's Badger Islay 2001 bourbon cask no. 27, dist Jun 01, bott Jul 07 **(91)** n23 t22.5 f23 b22.5. Like a badger, earthy and goes down beautifully... and do you know what? I doubt if this will be significantly better in six or eight years time... 46%. Milroy's of Soho. 398 bottles.

Pibroch Aged 12 Years (92) n23.5 a light, bright gristy nose but a balancing dryness makes for a pretty complex and seductive nose; t23 much sweeter than the nose foretells: juicy, gristy barley everywhere while the smoke comes in gentle layers, almost as an afterthought; f22 dry liquorice on the oak; b22.5 chugs along beautifully... 43%.

Port Askaig Aged 17 Years (89) n22 lightly oiled peat reek; t22.5 a citrussy sharpness for a second or two, then returns to its oily theme; a decent wave of black peppers hits the spot; f22.5 a touch of liquorice and hickory joins the unerring oily, peaty march; b22 what it does, it does rather attractively and with minimum fuss. 45.8%. Speciality Drinks.

Port Askaig Aged 25 Years (86) n22 t21.5 f21 b21.5. Distinctly Caol Ila in style, with big fat oils entirely running the show. The peat is curiously big and modest in the same show, but that has much to do with the sweet citrus and vanilla-enriched oils. Easy dramming. And perfect for keeping the most vicious of midges off you whenever sitting outside the Port Askaig hotel watching the ferry, as indeed I did when this was made 25 years ago... 45.8%.

⁙ **Port Askaig Aged 30 Years (81.5)** n19 t22.5 f20 b20. Some malts make it through to this age unscathed. Some don't. This falls into the latter category. Some exotic notes, but this always appears to work less well for Islays than mainlanders. The odd wonderful malt and caramel moment, even so. 45.8% Speciality Drinks Ltd

⁙ **Port Askaig Cask Strength (89)** n22 ash dry; t23.5 thumping peats which dominate until the sweet yam and muscovado muscles their way in on the soft oils; f21 bitters out; b22.5 surprisingly juicy after the nose. Profound. 57.1% Speciality Drinks Ltd

The Queen of the Hebrides Islay Single Malt Whisky (85) n22 t22 f20 b21. Big, rolling fat peats: any fatter and it'd be declared obese. 40%. Wine Shop, Leek; Islay Whisky Shop.

⁙ **Robert Graham's The Hoebeg Single Islay Malt (88)** n23 charming nose full of morning after the night before ashes of a peat fire; t22.5 fresh and chattering with all kinds of sugary smoke notes; f21 speedy fade leaving just sugars and smoky caramel behind; b21.5 what first appears to be a big, roaring Islay turns out to be a smoky kitten. 40%

Sainsbury's Single Islay Malt Aged 12 Years (90) n23.5 huge, clean peat: almost plastic mach-ish in its phenolic kick; t22.5 beautiful weight and depth; an uncompromising yet entirely comfortable degree of smoke and chewability with some toffee making the work harder for the jaws; f21.5 there really is a lot of toffee as its dries; b22.5 a classic of its type. 40%

Smokehead Extra Black Aged 18 Years (94) n23 what a softie....delicate layers of dry peat ash and oils intermingle; extra oaky-floral life added by gentle hickory and a sprig of prickly lavender; t24 juicy, rock-hard delivery which is entirely divorced from the nose; almost a bourbony rye-led fruitiness until the peat slowly, methodically and irrevocably takes over in that beautiful dry, ashy style; f23.5 dry smoked, coffee-stained and with enough molassed sugars to comfortably see off any threat of OTT oak; b23.5 doubtless some will prefer the in-your-face standard version. This is for those seeking a bit of grey-templed sophistication. 46%.

Smokehead Islay db **(92)** n24 even iodine doesn't come more iodiney than this. Also salty, youngish and bracing; t23 sweet grist at first, moves into sharp citrus and back into malt; f22 the complex peats begin to fade as vanilla and caramel kick on; b23 this company does this kind of whisky so well. A little gem. 43%. Ian Macleod.

Tesco Islay Single Malt 12 Years Old (89) n23 t23 f21 b22. Timeless whisky: this is like going back 25 years and onto the island when the peat was thick and caramel was thicker!! Had this been at natural colour, I think we'd have a malt closer to about 92: this has come from some wonderful casks. 40%. UK.

⁙ **Wemyss 1997 Single Islay "Autumn Leaves"** refill bourbon, bott Sep 09 **(75)** n18 t19 f19 b19. Technically, not quite the greatest whisky: one I will leaf well alone..... 46%

∵∵ **Wemyss 1996 Single Islay "Honey Smoke"** hogshead, bott Sep 09 **(85)** n21.5 t22 f20.5 b21. I was expected to find a smoked out hive. Instead, a rather salty dram where the sweetness is of a more muscovado sugar rather than honey variety. *59.6% 425 bottles.*

∵∵ **Wemyss 1997 Single Islay "Sandy Seaweed"** bott Apr 09 **(84)** n22 t22.5 f19 b20.5. In the artificial light of my tasting palnket, on picking this up I thought it was new make. To my astonishment, it's been around longer than the Euro. As is often the case when exhausted old casks are deployed, the nose and delivery are excellent (and new makey/gristy) but the finish is bitter and off key. *46% Malts Ltd. 342 bottles.*

Wemyss 1991 Single Islay "Smoked Sausages" bott Jan 07 **(88)** n22.5 t22.5 f21 b22. A surprise package with much less peat than the nose suggests. Charming stuff. *46%.*

∵∵ **Wilson & Morgan House Malt "Born on Islay"** cask no. 309928/309934, dist 2001, bott 2010 **(86)** n21.5 t22 f21 b21.5. A curious thick set Islay with a mildly industrial nose, revealing the oiliness of old workshops. The delivery is sweet but a little muted. *43%*

Wm Morrison Islay Single Malt Aged 10 Years **(84)** n21 t22 f21 b20. A uniform Islay which, though pleasant and initially sweet, fails to trouble the imagination or pulse. *40%.*

UNSPECIFIED SINGLE MALTS (Lowland)

Cadenhead's Classic Lowland Bourbon wood **(82)** n19 t21 f21 b21. Much juicier and fortified with rich barley than the nose suggests. *50%*

Cadenhead's Lowland Malt **(90)** n22 t23 f22 b23. One of the best lowlanders around. Fabulously fresh! *56.4%*

Dun Bheagan Lowland 8 Years Old **(81)** n19 t20 f21 b21. Recovers from a sweaty armpit nose to offer a bit of bite and juice on the palate. *43%. Ian Macleod Distillers.*

∵∵ **Master of Malt 12 Years Old Lowland 2nd Edition** **(86.5)** n22.5 t22 f20.5 b21.5. Lots of joined up aromas, with apple and liquorice character linking with drier elements quite effortlessly while the delivery offers attractive weaving between youthful maltiness and an older, slightly bourbony edge. *40%*

UNSPECIFIED SINGLE MALTS (Speyside)

Asda Extra Special Speyside Single Malt 12 Years Old **(76)** n18.5 t19 f19 b19.5. The last time I tasted this, some thug attacked my office and smashed up neighbouring property. If only there could be some similar violence to my taste buds, as this is as docile and nondescript as it comes. 40% ☉ ☉

∵∵ **Berrys' Reserve Speyside** **(88)** n21.5 some under-ripe fruit tangles with the barley; t22.5 silky, satisfying mouth feel, again with the barley dominating, though a little liquorice seeps in; f22 a curious coppery small still feel as the gentle vanillas grow; b22 entirely unspectacular, utterly lacking in star quality...and yet...a very pleasant, fault-free dram which hits the spot. *46% Berry Bros & Rudd*

Celtique Connexion Monbazillac Finish Aged 14 Years dist 94, bott 09 **(88)** n23 good grief...!! Is there any whisky in there? The grape dominates but on careful nosing something spicy and faintly barley-ish raises a white flag... t22.5 silky delivery, though the grape and spice does all the talking – loudly... f21 more grape, this time doused in molasses; b21.5 clean, fabulously sulphur-free and quite substantial whisky, but the Monbazillac has gone Monballistic... *46%. Celtic Whisky Compagnie.*

Celtique Connexion Sauternes Finish Aged 13 Years dist 95, bott 08 **(95)** n23.5 not as sweet as some Sauternes noses: dried orange peel and melted vanilla ice cream; t24 intriguing firm/soft body makes for a very different start: equally the sharp and sweeter notes also do battle as the spices get wilder; excellent barley for all the obvious fruit; f23.5 dry, spicy, complex and dignified. b24 top notch balance between spice and grape. Elegant. *46%.*

Celtique Connexion Vin de Paille du Jura Finish Aged 14 Years dist 94, bott 08 **(71)** n17 t19 f17 b18. It seems that many a whisky label with the word Jura on it is accursed: sulphur yet again! *46%. Celtic Whisky Compagnie.*

Dun Bheagan Speyside 8 Years Old **(85)** n22 t22 f21 b20. The fabulous malty-spice surge on delivery is arm-of-seat-gripping stuff! *43%. Ian Macleod Distillers.*

∵∵ **GlenParker Speyside Single Malt** **(86.5)** n21 t22.5 f21.5 b21.5. An enjoyable, bracing malt with plenty of backbone and bite. If you are looking for flavour and personality, you can do a lot worse. *40% Angus Dundee*

∵∵ **Macleod's Speyside** **(86)** n21.5 t22 f21 b21.5. Friendly, malty and juicy. *40%*

Master of Malt Speyside 30 Years Old Special Reserve **(87)** n22 t22 f21.5 b21.5. Shhhh. Stop whatever you are doing. Turn the radio off. And the central heating. Listen. Really listen. Hear that creaking...? It's this whisky... *40%. Master of Malt, UK.*

Master of Malt 30 Year Old Speyside 3rd Edition (88.5) n23 t23 f20.5 b22. A character malt, performing all kinds of stunning Speyside tricks, but with the odd one falling flat on its face. Great fun. 40%. Master of Malt, UK.

Master of Malt 40 Year Old Speyside 1st Edition (87.5) n22 t21.5 f22 b22. As the whisky changed in the glass – after 40 years in cask it deserves the longest outing it can possibly get – I was completely bemused by this one. At times it went through phases where it would struggle to get 77, while sometimes it peered into the possibilities of the 90s. But that was fleeting, and this is perhaps a mean score; to some in both senses... 40%.

⋯ **Master of Malt 40 Year Old Speyside 2nd Edition** (92.5) n23 t24 f23 b22.5. Brinkmanship doesn't quite cover it.....but the intense and multi-faceted sugars cope with the major splinters in there. 40%

Master of Malt Speyside 50 Years Old Special Reserve (95) n23 t24 f24 b24. A genuine masterpiece of an ancient malt showing improbable integrity and finesse. The only whisky tasted so far this year (and this is number 1,263) that I have not spat a single drop out. I don't know if this was a 1957 cask, or '58. On one hand I hope it was the '57, as that was the year I was born, and on that basis it should be stunning. On the other, a pang of regret that I didn't find this cask first and bottle it for my 50th birthday celebrations... 40%. Master of Malt, UK.

McClelland's Speyside (77.5) n20 t19 f18.5 b19. Remains stunningly inert. 40%.

Old Malt Cask Speyside's Finest Aged 40 Years sherry butt no. 3803, dist Dec 66, bott Aug 07 (88) n23 t21 f22 b22. Gets away with over-the-top oak thanks to some of the finest rum and raisin coffee I have ever tasted... 50%. nc ncf. Douglas Laing. 329 bottles.

⋯ **Old Malt Cask Speyside's Finest Aged 41 Years** sherry butt, cask no. 5515, dist Nov 67, bott Sep 09 (82) n22 t21 f19 b20. Salty biscuit and mocha. But buckles under the weight of oaky expectancy. 50% Douglas Laing & Co Ltd. 456 bottles.

Old Malt Cask Speyside's Finest Aged 41 Years sherry (94) n24 t22.5 f23.5 b24. My word! You need a bit of a sit down after a whisky like this. A dram to relax with? Hardly. Getting to the bottom of this, fair takes it out of you. But if you can think of a better way to spend an evening with a buxom 41-year-old from Speyside, let me know... 50%.

Old Malt Cask Speyside's Finest Aged 41 Years sherry cask (93) n23 tart gooseberries with a big vanilla topping; t24 no less tart barley which really does initially act with extraordinary vim for such an oldie; the oaks compensate by getting pretty heavy; f23 settles to a degree as some oils evolve and spread a cocoa-ish word; b23 for all its wrinkles, a malt with great charm and personality 50%. Douglas Laing.

⋯ **Old Malt Cask Speyside's Finest Aged 42 Years** sherry butt no. DL 6245, dist Nov 67, bott Jun 10 (88) n23 cherry fruitcake meets cherryade; a real touch of the cake shop about this one with a light spicy nip in the air; t21.5 friendly sumptuous fruit scores early but the hefty oaks fight back immediately to take the lead; f22 only late on do the fruit and oaks harmonise, though a touch of dry bitterness creeps in; b21.5 you know the elegant building in your town which is crumbling a bit and someone's tarted it up sllghtly in not quite the right colours....? 50% Douglas Laing. 385 bottles.

Old Malt Cask Speyside's Finest Aged 43 Years (83.5) n20 t22.5 f20 b21. A surprisingly juicy job for its age but not entirely flawless. 50%. Douglas Laing.

⋯ **Old Malt Cask Speyside's Finest Aged 43 Years** sherry butt, dist Jun 66, bott Oct 09 (96.5) n24 one of those improbably clean sherry butts (for its age) that offers as much medium roast Mysore/Java mix roast as it does fruit. Only rarely can a cask take such an oaky punch and not even flinch; t24.5 how does it do it after 43 years....? The first note is freshly pressed grape juice. Not far behind comes a whole army of subsidiary characters, led by mocha and hickory, then some pithy tannins, a little salt and muscovado....the column is endless; f24 ...still this ensemble marches on into the finish; and still the coffee has a big say, though now the big oaky vanillas have given it a slightly creamy texture....; b24 as near as damn it faultless.... 48.2% Douglas Laing for The Whisky Show 2009

Sainsbury's Single Speyside Malt Aged 12 Years (87) n22 fruity, fizzy and sharp; t22 lovely sweet delivery with some light muscovado sprinkled on the fruit; f21 tangy orange; slightly furry and bitters out; b22 gosh: behaving just like a Macallan! 40%

Spey Single Malt 1956 (87.5) n24 textbook ancient sherry cask single malt from the old school: even now the grape is intense, sweet, profound and yet calm, collected and controlled. Naturally the oaks are having a field day but in a quite acceptable toasty-liquorice manner. Classically beautiful; t21.5 after the tongue is bathed in soft, magnificent bourbon-tinged sherry the oak tries to run amuck. At first it is thwarted by the raisin, but finally succeeds as the woody waves continue to crash; f21 seriously burnt toast bitter, though it does move into a more stable cocoa style towards the death; b21 a case of a dram which has seen too much wood for its own good. Yet, as the magnificence of the nose shows, this cask still has something very special to offer. *45.8%. Harvie's of Edinburgh. Japanese market.*

Spey Single Malt 1991 (92) n23 beautifully presented fruit: clean save a hint of caramel, and some teasing spice; t24 now that is divine....!! The delivery makes the most of its impressive alcohol content to thump home once again the fruit with some really resounding barley pushing from behind – a further strata of sweetened mocha is just being flash; flattens on the middle; f22 quietens down towards a coffeed toffee, vanilla finale with the odd raisin here and there; b23 what a treat of an experience! Layered, complex and very high class. Those who enjoy the Glenfarclas style might enjoy this, too. *63.5%.*

Spey Single Malt Aged 12 Years (80) n20.5 t21 f18.5 b20. The over-ripe kumquat on the nose warns of some little imperfections to come, especially on the finish. *40%.*

Spey Single Malt Aged 15 Years (84) n22 t21 f20 b21. Soft and safe, there is not a bump in the tangy-caramel ride. *46%. Harvie's of Edinburgh. Japanese market.*

Spey Single Malt Aged 21 Years (92) n24 fabulous!! A controlled fruitfest from the obvious raisiny grape through to fat gooseberries with cooked apples in between; the oak is deep, sympathetic but not for a moment overbearing; t23 silky sultanas ensure a sweetness to the fruit arrival; the oak makes it mark slowly and with a degree of elegance befitting the overall charm and complexity; f22 long, delicate and still with fruit but with more toffee arriving and Madeira cake replacing the earlier Dundee style; b23 oh, had only this wonderful dram been bottled at at least 46%: it is like driving a Mercedes E class with an engine designed for a lawnmower... *40%. Harvie's of Edinburgh. Japanese market.*

Spey Single Malt 'Chairman's Choice' (90) n22 firm and oak-framed; a weak golden syrup attachment to barley; t23.5 brooding OTT oak at first but quickly pans out towards that same barley-golden syrup evident on the nose which morphs into light honey; f22 regulation vanilla; b22.5 my experience over the years is that most Chairmen haven't got a clue which end of a barrel is which. This does appear to be an exception, though... *40%.*

Tesco Speyside Single Malt 12 Years Old (88) n21 some stressed oak is becalmed by subtle smoke and firm barley; t22 outstanding delivery with a sheen to the barley as it glides over the palate; the spices mass as the oak concentrates; f22 a gentle return of smoke sits comfortably with the cocoa and barley; b23 no shrinking violet here: a Speysider with a touch of attitude – and class. *40%. Tesco, UK.*

⁓ **Wemyss 1990 Single Speyside "Toffee Apples"** dist 1990, bott Apr 09 (70) n17 t18.5 f17 b17.5. "Sulphured Casks 1990" *46% Wemyss Malts Ltd. 335 bottles.*

⁓ **Wemyss 1991 Single Speyside "Ginger Treacle"** dist 1991, bott Apr 09 (63.5) n16 t17.5 f15 b15. "Sulphured Casks 1991" *46% Wemyss Malts Ltd. 335 bottles.*

Wemyss 1995 Single Speyside "Chocolate Heaven" bott Jan 07 (86) n21 t22 f21.5 b21.5. Enjoyable for its fudgy-honey character. But chocolate...? I should cocoa.... *46%. 341 bottles.*

⁓ **Wemyss 1995 Single Speyside "Spiced Apples"** refill hogshead, bott Sep 09 (91) n22.5 thick treacle toffee and honey; t24 wonderful delivery and follow through: again, it's thick honey with a powering barley sub plot; beautifully lush mouth feel; f22.5 toffees out as the vanilla enters the fray; b22 a rich, satisfying, high quality dram. *46% 386 bottles*

The Whisky Agency Speyside Single Malt 39 Year Old dist 70, bott 09 (96) n24.5 as clean and juicy oloroso as the day the cask was filled; toffee apple, but so fresh the apple is still green... t25 staggering depth to the fruitcake delivery...retains a barley crispness amid the glowing oloroso while the spices are subtle and mount a stealthy attack; remains juicy and mouth-watering right through to the middle; f22.5 finally bitters out, as surely it had to, as the oak arrives with a certain vengeance yet still retains an overcooked Melton Hunt cake character; b24 no one has told me what this is. But anyone who knows a Glenfarclas at this age in full flow will understand the type of outstanding whisky this is. In a nutshell: old sherry at its blemish-free olde worlde pre-sulphur ruining finest. *54.4%. The Whisky Agency, Germany.*

UNSPECIFIED SINGLE MALTS (General)

McClelland's 12 Years Old Sherry Finish (86) n22 t21.5 f21 b21.5. Peachy, for once, to find a sherry finish not sulphur-tainted. Attractive, simple, clean and enjoyable for its simplistic charms. Don't expect the pulse to overly quicken but simply enjoy for its intense honesty. *40%. Morrison Bowmore.*

Rossend Castle 15 Years Old bourbon barrels, cask no. 3837 & 3838 (79) n21 t20 f19 b19. Malty, but pretty dull fare. *46%. Adelphi. 495 bottles.*

Wilson & Morgan Barrel Selection House Malt cask nos. 8586-8589 (92) n24 beautifully salted and coastal peats with enough youth to remain refreshing and profound; t22 lime juice lightens the smoke; f23 returns to a more gristy sweetness and depth; b23 a high quality (presumably) Islay of distinctive, compelling clarity. *43%*

Scottish Vatted Malts
(also Pure Malts/Blended Malt Scotch)
100 Pipers Aged 8 Years Blended Malt (74) n19 t20 f17 b18. A better nose, perhaps, and some spice on arrival. But when you consider the Speysiders at their disposal, all those mouth-wateringly grassy possibilities, it is such a shame to find something as bland as this. 40%

Altore Pure Malt matured in Corsican Muscat cask **(82.5) n21 t21.5 f19 b21.** Rounded with a decent sweetness. Such a short finish, though. 40%. Société Whisky Altore.

Altore Reserve Moresca Aged 8 Years matured in Cap Corse barrel **(86) n21.5 t22.5 f21 b21.** What a shame: evidence of some sulphur in the system here, otherwise this would have been quite a beauty. 40%. Société Whisky Altore.

Ballantine's Pure Malt Aged 12 Years bott code. LKAC1538 **(88.5) n22.5** spicy mixture of honey, light smoke and added orange; **t23** stupendous mouth-feel with the fruit re-inserted alongside the honey; **f21** pretty thin with almost a grainy feel alongside the bittering oak; **b22** no sign of the peat being reintroduced to major effect, although the orange is a welcome addition. Remains a charmer. 40% Chivas ⊙⊙

Barrogill (90) n22.5 t23 f22.5 b22. Prince Charles, who allows the name to be used for this whisky, is said to enjoy this dram. Hardly surprising, as its pretty hard not to: this is wonderful fun. Curiously, I have just read the back label and noticed they use the word "robust". I have employed "lusty". Either way, I think you might get the message. 40%

Barrogill North Highland Blended Malt Mey Selections bott code PO12630 **(79) n18 t21 f20 b20.** Recovers attractively – helped by a mighty dose of concentrated maltiness - from the disappointing nose. 40%. Inver House Distillers for North Highland.

⠂⠒ **Bell's Signature Blend Limited Edition** bott 2009, bott no. 42515 **(83.5) n19 t22 f21 b21.5.** The front label makes large that this vatted malt has Blair Athol and Inchgower at the heart of it as they are "two fine malts selected for their exceptionally rich character". Kind of like saying you have invited the Kray twins to your knees up as they might liven it up a bit. Well those two distilleries were both part of the original Bell's empire, so fair dos. But to call them both fine malts is perhaps stretching the imagination somewhat. A robust vatting to say the least. And, to be honest, once you get past the nose, good back-slapping fun. 40% 90,000 bottles.

Berrys' Best Islay Vatted Malt Aged 8 Years (82) n20 t21 f20 b21. Smoky, raw, sweet, clean and massive fun! 43%. Berry Bros & Rudd.

Berry's Best 14 Years Old Islay Vatted Malt bott 09 **(88) n22.5** takes a while for the peat to show – then it takes over; **t22** soft: excellently controlled sweetness and rolling, lightly oiled phenols; **f21.5** duller, a touch of spice but otherwise vanilla-led; **b22** a sleepy, clean vatting which talks in whispers. 43%. Berry Bros & Rudd.

Berry's Own Selection Blue Hanger 4th Release bott 08 **(87) n22** just so biscuity: German caramelized meets crushed garibaldi; elsewhere the oaks threaten the nostrils with the odd splinter; **t23** a malty dance – in slippers – on arrival then a gradual crescendo of fruit, toasty in part but also balanced by light brown sugars, spice but a nagging bitterness which hints at something just out of kilter; **f21** fruity sugars but the bitter note remains; **b21** its finest notes are very fine, indeed. 45.6%. Berry Bros & Rudd.

⠂⠒ **Big Peat (96) n25** magnificent array of salt and bitty peat; heavy yet light enough for the most delicate of citrus. Hard to find a nose which screams "Islay" at you with such a lack of ambiguity: it is, frankly, perfect. **t24** the delivery is constructed around a fabulous bourbon Demerara sugar and liquorice framework; the peat enters as soon as this is in place and in varying layers of oiliness and depth. The mid ground sees the re-emergence of the more complex Ardbeg and Port Ellen factions, a bourbon style, small grains busyness; **f23.5** long, softly oiled still and then a slow dissolving liquorice and spice; vanillas pop up very late, still accompanied by soft Demerara; **b23.5** I suppose if you put Ardbeg and Port Ellen together there is a chance you might get something rather special. Not guaranteed, but achieved here with the kind of panache that leaves you spellbound. The complexity and balance are virtually off the charts, though had the Caol Ila been reduced slightly, and with it the oils, this might well have been World Whisky of the Year. 46% ncf Douglas Laing

The Big Smoke 40 Blended Islay Malt (85) n22 t21 f21 b21. Much gristier than before with extra emphasis on oak and spice. 40% Duncan Taylor & Co. ⊙⊙

The Big Smoke 60 Islay Malt (86) n20 t23; f22 b21. Big and bolshy, the peats remorselessly thump anything in their path 60%. Duncan Taylor.

⠂⠒ **Black Face 8 Years Old (78.5) n18.5 t22 f19 b19.** A huge malt explosion in the kisser on delivery, but otherwise not that pretty to behold. 46% The Vintage Malt Whisky Co. Ltd

⠂⠒ **Burns Nectar (89.5) n22** honeycomb dipped in lime juice; **t22** glorious mouth feel to delivery: a soft, oily platform from which more honey can easily be detected; chewy toffee and vanilla, too; **f23** the lightest sprinkling of spice and some ginger cake to round off beautifully; **b22.5** a delight of a dram and with all that honey around, "Nectar" is about right. *40%*

Carme 10 Years Old (79) **n21.5 t20 f18.5 b19**. On paper Ardmore and Clynelish should work well together. But vatting is not done on paper and here you have two malts cancelling each other out and some less than great wood sticking its oar in. *43%*

⋅∷· **Castle Rock Aged 12 Years Blended Malt** (87) **n22.5** grassy, under-ripe gooseberry; **t23** every bit as fresh and juicy as the nose suggests **f19.5** a creeping bitterness; **b22** stupendously refreshing: the finish apart, I just love this style of malt. *40%*

⋅∷· **Cearban** (79.5) **n18 t21.5 f20 b19**. The label shows a shark. It should be a whale: this is massive. Sweet with the malts not quite on the same wavelength. *40% Robert Graham Ltd*

Clan Campbell 8 Years Old Pure Malt (82) **n20 t22 f20 b20**. Enjoyable, extremely safe whisky that tries to offend nobody. The star quality is all on the complex delivery, then it's toffee. *40%. Chivas Brothers.*

Clan Denny (Bowmore, Bunnahabhain, Caol Ila and Laphroaig) (94) **n24 t23 f23 b24**. A very different take on Islay with heavy peats somehow having a floating quality. Unique. *40%.*

Clan Denny Speyside (87) **n22** big, big malt: exceptionally clean and soft. Oily, too; **t22** a charming sweetness to the barley helps counter the more bitter aspects of the approaching oak; delicate oils help make for an exceptionally soft delivery **f21** no shortage of vanilla as it bitters out; **b22** a Tamdhu-esque oiliness pervades here and slightly detracts from the complexity. That said, the early freshness is rather lovely. *46%. Douglas Laing.*

Compass Box Canto Cask 6 bott Autumn/Winter 07 (86.5) **n20.5 t23 f21.5 b21.5**. The busy, rich, intense and honeyed delivery compensates for the surprising dullness elsewhere. The money from the sales of this go to Cancer Research, I hear. *53.1%. nc ncf.*

Compass Box Canto Cask 15 bott Autumn/Winter 07 (75.5) **n18.5 t20 f18 b19**. Despite the smear of honey, still something in the curiously sulphurous department appears intent on spoiling things. *46%. nc ncf. Between 200 and 250 bottles.*

Compass Box Canto Cask 17 bott Autumn/Winter 07 (87.5) **n21 t23.5 f21 b22**. Gosh, this really is a very strange whisky. The oak never quite finds its comfort zone on the nose, or finish, but there is a wonderful sweet, malty resonance. *53.4%. nc ncf. Between 200 and 250 bottles.*

Compass Box Canto Cask 20 bott Autumn/Winter 07 (86) **n22.5 t22 f20.5 b21**. Softly oiled, softly spiced, big oaked. *54%. nc ncf. Between 200 and 250 bottles.*

Compass Box Canto Cask 27 bott Autumn/Winter 07 (83.5) **n20 t22 f20.5 b20**. Decent malt explosion on entry, but the natural caramels appear to cancel each other out elsewhere. *52.5%. nc ncf. Between 200 and 250 bottles.*

Compass Box Canto Cask 35 bott Autumn/Winter 07 (85) **n21 t22 f21 b21**. Cream toffee and cocoa. Some major spice, too. *54.4%. nc ncf. Between 200 and 250 bottles.*

Compass Box Canto Cask 36 bott Autumn/Winter 07 (84.5) **n20.5 t21.5 f22 b21**. Delicious malt does its best to beat off some intrusive oak. Settles at the death for some sublime cocoa. *54.3%. nc ncf. Between 200 and 250 bottles*

Compass Box Canto Cask 37 bott Autumn/Winter 07 (89) **n23.5 t22 f21.5 b22**. A much better, richer version where the oak appears to know its place; *53.6%. nc ncf.*

Compass Box Canto Cask 46 bott Autumn/Winter 07 (88) **n22 t22 f22 b22**. Again, a canto that works, thanks to the oaks staying on a short leash; *53.2%. nc ncf*

Compass Box Canto Cask 47 bott Autumn/Winter 07 (82.5) **n20 t22.5 f20 b20**. Another entirely all-over-the-place, scattergun Canto bottling with little rhythm to be found. Musty nose, sensational delivery, muddled middle and then weird finale until the cocoa shines through. Fascinating, if frustrating whisky. *53.7%. nc ncf. Between 200 and 250 bottles.*

Compass Box Canto Cask 48 bott Autumn/Winter 07 (91.5) **n21 t24 f22 b23.5**. Easily the most beautifully constructed of the Canto range so far. Nose apart, perhaps, not a shred of awkwardness as the malts ignite on the palate. *54.4%. nc ncf.*

Compass Box Canto Cask 50 bott Autumn/Winter 07 (86.5) **n22.5 t22 f20.5 b21.5**. Sweeter than average with a distinct sugary gloss. *54.4%. nc ncf. Between 200 and 250 bottles.*

Compass Box Canto Cask 123 bott Autumn/Winter 07 (83) **n19 t22 f21.5 b21.5**. Toasty with some major oak contribution. *55.1%. nc ncf. Between 200 and 250 bottles.*

Compass Box Canto Cask 124 bott Autumn/Winter 07 (85.5) **n20.5 t21.5 f22 b21.5**. Plenty of oak, as usual, but the spices sizzle early on, accentuating the more refined finale. *55.1%. nc ncf. Between 200 and 250 bottles.*

Compass Box Canto Cask 125 bott Autumn/Winter 07 (79.5) **n18.5 t22 f19 b20**. And so endeth the first batch of Cantos. Canto, I presume, as in a poem. Too often, though, there were faltering stanzas here, and sometimes neither rhyme nor reason can be found. One or two work stunningly, the majority are good but refusing to show the brilliance normally associated with the Compass Box name. Perhaps this may have something to do with the brave use of

Dailuaine, apparently, as one of only three malts to make up these vattings. My own personal feeling is that, especially in such restricted company, you approach malt from this distillery in very much the way you might an unexploded bomb, and a ticking one at that: you prod at your peril. That said, if you are into big-oaked malt then this is the brand for you. *54.9%. nc ncf.*

Compass Box Eleuthera Marriage Married for nine months in an American oak Hogshead **(86) n22 t22 f20 b22.** I'm not sure if it's the name that gets me on edge here, but as big and robust as it is I still can't help feeling that the oak has bitten too deep. Any chance of a Compass Box Divorce...? *49.2%. Compass Box for La Maison du Whisky.*

Compass Box Flaming Hart second batch, bottling no. FH16MMVII **(95.5) n23.5 t24.5 f23 b24.5.** The Canto range was, I admit, a huge over-oaked disappointment. This, though, fully underlines Compass Box's ability to come up with something approaching genius. This is a whisky that will be remembered by anyone who drinks it for the rest of their lives as just about the perfect study of full-bodied balance and sophistication. And that is not cheap hyperbole. *48.9%. nc ncf. 4,302 bottles.*

Compass Box Juveniles 20th Anniversary Bottling bott 2007 **(85) n22 t21 f21 b21.** A Juveniles for Grown Ups: big, lordly with a hollering oaky-fruit theme. For all the fun, nothing like as delicate as the previous, more genteel bottling. As an after-dinner dram designed to blow away the last traces of the crepes suzettes, perfect! *53.9%. nc ncf. 246 bottles.*

⁖ **Compass Box Lady Luck** American white oak hogshead, bott Sep 09 **(91) n22** earthy; tree bark; dank woods; an irrigated Taiwanese tomato field; **t24** much lighter than the nose... and sweeter...and spicier....wow!!... **f23** pure chocolate mousse before some bitterness descends; **b22** just a shade too sweet for mega greatness like The Spice Tree, but quite an endearing box of tricks. *46% Compass Box Whisky Co*

Compass Box Morpheus bott Autumn/Winter 07 **(92.5) n23 t22 f23.5 b24.** Subtlety and balance the key here: just shows what magic can be performed with understatement. *46%*

Compass Box Peat Monster Reserve (92) n23 comfortable, thickish smoke and a dusting of peppers: complex and well balanced; **t23.5** silky soft malty oils cleverly disguise the big punchy peat which is to follow; lovely touch of golden syrup here and there, but mainly towards the delivery; **f22.5** smoky sweetened mocha; **b23** at times a bit of a Sweet Monster... beautiful stuff! *48.9%*

⁖ **Compass Box The Spice Tree** first-fill and refill American oak. Secondary maturation: heavily toasted new French oak **(95.5) n24.5** quite paradoxical. First sniff and you think: "whoa! That's a big-un." Then you nose again, slowly and carefully you realise that whilst the nose does seem superficially big, it is actually made up of dozens of tiny aromas ganging together. The main theme is delicate tangerine and vanilla – almost like tangerine yogurt – but there are weightier spices to note, all of them fragments, especially the watery allspice and ginger....sublime...; **t24.5** and now the palate continues with exactly the same theme: a million little flavour explosions, all timed to go off one after the other, but all on a sweet muscovado sugar bed created by the superb base malt of Clynelish; **f23** thins rapidly into a more basic vanilla, though there is still a spice pulse and glow; just a little bitter at the death; **b23.5** having initially been chopped down by the SWA, who were indignant that extra staves had been inserted into the casks, The Spice Tree is not only back but in full bloom. Indeed, the blossom on this, created by the use of fresh oak barrel heads, is more intoxicating than its predecessor – mainly because there is a more even and less dramatic personality to this. Not just a great malt, but a serious contender for Jim Murray Whisky Bible 2011 World Whisky of the Year. *46% Compass Box Whisky Co.*

Compass Box The Spice Tree Inaugural Batch (93) n23 t23 f23 b24. The map for flavour distribution had to be drawn for the first time here: an entirely different whisky in shape and flavour emphasis. And it is a map that takes a long time to draw... *46%. 4150 bottles.*

Co-operative Group (CWS) Blended Malt Aged 8 Years (86.5) n22 t22 f21 b21.5. Much, much better! Still a little on the sticky and sweet side, but there is some real body and pace to the changes on the palate. Quite rich, complex and charming. *40%*

⁖ **Douglas Laing's Double Barrel Ardbeg & Glenrothes Aged 10 Years** product no. MSW2685 **(92) n22** a salty breeze apart, the curiously inconspicuous Ardbeg allows the Speysider to dominate; **t24** but a different story on delivery where the malts are sharp, jagged and juicy while the smoke and oak, and even some rich dates from somewhere, hover in the background; with a metallic sheen and the nod spurt of honey here and there, this is different...and works a treat; **f23** a deft smoke edge to the vanilla; **b23** not what I was expecting. But a lovely experience nonetheless. *46% Douglas Laing & Co Ltd*

⁖ **Douglas Laing's Double Barrel Ardbeg & Glenrothes Aged 10 Years** product no. DBS0003 **(88.5) n23** great nose: delicate, playful smoke lightened by lime Rowntree's Fruit Gums; **t22** firm barley with virtually no give but a slow unveiling of juicy barley; the smoke is also firm but flighty; **f21.5** an oaky bitterness; **b22** an uncompromising but fun way to bring up New Whisky no. 750 for Bible 2011.... *46% Douglas Laing*

∵ **Douglas Laing's Double Barrel Braeval & Caol Ila Aged 10 Years (78) n18 t21 f20 b19.** The Mike and Bernie Winters of double barrelled whisky. *46% Douglas Laing & Co Ltd*

∵ **Douglas Laing's Double Barrel Caol Ila & Braeval Aged 10 Years (84.5) n21 t22 f20.5 b21.** It is probably impossible to find a malt which is more friendly and inoffensive. Or two malts which have done such a first class job of cancelling each other's personalities out. *46%*

∵ **Douglas Laing's Double Barrel Glenrothes & Ardbeg Aged 10 Years 4th Release (89.5) n21.5** surprisingly angular and sharp; **t23** and on delivery, too, though a soft caress of lightly oiled smoke helps. A few waves of honey hit the middle with some citrus thinning things down; **f22.5** lightly smoked custard; **b22.5** despite the average nose the charmingly effete palate is another matter entirely. *46% Douglas Laing.*

∵ **Douglas Laing's Double Barrel Highland Park & Bowmore (95) n23** pounding spices and dry smoke; **t24.5** a passionate embrace of honeyed peat followed by waves of juicy barley almost gives you the vapours; **f24** long, lip-smacking with the improbable degree of honey lasting the distance; the peat gives way to a stunning array of spices; **b23.5** the vital spark of fury to this one keeps the palate ignited. A standing ovation for such a magnificent performance on the palate. *46% Douglas Laing & Co Ltd*

∵ **Douglas Laing's Double Barrel Macallan & Laphroiag 5th Release (93) n23.5** rousing barley balances the light, flakey smoke; **t24** the ultra delicate theme continues, with a lovely jam Swiss Roll sweetness mixing it with the gristy peat; juicy with a slow building of oil; **f22.5** long with a sprinkling of grated chocolate in the vanilla and smoke; **b23** as if born to be together. *46%*

∵ **Douglas Laing's Double Barrel Macallan & Laphroaig Aged 9 Years (83.5) n21 t22 f20 b20.5.** Curiously muted. Sweet with the natural caramels outweighing the smoke. *46%*

Duncan Taylor Regional Malt Collection Islay 10 Years Old (81) n21 t22 f19 b19. Soft citrus cleanses the palate, while gentle peats muddies it up again. *40%.*

The Famous Grouse 10 Years Old Malt (77) n19 t20 f19 b19. The nose and finish headed south in the last winter and landed in the sulphur marshes of Jerez. *40%. Edrington Group.*

The Famous Grouse 15 Years Old Malt (86) n21 t22 f21.5 b21.5. Salty and smoky with a real sharp twang. *43%. Edrington Group.*

The Famous Grouse 15 Years Old Malt (86) n19 t24 f22 b21. There had been a hint of the "s" word on the nose, but it got away with it. Now it has crossed that fine – and fatal – line where the petulance of the sulphur has thrown all else slightly out of kilter. All, that is, apart from the delivery which is a pure symphony of fruit and spice deserving a far better introduction and final movement. Some moving, beautiful moments. Flawed genius or what...? *40%*

The Famous Grouse 18 Years Old Malt (82) n19 t21.5 f21 b20.5. Some highly attractive honey outweighs the odd uncomfortable moment. *43%. Edrington Group.*

The Famous Grouse Malt 21 Years Old (91) n22 candy jar spices, green apple and crisp barley. **t24** spot on oak offers a platform for the myriad rich malty notes and now, in the latest bottlings, enlivened further with an injection of exploding spice... wow! **f22** flattens slightly but muscovado sugar keeps it light and sprightly; **b23** a very dangerous dram: the sort where the third or fourth would slip down without noticing. Wonderful scotch! *43%. Edrington Group*

The Famous Grouse 30 Years Old Malt (94) n23.5 brain-implodingly busy and complex: labyrinthine depth within a kind of Highland Park frame with extra emphasis on grape and salt; **t24** yesssss!!!! Just so magnificent with the theme being all about honeycomb...but on so many different levels of intensity and toastiness; so juicy, too...; **f23** now the spices dive in as the barley resurfaces again; long, layered with spot on bitter-sweet balance; **b23.5** whisky of this sky-high quality is exactly what vatted malt should be all about. Outrageously good. *43%.*

∵ **Glenalmond 2001 Vintage (82.5) n22 t21.5 f19 b20.** Glenkumquat, more like: the most citrusy malt I have tasted in a very long time. *40% The Vintage Malt Whisky Co. Ltd*

∵ **Glenalmond "Everyday" (89.5) n21.5** mainly malt; **t23.5** soft delivery which increases in barley intensity at a remarkably even rate; excellent gristy sugar-vanilla balance; **f22** remains on its malty crusade to the death; **b22.5** they are not joking; this really is an everyday whisky. Glorious malt which is so dangerously easy to drink. *40%*

∵ **Glen Brynth Aged 12 Years Blended Malt (87) n22.5 t23 f19.5 b22.** Deja vu....! Thought I was going mad: identical to the Castle Rock I tasted this morning, right down to the (very) bitter end ..!!! *40% Quality Spirits International*

Glendower 8 Years Old (84) n21.5 t21 f20.5 b21 Nutty and spicy. *43%. J*

Glen Turner Pure Malt Aged 8 Years L525956A **(84) n20 t22 f22 b20.** A lush and lively vatting annoyingly over dependent on thick toffee but simply brimming with fabulously mouth-watering barley and over-ripe blood oranges. To those who bottle this, I say: let me into your lab. I can help you bring out something sublime!! *40%.*

Glen Orrin Six Year Old (88) n22 a bit sweaty but the oranges delight. Some delicate background smoke is a surprising complement; t23 big, chewy and rugged with outstanding soft-oiled lushness which helps to dissipate the youthfulness; f21 delicate spice and arousing coffee-cocoa: a bigger age signature than you might expect b22 a vatting that has improved in the short time it has been around, now displaying some lovely orangey notes on the nose and a genuinely lushness to the body and spice on the finish. You can almost forgive the caramel, this being such a well balanced, full-bodied ride. A quality show for the price. *40%*

Hedges and Butler Special Pure Malt (83) n20 t21 f22 b21. Just so laid back: nosed and tasted blind I'd swear this was a blend (you know, a real blend with grains and stuff) because of the biting lightness and youth. Just love the citrus theme and, err...graininess....!! *40%.*

Imperial Tribute (83) n19.5 t21.5 f21 b21. No, it's not a whisky paying homage to a silent Speysider. It's the first offerings of a new whisky company. It has been praised to the high heavens by others. And I'd like to give it a great mark for as truly fine a fellow as Mike Collings, but I can't. Without doubt a cask that shouldn't be here has snuck in. The result is a good whisky, but one which never quite finds its pitch or level, strains at the high notes and has croaks slightly at the lower. That said, there is enough fabulously intense barley during a purple period towards the very middle of the experience to make for some pleasing moments. And you can just feel the wonderful layering of fruit, barley and oak in clever measures just trying to impress with its sophistication. But that bothersomely bitter, dry residue (the signs of which can be spotted on both nose and delivery) does in some of the good work. I am sure – and sincerely hope – the next bottling will be cleaned up and the true Imperial Tribute can be nosed and tasted. Because this is what should be a very fine malt...but just isn't. *46%. Spencer Collings.*

Islay Trilogy 1969 (Bruichladdich 1966, Bunnahabhain 1968, Bowmore 1969) Bourbon/ Sherry (91) n23 t23 f22 b23. Decided to mark the 700th tasting for the 2007 edition with this highly unusual vatting. And no bad choice. The smoke is as elusive as the Paps of Jura on a dark November morning, but the silky fruits and salty tang tells a story as good as anything you'll hear by a peat fire. Take your time...the whiskies have. *40.3%. Murray McDavid.*

J & B Exception Aged 12 Years (80) n20 t23 f18 b19. Very pleasant in so many ways. A charming sweetness develops quickly, with excellent soft honeycomb. But the nose and finish are just so...so....dull...!! For the last 30 years J&B has meant, to me, (and probably within that old company) exceptionally clean, fresh Speysiders offering a crisp, mouth-watering treat. I feel this is off target. *40%. Diageo/ Justerini & Brooks.*

J & B Nox (89) n23 classy Speyside thrust, youthful and crisp with a wonderful strand of honey. Gentle oak balances pleasingly; t23 the nose in liquid form: exactly the same characteristics with some extra, gently peppered toast towards the middle; f21 dries just a little too much as the barley tires; b22 a teasing, pleasing little number that is unmistakably from the J&B stable. *40%. Diageo.*

John Black 8 Years Old Honey (88) n21 vanilla to the fore; t22.5 the promised honey arrives on delivery couched by fresh barley; f22.5 light, delicate back to vanilla; b22 a charming vatting. *40%. Tullibardine Distillery.*

John Black 10 Years Old Peaty (91) n23 salty and peaty; t23 soft and peaty; f22 delicate and peaty; b23 classy and er...peaty. *40%. Tullibardine Distillery.*

John McDougall's Selection Islay Malt 1993 cask no. 103 (94.5) n23.5 peek-a-boo peat can barely make itself heard above the honeyed barley and lightly salted oak. 'Delicate' barely covers it... t24.5 seductive beyond belief: the soft rounding off of the honey with a mint-chocolate peatiness, especially as it fills the middle ground, really is one for the collector's corner: unique and simply breathtaking, and with a Bowmore-ish Fisherman's Friend bite hitting for a couple of nano seconds, pretty intriguing, too; f22.5 drier with soft peat embers giving way to the milk coffee and vanilla; b24 complex, superbly weighted and balanced malt which just keeps you wondering what will happen next. *54.7%. House of Macduff.*

Johnnie Walker Green Label 15 Years Old (95) n24 kind of reminds me of a true, traditional Cornish Pasty: it is as though the segments have been compartmentalised, with the oak acting as the edible pastry keeping them apart. Sniff and there is a degree of fruit; nose again and there is the Speyside/Clynelish style of intense, slightly sweet maltiness. Sniff a third time, at last you can detect just a hint of smoke. Wonderful... t23.5 no compartmentalisation here as the delivery brings all those varying characters together for one magnificently complex maltfest. Weightier than previous Green Label events with the smoke having a bigger say. But the oak really bobs and weaves as the palate is first under a tidal wave of juicy malt and then the fruit and smoke – and no little spice – take hold...; f23.5 soft smoke and grumbling spice latch on to the fruit-stained oak; plenty of cocoa just to top things off; b24 god, I love this stuff...this is exactly how a vatted malt should be and one of the best samples I've come across since its launch. *43%. Diageo.*

Jon, Mark and Robbo's The Rich Spicy One (89) n22 t23 f22 b22. So much better without the dodgy casks: a real late night dram of distinction though the spices perhaps a little on the subtle side... 40%. *Edrington*

Jon, Mark and Robbo's The Smoky Peaty One (92) n23 t22 f23 b24. Genuinely high-class whisky where the peat is full-on yet allows impressive complexity and malt development. A malt for those who appreciate the better, more elegant things in life. 40%. *Edrington*

Matisse 12 Year Old Blended Malt (93) n23.5 a wonderful variation of fruit but with the accent on citrus-orangey notes. As astonishing as it is beautiful... t23 soft, delicate, melt-in-the-mouth delivery with those gentle fruits at the fore and the barley tagging on right behind; f22.5 a quieter finale placing the accent on milky custard; b23 succulent, clean-as-a-whistle mixture of malts with zero bitterness and not even a whisper of an off note: easily the best form I have ever seen this brand in. Superb. 40%. *Matisse Spirits Co. Ltd.*

Matisse Aged 12 Years (79) n17 t21 f20 b21. Not sure if some finishing or re-casking has been going on here to liven it up. Has some genuine buzz on the palate, but intriguing weirdness, too. Don't bother nosing this one. 40%. *The Matisse Spirits Co.*

⌁ **Milroy's of Soho Finest Blended Malt (76)** n18 t19 f20 b19. Full flavoured, nutty, malty but hardly textbook. 40% *Milroy's of Soho*

"No Age Declared" The Unique Pure Malt Very Limited Edition 16-49 Years (85) n22.5 t19.5 f22 b21. Very drinkable. But this is odd stuff: as the ages are as they are, and as it tastes as it does, I can surmise only that the casks were added together as a matter of necessity rather than any great blending thought or planning. Certainly the malt never finds a rhythm but maybe it's the eclectic style on the finish that finally wins through. 45%. *Samaroli*.

Norse Cask Selection Vatted Islay 1992 Aged 16 Years hogshead cask no. QWVIM3, dist 92, bott 09 **(95)** n24 a unique smorgasbord of dry, peat-reeky smoke and much oilier phenols. The interplay between sweet and dry is as startling and bamboozling is it is beautiful; t24 melts-in-the-mouth – and then explodes into something like phenolic fire: talk about being lulled into a false sense of security...the sugars – mainly muscovado style – go into overdrive while those oils ensure that the palate is fully coated and the tongue keeps smacking around the mouth in enquiry; f23 long, layered, not a single outbreak of anything even remotely bitter from the oak and still the phenols dance to varying tunes; b24 the recipe of 60/35/5 Ardbeg/Laphroaig/Bowmore new make matured in one cask is a surprise: the oiliness here suggests a squirt of Caol Ila somewhere. This hybrid is certainly different, showing that the DNA of Ardbeg is unrecognisable when mixed, like The Fly, with others. Drinkable...? Oh, yes...!! Because this, without a single negative note to its name, is easily one of the whiskies of the year and a collector's and/or Islayphile's absolute must have. 56.7%.

Norse Cask Selection Vatted Islay 1991 Aged 12 Years (89) n24 t23 f21 b21. Fabulous, but not much going in the way of complexity. But if you're a peat freak, I don't think you either notice...or much care...!! 59.5%. *Quality World, Denmark.*

Norse Cask Selection Vatted Islay 1992 Aged 15 Years hogshead ref no. QWVIM4, dist 92, bott 07 **(92)** n24 t23.5 f22 b22.5. Now that's more like it! Ardbeg 60%, Laphroaig 35%, Bowmore 5%...though that 5% feels two or three times bigger and on the finish especially. Big and serious fun. 57%. nc ncf.

Norse Cask Selection Vatted Islay 1988 Aged 19 Years hogshead ref no. QWVIM2, dist 88, bott 07 **(84.5)** n21.5 t21 f22 b21. Bowmore 55%, Laphroaig 40%, Caol Ila 5%. With full cough sweet characteristics on show, it seems more than just 555 Bowmore...!! 573%. nc ncf.

The Pot Still Scotch Vatted Malt Over 8 Years Old (90) n22 excellent oak sub plot to the ballsy barley; t24 goes down with all the seductive powers of long fingernails down a chest: the wonderful honey and barley richness is stunning and so beautifully weighted; f21 a lazier finale, allowing the chalky oaky notes to make folly of those tender years; b22 such sophistication: the Charlotte Rampling of Scotch. 43.5%. ncf. *Celtic Whisky Compagnie, France.*

Prime Blue Pure Malt (83) n21 t21 f21 b20. Steady, with a real chewy toffee middle. Friendly stuff. 40%

Prime Blue 12 Years Old Pure Malt (78) n20 t20 f19 b19. A touch of fruit but tart. 40%

Prime Blue 17 Years Old Pure Malt (88) n23 clever weight and a touch of something fruity and exotic, too; t21 thick malt concentrate; f22 takes a deliciously latte-style route and would be even better but for the toffee; excellent spicing; b22 lovely, lively vatting: something to get your teeth into! 40%

Prime Blue 21 Years Old Pure Malt (77) n21 t20 f18 b18. After the teasing, bourbony nose the remainder disappoints with a caramel-rich flatness. The reprise of a style of whisky I thought had vanished four or five years ago 40%

Sainsbury's Malt Whisky Finished in Sherry Casks (70) n18 t19 f16 b17. Never the greatest of the Sainsbury range, it's somehow managed to get worse. Actually, not too difficult when it comes to finishing in sherry, and the odd sulphur butt or three has done its worst here. 40% Sainsbury's, UK.

Scottish Collie (86.5) n22 t23 f20.5 b21. A really young pup of a vatting. Full of life and fun but muzzled by toffee at the death. 40%. Quality Spirits International.

Scottish Collie 5 Years Old (90.5) n22.5 teasing interplay between grassy young malts and something just a little more profound and vaguely phenolic; t23 more of the same on delivery; an engaging sharpness keeps the tastebuds puckered; f22 long, with the accent on that wonderfully clean ,sweet and sharp barley; even the soft toffee can't get much of a toe-hold; b23 fabulous mixing here showing just what malt whisky can do at this brilliant and under-rated age. Lively and complex with the malts wonderfully herded and penned. Without colouring and at 50% abv I bet this would have been given a right wolf-whistle. Perfect for one man and his grog. 40%. Quality Spirits International.

Scottish Collie 8 Years Old (85.5) n22 t21.5 f21 b21. A good boy. But just wants to sleep rather than play. 40%. Quality Spirits International.

Scottish Collie 12 Years Old (82) n20 t22 f20 b20. For a malt that's aged 84 in Collie years, it understandably smells a bit funny and refuses to do many tricks. If you want some fun you'll need a younger version. 40%. Quality Spirits International.

Scottish Leader Imperial Blended Malt (77) n20 t20 f18 b19. Now don't be confused here: this isn't Imperial malt from Speyside. And although it says Blended, it is 100% malt. What is clear, though, is that this is pretty average stuff. 40%. Burn Stewart.

Scottish Leader Aged 14 Years (80) n21 t21 f19 b19. A cleaner, less peaty version than the no-age statement vatting, but still fails to entirely ignite the tastebuds 40%. Burn Stewart.

Sheep Dip (84) n19 t22 f22 b21. Young and sprightly like a new-born lamb, this enjoys a fresh, mouthwatering grassy style wth a touch of spice. Maligned by some, but to me a clever, accomplished vatting of alluring complexity. 40%

·:· **Sheep Dip 'Old Hebridean' 1990** (94) n23 every aspect has the buoyancy of an anchor, the subtlety of Hebridean winter winds. Thick peat offering both smoke and a kippery saltiness is embraced by honey; t24 big, weighty delivery with an immediate spice and honey delivery; a butterscotch barley theme appears and vanishes like a small fishing craft in mountainous waves; f23.5 that honey keeps the pace and length, while a beautiful bourbon red liquorice beefs up the vanilla; b23.5 you honey!! Now, that's what I call a whisky....!! 40% The Spencerfield Spirit Co

·:· **The Six Isles Pomerol Finish Limited Edition** French oak Pomerol wine cask no. 90631-90638, dist 2003, bott 2010 (85.5) n19 t23 f21.5 b22. What makes the standard Six Isles work as a vatted malt is its freshness and complexity. With these attributes, plus the distinctive distilleries used, we consistently have over the world's great and truly entertaining whiskies. With this version we have just a decent malt. The wine finish has levelled the mountains and valleys and restricted the finish dramatically, while the nose doesn't work at all. Perfectly drinkable and the delivery is extremely enjoyable. But as a Six Isles, delighted it's a Limited Edition. 46% Ian Macleod. 3266 bottles.

Tambowie (84.5) n21.5 t21.5 f20.5 b21. A decent improvement on the nondescript bottling of yore. I have re-included this to both celebrate its newly acquired lightly fruited attractiveness....and to celebrate the 125th anniversary of the long departed Tambowie Distillery whose whisky, I am sure, tasted nothing like this. 40% The Vintage Malt Whisky Co. Ltd. ⊙⊙

·:· **Treasurer 1874 Reserve Cask** (90.5) n23 huge oak: pungent and salty with a soup on of peat; lightly molassed with a more telling imprint of maple syrup; t23 dense delivery: the wood is among the leaders, as is a pithy orange. But giant waves of malt break over the taste buds to claim control; the extra complexity is completed with busy spice; f22.5 toffee fudge and raisin; b22 some judicious adding has been carried out here in the Robert Graham shop. Amazing for a living cask that I detect no major sulphur faultlines. Excellent! 51% Robert Graham Ltd. Live casks available in all Robert Graham shops.

Vintner's Choice Highland 10 Years Old (88) n22 busy, herbal, with good oak backbone t22.5 salivating delivery with a big malty accent; a gentle spice tickle; f21.5 toffees out as the vanilla heads in; b22 light but with an attractive degree of complexity. 40%.

Vintner's Choice Island 10 Years Old (95) n24 serious coastal, seaweedy, strata to the smoke, enlivened further by a touch of honey and hickory; t24 sweet, molassed, softly oiled start; the peat appears to weave in and out with varying intensity and weight; f23 just so soft, with the sweetness retaining structure and direction; long, with the smoke pulsing and declaring a light, spicy interest; b24 not hard to guess which island... the complexity and layering of the peats is quite exemplary. An absolute gem of a vatted malt. 40%.

Vintner's Choice Lowland 10 Years Old (92.5) n22.5 green, clean and full of lemony promise; t24 just beautiful: one of the best deliveries of any vatted malt with the harmonization between the lemon sherbet freshness and the subtle oaks touching perfection; **f23** somehow retains its clarity and classy, grassy mouthwatering edge; loses a point for the toffee; **b23** as vatted malts go, this is a joy. As Lowland vatted malts go, it is about as good as I've ever known it. Just so refreshing and complex. It is as if someone has gone out to create a Rosebank. 40%. *Quality Spirits International.*

Vintner's Choice Speyside 10 Years Old (84) n21.5 t22 f20 b20.5. Pleasant. But considering the quality of the Speysiders Grants have to play with, the dullness is a bit hard to fathom. 40%. *Quality Spirits International.*

Waitrose Pure Highland Malt (86.5) n22 t22 f20.5 b22. Blood orange by the cartload: amazingly tangy and fresh; bitters out at the finish. This is one highly improved malt and great to see a supermarket bottling showing some serious attitude....as well as taste!! Fun, refreshing and enjoyable. 40%

⠿ **Wemyss Malts "Peat Chimney" 5 Years Old (82.5) n20.5 t21 f20 b21.** Rougher than the tongue of a smoking cat. 40% *Wemyss Malts Ltd*

⠿ **Wemyss Malts "Peat Chimney" 8 Years Old (85) n21.5 t21.5 f21 b21.** Delightful chocolate amid the attractively course peat. 40% *Wemyss Malts Ltd*

⠿ **Wemyss "Smooth Gentleman" 5 Years Old (80) n20 t21 f19 b20.** A bit of a schoolkid with an affectation. 40% *Wemyss Malts Ltd*

⠿ **Wemyss Malts "Smooth Gentleman" 8 Years Old (89) n21** sweet but a little bland; **t23.5** much better arrival with a gorgeous barley-toffee impact assisted, naturally, by a spoonful of acacia honey; **f22** returns to a more middle-of-the-road character, but still deliciously soft and rich...and a little juicy; **b22.5** more of a Kentuckian George Clooney than a Bristolian Cary Grant. 40% *Wemyss Malts Ltd*

⠿ **Wemyss Malts "Spice King" 5 Years Old (76) n18.5 t20 f18.5 b19.** A little on the mucky, tangy side. 40% *Wemyss Malts Ltd*

⠿ **Wemyss Malts "Spice King" 8 Years Old (87) n22** plenty of butterscotch and fudge; **t22** chewy toffee with a malty, honeyed strata; **f21.5** more toffee. Just when you start wondering where the spice is, it appears very late on through the trademen's entrance, though does the best it can not to disturb those at home; **b21.5** hard to believe this lush malt is in any way related to the 5-y-o...!! 40% *Wemyss Malts Ltd*

Wemyss Vintage Malt The Peat Chimney Hand Crafted Blended Malt Whisky (80) n19 t22 f20 b19. The balance is askew here, especially on the bone-dry wallpapery finish. Does have some excellent spicy/coffee moments, though. 43%. *Wemyss Vintage Malts Ltd.*

Wemyss Vintage Malt The Smooth Gentleman Hand Crafted Blended Malt Whisky (83) n19 t22 f21 b21. Not sure about the nose: curiously fishy (very gently smoked). But the malts tuck into the tastebuds with aplomb showing some sticky barley sugar along the way. 43%.

Wemyss Vintage Malt The Spice King Hand Crafted Blended Malt Whisky (84) n22 t22 f20 b20. Funnily enough, I've not a great fan of the word "smooth" when it comes to whisky. But the introduction of oily Caol Ila-style peat here makes it a more of a smooth gentleman than the "Smooth Gentleman." Excellent spices very late on. 43%. *Wemyss Vintage Malts.*

Wholly Smoke Aged 10 Years (86.5) n22.5 t22.5 f20 b21.5. A big, peaty, sweat, rumbustuous number with absolutely no nod towards sophistication or balance and the finish virtually disintegrates. The smoke is slapped on and the whole appears seemingly younger than its 10 years. Massive fun, all the same. *Macdonald & Muir Ltd. for Oddbins.*

Wild Scotsman Scotch Malt Whisky (Black Label) batch no. CBV001 **(91) n23.5** smoke hangs moodily in the glass; the atmosphere is heavy and humid with the oak in no mood to give way to the peat and the sugars in sticky, molassed form; even a separate layer of barley is thick and clearly means business...; **t23.5** sublime delivery with those molassed, sugary barley tones seeing to the form. But then the smoke comes crashing through followed shortly by some major oak. Elegant, soft, yet this is not a place for pussycats...; **f21** bitters out slightly as the oaks get a bit too cocky; **b23** the type of dram you drink from a dirty glass. Formidable and entertaining. 47%. *House of Macduff.*

Wild Scotsman Aged 15 Years Vatted Malt (95) n23 t24 f24 b24. If anyone wants an object lesson as to why you don't screw your whisky with caramel, here it is. Jeff Topping can feel a justifiable sense of pride in his new whisky: for its age, it is an unreconstituted masterpiece... 46% (92 proof). nc ncf. USA.

Mystery Malts

Chieftain's Limited Edition Aged 40 Years hogshead **(78) n22 t22 f16 b18.** Oak-ravaged and predictably bitter on the death (those of you who enjoy Continental bitters might go for this..!). But the lead up does offer a short, though sublime and intense honey kick. The finish, though... 48.5%. *Ian Macleod.*

Scottish Grain

I t's a bit weird, really. Many whisky lovers stay clear of blended Scotch, preferring instead single malts. The reason, I am often told, is that the grain included in a blend makes it rough and ready. Yet I wish I had a twenty pound note for each time I have been told in recent years how much someone enjoys a single grain. The ones that the connoisseurs die for are the older versions, usually special independent bottlings displaying great age and more often than not brandishing a lavish Canadian or bourbon style.

Like single malts, grain distilleries produce whisky bearing their own style and signature. And, also, some display characteristics and a richness that can surprise and delight. Most of the grains available in (usually specialist) whisky outlets are pretty elderly. Being made from maize and wheat helps give them either that Canadian or, depending on the freshness of the cask, an unmistakable bourbony style. So older grains display far greater body than is commonly anticipated.

Light whiskies, including some Speysiders, tend to adopt this north American stance when the spirit has absorbed so much oak that the balance has been tipped. So overtly Kentuckian can they be, I once playfully introduced an old single grain Scotch whisky into a bourbon tasting I was conducting and nobody spotted that it was the cuckoo in the nest ... until I revealed all at the end of the evening. And even had to display the bottle to satisfy the disbelievers.

Younger grains may give a hint of oncoming bourbon-ness. But, rather, they tend to celebrate either a softness in taste or, in the case of North British, a certain rigidity. Where many malts have a tendency to pulverise the taste-buds and announce their intent and character at the top of their voice, younger grains are content to stroke and whisper.

Scotch whisky companies have so far had a relaxed attitude to marketing their grains. William Grant had made some inroads with Black Barrel, though with nothing like the enthusiasm they unleash upon us with their blends and malts. And Diageo are apparently content to see their Cameron Brig sell no further than its traditional hunting grounds, just north of Edinburgh, where the locals tend to prefer single grain to any other whisky. And the latest news from that most enormous of distilleries...it is getting bigger. Not only are Diageo planning to up their malt content by building a new Speyside distillery, but Cameronbridge, never a retiring place since the days of the Haigs in the 1820s is set for even grander expansion. Having, with the now death-sentenced Port Dundas, absorbed the closure of a number of grain distilleries over the last 30 years something had to be done to give it a fighting chance of taking on the expansion into China, Russia and now, most probably, India. It is strange that not more is being done. Cooley in Ireland have in the last year or so forged a healthy following with their introduction of grain whiskies at various ages. They have shown that the interest is there and some fresh thinking and boldness in a marketing department can create niche and often profitable markets. Edrington have entered the market with a vatted grain called Snow Grouse, designed to be consumed chilled and obviously a tilt at the vodka market. The first bottling I received, though, was disappointingly poor and I hope future vattings will be more carefully attended to. All round, then, the news for Scottish grain lovers has not been good of late with the demolition of mighty Dumbarton and now, controversially, the pending closure of Port Dundas itself. With the expansion of Cameronbridge and a 50% stake in North British, Diageo obviously believe they have all the grain capacity they require.

The tastings notes here for grains cover only a few pages, disappointingly, due to their scarcity. However, it is a whisky style growing in stature, helped along the way not just by Cooley but also by Compass Box's recent launching of a vatted grain. And we can even see an organic grain on the market, distilled at the unfashionable Loch Lomond Distillery. Why, though, it has to be asked does it take the relatively little guys to lead the way? Perhaps the answer is in the growing markets in the east: the big distillers are very likely holding on to their stocks to facilitate their expansion there.

At last the message is getting through that the reaction to oak of this relatively lightweight spirit - and please don't for one moment regard it as neutral, for it is most certainly anything but - can throw up some fascinating and sometimes delicious possibilities. Blenders have known that for a long time. Now public interest is growing. And people are willing to admit that they can enjoy an ancient Cambus, Caledonian or Dumbarton in very much the way they might celebrate a single malt. Even if it does go against the grain...

Single Grain Scotch
CALEDONIAN

Clan Denny Caledonian Aged 44 Years dist Jan 65, bott Jul 09 **(94) n23** soft natural caramels caress the nose: toffee wafer with milk chocolate; **t23.5** velvety delivery of corn oil and custard pie; there is almost a bizarre hint of rye from the slightly harder fruity sub plot. Intriguing, if not impossible...; **f24** back to custard cream biscuits dunked in black coffee – and proceeds to melt in the mouth accordingly; **b23.5** I feared that after a gap ofour years since last seeing a Clan Denny Caledonian, time might have taken a fatal toll. Not a bit of it! Every bit as gentle as those great drams of yesteryear, even though the oak has, as to be expected, gone up an extra notch. Track a bottle down and cherish it!! 45.8%. Douglas Laing.

Scotch Malt Whisky Society Cask 93.1 Aged 29 Years refill barrel, dist May 78 **(93.5) n23 t24 f23 b23.5.** Another example of why old grains like these are among the finest whiskies found, not just in Scotland but the world. 60.1%

CAMERONBRIDGE

Celtic Heartlands Cameronbridge 1974 Aged 33 Years (88) n23 t22 f21 b22. I don't have the benefit of a label or any literature with this: I am nosing as I find....which is one effing weird single grain. Let's just say that if it was an antique, I would point out that there had been some restoration, mainly in the wood department, with oak where there was once walnut. And oak that has carried at various times fruit and peat. Not what you normally come to expect from a grain. It is 21 minutes past midnight and this was going to be the third to last whisky oa long and tiring day. It will instead be the last: my brain, after this assault, can take no more... 48.3%

⟨⠿⟩ **Duncan Taylor Collection Cameronbridge 1978** cask no. 391150 **(92) n23** corn bread with a touch of stem ginger cake and vanilla cream; **t23.5** succulent Demerara-infused oils effortlessly carry the corn and spices; **f22.5** long with very acceptable drying oak input; **b23** clearly from a first class cask. Pretty good grain, too. 54.6% Duncan Taylor & Co Ltd

Duncan Taylor Collection Cameronbridge 1979 cask no. 46 **(85) n23 t21 f20 b21.** The nose is a celebration of seriously delicate bourbon (not Canadian); a sliver of lime off the soft corn and leathery honeycomb; the delivery shows its age. 50.3%

Duncan Taylor Collection Cameronbridge 1979 cask no. 3582 **(85) n20 t23 f21 b21.** Almost pure Canadian in style but with the oak perhaps making too many inroads. There is a superb richness to the grain which dovetails wonderfully with the sweetened spices. 52.4%

Duncan Taylor Collection Cameronbridge 1979 cask no. 3585 **(86) n22.5 t22 f20.5 b21.** Oak pounds into the grain, at first making very little difference on the early sugars but then taking control. 51.9%

Duncan Taylor Collection Cameronbridge 1979 cask no. 3586 **(84) n22.5 t21 f20 b20.5.** For those who prefer their grain old and dry. 51.2%

Duncan Taylor Collection Cameronbridge 1979 cask no. 3587 **(82) n22 t22 f18 b20.** The fun and flavour is all front loaded. 51.3%

Scotch Malt Whisky Society Cask 94.1 Aged 29 Years refill barrel, dist May 79 **(93) n24 t23.5 f22.5 b23.** A sublime grain which does exactly what it says on the tin. 53%

CARSEBRIDGE

The Clan Denny Carsebridge Aged 45 Years cask no. HH4132 **(84) n19 t23 f21.5 b20.5.** Though the nose may be crumbling and there may be very shaky balance, the delivery is – almost literally, it seems – pure nectar. Sugary and watery, there is little form to this in true whisky terms. It is something of an old aged freak. Yet the enjoyment and wonderment derived from this ancient dram is unique and entirely priceless. Enjoy for what it is. 45.6%. Douglas Laing. 167 bottles.

Duncan Taylor Collection Carsebridge 1979 cask no. 33032 **(84.5) n20 t23 f20 b21.5.** Not quite in the same league as other DT Carsebridges othis run, due in no small measure to tiring, mildly embittered oak. Staggering about a little, not quite sure whether to clout or caress and ends up doing both. The great moments, though, are exactly that. 56%

Duncan Taylor Collection Carsebridge 1979 cask no. 33033 **(91) n23** real ye olde candy shop aroma: jars full oboiled fruit sweets and a dusty, wooden floor: takes me back nearly 45 years...; **t23** surprising degree of sugar evident from the kick off: superb gentle fruit and spice interplay; everything controlled and delicate **f22.5** chunky vanilla but its light sugar does a perfect balancing act; **b22.5** a fabulous dram from this lost distillery and about as relaxing as they come. Indeed, I found this Carsebridge the perfect antidote to when my beloved Millwall lost at Wembley against Scunthorpe... 54.9%

⋰ **Duncan Taylor Collection Carsebridge 1979** cask no. 33038 **(93.5) n23.5** a teasing aroma: powdered sugar on boiled fruit candy; a freshly opened bottle of lemon drops; **t24.5** crisp, brittle sugars and crunchy corn biscuit; a light topping of Demerara: just about perfect in grain whisky terms; **f22.5** fades with the usual chorus of vanillas; **b23** a Duncan Taylor Carsebridge bottling is usually one of the highlights of the whisky year. This one certainly doesn't disappoint. In fact, it's a belter...!!! *52.3% Duncan Taylor & Co Ltd*

Kingsbury Finest & Rarest Carsebridge 41 Years Old 1964 bourbon cask **(94) n24 t23.5 f23 b23.5**. Strange how some old grains get a Canadian passport, others a US. This is pure Kentucky...Oh, and by the way, it's a real stunner. *476%. nc ncf. Japan Import System Co. Ltd.*

Lonach Carsebridge Aged 43 Years distilled 1963 bottled 07 **(93) n23.5 t23.5 f23 b23**. Not a shred oevidence that the great age has damaged or reduced this in any way. Perhaps the least oak-ruined 40-something whisky you will ever taste. A freaky great and a real treasure for the US market. *43%*

Scotch Malt Whisky Society Cask 92.1 Aged 31 Years refill barrel, dist Nov 76 **(90) n22 t22 f23 b23**. Now here, from beyond the grave, is a wonderful example and object lesson in why it is a sin to add colouring to older blends (well, any blends, il was to get on my soapbox). Here is a whisky which has extracted from the wood all kinds of natural caramels. It works: it sits well in the scheme othings and balances out beautifully. Add some into the mix and then the balance vanishes. Grab some othis and see what I mean.. *56.6%*

DUMBARTON

Celtic Heartlands Dumbarton 1964 Aged 42 Years **(87.5) n20.5 t23 f21.5 b22.5**. Defies the odds for a charming dram. *46.7%*.

The Clan Denny Dumbarton Aged 43 Years cask no. HH3829 **(95) n23.5** lilacs? On a grain whisky...? 'Fraid so...Some real fizz and attitude as well as a hint of something from the high quality bourbon front; **t24** a near perfect landing on the palate: forget about spitting this one...the corn has perfect shape and body, the layering othe spice and vanillins − and even a minor blast of tannins; and as for the balance between sweet grist and the slightly, balancing drier oaks...it's off the scale... **f23.5** the vanilla mainstay of the finish is enriched by that continued gristy sweetness and some countering burnt toast bitterness; **b24** so I thought I'd celebrate tasting my 800th whisky for the 2009 Bible by showing an act of solidarity with Dumbarton, a great distillery needlessly lost to us, ritually slaughtered on an accountant's spreadsheet. *51.8%. Douglas Laing. 215 bottles.*

GARNHEATH

⋰ **The Clan Denny Garnheath Vintage 1969 Aged 40 Years** refill hogshead HH 5538 **(95) n25** a decidedly bourbony twist to this one with a blood orange, hickory and watered honey theme. On another level comes the berry fruits and apricot. Sensational...in every sense...!!! **t24** more bourbon on delivery and on the offshoot development: soft liquorice, the mildest honeycomb. It works so well because of the understatement and attention to elegance; **f22.5** bitters a little, with the odd flaw in the cask exposed as it enters its fifth decade. A soft red liquorice and vanilla depth, coupled with a charmingly tingling spice attack, does its best to compensate; **b23.5** one of the rarest experiences in Scotch whisky: even I have tasted different Garnheath only 30 to 40 times in my life. Few, though, have been as well rounded as this. The nose, especially, almost defies belief. Unquestionably grain of this and probably many a year... *47.9% Douglas Laing & Co Ltd*

GIRVAN

Berry's Own Selection Girvan 1989 bott 07 **(91) n22 t23 f23 b23**. A Steady-Eddie and eventually beautiful grain with no blemishes or fault-lines giving a good insight into why this make is so popular among blenders. *46%*.

⋰ **Berrys' Own Selection Girvan 1989** cask no. 37531 **(84) n21.5 t22 f20 b20.5**. Stodgy on both nose and delivery with the grainy sharpness coming through briefly but to excellent effect. *45.1% Berry Bros & Rudd*

Celtic Heartlands Girvan 1965 Aged 42 Years **(83) n21 t22 f20.5 b20.5**. I know that around about the time this was made some blenders in Scotland weren't over enamoured with Girvan − which is hardly the case today. Here you get a slight insight as to why some feathers were flying back then, with the sharpness of the firm grain at times biting pretty deep. However, after all these years, it is the oak making the loudest noise and the messages are mixed. Certainly the bitterness is entirely wood related. There is the odd window, though, especially just after initial delivery, through which the grain does show a rich shaft of golden promise. This is not a whisky without moments of great beauty. *45%*

The Clan Denny Girvan Vintage 1990 Aged 20 Years Bourbon Barrel hogshead no. 5794 **(88.5) n20.5** a touch of spice, otherwise non-committal; **t23** spice, indeed!! Sugared almonds add the balance as the oily spices take a delightful hold; **f22.5** lots of cocoa; **b22.5** the nose is quiet, but what happens on the taste buds is a joy. 59.3% 246 bottles

Scotch Malt Whisky Society Cask G7.1 Aged 18 Years refill barrel, dist Jul 90 **(86.5) n21 t23 f21 b21.5.** Subtly Canadian and slightly rich. Perhaps over indulges the caramels but weight, mouthfeel, degree of sweetness and spice impact are all very good. 54.2%

INVERGORDON

⋙ **Berrys' Own Selection Invergordon 1971 (79.5) n20 t20.5 f19 b20.** Buttery, but soapy and bitter, too. 48% Berry Bros & Rudd

Berry's Own Selection Invergordon 1971 bott 09 **(88) n22** just a slight twitch and twinge to an otherwise lifeless bowl of Canadian custard; **t22** melt-in-the-mouth vanilla, dissolving muscovado sugar; vanishing middle; **f22** drier and sharper with all the vicious bite of an enraged butterfly; **b22** steady as a rock; hard as a blancmange...; 48.2%. Berry Bros & Rudd.

The Clan Denny Invergordon Aged 42 Years cask no. HH4239 **(90) n23 t22.5 f22 b22.5.** How do grain whiskies like this be so effortlessly good? 49.8%. Douglas Laing. 155 bottles.

⋙ **The Clan Denny Invergordon Vintage 1965 Aged 44 Years** refill barrel HH 5576, dist 1965 **(90.5) n23** fat, absolutely dense corn with some jumbled, half-hearted fruit notes; **t23.5** how soft is that? The corn dissolves on arrival as it moves towards a lazy Canadian style. Almost one dimensional, but that is not a criticism as it does what it does superbly; **f22** more of the same, but now in a much more simpering, vanilla-led way; **b22** improbably simplistic and almost youthful for its age. You can't go wrong with this. 45.4% Douglas Laing

Duncan Taylor Collection Invergordon 1965 cask no. 15516 **(85.5) n21 t22 f21.5 b21.** Lively Lincoln biscuits with an extra sprinkling of sugar. 50.1%

Duncan Taylor Collection Invergordon 1965 cask no. 15517 **(94) n23.5 t24 f23 b23.5.** How strange that two casks can be outwardly so similar, but, on close inspection, so very different. This guy oozes class it has no right to possess after so many years. Perhaps it's the extra spice which does the trick. But just like when you meet two twins othe opposite sex, for one reason or other, one of them just has that special, almost indefinable, thing the other doesn't.... same here. 50.2%

Duncan Taylor Collection Invergordon 1965 cask no. 15518 **(88.5) n22.5 t22.5 f21.5 b22.** Charming, high quality, blemish-free ancient grain. 50.8%

Duncan Taylor Collection Invergordon 1965 cask no. 15519 **(94) n24.5** textbook complexity: yes it is a bit of a Canadian/bourbon hybrid. But it as if there are small grains at work here breaking up the more dominant vanillas into manageable pieces. A faultless treat of a nose with the bitter-sweet ratio as near as damn-it perfect; **t23** some genuine and surprising blood orange tones amid the regulation vanilla: complex and excellently weighted; small, busy spices prod and jab around the tastebuds; and the sub-plot is a cream-toffee/vanilla mix; **f23** long, relatively simplistic. But not a bad note from the cask and that means the spices and delicate sweet notes continue unsullied; **b23.5** DT obviously have obviously struck upon a rich seam of outstanding Invergordon. 100% most buy whisky. 51.6%

⋙ **Duncan Taylor Collection Invergordon 1965** cask no. 15528 **(94) n24** passion fruit and gooseberry neatly wrapped in custard....stunning!!... **t24** just the degree of melt-in-the-mouth yield you would expect from this distillery. Except here it not only shows its supine qualities, but a much more aggressive alter ego with first some punchy vanillas then a middle ground peppery spice; **f22.5** a lovely interplay between the elegant spices and delicate vanillas; **b23.5** it is very difficult to ask much more of a grain whisky of such advanced years, especially one that is determined not to go down the bourbony route. 50.8% Duncan Taylor & Co Ltd

Duncan Taylor Collection Invergordon 1965 cask no. 15532 **(85.5) n21 t22.5 f20.5 b21.5.** Good, simple entirely honest old grain. But here all the accent is on the vanilla and the complexity which wins heart and palate on 15519 is conspicuous by its absence. 52.7%

LOCH LOMOND

Loch Lomond 2000 Cask No. 37700 Aged in Organic French Wine Hogshead dist 24 Jul 00, bott 27 Apr 07 db **(94) n23.5 t24 f23 b23.5.** A brave decision to mature grain in grape, but this has worked so impressively well. On this evidence, who needs single malt when you can get grain this good....??? 45%. nc ncf. 475 bottles.

LOCHSIDE

Clan Denny Grain Lochside Aged 42 Years dist Nov 63, bott Nov 05 **(89) n23** I'm in deepest Kentucky and just opened up a 17-year-old barrel: it's tired and groaning but the hickory and muscovado sugar are such a treat; nice chestnuts, too; **t23** silky, mesmerising oak with splinters in every direction; lovely heavy roast Java coffee at the very centre; **f21** fades and becomes mildly bitter and tired with the coffee-bourbon theme continuing; **b22** a bit like clapped out bourbon on the nose and even more clapped out bourbon on the finish. My researcher put this under single malts, but as soon as I tasted it, I smelt (and tasted!) a rat. Proof positive that old grain Scotch can produce vintage bourbon!! *44.1%. Douglas Laing.*

NORTH BRITISH

Berry's Own Selection North British 2000 bott 09 **(78)** n19.5 t21 f18.5 b19. Pock marked by the occasional sulphurous North British house style – this is to do with distillation, not maturation – and for all its brightness on delivery has a bit of problem shaking off the dogged late bitterness. *46%. Berry Bros & Rudd.*

Celtic Heartlands North British 1974 Aged 33 Years (93.5) n23.5 t23.5 f23 b23.5. To be honest, it is rare that you find single malt whisky which stands the test of time with such panache. Women, in particular, are likely to fall for its honeyed charms. *47.4%.*

⋅⋅⋅ **The Clan Denny North British Vintage 1979 Aged 30 Years** refill butt HH 5557, dist 1979 **(90)** n22 pedestrian vanilla; corn oil with a sprinkling of icing sugar; **t24** absolutely everything you didn't expect from the nose: a flavour eruption of sharp, salivating corn and grass notes; vanilla towards the middle; **f22** bitters out as the cask begins to talk; **b22** I know a blender or two who will regret that such an effervescent cask for its age slipped through the net. *54.2% Douglas Laing*

Duncan Taylor Collection North British 1978 cask no. 38469 **(89)** n21.5 buttery corn oil and lightly sweetened; **t23** melt-in-the-mouth silk: again buttery with a fabulous flutter of golden syrup; **f22** slightly bitter vanilla and a dash of ice cream in cream soda; **b22.5** just charms you to death. *54.9%*

Duncan Taylor Collection North British 1978 cask no. 38472 **(84.5)** n21 t22 f20.5 b21. Many of the usual NB corn characteristics, but evidence of a mildly fatigued cask. *55.2%*

Duncan Taylor Collection North British 1978 Aged 29 Years cask no. 39889 **(91)** n23 t23.5 f22 b22.5. There is something about these better old grains which makes you want to applaud. A whisky with a bit of fight, but ends up relaxed and a picture of elegance: surely it is only a matter otime before these grandiose old grains are more widely appreciated. *54.5%*

Duncan Taylor Collection North British 1978 cask no. 39890 **(83)** n21.5 t20 f21.5 b21. Pleasantly stays the course. No great statements made, but doesn't veer out of control and crash, either. *55.6%*

Duncan Taylor Collection North British 1978 cask no. Q247 **(95)** n24 the jackpot..!! Well, nearly. Everything here I look for from this distillery at this kind oage: a complex, softly spiced layering to the usual corn field. Busy and gloriously three dimensional; **t24** what a delivery! Canadian from the top drawer in so many aspects! A real fizz to this as the spices move in and break up any corn mafia that's thinking about dominating proceedings: the starchy backbone also has light banana-vanillas and weak Demerara sugar to contend with; **f23** those soft spices spin on even as the corn oils begin to gain a belated foothold. The vanillas are faultless; **b24** golden proof that great grain is a match for anything. *54.7%*

Norse Cask Selection North British 1997 Aged 11 Years hogshead cask no. 18278, dist 97, bott 08 **(91)** n22.5 crisp, buttery, a Canadian flourish but without the caramel; **t23.5** firm, mouth-watering, on the edge of sweetness but distinctly sharp; **f22.5** long, lingering, excellent oak background to the mildly flinty grain; a bit of spice and mocha at the death **b22.5** an exemplary cask: exactly what you should expect from this distillery at this age. *64.9%. Qualityworld for WhiskyOwner.com, Denmark.*

Private Cellar North British 1992 bott 07 **(86)** n21 t22 f21.5 b21.5. Corn soup with a delightful sweet head and spicy tail. *43%. Speyside Distillers.*

Scotch Malt Whisky Society Cask G1.5 Aged 24 Years refill barrel, dist Apr 84 **(90.5)** n23 starchy corn oil with a dab of maple syrup sweetness...sure this isn't Canadian..? **t23.5** effortless grace on delivery: the soft corn oils envelop the mouth and custard and butterscotch sweetness is dispensed to all corners; better still, there is a fabulous juiciness, too; **f21** long, drying – as it should – but just not quite enough sweetness to counter the late bitter marmalade notes; **b23** even after nearly a quarter of a century, this a powering beauty. *60.7%*

NORTH OF SCOTLAND

⋅⋅⋅ **The Clan Denny North of Scotland Vintage 1974 Aged 35 Years** refill hogshead HH5562 **(80.5)** n21.5 t21 f18 b20. The more bitter elements of the cask have bitten deep but the Canadian style vanillas are shapely. *44.1% Douglas Laing*

Private Cellar North of Scotland 1970 bott 07 **(92) n24** stunning mixture of honey and stem ginger; **t23** lush, lusty corn with some amazing notches ohoney marked on the softest of oak; **f22** long, vanilla-clad, gently drying, a touch of the Canadians; **b23** this is the way old grain should be: slightly off the wall but radiating charm and class. *43%.*

PORT DUNDAS

Duncan Taylor Collection Port Dundas 1973 cask no. 128317 **(96) n24 t24 f24 b24.** Never have I seen a better example of a Coffey still in action: before I actually knew what I was nosing I had, in my mind, been transported back to Guyana and was nosing some Coffey still rum from there: the similarity is extraordinary!! And, believe me, this is one whisky I don't spit whilst working on this book!! A landmark whisky in my long experience. And an award winner osome type. *57.9%*

Duncan Taylor Collection Port Dundas 1973 cask no. 128321 **(77) n19 t20 f19 b19.** A previous bottling oa sister cask was a highlight othe year: in fact, the thing was in my taste offs for World Whisky othe Year. This one, though, might not quite make it that far. I suspect a sherry butt has been employed to liven it up and some sulphur has sneaked in. *54.5%*

Scotch Malt Whisky Society Cask G6.1 Aged 28 Years refill hogshead, dist Dec 80 **(89.5) n23** lavender and citrus head the cast for this most dainty aroma; **t22.5** the grain and vanilla feel inextricably linked: dense with a touch of the eggnog about this; **f22** some serious custard through to the end; **b22** about as friendly a dram as you will ever meet. *51%*

STRATHCLYDE

⟐ **The Clan Denny Strathclyde Vintage 1969 Aged 40 Years** refill hogshead HH 5741 **(86.5) n22** promising, thanks to some light citrus; **t23** big, marauding grains; less oils than its peers giving a fresher delivery and middle; **f21** thins and bitters out; **b21.5** delightfully textured and possessing a wonderfully rich and mouth-watering delivery. One of those grains which still turns up hidden at the back of hotel bars: definitely worth blowing the dust off. *51.7% Douglas Laing & Co Ltd*

Duncan Taylor Collection Strathclyde 1973 cask no. 74063 **(82.5) n20 t21.5 f20 b21.** How can something so old have so many teeth – and bloody sharp ones? Even the citrus stings. *55.5%*

Duncan Taylor Collection Strathclyde 1973 cask no. 74067 **(86) n22.5 t22 f20.5 b21.** An infinitely better cask than those previously in this series: the nose is almost identical to the Kentucky Tavern bourbon from the old Barton distillery a decade ago. *55.2%*

Vatted Grain

Compass Box Hedonism Maximus (93.5) n25 the kind of aroma your nose was invented for: lots orich bourbony swirls, with butterscotch, liquorice and chocolate-covered honeycomb arriving – big time! – on cue...; oh, and a few gooseberries and greengages tossed in for an extra dimension: it just doesn't get any better... **t22.5** the oak is a bit top heavy on arrival, but lush malt cushions its impact to a degree; still juicy and tongue-teasing; **f23** retains its overtly bourbony character to the end with massive chewy oak extract, but always enough sweetness in reserve to cope; **b23** Bourbon Maximus.... *46%*

Compass Box Hedonism Maximus bottling no. H25 MMVII **(88) n21.5** huge waves of vanilla and natural caramels help cover a wheaty sweetness; **t22.5** almost like dusted icing sugar on bread pudding; **f22** much more sedate with a soft oily lift; the sweetness remains a constant despite the slow oak arousal; **b22** sweet, gentle but with a wicked spice prickle. *50.1%. nc ncf. 2,400 bottles.*

Norse Cask Selection Inver Bridge Aged 29 Years hogshead cask no. QW-gr1108, dist 66 & 79, bott 08 **(88.5) n23** great age is apparent from the first moment: honeycomb/liquorice notes are there in mild, bourbony form, as well as a very light hint ofruit and several layers of vanilla. Yet for all the lightness of shades, the overall feeling is intense; **t23** silky mouthfeel with a touch onatural caramel sweetness, then a dose osomething much drier, more boldly oaky; **f21** perhaps too much oaky bitterness – like overly burnt raisin - at the death; **b21.5** hmmm, can't think which two distilleries this will have been made from... *46%. Qualityworld for WhiskyOwner.com, Denmark.*

The Snow Grouse (70.5) n17.5 t18 f17 b18. Served normally, a tedious nonentity oa whisky. What little flavour there is, is toffee-based. On both nose and finish there are distant offt notes, but in something so light louder than they might be. Surely...it just be...? Served chilled as instructed on bottle: **(79) n20 t21 f18 b20.** Much, much better. Very sweet and the 's' word is confined, especially on the vodka-ish nose. The finish is still a give away though. *40%.*

Scottish Blends

Doubtless, the odd eyebrow or two will be raised when it is announced that a blended scotch has again won Jim Murray's Whisky Bible World Whisky of the Year. For this means the award has gone to blends as many times over the last five years as single malts.

That implies blended scotch is as good as single malt. And, for my money, that is entirely the case; and if the blender is really doing his job, it should often be better. However, that job is getting a little harder each year. Once it was the standard joke that a sulphured sherry butt that had once been marked for a single malt brand would be dumped into a large blend where it would work on BP Chief executive Tony Hayward's "drop in the ocean" principle. However, there is now a lot more than just the odd sherry butt finding their way in and blenders have to take guard that their blends are not being negatively affected. Certainly, during the course of writing both the 2010 and 2011 Bibles I discovered this was becoming a much more common occurrence. Indeed, one or two brands which a few years back I would have expected to pick up awards on a regular basis have been hit badly: disappointing and a great loss to whisky lovers.

However, the fact that Ballantine's 17 – a blend that has been on a higher plane than most other world whiskies for the last decade – has finally managed to pick up the big one, after regularly knocking at the door, confirms that there are still a great number of stupendous blends out there to go and discover. It still amazes me, though, how many scotch whisky enthusiasts I meet worldwide who rarely taste blends more than a handful of times a year, if ever at all.

Perhaps it is a form of malt snobbery: if you don't drink malts, then you are not a serious Scotch whisky connoisseur ... or so some people think. Perhaps it is the fact that over 90 out of every 100 bottles of Scotch consumed is a blend, and therefore rather common, that has brought about this cold-shouldering. Well, not in my books. In fact, perhaps the opposite is true. Until you get to grips with blends you may well be entitled to regard yourself knowledgeable in single malts, but not in Scotch as a whole. Blends should be the best that Scotland can offer, because with a blend you have the ability to create any degree of complexity. And surely balance and complexity are the cornerstones of any great whisky, irrespective of type.

Of course there are some pretty awful blends created simply as a commodity with little thought going into their structure – just young whiskies, sometimes consisting of stock that is of dubious quality and then coloured up to give some impression of age. Yes, you are more likely to find that among blends than malts and for this reason the poorest blends can be pretty nasty. And, yes, they contain grain. Too often, though, grain is regarded as a kind of whisky leper – not to be touched under any circumstances. Some writers dismiss grain as "neutral" and "cheap", thus putting into the minds of the uninitiated the perception of inferiority.

But there really is nothing inferior about blends. In fact, whilst researching The Bible, I have to say that my heart misses more than one beat usually when I received a sample of a blend I have never found before. Why? Well, with single malts each distillery produces a style that can be found within known parameters. With a blend, anything is possible. There are many dozens of styles of malts to choose from and they will react slightly differently with certain grains.

For that reason, perhaps, I have marked blends a little more strictly and tighter than I have single malts. Because blends, by definition, should offer more.

The most exciting blends, like White Horse 12 (why, oh, why is that, like Old Parr 18, restricted mainly to Japan?) Grant's and this year's glorious Ballantine's show bite, character and attitude. Silk and charm are to be appreciated. But after a long, hard day is anything better than a blend that is young and confident enough to nip and nibble at your throat on its way down and then throw up an array of flavours and shapes to get your taste-buds round? Certainly, I have always found blends ultimately more satisfying than malts. Especially when the balance, like this year's Bible World Champion, Ballantine's 17, simply caresses your soul. And they do more: they paint pictures on the palate, flavour-scapes of extraordinary subtlety and texture. No two bottles are ever exactly the same, but they are usually close enough and further illustrate the fascination of a beautifully orchestrated variation on a theme.

With Blended Scotch the range and possibilities are limitless. All it takes is for the drinker not just to use his or her nose and taste-buds. But also an open mind.

Scottish Blends

"10 Years and a Bit" Blended Scotch (84) n21.5 t22 f20 b20.5. Matured in oloroso and finished in a Cognac quartercask. Explains why this blend lurches drunkenly all over the palate. Enough honeycomb, though, for a pleasant few minutes 42%. *Qualityworld, Denmark.*

100 Pipers (74) n18.5 t18 f19 b18.5. An improved blend, even with a touch of spice to the finish. I get the feeling the grains are a bit less aggressive than they were for so long were. I'd let you know for sure, if only I could get through the caramel. 40%. *Chivas.*

Aberdour Piper (88.5) n22 green apple and the most delicate smoke imaginable; t23 crisp malt and grain integrate so not a crack shows; juicy and mouth-cleansing; f21.5 vanilla concentrate and late, lethargic smoke; b22 always great to find a blend that appears to have upped the stakes in the quality department. Clean, refreshing with juicy young Speysiders at times simply showing off. 40%. *Hayman Distillers.*

Adelphi Private Stock Loyal Old Mature (88) n21 big grain overture; t23 golden syrup notes and bound tightly by firm grain; f22 delightful coffee with just the perfect degree of bite; b22 a very attractive number, especially for those with a slightly sweet tooth. 40%.

Antiquary 12 Years Old (92) n23.5 by some distance the smokiest delivery I have seen from this blend since my late dear friend Jim Milne got his hands on it. The last time I had hold of this it was Speyside all the way. Now peat rules; t23.5 immediate oils and smoke form a thick layer in almost Caol Ila style, but penetrating grains and juicier Speysiders ensure parity of style; f22 light with vanilla and echoes of peat; b23 a staggering about turn for a blend which, for a very long time, has flown the Speyside flag. I am not convinced that this degree of peatiness was intended. But it works! 40%. *Tomatin Distillery.*

Antiquary 21 Years Old (93) n23.5 as dense and brooding as an imminent thunderstorm: just a hint of a less than perfect sherry butt costs a point but manuka honey and crushed leaves, all helped along with a delicate peat-reek, ensure something sultry and wonderful; t23.5 improbably dense with a honeycomb maltiness you have to hack through; the grains offer lighter, bourbony touches; f23 softer vanillas and toffee, topped with the thinnest layer of molassed sugar and further bourbony notes; b23 a huge blend, scoring a magnificent 93 points. But I have tasted better, and another sample, direct from the blending lab, came with even greater complexity and less apparent caramel. A top-notch blend of rare distinction. 43%

Antiquary 30 Years Old (86) n22 t23 f20 b21. Decidedly odd fare: not only does the blend offer a greenish tinge, but the late waywardness of the finish suggests something odd has clambered aboard. That said, the endearingly eccentric nose and early delivery are sublime, with silky complexity tumbling all over the palate. 46%. *Tomatin Distillery.*

Antiquary Finest (79.5) n20 t21 f19 b19.5. Pleasantly sweet and plump with the accent on the quick early malt delivery. 40%. *Tomatin Distillery.*

Arden House Scotch Whisky (86) n19.5 t22 f22.5 b22. Another great bit of fun from the Co-op. Very closely related to their Finest Blend, though this has, for some reason or other, a trace of a slightly fatter, mildly more earthy style. If only they would ditch the caramel and let those sweet malts and grains breathe! 40%. *Co-Operative Group.*

⌐≥ **Asda Blended Scotch Whisky (76.5)** n19 t21 f17.5 b19. An early scattergun approach with sweet, syrupy notes hitting the palate early and hard. Beware the rather bitter finish, though. 40% *Asda*

Asda Extra Special 12 Years Old (78) n19 t21 f19 b19. Pleasantish but dragged down by the dreaded S word. 40%. *Glenmorangie for Asda.*

The Bailie Nicol Jarvie (B.N.J) (95) n24 the sharpest barley has been taken to a barley-sharpening shop and painstakingly sharpened; this is pretty sharp stuff...the citrus gangs together with the fresh grass to form a dew which is pretty well...er... sharp...; t24 mouth-watering, eye-closingly, mouth-puckeringly sharp delivery with the barley pinging off the tautest grain you can imagine; f23 softens with a touch of vanilla and toffee; the late run from the citrus is a masterpiece of whisky closing; b24 I know my criticism of BNJ, historically one of my favourite blends, over the last year or two has been taken to heart by Glenmorangie. Delighted to report that they have responded: the blend has been fixed and is back to its blisteringly brilliant, ultra-mouth-watering self. Someone's sharpened their ideas up. 40%.

Ballantine's Aged 12 Years (84.5) n22.5 t22 f19 b21. Attractive but odd fellow, this, with a touch of juniper to the nose and furry bitter marmalade on the finish. But some excellent barley-cocoa moments, too. 43%. *Chivas.*

Ballantine's 12 Years Old (87) n21 t22 f21 b23. The kind of old-fashioned, mildly moody blend Colonel Farquharson-Smythe (retired) might have recognised when relaxing at the 19th hole back in the early '50s. Too good for a squirt of soda, mind. 40%. *Chivas Bros.* ⊙

Ballantine's 17 Years Old (97.5) n24.5 deft grain and honey plus teasing salty peat; ultra high quality with bourbon and pear drops offering the thrust; a near unbelievable integration with gooseberry juice offering a touch of sharpness muted by watered golden syrup; **t24** immediately mouthwatering with maltier tones clambering over the graceful cocoa-enriched grain; the degrees of sweetness are varied but near perfection; just hints of smoke here and there; **f24** lashings of vanilla and cocoa on the fade; drier with a faint spicey, vaguely smoky buzz; has become longer with more recent bottlings with the most subtle oiliness imaginable; **b25** now only slightly less weighty than of old. After a change of style direction it has comfortably reverted back to its sophisticated, mildly erotic old self. One of the most beautiful, complex and stunningly structured whiskies ever created. Truly the epitome of great Scotch. To the extent that for the last year, I have simply been unable to find a better whisky anywhere in the world. *43%. Chivas Bros.* ⊙ ⊙

Ballantine's Aged 21 Years (93) n24 superbly intrinsic, relying on deft fruit and vanilla notes as the key; **t24** stunningly textured with subtle layers of honey, juicy grasses and refined, slightly subdued, bourbony notes from the grain; **f22** flattens somewhat as the toffee evolves; **b23** one of the reasons I think I have loved the Ballantine's range over the years is because it is a blenders' blend. In other words, you get the feeling that they have made as much, and probably more, as possible from the stocks available and made complexity and balance the keystones to the whisky. That is still the case, except you find now that somehow, although part of a larger concern, it appears that the spectrum of flavours is less wide, though what has been achieved with those available remains absolutely top drawer. This is truly great whisky, but it has changed in style as blends, especially of this age, cannot help but doing. *43%.* ⊙

Ballantine's Aged 30 Years (94) n23.5 satisfying interplay between spiced grape and vanilla-clad smoke; **t24** quite sublime: the delivery simply melts in the mouth. Mainly grain on show early, again with all the attendant vanilla, then a juicier network of sharper barley and fruit. The weight is outstanding; **f23.5** long, with a real grain-malt tug of war. Spices persist and the vanilla ups a gear; **b23.5** quite a different animal to that which I tasted last year....and the year before. Having come across it in three different markets, I each time noted a richer, more balanced product: less a bunch of old casks being brought together but more a sculpted piece from preferred materials. That said, I still get the feeling that this is a work in progress: a Kenny Jackett-style building of a team bit by bit, so that each compartment is improved where it is possible, but not to the detriment of another and, vitally, balance is maintained. *43%* ⊙ ⊙

Ballantine's Finest (96) n24 a playful balance and counter-balance between grains, lighter malts and a gentle smokiness. The upped peat of recent years has given an extra weight and charm that had been missing; **t24** sublime delivery: the mouthfeel couldn't be better had your prayers been answered; velvety and brittle grains combine to get the most out of the juicy malts: a lot of chewing to get through here; **f23.5** soft, gentle, yet retains its weight and shape with a re-emergence of smoke and a gristy sweetness to counter the gentle vanillas and cocoa from the oak **b24.5** as a standard blend this is coming through as a major work of art. Each time I taste this the weight has gone up a notch or two more and the sweetness has increased to balance out with the drier grain elements. Take a mouthful of this and experience the work of a blender very much at the top of his game. *40%. Chivas Bros.* ⊙

Ballantine's Limited 75cl royal blue bottle **(89) n22** beautifully clean barley and soft fruits; a touch of vanilla and smoke in the distant background; **t24** a sumptuous delivery of melt-in-the-mouth grain followed by a slow unfurling of complex malt notes, from sweet barley to spicier cocoa-oak. Lovely fruit and a dab of smoke in the middle; **f21** bitters out impatiently; **b22** hadn't tasted this for a little while but maintains its early style and quite glorious delivery. *43%.*

Ballantine's Master's (82) n21 t22 f19 b20. Excellent lively grain and chewy malt, but the always suspect, grain-drizzled finish has become even more nondescript in recent bottlings. *40%.*

⋰⋰ **Ballantine's Rare Limited (89.5) n23.5** busy and weighty: light smoke compliments the bananas and raisins; **t22.5** thick and soupy; the delivery and follow through are both lush and viscous and moderately juicy. Again we have bananas in custard plus a more aggressive muscovado-sweetened fruitiness; **f21.5** spices gather as do drier oaks; **b22** a heavier, more mouth watering blend than the "Bluebottle" version. *43% ncf Chivas*

⋰⋰ **Bell's Original (91) n23** superb, old fashioned stuff: a few biting grains (as there should be), but kept in good order by a confident, smoky tapestry. Plenty of caramel but still quietly assertive; **t22.5** delivery offers a two-pronged attack of grinding grain and more sumptuous oils and smoke; quick to sweeten though never too far; caramel and vanilla offers a fanfare to a middle spice surge; **f22.5** long with the smoke lengthening the tail further. Usual butterscotch and caramel, but everything charmingly well tailored; **b23** your whisky sleuth came across the new version for the first time in the bar of a London theatre back in December 2009 during the interval of "The 39 Steps". To say I was impressed and pleasantly surprised is putting it mildly. And with the whisky, too, which is a massive improvement on the relatively stagnant 8-year-old especially with the subtle extra smoky weight. If the blender asks me: "Did I get it right, Sir?" then the answer has to be a resounding "yes". *40%*

Bells 8 Years Old (85) n21.5 t22.5 f20 b21. Some mixed messages here: on one hand it is telling me that it has been faithful to some of the old Bells distilleries – hence a slight dirty note, especially on the finish. On the other, there are some sublime specks of complexity and weight. Quite literally the rough and the smooth. *40%. Diageo.*

Benmore (74) n19 t19 f18 b18. Underwhelming to the point of being nondescript. *40%.*

Berrys' Blue Hanger 30 Years Old 3rd Release bott 07 (90.5) n23 ye olde oake, as one might expect from this olde companye, manifesting itself in sweet exotic fruit; t22.5 bitter-sweet and tingly, from the very start the blend radiates fruit and big oak; f22.5 long, spiced, a dash of something vaguely smoky but never tries to disguise its great age; saved at the death by a lush sweetness which sees off any OTT oak; b22.5 much improved version on the last, closer to the original in every respect. Excellent. *45.6%. Berry Bros & Rudd.*

Big "T" 5 Years Old (75) n19 t20 f18 b18. Big, chunky and bitter. Still doesn't have the finesse of old and clatters about the tastebuds charmlessly. Enormous malt delivery early on, but doesn't compensate for the bitter finish. *40%. Tomatin Distillery.*

Black & White (91) n22 firm grin and a softer caramel surround; the second layer hints at smoke and oak; t23 the crispest of deliveries followed by a radiating softly malted sweetness; the bite is sensational and everything you could demand of a blend; f22.5 playful peat teases as the oaks gather and the grains carry on their stern, matronly way; b23.5 this one hasn't gone to the dogs: quite the opposite. I always go a bit misty-eyed when I taste something this traditional: the crisp grains work to maximum effect in reflecting the malts. A classic of its type. *40%. Diageo.*

Black Bottle (91) n22 some gnawing grains make the teasingly smoked malt work hard for its money; t23 a battling fizz reveals some youngsters having fun in there. Like the nose, the grain really does fight its corner and the fault line where it meets the malt is marked by a spicy, smoky sweetness; f23 the buzz continues and there is a touch of Demerara sweetness and coffee to the chewy smokiness; b23 it has taken me a bit of time to get used to this slight change in style for this persistently brilliant blend. This one's been reduced in smoke and roughed up a little: the intervening grain which restrain the battling malts has now become a bit of a bruiser in its own right. Ignore the nonsensical claim of "Original Blend" on the label: this is a very old brand that has gone through many changes in its lifetime and will be unrecognisable from the modest whisky concocted over a century ago in an Aberdeen shop. And there are any number of us who are so glad it is nothing like the seething firewater it was 20-30 years ago. But it has kept true-ish to its re-birth under Allied when they turned it into a peaty beast and is probably closer to that in style than Highland's subsequent, lush re-working of it. *40%. Burn Stewart/Gordon Graham & Co.*

Black Bottle 10 Years Old (89) n22 so age-weightedly peaty it could almost be a single malt: the grains make little discernible impact; t23 soft, deft malt and firmer grain. The peat arrives after a short interval; f22 more vanilla and other oaky tones; b23 a stupendous blend of weight and poise, but possessing little of the all-round steaming, rampaging sexuality of the younger version...but like the younger version showing a degree less peat: here perhaps even two. Not, I hope, a start of a new trend under the new owners. *40%.*

Black Bottle Original Blend (93.5) n23 a tad murky and confused, but the grumble of peat is compelling while the grains lighten without dispelling; t24 brilliant: the delivery appears sweet from a double whammy of barley and young grain then moves off into different flavour spheres, the peat being noticeable but by no means weighty and drier vanillas and nutty toast dig deep; thick stuff, vaguely fruity now and then, chewy, nipping here and there on the tongue and roof of mouth; no end of ballast and fabulous fun; f23 the smoke now begins to take a firmer grasp, but the peat element is multi-dimensional, from cough sweet to kippers; predictably furry as it fades; b23.5 I'll be honest with you, as always. Because of the large number of sulphured Bunnahabhain sherry butts I have seen over the last 25 years, I was a little bit apprehensive as to what I might find with this blend, having not tasted it for the best part of a year. Quite a few blends now have the tell-tale furry buzz of sulphur coming from them these days, a bit like that gray ring of pollution you see above the earth when flying. This has that dull buzz, but is certainly no worse than most other blends these days. Which is a relief, as this is a greatly improved dram where harmony has been restored. A thoroughly enjoyable whisky with just the right amount of bite and aggression when required, and it knows also when to relax and hold its quiet moments. A delight. *40%. Gordon Graham & Co.*

Black Dog 12 Years Old batch no. 015, bott Nov 05 (92) n21 distinctly nutty – especially walnuts – with no more than a hint of citrus lightening the deep vanilla and toffee. Gentle and attractively layered; t23 soft grains delve gently into the tastebuds offering light oak and a distinct toastiness. The barley sweetness is relaxed and clean; f24 traces of soft honey and a strand of marmalade welcome the visiting spices which cling to the subtle oils clamped to the roof of the mouth. Almost a near perfect finish for a blend this age. Stunning!; **b24** an altogether thinner style than Century but offering genuine sophistication and élan. This minor classic will probably require two or three glass-fulls before you take the bait... *42.8%.*

Black Dog Century (89) n21 a big nose displaying grainy teeth at first but chunky fudge and dried dates weigh in impressively; **t23** mouth-filling and distinctly viscous, chocolate fudge clamps itself to the roof of the mouth allowing a lighter, teasingly spicy pulse to do its work around the back of the tongue while, a well-mannered sweetness lurks around every corner ensuring the oak is on its best behaviour. Big and complex **f23** brilliantly long and chewy with the chocolate fudge **b22** I adore this style of no-nonsense, full bodied bruising blend which amid the muscle offers exemplary dexterity and finesse. What entertainment in every glass!! *42.8%. McDowell & Co Ltd, India. Blended in Scotland/Bottled in India.*

The Black Douglas bott code 340/06/183 **(84) n19 t20 f23 b22.** Don't expect raptures of mind-bending complexity. But on the other hand, enough chewability and spice buzz here to make for a genuinely decent whisky, especially on the excellent finish. Not dissimilar to a bunch of blends you might have found in the 1950s *40%. Foster's Group, Australia.*

The Black Douglas Aged 8 Years bott code 348/06/187 **(79) n20 t21 f19 b19.** Slightly lacking for an 8-y-o: probably duller than its non-age-statement brother because of an extra dollop of caramel. *40%. Foster's Group, Australia.*

The Black Douglas Aged 12 Years "The Black Reserve" bott code 347/06/188 **(87) n21 t21 f23 b22.** The toffee does its best to wreck the show – but there sre simply too many good things going on to succeed. The slight smoke to the nose delights and the honeycomb middle really does star. *40%. Foster's Group, Australia.*

Black Grouse (94) n23 outwardly a hefty nose, but patience is rewarded with a glorious Demerara edge to the malt and oak: superb, understated stature; **t24** again the smoke appears to be at the fore, but it's not. Rather, a silky sweet delivery also covers excellent cocoa and spice **f23** so gentle, with waves of smoke and oak lapping on an oaky shore. Brilliant... **b24** a superb return to a peaty blend for Edrington for the first time since they sold Black Bottle. Not entirely different from that brand, either, from the Highland Distillers days with the smokiness being superbly couched by sweet malts. A real treasure. *40%.*

Black Ram Aged 12 Years (85) n21 t23 f21 b20. An upfront blend that gives its all in the chewy delivery. Some major oak in there but it's all ultra soft toffee and molasses towards the finish. *40%. Vinprom Peshtera, Bulgaria.*

⁙ **Blend No. 888 (86.5) n20 t21.5 f23 b22.** Not to be confused with the Nantucket single malt by the same name (or number) – and by nose and taste cannot possibly be. Still, a good old-fashioned, rip-roaring, nippy blend with a fudge-honey style many of a certain age will fondly remember from the 60s and 70s. Love it! *40% The House of MacDuff*

⁙ **Broadford (78.5) n19 t19.5 f20 b20.** So boringly inoffensive, you could punch it. Toffee anyone? *40% Burn Stewart*

Buchanan's De Luxe 12 Years Old (82) n18 t21 f22 b21. Just don't recognize this as the usual ultra-classy blend you could put money on you'd normally get from this brand. The nose shows more than just a single fault and then the character simply refuses to get out of second gear. Certainly pleasant, and some of the chocolate notes towards the end are gorgeous. But just not the normal brilliant show-stopper! *40%. Diageo*

Buchanan's Red Seal (90) n22 clean with almost equal portions of grain, malt and oak; **t23** wonderful malt clarity guarantees a rare charm; the grains are crisp and amplify the barley sweetness; **f22** lovely sweet vanilla complements the persistent barley; **b23** exceptional, no-frills blend whose apparent simplicity paradoxically celebrates its complexity. *40%. Diageo*

Budgen's Scotch Whisky Finely Blended (85) n21 t22 f21 b21. A sweet, chunky blend offering no shortage of dates, walnuts, spice and toffee. A decent one to mull over. *40%..*

⁙ **Callander 12 Years Old (86) n21 t22 f21.5 b21.5.** Cheery stuff. No shortage of malt sparkle and even a touch of tangy salt. Very attractive and enjoyable without ripping up trees. *46.3% Burn Stewart*

Campbeltown Loch Aged 15 Years (88) n22.5 deft marzipan and smoke; **t22.5** firm, with ever-increasing oak but never at the cost of the honeyed malt; at times sharp and puckering; **f21** much grainier and firm; dries very slowly; **b22** well weighted with the age in no hurry to arrive. *40%. Springbank Distillers*

⁙ **Castle Rock (81) n20 t20.5 f20 b20.5.** Clean and juicy entertainment. *40%*

Catto's Aged 25 Years (87.5) n23 age pours from every molecule, but never in a negative way: teasing exotic fruit states that a significant part is played by the malts; there is toffee (I sincerely hope not from colouring for a 25-year-old whisky!!!) that dulls things a little – and turns it distinctly Canadian in style - but a kind of distant smoked bacon on the wind brings life back into things; **t22.5** a soft, juicy arrival is punctuated by deliciously teasing spice; again there is a caramel kick which flattens things as they get interesting; **f20.5** dull, toffee caramel... we have returned to the tundra of Canada; **b21.5** at once a hugely enjoyable yet immensely frustrating dram. The higher fruit and spice notes are a delight, but it all appears to be played out in a padded cell of cream caramel. One assumes the natural oak caramels have gone into overdrive. Had they not, we would have had a supreme blend scoring well into the 90s. *40%.*

Catto's Deluxe 12 Years Old (79.5) **n20 t21.5 f18 b20.** Strange how a standard blend can completely out-manoeuvre its 12-year-old brother. Refreshing and spicy in part, but still a note in there which doesn't quite work. *40%. Inverhouse Distillers.*

Catto's Rare Old Scottish (92) **n23.5** the young Speysiders leap from the glass with joyous abandon while the grain looks on benevolently; **t23.5** various shades of citrus and juicy grass make for a mouthwatering experience; a soft honey strand adds the slightest touch of weight and the most delicate of spices chime in; **f22** medium length, with gentle vanillas balancing the sweeter notes; remains refreshing to the death; **b23** currently one of my regular blends to drink at home. Astonishingly old-fashioned with a perfect accent on clean Speyside and crisp grain. In the last year or so it has taken on a sublime sparkle on the nose and palate. Of its style, an absolutely masterful whisky which both refreshes and relaxes. Just so understated and classy. *40%. James Catto & Co.*

Chequers Deluxe (78.5) **n19.5 t20 f19 b20.** Charm, elegance, sophistication....not a single sign of any of them. Still if you want a bit of rough and tumble, just the job. And make sure they serve it in a dirty glass... *40%. Diageo.*

Chivas Regal Aged 12 Years (83.5) **n20.5 t22.5 f20 b20.5.** Chewy fruit toffee. Silky grain mouth-feel with a toasty, oaky presence. *40%. Chivas.*

Chivas Regal Aged 18 Years (73.5) **n17.5 t20 f17.5 b18.5.** The nose is dulled by a whiff of sulphur and confirmation that all is not well comes with the disagreeably dry, bitter finish. Early on in the delivery some apples and spices show promise but it is an unequal battle against the caramel and off notes. I keep being told that this is Chivas' flagship brand. Well, it's been a very long time since I last tasted a good one – and I've tried a few over the years, believe me. Maybe I'm constantly unlucky. Or just maybe it's probable that it ranks among the most over-rated whiskies in the world. *40%*

Chivas Regal 25 Years Old (95) **n23** exotic fruit of the first order: some pretty serious age here, seemingly older than the 25 years; **t23.5** mesmerisingly two-toned, with a beautiful delivery of velvety grains contrasting stunningly with the much firmer, cleaner malts. Softly chewable, with a gentle spice fizz as the vanilla begins to mount; unbelievably juicy and mouth-watering despite its advanced age; **f24** long, wonderfully textured and deft; some cocoa underlines the oak involvement, but there is not once a single hint of over-aging; **b24.5** unadulterated class where the grain-malt balance is exemplary and the deft intertwining of well-mannered oak and elegant barley leaves you demanding another glass. Brilliant! *40%.*

Clan Campbell (85) **n20 t22.5 f21 b21.5.** Pleasing and for several exciting moments appears to be returning to its big Speyside roots...before being upended by a toffee surge. Some redeeming coffee notes up the complexity levels again. Always worth a second pour. *40%.*

Clan MacGregor (92) **n22** superb grains allow the lemon-fruity malt to ping around: clean, crisp and refreshing; **t24** as mouthwatering as the nose suggests with first clean grain then a succession of fruit and increasingly sweet malty notes. A brilliant mouthful, a tad oilier and spicier than of old; **f23** yielding grain; and now, joy of joys, an extra dollop of spice to jolly it along; **b23** just gets better and better. Now a true classic and getting up there with Grant's. *43%.*

Clan Murray Rare Old (84) **n18 t23 f21 b22.** The wonderful malt delivery on the palate is totally incongruous with the weak, nondescript nose. Glorious, mouth watering complexity on the arrival though. Maybe it needs a Murray to bring to perfection... *40%. Benriach Distillery.*

Clansman (80.5) **n20.5 t21 f19 b20.** Sweet, grainy and soft. *40% Loch Lomond*

The Claymore (85) **n19 t22 f22 b22.** These days you are run through by spices. The blend is pure Paterson in style with guts etc, which is not something you always like to associate with a Claymore. Even so, a livelier dram than it was with some delightful muscovado sugar at the death. Get the nose sorted (and do away with some toffee) and a very decent and complex whisky is there to be had. *40%. Whyte & Mackay Distillers Ltd.*

Compass Box Asyla Marriage married for nine months in an American oak barrel (88) **n22** a soup of a nose, though slightly over oaked for perfect harmony; **t23** a big, sweet cherry tart kick off with custard and spices galooped on top; **f21** warming, spiced vanilla; **b22** a lovely blend, but can't help feeling that this was one marriage that lasted too long. *43.6%. Compass Box Whisky for La Maison du Whisky in commemoration of their 50th Anniversary.*

Consulate (89) **n22 t22 f22.5 b22.5.** One assumes this beautifully balanced dram was designed to accompany Passport in the drinks cabinet. I suggest if buying them, use Visa. *40%.*

Co-operative Group (CWS) Finest Blend (93.5) n22.5 indelicate, salty smoke makes for a very traditional blend aroma, the sort a generation back favoured by breweries for their pubs; **t23.5** absolute silk as some top grade grain slithers around the palate, taking with it some hefty traces of smoke; **f24** now really goes to town with the peat becoming solid enough to chew and the sweeter elements balancing with the vanilla and toffee theme. Long, with lapping waves of soft smoke seemingly never ending; **b23.5** on first tasting it is hard to pick that many differences with Arden House. You even wonder if they are opposite ends of the same bottling run. They could be, theoretically; but the depth to the peat and clarity and balance of the sweetness makes this a much more complete dram which, frankly, I could drink any day. Forget about this being a supermarket brand: a must experience for all true whisky lovers out there. A classic is a classic, irrespective of age or label and had only this been caramel free, mostly likely some kind of award winner. Glorious and a cap doffed to tradition: ee, me old 'ostelries of Ancoats wud 'av been proud! What I'd give now for a pint of Chesters'... 40%

Co-operative Group Premium Scotch Aged 5 Years (93.5) n23 no doubt about the malts being present and correct here: good earthy weight; **t24** absolutely brilliant delivery: smoky, thick and lush, but a wonderful molassed sweetness ensures everything stays in harmony; **f23** lightly oiled, a touch of vanilla, but that weighty malt continues to glow... **b23.5** not exactly what you expect from a budget blend: a beautiful whisky fit to grace the home of any connoisseur... 40%

Craigellachie Hotel Quaich Bar Range (81) n20 t21 f20 b20. A delightful malt delivery early on, but doesn't push on with complexity as perhaps it might. 40%

Crawford's (83.5) n19 t21 f22 b21.5. A lovely spice display helps overcome the caramel. 40%.

⋰ **Cutty Black (83) n20 t23 f19 b21.** Both nose and finish are dwarfed and flung into the realms of ordinariness by the magnificently substantial delivery. Whilst there is a taint to the nose, its richness augers well for what is to follow; and you won't be disappointed. At times it behaves like a Highland Park with a toffeed spine, such is the richness and depth of the honey and dates and complexity of the grain-vanilla background. But those warning notes on the nose are there for good reason and the finish tells you why. Would not be surprised to see this score into the 90s on a different bottling day. 40% Edrington

Cutty Sark (86) n21 t22 f21 b22. The malt bursts around the palate in playful tandem with the crisp grain. Just a strange dull note to the nose and finale on this one. 40%.

Cutty Sark Aged 12 Years (92) n22 grain heavy, but crisp and clean; **t24** mountainous honey which had been hiding on the nose cascades onto the taste buds. The firm grain gives the honey and accompanying maple syrup a backbone while spices slowly gather; **f23** long and lush, toffee begins to absorb the honey; **b23** at last! Cutty 12 at full sail....and blended whisky rarely looks any more beautiful! 40% Edrington ☺ ☺

Cutty Sark Aged 15 Years (82) n19 t22 f20 b21. Attempts to take the honey route. But seriously dulled by toffee and the odd sulphured cask. 40% Edrington ☺ ☺

Cutty Sark Aged 18 Years (88) n22 much oakier output than before with only fragments of sherry; herbal; **t22** a safe delivery of yielding grain with out-reaching fingers of juicier malt; decent spice buzz as a bitter-sweet harmony is reached; **f22** cream toffee and custard creams; **b22** lost the subtle fruitiness which worked so well. Easy-going and attractive. 43%.

Cutty Sark Aged 25 Years (93.5) n23.5 the laziest smoke drifts aimlessly over rich honey-bourbon; **t23.5** for all the weight, a juicy maltiness sets the tone. Like the nose, a degree of bourbony richness pulses a honeycomb sweetness through that wonderfully silky body; **f23** late caramel brings a slightly premature halt but not before the most delicate wisps of smoke reveal themselves; very late cocoa re-lights the fire; **b23.5** outstanding whisky which does much of what you can ask of a 25-y-o blend. 45.7%. Berry Bros & Rudd.

Demijohn's Finest Blended Scotch Whisky (88) n21 strange, out of shape, but soft; **t22** salivating delivery with a wonderful firmness to the grain; the malts eventually mould into the style; **f23** remains tangy to the end, even with a touch of marmalade thrown in; **b22** a fun, characterful blend that appears to have above the norm malt. Enjoy. 40%. Adelphi

Dew of Ben Nevis Blue Label (82) n19 t22 f20 b21. A busier, lighter blend than the old Millennium one it replaced. The odd off-key note is handsomely outnumbered by deliciously complex, mocha tones with a touch of demerara. Ditch the caramel and you'd have a sizzler! 40%. Ben Nevis Distillery. Replacement for Dew of Ben Nevis Millennium Blend.

Dew of Ben Nevis Special Reserve (85) n19 t21 f23 b22. A much juicier blend than of old, still sporting some bruising and rough patches. But that kind of makes this all the more attractive, with the caramel mixing with some fuller malts to provide a date and nuts effect which makes for a grand finale. 40%. Ben Nevis Distillery.

Dew of Ben Nevis Supreme Selection (77) n18 t20 f20 b19. Some lovely raspberry jam swiss roll moments here. But the grain could be friendlier, especially on the nose. 40%.

Dewar's Special Reserve 12 Years Old (84) n20 t23 f19 b22. Some s... you know what... has crept onboard here and duffed up the nose and finish. A shame because elements of the delivery and background balance shows some serious blending went on here. *40%.*

Dewar's 18 Years Old (93) n23 confident and complex, the nose makes no secret that its foundations are solid grain. From it hang a succession of nubile malty notes, weighty and not without a minor degree of smoke. The fruit has a strawberry jam presence, and there are spices, of course... t24 entirely classical in its delivery: firm grain and rich, sweet malt linked arm in arm. Again the grain is bold and firm but tattooed into it is a buzzing busy maltiness, offering varying degrees of weight, sweetness and depth...; f22.5 a build up of caramel begins to lessen the degree of complexity, though not the body and weight; b23.5 here is a classic case of where great blends are not all about the malt. The grain plays in many ways the most significant role here, as it is the perfect backdrop to see the complexity of the malt at its clearest. Simply magnificent blending with the use of flawless whisky. *43%. John Dewar & Sons.*

Dewar's 18 Year Old Founders Reserve (86.5) n22.5 t22 f20.5 b21.5. A big, blustering dram which doesn't stint on the fruit. A lovely, thin seam of golden syrup runs through the piece, but the dull, aching finale is somewhat out of character. *40%. John Dewar & Sons.*

Dewar's Signature (93) n24 a stunning celebration of controlled grape: this is sweet-edged and of a distinctly sauturnes style. Elsewhere the oak offers a light vanilla haze and the barley is clean and relaxed. Just doesn't come much more sultry and elegant than this; t23.5 as luxuriant a mouthfeel as you could pray for, but with some spicy sparks flying. The fruit continues to dominate while the grain must be distilled satin; f22 some custard tart is about as aggressive as the oak gets, though there is an unwelcome buzz from a sherry cask or two; b23.5 a slight departure in style, with the fruit becoming just a little sharper and juicier. Top range blending and if the odd butt could be weeded out, this'd be an award winner for sure. *43%. John Dewar & Sons.*

Dewar's White Label (78.5) n19 t21.5 f19 b19. When on song, one of my preferred daily blends. But not when like this, with its accentuated bitter-sweet polarisation. *40%*

Dimple 12 Years Old (86.5) n22 t22 f21.5 b21. Lots of sultana while the spice adds aggression. *40%. Diageo.*

Dimple 15 Years Old (87.5) n20 simple; t21 a massive grain lead and with the shy malts all over the place at first, takes its time to get itself into any kind of order... f24 the late middle shows signs of extraordinary complexity, way above anything that has gone on before. The finish, though, takes it to the next level. All kinds of small flavour explosions with little smoke and barley notes popping about the palate; with so much grain, no surprise about the big cocoa finale; b22.5 only on the late middle and finish does this particular flower unfurl and to magnificently complex effect. The texture of the grains in particular delight while the strands of barley entwine. A type of treat for the more technically minded of the serious blend drinkers among you. *40%. Diageo.*

Drummer Aged 5 Years (83) n19 t22.5 f20.5 b21. The nose may beat a retreat but it certainly gets on a roll when those fabulous sharp notes hit the palate. However, it deserves some stick as the boring fudge finishes in a cymbal of too much toffee. *40%. Inver House.*

Duncan Taylor Auld Blended Aged 35 Years dist pre 70 (93) n23 a knife and fork nose appears too oaked but time in the glass allows some excellent marmalade and marzipan to appear; t24 glorious delivery: amazing silk, lots of gentle, natural caramel but topped with honeycomb; f22 chocolate malt and burnt toast; b24 only a handful of companies could come up with something like this. An infinitely better dram than previous bottlings, due mainly to the fact that the dangers of old oak appear to have been compensated for. *46%. 131 bottles.*

⚜ **Duncan Taylor Collection Black Bull 12 Year Old** (88.5) n22.5 like many a Black Bull, this is muscular and with no shortage of attitude; it is also a touch oily but the malt is well represented; t22.5 beautifully chewy with all kinds of natural toffees mixing well with the creaminess and hazelnut; even a light spice to add to the balance; f21.5 toffee and vanilla; b22 Black Bulls enjoy a reputation for being dangerous. So does this: once you pour yourself a glass, it is difficult not to have another...and another.... *50% Duncan Taylor & Co Ltd*

Duncan Taylor Collection Black Bull Deluxe Blend Aged 30 Years (93) n24 fantastically rich: a real mish-mash of fruit, barley, smoke and, of course, oak...really has hit the bullseye; t24 one of the creamiest-textured deliveries I've come across this year. Again the smoke leads, but there is so much else slushing around in these soft oils; the bourbony liquorice in the middle ground is sublime; f22 long with a real tapering spiciness amid the molasses and vanilla b23 this pedigree Black Bull doesn't pull its horns in.... *50%. Duncan Taylor.*

Duncan Taylor Collection Rarest of the Rare Deluxe Blend 33 Years Old (94) n24 a heady fusion of rich bourbon and old Canadian characteristics beefed up further with diced exotic fruit and a dash of ancient Demerara rum Uitvlught to be precise; t24 the bourbon hits the track running, closely followed by some silky barley couched in velvet grain; invariably some spices pitch in to ramp up the complexity even further; **f22** no great length, but no off notes, either. Instead the oak adds an unsweetened custardy grace; **b23** outstanding and astounding blended whisky. An absolute must for blend lovers....especially those with a bourbony bent. *43.4%*

⫶⫶ **Duncan Taylor Collection Black Bull 40 Year Old** batch 1 **(86.5) n23 t21 f21.5 b21.** Almost certainly whisky which had dipped below 40%abv in the cask has been included in this blend. That would account for the occasional spasm of ultra intense natural caramels, a kind of tell-tale fingerprint indicating this is likely to have been done. The nose is exotic fruit; the delivery is a battle to keep the oak at bay. One which is happily won. *40.2%*

The Famous Grouse (89) n22 a weightier aroma than Grouse once was. Not quite so clean and crisp; now a slight smoke can be detected, while honey threads, once audible, have to fight to be heard; once you get used to it, it is quite lovely...; **t23** a real surprise package for a Grouse, as this is no lightweight on delivery: the flavours come thick and fast – literally – though the intensity makes it hard to pick out individual notes; once acclimatised, there are distinct marmalade and custard qualities, but only after a brooding shadow of smoke moves out of the picture taking some honey with it; **f21.5** lots of mocha and cream toffee with the vanilla adding a dusty quality; **b22.5** it almost seems that Grouse is, by degrees, moving from its traditional position of a light blend to something much closer to Grant's as a middle-weighted dram. Again the colouring has been raised a fraction and now the body and depth have been adjusted to follow suit. Have to say that this is one very complex whisky these days: I had spotted slight changes when drinking it socially, but this was the first time I had a chance to sit down and professionally analyse what was happening in the glass. A fascinating and tasty bird, indeed. *40%. Edrington Group*

The Famous Grouse Bourbon Cask Finish (87.5) n21 pretty closed save for the caramel and light oak; **t23** bursts immediately into life with a major Speyside-style juice assault: sweet sugars melt into the malt – almost like a Milky Way candy bar; **f21.5** firm, grainy and finely textured; slow build up of spice; **b22** the extra oak sweetens things up pleasantly. *40%*

The Famous Grouse Gold Reserve (90) n23.5 ye gods! What an improvement on the last bottle of this I came across!! Really sexy complexity which, though showing decent weight, including delicate smoke, also celebrates the more citrussy things in life. At body temp the complexity of the structure and degree of layering goes through the roof...; **t23** honeyed to start, then an injection of lime and ground cherry; some caramel tries to interfere and to some extent succeeds; **f21.5** the toffee effect immediately curtails further complexity, but there is a slight spice rumble very late on and even a light sprinkling of barley grist; **b22** great to know the value of the Gold Reserve is going up....as should the strength of this blend. The old-fashioned 40% just ain't enough carats. *40%. Edrington Group*

The Famous Grouse Port Wood Finish (77) n20 t20 f18 b19. If anyone has tasted more different bottlings of Port Wood whisky, then I'd like to shake his hand: the sweaty armpit nose on this one really is unique. Pleasant, but first yawn, and then stupor-inducing as the fruit is lost without trace under the toffee. *40%. Edrington Group.*

The Famous Grouse Scottish Oak Finish bott Nov 05 **(95) n23** not dissimilar to the European oak of Czech whiskies, but better control. This seems to accentuate the smoke slightly and the grain is lost in a fusion of malt and butter. Really lovely – and very different: in fact unique to any blend I've come across; **t24** wow, wow, wow, wow, wow...!!! The mouth arrival is memorable and truly orgasmic: just wave upon wave of something beautiful, seamless and spicy. A kind of half-sweet honeycomb – all roast and chewiness – stars with the grains at last making themselves heard with a string of vanilla thrusts. Those spices pound the sides of the tongue and the roof of the mouth and the bitter-sweet balance is sensational. Just to make things better still, there is just the right degree of bite one desires in a blend; **f23** long, with mounting signs of oak dominance, but those glorious toasted-barley waves, now topped with muscovado sugar keep the blend honest. The final embers offer a surprising hint of juniper. Is that the oak...or the bottling hall?; **b25** what a stunner! What a one off....!!! Sadly, this is a limited edition blend...and once those 7,092 bottles have been drunk, that's it! I sincerely hope they are already planting new Caledonian oak to make this a fixture on the whisky shelves for future generations!! *44.5%.*

The Formidable Jock of Bennachie (82) n19 t22 f21 b20. "Scotland's best kept secret" claims the label. Hardly. But the silky delivery on the palate is worth investigating. Impressive roastiness to the malt and oak, but the caramel needs thinning. *40%. Bennachie Scotch Whisky.*

⫶⫶ **Fraser MacDonald (85) n21 t21.5 f21 b21.5.** Some fudge towards the middle and end but the journey there is an enjoyable one. *40% Loch Lomond Distillers*

⫶⫶ **Gairloch (79) n19 t20 f20 b20.** For those who like their butterscotch at 40%abv. *40%*

Glen Brynth (70.5) n18 t19 f16 b17.5. Bitter and awkward. 43%

Glen Lyon (85) n19 t22.5 f22 b21.5. Works a lot better than the nose suggests: seriously chewy with a rabid spice attack and lots of juices. For those who have just retired as dynamite testers. Unpretentious fun. 43%. Diageo.

Glenross Blended (83) n20 t22 f20 b21. Decent, easy-drinking whisky with a much sharper delivery than the nose suggests. 40%. Speyside Distillers.

Glen Simon (77) n20 t19 f19 b19. Simple. Lots of caramel. 40%. Quality Spirits Int.

The Gordon Highlanders (86) n21 t22 f21 b22. Lush and juicy, there is a distinctive Speysidey feel to this one with the grains doing their best to accentuate the developing spice. Plenty of feel good factor here. 40%. William Grant & Sons.

Grand Macnish (79) n19 t21 f19 b20. Welcome back to an old friend...but the years have caught up with it. Still on the feral side, but has exchanged its robust good looks for an unwashed and unkempt appearance on the palate. Will do a great job to bring some life back to you, though. 43% MacDuff International Ltd ⊙ ⊙

Grand Macnish 12 Years Old (86) n21 t22 f21.5 b21.5. A grander Grand Macnich than of old with the wonderful feather pillow delivery maintained and a greater harmonisation of the malt, especially those which contain a honey-copper sheen. 40% MacDuff ⊙ ⊙

Great MacCauley (81) n20 t20.5 f20 b20.5. Reminds me of another whisky I tasted earlier: Castle Rock, I think. Identical profile with toffee and spice adding to the juicy and youthful fun. 40% Quality Spirits International

Green Plaid 12 Years Old (89) n22 the smoke of old has been doused slightly, though mint comes through with the soft barley; t23 light oils coat the mouth with a gentle sweetness; f22 vanilla and a distant rumble of smoke; b22 a beautifully constructed, mouth-watering blend. 40%. Inverhouse Distillers.

Haddington House (85.5) n21 t21.5 f22 b21. Mouth-watering and delicate. 40%.

Haig Gold Label (88) n21 somewhat sparse beyond a vague grapey-graininess; t23 begins light and unimpressive, but about three flavour waves in begins to offer multi-layered spices and juice aplenty; the sweet-dry ratio as the oak arrives is brilliant; f22 classy fade with a touch of Cadbury's Fruit and Nut in the mix as the spices persist; b22 what had before been pretty standard stuff has upped the complexity by an impressive distance. 40%. Diageo.

Hankey Bannister (84.5) n20.5 t22 f21 b21. Lots of early life and even a malt kick early on. Toffee later. 40%. Inverhouse Distillers.

Hankey Bannister 12 Years Old (86.5) n22 t21.5 f21 b22. A much improved blend with a nose and early delivery which makes full play of the blending company's Speyside malts. Plenty of toffee on the finish. 40%. Inverhouse Distillers.

Hankey Bannister 21 Years Old (93.5) n22.5 a fruity ensemble, clean, vibrant and loath to show its age; t23.5 every bit as juicy as the nose suggests, except here there is the odd rumble of distant smoke; mainly a firm, barley-sugar hardness as the grains keep control; f23.5 the arrival of the oak adds further weight and for the first time begins to behave like a 21-y-o; long, now with decent spice and with some crusty dryness at the very death; b24 a beautifully balanced blend that takes you on a series of journeys into varying styles and stories. Does the blend movement a great service. 43%. Inverhouse Distillers.

Hankey Bannister 25 Years Old (91) n22.5 a slight bourbony honey-hickory edge, to where the 21-y-o has fruit; t24 a swooning delivery: just about everything in exactly the right place and showing sympathetic weight to the other. The grains are soft, the malts are sturdier and more energetic, the oak docile...for the time being; f21.5 some bitter cocoa notes reveal the oak to be a little more militant but the light oils help the grains recover the position and balance; b23 follows on in style and quality to 21-year-old. Gorgeous. 40%

Hankey Bannister 40 Years Old (89) n22 evidence of high malt levels here: pungent, nippy and lively. No shortage of over-ripe oranges, either.. t23 juicy, salivating delivery with a silky texture to the grain bringing out the best of the intense, sweet malt; the fruitiness is mixed, rich and blunted only by the toasty oaks; f22 pretty oak spattered with the grains continuing their soft theme. Enough barley remains to add another cushion against the age; b22 "This is some of the last whisky produced before England won the World Cup in 1966," Gareth Stanley of Inverhouse gleefully tells me. Yes, Gareth. Thanks for reminding me. But at least I can look Alex Salmond and his brothers straight in the eye and tell him: "Well, at least we once won the bloody thing..." This blend, though, has been put together to mark the 250th anniversary of the forging of the business relations between Messrs. Hankey and Bannister. And although the oak creaks like a ship of its day, there is enough verve and viscosity to ensure a rather delicious toast to the gentlemen. Love it! 44% Inverhouse

Hedges & Butler Royal (92) n22.5 curiously salty and coastal, yet peat-free; the grains couldn't get much crisper; t23.5 sharp, crisp grain working in complete harmony with the sprightly Speyside-style malts; all kinds of citrus, grassy notes; **f23** a lemon zesty liveliness refreshes and cleanses; some chattering, drier cocoa very late on; **b23** massively improved to become a juicy and charming blend of the very highest order. *40%.*

High Commissioner (88.5) **n22.5** beautiful weight with a touch of the old-fashioned English sweetshop about the subtle sugar input; something lightly rummy about this; **t22.5** star quality delivery and mouth-feel. Chewy with just the right degree of give. Again those sugars have a delightful say in proceedings; **f20.5** shame about the bitter fade; **b22.5** had to laugh. Picked up the wrong glass and nosed and tasted thinking it was Dewar's White Label. My notes read: "Bloody hell!!! White Label has suddenly become High Commissioner on steroids".....! Then I noticed the White Label bottle was still full and unopened. And yes, I had picked up what turned out to be the High Commissioner sample without realising it was one of the set of blends to be tasted. Now I admit I had a hand in cleaning this brand up a couple of years back, giving it a good polish and much needed balance complexity. But I don't remember leaving it in quite this good a shape. Just a bitter semi-off note on the finish, otherwise this guy would have been in the 90s. What a great fun, three-course dram this is... *40% Loch Lomond Distillers* ⊙⊙

⁘ **Highland Baron** (85.5) **n21 t22 f21 b21.5.** A very clean, sweet and competent young blend showing admirable weight and depth. *40% Loch Lomond Distillers*

Highland Bird (77) **n19 t19 f19 b20.** I've has a few of these over the years, I admit. But I can't remember one quite as rough and ready as this... *40%. Quality Spirits International.*

Highland Black 8 Years Old Special Reserve (83) **n21 t21 f20.5 b20.5.** I still maintain that if they stripped out the huge caramel input they would be left with a really stunning blend. Peering through the murk, there is enough on the nose and delivery to really enjoy, especially the muffled spicy kick. *40%. Aldi*

Highland Dream 12 Years Old bott Jan 05 (94.5) **n23.5** all the hallmarks of a married blend, with a genuine silkiness to the nose and absolutely no sign of a suture between the varying smoke, oak and fruit styles and the grain; **t24** lavish and lush, something, possibly the grains, appears a lot older than the minimum 12 years stipulated; wonderfully juicy and chewy at the same time, the smoke gives intermittent pulses; **f23** smoky and softly oiled; plenty of vanilla and butterscotch; **b24** now that is what I call a blend! How comes it has taken me two years to find it? A wet dream, if ever there was one... *43%. J & G Grant. 9000 bottles.*

Highland Dream 18 Years Old bott May 07 (88.5) **n22.5** huge sherry input; **t22.5** the silk you expect from this blend is there, as is a soft honey and fruit thread; **f21.5** light with the accent on vanilla and an attractive bourbony sweetness; **b22** perhaps doesn't get the marks on balance that a whisky of this quality might expect. This is due to the slight over egging of the sherry which, while offering a beautiful delivery, masks the complexities one might expect. Lovely whisky, and make no mistake: the type of which you'll find the bottle emptying very quickly during the course of a night before anyone quite realises. But, technically, doesn't match the 12-year-old for balance and brilliance. *43%. J & G Grant. 3000 bottles.*

Highland Earl (82) **n20 t21 f20.5 b20.5.** Much more emphasis on toffee these days but beneath that is a very firm grain. Simple, but attractive. *40%. Aldi*

Highland Gathering Blended Scotch Whisky (78) **n19 t20 f19 b20.** Attractive, juicy stuff, though caramel wins in the end. *40%. Lombards Brands.*

Highland Harvest Organic Scotch Whisky (76) **n18 t21 f19 b18.** A very interesting blend. Great try, but a little bit of a lost opportunity here as I don't think the balance is quite right. But at least I now know what organic caramel tastes like... *40%.*

Highland Piper (79) **n20 t20 f19 b20.** Good quaffing blend – if sweet - of sticky toffee and dates. Some gin on the nose – and finish. *40%.*

Highland Pride (86) **n21 t22 f21.5 b21.5.** A beefy, weighty thick dram with plenty to chew on. The developing sweetness is a joy. *40%. Whyte & Mackay Distillers Ltd.*

Highland Reserve (82) **n20 t21 f20 b21.** You'll probably find this just off the Highland Way and incorporating Highland Bird and Monarch of the Glen. Floral and muddy. *40%.*

Highland Warrior (77.8) **n19 t19 f19.5 b20.** Just like his Scottish Chief, he's on the attack armed with some Dufftown, methinks... *40%. Quality Spirits International.*

Highland Way (84) **n19 t20.5 f22.5 b22.** This lovely little number takes the High Road with some beautiful light scenery along the way. The finish takes a charming Speyside path. *40%.*

⁘ **Inverarity Limited Edition** cask no. 698, dist 1997, bott 2009 (84.5) **n20.5 t22 f21 b21.** A heady, heavy-duty blend where honeycomb rules on the palate and thick dates offer a more intense sweetness. But don't go looking for subtlety or guile: those whose palates have been educated at the Whyte and Mackay school of delicate sophistication will have a ball. *40%*

Iona Royale 25 Years Old (89) **n22** the rigid grain nails the malt to the glass. Yet there is something attractively of the dank forest about this; **t23** hold on to something tight: several tidal waves of oak-spattered malt crash about the palate; a second wave of barley remains fresh and salivating before drying with the warming grain; **f21** lots of burnt fudge and vanilla softened by an evasive sweetness; **b23** a massively malt-rich blend that piles on the complexity early on. 43%. J&G Grant.

Islay Mist 8 Years Old (84) n20 t22 f21 b21. Turned into one heavy duty dram since last tasting a couple of years back. This appears to absorb everything it touches leaving one chewy, smoky hombre. Just a little tangy at the end. 40% MacDuff International Ltd

Islay Mist 12 Years Old (90) n22 Bowmore-style cough sweet dominates over the most gentle of grains; **t23** decent smoke drive, intense at first then feathering out; remains sweet to the house style **f22** long, back to cough sweet and a long fade of gristy, muscovado sugar; **b23** adore it: classic bad cop - good cop stuff with an apparent high malt content. 40%. ☉

Islay Mist 17 Years Old (92.5) n22.5 reclusive peat can just be spotted amid the rich vanillas; **t23.5** silky, mouth-watering delivery: a dream of a start for any blend with the light muscovado, semi-buttery sugars keeping their shape; depth supplied by the shy peat and no less retiring oak; **f23** long finish with a late spice prickle and sugared almonds. The smoke continues to play a teasing role; **b23.5** always a cracking blend, this has improved of late into a genuine must have. 40% MacDuff International Ltd ☉ ☉

Islay Mist Delux (85) n21.5 t22 f21.5 b20. Remains a highly unusual blend with the youthful peat now more brilliant than before, though the sugar levels appear to have risen markedly. 40% MacDuff International Ltd ☉ ☉

Isle of Skye 8 Years Old (94) n23 Isle of Skye? Or Orkney? Honey and smoke play tag; the grain is firm and clean; **t24** just so beautiful. Honeycomb and light fudge form a rich partnership, the smoke is little more than ballast and a shy spice; the grains play a fabulous role in allowing the maltier notes to ping around and increase the salivating qualities; **f23.5** the spice is now pretty warming but the honeycomb and vanilla dominate the finale; **b23.5** where once peat ruled and with its grain ally formed a smoky iron fist, now honey and subtlety reigns. A change of character and pace which may disappoint gung-ho peat freaks but will intrigue and delight those looking for a more sophisticated dram. 40% Ian Macleod ☉ ☉

Isle of Skye 21 years Old (91) n21 sluggish: trying to work out its own stance; **t23.5** sweet chocolate raisin, sumptuously brushed with a layer of soft smoke and demerara; **f23** wonderfully deft spices nibble at the tastebuds like tiny fish at your feet in a rock pool; grains at last – soft and silky all the way; **b23.5** what an absolute charmer! The malt content appears pretty high, but the overall balance is wonderful. A belter of a blend. 40%. Ian Macleod.

Isle of Skye 50 Years Old (82.5) n21.5 t21 f20 b20. Drier incarnation than the 50% version. But still the age has yet to be balanced out, towards the end in particular. Early on some distinguished moments involving something vaguely smoked and a sweetened spice. 41.6%.

James Alexander (85.5) n21 t21.5 f21.5 b21.5. Some lovely spices link the grassier Speysiders to the earthier elements. 40%. Quality Spirits International.

James King (76.5) n20 t18 f20 b18.5. Young whiskies of a certain rank take their time to find their feet. The finish, though, does generate some pleasant complexity. 43%.

⋯ **James King Aged 5 Years (85) n21 t21.5 f21 b21.5.** Very attractive, old fashioned and well weighted with a pleasing degree of fat and chewy sweetness and chocolate fudge. Refreshingly good quality distillate and oak have been used in this: I'd drink it any day. 40%

James King 8 Years Old (78.5) n18.5 t21.5 f19 b19.5. Charming spices grip at the delivery and fine malt-grain interplay through the middle, even showing a touch of vanilla. But such a delicate blend can't fully survive the caramel. 43 %. Quality Spirits International.

James King 12 Years Old (81) n19 t23 f19 b20. Caramel dulls the nose and finish. But for some time a quite beautiful blend soars about the taste buds offering exemplary complexity and weight. 40%. Quality Spirits International.

James King 15 Years Old (89) n22 t23 f21.5 b22.5. Now offers extra spice and zip. 43 %. .

James King 21 Years Old (87.5) n20.5 curiously inferior nose to the 15, thanks to the missing peat. Some dusty fruit atones slightly but mildly off key; **t23.5** instant mouthwatering gait and a touch of exotic fruit and spice; the soft malt dovetails elegantly with the gentle vanillas; the starring role, though, goes to the wonderfully velvety grain which offers just enough backbone to help accentuate the malt; **f22** dries as the oak and caramel gather intensity. Some very late spice does puncture – and punctuate – the cream caramel; **b22** attractive blend, but one that could do with the strength upped to 46% and the caramel reduced if not entirely got rid of. One of those potentially excellent yet underperforming guys I'd love to be let loose on! 43 %. Quality Spirits International.

James Martin 20 Years Old (93) n21 egg custard; **t23.5** massive delivery as per the house style, but now we have a blend working in unison, with the malts having an unusually large say. The silky grains help accentuate the sweetness of the Speysidey barley and the milk chocolate middle holds up a hand of recognition to the oak and age; **f24.5** long and exceptionally clever, with the denouement heading in several directions before settling for something a little spicy and continuing on the cocoa theme; **b24** I had always regarded this as something of an untamed beast. No longer: still something of a beast, but a beautiful one that is among the most complex found on today's market. *43% Glenmorangie.*

James Martin 30 Years Old (86) n21.5 t22 f21 b21.5. Enjoyable for all its exotic fruitiness. But with just too many creaking joints to take it to the same level as the sublime 20-y-o. Even so, a blend worth treating with a touch of respect and allowing time for it to tell some pretty ancient tales... *43%. Glenmorangie.*

J&B Jet (79.5) n19 t20 f20.5 b20. Never quite gets off the ground due to carrying too heavy a load. Unrecognisable to its pomp in the old J&B days: this one is far too weighty and never properly finds either balance or thrust. *40%. Diageo.*

J&B Reserve Aged 15 Years (78) n23 t19 f18 b18. What a crying shame. The sophisticated and demure nose is just so wonderfully seductive but what follows is an open-eyed, passionless embrace. Coarsely grain-dominant and unbalanced, this is frustrating beyond words and not worthy to be mentioned in the same breath as the old, original J&B 15 which, by vivid contrast, was a malty, salivating fruit-fest and minor classic. *40%. Diageo*

J&B Rare (88.5) n21.5 the most youthful J&B nose ever: young malts and grain integrate well, but those grains really do appear still to have milk teeth; **t22.5** one thing about young whisky: it's packed with flavour. And here you go on salivatory overdrive as the sheer unopposed freshness gives the tastebuds goosebumps; **f22** clean, grain layered with soft vanilla; **b22.5** I have been drinking a lot of J&B from a previous time of late, due to the death of their former blender Jim Milne. I think he would have been pretty taken aback by the youthful zip offered here: whether it is down to a decrease in age or the use of slightly more tired casks – or both – is hard to say. *40%. Diageo.*

⁙ **Jim McEwan's Blended Whisky (86.5) n20 t22 f22.5 b22.** Juicy and eye-watering with clever late spices. *46% Bruichladdich*

John Barr (85.5) n20 t22 f21.5 b22. I assume from the big juicy dates to be found that Fettercairn is at work. Outwardly a big bruiser; given time to state its case and it's a bit of a gentle giant. *40%. Whyte & Mackay Distillers Ltd.*

Johnnie Walker Black Label 12 Years Old (95.5) n23.5 pretty sharp grain: hard and buffeting the nose; a buffer of yielding smoke, apple pie and delicate spice cushions the encounter; **t24.5** if there is a silkier delivery on the market today, I have not seen it: this is sublime stuff with the grains singing the sweetest hymns as they go down, taking with them a near perfection of weighty smoke lightened by brilliantly balanced barley which leans towards both soft apple and crème broulee; **f23.5** those reassuringly rigid grains re-emerge and with them the most juicy Speysidey malts imaginable; the lovely sheen to the finish underlines the good age of the whiskies used; **b24** here it is: one of the world's most masterful whiskies back in all its complex glory. A bottle like this is like being visited by an old lover. It just warms the heart and excites. *40%. Diageo.* ☉

Johnnie Walker Blue Label (88) n21 the old, cleverly peated nose has been lost to us and now the accent falls on fruit though this is hardly as cleanly endearing as it might be; **t24** but the magnificence of the mouth arrival is back with a bang with the most sumptuous marriage of over-ripened figs, volumous malt and lightly sprinkled peat all bound together and then expanded by a brilliant use of firm and soft old grains. Spices also sparkle and tease. Magnificent...; **f21** oh, so disappointing again, with the plot played on the arrival and there being insufficient reserve to see off the broodier elements of the slightly bitter oak; **b22** what a frustrating blend! Just so close to brilliance but the nose and finish are slightly out of kilter. Worth the experience of the mouth arrival alone. *43%. Diageo*

Johnnie Walker Gold Label The Centenary Blend 18 Years Old (96) n24 at first it seems a level nose with little happening. But look again...deeper. Stirring in the glass are diced apples and moist raisins, a squirt of something peaty, and a honey and golden syrup mix. Sweet yet weighty with just enough smoke and oak to anchor; **t24** the silky arrival magnifies the smoky edge to this: some Caol Ila here, I guess, doing what Caol Ila does best – buck up blends. But also that hallmark honey thread is there to savour, linking beautifully with soft grains carrying vanilla and fudge; meanwhile playful spices...play!; **f23** a beautiful denouement in which the vanilla-edged oak refuses to hide, but smoke and barley dovetail in wonderful counterbalance; **b25** at the moment I would say that the blending lab at Diageo is going through a kind of legendary period. In years to come people will look back at it fondly and with a healthy degree of awe and ask: "do you remember when?"; or they will point to this era and say: "that's when it all started." White Horse 12, Old Parr and Johnnie Walker Gold: three blends where the gauntlet has been laid down to all: blenders and drinkers alike. And also where I say to Scotch lovers: well, you might love malts, but just how many can match these for brain-exploding complexity? This is another astonishing whisky which just has to be included in people's must have lists. Some of you I was talking to at a tasting in San Francisco, I think, will remember when I answered a question about age and blends: how I said that Walker's Gold appears to have older whiskies than when it was launched. Well this is because it slipped my radar that it was now a 18-year-old, rather than the original 15. Sorry about that. Age, as I have often argued, is as likely to do a whisky down as improve it. Certainly, though, not in this case... 40%. Diageo/John Walker & Sons.

Johnnie Walker King George V db (88) n23 delicate smoke and honey with green tea. Unusual, but it works; t22 good weight and spice buzz on delivery; melting grains help lighten the oak; f21 gets lost in toffee. Pity... b22 One assumes that King George V is no relation to King George IV. This has genuine style and breeding, if a tad too much caramel. 43%

Johnnie Walker Red Label (87.5) n22 such a crisp delivery of grain; toffee apple, too...with young apples...; t22 juicy and hard delivery, much in keeping with the nose; toffee arrives early, then a welter of malty blows; f21.5 crisp grain again and the vaguest hint of smoke joins the vanilla; b22 the ongoing move through the scales quality-wise appears to suggest we have a work still in progress here. This sample has skimped on the smoke, though not quality. Yet a few months back when I was in the BA Business Lounge at Heathrow's new Terminal Five, I nearly keeled from almost being overcome by peat in the earthiest JW Red I had tasted in over three decades. I found another bottle and I'm still not too sure which represents the real Striding Man. 40%. Diageo.

Kenmore Special Reserve Aged 5 Years bott code L07285 (75) n18 t20 f19 b18. Recovers to a degree from the poor nose. A must-have for those who prefer their Scotch big-flavoured and gawky. 40%.

King Robert II (77) n19 t19 f20 b19. A bustier, more bruising batch than the last 40 per cent version. Handles the OTT caramel much better. Agreeably weighty slugging whisky. 43%.

Kings Blended 3 Years Old (83) n21 t21.5 f20 b20.5. A young, chunky blend that you can chew forever. 40%. Speyside Distillers.

King's Crest Scotch Whisky 25 Years Old (83) n22 t22 f19 b20. A silky middle weight. The toffee-flat finish needs some attention because the softly estered nose and delivery is a honey-rich treat and deserves better. 40%. Speyside Distillers.

Label 5 Aged 18 Years (84.5) n20.5 t22 f21 b21. A big mouthful and mouth-feel. Has changed course since I last had this one. Almost a feel of rum to this with its estery sheen. Sweet, simple, easy dramming. 40%. La Martiniquaise, France.

Label Five Aged 18 Years L606133A (87) n22 compare the nose with a fruit smoothie and try and spot the difference....! Some wonderful bourbony notes accentuate the age; t22 the oils could not have been better placed and the integration of the soft grain and the slowly pulsing malt is a joy: simple but sumptuous; f21 just loses its sure footedness with an overdose of flattening caramel; b22 a lovely little blend with a genuinely first-rate mouthfeel. 43%.

Label 5 Classic Black L617456A (75) n18 t20 f18 b19. The off-key nose needs some serious re-working. Drop the caramel, though, and you would have a lot more character. Needs some buffing. 40%. The First Blending for La Martiniquaise, France.

⋙ **Label 5 Reserve No. 55 Single Cask** sherry cask finish, bott code no. E-1067 (75) n19 t20 f18 b18. The cordite on the nose suggests fireworks. But somehow we end up with a damp squib. 43% La Martiniquaise, France

Lang's Supreme Aged 5 Years (93.5) n23.5 outstanding barley-grain interplay, with the vanillas in fine form; all this underpinned by the most delicate of smoky, mildly seaweedy notes; t23.5 a gushing early barley delivery confirms the relatively high malt content: Glengoyne's grassy fingers can be felt caressing the tastebuds before the gentle grain vanillas begin to soften things further; f23 the smoke which made no effort to interfere with the barley-grain love in, reinvents itself as a soft, purring spice; the finale is as deft as it is beautifully weighted though the odd fractious sherry note can be heard and brings the score down a point; b23.5 every time I taste this the shape and structure has altered slightly. Here there is a fraction more smoke, installing a deeper confidence all round. This is blended whisky as it should be: Supreme in its ability to create shape and harmony. It is the kind of whisky I like to have easily to hand around the home, a blend for every mood. 40%. Ian Macleod Distillers Ltd.

The Last Drop (96.5) n24 aromas don't get older than this: positively Jurassic yet such is the balance between the sweeter honeycomb and still fertile oak, you can barely bring your nose from the glass. The oak is as old and rounded as an ancient shore-line tree worn smooth by a million waves. The predominant notes are 99.9% bourbony rather than Scotch-style, which is hardly surprising...; t25 oh my gosh....this blended Scotch has transmogrified into the finest bourbon you can imagine: one assumes the grain content (which was then 100% corn-based) was high. And just as well because you will be hard-pressed to find something this glorious in all Kentucky. The intensity of the liquorice and honey is sublime, as are the lime and kumquat notes; the thinned out Demerara notes ensure just the right degree of sweetness....outright perfection....; **f23.5** miraculously there is not a single hint of bitterness for all the age though a firmness has developed which again points towards a significant grain contribution. Though the complexity may have lessened, there is no let up in overall quality. A touch drier, a hint of spice, a delicious layer of sweetened vanilla... **b24** how do you mark a whisky like this? It is scotch. Yet every molecule of flavour and aroma is pure bourbon. I think I'll have to mark for quality, principally, which simply flies off the graph. I'll dock it a point for not being Scotch-like but I feel a pang of guilt for doing so. This, by the way, is a blend that was discovered by accident. It had been put away many years ago for marrying – and then forgotten about in a warehouse. The chances of finding another whisky quite of this ilk are remote, though I'm sure the hunters are now out. It is a one off and anyone who misses this one will kick themselves forever. Astonishing. Unforgettable. A freak whisky at its very peak. *52%. The Last Drop Distillers Ltd.*

Lauder's (74) n18 t21 f17 b18. Well, it's consistent: you can say that for it! As usual, fabulous delivery, but as for the rest....oh dear. *40% MacDuff International Ltd* ⊙ ⊙

⌐ **Lauder's Aged 12 Years (93.5) n23** seemingly matured in an orange grove; blossom is everywhere; the grains are clean and crisp, the barley is unmolested and precise; **t24** that is stunning: the most delicate orange delivery melting in with the grassy barley; the grains are bright and act as a sublime mirror to the proceedings; **f23** soft oaky vanillas with some marzipan and Jaffa cake ensuring the controlled sweetness persists to the end; **b23.5** this is every bit as magnificent as the standard Lauder's isn't. A new whisky, as now at 43%, and with the extra alcohol has come a fresh, superbly balanced and quite elegant whisky. *43%*

Loch Lomond Blended Scotch (89) n22 beautiful balance: delicate with a simmering weightiness. Mainly grain apparent, but the malt chips in sweetly; **t22.5** excellent double thrust of crispness and velvety yield. Again the grains lead the way with toffee not far behind but the malt offers soft, barley-sharp contours; **f22** vanilla and caramel but so clean; **b22.5** a fabulously improved blend: now clean and precise and though malt is seemingly at a premium, a fine interplay. *40% Loch Lomond Distillers* ⊙ ⊙

Lochranza (83.5) n21 t21.5 f21 b20. Pleasant, clean, but, thanks to the caramel, goes easy on the complexity. *40%. Isle of Arran.*

Logan (78.5) n19 t19 f20 b19.5. Entirely drinkable but a bit heavy-handed with the grains and caramel. It appears Logan's run continues, despite the fact this was meant to have reached the end of the line. *40%. Diageo.*

Lombard's Gold Label (88) n22 t22 f22 b22. Excellently weighted with some wonderful honeycomb and spice making their mark. *40%. Lombards Brands.*

⌐ **Lord Hynett (88.5) n21.5** a bit messy, but there is hope... **t23** which is fully justified by the enormity of the delivery. A bare knuckle fighter of a blend with a sublimely haphazard, random deliciousness; honey and spices don't give shape but purpose; **f22** long, spiced toffee; **b22** just perfect after a shitty day. *40% Loch Lomond Distillers*

⌐ **Lord Scot (77.5) n18.5 t20 f19.5 b19.5.** A touch cloying but the mocha fudge ensures a friendly enough ride. *40% Loch Lomond Distillers*

Mackessack Premium Aged 8 Years (87.5) n21.5 t23 f21.5 b21.5. Claims a high Speyside content and the early character confirms it. Shoots itself in the foot, rather, by overdoing the caramel and flattening the finish. *40%. Mackessack Giovenetti. Italian Market*

Mac Na Mara Rum Finish (93) n22 as is often the case, the rum has hardened the aroma; **t24** beautifully crisp with fragile malts clashing with equally crisp barley; the touch of golden syrup works wonders; **f23** serious depth to the malt; the grains soften out with vanilla; **b24** this is high quality blending, and the usage of the rum appears to have retained the old Mac Na Mara style. Sublime. *40%. Praban na Linne.*

MacQueens (89) n21.5 a beautiful and very clever smudge of smoke gives backbone and vibrancy to an otherwise clean and delicate nose; **t22.5** lovely body and weight: voluptuous and silky, again with that delicate smoke intermingling with a caressing grain and sharper Speyside touch; **f22.5** long, beautifully structured with a soft, yielding oiliness that allows those soft sweeter notes to cling; **b22.5** I am long enough in the tooth now to remember blends like this found in quiet country hotels in the furthest-flung reaches of the Highlands beyond a generation ago. A wonderfully old-fashioned, traditional one might say, blend of a type that is getting harder and harder to find. I could drink this all day every day. Well, not really, but you know what I mean... *40%. Quality Spirits International.*

Master of Malt 8 Years Old (88) n22.5 t22.5 f21 b22. Understated and refined. 40%.

Matisse 12 Years Old (90.5) n23 vanilla and citrus make comfortable bedfellows; dry Lubeck marzipan perfects the balance; t23 mouth-watering with little grain evidence: the malt is clear, almost shrill; f22 gentle vanillas and caramels; the spices arrive late; b22.5 moved up yet another notch as this brand continues its development. Much more clean-malt oriented with a Speyside-style to the fore. Majestic and charming. 40%. Matisse Spirits Co Ltd.

Matisse 21 Years Old (86) n23 t22 f20 b21. Begins breathtakingly on the nose, with a full array of exotic fruit showing the older bourbon casks up to max effect. Nothing wrong with the early delivery, which offers a touch of honeycomb on the grain. But the caramel effect on the finish stops everything in its tracks. Soft and alluring, all the same. 40%.

Matisse Old (85.5) n20 t23 f21 b21.5. Appears to improve each time I come across it. The nose is a bit on the grimy side and the finish disappears under a sea of caramel. But the delivery works deliciously, with a chewy weight which highlights the sweeter malts. 40%..

Matisse Royal (81) n19 t22 f20 b20. Pleasant, if a little clumsy. Extra caramel appears to have scuppered the spice. 40%. Matisse Spirits Co Ltd.

McArthurs (89.5) n22 soft smoke rumbles about like distant thunder on a summer's day: the grains and light barley are bright; t22.5 silky delivery with a slow injection of peat as the storm moves overhead; the degree of sweetness to the soft vanillas is sublime; f22 gentle fade with the smoke rumbling though; b23 one of the most improved blends on the market. The clever use of the peat is exceptional. 40%. Inverhouse Distillers.

Michael Jackson Special Memorial Blend bottled 2009 (89) n24 superb fruit, both grapey and citrussy, controls the shape of the vanilla which is closely tucked in behind; soft but not for a second docile t22.5 full and fat, but never weighty, again there is a light touch to the juiciness; f20.5 a touch of bitterness; b22 whenever Michael and I had a dram together, his would either be massively sherried or equally well endowed with smoke. This is neither, so an odd tribute. Even so, there is more than enough here for him to savour, though I'm not sure what he would have made of the finish. 43%. Berry Bros & Rudd. 1000 bottles

Mitchell's Glengyle Blend (86.5) n21.5 t22 f21.5 b21.5. A taste of history here, as this is the first blend ever to contain malt from the new Campbeltown distillery, Glengyle. Something of a departure in style from the usual Mitchell blends, which tended to put the accent on a crisper grain. Interestingly, here they have chosen one at least that is soft and voluptuous enough to absorb the sharper malt notes. 40%. Springbank Distillers.

Monarch of the Glen (83) n20 t20 f22 b21. Elegant young whisky with a sweetish tinge and a lovely mixture of cocoa and barley at the death. 40%. Quality Spirits International.

❖ **Montrose** (74.5) n18 t20 f18 b18.5. A battling performance but bitter defeat in the end. A bad year for Montrose: first they finish ten points adrift of the rest of the Scottish Football League....and now this... 40% Burn Stewart

Morrisons The Best 8 Years Old (87) n21 a clumsier aroma than last year with the toast, grain and caramel still to the fore, but the vital honey and soft smoke now at a premium. Decent, but no longer great; t23 weighty stuff with the grains showing a touch of class but the malt really fighting to battle through the toffee; the spices are superb, though f22 long, pretty thick and chewy in places and at last some hints of oak amid the burnt fudge; some bitter notes where last year there had been none; b21 I could almost weep: last year this was a blend to delight and win over converts. It was the whisky I was telling everyone to go out and get. This year, some of the traces of its excellence are still there, it remains highly drinkable, but that greatness has been lost in a tide of caramel. Yes, there was caramel used last year, but it had not crossed that fine line: here it has and paid the price and all the high notes have been ruthlessly flattened. When oh when, are people going to understand that you can't just tip this stuff into whisky to up the colour – even minimally as in the case here - without causing a detrimental effect on the product? Is anybody listening? Does anyone care??? Someone has gone to great lengths to create a sublime blend – to see it wasted. Natural colour and this'd be an experience to die for. 40%

❖ **Morrisons Fine Blended Whisky** (77) n18.5 t21 f18.5 b19. Sweet, chewy but a few rough edges. 40% Wm Morrison Supermarket

Muirheads (83) n19 t22 f23 b21. A beautifully compartmentalised dram that integrates superbly, if that makes sense. 40%. MacDonald & Muir.

Northern Scot (68) n16 t18 f17 b17. Heading South bigtime. 40%. Bruce and Co. for Tesco.

Old Crofter Special Old Scotch Whisky (83) n18 t22 f21 b22. A very decent blend, much better than the nose suggests thanks to some outstanding, velvety grain and wonderfully controlled sweetness. 40%. Smith & Henderson for London & Scottish International.

Old Masters "Freemason Whisky" (92) n24 t23 f22 b23 A high quality blend that doesn't stint on the malt. The nose, in particular, is sublime. 40%. Supplied online. Lombard Brands

Old Mull (84.5) n22 t21 f20.5 b21. With dates and walnuts clambering all over the nose, very much in the house style. But this one is a shade oilier than most – and certainly on how it used to be – and has dropped a degree or two of complexity. That said, enjoyable stuff with the spices performing well, as does the lingering sweetness. 40%.

Old Parr 12 Years Old (91.5) n21.5 firm and flinty with the grains comfortably in control; t23.5 no surprise with the mouthwatering juice: the grains help the barley and soft fruit element hit top gear; delicate, light, teasing yet always substantial; f23 mocha dominates with the vaguest hint of gentle smoke; the weight, length and complexity are stupendous b23.5 perhaps on about the fourth of fifth mouthful, the penny drops that this is not just exceptionally good whisky: it is blending Parr excellence... 40%. Diageo

Old Parr Aged 15 Years (84) n19 t22 f21 b22. Absolutely massive sherry input here. Some of it is of the highest order. The nose, reveals, however, that some isn't... 43%.

Old Parr Classic 18 Years Old (84.5) n21 t21.5 f21 b21. Decent, yet in the Old Parr scheme of things, just doesn't do it for me. A real jumbled, mixed bag with fruit and barley falling over each other and the grains offering little sympathy. Enough to enjoy, but with Old Parr, one expects a little more... 46%. Diageo.

Old Parr Superior 18 Years Old batch no. L5171 **(97)** n25 here's a nose with just about a touch of everything: especially clever smoke which gives weight but allows apples and bourbon to filter through at will. Perfect weight and harmony while the complexity goes off the scales; t25 voluptuous body, at times silky but the grains offer enough jagged edges for a degree of bite and bourbon; mouthwatering and spicey with the peats remaining on a slow burner. Toasty and so, so chewey; f23 the vanilla is gentle and a counter to the firmness of the combined oak and grain. A flinty, almost reedy finish with spices and cocoa very much in evidence; b24 year in, year out, this blend just gets better and better. This bottling struck me as a possible Whisky of the Year, but perhaps only an outsider. Familiarity, though, bred anything but contempt and over the passing months I have tried to get to the bottom of this truly great whisky. Blended whisky has long needed a champion. This grand old man looks just the chap. This is a worthy, if unexpected (even to me), Jim Murray' Whisky Bible 2007 World Whisky of the Year. 43%. Diageo/MacDonald Greenlees.

Old Smuggler (85.5) n21 t22 f21 b21.5. A much sharper act than its Allied days with a new honeyed-maple syrup thread which is rather delightful. Could still do with toning down the caramel, though, to brighten the picture further. 40% Campari, France ☉ ☉

⋅∴⋅ **Old Stag (75.5)** n18.5 t20 f18.5 b18.5. Wants shooting. 40% Loch Lomond Distillers

The Original Mackinlay (83) n19 t21 f22 b21. Upped a gear since I last tasted this. Still a hard nose to overcome and the toffee remains in force for those addicted to fudge. But now a degree of bite and ballast appears to have been added, giving more of a story to the experience. Having said that, some 30 years ago this was my daily dram. In style it has moved away significantly. 40%. Whyte & Mackay Distillers Ltd.

Passport (83) n22 t19 f21 b21. It looks as though Chivas have decided to take the blend away from its original sophisticated, Business Class J&B/Cutty Sark, style for good now, as they have continued this decently quaffable but steerage quality blend with its big caramel kick and chewy, rather than lithe, body. 40%. Chivas.

v **Passport (91)** n23 crisp and clean, there are Speyside-style malts positively leaping from the glass. Salivating even before it reaches the lips, the grassy character absolutely exudes elegance; t23.5 spot on grain-barley integration, with the malts always in control; the clarity of the malt allows for a beautiful citrus, mildly strawberry fruitiness to thrive and the oaky vanillas to build into a mildly spiced middle; f22 drier, a little contribution from the caramel, but the vanillas hold out fine; b22.5 easily one of the better versions I have come across for a long time and impressively true to its original style. 40%. Bottled in Brazil.

v **Passport (91)** n22.5 classic grain nip; t22 firm, crisp Speyside-style juiciness; f23.5 beautiful development of spice and prickle; b23.5 a lovely version closer to original style with markedly less caramel impact and grittier grain. An old-fashioned treat. 40%. Ecuador.

Parkers (78) n17 t22 f20 b19. The nose has regressed, disappearing into ever more caramel, yet the mouth-watering lushness on the palate remains and the finish now holds greater complexity and interest. 40%. Angus Dundee.

Prince Charlie Special Reserve (73) n17 t20 f18 b18. Thankfully not as cloyingly sweet as of old, but remains pretty basic. 40%. Somerfield, UK.

Prince Charlie Special Reserve 8 Years Old (81) n18 t20 f22 b21. A lumbering bruiser of a dram; keeps its trademark shapelessness but the spices and lush malt ensure an enjoyable experience. 40%. Somerfield, UK.

Real Mackenzie (80) n17 t21 f21 b21. As ever, try and ignore the dreadful nose and get cracking with the unsubtle, big bruising delivery. A thug in a glass. 40%. Diageo.

Real Mackenzie Extra Smooth (81) n18 t22 f20 b21. Once, the only time the terms "Real Mackenzie" and "Extra Smooth" were ever uttered in the same sentence was if someone was talking about the barman. Now it is a genuine descriptor. Which is odd, because when Diageo sent me a sample of their blend last year it was a snarling beast ripping at the leash. This, by contrast, is a whimpering sop. "Killer? Where are you...???" 40%. Diageo.

Red Seal 12 Years Old (82) n19 t22 f20 b21. Charming, mouthwatering. But toffee numbs it down towards the finish. 40%. Charles Wells UK.

Reliance PL (76) n18 t20 f19 b19. Some of the old spiciness evident. But has flattened out noticeably. 43%. Diageo.

Robert Burns (85) n20 t22.5 f21 b21.5. Skeletal and juicy: very little fat and gets to the mouthwatering point pretty quickly. Genuine fun. 40%. Isle of Arran.

Robertson's of Pitlochry Rare Old Blended (83) n21 t20 f21 b21. Handsome grain bite with a late malty flourish. Classic light blend available only from Pitlochry's landmark whisky shop. 40%

The Royal & Ancient bott code L19.12.06 **(87)** n20 disappointing, dull toffee; t23 fat mouthfeel with a beautiful burnished honey follow-through; no shortage of burnt fudge and biting spice; f22 toffee has replaced the usual Demerara; the grain remains firm and friendly; b22 what a shame: just a shade of carelessness with the caramel has shaved off the finer points. Last year a staggeringly good blend; this year simply very good, indeed!! 40%.

Royal Castle 12 Years Old (84.5) n22 t22 f20 b20.5. Busy nose and delivery with much to chew over. Entirely enjoyable, and seems better each time you taste it. Even so, the finish crumbles a bit. 40%. Quality Spirits International.

Royal Household (90.5) n21.5 one is joyous of the occasion of the arrival of the smoke and all those other smaller, yet no less important constituents, such as the barley, grain and oak, which make such a pleasing experience; t23 my tastebuds and I are entirely delighted with the sophistication shown by the blenders by harmonizing the spices and soft peats to wonderful effect. One finds the sweetness towards the middle entirely to one's satisfaction; f23 once again one finds the soft sugars a pleasure and it is impossible not to be impressed with the length to which, quite literally, this whisky goes to prove its very good breeding; b23 we are amused. 43%. Diageo.

Royal Salute 21 Years Old (92.5) n23 has persisted the gentle, exotic fruit but less lush here with much more punch and poke; it even seems that the smoke which had been missing in recent years has returned, but in shadowy form only; t23.5 yep! Definitely more bite these days with the grains having a much greater input, for all the juiciness, and the vanilla striking home earlier. Makes for a decent sweet/dry middle, the sweetness supplied by boiled sweet candy; f23 plenty of cocoa and the very lightest dab of something smoky; b23.5 if you are looking for the velvety character of yore, forget it. This one comes with some real character and is much the better for it. The grain, in particular, excels. 40%. Chivas.

Royal Salute The Hundred Cask Selection Limited Reserve No. 3 (90) n22 t23 f22 b23 Can a blend be too charming and well behaved? Elegance, or what? 40%. Chivas Brothers.

Royal Salute The Hundred Cask Selection Limited Release No. 5 (93) n22.5 t23.5 f23 b24 This one reminds me of certain Japanese blends where there is a profound edge to the lighter malts which cut into the oak: a style rarely adopted in Scotland but employed here. A sophisticated blend impossible not to love. 40%. Chivas.

Royal Salute The Hundred Cask Selection Limited Release No. 7 (92) n22 a mixture of Caperdonich-esque exotic fruit and slightly over cooked, lactic oak masquerading as rice pudding; t23.5 the silky glide onto the palate you'd expect from the nose and previous experience; some groaning oak arrives pretty early on; f23 sweet, muscovado-sprinkled cocoa; b23.5 it would be rude to ask how old some of the whiskies that go into making this one up are...As blends go, its entire countenance talks about great age and elegance. And does so with a clipped accent. 40%. Chivas.

Royal Silk Reserve (93) n22 classically light yet richly bodied under the clear, crisp ethereal grains. The freshly-cut-grass maltiness balances perfectly; t24 crystal clear grains dovetail with intense, mouthwatering and refreshingly sweet malt to create a perfect pitch while the middle is heavier and livelier than you might expect with the very faintest echo of peat; f24 delicate oils and wonderful grainy-vanilla ensures improbable length for something so light. Beautiful spices and traces of cocoa offer the last hurrah. Sheer bliss; b23 I named this the best newcomer of 2001 and it hasn't let me down. A session blend for any time of the day, this just proves that you don't need piles of peat to create a blend of genuine stature. 40%. ☺

⋅⋅⋅ Sainsbury's Basics Blended Scotch Whisky (78.5) n19 t20.5 f19.5 b19.5. "A little less refined, great for mixing," says the label. Frankly, there are a lot of malts out there far less enjoyable than this. Don't be scared to have straight: it's more than decent enough. 40%

Sainsbury's Finest Old Matured Aged 8 Years bott code L7 109 **(83) n20 t21 f21 b21.** Reasonable fare with firm grain and a juicy depth. Lots of toffee. *40%*

Sainsbury's Scotch Whisky (82) n19 t21 f20 b22. Thinned out significantly over the last year allowing a pleasing degree of complexity amid the agreeable chewability. A great improvement: pretty good, indeed! *40%. Sainsbury's, UK.*

Sandy Mac (76) n18 t20 f19 b19. Basic, decent blend that's chunky and raw. *40%. Diageo.*

Scots Earl (76.5) n18 t20 f19 b19.5. It's name is Earl. And it must have upset someone in a previous life. Always thrived on its engaging disharmony. But just a tad too syrupy now. *40% Loch Lomond Distillers* ⊙⊙

Scottish Chief (77) n19 t19 f19 b20. This is one big-bodied chief, and not given to taking prisoners. *40%. Quality Spirits International.*

Scottish Collie (77) n19 t19 f19 b20. Caramel still, but a Collie with a bit more bite. *40%.*

Scottish Collie 12 Years Old (85) n22 t22 f20 b21. On the cusp of a really classy blend here but the bitterness on the finish loses serious Brownie points. *40%. Quality Spirits Int. UK.*

Scottish Collie 18 Years Old (92) n24 the most gentle honey-ginger theme delights; aided and abetted by evidence of some very old grain which radiates succulent, over-ripe exotic fruit amid the drier oaks and gathering spices: a real, rounded charmer; **t23** those sweeter notes apparent on the nose are at the vanguard of a sublime procession of silk-edged barley; myriad sugar-coated notes ranging from acacia honey to maple syrup and brilliantly balanced by the slow march of drier oakier tones; **f22** remains soft and free from the usual Scottish Collie bitterness, though the toffee apparent sits comfortably with the toasty oak; **b23** this, honey-led beaut would be a winner even at Crufts: an absolute master class of how an old, yet light and unpeated blend should be. No discord whatsoever between the major elements and not a single hint of over-aging. Superb. *40%. Quality Spirits International, UK.*

Scottish Glory dist 02, bott 05 **(85) n21 t21 f22 b21.** An improved blend now bursting with vitality. The ability of the grain to lift the barley is very engaging. *40%. Duncan Taylor. 960 bottles.*

Scottish Leader 3 Years Old (77) n19 t20 f18.5 b19.5. Still absolutely no pretensions about this from nose to finish. A bit rough and ready in places, but there is something attractively old-fashioned about it all. If anything, the toffee element has increased. *40% Burn Stewart.*

Scottish Leader Supreme 3 Years Old (83) n21 t20 f21.5 b20.5. Much spicier and weightier than of old. One of the most characterful, chewable blends around, and not just because of the extra toffee: there is even evidence of some smoke in there. Wonderful mocha at the death: love it! *40% Burn Stewart.*

Scottish Leader 12 Years Old (82.5) n19.5 t21.5 f20.5 b21. Had a bit of a character makeover of late. The early fruit gets a little lost in the at times sharp, then ultra soft confusion which follows On about fourth or fifth tasting of this – it needs that many to work out what is happening – it does begin to grow on you *40% Burn Stewart*

⸬ **Scottish Leader 30 Years Old (87) n23.5** stylish: fruit and honey in pretty even measures. Not only is it soft but there is neither spice nor an alcohol prickle to disrupt the silky passage; **t21.5** melt-in-the-mouth delivery with toffee and raisin theme; **f20.5** way too much caramel; a touch of bitterness creeps in; **b21.5** perhaps a little too docile ever to be a great whisky, but the nose is something rather special. A bit of attention on the finish and this could be a real corker. *40% Burn Stewart*

⸬ **Scottish Leader Select (91.5) n23** gorgeous honey with a buzzing spice accompaniment; **t23.5** beautiful delivery. Those honeys and spices gang together to make a delightful statement with the grains offering a beautiful custard-rich support; **f22.5** firmer, but the sweetness persists; **b22.5** had to do a James Finlayson double take on this one. Don't make the mistake of thinking this is just the 40% with three extra percentage points of alcohol. This appears to be an entirely different bottling with an entirely different personality the characters including a few handsome leads. A delight. *43% Burn Stewart. For the South African Market.*

⸬ **Scottish Leader Select (74) n18.5 t19 f18 b18.5.** I assume the leader is Major Disharmony. *40% Burn Stewart*

Scottish Piper (80) n20 t20 f20 b20. A light, mildly- raw, sweet blend with lovely late vanilla intonation. *40%.*

Scottish Prince (83.5) n21 t22 f20 b20.5. Muscular, but agreeably juicy. *40%.*

Scottish Reel (78.5) n19 t19 f20 b19.5. Non fussy with an attractive bite, as all such blends should boast. *40%. London & Scottish International.*

Scottish Rill (85) n20 t20.5 f22.5 b22. Refreshing yet earthy. *40%. Quality Spirits Int.*

Something Special (85) n21.5 t22 f20.5 b21. The marketing guys missed a trick here. If only they had teamed up with Waddington's and sponsored Cluedo. Colonel Plum. In the Library. With the Something Special Bottle. Let's face it, the one litre bottle of this has to be one of the most fearsome implements that one can legally buy over the counter today.

However, its contents could not be more different if it tried. Mollycoddled by toffee, any murderous tendencies seem to have been fudged away, leaving just the odd moment of attractive complexity. Enough to make you think that there is a hit man in there somewhere just trying to get out... 40%. *Chivas.*

Something Special Premium Aged 15 Years (89) n22 a vague, distant smokiness sits prettily with some fruity caramel; **t23** boisterous delivery with unshackled malt adding a wonderful, zesty spiciness amid much more mouth-watering Speyside-style fresh grass; the grain offers the desired cut-glass firmness; **f21** lots of vanilla and too much caramel, but remains busy and entertaining; **b23** a hugely enjoyable, fun whisky which pops around the palate like a crackerjack. Fabulous malt thread and some curious raisiny/sultana fruitiness, too. A blend-lover's blend. 40%. *Chivas/ Hill Thompson, Venezuela.*

Spar Finest Reserve (90.5) n21.5 fabulously clean, young grain offering butterscotch and toffee; elsewhere something earthy rumbles; **t22.5** brilliantly subtle delivery with silky grains ensnared in a sweet shell; towards the middle chocolate fudge and a distinctive smoky rumble forms; **f23.5** one of the best "supermarket" finishes to be found with a stunning array of clean, dapper smoke notes which cling, like softly oiled limpets, to the tastebuds for an improbably long time: lush and beautifully layered, this is masterful blending...; **b23** one of Britain best value for money blends with an honest (or as honest as any whisky with caramel can be) charm which revels in the clean high quality grain and earthier malts which work so well together. The mouthfeel and body are particularly impressive, especially the finish, complete with soft, smoky undertones. Greatly improved even on the last very good sample I came across. Very curiously, the buyer, or whoever, told us quite forcibly that he didn't want this whisky in my book and wouldn't send a sample. In fact he was so adamant about it his tone rather hurt and offended the feelings of my charming and good-natured researcher, Ali. Oh well, Mr. Buyer: isn't life full of disappointments! I'll bang the gong for this lovely whisky even if you won't, so that your customers and shareholders will benefit at least. 40%.

Stewart's Old Blended (93) n22.5 apples and date and walnut cake; clean and more delicate than the early weight suggests; **t24** sublime silky delivery with the slow erection of a fruity platform; the yielding grain cushions the juicy malt aspects; **f23** bitters out as some oak makes its play but firmer malt and molasses compensate superbly; **b23.5** really lovely whisky for those who like to close their eyes, contemplate and have a damned good chew. Voluptuous and as that chunky style goes, absolutely top of its league. 40%.

Swords (78) n20 t21 f18 b19. Beefed up somewhat with some early smoke thrusting through and rapier grains to follow. 40%. *Morrison Bowmore.*

Talisman 5 Years Old (85.5) n22 t22 f20.5 b21. Unquestionably an earthier, weightier version of what was once a Speyside romp. Soft peats also add extra sweetness. 40%.

Teacher's Highland Cream (90) n23 firm, flinty grain; a tad fruity with gently smoked malt-ensuring weight; **t23** mouth-filling with a tender sweetness; the grains seem softer than the nose suggests; **f22** toffee and lazy smoke; **b22** not yet back to its best but a massive improvement on the 2005 bottlings. So harder grains to accentuate the malt will bring it closer to the classic of old. 40%.

v **Teacher's Highland Cream (90) n23** grain dominates, but not the old-fashioned sharp Dumbarton style. This is softer, sweeter with a topping of thick vanilla and butterscotch and delicate barley...where's the famous smoke...??? It's there, but the most distant echo; almost a dull background throb – for some Teacher's diehards, it is too well integrated....; **t22.5** as silky a delivery as the nose promises. Again the grain comes through loud and clear with the playful malts hanging on to its coat-tails. Only towards the middle do the two combine, and rather attractively and with style; **f22** much more spiced with a decided vanilla twirl; still virtually no smoke worthy of the name other than a vague oiliness; **b22.5** a very curious, seriously high grade, variant. Although the Ardmore distillery is on the label (though for the life of me I don't recognize it!), it is the only place it can really be seen. Certainly - the least smoky Teacher's I've come across in 35 years of drinking the stuff: the smoke is there, but adds only ballast rather than taking any form of lead. But the grain is soft and knits with the malts with ease to make for a sweeter, much more lush version than the rest of the world may recognize. 40%

Tesco Scotch Whisky Finest Reserve Aged 12 Years (80) n19 t21 f20 b20. A thumping, thudding blend as hard as the granite rocks over which the waters ran to the Speyside distilleries used in the recipe. Value-for-money-wise, not a bad blend at all but for all the charm and mouth-watering properties of the malt, the grains are seismic. 40%.

Tesco Special Reserve (80) n16 t22 f21 b21. The sweaty armpit nose is relieved by the massively improved, rich, chewy and silky body. 40%. *Tesco UK.*

Tesco Value Scotch Whisky (83) n19 t21 f22 b21. Young and genuinely refreshing whisky. Without the caramel this really would be a little darling. 40%

⋰⋰ Traquair (78) n19 t21 f19 b19. Young, but offering a substantial mouthful including attractive smoke. 46% Burn Stewart

Ushers Green Stripe (85) n19 t22.5 f21.5 b22. Upped a notch or two in all-round quality. The juicy theme and clever weight is highly impressive and enjoyable. 43%. Diageo.

VAT 69 (84.5) n20 t22 f21 b21.5. Has thickened up in style: weightier, more macho, much more to say and a long way off that old lightweight. A little cleaning up wouldn't go amiss. 40%. Diageo.

White Horse (90.5) n22 busy, with a shade more active grain than normal. But the smoky depth is there, as is a gentle hickory, butterscotch and fruity thread; a few bruising malts can be picked up, too; t23 the usual sensual delivery, at first almost like a young JW Black, thanks to that soft billowing out towards the gentle honeys and juices; as it reaches the middle the clunking, muddied fist of some volumous malts can be easily detected; f22.5 gets no less complex or more subtle as it develops; playful spices dovetail with vanilla while the smoke reinforces the backbone; b23 a malt which has subtlety changed shape. Not just the smoke which gives it weight, but you get the feeling that some of Diageo's less delicate malts have been sent in to pack a punch. As long as they are kept in line, as is the case here – just – we can all enjoy a very big blend. 40%. Diageo.

White Horse Aged 12 Years (86) n21 t23 f21 b21. enjoyable, complex if not always entirely harmonious. For instance, the apples and grapes on the nose appear on a limb from the grain and caramel and nothing like the thoroughbred of old. Lighter, more flaccid and caramel dominated. Just don't recognize it from the glorious beast that so often sat within arm's length of me in my home. 43%. Diageo.

Whyte & Mackay 'The Thirteen' 13 Year Old (92) n22.5 a fruity barley edge to this one; soft and enticing; t23.5 a silky, mouth-watering delivery with some instant spices ensuring an immediate extra dimension. The sugars are muscovado toned, but with a pinch of molasses as a delicate bourbony sub plot develops below the tingling peppers; f23 drier with some beautifully integrated vanillas and mocha: clever stuff; b23 try this and your luck'll be in... easily the pick of the W&M blended range. 40%. Whyte & Mackay Distillers Ltd.

Whyte & Mackay Luxury 19 Year Old (84.5) n21 t22 f20 b21.5. A pleasant house style chewathon. Nutty, biting but with a tang. 40%. Whyte & Mackay Distillers Ltd.

Whyte & Mackay Supreme 22 Year Old (87) n21 t23 f20.5 b22.5. Ignore the nose and finish and just enjoy the early ride. 43%.

Whyte & Mackay Oldest 30 Year Old (87.5) n23 blackjack candy, punchy vanilla and apples: heavy booted but all rather sexy... t23 the usual W&M full throttle delivery with fruity flavours galore; f20 the usual W&M finale which is all a bit flat, tangy and furry; b21.5 what exasperating whisky this is. So many good things about it, but.... 45%.

Whyte & Mackay Original Aged Blended 40 Years Old (93) n23 anyone remember fruit fudge? Well, this is it in its toasted form; with burnt raisin and a Melton Hunt Cake. So yummy...!! t24 appears to have some Fettercairn in there: nonsense malt when young, but when older opens up and delivers the kind of sublime, intense juicy dates to chew on here; also the grains begin to show a gossamer touch and, finally, a soft pastel-shaded barley sweetens the proceedings as the oak arrives; f22 ultra-light and melt-in-the mouth b24 I admit, when I nosed and tasted this at room temp, not a lot happened. Pretty, but closed. But once warmed in the hand up to full body temperature, it was obvious that Richard Paterson had created a quite wonderful monster of a blend offering so many avenues to explore that the mind almost explodes. Well done RP for creating something that further proves, and in such magnitude, just how warmth can make an apparently ordinary whisky something bordering genius. 45%

Whyte & Mackay Special (84.5) n20 t23 f20 b21.5. This has to be the ultimate mood blend. If you are looking for a big-flavoured dram and with something approaching a vicious left uppercut, this might be a useful bottle to have on hand. The nose, I'm afraid, has not improved over the years but there appears to be compensation with the enormity and complexity of the delivery, a veritable orgy of big, oily, juicy, murky flavours and tones if ever there was one. You cannot but like it, in the same way as you may occasionally like rough sex. But if you are looking for a delicate dram to gently kiss you and caress your fever'd brow, then leave well alone. 40%.

William Grant's 12 Years Old Bourbon Cask (90.5) n23 lively and floral. The drier notes suggest chalky oak but the sweet spiciness balances beautifully; t22.5 flinty textured with both malts and grains pinging around the teeth with abandon; f22 remains light yet with a clever, crisp sweetness keeping the weightier oaks in check; b23 very clever blending where balance is the key. 40%

William Grant's 15 Years Old (85) n21 t23 f20 b21. Grain and, later, caramel dominates but the initial delivery reveals the odd moment of sheer genius and complexity on max revs. 43%.

William Grant's 25 Years Old (95.5) n23.5 some serious oak, but chaperoned by top quality oloroso, itself thinned by firm and graceful grain; t24 sheer quality: complexity by the shovel-load as juicy fruits interact with darting, crisp barley; again the grain shows elegance both sharpening increasingly mouth-watering malt and softening the oak; **f24** medium length, but not a single sign of fatigue: the sweet barley runs and runs and some jammy fruits charm. Just to cap it all, some wonderful spices dazzle and a touch of low roast Java enriches; **b24** absolutely top-rank blending that appears to maximize every last degree of complexity. Most astonishing, though, is its sprightly countenance: even Scottish footballing genius Ally MacLeod struggled to send out Ayr Utd. sides with this kind of brio. And that's saying something! A gem. *40%* ⊙ ⊙

William Grant's 100 US Proof Superior Strength (92) n23 sublime chocolate lime nose, decent oak; **t24** big mouth arrival, lush and fruity with the excellent extra grain bite you might expect at this strength, just an extra degree of spice takes it into even higher orbit than before; **f22** back to chocolate again with a soft fruit fade; **b23** a fruitier drop now than it was in previous years but no less supremely constructed. *50% (100 US proof).*

William Grant's Ale Cask Reserve (89) n21 t23 f22 b23. A real fun blend that is just jam-packed with jagged malty notes. The hops were around more on earlier bottlings, but watch out for them. Nothing pint-sized about this: this is a big blend and very true in flavour/shape to the original with just a delicious shading of grain to really up the complexity. *40%.*

William Grant's Family Reserve (94) n25 this, to me, is the perfect nose to any blend: harmonious and faultless. There is absolutely everything here in just-so proportions: a bit of snap and bite from the grain, teasing sweet malts, the faintest hint of peat for medium weight, strands of oak for dryness, fruit for lustre. Even Ardbeg doesn't pluck my strings like this glass of genius can; **t23** exceptionally firm grain helps balance the rich, multi-layered malty tones. The sub-plot of burnt raisins and peek-a-boo peat add further to the intrigue and complexity (if it doesn't bubble and nip around the mouth you have a rare sub-standard bottling); **f22** a hint of caramel can be detected amid returning grains and soft cocoa tones: just so clean and complex; **b24** there are those puzzled by my obvious love affair with blended whisky - both Scotch and Japanese - at a time when malts are all the rage. But take a glass of this and carefully nurture and savour it for the best part of half an hour and you may begin to see why I believe this to be the finest art form of whisky. For my money, this brand - brilliantly kept in tip-top shape by probably the world's most naturally gifted blender - is the closest thing to the blends of old and, considering it is pretty ubiquitous, it defies the odds for quality. It is a dram with which you can start the day and end it: one to keep you going at low points in between, or to celebrate the victories. It is the daily dram that has everything. *40%.*

William Grant's Sherry Cask Reserve (82) n20 t22 f20 b20. Raspberry jam and cream from time to time. Attractive, but somewhat plodding dram that's content in second gear. *40%.*

William Lawson's Finest (85) n18.5 t22.5 f22 b22. Not only has the label become more colourful, but so, too, has the whisky. However that has not interfered with the joyous old-fashioned grainy bite. A complex and busy blend from the old charm school. *40%* ⊙ ⊙

William Lawson's Scottish Gold Aged 12 Years (89) n22 t23 f22 b22. For years Lawson's 12 was the best example of the combined wizardry of clean grain, unpeated barley and good bourbon cask that you could find anywhere in the world: a last-request dram before the firing squad. Today it is still excellent, but just another sherried blend. What's that saying about if it's not being broke...? *40%* ⊙ ⊙

Windsor 12 Years Old (81) n20 t21 f20 b20. Thick, walloped-on blend that you can stand a spoon in. Hard at times to get past the caramel. *40%. Diageo.*

Windsor Aged 17 Years Super Premium (89) n23 a fabulous aroma which bombards the nose with both luxurious grain and a hint of something smoky above the butter-honey theme; **t22** sweet, as is the house style, with a Demerara coating to the crisp malt and gathering vanilla; silky and voluptuous throughout; **f22** a gentle, soft textured landing with an echo of spice; **b22** still a little on the safe side for all its charm and quality. An extra dose of complexity would lift this onto another level altogether. *40%. Diageo.*

Windsor 21 Years Old (90) n20 fruity and weighty but something a bit lactic and lethargic from some old bourbon casks has crept in; **t23** excellent oils surround the silk to help amplify the intensity of the fruit and drifting smoke; **f24** some spiciness that shows towards the middle really takes off now as drying vanilla counters the sweet grains; **b23** recovers fabulously from the broken nose and envelopes the palate with a silky-sweet style unique to the Windsor scotch brand. Excellent. *40%. Diageo.*

Ye Monks (86) n20 t23 f21.5 b21.5. Just hope they are praying for less caramel to maximize the complexity. Still, a decent spicy chew and outstanding bite which is great fun and worth finding when in South America. *40%. Diageo.*

Yokozuna Blended 3 Years Old (79.5) n18.5 t20.5 f20 b20.5. It appears the Mongols are gaining a passion for thick, sweet, toffeed, oily, slightly feinty whisky. For a nation breastfed on airag, this'll be a doddle... *40%. Speyside Distillers. Mongolian market.*

Irish Whiskey

As is the way with Empires, they grow then blossom and, finally, fall. And so it is now in Ireland.

Until the advent of the Cooley distillery in the late '80s, all Ireland's whiskey was made under the umbrella of Irish Distillers. And for a short period in the '90s it looked like it would be so again when ID tried to consume Cooley whole. But they choked on it and had to spit out when the Irish Government ruled against the move in the interests of competition. Cooley continues to this day as a maverick distiller helping forge new interest and markets in Irish whiskey.

That left Irish Distillers' owners, Pernod Ricard, with Ireland's two other distilleries. In the south they held Midleton, near Cork, where their stupendous pot still whiskey is made. And in the north, just two miles from the cliffs of Antrim, the malt distillery of Old Bushmills dating all the way back to 1784. That was until, as part of Great Whisky Merry-Go-Round following Pernod's acquisition of Allied and all the resultant sell-ons, Diageo parted with the stunning sum of £200 million and in return got The Old Bushmills Distillery (Established 1784) and all its satellite blends and brands.

Forever, it seemed, Irish Distillers' blender Billy Leighton had been travelling to Midleton and back to Bushmills in a dual role as blender for both companies, though of course being an Irish Distillers man through and through but helping Diageo create their own blending team. With job accomplished at his spiritual home of Bushmills he let go of the ties that had held him to the wonderful old distillery for most of his professional life. Though his input at Midleton has already seen some interesting and sometimes quite fabulous developments, with an apparent improvement in Midleton Very Rare and his putting together of the stunning Redbreast 15.....and already a marked improvement in Redbreast 12. Long have I wailed and gnashed my teeth that more was not done with their pot still stocks, as relatively low as I know they are. For 17 years I have been perching myself on the shoulder of every Irish Distillers executive I can find asking them to bring out pot still (that type of whiskey made from a mixture of malted and unmalted barley unique to Ireland - and now Midleton distillery in particular) as something above the usual Irish Distillers norm of 40% abv and at a variation of ages. Yes, I was told. Great idea. It would happen one day, I was reassured. Just needed the stock. And the market.

They at last responded, I am told, to a request from by Le Maison du Whisky in Paris who required something similar to sell. The result was Redbreast 15 and Jim Murray's Whisky Bible 2007 Irish Whiskey of the Year. And a lot of interest from drinkers who before rarely gave Irish a second glance. Or chance. Now, if I can get a result for my constant beseeching them to tone down - and one day remove - colouring from Midleton Very Rare and Powers in particular....

Of course Redbreast is a straight whiskey. The next significant input was with a blend - and what a blend! Jameson Vintage Reserve may have been launched to the improbable sound - or should that be silence? - of Sinead O'Connor forgetting her lines when singing "Nothing Compares 2 U" at Midleton Distillery. Fortunately for Irish Distillers, the Jameson 2007 Vintage Reserve didn't fluff its lines at all, was entirely word perfect and, frankly, nothing compared to it within the Irish whiskey industry for the remainder of the year. Billy Leighton had written a number one and, as he is way too talented to be a one-hit-wonder merchant, I look forward to his second. It is surely due any time now.

The highlight of the Irish whiskey year fell in March 2010 when one of the most beautiful whisk(e)y sites in the world, Locke's Distillery at Kilbeggan, changed from being a sealed-in-aspic working museum to actual whiskey producers, with their warehoused spirit reaching its third birthday and thereby becoming Irish whiskey. Wonderfully, owners Cooley are not remotely shy to correctly inform anyone that Locke's, dating back to 1757, is the oldest distillery in the world, a claim that Old Bushmills, for one, cannot remotely argue against. Certainly, a tour of the place – which should be on every whisk(e)y lover's to do once in their lifetime list – visually confirms it. Only the Mount Vernon distillery in Virginia, a stunning recreation of George Washington's 1797, and, nearer to home, the original Midleton distillery near Cork comes close.

On the whiskey front, for the second year running there have been few fireworks in new products. Well, except maybe one: I had no qualms in giving Irish Whiskey of the Dun Leire 8 Years Old. Remarkably, though, Cooley produce it for supermarket giant Sainsbury. So you won't be off your trolley buying an own label...

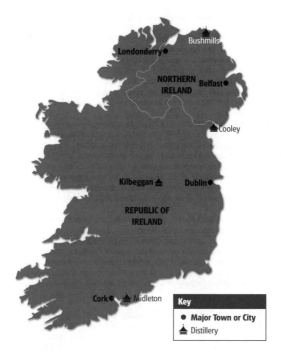

Bushmills

Londonderry●

NORTHERN
IRELAND   Belfast●

▲Cooley

Kilbeggan ▲   Dublin●

REPUBLIC OF
IRELAND

Cork●   ▲ Midleton

Key	
●	**Major Town or City**
▲	Distillery

Pure Pot Still
MIDLETON (old distillery)

Midleton 25-y-o Pot Still db **(92) n24 t24 f21 b23.** A really enormous whiskey that is in the truest classic Irish style. The un-malted barley really does make the tastebuds hum and the oak has added fabulous depth. Interesting when tasted against an American rye – the closeness of the character is there to be experienced, but also the differences. A subtle mature whiskey of unquestionable quality. Superb. *43%*

Midleton 30-y-o Pot Still db **(85) n19 t22 f22 b22.** A typically brittle, crunchy Irish pot still where the un-malted grains have a telling say. The oak has travelled as far as it can without having an adverse effect. A chewy whiskey which revels in its bitter-sweet balance. An impressively tasty and fascinating insight into yesteryear. *45%*

Midleton 1973 Pure Pot Still db **(95) n24 t24 f23 b24.** The enormous character of true Irish pot still whiskey (a mixture of malted and unmalted barley) appears to absorb age better than most other grain spirits. This one is in its element. But drink at full strength and at body temp (it is pretty closed when cool) for the most startling – and memorable effects. I have no idea how much this costs. But if you can find one and afford it ... then buy it!!

MIDLETON (new distillery)

Green Spot (94.5) n23.5 mouthwatering and fresh on one level, honey and menthol on another; **t24** crisp, mouthwatering with a fabulous honey burst, alarmingly sensuous; **f23.5** the caramel has receded, leaving the finer, sharper pot still character to battle it out with the honey. The spices are now much clearer too; **b23.5** this honeyed state has remained a few years, and its shar ness has now been regained. Complex throughout. Unquestionably one of the world's greatest branded whiskies. *40%. Irish Distillers for Mitchell & Son, Dublin.* ⊙ ⊙

Green Spot 12 Year Old Single Pot Still dist 91 **(93) n24** spices and zesty oranges abound, even a distant trace of coriander; uncompromising barley sugar and heather; **t24** a stunningly wonderful arrival: layers of sweet malt at first, but that takes a battering from much sharper, more prickly grains and spices. An enormous, vigorous mouthful; **f22** a degree of bourbon-style liquorice, vanilla and caramel; **b23** a single cask restricted to exactly 200 bottles to mark the 200th anniversary of the grand old man of Kildare Street, this is the first Middleton pot still I have seen at this strength outside of a lab. A one-off in every sense. *58%.*

Green Spot 10 Year Old Single Pot Still dist 93 **(92) n23** firm barley and orangey fruit with gentle hints of early bourbon: some serious ageing effect on this; **t22** mouthwatering and firm, then a gradual increase in the barley input and spices; **f24** shafts of honey throws a sweetening light on the bitter marmalade; **b23** launched to celebrate the 200th anniversary of this wonderful Dublin landmark, this is bottled from three mixed bourbon casks of Irish Pot Still. The extra age has detracted slightly from the usual vitality of the standard Green Spot (an 8-y-o) but its quality still must be experienced. *40%. Mitchell & Son. 1000 bottles.*

Redbreast 12 Years Old db **(96) n23.5** lively and firm, this one offering a gentle fruity swetness not too dissimilar to a rye, ironic as there is light bourbony kick off the oak, too; **t24.5** wonderfully clipped and correct in delivery: firm at first - very firm!!! - but slowly the barley melts and light muscovado sugars dovetail with a flinty fruitiness and pillow-soft vanilla; incorrigibly mouthwatering and the build up of spices is just showing off; **f24** remains spicy but clean, allowing a clear view of those varying barley tones drifting away; **b24** Yess...!!! Back to its classically classy, brilliant best. No sulphur casks this time (unlike last year). Just juicy pot still all the way. An old loved one has returned...more gorgeous than ever. *40%. Irish Distillers.*

Redbreast 15 Years Old db **(94) n23** seductive soft fruit wrapped in a hard barley shell. A slight soapy blemish, but minor; **t24** such enormity and depth fair takes the breath away; soft hints of citrus amid the pulsing grain. Stunning clarity and delicate spice. Extraordinary; **f23** multi-layered, panning out with barley-edged cocoa; **b24** for years I have been pleading for Irish Distillers to launch a pot still at 46%, natural colour and unchillfiltered. Well, I've got two out of three wishes. And what we have here is a truly great Irish whiskey and my pulse races in the certain knowledge it can get better still... *46%. ncf. France.*

OLD COMBER

Old Comber 30 Years Old Pure Pot Still (88) n23 t24 f20 b21. A classic example of a whiskey spending a few summers too many in wood: increasing age doesn't equal excellence. That said, always very drinkable and early on positively sparkles with a stunning mouthfeel. Out of respect for the old I have made the markings for taste cover the first seven or eight seconds... *40%*

Single Malt
COOLEY

Connemara bott code L7105 **(87.5) n22 t22 f21.5 b22.** Another Connemara where the style is very much subdued. *40%. Cooley Distillery.*

Connemara bott code L8065 **(89.5) n22.5 t22.5 f22 b22.5.** A superb bottling much closer to its old self with the peats remaining delicate but occasionally having much to say. *40%.*

Connemara bott code L9042 db **(88) n23** a bigger than usual salty, kippery tang; **t22.5** one of the more delicate and mouth-watering deliveries Connemara has given for a while: the peat is at once strident and meek but the subtle gristy sweetness is a constant and first class foil to the vanillas; **f20.5** rather short, toffeed and hurried; **b22** one of the softest smoked whiskies in the world which though quite lovely gives the impression it can't make its mind up about what it wants to be. *40%*

Connemara Aged 8 Years db **(85) n22.5 t21.5 f20 b21.** Another Connemara lacking teeth. The peat charms, especially on the nose, but the complexity needs working on. *46%*

Connemara Aged 12 Years bott code L9024 db **(85.5) n23 t21.5 f20 b21.** The nose, with its beautiful orange, fruity lilt, puts the shy smoke in the shade. *40%*

Connemara 1995 Sherry Cask cask no. V07/08 87, dist Oct 95, bott Oct 08 db **(76) n18 t20 f19 b19** Sulphured butts respect no international boundaries...and particularly love to hide behind peat. *46%*

Connemara Cask Strength bott code L7016 **(94) t21.5** prickly; the deft smoke is equalled by the oak input; **t24.5** gorgeous, nigh flawless delivery: every aspect from the mouth-watering grassy barley right through to the hickory and forever billowing smoke just melts in the mouth; **f24** long and even, the smoke hits every crevice whilst the bitter-sweet edge is stunningly sharp; **b24** a malt which, since its very first day, has always been at its best when at full strength doesn't disappoint. But for dud-oak nose, this would have been an award-winner. *57.9%. Cooley Distillery.*

Connemara Cask Strength bott code L9041 db **(90) n21.5** a shrill peatiness fends off a determined, off-key vanilla attack; **t23** fabulous delivery: it's juicy, sharp, eye-watering malt all the way, with the smoke prodding the tastebuds here and there; spices as the smoke becomes a little more hostile; **f22** finally the vanilla gets to have its say; **b22.5** a juicy negative of the standard bottling: does its talking on the palate rather than nose. Maybe an absence of caramel notes might have something to do with that. *57.9%*

⋙ **Connemara Distillers Edition** db **(86) n22 t22.5 f20 b21.5.** When I give whisk(e)y tastings around the world, I love to include Connemara. Firstly, people don't expect peated Irish. Secondly, their smoked whisky stock is eclectic and you never quite know what is going to come out of the bottle. This is a particularly tight, sharp style. No prisoners survived.... *43%*

Connemara Single Cask cask no. 4086, dist Aug 92, bott Mar 07 db **(88) n22.5** drier smoke than the norm for a Connemara despite the squeeze of citrus; **t22** sharp, chewy, at times tinderbox dry; **f21.5** some thumping oak takes the dryness down to new cocoa powder levels; **b22** a dry, peated Irish, anyone...? *46%*

⋙ **Connemara Single Cask** sherry finish, cask no. 112, dist Aug 92, bott Nov 09 db **(92.5) n23** allotment bonfires and freshly opened pack of dates; **t23.5** uncharacteristically silky for a Connemara! The fruit oozes around every crevice; the peat adds serious weight; decent flakey oak and grist through the middle; **f23** smoked chocolate dates; some wonderful oils spin it out; **b23** ladies and gentlemen: I have the pleasure of presenting to you Connemara wearing fruity clothes you may never have quite seen before. *46% Approx 300 bottles.*

⋙ **Connemara Turf Mór Limited Edition Small Batch Collection** cask no. 393, dist May 07, bott 2010 db **(94) n23.5** glorious lavender freshening the stodgy peat to ensure excellent balance; **t23.5** absolutely spot on delivery: the peat is thick and immediately filling the mouth with smoke, yet the barley juiciness oozes into every pore; **f23.5** long with hickory adding a firmer foundation to the smoke; fizzing peat tingles the tongue; **b23.5** defies belief that this is just a three year-old malt. Some bourbon aspects don't just prop up the act, they add fabulously to the proceedings. *58.2% To be released at the end of the year.*

Locke's Aged 8 Years bott code L9005 db **(88) n22.5** excellent, rousing citrus; **t22** begins bright fresh and sharp, clouds over slightly with caramel **f22** barley loses its toffeed marker from time to time to complete a juicy experience; **b21.5** a beautiful malt at probably this distillery's optimum age. *40%*

Locke's Aged 8 Years Crock (92) n23 pounding, intense, grassy-sweet barley; **t24** excellent mouth arrival and almost immediately a honey-rich delivery of lush, slightly oily malt: wonderful, wonderful stuff! **f22** soft oak tempers the barley and a degree of toffee digs in and flattens the .....; **b23** much, much better cask selection than of old: some real honey casks here. A crock of gold...! *40%.*

⋙ **Locke's Aged 9 Years Grand Crew** cask no. 696, dist Feb 00, bott Sep 09 db **(90.5) n23.5** some extra oak involvement here compared to cask 700. This one offers up a touch of ginger and very distant allspice – or is that Old Spice..??? – with the barley having to fight harder to get a foothold; **t22.5** fatter, silkier delivery with an immediate spice explosion. The sugars are more molassed and of a bourbon style; the barley wanders in almost as an afterthought; **f22.5** more soupy caramels and vanilla but a pleasing creamy mocha to finish; **b22** the cask this was filled into had seen less action in Kentucky than cask 700, so was itching to inject its character in this. The result is a whisky very different to its sister cask: this being heavier and less barley fresh. I have to admit I prefer cask 700, though i know some will think differently. Still, grabbing a bottle of each is a great way to teach yourself about the vagaries of the warehouse. And it's money to a great cause, too. *59.4% for The Irish Whisky Society. 216 bottles.*

⋙ **Locke's Aged 9 Years Grand Crew** cask no. 700, dist Feb 00, bott Sep 09 db **(91.5) n23** how delicate is that squeeze of lime juice on the crystal clear barley? **t23.5** that typically Cooley sharp barley thrust lightened by traces of honey; a wonderful silky sheen to the barley, yet a countering blue, too; **f22.5** a lovely, though brief, injection of ginger before the vanilla; **b22.5** this took me back a few years. Having the three new Locke's lined up was like the days when I went through the Cooley warehouses looking for casks to put into Knappogue. This wasn't far off the style I was searching for. The right age, too. *58.9% Cooley for The Irish Whisky Society. 233 bottles.*

⋙ **Locke's Aged 10 Years Premier Crew** cask no. 713, dist Feb 00, bott Jul 10 db **(88) n22** sharp barley, a bit of oak attitude; **t23** fabulous malt explosion: barley in several guises and varying weights; **f21** some cocoa but the hassle of the oak on the nose translates to a degree of bitterness; **b22** the cask does its best to try and spoil the barley fun. Here's a tip: stick to younger malts. Cooley is brilliant and relatively undiscovered at between seven and nine years. And there is less time for cask to bite back... *46% Cooley for The Irish Whisky Society. 292 bottles.*

The Tyrconnell bott code L9074 db **(86) n21 t22 f22 b21.** Sweet, soft, chunky and with a finely spice finale. *40%*

The Tyrconnell Aged 10 Years Madeira Finish bott code L8136 db **(91)** n23 a dull, rumbling marmalade bitter-sweetness; milk toffee and more delicate, twittering marzipan; t23 lush and fat, the sharpness is confined to the odd exploratory fizz of indeterminate fruit: purrs along very pleasantly; f22 toffee raisin; very late spiced apricot; b23 not quite the award-winning effort of a few years back, as those lilting high notes which so complimented the baser fruit tones haven't turned up here. But remains in the top echelon and still much here to delight the palate. 46%

The Tyrconnell Aged 10 Years Madeira Finish db **(95)** n24 apricots jelly, marzipan and orange-mango hybrid: just about unique; t24 supreme balance of oil to barley with intense malt spinning around the tastebuds, kept in company by an astonishingly thick oaky-fruity-milkycocoa backdrop; f23 banana milkshake and vanilla; b24 this has to be one of the finest Madeira finishes I've ever come across. The balance defies belief while the higher notes make one purr. I am quite astonished. 46%

The Tyrconnell Aged 10 Years Port Finish bott code L8167 db **(81.5)** n21.5 t21 f19 b20. Toffee all the way. 46%

The Tyrconnell Aged 10 Years Port Finish db **(93)** n23 puckering fruit with a hint of spicy menace; t23 firm body at first – to the point of shattering; oils out rather beautifully with a touch of raspberry preserve before going all solid again; f24 very soft spices and lots of fruity cocoa; b24 Cooley has excelled with its first serious foray into cask finishing. I didn't think this could be topped – until I came across the Madeira version. This, though, is like a fruit and nut chocolate bar – without the nuts. Wonderful. 46%

The Tyrconnell Aged 10 Years Sherry Finish bott code L8168 db **(84)** n22 t21 f21 b20. Like the Port Cask in this present series we have a thick malt that is friendly, toffeed and generally flat. This one, though, does have the odd peak of grapey richness, but you have to travel through a few plateaux to reach them. 46%

The Tyrconnell Aged 14 Years cask no. 3179, rotation K92/25 db **(93)** n23 apple blossom (no, honestly!), cedar wood and still remnants of ultra clean barley; t23 refreshingly rich barley offering a shard of golden syrup to its perfectly lush delivery; f23 long, soft vanilla, a touch of tannin and those continuing gentle oils....sigh, what bliss!! b24 By rotation, K92 means it was distilled in 1992. Which just proves this distillery really has come of age, because, make no mistake, this is a belter.... 46%

The Tyrconnell Aged 15 Years Single Cask cask no. 1854/92 db **(92.5)** n24 outstanding malt and vanilla interaction: the two poles have met and intertwined to offer maximum complexity; stunning, deft floral notes keep the odd squeak of citrus under control. One of the most beautifully structured Irish noses of the year; t23 like the nose, the weight is outstanding and the march of the juicy barley a treat; soft vanillas and engagingly shy spices fill in the middle ground; f22.5 biscuity sweetness before some exhibition cocoa; b23 infinitely more comfortable in its aging skin a similar malt I tasted in Canada last year. 46%

◦⫶◦ **The Tyrconnell Aged 17 Years Single Cask** cask no. 5306/92 db **(87)** n22 Lincoln biscuits; malty; t22 a frisson of sharpness to the simplistic barley; f21.5 soft caramel; b21.5 attractive barley all the way but barely deviates. 46%

The Tyrconnell Single Cask cask no. 351, casked 24 Jan 92, bott 9 May 07 db **(93.5)** n23.5 this is just showing off...excellent complexity with the fruity barley shining at so many different levels; t24 juicy to the point you drown in your own saliva: few 15-year-old malts show this degree of barley clarity, as if every grain has its own edge; f23 just wonderful spicing to add further structure and polish; soft boiled cooking apples offer an unexpected fruit edge; b23.5 stunningly juicy with the barley at its most intense and brittle. Bears absolutely no relationship to the average 15-y-o single malt. 46%

The Tyrconnell Single Cask cask no. 354, casked 24 Jan 92 db **(95.5)** n24 that morning-baked custard tart; that morning prepared lemon drizzle; malt shake - with extra malt; t24.5 you cannot but whimper and sigh on delivery, the tastebuds cannot but pucker; the saliva glands go into overdrive; layer upon layer of acacia honey and mollassed sugar, but all with a bold of barley through them; the overall intensity, even at 46% is near immeasurable; f23 a slow, rhythmic pulsing of spice, the higher notes of unfettered, ultra clean barley; slow, shuddering jolts of oaky vanilla; b24 lucky bloody Yanks!! What they have done to deserve a 15-year-old cask of whiskey of such age-defying magnitude, I can only imagine. I'll have to get my PA to book the next flight across The Pond, because this is unmolested Irish malt at its purest and finest. Just timeless brilliance: a classic in every definition. 46%. USA Market.

The Tyrconnell Single Cask cask no. 356, casked 24 Jan 92, bott 9 May 07 db **(87)** n22.5 vanilla and barley in dead equal measures; t23 a sumptuous fanfare of almost the most intense barley imaginable, all dusted by the most delicate layer of muscovado sugar; f20 the oaky caramel fights back gamefully; b21.5 lots of natural caramel amid the massive barley. 46%

The Tyrconnell Single Cask cask no. 359, casked 24 Jan 92, bott 9 May 07 db **(84) n21 t22 f20 b21.** Lively and juicy early on with the usual Cooley big malt. Refuses to up the pace complexity-wise, though the gentle spices excel. 46%. For Dugas, France.

The Tyrconnell Single Cask cask no. 360, casked 24 Jan 92, bott 9 May 07 db **(82) n21 t21 f19 b21.** The danger of older malts comes, usually, from within: the cask. This cask has offered lots of natural caramel. Hugely drinkable, even so. 46%

The Tyrconnell Single Cask cask no. 9571/1992 db **(85.5) n23 t21 f20.5 b21.** The wonderful citrus notes on the nose are swamped by the oak further down the line. There is no doubting the age of this Cooley! 46%

The Tyrconnell Willow Park Aged 15 Years cask no. 349/92 "The first private bottled single cask in North America" db **(87) n21** showing distinct signs of stress from age, but some excellent banana and barley notes impress; **t22** voluptuous mouth-feel but the oak arrives early straining at the leash; **f22** lots of caramel notes thankfully punctuated by citrus; a late malt surge helps; **b22** a beautiful whisky, in many respects due to the simplicity as the label says, but one on its way down. Remember: we are on a learning curve as regards Cooley. It is a new distillery and we just don't know how the malt will hold up. On this evidence it is reaching its limits and I suspect that had this been bottled two or three years earlier the points would have been considerably higher. That said, enjoy: it is still a delicious experience. 46%

Cadenhead's Cooley Aged 13 Years bott 05 **(93) n24** attractively smoked: orange and mango juice with the kippers; **t23** multi-shaded smoke fighting on varying levels with an influx of natural oaky-caramel and unusual oils; **f23** prickly spices and then a rerun to a semi-gristy sweetness; **b23** absolutely top-rate peaty Irish. 60.6%. 228 bottles.

Cadenhead's Cooley Aged 13 Years bott 05 **(93) n24** attractively smoked: orange and mango juice with the kippers; **t23** multi-shaded smoke fighting on varying levels with an influx of natural oaky-caramel and unusual oils; **f23** prickly spices and then a rerun to a semi-gristy sweetness; **b23** absolutely top-rate peaty Irish. 60.6%. 228 bottles.

Cadenhead's World Whiskies Cooley Aged 15 Years bourbon barrel, bott May 07 **(94) n23** perhaps as nonchalant a peat delivery as you are likely to find – kilny yet so clean! **t24** soft and silky oils carrying the most sensual, sweet and mildly gristy peat imaginable: sublime.. **f23** long fade with again those perfectly-weighted oily peats callings all the shots... **b24** perhaps the oldest Irish peated single barrel malt to hit the market for over a century, this is nigh on faultless and a revelation... 58.6%. 222 bottles.

Clonmel Peated Aged 8 Years (86) n22 t23 f20 b21. Take the toffee away and you would have one hell of an Irish. Claims to be "Pure Pot Still". It isn't (in Irish terms): it's malt. 40%. Celtic Whisky Compagnie.

Craoi na Mona Irish Malt Whiskey (68) n16 t18 f17 b17. I'm afraid my Gaelic is slipping these days: I assume Craoi na Mona means "Feinty, badly made smoky malt"... (that's the end of my tasting for the day...) 40%

Glen Dimplex (88) n23 solid malt with a hint of honey; charming, blemish-free; **t22** gentle development of the malts over simple dusty vanilla; **f21** quite dry, spiced and a little toffeed; **b22** overall, clean and classically Cooley. 40%.

Jon, Mark and Robbo's The Smooth Sweeter One Irish Malt (89) n22 a dry, oak-rich vanilla aroma with barley, dried pine nuts and distant honeybourbon to balance; **t23** much more fresh and mouthwatering than the nose suggests with a thick dollop of honey for the main theme: pretty young, almost embryonic, whiskey; **f22** decent spice, nut oils and then more vanilla and late cocoa-caramel; **b22** seriously enjoyable whiskey for all its youth, especially for those with a sweet tooth. 40%. Easy Drinking Whisky Co.

Knappogue Castle 1990 (91) n22 t23 f22 b24. For a light whiskey this shows enormous complexity and depth. Genuine balance from nose to finish; refreshing and dangerously more-ish. Entirely from bourbon cask and personally selected and vatted by a certain Jim Murray. 40%. nc. Great Spirits.

Knappogue Castle 1991 (90) n22 t23 f22 b23. Offers rare complexity for such a youthful malt especially in the subtle battles that rage on the palate between sweet and dry, malt and oak and so on. The spiciness is a great foil for the malt. Each cask picked and vatted by the author. 40%. nc. Great Spirits.

Knappogue Castle 1992 (94) n23 t23 f24 b24. A different Knappogue altogether from the delicate, ultra-refined type. This expression positively revels in its handsome ruggedness and muscular body: a surprisingly bruising yet complex malt that always remains balanced and fresh – the alter-ego of the '90 and '91 vintages. I mean, as the guy who put this whiskey together, what do you expect? But it's not bad if I say so myself and was voted the USA's No. 1 Spirit. Virtually all vanished, but worth getting a bottle if you can find it (I don't receive a penny – I was paid as a consultant!). 40%. nc. Great Spirits.

Knappogue Castle 1993 (see under Bushmills)
Knappogue Castle 1994 (see under Bushmills)
Magilligan Cooley Pure Pot Still Single Malt (91) n22 slightly waxy and honeyed: Cooley at its softest; t22 beautiful arrival of highly intense, spotlessly clean malt. The sweetness level is near perfect; f24 spiceless – unlike the previous bottling. Now just the longest fade-out of malt concentrate in Irish whiskey...and with a touch of honey for good measure; b23 ...or maybe not..!! 43%. Ian MacLeod.

Magilligan Irish Whiskey Peated Malt 8 Years Old (89) n21 old, blackening banana and peat; t23 lush, sweet barley, wonderfully oiled with the softest injection of smoke; f22 long, long fade with those oils working wonders. The smoke gathers in intensity considerably before dispersing; b23 such a different animal from the docile creature that formally passed as Magilligan peated. Quite lovely...and very classy. 43%. Ian Macleod Distillers.

Merry's Single Malt (83) n20 t22 f20 b21. Ultra-clean barley rich nose is found on the early palate. The finish is flat, though. 40%

Michael Collins Irish Whiskey Single Malt db (76) n20 t19 f19 b18. The sooner some people in this industry realize that Cooley is far too good and delicate a malt to withstand this insane degree of caramel, the better off everyone will be. 40% (80 proof).

Michael Collins Irish Whiskey Single Malt db (68) n17 t18 f17 b16. Bloody hell, I thought. Didn't anyone get my message from last year? Apparently not – and it's our fault as the tasting notes above were accidentally edited out before they went in. Sorry. But the caramel in the latest bottling has been upped to take the whisky from deep gold to bronze. Making this among the most over-coloured single malt I have tasted in years. Please guys. For the love of whiskey. Please let us taste exactly what a great malt this could be. 40% (80 proof).

Sainsbury's Single Malt Irish Whiskey bott code L8024/09 (89) n22.5 brilliant, crisp barley that signals a mouth-watering delivery.... t23 ...and is duly obliged! The malt is of the juiciest variety with fabulous strata of honeydew melon and eye-watering freshly cut grass; f21.5 a little vanilla and toffee get in on the act, which remains a pretty classy one; b22 just a little word to the wise: the back label says: "traditional distilled pot still Irish whiskey." It isn't. This is single malt. To my knowledge this is not a mixture of malted and unmalted barley, which constitutes traditional Irish pot still. Anyway, that apart, this is excellent stuff. 40%

Sainsbury's Single Malt Irish Whiskey bott code L9086/09 (93.5) n23 beautiful, multi-layered aroma with a soft, lilting barley note, but something more earthy and teasingly smoky forming the anchor; t24 mouth-watering and absolutely brimming with charm and depth; the clean barley sends the palate into super-salavating mode...and then comes that most delicate of smoky notes...what a darling, this is; f22.5 shortish, a tad furry and vanilla dried; b24 a real surprise package: you don't expect smoke on a whisky supplied by Cooley and I even contacted the guys in Ireland to find out where it came from. They don't know – it shouldn't be there. I am glad it is, if only in trace amounts because it really provides a fabulously balanced malt. 40%

❖ **Sainsbury's Dún Léire Aged 8 Years Single Malt** (95.5) n24 the score for this crept upwards as I investigated the aroma like the thermometer in my back garden on a bright summer's day. The first thing to throw itself at you is Seville blood orange, backed up by a clever layering of barley at varying intensity and sweetness; the delicate oak acts as no more than a buffer in between; t24 just about the perfect mouth feel: silky and melting on the palate. Again, it was an orangey citrus first to show, then again followed by some stunning malt. Everything dissolves: you don't have to do anything but close your eyes and enjoy, indeed: marvel...but it is hard work to stop yourself chewing; f23.5 dries slightly, but the bitterness threatened on the label fails to materialise...thankfully. The fruit and barley ride off into the sunset in tandem; b24 when I read "notes of bitter orange" on the label I feared the worst and expected a sulphurous whiskey. Well maybe there is a molecule or two hanging around, but so minor is it, it is impossible to tell exactly where it comes from. This is one of the great whiskeys from Cooley, ever. And as a supermarket Irish...unsurpassed. One of the surprise packages of world whisky for 2010. Magnificent. 40% Cooley for Sainsbury's Supermarket

Shannahan's (92) n23 beautifully young, fresh and zesty: this distillery's best style; t22 refreshing, clean barley that tries to be little else; f24 excellent late complexity as some first-class soft vanilla appears; b23 Cooley natural and unplugged: quite adorable. 40%

❖ **Slieve Foy Single Malt Aged 8 Years** bott code L9108 (88) n23 so delicate, you feel it could snap if you sniffed at it too hard: beautiful lemony malt with fudge and advocaat mix; t22.5 pure silk. Juicy young barley that just keeps you salivating. Fudge and vanilla begin to edge their way into the frame; f21 tame spices and toffee; b21.5 never deviates from its delicate touch. 40% Cooley Distillery for Marks & Spencer

The Spirit Safe & Cask Selection Cooley 1991 12 Years Old dist Sep 91, bott Oct 03 **(89) n22 t23 f22 b22.** Struggles to find a rhythm but the acacia honey holds it together. *43%. nc ncf. Celtique Connexion.*

Vom Fass Cooley 4 Years Old (82) n22 t21 f19 b20. Wonderfully clean; for a Cooley, actually has extra sheen and copper richness. Just fades towards the finish and lacks depth. *40%. Austria.*

Vom Fass Cooley Peated 8 Years Old (89) n22 gently smoked; lightly cured bacon; **t23** sweet delivery with a wonderful honey shadow to the smoke; **f22** oily liquorice and vanilla; **b22** much more recognisable. This is a treat from an above average cask, though the peating is subtle and subdued. *40%. Austria.*

The Whisky Fair Connemara Aged 15 Years bourbon barrel, dist 92, bott 07 **(94) n23.5** fresh ground black pepper nestled in peat ash; **t23** sweeter delivery than nose suggests, with superb layers of smoke. The spices are almost perfectly integrated; **f23.5** now the sweet, clean malts come out to play whilst the vanilla and smoke take a back seat; **b24** superbly balanced. *50.5%. Germany.*

The Whisky Fair Cooley Aged 15 Years bourbon barrel, dist 92, bott 07 **(90) n22** intense malt comfortably absorbs the booming oak; **t23** juicy, sweetened barley and puckering spice make for an eventful delivery; the oak tried to get a grip towards the middle but the astonishing freshness of grain, considering its age, comes to the rescue; **f22.5** predictable vanilla and cocoa but the balance with the barley excels; **b22.5** a malty gem. *56.4%. Germany.*

The Wild Geese Single Malt (85.5) n21.5 t21 f22 b21. "A Rare Blend of Pure Aged Irish Malt Whiskies" says the front label. Yet it is a single malt. Confusing. And very unhelpful to a whisky public already being totally bamboozled by the bizarre and misguided antics of the Scotch Whisky Association. It is not a blend. It is a mixing of Cooley malt whiskey, as I understand it. The back label's "Smoother Because We Distil it Longer" is also a bit of a blarney. It's made in a pot still and whilst it is true that if you distil faster (by higher temperatures) you could well end up with "hot" whiskey, I am not aware of this being distilled at a significantly slower rate than at either Bushmills or Midleton. Or do they mean the cut of the run from the spirit still is longer, which would impart more oils – not all of them great? Just ignore the Wild Goose chase the labels send you on and enjoy the malt, with all its failings, for what it is (and this is pretty enjoyable in an agreeably rough and ready manner, though not exactly the stiff of Irish whiskey purists): which in this case for all its malt, toffee and delicate smoke, also appears to have more than a slight touch of feints - so maybe they were right all along....!!! *43%. Cooley for Avalon.*

OLD KILBEGGAN

⋅:⋅ **Kilbeggan Distillery Reserve Malt** matured in quarter casks, batch no. 1, bott Jun 10 db **(89) n22.5** wonderfully delicate with a distinctive light nutty sweetness to the malt; the youth is well camouflaged behind a curious (considering you can't get any more inland than this distillery) coastal saltiness and a weak, nondescript fruit; **t22.5** a sugary delivery to boost the thin malty line; quick vanillas and toffee; **f22** mainly fudgy and flat but a light lemon postscript; a late spice buzz; **b22** an endearingly soft malt to see Kilbeggan distillery back into the whiskey world. Shame it has been reduced to 40%, as this one demanded to be at least 46% - indeed, preferably naked - and allowing those delicate, elegant but marginalised characters a chance to bloom. But welcome back...and I look forward to many an evening with me tasting you as you blossom, as I am sure you will. It has been nearly 20 years since I first discovered the beauty of Kilbeggan Distillery and I have countless times since dreamed of that moment. *40% 15000 bottles. Available only in the distillery gift shop.*

⋅:⋅ **The Spirit of Kilbeggan 1 Month (90.5) n22 t23 f23 b22.5.** Wow!! They are really getting to grips with the apparatus. Full bodied and lush small still feel to this but radiating complexity, depth, barley and cocoa in equal measures. The development of the oils really does give this excellent length. Impressed! *65.5%*

⋅:⋅ **The Spirit of Kilbeggan 1 Year (85) n20.5 t21 f22 b21.5.** A veritable Bambi of a spirit: a typical one year old malt which, as hard as it tries, just can't locate its centre of gravity. Even so, the richness is impressive and some highly sugared chocolate mousse near the end is a treat. *62.7%*

⋅:⋅ **The Spirit of Kilbeggan 2 Years (84) n20 t21 f22 b21.** A tad raw and a little thin. There is some decent balance between oak and malt, but the overall feeling is that the still has not yet been quite mastered. *60.3%*

OLD BUSHMILLS

Bushmills 10 Years Old matured in two woods db **(90) n22.5** for the first time in living memory there is real grape detectable on the nose; it appears to be of the crushed sultana school of fruitiness with a few minor honeyed notes also around; **t23** a fulsome delivery again with the grape at the vanguard; soft vanilla trundles along at Antrim speed; spices arrive with just a touch of cocoa for company; **f22** soft with the work being done by the grape and toffee; **b22.5** this malt has now changed character enormously....and certainly not for the worse. Until recently it was traditionally a chalky effort, dry-ish with the accent on the barley and oak. Now the sherry is the major shareholder in terms of all round shape and depth. And very good sherry butts they are, too. A great leap forward: this is lush and lovely whiskey. *40%*

Bushmills 12 Years Old Distillery Reserve db **(86) n22.5 t22.5 f20 b21.** This version has gone straight for the ultra lush feel. For those who want to take home some 40% abv fruit fudge from the distillery. *40%*

Bushmills Select Casks Aged 12 Years married with Caribbean rum cask db **(95) n23** unusual moist rum and raisin cake effect: effective and just enough spice to deliver extra complexity. Just the very slightest hint of bourbon, too; **t24** adorable malt richness; biscuity and stupendously seasoned yet always remains fresh and mouthwatering. The sweetness is very cleverly controlled; **f24** there are just so many layers to this: the oak is a growing force, but restricts itself to a vanilla topping; **b24** one of the most complex Bushmills in living memory, and probably since it was established in 1784. *40%*

Bushmills Aged 16 Years db **(90) n24.5** one of the most complex fruit aromas in the world: explodingly ripe greengage and gooseberry; those who love sauternes finishes will appreciate the spiced apricot and layered sweetness. Back to top form with a masterful brilliance; **t22.5** the arrival is pretty two-toned: on one hand is a juicy, sensual, fruit-tinged maltiness. By its side is a more bitter toffee kick; throughout is a fabulous spice rhythm; **f21.5** almost treacle tart toffeeness; **b21.5** a confusing malt: we have a nose that half the blenders of the world would give their right nostril for. And then we have a performance on the palate that promises but does not deliver to its expected potential. Lovely whisky, for sure, and it gets a 90, which means this really is the dbs – and I don't mean distillery bottlings. But I wonder if anything can be done about those duller toffee notes. *40%*

Bushmills Rare Aged 21 Years db **(95) n25** one of the cleanest fruit noses of any whiskey in the world and it needs to be: only then can you get a clear enough view and therefore a chance to see what the hell is going on. Grape notes come at you with different intensity in spice and sweetness; barley somehow makes the odd, firm guest appearance and there is a drifting medium roast Java to the oak. But it is the grape which intrigues and entirely seduces... **t23.5** silky, yet charismatic enough to confidently show you the spicier side to its personality early on; the grape ranges from burnt raisin to chocolate sultana; **f23** remains juiced and spiced to the end with a rummy-style bitterness to the sugars; **b23.5** I manage to get round to tasting this, socially, twice a year top whack. But whenever I do, I find myself spending more time nosing this than drinking it. And this sample is absolutely no exception. It almost redefines complexity. But, please, don't forget to taste it. I mean, you can have only so much foreplay.... there again, maybe not. *40%*

The Old Bushmills Single Cask 1989 Bourbon Barrel cask 7986 **(88) n22** big vanilla thrust; **t23** quite an outstanding intensity to the buttery malt with the sweetness almost on a precise curve upwards; some oak offers countering dryness; **f21** surprising toffee late on; **b22** perhaps a better malt than the early nose suggests, but very unusual in style for this distillery and would mark higher but for the debilitating toffee. *56.5%. ncf. Specially selected for Canada.*

The Old Bushmills Distillery Single Cask Bourbon Barrel 1989 cask 8139 db **(88) n21** fruity, but otherwise languid, with some dry, solid age apparent; **t23** juicy malt that really allows the barley to shine; **f22** long and revelling in its fresh barley richness; some very late, papery and dry oak at the death; **b22** Old Bushmills really springing a surprise with its depth for the age. *56.5%. USA.*

The Old Bushmills Distillery Single Cask Bourbon Barrel 1989 cask no 8140 db **(84) n20 t22 f21 b21.** Quite a fiery number, closed early on but with excellent cocoa finale. *56.5%. USA.*

The Old Bushmills Distillery Single Cask Bourbon Barrel 1989 cask no 8141 db **(88) n20** dry; soft barley; **t23** pure Bushmills in all its chalky yet oaky barley richness: distinctive and delightful with a bit of a nip; **f23** seriously impressive on the barley front with better balanced cocoa; **b22** the only one of the three bourbon casks to scream "Old Bushmills" at you for its unique style. *56.5%. USA.*

The Old Bushmills Distillery Single Cask Rum Barrel 1989 cask no 7110 db **(81) n21 t20 f20 b20.** Big, biting and hot but some serious malt. *53.7%. USA.*

The Old Bushmills Distillery Single Cask Rum Barrel 1989 cask no 7112 db **(84) n20 t21 f22 b21.** Sweet and attractively simple with excellent late malt. *53.7%. USA.*

The Old Bushmills Single Cask 1989 Rum Barrel cask no. 7115 **(93)** n22 delicate coating of sugar over malt; t24 a uniquely complex series of wonderful, prickly, banana-essence, liquorice-hinting waves of malt and spice: labyrinthine hardly does it justice; f23 the honied, mildly toffeed richness of the malt seems to multiply in intensity, as does the gentle hint of bourbon: a finish from near the top echelon; **b24** some in Canada may have seen me taste this for the first time with the country's most effortlessly beautiful and charming tv presenter Nancy Sinclair. I said then I thought we had a great malt on our hands, and a later tasting of it under more controlled – and private – conditions confirmed those initial suspicions. A real honey: elegant, deeply desirable, lip-smacking, memorable and something to get your tongue round and experience slowly at least once in your lifetime. And the whiskey's not bad, either.... *53.7%. ncf. Canada.*

The Old Bushmills Distillery Single Cask Sherry Butt 1989 db cask no 7429 **(90)** n22 passion fruit among the citrus. Sensual and gentle; t22 gets into a malty stride from go then a slow burning sherry fuse; f23 delightful finish that is long, vanilla-rich but with the most subtle interwoven fruit and barley and natural caramel; **b23** charismatic, charming, self-confident and supremely elegant. *53.7%. USA.*

The Old Bushmills Distillery Single Cask Sherry Butt 1989 cask no 7430 db **(91)** n21 slightly sweaty armpit but a good malt recovery t23 sweet, enormously malty for a sherry-influenced dram f24 mildly salty, with many layers of sweet malt and spice that go on almost endlessly **b23** this is a massively complex and striking Bushmills well worth finding: casks 7429 and 7430 could be almost twins...!! *53.7%. USA.*

Clontarf Single Malt (90.5) n23 barley concentrate with a squeeze of orange and distant juniper; t23 beautifully fresh barley, almost barley sugar, with light sinews of oak; f22 long, intense barley but with the vanilla standing tallest at the death as welcome spices finally gather; **b22.5** beautiful in its simplicity, this has eschewed complexity for delicious minimalism; *40%. Clontarf Irish Whiskey Co.*

The Irishman Single Malt bottle no. E2496 **(83)** n20 t21 f21 b21. Highly pleasant malt but the coffee and toffee on the finish underline a caramel-style whiskey which may, potentially, offer so much more. *40%. Hot Irishman Ltd.*

Knappogue Castle 1990 *(see Cooley)*
Knappogue Castle 1991 *(see Cooley)*
Knappogue Castle 1992 *(see Cooley)*

Knappogue Castle 1993 (91) n22 b22 f23 b24. A malt of exceptional character and charisma. Almost squeaky clean but proudly contains enormous depth and intensity. The chocolate finish is an absolute delight. Quite different and darker than any previous Knappogue but not dwarfed in stature to any of the previous three vintages. Created by yours truly. *40%. nc. Great Spirits.*

Knappogue Castle 1994 lot no. L6 **(89)** n23 f20 b22 A wonderful whiskey in the Knappogue tradition, although this one was not done by its creator. That said, it does have an Achilles heel: the finish. This is the most important bit to get right, especially as this is the oldest Knappogue yet. But not enough attention has been paid to getting rid of the oak-induced bitterness. *40%. Castle Brands.*

Knappogue Castle 1995 bott 07 **(88)** n23 banana skins and custard; soft barley but drier and dustier than any other Knappogue nose; t22 early mouthwatering barley fades; a sugary sheen is quickly usurped by an impatient oaky bitterness; f21 dry-ish and bitter but with a soft barley residue; some ultra late spices; **b22** a charming malt showing Old Bushmills in very unusual colours. Lacking the charisma, clarity and complexity of the first Knappogues simply because they were designed to extol the virtues of young (8-year-old) malt. Naturally, extra oak has crept in here, forcing out – as it must – the sharpness and vitality of the barley. A decent effort, but perhaps more should have been done to keep out the aggressive bitterness. *40%*

Single Grain
COOLEY

Cooley 1991 16 Years Old 1st fill bourbon cask no. 12441, dist Nov 91, bott Feb 08 **(89.5)** n22.5 some solid oak, but a fruity, soft oiliness smooths the ruffled feathers; t23 a sweet silkiness with bite: love it!! f22 gentle fade with the corn offering a sweeter edge to the oak; **b22** it hardly makes sense that Cooley grain appears to absorb the years better than their malt! Great stuff. *46%. Milroy's of Soho. 264 bottles.*

Greenore 6 Year Old bott code L9015 db **(89)** n23.5 even at such tender age this has more to do with bourbon than Irish: gentle, sweet red liquorice, toffee apple, and hot even the slightest hint of bitterness...; t22.5...but tastes of pure Canadian, especially with the over-enthusiastic caramels; sweet with an amazingly yielding texture; f21 lightly burnt toast and more toffee; **b22** very enjoyable whiskey. But two points: cut the caramel and really see the baby sing. And secondly, as a "Small Batch" bottling, how about putting a batch number on the label...? 40%. Cooley.

Greenore 8 Year Old bott code L8190 db **(86.5) n20 t22 f23 b21.5**. The vague hint of butyric on the nose is more than amply compensated by the gradual build up to something rather larger on the palate than you might have expected (and don't be surprised if the two events are linked). The corn oil is almost a meal in itself and the degree of accompanying sugar and corn flour is a treat. 40%. Cooley

Greenore 10 Years Old dist 97, bott 07 db **(87.5) n22** pretty standard Canadian style: plenty of corn digging in, a touch of toffee sweetness and a degree of bite; **t22** lightly oiled corn and vanilla; the oak dips in and out; **f21.5** pleasantly sweet at times yet amazingly docile, knowing what this grain is capable of... **b22** well made grain and always enjoyable but perhaps not brought to its fullest potential due to some less than inspired oak. 40%. 3000 bottles.

Greenore 15 Years Old bott code L8044 **(90) n23** the depth of ingrained oak mixed with corn heads you in the direction of Canada; a few spicy folds and golden syrup edges ensure a lovely simple elegance; **t22.5** just the right dosage of spice to counter the sugars; **f22** oaky bitterness outgunned by those marauding dark sugars; **b22.5** the advent of the Kilbeggan 15 reminded us that there must be some grain of that age around, and here to prove it is a superb bottling of the stuff which, weirdly, is a lot better than the blend. Beautiful. 43%

Blends

Bushmills 1608 anniversary edition **(94) n23.5** the grain barely gets a look in as the malt and oak dominates from the first whiff. Toasted oak and bread form a dense background, sweetened by muscovado sugar melting on porridge; **t23.5** now that's different: how many blends do you know kick off with an immediate impact of sweetness that offers about four or five different levels of intensity, and each accompanied by a toasted oakiness? Very, very different, charming, fascinating.....and delicious; **f23** long, mocha with the emphasis on the coffee and then, at the very end some firm grains at last get a toe-hold; **b24** this whiskey is talking an entirely different language to any Irish blend I have come across before, or any blend come to that. Indeed, nosed blind you'd not even regard it a blend: the malt calls to you like a Siren. But perhaps it is the crystal malt they have used here which is sending out such unique signals, helping the whiskey to form a thick cloak of roasty, toasty, burnt toffeed, bitter-sweetness which takes your breath away. What a fabulous whiskey! And whether it be a malt or blend, who cares? Genius whiskey is genius whiskey. 40%

❖ **Bushmills 1608 400th Anniversary (83) n21 t21.5 f20 b20.5**. Thin-bodied, hard as nails and sports a peculiarly Canadian feel. 46% Diageo

Bushmills Black Bush (91) n23 a firmer aroma with less evident malt and the spices have also taken a back seat. But the gentle, toffee apple and night garden scent reveal that the malt-grain interaction is still wonderfully alluring; **t23** busy delivery, much softer than the nose indicates with the malt first to show. The oak is no slouch either, offering excellent spices; some burnt, raisiny notes help confirm this is Black Bush on song; **f21.5** still over the top caramel interfering but not before some honeycomb makes a small stand; **b23.5** this famous old blend may be under new management and even better. But still the high quality, top-notch complexity rolls around the glass and your palate. As beautiful as ever. 40%

Bushmills Original (80) n19 t21 f20 b20. Remains one of the hardest whiskeys on the circuit with the Midleton grain at its most unflinching. There is a sweeter, faintly maltier edge to this now while the toffee and biscuits qualities remain. 40%

Cassidy's Distiller's Reserve bott code L8067 **(84.5) n21.5 t22 f20 b21**. Some salivating malt on flavour-exploding delivery, but all else tame and gentle. 40%. Cooley.

Clancey's bott code L8025 **(87) n22** sweet malt bounces off the firmer grain; young, lively and a touch floral; **t21** early toffeed delivery then a parade of vanilla and varied grains, barley most certainly included; **f22** burnt fudge and some teasing spice; **b22** remains an excellent blend for all the toffee. The spice balance excels. 40%. Cooley for Wm Morrison.

Clontarf Classic Blend (86) n18 t23 f23 b22. This has to be treated as a new whiskey. Many moons back I created this as a 100% grain from Cooley, a velvet-soft job of real subtlety. These days, with me having no involvement, the whiskies are from Irish Distillers. This is no longer all grain, though the malt content is no more than fractional. And it really underscores the difference in style between Midleton and Cooley grain. For every degree Colley is soft and yielding, Midleton is unremittingly rigid. The nose (though not the taste) is recognizable to devotees of White Bush and Paddy. Which means aroma-wise, with the caramel, it's pretty austere stuff. But you cannot fault the delivery which is crisp, salivating and offering surprising sweetness and big citrus. Not bad once you adapt: in fact, seriously entertaining. 40%.

Delaney's Special Reserve (84) n21.5 t20.5 f22 b21. An attractive blend with a big late spicy blast. The toffee dominates for long periods. *40%. Cooley for Co-operative Group.*

Feckin Irish Whiskey (81) n20 t21 f20 b20. Tastes just about exactly the feckin same as the Feckin Strangford Gold... *40%. The Feckin Drinks Co.* ⊙

Golden Irish bott code L7064 **(93)** n23 do I nose before me spice? And syrup-dripping coconut candy tobacco from childhood days? Yep, that and citrussy vanilla; t23 near perfect mouthfeel helps stoke up the malt intensity. The grain simply moulds into the palate bringing with it an odd twist of cocoa even by the middle; f23.5 milky chocolate and Demerara make for a long, pleasing, almost breakfast cereal-type finale; b23.5 by far one of the most enjoyable Irish blends around. Simple, but what it does, it does well – and deliciously well at that...!! *40%. Cooley.*

⁖ **The Irishman Rare Cask Strength** bott 2010 **(81.5)** n20 t22.5 f19 b20. Fabulous crescendo of weighty malt on delivery. But just too much bitterness and toffee hits this one. *53% Hot Irishman Ltd. 2850 bottles.*

The Irishman Rare Cask Strength bott 09 **(85.5)** n22 t21.5 f21 b21. A lovely, brawny malt which for all its strength feels that it has never quite slipped out of third gear. A chewy sweetness dominates but the caramel certainly has clipped this whiskey's wings. *56%. Hot Irishman Ltd. 1,800 bottles.*

The Irishman Rare Cask Strength (93.5) n23 a wonderful combination of soft bourbony notes and a light malty sub-plot. No shortage of honey and a lighter spinkling of the ginger which, if memory serves me correctly, is a feature of the mere mortal 40% bottling; t24 absolutely brilliant! It's not just the strength, although there are few whiskies that are so enormously affected. No, it's the immediate balance with the grains going in strong, but of such high quality and rich character that the gentle bourbon persuasion continues; softly oiled, very lightly malted, the arrival of the drier oak offers the perfect bitter-sweet foil; f23 long, chocolate rich and sophisticatedly spiced; b23.5 just so wonderful to come across a full strength blend. Better still when that blend happens to be as quite beautiful and characterful as this. A hot whisky alright: this should be burning a way into most blend lovers' homes. Quite exceptional, to be sure. *56%. Hot Irishman Ltd. 1400 bottles.*

The Irishman Superior Irish Whiskey bott code L6299L059 **(93)** n23 chunky caramel perhaps, but the apple is green and inviting; even an inclusion of soft manuka honey and ginger – most un-Irish; t23 lush, with a distinct malt charge before the caramel and oaky spice arrive; f23 those spices really tick, accentuated by the contrasting molasses and more honey but doused in vanilla; b24 what a quite wonderful blend: not of the norm for those that have recently come onto the market and there is much more of the Irish Distillers about this than most. Forget about the smoke promised in the tasting notes on the label...it gives you everything else but. And that is one hell of a lot!! *40%. Hot Irishman Ltd.*

Jameson (95) n24.5 Swoon....bizarrely shows even more Pot Still character than the Redbreast I tasted yesterday. Flinty to the point of cracking. The sherry is there but on reduced terms, allowing the firm grain to amplify the unmalted barley: truly brilliant; t24 mouthwatering delivery and then wave upon wave of diamond-hard barley and grain; the odd eclectic layer of something sweetish and honeyed, but this is eye-watering stuff; f22.5 an annoying touch of caramel creeps in, costing points, but even beyond that you still cannot other than be charmed by the layering of cocoa, barley and light grape; b24 I thought I had detected in bottlings I had found around the world a very slight reduction in the Pot Still character that defines this truly classic whiskey. So I sat down with a fresh bottle in more controlled conditions....and was blown away as usual. The sharpness of the PS is vivid and unique; the supporting grain of the required crispness. Fear not: this very special whiskey remains in stunning, truly wondrous form. *40%.*

Jameson 12 Years Old Special Reserve (88) n22 caramel, lazy sherry, musty; enlivened by a splash of sharper pot still; t23 the grape shows little sign of shyness, aided by a bitter-sweet element; good body and layering; f21 dulls out as the caramel arrives; dusty, drying; b22 much more sherry than of late and the pot still makes inroads, too. Just needs to lose some of the caramel effect; *40%*

Jameson 18 Years Old Limited Reserve eighth batch bott code JJ18-8 **(91)** n23 pure bourbon as oak dispenses myriad honey-leather-hickory notes with the Pot Still doing the job of the fruitier "rye"; t22.5 firm and juicy, gentle spice but a caramel-trimmed middle; f22.5 the redoubling of the juicier barley notes cuts through the vanilla and caramel to set up a long, delicately weighted finale; b22.5 the astonishing degree of bourbon on the nose thankfully doesn't make it to the palate where Ireland rather than Kentucky rules. *40%*

Jameson Gold Reserve (88) n22 a touch of menthol has crept into this much weightier nose: creaks with age as bourbony elements drift in and out of the grape; t23 sweet, sexily spiced delivery; hardens towards the middle but the grains are surprisingly lush and softly oiled; **f20** glutinous and plodding; **b22** enjoyable, but so very different: an absolute re-working with all the lighter, more definitively sweeter elements shaved mercilessly while the thicker oak is on a roll. Some distance from the masterpiece it once was. 40%

Jameson Rarest 2007 Vintage Reserve (96) n24.5 the crispest, cleanest, most beautifully defined of all the Jameson family: orange peel, hickory, spotted dog pudding, lavender – they're all there mushed around in near-perfect proportions; **t24** ditto the arrival with the mouth puckering under the onslaught of very old Pot Still: the bitter-sweet sharpness one would expect from this is there in spades; oak present and correct and edged in thin muscovado layer; **f23.5** vanilla by the barrel-load, pithy fruit and softly spiced barley **b24** is this the whiskey where we see a blender truly come of age. Tall green hats off to Billy Leighton who has, as all the better blenders did in the past, worked his way from quality-testing barrels on the dumping room floor to the lab. With this stupendous offering we have a blender in clover for he has earned his Golden Shamrocks. If the blending alone wasn't stellar enough, then making this a 46%, non chill-filtered offering really does put the tin hat on it (so Billy: you really have been listening to me over the years....!!!) This is truly great whiskey, among the pantheon of the world's finest. 46%

Jameson Signature Reserve (93) n23.5 adore the sharp citrus notes which bore, shrapnel-like, into the firm, though lighter than normal pure Pot Still: supremely balanced; the degree of honey is exemplary....and enticing; **t23.5** gossamer light delivery despite the obvious Pot Still presence. Some caramel momentarily dulls the middle but the flavours return for a beautifully constructed middle with alternating waves of citrus and pot still, occasionally honeyed, much as the nose predicts; the grains are softer than an Irish bog and simply dissolve without fuss: most un-Midleton **f22.5** beautiful: the vanilla does pulse with acacia honey; the Pot still stands firm and lightly fruity; **b23.5** be assured that Signature, with its clever structuring of delicate and inter-weaving flavours, says far more about the blender, Billy Leighton, than it does John Jameson. 40%. *Irish Distillers.*

Kilbeggan bott code L7091 **(86) n21 t22 f21.5 b21.5.** A much more confident blend by comparison with that faltering one of the last few years. Here, the malts make a significant drive towards increasing the overall complexity and gentle citrus style. 40%. *Cooley.*

Kilbeggan 15 Years Old bott code L7048 **(85.5) n21.5 t22 f21 b21.** My word! 15 years, eh? How time flies! And on the subject of flying, surely I have winged my way back to Canada and am tasting a native blend. No, this is Irish albeit in sweet, deliciously rounded form. However, one cannot help feeling that the dark arts have been performed, as in an injection of caramel, which, as well as giving that Canadian feel has also probably shaved off some of the more complex notes to middle and finish. Even so, a sweet, silky experience. 40%. *Cooley.*

Kilgeary bott code L8063 **(79) n20 t20 f19 b20.** There has always, and still proudly is, something strange about this blend. Cold tea on the nose and a bitter bite to the finish, sandwiches a brief flirtation with something sweet. 40%. *Cooley.*

Locke's bott code L8056 **(85.5) n21 t22 f21.5 b21.** Now, there you go!! Since I last really got round to analysing this one it has grown from a half-hearted kind of a waif to something altogether more gutsy and muscular. Sweeter, too, as the malts and grains combine harmoniously. A clean and pleasant experience with some decent malt fingerprints. 40%

Michael Collins A Blend (77) n19 t20 f19 b19. Michael Collins was known as the "big fellow". This pleasant, impressively spiced dram, might have enjoyed the same epithet had it not surrendered to and then been strangled by caramel on the finish. 40% (80 proof). *Cooley.*

Midleton Distillery Reserve (85) n22 t22 f20 b21. A whiskey which, for all its muscovado sweetness offers some memorable barley moments. 40%. *Irish Distillers Midleton Distillery only. Was once bottled as Jameson Distillery Reserve exclusive to Midleton. Changes character slightly with each new vatting. This one is some departure.*

Midleton Very Rare 1984 (70) n19 t18 f17 b16. Disappointing with little backbone or balance. 40%. *Irish Distillers.*

Midleton Very Rare 1985 (77) n20 t20 f18 b19. Medium-bodied and oily, this is a big improvement on the initial vintage. 40%. *Irish Distillers.*

Midleton Very Rare 1986 (79) n21 t20 f18 b20. A very malty Midleton richer in character than previous vintages. 40%. *Irish Distillers.*

Midleton Very Rare 1987 (77) n20 t19 f19 b19. Quite oaky at first until a late surge of excellent pot still. 40%. *Irish Distillers.*

Midleton Very Rare 1988 (86) n23 t21 f21 b21. A landmark MVR as it is the first vintage to celebrate the Irish pot-still style. 40%. *Irish Distillers.*

Midleton Very Rare 1989 (87) n22 t22 f22 b21. A real mouthful but has lost balance to achieve the effect. 40%. *Irish Distillers.*

Midleton Very Rare 1990 (93) n23 carrying on from where the '89 left off. The pot still doesn't drill itself so far into your sinuses, perhaps: more of a firm massage; t23 solid pot still again. There is a pattern now: pot still first, sweeter, maltier notes second, pleasant grains third and somewhere, imperceptibly, warming spices fill in the gaps; f24 long and Redbreast-like in character. Spices seep from the bourbon casks; b23 astounding whiskey: one of the vintages every true Irish whiskey lover should hunt for. 40%. Irish Distillers.

Midleton Very Rare 1991 (76) n19 t20 f19 b18. After the Lord Mayor's Show, relatively dull and uninspiring. 40%. Irish Distillers.

Midleton Very Rare 1992 (84) n20 t20 f23 b21. Superb finish with outstanding use of feisty grain. 40%. Irish Distillers.

Midleton Very Rare 1993 (88) n21 pot still with sub plots of honey and pepper; t22 the pot still makes use of the dry hardness of the grain; f23 beautiful elevation of the pot still towards something more complex and sharp balancing superbly with malt and bourbony-oak texture; b22 big, brash and beautiful – the perfect way to celebrate the 10th-ever bottling of MVR. 40%. Irish Distillers.

Midleton Very Rare 1994 (87) n22 pot-still characteristics not unlike the '93 but with extra honey and ginger; t22 the honeyed theme continues with malt arriving in a lush sweetness; f21 oily and a spurt of sharper, harder pot still; b22 another different style of MVR, one of amazing lushness. 40%. Irish Distillers.

Midleton Very Rare 1995 (90) n23 big pot still with fleeting honey; t24 enormous! Bitter, sweet and tart all together for a chewable battle of apple and barley. Brilliant; b21 some caramel calms proceedings, but Java coffee goes a little way to restoring complexity; b22 they don't come much bigger than this. Prepare a knife and fork to battle through this one. Fabulous. 40%. Irish Distillers.

Midleton Very Rare 1996 (82) n21 t22 f19 b20. The grains lead a soft course, hardened by subtle pot still. Just missing a beat on the finish, though. 40%. Irish Distillers.

Midleton Very Rare 1997 (83) n22 t21 f19 b21. The piercing pot still fruitiness of the nose is met by a countering grain of rare softness on the palate. Just dies on the finish when you want it to make a little speech. Very drinkable. 40%. Irish Distillers.

Midleton Very Rare 1999 (89) n21 malt and toffee: as sleepy as a nighttime drink; t23 stupendous grain, soft enough to absorb some pounding malt; f22 spices arrive as the blend hardens and some pot still finally battles its way through the swampy grain; b23 one of the maltiest Midletons of all time: a superb blend. 40%. Irish Distillers.

Midleton Very Rare 2000 (85) n22 t21 f21 b21. An extraordinary departure even by Midleton's eclectic standards. The pot still is like a distant church spire in an hypnotic Fen landscape. 40%. Irish Distillers.

Midleton Very Rare 2001 (79) n21 t20 f18 b20. Extremely light but the finish is slightly on the bitter side. 40%. Irish Distillers.

Midleton Very Rare 2002 (79) n20 t22 f18 b19. The nose is rather subdued and the finish is likewise toffee-quiet and shy. There are some fabulous middle moments, some of flashing genius, when the pot still and grain combine for a spicy kick, but the finish really is lacklustre and disappointing. 40%. Irish Distillers.

Midleton Very Rare 2003 (84) n22 t22 f19 b21. Beautifully fruity on both nose and palate (even some orange blossom on aroma). But the delicious spicy richness that is in mid launch on the tastebuds is cut short by caramel on the middle and finish. A crying shame, but the best Midleton for a year or two. 40%. Irish Distillers.

Midleton Very Rare 2004 (82) n21 t21 f19 b21. Yet again caramel is the dominant feature, though some quite wonderful citrus and spice escape the toffee blitz. 40%.

Midleton Very Rare 2005 (92) n23 t24 f22 b23. OK, you can take this one only as a rough translation. The sample I have worked from here is from the Irish Distillers blending lab, reduced to 40% in mine but without caramel added. And, as Midleton Very Rares always are at this stage, it's an absolute treat. Never has such a great blend suffered so in the hands of colouring and here the chirpiness of the pot still and élan of the honey (very Jameson Gold Label in part) show just what could be on offer given half the chance. Has wonderful natural colour and surely it is a matter of time before we see this great whiskey in its natural state. 40%

Midleton Very Rare 2006 (92) n22 real punch to the grain, which is there in force and offering a bourbony match for the pot still; t24 stupendously crisp, then a welter of spices nip and sting ferociously around the palate; the oaky coffee arrives early and with clarity while the barley helps solidify the rock-hard barley; f23 usually by now caramel intervenes and spoils, but not this time and again it's the grain which really stars; b23 the best Midleton for some time: as raw as a Dublin rough-house and for once not overly swamped with caramel. An uncut diamond. 40%. Irish Distillers.

Midleton Very Rare 2007 (83) n20 t22 f20 b21. Annoyingly buffeted from nose to finish by powering caramel. Some sweeter wisps do escape but the aroma suggests Canadian and insufficient Pot Still gets through to make this a Midleton of distinction. *40%. Irish Distillers*

Midleton Very Rare 2008 (88.5) n22 orange peel, pot still and a degree of bourbon...but too much caramel **t23** excellent big honey theme on delivery is augmented by a genuine, rock hard Pot Still juicy sharpness. An unusual coppery-metallic sheen gives the softly fruity proceedings polish; **f21.5** more caramel dulls the persistent pot still; **b22** a dense bottling which offers considerably more than the 2007 Vintage. Attractive, very drinkable and without the caramel it might really have hit the heights. *40%. Irish Distillers.*

Millars Special Reserve bott code L8069 **(86) n21 t22 f21.5 b21.5.** Now that's some improvement on the last bottling of this I found, with spices back with abandon and grains ensuring a fine mouthfeel. Even the chocolate fudge at the death is a treat. *40%. Cooley.*

⋰⋱ **Morrisons Irish Whiskey** bott code L10028 **(78) n19 t20 f19 b20.** Sweet, pleasant and inoffensive. *40% Wm Morrison Supermarket*

Paddy (74) n18.5 t20 f17.5 b18. Cleaned its act up a little. Even a touch of attractive citrus on the nose and delivery. But where does that cloying sweetness come from? As bland as an Irish peat bog but, sadly, nothing like so potentially tasty. *40%. Irish Distillers.*

Powers (91) n23 rugged pot still and beefed up by some pretty nippy grain; **t24** brilliant mouth arrival, one of the best in all Ireland: the pot still shrieks and attacks every available tastebud; **f22** pulsing spices and mouthwatering, rock-hard pot still. The sweetness is a bit unusual but you can just chew that barley; **b22** is it any coincidence that in this bottling the influence of the caramel has been significantly reduced and the whiskey is getting back to its old, brilliant self? I think not. Classic stuff. *40%. Irish Distillers.*

Powers Gold Label (87) n22 Powers? Really? I had to look twice and re-pour the sample to ensure this was the right stuff. Where is the clunking pot still? Soft, grainy caramel; **t22** attractively sweet with a distinct candy tobacco golden syrup but a serious departure from the ancient style. It's grain all the way, soft and silky as she goes; **f21** more lightness and caramel; maybe some semblance of pot still but you have to hunt to find it; **b22** the solid pot still, the very DNA of what made Powers, well, Powers is vanishing in front of our very noses. Yes, still some pot still around, but nothing like so pronounced in the way that made this, for decades, a truly one-off Irish and one of the world greats. Still delightful and with many charms but the rock hard pot still effect is sadly missed. What is going on here? *40%. Irish Distillers.*

Redbreast Blend (88) n23 some genuinely telling pot-still hardness sparks like a flint off the no less unyielding grain. Just love this; **t23** very sweet and soft, the grain carrying a massive amount of vanilla. Barley offers some riches, as does spice; **f20** a climbdown from the confrontational beginnings, but pretty delicious all the same; **b22** really impressed with this one-off bottling for Dillons the Irish wine merchants. Must try and get another bottle before they all vanish. *40%. Irish Distillers for Dillone IR (not to be confused with Kedbreast 12-y-o Pure Pot Still).*

St Patrick bott code L030907 **(77) n19 t20 f19 b19.** Good grief! No prisoners here as we have either a bitter oakiness or mildly cloying sweetness, rarely working in tandem. A few gremlins for the Kremlin. *40%. Cooley for Russia.*

Strangford Gold (81) n20 t21 f20 b20. A simplistic, exceptionally easy drinking blend with high quality grain offering silk to the countering spice but caramel flattens any malt involvement. *40%. The Feckin Drinks Co.*

Tesco Special Reserve Irish Whiskey bott code L8061 **(89.5) n21.5** gentle caramels try – and fail – to intervene as the vivid malts and seductive grains fuse; **t23.5** Irish blends don't come any softer: Cooley grain is as good as it gets anywhere in the word and here embrace and amplify the malts wonderfully; **f22** gentle, soft, sweet and clean; **b22.5** a cracker of a blend which allows the malts full scope to do their juicy bit. Possibly more malt than usual for a Cooley blend, but as they say: every little bit helps. *40%. Cooley.*

Tullamore Dew (85) n22 t21.5 f20.5 b21. The days of the throat being savaged by this one appear to be over. Much more pot still character from nose to finish and the rough edges remain, attractively, just that. *40%. Campbell & Cochrane Group.*

Tullamore Dew 10 Years Old (81.5) n21 t21.5 f19 b20. A bright start from this new kid on the Tullamore block. Soft fruit and harder pot still make some kind of complexity, but peters out at the death. *40%. Campbell & Cochrane Group.*

Tullamore Dew 12 Years Old (84.5) n21.5 t21.5 f20 b21.5. Silky thanks to some excellent Midleton grain: there are mouthwatering qualities here that make the most of the soft spices and gentle fruit. An improved whiskey, if still somewhat meek and shy. *40%. Campbell & Cochrane Group.*

Tullamore Dew Heritage (78) n20 t21 f18 b19. Tedious going with the caramel finish a real turn off. 40.0%. Campbell & Cochrane Group.

Walker & Scott Irish Whiskey "Copper Pot Distilled" (83) n20 t22 f20 b21. A collectors' item. This charming, if slightly fudgy-finished blend was made by Cooley as the house Irish for one of Britain's finest breweries. Sadly, someone put "Copper Pot Distilled" on the label, which, as it's a blend, can hardly be the case. And even if it wasn't a blend, would still be confusing in terms of Irish whiskey, there not being any traditional Irish Pot Still, that mixture of malted and unmalted barley. So Sam's, being one of the most traditional brewers in Britain, with the next bottling changed the label by dropping all mention of pot still. Top marks, chaps! The next bottling can be seen below. 40%. Sam Smith's.

Walker & Scott Irish Whiskey (85) n21 t22 f21 b21. Oddly, sharper grain has helped give his some extra edge through the toffee. A very decent blend. 40%.

The Whisky Fair Connemara 2001 bott 09 (90.5) n22 a golden toast dryness to the honeyed smoke; t23.5 goes into overdrive with some unexpected and unusual oils bulking up the sweetness; the drier points are hammered home with spicy intent; f22.5 vanilla and butterscotch with a hazelnut oil topping still can't quite master the powering phenols; b23 not your Irish bog-standard Connemara: extra doses of complexity and oil – not two things which normally go hand-in-hand. 59.2%. The Whisky Fair, Germany.

The Wild Geese Classic Blend (80.5) n20 t21 f19.5 b19. Easy going, pretty neutral and conservative. If you are looking for zip, zest and charisma you've picked the wrong goose (see below). 40%. Cooley for Avalon.

The Wild Geese Limited Edition Fourth Centennial (93) n23 sensationally clean and with the citrus really taking a starring role; vanillas abound, but in the soft, playful form; light and just so enticing; t23.5 barley notes peck around the tastebuds entirely unfettered by more tactile and heavier elements; lithe and lean, there is no fat on this goose and the vanilla lives up to its best expectation given on the nose while the mouth is drenched in salivating promises – simply stunning; f23 just so light, the clarity of the barley sugar and vanilla leaves you purring; b23.5 a limited edition of unlimited beauty. One of the lightest, subtle, intriguing and quite simply disarming Irish whiskeys on the market. As a bird and whiskey lover, this is one goose that I shall be looking out for. 43%. Cooley for Avalon.

The Wild Geese Rare Irish (89.5) n22 some toffee, yes, but the excellence of the vanilla is there to behold; just a light layering of barley but the gentle citrus caresses with the more exquisite touch... t23 superb arrival on the palate; the grain displays nothing other than excellence in both weight and control, and while the oaks and caramels are a tad bitter, the sweeter barley compensates wonderfully; f22 a silky, almost metallic sheen to the finale which complements the drying vanillins; b22.5 just love this. The Cooley grain is working sublimely and dovetails with the malt in the same effortless way wild geese fly in perfect formation. A treat. 43%. Cooley for Avalon.

Writers Tears (93) n23.5 a glossy Pot Still character: rather than the usual fruity firmness, the recognisable Pot Still traits are shrouded in soft honey tones which dovetail with lightening kumquat-citrus tones. Quite a curious, but always deliciously appealing animal...; t24 works beautifully well: the arrival is an alternating delivery of hard and soft waves, the former showing a more bitter, almost myopic determination to hammer home its traditional pot still standpoint; the sweeter, more yielding notes dissolve with little or no resistance, leaving an acacia honeyed trail; towards the middle a juicier malt element mingles with soft vanilla but the Pot Still character never goes away; f22 relatively short with perhaps the Pot Still, with an old-fashioned cough sweet fruitiness, lingering longest, though its does retain its honeyed accompaniment for the most part; b23.5 now that really was different. The first mix of pure Pot Still and single malt I have knowingly come across in a commercial bottling, but only because I wasn't aware of the make up of last year's Irishman Blend. The malt, like the Pot Still, is, I understand from proprietor Bernard Walsh, from Midleton, but the two styles mixed shows a remarkably similar character to when I carried out an identical experiment with pure pot still and Bushmills the best part of a decade ago. A success and hopefully not a one off. Which is more than I can say for the label, a whiskey collectors – sorry, collector's – item in its own right. There is a wonderfully Irish irony that a whiskey dedicated to Ireland's extraordinary literary heritage should be represented by a label, even a brand name, so punctually inept; it's almost brilliant. The reason for the Writers (sic) Tears, if from the spirits of James Joyce, Samuel Beckett, George Bernard Shaw, Oscar Wilde and perhaps even Maurice Walsh, whose grandson became a legendary blender at Irish Distillers, will be open to debate: we will never know whether they laughed or cried. As far as the actual whiskey is concerned, though, I am sure they, to a man, would have no hesitation but to pen the most luminous and positive critiques possible. 40%. Writers Tears Whiskey Co.

American Whiskey

Not that long ago American whiskey meant Bourbon. Or perhaps a very close relation called Tennessee. And sometimes it meant rye. Though nothing like often as it did prior to prohibition. Very, very rarely, though, did it ever get called single malt, because virtually none was made on the entire North American continent. That was a specialist - and very expensive - type left to the Scots and, to a lesser extent, the Irish. Or even the Japanese if a soldier or businessman was flying back from Tokyo.

I say "virtually" none was made because, actually, there was the odd batch of malt produced in America and, in my library, I still have some distilled at a rye distillery in Maryland in the early 1970s - indeed, I remember drinking the stuff there back in 1974. But it was hardly a serious commercial concern and the American public were never made greatly aware of it.

Now, though, at last count it appears that there are at least 25 distilleries doing their best to make whiskey mainly from malted barley but sometimes from rye and corn, too. Some still have much to learn, others have shown that they are well on their way to possible greatness. One distillery, Stranahan's in Colorado, has in a very short space of time managed to bring out a series of bottlings which left no doubt that they have joined McCarthy's of Oregon and Anchor of California in achieving it with another Portland distiller, Edgefield, not that far behind.

But as a collective movement it is by far the most exciting in the entire whisky world, despite what is happening in certain parts of Europe, especially Germany, Austria and Switzerland, where there is an even bigger movement. It appears to me that the better "micro distillers" are just a little more advanced in the US and have a stronger urge to grow. Some new wave American distillers, doubtless, will fall by the wayside while others will take their place. But those at the vanguard are likely to act as the spur to keep the others moving onwards and it is a situation I shall monitor very closely. There are squabbles about whether enzymes should be used for fermentation, a question I have been asked about many times. My view is that they should be avoided, although I can understand the reasons for their employment. However, when you are witnessing the birth of an entirely new whiskey life form it is always fascinating to see how it naturally develops. Usually the strongest live and the weakest die. In this survival of the fittest it will soon become apparent which methods are the ones that will succeed - and they tend to be the ones which have served distillers well over the last couple of centuries.

There is no little irony, however, that as we take a closer look at the alternative distilling world within the United States, it is the old order which is now really catching the eye. As I suspected, my award to Sazerac Rye 18 Years Old as Jim Murray's Whisky Bible 2010 World Whisky of the Year bemused quite a number of whisky lovers because it represents a style of whiskey they have never as much seen, let alone tasted. Doubtless Thomas Handy rye being named the world's second best for this 2011 Whisky Bible will also cause consternation in some quarters.

Once upon a time, though, rye whiskey was seen as the embodiment of indigenous American spirit and the preferred choice in the country. After falling out of favour following Prohibiton and then World War II the traditional rye distillers in Pennsylvania and Maryland closed, production of the spirit shrank to a week's fermentation a year, if that, in a few Kentucky distilleries and until recently it was seen only as a rare alternative to bourbon in American liquor stores, often hidden on the end of shelves, or at the bottom. And often, ignominiously, both - with giveaway prices to add insult to injury.

Rye whiskey, where a minimum 51 per cent of the mashbill is made from rye - as opposed to bourbon where 51 per cent must be from corn - has long been my favourite whisk(e)y style. What certainly isn't is the stuff which constitutes the flavoured "bourbons" which have been filling up valuable shelf space all over the USA. I was going to include them in the Bible – even though scores of less than 20 were not uncommon – but decided against it. For they are simply not bourbon whiskey, though the industry is watching sales go through the liquor stores' roof are not too upset to see the flavoured version standing shoulder to shoulder with traditional names. This, for me, is a major problem as it far from makes clear in the minds of drinkers exactly what bourbon is. But for the average liquor store manager, if cases of the stuff are selling each week: does he care? I can understand if he doesn't...

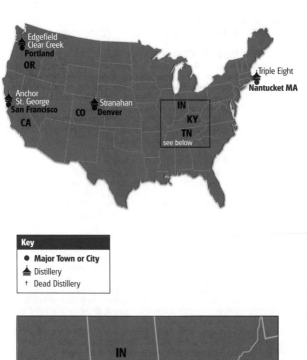

Key
- ● **Major Town or City**
- ▲ Distillery
- † Dead Distillery

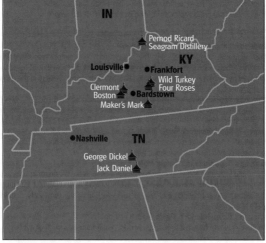

Bardstown
- ▲ Heaven Hill†
- ▲ Tom Moore

Frankfort
- ▲ Buffalo Trace

▲ Woodford Reserve

Louisville
- ▲ Early Times
- ▲ Bernheim
- ▲ Stitzel Weller

American Single Malt
ANCHOR DISTILLERY (see Rye)

CHARBAY DISTILLERY Napa Valley, California
Charbay Hop Flavoured Whiskey release II, barrels 3-7 (**91**) **n22** Sweet, intense barley wine with a rich floral seam; **t22** enormous. The malt is in concentrate form, which makes it sweet. But those hops provide a balancing bitter-sweet fruitiness. All this packed in at full strength. Wow!! **f23** quite bitter as the hops have the final say. The wood, though, forges a bourbon sheen to it all and adds to the all out assault on the tastebuds; **b24** being distilled from beer which includes hops, it can – and will - be argued that this is not beer at all. However, what cannot be disputed is that this is a rich, full-on spirit that has set out to make a statement and has delivered it. Loudspeaker and all. 55%

CLEAR CREEK DISTILLERY Portland, Oregon
McCarthy's batch W08-01, bott Oct 08 (**94.5**) **n24** the smokiest of kippers, phenols from the blackest of peat: it has to be McCarthy's! There is something quite farmyardy about this one, and the hog-theme continues with a salty smoked bacon edge. Hook me up to a mask so I can breathe this one in all day....! **t24** for all the posturing on the nose, the delivery is nothing short of gentlemanly and sedate. A coating of muscovado sugar clings to the juicy barley and the oak refuses to interfere other than to add a touch of vanilla; **f23** a long, long fade with the dryness slowly, almost imperceptibly replacing those astonishing sweet themes. Just so delicate, even at the death; **b23.5** the upping of the strength from 40% has done this whisky no harm whatsoever and at 46% it would be better still. Proof that consistent drams can come from small stills. An American masterpiece – and now an institution. 42.5%

McCarthy's Oregon Single Malt Aged 3 Years (**95**) **n23** kippery but also soft grist and spices and a hint of slightly overdone brown toast; **t24** jackpot hit as the sweetness is controlled and instead we have lush waves of ultra-clean smoke; the oiliness is there but defused enough to allow only a perfect coating of the palate; **f24** not far off the perfect finale. The oak adds a drier element but really it is the Port Ellen-style fresh gristiness that keeps your tongue working overtime as the finish refuses to fade; **b24** this is, unquestionably, the finest bottled whiskey I have tasted anywhere in the world from a small-batch distiller. Only Islay's very finest can out-complex this not so little chap. 40% (80 proof).

COPPER FOX DISTILLERY Sperryville, Virginia
Wasmund's Rappahannock Single Malt batch no. 2 (**82.5**) **n18 t20 f23.5 b21.** There are those who will struggle to get past the apple/cherry wood smoke, especially when it takes on this tobacco-like personality. A mixed bag of a malt, but one that deserves not to be dismissed by the nose alone. And curious, also, as it is the only distillery in the US which malts all its own barley. 48%

Wasmund's Rappahannock Single Malt batch no. 3 (**80**) **n17 t20 f22 b21.** Way more emphasis on the bitter-sweet here but the dry, bitter finale does overcompensate slightly for the gristy start. 48%

Wasmund's Rappahannock Single Malt batch no. 7 (**86.5**) **n19 t21 f24 b22.5.** . The nose is still a bit of a problem to a non-smoker like me but there is no doubting that this is a complex, well-crafted malt the moment it hits the palate. 48%

Wasmund's Rappahannock Single Malt batch no. 8 (**81**) **n17 t21 f22 b21.** Love it or loathe it – and I know whisky drinkers who do both – there is a consistency in style to these bottling which one has to admire. This one, however, suffers from some over indulgence in caramel (either natural or added it is hard to say) which trims the complexity significantly, especially at the finale. 48%

Wasmund's Rappahannock Single Malt batch no. 11 (**83.5**) **n16 t21 f24 b22.5.** Can't help thinking it would be great to see this whisky, made from its own floor malting, naked without any wood-smoke. 48%

Wasmund's Rappahannock Single Malt batch no. 13 (**89.5**) **n21.5 t23 f22.5 b22.5.** Either someone forgot to smoke the barley or apple and cherrywood was in short supply. Either way, this works genuinely well with tons of character and clarity. 48%

Wasmund's Rappahannock Single Malt batch no.14 (**87**) **n21 t23 f21.5 b21.5.** Exasperating intrusion of caramel – one assumes from the wood chips – spoils what might have been a beautiful story. 48%

Wasmund's Rappahannock Single Malt batch no. 18 (**84**) **n18 t21 f23 b22.** Back to original type, with plenty of fruit wood smoke to shape this intriguingly structured malt. I thought I had tasted this one before: I had, while chair judging for the American Distillers'

Institute in Kentucky. When I compared my scores, they were exactly identical. Absolutely 96% proof positive what a very distinctive style this whisky is. *48%*

Wasmund's Rappahannock Single Malt batch no. XIX **(84.5) n17 t22 f23 b22.5.** There appears almost to be a dollop of maple syrup to sweeten this one with the wood-smoke really performing a number here. Big, vanilla and caramel charged and even a hint of butterscotch trying to help smooth things over. Controlled spice ensures another layer of complexity. *48%*

⋅⋅⋅⋅ **Wasmund's Rappahannock Single Malt** batch no. 32 **(91.5) n22** you have to strain to find the tobacco note which used to kill me. Instead, we have a more subtle, nutty and delicate bonfire edge to the smoke; **t23** perfect mouth feel: after getting over the initial wobble on delivery we are met by a glorious fusion of Demerara sugar, hickory and a pulsing, lightly spiced smoke: beautiful....; **f23.5** spices up a notch and some honey begins to melt its way into the vanillas; **b23** one of the highlights since completing the 2010 Bible was driving over to Rick Wasmund's rambling Copper Fox distillery in Virginia. His was the first I had been to where they had turned chap maturation into an art form. Some of his earlier bottlings were testing. With practice, especially in the malting department, he appears to be getting the balance right. Batch 32 here, for instance, is a cracker by any standards. *48% (96 proof) ncf*

EDGEFIELD DISTILLERY Troutdale, Oregon

Edgefield Hogshead (94) n23.5 Lordy-me! No compromising or prisoners taken here: the oak and barley are upfront in equal measure and shouting for top attention; **t23.5** salivating to the point of improbability. A touch yeasty in part, but perhaps that accounts for the rolling fruitiness which takes grip as the barleywater intensifies; **f23** long, with a peppery robustness beginning to clobber anything half-hearted or lacking a spine. The enormity of the barley-oak theme takes some comprehending; **b24** this little distillery has very much come of age. This is fabulous malt that makes no attempt to confuse complexity with no-holds-barred enormity. Big, ballsy and just about flawless. No bottling or batch date, but believed to be bottled 2008. *46%*

NEW HOLLAND BREWING COMPANY Holland, Michigan

Zeppelin Bend Straight Malt Whisky (87) n19 intense malt but displaying a curious and disharmonious sweet and sour note; **t22** rare to find a malt with such spell-binding intensity: a sublime coating of grist helps see off some of the oils which should have not made the cut; **f23** much drier with the oak now throwing in liquorice and gentle spice which harmonise sublimely with those gristy/worty tones; **b23** an understandable and forgivable blemish here and there, especially on the nose, from this new distillery. But full marks for intrigue and entertainment! A brand to keep your eye on. *40%*

SAINT JAMES SPIRITS Irwindale, California

Peregrine Rock (83.5) n21 t20.5 f21.5 b20.5. Fruity and friendly, the wine and smoke combo work well-ish enough but the thumping oak injection highlights that maybe there isn't quite enough body to take in the aging. Perhaps less time in the barrel will reduce the bitter orange finale. *40%*

STRANAHAN DISTILLERY Denver, Colorado

Stranahan's Colorado Whiskey Batch No. 1 dist 9 Apr 04 db **(95) n25 t23 f23 b24.** This is ridiculous. No first-ever bottling has a right to be this good. If any lucky so-and-so still has a bottle of this...sit on it. Or drink it. You win either way. It is America distilling liquid gold and history in a glass. Beautifully distilled and crafted, the average quality of world, let alone American, malt whisky has just gone up a notch or two. *47% (94 proof).*

Stranahan's Colorado Whiskey Batch No. 2 dist 29 Apr 04 db **(89.5) n23 t22 f22.5 b22.** A beautiful whisky but lacks the improbable finesse and balance of Batch 1. *47% (94 proof).*

Stranahan's Colorado Whiskey Batch No. 3 dist 13 May 04 db **(95.5) n24 t23 f24.5 b24.** Back on song with another stunner. Just how do they get it this good....? *47% (94 proof).*

Stranahan's Colorado Whiskey Batch No. 4 dist 7 Jul 04 db **(88) n22.5 t21.5 f22 b22** Less busy than earlier bottlings, emphasising weight rather than dexterity. *47% (94 proof).*

Stranahan's Colorado Whiskey Batch No. 5 dist 9 Sep 04 db **(90) n23 t24 f21 b22** If the Rockies is where east meets west, then this first-ever Colorado whiskey is where bourbon meets single malt. The quality of the distilling is beyond reproach and this 3,608th, and final, whiskey to go into this 2007 Bible really is the perfect way to end six months' solid tasting. But if the whiskey does has a fault it is the enormity of the oak: for a two-year-old only Indian malt whisky matures faster. My instincts tell me that distillers Jake and Jess will benefit in future years from using a mixture of virgin and used casks to maximise the complexity lurking in the obvious riches found in this gold strike. But hey, this is Colorado. Where you don't mess with a man's woman...or his whiskey... *47% (94 proof).*

Stranahan's Colorado Whiskey Batch No. 6 dist 6 Oct 04 db **(91)** n23 t23 f22.5 b22.5 About as relaxed as you'll ever find this stuff! Also, nothing like as wide a cut as that found on Batch 5, the first from this distillery I tasted a couple of years back. *47% (94 proof).*

Stranahan's Colorado Whiskey Batch No. 7 dist 3 Nov 04 db **(90)** n23.5 t21.5 f22.5 b22.5 Almost aggressive in its oakiness the manner in which balance is achieved is as fascinating as it is enjoyable on the palate. *47% (94 proof).*

Stranahan's Colorado Whiskey Batch No. 8 db **(94)** n23.5 t23.5 f23 b24 Distilled not a million miles away from South Park, this is one Chef of a whiskey. Baby, get on down...! *47% (94 proof).*

Stranahan's Colorado Whiskey Batch No. 9 dist 17 Nov 04 db **(92.5)** n23 t24 f22.5 b23 Every bottling of this asks slightly different questions and gives you varying answers. This is such fun....!!! *47% (94 proof)*

Stranahan's Colorado Whiskey Batch No. 10 dist 3 Jan 05 db **(86)** n21.5 t22 f21.5 b21. Even when this fails to get going, still it is very drinkable whiskey. Here we have a thin'un. It never appears to gain its balance or poise and strains at the leash to recover. Some seriously delicate, kumquat-tipped moments which ensure a fine experience. But compared to the others... *47% (94 proof).*

Stranahan's Colorado Whiskey Batch No. 11 dist 12 Jan 05 db **(96)** n24 t24 f24 b24. Like batch 10, a lighter, more thoughtful version. Unlike Batch 10 it appears to hit a stride and rhythm. And as for the complexity....sighhhh. What a way to taste my 812th new whisky for this year, thereby eclipsing the 2008 Bible: it would have been hard to have chosen a finer malt. *47% (94 proof).*

Stranahan's Colorado Whiskey Batch No. 12 db **(89.5)** n23 t22.5 f22 b22 A departure from the norm: esters and spices kept to a minimum. *47% (94 proof).*

Stranahan's Colorado Whiskey Batch No. 13 db dist 10 Jan 05 **(88.5)** n22.5 t22 f22 b22 The second one on the trot where the natural caramels have played an important part. Here they almost dominate. *47% (94 proof).*

Stranahanís Colorado Whiskey Batch No. 14 dist 10 Oct 05 db **(77)** n18 t19 f21 b19. aggressive sweet bourbon characteristics try to disguise a degree of feintiness which has crept into this batch. The wide cut does ensure some major flavours to develop, though. Big and surly. *47%*

Stranahan's Colorado Whiskey Batch No. 15 dist 3 Mar 05 db **(80)** n19 t21 f20 b20. Fat, enjoyable, caramel-rich. But another wide cut wallah which doesn't quite have the standard Stranahan genius. *47% (94 proof).*

Stranahan's Colorado Whiskey Batch No. 16 dist 14 May 04 db **(92.5)** n22 t24 f23 b23.5. I was getting worried... *47% (94 proof).*

Stranahan's Colorado Whisky Batch No. 17 (95.5) n23 t24 f23.5 b25. How have they done it? How has a distillery come from nowhere and within a couple of years produced one of the best whiskies in the world? The only thing more stunning than the brilliance of their malt is the way in which a new whisky style has not only been invented, but seemingly perfected. For those who love bourbon and single malt, this really is the best of both worlds. *47%*

Stranahan's Colorado Whisky Batch No. 18 (89.5) n22 t23 f22 b22.5. Massive oak has tipped this over the edge slightly. Very enjoyable whiskey, but lacking the balance that made the Batch 17 a malt caressed by genius. *47%*

Stranahan's Colorado Whiskey Batch No. 19 db **(90)** n21.5 t23 f23 b22.5. Very odd, this one: juniper appears on both nose and delivery. Another slightly wider cut here, but does no great harm as the oranges make good. Big and boisterous until the effeminate cowboy of a finish. *47% (94 proof).*

Stranahan's Colorado Whiskey Batch No. 20 dist 14 Dec 05 db **(92)** n22 t23.5 f23 b23.5. Each bottle appears as a test: both for your tastebuds and the fledgling distillery in discovering what it is capable of achieving; *47% (94 proof).*

Stranahan's Colorado Whiskey Batch No. 21 dist 12 Apr 05 db **(89)** n22.5 t22 f22 b22.5. Tasting all these bottlings one after the other...it's kind of like looking at the same tree or building from a slightly different angle, or making love to a new (rather gorgeous) partner at a different pace or position... *47% (94 proof).*

Stranahan's Colorado Whiskey Batch No. 22 dist 27 Apr 05 db **(94.5)** n23 t24 f23.5 b24. Returns to something much closer to its original honeyed style sans the heavy natural caramel...and appears much more in tune and complex for it. *47% (94 proof).*

Stranahan's Colorado Whiskey Batch No. 23 db **(95)** n23.5 t23.5 f24 b24. If you could put a voice to this whiskey, it'd probably be Lee Marvin... *47% (94 proof)*

⁘ **Stranahan's Colorado Whiskey Batch No. 24** dist May 05 db **(87) n21.5** curious mixture of youth and age from the same date; but a few florals and botanicals apart, hi, honey: welcome home....; **t22** a real redneck this in that the spices really do go for the neck; soft oils help soften the countless blows until the middle ground settles with a joyous liquorice depth; **f21.5** some major toasty oak powers through but enough sugars for balance; **b22** hints of aggression from this guy, and then offers a bunch of honey-scented flowers to make amends... 47% (94 proof)

⁘ **Stranahan's Colorado Whiskey Batch No. 25** dist May 05 db **(93.5) n23.5** textbook Stranahan's: confident, thickly painted honey dovetailing with a sublime hickory and white pepper mix....wow!!...; **t24** hugely textured and muscularly structured, this batch goes for it big time, following the nose note by note but tipping in big vanilla and Demerara sugars for good measure; **f23** that fat body strings the finish out an extra minute or two. It gives the sugars and peppers extra time and space to gel; **b23** received a long phone call just prior to tasting this. At the end of it, grabbed the glass without thinking, brought to the nose momentarily forgetting what I had been tasting and thought: "Bloody hell! Stranahan's!!!" Unmistakable, unmissable, unique and truly gorgeous. 47% (94 proof)

⁘ **Stranahan's Colorado Whiskey Batch No. 26** dist May 05 db **(89.5) n22.5** the oak creaks a bit but there is some Jaffa Cake chocolatey-orangeyness to compensate; **t23** crunching, splintering oak might be too much for some whiskeys as it gatecrashes the third and fourth waves. But not this guy: bourbony-rich honey-hickory notes come flooding to the rescue; **f22** soft, sultry oils help crank up the vanilla; **b22** they obviously don't take prisoners in Colorado: you take this one on at your own peril... 47% (94 proof)

⁘ **Stranahan's Colorado Whiskey Batch No. 27** dist May 05 db **(94.5) n23** on the same lines as Batch 26 but now more oak and less Jaffa Cake; **t24.5** that is just awesome.... speechless....; absolutely every aspect of this whiskey is perfectly balanced. Death by chocolate meets life by honeycomb...and there is even very big wave upon wave of barley to give a juicy middle; the spices carried on the oils are polite and complex; **f23** thins out as the vanillas take charge but doesn't stint on the complexity; **b24** how do these guys do it? How can they produce a malt in which the flavours at times seem outlandishly big, but then you find everything has its place and time in this perfectly fitting jigsaw of sensations? How lucky am I to taste whiskeys of such magnificence? Talk about a gentle giant... 47% (94 proof)

⁘ **Stranahan's Colorado Whiskey Batch No. 28** dist Jun 05 db **(83) n20 t22 f20 b21.** A Beam...? No, just a fraction off beam... Attractive trademark honey, but perhaps too wide a cut. 47% (94 proof)

⁘ **Stranahan's Colorado Whiskey Batch No. 29** dist Jul 06 db **(86) n21 t22 f22 b21.** Another oily version. A thick layering of muscovado sugars and vanilla. 47% (94 proof)

⁘ **Stranahan's Colorado Whiskey Batch No. 30** dist Nov 06 db **(89.5) n22** thin layer of manuka honey on blackening toast; **t22** seeringly hot spices muffled by that persistent honey; **f23** settles attractively with some an unusual fruit thing going on, mainly on the plumy side; the honey continues its merry way for a ultra soft and sweet finale; **b22.5** plums? Where did they come from? An errant malt in some respects but the fruit and intense honey compensate outrageously well. 47% (94 proof)

⁘ **Stranahan's Colorado Whiskey Batch No. 31** dist Jul 05 db **(90.5) n23.5** here we go again: the full nine yards as the bourbon melts into the barley...; **t23** tangy small still: coppery – which is hinted at on the nose; plenty of roasted fat sultana, too; **f22** the coppery profile continues, offering an unusual crisp sheen to the finale; **b22** a show off whisky: everything it does it does big and vividly. Another beauty from the boys. 47% (94 proof)

⁙ **Stranahan's Colorado Whiskey Batch No. 32** dist Nov 06 db **(92.5) n23.5** they obviously grow roses in Colorado: Turkish delight with chocolate honeycomb; **t23.5** the kind of whiskey which grabs hold of your taste buds and gives them a damned good shake and lets them know who's in town: today it's the bourbon gang with juicy Demerara the leader. All kinds of hickory, liquorice and even juniper sidekicks are in force; **f23** lots of burnt fudge...a little creamy and even a touch Demerara rummy; **b23.5** I have to admit that tasting Stranahan's is one of the true highlights of my whiskey year. For pure entertainment value their whiskeys are in some ways unmatched. You kind of know what you are going to get. But it will always surprise you. Variations on a theme, maybe. But some of those variations can leave you drooling and chuckling to yourself because of the sheer fun of tasting this stuff. This is one such bottling.... and this is what enjoying whiskey or whisky should all be about. 47% (94 proof)

⁘ **Stranahan's Colorado Whiskey Batch No. 33** dist Nov 06 db **(85.5) n20.5 t22 f22 b21.** Lots of chocolate nougat....and chewing...!! 47% (94 proof)

⁘ **Stranahan's Colorado Whiskey Batch No. 34** dist Sep 06 db **(91.5) n22** another of those uniquely intriguing gin-bourbon styles, this one offering lots of lemon peel...; **t24** ...but not on the huge, mouth-engulfing lusciously fat delivery. So much Demerera- sweetened cocoa here...but hang on, a touch of juniper between my teeth....; **f23** ridiculously long. The light sugars have melted into the taste buds and their rays fade like a sun setting on a sea of oily vanilla barley; **b22.5** I haven't a clue what has gone on here. But whatever it is has you wanting to fill your glass with more. 47% (94 proof)

⁙ **Stranahan's Colorado Whiskey Batch No. 35** dist Jul 06 db **(88) n22** look at that: dead easy to interpret toasty, oaky, honeyed vanilla with a dash of barley water; **t22** the nose in liquid form...plus a few half-hearted spices; **f22** more thick vanilla with a dollop of hickory; **b22** one of the cleanest, least complicated Stranahan's for a long while. But the intensity means there is no chance of a dull moment. 47% (94 proof)

⁙ **Stranahan's Colorado Whiskey Batch No. 36** dist Sep 06 db **(89) n23** pretty close to all out bourbon character, including busy small grains and violets; **t23** fulsome, thick butterscotch and burned fudge with a honeyed thread; **f21.5** oils out allowing a soft vanilla, barley fade; **b21.5** delicious. But - unusually for this distillery - starts out at full throttle but reaches the finish line in third gear. 47% (94 proof)

⁙ **Stranahan's Colorado Whiskey Batch No. 37** dist Sep 06 db **(76.5) n20 t19 f18.5 b19**. A disappointing way to bring up my 400th new whisky for the 2011 Bible. This is thin and gruff; every sign of a still worked faster than usual. 47% (94 proof)

⁙ **Stranahan's Colorado Whiskey Batch No. 38** dist Sep 06 db **(88.5) n23** that leathery armchair bourbon character; red liquorice; just beautifully paced and relaxed; **t22** an aggressive delivery threatens a repeat of Batch 37, but fears are dispelled by several luxurious waves of ever intensifying fruitcake, increasingly well brown-sugared; **f21.5** softly oiled vanilla; **b22** excellent muscovado signature. Quite a clever whiskey without probably meaning to be. 47%

⁙ **Stranahan's Colorado Whiskey Batch No. 39** dist Oct 06 db **(87) n21.5** freshly baked plum pudding; **t23** the sugars of the barley and those extracted from the oak appear in harmonious control; the build up of spices is almost erotic; **f21.5** thins quickly towards vanilla.... and vanishes; **b21** how odd is that? I have heard that it happens to some men that they get so excited it's over in seconds. Appears the same thing happens with certain whiskeys... 47%

⁙ **Stranahan's Colorado Whiskey Batch No. 40** dist Feb 07 db **(81.5) n22.5 t22 f18 b19**. Excellent nose; loads of rich bourbon on delivery...then all gets rather bitter. And you don't find many from this distillery with an off-key finish. 47% (94 proof)

⁙ **Stranahan's Colorado Whiskey Batch No. 41** dist Jan 07 db **(94) n23.5** warm hazelnut oil and polished leather; **t24** myriad microwaves of sugared tannins spread across the palate; there is a second or two of light spice and then toffee-apple fills the middle; **f23** long, lightly oiled with a crème brulee touch to those brown sugars; **b23.5** so well behaved you are wondering when the rockets will fly. They don't, so just kick your shoes off and relax with this one. After a period of unusually ordinary batches by their own standards, we are back to something world class. With the emphasis on the class. 47% (94 proof)

⁙ **Stranahan's Colorado Whiskey Batch No. 42** dist Mar 07 db **(88) n22** a curious layer of pepper on the usual honeycomb tale; **t23** sharp, flinty with the barley really giving the taste buds a poke; usual sugar-rich display on delivery and middle; **f21** big vanilla; **b22** attractively angular in shape and delivery thanks to the lack of usual oils. 47% (94 proof)

⁙ **Stranahan's Colorado Whiskey Batch No. 43** dist Jun 07 db **(86) n21.5 t21 f22 b21.5**. Another very firm one with the grain and cocoa really chiselling its way about the mouth. This is one of the first where I have found a degree of youth shaping the style. The honeyed buzz is a trademark delight, though. 47% (94 proof)

⁙ **Stranahan's Colorado Whiskey Batch No. 44** dist Jun 07 db **(87.5) n22.5** vanilla and caramel line up alongside young malt; **t22** thick cream toffee with the usual Demerara sugar biz; **f21** lazy, long and toffee dependent; **b22** another bottling that feels as though it's holding back somewhat. On puberty, too. 47% (94 proof)

⁙ **Stranahan's Colorado Whiskey Batch No. 45** dist Apr 07 db **(90.5) n22.5** slightly less youth and more accent on spice and honey...where have you been, guys...? **t23.5** beautifully mouth-filling with varying textured honey, a hint or two of hickory...and a background spice buzz; **f22** lovely chocolate-covered fudge; **b22.5** much, much more on the money. Spices which had gone AWOL of late have returned to duty and the full meat and two veg Stranahan's is back singing its honeyed, complex, magnificent song. 47% (94 proof)

⁙ **Stranahan's Colorado Whiskey Batch No. 46** dist Jul 07 db **(89.5) n22** I could be in my Gentleman's Club breathing in the freshly polished Chesterfield....while enjoying honey on slightly burned toast; a slight hint of youth is overcome by an avalanche of bourbon sweetness; **t22** another youthful delivery, but again the big honey and hickory crushes it with great weight; **f23** long, a slow radiating of spices touches of barley; **b22.5** what an elegant whiskey. Doffs its cap to youth, but shows maturity in all the right places. 47% (94 proof)

⮑ **Stranahan's Colorado Whiskey Batch No. 47** dist Jul 07 db **(90.5)** n23 thick with the blossoming oak getting star billing; a curious hint of gin-like zesty fruitcake/citrus, too; t23 charming oils ensure a soft landing on delivery and an immediate coating of all the usual bourbon, honey-tinged suspects; still those botanicals persist, but on another level; f22.5 long with the spices and vanilla carving out the long road to the finale; b22 a real complex, mildly schizophrenic bottling which just entertains all the way. Superb! *47% (94 proof)*

⮑ **Stranahan's Colorado Whiskey Batch No. 48** dist Jun 06 db **(87.5)** n23 if this were bourbon, you'd describe this as small grainsy: wonderfully busy and bitsy; t21.5 the youthfulness is hugely apparent on delivery but then a big dose of liquorice and coppery sharpness; f22 settles with a dollop of butterscotch but the metallic sheen continues; b21 quite a different bottling. Great fun without ever really settling into a rhythm. *47% (94 proof)*

⮑ **Stranahan's Colorado Whiskey Batch No. 49** dist Oct 07 db **(94.5)** n23.5 it's back on the trail of thick, creamy mocha and honey...sure this isn't a bourbon....??? t24 that is fabulous: a mind-bendingly complex delivery with the key being the weight of oil against the drier vanillas and the deftness of touch from the muscovado sugars; f23.5 long and reverting back to the mocha promised on the nose; bitter oranges and just a touch of praline adds to the beauty; b23.5 when this distillery get it right, they get it very right. Required tasting for anyone thinking that great age is the key to great whiskey.... *47% (94 proof)*

⮑ **Stranahan's Colorado Whiskey Batch No. 50** Oct 07 db **(89)** n22.5 beefy with dense vanilla; t23 definitely a slightly different shape to the norm here with the sugar and spices outgunned by a vaguely fruity theme; f21.5 coppery, sharp, butterscotch and a touch of bitterness to the oak; b22 the most bitter-sweet yet. Chosen to represent the 50th batch, yet it seemed different? Or just the next one to be picked. A fascinating whiskey, but I would have had the previous batch to mark the half century....!! *47% (94 proof)*

⮑ **Stranahan's Colorado Whiskey Batch No. 51** dist Nov 07 db **(82)** n21 t22 f19 b20. Full bodied and not too bothered about frills and complexity. Good spice, though. *47% (94 proof)*

⮑ **Stranahan's Colorado Whiskey Batch No. 52** dist Jan 07 db **(81.5)** n20.5 t21 f20 b20. Evidence from nose to finish off a wider than normal cut. But enough sugars to give you a toothache. *47% (94 proof)*

⮑ **Stranahan's Colorado Whiskey Batch No. 53** dist Jan 08 db **(85.5)** n21 t21.5 f22 b21. Absolutely chock-a-block with honey-nougat. Everything dense and in concentrate. *47% (94 proof)*

⮑ **Stranahan's Colorado Whiskey Batch No. 54** dist Jan 08 db **(91.5)** n23.5 get a load of that barrow-full of oranges. It's like they have been peeled and dipped inside a barrel of bourbon; t23 beautiful delivery of weight and texture with the citrus still intact but the vanilla really begins to run the show; f22.5 long, lightly oiled, a building of spices and an understated liquorice flourish with a late return to tangy marmalade; b22.5 much more like it!!! *47% (94 proof)*

⮑ **Stranahan's Colorado Whiskey Batch No. 55** dist Mar 08 db **(88.5)** n22 forceful, spicy bourbon; t23 aggressive, sweet delivery: almost a small grain rye style due to the busy spices and semi-developed fruit. Then goes off on a silky, almost sulky, oily vanilla trip; f21.5 light honeycomb; b22 good cop, bad copy whiskey with it one moment giving your taste buds a good slap, the next offering them a gentle dusting down. *47% (94 proof)*

TRIPLE EIGHT DISTILLERY Nantucket, Massachusetts

Triple 8 Notch db **(94)** n22 t24 f23 b23. This is the malt that was presented at table to the guests at the launch of the distillery's first-ever commercial bottling. However, it is likely that a bottle or two has been purloined and will end up at some stage on eBay or an auction somewhere. This was blended by distiller Dean Long and has immediately catapulted this distillery to the top echelons of American malt whisky – and many other countries' besides. What a fabulous and exciting start. *45%*

⮑ **The Notch Aged 8 Years** dist 2000, bott Aug 08 db **(93)** n24 the intermingling of dusty oak and delicate malt is simply wonderful. But probably no better than the soft fruit and saline thread which appears to be the early house style; t23.5 sharp, almost playfully nipping at the tongue and taste buds, the barley is juicy, rich and collides with the oak head on to create a big statement towards the middle; f22.5 subsides with a slightly salty flourish; a seam of heavy oaked bitterness is apparent, but is superbly supported by a touch of mocha and more maltiness on the chalk; b23 very few distilleries make their international bow with a single malt this sublime and superbly constructed. $888 dollars a bottle it may be, but for a taste of America's very first island malt....well, is there really a price? A head turner of a whisky, and every time it's towards the glass. Do we have a world classic distillery in the making...? *44.4% (88.8 proof)*

∴ **The Notch Aged 8 Years** db **(95.5)** n24.5 a veritable fruitfest: name one, look hard enough and you'll find it. Topping the bill, though, are apricots and peaches in full juicy ripeness. A sprinkle of salt reminds you this is an island whisky and traces of vanilla underscores the aging. Oh, and you can't help but trip over the malt; t24.5 as juicy fruits tend to do, this just melts in the mouth. The malt is phenomenal in its clarity and intensity and, like the fruit, mouth-watering to an improbable degree; a very fine oil embraces the taste buds and ensures the structure and layering stay in place; f23 a dignified exit, full of toasty oakiness, the drier balancing act to the juicy opera of before; b23.5 only six bottles of this were produced for a special dinner at the distillery. It is possible one escaped. I admit I had a hand in putting this one together, selecting samples from about half a dozen casks on the warehouse and blending them to certain percentages. Perhaps the closest it might be compared to is a Cardhu, though with a touch extra fruit. For the doubters, proof that this distillery is quite capable of whisky of the very highest calibre. *40% (80 proof)*

∴ **Triple Eight Distillery** db **(90)** n23 a sprig of mint mingles with the salt and a light sawdusty oakiness; distant fruits sweetens things: delicate enough to snap in two...; t23 immediately juicy and though thin in body by Notch standards still churning out pristine malt to an intense degree; a little chalky towards the middle but a dilute maple syrup sweetness blends well with a late gristy sugariness; f21.5 remains on the chalky theme though a touch of salt sharpens; some late oaky spices buzz in... b22.5 a beautifully-made malt but keeps very much to a lighter style. Almost classically elegant. *44.4% (88.8 proof)*

WOODSTONE CREEK DISTILLERY Cincinnatti, Ohio

Woodstone Creek Single Barrel #1 (92) n24 earthy, salty peat much more rendolent of Islay than Cincinnati. Just beautifully constructed with excellent layering of gentle smoke, grapey fruit and toasted oak: glorious! t23 the silkiness on the palate stuns: all is understated yet the clarity of the riches never fades. Lots of fruit, but the even sweeter peat circles in clouds and dovetails with drier oak-led incursions; a tantalising saltiness gives this a coastal dimension which belie the distillery's position some 1,000 miles inland...; f22 surprisingly brittle at the finish, but the smoke shows little sign of abating; b23 what a wonderful whisky! Islayphiles will be confused by this one because it displays so many coastal characters. A massive well done for a first bottling from this new distillery! *47%*

Bourbon Distilleries

Bourbon confuses people. Often they don't even realise it is a whiskey, a situation not helped by leading British pub chains, such as Wetherspoon, whose bar menus list "whiskey" and "bourbon" in separate sections. And if I see the liqueur Southern Comfort listed as a bourbon one more time I may not be responsible for my actions.

Bourbon is a whiskey. It is made from grain and matured in oak, so really it can't be much else. To be legally called bourbon it must have been made with a minimum of 51% corn and matured in virgin oak casks for at least two years. Oh, and no colouring can be added other than that which comes naturally from the barrel.

Where it does differ, from, say Scotch, is that the straight whiskey from the distillery may be called by something other than that distillery name. Indeed, the distillery may change its name which has happened to two this year already and two others in the last three or four. So, to make things easy and reference as quick as possible, I shall list the Kentucky-based distilleries first and then their products in alphabetical order along with their owners and operational status.

TOM MOORE Bardstown. Sazerac. Operating.
BUFFALO TRACE Leestown, Frankfort. Sazerac. Operating.
BROWN-FORMAN Shively, Louisville. Brown-Forman. Operating.
FOUR ROSES Lawrenceburg. Kirin. Operating
HEAVEN HILL BERNHEIM DISTILLERY Louisville. Heaven Hill. Operating.
JIM BEAM Boston and Clermont. Fortune Brands. Operating.
WOODFORD RESERVE Near Millville. Brown-Forman. Operating.
MAKER'S MARK Loretto. Fortune Brands. Operating.
WILD TURKEY Lawrenceburg. Campari Group. Operating.

Bourbon

Ancient Age (72) n18 t19 f17 b18. Pleasant in part: don't go complexity hunting. *40%*

Ancient Ancient Age 10 Star (91.5) n23.5 a different, massively bourbon, world from the standard AAs. Here the oak makes a speech to announce its arrival and there is plenty of rye and honey-coated corn in attendance, too; t23 a deliciously satisfying delivery: the texture of the rye element almost makes you groan with pleasure whilst the genteel quality of the vanilla simply makes you purr.; **f22** some unexpected spiced coconut notes turn up towards the death, complete with chocolate; **b23** a marked improvement on recent bottling, though this has never been a harbinger of shoddy work. The delicate nature of the rye really does charm. 45%

Ancient Ancient Age 10 Years Old (95) n24.5 unreal: almost a portrait of how a delicate, well-aged bourbon should be. A basket of mixed fruits, plus sultanas and buttered oatcake, oddly. The vanillas add nothing more than the softest background noise while the most subtle liquorice and hickory confirms the age; **t24** at once delicate and understated, and on another level sharp and mouthwatering; the rye perhaps takes the most significant lead, rounding up honey and Demerara, but the cream toffee allows it to go only so far; **f23** relatively simplistic with a late lemon jelly (I mean the sweet, not the band) surge as those small grains continue to loiter; **b23.5** this was once my standard whiskey when in Kentucky. Then they began using over-matured whiskeys which masked the complexity. Now it is back to its mesmerising best. Bourbon rarely comes more subtle or gentle than this: one to take a good half hour over for each glass. 43%

Ancient Age Preferred (72.5) n17 t18 f19.5 b18. Curious saccharine sweetness. The oak and corn haven't really forged a partnership here, though some late spices break up the monotony. 40%

Baker's Aged 7 Years batch B-90-001 **(81.5) n21 t22.5 f18 b20.** Complex, if a little lethargic, with some surprising youthfulness in evidence. The delivery promises untold complexity and then....disappointment for the most part, and, despite the crisp, precise and firm early delivery, there is an overall imbalance with the oak never quite gelling with the grains, especially in the car-crash of a finish. 53.5%

Barton Two Bobs Kentucky 13 Years Old cask no. 64, dist Jun 94 **(86) n21.5 t22 f21 b21.5.** Seriously odd: the nose was identical to a Glenugie I tasted in the shell of the distillery back on the early 1980s. Must have something to do with Barton's notorious grain character, in this case barley, and the lightness of the Glenugie malt allowing in the oak. Pleasant, though a tad hot. 64%. Ian Macleod Distillers.

Barton Two Bobs Kentucky 13 Years Old cask no. 65, dist Jun 94 **(93) n23** spot on, classy bourbon of the rich rye variety; enhanced by some hazy fruit and more distinct cocoa powder; **t23** massive delivery but the enormity is couched slightly by the sophisticated layering of the rye, corn and liquorice; **f24** long, near perfectly weighted with the oils deftly gilding a sherry fruitcake depth; strands of honey and lime do the trick balance-wise, as do the late spices; **b23** whether matured in Kentucky or Scotland, Barton rarely reaches 13 years of age. So this is a fascinating brand. Of those I have encountered, though, this captures the busy Barton style in the finest detail. 63.6%. Ian Macleod Distillers.

Barton Two Bobs Kentucky 13 Years Old cask no. 66, dist Jun 94 **(88.5) n20 t23.5 f22 b23** Unmistakably Barton in style, for all the age. 63.7%. Ian Macleod Distillers.

Basil Hayden's 8 Years Old (78) n20 t20 f19 b19. A thin bourbon which never quite finds anchor. Certainly one of the most citrusy bourbons around, but, overall, more Basil Fawlty as this is a bit of a strange, mildly neurotic character. 40%

Benchmark (86) n21 t22 f21.5 b21.5. Unquestionably a better whiskey than once it was with now an entirely well constructed vanilla-sugar depth adding ballast where once there was none. Lovely unexpected spices, too. A real surprise after not having tasted for a couple of years...as, frankly, it hadn't been worth it. Now it is... 40%

Benchmark No. 8 (79) n20 t21 f19 b19. Conspicuously thinner in body and character than the standard Benchmark. Papery aspects to the sweetness, but little of the balancing spice of its stablemate. 40%

Blanton's Gold Single Barrel (93) n23.5 as near as damn it a rye in style, the fruitiness and spice generated by that grain veritably glows in the glass; **t24** big rye again. It absolutely glitters about the palate offering salivating fruit notes against a background of cane juice. Wonderful; **f22.5** softens as the vanilla makes its mark, but the rye still pulses; **b23** looks as though someone tipped a few extra sacks of rye into the recipe by mistake. Not that I'm complaining... 41.5% (103proof)

Blanton's Red (90) n23 busy, supremely complex with outstanding small grain interaction: classic; **t22** corn oils abound but there is also a pleasant, controlled bitterness as the oaks gain confidence; **f22.5** clever spices ensure life is retained; **b22.5** a bourbon for those who like to think about what it is they are drinking. 40%

Blanton's Silver (85.5) n20.5 t22 f22 b21. Useful spices early on but the development peters out as the sweetness gathers. 49%

Blanton's Single Barrel (77) n18.5 t20 f19.5 b19. Limited in scope. Plenty of corn but otherwise same old, same old from start to finish. Disappointing. (93 proof)

Blanton's Single Barrel Green Label barrel 139 dumped 10-1-05 **(89) n23** kumquats and blood orange abound; **t23** a big rye presence on delivery which shows some delicate touches amid the odd punch; **f21** drier vanilla; **b22** deliciously fruity and rye proud. *40%*

Blanton's Single Barrel 7 Years Old (86) **n22 t22 f21 b21.** Enjoyable, but not exactly what I expected. The bourbon and oak haven't quite gelled: a teen beauty with a few unsightly spots. *51.5%. Buffalo Trace. 1500 bottles for readers of the Suddeutsche Zeitung Magazin, Germany.*

Blanton's Single Barrel No. 18 warehouse H, rick 14 **(85) n22.5 t20.5 f21 b21.** Delicate, complex tangerines and sawdust on the nose; the delivery, though sweet, feels a little shackled. *40%*

Blanton's Single Barrel No. 28 warehouse H, rick 50 **(88) n22.5** soft spices enliven an otherwise ultra-soft vanilla and liquorice aroma; **t23** lands without a bump with the liquorice to the fore. Butterscotch and molasses battle it out for the sweet heart; **f21** a little short and vanilla packed; **b21.5** fulsome yet friendly. *46.5% (93 proof)*

Blanton's Single Barrel No. 53 warehouse H, rick 28 **(94) n24** talk about fruity....first we have kumquats and banana...and then pure strawberry. Wow!! That is one very different aroma. Somewhere, if you get over the shock, you'll also find red string liquorice and a dab of honey; **t23** typical BT delivery: the mouthfeel has just that spot degree of oils and then a processions of busy, roast-honeyed waves...with a hint of strawberry topping it off; **f23.5** top rate light sugars coating the roastier oaks...and still those rye-induced fruits keep up their good work; **b23.5** when you realise that a score of 94 is pretty average for this particular version of this brand, you are getting some idea of the quality we are talking about here. And as for the strawberries...don't ask....!! *(127 proof)*

Blanton's Single Barrel No. 56 warehouse H, rick 200 **(90.5) n23** molasses and liquorice by sober degree; **t23** bitter-sweet delivery: the bitterness appears to be a rye-packed fruity hardness; the sweetness is the usual molassesed and honey suspects; spices swell the middle ground; **f22** much drier than normal, again with the rye happy to make itself heard; **b22.5** confident and bold. *46.5% (93 proof)*

Blanton's Single Barrel No. 83 warehouse H, rick 43 **(84.5) n21.5 t21 f21 b21.** Good cocoa and spice. *40% (80 proof)*

Blanton's Single Barrel No. 86 warehouse H, rick 43 **(93.5) n24** classic...the nose trumpets Buffalo Trace like a corny Hollywood blockbuster would fanfare the opening scenes of a Roman games. Stunning honey/molasses mix; salty like sweaty saddle leather; **t23.5** improbably good on the palate also, with those molassed-honeyed notes following through with dexterity, allowing the vanillas all the space they require; **f23** relaxed, light liquorice and still that hint of molasses are happy to ensure not a single trace of bitterness enters the fray from nose to finish; **b23** a big thumbs up. *40% (80 proof)*

Blanton's Single Barrel No. 183 warehouse H, rick 23 **(88.5) n22.5** unusual hint of sugared carrot cake amid the acacia honey and vanilla; **t22.5** the corn dissolves along with muscovado sugar and honey; **f22** light flecks of vanilla and bitter-free marmalade on toast; **b22** what a sweetie!! *40% (80 proof)*

Blanton's Single Barrel No. 223 warehouse H, rick 47 **(79.5) n19 t21 f19.5 b20.** Lashings of cream toffee. Emboldened only by minor spice. *46.5% (93 proof)*

Blanton's Single Barrel No. 250 warehouse H, rick 1 **(90) n23.5** beautiful rye and small grain lead, the rest falls naturally into place; **t22** juicy, firm, salivating rye – as to be expected from the nose - doused by a delivery of natural caramels; **f22** spices pick up the rye thread; the fade is one of red liquorice; **b22.5** effortlessly beautiful. *46.5% (93 proof)*

Blanton's Single Barrel No. 349 warehouse H, rick 33 **(95.5) n24.5** surprisingly fruity and floral in a not dissimilar way to the botanicals found in gin; again the small grains from this batch are busy, at times almost mesmerizingly so; **t23.5** soft delivery with an initial feel of kumquat and pith, then a quiet zap of rye; salivating and lively, the small grains begin to make mischief again towards the delicately-spiced middle; **f24** spices in full flow, but still contained and in sync with those lively rye pulses and now a demarara-sweetened mocha fade; **b24.5** more like Buffalo Treats: stunning...!!! *46.5% (93 proof)*

Blanton's Single Barrel No. 368 warehouse H, rick 37 **(86) n21 t22 f21.5 b21.5.** Slightly over emphatic oak makes for good spice but shouts down many of the other notes. *40%*

Blanton's Single Barrel No. 477 **(94) n23.5** significant degrees of honey and even rye **t24** lordy, lordy: it's as though we have a role call of every flavour value that constitutes excellent bourbon... a delivery and a half: how honeyed and liquoricy can you get....? **f23** drier with the earlier honey fading but more emphasis on liquorice and demerara sugar; **b23.5** the racehorse on the bottle top says it all: a pure thoroughbred... *(129 proof)*

Blanton's Single Barrel Barrel Proof No. 7 warehouse H, rick 23 **(93.5) n23** caramelized biscuit, as much liquorice-rimmed rye as you can shake a barrel gauge at; improbably malty in part; **t24** thumping citrus: sexy, bitter-sweet spice-sprinkled corn and again there is an unmistakable and puzzling barley effect towards the middle; **f23** perhaps overdoes the natural caramels and corn oils, which together are immense, but a lovely cocoa thread at the finish does the trick; **b23.5** the massive strength does nothing to hinder the enjoyment. Curiously, this is one that will appeal to single malt lovers yet to be converted to the greatness of bourbon. *65% (130 proof)*

Blanton's Single Barrel Gold No. 174 warehouse H, rick 44 **(81) n20 t21 f20 b20.** Fools' gold.... *51.5% (103 proof)*

Blanton's Single Barrel Gold No. 201 warehouse H, rick 25 **(93.5) n23** a big rye-liquorice, mildly minty thing; **t24** text-book complexity on delivery: brilliantly layered with those rye tones forming the intermediate backbone while an almost phenolic, cough sweet tang develops around it; **f23** lots of small grain charm **b23.5** distinctly different. *51.5%*

Blanton's Single Barrel Gold No. 316 warehouse H, rick 10 **(89) n24** yet another mammoth rye kick on the nose: it feels like a 51/39/10 corn/rye/malted barley mash bill; so firm is the small grains, with their elegant kumquat charm, the oaks actually offer a softening impact with a light, friendly custard tart element; sublime spices completes the score; **t23** a flinty firmness as the rye cuts to the quick; then appears to become entangled with caramel; **f21** big caramel fade: a relative non-finish compared with the might of before; **b21** a superb bourbon on which the curtain comes down all rather too quickly. *51.5% (103 proof)*

Blanton's Single Barrel Gold No. 678 warehouse H, rick 44 **(86.5) n22.5 t22 f21 b21.** Juicy, occasionally barbed with sharp rye; natural caramels are out in force, though. *51.5%*

Blanton's Single Barrel Silver No. 59 warehouse H, rick 22 **(89) n22** excellent corn-rye interplay; **t23** juicy: a steady stream of almost barley-rich notes surface but not far below if the firmer rye. A light hickory sweetness compliments; **f22** a light flutter of spices return the rye to pole position; **b22** sturdy and sound. *49% (98 proof)*

Blanton's Single Barrel Silver No. 316 warehouse H, rick 28 **(96.5) n25** faultless: just so rare to come across a bourbon where the rye sparkles like this on the nose. The corn plays its part, but only as a soft, delicately sweetening buffer between the firm, fruity rye tones and the oak-led butterscotch, fudge candy and custardy vanillins. Just a light sprinkle of muscovado sugar on old-fashioned bitter English marmalade, but the colonel of the sweetness is corn-based; **t24** much sweeter delivery, with the marmalade making an early statement. A real buzz of rye-enriched spice; the liquorice-honey signature of ripe bourbon is there in several strands, but it's that rye firmness which really catches the eye – and tastebuds; **f23.5** long, soft corn oils enforce a never-ending tail. Chewy with shards of firm rye, but the oak plays a greater role now with a coffee-liquorice depth and a playful spice buzz. Elsewhere a gentle, sweet haze ensures nothing the oak can do will get out of hand; **b24** rarely does a bourbon resonate with such astonishing rye tones. I have comes across some straight ryes showing less character and I would not be surprised to learn that this batch was worked from a slightly altered formula. An absolute must for those who love their bourbon the really old-fashioned way. Blanton's Silver? This is pure gold.... *49% (98 proof)*

Blanton's Uncut/Unfiltered (96.5) n25 t24 f23.5 b24. Uncut. Unfiltered. Unbelievable. *65.9%*

Booker's 6 Years 7 Months batch C00-K-15 **(93) n23** wonderfully roasty with Colombian/Java coffee mixing with singed-toast black peppers; older in character than its allotted years; **t23.5** huge delivery, not just in terms of alcohol strength but by that roasty signature chugging through; delightfully bitter-sweet with butterscotch and vanilla playing a useful role; **f23.5** impressive rye signature to the finale with marauding honeycomb and muscovado sugar against darker, oaky forces; **b23** a combative bourbon with all its considerable personality at full volume. Striking stuff. *63.2%*

Buffalo Trace (93.5) n23.5 a restrained nose for a BT with the rye hiding behind a curtain of corn. A complex procession of vanillas with the usual citrus presence offering a thin veneer; **t23.5** a series of soft explosions lights up the tastebuds but again it is the corn which dominates, its soft oils acting as a buffer for the rye and spice; **f23** long and improbably elegant with the smaller grains at last finding a coherent voice; the sweeter vanilla is joined by a dry, toasty oakiness. Unquestionably a more easy-going sample than some recent bottlings I have tasted; **b23.5** as an everyday bourbon there is little to match this one. It's all about balance and complexity and injections here and there of the elements that make bourbon unique. *45%*

👉 **Buffalo Trace Experimental Collection 1993 Double Barrelled** charred white oak, dist Apr 93, bott Sep 09 **(92) n23.5** classically brooding. Chocolate fudge integrates handsomely with a vaguely fruity, rye-like sharpness; **t24** mouth-filling; wonderful volley of spice and a cluster of small grains; busy and exhilarating; **f22.5** calms down as the caramels wade in, but remains sweet; **b22** this thoroughbred swapped horses in midstream (if you get my drift) by spending about eight years in one virgin oak cask before being transferred to another. If you think any whisky can't take that kind of treatment, think again... 45% (90 proof) Buffalo Trace

‑‑ **Buffalo Trace Experimental Collection 1997 Double Barrelled** charred white oak, dist Nov 97, bott Sep 09 (86) n22.5 t22 f20.5 b21. Quite a curious one, this. The kumquat-tangy nose offers a honeycomb sweetness which never wholly forms on the palate. Instead, we are treated to a welter of rich natural caramel, ensuring a soft, easy ride throughout. 45%

Buffalo Trace Experimental Collection Course Grain Oak rick/row/slot 1/1/2, 62% evaporation, dist Dec 94, bott Jul 09 (96) n24 almost the burnt raisin aroma of a very old sherry cask, but obviously can't be; also very toasty but here a balancing sweetness hits the oak head on; t24.5 a commanding yet restrained demerera sweetness is superbly layered between those biting, toasty oak notes: complex and very comfortable with itself; once more the mouth feel is faultless; f23.5 takes its foot off the pedal, as if having proved just what it can do: everything slows down, but soft liquorice and demerara-sweetened coffee hang around for a while; b24 just appears to have another gear by comparison to the Fine Grain and ups into it effortlessly. One of the whiskey – and whisky – experiences of the year. 45%

Buffalo Trace Experimental Collection Fine Grain Oak rick/row/slot 1/1/1, 51% evaporation, dist Dec 94, bott Jul 09 (91.5) n22 toasty, major oak influence but strangely devoid of the usual sweetness one might reasonably associate with a 15-y-0 bourbon. Perhaps a hint of some dried orange peel; t23 mixed bag on delivery: a minor movement towards fruity sweetness is ruthlessly crushed underfoot by thick oak. This is big and for a while too much. But the middle ground become occupied by varied and complex citrus, some of which was seen on delivery and sublime spices. The body and mouth feel are exceptional; viscous almost; f23.5 the spices twitter merrily away with the ever-sharpening citrus now on safer ground and unmolested. A charming degree of latte drifts in for the finale; b23 one of those whiskeys you have to stand up, walk away from the table and start again with. On first tasting you think: woah!! Way too old...!!! Then you look again and suddenly you find that vaguest hint of orange peel on the nose is actually the one things that stands up to the oak in character on the palate. And what's more, fights back.... 45%

Cadenhead's World Whiskies Heaven Hill Aged 15 Years bourbon, bott Sep 07 (87.5) n22 t21 f22.5 b22 A very odd bourbon in that it doesn't fall into any one distillery's particular character. An attractive, if abrasive, stand-alone bourbon for all that. 57.2%. 150 bottles.

Charter 101 (89) n22 the accent on evening flowers and nose-prickling spices; t23 big, bold and honeyed. Some glorious sweet oils help transport the busy oaky-vanilla tones to the furthest points. Everything slapped on with a thick brush – but it's great fun...; f22 settles down to a no less simplistic but much more gentle finale; b22 a straight as a die bourbon with no interest in veering off its set course. Gathers just enough complexity along the way to make for a delicious, want again experience. 50.5%

Corner Creek Reserve (86) n22 t22 f21 b21. Honeyed with some striking small grain action. 44%. Corner Creek Distilling Company.

Cougar Bourbon Aged 5 Years bott code 038/07/13 (95) n25 light, fruity rye offers an aroma I have only ever encountered in an Alpine meadow with myriad flowers popping up through the earthy moss; this is probably the best rye in the world diffused to perfection; t24 soft, sweet delivery with again the rye taking central command, directing fruity, rooty elements in all directions; f23 dries agreeably with vanilla subduing the fruity freshness b23 if Karl Kennedy of Neighbours really is the whisky buff he reckons he is, I want to see a bottle of this in his home next to Dahl. By the way: where is Dahl these days...? (And by the way, Karl, the guy who married you and Susan in London is a fan of mine. So you had better listen up...!) 37% (74 proof). Foster's Group, Australia.

Daniel Stewart 8 Years Old (92.5) n22 bubbling small grains, rye in particular. A hint of celery complements the polished leather; t23 busy and quite beautifully crafted. The sweetness is a delight, perfectly balanced by rich, marauding ryes. Burned cream toffee acts as delightful ballast; f23.5 back to the small grains and lashings of muscovado sugar. Long and gloriously elegant, with a late dash of sweetened milked coffee; b24 stellar sophistication. Real complexity here, and, as 8-year-olds go, probably among the most complex of them all. A deep notch up on the previous bottling I encountered. 45%

Eagle Rare Aged 10 Years Single Barrel Mac Y 10th Anniversary (93) n23 unmistakable Buffalo Trace whiskey with the vanilla revealed in so many textured layers; t23 surging oaks on delivery. Then a backing off to allow a more measured, mildly molassed sweetness to interlink with some orangey citrus; f23 slow spice arrival, a brushing of hickory and some developing rye fruitiness; b24 beautiful bourbon from the school of complex shades and inferences. 45%. Denmark.

Eagle Rare Kentucky Straight Bourbon 17 Years Old bott fall 07 **(91)** n23.5 just the right amount of honey works wonders; t22 rich, roasty with a satisfying combination of small grain bite and oaky menace; f23 long, tons of natural caramels and late liquorice; b22.5 a bourbon growing old gracefully but not beyond displaying its seniority at crucial moments. Superb. *45%*

Eagle Rare Kentucky Straight Bourbon 17 Years Old bott fall 08 **(87.5)** n23.5 anyone who has romped in a hayloft will recognize this one: new mown hay; bales of it sweating in the barn. Light, sweet, a dab of acacia honey and lots of natural caramels; t22 silky, sweet delivery with a quick jolt of rye then a drift towards light oaky sugars; f21 flattens dramatically as the caramels take command; b21 attractive, but after the great nose I expected considerably more. *45% (90 proof)*

Eagle Rare Single Barrel (86.5) n21.5 t22 f22 b22. For those who like their bourbons seriously sugary: loads to get the tastebuds round, but the sweetness encroaches on the complexity. *45%*

Elijah Craig 12 Years Old (86) n21 t22 f21 b22. Well, we wondered what would happen when the EC12 switched to a new distillery, following the loss of the mother ship in 1996. Perhaps this is Bardstown bourbon, but older than 12. I don't think so. That slightly yeasty character is in evidence on the nose and a syrupy feel masks the greater complexity. Enjoyable, but... *47%*

Elijah Craig 18 Years Old Single Barrel barrel no. 2202, barrelled on 8-31-89 **(93.5)** n23 riddled with seams of rich rye, a coppery element ensures the honey does not escape the heady atmosphere; t24 close your eyes and just allow the stunning rich corn and vivid rye to overwhelm the senses. Liberally spiced, but couched in oily shock-absorbers; all the soft liquorice notes you would demand of this vintage are there; f23.5 long, with wonderful strands of strawberry preserve and other tart fruits. The vanillas cushion the impact; b23 now this is more like it. Screams Bardstown. Sings lullabies. Sheer class. *45%*

⌐ **Elmer T. Lee 90th Birthday Limited Edition (93.5)** n23.5 a vanilla special: soft, friendly and interspersed with the most delicate tangerine and cherry notes; t23.5 slightly more upfront oak and rye sharpness on delivery, then a slightly puckering surge of oak and vanilla before those playful rues nip back; f23 like the nose, the softest vanilla imaginable; b23.5 age has mellowed the whiskey's top class, complex, slightly fiery character....a bit like an old friend and bourbon legend I could name. This sample has come directly from the bottle Elmer gave me after I had the honour of sitting beside him at his 90th birthday bash. Sadly, a member of my staff opened it by mistake for my sampling. Though it was the first new whisky I tasted after completing the 2010 Bible, I have made this the 1,056th whisky to officially taste for the 2011 Whisky Bible. Because tell me: how can you follow an Elmer T Lee....? *45%*

Elmer T Lee Single Barrel (87.5) n22 dense, with a touch of latte coffee, but lightened by a squeeze of something citrusy; t22 oily, yet busy, with increasing weight towards vanilla; f21.5 simplistic and sweet at first but with a very late spice arrival; b22 a steady bottling by ETL's usual standards. *45%*

Evan Williams (76.5) n18 t20 f19 b19.5. Unrelentingly sweet and simplistic. *43.3%*

Evan Williams 12 Years (90) n21.5 a touch of the new HH Character, but compensated by a real old fruitcake kick; t23.5 brilliant mouth arrival with the spices boldly leading the way. Juicy, fruity rye isn't too far behind and the liquorice notes begin to up the ante at just the right time; f22.5 varying dark sugar tones are sprinkled over the drier vanillins and chalky oakiness; b22.5 perhaps not the force it recently was, but enough grunt here to emphasise the important bits. Namely the enormity of the rye and the sharp spices. Much more at home than, say, the 12-year-old Elijah Craig, for so long its match for quality. *50.5%*

Evan Williams 23 Years Old (95.5) n24 unreal: this is really 107 proof? Well, I've just popped open a fresh bottle, so it must be...Not a single harsh or unkind note on the nose: not even spirit attack. Just the patter over the nosebuds of exceptionally well behaved toffee-rye notes, the odd kumquat and kiwifruit and....oh, some liquorice, as befitting its grand age; t24.5 a sultry delivery....at first. Then a cavalry charge of spices, with rye and demerara at the rear; the fingerprint of the old Bardstown distillery is so firm and clear I could weep: glorious! f23.5 now starts to get a bit flash with the acacia and manuka honey making equal inroads into the drier vanilla. Just works so well with almost effortless grace; b24 easily the best EW23 I have come across, and by a distance. Sadly not a single marking on the bottle to show which batch this may be. But if I were in commodities, my message would be: buy, buy, buy...!!! *53.5%* ⊙

Evan Williams 1783 (71.5) n17 t18 f18.5 b18. A struggle to get beyond the nose. *43%*

Evan Williams Single Barrel Vintage 1996 barrel no. 1, bott 4 Oct 05 db **(92)** n24 t23 f22 b23 Up to the usual superb standards. *43.3% (86.6 proof).*

Evan Williams Single Barrel 1999 barrel no 1 **(88.5) n24** sensational honeycomb: it just doesn't get more honeyed...or more burnt. It's as though the barrel has spent its entire life at the top of the warehouse and the light eucalyptus note really does suggest a whiskey twice the age it actually is; **t22** initial manuka honey delivery and then roasty oak....big time; **f21** marmalade bitterness and a huge wave of caramels; **b21.5** technically too old: the oak really has got its fingers and thumbs around the neck of the grain. But those moments when it's got it right....boy, oh, boy...!!! *43.3% (86.6 proof)*

⋰ **Evan Williams Single Barrel Vintage 2000** dist Mar 00, bott Oct 09 **(90) n24** if you could write a list of every aroma that signals old aged bourbon, each one would be ticked here. The most overwhelming is a combination aroma: kumquat, pine, lavender and honeycomb...all arm in arm. Amazing...; **t23** bizarrely lightweight delivery after such a fomenting nose; for a moment Demerara sugar-led, then liquorice takes command. Low level spices pop up; **f21.5** a relatively thin finale, with the liquorice still offering the majority of weight; **b21.5** beautiful bourbon for sure. But when you get that type of aroma and this kind of strength.... Well, let's say that it's like owning a Corvette and finding a lawnmower engine under the hood. *43.3% (86.6 proof)*

Fighting Cock Aged 6 Years (85.5) n20 t22 f22.5 b22. The classic old aroma of the first bottling may have been cock-olded, but the arrival on the palate makes for a stunner. Just heaps of small grain bristle around the palate and their combined intensity and assertiveness ensure a chewy, mildly waxed experience. A big cock, indeed... *51.5%*

Four Roses Barrel Strength Aged 12 Years 120th Anniversary Limited Edition (88) n21 firm, dry, toasty; **t22** immediate spice explosion, then hickory and fruit; **f22.5** more controlled, corn-rich, chewy and oily; **b22.5** typically understated and charming. *55.4%*

Four Roses 120th Anniversary 12 Years Old Single Barrel (91.5) n22.5 lots of vanilla; no little spice; **t24** an improbably refined delivery for all the huff and puff of the alcohol: a small grain extravaganza with the rye leading the way, peppering the tastebuds like so much shot; **f22** waves of blunted sweetness crash against an extraordinary French toast finale; **b23** twelve year old bourbons are just so meant to be more in your face than this...An essay in understatement and subtlety. Four Roses is beginning to make its mark as Kentucky's most delicate bourbon. *(110.5 proof)*

Four Roses Barrel Strength Aged 13.5 Years (86.5) n21 t21.5 f22.5 b21.5. Relatively closed by FR standards with the liquorice and spices on top form. *52.1% (104.2 proof).*

Four Roses (Black Label) (88) n20 unhappy, with some off-key lactic moments; **t23** recovers supremely with a fabulous complexity to the rye-oak interchange. Really chewy, with awesome soft oils and spices that pepper the mouth – literally! **f23** a sustained sweetness draws upon the central corn character and is backed by a profusion of late liquorice and honey; **b22** a whiskey which starts falteringly on the nose recovers with a sublime delivery of all things bourbon. *40%*

Four Roses Marriage Collection 2008 (92.5) n23 a trifle pugnacious. The oak is having much to say, throwing down big weight to out punch the evident rye and light botanical (including delicate juniper) feel. Muscular and happy to deliver the odd punch; **t23** as dry as the Single Barrel I tasted was sweet: again it's all about the oak. Very toasty, mild hickory but a subtle coating of molassed sugar ensures there is no oaky excess; **f23** long, complex, with outstanding interweaving between the lightly burned coffee and sweeter liquorice; **b23.5** sophisticated, bourbon lovers' bourbon. *53.9% (107.8 proof)*

Four Roses Marriage Collection 2009 (88.5) n23.5 pretty big by Four Roses standards with an emphasis on caramelized orange-mint; the oak, though, broods; **t22** it's the oak which really makes the impact, ensuring a dry, spicy delivery with a surprising degree of oils; **f21.5** toasty and dry with the caramelized sugars hyper caramelized; **b21.5** not sure of the barrel number for this one, but could do with a little less toastiness if in search of true greatness. Even so, lovely stuff. *58% (116 proof)*

Four Roses 2009 Limited Edition (88) n22 chunky, perhaps slightly over fried in barrel; **t23** it doesn't take long for spices to make their mark, actually lightening the big oaky delivery along with a few spoon-fulls of molasses and liquorice; **f21** enormous amounts of natural caramels have been let loose, too; **b22** attractive bourbon, but perhaps the nagging feeling that this barrel may have been very slightly over-aged. *58.4% (116.8 proof)*

Four Roses Single Barrel warehouse BS, barrel 36-5R **(89) n22** fingers of citrus gently massage the nose buds; floral and delicate; **t22.5** traces of maple syrup throughout; the vanilla alternates between toasty and custardy; **f22** long, still with that distinctive sweet edge but a delicate toastiness; **b22.5** for those who prefer their bourbons soft and very sweet: much more of a sissy than some of the others from this distillery I have tasted of late and, to be honest, much more of the style traditionally associated with Four Roses. *50% (100 proof)*

Four Roses Single Barrel (84) n21 t22 f20 b21. Juicy to the Nth degree early on; perhaps on the flat and oily side at the death. 43%

Four Roses Single Barrel warehouse KE, barrel no. 9-6A **(93.5) n22 t25 f23 b23.5** A supremely well assembled and deft bourbon of the highest order. The delivery is near enough perfection as damn it. 50%

Four Roses Small Batch (86.5) n18.5 t22 f24 b22. Lightweight and delicate, this is as juicy and mouth-watering as bourbon gets. A touch tart, perhaps, but a treat for those looking for the ultimate in small gain complexity. The finish, which rumbles like an Evansville earthquake, is nothing short of breathtaking. Such a pity about the off-key nose. (90 proof)

Four Roses Super Premium (90.5) n23 t23 f22 b22.5. This distillery's whiskey is amongst the hardest to judge in the world: on the one hand it is light and sophisticated, on the other it sometimes misses out on the riches and balance that truly great bourbon demands. This bottling, however, successfully accumulates ticks in every department. (86 proof)

Four Roses (Yellow Label) (84) n21 t22 f20 b21. A straight as a die bourbon that for all its effete lightness and mannerisms still conjures enough weight and charisma to entertain. On nose and palate, as citrusy as the colour of the label suggests. However, it is the backbone rye that stars early on, though it fades towards the ultra light finish. 40%

⸫ **George T. Stagg (96) n24** crisp, fruity, almost smoky in its toastiness; the corn offers a subtle oil despite the mega aroma; **t24.5** puckeringly sharp delivery as a double whammy of oak and sharp rye-style notes both strike gold: one of the finest deliveries of the year; manuka honey and liquorice entangle deliciously for the middle ground; **f23.5** long, with vanilla storming the ramparts having seemingly waited its moment; **b24** on first tasting this at the distillery last year, my knee-jerk reaction was that this was a fair distance behind the Weller. However, with whiskey this massive, it takes four or five hours to unravel its mysteries. Taste this only if you can give it the time. 70.7% (141.4 proof) ncf

George T Stagg (96.5) n24.5 t24.5 f23.5 b24. Pretty close to perfection with the finale missing a spicy riposte. But that is being churlish: the elegance topples off the scales and the complexity, once the palate adjusts to the powering alcohol, appears to set new standards. One of the whiskeys of the year, easily. (144.8 proof)

Hancock's Reserve Single Barrel (93.5) n24.5 almost erotic in the way the rye and vanilla tease the senses: a gentle, small-grained attack that is busy, alluring and almost showing off. Changes shape slightly as the temperature alters and the odd orangey note can be detected. But it is the charm of the rye which perhaps excites most; **t23** every bit as busy as the nose with the rye really making itself known. But all done in a casual, relaxed way that allows a custard-cream cream-caramel element to evolve and delight; **f22.5** long, though the vanillas start to take a grip; **b23.5** sticks to its trademark cream caramel signature. But this time far greater emphasis on the firm rye outcrops. Impressively balanced all round: bourbon at its most sophisticated. 44.45% (88.9 Proof)

Heaven Hill Old Style Bourbon (78) n21 t19 f19 b19. Much better nose but the body thins out dramatically. Decent dose of sweetness, though. 40%

Heaven Hill Old Style Bourbon Bottled in Bond (81) n20 t21 f20 b20. An entire role reversal from the standard bottling with the shy nose showing absolutely no sign of the rye-led riches that follow. Some decent Demerara cuts in, too. 50%

Heaven Hill Old Style Bourbon 6 Years Old (66) n17 t17 f16 b16. Very strange bourbon with a weird yeastiness/fermentation residue. Never finds a rhythm or settles. An uncomfortable and very un-Heaven Hill-like ride. 45%

Heaven Hill 6 Years Old (83) n20 t20 f22 b21. An infinitely more satisfying bourbon than its Old Style stable mate at this age. The battle between crisp rye and compact caramel is intriguing and pretty tasty to boot. 40%

Heaven Hill Mild and Mellow (80) n18 t20 f21 b21. Also known as the 86 proof, this has changed markedly in recent years. Firm and oily, the corn dominates where once barley had such an unusually large say. Since moving distillery(-ies) the house style has chopped and changed a little and again the nose is the weak spot. Pleasant otherwise. 43%

Heaven Hill Ultra Deluxe Aged 36 Months (86.5) n20 t22.5 f22 b22. Another Heaven Hill that has changed tack considerably over the last year or so. And possibly age. For all its baby fat, this youngster is something of a beauty in that few bourbons are quite so mouth-watering and fresh. The rye pulses on the tastebuds and there is even an injection of something vaguely of the liquorice family: amazing for its tender years. Simply, pure fun whiskey with zero pretensions but maximum effect. Just love it!! 40%

Henry McKenna Aged 10 Years Single Barrel bottled in bond barrel no. 327, barrelled Dec 97 **(81.5) n19 t21 f21 b20.5.** Sweet, pleasant, corn-rich, a touch syrupy in parts and never begins to extend itself...or the imbiber. 50%

Hudson Baby Bourbon bear 08, batch 3 **(71)** n15 t17 f19 b18. Hard to make it past the butyric-riddled nose. Some wonderfully intense fruity notes to ensure a degree of pleasantness. But this is an early attempt from a fledgling distillery and a journey back to the drawing board is required. 46%

Hudson Four Grain Bourbon bott 08, batch 3 **(78.5)** n17 t20 f21.5 b21. Neither for the feint nor faint hearted. The nose is a problem, but there is no shortage of sharp and puckering complexity to concentrate the mind thanks to the intense and, it has to be said, wonderfully entertaining palate. Sort out a few gremlins and this promises to be a whisky to watch. 46%

Jefferson's Reserve batch no. 84 **(91)** n23 solid as a rock: the rye forms an almost impenetrable barrier to the softer, oilier corn. But not quite..; t23.5 lush and full bodied, the sweetness gallops off in every direction unmolested until several thick waves of vanilla and spice intervene. Sugar-coated liquorice fills the middle; f22 much more genteel, with the drier vanillas taking charge; b23 once a 15-year-old, no age statement here. But this has seen off a few summers, and sweetened with each passing one. 45.1%. 2400 bottles.

Jim Beam (83) n20 t20 f22 b21. A notch or two lighter than recent years with a noticeably less oaky backbone. A complex finish after a sluggish start, though, with some playful brown sugar stirring things up attractively. 40%

Jim Beam Black Aged to Perfection (89.5) n22 softer, less pungent than the 8-y-o version; t23 the accent on the sugars with the usual rye boldness taking a back seat behind the sweeter corn, though by no means invisible; f22.5 gentle vanilla and more molasses with some puckering liquorice towards the finale; b22.5 Jim Beam Black. But, teasingly, with no age statement! Does it live in the shadow of the sublime 8-years-old? Well, perhaps not quite. Lacks the lushness and the peaks and troughs of complexity. But, though a lot more even in temperament, it never fails to delight, even if the standard rye kick is conspicuous by its absence. As a bourbon, excellent. As a Jim Beam Black, a little disappointing. 43% (86 proof)

Jim Beam Black Aged 8 Years (94) n23 the layering here is exemplary: we are talking well aged fruitcakes (of the burnt raisin and cherry on the crust variety) here, not to mention mild ginger cake moistened by subtle oils and a sub layer of fruity rye. Garnish that with the usual leathery liquorice and ... mmmmmm....!!! t24 begins deftly with the corn and oak delivering polished, gentle beats hand in hand; then the sweetness begins to build as do the playful spices. Silky hints of rye on a bed of bitter-sweet oak and a trace of hickory; f23 mouth-watering rye shows no shyness here and the engrossing dryness never outweighs the Demerara sub-plot. Engrossing, charming and almost hypnotic in its delicacy and balance; b24 it is if, at last, the guys behind the barrel selection and dumping of this product are now truly believing in what they are doing. As each year comes and goes, so, it seems, this bourbon gets better and better. The jump in quality between this and the standard "white" Beam has shifted from gap to chasm in the last decade, with the pace widening and increasing over the last four years. Unquestionably one of the great bourbons, this is an everyday whiskey with which I win more converts to the bourbon cause than any other. A big whiskey, yet one that openly revels in its finesse and complexity. A Kentucky classic. 43%

Jim Beam Choice Aged 5 Years (89) n22 those who remember the stuttering, faltering nose of the Choice a year or two ago will be taken aback: now firm, almost brooding with a classic red and black liquorice depth; t22 sweet delivery shows an impressive harmony between corn and oak; f23 lush, chewy and offering increasing degrees of spice. Superbly structured and layered and improbably confident for its age; b22 a hugely improved whiskey which is no longer betwixt and between but now strikingly makes its own bold statements. Makes noises on both nose and palate way above its five years. A bourbon to grab whilst in this expansive and impressive mood. 40%

Jim Beam Premium Aged 7 Seven Years Old (White Label) db **(82)** n21 t21 f20 b20. Hard, uncompromising and showing little of what is to come with a stunning 8-years-old. Young in character even to the point of the Old Taylor from the same stable entirely outflanking this for complexity and riches. That said, good crispness and a lovely – and unexpectedly – malty tail- off in middle. Decent but disappointing. 40% (80 proof).

Kentucky Supreme Number 8 Brand (76) n18 t19 f20 b19. Simplistic and undemanding with massive emphasis on a barley sugar-style tartness and sweetness. 40%

Kentucky Tavern (84) n20 t22 f21 b21. Another juicy little number which appears almost to have a young malt feel to it. Clean, with just the right amount of rye sparkle to offer buzz and complexity. 40%

Kentucky Vintage (91.5) n23 a slight yeasty kick to the classic honeycomb-liquorice fanfare; t24 sublime: mouth-watering grains strike a great rapport with copper-sheened molassed notes; light spices keep the tastebuds working overtime; f22 a lovely amalgamation of dried and juicy dates; b22.5 damned fine bourbon! 45%

Knob Creek Aged 9 Years (94) n23.5 almost stereotypical of what a chunky and very good bourbon should be: firm yet yielding with excellent honeycomb and cocoa amid vanilla and honey. At times almost old Jamaican pot still rum-like; **t23.5** sweet delivery – rummy again! – then a delivery of oily corn and spices and wonderful layering of vanilla-fed oak; **f23.5** long and powerful and fabulously lush with a return to honeycomb topped by a sugared rye-spice climax; **b23.5** no whiskey in the world has a more macho name, and this is not for the faint-hearted. Big, hard in character and expansive, it drives home its point with gusto, celebrating its explosive finish. *50%* ⊙ ⊙

Maker's Mark (Red Seal) (88.5) n21 a little spicier than the norm but those fruit and honey strands are tightly bound; a touch of lactose from the oak surprises; **t23.5** the wax is confined not just to the seal as a wonderful coating encrusts every solitary tastebud. A wonderful honey theme plays alongside the busy wheat-induced spices; **f22** thins as the crème brulee gets a grip; **b22** just as the distillery is an official historic landmark of Kentucky, then so too should be the remarkably consistent character of its whisky. By rights, any whisky that boasts no more than 19 casks should jump around pretty spectacularly from bottling to bottling. With MM you do get variance, of course, but the style is so tight and consistent, it is pretty easy to spot even when tasted blind. *45%*

Most Wanted Kansas Bourbon Mash Whiskey (83) n18 t20 f23.5 b21.5. A sweaty armpit nose is the unlikely overture for an attractively flavoursome and delicately sweet bourbon. Highly unusual and rather gristy in style, the superb finish offers hugely attractive chocolate. One that really grows on you. *40%*

Old 1889 Royal Aged 12 Years (78) n19 t20 f19 b20. A curiously ineffectual and ultimately frustrating bourbon which still needs to feel loved for its small grain complexity but succeeds only in demanding a slap for being so lily-livered. In the end it falls between the delicate and full-blown fruity stools. *43%*

Old Charter 8 Years Old (78) n21 t20 f19 b19. Remains dull and overly toffeed. *40%*

Old Charter 10 Years Old (83) n20.5 t21 f21.5 b21. From having blazed a glorious trail for a brief time in the recent past, it has returned to type. Plods about the palate like a dazed brontosaurus: big, but no serious bite and too unwieldy ever to be a beauty. Pleasant, though, and just the odd busy sugar-vanilla moment helps it along. *43%*

Old Crow Aged 3 Years (85.5) n21 t21.5 f21 b22. Maintained its youthful style solidly with the aroma upping a gear or two. Still a minty freshness to the nose, but now aided and abetted by the first strands of young liquorice. A real surprise package. *40%*

Old Fitzgerald (83.5) n19 t21 f22 b21.5. A greatly improved bourbon that is beginning to feel more at home in its sweet, vaguely spicy surroundings. *43%*

Old Fitzgerald's 1849 (74) n18 t19 f18.5 b18.5. Cloying, shapeless and hugely disappointing: as a corn whiskey it'd do better. "Its quality unchanged since 1849", shrills the label. Well, it's dropped 16 points since 2006 in my book... *45%*

Old Fitzgerald Very Special 12 Years Old (93.5) n23 slightly sluggish and off-colour in parts but some oaky zeal manages to get some spicy banana custard into play; allow the glass to sit for a while, or nose when empty and you get a very clear picture of something very different and beautiful; **t24** soft, entirely melt-in-the-mouth stuff. Sweet, but the sugars are layered, as are the receiving vanillas. Delicate and impressive and the spices genuinely add guile; **f23** many more vanilla-charged layers complete the complexity; **b23.5** in the topsyturvy world of Old Fitz, the 1849 has sunk without trace whilst this has improved beyond all recognition. I suspect some of the bourbon from the old 1849 8-year-old is now making its way into this impressive and highly distinguished little number. The best Old Fitz I've encountered for some 20 years. *45%*

Old Forester Birthday Bourbon distilled spring 93, bottled 05 **(94) n24 t23 f23 b24** One of the most rye-studded stars in the bourbon firmament and wholly in keeping with the fabulous quality for which this brand has now become a byword. *40%*

Old Grand-Dad (90.5) n22 a nose that screams small grains at you, with the rye and even barley having an unusually hefty say. Seriously complex and one that needs a few minutes to get to know; **t23** fabulous marriage of aged weight and grainy complexity. The tastebuds are bombarded with myriad juicy notes as the soft ryes and molassed sugars weave a course through the building vanilla; **f23** light, almost lofty, as those busy grainy notes begin to head towards something a little more traditional in weight and oiliness; not before some mocha creeps in for good measure, though; **b23.5** this one's all about the small grains. A busy, lively bourbon, this offers little to remind me of the original Old Grand-Dad whiskey made out at Frankfort. That said, this is a whisk(e)y-lover's whiskey: in other words the excellence of the structure and complexity outweighs any historical misgivings. Enormously improved and now very much at home with its own busy style. *43%*

Old Grand-Dad Bonded 100 Proof (88) n21.5 t22 f22.5 b22. A punchy, weightier version than the standard Grand-Dad. This appears to have greater age and the encroaching oak manages only to strike out some of the complexity so gloriously relevant in the lighter bottling. Still good whiskey, and with a much more intense cocoa delivery. *50%*

Old Heaven Hill Bottled in Bond (79) n17 t21 f21 b20. A bourbon which grows in stature the longer it stays on the palate with spice/rye/muscovado sugar interplay particularly delightful. The nose, though, does it little justice. *50%*

Old Heaven Hill Very Rare Old Aged 8 Years (84) n20 t22 f21 b21. Fruity and light, there is a decent rye-style surge early on in the delivery which offers a gripping intensity. *43%*

Old Heaven Hill Very Rare Old Aged 10 Years Bottled In Bond (88) n21 Shall we call it the Heaven Hill Character? Certainly an entirely different aroma from the days when distilled back in Bardstown. An amalgam of rye and brown sugars offers something decent and weighty, but a light, fruity sub-stratum undermines the plans. t22.5 Entirely nonsensical and out of sync, the manner in which the different elements crash blindly about the palate actually makes for serious entertainment. Again it is the rye which totally dominates proceedings, but without ever keeping control. Powering vanillas stir things up like a naughty schoolboy; f22.5 a degree of sanity is restored and even a touch of finesse injected. The caramel/vanilla/rye trilogy is an intense one; b22 a mad professor of a bourbon, heading off in every direction without any apparent sense. But then works out beautifully. *50%*

Old Rip Van Winkle 10 Years Old (81.5) n19 t21 f20.5 b21. Oily, soft and slightly effete. *45% Buffalo Trace*

Old Rip Van Winkle Bourbon Aged 13 Years (87) n22 t22 f21 b22 very different: in fact I have never seen a Buffalo Trace whiskey like it. There are restaurants in Stockholm's Old Town whose owners would offer major favours to have a house acavuit like this. *53.3%*.

Old Taylor Aged 6 Years (present bottling) (89) n23 marzipan and Seville orange offer a delightful lightness of touch and teasing complexity; t23 almost a hint of single malt about the lightness of touch to the honey here; the arrival is sweet and busy with just enough oaky depth to add ballast; f21 almost vanishes off the palate though the rye and spice stick around to impress; b22 the curiously thin finish is in telling contrast to the superbly honeyed middle that simple dances with small-grain charm. So much lighter than the original Old Taylor (see below) of McCracken Pike. But certainly has enough weight and fruit punch to make this better than the cheap brand it is perceived to be. *40%*

Old Taylor Aged 6 Years (old bottling) (94) n24 t23 f23 b24 Just a mile from my home in Kentucky stands, or perhaps I should say stood, the Old Taylor distillery. It may not still be there because the widow of my close and dearly missed friend, Cecil Withrow, finally sold it and the old place where Cecil once worked and, until his untimely death, harboured dreams of distilling again, faces the almost certain prospect of the demolition ball. I thought it fitting, then, that for my 1,000th whiskey tasted from the 2007 edition of the Bible it should be an original Old Taylor six-years-old which I found in a back street liquor store in Verona, Italy. In fact there are still many bottles of this truly classic bourbon to be found in that country and if visiting Italy for its architecture and food isn't enticing enough, then here must be the ultimate reason. And just to put a strange and fitting twist to this tale, how about this: as I was tasting and writing these notes a delivery van turned up. Nothing unusual there: we get four or five deliveries of samples every day. This, though, was a special shipment from Peru: the very first copy of a special edition of the Whisky Bible I produced for the 2006 US Christmas market. And the book had been specially dedicated to... the memory of Cecil Withrow... *40%*.

Old Virginia Aged 6 Years (79) n20 t21 f18.5 b19.5. Old Virginia because of the drying tobacco leaf on the aroma? Sweet, but a lot flatter than the state... *40%. La Martiniquaise,*

Old Virginia Aged 8 Years L434401A (85) n22 t21 f21 b21. Vanilla-rich and never quite lives up to the bold nose. *40%. La Martiniquaise, France.*

Pappy Van Winkle's Family Reserve 15 Years Old (93.5) n23.5 classic corn-rye whiskey with a bit of an edge. Blood oranges and something meaty, too; t24 the mouth puckers under the onslaught of sharp rye and toast-dry vanilla. Yet this is nowhere near over the top and the marmalade fruitiness charms and endears as the spices hit home. Woomphh...!! f22.5 with the battle over, the waves of juicy rye lap kindly on the palate, though the amount of yield remains minimal; b23.5 big whiskey making a big statement. Delightful on numerous levels and pappy as it should be. *(107proof)*

Pappy Van Winkle's Family Reserve 20 Years Old (78.5) n21 t20 f18.5 b19. Flat for the most part and bitter at the end. Just doesn't click as you'd hoped it might. *(90.4 proof)*

Pappy Van Winkle's Family Reserve 23 Years Old (86.5) n23 t21.5 f21 b21. Massive bourbon but the oak, in true PVW style, has become something of a problem. Lots of lavender hickory, but not even close to being a classic bourbon. *(95.6 proof)*

Parker's Heritage Collection (94.5) n22.5 t24 f24 b24. A bourbon for men – and probably women – with hairs on their chests. The bottle suggests you add water to this. Yeah, if you're a gutless wimp. I have known Parker Beam since before the barrels selected for this was a wicked glint in the old distiller's eye. And I can't believe he didn't pass many a barrel by before he chose those which have given us one of the best new whiskeys of the year. An instant classic. And a new must have bourbon is born. *64.8% (1296 proof)*

Parker's Heritage Collection barrelled 26 Apr 96 (91.5) n23 a thudding, no holds-barred aroma, full of peppered celery. Leathered armchair stuff: both on nose and countenance. Sophisticated and at times delicate for all its oomph; t23 boiled apple and soft rye and corn oils combine tactfully; f22.5 brown sugars and vanillas collide with surprising grace; b23 big full-on bourbon at first, then simmers down for something unashamedly fragile towards the end. Superb. *122.6 proof. Heaven Hill.*

Parker's Heritage Collection Second Edition Aged 27 Years bott 08 (93) n23 t23 f23.5 b23.5. An improbably excellent bourbon from the oldest commercial bottling I can remember ever seeing. To be honest, I expected the worst and if someone was to ask me prior to tasting this what hope I would have for bourbon of this age hitting the heights, my answer would not have been particularly positive. However, I have now known Parker Beam for more years than I care to admit and am 100% confident in this sound values: he is without a shadow of doubt in the highest echelon of whiskey and whisky men there have been in our generation. It was he who selected the casks so I was intrigued (also in why they didn't bring out 100 single barrel bottlings rather than dump them together for a one-off, but that's another story), to put it mildly. And the result of 27 years in the barrel is an entirely unique experience not even close to being similar to any other whisky in the world. Indeed, it as if it has not so much entered another whisky world but a parallel universe. Normally I'd shudder at the thought of so much oak. However, this works - and some! I hear it's going for 200 bucks a bottle. I don't normally comment on price but, believe me, for its uniqueness of style alone it's a snip. *48% (96 proof)*

Parker's Heritage Collection Third Edition 2009 "Golden Anniversary" (96.5) n24.5 super rich nose with massive orange current riding high on the mountainous oaky waves: almost like controlled anger for having to wait in a barrel for so many decades before being let out; t24 again, absolutely huge: cocoa is normally a characteristic found at the back end of a whisk(e)y as the oaks bite. Here it is the first personally to be heard and is followed close behind by that concentrated, spicy kumquat note you knew would be lurking somewhere and the inevitable honeycomb; yet between the cocoa and kumquat look out for a brief pulse of palma violet. Just so complex and beautifully oiled to (leathery) boot; f23 the tangy Jaffa gives way to some distant oaky bitterness but there's an assured layer of muscovado sugar to ensure the oaks bow out with grace and natural caramels also help put on the brakes; b24.5 if you are looking for a quiet whiskey with minimum personality, something which ice actually livens up, then don't waste your time here. This is creaking under the oaky strain, hardly surprising as some of what's in your glass is over 40 years old...or about 80 in Scottish years. But the layering and depth is as monumental as it wondrous. How has old timer Parker Beam managed to restrain so much oak? And, better still, harness it into something radiating such unlikely riches. Probably only he knows: he has a few tricks up his sleeve after 50 years in the game. The best commercially available bourbon I have tasted this year and easily one of the top five whiskies in the world. A whiskey entirely befitting Parker, a quiet colossus not just in the bourbon industry but the world whisky stage. This whiskey, like the man, is the real deal. *50% (100 proof) Heaven Hill.*

⦂ **Parker's Herritage Collection Fourth Edition Aged 10 Years** wheated bourbon (95.5) n25 huge. And I mean like....H-U-G-E!! Wondered how all those peppers were managing to penetrate the massive liquorice-honey with such ease. Then realised it is from a wheated recipe, not rye. In many ways, it appears way above its 10-y-o statement, especially considering the toastiness of the Demerara sugars. A tad floral too, but no shrinking violet; t24 sweetly salivating, succulent and yet there is an immediate sugary firmness which borders on crunchy. All the usual high class suspects are there in buckets, especially the molasses and hickory, though the honeycomb almost borders on delicate; f23 cooling, minty dryness allows the vanillas to gain a foothold against the more macho notes; long fade with the sugars still in force; b23.5 here we go again: you know if a whiskey has Parker's name on it, you have to strap yourself in and go for the long haul. One of those bourbons which starts off as though it is going to overwhelm you, but calms down to show it's just a good, well-mannered boy at heart and the epitome of great bourbon. A bit like Parker, I guess... *63.9% (1278 proof) Heaven Hill. 4800 bottles.*

Peach Street Bourbon (86) n19 t22 f23 b22. The nose, though the weak link, is not without its charms; the delivery offers excellent spice and a real fruit cake quality, complete with juicy dates. The finish, as the oak finds a home, really is a joy. Impressive stuff from a small batch distiller and a two-year-old bourbon. *43%. Peach Street Distillers, Colorado.*

Pritchard's Double Barrelled 9 Years Old (92) n23 classy, effortless delivery. The corn-rye integration oozes sophistication and the vanilla-themed oak offers the perfect background; t24 immediate bitter-sweet character celebrates both a raisin-fruity juiciness and a much firmer, burned-honeycombed middle; complex, classy and challenging; f22 thuddingly firm with limited yield. Spices from the rye try to probe the wall, but this is the metalled hoof of a Kentucky thoroughbred; b23 a very different bourbon that ticks the boxes as they should but throws in a few curve balls for the palate to negotiate. *43%*

Ridgemont Reserve 1792 8 Years Old (92.5) n23 t23.5 f22.5 b23.5. A shade heavier than when I first tasted this one with the oak showing a burlier attitude. However, the unique rye fizz ensures a delightful and by no means understated degree of charm. Fabulously different and wholly adorable. *(93.7proof)*

Rock Hill Farms Single Barrel (84.5) n20 t22 f21 b21.5. The stodgy, flat nose is rescued by the well-mannered sweetness of the delivery. All just a tad too oily and corn-rich for anything approaching greatness, though. *50%*

Speakeasy Select dist 1/28/93 **(87)** n22 honeyed grains with a rye-led fruitiness battling off the encroaching oak; t22.5 firm, juicy, pleasantly spiced but the corn spends more time fending off the oak than it might; f21.5 genuinely dry with strands of liquorice and hickory softened by a hint of Demerara; b21 pleasant, but one or four summers too long for this barrel. *58.1%. Steelbach Hotel, Louisville, Kentucky.*

Ten High (68) n17.5 t16.5 f17 b17. Always one of the lighter bourbons, now sporting a curious sweetness which does little to engage. Still a good mixer, though. *40%*

Tom Moore (83) n19 t21 f22 b21. Gloriously consistent, there is s certain something about the rye attack and the general complexity which I just love. *40%*

Van Winkle Special Reserve 12 Years Old lot B **(77.5)** n21 t19.5 f18 b19. Some ryes make for an interesting interlude. But misfires for the most part. *(90.4 proof)*

⋇ **Van Winkle 23 Years Old (89.5)** n23 big oak impact but still breathing with some soft coffee notes; a freshly opened bag of Liquorice Allsorts candy; t23 sweet muscovado sugars help the liquorice see off some probing pine notes; pulsing spices and diced, slightly burnt apple pie; f21.5 burnt French toast; b22 more of a Van Wrinkle: this is showing a lot of age. But enough of a pulse for one last enthralling show. *57% (114 proof) Buffalo Trace*

⋇ **Very Old Barton (85.5)** n21 t22 f21 b21.5. A fair slab of vanilla to go with the busy-ish spice. Attractive, but nothing like as complex as the 6-y-o label. *40% (80 proof)*

Very Old Barton 6 Years Old (90.5) n22.5 the ryes are not shy, displaying their fruity, peppery intent. Fresh, and a hint of Sahara camp fires with green tea on the brew; t23 darting, firm fruit makes for maximum salivation. You could swear some barley gets in on the action, too; f22 slightly more imperious in its vanilla delivery than of old but the rye hangs around to the end; b22.5 a unique style of bourbon with its emphasis on small detail and business around the palate. Always satisfying and fun. *43%* ⊙

Virgin Bourbon 7 Years Old (82.5) n19 t21 f21.5 b21. Firm and crisp from the moment it hits the palate. Even a touch of sophistication to the slow unfurling of the vanillas. Not the whiskey it was, but the astonishing chestnut colour stays the same. *50.5%*

Virgin Bourbon 15 Years Old (92.5) n23.5 mesmeric in its copper-rye depth. Some decent honey combined with maple syrup adds only a degree of lustre to the vanilla and red liquorice. Sumptuous. t23 stately in its elegance and demeanour: this is serious bourbon doing seriously bourbon things. Like pulsing with raisin-rich, spiced honey notes, for instance. f23.5 long, with clever intermingling of oak-studded vanilla and firm rye. b23 the kind of bourbon you want to be left in a room with. *50.5%*

Walker's DeLuxe 3 Years Old (86) n22 t22 f21 b21. Excellent by 3-y-o standards. *40%*

Weller Special Reserve 7 Years Old (83) n20 t21 f21 b21. Pleasant stuff which sings a fruity tune and is ably backed by subtle spice. Perhaps a little too sweet, though. *45%*

Weller 12 Years Old (93.5) n23.5 honeydew melon, apple and liquorice are all there in abundance, but with a glossy Demerara coating; t23.5 the oily corn leads, the honey follows; f23 drier, as the vanillas try to get a foothold; b23.5 seismic in its ability to send giant waves of all those rich, honeyed fingerprints one usually associated with old, high quality bourbon. Such an improvement on previous bottlings and a wheated to set the pulse racing. *45%*

Weller Antique (86.5) n21.5 t22 f21.5 b21.5. The firm nose offers dried dates; the palate is the prickly spice that one so often associates with wheated whiskey with a late waxy lustre. Attractive stuff. *53.5%*

Wild Turkey (77) n19 t19 f20 b19. As sweet and simple as bourbon gets. Shows few of the qualities that make it such astonishing whiskey when older. *(80 proof)*

⠿ **Wild Turkey Tradition Aged 14 Years** db **(89) n23** thick and indulgent: the oak makes a big statement but there is enough high cocoa chocolate and shards of honeycomb to impress; **t21.5** for the first few waves, the harsh oak has control; some time elapses before the sugars and liquorice compose themselves and realign with the recovering honeycomb; milky chocolate fills the middle ground; **f22.5** more cocoa and a little toffee to go with it; **b22** something of a departure in style for a Wild Turkey (which is why it is a little odd it is called "Tradition"): this one makes a point of being an old bird. *50.5% (101 proof)*

Wild Turkey American Spirit Aged 15 Years (92) n24 almost the full gambit. The extra year or two on rare Breed means that the oak has subtracted from the overall complexity. But there is enough going on in the fruitcake and custard pie department to know that we have some major complexity and balance here; **t22.5** sharp delivery: the rye appears first but the essence of liquorice that forms a hint on the nose makes a soft landing here; butterscotch is ladled on and the drier oaky and deft honey notes do the rest; a sweeter Turkish delight edge can be located at the death; **f22.5** a touch thinner than might be expected, but the adroitness of the spices is stunning. Vanilla and toffee apple complete the romp; **b23** a delightful Wild Turkey that appears under par for a 100 proofer but offers much when you search those nooks and crannies of your palate. *50.0% (100 proof)*

Wild Turkey 101 (88) n20 surprisingly dull; **t23** full bodied from the first with soft oils helping to lift and then maintain the ever-increasing spice assault. Chewy and entirely wonderful! **f22.5** long, with no shortage of deep chocolatey sugar cane notes; **b22.5** a lively bird that has gone up the pecking order over the last year or so. The delivery really does have a genuine lustre to it, which comes as a bit of a shock after the so-so nose. It's the spices, though, that steal the show, together with the long finale. *55.5%*

Wild Turkey Rare Breed bottle no. L8002FH **(96) n25** one of the wonders of the whisky and whiskey world....the complexity, the brain-exploding perfection of it all is almost frightening. The trick is the understatement of all that's happening on the nose: the apples, the citrus, the lychees, the cherries...All these elements are there, but fusing with the soft rye (or are those fruit notes part of the rye fingerprint?), and then comes the butterscotch, the odd dollop of honey and that glorious hint of the corn fermenting. Just too good to be true and an aroma that has previously non-lovers of bourbon rethinking their whiskey life; **t24** fabulous, yet after the nose almost a letdown....almost. Silkily structured with an immediate spice, corn and vanilla input. The old liquorice of yore has receded on this bottling, replaced by a bitter-sweet rye presence; **f23.5** long, genuinely soft and again playful with so many notes criss-crossing the palate and offering peek-a-boo sightings of all the things you thought you had detected on the nose; **b24.5** a bourbon that almost teases and tortments you with its complexity. A world great. Note: the sample I officially tasted was from a bottle marked at the neck Batch WT-03RB. Every Rare Breed I have ever tasted has boasted this batch number. More relevant is the bottling number. *54.1%*

Wild Turkey Russell's Reserve 10 (94) n23 fascinating layering of diverse aromas: something almost smoky to this one, perhaps from extracting a peculiar, heavy-ish character from the oak; thinned by a delicate gooseberry note (yes, really!) - as opposed to the usual citrus - which itself is sandwiched between subtle Demerara sugar and vanilla; the rye also makes itself heard; **t23** the body flexes muscles enough to compound the rich brown sugar/liquorice background and intense rye fruitiness. Serious chewing required; **f24** excellent depth, with the oaks now offering impressive soft bitter balance; remains long and consistent as the spices amplify; **b24** unquestionably an upgrade on the last bottling I examined and shows the complexity of this world great distillery. But I still cannot even begin to get my head around the fact that a whiskey named after bourbon legend Jimmy Russell is bottled at 90 proof and not his own preferred 101. One of the true wonders of the whiskey world, that... *45%*

Willett Straight Kentucky Bourbon Aged 11 Years barrel no. 105, bott 08 **(92) n22.5 t23 f23.5 b23.** A very different bourbon eschewing the usual honeyed path and offering something that more than borders on deep sophistication. *54.4%. Special bottling for Heinz Taubenheim, Germany. 192 bottles.*

Willett Straight Kentucky Bourbon Aged 15 Years barrel no. 2, bott 08 **(86) n21 t21.5 f22.5 b21.** A crisp bourbon, hard edged and determined to develop certain themes only so far before abandoning them. Deliciously crunchy and the brief honeyed radiance is a winner. At times hot and raw. *50%. Special bottling for Heinz Taubenheim, Germany. 182 bottles.*

Willett Straight Kentucky Bourbon Aged 15 Years barrel no. 84, bott 08 **(92.5) n22 t23 f23.5 b24.** Survives the obvious battering it took in the higher parts of the warehouse. The balance is the key and after the threatening nose, it never fails once it hits the tastebuds. Don't expect to enjoy on either first, third or fourth tasting. And don't swallow, either.

Remain sober to get and appreciate the full works. Even so, another summer or two and this would have gone down hill very quickly, indeed. *64.7%. Special bottling for Heinz Taubenheim, Germany. 93 bottles.*

·:·· **Willett Straight Kentucky Bourbon Aged 17 Years** white oak barrel no. 1599, bott no. 9 of 36, dist Apr 91 **(86) n22 t22 f21 b21.** An overdose of natural caramels puts a cap on the complexity. Thoroughly enjoyable, but follows few trails. *53.6% Heinz Taubenheim*

·:·· **Willett Straight Kentucky Bourbon Aged 17 Years Barrel Proof** white oak barrel no. 1598, bott no. 6 of 72, dist Apr 91 **(95) n23.5** beautiful kumquat marriage to the sweet liquorice; excellent weight but some lighter touches when required; **t24.5** now that is quite staggering: ask me to draw a picture in my mind of great bourbon on the palate...and here it is. Like a Merc E320: awesome power, so beautifully handled, just gliding, quietly, to its destination, the huge citrus-liquorice-honey makes not a single false move as it reaches its many destinations; **f23.5** and so it continues, except now the drier hickory arrives, backed up by Demerara sugars to ensure balance and grace; **b24** truly great, memorable bourbon. No argument. *60.5% (121 Proof) Heinz Taubenheim*

·:·· **Willett Straight Kentucky Bourbon Aged 19 Years Barrel Proof** white oak barrel no. 8552, bott no. 5 of 5, dist Mar 90 **(77) n21 t18 f20 b17.** Seriously folks: like taking a mouthful of medicine. This is so outrageously over oaked it nearly pulls it off! When it came to the age I think they got the numbers "1" and "9" in the wrong order... After about the fifth mouthful your palate adapts. And you pick out some mocha to go with the minty aroma. But still so OTT..... *63.9% (127.8 Proof) Heinz Taubenheim*

·:·· **William Larue Weller (97) n24** stunning potpourri of ginger, crystallized Demerara sugar, milk coffee and caramelized biscuit; the mingling and interplay is the stuff of wizardry; **t24** immediately mouth-enveloping with a semi-sweet, thick liquorice slick followed swiftly by superb, controlled spices on a major scale. Tannins begin to fill the middle ground but liquorice and burnt honeycomb ensure balance and civility; **f25** long, with the darker, more intense toastier notes gathering weight. A later bitter-ish marmalade secures the balance but it is the death by chocolate which makes this something it is very likely you have never experienced before. It is if they have distilled from chocolate mousse (as opposed to Stag); **b24** among the best wheated mash bill bourbon I have ever encountered. Why some whiskeys work better than others is the stuff of long debate. The reason for this particular bottling is relatively simple: you have an almost breathless intensity, yet somehow the constituent parts of the complexity can be individually identified and savoured. That is quite rare in any whiskey with this degree of weight. *67.4% (134.8 proof) ncf*

William Larue Weller bott 07 **(89) n22.5 t23 f21.5 b22** Just a bit too old and OTT for greatness. The oak has made almost violent inroads into every facet, but there is just enough quality to stand its ground. A pitched battle on the tastebuds – and fun for all that! *58.9% (117.9 proof)*

William Larue Weller (92) n22 t23 f24 b23. Lovely and quite different whiskey here – takes about four or five mouthfuls before you start getting the picture - with a clever build up of sugars. Relatively spiceless for a wheated bourbon but its all about structure and form. Even straight, the strength never overwhelms. *60.95%. (121.9 proof). nf*

William Larue Weller (93) n23.5 spices often associated with wheat recipe bourbon are here in force and make dazzling inroads into the toasty oaky: complex, sturdy, very well weighted and with impressive bitter marmalade for further balance; **t23** massive arrival with the alcohol playing only a minor part in the intensity. The flavours are already well defined through serious time in the oak. The vanilla forms the background but the backbone has to be thick hickory, with a fabulous interplay between those peppery spices and more playful overcooked plum tart fruit tones; a light dusting of muscovado sugars are present throughout to keep control; **f23.5** much more delicate with strands of mocha overtaking the hickory for lead role. Mild buttery tones to the vanilla; **b23** now that's much more like it. The 2007 version was simply too dependent on the older oaks. Here we have an intelligent balance where the wheat really gets to have a say. Beautiful: a mercurial bourbon that you should track down and bring home dead or alive. Because, as a life-long Millwall supporter, I can tell you there will be a Posse after this Weller.... *62.65% (125.3 proof)*

Woodford Reserve Master's Collection Four Grain (95) n24 t24 f23 b24. Sod's law would have it that the moment we removed this from the 2006 Bible, having appeared in the previous two editions without it ever making the shelves, it should at last be belatedly released. But a whiskey worth waiting for, or what? The tasting notes are not a million miles from the original. But this is better bourbon, one that appears to have received a significant polish in the intervening years. Nothing short of magnificent. *46.2%*

Tennessee Whiskey
GEORGE DICKEL

George Dickel Superior No 12 Brand (90) n21 so floral and perfumy that I actually sneezed! Otherwise a bit lazy and over-relaxed; **t22** varying intensity throughout; sweetened by a barley-sugar richness unusual in American whiskey. However, resonating rye refreshes the palate and steers it back on course; **f24** goes into overdrive with astonishing length and stupendous oak: the complexity has earned its corn, so to speak, with the drying oak offering a get-out clause for the developing sugars; **b23** like watching a sea eagle take to flight after catching a larger fish than anticipated: a lumbering take off that at times looks doomed to failure but finally lift off is achieved with spell-binding grace and beauty. Welcome back to a great whisky after years in the doldrums! *45%*

JACK DANIEL

Gentleman Jack Rare Tennessee Whiskey (77) n19 t20 f18 b19. A Tennessee that appears to have achieved the impossible: it has got even lighter in character in recent years. A whiskey which wilfully refuses to say anything particularly interesting or go anywhere, this is one for those prefer their hard liquor soft. *40%. Brown-Forman.*

Jack Daniel's (Green Label) (84) n20 t21 f22 b21. A light but lively little gem of a whiskey. Starts as a shrinking violet, finishes as a roaring lion with nimble spices ripping into the developing liquorice. A superb session whiskey. *40% (80 proof).*

Jack Daniel's Old No. 7 Brand (Black Label) (87) n21 thick, oily, smoky, dense, corn syrupy ... it's Jack Daniel; **t23** sweet, fat, chewy, various types of burnt notes: tofffee, toast etc. etc; **f21** quite a sweet, fat and toffeed finale; **b22** a quite unique whiskey at which many American whiskey connoisseurs turn up their noses. I always think it's worth the occasional visit; you can't beat roughing it a little. *40% (80 proof). Brown-Forman.*

Jack Daniel's Single Barrel barrel no.7-3915, bott 28 Sep 07 **(87) n21.5** like opening the larder on a warm summer's day: a soft background noise of spices and sugar-sprinkled cookies; **t22** soft and buttery, again with brown sugars at the fore; **f22** creamy corn and thickening vanilla; **b21.5** pleasant, yet perhaps not the most inspiring single cask I have come across from JD. This one refuses to offer up the usual oily weight. *45%. Brown-Forman.*

Corn Whiskey

Dixie Dew (83) n19 t21 f22 b21. A few years back at a New York whisky festival some bore or other buttonholed me. "Hey, Mr Whiskey Expert" he sneeringly greeted me. "You reckon you know everything about whiskey, right? Well, why then in your 'Bi-ble' do you go and say that all them corn whiskies taste different? We all know they are made at the same distillery and taste exactly the same. Fact is, you know shit about whiskey, you limey faggot." When patiently I pointed out to this charmless, dosed-up fan of mine that yes, I was aware that the corn whiskeys were made at the same place and, indeed, bottled at the same strength, he smirked. However this was slowly wiped off his face when I further explained that different bottlings, using different casks at slightly varying ages, carrying different spirit from a different wash, would easily account for the variance in styles – and I had certainly been sent different batches. This time round, though, the Dixie Dew is so similar to the Mellow Corn, they could, indeed, be identical twins. Like my dear friend and his wife. *50%*

Georgia Moon Corn Whiskey aged less than thirty days **(84) n20 t22 f21 b21.** Agreeable, sweet, mildly syrupy white dog. Would love to see this at full strength. *40%. Heaven Hill.*

J W Corn (92) n23 firm, solid base despite the dry, oily surround, even a hint of rye here, easily the most sophisticated corn nose I've yet encountered; **t22.5** initially sweet then a crackerjack delivery of spice; oak and vanilla also make a big effort for centre place; **f23** refuses to buckle under the oily attack and allows the oak to offer wave upon wave of dry, cocoa-crusted depth; **b23.5** appears significantly older than the norm: wouldn't be surprised if the odd very over-aged barrel was added to this dumping. Unusual and complex. Oh, and totally brilliant. Cornutopia! *50%*

Mellow Corn (83) n19 t21 f22 b21. Dull and oily on the nose, though the palate compensates with a scintillating array of sweet and spicy notes. *50%*

Single Malt Rye
ANCHOR DISTILLERY

Old Potrero 18th Century Style Whiskey Essay 10-RW-ARM-3-C (90) n20 t23 f24 b23 Always remember something about wide cuts. The nose will be off beam. But the flavours hitting the tastebuds will be off the Richter scale. After tasting this I need to lie down somewhere and rest. Because so few whiskeys in the world are half as big as this, or more fun. Forget about descriptors: this one writes its own book... *62.55% (125.1 proof).*

Old Potrero Single Malt Hotaling's Whiskey Aged 11 Years Essay MCMVI-MMVI (96) n24 t25 f23 b24 This may sound coarse (and I apologise, but it is relevant), but I belched (twice) whilst tasting this. Oddly enough, that never happens when I taste whisky...only gin... And I was spitting. I think gin lovers will be converted and whiskey drinkers truly amazed. Let's make no bones here: this is one of the world's true great whiskies, which just shows the quality of Ritttenhouse barrel 28. Even so, rarely have I encountered complexity like it. I admit rye whiskey is my favourite genre. And no rye in the world offers anything like this. A must have bottling: there is nothing even close in style. *50% (100 proof).*

Old Potrero Single Malt Hotaling's Whiskey Aged 12 Years Essay MCMVI-MMVII (96) n24 t25 f23 b24. I have tasted this Essay against the previous one, and whilst there are the odd subtle differences, this is the closest in style I have ever found two Potreroes to be: their likeness, in general terms, is uncanny. This one has perhaps the slightly drier finish but on the complexity front there is nothing to compare in the whisky world. I am not, remotely, an advocate of whisky and food. But I could murder a beautifully marbled T bone at my third favourite steak joint in the world, Harris's of San Francisco (still has a little way to go to match the incomparable The Ring in Portland, and, at a shorter distance, Barbarian's in Toronto), and follow after a delicate pause with a glass of this local super whisky. Life rarely, if ever, gets better than that. *50% (100 proof).*

Old Potrero Single Malt Straight Rye Whiskey Essay 10-SRW-ARM-E (94) n24 t23 f24 b23 The whiskey from this distillery never fails to amaze. *45% (90 proof).*

Straight Rye

Cougar Rye (95) n25 OK. I have died. I have gone to heaven...what next...? t24 the nose, an impossible jumble of fruity, spicy elements, is nearly perfectly translated onto the palate with the added extra of burnt toast and impressively cindered fruitcake; f23 the spices prevail as does a liquorice and vanilla dryness; b23 if I gave World Whisky of the Year to a rye that's 37% I'd be taken out by Malt Extremists who'd have issued a fatwa on me. It's bloody tempting mind... had it been at full strength of about 50% abv, I don't think there would have been much debate. And to think this is from yet another distillery (Lawrenceburg, Indiana) that had been closed and was under threat of extinction is almost beyond belief. However, word reached me this year that the Lawrenceburg distillery will not just continue to produce gin, but also whiskey: some of the most heart-warming intelligence to come from the United States this year. Surely someone will recognise the utter brilliance of both the bourbon and rye - especially the rye - which is produced here and come up with a plan for it to conquer the world. At the moment only Australia and a few pockets in the home market are lucky enough to find whiskey from this distillery on a regular basis. If any distillery should be given a world stage, then this is it. *37%. Foster's Group, Australia.*

Devil's Bit Seven-Year-Old Single Barrel (93.5) n22.5 gloriously floral as well as fruity; the oak dampens the peppery spice but enough only to keep it in harmony; t24 every bit as juicy and mouth-watering as a great rye should be. The grains are crisp and bounce about the palate brewing up a big spicy storm; the oils are spontaneous and spot on, coating the palate instantly, but never overly so; f23 oak time as the age plays its part with a switch to sweet fruits to drier vanilla. Chewy and warming to the death; b24 I am stunned. A few years back I inspected a barrel or two of rye at the distillery and told the guys there that their rye was top quality. This, though, is even better than I remember it: much better, in fact. Brilliantly made, not a single off note or blemish and complexity oozing from every pour. Just hope they start batch-numbering the bottles if they intend to carry on bringing out single cask expressions. This one gives no clue to its age. A must-find rye from one of the most impressive small distilleries in the world. *47.7%. Edgefield Distillery.*

High West Rendezvous Blend of Straight Rye Whiskies Batch No. 4 (93) n24 brilliant! Unambiguous age here with a compelling mixture of bluebells and cinnamon taking the lead. Muscovado sugar sweetens the pot pourri; t24 shrieking rye dovetails between fresh, juicy rye and something altogether fuller and more sinister. Complex and demanding full attention; f22.5 lots of natural caramel again suggests age but the buzzing fruity spices work hard to the end; b22.5 a very different rye, and no wonder why: it turns out this is a mixture of 6- and 17-year-old, which accounts for the at times bipolar personality. Absolutely seething with character and charisma. *46%*

Hudson Manhattan Rye bott 08, batch 1 (76.5) n16 t20 f21.5 b19. Fruity rye meets fruity butyric. Unbalanced and ungainly on the nose, it is instantly obvious that there are properties here that perhaps shouldn't be about. Still unmistakably a rye though, and on the palate a real juicy flavour-fest. Again, the oils and properties which make the nose something of a car crash add positively to overall character with the finish having much to celebrate in its spicy demeanour. Batch one and a real juicy work in progress that is very drinkable providing you take on at body temperature. 46%

Jim Beam Rye (88) n23 firm and flowery with lavender amid the cinnamon-encrusted sultanas; **t22** an immediate explosion of almost candy-like tartness and spice. Dulls quickly, though; **f21** soft vanilla begins to outweigh the natural fruity-juiciness; **b22** lost a significant degree of its trademark sharpness and zest for all its charm. 40%

Old Overholt Four Years Old (85) n22 t21 f21 b21. Still little sign of this returning to its old rip-roaring best. Duller and less challenging even than a year back with a frustrating dustiness to the procedings. 40%

Pappy Van Winkle's Family Reserve Rye 13 Years Old (94) n24 outwardly, the aroma basks in a crisp rye flourish; scratch below the surface and there are darker, more sinister oaky forces at work; **t23.5** crisp, almost crackling rye offers both the fruity-clean and burned fruitcake options; **f23** dulls out a bit as the liquorice/toffee oak takes hold but remains alluringly spicy and sensual; **b23.5** uncompromising rye that successfully tells two stories simultaneously. A great improvement on the Winkle rye of old. 47.8%

Pikesville (92.5) n23 one of the liveliest and cleanest rye noses around. Still retains its unique scrumpy and new car interior mix but now the rye is really pitching up with something quite firm, too; **t23.5** sublime clarity in the way the old Jim Beam Yellow Label went about its business until quite recently. The rye is polished and sparkling and helped along by some unrefined sugar; **f22.5** it takes a while for the vanilla to find its range. Even when it does, it is outgunned by the rye; **b23.5** the most improved standard rye on the market place. And none around where the grain is delivered with such unabashed, crystal clarity. 40%

Rathskeller Rye dist 83 **(95) n24** big, firm, with an almost metallic hardness, yet something soft and yielding beneath. Quite beautiful, and, once placed in front of you, is quite impossible not to explore without a degree of excitement. At its very best in the romantic semi-darkness of the uniquely atmospheric Steelbach bar, a whiskey Eden created by the Gods of grain. And in intensity even capable of overcoming the bizarre and daunting polished leather aroma of the hotel's Rathskellar itself where it also reveals itself seductively and memorably; **t24** the tongue cannot help but explore that double layered soft-hard signature. And as the tongue delves into the tempting fruitiness, so everything hardens yet becomes juicier. Absolutely classic Kentucky rye and a lot younger in body than you might be given to think given the label; **f23.5** chewy, chocolate and cherries and brilliantly controlled spice on the oak; **b23.5** a beguiling rye of genuine beauty and charm which electrifies and excites; that complex, yielding hardness so typical of a great rye is something the tongue was invented for. Further exploration needed on my return to the hotel: just hope the bar still has it! 65%. *Steelbach Hotel, Louisville, Kentucky.*

Rittenhouse (86) n21 t23 f21 b21. The only Kentucky rye I know spelt "whisky" has upped its rye character in recent bottlings. However, this one's all about the first few seconds of delivery, which are exquisite. The rest is relatively routine. 40%

Rittenhouse 100 Proof Bottled in Bond (94) n22.5 sampled blind I would swear this to be a mixture of pot and column still rum, with some Barbadian and Guyanan taking the lead; **t24** the tastebuds are left to wave the white flag as they are over-run by marauding rye notes. These are firm, fruity and flighty one moment, duller and weightier the next; always salivating, you are left to drown in your own juices as the spices begin to kick in with aplomb; **f23.5** fantastic marriage between high cocoa chocolate and burnt toffee. Long and chewy until your jaw aches; **b24** staggering whisky. Rye like this, as I predicted long ago, will win a worldwide following which is unlikely to go away: the flavours are delivered with abandon and complexity. No serious whisky lover can be without this guy on his shelf. 50%

Rittenhouse Very Rare Single Barrel 21 Years Old (91) n25 Incredible. Intriguing. Unique. Such is the punch to the super-ripe fruit, so intense is the oak that has fused into it, that it takes literally hours to try and make sense of what is happening here. There is no other aroma in the whisky or whiskey world that matches, the closest relation being ancient pot still whiskey from Ireland for reasons I will explain later. It perhaps needs a whisky lover with the mind of an archaeologist to understand this one, because the nose is a series of layers built up over time. The key is to dig deeper than the surface spices and burnt honeycomb. In there, in varying strata, are diffused mint and lemon zest and a fruity intensity to the rye grain normally found only when malted. Astonishing and almost too beautiful for words; **t23** impatient oak rampages through the early, oily arrival of rye concentrate. Then waves of spice, of steadily increasing intensity crash lip-smackingly into the tastebuds. But such is the magnitude of the rye it absorbs the oak without too much early damage and only towards the middle does it begin to lose the battle; **f21** a dry finale as the come-of-age oak demands the last say; **b22** I may be wrong, but I would wager quite a large amount that no-one living has tasted more rye from around the world than I. So trust me when I tell you this is different, a genuine one-off in style. By rights such telling oak involvement should have killed the whisky stone dead: this is like someone being struck by lightning and then walking off slightly singed and with a limp, but otherwise OK. The closest style of whisky to rye is Irish pot still, a unique type where unmalted barley is used. And the closest whiskey I have tasted to this has been 35 to 50-year-old pot still Irish. What they have in common is a massive fruit base, so big that it can absorb and adapt to the oak input over many years. This has not escaped unscathed. But it has to be said that the nose alone makes this worthy of discovery, as does the glory of the rye as it first melts into the tastebuds. The term flawed genius could have been coined for this whisky alone. Yet, for all its excellence, I can so easily imagine someone, somewhere, claiming to be an expert on whiskey, bleating about the price tag of $150 a bottle. If they do, ignore them. Because, frankly, rye has been sold far too cheaply for far too long and that very cheapness has sculpted a false perception in people's minds about the quality and standing of the spirit. Well, 21 years in Kentucky equates to about 40 years in Scotland. And you try and find a 40-year-old Scotch for £75. If anything, they are giving this stuff away. The quality of the whiskey does vary from barrel to barrel and therefore bottle to bottle. So below I have given a summary of each individual bottling (averaging (91.1). The two with the highest scores show the least oak interference...yet are quite different in style. That's great whiskey for you. *50% (100 proof). ncf. Heaven Hill.*

Barrel no. 1 (91) n25 t23 f21 b22. As above. *50%*
Barrel no. 2 (89) n24 t23 f20 b22. Dryer, oakier. *50%*
Barrel no. 3 (91) n24 t23 f22 b22. Fruity, soft. *50%*
Barrel no. 4 (90) n25 t22 f21 b22. Enormous. *50%*
Barrel no. 5 (93) n25 t23 f22 b23. Early rye surge. *50%*
Barrel no. 6 (87) n23 t22 f20 b22. Juicy, vanilla. *50%*
Barrel no. 7 (90) n23 t23 f22 b22. Even, soft, honeyed. *50%*
Barrel no. 8 (95) n25 t24 f23 b23. The works: massive rye. *50%*
Barrel no. 9 (91) n24 t23 f22 b22. Sharp rye, salivating. *50%*
Barrel no. 10 (93) n25 t24 f22 b22. Complex, sweet. *50%*
Barrel no. 11 (93) n24 t24 f22 b23. Rich, juicy, spicy. *50%*
Barrel no. 12 (91) n25 t23 f21 b22. Near identical to no.1. *50%*
Barrel no. 13 (91) n24 t24 f21 b22. Citrus and toasty. *50%*
Barrel no. 14 (94) n24 t24 f22 b23. Big rye and marzipan. *50%*
Barrel no. 15 (88) n23 t22 f21 b22. Major oak influence. *50%*
Barrel no. 16 (90) n24 t23 f21 b22. Spicy and toffeed. *50%*
Barrel no. 17 (90) n23 t23 f22 b22. Flinty, firm, late rye kick. *50%*
Barrel no. 18 (91) n24 t24 f21 b22. Big rye delivery. *50%*
Barrel no. 19 (87) n23 t22 f21 b21. Major coffee input. *50%*
Barrel no. 20 (91) n23 t24 f22 b22. Spicy sugar candy. *50%*
Barrel no. 21 (94) n24 t23 f24 b23. Subtle, fruity. *50%*
Barrel no. 22 (89) n24 t23 f22 b22. Mollased rye. *50%*
Barrel no. 23 (94) n24 t23 f24 b23. Soft fruit, massive rye. *50%*
Barrel no. 24 (88) n23 t22 f21 b22. Intense oak and caramel. *50%*
Barrel no. 25 (93) n25 t22 f23 b23. Heavy rye and spice. *50%*
Barrel no. 26 (92) n23 t23 f23 b23. Subtle, delicate rye. *50%*
Barrel no. 27 (94) n25 t23 f23 b23. Delicate rye throughout. *50%*
Barrel no. 28 (96) n25 t24 f23 b24. Salivating, roasty, major. *50%*
Barrel no. 29 (88) n23 t22 f21 b22. Hot, fruity. *50%*
Barrel no. 30 (91) n24 t23 f22 b22. Warming cough sweets. *50%*
Barrel no. 31 (90) n25 t22 f21 b22. Aggressive rye. *50%*

Rittenhouse Rye Single Barrel 23 Year Old barrel no. 8 **(96) n24** singes the nose hairs with its forceful exuberance; the oak tries to dominate totally but there is enough fruit in reserve to stand its ground. Still, strangely phenolic with something of the dental surgery about it all; elsewhere bluebells in the dankest and darkest of Surrey woodlands; brooding honeycomb; **t23.5** the exotic fruit you find in some exceptionally old old Scotch appears to be having a convention of its own here: some of it is the rye, but the massive oak must have some say in this. Wonderfully spiced and lush, the high roast Java towards the middle works rather well; **f24** long, with a viscosity that belies the years; those eye-watering spices stay the distance and then the most bitter of cocoa arrives; throughout, though, the fruity rye adds a consistent and improbably clean voice; **b24.5** it has been 34 years now since I fell in love with rye whiskey.

And I can tell you I have never tasted anything quite like this. In most whiskies around the world an injection of oak to this degree would kill it stone dead. Here, however, it survives and somehow appears to turn the very points that should be the whiskey's downfall into its strengths. A freak of a whiskey. But, my God, a fabulous one! *50% (100 proof). Heaven Hill.*

⋰⋰ **Rittenhouse Rye Single Barrel Aged 25 Years** bott Nov 09 **(93.5) n24.5** cinnamon on apple crumble. That's perhaps the easy way of describing something which is almost too astonishingly complex for words. Remember how, with very good justification, I was blown away by the 21-year-old a few years back....? Well this has actually upped the game and taken the rye, nose-wise into a new dimension. When you are playing with old whiskies like this it is too easy for the cask to run away with itself; for an off note or a sign of tiredness to begin an unstoppable journey of destruction. It simply hasn't happened here: what we have is one of the ultimate experiences of truly great spirit being filled into entirely compatible top-drawer barrels and time being allowed to coax every last degree of complexity and beauty possible. Beyond that cinnamon, away from that apple crumble, we have so much more. Like ultra high quality Jamaican medium high ester pot still of advanced years from Long Pond; or lighter efforts from Hampden. There is a golden honey and coconut thread to this, a touch of leathery hickory, too. But we keep getting back to that rye-ramped fruitiness, the key to aroma puzzle....it really is a thing of ridiculous complexity and beauty. And, frankly, mystery... **t24** an immediate arm locking of firm, rock-hard rye in the form of a candy-like fruited, crystalline Demerara sugar, and much more aggressive oak with a real thick hickory/camp coffee assertiveness: one heck of a confrontation; **f22** long with a definite oak drawl but still a fruity juiciness fighting off the worst of the aging; **b23** this is principally about the nose: a thing of rare beauty even in the highest peaks of the whiskey world. The story on the palate is much more about damage limitation with the oak going a bit nuts. But remember this: in Scottish years due to the heat in Kentucky, this would be a malt well in excess of 50 years. But even with the signs of fatigue, so crisp is that rye, so beautifully defined are its intrinsic qualities that the quality is still there to be clearly seen. Just don't judge on the first, second or even third mouthful. Your taste buds need time to relax and adjust. Only then will they accommodate and allow you to fully appreciate and enjoy the creaky old ride. At this age, though, always worth remembering that the best nose doesn't always equal the best tasting experience... *50% (100 proof) Heaven Hill*

⋰⋰ **Barrel no. 1 (93.5) n24.5 t24 f22 b23.** As above. *50%*
⋰⋰ **Barrel no. 2 (88) n22 t24 f20 b22.** Intense. Crisp, juicy; a tad soapy, bitter. *50%*
⋰⋰ **Barrel no. 3 (89.5) n23 t23.5 f21.5 b21.5.** Fabulously crisp. Fruity. Mollassed. *50%*
⋰⋰ **Barrel no. 4 (85) n21.5 t21.5 f21 b21.** Subdued fruit. Massive oak. *50%*
⋰⋰ **Barrel no. 5 (90.5) n25 t22.5 f21.5 b21.5.** Complex. Mega oaked but spiced, fruity. *50%*
⋰⋰ **Barrel no. 6 (91.5) n24.5 t22 f23 b22.** Tangy. Honeyed and hot. Spiced marmalade. *50%*
⋰⋰ **Barrel no. 7 (83.5) n20 t22 f20.5 b21.** Treacle toffee amid the burnt apple. *50%*
⋰⋰ **Barrel no. 8 (90) n23.5 t23.5 f21 b22.** Flinty, teeth-cracking rye. Crème brulee. *50%*
⋰⋰ **Barrel no. 9 (91) n23.5 t23.5 f22 b22.** Massive ryefest. Mocha coated. *50%*
⋰⋰ **Barrel no. 10 (86.5) n22 t23 f20 b21.5.** Early zip and juice. Tires towards caramel. *50%*
⋰⋰ **Barrel no. 11 (89) n24 t22 f21 b22.** Honeycomb. Hickory. Caramel. Oil. *50%*
⋰⋰ **Barrel no. 12 (84.5) n22.5 t21 f20 b21.** Delicate. Vanilla and caramel. Light. *50%*
⋰⋰ **Barrel no. 13 (89.5) n22.5 t23 f22 b22.** Succulent. Yet rye remains firm. *50%*
⋰⋰ **Barrel no. 14 (88) n22 t23 f21 b22.** Very similar to 13 but with extra caramel. *50%*
⋰⋰ **Barrel no. 15 (86) n21 t23 f20.5 b21.5.** Lazy grain. Warming but flat. Caramel. *50%*
⋰⋰ **Barrel no. 16 (92) n23 t23 f23 b23.** Sculpted rye: sugared fruit; a twist of juniper. *50%*
⋰⋰ **Barrel no. 17 (86.5) n22.5 t21.5 f21 b21.5.** Fizzy fruity spice calmed by caramel. *50%*
⋰⋰ **Barrel no. 18 (91) n23.5 t23.5 f21.5 b22.5.** Pristine rye. Spice. Juicy molasses. Crisp. *50%*
⋰⋰ **Barrel no. 19 (96) n24 t23.5 f24.5 b23.5.** Concentrated honeycomb and chocolate. *50%*
⋰⋰ **Barrel no. 20 (89.5) n23 t22 f22.5 b22.** Cream toffee. Fruit and spice. *50%*
⋰⋰ **Barrel no. 21 (85) n21 t20 f23 b21.** Severe oak delivery. Recovers with mocha toffee. *50%*
⋰⋰ **Barrel no. 22 (81) n20 t20 f21 b20.** Mild sap. Fruity. Oily. *50%*
⋰⋰ **Barrel no. 23 (94) n23.5 t24 f23.5 b23** Rich. Fruity. Juicy. Clean. Corn oil. Cocoa. *50%*
⋰⋰ **Barrel no. 24 (88.5) n22.5 t22 f22 b22.** Huge vanilla. Slow spice. *50%*
⋰⋰ **Barrel no. 25 (88) n22.5 t21.5 f22 b22.** Custard and sugared fruit. Sharpens. *50%*
⋰⋰ **Barrel no. 26 (90.5) n22 t23 f23 b22.5.** Classic crisp rye. Big, manageable oak. *50%*
⋰⋰ **Barrel no. 27 (88) n23 t22 f21.5 b21.5.** Huge, honeyed oak. Oily. Dries at end. *50%*
⋰⋰ **Barrel no. 28 (91) n22.5 t23.5 f22.5 b22.5.** Exemplary honeycomb-rye delivery. Spices. *50%*
⋰⋰ **Barrel no. 29 (94) n23.5 t24 f23 b23.5.** Juicy rye; crisp sugar-vanilla-hickory fade. *50%*
⋰⋰ **Barrel no. 30 (94.5) n23 t24 f24 b23.5.** Thick rye. Cocoa. Spices. *50%*
⋰⋰ **Barrel no. 31 (79) n21 t20 f19 b19.** Lethargic. Bitter. *50%*

⁘ **Barrel no. 32 (88)** n21.5 t22.5 f22 b22. Relaxed honeycomb. Hint of mint. *50%*

⁘ **Barrel no. 33 (88.5)** n22.5 t22 f22 b22. Powering oak-rye battle. *50%*

⁘ **Barrel no. 34 (84)** n23 t21 f20 b20. Thick oak throughout. Corn oil. *50%*

⁘ **Barrel no. 35 (93.5)** n22.5 t23.5 f24 b23.5. Big rye. Demerara-hickory. Complex. *50%*

⁘ **Barrel no. 36 (77)** n21 t19 f18 b19. Bitter oak. *50%*

Sazerac Rye 6 Years Old (91) n22.5 firm, unambiguous rye with minimum yield and complexity; t23 much juicier, showing little oak interference. Almost candy-like in its sugar and spice qualities; f23.5 again the rye dominates with minimal restraint but at least offers several paths, the longest being slightly dry with butterscotch off-shoots; b22 rye perhaps at its least complicated. But horny stuff, nonetheless. *45%*

Sazerac Rye 18 Years Old bott Fall 2007 **(95.5)** n24.5 t24 f23 b24. Remains among the ultimate Kentucky rye experiences with its uncompromising strength and beauty. A true world classic. *45%*

Sazerac Rye 18 Years Old bott Fall 2008 **(97.5)** n25 simply gorgeous outpouring of clean rye notes: crisp, fruity, saliva-inducing boiled candy. The oak weighs in with a confident but reverently restrained minty sweetness, perhaps with a degree of lavender, too. The overall effect is absolutely perfect balanced; t24.5 demi-sec fruit, crisp and brittle as a great rye should be. The oak again take a leading role with a buzzing spice and dry, bitter marmalade on burnt toast qualities which again counter the rye with almost playful panache; a thin layer of molasses provides the balance without ever detracting from the complex battles raging; f23.5 some inevitable caramels thin out the complexity slightly. But still can't stop those spice pulses or the last juicy remnants of the rye; b24.5 there are very few greater treats in my life than to see how the latest bottling of Sazerac has turned out. This one, with its cleverly disguised sophistication coupled with its extraordinary maintenance of a unique style, is a classic even by its own Himalayan standards. This radiated possible World Whisky of the Year from the very first nosing: it did not lie. *45% (90 proof)*

⁘ **Sazerac Straight Rye** bott Fall 2009 **(95.5)** n24 floral and fruity: dense interplay between fabulous lavender and kumquat concentrate; the most tangy, almost bizarrely coastal of the Sazerac 18s yet; t24 tight and dry delivery with the oaks diving in early and with intent; juicy rye quickly wades in to compensate. The more complex elements take a little time to extract themselves from the quick vanillas and caramel, but they arrive as a lightly spiced procession, this time offering mildly salted celery, muscovado sugars, red liquorice and a wonderful fruited tang; f23.5 long with a more relaxed and stretched breakdown of characters and flavours. The oaks have been tamed and vanillas dominate despite the best efforts of the fizzy spices; b24 another year, another dip into the metal vats...and another different result. Fabulous whiskey worthy of the finer moments in your life, though somehow not quite matching the genius and improbable freshness of the Fall 2008 version. *45% (90 proof)*

Templeton Prohibition Era Recipe Rye batch 2, barrel 122, bott 08 **(93)** n24 huge, unmistakable rye: almost in concentrate or candy form with a dollop of manuka honey for good measure. Different yet familiar in that the style is unique but painted in a way that is familiar to those of us who know the excellence of a certain distillery which, in my humble opinion, pushes out the best rye whisky in the world; t23.5 rock-hard barley crunches into the taste buds, ricocheting around the palate to astonishing effect. A softer sub-plot involves soft fruits and even a gentle barley grandeur, but that is fleeting and it is principally about the ultra-firm rye; f22.5 a surprising austerity punctured by a very late show of delicate spice; b23 unique rye that never quite lives up the brilliance of the nose, but offers enough singular entertainment throughout to make this a must have for rye lovers. The mashbill, I have since discovered since writing the notes above is a mixture of rye and malted barley alone. And it is not, as I very much suspected, made at the Templeton distillery in Chicago: I would have been astonished and given up my job as a whisky critic if it had. The actual distillery where it is made, outside Kentucky, is being kept secret by Templeton. But there is no doubt that whoever made this knew exactly what they were doing, and were doing it in stills that needed no proving. Wonderful and truly singular. *40%*

⁘ **Thomas H Handy Sazerac Straight Rye Whiskey (97)** n24 seriously heavy duty: thick enough to use for armour plating. Takes time, but slowly the notes become identifiable, the dense, obvious rye apart. On hand warming, concentrated cocoa notes emerge, as well as spiced kumquat. But that is only the beginning: light cloves and molasses confirm the oak's impact; t25 massively thick with the oils of rye and corn forming a surprisingly lush field. The cocoa on the nose is re-introduced, this time as molten chocolate while the juicy fruity rye fizzes and forms mini lakes as the salivation factor goes through the roof (of the mouth); massive infusion of Demerara sugar, but these do no more than balance the gathering spice intensity: perfection...; f24 calms down quite dramatically as the natural caramels and vanillas begin to impact. But still those heady chocolate-rye notes continue their delicious seduction of the taste buds; **b24** it has taken me over three hours to taste this. Were all whiskies and whiskeys like this, the Bible, quite simply, would never see the light of day. Beyond enormous. A whiskey which located taste buds I had no idea I actually possess... Just like his near namesake, Thomas Hardy, Thomas Handy has come up with a rambling, immortal classic. *64.5% (129 proof) ncf*

Thomas H Handy Sazerac Straight Rye Whiskey (94.5) n24 t24 f23 b23.5. Any crisper and the....I think you may have got the idea...... *67.4% (134.8 proof). ncf.*

Wild Turkey (89) n22 fresh layers of rye topped by a vanilla coating; **t23** sharp, crashing rye blundering into the tastebuds with serious juiciness; a genuine liquorice backbone to this one upping the intensity and weight another degree; **f22** chewy, almost bourbonesque in its fade with a late firm rye resurgence; **b22** true to type but with less natural caramel and more assertiveness from the grain. A grand improvement. *50.5%*

Wild Turkey Russell's Reserve Rye Aged 6 Years (91) n23 rye at its juiciest; a hint of spearmint; sweet, with just enough oak to work beautifully; **t23.5** immediate spice impact, then a spreading of soft brown sugar and honey; **f22.5** soft oils embrace the growing vanilla and soft liquorice; long and luxuriant; **b22.5** a much cleaner, more vibrant version of the standard Turkey rye. Seriously delicious. *45.0% (90 proof)*

Straight Wheat Whiskey

Bernheim Original (91.5) n22 smouldering toast from that-day-baked bread. Mealy, too with a little salt added for effect; **t23** that peculiar salty tang on the nose transfers with little difficulty to the palate. It joins a citrusy throng and a delightful sharpness which counters the sweeter, oilier nature of the beast; **f23** a classy finale where we are back to toast, if a little burned, and dissolving sugars but, mainly, a crackling firmness which appears to be a stand off between the wheat and the oak; **b23.5** by far the driest of the Bernheims I have encountered – and this is about the 10th – showing greater age and perhaps substance. Unique and spellbinding. *45%*

Kentucky Whiskey

Early Times Kentucky Whisky (74) n19 t19 f18 b18. Slightly improved with some extra beefing up, but still light and over sweet. *40% (80 proof). Brown-Forman*

Medley's Kentucky Whiskey bott code L6114 **(81)** n21 t21 f19 b20. Very tight grains. Pleasant, but limited complexity. *40%. Berentzen Distillers.*

American/Kentucky Whiskey Blends

Charter Private Reserve (72.5) n18 t18.5 f19 b17. Molten sugar sprinkled with vanilla. *40%*

Other American Whiskey

❖ **Buffalo Trace Experimental Collection 1995 American Oak Chips Seasoned** dist Apr 95, bott Aug 10 **(92)** n24 a glass of assorted citrus concentrate, mainly kumquat but no shortage of lemon sherbet candy, either, plus a liberal sprinkling of chopped mint. A dull allspice and clove note hovers in the far background; **t23** a resounding early rye firm, fruitiness delivery but notable for its limited sweetness: liquorice (without the usual Demerara sugars) leading to hickory; **f22.5** remains dry with a light oiliness to the hickory and light tannins before reverting to that playful mintiness found on the nose; **b22.5** absolutely fascinating. BT as you will never have quite seen it before. The muted sugars gives us a rare insight to the other, firmer aspects of the whiskey. *45%*

❖ **Buffalo Trace Experimental Collection 1995 French Oak Barrel Aged** dist Apr 95, bott Jul 10 **(94.5)** n23.5 one of the biggest Guyanan rum noses to an American whiskey I have yet encountered; myriad dark sugar notes bludgeoning any half-hearted spices which think twice about showing themselves; the oak infusion is considerable but in balance; **t24.5** fabulously rich chocolate delivery then a massive outpouring of spices: quite astonishing layering of thick tannins, leading from cocoa to mocha; the middle ground is a huge liquorice convention and, at last, some throbbing spices; **f23** a building of oils adds further depth to the spices and vanillas on the long finale; **b23.5** a memorable knife and fork job which is required drinking for anyone who prefers their whiskey to take your taste buds to the limit. Just outlandish fun! *45%*

Nor'Easter "Bourbon" (85.5) n22 t22 f20 b21.5. A pretty whiskey with an attractively perfumed nose. The finish is thin and scant but the body delves into sugary recesses in which the odd strip of liquorice can be found. *44.4%. Triple Eight Distillery.*

Old Virginia Extra Rare American Whiskey Aged 12 Years L530133A **(90)** n22 t23 f22 b23. Good grief: this is damn good stuff. The most honeyed and high-class non-bourbon on the market. *40%. La Martiniquaise, France.*

Canadian Whisky

It is becoming hard to believe that Canadian was once a giant among the world whisky nations. Dotted all over its enormous land large distilleries pumped out thousands upon thousands of gallons of spirit that after years in barrel became a clean, gentle whisky.

It was cool to be seen drinking Canadian in cocktail bars on both sides of the pond. Now, sadly, Canadian whisky barely raises a beat on the pulse of the average whisky lover. It would not be beyond argument to now call Canadian the forgotten whisky empire with column inches devoted to their column stills measured now in millimetres. It is an entirely sad, almost heartbreaking, state of affairs though hopefully not an irreversible one. The finest Canadian, for me, is still whisky to be cherished and admired. But outside North America it can be painfully hard to find.

Especially seeing how whiskies containing the permitted 9.09% of non-Canadian whisky (or whisky at all) had been barred from the European market. So just to ensure Jim Murray's Whisky Bible remained on the ball I spent two spells last year in Canada tasting every Canadian whisky I could find on the market. The result, as ever, was illuminating. This latest blitz reconfirmed there was now a clear divergence of styles between traditionalist whisky like Alberta Premium and a more creamy textured, fruit-enhanced product once confined to the USA but now found in Canada itself.

BRITISH COLUMBIA

ALBERTA

MANITOBA

Vancouver

Alberta
Calgary

Okanagan †

Palliser

Gimli

Key

● Major Town or City
▲ Distillery
† Dead Distillery

However, there is no doubt that we are seeing a change in the perception of Canadian by drinkers who had previously confined themselves to top quality Scotch malt. Following my award of Jim Murray's Whisky Bible Canadian Whisky of the Year 2006 to Alberta Premium, I had the chance to spend time in television and radio studios around the country talking about the exceptionally high quality of top Canadian whiskies. It led to a string of emails from readers telling me they had since tasted Alberta and been somewhat shocked to find a world classic whisky lurking so unobtrusively - and cheaply - on their shelves. For many, this had led to further exploring of Canadian, and uncovering of further gems. One of those to really light up the Canadian scene was Danfield's 21-year-old but last year the Award went to another showing great complexity and balance: Wiser's Red Letter. For the Jim Murray's Whisky Bible 2011 it is Crown Royal Reserve. The Wiser's had taken advantage of a rare form blip from Alberta Premium. This year, though, Alberta was back to its brilliant self, showing just how good the Crown Royal Reserve had to be to get top billing. Working out which thrilled me most was one of the highlights of my whisky year.

Perhaps one of the things that makes Canadian whisky compelling is its ever-changing face. Many brands do have a tendency to move around in style slightly more than you might expect. However, there is an interesting development from Kentucky which contradicts that in an unorthodox manner. Buffalo Trace have decided to bottle some casks of Canadian in their inventory as a single barrel product. They sent me and others some samples back in their developmental stage and asked us for our input. Now, contrary to what anyone tells you, or claim they know, a Canadian single cask whisky called Bush Pilot was around some 15 years ago, the product of Canadian Club's Okanagan distillery. And each bottling was natural and fascinatingly different. The same can't quite be said for the new Caribou Crossing, a pleasant enough whisky which sports a thumping degree of unionizing caramel while the Canadian whisky lover, or potential convert, is little helped by every bottle looking identical with no cask details. BT have done little wrong in the last decade; indeed, in that time have become the most consistently excellent and exciting distillers in the world taking both bourbon and rye to new heights in my lifetime, and in Drew Mayville (a Canadian, incidentally) they have a blender at the top of his game. But the usual BT sure-footedness appears to have found a hole in the ice - for you can't help thinking that this perfect chance to win over hearts and minds to Canadian has not been fully grasped. Both Drew and I learned our Canadian from the very same school of past Canadian blending masters – and I use the term carefully – so we tend to have very similar views on matters Canadian/Canadien. But when I am back in Frankfort I am looking forward to locking friendly Caribou horns with him on this one...

ONTARIO

QUEBEC

🌲 Glenora

NOVA SCOTIA

●**Quebec**

Valleyfield ●**Montreal**

Canada Mist 🌲 ●**Toronto**

🌲 Kittling Ridge

🌲 Walkerville

Canadian Single Malts
GLENORA

Glen Breton db (81) n19 t21 f20 b21. Enormously sweet malt, in almost concentrated form with a tantalising whiff of smoke hanging around; mildly spiced and slightly oily, soapy finale. 43%

Glen Breton Rare db (73) n14 t21 f19 b19. This is a version – probably a very early one – I had not seen and it makes for exceptionally grim nosing. However, after that very unpleasant, feinty experience, it comes back to life on the palate with remarkable honey and copper input. A right mixed bag. 40%

Glen Breton Rare db (80) n18 t21 f20 b21. Caramel nose a bit soapy but the buttery, sweet malt, with its vanilla fizz, makes for a pleasant experience. 43%

Glen Breton Rare Aged 10 Years (75) n15 t21 f20 b20. Lashings of butterscotch help put out of the mind the feinty nose (those who tasted the original Sullivan's Cove from Australia will be suffering serious déjà vu here...). Full bodied, as wide-cut whiskies tend to be, and for all the cuts, bruises and plasters, there is enough complexity here to make for an entertaining Canadian - once the nose has been negotiated. 40%

Glen Breton Ice Aged 10 Years (85.5) n21.5 t21 f22 b21. Tasting both a full strength bottled Canadian, and one that had been matured in Icewine barrels, I was nearly blown through the back of my seat and into the wall. One of the biggest shocks to hit you on the Canadian whisky scene today, there is no denying that this whisky offers sufficient panache and lucidity to genuinely impress. Hardly an exercise in perfect balance, it certainly celebrates the art of surprise and, late on, charm. The cocoa-dusted butterscotch really is a rare treat and, thanks to the fruity world it finds itself in, a truly unique and enjoyable experience. 57.2%

OKANAGAN

Long Wood 8 Years Old Malt db (74) n19 t20 f17 b18. There are no discernable off notes and a pleasant liquorice-spice prevails. But the true life has been strangled out if it by caramel. A tragedy, in whisky terms, as this is very rare malt from a lost distillery. 40%. Germany.

Canadian Blended Whisky

Alberta Premium (95.5) n24 throbbing, pulsing rye on a variety of levels: full and juicy, dull and dusty, firm and flinty. Unique and unmistakable; t25 my first whisky of the day – and it needs to be. The tastebuds are given such a working over that they need to be fully tuned and fit to take this on. Again it is all about the rye: the first, second and third flavours to pound the mouth are all rye-related. The very first are juicy with a minute sweetness. The second, hanging onto the coattails of the first are Rockies hard and brittle, clattering into the tastebuds with zero yield. Next comes a quick follow through of explosive peppers, but again leaving in their wake a semi-sweet juicy, fruitiness, almost certainly from the malted rye. No other whisky in the world unleashes this combination of grainy punches around the palate in this way. Beautiful and complex: just words, and ones that don't even begin to do this whisky justice; f22.5 dulls down, probably because of the needless caramel added, but there is slightly more depth than before thanks most probably to the malted rye. The spices continue to fizz as the Demerara-tipped vanillas make their mark; b24 it has just gone 8am and the Vancouver Island sky is one of clear blue. My windows are open to allow in some chilly, early spring air and, though only the first week of March, an American robin sits in the arbutus tree, resplendent in its new two-toned leaves, calling for a mate, as it has done since 5.15 this morning, his song blending with the lively trill of the house finches and the doleful, maritime anthem of the gull. It seems the natural environment of Alberta Premium, back here to its rye-studded best after a couple I tasted socially in Canada last year appeared comparatively dull and restrained. (Indeed, I am tasting this from Bottle Lott No L93300197: it is classic, generating all I expect and now demand. Another bottle here, L00180007 offers something caked in caramel and is by, AP standards, inert and scores only 88.) Now L933 is calling from the glass, like the robin and finches from the Arbutus, true to nature: it is a true rye whisky, not a misnomer like the rest. The 100% rye grain used, fortified in its mouth-watering delivery by the usage of a degree of malted rye, offers flavours unlimited. Alberta Premium is no longer just a great Canadian whisky. It has become a national treasure. 40% ⊙ ⊙

Alberta Premium 25 Years Old (95) n24 t23 f23 b25. Faultless. Absolutely nothing dominates. Yet every aspect has its moment of conquest and glory. It is neither bitter nor sweet, yet both. It is neither soft nor hard on the palate yet both elements are there. Because of the 100% rye used, this is an entirely new style of whisky to hit the market.

No Canadian I know has ever had this uncompromising brilliance, this trueness to style and form. And, frightening to think, it could be improved further by bottling at least 46% and un-chillfiltered. For any whisky lover who ever thought Canadian was incapable of hitting the heights among the world's greats, I have previously recommended Alberta Premium. I still do. But if they want to taste something that will amaze then they can do worse than this. The question will now rage: which is the better of the two? For me, perhaps the Premium, because it also has bite as well as guile and slakes thirsts as well as outrageously entertains. Having made love to a young vixen this, though, is perhaps closer to spending a night in the arms of a sultry lady of greater experience. Passion or elegance? We are back to whisky being a mood thing. And if this doesn't get you in the mood, nothing will. *40%. Alberta Distillers.*

Alberta Springs Aged 10 Years (88) n23 busy and rye rich, there are also icing sugar and green tea elements to this; **t23** voluptuous, mouth-watering and gentle, the rye displays impeccable behaviour choosing only to offer its fruitier element, until the very middle when it hardens out; **f20** a slow development of spices, but the OTT vanilla and caramel really do make things awkward; **b22.5** the intense, disappointing vanilla-toffee fade, plus a curious candy sweetness, robs this otherwise delicious whisky of greatness. 40% ⊙

Barton's Canadian 36 Months Old (78) n19 t20 f19 b20. Sweet, toffeed, easy-going. *40%. Barton.*

Black Velvet (78) n18 t20 f20 b20. A distinctly off-key nose is compensated for by a rich corn and vanilla kick on the palate. But that famous spice flourish is a distant memory. Another big caramel number. 40%

⋅⋅ Campbell & Cooper Aged a Minimum of 36 Months (84.5) n21.5 t22 f20 b21. Huge flavour profile. An orchard of oranges on the nose and profound vanilla on delivery. 40%

Canadian Club 100 Proof (89) n21 t23 f22 b23. If you are expecting this to be a high-octane version of the standard CC Premium, you'll be in for a shock. This is a much fruitier dram with an oilier body to absorb the extra strength. An entertaining blend. 50%.

Canadian Club Premium (78.5) n19 t21.5 f18 b20. The ashy nose is hardly a come on, but the delivery – remaining on the fruity course it has taken of late – compensates. The bitter, unhappy finish is dried further by heavy caramel. 40% ⊙⊙

Canadian Club Aged 6 Years (88.5) n21.5 t22 f22.5 b22.5. Not at all bad for a Canadian some purists turn their nose up at as it's designed for the American market. Just brimming with mouth-watering enormity and style. Dangerously moreish. 40%

Canadian Club Reserve 10 Years of Age (93) n22.5 no shortage of grapes and apples here; also there is a clear message coming from the oaky vanilla and Java at work; **t24** outstanding: for the first time the 10 year old kicks off the proceedings with a sublime peppery fanfare. Then we are back to normal with the trademark soft, oily body but now a degree of lush honey. A mishmash of unidentifiable fruity notes drift in and out, but the honey and spice prickle teases and delights; **f23** moves much more towards a muscovado sugar theme with crystallised pears; the vanillas move in with gentle authority as the age begins to count; **b23.5** the perfect antidote after the disappointing standard CC I have just tried. This is a real charmer of a Canadian; the sweetness, though profound, is always controlled and kept in line by that fabulous spice. A surprise package to the natives not least because of the clever interplay between fruit and oak. I suppose the law of averages dictates that one fruited Canadian is going to be pretty damn good: well, this is it! 40% ⊙⊙

Canadian Club Classic Aged 12 Years (91.5) n22 fruity, firm, a sprinkle of cinnamon yet a touch closed, even with maximum coaxing; **t24** beautifully coated with honey and grain oils, allowing for a juicy chewiness to gain momentum before delicate spices strike. they don't come much more luxuriant than this; **f21.5** long with a similar copper-honey character to the standard CC. Crushed sultana and sharper raisin, but it's not all fruit as some grains deliver some more fiddly, intrinsic notes. Lots of chalky vanilla confirms the age; a point dropped for the slight furry bitterness at the death; **b23.5** a confident whisky which makes the most of a honeycomb theme. 40% ⊙⊙

Canadian Club Aged 20 Years (92.5) n24 bread pudding and sherried fruit cake combine. Some real fizzle and entertainment – oh, and some class – make for one of the best Canadian noses around; **t21** a very tame delivery, with soft oils confused by the fruit; pleasant enough but almost a cancelling out of character; **f23.5** readjusts and reinvents itself brilliantly and we are back to the same bread pudding my mum used to make; as those spices settle, some marauding cocoa also goes for it...and then a return to soft corn oil...it's bitter sweet all the way and, as finishes go, this is a bloody long way...!! **b23** in previous years, CC20 has ranked among the worst whiskies I have tasted, not just in Canada, but the world. Their current bottling, though, is not even a distant relation. Sure, it has a big sherry investment. But the sheer elan and clever use of spice make this truly magnificent. Possibly the most pleasant surprise in my latest trawl through all Canada's whiskies. *40%*

Canadian Club Sherry Cask batch no. SC-018 **(76) n18 t20 f20 b18.** Question. Am I in my usual suite at the Empress Hotel, Victoria, that emblem of Canada's finest traditions? Or am I in a dusty bodega in Jerez, Spain, sticking my nose into a freshly opened sherry butt? My eyes tells me the sun is setting beyond the flowering arbutus tree and over the ancient, purpling volcanic mountains of British Columbia. My nose sends clear messages of freshly crushed grape, the first part of the wine making process that leads to Portugal's finest export. How do I mark it as a whisky? On the nose where is the grain? Where is the oak? As fruity Canadians go, this has to be the ultimate olfactory experience....In the end I have marked somewhere between the two. Doubtless the blender will be shaking his head, as will the CC execs. But I have to ask them this: what was the point of this whisky? To make it nose and taste like sherry? Then it has succeeded. To make it nose and taste like whisky? Then it has failed. As a fruited Canadian, it is superior because the grape is rich and clean to the point of faultlessness. And anyone into that kind of thing will find the whole thing orgasmic. As a sherry: well, it's twice as strong as you can normally buy it yet somehow has only half the body. As I say, I really don't know what to make of this. Nor do I get the point. *41.3%*

Canadian Five Star Rye Whisky (83) n21 t22 f20 b20. An entirely tame, well behaved Canadian which celebrates the inherent sweetness of the species. That said, the immediate impact on the palate is pretty delicious with a quick, flash explosion of something spicy. But it is the deft, satin-soft mouthfeel which may impress most. *40%* ☉

Canadian Hunter (83.5) n22 t21.5 f20 b20. Tasted blind you'd spot this as a Canadian 99/100 times. With the vanilla, toffee and oak having such a pleasant say, could it be anything else? *40%*

Canadian Mist (78) n19 t20.5 f18.5 b20. Much livelier than previous incarnations despite the inherent, lightly fruited softness. *40%* ☉ ☉

Canadian Pure Gold (82) n21.5 t20.5 f20 b20. Full-bodied and still a notably lush whisky. The pure gold may have more to do with the caramel than the years in cask but the meat of this whisky still gives you plenty to chew over. I especially enjoy the gradual building of spices. *40%*

Canadian Spirit (78) n20 t20 f19 b19. A real toffee-fest with a touch of hard grain around the edges. *40%. Carrington Distillers (Alberta Distillers).*

⸰⸰⸰ **Caribou Crossing Single Barrel (84) n20 t22.5 f20 b21.5.** While the nose offers an unholy battle between some apple-fruity rye notes and dry, dusty caramel, there is a real pulsating delivery with the sharper spices helped along the way by the silkiness of the body. Though the caramel offers a toffee-fudge backdrop, a countering dry date sweetness does more than enough to keep it at bay. However, the finish dulls out as the caramel gains the upper hand, though the twitching spices do ensure a light, throbbing beat. An enjoyable Canadian, undoubtedly, I am somewhat perplexed by it. There is no reference to the barrel number so you won't know if you are buying from different casks. Also, if it is single barrel what is the point of the caramel? If it is to make all the casks taste the same, or similar, then why not just blend them together. A badly missed opportunity. *40% Sazerac*

Centennial 10 Year Limited Edition (88.5) n21.5 light, oaky sawdust with a gentle powdering of sweet vanilla; **t23** clean with a beautifully complex, delicate spice and honey chorus; **f22** the spices continue their trademark buzz; **b22** retains its usual honey-flavoured breakfast cereal style, but the complexity has unquestionably increased. A busy and charming whisky throughout. *40%* ☉ ☉

Century Reserve 8 Years Old Premium (82) n20 t21 f20 b21. Clean vanilla caramel. *40%.*

Century Reserve Custom Blend 15 Years Plus (88.5) n21.5 t22 f23 b22. After two days of being ambushed in every direction, or completely steamrollered by Canadian caramel, my tastebuds are in total shock. Caramel kept to an absolute minimum so that it hardly registers at all. Charming and refined drinking. *40%*

⸰⸰⸰ **Century Reserve 21 Years Old (91.5) n23.5** a beautiful mix of banana and soft oak; a teasing spice prickle is offset by a light liquorice and sugar cane juice sweetness: impressively delicate and refined; **t23** the slight hint of rum on the nose is emphatically underscored on delivery: back to sugar cane and the inevitable Highwood distillery spices; **f23** continues on the vanilla-spice theme and, for all the obvious age present, that rum character continues throughout. Lovely strands of honey and even coconut balance the drier elements; **b22** quite beautiful, but a spirit that is as likely to appeal to rum lovers as whisky ones. *40%*

⸰⸰⸰ **Century Reserve Custom Blend** lot no. 1525 **(87) n21.5** light buttery grains tangle with a delicate, yet still more forceful fruitiness; **t22** a gorgeous mouth-feel: the weight is excellent and the grains clean and confident; a wheaty spiciness gets the buzz going..; **f21.5** the spices dominate on an otherwise arid, grainy backdrop; a touch of caramel helps reduce further complexity; **b22** an enjoyable whisky which doesn't quite reach its full potential. *40%*

Corby's Canadian 36 Months Old (85) n20 t21 f22 b22. Attractive with fine bitter-sweet balance and I love the late spice kick-back. *40% Barton. Interesting label: as a keen ornithologist, I had no idea there were parrots in Canada. Must be related to the Norwegian Blue.*

Crown Royal (87) n20 dry and grapey, like a puckering fino. The grains, once the fluttering flag of the old CR nose, are hardly anywhere to be seen; **t22** the grain wizardry which once mapped out every nuance on the palate has now completely vanished. This is about fruity contours peaked by busy, chattering spices; **f22.5** dries and bitters out; pithy and sharp; **b22.5** it looks as though we have waved goodbye to the old multi-layered rich grained CR for ever: I'll have to pop over to Vancouver and raid the library of Mike Smith for those. But this brand has come a long way in the last year or so and there is now a confidence and shape to the blending that had been badly missing. Still a bit of a shock to us long-time (and I'm talking decades here) CR lovers, but a very decent whisky nonetheless. *40%* ☉ ☉

Crown Royal Cask No 16 Finished in Cognac Casks (85.5) n21.5 t21 f22 b21. Clean cut and exceptionally grapey. The nose is unique in the whisky world: it is one of Cognac. But otherwise this struggles to really find its shape and rhythm. A perfect Canadian for those who prefer theirs with an air of grace and refinement but very limited depth. In fact, those who prefer a Cognac. *40%* ☉

Crown Royal Limited Edition (88) n22 dry, dusty caramels and fudge but perked up with a vanilla and apple topping; **t22.5** a much firmer mouth-feel than of old, though the buttered toffee character remains. This is joined now by a vaguely toasty grain component and scattered spices; **f21.5** remains on that attractively bitter-sweet road with a mild overdependence on the spice; **b22** a much happier and productive blend than before with an attractive degree of complexity. *40%* ☉ ☉

Crown Royal Special Reserve (96) n24 a clean and attractively spiced affair with cinnamon and the faintest pinch of allspice leading the way: rye at work, one presumes; the fruit is clean and precise with weightier grape overshadowing a green apple freshness; **t24** a spicier element to the usual rye and fruit delivery, much more in keeping with the nose, but that fabulous, contrary mouth-feel of harder grain and softer fruit continues to do the business. The spices build slowly but with an impressive evenness and determination: one of the most outstanding Canadians on the palate of them all; **f24** the finish has been tidied up and with stunning effect: no more sawdust and eye-watering dryness. Both grain and soft fruit ensure a magnificently mouth-watering end to an amazing journey; **b24** complex, well weighted and simply radiant: it is like looking at a perfectly shaped, gossamer clad Deb at a ball. The ryes work astonishingly well here (they appear to be of the malted, ultra-fruity variety) and perhaps to best effect after Alberta Premium, though now it is a hard call between the two. *40%* ☉ ☉

⋯ **Crown Royal XR Extra Rare** lot no. L7064 N4 **(93.5) n24 t23 f23 b23.5.** Just about identical to the previous bottle above. The only difference is on the finish where the rye, fortified with spice, decides to hang back and battle it out to the death; the toffee and vanilla make a controlled retreat. Either the same bottling with a slightly different stance after a few years in the bottle, or a different one of extraordinary high consistency. *40%*.

Danfield's Limited Edition Aged 21 Years (95) n24 forgive me if I'm wrong, but isn't that rye absolutely pouring from the nose? And probably some malted rye, such is its sweet intensity. God! This is how I dream Canadian whisky should be: rich yet complex and layered, the only discernible fruitiness being rye generated. And if it isn't rye, then well done for finding some fruit that gives it an almost identical character! **t24** fabulously layered with the softer notes proffering rich acacia honey and Demerara, the firmer again accentuating a rye core **f23.5** a busy buzz of spice and building vanillas and tannins; strands of honey soften the burnt-toffee late bitterness; **b23.5** a quite brilliant first-time whisky. The back label claims this to be small batch, but there is no batch number on the bottle, alas. Or even a visible bottling code. But this is a five star performer and one of this year's whiskies of the world. *40%*

Danfield's Private Reserve (84.5) n20 t21.5 f22 b21. A curious, non-committal whisky which improves on the palate as it goes along. An overdose of caramel (yawn!!) has done it no favours, but there is character enough for it to pulse out some pretty tasty spice. Seamless and silky, for all the toffee there underlying corn-rich clarity is a bit of a turn on. *40%*

⋯ **8 Seconds Small Batch (86) n20 t22 f22.5 b21.5.** Fruity, juicy, luxurious. And perhaps one of the few whiskies on the market anywhere in the world today which could slake a thirst. *40% Frank-Lin Distillers*

Forty Creek Barrel Select (75) n20 t21 f16 18. Sadly, still appears to be sulphur-tainted, especially at the death. The nose, though, is better than of old and the delivery really does give you a rich lift....then the dreaded S-word strikes. Blast!!! 40% ⊙⊙

⨀ **Forty Creek Double Barrel Reserve** lot no. 242 (83.5) n20 t21.5 f21 b21. One of those whiskies which has that James Finlayson double-take moment. At first you think: hmmmm, bubble gummy, fruity but flat. But then the spices begin to gather with intent and before you know it you are on your fifth mouthful trying to find exactly what is going on here. Certainly there is oak and there is fruit. And for all the softness and palate caressing there is a grainy trail-off harder than silicon. 40%

⨀ **Forty Creek Port Wood Reserve** lot no. 60 (88) n21.5 the usual Kitling Ridge fruit fest in full flow, the grape displaying a mildly shrivelled, sweet character while the vanilla and spice somehow find space to breathe; a distinctive Spanish-style brandy character kicks in; t22.5 for all the soft juiciness, this is not shy on the palate, as spices literally pepper the taste buds. A light viscosity allows these spices to gain a decent foothold as the chocolate raisin middle develops; f22 soft waves of spice continue but now the vanilla gets a late say; b22 a strange though thoroughly entertaining beast with as many elements of brandy as there are whisky. 45%

Forty Creek Small Batch Reserve lot 104 (91.5) n23.5 seriously chunky with an enticingly complex cereal depth softened by chocolate raisin candy. Charming and charismatic; t22 initially lighter delivery than the nose suggests. But still mouth-filling and continuing that cereal-fruit theme: liquid breakfast...; f23 a really excellent panning out of those intense flavours into more easily defined factions. Most delightful has to be the delivery of the spice and the oak-grain balance and a lingering cocoa note; b23 great stuff, this, not least because the path it follows on the palate is an unusual one with fascinating by-ways and occasional dead-ends. A quality whisky from a distillery now showing obvious self-confidence in its product. 40%

Forty Creek Three Grain (76) n19 t20 f18 b19. Not quite as well assembled as some Three grains I have come across over the last few years. There is a lopsidedness to this one: we know the fruit dominates (and I still haven't a clue why, when surely this of all whiskies, just has to be about the grains!) but the bitterness interferes throughout. If there have been sherry casks used here, I would really have a close look at them. 40%

Gibson's Finest Aged 12 Years (79) n19 t20 f20 b20. You can't help getting the feeling that here is a decent whisky sitting on the fence, just not knowing which way to go. Pleasant, but in the same way as that boring neighbour you are happy to offer a cheery hullo to but not invite round for dinner. Bitter-sweet, but strangely lacking complexity or depth. Has fallen behind sterling for entertainment value. 40% ⊙⊙

Gibson's Finest Rare Aged 18 Years (95.5) n24 close your eyes and sniff and you would swear you have a bourbon-rye mix: simultaneously crisp and soft, the sharpness of the rye and apple-style fruitiness is sublime and as enticing as it gets; t24.5 and a perfect transfer onto the palate: spectacularly juicy with all kinds of clean rye and corn notes bobbling around in a gorgeous gentle Demerara sugar backdrop; f23.5 impressive vanilla and long strands of grain and bitter liquorice; b23.5 so far ahead of both Sterling and the 12, it is hard to believe they are from the same stable. But make no mistake; this is pure thoroughbred: truly world class. 40% ⊙⊙

Gibson's Finest Canadian Whisky Bourbon Cask Rare Reserve (89) n23 t21 f23 b22. A much better version than the first bottling, the depth this time being massively greater. 40%

Gibson's Finest Sterling (81) n20 t20 f20.5 b20.5. Lightened and loosened up dramatically of late. There are even strands of corn detectable amid the surprising complexity. Even the old off-key bitterness has changed to something far more tangible and attractive: in this case sharp marmalade. 40% ⊙⊙

Gibson's New Oak (88) n22 t21 f23 b22. Distinctly different from any other Canadian doing the rounds: the oak influence makes a wonderful and clever impact. 40%

Highwood Pure Canadian (84) n20 t21 f22 b21. A decent, ultra-clean Canadian with markedly more character than before. Certainly the caramel has been seriously reduced in effect and the wheat ensures a rather attractive spice buzz while the cane juice sweetness harmonises well. Perhaps most delightful is the wonderful and distinct lack of fruit. Yippee!! Impressive for all its simplicity. 40%

Hiram Walker Special Old (93) n22.5 granite-hard with softer, oilier, more citrusy notes being trampled underfoot by almost impermeable grain; t24 textbook delivery with the rye offering both yielding juice and granite. Absolutely no let up in the spice development which works outstanding well with the hard skeleton. The sweetness is more upfront now with the honey petering out towards the late middle; just gone up an impressive notch; f23 drier now with the grain offering rich vanilla though the muscovado sugar signature subtlety remains; the caramel is present but doing a little less damage b23.5 even with the extra degree of all-round harmony, this remains the most solid, uncompromising

Canadian of them all. And I love it! Not least because this is the way Special old has been for a very long time with obviously no intentions of joining the fruity bandwagon. Honest, first class Canadian. 40% ☉ ☉

Lord Calvert (72.5) n19 t18.5 f17 b18. Truly eccentric aristocracy, this. Comes from the most noble of homes, Alberta Distillery, and the pedigree of the rye is evident in patches on both nose and delivery. Then marries something very fruity well beneath its class. 40%

McGuinness Silk Tassel (79.5) n20 t21 f19.5 b19. Silk or satin? The corn oils offer a delightful sheen but still the caramel is over enthusiastic. 40% ☉

Wm Morrison Imported Canadian Rye (87.5) n22 lavender and still a hint of something in the area of rye. Certainly bold and big; t22 firm, big and chewy but the caramels deliver much earlier these days; f21.5 a touch of oak-spice buzz; the toffee dominates the death; b22 still a lovely Canadian, though the toffee needs toning down. Not sure what "Full Strength" is doing on the label when bottled at 40%, though.... 40%.

Mountain Rock (87) n22 t20.5 f22.5 b22. Still a soft Canadian cocking a melt-in-the-mouth snook at its name. But this time the fruit is just over anxious to be heard and a degree of its old stability has been eroded. 40%. Kittling Ridge.

Pendleton Let'er Buck (91.5) n22.5 firm and dry with the accent on a grain-oak bite; t23 an immediate grain pinch, then a delicious mouth-watering crescendo; the sweetness is controlled and regulated by spice; f22.5 some corn oils and building oak make for an excellent bitter-sweet finale of some length and style; b23.5 a significantly improved whisky from the ultra-sweet, nigh on syrupy concoction of before. Here the surprisingly complex and sensual grains take star billing, despite the caramel: it almost makes a parody of being Canadian, so unmistakable is the style. For those who affectionately remember Canadian Club from 20-30 years ago, this might bring a moistening of the eye. 40% (80 proof). Hood River Distillers.

⠶⠶ **Potter's Crown** (83) n19 t21.5 f21.5 b21. Silky and about the friendliest and most inoffensive whisky on this planet. The dusty aroma and thick, chewy toffee backbone says it all but still impossible not to enjoy! 40%

Potter's Special Old a blend of 5 to 11 year old rye whisky (91) n23.5 t23 f22 b22.5. More Canadian than a hockey punch-up – and, for all the spice, somewhat more gentle, too. 40%

Potter's Special Old Rye (85.5) n21 t23.5 f20 b21. Not quite the force majeure of a year or two back, the grains are now thinner and starker despite the beautifully striking delivery on the palate. The soft honey tones are an attractive compensation but the austerity on nose and finish takes a little getting used to when remembering previous incarnations. 40% ☉ ☉

Rich and Rare (79) n20 t20 f20 b19. Simplistic and soft. One for toffee lovers. 40%

Royal Canadian (78) n18.5 t19 f21.5 b19. Much better than the nose predicts thanks to an injection of late spice. Some abstract fruitiness dotted around. 40%

⠶⠶ **Royal Canadian Small Batch** (88) n22 intense, thickly oaked, big caramels and spices; t22.5 rich and silky, the honeycomb leads from the front; the spices cut through the toffee and firmer grains; f21.5 bitters dramatically under those oaks and caramels; b22 a big Canadian with a pleasing silk and steel pulse. 40% Sazerac

Royal Reserve (84.5) n19 t22.5 f21.5 b21.5. No question that the delivery is much richer, fresher and entertaining than before with the spices, dovetailing with subtle fruit, ensuring a complexity previously lacking - especially at the death. Frustratingly, the caramel seems to be biting deeper on the nose, which has taken a backward step. A much more enjoyable and satisfying experience, though. 40% ☉ ☉

Royal Reserve Gold (94.5) n24 this was already one of the better Canadian noses. And with this latest bottling the grain complexity has moved up a gear. Bereft of the tacky toffee which dulls so many Canadian whiskies, we have here a joyous mixture of rye and citrus notes beautifully embedded in decent, vanilla-clad oak and the most tantalising of light honey tones; t23.5 a glorious composition of juicy, salivating rye in tandem with a honey-biscuit note gets this off to a stupendous start. It gets better still as the spices lift off and that honey begins to stick to the roof of the mouth; f23 magically light: a dusting of oak gives a nod towards a respectable, aged dryness but then this acts only as a foil to the delicate lime and Fruit Pastille juiciness and late, radiating rye; b24 retains its position as a classy, classy Canadian that is an essay on balance. Don't confuse this with the much duller standard bottling: this has been moulded in recent years into one of the finest – and among its country's consumers - generally most underrated Canadians on the market. 40% ☉ ☉

Sam Barton Aged 5 Years (83.5) n19 t21.5 f22 b21. Exceptionally sweet session whisky with a lovely maple syrup glow and some complexity on the finish. Friendly, hospitable and impossible not to like. 40%. La Martiniquaise, France.

Schenley Golden Wedding (92) n22 caramel, figs and honey; t24 now that really is brilliant: full complexity between grains and oak. Still the satin-skinned Canadian of old, but now with the spices more up front and the honey and vanillins enjoying a more confident interplay; a gentle sultana sweetness also adds to the charm; **f22** much drier and its vanilla all the way; **b23** like a rare, solid marriage, this has improved over time. Always been a consistent and pleasant whisky, but now there appears to be a touch of extra age and maturity which has sent the complexity levels up dramatically. Quite sublime. 40%

Schenley OFC (90) n22 well balanced with drier oaks arriving early. There is a honey thread, though; **t22.5** a sublime viscosity really does ensure that the sweet, softly-spoken corn is amplified: superb texture **f23** long, with some glorious brown sugars tangling with the drier, slightly embittered oak **b22.5** notice anything missing from this whisky? Well the 8-year-old age statement has fallen off the label. But this is still a truly superb whisky which would benefit perhaps from toning down the degree of sweetness, but gets away with it in spectacular fashion thanks to those seductive oils. Not as complex as the magnificent old days, but a whisky that would have you demanding a refill nine time out of ten. 40%

Seagram's Canadian 83 (86.5) n21 t22 f21.5 b22. A vastly improved blend which has drastically cut the caramel to reveal a melt-in-the-mouth, slightly crisp grain. There are some citrusy edges but the buttery vanilla and pleasing bite all go to make for a chic little number. 40%

Seagram's VO (91) n22 dried banana skin, a touch of waffle and a complex layering of drier, oaky notes; **t23.5** mouth-filling, lush corn oil and a slow, sensual build up of brown sugar and spice; **f22.5** back to its oaky promise on the nose as it dries with a mixture of niggly spice and vanilla; **b23** with a heavy heart I have to announce the king of rye-enriched Canadian, VO, is dead. Long live the corn-dominant VO. Over the years I have seen the old traditional character ebb away: now I have let go and have no option other than to embrace this whisky for what it has become: infinitely better than a couple of years back; not in the same league as a decade ago. But just taking it on face value, credit where credit is due. This is an enjoyably playful affair, full of vanilla-led good intention, corn and complexity. There is even assertive spice when needed and the most delicately fruity edge...though not rye-style. Thoughtfully blended and with no little skill, I am impressed. And look forward to seeing how this develops in future years. A treat which needs time to discover. 40% ⊙ ⊙

Tangle Ridge Aged 10 Years (69) n18.5 t19.5 f15 b16. Decidedly less in your face than of old, unless you are thinking custard pies. For all the cleaned up aroma and early injection of spiced sultana, the uncompromisingly grim finish remains its usual messy self. An unpleasant reminder as to why I only taste this when it's Bible time... 40% ⊙ ⊙

Tesco Canadian Whisky (75) n18 t18 f20 b19. Sweet, clean, uninspiring. 40%

⠶ **White Owl (77.5) n19 t19.5 f20 b19.** White whisky: in others words, a whisky the same colour as water. To both nose and taste somewhat reminds me of the long gone Manx whisky which was casks of fully matured scotch re-distilled and bottled. Sweet and pleasant. But I doubt if connoisseurs will give two hoots.... 40%

Windsor (85.5) n21 t22 f21 b21.5. A whisky you could usually bet your week's wages on for consistency and depth. Here, though, the usual rye fruity, crispness has been dumbed down and though there are enough spices to make this a pleasant affair, the impact of the caramel is a tad too significant. The usual custard sweetness has also changed shape and dry vanilla at the death is the compromise. 40% ⊙ ⊙

Windsor (86) n20 t21 f23 b22. Pleasant but with the majority of edges found on the Canadian edition blunted. Some outstanding, almost attritional, spice towards the middle and finale, though. Soft and desirable throughout: a kind of feminine version of the native bottling. 40% for US market.

⠶ **Wiser's 18 Years Old Limited Release (93.5) n24** a variation on a wonderful, familiar theme: the green apples and sultana are there in abundance but a firmer, grainier note keeps it all anchored. The usual clarity remains and now there appears an extra degree of delicacy; **t24** quite brilliant: the grains now cut loose to bombard the taste buds with myriad crisp, peppery notes. Less rye apparent than before but a significant upping in the Demerara coating; **f22.5** cleaner and grainier, with the fruit jettisoned for a more minimalist finale, concentrating on the vanilla and corn; **b23** like most of the Wiser's family, an improved, more carefully thought out blend than of a year or two back. Thoughtful, top quality blending resulting in a whisky which holds its head high on the world stage. 40% 3500 bottles

Wiser's Very Old 18 Years Old (90.5) n24 truly fabulous: one of the great Canadian noses with a stunning tapestry of rye and sherry style fruits combining with maple syrup and green apple: clean, precise and radiating class; **t3** that clarity on the nose comes across brilliantly in the rye-studded delivery: firm and crisp with a Demerara coating; **f21.5** pleasant but a touch mangled with a bitter note encroaching from some grape or oak – probably both; **b22** much better than the last bottling I encountered, which in itself was no slouch. Here, though, the blender has written bolder what he is trying to achieve. 40%

Wiser's De Luxe (86) n20 t22.5 f21.5 b22. A whisky which never sits still: I have noticed over the last few years that the shape of this whisky has changed and changed again. Once, it was my everyday drinking Canadian: pale coloured though 10 years old and absolutely brimming with grain-oak complexity. Then the age guarantee vanished. And the colour got darker and darker until today it is unrecognisable. Still nothing like the classic, ultra-charming and almost fragile-delicate Wiser's of old. But this present bottling has got its head partly out of the sand by injecting a decently oaked spiciness to the proceedings and one might even fancy detecting shards of fruity- rye brightness beaming through the toffeed clutter. Definitely an impressive turn for the better and the kind of Canadian with a dangerous propensity to grow on you. If they had the nerve to cut the caramel, this could be a cracker... 40% ⊙ ⊙

⋰∷⋰ **Wiser's Legacy (95)** n24 even by Canadian standards, a little different: coriander and juniper give a slight gin-style edge to this, though waiting in the wings is a subtle, spicy wine quality. The teasing sweetness, not entirely without a bourbon style new-oakiness and hint of rye-fruitiness, has all the intensity of Mona Lisa's smile...; t24.5 there is a crystalline quality to the nose, and it transfers immediately to the palate. One is reminded of absolutely unblemished First Growth Bordeaux in the way the grape–fruitiness announces itself before progressing into greatness. After that, it takes, thankfully, a very different course except perhaps in the way the spices unfold: first no more than a shadow, then blossoming out into something profound, deep and always in sync with all else that is going on. Cocoa notes arrive early and stay while the grains offer a salivating edge...nothing short of glorious...; f22.5 serious but high quality and contained oak: dry and toasty but always a light dusting of slightly sweetened vanilla; b22.5 when my researcher got this bottle for me to taste, she was told by the Wiser's guy that I would love it, as it had been specially designed along the lines of what I considered essential attributes to Canadian whisky. Whether Mr Wiser was serious or not, such a statement both honoured and rankled slightly and made me entirely determined to find every fault with it I could and knock such impertinence down a peg or two. Instead, I was seduced like a 16-year-old virgin schoolboy in the hands of a 30-year-old vixen. An entirely disarming Canadian which is almost a whisky equivalent to the finest of the great French wines in its rich, unfolding style. Complex beyond belief, spiced almost to supernatural perfection, this is one of the great newcomers to world whisky in the last year. It will take a glass of true magnificence to outdo this for Canadian Whisky of the Year. 45%

Wiser's Red Letter (95) n24 the complexity is enough to make you weep: the accent is on elegance, achieved by offering near perfect servings of all you hope to see in a great Canadian. An orangey citrus element is in turn caressed by small grain embedded in a field of soft-oiled corn, which sports a light grape hillside. The toffee-caramel has a flattening effect, sadly: otherwise near perfection in complexity; t24 a wave of soft corn oil spreads over the roof of the mouth; both juicy and chewy in equal measure, the vanilla starts making delightful speeches while the most delicate of rye injections cranks up the complexity further; f23.5 the caramel which builds on the nose does likewise on the finale to form a toffee-dam. At least some spices filter through; b23.5 the recent trend with Canadian whisky has been to do away with finesse and cram each bottle with fruit. This returns us to a very old fashioned and traditional Canadian style. And had the rye been upped slightly and the caramel eschewed entirely it might have been a potential world whisky of the year...Even in this form, however, it is certainly good enough to be Jim Murray's Whisky Bible Canadian Whisky of the Year 2010 45%

Wiser's Reserve (75) n19 t20 f18 b18. Something very strange has happened to this. The nose offers curious tobacco while the palate is uneven, with the bitterness out of tandem with the runaway early sweetness. In the confusion the fruit never quite knows which way to turn. A once mighty whisky has fallen. And I now understand it might be the end of the line with the excellent Wiser's Small Batch coming in to replace it. So if you are a reserve fan, buy them up now. 43%

Wiser's Small Batch (90.5) n21.5 much bigger in the fruit department than of yore with the grains struggling to be heard; soft to the point of borderline flat; t24 that's more like it!! Back online with the huge, salivating, juicy, mouth-enveloping delivery. The spices spark and ark around the palate for a while the fruits are lost. Layers of grain dominate and the balance between the brown sugar sweetness and the pounding peppers is sublime; f22 much harder and crisp with the fruit having now fallen by the wayside. Even the spices burn out leaving firm vanilla; b23 a real oddity with the nose and taste on different planets. The fruity onslaught promised by the drab nose never materialises – thankfully! – and instead we are treated to a rich, grainy explosion. It's the spices, though, that take the plaudits. 43.4% ⊙ ⊙

Wiser's Special Blend (78) n19 t20 f19 b19. A plodding, pleasant whisky with no great desire to offer much beyond caramel. 40% ⊙

Japanese Whisky

At Edinburgh Castle this year a fanfare of pipes heralded the launch of the first 70-year-old whisky certainly within living memory. A Speyside scotch single malt, it deservedly brought great acclaim and an enormous degree of publicity. Elsewhere, sneaking in through the back door, came a Japanese single malt bottled by the Whisky Exchange in London as part of their 10th anniversary celebrations. It was 42 years old and from the Karuizawa distillery.

Now Japan tends to get hot...very hot. Certainly a lot hotter than anywhere in Scotland. And though the winters can sometimes be equally if not more cold than Speyside, I would be quite confident in saying that 42 Japanese summers is worth at least 70 Scottish in terms of whisky maturation. Ironically, I sat next to WE's owner, Sukhinder Singh, at the Edinburgh event but didn't have time to chat about the Karuivawa. Perhaps the Mortlach edges it in terms of finesse and overall star quality, but for sheer fun the freaky Karuivawa 1967 wins hands down and, for me, and despite its obvious oaky input, was the Japanese Whisky of the Year. I am not the only one praying that this has opened the door for other grandiose Japanese malts to follow.

Yet still there is a great frustration that the myriad types of Japanese whisky is unlikely to be seen outside the mother country, so slow has been the expansion of their whisky empire.

I have met a number of whisky shop owners around the world who will stock only a handful of Japanese simply because they cannot get assurances that what they are being sent does not contain Scotch. Certainly, these mind-blowing single malts which had lorded it with the world's elite were 100% from the land of the rising sun. But until exchanging whiskies within Japanese companies becomes a natural part of their culture it is hard to see how the confidence generated by the excellence of the single malt and grains available as singletons can be extended to the blends.

Part of the problem has been the Japanese custom of refusing to trade with their rivals. Therefore a Japanese whisky, if not made completely from home-distilled spirit, will instead contain a percentage of Scotch rather than whisky from fellow Japanese distillers.

This, ultimately, is doing the industry no favours at all. The practice is partly down to the traditional work ethics of company loyalty and an inherent, and these days false, belief that Scotch whisky is automatically better than Japanese. Back in the late 1990s I planted the first seeds in trying to get rival distillers to discuss with each other the possibility of exchanging whiskies to ensure that their distilleries worked more economically.

In the meantime word is getting round that Japanese whisky is worth finding. It is now not uncommon for me to discuss with whisky lovers at a fair or book signing the merits and differences of Yoichi and Hakushu, two distilleries which are now being correctly recognised for their world-class brilliance. And, increasingly, Yamazaki which has moved away from a comfort zone it operated in for many years and is now offering malts of great magnitude: indeed, it was recently the producer of one of the two Japanese whiskies which was considered as a possible Whisky Bible World Whisky of the Year. And I still get a small thrill when I hear Yoichi's name mentioned around the world: I'm proud to have first brought it to the world's attention way back in 1997 – though these days the distillery, like all others in Japan, has to be a little more careful with their use of sherry.

Mind you, the same didn't have to be said about the Karuivawa 1967. That may have been matured in a sherry butt, but it was filled in the good old days when they were sent from Jerez to Japan still full of the fortified wine, so arrived fresh. Further evidence that there is just no beating the old traditions...

Single Malts
CHICHIBU

Golden Horse Chichibu db **(80)** n19 t21 f20 b20. Light, toasty and delicate yet the oak is prominent throughout. Good balancing sweet malt, though. *43%. Toa.*

Golden Horse Chichibu 10 Years Old Single Malt db **(82)** n19 t22 f21 b20. Developing citrus notes lighten the weight as the oak and sweet malt go head to head. *43%. Toa.*

Chichibu 14 Years Old Single Malt db **(89)** n20 tangerine peel and rice: two years older than the 12-y-o, that hint of bourbon has now become a statement; t23 brilliantly eclectic arrival on the palate with no organisation at all to the flurry of malt and bourbony oak and tangerine-fruity spices that are whizzing around; f23 pretty long with firm vanilla and a distinctive oiliness. Something approaching a whiff of smoke adds some extra ballast to the oak; b23 we are talking mega, in-your-face taste explosions here. A malt with a bourbony attitude that is unquestionably superb. *57%. Toa.*

⋯⋯ **Chichibu Single Malt Newborn Double Matured** cask no. 447, dist 2008, bott 2009 db **(81)** n18.5 t22.5 f20 b20. A toffee fest. Seeing as it was distilled only a year or two ago, I'm amazed it is quarter matured, let alone double matured... *61.3%*

⋯⋯ **Chichibu Single Malt Newborn Heavily Peated** cask no. 451, dist 2009, bott 2009 db **(84)** n21.5 t22 f20.5 b20. Chewy, peaty toffee. *61.3%*

Ichiro's Malt Chichibu Newborn cask no. 127, dist 08, bott 08 **(80)** n18.5 t21 f20.5 b20. A fierce, juicy, fruity, barley-oil intense semi new make which appears to have spent a limited time in cask. Not entirely free of feints, it is not lacking in character for that and while technically challenged, is flavourful fun. *62.5%. Number One Drinks Co.*

FUJI GOTEMBA 1973. Kirin Distillers.

The Fuji Gotemba 15 Years Old db **(92)** n21 diced nuts, especially pistachio with vanilla and a sprinkling of sugar; t23 mouth watering from the start with a sensational development of sweet malt; f24 plateaus out with textbook spices binding sweet malt and dry oak. The length is exemplary; b24 quality malt of great poise. *43%. Kirin.*

The Fuji Gotemba 18 Years Old db **(81)** n20 t19 f21 b21. Jelly-baby fruitiness, complete with powdered sugar. Big, big age apparent. *43%. Kirin.*

Fuji Gotemba 20th Anniversary Pure Malt db **(84)** n21 t20 f22 b21. The nose is a lovely mixture of fruit and mixed oak; the body has a delightful sheen and more fruit with the malt. Handsome stuff. *40%. Kirin.*

HAKUSHU 1973. Suntory.

Hakushu Heavily Peated Aged 9 Years bott 09 db **(92.5)** n22.5 lightly heavily peated with a now lost Port Ellen style gristy sweetness; t23.5 ultra sweet barley bang on cue and a slow radiation of spice, citrus and sympathetic oak; f23 drier, oakier but still some sugared lime for balance and freshness. The smoke is distant and barley involved; b23.5 nothing like as heavily peated as some Hakushus it has been my pleasure to sample over the years. But certainly superbly orchestrated and balanced. *48%*

Hakushu Single Malt Whisky Aged 10 Years bott 09 db **(87.5)** n22 a much more lumbering gait with both barley and oak; t23 sprightly barley at first, which immediately sweetens deliciously. The oak and toffees become a brooding presence; f20.5 pretty flat and oak-fuelled; b22 duller than of old. *40%*

Hakushu Single Malt Whisky Aged 12 Years db **(91.5)** n22.5 t23.5 f22.5 b23. Just about identical to the 43.3% bottling in every respect. Please see those tasting notes for this little beauty. *43.5%*

Hakushu Single Malt Aged 12 Years db **(91)** n22 revitalising barley with smoke as distant as a cloud over Fuji; t23 multi-layered barley with so many levels of sweetness; the very faintest hint of smoke on the middle; f23 long with the accent now on vanilla and soft, developing oil and spice; b23 an even more lightly- peated version of the 40%, with the distillery's fabulous depth on full show. *43.3%.*

The Hakushu Single Malt Whisky Aged 15 Years Cask Strength db **(95)** n24 pure, unmistakable Hakushu: intense, powering, yet clean and refined. Loads of citrus to lighten matters but the local oak ensures enormity; t23 big, initially oak-threatened but the barley comes flooding back with light oils helping to soften the early scratchiness; first mouthful is dry, the second shows a much truer picture; f24 now goes into complexity overdrive as all those fruity-barley-oaky- elements continue to jostle for supremacy, only for late spices and gorgeous milky mocha to come in and steal the thunder; b24 last time round I lamented the disappointing nose. This time perhaps only a degree of over eagerness from the oak has robbed this as a serious Whisky of the Year contender. No matter how you look at it, though, brilliant!! *56%*

Hakushu Single Malt Whisky Aged 18 Years bott 09 db **(86) n**20 **t**23.5 **f**21 **b**21.5. Wow! Where has all this oak come from? Appears to have gone gray overnight...The delivery, though, makes this a malt worth finding because for 20 seconds or so we have absolutely everything in complete harmony, and the degree of barley sweetness is just about perfect. Then all is lost to the duller oak tones again. *43%*

The Hakushu Single Malt Whisky Aged 25 Years db **(93) n**23 some blowhard oak is pegged back by an intense barley-fruit mix; thick yet complex; **t**24 a wonderful combination of silk and barley sheen juxtaposed with busy but light spice; soft fruits adorn the higher places within the palate while a subtle earthiness rumbles below; **f**23 improbably long. Even though some serious extraction has taken place from the oak, the integrity of the barley makes you sigh with pleasure. Now the spices change in nature to soft and playful to warm and rumbling; **b**23 a malt which is impossible not to be blown away by. *43%*

Hakushu 1984 db **(95) n**22 delicate banana and malt with a gentle fly-past of peat. The oak is unbowed but sympathetic; **t**25 staggeringly beautiful: wave upon wave of astonishing complexity crashes against the tastebuds. The malt is intense but there is plenty of room for oak in varying guises to arrive, make eloquent speeches and retire. The intensity of spice is spot on – perfect; **f**24 long, more spice and greater malt intensity as the oak fades. Only the softest hints of smoke; mouthwatering to the last as mild coffee appears; **b**24 a masterpiece malt of quite sublime complexity and balance. The sort of experience that gives a meaning to life, the universe and everything... *61%*

Hakushu 1988 db **(92) n**21 overtly peaty and dense, pleasant but lacking usual Hakushu complexity; **t**24 mouthwatering start with massively lively malt and fresh peating hanging on to its coat-tails. Some amazing heather–honey moments that have no right to be there; the peat intensifies then lightens; **f**23 lots of rich peat and then intense vanilla; crisp and abrupt at the finale with late bitter chocolate; **b**24 like all great whiskies this is one that gangs up on you in a way you are not expecting: the limited complexity on the nose is more than compensated for elsewhere. Superb. If this were an Islay malt the world would be drooling over it. *61%*

⋯ **Hakushu 1989 Sherry Cask** bott 2009 **(88) n**22 there must be some whisky in there somewhere.... **t**22 ....yep...no...yep...there it is: just seen it coming up for the second time.... **f**22 ...no gone for good now.... **b**22 a malt whisky drowned in a sea of thick sherry. Enjoyable, though! *62% Speciality Drinks Ltd bottled for TWE's 10th Anniversary*

Hakushu Vintage Malt 1990 db **(89) n**22 firm barley and firmer oak; **t**23 serious intensity on delivery, this time with all the action being enjoyed by the concentrated, grassy barley; **f**22 layers of vanilla add balance to the fade; **b**22 warming in places with the tastebuds never getting a single moment's peace. *56%. Suntory.*

The Cask of Hakushu 1993 Spanish oak Bota Corta, dist 93, bott 08 db **(80.5) n**20 **t**22 **f**18 **b**20. Grape influence rarely gets any bigger than this without taking over entirely. However, this falls on a sulphurous sword which doesn't exactly ruin the experience, but certainly has you looking for a hanky to weep into. *60%. 571 bottles.*

The Cask of Hakushu 1993 Heavily Peated Malt cask no 3B40574 white oak hogshead, dist 93, bott 08 db **(96) n**23.5 subtle smoke is almost – though not quite – out-muscled by the oak; bonfires and rain on warm ash give this an earthy, outdoor feel; **t**24 brilliant delivery: the peats are pent up but holding back, allowing a really juicy barley theme to develop. Slowly the smoke is unleashed... **f**24 long with a wondrous development of spot on oils which offer almost perfect sweetness and depth to the smoke; spices arrive late to tingle and tease; a slight vegetable feel, too, as if going along with the earthy-garden-allotment feel; **b**24.5 it's bottlings like this which underline Hakushu's position as one of the world's great distilleries. I just think they got the title on the label wrong: I think they meant "Heavenly Peated Malt"... *58%. 232 bottles.*

⋯ **Scotch Malt Whisky Society Cask 120.05 Aged 17 Years** 1st fill barrel, dist Dec 91 **(94) n**23 subtly peated in a way Hakushu possibly does best of all; **t**24 it's all there: the most deft smoke; firm, eye-watering barley; explodingly over-ripe cherries; an Arbroath Smokie saltiness; oil laced with honey....; **f**23.5 remains bullet hard and mercurially smoky to the last departing atom; **b**23.5 amazingly, this is a less than perfect cask deployed. But so absurdly good was the spirit filled into it, you barely notice....or care. *59% 104 bottles.*

Suntory Pure Malt Hakushu Aged 20 Years db **(94) n**23 fresh, mildly grapey fruit combined with subtle waves of peat; **t**24 the peat is now less subtle: wave upon wave of it bringing with it flotsam of drifting oak and then a very sharp malt tang; **f**23 long, sweet spice but the oak forms a chunky alliance with the firm peat. The bitter-sweet compexity almost defies belief; **b24** a hard-to-find malt, but find it you must. Yet another huge nail in the coffin of those who purport Japanese whisky to be automatically inferior to Scotch. *56%*

HANYU

Hanyu 1990 cask no. 9511, dist 90, bott 07 db **(91) n23 t23 f22 b23.** Leaves you in no doubt how outstanding this stuff can be when found nowhere near a sherry butt... *55.5%.*

Full Proof Europe Hanyu 1988 butt no. 9307, bott 08, **(74.5) n19 t20.5 f18 b18.** Some bright honeyed moments can't quite entirely contain the sulphur. *55%. nc ncf. 534 bottles.*

Ichiro's Card "Ace of Diamonds" 1986 cream sherry butt finish, cask no. 9023, dist 86, bott 08 **(94.5) n24** pretty sound sherry: deep, fruitcakey and well spiced; that would normally be enough, but there is a distinct bourbon sub plot here; **t23.5** fine arrival: juicy grape and spice in equal portions and remains clean right through to the barley, muscovado sugars and butterscotch entering the fray; an injection of hickory is respectful nod to the oak; **f23** slightly dry and dusty, but those spices keep coming...; **b24** another big sherry finish. But again sulphur free and here provides sufficient spice to make the whole thing rock. High grade Japanese. And even higher grade finishing... *56.4% Venture Whisky Ltd*

⁜ **Ichiro's Card "Eight of Diamonds"** Spanish oak oloroso sherry butt finish, dist 1991, bott 2009 **(77.5) n20 t21 f18 b18.5.** Wild cherry with some fizz and bite. But bitter and off key, too. *57.1% Venture Whisky Ltd*

Ichiro's Card "Eight of Spades" 2000 cask no. 9301, dist 00, bott 08 **(66.5) n16 t18 f16 b16.5.** The sulphur reduces this to a deuce. *58% Venture Whisky Ltd*

⁜ **Ichiro's Card "Five of Clubs"** Mizunara hogshead finish, dist 1991, bott 2009 **(84.5) n22 t21.5 f20 b21.** A fruitier number but with a blemish on the finish. *57.4% Venture Whisky Ltd*

⁜ **Ichiro's Card "Four of Spades"** Japanese oak "Mizunara" puncheon finish, dist 2000, bott 2010 **(95) n24** big bourbon character: not just honey and liquorice, but an almost rye-like fruity (cherry) hardness, too; **t24.5** glorious arrival with a manuka and clear honey mix plus a landslide of warming spices. Then it's back to pure bourbon again with the liquorice, molassed and succulent, kicking in; **f23.5** long, at last with an element of maltiness but the butterscotch and vanilla hints at honeycomb, too; **b23.5** I have often heard the Japanese accused of trying to mimic scotch whisky. On this evidence, it's the Kentuckians who should be looking over their shoulder.... *58.6% Venture Whisky Ltd*

Ichiro's Card "Jack of Diamonds" 1988 cask no. 9103, dist 88, bott 08 db **(92) n22** no going easy on the oak...; the smoke is much more delicate; **t23. 5** brilliant delivery: the spices rage as the barley sings; the oak is definitely of grey-beard persuasion, but there are enough phenols in there to give the weight a certain energy and shape; some citrus lightens matters – but only by a fraction; **f23** exceptionally long with a sublime mocha fade; **b23.5** a malt which takes the oaks to the very limit and somehow comes out as an ancient classic. *56%*

⁜ **Ichiro's Card "Jack of Hearts"** red oak hogshead finish, dist 1991, bott 2010 **(86) n22.5 t22 f20.5 b21.** A knave of a dram. Lulls you into thinking this is going to be a honeyed gem, then mugs you with its rock hard, biting malt. *56.1% Venture Whisky Ltd*

⁜ **Ichiro's Card "King of Hearts"** Pedro Ximenez sherry butt finish, dist 1986, bott 2009 **(95.5) n23.5** big and fruity: strawberry and figs; more than a trace of smoked oak; some ginger and clove sprinkled in, too; **t24** superb spice delivery, accompanied by soft peat, followed by a salivating salvo of ultra sharp greengages. Finally the barley begins to soak into the middle ground accompanied by that luxurious smoke; **f24** smoked chocolate mousse; **b24** this King of Hearts had some smoky tarts...delicious and complex almost beyond measure! *55.4%*

Ichiro's Card "King of Spades" 1986 cask no. 9418, dist 86, bott 07 db **(91) n22 t23 f23 b23.** Another little belter from this excellent distillery showing confidence at this age to the point of arrogance. *57% Venture Whisky Ltd*

Ichiro's Card "Queen of Clubs" 1988 cask no. 7003, dist 88, bott 08 db **(84.5) n20.5 t22 f21 b21.** Is it a rum? Is it a bourbon? No...it's a malt!! Enormous in every respect and a bit of bite and attitude, too; not entirely blemish-free. *56% Venture Whisky Ltd*

⁜ **Ichiro's Card "Queen of Spades"** port pipe finish, dist 1990, bott 2009 **(83.5) n22.5 t22 f19 b20.** Lots of toffee; the finish is furry and bitter. *53.1% Venture Whisky Ltd*

⁜ **Ichiro's Card "Six of Clubs"** cream sherry butt finish, dist 2000, bott 2009 **(66) n17 t18 f15 b16.** A sulphurous deuce. *57.9% Venture Whisky Ltd*

Ichiro's Card "Ten of Clubs" 1990 sherry butt finish, cask no. 9032, dist 90, bott 08 **(85) n22.5 t21.5 f21 b20.** Tempted to give this one extra marks just for finding a non-sulphured cask. But also have to say that the sherry here, though profound and clean, is having too big a say. Some of the grape is formidably beautiful. But there is too much of a good thing, and vital complexity is lost. That said, a whisky worth investigating. *52.4% Venture Whisky Ltd*

Ichiro's Card "Two of Clubs" 2000 cask no. 9500, dist 00, bott 07 db **(92)** n22 t24 f23 b23. Beautifully made and full of malty gusto. A genuine treat – especially for a malt so young. Two of Clubs, maybe. A Full House in anyone's books, though. *57% Venture Whisky Ltd*

⠞ **Ichiro's Card "Two of Hearts"** Madeira hogshead finish, dist 1986, bott 2009 **(86)** n22 t23 f20 b21. Big, sweeping, delicious statements: some malty, some bourbon. But, overall, just a shade on the hot and rough and ready side. *56.3% Venture Whisky Ltd*

⠞ **Ichiro's Malt Aged 15 Years** 4th bottling **(89.5)** n23.5 lively, saline tang to the spicy marmalade; t23 another, typically Hanyu, sugar-malt juicy salvo; f21 a degree of tangy buzz; b22 oozes character and quality. *46% Venture Whisky Ltd*

⠞ **Ichiro's Malt Aged 23 Years (92.5)** n23 salty; obvious age and some less obvious smoke; t23.5 beautifully salivating delivery with rich, focussed barley; f23 long, with a stream of ever-sweetening vanilla; b23 a fabulous malt you take your time over. *58%*

⠞ **Ichiro's Malt The Final Vintage of Hanyu Aged 10 Years** cask no. 6067 **(89.5)** n22.5 slight vegetable edge to the thick malt; t24 wow! That malt is thick! Beefed up with plenty of oak and maple syrup; f21.5 on the bitter side; b21.5 if it's a quiet glass of whisky you're after, give this one a miss... *60.8% Venture Whisky Ltd*

⠞ **One Single Cask Hanyu 1990** cask no. 9305, bott 2009 **(90.5)** n23 an injection of orange peel where and when needed; t23 powering barley/oak mix: the intensity of the sweetly sapped oak is every bit as mouth-watering as fresh barley; f22.5 an enormous surge of sharp vanilla; b22 huge whisky but borderline OTT oak. The infused sugars do the trick. *53.4%*

⠞ **One Single Cask Hanyu 1991** Japanese oak, cask no. 370, bott 2009 **(91.5)** n22 spices nestle amid the dry oak; t23.5 glorious delivery: honeycomb in its densest form with some marauding spices intensifying by the second; f23 long, a catwalk for varying types of vanilla, but decent sugars offer balance; b23 unmistakable style: I found myself muttering " ah, local oak!" to myself (tasting close on 800 malts in a couple of months does that to you....) before I spotted the label. Quite beautiful. *57.3% Number One Drinks Co*

KARUIZAWA 1955. Mercian.

⠞ **Karuizawa 1967 Vintage** sherry cask, bott 2009 **(96)** n24 spiced Mysore coffee sweetened with Demerara; a little hickory and peat thing going on, too; remarkably, for its age, not an off note in sight.... t24.5 back to that style I have encountered so many times over the years from this distillery: grape and malt followed by waves of burnt raisin, yet somehow drenching the palate in salivating barley and green grape, too : is this for real...????? f23.5 seemingly infinitely long, with a playful liquorice finale, giving way to some improbably late Demerara; b24 another engaging, engrossing and, frankly, brilliant malt from this distillery, equalling the oldest I have ever encountered from Karuizawa. If you find it, sell your body, sell your partner's body... anything...just experience it! *58.4% Bottled for TWE's 10th Anniversary*

Karuizawa 1971 cask no. 6878, dist 71, bott 08 **(94)** n24 solid as a rock: firm barley with all kinds of south Pacific fruits plus leather armchairs and honeycomb to underline the age just in case you hadn't got the message; oh and overcooked raisins, just in case you hadn't sussed the barrel type, either... t23.5 entangled delivery: another bottling where you need some serious time and a brain capable of sorting out Chinese puzzles – or in this case, Japanese. The intensity of the aged oak makes for a puckering start, but beyond that we are into the land of badly burnt raisins (confirming the nose), sultanas that have gone all squidgy and juicy; massive Christmas pudding character with trifle for good measure. Suewth! as they may say a bit further south-east of this distillery; decent esters help give this a slightly rummy edge, too; f23 long, with some custard powder helping tone things down slightly; the glazed sugar/caramelised biscuit effect is impressive and those toasted raisins remain alluring; b23.5 it's not just Scotch which goes all exotic fruity on us when it gets towards being an antique malt. By the time you have grappled and overcome this one your tastebuds and brain are pretty knackered. But it's so worth the battle....! *64.1%. Number One Drinks Company.*

Karuizawa 1972 Aged 31 Years cask 5530 db **(78)** n19 t18 f21 b20. Oaky and hot with just a bit too much age.

Karuizawa 1972 sherry butt finish, cask no. 7290, dist 72, bott 08 **(87.5)** n24 ultra clean grape punctuated by even cleaner barley. A nutty colonel offers dry Lubeck marzipan. Almost too beautiful for words... t20 thin delivery. All spirit and limited malt development... f22 settles – kind of - and barley and fruit come through loud and clear; b21.5 a bizarre whisky, not helped by its strength and spirit-driven punch. But clean and hammers home its finer points if you are able to listen. It's the nose, though, which stars. *65%. Number One Drinks Co.*

Karuizawa 1973 Aged 30 Years cask 6249 db **(84) n20 t21 f22 b21.** Sweet barley and very silky oaky vanilla. Plucked from the cask just in time.

Karuizawa 1974 Aged 29 Years cask 6115 db **(91) n23** brilliant complexity: juicy dates and figs wrapped around a theme of richly oaked barley; **t22** much sweeter arrival on the nose with burnt fudge and toast arriving for the middle; **f23** slightly salty, the barley seems both sweet and roasty. Soft liquorice makes this one you can chew for hours; **b23** an exhibition of bitter-sweet enormity.

Karuizawa 1975 Aged 28 Years cask 4066 db **(85) n20 t21 f23 b21.** Much more relaxed late middle and finish with they honey thread soothing the singed taste buds; loud at first, it sings sweet lullabies at the death. Always complex.

Karuizawa 1976 Aged 27 Years cask 6949 db **(83) n19 t20 f23 b21.** Big, mouthfilling but just a touch too much oak among the honey.

Karuizawa 1977 Aged 26 Years cask 7614 db **(74) n17 t20 f19 b18.** Some decent sweetness but doesn't quite work.

Karuizawa 1978 Aged 25 Years cask 2368 db **(87) n21** seaweedy and shoreline, but without the peat; **t20** almost violent arrival of searing sherry and vicious oak: hang on to your chair; **f23** calms down stupendously with soft smoky peat to be found in the many strata of clean fruit and barley; **b23** extra dry sherry, biting, salty and with a big coastal tang.

Karuizawa 1979 Aged 24 Years cask 8835 db **(94) n23** much more fruit than is usual for this distillery with apples and fresh pear; lots of barley survives despite the age; **t23** the barley is drinking in gentle honey and cocoa-enriched oak; **f24** marvellously long with teasing, toasted caramelised oak adding a glorious repost to the rich, Demerara-sweetened barley; **b24** one of those rare casks that appears to have had a magic wand waved at it and stardust sprinkled liberally.

Karuizawa 1980 Aged 23 Years cask 7614 db **(89) n22** solid age but the softness of the toffee-apple and barley sugar is first class; attractive bourbony notes develop; **t21** gripping, wild and hot at first, then a series of soothing waves of malt and liquorice; **f24** peppery and estery; the honey-malt mouthfeel is long, lush and fabulous; **b22** a classy Japanese malt that relishes the battle against advancing oak.

Karuizawa 1981 Aged 22 Years cask 8280 db **(73) n17 t19 f19 b18.** Sharp redcurrants but too obvious off-notes abound.

⁘ **Karuizawa 1982** sherry, bott 2009 **(90) n23** latticed cherry tart; a light spice and smoke dart around the periphery; **t24** profound grape, sharp at first, then a quite enthralling, shocking, almost unique, wave of ultra-rich malted vanilla...."beautiful" doesn't quite do it justice; **f22** bitters out slightly; **b22** forget the sherry. Forget the distant, nagging "S" word. Just home in on that astonishing middle: like a million Maltesers dissolving in your mouth all at once....there is nothing else like it in the whisky world. And no other distillery is capable. Alas. *56.1% Speciality Drinks Ltd bottled for TWE's 10th Anniversary*

Karuizawa 1982 Aged 21 Years cask 8527 db **(85) n21** a forest full of honey bees; **t21** deep honey and toasted fudge; the middle erupts with strangely enjoyable sap; **f22** gentle malt with a pinch of moscavado sugar and liquorice; **b21** a mature whisky showing some sag but just hanging onto its sexy, alluring figure.

Karuizawa 1983 Aged 20 Years cask 8609 db **(88) n20** slightly estery; chocolate honeycomb and a slice of pine; **t24** estery, rich enormous copper presence; **f22** medium length with elegant wisps of honey and toffee; **b22** tasted blind you would bet your own grandmother that this was pot still Jamaican rum. And one probably older than your gran.

Karuizawa 1984 Aged 19 Years cask 2563 db **(78) n17 t20 f21 b20.** Some quality touches of grape against smoky grist, and the mild peat is a redeeming and unexpected surprise, but what a shame that minor sulphury blemish.

Karuizawa 1985 Aged 18 Years cask 6885 db **(90) n22** honey as a side dish on butterscotch tart; **t22** mouth filling, oilier than usual with sumptuous malt and oak; **f23** wonderful tones of butterscotch sweetened over the broadening oak. Just a slight sprinkling of cocoa; **b23** whisky that celebrates its middle age with a show of complex intensity.

⁘ **Karuizawa 1985 Vintage Single Cask** cask no. 7017, bott 2009 db **(78.5) n19 t22.5 f18 b19.** Sherry preserve spread over slightly burnt toast. Pity about that sulphur. *60.8%*

Karuizawa 1986 cask no. 7387, dist 86, bott 08 **(82.5) n20 t22 f20 b20.5.** For a malt so obviously trying to overcome a sulphurous handicap it holds its head high with a vivid barley thrust. Lots of caramel on the finish, too. *60.7%. Number One Drinks Company.*

Karuizawa 1986 Aged 17 Years cask 8170 db **(94) n23** full-frontal, naked sherry. And spicy, too; **t23** massive, almost uncontrollable sherry-malt explosion; dried dates and vanilla concentrate form an unlikely but delicious alliance; **f24** long, fruity with hidden spices; the malt ducks in and out playfully; **b24** find a faultless sherry butt and place in it a whisky of the very finest quality and complexity. This is the result.

Karuizawa 1987 Aged 16 Years cask 8694 db **(93) n23** amazingly soft malt with just a touch of far-away, background smoke; **t23** brilliant malt arrival: the barley sings from every direction; **f24** surprising lack of development as the oak remains shy and the barley rules unhindered; just the faintest wisp of smoke here and there; **b23** almost like a malt-shake in its barley intensity. No complaints here, though.

Karuizawa 1988 Aged 15 Years cask 691 db **(88) n20** malty banana and custard; **t22** drying oak at first and then the most teasing build-up of honey imaginable; **f23** this creeping effect continues with a crescendo of acacia honey and green-grassy barley in total control of the oak; **b23** quite fabulous whisky that exudes confidence and charisma.

Karuizawa 1988 Single Cask No. 3397 dist 88, bott 07 db **(90) n21 t23 f23 b23.** Technically a slightly flawed dram. But there is no denying its drama. 59.8%

Karuizawa 1991 cask no. 3318, dist 91, bott 07 **(85) n19 t21.5 f22.5 b22.** Aggressive barley tries to help compensate for the over extraction from the oak. Never less than high quality, though, and blessed with delicious molasses all the way. 62.5%.

Karuizawa 1992 cask no. 3330, dist 92, bott 07 **(92) n23 t22.5 f23.5 b23.5.** Flawed, certainly. But in genius, it's just about forgivable.. 61.5%. Number One Drinks Company.

Karuizawa Pure Malt Aged 12 Years (85) n18 t23 f22 b22. A recent Gold Medal Winner at the IWSC, but surely not by sporting a fractured nose like this. Thankfully the delivery is quite superb with the emphasis on silky honeycomb. 40%

Karuizawa Pure Malt 15 Years (76) n17 t21 f20 b18. Some vague sulphur notes on the sherry do no favours for what appears to be an otherwise top-quality malt. (Earlier bottlings have been around the 87–88 mark, with the fruit, though clean, not being quite in balance but made up for by an astonishing silkiness with roast chestnut puree and malt). 40%

Karuizawa Single Malt Aged 17 Years (87.5) n23 juicy dates in the rich, molassed fruitcake; **t23** almost ridiculously soft on delivery: it's all about fruit, for sure, but the roast coffee and dark molassed sweetness do give it a required dimension; **f20** despite the clarity of grape, still a dry, bitter note develops; **b21.5** a beautiful malt in so many ways, but one less-than-wonderful sherry butt has robbed this of greatness. How many times has this happened this year....? 40%

Karuizawa Pure Malt Aged 17 Years (90) n20 bourbony, big oak and pounding fruit; **t24** enormous stuff: the link between malt and fruit is almost without definition; **f23** amazingly long and silky. Natural vanilla melts in with the almost concentrated malt; **b23** brilliant whisky beautifully made and majestically matured. Neither sweetness nor dryness dominates, always the mark of a quality dram. 40%

⟐ **Noh Whisky Karuizawa 1976** cask no. 6719, bott 2009 **(91) n22** tight, spiced grape; **t24** enveloping grape dovetailing with thick stratum of malt; impressive early sugars and a mouth feel to die for; the laid back juiciness is a treat; **f22.5** delicate hickory and plenty more rich barley; **b22.5** sticks religiously to the malty house style despite the grape trying to enter from every angle. A beautiful whisky, reminding me what a special year 1976 was for Japan. Happy 35th in April.....x. 63% Number One Drinks Co.

⟐ **Noh Whisky Karuizawa 1977** cask no. 4592, dist 1977, bott 2010 **(75) n19 t19 f18 b19.** The bizarre dark colour and aggressive sharpness of nose and flavour suggests a small iron nail dropped into the cask at some time in its long life. Pity, for the grape is quite wholesome. 60.7% Number One Drinks Co.

Noh Whisky Karuizawa 1995 Japanese wine cask finish no. 5004, dist 95, bott 08 **(93.5) n23.5** a touch of cherry stone brandy: hard, uncompromising, full of nutty fruit...and glorious... **t23** for the enormity of the malt, the salivatory experience goes off the scale as those cherries, now accompanied by liquorice and raspberry jam go into overdrive; **f23.5** much more sedate: but still the mouth-watering barley and fruit carry on regardless of a half-hearted oaky intervention; **b23.5** seatbelts needed for this enormous ride. An unusual malt which doesn't entirely add up....but comes to the right numbers!! 63%. Number One Drinks Co.

The Whisky Fair Karuizawa Aged 19 Years refill sherry, dist 88, bott 07 **(84) n21 t22 f20 b21.** Softly oiled with the accent on barley and caramel. 58.3%. Germany.

The Whisky Fair Karuizawa Aged 19 Years sherry, dist 88, bott 07 **(89.5) n22.5 t23 f22 b22.** A fuller, happier malt than the refill version. 60.6%. Germany.

KIRIN

Kirin18 Years Old (86.5) n22 t22 f21.5 b21. Unquestionably over-aged. Even so, still puts up a decent show with juicy citrus trying to add a lighter touch to the uncompromising, ultra dense oak. As entertaining as it is challenging. 43%. Suntory

KOMAGATAKE

Komagatake 10 Years Old Single Malt db **(78)** n19 t20 f19 b20. A very simple, malty whisky that's chewy and clean with a slight hint of toffee. *40%. Mars.*

Komagatake 10 Years Old Sherry Cask db **(67)** n16.5 t17 f16.5 b17. Torpedoed by sulphur. Gruesome. *40%. Mars.*

Komagatake 1988 Single Cask sherry cask, cask no. 566, dist 88, bott 09 db **(62.5)** n15 t16.5 f15 b16. I can assume only that this has been "finished" in a relatively recent sherry butt. "Finished" is putting it mildly. A sulphur horror show. *46%. Mars.*

Komagatake 1989 Single Cask American white oak cask, cask no. 617, dist 89, bott 09 db **(88)** n23 candy stores of the 50s and 60s...dentine and waxed floors. Beautiful... t22.5 sugary beginnings, a livid barley scream and then vanilla; f21 bitters out as oak attacks; b21.5 a fine but bitty malt which feels its age at times. *46%. Mars.*

Komagatake 1992 Single Cask American white oak cask, cask no. 1144, dist 92, bott 09 db **(93.5)** n24.5 one of the noses of the year: cartful of apples, some of the toffee apple variety; dentine and molassed rum; t23 firm, teeth-cracking malt which really piles on the malty style; caramel as well, but it appears fresh and breathing - as though extracted from the oak; f22.5 rumbling spice carries on indefinitely; vanilla and walnut oil; b23.5 you know when you've had a glass of this: beautiful and no shrinking violet. *46%. Mars.*

MIYAGIKYO (see Sendai)

SENDAI 1969. Nikka.

Miyagikyo batch 24H20B db **(89)** n22 sweet chestnut and marzipan share the nutty honours; t23.5 beautiful delivery, superbly weighted: the malt really has some backbone and some toffee liquorice makes for a chewy middle ground; f21.5 perhaps a touch too much toffee; b22 another high quality malt from this improving distillery. *43%*

Miyagikyo 10 Years Old batch 06I08C db **(83)** n19 t22 f21 b21. Much better than the sharp nose warns, with some juicy, fruity moments. A little flat, though. *45%*

Miyagikyo 12 Years Old batch 08I28A db **(89)** n22.5 that familiar gooseberry nose with barley and custard; t23 juicy and sweetens superbly mainly with gristy barley, though that oaky vanilla lurks nearby; f21 drier, a hint of bitterness, but that persistent sweet barley compensates; b22.5 in many ways, absolutely 100% recognisable as the distillery house style; in another this has much more confidence and charisma than of old. *45%*

Miyagikyo 15 Years Old batch 02I10D db **(91.5)** n23 fruity, as is the expression's style. But now lighter with much more emphasis on a Sauternes-style sultana; t23.5 pulsing fruit, but the barley is sharp and wonderfully juicy; f22 vanillas balance the barley and still a residual sweet grape can be found; a mild degree of very late bitterness; b23 a much lighter, more refined and elegant creature than before. Despite a minor sherry butt blemish, fabulous. *45%*

Miyagiko Key Malt Aged 12 Years "Fruity & Rich" db **(90)** n22 fruit biscuits with burnt raisin and sugar; t23 wonderful lift-off of sultana and burnt raisin on a sea of chewy barley. Towards the middle, a brief expression of oak and then much sweeter – and oilier – barley. Fruity; f22 rich! b23 a very comfortable whisky, much at home with itself. *55%. Nikka.*

Miyagiko Key Malt Aged 12 Years "Soft & Dry" db **(85)** n22 t21 f21 b21. Perhaps needs a degree of sweetness.... *55%. Nikka.*

Miyagikyo 15 Years Old batch 20C44C db **(84)** n20 t21 f22 b21. Very typically Sendai: light body and limited weight even with all the fruit. Clean and gathers in overall enjoyability, though. *45%*

Sendai 12 Years Old code 06C40C db **(83)** n17 t22 f23 b21. To put it politely, the nose is pretty ordinary; but what goes on afterwards is relative bliss with a wonderful, oily, fruity resonance. For those thinking in Scotch terms, this is very Speysidey with the malt intense and chewy. *45%. Nikka.*

Sendai Miyagikyo Nikka Single Cask Malt Whisky 1986 dist 16 May 86 bott, 5 Dec 03 db **(88)** n22 t20 f24 b22. Little to do with balance, everything about effect. *63.2%*

Sendai Miyagikyo Nikka Single Cask Malt Whisky 1992 dist 22 Apr 92, bott 5 Dec 03 db **(84)** n19 t20 f24 b21. Very strange whisky: I would never have recognised this as Sendai. I don't know if they have used local oak on this but the fruity, off-balance nose and early taste is compensated by an orgy of mouth-watering, softly smoked barley that sends the taste buds into ecstasy. A distinct, at times erratic, whisky that may horrify the purists but really has some perzaz and simply cannot be ignored. *55.3%*

SHIRAKAWA

Shirakawa 32 Years Old Single Malt (94) n23 ripe mango meets a riper, rye-encrusted bourbon. We are talking a major aroma here; t24 the most intense malt you'll ever find explodes and drools all over your tastebuds. To make the flavour bigger still, the oak adds a punchy bourbon quality. Beautiful oils coat the roof of the mouth to amplify the performance; f23 long, sweet and malty. Some fruitiness does arrive but it is the oak-malt combination that just knocks you out; b24 just how big can an unpeated malt whisky get? The kind of malt that leaves you in awe, even when you thought you had seen and tasted them all. 55%. Takara.

WHITE OAK DISTILLERY

White Oak Akashi Single Malt Whisky Aged 8 Years bott 07 db (74.5) n18.5 t19.5 f17.5 b19. Always fascinating to find a malt from one of the smaller distilleries in a country. And I look forward to tracking this one down and visiting, something I have yet to do. There is certainly something distinctly small still about his one, with butyric and feintiness causing damage to nose and finish. For all the early malty presence on delivery, some of the off notes are a little on the uncomfortable side. 40%

YAMAZAKI 1923. Suntory.

Yamazaki Vintage 1979 db (78) n20 t21 f18 b19. Spicy and thick malt. But this has plenty of wrinkles and a stoop, too. 56%. Suntory.

Yamazaki Vintage Malt 1980 db (75) n19 t19 f18 b19. Some lovely blood oranges, but no whisky can survive this amount of oak unscathed. 56%

Yamazaki Vintage 1982 db (84) n20 t22 f21 b21. Big, muscly malt with some sexy spices. 56%. Suntory.

Yamazaki 1984 bott 09 db (94) n24 masive: more dates and walnut – the occasional distillery style - only here in concentrate form; t24 big. But you'd never know it. Superbly weighted grape is full, buxom and ripe. But gathers in with almost honeycomb-bourbony oak with something approaching tenderness. Juicy and weaving between bourbony and sherried channels with aplomb; f22.5 a slight buzz to the finale shows we don't have perfection, but the vanillas remain intact; b23.5 if you like your whisky boringly neutral, lifeless and with nothing to say other than that it has been ruined by sulphur, then this will horrify you. Though there is a little blemish at the very death, there is still no taking away from this being a sublime 25-year-old. When this distillery is on form it makes for compelling whisky and here we have a bottling showing Yamazaki at its brightest. 48%

Yamazaki Sherry Wood Vintage 1986 db (93) n24 a sherry butt found in heaven: clean, absolutely dripping in grapejuice yet light enough to allow further complexity from bright malt and a touch of smoke; t23 mouthwatering fruit clings, thanks to the estery malt, to every crevice in the mouth; f23 exceptionally long fade with a chocolate and sultana finale, topped with a puff of smoke; b23 something here for everyone; one of the most outstanding "new" sherry casks of the year. 45%. Suntory Whisky.

Yamazaki Vintage 1991 db (88) n23 a curious mixture of peat reek and Golden Graham breakfast cereal; t23 soft smoke at first and then the grain hardens and takes a stranglehold; f21 honied yet remaining firm; b21 hard and tough as nails towards the finish: a surprising conclusion after such a yielding start. 56%. Suntory.

Yamazaki 1991 db (88) n21 bourbony and light with a substratum of soft malt; t23 astonishing unfurling of mouthwatering malt tones that spreads over the mouth revealing a subtle hint of smoke and beautifully graceful oak; t22 long, lashings of cocoa powder and again soft barley hand-in-hand with gentle oak; b22 closed when cold, improves dramatically when warmed on the hand. But the mouth arrival really does deserve a medal. 61%

Yamazaki 1993 db (87) n23 smoky and clean; gristy and Port Ellen-ish with a bit of extra exotic oak; t23 sweet, spicy, vaguely Islay-ish start with the peats developing but not at the expense of dense malt. The oak is refined and there is something unusually coastal for a non-Scottish peated malt; f20 rather hard, closed and brittle. Metallic malt scrapes against rock-like peat; b21 a real surprise package. At times quite Islay-ish in style – Port Ellen in particular – but the finish is more realistic. A really delicious experience nonetheless.

Yamazaki Vintage 1994 db (91) n23 butterscotch and cedarwood; t24 intense, ultra-clean malt and honey; soft oak and spice add balance; f22 drier, toasty with residual malt; b22 very high quality whisky without a single blemish. 56%. Suntory.

The Yamazaki Single Malt Whisky Aged 10 Years bott 09 db (87.5) n21.5 a mixed bag of big vanilla, barley and plummy bananas; t22 whisky doesn't come softer on delivery but there is a price; the toffees seem to flatten any higher notes but there is still a tangible fruitiness drifting on from somewhere which is very attractive; **f22** remains lightly sweet, with raisins and vanilla the softness continues; **b22** returned to some of its fruitier root. But if it's silky whisky you want, look no further. *40%*

The Yamazaki Single Malt Whisky Aged 10 Years db **(89) n22** subtle vanilla; clean, grassy barley – for those into Speyside style malts; **t23** mouth-watering and wonderful display of barley offering a golden syrup counter to the drier oaks; **f22** more strands of syrup but never over the top as the vanilla pods crank up the intensity **b22** a beautifully improved, charismatic malt displaying a voluptuousness and understanding between clean barley and drier oak that had been lacking. Nothing like so fruity and a very charming experience. *40%*

The Yamazaki Single Malt Whisky Aged 12 Years bott 09 db **(93.5) n23** a seriously "married" nose, as though the many styles and riches have had time to mix: a real sherry trifle feel to this, but so clean it almost sparkles; **t24** brilliant arrival: the fruit and barley unite to form an enormous juicy front. Light milky cocoa follows behind while the sugars are on the lightly molassed side. Dazzling.. **f23** long, retains its sweetness and offers chocolate raisin finale; **b23.5** one of the cleanest and most beautifully integrated whiskies I've tasted for a while. Unlike the 10-y-o, nothing so dominates that the more complex notes are trimmed or flattened. One to find. *43%*

The Yamazaki Single Malt Whisky Aged 12 Years db **(83) n21 t21 f20 b21.** The flattest Yamazaki 12 I have ever tasted. Partly due, I'd say, to an increase in oak and caramel levels, as the toffee is a driving force. Also, perhaps to a degree of extra oil. Some butterscotch around, but it's an uphill battle. *43%*

The Yamazaki Single Malt Whisky Aged 15 Years Cask Strength db **(94) n23** just a hint that its gone OTT oak-wise, but there is a wisp of smoke to this, too. All in all, wonderful brinkmanship that pays off; **t24** stunning: a massive injection of bourbon-style liquorice and honeycomb plays perfectly against the softer malts. The most controlled of malty explosions... **f23** long, lascivious, the tastebuds are debauched by ingots of honeycomb, molasses and dark sugary notes balanced by the drier oaks; **b24** an extraordinary bottling that far exceeds any previous version I have encountered. Stunning. *56%*

The Yamazaki Single Malt Whisky Aged 18 Years db **(88.5) n22** from the date and walnut school of bigness; **t23** surprisingly early signs of chocolate: melts in beautifully with the raisin and nuts; **f21.5** dries in rather too sharp a way, meaning that oak alone isn't responsible. But still malty echoes to enjoy; **b22** a towering recovery from last year's disappointing bottling. I certainly wouldn't wager that every sherry butt is unmolested by sulphur, but overall quality shines through like a rising sun. *43%*

The Yamazaki Single Malt Whisky Aged 25 Years db **(87) n23** no sulphur here – just sherry and more sherry....!! Once you get below the grapey surface the degree of complexity is bewitching, with the bitter-sweet spices and bourbons really going to town; **t22** good grief; the tastebuds are flattened by the oak and sherry-weighted steamroller; **f20** pretty bitter as what seems like highly aged oloroso and extremely old oak kick in with a vengeance; **b22** it has taken me over an hour to taste this. And still I don't know if I have marked it too high. You'll either love it or hate it – but you'll find nothing else like it..!! *43%*

The Yamazaki Sherry Cask Aged 10 Years bott 09 db **(82.5) n21 t22 f19.5 b20.** Very tight. The grape, initially impressive, is domineering leaving the malt's wings clipped. There are those who will adore this. But, technically and balance-wise, not quite right. *48%*

The Cask of Yamazaki 1990 Sherry Butt cask no. 0N70646, dist Feb 90, bott Jun 08 db **(97) n24.5** massive, elegantly spiced, sherry. Huge almost Demerara rum molasses, pithy apples, liquorice and hickory, too. Ye olde Macallan lovers – and I mean those of us who used to worship the stuff over 30 years ago – will weep at its flawless beauty and enormity....; **t24** fills the mouth with successive layers of spiced brilliance. Seriously bitter-sweet with a sharp, piercing sugar-coated edge to the malt. The grape crashes into the rock-firm body to produce a juicy element; **f24** just so much coffee – or is it mocha? – with a light sprinkling of Demerara sugar. Long, silky yet crisp; **b24.5** such is the state of sherry butts today – including in Japan – that the first thing to report is that it is entirely sulphur-free....and some!! Without blemish, this is a rare treat. Once, slightly over the top grape-wise. These days a joyous relief! Beyond that, it is gargantuan. Few whiskies this year have covered such a wide variety of flavours and aromas with such panache: the structure and complexity for its type are close to perfection. Even more telling, is the fact that it is hard to believe that one of this company's Scottish distilleries could have come up with something quite so brilliant. *61%. 506 bottles.*

The Cask of Yamazaki 1993 Heavily Peated Malt white oak puncheon cask, dist May 93, bott Oct 07 db **(95) n23.5 t25 f23 b23.5.** When they say "Heavily Peated" they mean heavily.

Like some kind of new phenol isotope, this is heavy peat whisky. Like probably twice as thick as the average peaty whisky you come across. It is, shall we say....peaty. Strap yourself in for the ride: only the fittest will survive... *62%. 574 bottles.*

The Cask of Yamazaki 1993 Heavily Peated Malt white oak puncheon cask no. 3Q70048, dist May 93, bott Jun 08 db **(89) n22** dry, peat cinders blowing in the wind; **t21.5** oily, thick delivery reveals little early on; blossoms out with some welcome lemon thinning out the peat until the maltiness is juicy and lively; **f23** long with crashing waves of peat and citrus – easily the best phrase of the story. Glorious bitter-sweet notes, including cocoa (by the spadeful) and chocolate lime candy (by the bagful); **b22.5** takes a long time to get going thanks to an initially unattractive oily coating. But on finding its feet becomes a cracker. *62%. 503 bottles.*

Suntory Pure Malt Yamazaki 25 Years Old db **(91) n23** quite intoxicating marriage between grapey fruitiness and rich oak: supremely spiced and balanced with a wave of pure bourbon following through; **t23** big, big oloroso character then an entrancing molassed, burnt raisin, malty richness; **f22** subtle spices, poppy seed with some late bitter oak; **b23** being matured in Japan, the 25 years doesn't have quite the same value as Scotland. So perhaps in some ways this can lay claim to be one of the most enormously aged, oak-laden whiskies that has somehow kept its grace and star quality. *43%*

Suntory Single Malt Yamazaki Aged 12 Years db **(87) n22** delicate, chalky vanilla with a squeeze of kiwifruit and butterscotch; **t23** a wonderfully light touch with fresh house-style mouth-watering barley and transparent fruit setting up the busy middle spice; **f20** pretty dry with oak and toffee; **b22** this was the 2006 bottling which somehow missed entry into the Bible, although tasted. A fruity little babe. *43%*

YOICHI 1934. Nikka.

Hokkaido 12 Years Old db **(87) n23 t22 f21 b21.** Full-flavoured malt with absolutely zero yield. Just ricochets around the palate. *43%. Nikka.*

Yoichi batch 04H10D **(87.5) n22.5 t22 f21.5 b21.5.** Very drinkable, though you get the feeling it is performing well within itself. *43%*

Yoichi batch 04I10D db **(81.5) n21.5 t21.5 f18.5 b20.** A very hard malt: crisp, sweet at first but with limited yield. The apparent sulphur on the finish doesn't help. *43%*

Yoichi 10 Years Old batch 08I16C db **(83.5) n21.5 t21 f20.5 b20.5.** Good grief! What has happened to this whisky? Actually, I think I can tell you: too much sherry and caramel makes for a dull malt. Pleasant. Drinkable. But dull. *45%*

Yoichi 10 Years Old batch 12I32, old Hokkaido "Yoichi" distillery label db **(91) n22 t23 f23 b23.** Yet another teasing, unpredictable dram from Yoichi. *43%. Nikka.*

Yoichi 10 Years Old batch 14I16A db **(75) n19 t19 f18 b19.** Proof that sulphur can detract even from a great like Yoichi. *45%*

Yoichi 10 Years Old batch 14B22, new "Yoichi" distillery label db **(88) n18 t23 f23 b24.** Typical Yoichi. Even when it shows a flaw it recovers to an unbelievable degree: like a champion ice skater who falls at the first leap and then dances on as if nothing happened. Keeps you guessing to the very last about what is to happen next. Fabulous verve and complexity. *45%. Nikka.*

Yoichi 10 Years Old batch 14H62A, old Hokkaido "Yoichi" distillery label db **(91) n23 t23 f22 b23.** The crispness and bite of this whisky makes it almost blend-like in style – which goes to underline the complexity. *43%. Nikka.*

Yoichi 10 Years Old batch 14H62B, old Hokkaido "Yoichi" distillery label db **(89) n23 t21 f22 b23.** Soft and delicate with beautifully chewy peat throughout. *43%. Nikka.*

Yoichi 10 Years Old batch 24G48C, old Hokkaido "Yoichi" distillery label db **(93) n23 t23 f24 b23.** A Yoichi in its "Old Speyside" phase, with just a waft of peat-reek to add some ballast to the enormous, clean malt. The fade is nothing short of fabulous. A Japanese version of Ardmore: whisky for grown-ups. *43%*

Yoichi 10 Years Old batch 24H18C, old Hokkaido "Yoichi" distillery label db **(89) n20 t23 f23 b23.** Another bottle of understated genius. *43%. Nikka.*

Yoichi Single Malt 10 Years Old batch 12F04C db **(89) n21 t24 f21 b23.** Mildly dodgy nose, overly toffeed finish... and still it's a lightweight treat! *45%*

Yoichi 12 Years Old batch 06C14, new Yoichi label with distillery drawing db **(91) n21 t24 f22 b24.** Absolutely magnificent malt with a no-holds-barred intensity of fruit and malt. *45%.*

Yoichi 12 Years Old batch 08I18B db **(75.5) n19 t19 f18.5 b19.** fruity but flat and sulphury; some smoke perhaps, but all rather hush-hush...and very disappointing, though had you been at the distillery some dozen years ago not entirely surprising. One feared this day might come....and it has. *45%*

Yoichi 12 Years Old batch 16J32, new Yoichi label with distillery drawing db **(87)** n20 t22 f23 b22. A pretty light Yoichi almost devoid of peat. After getting over a toffee-led lull the malt comes to life with impressive results. 45%. Yoichi.

Yoichi Key Malt Aged 12 Years "Peaty & Salty" db **(95)** n23 the peat rumbles like distant thunder, difficult to pinpoint but letting you know that it is there. The oaky tones suggest a mixing of Kentucky and something local; soft fruits make an almost apologetic appearance; t25 there is perfect distribution of peat. It rumbles around the palate offering bitter-sweet depth, and a salty, coastal tang emphasises the richness of the malt; f23 waves of vanilla begin to outflank the soft peat: the finish is long and there is no victor between the sweet malt and the more bitter, salty oak; b24 of all the peated whiskies of the world, only Ardbeg can stand shoulder to shoulder with Yoichi when it comes to sheer complexity. Here is an astonishing example of why I rate Yoichi in the best five whiskies in the world. Forget the odd sulphur-tarnished bottling. Get Yoichi in its natural state with perfect balance between oak and malt and it delivers something approaching perfection. And this is just such a bottling. 55%. Nikka.

Yoichi Key Malt Aged 12 Years "Sherry & Sweet" db **(80)** n19 t22 f19 b20. Sad to report that this should be called "Very Slight Sulphur and Sweet". A real pity because it is obvious that had the Spaniards not molested these butts, they would have been absolutely top-of-the-range. And probably would have scored in the low to mid 90s. I could weep. 55%. Nikka.

Yoichi Key Malt Aged 12 Years "Woody & Vanillic" db **(83)** n21 t22 f20 b20. Pretty decent whisky. Not sure about creating one that sets out to be woody: that means balance has been sacrificed to concentrate on a particular essence to the whisky that should be used only as a component of complexity. Still, there is enough sweet malt on arrival to make this a dram to be enjoyed. 55%

Yoichi Single Malt 12 Years Old batch 14F36A db **(91)** n22 soft smoke and under-ripe fruit; t23 profound, chewy barley; lots of small still coppery sharpness and then a gentle awakening of peat; f23 sweet peats dusted with demerara; it takes some time for the chalky oak to finally have a say; b23 best when left in the glass for 10-15 minutes: only then does the true story emerge. 45%

Yoichi 15 Years Old batch 06I08B db **(91.5)** n22 surprisingly quiet and well behaved considering the light smokiness drifting about; t23.5 nutty, chewy and with lots of early toffee. Juices up to puckering effect as the barley and phenols strikes home; f23 sweet and spicy in the right places as the malt begins to find its legs and goes up a notch or two b23 for an early moment or two possibly one of the most salivating whiskies you'll get your kisser around this year. Wonderfully entertaining yet you still suspect that this is another Yoichi reduced in effect somewhat by either caramel and/or sherry. When it hits its stride, though, becomes a really busy whisky that gets tastebuds in a right lather. But I'm being picky as I know that this is one of the world's top five distilleries and am aware as anyone on this planet of its extraordinary capabilities. Great fun; great whisky – could be better still, but so much better than its siblings... 45%

Yoichi Single Malt 15 Years Old batch 04F44D db **(86)** n22 t22 f20 b22. Zesty and tangy; most peculiar by Yoichi standards. But still big, rich and lip-smacking. 45%

Yoichi 20 Years Old batch 06I06A db **(87)** n22 an enormous statement from the glass. Immediately the odd sulphur note is detected, but the grape and high roast Java (possibly with medium Mysore) comes to its aid. The result is thick and very warehousy; t22.5 much lighter delivery than nose: the barley actually shows first and juices up. Soon after though, the dark coffee clouds form; spicy in part, but something niggles away... f20.5 that off key note gains strength amid a mocha recovery; b22 bitter-sweet experience, both in taste and perception. Not unusual to find sulphur on this guy, but a shame when it alters the course of the malt. 52%

Yoichi 20 Years Old db **(95)** n23 magnificently intense oloroso (a tiny fleck of sulphur burns off in about 10 minutes when warmed), the background malt oak-laden; t23 again it's oloroso that leads the way, apparently too intensely at first but quickly settling to allow some stupendous spices to unravel and create balance. Fabulous bitter-sweet harmony; f25 Okay, guys, help me out here. Spot the fault. I can't. The fruit is now spotlessly clean and displaying a grapey complexity, the spices are warming but not entirely engulfing, the oak is firm and adds no more than a hint of dryness and at last the malt comes into full play to offer both mouthwatering barley and something slightly smoky. If you can pick a defect, let me know; b24 I don't know how much they charge for this stuff but either alone or with mates get some for one hell of an experience. What makes it all the more remarkable is that there is a slight sulphury note on the nose: once you taste the stuff that becomes of little consequence. 52%. Nikka.

Yoichi 1987 batch 22G26B **(89.5)** n22 juicy grape somehow outperforms the delicate peats; t23.5 again the grape is first to show: sweet and juicy and then gives way slightly as some peated chocolate arrives – almost like a smoked fruit chocolate bar: delicious... f21.5 a few signs of the cask tiring, but the fruit and smoke provide the required sticking plaster; b23 having tasted from quite a number of casks from this year at the distillery itself, I was a bit worried when I saw that sherry butts had been used. However, no great signs of sulphurous ruination here and the marriage of the varying styles of peat and grape has created the desired degree of complexity. 55%

Nikka Whisky Yoichi (78) n18 t20 f21 b19. Not often I'm lost for words...but this one left me stunned. Nothing like I expected. Not least because it seems either very young. Or not remotely short of feints. Or both. And the whole thing is propped up by caramel. The best bit is the late spice attack....but this is like nothing I would have expected from one of the top five distilleries in the world. As my one time Japanese girlfriend would have said: "I am shocked..." 43%

Nikka Whisky Yoichi 1986 20 Years Old (94) n23 age, the salty sea air of Hokkaido and sweet oak have accounted for the more exceptional possibilities of the peat: weighty but restrained; t24 no holding back here, though, as the delivery is one first of juicy fruit and then silky waves of peat; chunky heavy-duty stuff which, for some reason, appears to float about the palate; the spices shoot on sight; f23 a sweeter, more sober finale with liquorice and molasses joining forces with the salty oakiness to keep the lid on the smoke; b24 now this is unambiguous Yoichi :exactly how I have come to know and adore this distillery. 55.0%

Scotch Malt Whisky Society Cask 116.12 Aged 21 Years refill hogshead, dist Jul 86 **(87.5)** n22 soft smoke and cocoa; t22 the peat is thinly spread around the sweet barley; gentle oils and Party Ring biscuits; f21 bitters out with the cask; b22.5 attractive and works to the limitations of the cask itself. 54.2%

Scotch Malt Whisky Society Cask 116.14 Aged 25 Years 1st fill hogshead, dist Sep 83 **(96.5)** n23.5 very big, indeed: the oak is creaking yet somehow doesn't make even a hint of threat. Some really dank, floral notes – bluebells in a dark forest – earthy but not peaty. Weighty stuff... t24.5 very, very big...!!! The delivery, helped along by the big alcohols, really is monumental with, in the space of three of four tsunami-size waves, we cover barley at its most heavy and concentrated, oak at its bourbony sweetest yet controlled by a sprinkling of cocoa, and a disingenuous fruitiness, that is one minute there...then not. The middle is all the above points to greater or lesser degrees. This is whisky and a half; f24 big, but very, very, very discreet: perhaps more emphasis on the chocolate, though some muscovado has got into the mix. Not a single note of bitterness, or a groan against so many years in the cask...awe inspiring... b24.5 what a bloody whisky....!!! There are times, when tasting one sulphur-stuffed whisky after another, I wonder why I do this. Then something as beautiful as this comes along and you remember the exact reason. Whisky can be, and should be, the dark matter of our appreciation of the senses. The reason why so many millions of people worldwide have switched on to whisky is because they have discovered that, if made, matured or mixed the right way, it can bring sensations of joy that we previously thought only possible on a bed, or swinging from a chandelier. So whiskies like this have an exotic and erotic element to them, but to make them sexier still there has to be a cerebral quality, too. In other words, all your senses are being stimulated. Few whiskies stimulate them quite as well as this one. 59.4%

Scotch Malt Whisky Society Cask 116.15 Aged 25 Years Japanese oak, dist Sep 83 **(89)** n23.5 denser than a Japanese rain forest. The oak has a slightly different call to normal European oak, and at this age is offering quite another alternative. Sweet chestnut and reduced Jaffa cake make for an interesting combination... t22 big on the kumquaty citrus, and a roll of thick barley. But this disappears beneath a cloak of uncompromising oak for a few moments before some cocoa appears; f21.5 powdery dry but the oddly-flavoured vanillas succeed in adding a modicum of sweetness; in the end it is the 90% cocoa chocolate which closes the experience; b22 one of the problems with Japanese oak is that whilst it can add an extra, and quite unique, zing to a malt at conventional Japanese ages, when it gets to 25 years it has perhaps added a little too much. Here is a case of a Japanese oak not exactly doing Japanese oaky sort of things. All that said....a really delightful whisky and one which takes you into fascinating, unexplored lands...!!! 58.9%

Unspecified Malts

"Hokuto" Suntory Pure Malt Aged 12 Years (93) n22 trademark delicate lightness; fleeting barley chased by soft vanilla; t24 melt-in-the-mouth malt arrival; hints of honey work well with the loftier barley and earthier oak; **f23** honey on toast with just a little toffee; **b24** another example of Suntory at its most feminine: just so seductive and beautiful. Although a malt, think Lawson's 12-y-o of a decade ago and you have the picture. *40%*

Nikka Whisky From the Barrel (89) **n20** carries some weight; good age and subtle malty sugars; **t23** exemplary mouthfeel: delightful oils and nipping spices but the malt remains clean and very sweet; **f22** some dryer oakiness but the malt keeps its balancing sweetness; **b24** a whisky that requires a bit of time and concentration to get the best out of. You will discover something big and exceptionally well balanced. *51.4%. Nikka.*

Nikka Whisky From the Barrel batch 02F26A (82) **n20 t22 f20 b20.** Some attractive honey notes and caramel, but a bit laboured. *51.4%*

Nikka Whisky From the Barrel batch 12F32C db (91) **n22** date and brazil cake; **t24** monumental delivery with soft smoke melting into the most glorious honeycomb known to man; tingly spices and toffee-apple, too; **f22** caramel kicks in slightly but some butterscotch rounds it off wonderfully; **b23** truly great whisky that mostly overcomes the present Japanese curse of big caramel finishes. *51.4%*

Nikka Whisky Single Coffey Malt 12 Years (97) **n23.5** forget all about the malt: it's the big bourbony, hickory and honey sweet oak which wins hands down; **t25** hold on to your hats: it's flavour explosion time....on first tasting it's simply too much to comprehend. Only on third or fourth mouthful do you really get an idea. First, the delivery is pretty close to perfection: the soft oils seem to draw every last nuance from the barley; then when it has done that, it manages to mix it with myriad delicate sweet notes radiating from the oak. This includes some of those allied to bourbon, especially chocolate honeycomb and very deep molassed notes usually associated with Demerara Coffey still rum; a unique combination absolutely perfectly displayed; **f24** long...just so long. One mouthful, especially at 55%, last for about six or seven minutes. So impressive here is the delicacy of the fade: after a delivery so large, the finesse is extraordinary. The flavours in effect mirror the earlier delivery. Except now some vanilla does come in to dry things a little; **b24.5** the Scotch Whisky Association would say that this is not single malt whisky because it is made in a Coffey still. When they can get their members to make whisky this stunning on a regular basis via their own pots and casks, then perhaps they should pipe up as their argument might then have a single atom of weight. *55%.*

Vatted Malts

All Malt (86) **n22 t21 f21 b22.** The best example by a mile of an almost unique style of vatted whisky: both malt and "grain" are distilled from entirely malted barley, identical to Kasauli malt whisky in India. Stupendous grace and balance. *40%. Nikka.*

All Malt "Pure & Rich" (89) **n22** honeycomb and liquorice with some thumping oak; **t24** beautifully mouthfilling. and "rich" is an understatement. Barley sugar and molten brown sugar combine and then there is a soft gristiness. Big...; **f21** vanilla and caramel with some residual malt; **b22** my word, this has changed! Not unlike some bottlings of Highland Park with its emphasis on honey. If they could tone down the caramel it'd really be up there. *40%. Nikka.*

All Malt Pure & Rich batch 14F24A (77) **n19 t20 f19 b19.** My former long term Japanese girlfriend, Makie (hope you enjoyed your 30th birthday in April, by the way), used to have a favourite saying, namely: "I am shocked!" Well, I am shocked by this whisky because it is much blander than the previous bottling (04E16D), with all that ultra-delicate and complex honeycomb lost and lovely gristiness removed. For me, one of the biggest surprises – and disappointments - of the 2007 Bible. But proof that, when using something so potentially dangerous as caramel, it is too easy to accidentally cross that fine line between brilliance and blandness. Because, had they gone the other way, we might have had a challenger for World Whisky of the Year. *40%. Nikka.*

Hokuto Pure Malt Aged 12 Years (86) **n20 t22 f22 b22.** An oaky threat never materialises: excellent mixing. *40%. Suntory.*

⋄ **Ichiro's Malt Double Distilleries** bott 2010 (86.5) **n22.5 t22 f21 b21.** Some imperious barley-rich honey reigns supreme until a bitter wood note bites hard. *46% Venture Whisky Ltd*

⋄ **Ichiro's Malt Mizunara Wood Reserve** (76) **n19 t21 f18 b19.** I have my Reservations about the Wood, too... *46% Venture Whisky Ltd*

Malt Club "Pure & Clear" (83) **n21 t22 f20 b20.** Another improved vatting, much heavier and older than before with bigger spice. *40%. Nikka.*

Mars Maltage Pure Malt 8 Years Old (84) **n20 t21 f21 b22.** A very level, intense, clean malt with no peaks or troughs, just a steady variance in the degree of sweetness and oak input. Impossible not to have a second glass of. *43%. Mars.*

Nikka Malt 100 The Anniversary Aged 12 Years (73) n18 t19 f18 b18. The depressing and deadly fingerprint of sulphur is all over this. Shame, as the spices excel. *40%*

Nikka Pure Malt Aged 21 Years batch 08I18D db (89) n23 profound, clean, over-ripe grape with some lovely nip and prickle; weighty with a liquorice bourbony element, too; t22.5 soft at first then a steady build up of malt and spice. The fruit is never far away; f21.5 toasty vanilla and a light buzz from the sherry; b22 by far the best of the set. *43%*

Nikka Pure Malt Aged 17 Years batch 08I30B db (83) n21 t21 f20 b21. A very similar shape to the 12-years-old, but older - obviously. Certainly the sherry butts have a big say and don't always do great favours to the high quality spirit. *43%*

Nikka Pure Malt Aged 12 Years batch 10I24C db (84) n21.5 t21 f20 b21.5. The nose may be molassed, sticky treacle pudding, but it spices up on the palate. The dull buzz on the finish also tells a tale. *40%*

Pure Malt Black batch 02C58A (95) n24 an exquisitely crafted nose: studied peat in luxuriant yet deft proportions nestling amid some honeyed malt and oak. The balance between sweet and dry is faultless. There is neither a single off-note nor a ripple of disharmony. The kind of nose you can sink your head into and simply disappear; t23 for all the evident peat, this is medium-weighted, the subtlety encased in a gentle cloak of oil; f23 long, silky, fabulously weighted peat running a sweet course through some surging malt and liquorice tones with a bit of salt in there for zip; b25 well, if anyone can show me a better-balanced whisky than this you know where to get hold of me. You open a bottle of this at your peril: best to do so in the company of friends. Either way, it will be empty before the night is over. *43%. Nikka.*

Pure Malt Black batch 06F54B (92) n24 great balance to the nose with a careful sprinkling of barley, honey, peat and oak – but never too much of any; t24 massive, ultra-intense sweet malt with a delicate sub-stratum of smoke; a spiced fruitiness also cranks up the weight and depth; f21 vanilla kicks in as it thins surprisingly fast; b23 not the finish of old, but everything else is present and correct for a cracker! *43%. Nikka.*

Pure Malt Red batch 02C30B (86) n21 t21 f22 b22. A light malt that appears heavier than it actually is with an almost imperceptible oiliness. *43%. Nikka.*

Pure Malt Red batch 06F54C (84) n21 t22 f20 b21. Oak is the pathfinder here, but the oily vanilla-clad barley is light and mouth-watering. *43%. Nikka.*

Pure Malt White batch 02C30C (92) n23 massive, Islay-style peat with a fresh sea kick thanks to brine amid the barley; t24 again, the peat-reek hangs firmly on the tastebuds from the word go, the sweetness of the barley tempered by some drying oaky notes suggesting reasonable age. Lots of subtle oils bind the complexity; f22 liquorice and salt combine to create a powerful malty-oak combo. An oily, kippery smokiness continues to the very end; b23 a big peaty number displaying the most subtle of hands. *43%. Nikka.*

Pure Malt White batch 06J26 (91) n22 soft peat interrupted by gentle oak; t23 biting, nippy malt offering a degree of orangey-citrus fruit amid the building smoke; f22 sweet vanilla and light smoke that dries towards a salty, tangy, liquorice finish; b24 a sweet malt, but one with such deft use of peat and oak that one never really notices. Real class. *43%.*

Pure Malt White batch 10F46C (90) n23 the quality of the delicate peat is beyond reproach; some attractive kumquat juices it up nicely; t23 wonderful balance between silky-soft and nail-hard malts with some tasty local oak getting in on the act; f22 the smoke lessens to allow vanilla and toffee dominance; a sawdusty dryness brings down the curtain; b22 there is a peculiarly Japanese feel to this delicately peated delight. *43%*

Southern Alps Pure Malt (93) n24 bananas and freshly pooled lemon skin. one of the world's most refreshing and exhilarating whisky noses; t23 crisp youngish malts, as one might suspect from the nose, mouthwatering and as a clean as an Alpine stream; f22 some vanilla development and a late slightly creamy flourish but finished with a substantial and startling malty rally boasting a very discreet sweetness; b24 this is a bottle I have only to look at to start salivating. Sadly, though, I drink sparingly from it as it is a hard whisky to find, even in Japan. Fresh, clean and totally stunning, the term "pure malt" could not be more apposite. Fabulous whisky: a very personal favourite. *40%. Suntory.*

Super Nikka Vatted Pure Malt (76) n20 t19 f19 b18. Decent and chewy but something doesn't quite click with this one. *55.5%. Nikka.*

Taketsuru Pure Malt 12 Years Old (80) n19 t22 f19 b20. For its age, heavier than a sumo wrestler. But perhaps a little more agile over the tastebuds. Lovely silkiness impresses, but lots of toffee. *40%. Nikka.*

Taketsuru Pure Malt 17 Years Old (89) n21 firm oak, but compromises sufficiently to allow several layers of malt to battle through with a touch of peat-coffee; t22 massive: a toasted, honeyed front gives way to really intense and complex malt notes; **f23** superb. Some late marmalade arrives from somewhere: the toast is slightly burnt but the waves of malty complexity are endless; **b23** not a whisky for the squeamish. This is big stuff – about as big as it gets without peat or rye. No bar shelf or whisky club should be without one. *43%. Nikka.*

Taketsuru Pure Malt 21 Years Old (88) n22 middle-aged bourbon with a heavy, vaguely honeyed malt presence; **t21** the oak remains quite fresh and chewy. Again, the malt is massive; **f22** sweet, oily and more honey arrives; **b23** a much more civilised and gracious offering than the 17-y-o: there is certainly nothing linear about the character development from Taketsuru 12 to 21 inclusive. Serious whisky for the serious whisky drinker. *43%. Nikka.*

Zen (84) n19 t22 f22 b21. Sweet, gristy malt; light and clean. *40%. Suntory.*

Japanese Single Grain

Nikka Single Cask Coffey Grain Whisky Aged 12 Years "Woody & Mellow" (93) n22 delicate vanalins and tannins; **t24** sweet and yielding (probably corn) with layers of drying spices. Stupendous; **f23** long, with subtle oils lengthening the grain effect and spice; more vanilla at the very death...eventually. Vague bourbony tones towards the finale; **b24** exceptional grain whisky by any standards – and helps explain why Japanese blends are so damn good!! *55%. Nikka.*

Nikka Single Cask Coffey Grain 12 Years Old 70th Anniversary (85) n20 biting, nose, tingling oak; **t22** massive oak delivery sweetened and soothed by the rich grain; lush and brilliantly weighted throughout; **f22** long liquorice and cocoa tones are met by some bitter, zesty, oaky notes; **b21** more woody than the "woody and mellow". *58%. Nikka.*

Nikka Single Cask Coffey Grain Aged Over 13 Years batch 20 116399, dist 1992, bott 2005 db **(85) n22 t23 f20 b20.** Distinctly subdued by this brand's normal high standards, though the early bourbon riches are mesmerizing. The finish, though attractive, is too simplistic. *62%. sc.*

Nikka Single Cask Coffey Grain Whisky 1991 dist 1 Oct 91, bott 12 May 03 db **(93) n22 t24 f23 b24.** I have tasted much Japanese straight grain over the years but this is the first time in bottled form for public consumption. And Nikka have exceeded themselves. Forget the word "grain" and its inferior connotations. This is a monster whisky from the bourbon family you are unlikely ever to forget. Use the first couple of mouthfuls for a marker: once you get the idea, life will never quite be the same again. Track down...and be consumed. *61.9%*

Nikka Single Cask Coffey Grain 1992 dist 31.2.92, bott 25.7.06 db **(95) n24** a curious mixture with hints of Japanese oak (from the cask heads?) and a bourbony, hickory edge. Rich and rousing; **t24** sweet, flushed with maize and a silky body, almost verging on demerara. Honeyed and revelling in its bourbon theme; **f23** vanilla layers, again with a deep, delicious touch of molasses; **b24** make no mistake: this grain is as entertaining as any malt. Those loving high-class bourbon will be thrilled. *57%. France.*

Blends

Ajiwai Kakubin (*see Kakubin Ajiwai*)

Black Nikka Aged 8 Years (82) n20 t21 f21 b20. Beautifully bourbony, especially on the nose. Lush, silky and great fun. Love it! *40%. Nikka.*

The Blend of Nikka (90) n21 a dry, oaky buzz infiltrates some firm grain and sweeter malt; **t23** brilliant! Absolutely outstanding explosion of clean grassy malts thudding into the tastebuds with confidence and precision: mouthwatering and breath-catching; **f22** delightful grain bite to follow the malt; **b24** an adorable blend that makes you sit up and take notice of every enormous mouthful. Classy, complex, charismatic and brilliantly balanced. *45%*

Evermore (90) n22 big age, salt and outstanding malt riches to counter the oak; **t23** more massive oak wrapped in a bourbony sweetness with glorious malts and a salty, spicy tang; **f22** long, sweet malt and crisp grains: plenty to chew on and savour; **b23** top-grade, well-aged blended whisky with fabulous depth and complexity that never loses its sweet edge despite the oak. *40%. Kirin.*

Ginko (78.5) n20.5 t20 f19 b19. Soft – probably too soft as it could do with some shape and attitude to shrug off the caramel. *46%. Number One Drinks Company.*

Golden Horse Busyuu Deluxe (93) n22 some decent signs of age with some classy oak alongside smoke: sexy stuff; **t24** enormous flavour profile simply because it is so fresh: massive malt presence, some of it peaty, bananas and under-ripe grapes; **f23** clean malt and some sharpish grain with a touch of bite, continuing to tantalise the tastebuds for a long time; **b24** whoever blended this has a genuine feel for whisky: a classic in its own right and one of astonishing complexity and textbook balance. *43%. Toa. To celebrate the year 2000.*

Hibiki (82) n20 t19 f23 b20. The grains here are fresh, forceful and merciless, the malts bouncing off them meekly. Lovely cocoa finale. A blend that brings a tear to the eye. Hard stuff – perfect after a hard day! Love it! *43%. Suntory.*

Hibiki 12 Years Old (89) n21.5 lots of vanilla and boiled yam; **t22** a fizzing delivery with an impressive, slightly juicy marriage between barley and oak. The grains offer a light oily diversion; **f22.5** the spices begun in the middle ground begin to really take effect and work well with the lightly sugared oaks; **b23** a thoughtful blend which improves greatly and develops a rhythm the longer it goes on. *43%. Suntory.*

Hibiki 17 Years Old (85.5) n22 t22 f20 b21.5. Much richer and honeyed than before: the degree of oak on the nose and molasses half way through are a delight. If they can just inject some life into the toffeed finish, this'd quite superb. *43%. Suntory.*

Hibiki 21 Years Old (89.5) n24 big signature as always. Those big cherry and kumquats I always associate with this blend are there in force, as the sweet richness of the old bourbony character. But the smoke appears to be missing, though no damage done to the balance, though the weight is down slightly; **t23** not surprisingly, it's the bourbon style first out of the traps – and with some grace, too: as soft and silky as you like; **f20.5** buttery cocoa but the sherry involvement is represented by a slight sulphurous buzz; **b22** a change of character from last time; the smoke has drifted away, a bit of extra fruit and although nothing like so great a finish, still a charmer. *43%. Suntory.*

Hibiki 50.5 Non Chillfiltered 17 Years Old (84) n22 t22 f20 b20. Pleasant enough in its own right. But against what this particular expression so recently was, hugely disappointing. Last year I lamented the extra use of caramel. This year it has gone through the roof, taking with it all the fineness of complexity that made this blend exceptional. Time for the blending lab to start talking to the bottling hall and sort this out. I want one of the great whiskies back...!! *50.5%. Suntory.*

Hibiki 21 Years Old (93) n24 fruitier notes of cherry and sherry with a triumphal triumvirate of intense malt, the subtlest of peat smoke and leathery oak combining for maximum, stupendous complexity, also a dash of kumquats; **t22** fat and oily, like the nose hinting slightly at bourbon but the grains thin the middle out sufficiently to let the malt, mildly peaty and otherwise, through; **f23** long and intense with more lightly orchestrated smoke and lashings of late, grapey fruit and a build-up of, first, sweet malts, then a drier, spicier oak; **b24** when people refer to Yoichi as the exception that proves the rule about Japanese whisky, I tend to point them in the direction of this. If I close my eyes and taste this, cherry blossom really does form in my mind's eye. *43%. Suntory.*

Hibiki 30 Years Old (88) n21 less smoky than before, a touch of soap and no shortage of bourbon honeycomb; **t22** sweet delivery with that Kentuckian drawl to the middle; **f22** long, with some extra molasses to the finale; a few extra splinters of oak, too; **b23** still remains a very different animal from most other whiskies you might find: the smoke may have vanished somewhat but the sweet oakiness continues to draw its own unique map. *43%. Suntory.*

Hibiki 30 Years Old (87) n21 curious mix of peat and bourbon; **t22** sweet, fat oak: bourbon all the way; **f22** the glorious rich-textured sweetness continues forever; **b22** Kentuckians would really go for this one: the smoke might confuse them a little, though. Pretty unique the world over. *43%. Suntory.*

Hokuto (86) n22 t24 f19 b21. a bemusing blend. At its peak, this is quite superb, cleverly blended whisky. The finish, though, suggests a big caramel input. If the caramel is natural, it should be tempered. If it is added for colouring purposes, then I **don't see** the point of having the whisky non-chillfiltered in the first place. *50.5%. ncf. Suntory.*

⋯ **Ichiro's Blend Aged 33 Years (84) n20 t22 f21 b21.** Silky and sweet. But the creamy fudge effect appears to wipe out anything important the oak may have to say. Pleasing spices towards the end, though. *48% Venture Whisky Ltd*

Imperial (81) n20 t22 f19 b20. Flinty, hard grain softened by malt and vanilla but toffee dulled. *43%. Suntory.*

Kakubin (92) n23 lemon zest and refreshing grain: wonderful; **t23** light, mouthwatering, ultra-juicy with soft barley sub-strata; true melt-in-the-mouth stuff; **f22** long, with charming vanilla but touched by toffee; **b24** absolutely brilliant blend of stunningly refreshing and complex character. One of the most improved brands in the world. *40%. Suntory.*

Kakubin Ajiwai (82) n20 t21 f20 b21. Usual Kakubin hard grain and mouthwatering malt, with this time a hint of warming stem ginger. *40%. Suntory.*

Kakubin Kuro 43° (89) n22 a confusing but sexy mix of what appear to be old oak and burnt toffee; **t23** fabulous weight on arrival with again the oak in the vanguard but controlled by a malty, chewy-toffee arm; **f22** long with soft vanillins and toffee; **b22** big, chewy whisky with ample evidence of old age but such is the intrusion of caramel it's hard to be entirely sure. *43%. Suntory.*

Kakubin New (90) n21 gritty grain with very hard malt to accompany it; **t24** stunning mouth arrival with heaps of mouthwatering young malt and then soft grain and oil. Brilliant stuff; **f21** some beautiful cocoa notes round off the blend perfectly; **b24** seriously divine blending: a refreshing dram of the top order. *40%. Suntory.*

Kirin Whisky Tarujuku 50° (93) n22.5 some prickly oak and prickly pear; **t24** what a delight...! A delivery from the heavens: the combination of malt, grain and oak all appear to be equally divided here, but rather than arriving in layers they erupt upon the palate together. The shockwaves are sweet ones, with subtle molasses infiltrating the oak; **f23** long, cleverly oiled and still with those lightly sugared vanillas having much to say. The balance isn't for one second compromised; **b23.5** a blend not afraid to make a statement and does so boldly. A sheer joy. *50%. Kirin Distillery Co Ltd.*

Master's Blend Aged 10 Years (87) n21 t23 f22 b21. Chewy, big and satisfying. *40%. Mercian/Karuizawa.*

New Kakubin Suntory *(see Kakubin New)*

Nikka Master Blend Blended Whisky 12 Years Old 70th Anniversary (94) n24 nothing shy or retiring here: big oak, big sherry. A little nervousness with the smoke, maybe; **t23** lush, silky grain arrives and then carries intensely sweet malt and weightier grape; **f24** dries as the oak takes centre stage. But the peripheral fruit malt, gentle smoke and grain combine to offer something not dissimilar to fruit and nut chocolate; **b23** an awesome blend swimming in top quality sherry. Perhaps a fraction too much sweetness on the arrival, but I am nit-picking. A blend for those who like their whiskies to have something to say. And this one just won't shut up. *58%. Nikka.*

The Nikka Whisky Aged 34 Years blended and bottled in 99 **(93) n23 t23 f24 b23.** A Japanese whisky of antiquity that has not only survived many passing years, but has actually achieved something of stature and sophistication. Over time I have come to appreciate this whisky immensely. It is among the world's greatest blends, no question. *43%. Nikka.*

Nikka Whisky Tsuru Aged 17 Years (94) n23 the usual fruity suspects one associates with a Tsuru blend, especially the apple and oranges. But the grains are now making a bourbony impact, too; **t24** advanced level textbook delivery here because the marriage between fruit, grain and oak is about as well integrated as you might wish for; simperingly soft yet enough rigidity for the malts to really count and the palate to fully appreciate all the complexities offered; **f23** brushed with cocoa, a touch of sultana and some gripping spices, too; only the caramel detracts; **b24** unmistakingly Tsuru in character, very much in line, profile-wise, with the original bottling and if the caramel was cut this could challenge as a world whisky of the year. *43%*

Robert Brown (91) n22.5 the grain really has kicked this one on towards a leathery bourbon; **t23** clean, sweet, brown sugars with a juicy sub plot; **f22.5** lovely spices accompany the custardy vanilla; **b23** just love these clean but full-flavoured blends: a real touch of quality here. *43%. Kirin Brewery Company Ltd.*

Royal 12 Years Old (91) n23 chalky and dry, but malt and oranges – and now some extra juicy grape - add character; just a soupcon of smoke adds the perfect weight; **t23** fabulously complex arrival on the palate with some grainy nip countered by sparkling malt and where once there was smoke there is now ultra clean sherry; **f22** the grains and oak carry on as the spice builds; **b23** a splendidly blended whisky with complexity being the main theme. Beautiful stuff that appears recently to have, nose apart, traded smoke for grape. *43%*

Royal Aged 15 Years (95) n25 soft ribbons of smoke tie themselves to a kumquat and sherry flag; supremely well weighted and balanced with the grains and malts united by invisible strands; **t24** few whiskies achieve such a beautifully soft and rounded delivery: there is no dominance on arrival as the tastebuds are confronted by a silky marriage of all that is found on the nose, aided and abetted by luxurious grain; **f22** a degree of toffee slightly hinders the fade but the lightness of touch is spellbinding; **b24** unquestionably one of the great blends of the world that can be improved only by a reduction of toffee input. Sensual blending that every true whisky lover must experience: a kind of Japanese Old Parr 18. *43%. Suntory.*

Shirokaku (79) n19 t21 f20 b19. Some over-zealous toffee puts a cap on complexity. Good spices, though. *40%. Suntory.*

Special Reserve 10 Years Old (94) n23 magnificent approach of rich fruit buttressed by firm, clear grain. Some further fruity spices reveal some age is evident; **t24** complex from the off with a tidal tsunami of malt crashing over the tastebuds. The grain holds firm and supports some budding fruit; **f23** a touch of something peaty and pliable begins to take shape with some wonderful malty spices coating the mouth; **b24** a beguiling whisky of near faultless complexity. Blending at its peak. *43%. Suntory.*

Special Reserve Aged 12 Years (89) n21 peaches and cream with a dollop of caramel; **t24** luxurious delivery of perfect weight and softness to body; the barley sweetness works beautifully with the buzz of oak and yielding grains; **f21** caramel-coffee crème from a box of chocs; **b23** a tactile, voluptuous malt that wraps itself like a sated lover around the tastebuds, though the complexity is compromised very slightly by bigger caramel than the 10-y-o. *40%. Suntory.*

Suntory Old (87) n21 dusty and fruity. Attractive nip and balance; **t24** mouthwatering from the off with a rich array of chewy, clean fresh malt: textbook standard, complete with bite; **f20** thins out far quicker than it once did leaving the vanilla to battle it out with toffee; **b22** a delicate and comfortable blend that just appears to have over-simplified itself on the finale. Delicious, but can be much better than this. *40%*

Suntory Old Mild and Smooth (84) n19 t22 f21 b22. Chirpy and lively around the palate, the grains soften the crisp malts wonderfully. *40%*

Suntory Old Rich and Mellow (91) n22 very lightly smoked with healthy maltiness; an extra touch of older oaks in the most recent bottling helps the balance and works wonders; **t23** complex, fat and chewy, no shortage of deep malty tones, including a touch of smoke; **f23** sweeter malts see off the grain, excellent spices; **b23** a pretty malt-rich blend with the grains offering a fat base. Impressive blending. *43%*

Super Nikka (93) n23 excellent crisp, grassy malt base bounces off firm grain. A distant hint of peat, maybe, offers a little weighty extra; **t23** an immediate starburst of rich, mouthwatering and entirely uncompromising malt that almost over-runs the tastebuds; **f23** soft, fabulously intrinsic peaty notes from the Yoichi School give brilliant length and depth. But the cocoa notes from the oak-wrapped grain also offer untold riches; **b24** a very, very fine blend which makes no apology whatsoever for the peaty complexity of Yoichi malt. Now, with less caramel, it's pretty classy stuff. However, Nikka being Nikka you might find the occasional bottling that is entirely devoid of peat, more honeyed and lighter in style (21-22-23-23 Total 89 – no less a quality turn, obviously). Either way, an absolutely brilliant day-to-day, anytime, any place dram. One of the true 24-carat, super nova commonplace blends not just in Japan, but in the world. *43%. Nikka.*

Super Nikka Rare Old batch 02I18D **(90.5) n22** toffeed but no shortage of lively barley bouncing against firm grain; some playful fruit, mainly greengages, ensures extra freshness; **t23** superb arrival with a shimmering barley sweetness fending off the drier vanillas: the balance is spot on here. Remains delicately mouth-watering though it is milky mocha which arrives, not the peat I normally find here; **f22.5** remains happily on its vanilla course but some soft cocoa and fruit also plays along; **b23** beautiful whisky which just sings a lilting malty refrain. Strange, though, to find it peatless. *43%. Nikka.*

Torys (76) n18 t19 f20 b19. Lots of toffee in the middle and at the end of this one. The grain used is top class and chewy. *37%. Suntory.*

Torys Whisky Square (80) n19 t20 f21 b20. At first glance very similar to Torys, but very close scrutiny reveals slightly more "new loaf" nose and a better, spicier and less toffeed finale. *37%. Suntory.*

Tsuru (93) n23 apples, cedar, crushed pine nuts, blood oranges and soft malt, all rather chalky and soft – and unusually peatless for Nikka; **t24** fantastic grain bite bringing with it a mouthwateringly clean and fresh attack of sweet and lip-smacking malt; **f22** a continuation of untaxing soft malts and gathering oak, a slight "Malteser" candy quality to it, and then some late sultana fruitiness; **b24** gentle and beautifully structured, genuinely mouthwatering, more-ish and effortlessly noble. If they had the confidence to cut the caramel, this would be even higher up the charts as one of the great blends of the world. As it is, in my house we pass the ceramic Tsuru bottle as one does the ship's decanter. And it empties very quickly. *43%. Nikka.*

The Whisky (88) n22 t22 f21 b23. A really rich, confident and well-balanced dram. *43% Suntory.*

White (80) n19 t21 f20 b20. Boring nose but explodes on the palate for a fresh, mouth-watering classic blend bite. *40%. Suntory.*

Za (79) n19 t21 f19 b20. Some lively boisterous grain offers a suet-pudding chewiness. A little bitter on the finish. *40%. Suntory.*

European Whisky

The beaurocrats at the EU will be delighted: Europe is expanding. Well, at least in terms of whisky. For a start, England now boasts a commercially available malt whisky and Denmark is not very far behind. While the number of distilleries operating in Germany, Switzerland and Austria appears forever on the increase.

It means that this section of the Whisky Bible has been expanded for the second year running, though it still has to be said that most of the whiskies remain devilishly hard to find. Indeed, have you ever tasted a European mainland whisky – or an island one, like St George's from Norfolk? I thought not. Do you know anyone who has? No? Hardly surprising. For all the new distilleries springing up in so many countries, and considering the high quality of a good many, tracking down and drinking them is as much an art form as the whisky actually being made.

The problem is that the vast majority of these whiskies come from such small stills that the limited output rarely gets beyond local bars and restaurants or visitors who make the pilgrimage to whichever of these tiny distilleries they can find. In some ways this is part of the charm. Some of the distilleries you find in Switzerland and Austria in particular are almost throwbacks to the Scottish highlands of 200 years ago, or Virginia, Pennsylvania and Kentucky of the same period, when farms would include a still to make the most of the surplus grain. And, just like those embryonic distilleries of the early 19th century, they would make their whisky from whichever grain they could grow. Distilleries where the land and spirit were as one.

The most vivid example of this is probably in Sweden. So it is always a magnificent and heart-warming experience to get over to Mackmyra to see how they had turned what had been among the most sub atomic of micro distilleries into something that you would expect to find somewhere in a Scottish glen. It is a distillery which every single small distiller in Europe should take the time to see. And a whisky they must taste. Not for the first time they have carried off the Jim Murray's Whisky Bible European Whisky of the Year Award: for this 2011 edition with their Brukswhisky, which is about their most delicate and sophisticated bottling yet – a long way removed from their early, slightly bludgeoning style.

So that means no award this time round for the outstanding St George's distillery, which launched its first whisky in December 2009 to enormous national and international interest. Their entire stocks sold out in days. To be honest, despite the publicity and hype, in 2010 England was not even close in quality to take on the world and get gold, and by 2012 there is still pretty little chance of getting the European award. Well, so much for its abysmal football team. But as for its whisky, being best in Europe by then is a distinct possibility. A few hours tasting away in their warehouse convinced me they had the diversity and quality in stock to make people sit up and take note for some while to come; without question their peated spirit, the first year's stock made by legendary Laphroaig distillery manager Iain Henderson...and it shows.

The year 2012 will also be when the Stauning Distillery in Denmark will launch their first single malt. Having popped along there last March to view one of the most exciting developments in European whisky since the building of St. George's, it is hard to be other than impressed with their set up, especially their maltings, and maturing spirit which, like Mackmyra, St. George's and Penderyn in Wales, enjoys an excellent middle cut. By contrast, one of the things that is instantly noticeable with many of the European whiskies from smaller distilleries is the amount of feints kicking about the glass after the whisky has been poured. This is usually a result of the cut being too wide, often because the stills are so small. But to enjoy the whiskies at their best you could do worse than leave them in an open glass in a very warm room to allow the higher alcohols to evaporate. You will usually be pleasantly surprised by the results. If an hour of that hasn't done the trick, you – and the whisky – might have a problem. And that is probably the rub: with the bigger new distilleries comes consistency, with the smaller throughout Europe often comes flashes of brilliance.

As I pointed out last year, some of these distillers may decide to take that extra step and expand. Or they might stick with what they know, keep expenditure and investment down and carry on as they are going. There really is no right or wrong way. At Stauning one of the founders has now gone full time and that bodes well for them, as this was the path taken at Mackmyra, Penderyn and St George.

Meanwhile, my friend Julia Nourney has continued her sojourn to the new frontiers of the Germany and the Alpine countries, bringing me back for me samples which fascinate, entertain and frustrate in equal measures. How I envy her....

AUSTRIA
ACHENSEE'R EDELBRENNEREI FRANZ KOSTENZER Maurach. Working.

Whisky Alpin Grain Whisky Hafer bott code L1/2005 db **(92) n24** one of the firmest, cleanest oat noses I have come across for a year or two: porridge with muscovado sugar melting on top and even gooseberries offering a fruity respite; **t22** a bit too firm and oaky at first, maybe, though the sweetness and spices try to confirm complexity; **f23** even better as the spicy oats and butterscotch tart find a tasty compromise; **b23** if you are looking for a whisky with a personality, you've just found it... 44%

Whisky Alpin Rye & Malt bott code L1/2005 db **(87.5) n21.5** the fruity rye dominates; **t23** brilliant delivery where the brain can barely cope with the complexity: sweet, juicy lush rye abounds but there are much darker, spicier notes to contest their dominance; **f21** over bitters out; **b22** despite the feinty sub plot, this is one very impressive distillery. 40%

BRENNEREI EBNER Absam. Working.

Absamer Whisky bott code L2305 db **(79.5) n23 t17 f21.5 b18.** This job of mine prepares you for most things. But not this. What the bloody hell has just hit me....? It was going so well with the nose: punchy oak, but not a normal oak varietal, it seemed to me. Some kind of rare European species, I wondered? Whatever it was, the balance between sweet and dry was pretty bang-on and the complexity levels were falling off the page. And then, on delivery, it seared my tastebuds like a blowtorch. Not from the strength, but simply the sheer viciousness of the oak – which arrives only after a few lovely nanoseconds of sweetness lulls you into a completely false sense of security. A liquorice, walnut oil and maple syrup (more wood) sweetness salvages the job. 50%

BRENNEREI LAGLER Kukmirn. Working.

Best Korn Burgenland bott 2007 db **(84) n20 t22 f21 b21.** A strange paprika and hop nose, though the body is fruity and sweet. 43%

Pannonia Korn Malt bott 2007 db **(85.5) n21.5 t21.5 f21 b21.5.** Easy drinking whisky with a charming, stimulating sweetness and light though lush finish. 40%

Pannonia Blend bott 2008 db **(83.5) n19 t22 f21 b21.5.** The strength means this is not actually whisky by native European standards. And you fear the worst with the feinty nose. But pans out pleasantly and sweetly, as is the house style. 38.5%

DESTILLERIE GEORG HIEBL Haag. Working.

George Hiebl Mais Whisky 2004 db **(93) n23** the corn is unmistakable and the cask must be pretty new oak, too: a few spices flit around whilst the lighter of the varied sweetness looks like a delicate dose of maple syrup; best of all though is the unmistakable aroma of newly bound and laid hay bales...just fabulous...**t23.5** melt-in-the-mouth corn and treacle with a real sheen to the coppery, honey notes; light red liquorice dissolves in with the ascending vanilla; **f23** chewy toffee, a touch of cocoa and molasses...and more small still copper; **b23.5** more bourbon in character than some American bourbons I know...!! Beautifully matured, brilliantly matured and European whisky of the very highest order, Ye.. haahhhh!! 43%

George No. 1 Aged 5 Years db **(86) n22 t22 f20 b22.** Much more perfumy and oily with honeycomb rather than honey. 40%

George No. 2 Aged 5 Years bott code L1/09 db **(84.5) n21.5 t21 f22 b20.** Very pleasant in part. But much of its bourbony personality seems to be shaped from laying in a bed of caramel....making it rather Canadian 41.8%

DESTILLERIE KAUSL Mühldorf, Wachau. Working.

Wachauer Whisky "G" Single Barrel Gerste (Barley) bott code L6WG db **(90.5) n22** sweet, soft, clean, mildly buttery; **t23** impressive mouth-feel: the light oils work superbly, and the arrival of sweet barley is without fanfare...very natural, indeed; **f22.5** long, retains a gristy sweetness as the vanillas build; **b23** absolutely charming and well made malt. 40%

Wachauer Whisky "H" Single Barrel Hafer (Oat) bott code L1WH db **(88) n21.5** chunky with good oak but a touch of drying tobacco, too. The oats offer a sweet respite in the strange, smoky atmosphere; **t21.5** a confused delivery, with some very sweet and very bitter notes not quite on talking terms. The bitterness heads towards bitter cherry, the sweetness is rather more molassed. By the middle, they have relaxed delightfully; **f23** the best part of the experience with sweetened liquorice heading towards a slight milky cofffe finale; **b22** I can safely say that no whisky in the world has quite this signature. A unique and ultimately very enjoyable whisky. 40%

Wachauer Whisky "R" Single Barrel Roggen (Rye) bott code L2WR db (**86.5**) **n21 t22 f23.5 b21.** A real eyebrow-raiser. Bloody hell!! Where do I start...? OK: butyric nose...not good. Way, way too much oak...not good. Yet...also on the nose: superb fruitiness to the unmistakable rye; ditto the sharp juiciness on delivery. This really is rye whisky with knobs on. Like others from this distillery, there is a lovely mocha-coffee slant to the, frankly, astonishing finish. Technically, an absolute nightmare that should be taken out and shot. In effect – and as much as I hate to say it....bloody delicious...!!! 40%

Wachauer Whisky "W" Single Barrel Weizen (Wheat) bott code L1WW db (**76.5**) **n19 t18.5 f20.5 b18.5.** A feinty heavyweight which has real problems finding its direction and balance. Only when some molasses and cocoa form towards the end does it take shape. 40%

DESTILLERIE ROGNER Rappottenstein. Working.

Rogner Waldviertel Whisky No. 2 db (**86**) **n21.5 t21 f22 b21.5.** Toasted almonds and light molasses make for enjoyable and oily whisky. I wish more of their whiskies were as good as this. 42.7%

Rogner Waldviertel Whisky 3/3 db (**77.5**) **n17.5 t20 f21 b19.** Once you get past the startling nose, which is more akin to certain forms of Scandinavian aquavit than whisky, the rest of the journey is sweet and easy. Though still pretty unwhisky-ish. 42%

Rogner Waldviertel Whisky 3/3 Malz db (**87.5**) **n19.5** hmmm. A few technical hiccups here, but if you are fan of chocolate nougat... **t23.5** massive oily delivery with sweet, nutty flavours on full throttle. Loads of mocha comes screeching through early on and you have to admit that this is fun stuff; **f22** all kinds of sharp cherry candy while the milky mocha continues; **b22.5** hang on to your hats: this one plays for shocks. Look forward to visiting this distillery to work out what the hell they are up to there. Absolutely love it! 65%

Rogner Waldviertel Rye Whisky No. 13 db (**83**) **n20 t21.5 f20.5 b21.** Drying tobacco nose and not quite the cleanest delivery. But an attractive rye fruitiness does has something to say, aided and abetted by some toffee and oil. 41%

DESTILLERIE WEUTZ St. Nikolai im Sausal. Working.

Hot Stone Single Malt db (**88**) **n21.5** reminds me of a spiced biscuit I've come across from time to time in Eastern Europe, the name of which, annoyingly, escapes me; **t23** wonderful with burnt honeycomb and fudge all over the place; the bitter-sweet ratio just couldn't be better; **f21.5** technically unsound, but really so much beautiful malt-vanilla-walnut interaction, you have to give it a tick; **b22** the Arnold Schwarzenegger of Austrian whisky: huge, muscle-bound....and a bit of a friendly giant. Technically, the finish needs some attention; and it could do with a tweak here and there from onwards, really. But just one of those drams that demands a second glassful – even when you are still like to be in a state of wonder and shock from the very first arrival. Delicious! 67.1%

Hot Stone Single Malt Single Cask db code L 041411/01 db (**88.5**) **n21** forensically flawed, but effectively attractive nougat amid rich barley; **t23** seems to be wrapped in caramel, but this is big malt, expanding forever, moving into sweeter, fatter territory; **f22** really kicks in with a coppery screech that gets young tongue working flat; for a second something slightly smoky kicks in; **b22.5** exhausting to taste, as the brain has to go into overdrive to work out what the hell is going on! 42.1%

REISETBAUER Axberg, Thening. Working.

Reisetbauer Single Malt 7 Years Old Chardonnay and sweet wine cask, bott code LWH 099 db (**85.5**) **n19 t21 f23.5 b22.** Well it takes some time. But it gets there in the end. A less than impressive nose is followed by a rocky delivery. But the panning out is truly spectacular as harmony is achieved with a rich honey and nougat mix, helped along the way with pecan nuts and figs. The finish is like a top rank trifle and fruitcake mix. A whisky of two halves. 43%

Reisetbauer Single Malt 12 Years Old Limited Edition db (**85**) **n18.5 t21.5 f23 b22.** A remarkably similar story to the 7-y-o, though a touch silkier, with less sweetness and not quite so much complexity at the death. Even so, a dram to find. 48%

Reisetbauer Single Malt Whisky 1998 Destilliert db (**86.5**) **n20.5 t21 f22.5 b22.5.** A large, rambling malt bursting at the seams with character and charm. Ten years in the cask appears to have seen off the worst of the odd distilling blemish. Bravo for bottling at full strength, because the spices are seen to best effect, as is the barley which tries to find a sugared course, but narrowly fails. Substantial weight throughout and an excellent length to the finish. The toasty dryness is also a delight. I can't wait to see further bottlings from this obviously polished distillery. Impressive and desirable. 56%

WHISKY-DESTILLERIE J. HAIDER Roggenreith. Working.

⟐ **Single Malt J.H.** bott code L 3/03 db **(86) n21 t21.5 f22.5 b21.** Rich and robust, for the odd brief moment it displays the character of a malt heading somewhere towards its 40th birthday: the oak certainly makes an impact here. Plenty of honeycomb to delight. *41%*

⟐ **Special Single Malt "Karamell" J.H.** bott code L 2/03 db **(80.5) n19 t21 f20.5 b20.** The sugars, most of them dark and rich, appear to be welded on to the malty body. I am sure I have grown a few extra hairs on my chest, taking on this oily slugger. *41%*

Single Malt Selection J.H. L7/02 db **(86) n22 t21 f21.5 b21.5.** A pretty, layered, nose, sporting excellent oak integration. Doesn't quite hit the same heights on the palate where sugars and certain oils, some bitter, dominate. Good biscuity tail off, alternating between caramelized dunking fare and sweet digestive. Molasses abounds. Deceptively enjoyable. *46%*

Original Rye J.H. L2/02 db **(82) n20.5 t21 f20.5 b20.** Some quiet spice and aggression amid the sleepy toffee. *41%*

⟐ **Original Rye-Whisky J.H.** bott code L 5/03 db **(93.5) n24** one of the cleanest rye noses ever from the distillery: I could be in Kentucky!! Beautifully fruity and entirely unambiguous; **t23.5** mouth-watering rye that's just a little softer on delivery than you'd expect. Reigns supreme for a comparatively short time before the oak enters with an egg-custard flourish; **f23** long finish with some spicy candy balls **b23** a masterpiece from a distillery located in an area named after rye...how fitting! *41%*

⟐ **Pure Rye Malt J.H.** bott code L 6/03 db **(83) n18.5 t22 f21 b21.5.** Here's a "Nougat" one, too, though they've advertised "caramel"! Butyric in part, there is still enough wholesome rye percolating through to give the taste buds a charming, sugar-crisp rye platform from which to watch the developing vanillas, mochas and caramels. After the shock of the nose, enjoyable. *41%*

Pure Rye Malt J.H. L14/02 db **(92) n23** a sprig of lavender bolsters the fruity intensity; **t23.5** clean, intense rye. Mouth-watering firm, hard, flinty – exactly how it should be; **f22.5** grains of brown sugar spike up the rye's fruity finale; **b23** some of the most beautifully made whisky I have come across for a little while. This is absolutely top grade European rye whisky. And all the better when left in the glass for 20 minutes before drinking. *41%*

⟐ **Special Rye Malt "Nougat" J.H.** bott code L 1/03 db **(77.5) n17 t21 f19.5 b20.** A huge, oily beast of a whisky. For "Special" and "Nougat" read feinty... *41%*

Pure Special Rye Malt "Nougat" J.H. L13/02 db **(78) n19.5 t20 f20 b19.5.** A little fat. A little feinty. A little bitter. *41%*

Special Single Malt "Karamell" J.H. L15/02 db **(74) n18 t19.5 f17.5 b19.** Just too many feints to work. *41%*

Special Single Malt Selection J.H. L15/02 db **(84.5) n20.5 t22 f21 b21.** Attractively simplistic. The malt has the upper hand throughout and there is extra weight and fizz from the slightly feinty oils. *46%*

DESTILLERIE WEIDENAUER Kottes. Working.

Waldviertler Single Malt db **(75) n18 t19 f19 b19.** Heavy, lush oily and with a big oak signature. The feel is that the cut taken has been very wide, indeed. *42%*

Waldviertler Dinkelmalz (2008 award label on neck) db **(77.5) n18.5 t21 f19 b19.** A bit rough round the edges from time to time, though the citrus on delivery charms. *42%*

Waldviertler Dinkelmalz (A La carte label on neck) db **(89) n22.5** a clean, fascinating battle between the malt and oak. Vanilla appears to just about win out; **t23** like on the nose, two factions battle it out for supremacy, ensuring a lovely degree of complexity. An adroit sweetness ensures a fresh, gristy feel; **f21.5** bitters out slightly, but there's a touch of chocolate mint chip to compensate; **b22** now that's far more like what I expect from this usually excellent distillery. *42%*

Waldviertler Dinkel (2008 Silber Medaille label on neck) db **(90) n19.5** ooops. Promises much but the stray butyric note pegs this one back; **t23** a beautiful concoction of pulpy apple, the lightest sprinkling of muscovado sugar all glued together by outstanding oils. While the grain simply pulses in happy tandem with the oak; **f23.5** actually ups the anti complexity-wise and now those extra feints are actually piling on the depth and length: what a treat...!! **b24** the nose apart, the odd feint note here and there can't seriously detract from this majestically attractive whisky and towards the end even helps! Classy, classy whisky...!!! *42%*

Waldviertler Hafer (2007 Silber Medaille label on neck) db **(83.5) n19 t22 f21 b21.5.** A unique flavor profile from these oats. A touch more bitter than usual, perhaps, but there is a superb mouthwatering quality which counters the woody impact. *42%*

Waldviertler Hafer-Malz (2007 Gold Medaille label on neck) db **(91) n22** a curious aroma of old steam trains back in the 1960s: a little oily, coal smoky and dank; **t22.5** the palate is greeted with a wonderful luster to the arrival: a distinctive, metallic small still copperiness which is coated with the soft sweetness of the oats; **f23** wonderful finish which is displayed in many layers but always that perfect setting of light sweetness if never altered and the grains the oak gel with amazing ease; **b23.5** one of those whiskies that just gets better the longer it stays on the palate. Also, a master class in achieving near perfection in the degree of sweetness generated. *42%*

Waldviertler Hafer-Malz (2008 award label on neck) db (**76.5**) **n20 t19.5 f18 b19**. The big oaks do their best to compensate. But the damage has been done by making the cut here a little too wide and flooding the usual complexity with heavy oils. *42%*

BELGIUM
THE BELGIAN OWL

⬡ **The Belgian Owl Single Malt** 1st fill bourbon cask, bott Oct 09 db (**89.5**) **n22** some early feints, so minor the worst burns off quickly in a warm room or glass, cannot upstage the lemon peel and barley theme; **t22.5** the lightest delivery yet with sweet malt flooding into the taste buds; a really lovely sweet-dry undulation to the barley-vanilla middle; **f22.5** a hint of chocolate nougat; **b22.5** one very relaxed owl. An easy-drinking joy with no shortage of charisma. *46%*

The Belgian Owl Single Malt first fill bourbon cask, bott 09 db (**90.5**) **n22** just a slight catch of feints, but nothing untoward, though it ensures a drier edge to the malt; **t23.5** a real weighty thump to the tastebuds from thick, uncompromising malt which is helped along by the small still, wider cut oiliness. Works blindingly well thanks to the slow but delightful build up of high-grade marzipan, which injects a controlled, delicate, mildly nutty and oily sweetness..., but all the time the malts are singing sweetly in the background; **f22.5** a light, fizzing spice embraces the drier oaks. Still the malt is never far away from the horizon; **b22.5** just one of those malts which are a sheer joy to experience. *46%*

The Belgian Owl Single Malt Spirit New Make db (**90**) **n22 t22 f23 b23**. Beautiful small still spirit where the barley content appears to be in concentrate form towards the finish. Excellent sweetness and just the right degree of soft oil. *46%. nc ncf.*

The Belgian Owl Single Malt Spirit Aged 7 Months cask no. 42759.76 db (**77**) **n18 t21 f19 b19**. Usual lack of balance at this age. Sweet, intense malt, but a touch feinty as well. *46%. ncf.*

The Belgian Owl Single Malt Spirit Aged 12 Months cask no. 427 58 72 db (**88**) **n22 t22 f22 b22**. Remarkably even for its age. The oak has fused well but has not the spirit of its high grade malty style. Entirely charming and eminently drinkable. *46%. nc ncf.*

The Belgian Owl Single Malt Spirit Aged 13 Months cask no. 4018741 db (**84.5**) **n20 t22 f21.5 b21**. Much firmer in style than most. The oak and barley are hacking lumps out of each other. Lots of good sugars and spices, though. *46%. ncf.*

The Belgian Owl Single Malt Spirit Aged 18 Months cask no. 4275877 db (**85**) **n22.5 t21 f21.5 b20**. Another hugely tasty but obviously unstable fledgling. Massive natural caramels are thumping home; the malt tries to get a word in edgeways but fails every time. Even so, this is well made spirit and you help to enjoy the spectacle. *46%. nc ncf.*

The Belgian Owl Single Malt Spirit Aged 18 Months cask no. 4276017 db (**89**) **n21 t23 f22 b23**. A fizzing beauty with salivating barley at every turn. The juices are required to help douse the mental spices. Chewy, delicious – even with a surprising mocha character – and a quite freaky balance for its age. *46%. ncf.*

⬡ **The Belgian Owl Single Malt Spirit Aged 24 Months 1st Fill Bourbon** cask no. 4275997, bott Feb 10 db (**89**) **n22.5 t22 f22.5 b22**. Some of the best spirit to have come from this distillery. Signs that the distiller and apparatus have a better understanding of each other. Not just malty, but the cut, and therefore weight, appears more in tune with the spirit's capabilities even though it remains a little on the hefty side. *46%*

The Belgian Owl Limited Edition Single Malt Aged 36 Months cask no. 4275873 db (**90.5**) **n21.5 t22.5 f23.5 b23**. So here it is: the first-ever dedicated malt whisky produced in Belgium. I first tasted this at the distillery alongside distiller Etienne Bouillon, but decided to mark it in the less romantic environs of my tasting room. Really, it doesn't matter where you drink this malt: absolutely brimming with character and after a short while settling in, announces its brilliance. Magnifique!! *46%. ncf.*

⬡ **The Belgian Owl Single Malt Spirit Aged 44 Months** 1st fill bourbon cask no. 4275966, bott Oct 09 db (**95.5**) **n23.5** massive bourbon theme on the nose; liquorice and spiced honey blows hot and sweet; **t23.5** near perfect weight on delivery. Those oils make the landing of a 74%abv whisky just about painless. But what works so well is the degree of sweetness: the muscovado sugars are balanced with just-so degrees of vanillas to ensure an improbable degree of balance and complexity to a whisky quite so enormous; **f24.5** now goes into owly overdrive and benefits from the slightly wider than normal cut. Especially when the nougat-mocha notes kick in. Again the sugars remain in total sync and harmony and allow the barley the clearest of paths to make a late, juicy stand. Astonishingly beautiful... **b23.5** this owl is hunting every taste bud you have. What a wonderful experience....and whatever species this may be, a Little Owl, it isn't... *74.2%*

DESTILLERIE RADERMACHER
Lambertus Single Grain Aged 10 Years db **(44) n12 t12 f10 b10.** This is whisky....? Really???!!!????? Well, that's what it says on the label, and this is a distillery I haven't got round to seeing in action (nor am I now very likely to be invited...). Let's check the label again.... Ten years old....blah, blah. Single grain... blah, blah. But, frankly, this tastes like a liqueur rather than a whisky: the fruit flavours do not seem even remotely naturally evolved: synthetic is being kind. But apparently, this is whisky: I have re-checked the label. No mention of additives, so it must be. I am stunned. *40%*

FILLIERS DISTILLERY
Goldly's Belgian Double Still Whisky Aged 10 Years db **(88) n21.5** bristling grain and a lovely cameo rye touch. But toffee dictates the overall shape; **t23** beautiful delivery and then explosion of complexity. Three grain types are present here and they each show their paces with the rye having the loudest say; the malt adds the comforting sweetness; **f21.5** again toffee returns, though late spices try to inject extra life; **b22** having actually discovered this whisky before the distillers – I'll explain one day...!! – I know this could be a lot better. The caramel does great damage to the finish in particular, which should dazzle with its complexity. Even so, a lovely, high-class whisky which should be comfortably in the 90s but falls short. *40%*.

CZECH REPUBLIC
Single Malt
STOCK PLZEN - BOZKOV S.R.O.
⠶ **Hammer Head 1989** db **(88.5) n22** light with as much accent on the clean oak as there is the crystal clear barley; **t22.5** a re-run of the nose, except here the malt is richer, biscuity and much more intense; **f22** a lovely oily malt film clings to the palate...and lasts... **b22** don't bother looking for complexity: this is one of Europe's maltiest drams...if not the maltiest... *40.7%*

Blends
⠶ **Printer's Aged 6 Years (86.5) n21.5 t22.5 f21 b21.5.** Blended whisky is something often done rather well in the Czech Republic and this brand has managed to maintain its clean, malty integrity and style. Dangerously quaffable. *40%*

ENGLAND
ST. GEORGE'S Rowdham. Working.
English Malt Spirit New Make dist 20 Jul 08 db **(92) n23 t24 f22 b23.** Exceptionally high quality new make. The peat comes across in coke-ash, cindery terms while the sweetness and clarity of barley ticks every box. Top rate. *46%*

English Malt Spirit New Make dist 6 Aug 08 db **(93.5) n22.5 t23 f24 b23.** Even without the peat we have a gloriously characterful new make. Indeed, the lack of smoke lets us see the wonderful juicy qualities of this spirit and the extent of the spice and balance. Naturally, with a new still the copper-richness is there in abundance and this is likely to tone down over time. But providing this has been filled into first class new bourbon (please, god, not sherry!) casks, this first dedicated English distillery for over a century is likely to gain a name for exceptional quality. *46%*

English Malt Spirit Cask 30, 31, 32 dist 5 Mar 07 db **(85.5) n22 t22 f21.5 b20.** It is a curious fact of whisky nature that spirit matured for a year or two in cask often tastes a lot inferior to new make. Here is a classic example. Entirely respectable and enjoyable. And clearly well made. But there is a Bambi-like effect as the balance stutters all over the place as the oak makes its first incursions and the barley appears ill-prepared to take it on. This is normal for virtually every malt distillery in the world and in no way reflects on the quality of this distillery's malt. I am tasting this one a month or so ahead of its bottling date in September 2008, so there is room for it to improve...or get worse...!!! *46%*

⠶ **The English Whisky Co. Chapter 6 English Single Malt** (unpeated) batch no. 001 **(90) n22.5** youthful, delicate barley. The occasional catch of new make disappears behind a weightier vanilla and citrus blast; this screams at you that despite its youth, it is exceptionally well made; **t23** melts in the mouth on contact. A plethora of barley notes mingle with a vanilla-caramel spine. Barley juices continue to flow; **f22.5** surprisingly long and chewy. The faintest move towards spice and then a very late honey-toffee sweetness; **b22** we had to wait over 100 years for it to happen. But, at last, another English whisky on the market. Was it worth the wait? On the evidence of this first-ever bottling, then unquestionably. The firm and expert hand of former Laphroaig distillery manager Iain Henderson was on the tiller when this spirit was made three years ago and his fingerprints are all over this precocious and ultra high quality bottling. Adorable clarity to this malt which is, considering its youth, without weakness or blemish and, for its tender years, an uncommonly fine whisky. The 1,000th new whisky for the 2011 Bible. As an Englishman, could there have been any other? *46%. nc ncf.*

⁘ **The English Whisky Co. Chapter 6 English Single Malt** (unpeated) cask no. 163/165/171/173, dist May 07, bott Jun 10 db **(91) n22** much firmer and flintier barley than the previous bottling; less evident oils. The citrus is now closer to tangerine than lemon; **t23** crisp, sharp and brimming with fresh barley...as you might expect. Even room for a hint of milky mocha to come through on the middle. But it is the juicy barley quality and a light spicy touch which steals the show; **f23.5** superb interplay between the continuing crisp barley and polite vanilla, though what oils there are now assemble to stretch the finish: fabulous; **b22.5** further confirmation that this distillery is on course for true excellence. Here, by comparison to earlier bottlings, the distillate shows some evidence that the stills have been run just a little faster and the cut thinned a tab, meaning a laser-sharp crispness to the barley. So reminds me of Glen Grant at this age. *46%*

⁘ **The English Whisky Co. Chapter 9 English Single Malt** (peated) cask no. 102/115/124/144, dist May 07, bott May 10 db **(93.5) n23** the softest vanillas imaginable vanish into a delicate, beautiful peat reek; exceptional in its clarity; **t23.5** quite fabulous delivery and follow through: a surprising hickory note thickens the peat; gristy notes offer a near perfect degree of sweetness; **f24** lengthens as the oils gather and spices begin to bubble and nip. Demerara sugars arrive from somewhere...and still that peat persists; **b23** frankly, it would be churlish to ask any more of a malt whisky of this age. Three years old only, yet going through the gears of complexity like an old 'un. The secret, though, is in the quality of the distillation and the very decent casks used. So exceptional is this, you would almost think that this was created by the guy who made Laphroaig for many a year.... *46%*

⁘ **The English Whisky Co. Limited Edition "Ibisco Decanter"** bourbon cask, dist Nov 06, bott Dec 09 db **(91.5) n22** decidedly childish: the nose is still in short trousers as the oak makes limited headway into the slightly citrusy, juicy barley, but it's well-made stuff; **t24** forget the first mouthful, which gives you only beefed up new make: put all your energy into concentrating on the second onwards which is the most refreshing barley you will taste in a long while. Soft oil helps with the intensity, while a squeeze of lemon juice underscores the freshness and creates a subtle layering; **f23** remains clean and uncomplicated as some half-hearted vanilla inches into the picture; **b22.5** quite adorable. Beautifully made whisky from stills small enough to add almost invisible but vital weight. One of the true fun whiskies of the year which further raises the expectations of what this distillery is capable of. And mark my words: it will be a lot.. *46%*

FINLAND
PANIMORAVINTOLA BEER HUNTER'S Pori. Working.

Old Buck first release, cask no. 2, dist 25 Nov 01, bott Nov 04 db **(93.5) n23 t24 f23 b23.5.** What an unexpected treat! *70.6%. nc ncf sc.*

Old Buck second release, cask no. 5, dist 25 Feb 03, bott Jul 07 db **(96) n24** I assume Finland is a part of Kentucky. Pure bourbon: with the nose offering every degree of honeycomb-liquorice imaginable... **t24** I am no longer in my chair...I have been catapulted to the furthest recess of my tasting room...the delivery nigh defies description, other than that we are talking huge – and I mean bloody gargantuan – degrees of manuka honey and oak on its sweetest, toastiest form... **f24** long, so enormously long. Just carries on the bourbon theme with the oak throbbing out waves of liquorice and hickory and the spices just pulse merrily away and never for one moment either losing balance or dredging up unwanted notes from either cask or still... **b24** it's as though they have been distilling George T Stagg...!!! Quite amazing: perhaps the surprise package of the year. I thought the first bottling was a freak. This really does send you not so much into another orbit but an entirely parallel universe. Buck me...!! *70.6%. nc ncf sc.*

⁘ **Old Buck** cask no. 4, dist Mar 04, bott Apr 10 db **(95) n24 t23 f24 b24.** Just read the tasting notes to the second release because, a dose of what almost seems like corn oil and ancient Demerara rum combined apart, oh - and an extra dose of oak, there is barely any difference. I will never, ever forget how I got this sample: I was giving a tasting in Helsinki a few months back to a horseshoe-shaped audience and a chap who had been sitting to my right and joining in with all the fun introduced himself afterwards as I signed a book for him as non other than Mika Heikkinen, the owner and distiller of this glorious whisky. I had not been told he was going to be there. His actual, touchingly humble words were: "You might be disappointed: you may think it rubbish and give it a low score. It just means I have to do better next time." No, I am not disappointed: I am astonished. No, it isn't rubbish: it is, frankly, one of the great whiskies of the year. And if you can do better next time, then you are almost certainly in line for the Bible's World Whisky of the Year award. *70.6%*

TEERENPELI

Teerenpeli Single Malt Whisky Aged 5 Years db (86) n21.5 t22 f21 b21.5. No shrinking violet, this impressive first bottling from Teerenpeli. It radiates the chunkier qualities often found with smaller stills, yet still manages to harness the richer barley notes to enjoyable effect. Weighty and a touch oily, the sweet barley which is briefly announced on arrival soon makes way for a more rumbustious combination of oak and higher oils. I look forward to getting there at last to see how it is done...though I think I can already imagine...!! *43%*

FRANCE
Single Malt
DISTILLERIE BERTRAND

Uberach db (77) n21 t19 f18 b19. Big, bitter, booming. Gives impression something's happening between smoke and grape... whatever it is, there are no prisoners taken. *42.2%*

DISTILLERIE DES MENHIRS

Eddu Gold db (93) n22 greater harmonization than the silver; still a hint of tobacco but now a richer, honeyed tone compensates and flourishes; t23 big, bulging arrival. There is a real pulse to the grain, a sturdiness which helps intensify the controlled Demerara sweetness. Big yet elegant; f24 now goes into overdrive as the oak adds further weight and spices. Yet the satin effect remains intact; b24 rarely do whiskies turn up in the glass so rich in character to the point of idiosyncrasy. Some purists will recoil from the more assertive elements. I simply rejoice. This is so proud to be different. And exceptionally good, to boot!! *43%*

DISTILLERIE GLANN AR MOR

Glann Ar Mor Aged 3 Years 1st fill bourbon barrel db (85) n21.5 t22 f20.5 b21. The slight feints, so typical of European small still whisky, works well in upping the weight, structure and chewability. Juicy barley and cocoa dominate, but tasting after it has sat in an open glass for half an hour works wonders. *46%. Celtic Whisky Compagnie.*

Glann Ar Mor Taol Esa Ian Gwech 08 db (92) n22 a hint of pear lightens the obvious small still weightiness; barley sugar and gentle vanillas do likewise; t23 stunning silky delivery. A beautiful interwoven barley and soft fruit lead is supported ably by the distinctive coppery sheen: the mouth-feel is exceptionally good; f23.5 fabulous mocha and mint fade, still with that lovely coppery richness to the texture; the vanillas do become more compelling but the oaks are always at their most gentle; b23.5 I have been impressed by this distillery in the past and I am impressed again. This is honest whisky, where its character can be charted and defined needing nothing more than a clear mind and palate. It is entirely appropriate that this distillery faces an old lighthouse: because this is a beacon for those in search of excellent malt. These Bretons are keeping the Celtic tradition of making fine whisky flying from the very highest point they can find... *46% Celtic Whisky Compagnie. France*

⁖ **Glann Ar Mor Taol Esa Ian Gwech 09** db (88) n21 dank hay; decidedly grassy; t22 a wider spectrum of oil on delivery and with it a thick surge of buttery malt; f23 long and the now familiar mocha arrives in good shape; just a squeeze of citrus barley very late on; b22 not quite as cleanly made and technically brilliant as their last bottling, but still a whisky to be reckoned with. Even with a slightly wider cut, remains delicate and engrossingly structured. *46% Celtic Whisky Compagnie, France*

⁖ **Kornog Taouarc'h Kentan** db (94.5) n24 now, when was the last time I came across peat this delicate yet profound? A glorious chocolate note mixes imperiously with the drifting smoke; the sweet-dry ratio cannot be bettered; t24 sizable oil on delivery but it brings with it malt on two fabulous levels. Just ahead of the other is a standard juicy, biscuit barley, then directly behind arrives the charmingly weighted peat; the middle ground is filled with a chocolate toffee biscuit...but enveloped in light smoke; f23 a few vanillas build up and there is a light treacle flourish to the lingering smoke; b23.5 not sure there has been this number of perfectly rhapsodic notes coming out of France since Saint Sans was in his pomp.... *57.1%*

DISTILLERIE GUILLON

Guillon No. 1 Single Malt de la montagne de Reims db **(87) n22** slight tobacco kick from, presumably, the still. But the crushed (slightly jaded) orange works well with the malt; **t21** lively malt, not entirely clean, has enough in fruity-doughy reserve genuinely to attract; **f22** dry with a shortcake butteriness; the sugarless custard tart finish is excellent **b22** right. I'm impressed. Not exactly faultless, but enough life here really to keep the tastebuds on full alert; By and large well made and truly enjoyable. Well done, Les Chaps! *46%*

DISTILLERIE MEYER

Meyer's Whisky Alsacien Blend Superieur db **(88.5) n22.5** a complex nose showing excellent distilling technique and clarity to the lightly honeyed grain and even a delicate fruitiness; **t22.5** those fruits on the nose, a kind of light raspberry jam, arrive early and complement the soft vanillas and barley; **f21.5** a parting slight toasty bitterness from the oak; **b22** impressively clean, barley-thick and confident: a delight. *40%*

DISTILLERIE WARENGHEM

Armorik db **(91) n23** alluringly spicy and biting, the oak jabs with limited venom whilst the malt takes the blows with ease. Highly attractive and complex; **t22** sweet, easily recognisable malt glides over the palate charmingly; some serious gristy notes develop early; **f23** a long, exceptionally malty finish, again with the barley in the ascendancy and with few challengers; **b23** I admit it; I blanched, when I first nosed this, so vivid was the memory of the last bottling. This, though ,was the most pleasant of surprises. Fabulous stuff: one of the most improved malts in the world. *40%*

⠸ **Armorik Single Malt 5 Years Old** bourbon casks & Breton oak casks, sherry finish, bott 2009 db **(83) n18 t21.5 f22 b21.5.** The standard Armorik is a rewarding whisky to find. This version, though attractively juicy and chewy in part, is a reminder that playing with sherry butts, even good ones, can result in a levelling of the higher points and an ultimately duller whisky. *42%*

⠸ **Breizh Whisky Blended** 50% malt/50% grain db **(85.5) n22 t21 f21 b21.5.** A safe, pleasant whisky which happily remains within its sweet, clean and slightly citrusy parameters. *42%*

DOMAINE MAVELA DISTILLERIE ARTISANALE

P&M Pure Malt Whisky bott 05 db **(91) n23** an extraordinary injection of kumquats makes for a pleasing – and individualistic – aroma; **t23** amazingly sharp and mouthwatering. There are flavours new to me here – and that doesn't happen often; **f22** almost bitter at times; **b23** an outstanding whisky which, being French, seems to offer a style that is entirely different from anything else around. I have been told there is chestnut within the grist which, strictly speaking, means this is not whisky as we know it. My French is not good enough to discover the truth of this. Between now and the 2008 Bible I shall travel to the distillery in Corsica to get to the bottom of this. In the meantime, though, I shall occasionally enjoy this delicious dram! *42%*

WAMBRECHIES DISTILLERY

Wambrechies Single Malt Aged 3 Years db **(78.5) n19 t19 f21 b19.5.** Sweet with a Malteser candy touch. A few feints just dampen the overall effect. There is also an aroma on the nose I kind of recognize, but... *40%*

Wambrechies Single Malt Aged 8 Years db **(83) n20 t21 f21 b21.** ....and there's that aroma again, just like the 3-y-o. Except how it kind of takes me back 30 years to when I hitchhiked across the Sahara. Some of the food I ate with the local families in Morocco and Algeria was among the best I have ever tasted. And here is an aroma I recognize from that time, though I can't say specifically what it is (tomatoes, maybe?). Attractive and unique to whisky, that's for sure. I rather like this malt. There is nothing quite comparable to it; there is obviously some kind of feinty note, but nothing disastrous. And the curious malty-fruity bit is charming. One I need to investigate a whole lot more. *40%*

Blends

P&M Blend Supérieur (82) n21 t21 f20 b20. Bitter and botanical, though no shortage of complexity. *40%. Mavela Distillerie.*

P&M Whisky (89) n22 light, lemony, mildly Canadian wheated in style; **t23** beautiful, sharpish citrus ensures a salivating experience; **f22** soft oak lowers the sweetness levels; **b22** no mistaking this is from a fruit distillery. Still quite North American, though. *40%.*

GERMANY
AV BRENNEREI ANDREAS VALLENDAR Wincheringen. Working.

Threeland Single Malt 2006 db **(93) n23** green, newly mown grass and hay: beautifully fresh, enticing and with that juicy, just-so degree of sweetness; **t23.5** mouthwatering, slightly sweeter than the nose suggests; gristy but always intense; **f23** an elegant vanilla and barley fade; **b23.5** on this evidence, one of the technically best distillers of malt on mainland Europe. Sensational...!!! 46%

⁖ **Threeland Whisky** dist 2007, bott code L-Wtr200701 db **(83) n19.5 t22.5 f20 b21.** Whilst pleasant and malty enough in its own right, my eyes opened up at this one, as I remember last year's bottling as being one of the best from anywhere in Europe. That, I recall, was so wonderfully fresh and clean. This one, sadly, is bigger and oilier with evidence that the distiller has included some heads and tails which were excluded last time out. Still malty and mouth watering. But a useful lesson in learning the vital difference between good and great whisky. 46%

⁖ **Threeland Whisky Sherry Fino Finish** dist 2007 db **(88.5) n22.5** beautifully malty and clean with the Fino having a very limited input; **t22** virtually sleep walks over the taste buds, soft and quiet but with some heavier oils and dates meeting at the midpoint; **f22** much more assertive now with a spiciness chattering in the fruity distance; all kinds of fudge, some with a vague hint of cocoa; **b22** again not exactly a picture of technical perfection, but the relationship between the malt and fruit makes for very enjoyable tasting. 52.5% 352 bottles.

BIRKENHOF-BRENNEREI Nistertal. Working.

⁖ **Fading Hill 4 1/2 Years** American and French oak, cask no. 09 & 11, dist Nov 05, bott Apr 10 db **(74) n18 t20 f17.5 b18.5.** One of those peculiar malts which sends out mixed messages. On one hand, there is a curiously attractive damp hay character and for the more fanciful, orange blossom. On the other, signs, confirmed by the finish, that not all is right or happy. 45.7%. 680 bottles.

BOSCH EDELBRAND Unterlenningen. Working.

Bosch Edelbrand Schwäbischer Whisky lot 9105 db **(83.5) n19 t22.5 f21 b21.** Needs to make the cut a little more selective: has the promise to become a pretty high quality whisky. This shows some outstanding depth and honey for some time after the first, impressive delivery. 40%

BRANNTWEINBRENNEREI WEINBAU ADOLF KELLER Ramsthal.

A.K Whisky bott code L10209 db **(89.5) n22** a beautiful Sauternes-style sweetness picks up some extra spices and overcomes a hint of feints; **t23** a very sweet whisky, yet somehow doesn't cross the point of no return: still a slight distilling blemish can be detected, but that appears to offer slightly extra oil for the grape and grain to intensify their battle; **f22** much more emphasis on the dull, throbbing spice, but still that Sauternes/noble rot lushness holds sway, despite a real custardy-vanilla arrival; **b22.5** hardly faultless from a technical point of view. But if you can't enjoy something as raunchy and ribald as this, you might as well stop drinking whisky. 40%

⁖ **A.K Whisky** bott code L11110 db **(67) n15 t18 f17 b17.** I think the A.K. stands for the rifle which is required to shoot this ultra fruity, bizarrely scented whisky.... 40%

BRENNEREI ANTON BISCHOF Wartmannsroth, Working.

Bischof's Rhöner Whisky bott code L-12 db **(75.5) n18 t19.5 f19 b19.** Rich and chewy, especially the toffee, but all a tad too feinty. 40%

⁖ **Bischof's Rhöner Whisky** bott code L-24 db **(75.5) n17.5 t20 f18 b19.** That unique blend of feints and intense, biscuity grains. Just checked: I see I gave it the same score as last year. Not only unmistakable, but consistently so! 40%

BRENNEREI DANNENMANN Owen. Working.

⁖ **Danne's Schwäbischer Whisky** dist 2002 db **(89) n22** crisp, clean and obviously well made. A light, grainy exoskeleton protects the delicate fruit; **t23** superb mouth feel with a textbook countering of a sweet, juicy lushness and a much firmer, well spiced character not so much a sub plot, but more an entirely different story; **f22** the usual bitterness, but aided by some playful spices; **b22** an exhausting whisky to try and understand. You crack the code only when you fathom that there are two entirely different songs being played at the same time. 54.6%

👁️ **Danne's Schwäbischer Whisky** dist 2002 db **(78)** n19 t21.5 f18.5 b19. A recognisable style of pungent, full-flavoured central and northern European spirit I have experienced over the many years, though not always associated with whisky. There is both a fruit and vegetable character here but the begrudging and short-lived juicy sweetness is, I assume, the brief bow towards the grain. The finish could almost be a full blown, old-fashioned Swedish or Norwegian aquavit. *43%*

Schwäbischer Whisky vom Bellerhof db **(88)** n21 European-style Kentucky dry tobacco with a vaguely honeyed edge; **t22** soft, entirely melt-in the-mouth barley with dissolving brown sugars; **f23** the most butterscotchy finish of all time with wonderful elements of the softest oak and honey imaginable; **b22** easy drinking clean and deliciously sweet malt with that indelible touch of class. *43%*

Schwäbischer Whisky vom Bellerhof db **(88)** n23 subtle honey and vanilla: exceptionally clean; **t22** more melt-in-the mouth malt just as before; **f21** dries until the oak bites; **b22** an entirely different route to the same high quality whisky...! *47.4%*

BRENNEREI ERICH SIGEL Dettingen. Working.
Original Dettinger Schwäbischer Whisky db **(88)** n21.5 sharp; egg-custard tart and a supine touch of pine; **t22.5** sugared almonds; body is silky and sweetens gently; **f22** heaps of vanilla and a slow build up of juicy barley notes and spice **b22** softly sophisticated. *40%*

BRENNEREI FABER Ferschweiler. Working.
👁️ **Whisky aus der Eifel Aged 6 Years** American oak, dist 2003 db **(91)** n23 mint and lavender crushed in the fingers; a little orange peel, too; **t23** exceptional weight with the barley forming a sweet layer at the top and more solid cocoa, caramel and tannin in the sediment; **f22.5** long, lightly oiled, subtly fused with a citrus sweetness and weightless spices; **b22.5** a riveting whisky of uncommonly high quality. *46%*

BRENNEREI FRANK RODER Aalen - Wasseralfingen. Working.
👁️ **Frank's Suebisch Whisky** dist 2005 db **(86)** n21 t22.5 f21 b21.5. Impossible not to be charmed by the disarming citrus note. Every aspect of this whisky is low key and delicate. *40%*

BRENNEREI HACK Pinzberg. Working.
👁️ **Walburgis Franken** db **(78)** n17 t20 f21 b20. While the nose puts the 'aahhhh!' in nougat, the sweet walnut-cake nuttiness on delivery and beyond makes some amends. *40%*

BRENNEREI HÖHLER Aarbergen, Kettenbach. Working.
👁️ **Whesskey Caramell-Malz** bott code 2 db **(83)** n18 t21.5 f22 b21.5. This distillery makes whisky of remarkably consistent quality, even though the styles are slightly different This one uses all the extra alcohol to give the grain extra spice and momentum to push through the rich cream caramel. *58%*

👁️ **Whesskey Hessischer Blended Whiskey** bott code 114/150, dist Spring 07, bott May 10 db **(82)** n18 t21 f22 b21. A substantial jump in quality from Hohler's blend of last year. Curiously enough, reminded me of the Loch Lomond single malt I tasted earlier in the day, but gets over the feinty hump more easily and with a better display of controlled sugars. Cream toffeed and enjoyable. *42% 150 bottles.*

👁️ **Whesskey Hessischer Mais Whisky** bott code 62/250, dist Feb 07, bott May 10 db **(82.5)** n19 t22 f20.5 b21. Intriguingly dense whisky with stewed nettles and celery on the nose and a curiously metallic delivery despite the pea soup consistency of the grain. Not for one second dull.... *44% 250 bottles.*

Whesskey Special Blend db **(77)** n17.5 t21 f19.5 b20. One of those odd creatures which surface from time to time in this part of the world. The flavor profile – even taking into account the massive cream toffee caramel style – isn't quite like anything you've encountered before. You kind of like it, admire the deft spice delivery, but..... *41%*

BRENNEREI HÜBNER Stadelhofen, Steinfeld, Working.
Fränkischer Whisky db **(67.5)** n15 t17.5 f18 b17. Well, that was different. Can't really give you tasting notes as such, as I don't really have a reference point as to where to start. Quite simply, a bunch of bizarre aromas and flavours, the vast majority of which I have never encountered before. Another distillery I must seek and visit to find out what all this is about... *40%*

Hubner Los Nr 3 db **(80.5)** n20 t22.5 f18 b20. Overwhelmed by fruit as far as complexity is concerned, but there is a distinctive smoky, salivating theme to this nonetheless. The balance has been trashed and if it were a novel, you'd have to read it three times...and still make no sense of it. A David Lynch film of a whisky...and I love it, though I have no idea why. 40%

BRENNEREI LOBMÜLLER Talheim. Working.

Schwäbischer Whisky Single Grain cask no. 6 db **(83) n20 t22 f20.5 b20.5.** A big toffee presence softens the impact and helps steer this towards a gentle, pleasantly sweet whisky. 41%

⋯⋙ **Schwäbischer Whisky Single Grain** cask no. 7 db **(86.5) n20 t22.5 f22 b22.** A friendly, big-hearted, soul full of toffee-chocolate chewiness. Highly enjoyable. 41%

BRENNEREI MARTIN MEIER Neuravensburg. Working.

⋯⋙ **Mein 9. Fass** db **(84) n19 t21.5 f22 b21.5.** The light spices and dissolving sugars melt beautifully into the malt. Nose apart, this is a ja, nicht ein 9.... 42%

BRENNEREI MARTIN ZIEGLER Baltmannsweiler. Working.

Esslinger Single Malt Aged 8 Years db **(85) n20.5 t22 f21 b21.5.** Malty, nutty, a decent degree of sweetness and toffee marzipan. A well-made malt which you appreciate more as you acclimatise to its compact style. 42%

BRENNEREI RABEL Owen. Working.

⋯⋙ **Schwäbischer Whisky** db **(76.5) n17 t21.5 f18 b20.** Here's something different. While the nose, or at least the getting it right, is a work in progress, the delivery and body are much more on the ball thanks mainly to a rich treacle and prune element which sees off the thicker distillate. The finish, though, confirms the fault lines. 40%

BRENNEREI VOLKER THEURER Tübingen-Unterjesingen. Working.

Black Horse Ammertal db **(83) n21 t21.5 f20 b20.5.** A big puncher, this, with a coastal saline, phenolic uppercut amid the sugary jabs. 40%

⋯⋙ **Black Horse Ammertal** bott code BL-2010 db **(79) n18.5 t21 f19 b20.5.** The wider cut used in the distilling means this Black Horse has put on a little bit of weight from the BL2008 I tasted last year. The light phenols have gone but the sugars have increased. 40%

⋯⋙ **Sankt Johann Single Barrel Aged 8 Years** bott code BL-2010 db **(85) n19.5 t22 f21.5 b22.** Fabulous fun. Once it gets over the drying tobacco nose the inevitable nougat is delivered. But it comes with a milk-creamy mocha which develops in intensity and with just the right doses of treacle to keep the sweetness at desired levels. Good background spices too. A very likeable character, this Saint Johann. 46.5%

BRENNEREI ZAISER Köngen. Working.

Zaiser Schwäbischer Whisky db **(83) n23 t21.5 f19 b19.5.** Surprisingly dry and constricted in development considering the beautiful soft sugars on the nose which also boast excellent clarity. 40%

DESTILLERIE DREXLER Working.

⋯⋙ **Drexler Arrach No. 1 Bayerwald Single Cask** cask no. 262, dist May 07, bott May 10 db **(88.5) n21** a tad confused with a hint of kumquat and spices more recognisable at the local Indian takeaway; **t23** much more at home on the palate where the grain and oak appear to harmonise pretty effortlessly, **f22** fades pleasantly, **b22.5** very good bitter-sweet marriage, but better still is the luxuriant mouth-feel. A well constructed malt. 46% 210 bottles

DESTILLERIE HERMANN MÜHLHÄUSER Working.

⋯⋙ **Mühlhäuser Schwäbischer Whisky aus Korn** db **(90.5) n23** as usual with Herman's whisky I am taken back to a farm. This time it is like when the freshly harvested corn is being unloaded into the silo and the dust of summer is floating in the air...; **t23** mouth wateringly fresh (and cleaner than last year) the grains and oak appear to harmonise instantly; the delicate nature of the sweetness wants to make you applaud; **f22** at last a few stray feints gather, but they also help ramp up the spices; **b22.5** another stunning bottling from this excellent distiller. You have to admire the subtlety of the complexity of this whisky. 41%

Mühlhäuser Schwäbischer Whisky aus Korn db **(90) n22.5** good grief: distilled haystacks...the closest aroma to working on a farm stacking bales since my early youth...; **t23** gorgeous gristy wholemeal liberally sugared; **f22** some slight feinty oils mix with a light saltiness and drying oak **b22.5** so different! If you are into this, it'll be pastoral perfection. 40%

WHISKY-DESTILLERIE ROBERT FLEISHMANN Eggolsheim. Working.

Austrasier Single Cask Grain cask no. 3, dist Jun 94, bott Jun 08 db **(89.5) n21 t22 f23.5 b23.** Beautifully weighted whisky with a glorious liquorice development – some finer bourbon notes at play here. High quality whisky. 40%

Blaue Maus Single Cask Malt db **(84.5) n18 t22 f22.5 b22.** Beautifully molassed with a big burnt fudge finale. 40%

-ᕽᕽ- **Blaue Maus Single Cask Malt** cask no. 2, dist Jun 98, bott May 10 db **(86) n22 t22 f21 b21.** For those who love their fruitcake to have something of the sherry trifle about it. Brimming with clean grape, though curiously out of sync with the body of the spirit. The bitterness at the death is unexpected. 40%

-ᕽᕽ- **Blaue Maus 2. Fassfüllung Single Cask Malt** cask no. 1, dist Jun 97, bott May 10 db **(84) n20 t22 f21 b21.** Thick and soupy on both nose and palate, the malt showing juicy personality despite the weight. Decent exploitation of delicate brown sugar trait. 40%

Blaue Maus Single Malt cask no. 2, dist Oct 97, bott Jun 08 db **(85.5) n20 t21.5 f22.5 b21.5.** Substantial whisky which, as this distillery's style dictates, just gets better as it goes along. The usual burnt sugar effect is in full flow and the spices evolve with a degree of sophistication. 40%

Blaue Maus Single Malt 20 Jahre cask no. 1, dist Jul 88, bott May 08 db **(91) n22 t23 f22.5 b23.5.** Complex and superbly balanced, the age is never in doubt while the management of the old oak is sublime. 40%

Blaue Maus Single Malt 25 Jahre dist 83, bott 08 db **(95.5) n24 t24 f23.5 b24.** My 1,400th whisky for the 2009 Bible. And what better way to celebrate than by tasting Robert Fleishmann's special bottling to mark his 25th anniversary as a whisky distiller. I first tasted it with Robert earlier in the year at the Munich Whisky Festival. Back on neutral territory it tastes no worse than the stunning whisky he poured for me then. Quite dazzling and a magnificent way to mark this momentous anniversary. Because if a better German single malt has ever been bottled, then I have missed it. Which is rather unlikely... 40%

Blaue Maus Single Cask Malt 2 Fassfüllung cask no. 1, dist Jul 96, bott Jun 08 db **(86.5) n18.5 t22 f23.5 b22.5.** The strange, house-style nougat nose is an unworthy fanfare to a really dogged and eventually sophisticated malt. The way in which it grows on the palate in both style, complexity and overall quality is wonderful. The intensity of the lingering malt at the end is almost worthy of applause. 40%

Blaue Maus Single Cask Malt Fassstärke cask no. 1, dist Apr 92, bott May 08 db **(89) n20 t23 f23 b23.** A massive experience: The Blaue Max. 58.6%

Blaue Maus Single Cask Malt Fassfüllung cask no. 1, dist Jun 97, bott Jan 09 db **(85) n18.5 t21.5 f23 b22.** A steady-as-she-goes whisky: safe, attractive, a touch drier and with a juicy element to the malt and some genuine sophistication to the vanilla-led finale. 40%

Blaue Maus Single Cask Malt Fassstärke db **(91.5) n19.5** another nose with all kinds of faults...and yet it somehow carries countless positives especially with that big fruity cocoa signature, a kind of distillery trademark these days... **t24.5** one of the best deliveries found in the world this year: sweet, molassed, plenty of cocoa but also ripe figs and dates getting in on the act....I am salivating so much from this I'm in danger of drowning... **f23.5** exactly the kind of oaky bite I'd want from something of this age. Burnt raisin, traditional fruitcake sweetened with molasses...it's all there in spades... **b24** tasting whisky from this unique distillery is always fun. And it appears distiller Robert Fleishmann is really doing this with a smile on his face. This is really what world whisky is all about: what entertainment...what fantastic bloody fun....!!!! 56.3%

Blaue Maus Single Malt Münchner Whiskyfestival 4-6 Februar 2005 cask no. 1, dist Jul 90 db **(93) n23** minty, lavender, faintly herbal; **t24** dry and toasty at first, there is a mad rush of malt before the soft liquorice, oaky notes begin to arrive in numbers, as does the deep honey; **f22** cream toffee and wonderful honeycomb; **b24** tasted blind this could so easily be mistaken for a bourbon. The oldest European mainland whisky I have ever come across. 40%

-ᕽᕽ- **Elbe 1 Single Cask Malt** cask no. 1, dist Jul 96, bott May 10 db **(77) n19 t19 f18 b19.** A long way removed from the normal house style, the accent decidedly floral and dry: almost London gin-like. 40%

Grüner Hund Single Cask Malt cask no. 2, dist Aug 96, bott Jan 09 db **(91) n21** chocolate nougat: fat, sweet and nutty; **t23.5** beautiful delivery of toffee raisin again with plenty of cocoa to add to the mix; more juicy fruits abound with fat sultanas, fig and exploding ripe plums at the head; **f23.5** goes into complexity overdrive with the cocoa notes mingling with vanilla and molasses; **b23** Blaue Maus at its irrestistable best. 40%

Grüner Hund Single Cask Malt cask no. 2, dist Aug 97, bott Jun 08 db **(79) n18 t20 f21 b20.** Some bitter oak arrests the usual malt development. *40%*

⁖ **Grüner Hund Single Cask Malt** cask no. 3, dist Aug 97, bott May 10 db **(92.5) n23.5** bakery ginger cake...of a very European style; **t24** and that ginger isn't shy on delivery: again almost like a central European cake you find seasoned with ginger but with a soft honey and treacle filling on the inside; a touch of nougat fills the middle ground, but still the feel of the bakery persists; **f22.5** long, lightly oiled with growing spices; **b22.5** somehow you get a feeling that here is a man enjoying the making of whisky. And I am certainly a man who enjoys tasting it...especially when it reaches these fun-filled heights. *40%*

⁖ **Grüner Hund Fassstärke Single Cask Malt** cask no. 1, dist May 96, bott May 10 db **(81.5) n21.5 t21 f19 b20.** Dry with plenty to chew over. But then when the cut has been made this wide, letting the nougat-rich feints surge in, that is hardly a surprise. *48.9%*

Krottentaler Single Cask Malt cask no. 1, dist Jul 96, bott Jun 08 db **(80.5) n18 t19 f22 b21.5.** Another which struggles to find either a rhythm or style until late on when those stunning sugars come into their own. *40%*

Krottentaler Single Cask Malt cask no. 1, dist Mar 97, bott Jan 09 db **(77.5) n17 t21 f19.5 b20.** Loads of sweet cocoa for all its obvious weaknesses. *40%*

⁖ **New Make** lott no. 1, dist Mar 09, bott May 10 db **(89) n22.5 t23 f21.5 b22.** High quality new make where, despite the strength, the malt goes on a salivating route. Better than one or two scotch single malt commercially sold. And excellent for dissolving your plaque.....and probably enamel. *85.2%*

Old Fahr Single Cask Malt cask no. 1, dist Jul 00, bott Jan 09 db **(89) n19.5** delicate hickory and cocoa amid the nougat-feints; **t23.5** plenty of mint chocolate on a whisky very similar in style to the Fassfullung, except with a touch of extra sweetness and a dose of busy spice; **f23** long, with a dramatic build up of rich demerara; **b23** quite simply a beautiful whisky. *40%*

⁖ **Old Fahr Single Cask Malt** cask no. 3, dist Jul 00, bott May 10 db **(89.5) n22.5** less nougat than of old and much more hickory and toffee fudge; **t22** drier than expected with a real silky body. There is a subdued honeycomb, the sweeter edges rounded by vanillin; **f23** the perfect finale for those who prefer the chocolate-flavoured Liquorice Allsorts; **b22** beautifully complex and delightfully weighted with the odd technical imperfection which works in its favour. A late night treat. *40%*

⁖ **Otto's Uisge Beatha** cask no. 1, dist Mar 07, bott May 10 db **(88.5) n22** the Scottish malt is more than evident with some thick, crusty smoke flying about; **t23** very different and damned tasty: gristy, smoky and roasty, but with a bizarre semi-nougat attachment; sweet, lusty and busty....; **f21.5** the bawdiness of the delivery calms as the vanilla and nougat toffee get a grip; **b22** Germany meets Scotland. Just as well it's in whisky and not football, otherwise this could have been embarrassing. Or something as grim as the days of Berti Vogts. *40%*

Schwarzer Pirat Single Cask Malt cask no. 1, dist Mar 97, bott Jun 08 db **(89) n21 t23 f22.5 b22.5.** Hugely enjoyable *40%*

Schwarzer Pirat Single Cask Malt cask no. 2, dist Jun 96, bott Jan 09 db **(86.5) n20 t22.5 f22 b22.** Honey and nougat all the way. *40%*

Spinnaker Single Cask Malt cask no. 1, dist Apr 98, bott Jun 08 db **(84) n18.5 t22 f22.5 b21.** Muscovado sugar on heat. *40%*

Spinnaker Single Cask Malt cask no. 1, dist Aug 93, bott Jan 09 db **(89) n19.5** molassed toffee; **t23** exemplary delivery: pure silk as delicate spices try to make an impact on the marzipan-cocoa theme; **f23.5** brilliant butterscotch and vanilla melt-down, with molasses and cocoa just around the corner. brilliant. !!! **b23** stunning chocolate fudge. *40%*

Spinnaker Single Cask Malt 2 Fassfüllung cask no. 1, dist Jun 95, bott Jan 09 db **(86.5) n18 t23.5 f22.5 b22.5.** Ignore the nutty nougat/butyric nose and you have a sublime malt absolutely bursting out of the glass with cocoa-laden barley. Fabulously beautiful in every department, other than the aroma. (Note: all Blaue Maus whiskies can be improved by allowing the whisky to stand in heat for a while to burn off the feints) *40%*

Spinnaker Single Cask Malt Fassstärke cask no. 1, dist Jul 99, bott Apr 08 db **(80) n17 t19 f23 b21.5.** This one is holed very early on with the nose and delivery being way out. But, as is so often the case with this unique distillery, we have here a malt which somehow manages to bounce back with an irresistible finish that appears to explore previously unknown avenues of sweetness and chewability. *48.2%*

EDELBRENNEREI PETER HOHMANN Nordheim, Rhön. Working.

⁖ **Rhöner Grain Whisky Aged 6 Years** db **(89) n21** heady and bready. A distinct spice buzz; **t22.5** delicate body with wispy strands of treacle and spice; **f23** the peppery spices hit full flow as the vanillas enter; the late liquorice, honey and hickory is superb; **b22.5** impressively made and matured with a quite lovely marriage between the sugars and spices. *40%*

EDELOBST-BRENNEREI ZIEGLER Freudenberg. Working.
⪼ **AVREVM** db (83) **n21.5 t21 f20 b20.5**. A most peculiar, though not unattractive, marriage of marmalade and hops. *43% 1000 bottles.*

FEINBRENNEREI SEVERIN SIMON Alzenau-Michelbach. Working.
⪼ **Simon's 10 Years Old Bavarian Pure Pot Still** db (86.5) **n21.5 t21.5 f22.5 b21**. Not a whiskey to rush. Takes several hours to get to know this chap. When they say Pure Pott Still, I am sure they mean a mixture of malted and unmalted barley. Because that is the only style that offers a whiskey as rock hard as this with virtually no give on the palate. If there is any yield, it comes in a vaguely fruity form but this is a whiskey which sets up an impenetrable barrier and defies you to pass. Fascinating and very different. *40%*

GUTSBRENNEREI AGLISHARDT Nellingen. Working.
HFG Gutsbrennerei Aglishardt db (86.5) **n22 t21 f22 b21.5**. Clean, fruity and not entirely without some Fisherman's Friend phenol. A real juicy job. *40%*
⪼ **HFG Dinkelwhisky Single Cask No 2** db (87.5) **n21.5** well weighted oak with light layers of honey and nougat; **t22** mouth watering and immediately chewy. Gristy sugars hold control; **f22** long with a light spice addition to the vanilla; **b22** good, honest whisky with plenty of charm from the grain. *41.5%*
⪼ **HFG Schwäbischer Whisky** db (72.5) **n18 t19 f17.5 b18**. Dry and spicy. But let down by the cask. *40%*

HAMMERSCHMIEDE Zorge. Working.
⪼ **Glen Els Single Hercynian Malt** dist May 06, bott May 10 db (86.5) **n22 t22.5 f20.5 b21.5**. Loads of baked yam and fresh barley on nose; clean and a touch of the Malteser candy on palate. Thoroughly enjoyable, and doubtless the SWA will love it even more... *51% 570 bottles.*

HELMUT SPERBER Rentweinsdorf. Working.
⪼ **Sperbers Destillerie Malt Whisky** dist 2002 db (76.5) **n17.5 t19 f21 b19**. Great finish with the house cocoa/mocha style. But some of the other characteristics seem other worldly. *46%*
⪼ **Sperbers Destillerie Malt Whisky** dist 2002 db (77.5) **n17.5 t20 f21 b19**. Very similar to the 46% except the sugars are much more eccentric. *59%*
⪼ **Sperbers Destillerie Single Grain Whisky** dist 2002 db (76) **n17 t21 f19 b19**. Once you get past the butyric nose the mouth feel and slow cocoa development is rather lovely. *40%*

KINZIGBRENNEREI MARTIN BROSAMER Biberach. Working.
⪼ **Kinzigbrennerei Martin Brosamer Single Malt** oak cask, dist Apr 05, bott Sep 08 db (84) **n20.5 t21 f21.5 b21**. For all the obvious nougat, the barley is given a clear stage from which to make its sweet speech. *42% 120 bottles.*

KLEINBRENNEREI FITZKE Herbolzheim-Broggingen. Working.
⪼ **Schwäbischer Whisky 4-Korn-Malz** db (75) **n18 t19.5 f18.5 b19**. Hard to have fun picking out the various ingredients when the distillate is this heavy. A thinner cut would have given us a better chance. *43%*
⪼ **Schwäbischer Whisky Buchweizen** db (83) **n22 t21 f19 b21**. With buckwheat being a plant and not a cereal crop, the spirit distilled from it cannot be called a whisky....whatever the label says. The spirit here is pleasant enough with an attractive vegetable nose and plenty of spices ducking in and out of the sugars. *43%*
⪼ **Schwäbischer Whisky Dinkelmalz** db (85.5) **n22 t21 f21.5 b21**. A fabulous whisky to find. The style is uncompromisingly different and it takes a little while for one's nose and taste buds to fall into line. But once you get into stride with it, the brittleness is a joy as is the attractively sour-sweet grain note and the light cocoa finale. *43%*
⪼ **Schwäbischer Whisky Hirse** db (88.5) **n22** unique. A touch of the chewing gum about this. A mixture of molten sugar, prune juice and kind of stewed leaf concoction I had in Africa once; **t22** wow! So intense: a green tea bitterness to this but elsewhere a dense sugar and spice counters quite forcefully; **f22** exactly more of the same, but just fading with those tealeaves hanging in to the end; **b22.5** not every day you come across a whisky distilled from sorghum (if, indeed, it officially can be), though I am no stranger to Maotai, China's equivalent which does not taste remotely like this. A pity. *43%*

KORNBRENNEREI WAGNER Dauborn. Working.

⋯ **Golden Ground Grain Whisky Original Dauborner** dist 2005 db (84) n21 t21.5 f21 b20.5. Lots of latent honey, yet the sum total offers a pretty dry experience. 40%

⋯ **Golden Ground Grain Whisky Original Dauborner** dist 2005 db (88) n21 wide cut but sweet and spicy; t23 superbly weighted with genuine honey attaching to an almost pasty graininess which works through the complexity gears with ease; f22 late spices work well with the drier distillate and oak; b22 a little extra feints has worked well for the rich and complex body. 46%

KOTTMANN´S EDELDESTILLAT-BRENNEREI Bad Ditzenbach. Working.

Schwäbischer Whisky lot no. 120705 (78.5) n19 t20 f19 b19.5. Heavy, oily and with much nougat to chew on. 40%

NORBERT WINKELMANN Hallerndorf. Working.

⋯ **Fränkischer Rye Whisky** db (93.5) n24 classic rye. The crisp fruitiness is refreshing, light and heavy, sweet and spicy. Magnificent....; t24 the excellence of the nose, which suggested ultra high class, feint-free distilling, is confirmed here. The grain is classically crunchy, with the sugar candy sweetness and the contrasting fruit juiciness enough to set you on a jig of delight; f22.5 spices pound and buzz though there are shades of feinty, oily bitterness that are apparent for the first time as the intensity of the rye fades; b23 for the record, the nose is so good to this that I kept it with me one evening after a badly sulphured cask from another distillery had ruined my tasting for the day. The fruity beauty of this was not just balm, but a reminder of just how wonderful whisky should touch you. 42%

⋯ **Fränkischer Whiskey Strong Single Malt** db (78) n17.5 t20.5 f20 b20. A huge whisky, but mainly because the cut has been nothing like so judicial as the rye. 48%

PRIVATBRENNEREI SONNENSCHEIN Witten-Heven. Demolished

Sonnenschein 15 db (79.5) n19.5 t21 f19 b20. So, it's back!! In its youth, this was a tough whisky to entertain. Many years on and some of the old faults remain, but it has picked up a touch of elegance along the way. 41%

BRENNEREI REINER MÖSSLEIN Zeilitzheim. Working.

⋯ **Fränkischer Whisky** db (91) n23 quite extraordinary: stick your head in a dank, warm bale of hay and you won't be far off this; on the other side, there is hint of emulsion paint, too....; t23 the lightest possible coating of maple syrup helps balance the intense oak statement of intent; the weight and body are exemplary; f22.5 long, clean; a more pronounced liquorice edge and just a hint of spice; b22.5 rich, earthy, pungent, full of unique character and quite adorable. Might be an acquired taste for single malt stick-in-the-muds, though... 40%

SLYRS Schliersee-Neuhaus. Working.

Slyrs Bavarian Single Malt 2004 lot no. L26143 db (92.5) n22.5 really expansive oak leaning enticingly towards floral; t23 the oaks stake their claim on delivery but soon allow malty and then honeyed settlers to flourish; the early middle becomes wondrously juicy for a malt which starts so dry – real class at work...; f23.5 now really hits top gear as both oak and barley scuttle off into varying degrees of bitter-sweet complexity; for a while the juicy barley stays the course but fades as the vanillas thicken; b23.5 by far the best malt I have encountered in bottled form from this distillery. Also probably the driest as oak and barley form a happy alliance to create maximum balance. This is the bottling which announced this distillery's greatness. A German treasure. 43%

Slyrs Edition Dallmayr 2004 bott 2007 db (92) n22 t23.5 f23.5 b23. Another quite stunning offering from this distillery found in the heart of Bavaria. The spices, aided by the full strength, really are majestic. But it's not all about Wagnerian drama: the charm, subtlety and near romance of barley is pure Richard Strauss. 55%

Slyrs Bavarian Single Malt 2005 lot no. L13157 db (80.5) n20 t20 f21.5 b19. Oily and off centre, an injudicious cut at the stills has taken away any chance of repeating the elegance and excellence of the previous bottling. Big barley ensures it remains drinkable and towards the finish is particularly enjoyable. 43%

⋯ **Slyrs Bavarian Single Malt 2006** lot no. L26752, bott 2009 db (87.5) n22 malt thick enough to cut with a knife; a slightly sharp fruity, yeasty note, too; t22 friendly sugars join the melt-in-the-mouth gristy barley; f21.5 some oils and oaky dryness; b22 a very friendly, malty and well made greeting from Bavaria. 43%

SPREEWALD-BRENNEREI Schlepzig. Working.

Sloupisti 4 Years db (88.5) n22 some kind of wine cask – gloriously unsulphured!! – is working overtime to outdo the grain for the cleanest hit on the nose; t22 mouthwatering and chewy, there is an immense, clean fruitiness to this which is accompanied by sympathetic spices f22 a cherry-chocolate finale; b22.5 very much grows on you: it is obvious the distillers have worked very hard to get both distillation and maturation right. 40%

Sloupisti 4 Years (Cask Strength) db (94) n23 huge...some of you who were tasting whisky over 20 years ago might remember a sherry cask Glengarioch showing just this kind of massive and compelling personality; t24 the enormity of this whisky hints towards almost something vaguely phenolic mixing in with the lush grape (Glengarioch again!) f23 chocolate and raisins in concentrated form; b24 a mind-blowing fruitfest. Just love the clarity to the flavours. This is such great fun....!! 64.8%

⠴ **Spreewälder "Sloupisti" Single Malt No. 1** db (89.5) n23 complex and busy. The vaguest hint of pine amid the citrus and diluted muscovado; t22.5 sweetened tangerines; a couple of sugars in the mocha; f22 thin but with an attractive malty-sweet, slightly buttery fade; b22 very clean malt which refuses to venture into the realms of bitterness despite the early threat of oak. 40%

⠴ **Spreewälder "Sloupisti" Single Malt No. 1** db (88) n22.5 a slight touch of air freshener about this one but a little nip and spice and extra muscovado gives the nose the come hither treatment; appears rather wet-behind the ears...; t22 big, young, brash new-make-type maltiness; f21.5 remains strictly pre-pubescent, malty but lacking the usual oaky signature; b22 usually, whisky is easy to interpret yet I have to admit it: I'm entirely confused. Both labels are identical, except the strength. And they have both been marked as single Malt No 1. Yet the 62.2%, though beautifully made, strikes me as a youngster whilst the weaker version offers some evidence of maturity. Another point: how can the same malt, 50% weaker in strength than its twin, actually have more colour....? Really lovely whisky, but an enigma. 62.2%

STAATSBRAUEREI ROTHAUS AG Grafenhausen-Rothaus. Working.

⠴ **Black Forest Single Malt Whisky** dist Sep 06, bott Mar 10 db (74.5) n19 t20 f17.5 b18. Black Forest...Green Whisky. In fact I haven't seen anything with this green a tinge since I discovered those now legendary Green Whiskies in the warehouse of Springbank some 20 years ago, and the stuff at the Murree distillery in Pakistan about six years later. Just like the Springbank there is a sugary rum-like sheen to this, except here we are treated to a peculiar hoppy note, too, on both nose and finish. 43%

STEINWÄLDER BRENNEREI SCHRAML Erbendorf. Working.

Stonewood 1818 dist. 1999 db (91) n22.5 delicious lemon curd tart and egg custard tart mix, t23 sharp as a knife citrus cuts through any oak trying to make a showing: refreshing and with a spot-on degree of sweetness to balance; f22.5 a touch of spice kicks in, as does a mild degree of oily feints on which the vanillas thrive; b23 consistant throughout with a superb and endearing degree of sweetness. High quality stuff. 45%

⠴ **Stonewood 1818 Bavarian Grain Whisky 10 Jahre** dist 2000 db (84) n19 t22 f21.5 b21.5. Comes out all guns blazing spraying juicy citrus in every direction. 45%

UNIVERSITÄT HOHENHEIM Working.

Hohenheim Universität Single Malt (82) n21 t20 f20 b21. The aroma is atractively nutty, marzipan even, and clean; the taste offers gentle oak, adding some weight to an otherwise light, refreshing maltiness. Pleasant if unspectacular. 40%. Made at the university as an experiment. Later sold!

WHISKY DESTILLERIE LIEBL Bad Kötzting. Working.

⠴ **Coillmór American Oak Single Cask** cask no. 45, dist Sep 06 db (71) n17 t18 f18 b18. If you are smoker – which I have never been – you might enjoy this one: stale cigarette smoke amid the sharp barley. 43%

⠴ **Coillmór American Oak Single Cask** cask no. 45, bott code LA0110, dist Dec 06 db (72) n17 t18 f19 b18. Well, 10/10 for consistency. Another cask which fails to work on many levels. That period in 2006 will not go down as the distillery's finest. 46%

Coillmór Bavarian Single Malt American white oak cask, distilled Mar 06 db (82) n17.5 t22 f21 b21.5. The superb honey delivery on the palate goes some way to make up for the drying tobacco aroma. 43%

Coillmór Bavarian Single Malt Bordeux cask, dist 18 Mar 06, bott code LB0109 db (40) n10 t10 f10 b10. The French wine industry should never be let anywhere near any country's whisky, unless under the strictest supervision. Absolutely appalling degree of sulphur...about as bad as it gets... *43%. 380 bottles.*

Coillmór Bavarian Single Malt sherry cask, dist 05 May 06, bott code LB0109 db **(89)** **n21** a slight feinty note does its best to knock the superb grape off course...and fails; **t22.5** silky barley copes with the feints efficiently, leaving the grape to move in for the juicy kill; **f23** a beautiful sweetness to the finale, with gristy malt and sultanas hand-in-hand while the spices seep in from the oak and feints; **b23** far from flawless. But you can't ignore the beauty of much of what happens here. *43%. 900 bottles.*

Coillmór Bavarian Single Malt sherry cask, dist May 06 db **(90)** **n21.5** the flawless richness of the grape does all that is possible to overcome the poor nose to the distillate; a strange kind of oily praline cocoa note is the very acceptable hybrid... **t23.5** sweet and oily delivery blossoms out into a real old-fashioned fruitcake complete with seriously burnt raisin; beautiful weight and mouth-feel and the gathering spice is a perfect compliment; **f22** those slight flaws from the distillate gather at the back of the throat but elsewhere the fruit remains luxurious and high class; **b23** excellent: that seriously works....!!! Oh, if only the Scots could come up with a sherry butt of such faultless beauty... *55%*

⋰ **Coillmór Peat & Smoke Aged 3 Years** db **(79.5)** **n19 t20 f20.5 b20.** Major novelty value: peat and cigarette smoke...? *46% 920 bottles.*

⋰ **Coillmór Sherry Single Cask Aged 3 Years** cask no. 81 db **(87.5)** **n21.5** seriously thick grape; **t22.5** huge grain again, but just a little marzipan, too, like the inside of a fruitcake; **f21.5** a little furry dryness; **b22** moments of delightful revelation. *46%*

LATVIA
LATVIJAS BALZAMS Riga. Working.
L B Lavijas Belzams db **(83)** **n20 t22 f20 b21.** Soft and yielding on the palate, this is said to be made from Latvian rye, though of all the world's rye whiskies this really does have to be the softest and least fruity. I'll be astonished if there isn't a fair degree of thinning grain in there, too. *40%*

LIECHTENSTEIN
TELSER Triesen. Working.
Telsington db **(94)** **n23** rarely are Pinot Noirs particularly salty. And never, in my experience, smoky. Yet salt and light iodine abound in a seaweedy coastal romp. The fruity does turn up, but only once the nose has accustomed itself to the massive onslaught its has faced. Welcome to whisky from Lichtenstein...and it has not arrived quietly... **t23.5** the tastebuds are immediately enveloped in the most slinky of fruity gloves – and yet at the same time a fruit rock-hard one... Pinot at play..!! To complicate matters, the vague smokiness drifts around, landing feeble slaps and punches. And on another layer altogether a juicier barley note abounds: what a delight... **f23.5** although a certain bitterness from the oak comes into play, it is supremely controlled by the deft fruit and barley which play a similar tune to earlier, except now more softly **b24** now here's a conundrum if not irony. The first ever whisky from probably the most land-locked country in the whole of Europe, and it has the aroma of a rock pool found on a Hebridean island of about the same, tiny size. As for the whisky? What can I say? The last time I stayed in this beautiful, idiosyncratic country I had no option other than to spend the night in the worst hotel I have encountered in the western world. Thankfully the new distillery does not perform to such pitiful standards. This is not just good whisky, it is outstanding: far, far better than it has any right to be at first attempt. Obviously a fourth visit to Vaduz is now called for: this whisky is worth another night of misery and rudeness. I seriously need to shake the hand of the distiller...this is the most entertainingly delicious whisky I have tasted from mainland Europe this year. *40%*

THE NETHERLANDS
US HEIT DISTILLERY Bolsward. Working.
Frysk Hynder Frisian Single Malt Whisky dist 05 Nov 03, bott 01 Dec 06 db **(87)** **n22.5** elegantly malty and delicately oaked; **t21.5** again the malts pack the punch and after a rather off-balanced delivery, it steadies itself for a wonderfully rich middle; **f22** back to the same malt-oak mix as on the nose, though the oak has the bigger say here; **b21.5** doesn't even begin to try to be complex. Almost opulently simplistic with its thick barley-oak theme. But well made and perhaps too easily quaffable. *40%.*

SPAIN
DYC Aged 8 Years **(90)** **n22** a charming meeting of delicate barley and equally light vanilla; **t23** more of the same, with a silky soft grain element totally in tune with the clean juiciness

of the malt; **f22.5** more of the same, with a Victoria sponge creamy strawberry note; **b22.5** I really am a sucker for clean, cleverly constructed blends like this. Just so enjoyable! 40%

DYC Pure Malt (84.5) n20 t21 f21.5 b21. I admit it's been a few years since I visited the distillery, but from what I then tasted in their warehouses I am surprised that they have not brought out their own single malt to mark the 50th anniversary of the place. This, which contains a percentage of Scotch, I believe, is OK. But no better than what I remember sampling. 40%

DYC Selected Blend (86) n21.5 t22 f21 b21.5. Although still a bantamweight and remains its old refreshing self, has definitely muscled out slightly on nose, delivery and finish....with a distinct hint of smoke. Unquestionably a bigger DYC than before. 40%

⋅❖⋅ **MAG'5 (80.5)** n19 t21.5 f20 b20. Much more Alonso than Puyol.... 40% Destillerias MG

SWEDEN
MACKMYRA Gästrikland. Working.

⋅❖⋅ **Mackmyra Brukswhisky** db **(95.5)** n24 deceptively heavy nose, or deceptively light? At first thin golden syrup, but a lovely rumbling counterweight of light oil, toasty grain and red liquorice; **t24** just fabulous: so delicate and complex as varying levels of busy oak pop around the palate. Bourbony in some senses but the juiciness of the grain has an entirely different character. The molten honeycomb and drier hickory has a familiar feel; **f23.5** long, spicy, chocolatey, honeyed, vanillary; **b24** one of the most complex and most beautifully structured whiskies of the year. A Mackmyra masterpiece, cementing the distillery among the world's true greats. 41.4%

Mackmyra Preludium 04 Svensk Single Malt Whisky bott 11 Apr 07 db **(91)** n22 t23 f23 b23. Most distilleries have a trademark character: Mackmyra's is entirely unique. What is clear now is a density to the malt matched nowhere else. I admit: I adore it...! 53.3%

Mackmyra Preludium 05 Svensk Single Malt Whisky bott 08 Aug 07 db **(87)** n22 t21 f22 b22. A thinner, more metallic beast but still an enormous mouthful that never seems to taste the same twice. 48.4%

Mackmyra Preludium 06 Svensk Single Malt Whisky bott 06 Nov 07 db **(87.5)** n22 t22.5 f21 b22. Always pleasant, always showing a good mouthfeel yet somehow – by Mackmyra standards – doesn't quite get out of third gear. 50.5%

Mackmyra Privus 01 Topp Tunnor bott 06 Mar 07 db **(91)** n24 t24 f21 b22. No other whisky on the planet matches this in style. Takes some getting used to....but it's worth it! 54.5%

Mackmyra Privus 02 Näsa För Sprit bott 07 Mar 07 db **(94)** n23 t24 f23 b24. Excellent balance from first to last, poise, charm and idiosyncrasy are there in equal measures. Quite simply makes my whisky tasting year complete to find something so unique – and astonishing. 54.5%

Mackmyra Privus 03 Rökning Tillåten bott 08 Mar 07 db **(96)** n24 t24 f24 b24. Previously at Mackmyra: fruity, then nutty. Now this. Sensational. Because this is no "me too" whisky. It challenges, asks questions, makes statements. Every expression appears to further and expand my own experience and expectations of whisky, which really is saying something. 56%

Mackmyra Privus 04 Ratta Virket bott 28 Jan 08 db **(95)** n24 t24 f23 b24. Wonderfully raw, almost untamed, around the edges and quite impossible not to love. 55%

Mackmyra Privus 05 Reserve Svensk Single Cask Malt Whisky bodas gruvlager, flask nr. 17/49 db **(93)** n22.5 t23 f23.5 b24. It is entirely impossible not to be head over heals in love with this whisky. This is a malt which makes one bold statement after another: the only thing it has in common with sitting on the fence is the degree of splinters you get. Big oak, yes. But even bigger flavour development from elsewhere. 54%

Mackmyra Privus 06 I Bergakungens Sal bott 28 Jan 08 db **(93.5)** n22.5 a complex interweaving of fruity and salty notes: something wonderfully coastal about this in the manner old, peatless Bunnhabhain so often used to be; **t23.5** juicy at first then a bombardment of spices (including a brief puff of smoke), again pepped by salt, followed by several layers of rich barley of varying degrees of sweetness; the degree of soft oils is exemplary; **f23** long with a withering vanilla kick showing some age coming through; light mocha in this most delicate finale... **b24.5** sober and sultry by Mackmyra standards. No grand statements, no sweeping aromas or flavours taking all before it. Thoughtful, sophisticated and very high class whisky. 54.5%

Mackmyra Reserve "The Smokey Duck" cask no. 36/48, dist Sep 03, bott Sep 07 db **(93)** n22.5 the smoke is browbeaten by the chunky oak; even so citrus makes waves as does soft barley; **t23.5** massive delivery making no apology for its startling oak theme: lazy oils help spread the weight about but the slow build up of spices is simply dazzling, seeming to magnify, somehow, the thick marmalade/citrus strands; **f24** drier oaks now, as to be expected, but the build up of the cocoa is simply brilliant. Very unusually the sweetness appears to re-enter the mix with a smoky farewell that stokes up the brown sugars and honeyed bourbon; **b23.5** back in my own tasting rooms this comes across as a far better dram than when I first tasted it in Sweden. This is a private bottling to be found in Avesta, Sweden: on first taste (as in Sweden) the oak appears simply too inelegant, almost brutal. However, twenty minutes alone with this one with no other distractions other than a spittoon and you'll be amazed how the complexity crystalises and it all makes sense. Superb. *57%*

⁜ **Mackmyra Special: 01** eminent sherry, bott winter 2008 db **(87.5) n21.5** firm, almost a little brusque with limited development; **t22.5** loosens on delivery with a soft fruit fanfare but with a surprising degree of caramels swamping the middle ground; **f22** some half-hearted spices try to liven up the thick vanillas; **b21.5** enjoyable and chewy, but you feel the whisky tries to break free of the dull grape. *51.6%*

⁜ **Mackmyra Special: 02** bott Summer 2009 db **(78.5) n20 t20.5 f18 b20.** Feinty. Some barley and cocoa. But simply nowhere near up to this distillery's usual, brilliant standard. *50.6%*

⁜ **Mackmyra Special: 03** bott Jul 09 db **(91) n23** a compelling mixture of the lightest smoke, wine gums, a rather thicker than technically demanded cut from the stills (though it works!!), marmalade, and much more besides make for a slightly eclectic aroma, but one so beguiling you almost forget to taste the thing....; **t23.5** a creamy, sweet bourbon edge to the delivery. Muscovado sugars do battle with the liquorice, then the grains battle their way in; **f22** just a touch of marmalade bitterness; **b23** after the last two less than special Specials, it's great to see Mackmyra right back on track with this glorious, typically characterful whisky which simply blows you away. *48.2%*

⁜ **Mackmyra Special: 04** double dip bourbon, bott Summer 2010 db **(89.5) n23** the kumquat school of bourbony oak: busy, spicy, bitty, malty. Just never sits still; **t22.5** sharp, bubbling delivery soon gives way to a more relaxed, natural cream toffee; **f22** pretty even though the oak begins to show a marked tannin-bitter persona; **b22** for those who like big oak but without the feeling of over aging: a very different style of whisky. *53%*

Mackmyra Whisky Svensk Single Malt Den Forsta Utgavan bodas gruva, batch no. 08-01 db **(91) n22.5** salted buttered toast, a diced, wet vanilla pod and a non-specific sweetness – not quite honey, not quite syrup, not quite honey, not quite barley (well, maybe a touch of barley)...just sweet; **t23** gentle, well-mannered, barley driven...just so un-Mackmya...!! **f22.5** light, mainly oak oriented with the accent of delicate barley edging towards a late, surprising juiciness – all with a touch of cocoa; **b23** how ironic that after all the Privus (or should that be Previ...?) and Preludiums, each howling wolves which blew your socks off, the first whisky to be produced for relative mass market by Mackmyra standards should be pure, playful pussy. That said, when it comes this elegant and demure, and just sings and purrs prettily to you - is there anything more sexy....? *46.1%*

Mackmyra Whisky Svensk Single Malt Den Forsta Utgavan bodas gruva, batch no. 08-02 db **(90) n21.5** unusual tobacco smoke amid the malt and vanilla: small still character yet surprisingly light for the distillery; **t23** returns to heart-winning ways with a genuinely juicy delivery bordered by the vaguest smoke and a marmalade sharpness; the honey notes are thick and barley rich; **f23.5** magnificently well weighted and balanced with stunning bitter-sweet echoes. Loads of cocoa dust which just puts the perfect cap on the rich barley, which has to be among the most intense I have ever tasted this year. The oak also offers a lively chewiness and vanilla depth; **b23** taste two or three times before getting into the rhythm of this malt. Once there, you'll be hooked. More greatness from Mackmyra. *46.1%*

SWITZERLAND
BRAUEREI LOCHER Appenzell. Working.
Säntis Malt Swiss Highlander Edition Dreifaltigkeit db **(96.5) n24** fantastic mixture of apple-wood style smoke (this is very similar, almost identical in fact, to the smell from the bonfires burned by my late father at his Surrey allotment in the early 60s, and, yes, I think old branches from our apple tree often went up in smoke) and something a bit earthier – obviously the peat. Like a Rupp Cheese of malty heat; **t24.5** this is truly astonishing: the weight of oil on the palate is gentle but sufficient to coat the mouth; next comes a layer of mixed smoke, both woody and earthy; this is followed by a layering of caramelized molasses; an indecipherable fruitiness makes itself heard, while spices pepper the palate like so many small asteroids hitting a small planet.... **f24** a near faultless finale (perhaps a degree of overenthusiastic bitterness), though the experience is so long and seamless, it is hard to know where the main body of the flavours are and when the finish begins... **b24** this is one of the whiskies of the year, without question. Such is the controlled enormity, the sheer magnitude of what we have here, one cannot help taste the whisky with a blend of pleasure and total awe. *52%*

Säntis Malt Swiss Highlander Edition Säntis oak beer casks db **(88)** n22.5 charming, delicate, smoked apple wood; t23 clean, mouthwateringly fresh. A hint of green fig on the silky texture, sweetened slightly by diluted golden syrup; a light touch of phenols hang in the background; f20.5 a touch of oaky, toasty bitterness; b22 light, fruity and impressive. 40%

Säntis Malt Swiss Highlander Edition Sigel oak beer casks db **(91.5)** n23.5 though matured in oak beer casks, this appears to be screaming grape from the glass: one sniff of this cleanest of aromas and you simply can't stop salivating t23 beautiful again: clean, melt-in-the mouth malt combined with a juicy fruitiness and light spice; f22 lots of vanillas represents the oak in the friendliest manner; the spice has intensified and now adds some welcome prickle; b23 high quality whisky which balances with aplomb. 40%

BRENNEREI HOLLEN Lauwil. Working.
Hollen Single Malt Aged Over 6 Years matured in red wine casks db **(89)** n23 another sublime fruit-riddled number. Not a single degree of sulphur or off-note from the distillate makes this a joy. The most distant echo of something vaguely smoky; t22.5 stunning delivery on the palate again with a vague phenol to be detected with the ultra-clean grape; a soft spice buzz delivers into the middle ground f21.5 some natural caramel kicks in to blot out the juices; b22 perhaps the fruit is rather too emphatic and, a late show of spice apart, some of the other forms of character development you might wish to see are lacking. Apparently peatless. Possibly, but not entirely convinced. 42%

Hollen Single Malt Aged Over 6 Years smoke malt, matured in white wine casks db **(92)** n23.5 highly complex: the faintest of peaty touches wrestles for a leading spot amid the vanilla and crisp barley...and if that wasn't enough a soft grape presence muddies the waters further; t23 this must have been one very juicy bunch of casks they found: sweet grape abounds, though a bit of tannin bitterness present, too; a light smokiness on delivery vanishes under the grapey onslaught; f22.5 pretty long with a butterscotch-truffle fade; b23 you just can't really fault this stuff. 42%

Hollen Single Malt Aged Over 6 Years matured in white wine casks db **(90.5)** n23 rum, anyone? Especially if you fancy a Jamaican pot still; t23.5 be prepared to drown in your own saliva...one of the juiciest whiskies ever. And I mean ever...the fruit is so ridiculously clean, it could be some fruit candy f21.5 to many a purist so clean and flat; almost a chewy fruit toffee element; b22.5 many facets to its personality, the nose especially, shows more rum characteristics than malt. A won't-say-no glassful if ever there was one, though, and made and matured to the highest order. Indeed, as I taste and write this, my BlackBerry informs me that Roger Federer is on his way to another Wimbledon title: the similarities in the quiet dignity, elegance and class of both Swiss sportsman and whisky is not such a corny comparison. 42%

Hollen Single Grain Aged Over 6 Years db **(86.5)** n22.5 t21.5 f21 b21.5. Big, sharp and bruising. The odd feint kick here and there, but there is a pleasing chocolate fruit and nut touch to this one, too. 51.6%

Hollen Single Wheat Malt Aged Over 6 Years db **(74)** n18 t19.5 f18 b18.5. Oooops! Bitter, off-key...Even Federer has his off days....and I've just read that over at Wimbledon Roddick is storming to the fourth set...these things happen. (see Hollen White Wine Cask) 42%

BRENNEREI SCHWAB Oberwil. Working.
Bucheggberger Single Malt cask no. 23, bott no. 10 db **(74)** n17 t21 f17 b19. Decent malty lead, but the intensely bitter finish makes hard work of it. 42%

BRENNEREI URS LÜTHY Muhen. Working.
Dinkel Whisky pinot noir cask db **(92.5)** n23 lusty, clean fruit: the grapes appear to be sultana-sweet and beautifully spiced; clean and complex t24 lush, warmingly-spiced grape – as promised on the nose – medium-thick oils and a wonderful transformation into a coffee and fruit cake mix; the barley scuttles out from this enormous mix to make its mark near the middle ground; f22 a touch of bitterness creeps in, but some mocha-grape holds firm; b23.5 a big, striking malt which is not afraid to at times make compellingly beautiful statements. 61.5%

Wyna Whisky Original No. 2 dist Apr 06, bott Apr 09 db **(79)** n21 t21 f18 b19. Fruity, but seriously overcooks the bitterness. 43%. 489 bottles.

BURGDORFER GASTHAUSBRAUEREI Burgdorf.
Reiner Burgdorfer 5 Years Old cask no. 4 db **(82.5)** n18 t22 f21 b21.5. Recovers from the mildly feinty nose to register some wonderfully lush cocoa notes throughout the coppery, small still development on the palate. 43%

DESTILLERIE EGNACH Egnach. Silent.

Thursky db **(93)** n24 all kinds of big fruit-edged bourbon notes; liquorice and honeydew melon; some lychee and marzipan add wonderfully to the mix; even a slightly rummy style to this; **t23.5** silky, estery with a controlled sweetness; again there is a lovely bourbon-fruit interaction, perhaps more on the red liquorice honeycomb bourbon style; **f22.5** some oak begins to bite but the honeyed sheen and light mint-cocoa dusting keeps the whisky honest; **b23** beautifully even whisky! I am such a sucker for that clean fruity-spice style. Brilliant! 40%

BRENNEREI-ZENTRUM BAUERNHO Zug. Working.

Swissky db **(91)** n23 young, clean, fresh malt which sparkles with a hint of apple: one of the best noses on the European scene; **t23** stunningly clean arrival and then the most delicate of malty displays that all hinges around a juicy youth to the barley. The sweetness is controlled, refined and evenly distributed; a soft oiliness helps to lubricate the tastebuds; **f22** no less soft and simple with the oak offering the kind of weight that can barely be detected; **b23** while retaining a distinct character, this is the cleanest, most refreshing malt yet to come from mainland Europe. Hats off to Edi Bieri for this work of art. Moving stuff. 42%

Swissky Exklusiv Abfüllung L3365 db **(94)** n23 t23 f24 b24. A supremely distilled whisky with the most subtle oak involvement yet. Year after year this distillery bottles truly great single malt, a benchmark for Europe's growing band of small whisky distillers. 40%

HAGEN DISTILLERY Hüttwilen. Working.

Hagen's Best Whisky No. 2 lot no. 00403/04-03-08.08 db **(87)** n19 heavy, toffee; **t23.5** rich textured malt with a delightful touch of muscovado sugar and a main theme of chocolate nougat; purposeful and confident; **f22** a slight bitterness, but competently handled by those delicate sugars and gristy malt; **b22.5** much more Swiss, small still style than previous bottling and although the nose isn't quite the most enticing, the delivery and follow through are a delight. Lovely whisky. 42%

Hagen's Best Whisky Oak Special lot no. 3031/03.03 -12.07 db **(84)** n21 t21.5 f20.5 b21. A very well made, sweet, uncomplicated malt matured in a thoroughly used bourbon barrel – or so it seems. Not sure if this is a compliment or not, but could easily be mistaken for some kind of Speyside single malt whisky destined for a young blend. 42%

HR Distillery lot no. 10099, dist Dec 99, bott Jan 05 db **(88)** n21 clean, fine malt. Crisp with a degree of fruit, especially freshly bitten green apple. Some soft dough adds the extra depth; **t23** mouthwatering and deft, this offers a butterfly delivery of sweet young malt backed again by that apple-fresh fruitiness; **f22** lovely delivery of vanilla which balances just so well with the barley; **b22** again we have an enormously impressive whisky from Switzerland. Here we have a classic case of a whisky that has matured for a few years side by side with fruit spirit (probably apple) and has breathed in some of those delicate elements. 42%

HUMBEL SPEZIALITÄTENBRENNEREI Stetten. Working.

Farmer's Club Finest Blended db **(85.5)** n22 t22 f20.5 b21. Clean, well made, astonishingly Scotch-like in its style. In fact, possibly the cleanest whisky made on mainland Europe. Lashings of butterscotch and soft honey; even a coppery sheen while the oak makes delightful conversation. But there appears to be lots of caramel which dulls things down somewhat. 40%

Ourbeer Single Malt db **(84)** n21 t20.5 f21.5 b21. Once more very well made with some entertaining spice. But the caramels have way too much to say for themselves 43%

SPEZIALITÄTENBRENNEREI ZURCHER Port. Working.

Zürcher Single Lakeland 3 Years Old dist Jul 06, bott Jul 09 db **(88.5)** n21.5 thickset and quite handsome in a rugged, yeasty, honeycombed way; **t23** comes into its own with a real red liquorice and nougat middle; oily, nutty with a touch of redcurrant jam towards the middle; **f21.5** mainly vanilla, but the nutty nougat hangs around **b22.5** this distillery never fails to entertain. Not as technically perfect as usual, but none of the blemishes are seriously damaging and even add a touch of extra character. 42%

Zürcher Single Lakeland Malt Whisky 3 Years Old dist Sep 04, bott Sep 07 db **(83)** n21 t22 f20 b20. Enjoys some highly attractive moments when that famous grape-barley gets into full swing. But a sub-standard barrel has done a little damage here. 42%

Zürcher Single Lakeland Malt Whisky 3 Years Old dist Jun 05, bott Jun 08 db **(91.5)** n23 t23 f22.5 b23. Stunning clarity to the fruit ensures a malt which simply sings on the palate. The fruit-barley balance is quite exceptional, though not surprising from this highly impressive distillery. 42%

WHISKY CASTLE Elfingen. Working.

8820 Whisky 1378 days in cask db **(87) n20 t22 f23 b22.** One of those whiskies that grow on you once you understand that it has a different viewpoint. Hugely entertaining. *55%. For Wadi Brau Wadenswil.*

∴ **Castle One Single Malt Edition Käser** cask no. 455, dist Jan 05 db **(86) n19 t22 f23 b22.** Technically, not the best from this distillery with the nose an OTT clash between feints and withering oak . But the extra weight from the extended cut has given the spirit enough muscle to take the weight of the enormous wood influence. The result is demanding, especially at full 68%abv throttle, but ultimately delicious when the Demerara sugars kick in. *68%*

Double Wood Castle Hill Single Malt cask no. 400 db **(83) n21 t20 f21 b21.** Oily, fruity, a tad feinty. *43%*

Edition Käser Castle One Single Malt cask no. 406 db **(94) n23** chocolate nougat, complete with fruit and nuts... and a few green figs thrown in for good measure; **t23.5** big, grapey, quasi-smoky take off, exploding with massive juice and barley on impact with the tastebuds: mind-bogglingly mouthwatering; **f23.5** some cocoa coats the light fruit and soft vanillas; as seemingly unending as a Federer finish at Wimbledon; **b24** another astonishing whisky from this top-rate distillery. *70.6%*

Smoke Rye Whisky Castle Single Malt cask no. 338 db **(90.5) n21.5** the apple-fruity ryes take off in the glass as the heavier of the light feints evaporate in the open air; the smoke appears to a woody – as in smoked cheese - rather than peaty type; **t23.5** juicy, lush and crisp rye of the top order: seriously salivating. Its stretching wings are clipped though by the brooding phenols; **f22.5** some serious cocoa notes dig in and an outbreak of vanilla adds a drying balance; **b23** this will not be to everyone's liking: the distinctive nose alone is not entirely blemish free (though leave a glass of it in a very warm room for about half an hour and most of those blemishes will have vanished) but, like the tale which unfurls on the palate, it is very different, never less than fascinating and sometimes hits the point of high deliciousness. *43%*

Smoke Spelt Whisky Castle Single Malt cask no. 336 db **(71) n16 t19 f18 b18.** Never, ever, have I smelt the countryside so emphatically in a glass than with this whisky. Fusty hay. In concentrate. Amazing: liquid Constable. Also parts of the aroma is pure malting floors. Sadly, though, I am not convinced all this is entirely intentional: it also appears like some kind of infection has got in somewhere during the brewing process. If there is confirmation, it is from the slightly rancid nut oil on the taste. Yet for all the low scores and negatives, I also recognize certain elements on both nose and taste which are beautiful, or at least potentially so. Certainly unique. There again, I can't remember the last time I came across smoked spelt.... I really want to see these guys try this one again and see what happens. Maybe this is the way it does turn out. Or maybe it will prove to be an invaluable and idiosyncratic addition to the whisky lexicon. The earth may or may not move for you with this one. But at least there is proof that it is still going round.... *43%*

∴ **Whisky Castle Terroir** cask no. 477, dist Sep 06 db **(71.5) n16 t18 f19 b18.5.** Butyric and wildly off target. *43%*

∴ **Whisky Castle Vintage** cask no. 485, dist Sep 06 db **(90.5) n22** wonderfully seasoned and spiced with a degree of stewed celery, hob-nobbing with the wood-injected barley; **t23** good grief....! That is an exceptionally silky landing. There is a sweetness and fruit edge which just doesn't manifest itself on the nose: a genuine surprise; **f23** as it dries the mouth feel becomes courser. And as it does the cocoa character is raised a notch or two; **b22.5** imagine a whisky angel gently kissing your palate....this is all about very good spirit (with a slightly wide cut) spending time in what appears to be either a high quality virgin cask, or something very close to one. Brimming with character and charisma. *43%*

WALES
PENDERYN Penderyn. Working.

Penderyn bott code Jan 07 db **(88) n21 t23 f22 b22.** The flavour profile is all upfront. Quite charming, though. *46%. ncf.*

Penderyn bott code Feb 07 db **(89) n22 t22 f22 b23.** Elegant and understated all the way. *46%. ncf.*

Penderyn bott code Mar 07 db **(90) n21 t22 f24 b23.** High quality, softly spoken malt. *46%. ncf.*

Penderyn bott code Apr 07 db **(76) n18 t21 f18 b19.** Hmmm. Oily, a touch hot, bitter and even an unusual hint of feint. Hardly your classic Penderyn. *46%. ncf.*

Penderyn bott code May 07 db **(92) n21 t23 f24 b24.** Normal, quite beautiful service has been resumed...! *46%. ncf.*

Penderyn bott code Jun 07 db **(95)** n23.5 t24.5 f23 b24. Quite simply the best standard bottling yet. An all day every day dram. Welsh gold, indeed. *46%. ncf.*

Penderyn bott code Jul 07 db **(91)** n22.5 t23 f23 b23.5. A rich vein of form as well as Welsh Gold. There is a real confidence to this malt. *46%. ncf.*

Penderyn bott code Aug 07 db **(88)** n22 t22.5 f21.5 b22. A bit brooding and sulky. Takes some work to coax out its more gentle nature. *46%. ncf.*

Penderyn bott code Sep 07 db **(88.5)** n22 t23 f21.5 b22. Fruity and spicy. *46%. ncf.*

Penderyn bott code Oct 07 db **(88.5)** n22.5 t22 f22 b22. The third of perhaps the three most consistent bottlings in terms of style and quality since the distillery began bottling. *46%. ncf.*

Penderyn bott code Nov 07 db **(87)** n21 t22.5 f22 b21.5. A bits and pieces rendition which in the end works attractively though it is a bit parsimonious early on when dealing out the complexity. *46%. ncf.*

Penderyn bott code 1 Dec 07 db **(92.5)** n23.5 t23.5 f22.5 b23. This one pulls out the stops to get the Madeira into full swing. *46%. ncf.*

Penderyn bott code 2 Dec 07 db **(92.5)** n23 t24 f22 b23.5. Truly magnificent in its complexity. *46%. ncf.*

Penderyn bott code 3 Dec 07 db **(85.5)** n22 t21.5 f21 b21. Rounded and soft. But rather too much fudge to make it a great malt. Unless you are fudge dependent... *46%. ncf.*

Penderyn bott code Jan 08 db **(94)** n24 t23 f23 b24. Just gripping with class. *46%. ncf.*

Penderyn bott code Feb 08 db **(91)** n23 t23 f22.5 b22.5. Yet another high performance malt from this distillery, though this one has much more a sherry than Madeira feel. *46%.*

Penderyn bott code Mar 08 db **(88.5)** n23 t23 f21 b21.5. A very pleasant ride, but doesn't offer the scenery promised by the nose. *46%. ncf.*

Penderyn bott code Apr 08 db **(90)** n23 t23 f21.5 b22.5. Such a relaxing dram. You've heard of an Indian Head Massage: well, this is a Welsh one. *46%. ncf.*

Penderyn bott code May 08 db **(92.5)** n24 t23 f22.5 b23. There is something about every second or third bottling that just makes you close your eyes and emit an involuntary groan of satisfaction. Here's another one... *46%. ncf.*

Penderyn bott code June 08 db **(86.5)** n21 t22.5 f21.5 b21.5. A touch thinner than usual, allowing a lovely bite amid the blossoming fruity honey. *46%*

Penderyn bott code Jul 08 db **(94.5)** n24 light cocoa adds a drier texture to the plummy fruit; **t24** lush with a demure, stewed fruit sweetness; no surprise about the milky chocolate found in the middle ground; **f24** lengthy with enough gentle oil to keep those dreamy fruit notes gripped to the roof of the mouth. The butterscotch is lightly laced with cocoa, the complexity actually increasing with time, rather than dropping off; **b24** one of the finest Penderyns of them all: as complex, dark and intriguing as a Christian Bale character. *46%*

Penderyn bott code Aug 08 db **(91)** n22 much more of a bourbony statement made; **t23** juicy and salivating; the oaks nip and bite; **f23** more relaxed and positively grapey; the custardy notes are sweet and mildly sticky; **b23** in a month this whisky shows yet another fascinating said of its character. This is really fun stuff. *46%*

Penderyn bott code Sept 08 db **(86)** n21.5 t22 f21 b21.5. Lots of fruity substance, at times lively, with a bigger say from drier vanillins. *46%*

Penderyn bott code Oct 08 db - no issue

Penderyn bott code Nov 08 db **(89.5)** n22 heavy, lush fruit, some of it citrusy, invigorated with the softest sprinkling of Demerara; the vanillas aren't remotely shy; **t23** sublime, mouth-filling delivery: a chewy experience with a distinct candy feel; a delicate throb of spice ups the complexity; **f22** surprisingly bitters out for a while. Bitter marmalade softened by cream toffee; **b22.5** a busy, slightly off the wall bottling by Penderyn standards but a belter all the same. *46%*

Penderyn bott code Dec 08 db **(90)** n22 the citrus and grape are seen in a clearer perspective than normal; **t23** the influence of the Madeira comes into play from the first nanosecond – and stays right through, despite several gear changes in fruit intensity; a light milky, mocha sweetness towards the middle; **f22** old fashioned English (!) marmalade (sorry, Welsh people) with thick cut fruit, a persistent zesty bitterness and spices; **b23** the perfect breakfast malt... *46%*

Penderyn bott code Jan 09 db **(89.5)** n22 pretty sharp with a distinct nip in the air for the fruitier notes; **t23** the usual lushness on delivery, except here the fruit appears to have a wider remit to offer juicier, more bitter-sweet characteristics; an almost cleaner development showing some real fresh barley notes, too; **f22** the developing house style of bitter marmalade is with us again and it remains a treat; **b22.5** a zingy, lively bottling where the fruits really do get a free hand. *46%*

Penderyn bott code Feb 09 db (**93**) n22.5 vanilla and custard enjoy a surprising dominance: a serious touch of Madeira trifle.. t24 a fabulous clarity to the fruit: salivating on both a grapey-orangey score and with sublime barley and cocoa making the middle ground a complex place to be; f23 a buzzy, busy spiciness. Again, the fruit which really impresses with its see-through juiciness over such a long period; b23.5 a delicious malt which enjoys the clarity you sometimes feel after a heavy downpour. 46%

Penderyn bott code Mar 09 db (**88**) n21.5 a touch flatter than recent bottlings, clean but with mildly less definition; t22.5 zingy for a split second, then one of the softest Penderyn deliveries: pure silk on the lazy fruits; f22 straggly vanillas amid the late, tangy fruit; b22 another lovely bottling, but less inclined towards the dazzling complexity of late. 46%

Penderyn bott code Apr 09 db - no issue

Penderyn bott code May 09 db (**84.5**) n20 t21 f22 b21.5. Pleasant, and softly fruited – like a chewy candy. But the complexity levels are down and relatively ordinary by the outstanding distillery's own high standards. 46%

⋰⋰ **Penderyn** bott code Jul 09 db (**94**) n23.5 juicy apricots by the spoonful...some shimmering malt and vanilla, too; fruit stones and coal-dust add an extra, earthy dimension; t24 wonderfully two-toned; at first crisp barley and within a split second this is enclosed in a softer, fruitier casing; both fabulously sharp and chewy at the same time; f23 powdered cocoa on butterscotch; b23.5 in many ways the essential Penderyn, showing its true colours and at times perplexing complexity. 46%

⋰⋰ **Penderyn** bott code Aug 09 (**77**) n19 t21 f18 b19. Not sure what happened here. The Edward Hyde to the July 09's Henry Jekyll. Hot and thin, the usual charm and complexity is in very short supply. 46%

⋰⋰ **Penderyn** bott code Sep 09 db (**89.5**) n22 interesting, if slightly harsh, mixing of crushed hazelnut and almond; t23 attractive, understated sweetness reveals the Madeira in its most supine mood; the middle ground is gently lit with spice; f22.5 tangy marmalade with a touch of vanilla and cocoa; b22.5 much more like it. A seductive, silky glove glides around the palate. 46%

⋰⋰ **Penderyn** bott code Oct 09 db (**91**) n22.5 Madeira. Madeira. And...errr Madeira.....; t23.5 one of the cleanest whiskies I have tasted in the world this year. The grape is almost transparent but radiates a feisty spiciness which is actually calmed by some soothing vanilla; f22.5 much more quiet with a pithy fruitiness poking tetchily at the vanilla; b22.5 good grief! The most Madeira dominated standard bottling of them all. 46%

⋰⋰ **Penderyn bott** code 01 Nov 09 db (**92.5**) n22 a little thin but some almost virgin oaky bourbony traits waft through...; t24 now that is ridiculously good: the delivery immediately hits a sublime balance between the fruit and oak, the sweet and the dry. But there is an unusual degree of oil to this, too....probably from the Madeira cask. And it's juicy.... f23 for all the obvious fruit, the barley is right up there and singing proud like you'd expect a son of Wales to sing.. b23.5 my, oh my: what a treat this is! The consistency of bottling after bottling, not so much in style but quality, almost defies belief: this is the Golden Age of Welsh whisky.. 46%

⋰⋰ **Penderyn** bott code 02 Nov 09 (**85**) n21.5 t22 f20 b21.5. Fat with varying layers of grape; vanilla hits the middle ground running. 46% ncf

⋰⋰ **Penderyn** bott code Nov 09 db (**88**) n22 Tunnock's mallow and jam... t23.5 succulent, virile grape. Sharp, mouth-watering barley forms a delicious ally; f21 late oaky bitterness; b21.5 disappointing fade but the delivery is pure Welsh magic. 46%

⋰⋰ **Penderyn** bott code 01 Dec 09 db (**88**) n22 varying shades of clean vanilla; t23 wow! One of the sweeter deliveries with some muscovado sugar appending itself to the sharp, eye-watering grape; the middle ground pleasantly alternates between gristy barley and the softest fruit echoes; f21 cream toffee and vanilla; b22 the dullish finish cannot eclipse the bright, complex delivery. 46%

⋰⋰ **Penderyn** bott code Dec 09 db (**86.5**) n22.5 t22 f21 b21. Toffee and vanilla. 46%

⋰⋰ **Penderyn** bott code Jan 10 db (**78**) n19 t21 f19 b19. Pleasant. But a few cylinders failing to fire. 46%

⋰⋰ **Penderyn** bott code Feb 10 db (**85.5**) n21 t22.5 f21 b21. Chubby, attractive spices and fruitily simplistic. 46%

Penderyn bottle code 0411208 (750ml) db (**89**) n23 t23 f21 b22. A safe version that is performing elegantly but within itself. 46% (92 proof). ncf.

⋰⋰ **Penderyn** bott code 092909 (**93.5**) n23 here we go: soft traces of apricot and distilled fruit stone, caressed by vanilla and with the most delicate of bourbon-sweet edges; t23.5 mouth watering, lush, an early sprig of mint and then onto a much more powdery middle where both fruit and oak are eyeing each other up warily; f24 decides on the course it wishes to take, then rumbles along forever. Just a continuous interplay between sweet fruit and drier vanilla, but a light molassed caress to ensure the fruit stones never quite bitter out; the raisin dusted in cocoa powder on the finish is almost being cocky; **b23** just couldn't have been more Welsh than any potential offspring of Catherine Zeta Jones by Tom Jones, conceived while "How Green Is My Valley" was on the DVD player and a Shirley Bassey CD playing in the background. And that after downing three pints of Brains bitter after seeing Swansea City play Cardiff City at the Liberty Stadium, before going home to a plate of cawl while watching Wales beating England at rugby live on BBC Cymru. Yes, it is that unmistakably Penderyn; it is that perfectly, wonderfully and uniquely Welsh. *46% ncf Imported by Sazerac Company*

Penderyn bott code 1131008 (750ml) db **(93.5) n22.5** a dark, baritone undercurrent to this one: the mushy fruit occasionally flies off on a high one but elsewhere there is more persistent deep murmur of beautifully fused grape and cocoa; **t23.5** exactly the same on delivery: not often outside fresh oloroso that the evident fruit offers such deep base; the odd sparkier high notes carrying both grape and vanilla with aplomb. The middle ground fills in beautifully, shaped by soft oils and embracing the lightest of praline chocolate wafers; **f23.5** no high notes at all here: a long, persistent rumble of fruit and praline with a spot-on degree of sweetness. A creaseless experience: a gentle, almost erotic massaging of the tastebuds ...; **b24** the light cocoa infusion just tops this off perfectly. A truly classic Penderyn; more charm than Tom Jones, hitting just as many pure notes...and just being a fraction of his age *46% US Market.*

⠿ **Penderyn 41** db **(91.5) n22** delicate peach and bitter almond; a touch of apricot, too; **t23** the Madeira coats the palate with first a light layer of soft grape, then a heavier one of skin and stone. Against the drier vanillas, the gristy sweetness of the barley is supported by the constant grape; **f24** a charming fade of spiced butterscotch and lightly sweetened cocoa; **b22.5** don't think for one moment it's the reduction of strength that makes this work so well. Rather, it is the outstanding integration of the outlandishly good Madeira casks with the vanilla. At usual strength this would have scored perhaps another couple of points. Oh, the lucky French for whom this was designed... *41%*

⠿ **Penderyn 41** bott code Sep 09 db **(91.5) n22** dry vanilla ice cream with peach and apricot ripple; **t23.5** luxurious delivery with a splendid diversity of delicately sweetened vanilla and soft fruit notes. Complex and sublimely balanced with a playful peppering of spices; **f23** varying levels of fruit and nut chocolate; **b23** tells a slightly different story to the first version of the "41", but tells it no less brilliantly. *41%*

⠿ **Penderyn 41** code Feb 10 db **(89.5) n21** crushed fruit stones; **t23.5** soft and fruity delivery with a slow growth of sweeter sugars to spar with the spices; **f22.5** excellent oil development hangs on the gristy and dilute treacle sweetness to the not so bitter end; **b22.5** this sweeter bottling opts for a much more understated and easy-going approach with a notably more emphatic fruit input. A hat-trick of ultra-complex stunners from Penderyn...astonishing! *41%*

Penderyn Cask Strength Rich Madeira db **(96.5) n24.5 t24 f24 b24.** Sadly, only three bottles of this were produced. Two were presented to directors of the company, the third to Prince Charles on the occasion of his visit to the distillery to officially open the Visitors' Centre. The remainder of this cask will eventually be bottled, though if quite as sublimely balanced as this I'll be surprised: I suspect this was a whisky plucked in full ripeness. Some of you may have seen on television a certain whisky writer enjoying this with Prince Charles and Penderyn blender Dr Jim Swann. I can tell you we were all genuinely stunned by it – even Jim Swann! Now having had time to study it in my own tasting lab, away from the lights, cameras and the principality's most expensive aftershave and perfume....well, it's even better than I remember it. If finer whisky has been bottled in Wales, then I wasn't alive at the time to see it. A prince of a Welsh whisky truly fit for the Prince of Wales. *57.7%. ncf. nc.*

Penderyn Grand Slam 2008 Edition db **(88.5) n23 t23 f21 b21.5**. You'd think that to mark the winning of a Grand Slam, they'd bring out a real hefty, hairy-arsed dram full of spice and vim. But no: it's a gentle giant. Are they trying to suggest the Championship was won by craft, guile and an understated touch of class...? *46%. ncf.*

⠿ **Penderyn Madeira** bott code Mar 10 db **(88.5) n22.5** docile bourbony oak with a full gamut of citrus fruits and spice: a Welsh gentlemen's Cologne (or an Aberfeldy, I think they call it)... **t23** hard as Welsh slate on delivery and then a fabulous eruption of varying coffee notes; **f21** mocha with strictly no sugar...; **b22** oh, if only they had managed to inject some sweetness into the finish of this one, it would have been one for the collection. *46%*

⠿ **Penderyn Madeira** bott code Apr 10 db **(94.5) n24** now that is one of the most upfront Madeira finishes I have come across from this distillery for a little while: while the fruit is dripping from the glass, there is much more bourbon influence, too, with a serious touch of the Kentuckys about this...; **t23.5** mouth-filling and lusciously malty, it is no time at all before the spices explode, lighting up the rich fruit middle. All around cocoa notes fly, as do some strategic muscovado sugars and delicate liquorice, underlining the big bourbon thread on this; the degree of accommodating oils nears perfection; **f24** almost ridiculous in its length and complexity. Those oils which develop mid range can go on for many minutes more, carrying with them the light sugars and soft spearmint which so well matches that delicate mocha. Long, flakey and wonderfully complex; **b23** now that IS a classic! Does what all the previous bottlings tried to do, but much more thoroughly and with confidence abounding. Big whisky, for something so seemingly delicate. *46%*

⊸ **Penderyn Madeira** bott code May 10 db **(90) n21** lots of Kentucky again, on the nose through drying tobacco leaves; **t23.5** much better assembled: in fact, pure entertainment! Seriously complex, at first just needing a slightly more telling degree of early sweetness to achieve excellence and then getting there with the super slow-motion assembling of juicy grape notes and then a hickory/Demerara ensemble....makes you purr like a contented dragon... **f23** that softly fruited and big-spiced personality powers through for a superb – and very long - finale; **b22.5** when at last the sweetness of the Madeira and malt can be heard we have an exceptionally complex whisky on our hands. *46%*

⊸ **Penderyn Madeira** bott code Jun 10 db **(84.5) n21.5 t22 f20.5 b21.** Perfectly enjoyable, if somewhat dry, whisky for stirring the bones on getting home in the evening from the pits and clearing the coal dust from the taste buds. Or having just seen your football team lose. But for a Penderyn, even for a wonderful mid-range surge of Madeira, it just doesn't hit the right notes at the end with the early promise never quite being fulfilled. Still, should provide the kind of jolt back to life Swansea City fans will probably need on the dank, chilly evening of Saturday 11th December 2010. Mind you, not sure how they feel about things associated with Portugal right now... *46%*

Penderyn Peated Edition bott code Sep 07 db **(92.5) n23 t24 f22.5 b23.** Not one for those who want their peat naked, but rather wearing something that is vaguely see-through in the soft light. *46%. ncf.*

Penderyn Peated Edition bott code Dec 07db **(86.5) n21.5 t22.5 f21 b21.5.** Let's all play "Spot the Peat". It is there, of course, but rather than add an extra dimension, it appears to shield some of the usually more complex notes. Or is that the toffee on the finale...? *46%. ncf.*

Penderyn Peated Edition bott code Apr 08 db **(78) n18.5 t20 f19.5 b19**. Oily, clanking, thick whisky. Pleasant in part but something here just doesn't add up – on the nose especially. The most unsubtle Penderyn of them all. *46%. ncf.*

Penderyn Peated Edition bott code May 09 db **(92) n23.5** that distinctive, light, clean coating of peat enjoys an improbable degree of balance between the sweeter and drier, chalky vanilla tones: the kind of aroma that temps you to keep your nose buried in the glass most of the day... **t23** the delivery is one of pure silk; eventually a juicier grassy barley element emerges with an almost apologetic smokiness hanging on to its coat-tail; **f22** that cocoa/mocha note found from time to time with Penderyn can be spotted here, too. Despite the rumble of spiced peat... **b23.5** for those not of a peaty disposition, don't let the nose worry you: it plays only a character rather than leading role on the palate. Beautiful, anytime whisky. *46%*

⊸ **Penderyn Peated Edition** bott code Sep 09 db **(93.5) n23** you can almost count the peat molecules... **t24** a tantalising dusting of smoke over the juicy Chinese pear and an oilier malt thread; reaches its zenith at the midpoint when all these flavour profiles are still in play but joined also by mocha and raspberry jam; youthful and lithe; **f23** very long finish for a whisky which, for all its delicate smoke, always remains light and dextrous; **b23.5** a definitive case of where less is more: just the lightest smoke infusion helps cloak any disjointed notes, but is never heavy enough to allow the main flavour players full run. Fabulous. *46%*

⊸ **Penderyn Peated Edition** bott code Dec 09 db **(86) n21 t21 f22.5 b21.5.** Shows attitude throughout and an early over sweetness. Some rough edges are never quite blunted by the smoke and though the finish in particular keeps you entertained, it never gets close the magnificence of the September peated version. *46%*

⊸ **Penderyn Peated Edition** bott code May 10 db **(84) n21 t20 f22 b21.** The smoke at times can barely bother registering. When it does it tends to rail against fruits and oak to create a heated whisky in every sense. Stirring, enjoyable, roughhouse stuff and never for a moment a glass you can relax with. *46%*

Penderyn Port Wood Edition cask no. PORT 13 db **(96.5) n24** dark and intriguing: the Port character is in a form that will not be easily recognised to usual Port Finish lovers. This one has a brooding, though not quite forbidding presence. And seems to work alongside the bourbony subtext with almost arrogant ease. The result is a stunning, almost rummy experience of the highest Guyanese variety.. **t24** the Port batters open the tastebuds almost ruthlessly for a second or two, as if forgetting its own strength. Shortly, though, it has calmed and the layering of softer, juicier fruit and a more bitter oak infusion has begun; **f24** now blithely enters superstar status with an extraordinary complexity that becomes seductively apparent. Again the grape is there, rich textured and fat, but the bourbony notes are not shy, either, and melt into the story with a burnt honeycomb and medium roast Jamaican Blue Mountain coffee signature. The sweeter notes need to be provided by a molassed/muscovado style for balance - and is, right on cue..... **b24.5** if you have five minutes to try a great whisky, don't bother with this one. This is a full half hour job. At least. One of those malts which never sits still, changing shape and form and refuses to tell quite the same story twice. Classic doesn't quite cover it....I doubt if even Swansea's much vaunted beautiful football is quite as beautiful as this: that was Spanish inspired...this is Portuguese perfection. *60.4%*

⌬ **Penderyn Port Wood Edition** cask no. PT26 db **(81) n18 t22 f21 b20.** Enormous, eye-watering, fruit delivery which all but bludgeons the taste buds into submission. Tightens alarmingly on arrival and then again towards the middle ground and finish. For all its might and magnitude, and occasional lip-smacking deliciousness, at times bitter, grouchy, cramped and, overall, just not in the same league as the previous, legendary, Port Wood Penderyn. Having said all that, so different you just have to try it...!! One for the world's Whisky Clubs: I'd love to be a fly on the fall of the debates around this one... *60.6%*

Penderyn Rich Madeira Limited Edition cask no. M3 **(96) n24.5** certain elements here are not dissimilar to an exceptionally fine old Malmsey I keep in my cellar. But, as with all truly great whisky noses, it's not just about the star attraction: it is about complexity, integration and balance. And here we have some major oak influence manifested in finest Niederegger marzipan, liberally doused in dark chocolate as well as fabulous bitter marmalade and a peppery, spicy nip for good measure...and a bit of matching salt, too. And, of course the apricots so resplendent in the Prince Charles bottling are still there, but not quite as sweet as before; **t24.5** the mouth-feel and delivery oozes complexity: in a fraction of a second the tastebuds are encountered by an eye-wateringly dry bite on one level, and juicy, chewy fruits on another. The barley, silent on the nose, is at last heard but only for a few moments before the grapey-marmaladey fruit signature arrives in the silkiest of fashions. The middle ground is filled with fruit and oak playfully squabbling to be top dog, but eventually allowing each other turns; again there is a light sprinkling of salt to the oak; **f23** the fade has shortened slightly, but now we have a weak milky chocolate attaching to the light oils which is pulsed out alongside the returning apricot and mushy grape. Gentle spices represent the oak with a delicate grace. **b24** this whisky has moved on since that extraordinary bottling was presented to Prince Charles. In some ways it has gained, in others lost. But, quality-wise, it is impossible to separate them by anything wider than the width of a grape skin. Unquestionably one of the world whiskies of the year, and if anything crops up better in Europe we will have found something truly exceptional. This is the kind of whisky where if you can only get a bottle by swearing allegiance to the Principality of Wales, I for one would re-name my house Yaki Dah, eat nothing but leak soup and go back to find that girl I knew in Maesteg and have lots of Welsh-born sprogs. Second thought.... giving up my Millwall season ticket for a Swansea one...now you're asking a bit too much... *54.3%*

Penderyn Sherrywood Edition bott code Jun 08 db **(91) n22.5 t23 f22.5 b23.** A beautifully constructed and weighted malt which fills every crevice in the palate *46%. ncf.*

⌬ **Penderyn Sherrywood Edition** bott code Dec 09 db **(94.5) n22** firm; maybe a subtle hint of bitter cherry; **t24.5** envelops the mouth with a bosomy embrace: fat, succulent and something to alternately nibble and chew...; fruits pop into every crevice and spices aren't far behind; **f24.5** a quite beautiful spice pulse beats to the lip-smacking, cocoa encrusted end; no bitterness, no off notes, just wave upon wave of unbelievable complexity: one of the greatest finishes in Wales since Ivor Allchurch was strutting his stuff at The Vetch; **b23.5** one of those whiskies which on first taste you think: Hmmm, a bit quiet. Ordinary..." On second taste you think: "hang on...what's going on here...?" Third taste: "ooh, I say..." Funny how it's the quiet ones you have to watch... *46%*

Penderyn Welsh Rugby Union 125th Anniversary Edition Madeira finish db **(95) n23** dripping in lightly spiced grape, the vanilla-barley sub-plot adds just the right weight; **t24** My word! There'll be a few people in Madeira surprised that their fortified wine can be quite this good...the spice-fruit balance is now the stuff of Welsh legend; **f24** the accent falls on the oak but so many layers of grape and barley and black-peppered spice wash over it that you wonder if it will ever end. Even a tendency towards bitterness works in its favour as that honeycomb arrives to absorb it. Stunning; **b24** lamb apart, the best thing from Wales I have ever got my lips round... (!) And I say that with full apologies to a young lady from Maesteg, but it's true, you see... *50%. 1250 bottles.*

World Whiskies

I have long said that whisky can be made just about anywhere in the world; that it is not writ large in stone that it is the inalienable right for just Scotland, Ireland, Kentucky and Canada to have it all to themselves. And so, it seems, it is increasingly being proved. Perhaps only sandy deserts and fields of ironstone can prevent its make physically and Islam culturally, though even that has not been a barrier to malt whisky being distilled in both Pakistan and Turkey. While not even the world's highest mountains or jungle can prevent the spread of barley and copper pot.

Outside of North America and Europe, whisky's traditional nesting sites, you can head in any direction and find it being made. South America may be well known for its rum, but in the south of Brazil, an area populated by Italian and German settlers many generations back, malt whisky is thriving. In even more lush and tropical climes it can now also be found, with Taiwan and Thailand leading the way.

Japan has long represented Asia with distinction and whisky-making there is in such an advanced state and to such a high standard Jim Murray's Whisky Bible has given it its own section. But while neighbouring South Korea has ended its malt distilling venture, further east, and at a very unlikely altitude, Nepal has forged a small industry to team up, geographically, with fellow malt distillers India and Pakistan. The one malt whisky from this region making inroads in world markets is India's Amrut single malt. Actually, inroads is hardly doing them justice. Full-bloodied trailblazing, more like. So good now is their whisky they have, with their fantastically complex brand, Fusion was deservedly awarded Jim Murray's Whisky Bible 2010 Third Finest Whisky in the World. That represented a watershed not just for the distillery, but Indian whisky as a whole and in a broader sense the entire world whisky movement: it proved beyond doubt that excellent distilling and maturation wherever you are on this planet will be recognised and rewarded.

Africa is also represented on the whisky stage. There has long been a tradition of blending Scotch malt with South African grain but now there is single malt there, as well. Two malt distilleries, to be precise, with a second being opened at the Drayman's Brewery in Pretoria. I was supposed to have visited it a little while back, but the distiller, obviously not wanting to see me, went to the trouble of falling off his horse and breaking his thigh the actual day before. Wimp.

One relatively new whisky-making region is due immediate further study: Australia. From a distance of 12,000 miles, the waters around Australia's distilleries appear to be muddied. Quality appears to range from the very good to extremely poor. And during the back end of 2004 I managed to discover this first hand when I visited three Tasmanian distilleries and Bakery Hill in Melbourne which perhaps leads the way regarding quality malt whisky made south of the Equator. Certainly green shoots are beginning to sprout at the Tasmania Distillery which has now moved its operation away from its Hobart harbour site to an out of town one close to the airport. The first bottlings of that had been so bad that it will take some time and convincing for those who have already tasted it to go back to it again. However, having been to the warehouse – and having tasted samples from every single cask they have on site – I reported in previous Bibles that it was only a matter of time before those first offerings would be little more than distant – though horrific – memories. Well, as predicted, it is now safe to put your head above the parapet. The last cask strength bottling I tasted was a bloody beaut. For this year's 2011 Bible, I have managed to taste for the first time Australian whiskies from the Timboon Railway Shed, The Nant and the Great Southern distilleries, each of which managed to offer something which scored above 90, as did the old mainstays of Lark and Bakery Hill. That is a quite staggering achievement and one which means that I now have no option but to start thumbing through an Atlas and flight timetable to get back over there pronto. The remaining casks of Wilson's malt from New Zealand are disappearing fast and when in New Zealand I discovered the stills from there were not just making rum in Fiji but whisky as well. We are all aware of the delights of island whisky, but a Pacific Island malt? Which leaves Antarctica as the only continent not making whisky, though what some of those scientists get up to for months on end no one knows.

ARGENTINA
Blends
Breeders Choice (84) n21 t22 f21 b20. A sweet blend using Scottish malt and, at the helm, an unusually lush Argentinian grain. *40%*

AUSTRALIA
BAKERY HILL DISTILLERY 1999. Operating.
Bakery Hill Classic Malt db **(83)** n19 t22 f21 b21. Lots of serious attitude and gristy sweetness, but a tad feinty. *46%*

Bakery Hill Classic Malt cask no. 2308 db **(87)** n22 flaky oak forms a dry layer over the barley; t22 a lush malt slowly increases the sugary tempo; a touch of cocoa fattens things out; f21.5 slightly short with the vanillas and cocoa lording it over the barley; b21.5 enjoyable. But not a patch on its cask strength version. *46%*

Bakery Hill Classic Malt cask no. 2707 db **(84)** n19 t22 f21 b22. Bizarre. Just checked – and found I have given almost identical marks to last year's version – and the tasting notes remain spot on. *46%*

⋙ **Bakery Hill Classic Malt** cask no. 3009 db **(81)** n21 t21.5 f18.5 b20. Malty and sawdusty. Feints inject some weight and bitters. *46%*

Bakery Hill Classic Malt cask no. 3108 db **(82)** n20 t21 f20.5 b20.5 More than a hint of feints amid the oily barley. *46%*

Bakery Hill Classic Malt Cask Strength db **(86)** n20 t22 f23 b21. A shadow of something feinty, but nothing like the 46% version. The result, though, is about as big a whisky as you'll get for something theoretically unsmoked...! *60.1%*

Bakery Hill Classic Malt Cask Strength cask no. 2308 db **(92)** n23 the oak is full and confident but the light liquorice fits in well with the barley; t23.5 rich barley offers a mouth-watering impact. A drizzle of muscovado sugar links directly in with the growing cocoa; f22.5 long, softly oiled and daintily spiced. Still the cocoa lingers and tapers towards a chocolate and vanilla ice mix; b23 here's incontrovertible proof that whisky does not necessarily improve with the addition of water. Where the 46% version of this is bitty and just keeps itself together for a decent innings, this one has all the oils in full flow ensuring something rich and magnificent. *60.2%*

Bakery Hill Classic Malt Cask Strength cask no. 2606 db **(94)** n23 t24 f24 b23. There are about 20 distilleries in Speyside that would die to be able to make a whisky this stunningly integrated. Young, barely pubescent but sheer, unadulterated, class... *60.1%*

Bakery Hill Classic Malt Cask Strength cask no. 2707 db **(86)** n20 t22 f22 b22. A big malty march from delivery to finish aided by some enthusiastic oils that slightly undid the nose. *58%*

Bakery Hill Classic Malt Cask Strength cask no. 3108 db **(82.5)** n20.5 t21 f20.5 b20.5 Cask strength feintiness. *60.2%*

⋙ **Bakery Hill Classic Malt Cask Strength** bourbon cask no. 4510 db **(89)** n23 big barley with a thick liquorice and caramelised ginger strata; t22.5 crystallised barley sugar on delivery; fattens as the oils arrive, as does the light honey and spice; f22 a thick coating of malt clings on forever; b22 talk about going back in time: it is 1994 and I am in a warehouse in Dunedin going through the earliest existing casks of Lammerlaw New Zealand malt. The closest thing to it. *60.5%*

⋙ **Bakery Hill Classic Malt Cask Strength** bourbon cask no. 5710 db **(83)** n21.5 t21.5 f19.5 b20.5. One seriously sweet bottling. Plenty of nougat and honey. *60.5%*

Bakery Hill Double Wood db **(84)** n21 t22 f20 b21. Attractively chewy, juicy in places but ultimately heavy duty and a tad fey on the finish. *46%*

Bakery Hill Double Wood cask no. 2719 db **(92)** n22 some major citrus and grape makes inroads into the oaky malt; a wisp of smoke, or my imagination...? t23 more of the same with a fruitcakey feel now, complete with a slight doughyness to the malt; big, busy middle; f23 long, classy finish with some chocolate adding to the fruitcake and some smoke ensuring, with the delicate oils, depth, further length and weight; b24 high class whisky is high class whisky wherever its made. Get up to body temp – and marvel..! *46%*

Bakery Hill Double Wood cask no. 3536 db **(78.5)** n21 t20 f18 b19.5 Citrus and feints. *46%*

⋙ **Bakery Hill Double Wood** bourbon & French oak cask no. 5855 db **(86.5)** n22.5 t22.5 f20.5 b21. Substantial whisky with a delightful chocolate fruit and nut core. Chewy and enjoyably macho. *46%*

Bakery Hill Peated Malt db **(89)** n21 ultra delicate: the very lightest smoke and vanilla; t22 delightful barley sugar lead with peat tagging along as a faint shadow; f23 the peats begin to gather and some spices arrive; b23 restrained and delicate from first to last. *46%*

Bakery Hill Peated Malt cask no. 1307 db **(90) n22** half Bowmore-half Laphroaig-style kippery, Fisherman's Friend cough sweet element to this – the most Islay style from this distillery yet; **t23** perfect weight on the oils ensure the delivery is soft and, at first malty. The smoke gathers density... **f23** a sharp, citrus kick to the lightly-oiled finish – smoked marmalade on toast... **b22** well made and simply lovely whisky. 46%

Bakery Hill Peated Malt cask no. 2408 db **(86.5) n22 t21.5 f21.5 b21.5**. Very lightly peated, this actually has more of a Cadbury's Whole Nut character than an all out smoky one. Chewy and very enjoyable. 46%

Bakery Hill Peated Malt cask no. 2507 db **(83) n21 t22 f19 b21**. Another big mouth filler with the smoke little more than a distant cloud. Pretty bitter at the death. 46%

⋅⋰⋅ **Bakery Hill Peated Malt** bourbon cask no. 6209 db **(88.5) n22** firm, flinty phenols; **t23** crisp barley; crunchy brown sugars alongside the peat; **f21** over-baked caramelised biscuit **b22.5** spic and span, matter of fact malt. 46%

Bakery Hill Peated Malt Cask Strength db **(89) n23** clean, the usual citrus house-style; the peats are a bit laid-back but charming; **t23** stunningly refreshing with superb soft oils for the sweet peat to melt into; **f21** a minor vanilla fest and some coppery sharpness; **b22** another really lovely malt from this outstanding distillery. 60.1%

Bakery Hill Peated Malt Cask Strength cask no. 1307 db **(93) n23 t24 f23 b24**. No surprise: it is just like the 40% version (being from the same cask), except the bigger notes are huge and there is just a greater degree of harmony to assist the overall balance. More absolutely outstanding distilling from that true master distiller, David Baker....someone so deserving of an overused and lately cheapened nomenclature. 59.8%

Bakery Hill Peated Malt Cask Strength cask no. 2507 db **(84.5) n20.5 t22 f20.5 b21.5**. Again a much more rotund and confident malt at this strength with a sweetness that falls between chocolate-liquorice and light molasses. But the nose, like the finish, has some unresolved issues. 60.7%

⋅⋰⋅ **Bakery Hill Peated Malt Cask Strength** French oak cask no. 6009 db **(92.5) n23.5** heavyweight stuff: fruity and phenolic; a few spices march around; **t24** and those spices come up trumps on delivery: a huge arrival with a big soft juicy backdrop acting as a stark contrast; the smoke resurfaces gingerly; **f22.5** elegant fade with the fruit having been vanquished by the vanilla, spices and soft smoke; **b22.5** I remember when Talisker had this kind of spice attack. Virtually every phase of this malt works fabulously: a truly wonderful piece of distilling and maturation. 60%

⋅⋰⋅ **Bakery Hill Peated Malt Cask Strength** bourbon cask no 6810 db **(87) n22.5** the peat is so distant, it could be on the other side of the world....; **t22** the mouth is washed in sweet barley. Some smoke nonchalantly hangs around; **f21** bitter oak; **b21.5** not the kindest cask, but the peat is intriguing. 60%

BOOIE RANGE DISTILLERY

Booie Range Single Malt db **(72) n14 t20 f19 b19**. Mounts the hurdle of the wildly off-key nose impressively with a distinct, mouth watering barley richness to the palate that really does blossom even on the finish. 40%

LARK DISTILLERY

The Lark Distillery Single Malt Whisky cask LD38, bott Apr 09 db **(88.5) n22.5** a few feints, but some sexy mocha is the bait... **t22** oily (no surprise there given the nose) but a real ramping up of intense barley and cocoa; **f22** sweetens with a touch of dry molasses with an oily vanilla-barley fade; **b22** distiller Kristy Lark has taken a liberty or two here with her cut...and somehow got away with it. That's women distillers for you... 43%

The Lark Distillery Single Malt Whisky cask LD46, bott Apr 07 db **(86) n20 t22 f22 b22**. Some serious malty oomph to the middle and latter stages of this one with heaps of natural caramel. 40%. sc.

The Lark Distillery Single Malt Whisky cask LD48, bott Jan 07 db **(88) n21 t23 f22 b22**. Knife and fork whisky – and a spoon wouldn't go amiss. 58%. sc.

The Lark Distillery Single Malt Whisky cask LD60, bott 08 db **(86.5) n21 t21.5 f22 b22**. Celebrates all things malty. The odd touch of butterscotch infiltrates, but really it's all about sweet barley almost in mash form. Charming. 43%

The Lark Distillery Single Malt Whisky Cask Strength cask LD31, bott 08 db **(89.5) n22** salted – and peppered! – celery stick; **t23** dry, prickly-spiced and beautifully fruit and barley layered; **f22.5** puckeringly dry in places but a big Demerara and spice statement rekindles the flame just when it appears to be flickering out; **b22** well made, complex whisky which really does take the sweet-dry balance to a new level.... 58%

The Lark Distillery Single Malt Whisky Cask Strength cask LD58, bott 07 db (90.5) n23.5 t22 f22.5 b22.5. A massively enjoyable, beautifully made, in your face dram which never thins out or even remotely takes its foot off the gas. 58%

The Lark Distillery Single Malt Whisky Cask Strength cask LD68 db (84) n21 t20 f21.5 b21.5. Another well made malt from Lark's which again really zaps up the barley content. Some major small, still notes here which engineer a hefty weight to the proceedings. 58%

⁓ The Lark Distillery Single Malt Whisky Cask Strength cask no. LD100, bott Oct 08 db (93.5) n23.5 I remember celery was part of the profile a little while back: here it is again, peppered rather than salted; t24 fabulous fruit take off: juicy from a grape as well as a barley perspective, roasty and a late build up of intense spice; f23 vanilla injection but the white peppers hangs around the tongue for quite some while... b23 a stupendous bottling from Larks, brimming with impossible character and probably the best of theirs I have ever encountered. Did Kristy accidentally leave a pepper pot in the still or something....? 58%

⁓ The Lark Distillery Single Malt Whisky Cask Strength cask no. LD140, bott Feb 10 db (80) n19.5 t18.5 f22 b20. From tip to tail there is a note on this I can't quite put my finger on, or say I much approve of. But there is also a real coppery small still feel to this, bolstered by a late-developing honeycomb and Demerara sheen. 58%

The Lark Distillery Single Malt Whisky Distillers Selection cask LD51, bott May 07 db (91) n22 t23 f23 b23. One very big malt that keeps your tastebuds guessing all the way. A treat of a whisky. 46%. sc.

The Lark Distillery Single Malt Whisky Distillers Selection cask LD59, bott 08 db (80) n19 t21 f20 b20. Hmmm. I just hope distiller Kristy Lark's brand new husband is a bit better than this... 46%

The Lark Distillery Single Malt Whisky Distillers Selection cask LD99, bott Feb 09 db (82) n21 t19 f21 b21 Well there's one to get your kisser round! The nose has almost a toothpaste-y, minty edge and though the delivery doesn't seem quite on the button it recovers impressively enough for a real ol' oak and cocoa dust up further down the track. Not quite up to this distillery's usual high standards, though. 46%

⁓ The Lark Distillery Single Malt Whisky Distillers Selection cask no. LD109, bott Apr 10 db (86.5) n21.5 t21 f22.5 b21.5. A chunky affair with some attractive nougat and orange; the star turn is the Rolo candy finale. 46%

LIMEBURNERS

⁓ Limeburners Single Malt Whisky Barrel M23 bott no. 78 db (90.5) n22.5 firm, grapey brandy with a wine gum sweetness; on another level, young barley pulses its malty theme; t23.5 beautiful mouth feel: my word, this is well made spirit! Silky and no spirit burn despite the strength, with the taste buds bathed in uncluttered grape and powering malt; f22 long with a dash of liquorice to thicken the grape further; b22.5 first time I've tasted anything from this Western Australian mob. G'day fellas! I have to admit, thought it might have been from France at first, as the aroma on nosing blind reminded me of brandy. And not without good reason, it transpires. This no age statement malt spent an unspecified amount of time in American brandy cask before being finished in bourbon casks. Does it work? Yes it does. But now that's torn it lads. You are supposed to start off with a bloody horrible whisky and get better. Now you have gone and made a rod for your own back. Good on you! 61%

⁓ Limeburners Single Malt Whisky Barrel M27 bott no. 47 db (73) n18 t19 f17 b19. Malty, but feinty, too. Probably not had the happiest fermentation, either. 43%

⁓ Limeburners Single Malt Whisky Barrel M31 bott no. 293 db (85.5) n21.5 t22 f21 b21. Pouting, semi-spiced up sultana fruitcake, complete with a delicate nuttiness; full on in part, yet curiously weightless. 43% Great Southern Distilling Co. ncf

THE NANT DISTILLERY

⁓ The Nant Single Malt First Release bott 2010 db (91.5) n24 all the hallmarks of virgin oak giving it large; beautifully supported by medium roast Java and dreamy fruit: there's a statement of intent for you....; t23 juicy, intense....and yet that big oak only serves to whip the complexity, with a kumquat and liquorice thread tying in to that persistent coffee perfectly; f22 some fizzing spice and vanilla; b22.5 beyond excellent for a first go. The flavours and style could not be more clearly nailed to the mast. I'll be watching this distillery closely. 43%

SMALL CONCERN DISTILLERY

Cradle Mountain Pure Tasmanian Malt db (87) n21 curiously vivid bourbon character; sweet vanilla with hints of tangerine and hazelnut. Really very, very attractive; t22 an almost perfect translation onto the palate: gloriously sweet and gently nutty. The mouthfeel and body is firm and oily at the same time, the barley sparkles as the oak fades. Exceptionally subtle, clean and well made; **f21** pretty long with some cocoa offering a praline effect; **b23** a knock-out malt from a sadly now lost distillery in Tasmania. Faultlessly clean stuff with lots of new oak character but sufficient body to guarantee complexity. *43%*

Cadenhead's World Whiskies Cradle Mountain Aged 11 Years bourbon, bott Sep 07 db **(72) n16 t18 f20 b18.** If memory serves me correctly, the last sample I had from this distillery was a bit of a weirdo. On that score we have consistency. Without spoiling the fun and looking back on my own notes, the previous one – I think!! – bore all the hallmarks of rum. This one, bizarrely, has some of the traits found on Brazil nuts left a year or two too long...Some surprisingly charming barley does hoist a flag at the finale. *55.3%. 204 bottles.*

TASMAN DISTILLERY

Great Outback Rare Old Australian Single Malt db **(92) n24** I could stick my nose in a glass of this all day. This is sensational: more a question of what we don't have here! The malt is clean, beautifully defined and dovetails with refined, orangey-citrus notes. The oak is near perfection adding only a degree of tempered weight. I don't detect peat, but there is some compensating Blue Mountain coffee; **t24** just so beautifully textured with countless waves of clean, rich malt neither too sweet nor too dry. This is faultless distillate; **f21** lightens considerably with the oak vanilla dominating; **b23** What can you say? An Australian whisky distillery makes a malt to grace the world's stage. But you can't find it outside of Australia. This will have to be rectified. *Strength not known.*

TASMANIA DISTILLERY

Old Hobart db **(69) n16 t19 f17 b17.** The nose still has some way to go before it can be accepted as a mainstream malt, though there is something more than a little coastal about it this time. However, the arrival on the palate is another matter and I must say I kind of enjoyed its big, oily and increasingly sweet maltiness and crushed sunflower seed nuttiness towards the end. Green (and yellow) shoots are growing. The whisky is unquestionably getting better. *60%*

Sullivan's Cove db **(61) n13 t15 f17 b16.** Some malt but typically grim, oily and dirty; awesomely weird. *40%. Australia.*

Sullivans Cove Cask Strength bourbon maturation, barrel no. HH0270, dist 22 Apr 00, bott 22 Jun 07 db **(94.5) n23 t24 f23.5 b24.** Rarely do malts balance out quite this beautifully. Drampiodean genius. *60%. 167 bottles.*

Sullivans Cove Cask Strength port maturation, barrel no. HH0544, dist 10 Nov 00, bott 25 Jun 07 db **(92) n24 t22 f23 b23.** One of the best wine-matured whiskies I have tasted for a long while – and simply because the balance and complexity are never lost for a second. *60%.*

Sullivans Cove Cask Strength port maturation, barrel no. HH0548, dist 14 Nov 00, bott 14 Feb 07 db **(93) n23 t24 f23 b23.** Nosed blind I might have mistaken this for a Demerara rum! Big and ballsy. *60%. 427 bottles.*

Sullivan's Cove Double Cask bourbon & port oak db **(87) n20** off- key oils are rounded off by fruit with chocolate-y results; **t22** excellent body and weight with a malty flourish; **f23** excellent finale, most probably thanks to the oils that shouldn't be there adding chewiness to the fruit and malt. Long, as one might expect; **b22** right: here's a bet – any money you like. Take a glass of this malt. Leave it by a fire/radiator and come back to it in about an hour. I am sure those off notes will have vanished and you'll have a malt in the 90s displaying the honey notes just dying to get out. Not had time to do it myself, but as soon as the Bible's complete... *40%*

Sullivans Cove Single Malt Whisky 6 Years Old bourbon maturation cask no. HH0274 db **(95) n23** rich and intense, there is a lovely jammy fruitiness attached to the big barley; **t24** barley concentrate with a dab of golden syrup and raspberry jam towards the middle. The body and weight are nigh perfect. Sensational!!; **f24** lovely strands of vanilla interplay with the barley and then cocoa to see out the lightly oiled finish; **b24** great on these guys. This must be the biggest Australian comeback since Larwood and Voce taught them how to bowl. A distillery once understandably a byword for less than brilliant whisky has come up with something that is truly beautiful. When I was in their warehouse a few years back, I detected the odd cracking cask, so knew their future could be bright. But perhaps not quite this brilliant...! *60%*

Sullivans Cove Single Malt Whisky 6 Years Old port maturation cask no. HH0571 db **(90) n23** so much grape but enough room for lots of natural caramel and vanilla; **t23** lush, grapey delivery, which is no surprise. Excellent spice burst in the middle; **f22** those caramels begin to spread; **b22** high quality whisky helped by some pretty top dog casks. *60%*

Sullivans Cove Single Malt Whisky 6 Years Old matured in port and bourbon casks db (**88**) **n22** butterscotch tart, grape juice and barley in just-so portions; **t23** oak-led and dry with just enough clean barley to sweeten the edge; **f21** vanilla and toast breeze through to the finish; **b22** subtle and sensuous. A bit like your average Tasmanian... 40%

TIMBOON RAILWAY SHED DISTILLERY
⌁ **Timboon Single Malt Whisky** port cask, dist May 08, bott Jun 10 db (**85**) **n22.5 t20.5 f21 b21.** Fruity and edgy, almost closer to the botanicals in gin (minus juniper) than single malt. There is a background rumble which is quite unique. Ever seen those war films where the guy manning the radar on the sub detects something, yet despite all his experience cannot quite fathom what it is that ping is telling him? Well that's me with this whisky: I need to get out there to find out what this one is all about. In the meantime, not to be confused with Tim Boon, the England cricket coach who helped plot the downfall of the Aussies in the 2005 Ashes series... 40%

YALUMBA WINERY
Smith's Angaston Whisky Vintage 1997 Aged 7 Years db (**88**) **n20** an attractive, if not entirely faultless, combination of barley and fruit sewn together by honey; **t22** an almost implausible silkiness to this: the barley and honey tip-toe over the tastebuds using a touch of oil to help them glide as well; **f23** now we have some serious complexity with the fruits showing a berry-like sharpness, but it's all very effete; **b23** easily one of the most delicate whiskies of the year and one that puts Samuel Smith on the map. Perfect for the hipflask for a night at the ballet. 40%

Smith's Angaston Whisky Vintage 1998 Aged 8 Years db (**86**) **n20 t22 f22 b22.** Perhaps conscious that their first offering, a genuine touch of culture that it was, wasn't quite Bruce enough to called Australian, this one's showing bit of aggression. And I mean a bit, as this is no tackle from Lucas Neil. Because after the delivery it's back to the girlie stuff with some admittedly delicious Swiss Roll filling fruitiness. Lovely malt from a distillery I'm going to have to keep my eyes on. 40%

Vatted Malts
⌁ **Tasmanian Double Malt Whisky Unpeated** (**87.5**) **n22** muscovado sugar and vanilla; **t22** delightfully slick mouth with feel egg yolks and sugar: half way to a cake mix...; **f21.5** powdery oak with a spurt of lemon; **b22** not a chance of getting bored with this guy. A sweet tooth would be useful. 43% The Nant Distillery

BRAZIL
HEUBLEIN DISTILLERY
Durfee Hall Malt Whisky db (**81**) **n18 t22 f20 b21.** Superbly made whisky; the intensity of the malt is beautifully layered without ever becoming too sweet. Very light bodied and immaculately clean. Good whisky by any standards. 43%

UNION DISTILLERY
Barrilete db (**72**) **n18 t19 f18 b17.** Nothing particularly wrong with it technically; it just lacks vitality. Thin but extremely malt intense. 39.1%

Blends
Cockland Gold Blended Whisky (**73**) **n10 t18 f19 b18** Silky caramel. Traces of malt there, but never quite gets it up. 38%. Fante.

Drury's Special Reserve (**86.5**) **n21.5 t22 f21 b22** Deceptively attractive, melt-in-the-mouth whisky; at times clean, regulation stuff, but further investigation reveals a honeycomb edge which hits its peak in the middle ground when the spices mix in beautifully. One to seek out and savour when in Brazil. 40%. Campari, Brasil.

Gold Cup Special Reserve (**84.5**) **n21 t22.5 f20 b21** Ultra soft, easily drinkable and, at times, highly impressive blend which is hampered by a dustiness bestowed upon it by the nagging caramels on both nose and finish. Some lovely early honey does help lift it, though, and there is also attractive Swiss roll jam towards the finish. Yet never quite gets out of third gear despite the most delicate hint of smoke. 39%. Campari, Brasil.

Gran Par (**77**) **n19.5 t22 f17.5 b18.** The delivery is eleven seconds of vaguely malty glory. The remainder is thin and caramelled with no age to live up to the name. And with Par in the title and bagpipes and kilt in the motif, how long before the SWA buys a case of it...? 39%

Green Valley Special Reserve batch 07/01 **(70)** n16 t19 f17 b18. A softly oiled, gently bitter-sweet blend with a half meaty, half boiled sweet nose. An unusual whisky experience. 38.1%. Muraro & Cia.

Malte Barrilete Blended Whisky batch 001/03 **(76)** n18 t20 f19 b19. This brand has picked up a distinctive apple-fruitiness in recent years and some extra oak, too. 39.1%.

Natu Nobilis (81.5) n22.5 t20 f19 b20 The nose boasts a genuinely clean, Speyside-style malt involvement. But to taste is much more non-committal with the soft grain dominating and the grassy notes restricted the occasional foray over the tastebuds. Pleasant, but don't expect a flavor fest. 39%. Pernod Ricard, Brasil.

Natu Nobilis Celebrity (86) n22.5 t22 f20.5 b21 A classy blend with a decent weight and body, yet never running to fat. Some spice prickle ensures the flavor profile never settles in a neautral zone and the charming, citrus-domiated malt on the nose is immediately found on the juicy delivery. A cut above the standard Natu Nobilis and if the finish could be filled out with extra length and complexity, we'd have an exceptionally impressive blend on our hands. Another blend to seek out whenever in Brazil. 39%. Pernod Ricard, Brasil.

O Monge batch 02/02 **(69)** n17 t18 f17 b17. Poor nose but it recovers with a malty mouth arrival but the thinness of the grain does few favours. 38.5%. Union Distillery.

Old Eight Special Reserve (85.5) n20 t21 f22.5 b22 Traditionally reviled by many in Brazil, I can assure you that the big bite followed by calming soft grains is exactly what you need after a day's birding in the jungle. 39%. Campari, Brasil.

Pitt's (84) n21 t20 f22 b21. The pits it certainly aint!! A beautifully malted blend where the barley tries to dominate the exceptionally flinty grain whenever possible. Due to be launched later in 2004, this will be the best Brazil has to offer – though some fine tuning can probably improve the nose and middle even further and up the complexity significantly. I hope, when I visit the distillery early in 2005, I will be able to persuade them to offer a single malt: on this evidence it should, like Pitt's, be an enjoyable experience and perfect company for any World Cup finals. 40%. Busnello Distillery.

Wall Street (84) n23 t22 f19 b20 Fabulous nose with a sexy citrus-light smoke double bill. And the arrival on the palate excels, too, with a rich texture and confident delivery of malt, again with the smoke dominating. But falls away rather too rapidly as the grains throw the balance out of kilter and ensures too much bitter oak late on. 38%. Pernod Ricard, Brasil.

INDIA
AMRUT DISTILLERY

Amrut Single Malt bott 08 db **(91.5)** n22.5 distinctly confidant liquorice-bourbon notes with near perfect bitter-sweet balance; burnt honeycomb and toffee also abound; t23.5 outstanding richness and sheen to the enormous barley-oak sweetness; again there is a big bourbony cut to the cloth with all the liquorice and molassed sugar normally associated; but the barley adds that extra dimension; f22.5 long, wonderfully layered oak offering variations of a sweet-dry theme; a touch silky with some cream toffee at the death; b23 taking it up that extra 6% abv has made a significant difference as this is stupendous stuff. I had a little moan with the distillers about the slight use of caramel here which helps neither the nose nor finish. They called back the next day to tell me they had considered my comments and decided to drop the use of caramel in all future bottlings of Amrut altogether: Power to the Bible! 46%

⁙ **Amrut Cask Strength** oak barrels, bott no. 01, bott Jul 09 db **(89.5)** n23 some alpha oak whips up an orangey lead and some major caramels; t22.5 surging, eye-watering barley: sharp, grassy and youthful at first. Then onrushing caramels make for a much softer second half; f22 sweet, with a relatively simple barley-caramel fade; b22 another big malty tale from India. But there is a big surge of natural, oily caramels to this one which keeps the complexity levels marginally down. 61.8%

Amrut Cask Strength Limited Edition bott Sep 07 db **(93.5)** n23.5 t23 f23 b24. Bottlings such as these are beginning to help cement Amrut's position as one of the great and most consistent distilleries of the world. 61.9%

⁙ **Amrut Double Cask** ex-bourbon cask no. 2874/2273, bott no. 44, bott Feb 10 db **(96)** n23 a parade of delicate, natural caramels does not detract from the complexity: dried dates and figs offer a thickening sweetness; there is even room for a more floral note...perhaps befitting how this is from the India's garden city....; t24.5 now defies belief: a combination of thumping, heady oaks but miraculously offset by the softest yet juiciest barley and intense vanilla and biscoito de polvilho so you barely notice the impact; the spices are pandering to the taste buds by offering a playful excursion from the growing sweetness; some quietly chattering orangey notes add further complexity and balance; f24 long, not a shard of bitterness as might be expected from the demands upon the barrels, which means those vanillas, increasingly nutty and oily, have a perfect chewy journey to the finish; **b24.5** frankly, a malt I thought I'd never see: how can a whisky survive seven years under the unremitting Bangalore sun? I am proud of the very small part I played in seeing this wonderful whisky see the world: I tasted both casks, containing the oldest whisky Amrut had ever produced, in a cellar at the distillery earlier in the year and passed both not only fit but exceptional. But I made the observation that they would certainly be better still if mixed together as the personalities of both casks very much complimented the other. On the day the younger of the two casks turned seven years old, this they did and bottled it. And just to show how wonderful this whisky is, from now what must surely be from one of the top two or three malt whisky distilleries in the world, simply leave an empty glass of it by your bedside table and smell it first thing in the morning. *46% 306 bottles*

Amrut Fusion batch no. 01, bott Mar 09 db **(97) n24** heavy, thickly oaked and complex: some curious barley-sugar notes here shrouded in soft smoke. Big, but seductively gentle, too... **t24** the delivery, though controlled at first, is massive! Then more like con-fusion as that smoke on the nose turns into warming, full blown peat, but it far from gets its own way as a vague sherry trifle note (curious, seeing how there are no sherry butts involved) – the custard presumably is oaky vanilla - hammers home that barley-fruitiness to make for a bit of a free-for-all; but for extra food measure the flavours develop into a really intense chocolate fudge middle which absolutely resonates through the palate; **f24** a slight struggle here as the mouthfeel gets a bit puffy here with the dry peat and oak; enough molassed sweetness to see the malt through to a satisfying end, though. Above all the spices, rather than lying down and accepting their fate, rise up and usher this extraordinary whisky to its exit; **b25** one of the most complex and intriguing new whiskies of the year that needs about two days and half a bottle to get even close to fathoming. Not exactly a textbook whisky, with a few edges grinding together like tectonic plates. And there is even odd note, like the fruit and a kind of furry, oaky buzz, which I have never seen before. But that is the point of whiskies like this: to be different, to offer a unique slant. But, ultimately, to entertain and delight. And here it ticks all boxes accordingly. To the extent that this has to be one of the great whiskies found anywhere in the world this year. And the fact it is Indian? Irrelevant: from distillation to maturation this is genius whisky, from whichever continent... *50%*

⁝⁝∴ **Amrut Intermediate Sherry Matured** bott no. 01, bott Jun 10 db **(96.5) n24.5** instead of the usual biscuit aroma, we now get moist cake. And my word: is it fruity and spicy!! Love the freshly waxed oak floor, too. Brain-explodingly complex and multi-layered with one of the most intriguing sherry-style-bourbon-style marriages on the market; **t24** cracking delivery and entirely unique in form. The structure is decidedly oak-based, but acts as no more than a skeleton from which the juicy sultana and spices drape. Salivating, too, as the barley kicks in powerfully. But the liquorice-orangey-honeycomb bourbon theme quietly shapes the flavour profile; the spices pulse and glow; **f23.5** quite a chunk of natural caramel quietens the more exuberant characteristics; long and elegant; **b24.5** how do you get three freshly emptied oloroso butts from Jerez to Bangalore without the casks spoiling, and not use sulphur? Answer: empty two cases of Amrut cask strength whisky into each of the butts before shipping them. Not a single off note. No bitterness whatsoever. And the fruit is left to impart its extraordinary riches on a malt matured also in American oak. Amrut is spoiling us again... *57.1%*

Amrut Peated batch no. 1, bott Sep 08 db **(94) n23** unusually dry peat; not dissimilar to peat reek absorbed by an old leather armchair; a hint of citrus, too; **t24** despite the nose, the immediate sensation is one of being caressed by molassed sugar and then a ratching up of the peat notes. As they get more forceful, so the experience becomes that little bit drier and spicier, though not without the molasses refusing to give way; **f23.5** you can tell the quality of the distillate and the barrels it has been matured in by the crystalline depth to the finish. Everything is clear on the palate and the butterscotch vanillas wrap the phenols for a comfortable and clean finale; **b23.5** absolutely everything you could ask for a peated malt at this strength. The length and complexity are matched only by a train journey through this astonishing country. *46%*

Amrut Peated Cask Strength bott Apr 08 db **(92) n22** gristy smoked barley, kippers with a salted butter, peppered bite; **t22.5** the delivery is youthful and barely reaching puberty then suddenly an intensely malty ascendancy followed by a healthy dose of drier oaks; **f24.5** a sublime finale for its sheer delicacy and elegance; the peat no more than oozes, there are cups galore of sugarless medium roast Mysore and finally, as a bourbony trail is discovered, soft liquorice and molassed sugar – easily the highlight of the experience: one of the best finishes of the year... **b23** a touch of youth to this guy but the finish, entirely uncluttered by unnatural caramel or deprived by filtration, confirms a degree of greatness.

By the way: if you want to experience something really stunning, trying mixing the 2007 and 2008 peated. When you get the proportions right...well, watch out Islay...!! 62.78%

Amrut Peated Cask Strength Limited Edition bott Sep 07 db (94) n23.5 t23.5 f23 b24. A split personality of a dram which offers drama and serenity in equal measures: a peat whisky lover's dream. 61.2%. 480 bottles.

⊸ **Amrut Single Cask** oak barrels, bott no. 15, bott Feb 10 db (93.5) n23 Malted Milk biscuits dunked in coffee; the distinctive aroma of melting Demerara sugar adds a piquancy to the sweetness, as do the sharp kumquats; t24 that is so beautiful: about as relaxed and confident a malt as you'll find anywhere in the world. The malt is refreshing, though in concentrated malt shake form, but this is punctuated by a busy but understated oak infusion, led again by that distinctive orangey-citrus note found on the nose; f23 long, with a late bourbon liquorice flourish, but creamy and light with those sugars lasting the distance with ease; b23.5 as good as their word: Amrut with no colouring as promised following a campaign by the Whisky Bible. And it pays off as the astonishingly intrinsic qualities of this fine whisky, fudgeless for the first time, is now there for all to see. Incredibly similar to their cask strength bottling of a year or two ago, proving there really is a formulated house style. 46%

Amrut Two Continents Limited Edition bott Feb 09 db (95) n23.5 a classy nose: the oak is abundant, but entirely controlled. It allows those blood orange and kumquat notes that are no stranger to this distillery to flourish, as well as a mildly bourbony dry liquorice; t24 such a soft landing....the barley is intense, sweet yet never overly so while the oaks again have a presence yet keep their distance, being happy to inject a busy spice kick into the middle ground; the oils are soft, lightly sweetened and lingering; f23.5 delicate. Some over-ripe, dry banana and a light dusting of muscovado sugars; b24 here we have a malt distilled in India and matured first on the sub-continent and then Scotland. Let's just say that it is a malt which has travelled exceptionally well...and arrived at greatness. This is exactly how I like my whisky to be. 46%. 786 bottles.

⊸ **Amrut 100 Peated Single Malt** ex-bourbon/virgin oak barrels db (92) n23 youthful barley integrates effortlessly with the hickory and smoke: outrageously delicate for a nose so big; t23 the virgin oak used has injected some major Demerara sugars. The smoke is not quite big enough to keep it all under control, nor the rising tide of vanillins; f23.5 all kinds of milky mocha notes work well with that soothing smoke; b22.5 ironically, though one of the older whiskies to come from this distillery, the nose shows a little bit of youth. A quite different style from Amrut's other peated offerings and it was obviously intended. Further proof that this distillery has grown not only in stature but confidence. And with very good reason. 57.1% nc ncf

Milroy's of Soho Amrut 2003 cask no. 08/08/30-1, dist Jul 03, bott Jan 09 (84) n21 t22 f20 b21. Juicy in part and very malty. But this whisky struggles at this kind of age with the oak, especially through the flattening natural caramels, dumbing the beauty down. 46%. 210 bottles.

The Ultimate Amrut 2003 Cask Strength cask no. 348, dist 25 Jul 03, bott 11 Jun 08 (91) n21.5 t22.5 f24 b23. When they say Ultimate, they aren't joking. They have taken this cask to close on five years. And in India that is Gandhi old. The oak is straining and creaking at every turn, yet somehow – and against the odds – it remains intact. Indeed, at times the experience is nigh transcendental. Other times you are searching for the tweezers...a ridiculous whisky which breaks all the rules. And yet is just so outstanding... 61.6%. nc ncf. 275 bottles. Ultimate Whisky Co. Holland.

⊸ **The Ultimate Amrut 2005 Cask Strength** bourbon barrel no. 1641, bott no. 174, dist Dec 05, bott Apr 10 db (94.5) n23.5 high phenols and proud of it: dank and earthy, bluebells in full bloom; slightly musky with neither the sweet or dry notes enjoying the upper hand; t24 eye-closingly beautiful: the waves of sweet peat roll uncontainably over the taste buds; the gristy sweetness merge with Demerara sugars and other sub bourbon notes; meanwhile the prickly peat continues its quiet rampage; f23.5 long, a smoky spice buzz and countless strands of vanilla; b23.5 it makes no difference whether made and matured in Islay or India, great malt whisky is just that. And this is near faultless. And, what's more, it appears to have a character and personality all its own. 62.8%

PONDA DISTILLERY

Stillman's Dram Single Malt Whisky Limited Edition bourbon cask no. 11186-90 (94) n23 beautifully soft peats fuse with lime-led citrus notes. At once delicate and enormous; t23 softly smoked malts dissolve into honeyed pools on the palate. Sexier and more relaxing than a Goan foot massage; f24 the way the delicate oak washes gently against the palate, the manner in which the soft peats build to a crescendo - and yet still refuse to overpower – the entrancing waves of muscovado-sweetened coffee, all make for a sublime finale; **b24** well, I thought I had tasted it all with the Amrut cask strength. And then this arrived at my lab...!! I predicted many years back that India would dish out some top grade malt before too long. But I'd be stretching the truth if I said I thought it would ever be this good... 42.8%. McDowell & Co Ltd, India.

Blends

Antiquity blend of rare Scotch and matured Indian malts, bott Feb 06 **(79) n20 t21 f19 b19**. Uncluttered but clever in places with a silky and distinctly malty delivery on the palate; the oak – not noticeable on the nose - dominates the finish intertwined with toffee-caramel. Attractive, but never quite works out which direction it is going. 42.8%. Shaw Wallace Distilleries, India. No added flavours.

Peter Scot Malt Whisky (84) n20 t21 f22 b21. Enjoyable balance between sweetness and oak and entertainingly enlivened by what appears to be some young, juicy malt. 42.8%.

Royal Stag a blend of imported Scotch malts and select Indian grain spirits, batch no. 068, bott Feb 06 **(90) n20** firm, clean good oak and barley presence; **t23** crisp, refreshing Speyside-style malt dominates early; **f24** attractive drying cocoa and spice prickle; gathering sweetness and even a touch of something very vaguely smoky; **b23** thoroughly attractive, well-balanced and rewarding whisky by any standards: the finish is fabulous. Average nose part, just love it! 42.8%. Seagram's/Gemini Distilleries, India.

NEW ZEALAND
THE SOUTHERN DISTILLING CO LTD

The Coaster Single Malt Whiskey batch no. 2356 **(85) n20 t22 f21 b22**. Distinctly small batch and sma' still with the accent very much on honey. Nosed blind I might have mistaken as Blue Mouse whisky from Germany: certainly European in style. Recovers well from the wobble on the nose and rewards further investigation. 40%

The MacKenzie Blended Malt Whiskey (85) n20 t22 f21 b22. A vaguely spicier, chalkier, mildly less honeyed version of Coaster. Quite banana-laden nose. I have flown over Timeru many times, half way as it is between Christchurch and Dunedin. By the time you read this, there is more than even chance I shall have driven there and visited this distillery. I'll let you know on the website. 40%

WILSON DISTILLERY

Milford Aged 10 Years batch 321M42, dist 93, bott 04 db **(89) n20** less than impressive with a touch of soap; **t23** fresh, grassy barley with a mildly metallic hardness; **f23** waves of vanilla, soft spices and that continuing grassy, metallic theme; **b23** what a shame that the Wilson distillery is not still extant and rich new make was being filled into some high quality bourbon casks. 43%. 4780 bottles.

Milford Aged 15 Years batch 89M414, dist 88, bott 04 db **(91) n21** battling, lively vanilla with the barley. Even the most distant hint of coal smoke; **t24** beautiful barley delivery that shows remarkable freshness and zest. Lubeck marzipan offers a mild nutty sweetness, bringing with it some soft oaks which cranks up the complexity towards the middle; **f23** light with strands of vanilla and a touch of citrus; **b23** quality whisky though slightly flattened by age but shows enough early on to confirm its class. 43%. 1878 bottles.

Cadenhead's World Whiskies Lammerlaw Aged 10 Years bourbon, bott Sep 07 **(91.5) n22 t23.5 f23 b23**. Stunning bottlings like this can only leave one mourning the loss of this distillery. 48.9%. 198 bottles.

Blends

Kiwi Whisky (37) n2 t12 f11 b12. Strewth! I mean, what can you say? Perhaps the first whisky containing single malt offering virtually no nose at all and the flavour appears to be grain neutral spirit plus lashings of caramel and (so I am told) some Lammerlaw single malt. The word bland has been redefined. As has whisky. 40%. Ever-Rising Enterprises, NZ, for the Asian market.

Wilson's Superior Blend (89) n22 stupendously clean and malt rich. Imperiously mouthwatering and enticing; **t23** brilliant, almost dazzling clean malt arrival sharpened even further with mildly though distant crisp grain. One of the world's maltiest, most salivating blends, perhaps a touch simplistic but the charm of the malt endures while the ultra-delicate oak offers a teasing weight; **f21** loses marks only because of a caramel-induced toffee arrival, but still the malt and grain are in perfect sync while the drying oak offers balance; **b23** apparently has a mixed reception in its native New Zealand but I fail to see why: this is unambiguously outstanding blended whisky. On the nose you expect a mouthwatering mouthful and it delivers with aplomb. Despite this being a lower priced blend it is, intriguingly, a marriage of 60% original bottled 10-y-o Lammerlaw and 40% old Wilson's blend, explaining the high malt apparent. Dangerous and delicious and would be better still at a fuller strength... and with less caramel. *37.5%. Continental Wines and Spirits, NZ.*

SOUTH AFRICA
JAMES SEDGWICK DISTILLERY
Three Ships 10 Years Old (db (83) n21 t21 f20 b21. Seems to have changed character, with more emphasis on sherry and natural toffee. The oak offers a thrusting undercurrent. *43%*

Blends
Drayman's Solera (86) n19 t22 f23 b22. For a change, the label gets it spot on with its description of chocolate orange: it is there in abundance. If they can get this nose sorted they would be on for an all round impressive dram. As it is, luxuriate in the excellent mouthfeel and gentle interplay between malt and oak. Oh and those chocolate oranges... *43%. Drayman's Distillery. South African/Scotch Whisky.*

Harrier (78) n20 t20 f19 b19. Not sure what has happened to this one. Has bittered to a significant degree while the smoke has vanished. A strange, almost synthetic, feel to this now. *43%. South African/Scotch Whisky.*

Knights (83) n20.5 t21 f20 b20.5. While the Harrier has crashed, the Knights is now full of promise. Also shows the odd bitter touch but a better all-round richer body not only absorbs the impacts but radiates some malty charm. *43%. South African/Scotch Whisky.*

Three Ships 5 Years Old (88.5) n21.5 the trademark soft grist peat remains but burnt toast has replaced the Columbian coffee – drat! **t22.5** a curiously soft yet chunky delivery with the smoke not taking too long to make its mark; elsewhere there are attractive sweet layers of vanilla and barley; **f22** soft oils ensure a silky touch to the finish; **b22.5** a more gentle and mildly austere bottling than of old but the clever use of smoke lifts it into a pretty high league. Really delicious stuff! *43%. South African/Scotch Whisky.*

Three Ships Bourbon Cask Finish (90) n22 unfazed by the big oak, the soft, nutty undertone melts into the even softer grain; **t23** melt-in-the-mouth with strands of juicy barley kissing gently a, presumably, grainy lushness; ice-cream style vanilla begins to fill the middle; **f22.5** delicate and not quite docile, the barley re-emerges with a vague honeyed sheen; the vanillas and the gentlest spice head towards the sunset; **b22.5** a soft, even whisky which enjoys its finest moments on delivery. Clean with a pressing, toasty oakiness to the sweeter malt elements. Always a delight. *43%.*

Three Ships Original (82) n19 t22 f21 b20. Not sure if this is meant to be the 3-yo. Certainly has different character, being smokeless save perhaps some late, late spice. Great grains, though. *43%*

TAIWAN
KAVALAN DISTILLERY
⌐◈⌐ **Kavalan** db (91) n23 predominantly fruity: plums and raisins topped by mint; a lovely dried date background; **t23** firm, flinty, juicy delivery with thudding malts soothed and comforted by lighter fruits; the mid ground moves towards a more lush, velvety texture and the first signs an oaky weight; **f22** a light buzz on the tongue points to a less than perfect sherry butt somewhere, but the compactness of the barley against the expansiveness of the delicate fruit remains a source of enjoyment; **b23** a high quality, confident malt which underline's this distillery's enormous potential. *40%*

Kavalan Concertmaster Single Malt Port cask finish db (87) n22 proud, juicy grape spread over some toasty vanilla; a slight, dull hint of a lesser cask; **t23** voluptuous entry: the silkiness of the malt is matched by the salivating, sharper tones of fruit; the middle ground is diminuendo and more introspective; **f20.5** a familiar buzz of an off-key cask; **b21.5** a malt which will split its audience. In Germany, for instance, the light sulphur note will win all kinds of standing ovations; however, to the purist there will be a preference that it was not there. Because this piece has many moments of beauty as the malt and grape mingle and interlink: together they are company, anything else is a crowd. Even so I envisage many an encore for this... *40%*

⌐◈⌐ **Kavalan Solist Fino Sherry Cask** db cask no. S060814045, bott no. 079/500 (95) n24.5 textbook aroma: one of those almost now extinct species of sherried malt where the grape neither dominates nor offers sulphur in any degree. Being a fino there is an underlying dryness to the entire nose, yet as the malt and a bourbon-esque oak both have a say, there is a countering sweetness, too. The result is a rich texture, but one never straying towards heavy.

The fruits aren't just white grape, either, but tomato and papaya, too. To add to the fray, delicate spices, most notably white pepper; pulse; **t24.5** one of the great deliveries of the year: how can something so seemingly clean be teaming with such extraordinary life? The taste buds go through about half a dozen flavour gear changes in the space of about a minute, yet there is no lurching or power surging: it's just one graceful glide all along the way. It is instantly juicy, the salivation factor going through the roof as a fabulous combination of fresh malt and grape offer a monumental double whammy. Next comes several layers of oak of varying degrees of intensity and sweetness; indeed at times we are on a roller-coaster ride of sweet-dry-sweet-dry with the sweeter notes offering a strata of bourbon brown sugars, the drier, a chalkier counter balance. But always in the background is that soft, regal grape; **f22.5** perhaps distilled before they widened the cut a little, the finish isn't quite as long as the glorious nature of the delivery might have you expect. The oils present seem to prefer the oak to the fruit, but the tailing off is as gradual as it graceful; **b23.5** when Dr Jim Swan, the distillery's consultant, told me he thought he'd found a cask which could well be a world-beater, I had mixed feelings. On one hand he'd been right when he'd said the same thing when he found a port pipe for Penderyn which has now entered Welsh whisky folklore. But, on the other, there are many times during the year when those I have long known in the game, including some good friends, have called me after reading my review and asked why I had marked their Great Hope down. Jim, though, has got this one spot on. The natural colour is astonishingly un-fino-esque and the overall experience is one that you come across only too rarely in life – especially with sherry butts. The marriage between the sweeter malt and drier grape notes is a thing of not just beauty, but awe. This is a bottling which will place the King Car Yuan-Shan distillery on the world map of truly great distilleries. Because having an exceptional cask is one thing. You also have to have a spirit excellent enough to maximize the potential of that cask and not be overwhelmed by it. That is exactly what you have here. A great new whisky dynasty has been born... *58.5% ncf nc*

Kavalan Solist Single Cask Strength ex-Bourbon Cask cask no. B070319060 db **(90.5) n23** an unusual array of dry toast, walnut oil, grated chocolate and even dried banana skin: an attractive compilation; **t23** beautiful delivery with a multi-faceted richness. The oils are soft and wonderfully useful for getting the vanilla-driven complexity across. Fabulous, prickly spices abound while the sweet, juicy malts play the perfect foil; **f22** returns to its drier self; the vanillas now really going into an almost chalky overdrive; a vague bitter marmalade on slightly burned toast bites home as a late surprise; **b22.5** wow....!!! The first single cask from this excellent new distillery has much to say for itself. And most are seriously worth listening to. Much more of a soloist than a solist, I'd say. What's more how can you not adore the natural Eastern Cattle Egret breeding colour of the whisky...? *57.3% ncf nc*

Kavalan Solist Single Cask Strength Sherry Cask cask no. S080821033 db **(92) n22.5 t24 f22.5 b23.** One of those fabulous sherry butts marked by a mild sulphury shadow but has so much else going on, that much, if not all, can be forgiven. *57.3%*

Other Brands Available In Taiwan

⸭ **Eagle Leader Storage Whisky** (81.5) **n20 t21 f21 b20.5.** Attractively smoky with a surprisingly long finish for a whisky which initially appears to lack body. By no means straightforward, but never less than pleasant. *40%*

⸭ **Golden Hill Single Malt** (75) **n18 t20 f19 b18.** An unwieldy heavyweight. *40%*

⸭ **Golden Knight All Malt** (61) **n17 t16 f12 b16.** Amazingly thin for a malt with all the weight provided by caramel. *40%*

⸭ **Golden Shield Storage Whisky** (62.5) **n17.5 t16 f14 b15.** Tarnished gold. Grim. *40%*

Good Door (in Chinese Characters) see McAdams

⸭ **Louis Dynasty** (66.5) **n16 t16 f17.5 b17.** A very strange concoction. Certain elements leave much to be desired, offering a most peculiar mouth feel. Yet there is also the odd smoke note which beds down the sweeter, firmer notes. *40%*

⸭ **McAdams Rye Whisky** bott Nov 09 (85.5) **n21 t22 f21.5 b21.5.** Thoroughly delicious stuff absolutely brimming with juicy, crisp grain notes. The body is lightly oiled and shapely while the finish is sweet and attractive. The odd green apple note, too. *40% Note: Says it's made in Taiwan, but possesses a maple leaf on the label.*

⸭ **Sea Pirates** (77) **n18 t21 f19 b19.** More Johnny Depp than Errol Flynn. Attractive smoke, though. *40%*

MISCELLANEOUS

Jaburn & Co Pure Grain & Malt Spirit (53) **n14 t13 f13 b13.** Tastes like neutral grain and caramel to me. Some shop keepers, I hear, are selling it as whisky though this is not claimed on the label. Trust me: it isn't. *37.5%. Jaburn & Co, Denmark.*

House of Westend Blended Whisky (67) n17 t18 f16 b16. No more than OK if you are being generous; some tobacco-dirty notes around. Doesn't mention country of origin anywhere on the label. 40%. *Bernkasteler Burghof, Germany.*

Prince of Wales Welsh Whisky (69) n17 t18 f17 b17. Syrupy aroma is compounded by an almost liqueurish body. Thin in true Scotch substance, probably because it claims to be Welsh but is really Scotch with herbs diffused in a process that took place in Wales. Interestingly, my "liqueur" tasting notes were written before I knew exactly what it was I was tasting, thus proving the point and confirming that, with these additives, this really isn't whisky at all. 40%

Shepherd's Export Finest Blend (46) n5 t16 f12 b13. A dreadful, illdefined grain-spirit nose is softened on the palate by an early mega-sweet kick. The finish is thin and eventually bitter. Feeble stuff. 37.2%. *"A superb blend of Imported Scotch Malt whiskies and Distilled N.Z. grain spirit", claims the label which originally gives the strength as 40%, but has been over-written. Also, the grain, I was told, was from the USA. Southern Grain Spirit, NZ.*

CROSS-COUNTRY VATTED MALT

Celtic Nations (Bruichladdich 1994 & Cooley Irish 1999) (82) n20 t22 f20 b20. Pleasant enough, very softly smoked, but a degree of inter-country bickering. 46%. *Bruichladdich Distillery.*

Cradle Mountain db (77) n19 t21 f18 b19. Doesn't quite gel for me, though it has some delicious malty moments. 46%. *Aussie malt from Cradle Mountain and Springbank single malt.*

Cradle Mountain Double db (88) n20 t23 f23 b22. This appears to be a different vatting to the 46% with greater Tasmanian whisky evident – although it isn't! Much more poise and zest and no shortage of charisma. Brilliant stuff. 54.4%. *Aussie malt from Cradle Mountain and single malt scotch from Springbank.*

Jon, Mark and Robbo's The Smooth Sweeter One a vatting of Scottish and Irish malt (92) n24 t22 f23 b23. A beautiful whisky. Intriguing as it may be, claims I have heard of this being the first such whisky of its type are way off mark – not to mention Jon and Robbo. A hundred years ago and more it was not uncommon to find bottled malt whisky being a combination of Scotch and Irish. It would have come under the general title "whisky" and brought together by merchants procuring whiskies at the best prices they could get. In my library somewhere I have old labels of these forebears. That said, those whiskies of a century ago would have been hard pushed to better it. 40%. *Edrington.*

Premium Bottlers Pure Malt Whisky Aged 10 Years LINK cask no. 1013 (marriage of Linkwood Single Malt and Canadian Single Malt) (86) n21 t23 f21 b21. Gallops off at a brisk, juicy, malty pace but tires as the natural caramels take hold. 46%. nc ncf.

Premium Bottler Vatted Malt Whisky Aged 10 Years SCAP 101 (99% Scapa Scotch, 1% Glenora Canadian) (90) n23 t23 f22 b22. Absolutely amazing malt. This Scapa, from a third-fill bourbon cask one assumes, appears half its age and simply glories in its natural brilliance. If this doesn't prove what world-great whisky this distillery conjures up in its most simple form, nothing will. 46%. nc ncf.

Premium Bottler Vatted Malt Whisky Aged 10 Years STRT 101 (99% Strathisla Scotch, 1% Glenora Canadian) (86) n20 t22 f23 b21. Early evidence, on the nose particularly, of an over-tired cask but the natural exuberance and lustre of the distillate carries it through. Wonderfully chewy in part. 46%. nc ncf.

Premium Bottler Vatted Malt Whisky Aged 10 Years ACHN 102 (99% Auchentoshan Scotch, 1% Glenora Canadian) (84) n21 t22 f20 b21. Very young, enormously citrussy effort with all the usual Auchtoshan foibles. Coming from a third fill makes for interesting dramming. 46%. nc ncf.

Premium Bottlers Pure Malt Whisky Aged 11 Years BLAT cask no. 1011 (marriage of Blair Athol Single Malt and Canadian Single malt) (84) n19 t22 f21 b22. After a disaster at the first fence, picks itself up for a deliciously malty comeback. 46%. nc ncf.

Premium Bottlers Pure Malt Whisky Aged 11 Years RLOC cask no. 1015 (marriage of Royal Lochnagar Single Malt and Canadian Single Malt) (89) n21 t22 f23 b23. After a slow, cumbersome start finishes the course with surprising strength and grace. 46%. nc ncf.

Premium Bottler Pure Malt Whisky Aged 12 Years BRIN cask no. 1009 (marriage of Benrinnes Single Malt and Canadian Single Malt) (76) n18 t20 f19 b19. A tad feinty and falls at the first hurdle. 46%. nc ncf.

Premium Bottler Vatted Malt Whisky Aged 12 Years GLLS 101 (99% Glen Lossie Scotch, 1% Glenora Canadian) (86) n21 t22 f22 b21. Very drinkable, pre-pubescent Lossie. Beware the false finale: it appears to vanish for a short finish and then reappears even more intensely than before. 46%.

Premium Bottler Vatted Malt Whisky Aged 12 Years MRTL 101 (99% Mortlach Scotch, 1% Glenora Canadian) (83) n21 t20 f21 b21. Very decent heavyweight despite the lack of oak involvement. Excellent natural oils. 46%. nc ncf

Slàinte

It seems as though you can't have a Bible without a whole lot of begetting. And without all those listed below – shimmering shoals of the all the world's whisky people – this Jim Murray's Whisky Bible 2011 would never have been begot at all. Especially without Birgit Bornemeier, for whom I reserve the most humble and heartfelt thanks. A huge amount of blood, sweat and tears go into the production of each edition, more than anyone not directly involved could ever even begin to comprehend. So I must again thank my amazing team: James Murray, Billy Jeffrey, Judith Lill, Mark Hunt, David Rankin and, of course, Dani Dal Molin, whose Vulcan Latino hyperactivity makes it possible to get two jobs covered while paying only one salary. Also, special thanks to Julia Nourney for traipsing around Europe on my behalf finding obscure samples; and the management and staff of my second home, The Empress Hotel, Victoria, BC, where I carry out my Canadian research. And, as ever, my wonderful friends and supporters Heiko Theime and Mike Smith. Thanks are also in order to all the whisky companies around the world who fearlessly(?) send their brands in for scrutiny. And finally my thanks to you, cherished reader, for buying this book and ensuring that the considerable efforts and sacrifices of all the above, as well as your most obedient servant, have not been in vain.

Tomo Akaike; Esben Andersen; Ichiro Akuto; Iain Allan; Jens-Uwe Altmann; Justin Apthorp; Raymond Armstrong; Paul Aston; Sarah Bailey; David Baker; Duncan Baldwin; Nicola Ball; Melanie Balmer; Kevin Balmforth; Hazel Barnes; Liselle Barnsley; Rachel Barrie; Edward Bates; Keith Batt; Michael Beamish; Lars Benjaminsen; Barry Bernstein; Jim Beveridge; Marilena Bidaine; John Black; Frank Michael Böer; my beautiful Borat, RIP; Etienne Bouillon; Neil Boyd; Shane Braniff; Jens Breede; Stephen Bremner; David Brisset; Ken Bromfield; Marie Broomer; Morag Brotherton; Karen Brown; Kim Brown; Mike Brown; Sara Browne; Alex Bruce; Corinne Bucchioni; Mikki Burgers; Andy Burns; Jim Busuttil; Emily Butcher; Bill Caldwell; John Campbell; Jenny Cantrell; Tina Carey; Chris Carlsson; Alex Carnie; Mark Carpenter; Ehrlich Carsten; Ian Chang; Ian Chapman; Candy Charters; Suzanne Chester; Ashok Chokalingam; Duncan Chisholm; Ashok Chokalingam; Julie Christian; Karen Christie; Ricky Christie; Nick Clark; Margaret Mary Clarke; Melissa Colman; Susan Colville; Kris Comstock; Rick Connolly; Andy Cook; Robin Cooke; Paula Cormack; Andy Cornwall; Silvia Corrieri; Isabel Coughlan; Graham Coull; James Cowan; David Cox; Ronnie Cox; Jason Craig; Georgie Crawford; Fergal Crean; Katherine Crisp; David Croll; Andy Crook; Andrew Currie; Peter Curry; Ewa Czernecka; Bob Dalgarno; Andre Dang; Craig Daniels; John Dannerbeck; Kimberley Davenport; Jancine Davies; Stephen Davies; Mark Dawkins; Martin Dawson; Zara D'Cotta; Herbert Debbeler; Jürgen Deibel; Alex Delaloye; Nathalie Desmedt; Eve Dewar; Marco Di Ciacca; Steve Dobell; Gordon Doctor; Ed Dodson; Aleta Donaldson; Chris Donaldson; Jean Donnay; Simon Downins; Lucy Drake; Jonathan Driver; Hayley Dunn; Peter Dunne; Charles Du Pré; Colin Dunn; Peter Dunne; Frances Dupuy; Gavin Durnin; Lucy Egerton; Carsten Ehrlich; Ben Ellefsen; Brent Elliot; Pat Ellis; Duncan Elphick; Per Eriksson; Richard Evans; Roy Evans; Lucy Evrington; Tracy Ewart; Lucy Farber; Bruce Farquhar; Joanna Fearnside; Bernie Fennerty; Angus Ferguson; David Findlay; Giles Fisher; Alex Fitch; David Fitt; Keira Fitzpatrick; Robert Fleischmann; Aude Florentin; Sally Forbes; Mary Forest; Angela Forsgren D'Orazio; Seth Fox; Georgina Fowler; Tim French; Barry Frieslander; Alan Galloway; Luis Garcia Burgos; Stephen Gardiner; Nick Garland; Keith Geddes; Emma Gill; Fiona Gittus; John Glaser; Gregg Glass; John Glass; Alyson Goodenough; Jim Gordon; Richard Gordon; Jess Graber; Ed Graham; Isabel Graham-Yooll; George Grant; Lynn Grant; Miaochen Gray; Virginia Gray; Jonathan Greene; Hardus Greyling; Ken Grier; Christian Gruel; Jasmin Haider; Johann Haider; Monika Haider; Olga Haley; Anna Hall; Archie Hamilton; Claudia Hamm; Wendy Harker; Jay Harman; David Harper; Wendy Harries Jones; Mark Harris; Susan Harris; Alistair Hart; Andy Hart; Donald Hart; Lily Hassan; Julian Haswell; Christopher Hayman; Michael Heals; Mika Heikkenin; CJ Hellie; Jim Helsby; Lincon Henderson; Irene Hemmings; Anne Hempstock; John Hempstock; William Henderson; Robert Hicks; Vincent Hill; Aaron Hillman; Sarah-Jane Hodson; Karl-Holger Hoehler; Alexa Hopkins; Gillian Howell; Steve Hoyles; David Hudson; Mark Hunt; Ford Hussain; David Hynes; Sandy Hyslop; Kai Ivalo; Sean Ivers; Ily Jaffa; Dee Jacques; Vivienne Jawett; Kate Johansen-Berg; Richard Joynson; Ben Kagi; Joanne Kain; Sonia Kalia-Sagoo; Shane Kalloglian; Naofumi Kamaguchi; Lara Karakasevic; Larry Kass; Caitriona Kavanagh; Halley Kehoe; Jaclyn Kelly; Bob Kennedy; Sheila Kennedy; Keiko Kinoshita; Brian Kinsman; Phillip J. Kirk; Daniel Kissling; Dennis Klindrup; Mana Kondo; Sare

Kotze; Lex Kraaijeveld; Peter Krause; Libby Lafferty; Cara Laing; Fiona Laing; Fred Laing; Stuart Laing; Hannah Langdon; Bill Lark; Kristy Lark; Lynne Lark; Liske Larsen; David Larsson; Rohna Lawson; Megan LeBoeuf; Walter Lecocq; Patricia Lee; Harvey Lees; Anne Marie Le Lay; Guy Le Lay; Billy Leighton; Darren Leitch; Gilles Leizour; Lars Lindberger; Graeme Lindsay; Lochy; Andrew Long; Jim Long; Martin Long; Alistair Longwell; Linda Love; Jason Low; Andreas Lübberstedt; Bill Lumsden; Jane MacDuff; Stuart MacDuff; Frank MacHardy; Dominique Mackay; Roderick Mackenzie; Lorne Mackillop; Sharon Maclaughlin; Stephanie Macleod; Grant MacPherson; Rosalyn MacRae; Iseabail Mactaggart; Lesley-Ann Maguire; Patrick Maguire; Chris Maile; Dennis Malcolm; Ellen Malinski; Pekka Marjamaa; Tracy Markey; Linda Marks; Gillian Marshall; Tim Marwood; Elaine Masson; Norman Mathison; Larry Mattingly; David Maxwell-Scott; Iain McCallum; Antony McCallum-Caron; Steve McCarthy; Tom McCulloch; Mhairi McDonald; John McDougall; John McDonough; Barbara McEwan; Jim McEwan; Lynne McEwan; Julie McFadden; Sarah McGhee; Paul McGinlay; Helen McGinn; Alister McIntosh; Doug McIvor; Dominic McKay; Anne McKerrow; Thomas McKenzie; Jaclyn McKie; Margaret McKie; Lorne McKillop; Morna McLelland; Kirsty McLeod; Fred McMillan; Janice McMillan; Steven McNeil; Alan McConnachie; Laura McVicar; Lee Medoff; Clare Meikle; Jon Metcalf; Rick Mew; Stephanie Middleton; Paul Miles; Robbie Millar; Ann Miller; Bill Miller; Ester Miller; Patrick Millet; Tom Mills; Jack Milroy; John Milroy; Tatsuya Minagawa; Andre Miron; Elaine Mitchell; Euan Mitchell; Matthew Mitchell; Michael Moane; Jürgen Moeller; Takeshi Mogi; Zubair Mohamed; Rainer Mönks; Glen Moore; Les Morgan; Chris Morris; Jemma Morris; Ian Morrison; Joanna Morrow; Mary Morton; Edelle Moss; Gordon Motion; Arthur Motley; Helen Mulholland; Malcolm Mullan; Anna Murby; Jayne Murphy; Alison Murray; Andrew Murray; Bert Murray; Charles Murray; David Murray; Karen Murray; Stacey Murray; Elaine Mutch; Arthur Nagale; Kamiguchi Naofumi; Shin Natsuyama; Marc Neilly; Jill Nelson; Andrew Nelstrop; Alie Newton; Mark Newton; Alex Nicol; Margaret Nicol; Graham Nicolson; Thrivikram G Nikam; Micke Nilsson; Kate Nimmo; Edel Nørgaard; Johannes Nørgaard; Lis Nørgaard; Søren Nørgaard; Jake Norris; Tom O'Connor; Gerry O'Donnell; Catherine O'Grady; Deirbhile O'Grady; Aoife O'Sullivan; Barbara Ortner; Wolfram Ortner; Linda Outterson; Bill Owens; Ian Palmer; C R Parker; Richard Parker; Micheal Patterson; Robert Patterson; Richard Paterson; Rupert Patrick; Siobhan Payne; Nadège Perrot; John Peterson; Plamen Petroff; Justin Petszaft; Stefan E. Petszaft; Catharine Pickering; Edi Pierri; Simon Pointon; Alex Polasek; Dorothea Polasek; Nick Pollachi; Steve Poore; Henry Pratt; Amy Preske; Ashley Presser; Warren Preston; Sabina Pringle; Lucy Pritchard; Annie Pugh; Scott Pugh; Roland Puhl; Bernadette Quinn; David Radcliffe; John Ramsay; Caroline Randu; David Rankin; Robert Ransom; Aaron Rasmussen; Kaye Rawlings; Kelly Rayney; Alan Reid; Clémence Réveilhac; Mark Reynier; Kay Riddoch; Jeannie Ritchie; Christine Roberts; Patrick Roberts; Allan Robertson; Jennifer Robertson; Pamela Robertson; Maureen Robinson; Geraldine Roche; Jim Rogerson; Johanne Rolland; Claire Ross; Colin Ross; Duncan Ross; Fabio Rossi; Ronnie Routledge; Jim Roy; Leonard S Russell; Suzy Russell; Jim Rutledge; Caroline Rylance; Richard Salmond; Silvano S. Samaroli; Courtney Sandora; Christine Sandys; Jacqui Sargeant; Virginie Saudemont; Trish Savage; John Savage-Onstwedder; Leander Schadler; Gerd Schmerschneider; Yossi Schwartz; Kendra Scott; Tara Serafini; Euan Shand; Rubyna Sheikh; Yuko Shimoda; Naomi Shooman; Joy Simpson; Alistair Sinclair; Fred Sinclair; Sukhinder Singh; Michael Slevin; David Sloan; Ian Smart; Allan Smith; Barbara Smith; Michelle Smith; Mike Smith; Robert Hill Smith; Isa Sneddon; Emanuel Solinsky; Squeak Sparrow; Jeremy Speirs; Sue Stamps; Rory Steel; Barry Stein; Florian Stetter; Tamsin Stevens; David Stewart; Karen Stewart; David Stirk; Kathleen Stirling; Katy Stollery; Kaj Stovring; Derek Strange; Johanna Strasser; Ivar Svensson; Noel Sweeney; Kier Sword; Shogo Takagi; Katsuhiko Tanaka; James Tanner; Michelle Tansley; Graham Taylor; Elizabeth Teape; Jack Teeling; Jo Terry; Celine Tetu; Volker Theurer; Heiko Thieme; Jens Tholstrup; Corinna Thompson; Stuart Thompson; Terry Threlfall; Drew Tiffin; Nick Tilt; Margrat Mary Timson; Una Tomnay; Jeff Topping; Hamish Torrie; Angela Traver; Sarah True; Rob Tuer; Matthew Turner; Ben Upjohn; Ian Urquhart; Mr Vannan; Johan Venter; Stefanu Venturini; Kenneth Vernon; Alistair Viner; Christine von Allwörden; Hans von Essen; Alistair Walker; Billy Walker; Jamie Walker; Karen Walker; Leesa Walker; Barry Walsh; Bernard Walsh; Christopher Watkin; Claire Watson; Joanna Watson; Mark Watt; Andy Watts; Susan Webster; Peter Wheeler; Oswald Weidenauer; Ian Weir; Isabella A Wemyss; Jan H Westcott; Kerry White; Nick White; Sian Whitelock; Jack Wiebers; Lars-Göran Wiebers; Alex Williams; David Williamson; Anthony Wills; Pamela Wils; David Wilson; Lisa Wilson; Arthur Winning; Lance Winters; Tony Wise; David Wood; Léonie Wood; Steve Worrall; Gordon Wright; Graham Wright; Kate Wright; Vanessa Wright; Chi-Min Wu; Junko Yaguchi; Venita Young; Daniel & Ursula Zurcher.